The Very Best Coaching and Study Course for the

ACT
A S S E S S M E N T

5th EDITION
with New Writing Test

with CD-ROM for both Windows & Macintosh
REA's Interactive ACT TEST*ware*®

Charles O. Brass
Office of Special Programs
University of Chicago, Chicago, IL

Jean O. Charney, Ph.D.
Jean Charney Editorial Services
Fort Collins, CO

Suzanne Coffield, M.A.
Department of English
Northern Illinois State University,
De Kalb, IL

Joseph T. Conklin
Meteorologist
Red Bank, NJ

Anita Price Davis, Ed.D.
Chair, Education Department
Converse College, Spartanburg, SC

Slim Fayache, Ph.D.
Department of Physics and Astronomy
Rutgers University, New Brunswick, NJ

Mitchel Fedak
Department of Chemistry
Community College of Allegheny,
Monroeville, PA

Bernice E. Goldberg, Ph.D.
Educational Consultant
Falmouth, ME

Kevin James Hanson
Science Instructor
Foley Intermediate School, Foley, MN

Kai Miao, Ph.D.
Department of Mathematics
Rutgers University, New Brunswick, NJ

Lina Miceli, M.A.
Guidance Counselor
Piscataway High School, Piscataway, NJ

Pamela K. Phillips
Science Instructor
Hayden High School, Hayden, AL

Elizabeth M. Powell, M.S.
Science Writer, Edison, NJ

Michael Sporer
Meteorologist, Edison, NJ

Corinna Siebert Ruth, M.A.
Department of English
Reedley High School, Reedley, CA

Marjorie Wexler, Ph.D.
Science Writer, Chappaqua, NY

Research & Education Association
61 Ethel Road West
Piscataway, New Jersey 08854

The Very Best Coaching and Study Course for the
ACT ASSESSMENT with CD-ROM for both
Windows & Macintosh–REA's Interactive ACT TEST*ware*®

Printed in the United States of America

Library of Congress Control Number 2004111867

International Standard Book Number 0-7386-0073-3

REA supports the effort to conserve and
protect environmental resources by
printing on recycled papers.

I04-0102

CONTENTS

* The writing test is optional; check with your college of choice to determine whether you should take it.

INDEPENDENT STUDY SCHEDULE

ACT INDEPENDENT STUDY SCHEDULE

This study schedule is designed to systematize your preparation for the ACT. Although it is designed for 10 weeks, it can be compressed into a five-week course by collapsing two weeks into one. If you are not enrolled in a structured course, be sure to set aside at least two hours each day to study. No matter which study schedule works best for you, the more time you spend studying, the more prepared and relaxed you will feel on the day of the exam.

Week	Activity
1	Read through Chapter 1 to acquaint yourself with the ACT. Next, take the Diagnostic Exam to pinpoint your strengths and weaknesses. Score each section by using the chart in Chapter 1.
2	Study the English Review and—if you're taking the optional ACT Writing Test*—the Writing Test Review. Be sure to thoroughly work through the grammar and rhetorical skills review sections, and complete all the drills. If you have particular trouble with any of the drill questions, go back and study the corresponding section of the review.
3	Study the Mathematics Review. If any particular type of question gives you trouble, review that section again.
4	Study the Reading Review. Read the sample passages and answer all the practice questions, using the tips and techniques you have learned.
5	Study the Science Reasoning Review and the individual subject reviews. Answer each drill using the methods you have learned in the review.
6	Take ACT Diagnostic Software Exam I. This is the same as Exam III in the book, but it is highly recommended that you take the exam first on computer for maximum study benefits. After the computer scores your exam, carefully review all incorrect answer explanations. If there are any types of questions that are particularly difficult for you, review those subjects by studying the appropriate section again. At the end of every explanation, a page reference to the appropriate subject area in the Review section is displayed on the computer screen.

* Check with your college of choice as to whether it requires the ACT Writing Test.

Week	Activity
7	Take ACT Diagnostic Software Exam II. This is the same as Exam IV in the book, but it is highly recommended that you take the exam first on computer for maximum study benefits. After the computer scores your exam, carefully review all incorrect answer explanations. If there are any types of questions that are particularly difficult for you, review those subjects by studying the appropriate section again. At the end of every explanation, a page reference to the appropriate subject area in the Review section is displayed on the computer screen.
8	Take Exam I in the book and, after scoring your exam, carefully review all incorrect answer explanations. If there are any types of questions that are particularly difficult for you, review these subjects by studying the appropriate section again.
9	Take Exam II in the book and, after scoring your exam, carefully review all incorrect answer explanations. If there are any types of questions that are particularly difficult to you, review these subjects by studying the appropriate section again.
10	To be sure that you will be comfortable on the day of the exam, read through the test-taking tips given in each review once again. If there are any subject areas that are still difficult for you, study the appropriate section once more, and look over all the practice test questions and explanations on that topic.

ABOUT RESEARCH & EDUCATION ASSOCIATION

Founded in 1959, Research & Education Association (REA) is dedicated to publishing the finest and most effective educational materials—including software, study guides, and test preps—for students in middle school, high school, college, graduate school, and beyond.

REA's Test Preparation series includes study guides for all academic levels in almost all disciplines. Research & Education Association publishes test preps for students who have not yet completed high school, as well as high school students preparing to enter college. Students from countries around the world seeking to attend college in the United States will find the assistance they need in REA's publications. For college students seeking advanced degrees, REA publishes test preps for many major graduate school admission examinations in a wide variety of disciplines, including engineering, law, and medicine. Students at every level, in every field, with every ambition can find what they are looking for among REA's publications.

While most test preparation books present only a few practice tests that bear little resemblance to the actual exams, REA's series presents tests that accurately depict the official exams in both degree of difficulty and types of questions. REA's practice tests are always based upon the most recently administered exams, and include every type of question that can be expected on the actual exams.

REA's publications and educational materials are highly regarded and continually receive an unprecedented amount of praise from professionals, instructors, librarians, parents, and students. Our authors are as diverse as the subject matter represented in the books we publish. They are well-known in their respective disciplines and serve on the faculties of prestigious universities throughout the United States and Canada.

ACKNOWLEDGMENTS

In addition to our authors, we would like to thank John Paul Cording, Manager of Educational Software, for coordinating the design, development, and testing of the software; Larry B. Kling, Manager, Editorial Services, for his editorial direction; Pam Weston, Production Manager, for ensuring press readiness; Gianfranco Origliato, Project Manager, for coordinating revisions; Jeff LoBalbo, Senior Graphic Designer, for coordinating pre-press electronic file-mapping; Bernadette Brick, Brian Dean, and Jeff Karnicky for their editorial contributions; and Wende Solano for typesetting the manuscript.

ACT
ASSESSMENT

CHAPTER 1

Scoring High
on the
ACT Assessment

Chapter 1

SCORING HIGH ON THE ACT ASSESSMENT

ABOUT OUR BOOK AND ACT TEST*ware*®

This book, along with our accompanying ACT TEST*ware*® software, has been designed to effectively prepare you for the ACT Assessment. It contains five full-length practice exams complete with answer keys and detailed explanations for each question, and a review for each ACT test. Practice exams III and IV are available in our book and on CD-ROM as part of our exclusive interactive ACT TEST*ware*®. By taking the exams on computer, you will gain the additional benefits of enforced timed conditions, individual diagnostic analysis of what subjects need extra study, and instant scoring. All practice exams are based on the most recent ACT test administrations and contain every type of question that you may encounter on the actual exam.

For your convenience, our ACT TEST*ware*® has been provided for you in both Windows and Macintosh formats. Many useful features are included to help you prepare for the ACT. Some of these features include automatic scoring (you will receive both raw and scaled scores for each test and subscore area), and guidance on what page in our book to study if you answer a question incorrectly. In addition, our Verbal Builder software will help you build your vocabulary with crossword puzzles and match-and-link games. Improve your reading comprehension skills with the reading builder/speed reader exercises. For instructions on how to install and use our ACT TEST*ware*® and ACT Verbal Builder software, please refer to the appendix at the back of this book.

ABOUT THE ACT

Who Takes the ACT and What is It Used for?

The ACT is usually taken by high school juniors and seniors. The exam is used by college admissions officers as a way to fairly judge all the students who apply to their school. Because high schools across the United States use many different grading systems, ACT scores put everyone on more of an equal footing.

Your ACT scores, along with other information provided by you and your high school, help colleges predict how well you will do at the college level.

If you don't do well on the ACT, don't panic! The exam can be taken over so that you can work on improving your scores. It's also not the be-all and end-all that you might think it is. Admissions officers use a number of criteria to judge applicants: Grade-point average, extracurricular activities, on-campus interviews, and the degree to which you've been taking challenging courses in high school are all factors that go into the mix. REA believes you have every reason to believe that, with enough of the right preparation, you can and should score well on the ACT. Nonetheless, you shouldn't think that not doing so will necessarily jeopardize your chances of attending the college of your choice. The very fact that you picked up this book, however, means that you're not one to leave much to chance. Having our test prep at your side as you approach test day will give you the extra shot of confidence we all sometimes need to climb the ladder of success.

Who Administers the ACT?

The ACT is developed and administered by ACT, Inc., and involves the assistance of educators throughout the country. The development process is designed and implemented to ensure that the content and difficulty level of the exam are appropriate.

When and Where is the ACT Given?

You should try to take the exam early in your junior or senior year so that you will have another opportunity to take it if you are not satisfied with your performance. Taking our practice exams will familiarize you with the types of questions and format of the ACT so that you do not have to go through the anxiety of learning about the ACT during the actual exam.

The ACT is usually administered five times a year throughout the country. It is given at hundreds of locations, including high schools. The usual testing day is Saturday but the exam may be taken on an alternate day if a conflict, such as a religious obligation, exists.

To receive information on upcoming administrations of the ACT, consult the ACT Registration Bulletin, which can be obtained from your guidance counselor, or contact ACT, Inc., directly at:

ACT Registration
P. O. Box 414
Iowa City, IA 52243-0414
Phone: (319) 337-1270 (weekdays 8 A.M. to 8 P.M. CT)
Website: http://www.act.org

To take the ACT, you must pay a registration fee. A fee waiver may be granted in certain situations. To find out if you qualify, ask your guidance counselor.

HOW TO USE THIS BOOK AND SOFTWARE

What Do I Study First?

Begin your studies by first taking our written diagnostic exam. The tables that follow include an answer key to score your exam, and also explain what review material you need to study if you answered a question incorrectly.

After taking the written diagnostic exam, you may wish to continue your preparation by moving on to our software. Or, if you prefer, first study our reviews which are designed to provide you with the information and strategies you need to do well on the ACT.

Complete your preparation by taking the remaining two practice exams. For the most benefit, be sure to simulate actual testing conditions. Sit at a table in a quiet room and be sure to time yourself. Doing so will help you become familiar with the format and procedures involved with taking the actual ACT, and should help alleviate some of your test-taking anxiety.

To best utilize your study time, follow our ACT Independent Study Schedule located in the front of this book. The schedule is based on a ten-week program, but can be condensed to five weeks if necessary.

When Should I Start Studying?

It is never too early to start studying for the ACT. The earlier you begin, the more time you will have to sharpen your skills. Do not procrastinate! Cramming is *not* an effective way to study, since it does not allow you the time needed to learn the exam material. The sooner you learn the format of the exam, the more time you will have to familiarize yourself with it.

FORMAT OF THE ACT ASSESSMENT

Test	Question Type	Number of Questions
English	Usage/Mechanics:	
45 minutes	Punctuation 13%	10 multiple-choice
75 questions	Basic Grammar & Usage 16%	12 multiple-choice
	Sentence Structure 24%	18 multiple-choice
	Rhetorical Skills:	
	Strategy 16%	12 multiple-choice
	Organization 15%	11 multiple-choice
	Style 16%	12 multiple-choice
Mathematics	Pre-Algebra / Elem. Algebra:	
60 minutes	Pre-Algebra 23%	14 multiple-choice
60 questions	Elementary Algebra 17%	10 multiple-choice
	Int. Algebra / Coord. Geometry:	
	Intermediate Algebra 15%	9 multiple-choice
	Coordinate Geometry 15%	9 multiple-choice

	Plane Geometry / Trigonometry:	
	Plane Geometry 23%	14 multiple-choice
	Trigonometry 7%	4 multiple-choice
Reading	Social Studies/Sciences:	
35 minutes	Social Studies 25%	10 multiple-choice
40 questions	Natural Sciences 25%	10 multiple-choice
	Arts/Literature:	
	Prose Fiction 25%	10 multiple-choice
	Humanities 25%	10 multiple-choice
Science Reasoning	Data Representation 38%	15 multiple-choice
35 minutes	Research Summaries 45%	18 multiple-choice
40 questions	Conflicting Viewpoints 17%	7 multiple-choice

The breakdown of questions may appear as follows:

Test 1: English
(45 minutes)

5 passages each followed by 15 questions

Test 2: Mathematics
(60 minutes)

60 regular math questions

Test 3: Reading
(35 minutes)

4 reading passages with 10 questions on each passage

Test 4: Science Reasoning
(35 minutes)

7 passages each followed by between 5 and 7 questions

Note:

On certain test dates, a fifth test is administered for developmental purposes. This test will not be counted toward your score.

Total questions: 215
Total Testing Time: 2 hours, 55 minutes

All of the questions on the ACT are in multiple-choice format and provide four answer choices, except those in the Mathematics test which present five choices.

English Test

There are two types of English questions on the ACT, for which you will receive separate subscores:

- *Usage/Mechanics:* (40 questions) You will be required to review sentences from the passages for proper grammar. These questions test your knowledge of punctuation, your understanding of basic grammar and usage, and your recognition of proper sentence structure.

- *Rhetorical Skills:* (35 questions) You will be tested on your ability to recognize the strategy of a piece of writing, and to choose expressions and sentences which will support that strategy. Your skill level in organizing ideas and judging statements in context will also be tested. Finally, your ability to select precise and appropriate words and images, avoid ambiguous or ineffective writing, and write economically will be tested.

Mathematics Test

In the Mathematics test, you will encounter standard multiple-choice questions. The test covers five areas, but you will receive three subscores based on the following topics:

- *Pre-Algebra/Elementary Algebra:* (24 questions) These questions test your knowledge of whole numbers, decimals, integers, fractions, linear equations, algebraic equations, and your ability to solve a quadratic equation.

- *Intermediate Algebra and Coordinate Geometry:* (18 questions) You will be tested on graphing in the coordinate plane, operations with integer exponents, radical and rational expressions, the quadratic formula, linear inequalities in one variable, and systems of two linear equations in two variables.

- *Plane Geometry/Trigonometry:* (18 questions) These questions evaluate your knowledge of the properties and relations of figures on the geometric plane, right triangle trigonometry, graphing trigonometric functions, and basic trigonometric identities.

Reading Test

The Reading passages cover topics in social studies, the natural sciences, prose fiction, and the humanities. You will receive two subscores based on the following areas:

- *Social Studies/Natural Sciences:* (20 questions) The Social Studies questions will evaluate your understanding of a passage that may be drawn from history, political science, anthropology, psychology, or sociology. The Natural Science questions will test you on a passage from biology, chemistry, physics, or the physical sciences.

- *Arts/Literature:* (20 questions) Questions on the Arts will be based on a passage covering art, music, philosophy, theater, architecture, or dance. The Literature questions will evaluate you based on a passage that is a complete short story, or an excerpt from a short story or novel.

Science Reasoning Test

The Science Reasoning test has seven passages, which are taken from the fields of biology, chemistry, physics, and the physical sciences (this includes astronomy, geology, and meteorology). Rather than test your recall of scientific content, or your skill in mathematics or reading, these questions seek to evaluate your ability to reason scientifically. The information will be conveyed in one of three formats:

- *Data Representation:* (15 questions) These questions ask you to read tables, graphs, or scatter plots. Your ability to read and interpret information presented in this format will be measured.

- *Research Summaries:* (18 questions) You will be presented with descriptions of one or more related experiments. Questions in this format will focus on experimental design and ask you to interpret the experimental results.

- *Conflicting Viewpoints:* (7 questions) These questions will be based on a reading passage that presents several hypotheses or views that are inconsistent with each other. You will be asked to understand, analyze, and compare these conflicting viewpoints or hypotheses.

ABOUT THE REVIEW SECTIONS

The reviews in this book are designed to help you sharpen the basic skills needed to approach the ACT as well as provide strategies for attacking each type of question. A separate review is presented for each ACT test: English, Mathematics, Reading, and Science Reasoning. Drills are provided to reinforce what you have learned. By using the reviews in conjunction with the practice tests, you will better prepare yourself for the actual exam.

SCORING THE ACT

How Do I Score My Practice Exam?

In scoring your exams, you will be determining three different scores: a raw score, a scaled score, and a composite score. Your raw scores will be used to determine your scaled scores, and your scaled scores will be used to determine your composite score. These scores should be recorded in our "Scoring Worksheet" on page 9. You may want to photocopy the worksheet so that you will have a separate worksheet for each practice exam.

How Do I Calculate My Raw Score?

Raw scores for each practice exam are, simply put, the number of questions you answered correctly. These scores will be broken down so that a raw score will be calculated for each test within that exam. In addition, a raw score will be calculated for the subscore areas within each test, save for the Science Reasoning Test, which is not divided into subscore areas.

To determine your raw scores, first check your answers against the answer keys at the end of each exam. As you will see, the answer keys note both the correct answer for each question and the question's subscore area (except for Science Reasoning). Count the number of correct answers for each test and for each subscore area within each test. These are your raw scores. Record them on the Scoring Worksheet.

How Do I Calculate My Scaled Score?

In order to determine your scaled scores, refer to the tables following the Scoring Worksheet. A separate table is provided for the tests and for the subscore areas. Since separate tables are used, you cannot simply add together your scaled scores for the subscore areas in order to determine the scaled score for each test. Scaled scores for each test will range from a low of "1" to a high of "36," while scaled scores for the subscore areas will range from a low of "1" to a high of "18."

To determine your scaled score for each test, look at the Raw Score Conversion Chart and find the column which corresponds to the test you are scoring (i.e., English, Mathematics, Reading, or Science Reasoning). Next, locate your raw score under that column. Then, look under the scaled score column to find the number that corresponds to your raw score. This number is your scaled score for that test, and it should be recorded on the Scoring Worksheet.

To determine your scaled score for each subscore area, look at the Subscore Conversion Chart and find the column which corresponds to the subscore area you are scoring. Locate your raw score under that column and then find its corresponding number in the scaled-score column. Record this number on the Scoring Worksheet.

How Do I Calculate My Composite Score?

Finally, you will need to determine a composite score for your practice exam. The composite score is the average of the four scaled scores for the exam (English, Mathematics, Reading, and Science Reasoning). Add together your four scaled scores and divide this number by four. This is your composite score and should be recorded on the Scoring Worksheet. Composite scores for your exam will range from a low of "1" to a high of "36."

When Will I Receive My Score Report and What Will It Look Like?

You will receive your score report four to eight weeks after you take the test. Aside from you, only your high school, the colleges you indicated on your answer sheet, and scholarship services will see your scores.

Your score report will contain your scaled scores for each of the four tests, and your composite score. Your subscores for the English, Mathematics, and Reading tests will also be noted. As mentioned, because each section is scored independently, the subscores will not necessarily add up to the scaled score for each test. For example, the three Mathematics subscores will not necessarily add up to your scaled score in Mathematics. The score report will also denote percentiles for each scaled score, subscore, and your composite score. This information tells you the number of students who took the same administration of the ACT and received scores equivalent to or lower than yours. Your composite score will also be ranked with those of enrolled first-year students at the colleges you indicated on your answer sheet.

SCORING WORKSHEET

	Raw Score (Total Correct)	Scaled Score
English Test	_____	_____
Usage/Mechanics (UM)	_____	_____
Rhetoric (RH)	_____	_____
Mathematics Test	_____	_____
Pre-Alg./El. Alg. (EA)	_____	_____
Int. Alg./Coord. Geo. (AG)	_____	_____
Plane Geom./Trig. (GT)	_____	_____
Reading Test	_____	_____
Soc. Stud./Sci. (SS)	_____	_____
Arts/Literature (AL)	_____	_____
Science Reasoning Test	_____	_____

Subscore area labels appear beside the English, Mathematics, and Reading subscore groups.

Composite Score _____

(English Test Scaled Score + Mathematics Test Scaled Score + Reading Test Scaled Score + Science Reasoning Test Scaled Score) ÷ 4 = Composite Score

RAW SCORE CONVERSION CHART*

TEST 1 Your English Raw Score	TEST 2 Your Mathematics Raw Score	TEST 3 Your Reading Raw Score	TEST 4 Your Science Reasoning Raw Score	YOUR SCALED SCORE
75	60	39-40	40	36
—	—	38	—	35
74	59	—	39	34
73	58	37	—	33
72	57	—	38	32
71	55-56	36	37	31
69-70	53-54	35	36	30
68	50-52	34	35	29
66-67	48-49	—	34	28
64-65	45-47	32-33	32-33	27
61-63	43-44	31	31	26
59-60	40-42	30	29-30	25
56-58	38-39	29	27-28	24
54-55	35-37	28	26	23
52-53	33-34	27	24-25	22
49-51	31-32	25-26	22-23	21
46-48	28-30	24	20-21	20
44-45	26-27	23	18-19	19
41-43	23-25	21-22	16-17	18
39-40	20-22	20	15	17
36-38	17-19	19	13-14	16
33-35	15-16	17-18	12	15
30-32	13-14	16	10-11	14
28-29	11-12	14-15	9	13
25-27	9-10	13	8	12
23-24	7-8	11-12	6-7	11
20-22	6	9-10	5	10
17-19	5	8	4	9
14-16	4	7	—	8
12-13	—	6	3	7
9-11	3	5	2	6
7-8	2	4	—	5
5-6	—	3	1	4
4	1	2	—	3
2-3	—	1	—	2
0-1	0	0	0	1

* The conversion scale used in this chart does not necessarily reflect the scale that will be used by ACT, Inc., in scoring the ACT. Used in conjunction with our subscore-coded answer sheets, however, it will enable you to strongly approximate the ACT scoring system.

SUBSCORE CONVERSION CHART: RAW SCORE TO SCALED SCORE*

RAW SCORES

Scaled Subscore	Test 1 - English		Test 2 - Mathematics			Test 3 - Reading	
	Usage/ Mechanics	Rhetorical Skills	Pre-Algebra/ Elem. Algebra	Inter. Algebra/ Coord. Geometry	Plane Geometry/ Trigonometry	Social Studies/ Sciences	Arts/ Literature
18	39-40	35	24	18	18	20	20
17	38	—	22-23	17	—	19	19
16	36-37	33-34	21	16	17	18	18
15	34-35	32	20	14-15	16	17	17
14	32-33	30-31	18-19	13	14-15	16	—
13	30-31	28-29	17	11-12	13	15	16
12	28-29	26-27	15-16	10	11-12	13-14	15
11	26-27	24-25	14	8-9	9-10	12	14
10	24-25	22-23	12-13	7	8	11	13
9	22-23	19-21	10-11	5-6	6-7	9-10	12
8	19-21	16-18	9	4	5	8	11
7	17-18	14-15	7-8	3	4	7	9-10
6	15-16	12-13	6	—	3	6	8
5	12-14	9-11	4-5	2	—	5	7
4	9-11	7-8	3	—	2	4	6
3	7-8	5-6	2	1	—	3	5
2	5-6	3-4	1	—	1	2	3-4
1	0-4	0-2	0	0	0	0-1	0-2

* The conversion scale used in this chart does not necessarily reflect the scale that will be used by ACT, Inc., in scoring the ACT. Used in conjunction with our subscore-coded answer sheets, however, it will enable you to strongly approximate the ACT scoring system.

STUDYING FOR THE ACT

It is very important to choose the time and place for studying that work best for you. Some students may set aside a certain number of hours every morning, while others may choose to study at night before going to sleep. Other students may study during the day, while waiting on line, or even while eating lunch. Only you can determine when and where your study time will be the most effective. But be consistent and use your time wisely. Work out a study routine and stick to it!

When you take our written practice exams, try to make your testing conditions as much like the actual exam as possible. Turn your television and radio off, and sit down at a quiet table free from distraction. Make sure to time yourself. Start off by setting a timer for the time that is allotted for each test, and be sure to reset the timer for the appropriate amount of time when you start a new test.

As you complete each diagnostic and practice exam, score your exam and thoroughly review the explanations to the questions you answered incorrectly; however, do not review too much at one time. Concentrate on one problem area at a time by reviewing the question and explanation, and by studying our review until you are confident that you completely understand the material.

Since you will be allowed to write in your test booklet during the actual ACT, you may want to write in the margins and spaces of this book while practicing; however, do not make miscellaneous notes on your answer sheets. Mark each answer clearly and make sure the answer you have chosen corresponds to the question you are answering.

Score your exams using the Scoring Worksheet and keep track of them. By doing so, you will be able to gauge your progress and discover general weaknesses in particular sections. You should carefully study the reviews that cover your areas of difficulty, as this will build your skills in those areas.

TEST-TAKING TIPS

Although you may not be familiar with standardized exams such as the ACT, there are many ways to acquaint yourself with this type of examination and help alleviate your test-taking anxieties. Listed below are ways to help you become accustomed to the ACT, some of which may be applied to other standardized tests as well.

Become comfortable with the format of the ACT. When you are practicing, simulate the conditions under which you will be taking the actual exam. Stay calm and pace yourself. After simulating the exam a couple of times, you will boost your chances of doing well, and you will be able to sit down for the actual ACT with much more confidence.

Read all of the possible answers. Just because you think you have found the correct response, do not automatically assume that it is the best answer. Read through each choice to be sure that you are not making a mistake by jumping to conclusions.

Use the process of elimination. Go through each answer to a question and eliminate as many of the answer choices as possible. By eliminating two answer choices, you have given yourself a better chance of getting the item correct since there will only be two or three choices left from which to make your guess. Guess only if you can eliminate at least two answers.

Be careful if you use a calculator. Calculators are now permitted on the mathematics portion of the test. However, all the questions can be solved without the use of a calculator. Use your judgment on when and where you should use a calculator. You may find that some questions are more easily solved without the use of a calculator. A good rule of thumb is to use a calculator only if you use it regularly in your classwork and homework. You should note that not all types of calculators are permitted. Unacceptable calculators include handheld or laptop computers, electronic writing pads or pen-input devices, pocket organizers, models with typewriter-style keypads, noisy or paper-tape calculators, and calculators that require a powercord. You should make sure your calculator has fresh batteries and remember that sharing of calculators is prohibited.

Answer every question. You are not penalized if you answer a question incorrectly. Try to use the guessing strategy even if you are truly stumped by a question, since there is still a possibility you will select the correct answer.

Work quickly and steadily. You will have only 35 to 60 minutes to work on each test, so avoid focusing on any one problem too long. Take our practice exams to help you learn to budget your precious time.

Learn the directions and format for each test. Familiarizing yourself with the directions and format of the different tests will not only save time, but will also help you avoid anxiety (and the mistakes caused by getting anxious).

Work the easier questions first. If you find yourself working too long on one question, make a mark next to it in your test booklet and come back to it. After you have answered all the questions that you can, go back to the ones you have skipped.

Be sure that the answer oval you are marking corresponds to the number of the question in the test booklet. Since the tests are graded by machine, marking one wrong answer can throw off your answer key and score. Be extremely careful.

Eliminate the obviously wrong answers. Sometimes an ACT question will have one or two answer choices that are a little odd. These answers will stick out as being wrong for one of several reasons: they may be impossible given the conditions of the problem, they may violate mathematical rules or principles, or they may be illogical. Being able to spot answers that are clearly wrong before you finish a problem gives you an advantage because you will be able to make a more educated guess from the remaining choices if you are unable to fully solve the problem.

Work from the answer choices. One of the ways you can use a multiple-choice format to your advantage is to work backwards from the answer choices to solve a problem. This is not a strategy you can use all of the time, but it can be helpful if you can just plug the choices into a given formula or equation. The answer choices can often narrow the scope of the responses. You may be able to make an educated guess based on eliminating choices that you know do not fit into the problem.

THE DAY OF THE EXAM

Before the Exam

On the day of the exam, you should wake up early and have a good breakfast. Make sure to dress comfortably, so that you are not distracted by being too hot or too cold while taking the tests. Also, plan to arrive at the test center early. This will allow you to collect your thoughts and relax before the exam, and will also spare you the anguish that comes with being late. As an added incentive to make sure you arrive early, keep in mind that no one will be allowed into the test session after the test has begun.

Before you leave for the test center, make sure that you have your admission ticket and another form of identification, which must contain a recent photograph, your name, and signature (i.e., passport, driver's license, recently published photo, or a letter of identification from your school with photo attached). Check with your guidance counselor or ACT, Inc., if you have any questions about proper identification, since you will not be allowed in the test center without it. You must also bring several sharpened No. 2 pencils with erasers, as none will be provided at the test center.

If you would like, wear a watch to the test center. However, you may not wear one that has an alarm, as it may disturb other test-takers. You also will not be allowed to wear a watch that has a built-in calculator. As we said, calculators *are* allowed for the math portion of the test, but consult the latest registration bulletin for restrictions. Other than your calculator, only your pencils and admission ticket will be permitted into the testing area. (No dictionaries, textbooks, notebooks, briefcases, or packages will be permitted and drinking, smoking, and eating are prohibited.)

During the Exam

Once in the test center, follow all of the rules and instructions given by the test supervisor. If you do not, you risk being dismissed from the test and having your ACT scores canceled. When all of the exam materials have been passed out, the test supervisor will give you directions for filling out your answer sheet. You must fill out this answer sheet carefully. Write your name exactly as it appears on your identification documents and admission ticket, unless otherwise instructed.

Remember that you can write in your test booklet, as no scratch paper will be provided. Mark your answers in the appropriate spaces on the answer sheet. Each numbered row will contain four or five ovals corresponding to each answer choice for that question. Fill in the oval which corresponds to your answer darkly, completely, and in a neat manner. You can change you answer, but remember to completely erase your old answer. Only one answer should be marked. As your answer sheet will be machine-scored, stray lines or marks may cause the machine to score your answers incorrectly.

After the Exam

Once your exam materials have been collected, you will be dismissed. Your score report should be mailed out in four to eight weeks.

ACT
ASSESSMENT

CHAPTER 2

Choosing a College: Advice from a High School Guidance Counselor

Chapter 2

HOW TO CHOOSE A COLLEGE

By Lina Miceli, M.A.

As a guidance counselor for a large suburban high school in Central New Jersey, Lina Miceli has helped countless students with one of life's biggest choices—selecting the right college.

As junior year comes to an end, and graduation is approaching, many students ask themselves, "Where do I go from here?" All students, especially those interested in furthering their education, will be faced with many questions, options, and decisions.

Selecting a college may not be the most important decision in your life, but it will have a big impact on your future. This process will be exciting, frustrating, confusing, and overwhelming, but once it is complete, you will have a great sense of satisfaction and relief.

To ensure that you end up with the "right" school, you must devote both time and energy to this process. It is best to begin your search in your junior year because this will provide the maximum amount of time to complete all of the steps.

Your biggest challenge in making this decision is to understand what is important to you and what you hope to accomplish in the future. The first step might be to think about your values, goals, dreams, expectations, and career plans. As you start your search, ask yourself these questions:

- ❒ "Why do I want to go to college?"

- ❒ "What are my career plans?"

- ❒ "Am I ready to handle a college program?"

- ❒ "Am I willing to work hard?"

- ❒ "Am I applying to college because my friends are?"

In answering these questions, did you determine that going to college is truly one of your goals? If so, you are ready to identify what you desire in a university or college. Let's explore some factors that will help you in your search.

HOW DO I FIND COLLEGE INFORMATION?

A valuable source of information is your high school guidance counselor and the counseling office. A guidance counselor can assist you in identifying your goals and strengths, and can direct you towards gaining further information. Guidance counselors are equipped to help you assess your chances of gaining admission to a particular school. A guidance counselor can also pass along information to you about schools from previous graduates.

College catalogs, videos, and handbooks are excellent sources of information. These resources are available in the high school guidance office as well as at in-school and public libraries. Once you know which Web sites are worth your time, the Internet is an invaluable tool in assisting your research. A brief list of informative sites is listed at the end of the chapter, with more at REA.com.

Also available are software programs that allow students to take inventories of their values, interest, abilities, and personality and match the results with a list of possible careers and colleges. These computer programs offer information about majors, cost, location, and admissions requirement that fit the description of the type of school you wish to attend.

Most colleges have their own Web sites that provide the most current information about their school. Many colleges offer either an electronic application, which you complete on-line, or the opportunity to download the application for completion.

There are other ways to obtain information about colleges. High schools often sponsor college fairs where admission counselors from colleges can meet with students. In addition, most colleges hold an "open house," providing an excellent opportunity for students to speak with alumni and those that presently attend the college. Also, virtual tours of colleges are available at www.campustours.com.

TYPES OF INSTITUTIONS

There are over 3,500 institutions of higher education throughout the U.S. Each has its own unique and distinctive features. Now, let's look at information that will help you determine which type of institution you want to explore.

A **college** offers instruction beyond high school; its programs satisfy the requirements for an associate, baccalaureate, or graduate degree. A **university** offers instruction beyond high school; its programs satisfy requirements for a baccalaureate and graduate levels. Universities also generally have several colleges and professional schools.

Private vs. Public

Private colleges and universities are either run by a board of trustees or are church affiliated. Some church-related schools have a strong affiliation that affects curriculum and regulations, while others are less stringent. Privately controlled institutions are usually more expensive, but have larger endowments and offer larger financial packages to overcome this difference.

Public colleges are usually controlled by a state, county, or municipality. These schools are publicly supported and, consequently, less expensive. Also, tuition is lower for in-state students than for out-of-state students.

Types of Colleges and Universities

Two-Year Colleges—These institutions offer an Associate degree. The aim of a two-year college is to provided preparation for students who want to transfer to a four-year college or university, or provide specialized training for a career in a specific field. Community colleges have open admission.

Liberal Arts Colleges provide students with a broad foundation in arts and sciences. Students at liberal arts colleges usually major in humanities, social sciences, natural sciences, or fine or performing arts. The degree offered is usually a Bachelor of Arts or a Bachelor of Science.

Technical Institutes are colleges that offer intensive training in engineering and other scientific fields. Some schools of technology coordinate their programs with liberal arts colleges.

Nursing Schools—There are several avenues that lead to preparation in nursing. Some hospitals offer three years of intensive training, leading to state certification as a Registered Nurse. Many junior or community colleges—in conjunction with local hospitals—offer a two-year nursing program, leading to an Associate of Science degree with R.N. state certification. Many colleges and universities offer a four-year program of liberal arts and nursing training, leading to a Bachelor of Science degree with R.N. state certification.

Service Academies are four-year colleges that offer a baccalaureate degree. Their primary purpose is to develop officers for the military. Admission is highly competitive. If you're interested in applying to the service academies, start planning with your guidance counselor in the spring of your junior year.

Career Schools—These are generally private, non-college professional schools that offer specialized training for specific careers such as photography, culinary arts, court reporting, and business. Other career schools offer technical programs such as computer technology, diesel, chemical, and electrical careers.

WHAT AM I LOOKING FOR IN A COLLEGE?

College Majors and Academic Strengths

What do you want to study? This question should guide you in your initial search for a college. Are you looking to enter a liberal arts program, or are you looking for a more specific program such as engineering or pharmacy? Obtain information from colleges that offer a major in this area. If you are not sure what college major you would like to pursue, collect information from any college you think you may want to attend. Look for colleges that offer programs that mesh with your interests.

It is also a good idea to keep in mind whether or not it will be a big problem to change your major. Statistics show that over two-thirds of students change their major; if you decide to do so, you'll want this process to be as easy as possible. This is especially important if you are not sure what major you would like to pursue.

If you are undecided about a major, an institution with a sound liberal arts program is a good choice. Most colleges do not require students to select a major until their junior year. If you are not sure now, you will have plenty of time to experiment and decide what you want to major in.

Do not assume that the harder a college is to get into, the better its quality. Colleges with higher admission standards usually have high academic standards, but many schools that are academically strong may appear more lenient on admissions in order to attract a diverse student body. You should select a college that will be academically challenging, but will also provide an environment in which you can achieve academic success.

You may also want to find out the number of students who go on to graduate school from a college or what the school's academic focus is. This information may be important should you choose to further your education.

Location

If you plan to live at school, you may want to look at schools within a five hundred mile radius from your home. This will ensure that travel cost and time allowance will not inhibit you from coming home, but will eliminate the temptation to return home often.

You should also take the location of the college into consideration. Is the college in a city, suburban area, or rural area? You should choose a location where you feel at ease, because the school's location may play an important role in your college experience. There are excellent colleges in all parts of the country, but you need to find one where you will feel most comfortable and will provide you with the best setting to get an education.

Size

The size of the prospective institution should be considered carefully. Smaller colleges tend to be centered more upon the student as an individual. Because of their size, these types of colleges can often provide the opportunity for closer relations with faculty and professors and can offer a sense of community and belonging.

Larger schools tend to have a wider focus and diversity of programs, activities, faculty, and social opportunities. Classes at these schools tend to be larger and often held in lecture halls.

You need to decide where you think you can get the best experience. Would you feel more comfortable in a small, medium, or large school? Think about it and keep this factor in mind when deciding where you would like to attend college.

Faculty

Quite often the college catalog proves to be the most informative listing of faculty members and their backgrounds. You should examine this list to see what types of degrees most of the professors have obtained and the amount of experience they have. Also, you might want to find out the ratio of faculty to undergraduate students, the percentage of time devoted to undergraduate teaching and advising, and if the professors make themselves readily available to assist students through seminars, after-class meetings, and office hours.

Cost

In estimating the cost of attending college you should take into account tuition, room and board, additional fees, books, traveling expenses, and personal needs. Just because a school is expensive does not mean it is good; strong colleges exist at all levels of price.

You should place more emphasis on a college's curriculum than its cost. Loans, scholarships, and financial aid are available, and colleges often offer a variety of alternative financing resources. One example of this is cooperative education, which allows students to alternate semesters of work and school.

A high quality education does not have to be expensive. Attending a community college for a year or two may help reduce tuition expenses and still provide a good education. If you are planning on taking this route, however, it is a good idea to make sure that your credits will transfer to your next school.

Do not let the cost of a college discourage you from applying!

Social Life

Surprisingly, the same number of students transfer out of a college because of its social atmosphere as do students who transfer for academic reasons. It is important to locate a school which seems to have a personality comparable to your own. Select a school where you think you will feel comfortable for four years.

Look into whether or not the majority of students go home on the weekend, and if so, are there activities planned on the weekend that might interest you.

Other things to consider are the rules and regulations governing campus and dormitory life, and the influence of fraternities and sororities on campus. Also, find out if the school provides for the fulfillment of religious obligations.

WHAT DO COLLEGES LOOK FOR?

Knowing the criteria used for college selection may help you in your planning. Colleges will base their decision, in part, on the following information:

- **Your high school record:** This includes your grades as well as the courses you have taken in grades nine through twelve. The recommended guideline is as follows:

→ 4 years of English

→ 3 years of social studies

→ 3 or 4 years of mathematics

→ 2 or 3 years of science

→ 2 or 3 years of a foreign language

Your high school program helps admission officers determine your level of motivation, and shows if you have taken a challenging curriculum. Since entrance requirements vary among colleges, it is best to take the strongest academic program possible, especially if you seek admission to a highly selective college.

- **Class rank:** This is a comparison of your grade point average to that of every other student in your class.

- **Entrance examinations:** An example of an entrance exam is the ACT. Acceptable scoring ranges will vary from school to school. The scores on these tests add another dimension to your high school record.

- **Extracurricular activities:** These include hobbies, community group involvement, sports, and clubs. Colleges are interested more in the quality and depth of your involvement than in the quantity.

- **Recommendations:** These can come from counselors, teachers, employers, or people who know you very well and can write about your special traits and abilities.

- **Essay or personal statement:** This portion of the admission application allows you to express yourself and explain your goals. The essay provides information that does not appear in grades or test scores. It can reveal many things about you which can help an admissions officer determine if you are right for their college.

The college essay is an opportunity to express your viewpoint, to be creative, and to demonstrate your writing ability. Your essay can provide the admission officer with insight into how well you think, write, and who you are.

VISITING COLLEGES

Should you visit a college campus before applying for admission?

Yes!

Although catalogs and brochures introduce you to a college, there is nothing like the experience of seeing it for yourself. A visit to your college choices can be enjoyable and worthwhile. Write to or call the college for an appointment and try to visit on a day when regular classes are in session, as this will give you a realistic picture of the campus. Allow plenty of time for your visit and try to arrange to visit a class and eat at the dining hall if possible.

Before you visit, study the school's literature and write down questions you may have about it. During your visit, don't ask questions that can be answered by reading the catalog.

Try to talk to some students, not just your assigned tour guide. Find out if you can speak with a student or faculty member in a field in which you are interested. Gather as much information as possible and don't be afraid to ask questions. This is an important decision and the more informed you are, the better equipped you will be to make your decision.

Here's a list of questions you should consider regarding the facilities and services the campus may have:

- Are academic, financial, personal, and career counseling available?

- What health services are available to students?

- Are tutorial and writing labs available for students?

- Is there Internet access throughout the academic and residential centers?

- Are the science labs equipped with the latest science and technology equipment?

- How extensive are the library's resources, including professionally trained staff to help students with their research?

- What athletic facilities are offered for men and women?

- What intercollegiate and intramural sports are offered?

- What are the quality, nature, and availability residential housing?

- How are roommates selected?

- Is housing guaranteed for all four years?

- What services are available for career development and job placement?

Look at the campus facilities, walk through as many buildings as you can, and take a tour of the library, dorms, and student centers. You should consider the location of the school. Can it be reached by public transportation? Will traveling to and from school be a problem?

When talking to the students at the college, you should ask how demanding the academic environment is, and also inquire about the social life and contact with faculty and staff. Find out how many first-year students usually return for the next year.

You should pick up an application, scholarship material, and financial aid information. If you do a thorough job, your campus visit can be vital in telling you if this college seems right for you.

After your visit, you should jot down some notes to yourself about the school; use them when evaluating other schools.

The Interview

Although most colleges still grant interviews, very few require them and many do not consider them in their admission decision. All of the applicants cannot be interviewed, so most colleges have done away with using them to avoid giving an unfair advantage. Even so, you may want to request an interview if you feel that your application does not convey your real strengths and personality, or if you need to explain some personal information that might have affected your scholastic record.

If you wish to be interviewed, you should contact the school and request an appointment. On the day of your interview, be sure to arrive on time and dress neatly and appropriately. Make a list of specific questions you would like to ask, and be prepared to answer some questions about yourself. You should answer all questions completely and honestly. Interviewers often know when someone is exaggerating the truth in an attempt to impress them. You will probably be nervous, but try to relax.

ATHLETICS

No matter how or where you are going to compete in college, you have to start planning your path while you are in high school.

When you hear about NCAA athletics, the references are to Division I athletics and the schools that generally captivate the media. The NCAA is the major governing body of collegiate athletics. This means that you need to learn its rules and live by them.

Most colleges belong to the NCAA in Division I, II, or III. If you are not being actively recruited or contacted by a certain institution, there are ways you can market and promote yourself to let coaches know that you are interested in competing at their schools.

You need to identify your needs and desires and match them first of all with the academic program and then with the athletic program. You need to base your decision on a combination of both factors.

Learning to market yourself as an athlete is essential. For each school you are considering, ask yourself whether you would be happy at that school if, say, you were injured and could no longer play sports.

The NCAA's requirements change every two years or so; it's important to find out how the current eligibility requirements apply to you. Be sure to check the NCAA's Web site, www.ncaa.org, for the latest eligibility requirements.

Your high school coach can serve as a great resource for college coaches to find out about your training habits, goals, and ability to fit in their program successfully.

The NCAA is known as the governing body of college sports. They are responsible for all sorts of issues such as recruiting, financial aid, scholarships, and academic standards.

Division I and II Requirements

- Graduation from high school

- Successful completion of a required course curriculum consisting of a minimum number of courses in specified subjects

- Specific minimum SAT or ACT scores

Other Athletic Governing Associations

- National Association of Intercollegiate Athletes (NAIA), www.naia.org

- National Junior College Athletic Association (NJCAA), www.njcaa.org

- NCAA Initial-Eligibility Clearinghouse

If you are planning to enroll in college as a freshman and want to play on a Division I or Division II team, the NCAA Initial-Eligibility Clearinghouse must certify you before you can play. It is your responsibility to make sure the Clearinghouse has everything it needs to certify you, such as the student release form, an application fee, an official high school transcript, and SAT or ACT score reports.

Marketing Yourself

Be honest with yourself about your abilities both academically and athletically. Take a close look at your strengths and weaknesses and how they pertain to playing sports in college. Talk to your high school coach and find out what s/he thinks of your potential.

Over the summer between your junior and senior year, send letters to the coaches of teams for which you are interested in playing. Include a packet and make sure you list your upcoming competitions so they know where and when to look for you in action. Send updates during the year to every coach who has indicated interest in you. Ask your high school coach to call the college coaches on your behalf. Send a videotape of your performances.

Your athletic packet should include information about yourself and your athletic achievements, GPA, SAT/ACT and other standardized test scores, high school transcript, school profile, and a list of relevant references (e.g., coaches, teachers, members of the community). Include their phone numbers and addresses, but remember to ask their permission to use them as references.

Also, include your schedule and your athletic resume.

HOW TO APPLY

After you have made a list of colleges that you feel are right for you, narrow down the list and carefully include one or two colleges for which your scholastic record indicates that you have an excellent chance for admission. Your final choices, probably no more than five colleges, should be schools that you believe you will be happy attending.

Many colleges give students the option of applying on-line or completing a hard copy application. The Common Application is a single application for undergraduate college admission used by a consortium of selective colleges and universities. There are currently 240 member colleges and universities who accept it. You can find the member list on the Common Application Web site, www.commonapp.org.

Whatever you choose, do so early in your senior year. Allow yourself plenty of time to complete the application. Be sure to tell your counselor which schools you are applying to and request your transcript to be sent to those colleges.

Here are some hints for applying to a college:

- Read the application thoroughly before completing it.

- Make a copy of your application and complete a rough draft. When you fill out the actual application, be neat—type it if you can.

- Answer all of the questions accurately and get help from your counselor if you are not sure how to answer a question.

- If an essay is required, make a rough copy before putting it on the application.

- Follow the guidelines given on the application for the essay. Try to be brief but fully answer the question.

- Be sure to check your essay for correct spelling, grammar, punctuation, and clarity.

- Review your completed application with your counselor. Your high school transcript will be sent to colleges you apply to also, so if you have any questions about it or what it includes, you should ask your counselor.

- Be sure to give your counselor the application well before the deadline so that all of the necessary forms can be completed and mailed to the college.

- Your school record can be sent with your application or it can be mailed separately.

After You Apply

Each college you apply to will send you a letter indicating that you have been accepted, denied admission, or put on the waiting list.

Early decision candidates will usually be notified in December. If you are not accepted during the early decision period, your application will be reconsidered for admission later in the school year. Once you have been accepted to a school and have made a decision to attend, you should withdraw any applications filed at other schools.

If you have been accepted, most colleges require a tuition deposit for enrollment. This fee must be submitted by the candidate's reply date, usually May 1, to secure your place in the entering class. Most acceptances are contingent upon satisfactory completion of senior year course work. Acceptances have been revoked due to failure to maintain academic standards during the remainder of the senior year, so don't slack off.

You may find that you have been put on a waiting list. If so, find out exactly what that means at that particular school. Do not count on being accepted at a school that has wait-listed you. You should try and hold your place at a school where you have been accepted to guarantee a place for you come September.

If you have been denied admission to all the schools to which you have applied, see your guidance counselor. You may still be able to apply at other schools that can meet your educational needs. Do not give up!

When it comes to making your final decision, your best choice is to go with the school that feels most comfortable to you. Be sure to let your guidance counselor know which school you are planning to attend so that your final school records can be sent to your new school.

Good luck!

Visit REA.com for a handy pre-college calendar and checklist, and a bevy of Web sites to help you with your college plans. Below you'll find some top picks from this section's author, Lina Miceli, M.A.

FastWeb College Search	www.fastweb.com
Yahoo College Directory	www.dir.yahoo.com/Education/Higher
Campus Tours	www.campustours.com
College Source	www.collegesource.org
Common Application	www.commonapp.org
ECollegeApps	www.ecollegeaps.com
Wired Scholar	www.wiredscholar.com
GoCollege	www.gocollege.com

CHAPTER 3

A Diagnostic
Exam

Chapter 3

A DIAGNOSTIC EXAM

Now that you have some background information concerning the ACT Assessment, you are ready to take the diagnostic exam. This exam is designed to help you identify where your strengths and weaknesses lie. You will want to use this information to help you study for the ACT. It is a complete exam, so take this diagnostic exam in the same way you would take the actual ACT. Situate yourself in a quiet room so there will be no interruptions, and keep track of the time allotted for each test. When you are finished with the exam, refer to the charts that follow to evaluate your performance. The entries in each chart refer to the questions you answered incorrectly, and will direct you to the pages in this book that discuss the material covered in that type of problem.

ACT ASSESSMENT DIAGNOSTIC EXAM

(An answer sheet for this test appears in the back of this book.)

Test 1: English

Time: 45 Minutes
75 Questions

DIRECTIONS: This test consists of five passages. In each passage, certain words and phrases have been underlined and numbered. The questions on each passage consist of alternatives for these underlined segments. Choose the alternative that follows standard written English, most accurately reflects the style and tone of the passage, or best relays the idea of the passage. Choose "NO CHANGE," if no change is necessary.

In addition, you will also encounter questions about part of the passage, or the passage as a whole. These questions are indicated by a number in a box at the end of the section, rather than an underlined portion.

Once you have selected the best answer, fill in the appropriate oval on the answer sheet for the correct choice.

Passage I

[1]

One can usually see undisturbed territory for about twelve miles. <u>Standing</u> on the fire tower on Bear Swamp Hill, located in Washington
₁
<u>Township; Burlington County, New Jersey.</u> <u>Primarily you sees</u> pines and oaks.
₂ ₃
Here and there <u>stands long, dark</u> patches of Atlantic white cedars, tall and close
₄
to each other. <u>Looking eastward,</u> a similar view of miles of dwarf trees, forests in
₅

which a person can stand and be seen above tree tops for miles. To the west, one can see Apple Pie Hill; to the south, the view is disturbed by a lake and a cranberry bog.

[2]

6 And so it is that this area called the Pine Barrens, is so beautiful yet so
                                    7
different from the transportation corridor situated beside it. One finds along this corridor the sounds of industry as well as smells to make one's hair stand on end,
                                                            8
both signs of progress. One day we'll find one continuous city that stretches from Boston to Richmond; this section of that urban area has already been filled in along this route.

[3]

Needless to say, the Pine Barrens covers about 650,000 acres, making it
            9
really the size of Yosemite. New Jersey has a population of about a thousand people per square mile, no other state in the Union has so great
                        10
a density. However, in the central Pine Barrens the land carries about fifteen people per square mile. These fifteen people usually congregate in tiny small
                                                                    11
forest towns so that in a single particular area of more than 100,000 acres, one
    11
will find twenty-one people.

[4]

Today the Pine Barrens is not nearly so large as the original wilderness area
                            12
that it once was. Indeed, the signs of civilization are moving into the area so that a person may be in the Pine Barrens but still find that a metropolis is quite close by.
                                                        13

In fact, on a clear night a person standing atop the Empire State <u>Building in New York City could</u> see a light in the middle of the Pine Barrens. And if a person
₁₄

drew on a map a straight line from Boston to <u>Richmond; the epicenter</u> of this
₁₅

sprawling megalopolis <u>fallen</u> in the northern part of these very woods, some
₁₆

twenty miles from Bear Swamp Hill.

1.   A. NO CHANGE   C. miles standing

     B. miles. While standing   D. miles; while standing

2.   F. NO CHANGE

     G. Township; Burlington County New Jersey.

     H. Township, Burlington county, New Jersey.

     J. Township, Burlington County, New Jersey.

3.   A. NO CHANGE   C. Primarily the visitor sees

     B. Primarily we see   D. Primarily you see

4.   F. NO CHANGE   H. stands long dark

     G. stand long dark   J. stand long, dark

5.   A. NO CHANGE

     B. Looking eastward, one perceives

     C. Looking eastward one perceive

     D. Looking eastward from the tower,

6.   Which of the following sentences makes the best introduction to Paragraph 2 and the best transition from Paragraph 1?

     F. NO CHANGE

     G. Twentieth century transportation problems permeate all of the state.

     H. Cranberry bogs are, indeed, a sweet surprise for the unsuspecting visitor.

     J. Certainly, industry is a consideration for this busy east coast state.

7. A. NO CHANGE
   B. called the Pine Barrens is
   C. , called the Pine Barrens is
   D. called by the name of Pine Barrens

8. F. NO CHANGE
   G. its visions of urban destruction
   H. the affected air of its smokestacks
   J. the smells of industry

9. A. NO CHANGE
   B. Therefore, the Pine Barrens
   C. On the contrary, the Pine Barrens
   D. Surprisingly, the Pine Barrens

10. F. NO CHANGE   H. mile; and yet, no other
    G. mile; no other   J. mile; while no other

11. A. NO CHANGE
    B. small forest towns
    C. unbelievably tiny small forest towns
    D. tiny, small forest towns

12. F. NO CHANGE   H. not nearly so large when
    G. not nearly larger if   J. no more larger then

13. A. NO CHANGE
    B. still be close to a metropolis.
    C. may still find a metropolis quite close by.
    D. still a metropolis may be very close in proximity.

14. F. NO CHANGE
    G. Building, in New York City could
    H. Building in New York City, could
    J. Building in New York City could,

15. A. NO CHANGE
    B. Richmond; however, the epicenter
    C. Richmond, the epicenter
    D. Richmond. The epicenter

16. F. NO CHANGE   H. falling
    G. fell   J. would fall

Passage II

[1]

[1] The bicycle, with a history that spans nearly two <u>centuries, has</u> fre-
17
quently looked upon in the United States as a <u>childs plaything</u>. [2] During the late
18
nineteenth century, the cycle's greatest <u>use were</u> likewise among adults, and this
19
use sparked the early good-roads movement. [3] Of equal importance was the
role of the bicycle in demonstrating the possibilities of independent personal
transportation, thus creating a demand that facilitated the introduction of the
automobile. [4] In a natural progression, children seem to move directly from the
crawling to the toddling to the walking to the bicycling stage. [5] Despite having
but two wheels, this early bicycle truly was the inspiration for today's motor
vehicles and superhighways. ☐ 20

[2]

The first known bicycle was shown by the <u>Comte de Sivrac whom</u> in 1791
21
was seen riding a two-wheel "wooden horse" in the gardens of the Palais Royal
in Paris. Called a "celerifere," the machine had two rigidly mounted <u>wheels. So</u>
22
that it was incapable of being steered. To <u>change direction, reverse, or go the</u>
23
<u>other way, it</u> was necessary to lift, drag, or jump the front wheel to one side. In
23

1793 the name was changed to <u>velocifere, and, as</u> these machines became in-
24
creasingly popular among the sporting set of Paris, clubs were formed, and races
were run along the Champs Elysses.

[3]

A revolutionary improvement in the "velocifere" occurred in
<u>1817. When</u> Charles, Baron von Drais, of Saurerbrun, devised a front wheel
25
capable of being steered. As chief forester for the Grand Duke of <u>Baden; von</u>
26
Drais found the machine useful in traversing the forest land under his supervision. He also <u>has given it</u> a padded saddle and an armrest in front of his body,
27
which assisted him in exerting force against the ground. Granted a patent in
1818, he took his "Draisienne" to Paris, where it was again patented and acquired
the name of "velocipede," a term that was to continue in use until about 1869
when the word "bicycle" came into use.

[4]

The velocipede gained rapid popularity in France and almost immediately
migrated to <u>England. Where</u> it was known variously as a Draisene, Swiftwalker,
28
Hobby Horse, Dandy Horse, or Pedestrian Curricle. Riding academies were
<u>established, with the concept of teaching</u> the fine points of balance and manage-
29
ment, and soon many riders were seen in the streets and parks about London<u>; yet it</u>
30
declined almost as rapidly as it had risen, and after the early 1820s velocipedes
were rarely seen.

17. A. NO CHANGE   C. centuries has been

    B. centuries has   D. centuries, has been

18. F. NO CHANGE
    G. childrens plaything
    H. child's plaything
    J. childs' plaything

19. A. NO CHANGE
    B. use was
    C. use are
    D. uses are

20. For the sake of unity and clarity, Sentence 4 should be
    F. placed where it is now.
    G. placed after Sentence 1.
    H. placed before Sentence 3.
    J. placed after Sentence 5.

21. A. NO CHANGE
    B. Comte de Sivrac, whom
    C. Comte de Sivrac who's
    D. Comte de Sivrac, who

22. F. NO CHANGE
    G. wheels so
    H. wheels
    J. wheels; so

23. A. NO CHANGE
    B. change direction, one would find that it
    C. change direction one would find that it
    D. change direction, it

24. F. NO CHANGE
    G. velocifere and, as
    H. velocifere and as
    J. velocifere; and, as

25. A. NO CHANGE
    B. 1817 when
    C. 1817; when
    D. 1817, however,

26. F. NO CHANGE
    G. Baden von Drais
    H. Baden, von Drais
    J. Baden von Drais,

27. A. NO CHANGE
    B. had given them
    C. gave it
    D. would have given it

28. F. NO CHANGE
    G. England where,
    H. England; where
    J. England, where

29. A.   NO CHANGE

     B.   established to teach

     C.   established in order to teach

     D.   established, to instruct in the art of teaching

30. F.   NO CHANGE   H.   ; yet, it

     G.   , yet, the pastime   J.   ; yet, the pastime

Items 31 and 32 pose questions about Passage II as a whole.

---

31. As a publisher assembling essays for a textbook, you would most logically place this article in the section containing essays on:

     A.   French nobility's rise to power.

     B.   hobbies in the early twentieth century.

     C.   inventions in sports equipment.

     D.   garden paths in continental Europe.

32. Which of the following sentences added to the end of Paragraph 4 would best relate to Paragraph 1, thus unifying the essay as a whole?

     F.   However, the process of improving and popularizing the bicycle in Europe was exhilarating, albeit disappointing, in its early demise.

     G.   Nevertheless, the velocipede would not be just a pastime forgotten, but an inspiration to those would-be inventors eager to make their mark on society.

     H.   But even with the velocipede's decline in popularity, its cousin, the American bicycle, rapidly rose in public use and adoration, thus giving Americans the taste for truly independent transportation.

     J.   There is no clear evidence that these velocipedes really gained popularity when American entrepreneurs imported them into the United States in early 1819.

Passage III

[1]

Three simple questions can sum up three areas that mystified the great Albert Einstein in his lifetime: what is space, what is time, what is gravity.

Since Einstein discovered unsuspected connections among these questions. One
    33
of those concerned a common part of everyday life for everyone on the face of
      34
the Earth: gravity. Even today Einstein's theory of gravity remains the

profoundest of concepts where logic in natural philosophy is concerned. In fact,

gravity itself is one of science's more intriguing puzzlements.

[2]

Gravity is unique in that it possesses traits that other natural forces don't

have. Gravity cannot be turned off or on as, say, our electricity can. We can

control the path of an electrical current with switches. In fact, gravity abnegates

its effects to no force, passing through absolutely anything and everything. No

force on Earth opposes it. ⟨35⟩

[3]

Since gravity always exists on Earth, and exists unaffected, we

usually pays no mind to it. Even so, it touches our lives in every way. We might
      36
of even thought of our relationship with gravity as a daily competition. We
    37
manage to triumph over it each time a baby lifts its head or takes a step. We win

when we ride a bike, or throw a football. But gravity wins when we fall down
          38
steps, slide down a snow bank, or plunge over the side of a pool.

[4]

Gravity forms a never ending cycle. The cycle begins as we rise each
              39
morning and feel an insurmountable pull as we strive to get rolling on a new day.

We'll spend time climbing stairs, moving equipment, rising and lowering things.
                                                   40

As we do, the blood in <u>one's</u> veins works against gravity as it moves upward
41

through our bodies. This battle occurs each day of our lives until finally we

<u>die and</u> give in to the gravity in the grave.
42

[5]

Gravity works not only in our lives but in the natural processes in the world

around us. It provides the <u>adhesives that holds</u> our globe together. It propels
43

streams and rivers while pulling water from the sky and leaves from trees. It

shapes the stars and galaxies, the planets' orbits, the expanding universe itself.

33. A. NO CHANGE   C. Inasmuch as Einstein

     B. However, Einstein   D. Therefore, Einstein

34. F. NO CHANGE

     G. of these concerned

     H. of those connections concerned

     J. OMIT the underlined portion.

35. Which of the following sentences would most logically support Paragraph 2's assertion that "Gravity is unique in that it possesses traits that other natural forces don't have"?

     A. Unlike magnetism, which can be shielded with a surface between the magnet and the object it attracts, gravity is undisturbed by intervening objects.

     B. The specific gravity varies from that which we experience here on Earth to that, say, the astronauts felt on the moon, as films of Neil Armstrong and his first walk on the moon will attest.

     C. The theory of gravity was discovered by Sir Isaac Newton.

     D. It is gravity which forms an integral and definitive part of our every-day existence.

36. F. NO CHANGE

     G. , usually pay no mind

    H.   usually pay no attention

    J.   never give it a second thought

37. A.   NO CHANGE   C.   even think

      B.   even of thought   D.   have even thought

38. F.   NO CHANGE   H.   bike; or

      G.   bike or   J.   bike or,

39. Which of the suggested sentences makes the best introduction to Paragraph 4 and the best transition from Paragraph 3?

    A.   NO CHANGE

    B.   We encounter gravity's unique qualities throughout the solar system.

    C.   These contests with gravity form a never-ending cycle in our personal routines.

    D.   Nevertheless, Einstein's discovery has had amazing repercussions in our modern workaday world.

40 F.   NO CHANGE   H.   raising

      G.   in rising   J.   raise

41. A.   NO CHANGE   C.   our

      B.   ones   D.   everyones'

42. F.   NO CHANGE   H.   die; and

      G.   die, and   J.   die; and thus

43. A.   NO CHANGE   C.   adhesive that hold

      B.   adhesive that holds   D.   adhesive that has been holding

---

Items 44–46 pose questions about Passage III as a whole.

---

44. If the writer wanted to strengthen the passage by incorporating new material on gravity's effects on the human physique, it would be most logical to place this new data:

    F.   in Paragraph 1 because this first paragraph must mention all vital information to follow in an essay.

G. in Paragraph 2's place since that paragraph is unimportant in that it notes we forget gravity even exists.

H. following Paragraph 4 because it dealt with gravity's effects on our human routines and could easily lead to human anatomy.

J. after Paragraph 5 because ending with the human body gives the essay a link back to the first paragraph and thus creates cohesiveness.

45. Which of the following sentences, if added to the end of Paragraph 5, would best relate Paragraph 5 to Paragraph 1 in order to tie together the passage as a whole?

A. Gravity is particularly evident in the orbital pattern of Jupiter.

B. As a shaper of stars and galaxies, gravity's impact is immense.

C. This mystery of gravity, vast as the universe, still serves to intrigue and puzzle humankind.

D. Albert Einstein is known worldwide as one of the most gifted, original thinkers of our time.

46. The writer wants to support the assertion in Paragraph 1 that gravity remains the profoundest of concepts where logic in natural philosophy is concerned. Which of the following strategies would best accomplish that goal?

F. Citing several mysteries of the process of gravity

G. Explaining how the study of philosophy originated

H. Explaining why we as human beings should be concerned about gravity

J. Comparing less profound concepts of logic and natural philosophy to that of gravity

Passage IV

[1]

A submarine was first used as an offensive weapon during the Revolutionary War. The Turtle, which was a one-man submersible was designed by an
47
American inventor named David Bushness and hand-operated by a screw propeller. It attempted to sink a British man-of-war the H.M.S. *Eagle,* in New York
48

Harbor. <u>Since</u> the attack was unsuccessful, it caused the British to move their
49
blockading ships from the harbor to the outer bay, <u>out of harm's way.</u>
50

[2]

The submarine first became a major component in naval warfare during World War <u>I; when</u> Germany demonstrated <u>it's</u> full potential. Wholesale sinking
51   52
of Allied ships by the <u>German. U-boats</u> almost swung the war in favor of the
53
Central Powers. Then, as now, the submarine's greatest advantage was that it could operate beneath the ocean surface where detection was difficult. Sinking a submarine was comparatively easy, once it was found—but finding it before it could attack was another matter.

[3]

During the closing months of World War I, England and the United States formed the Allied Submarine Devices Investigation Committee<u>, whom was</u> to
54
obtain from science and technology <u>real</u> effective underwater detection equip-
55
ment. The committee developed a trainable hydrophone<u>, a reasonably</u> accurate
56
device for locating a submerged submarine. Attached to the bottom of the ASN ship, it was used to detect screw noises and other sounds that came from a submarine. Although the committee disbanded after World War I, the British made improvements on the locating device during the interval between then and World War II and named it ASDIC after the committee. American scientists further improved on the device, calling it SONAR, a name derived from the bold-faced initials of the words **so**und **na**vigation and **r**anging. Consequently, the U.S.-made submarines could detect <u>additional</u> submerged subs than the Axis
57
forces.

[4]

[1] At the end of World War II, the United States improved the snorkel (a device for bringing air to the crew and engines when operating submerged on diesels) and developed the Guppy (short for greater underwater propulsion power), a conversion of the fleet-type submarine of World War II fame. [2] Performance increased greatly with the improved electrical <u>equipment, additional</u>
58
battery capacity and <u>the fact of the extra addition of the snorkel</u>, making the
59
submarine a truly formidable craft. [3] The superstructure was changed by reducing the surface area, streamlining every protruding object, and enclosing the periscope shears in a streamlined metal fairing. | 60 |

47. A. NO CHANGE
     B. Turtle which was a one-man submersible
     C. Turtle, which was a one-man submersible,
     D. Turtle which was a one-man submersible,

48. F. NO CHANGE   H. war, the HMS *Eagle*
     G. war, the HMS *Eagle*, J. war, the HMS *Eagle*—

49. A. NO CHANGE   C. Because
     B. Although   D. Inasmuch as

50. F. NO CHANGE
     G. without a doubt out of harm's way.
     H. completely out of harm's way.
     J. out of danger.

51. A. NO CHANGE   C. I. When
     B. I; just when   D. , when

52. F. NO CHANGE   H. its
     G. its'   J. there

53. A. NO CHANGE   C. Germans U-boats
     B. German U-boats   D. Germans; U-boats

54. F. NO CHANGE   H. , which was
     G. , who was   J. who was

55. A. NO CHANGE   C. less
     B. more   D. least

56. F. NO CHANGE   H. , which was a reasonably
     G. ; a reasonably   J. a reasonably

57. A. NO CHANGE   C. repeated
     B. extended   D. more

58. F. NO CHANGE   H. equipment additional
     G. equipment; additional   J. equipment, additional,

59. A. NO CHANGE

     B. the modified snorkel,

     C. the snorkel, a modified and redesigned attachment

     D. the redesigned snorkel which they had revised,

60. For the sake of unity and coherence, Sentence 2 should be placed

     F. where it is now.   H. at the beginning of Paragraph 4.

     G. after Sentence 3.   J. at the end of Paragraph 3.

Item 61 poses a question about Passage IV as a whole.

---

61. Suppose the writer wanted to add the following sentences to the passage:

> The plan was to attach a charge of gun powder to the ship's bottom with screws and explode it with a time fuse. After repeated failures, the submarine gave up and withdrew, exploding its powder a short distance from the British ironclad.

The new sentences would most logically be placed in which of the following paragraphs?

A. Paragraph 1, because that is where a specific unsuccessful submarine attack of an ironclad is mentioned.

B. Paragraph 2, because the sinking of Allied ships is discussed here.

C. A separate paragraph following Paragraph 2, because important new material must be placed alone so it stands out.

D. Paragraph 4, because it is best to end an essay with a strong visual image.

Passage V

[1]

Cacti and other succulent plants originate in <u>areas, where</u> water is only
62
occasionally available and are, therefore, conditioned to deal with long periods of drought. They <u>give evidence of incorporating a variety of structural modifica-</u>
63
<u>tions and adjustments which enable</u> them to store moisture for use in times of
63
scarcity.

[2]

Such adaptations may be similar in both succulents and <u>cacti. Cacti are a</u>
64
<u>subspecies of succulents.</u> Storage areas include thickened leaves, stems, and
64
corms. Leaves which transpire precious moisture may be eliminated altogether, or the moisture in the leaves may be protected from evaporation by a leathery <u>surface, wiry or velvety hairs, thick spines, or a powdery coating.</u> The very shape
65
of many succulents <u>provide</u> the same protection; globular and columnar forms
66
offer the least exposed area to the drying effects of the sun and wind.

[3]

<u>The areole, a feature that is possessed by cacti alone, consists</u> of cushion-
67
like modifications on the body of the cactus from which <u>arises</u> spines, hairs (and
68

the barbed hairs or spines of "Opuntia"), flowers, fruit, and often new growth. The flowers of the cacti <u>usually stick out like a sore thumb</u> and most often appear
69
from areoles near the tip of the plant. In other succulents they are inclined to be less showy and more likely to emerge from between the leaves or from the base.

[4]

Many times there are "look-alikes" in the two groups. Certain cacti coming from the New World closely resemble counterparts in the Euphorbias of Africa. <u>The cost of a trip to Madagascar can be rather reasonable or astronomical.</u> How
70
do we then differentiate between cacti and other succulents? It is not always <u>easy. Because</u> the presence or absence of leaves can be helpful, as can the size
71
and brilliance of flowers, the real test comes by learning to recognize the areole.

[5]

In addition, with a very minor possible exception (a form of Rhipsalis), all cacti are native to the Western Hemisphere. It is sometimes hard to believe this because of the vast areas of escaped cactus in many parts of the world today. The majority of other succulents (excluding Agave, Echeveria, Sedum, Sempervivum, and a few others) <u>are being</u> indigenous to Africa and a few scattered areas in the
72
Eastern Hemisphere.

[6]

Both cacti and other succulents are excellent subjects for the outdoor garden, greenhouse, or windowsill. They require a minimum of <u>care. Provided that</u>
73
they have a requisite amount of sunlight and that their condition of hardiness is respected.

62. F. NO CHANGE
    G. lands, where
    H. a variety of areas in which
    J. areas where

63. A. NO CHANGE
    B. possess structural modifications, and adjustments which enables
    C. possess structural modifications enabling
    D. give evidence of incorporating a variety of structural modifications, which enable

64. F. NO CHANGE
    G. cacti, a succulent subspecies.
    H. cacti, in that all cacti are succulents, but not all succulents are cacti.
    J. cacti the latter of which is a subspecies of the former.

65. A. NO CHANGE
    B. surface or covered with wiry or velvety hairs, thick spines, or even with a powdery coating.
    C. surface: wiry or velvety hairs; thick spines, or a powdery coating.
    D. surface; wiry or velvety hairs, thick spines, or even a powdery coat.

66. F. NO CHANGE
    G. has provided
    H. is providing
    J. provides

67. A. NO CHANGE
    B. The areole which is possessed solely by the cactus alone consists
    C. Possessed by cacti alone, the areole consists
    D. Possessed by the areole alone the cacti consists

68. F. NO CHANGE
    G. arise
    H. has arisen
    J. arose

69. A. NO CHANGE
    B. are usually more conspicuous
    C. are usually scarce as hens' teeth
    D. usually stick out, like a sore thumb,

70. F.   NO CHANGE

    G.   The cost of a trip to Madagascar can be rather reasonable, or astronomical.

    H.   It is quite an expensive undertaking to visit Africa.

    J.   OMIT the underlined portion.

71. A.   NO CHANGE   C.   easy. Although

    B.   easy; nevertheless   D.   easy although

72. F.   NO CHANGE   H.   will have been

    G.   are   J.   having been

73. A.   NO CHANGE   C.   care, provided, that

    B.   care, provided that   D.   care provided, that

Items 74 and 75 pose questions about Passage V as a whole.

---

74. For the sake of unity and coherence, Paragraph 3 should be placed:

    F.   where it is now.   H.   after Paragraph 4.

    G.   after Paragraph 1.   J.   after Paragraph 5.

75. In discussing succulents and cacti, the writer is:

    A.   arguing the advantage of owning cacti rather than succulents.

    B.   revealing the evolutionary process of succulent development.

    C.   comparing and contrasting succulents and cacti.

    D.   contrasting cacti and succulents to indigenous North American flora.

THIS IS THE END OF TEST 1.

Test 2: Mathematics

Time: 60 Minutes
60 Questions

DIRECTIONS: Solve the following problems, and fill in the appropriate ovals on your answer sheet.

Unless otherwise indicated:

1. Figures may not have been drawn to scale.
2. All geometric figures lie in a plane.
3. "Line" refers to a straight line.
4. "Average" refers to arithmetic mean.

---

1. The following $A = \dfrac{\pi \times \sqrt{2} \times 2.17}{6.83^2 + 1.07^2}$ is approximately

   A. 0.2.   D. 3.0.

   B. 1.0.   E. 8.0.

   C. 11.5.

2. If one root of $x^2 - ax + 12 = 0$ is 6, then the other root is

   F. 2.   J. 8.

   G. −4.   K. 12.

   H. −6.

3. A man buys a book for $20 and wishes to sell it. What price should he mark on it if he wishes a 40% discount while making a 50% profit on the cost price?

   A. $25   D. $50

   B. $30   E. $55

   C. $40

4. If a and b are positive integers such that $c = 12a + 54b$, then c must be divisible by which of the following?

   F. 4   G. 6

H. 8   J. 9

K. 27

5. If $a = 4$ and $b = 7$, then $\dfrac{a + \dfrac{a}{b}}{a - \dfrac{a}{b}}$ equals

A. $\dfrac{3}{4}$.   D. $\dfrac{4}{3}$.

B. $\dfrac{3}{7}$.   E. $\dfrac{7}{3}$.

C. 1.

6. Given the equation $\dfrac{7}{3}x = (a^4 + 1)^3$, and $a = -1$, solve for x.

F. 16   J. $\dfrac{20}{3}$

G. $\dfrac{24}{7}$ K. 0

H. 24

7. $\sqrt{108} + 3\sqrt{12} - 7\sqrt{3} =$

A. $3 - 3\sqrt{3}$.   D. $5\sqrt{3}$.

B. 0.   E. $10\sqrt{3}$.

C. $4\sqrt{3}$.

8. Find the solution set of the following equation:

$|3x - 2| = 7$.

F. $\left\{-\dfrac{5}{3}\right\}$ J. $\left\{-\dfrac{7}{3}, 3\right\}$

G. $\left\{-\dfrac{5}{3}, -\dfrac{7}{3}\right\}$ K. $\left\{3, -\dfrac{5}{3}\right\}$

H. $\{3\}$

9. What is the biggest positive integer k for which the product of $7 - k$ and $18 - k$ will be non-zero and the quantities will have opposite signs?

   A. 8   D. 17

   B. 0   E. 18

   C. 7

10. If $c = 18a + 24b$, where a and b are positive integers, then c must be divisible by which of the following?

    F. 4   J. 12

    G. 6   K. 72

    H. 9

11. If A can do a job in 8 days and B can do the same job in 12 days, how many days would it take the two men working together to complete the job?

    A. 3   D. 5.8

    B. 4.8   E. 6

    C. 10

12. Find $\left\{ x \left| \dfrac{2}{x+1} - 3 = \dfrac{4x+6}{x+1} \right. \right\}$.

    F. $x = -2$ J. $x = 7$

    G. ϕ K. $x = -7$

    H. $x = 1$

13. If $\dfrac{a+3}{3a+5} = \dfrac{2}{3}$, then $a =$

    A. $-\dfrac{2}{3}$.   D. $\dfrac{1}{3}$.

    B. $-\dfrac{1}{3}$.   E. $\dfrac{2}{3}$.

    C. 0.

14. If $x = (y + 4)^2$ and $y = -7$, then what is x?

    F. 7   G. 9

H.   10   J.   11

K.   13

15. Simplify $\dfrac{4x^3 + 6x^2}{2x}$.

A. $x + 1$ D. $2x + 1$

B. $x + 3$ E. x

C. $2x^2 + 3x$

16. If $abc \neq 0$, then $\dfrac{6a^3bc^4}{18a^2b^3c^2} =$

F. $\dfrac{ac^2}{3b^2}$.   J. $\dfrac{a^2}{3b^2c}$.

G. $\dfrac{a^3b}{3c^2}$.   K. $\dfrac{a^2c^3}{3b^2}$.

H. $\dfrac{3b^2}{ac^2}$.

17. The equation $x^2 + 2(k + 2)x + 9k = 0$ has equal roots. k is therefore equal to

A.   4.   D.   −1 and 4.

B.   1 and 4.   E.   2 and −4.

C.   0 and 4.

18. If $x - 1$ is a factor of $3x^2 - 2kx + 1$, then $k =$

F.   −1.   J.   1.

G.   0.   K.   2.

H. $\dfrac{1}{2}$.

19. Given the expression $\dfrac{3}{x + 4} + \dfrac{5}{x - 4} = \dfrac{8}{x^2 - 16}$, solve for x.

A.   4   D.   1

B.   5   E.   2

C.   0

20. Evaluate $p = \dfrac{(a-b)(ab+c)}{(cb-2a)}$ when $a = 2$, $b = -\dfrac{1}{2}$, and $c = -3$.

    F. 3

    G. 2

    H. 0

    J. 1

    K. 4

21. Change 125.937% to a decimal.

    A. 1.25937

    B. 12.5937

    C. 125.937

    D. 1,259.37

    E. 12,593.7

22. Simplify $\dfrac{1+\dfrac{1}{x}}{1-\dfrac{1}{x}}$.

    F. $\dfrac{x-1}{x+1}$

    G. 1

    H. $\dfrac{x+1}{x-1}$

    J. $\dfrac{x-1}{2-x}$

    K. 2

23. Find the roots of the following equation:

    $x^2 - 5x + 6 = 0$.

    A. 1 and 5

    B. 1 and 6

    C. 2 and 3

    D. 2 and 5

    E. 3 and 5

24. If $\dfrac{a}{b} = 5$, then $a^2 - 25b^2 =$

    F. −25.

    G. −16.

    H. 0.

    J. 16.

    K. 25.

25. Solve the following inequality:

    $4(2x - 6) - 10x \leq -28$.

    A. $x < 2$ D. $x \geq 26$

    B. $x > 2$ E. $x \leq 26$

    C. $x \geq 2$

26. If $abc \neq 0$, then $\dfrac{25\left(\dfrac{a}{b}\right)^{3}\left(\dfrac{c}{a}\right)^{4}}{125\left(\dfrac{a}{c}\right)^{7}\left(\dfrac{b}{c}\right)^{-2}} =$

    F. $\dfrac{a^{8}b}{5c^{9}}$.   J. $\dfrac{c^{6}}{5a^{2}b^{4}}$.

    G. $\dfrac{c^{9}}{5a^{8}b}$.   K. $\dfrac{c^{10}}{5ab^{5}}$.

    H. $\dfrac{c^{7}}{25a^{7}b^{2}}$.

27. If $x^{2} - 3x - 4 < 0$, then the solution set is

    A. $-4 < x < 1$.   D. $-1 < x < 0$.

    B. $-4 < x < -3$.   E. $-1 < x < 4$.

    C. $-3 < x < 0$.

28. If a function is defined as $|\,2 \quad 5x\,| < 3$, then the interval which does not contain any solution for x is

    F. $0 < x < 1$.   J. $-\dfrac{3}{5} < x < -\dfrac{1}{2}$.

    G. $0 < x < 2$.   K. $-1 < x < 1$.

    H. $-\dfrac{1}{25} < x < 0$.

29. If $x - 2$ is a factor of $x^{3} - 7x^{2} + kx - 12$, then k is

    A.   32.   D. -32.

    B.   16.   E. -16.

    C.   2.

30. The solution set to the system $\begin{cases} 2x + 3y = 6 \\ y - 2 = -\dfrac{2x}{3} \end{cases}$ is

   F. $\{0, 2\}$.

   G. $\{0, 0\}$.

   H. $\left\{\dfrac{1}{3}, 5\right\}$.

   J. $\{8, 3\}$.

   K. There are an infinite number of solutions.

31. The solution to the pair of equations

   $\begin{cases} kx + my = 7 \\ mx + ky = 5 \end{cases}$

   is $x = 3$ and $y = 2$. What are the values of k and m?

   A. $m = \dfrac{1}{5}$ and $k = \dfrac{11}{5}$

   B. $m = \dfrac{1}{3}$ and $k = \dfrac{11}{3}$

   C. $m = \dfrac{1}{3}$ and $k = \dfrac{1}{5}$

   D. $m = \dfrac{1}{5}$ and $k = \dfrac{11}{3}$

   E. $m = 0$ and $k = 0$

32. Simplify the complex fraction $\dfrac{\dfrac{1}{x} - \dfrac{1}{y}}{\dfrac{1}{x^2} - \dfrac{1}{y^2}}$.

   F. $\dfrac{xy}{y + x}$

   G. xy

   H. $\dfrac{xy}{x^2 + y^2}$

   J. $\dfrac{xy}{x - y}$

   K. $x - y$

33. If $\dfrac{2}{x} = \dfrac{\dfrac{1}{3}}{y}$, then $1 < x < 10$ if and only if

A. $10 \geq y \geq 1$.   D. $10 > y > -10$.

B. $6 > y > \dfrac{3}{5}$.   E. $\dfrac{1}{6} < y < \dfrac{5}{3}$.

C. $6 \geq y \geq \dfrac{3}{5}$.

34. What are the coordinates of the midpoint between the points $(-2, 3)$ and $(4, -5)$?

    F. $(2, -1)$ J. $(1, 1)$

    G. $(1, -1)$ K. $(1, 2)$

    H. $(0, -1)$

35. What is the distance between $(0, -2)$ and $(7, 0)$?

    A. $\sqrt{43}$ D. $\sqrt{53}$

    B. $\sqrt{45}$ E. $\sqrt{55}$

    C. $\sqrt{47}$

36. If a line contains the points $(1, 3)$ and $(-2, -4)$, then its slope is

    F. 3.   J. 1.

    G. $\dfrac{7}{3}$.   K. $\dfrac{2}{3}$.

    H. $\dfrac{5}{3}$.

37. Which of the following inequalities has a solution set on the real axis?

    A. $x^2 < -1$ D. $x^2 < -4$

    B. $x^2 + 2x + 2 > 0$ E. None of the above.

    C. $-3x^2 + x - 1 > 0$

38. The measure of an inscribed angle is equal to one-half the measure of its inscribed arc. In the figure shown, triangle ABC is inscribed in circle O, and line BD is tangent to the circle at point B. If the measure of angle CBD is $70°$, what is the measure of angle BAC?

F.   110°

G.   70°

H.   140°

J.   35°

K.   40°

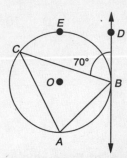

39. If $f(x) = 7x + 3$ for all x, then the y-intercept of the line given by $y = f(x + 1)$ is

A.   3.

B.   5.

C.   7.

D.   10.

E.   15.

40. The coordinates of the point of intersection of the lines having equations $3x + 2y = 5$ and $x - 4y = 1$ are

F. $\left(-\dfrac{11}{7}, \dfrac{-1}{7}\right)$.

G. $\left(-\dfrac{11}{7}, \dfrac{-2}{7}\right)$.

H. $\left(\dfrac{11}{7}, \dfrac{1}{7}\right)$.

J. $\left(\dfrac{11}{7}, \dfrac{2}{7}\right)$.

K. $\left(\dfrac{11}{7}, \dfrac{16}{7}\right)$.

41. Find the mean of the following scores:

5, 7, 9, 8, 5, 8, 9, 8, 7, 8, 7, 5, 9, 5, 8, 5, 9, 6, 5.

A.   5

B.   6

C.   7

D.   8

E.   9

42. Find the slope of a line whose equation is $y = -6x + 3$.

F. $-\dfrac{1}{6}$

G.   6

H.   3

J. -6

K. -3

43. From a point 336 feet from the base of a building, the angle of elevation to the roof is 30°. Find the height of the building.

    A.   112

    B. $112\sqrt{2}$

    C. $112\sqrt{3}$

    D.   168

    E. $168\sqrt{2}$

44. Given the quadrilateral *ABCD* with vertices at *A*(–3, 0), *B*(9, 0), *C*(9, 9), and *D*(0, 12), find the area of quadrilateral *ABCD*.

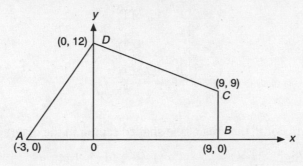

    F.   94.5

    G.   112.5

    H.   99

    J.   105

    K.   Cannot be determined.

45. From a certain point on a level plain at the foot of a mountain, the angle of elevation of the peak is 45°. From a point 50 feet farther away, the angle of elevation of the peak is 30°. What is the height of the peak above the foot of the mountain?

    A. $\dfrac{50}{\sqrt{3}}$

    B. $50(\sqrt{3}-1)$

    C. $\dfrac{50}{\sqrt{3}-1}$

    D. $50\sqrt{3}$

    E. $50\sqrt{3}+1$

46. A square has a diagonal = 2*x*. A second square has twice the area of the first square. The perimeter of the second square is

    F. $2\sqrt{x}$.

    G.   2*x*.

    H. $x^2\sqrt{4}$.

    J.   8*x*.

    K. $4x^2$.

47. A rhombus has consecutive sides of measure $3x + 10$ and $2x + 15$ with included angle $12x$. What is the length of its shorter diagonal?

A. $\dfrac{25}{2}$

B. 5

C. 10

D. 18

E. 25

48.

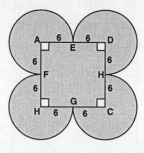

Find, in terms of π, the area of the shaded region in the diagram.

F. $6\pi + 36$

G. $108\pi + 144$

H. $144\pi + 36$

J. $144\pi + 144$

K. $36\pi + 144$

49. In the figure, $\triangle ABC$ is equilateral of side S. If point G joins the medians of the triangle together, then distance $\overline{GF_x}$ is

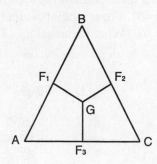

A. $\dfrac{\sqrt{2}}{2}S.$

B. $\dfrac{S}{2}.$

C. $\dfrac{\sqrt{3}}{6}S.$

D. $\sqrt{3}S.$

E. $\dfrac{S}{3}.$

50. If △ABC is an equilateral triangle with side *S*, the diameter of the circle is

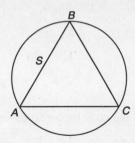

    F.   *S*.   J. $3\sqrt{3}S$.

    G. $\dfrac{2\sqrt{3}}{3}S$.   K. $\dfrac{3}{4}S$.

    H.   3*S*.

51. In the figure, which of the following must be true for $\overline{BD} \parallel \overline{AE}$?

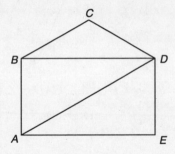

    I. $\angle BAD = \angle ADE$

    II. $\angle BDA = \angle DAE$

    III. $\angle CBD = \angle BDC$

    A.   I only.   D.   II only.

    B.   I and II only.   E.   III only.

    C.   II and III only.

52. If a figure has exterior angles that all measure 72°, then the figure is a

    F.   triangle.   J.   hexagon.

    G.   square.   K.   octagon.

    H.   pentagon.

53. Of all rectangles with a given perimeter, the square has maximum area. What is the maximum area of a rectangle with perimeter 36?

   A. 36   D. 121

   B. 81   E. 80

   C. 64

54. If the measure of an angle exceeds its complement by 40°, then its measure is

   F. 65°.   J. 40°.

   G. 50°.   K. 30°.

   H. 45°.

55.

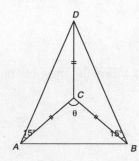

   In the figure, if $\overline{AC} = \overline{BC} = \overline{CD}$ and $\angle CAD = \angle CBD = 15°$, then $\theta =$

   A. 15.   D. 60.

   B. 30.   E. 75.

   C. 45.

56. A man encloses a rectangular area of 30,000 square feet with 800 feet of fencing. What is the maximum rectangular area he can enclose?

   F. 60,000   J. 40,000

   G. 55,000   K. 72,000

   H. 50,000

57. Which of the expressions below is equivalent to $csc^2 x$?

   A. $-\tan^2 x + \sec x$ D. $-\dfrac{1}{\sin^2 x}$

   B. $1 - \cot^2 x$ E. $-\dfrac{1}{\cos^2 x}$

   C. $1 + \cot^2 x$

58. In the triangle shown below, cosω is equal to

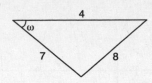

F. $\dfrac{1}{16}$.

J. $\dfrac{\sqrt{3}}{3}$.

G. $\dfrac{\sqrt{2}}{2}$.

K. $\dfrac{1}{56}$.

H. $\dfrac{1}{28}$.

59.

In this right triangle, tanθ is equal to which of the following?

I. $\dfrac{a}{b}$

II. $\dfrac{\sin\theta}{\cos\theta}$

III. $\dfrac{a}{\sqrt{a^2+b^2}}$

A. I only.

D. I and II.

B. II only.

E. I and III.

C. III only.

60.

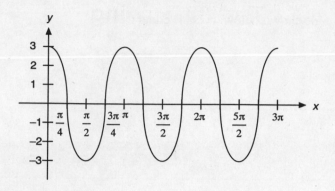

The above graph represents the function

F. $y = 2 \sin 3x$.

G. $y = 3 \sin 2x$.

H. $y = 3 \cos 2x$.

J. $y = 3 \cos 3x$.

K. $y = \cos 2x$.

THIS IS THE END OF TEST 2.

Test 3: Reading

TIME: 35 Minutes
40 Questions

Passage I

Mrs. Margery Pinchwife, *and* Alithea: *Mr.* Pinchwife *peeping behind at the door.*

Mrs. Pin. Pray, Sister, where are the best Fields and Woods, to walk in *London*?

5   *Alith.* A pretty Question; why, Sister! *Mulberry Garden,* and *St. James's Park*; and for close walks the *New Exchange.*

Mrs. Pin. Pray, Sister, tell me why my Husband looks so grim here in Town? and keeps me up so close, and will not let me go a walking, nor let me wear my best Gown yesterday?

10 *Alith.* O, he's jealous, Sister.

Mrs. Pin. Jealous, what's that?

Alith. He's afraid you shou'd love another Man.

Mrs. Pin. How shou'd he be afraid of my loving another man, when he will let me see any but himself?

15 *Alith.* Did he not carry you yesterday to a Play?

Mrs. Pin. Ay, but we sat amongst ugly People, he wou'd not let me come near the Gentry, who sate under us, so that I cou'd not see 'em: He told me, none but naughty Women sate there, whom they tous'd and mous'd; but I would have ventur'd

20 for all that.

Alith. But how did you like the Play?

Mrs. Pin. Indeed I was aweary of the Play, but I lik'd hugeously the Actors; they are the goodliest, proper'st Men, Sister.

Alith. O, but you must not like the Actors, Sister.

25 *Mrs. Pin.* Ay, how should I help it, Sister? Pray, Sister, when my Husband comes in, will you ask leave for me to go a walking?

Alith. A walking, hah, ha; Lord, a Country Gentlewoman's leasure is the drudgery of a foot-post; and she requires as much

30 airing as her Husband's Horses. [*Aside.*

Enter Mr. Pinchwife to *them.*

But here comes your Husband; I'll ask, though I'm sure he'll not grant it.

35   *Mrs. Pin.* He says he won't let me go abroad, for fear of catching the Pox.

Alith. Fye, the small Pox you shou'd say.

Mrs. Pin. Oh my dear, dear Bud, welcome home; why dost thou look so fropish? who has nanger'd thee?

40   *Mr. Pin.* Your a Fool.

Mrs. Pinch. *goes aside, & cryes.*

Alith. Faith, so she is, for crying for no fault, poor tender Creature!

Mr. Pin. What, you wou'd have her as impudent as your-
45   self, as errant a Jilflirt, a gadder, a Magpy, and to say all a meer notorious Town-Woman?

Alit[h]. Brother, you are my only Censurer; and the honour of your Family shall sooner suffer in your Wife there, than in me, though I take the innocent liberty of the Town.

50   *Mr. Pin.* Hark you Mistriss, do not talk so before my Wife, the innocent liberty of the Town!

Alith. Why, pray, who boasts of any intrigue with me? what Lampoon has made my name notorious? what ill Women fre-
quent my Lodgings? I keep no Company with any Women of
55   scandalous reputations.

Mr. Pin. No, you keep the Men of scandalous reputations Company.

Alith. Where? wou'd you not have me civil? answer 'em in the Box at the Plays? in the drawing room at *Whitehal*? in *St.*
60   *James's Park? Mulberry garden?* or—

Mr. Pin. Hold, hold, do not teach my Wife, where the Men are to be found; I believe she's the worse for your Town documents already; I bid you keep her in ignorance as I do.

Mrs. Pin. Indeed be not angry with her Bud, she will tell me
65   nothing of the Town, though I ask her a thousand times a day.

Mr. Pin. Then you are very inquisitive to know, I find?

Mrs. Pin. Not I indeed, Dear, I hate *London*; our Place-
house in the Country is worth a thousand of't, wou'd I were there again.

70   *Mr. Pin.* So you shall I warrant; but were you not talking of Plays, and Players, when I came in? you are her encourager in such discourses.

Mrs. Pin. No indeed, Dear, she chid me just now for liking the Player Men.

75   *Mr. Pin.* Nay, if she be so innocent as to own to me her liking them, there is no hurt— [*Aside.*

Come my poor Rogue, but thou lik'st none better than me?

Mrs. Pin. Yes indeed, but I do, the Player Men are finer Folks.

80   *Mr. Pin.* But you love none better than me?

            Mrs. Pin. You are mine own Dear Bud, and I know you, I
      hate a Stranger.

            Mr. Pin. Ay, my Dear, you must love me only, and not be
      like the naughty Town Women, who only hate their Husbands,
85   and love every Man else, love Plays, Visits, fine Coaches, fine
      Cloaths, Fidles, Balls, Treates, and so lead a wicked Town-life.

            Mrs. Pin. Nay, if to enjoy all these things be a Town-life,
      London is not so bad a place, Dear.

            Mr. Pin. How! if you love me, you must hate *London*.

90   *Ali[th].* The Fool has forbid me discovering to her the plea-
      sures of the Town, and he is now setting her a gog upon them
      himself.

            Mrs. Pin. But, Husband, do the Town-women love the
      Player Men too?

95   *Mr. Pin.* Yes, I warrant you.

            Mrs. Pin. Ay, I warrant you.

            Mr. Pin. Why, you do not, I hope?

            Mrs. Pin. No, no, Bud; but why have we no Player Men in
      the Country?

100   *Mr. Pin.* Ha—Mrs. Minx, ask me no more to go to a Play.

            Mrs. Pin. Nay, why, Love? I did not care for going; but
      when you forbid me, you make me as 't were desire it.

            Alith. So 'twill be in other things, I warrant. [*Aside.*

            Mrs. Pin. Pray, let me go to a Play, Dear.

105   *Mr. Pin.* Hold your peace, I wo' not.

            Mrs. Pin. Why, Love?

            Mr. Pin. Why, I'll tell you.

            Alith. Nay, if he tell her, she'l give him more cause to
      forbid her that place. [*Aside.*

110   *Mrs. Pin.* Pray, why, Dear?

            Mr. Pin. First, you like the Actors, and the Galiants may
      like you.

            Mrs. Pin. What, a homely Country Girl? no, Bud, no body
      will like me.

115   *Mr. Pin.* I tell you, yes, they may.

            Mrs. Pin. No, no, you jest—I won't believe you, I will go.

From William Wycherley, *The Country Wife.*

1.   The character named Alithea is

      A.   an actress in the play.   C.   the sister-in-law of Mr. Pinchwife.

      B.   the wife of Mr. Pinchwife.   D.   a family friend of Mrs. Pinchwife.

2. Mrs. Pinchwife said she yearned to go to the play because

   F. she wanted to add to her culture.

   G. she wanted to walk among the gentry.

   H. she wanted to accompany her husband.

   J. her husband would not allow her to go.

3. In its context, "why dost thou look so fropish" suggests that the husband

   A. enters the house in a bad mood.

   B. has heard the people gossip about his sister.

   C. wants nothing more than to be left alone.

   D. frequents bars and play-houses.

4. It can be inferred from her lines that Mrs. Pinchwife is a(n)

   F. totally arrogant snob.

   G. somewhat naive young woman.

   H. immoral, adulterous wife.

   J. victim of idle social gossip.

5. Because Alithea defends her honor so quickly, it can be inferred that

   A. she has actually been keeping company with men of dubious reputation.

   B. many wives suspect her of having an affair with their husbands.

   C. this is a conversation she has had many times with her brother.

   D. she is afraid her sister-in-law will get the wrong impression of her.

6. The humor in this conversation is created by which of the following?

   I. Alithea has already shown her sister-in-law some of the pleasures of town life.

   II. The husband, while trying to explain what his wife should avoid, shows her what to look for.

   III. It is obvious the wife does not want to be kept ignorant by her husband.

   F. I only.   H. I and II only.

   G. II only.   J. I, II, and III.

7. Mr. Pinchwife's first reaction to his wife's admission to liking the Player Men was an expression of

    A. intense jealousy.

    B. mistrust of her morals.

    C. confirmation of her innocence.

    D. uncontrollable outrage.

8. Mr. Pinchwife's reference to his wife as a "minx" indicates that he considers her

    F. past her prime.   H. pert and saucy.

    G. an unattractive animal.   J. matronly and motherly.

9. Mr. Pinchwife does not want his wife to attend plays because he is afraid she will

    A. become used to spending too much of her time away from home.

    B. have an affair with one of the actors.

    C. spend more money than he can afford.

    D. catch him having an affair with one of the actresses.

10. What conditions did Mr. Pinchwife set for loving his wife?

    I.   Dislike the country

    II.   Dislike London

    III. Love him

    IV.   Love none better

    F. I and II only.   H. I, II, and III.

    G. II and III only.   J. II, III, and IV.

Passage II

The great fault of a modern school of poetry is that it is an experiment to reduce poetry to a mere effusion of natural sensibility; or, what is worse, to divest it both of imaginary splendour and human passion, to surround the meanest objects with the

5   morbid feelings and devouring egotism of the writers' own minds. Shakespeare did not so understand poetry. He did not do interpretation both to nature and art. He did not do all he could to get rid of the one and the other, to fill up the dreary void with the

Mood of his own Mind. He owes his power over the human
10 mind to his having had a deeper sense than others of what was
grand in the objects of nature, or affecting in the events of human
life. But to the men I speak of there is nothing interesting, nothing heroical, but themselves. To them the fall of gods or of great
men is the same. They do not enter into the feeling. They cannot
15 understand the terms. They are even debarred from the last poor,
paltry consolation of an unmanly triumph over fallen greatness;
for their minds reject, with a convulsive effort and intolerable
loathing, the very idea that there ever was, or was thought to be,
anything superior to themselves. All that has ever excited the
20 attention or admiration of the world, they look upon with the
most perfect indifference; and they are surprised to find that the
world repays their indifference with scorn. "With what measure
they mete, it has been meted to them again."

Shakespeare's imagination is of the same plastic kind as his
25 conception of character or passion. "It glances from heaven to
earth, from earth to heaven." Its movement is rapid and devious.
It unites the most opposite extremes; or, as Puck says, in boast-
ing of his own feats, "puts a girdle round about the earth in forty
minutes." He seems always hurrying from his subject, even
30 while describing it; but the stroke, like the lightning's, is sure as
it is sudden. He takes the widest possible range, but from that
very range he has his choice of the greatest variety and aptitude
of materials. He brings together images the most alike, but
placed at the greatest distance from each other; that is, found in
35 circumstances of the greatest dissimilitude. From the remoteness
of his combinations, and the celerity with which they are effected, they coalesce the more indissolubly together.

The more the thoughts are strangers to each other, and the
longer they have been kept asunder, the more intimate does their
40 union seem to become. Their felicity is equal to their force. Their
likeness is made more dazzling by their novelty. They startle,
and take the fancy prisoner in the same instant. I will mention
one which is very striking, and not much known out of *Troilus
and Cressida*. Aeneas says to Agamemnon:

45 "I ask that I might waken reverence,
And bid the cheek be ready with a blush
Modest as morning, when she coldly eyes
The youthful Phoebus."

Shakespeare's language and versification are like the rest of
50 him. He has a magic power over words; they come winged at his

bidding, and seem to know their places. They are struck out at a heat on the spur of the occasion, and have all the truth and vividness which arise from an actual impression of the objects. His epithets and single phrases are like sparkles, thrown off from
55 an imagination fired by the whirling rapidity of its own motion. His language is hieroglyphical. It translates thoughts into visible images. It abounds in sudden transitions and elliptical expressions. This is the power of Shakespeare, and it goes unequalled in the modern age.

From William Hazlitt, *On Shakespeare and Milton.*

11. The primary distinction made in the first paragraph is one between

   A.   the poetry of the senses and the poetry of imagination.

   B.   the modern school of poetry and that of Shakespeare.

   C.   the poetry of egotism and the poetry of sensibility.

   D.   the modern school of poetry and the poetry of human mood.

12. The critic cited here seems particularly upset by what he terms the modernist's

   F.   "morbid feelings."   H.   "human passion."

   G.   "egotism."   J.   "intolerable loathing."

13. In context, the sentence "He did not do interpretation both to nature and art" (lines 6–7) suggests which of the following?

   A.   Shakespeare did not espouse the political conservatism of the modernists.

   B.   Shakespeare was tolerant in matters concerning nature and art.

   C.   Shakespeare did not understand poetry in the same way as the modernists.

   D.   The modern age is one of egotism.

14. The passage suggests that Classical Tragedy would not be of interest to the "modern school" because they

   F.   do not see any difference between "the fall of the gods or of great men."

   G.   hate anything that holds the "admiration of the world."

   H.   cannot deal with the criticism the world has for them.

   J.   feel compelled to substitute their own "dreary world" for the real thing.

15. The author brings closure to his first paragraph by

    A.   stating that the modernists are as surprised at their reception as he is at their views.

    B.   implying that the rest of the world is as indifferent to the modernists as the modernists are to the idea of something being superior than themselves.

    C.   implying that the rest of the world scorns the modernists as much as he does.

    D.   stating that there is nothing "heroical" in the modernist position.

16. The "girdle round about the earth" (line 28) is best understood as

    F.   Shakespeare's universal appeal.

    G.   Shakespeare's ability to discuss all topics.

    H.   Shakespeare's capacity to bring together extremes.

    J.   Shakespeare's ability to communicate quickly using appropriate symbols.

17. The critic suggests light criticism of Shakespeare for his

    A.   almost "plastic" conception of character.

    B.   need to bring dissimilar images together.

    C.   deviousness in character portrayal.

    D.   hurrying from one subject to another.

18. At the end of the second paragraph, the critic distinguishes between similar images and

    F.   dissimilar meanings.   H.   dissimilar ranges.

    G.   indissoluble materials.   J.   dissimilar circumstances.

19. The author can best be described as being

    A.   highly critical of Shakespeare and his works.

    B.   somewhat disconcerted by the works of Shakespeare still being in prominence today.

    C.   one who recognizes Shakespeare's continued greatness.

    D.   highly antagonistic toward Shakespeare's hieroglyphical writing.

20. According to the author, Shakespeare can best be described as

   I.   comprehending poetry and its forms.

   II. able to interpret for others the art of poetry and the natural world about him.

   III. preoccupied with mood and feeling.

   IV. adept at recognizing both significant events and majesty in nature.

   F.   I and II only.   H.   I, II, and III.

   G.   II and III only.   J.   IV only.

Passage III

A good scientific law or theory is falsifiable simply because it makes definite claims about the world. For the falsificationist, it follows readily that the more falsifiable the theory, the better. The more claims a theory makes, the more
5   potential there is for showing that the world does not, in fact, behave in the way laid down by that theory. A very good theory is one that makes very wide-ranging claims about the world, and which is, consequently, highly falsifiable. This is a theory that resists falsification whenever it is put to the test.
10   This point can be illustrated by means of a trivial example. Consider the two laws:
    (a) Mars moves in an ellipse around the Sun.
    (b) All planets move in ellipses around their Sun.
It is clear that (b) has higher status than (a) as a piece of
15   scientific knowledge. Law (b) tells us what law (a) tells us and more. Law (b), the preferable law, is more falsifiable than (a). If observations of Mars should turn out to falsify (a), then they would falsify (b) also. Any falsification of (a) will be a falsification of (b), but the reverse is not that case. Observation state-
20   ments referring to the orbits of Venus, Jupiter, etc. that might conceivably falsify (b) are irrelevant to (a). If we follow Popper and refer to those sets of observation statements that would serve to falsify a law or theory as potential falsifiers of that law or theory, then we can say that the potential falsifiers of (a) form a
25   class that is as subclass of the potential falsifiers of (b). Law (b) is more falsifiable than law (a), which is tantamount to saying that it claims more, that it is the better law.
A less-contrived example involves the relation between Kepler's theory of the solar system and Newton's theory of the
30   solar system. Kepler's theory consists of three laws of planetary motion. Potential falsifiers of this theory consist of sets of state-

ments referring to planetary positions, relative to the Sun, at specified times. Newton's theory, a better theory that supersedes Kepler's, is more comprehensive. It consists of Newton's law of
35 motion, plus his law of gravitation, with the latter asserting that all pairs of bodies in the universe attract each other with a force that varies inversely as the square of their separation. Some of the potential falsifiers of Newton's theory are sets of statements of planetary positions at specified times, but there are many oth-
40 ers. These include those referring to the behavior of falling bodies and pendulums, the correlation between the tides and the locations of the Sun and the Moon, and so on. There are many more opportunities to falsify Newton's theory that there are to falsify Kepler's theory. As the falsificationist's theory goes,
45 Newton's theory is able to resist falsification attempts, thereby establishing its superiority over Kepler's theory.

Highly falsifiable theories should be preferred over less falsifiable ones, provided they have not, in fact, been falsified. This qualification is important to the falsificationist. Theories
50 that have been falsified must be ruthlessly rejected. The enterprise of science consists in the proposal of highly falsifiable hypotheses, followed by deliberate and tenacious attempts to falsify them.

"We learn from our mistakes. Science progresses by trial
55 and error." Falsifications become important landmarks, striking achievements, and major growing-points in science because of this logical process. This renders impossible the derivation of universal laws and theories from observations, but makes possible the deduction of their falsity.

From A.F. Chalmers, *What Is This Thing Called Science?*

21. According to the author, the most important advances in science occur by

    A. proposing highly falsifiable theories.

    B. falsifying existing theories.

    C. finding general theories of motion.

    D. identifying theories of planetary motion.

22. The author's example in paragraph two is intended to

    F. inform the reader of the shape of Mars' orbit.

    G. describe how all planets move about the Sun.

    H. show how a theory can be falsified.

    J. illustrate how a theory can be more falsifiable.

23. Based on the passage, which of the following is a potential falsifier?

    A. An observation statement that falsifies an existing theory

    B. A description of a general theory

    C. A statement describing a narrowly defined theory

    D. A statement describing the shape of Mars' orbit

24. Based on the passage, it can be reasonably inferred that a bad scientific theory does which of the following?

    F. Limits the advances of scientific knowledge

    G. Fails to make definite claims about the world

    H. Has been falsified

    J. Inaccurately describes planetary motion

25. According to the author, Newton's theory is superior to Kepler's because of which of the following?

    A. Kepler's theory was proven false.

    B. Kepler's theory inaccurately describes the motion of Mars.

    C. Newton's theory makes broader claims than Kepler's.

    D. Newton's theory makes specific claims.

26. According to the author, one scientific theory is considered better than another if it does which of the following?

    F. Makes more claims about the world

    G. Has been falsified

    H. Is limited to descriptions of planetary motion

    J. Contains a subset of Newton's theory

27. Based on the passage, which of the following would a falsificationist consider necessary for a very good scientific theory?

    I.   A theory making wide-range claims about the world

    II.   A theory that resists falsification

    III. A theory containing false claims

    A. I only.   C. I and III.

    B. I and II.   D. II and III.

28. The author's suggestion that we learn from our mistakes refers to

    F. the way habits are formed.

    G. learning to propose broader theories.

    H. the preference for highly falsifiable theories.

    J. the trial and error nature of scientific progress.

29. Based on the passage, which of the following is the most falsifiable theory?

    A. Judges make decisions based on a small number of environmental cues.

    B. Supreme Court justices make decisions based on a small number of environmental cues.

    C. Appellate judges make decisions based on a small number of environmental cues.

    D. People make decisions based on a small number of environmental cues.

30. According to the passage, which of the following would not be considered a potential falsifier of Kepler's theory?

    F. An observation that Mars was not in the correct place at a given time

    G. An observation that neither Mars nor Venus were in the predicted places at a specified time

    H. An observation that there was no correlation between the tides and the positions of the Sun and Moon

    J. An observation that none of the planets in the Solar System conformed to their predicted positions at any point in time

Passage IV

Mr. E. W. Hawkes has lately published a valuable account of the ceremonies of the two Eskimo tribes, of the Unaligmiut and Unalaklit on the Isle of St. Michael, at the mouth of the Yukon River. In the months of November and December are
5   held local rites, termed the Aiyaguk or "Asking" festival, and the Teauiyuk ("Bladder feast"), the last of which is to placate the spirits of animals already slain. But still more important is the Aithukaguk or "Inviting-In" feast, for it is an appeal to the spirits represented by the masks—the totemic guardians—for
10 future success in hunting. In the Eskimo ritual this festival is only equalled in importance by the Great Feast of the Dead: "One supplies the material wants of the living, the other the spiritual needs of the dead." In St. Michael the "Inviting-In"

15 feast has lost much of its religious character and is now maintained chiefly for its social utility and as offering an opportunity for trade between two friendly tribes. An old chief remarked that they did not dance for pleasure alone, but to attract the game so that their families might be fed. If they did not dance, the spirits (*inua*) who attended the feast would be angry
20 and the animals would stay away. The shades of their ancestors would go hungry since there would be no one to feed them, and their own names would be forgotten if no namesake could sing their praises in the dance. There was nothing bad about their dances, which made their hearts good towards each other and
25 tribe friendly with tribe.

Dances and Songs. When a feast is arranged, the people gather nightly in the Kazgi, the communal house where tribal meetings are held, to rehearse the songs, which are taught to them by an old man, whom they requite with gifts. The people sit
30 in darkness, in order that any spirit which may be attracted by the songs may not be frightened away by the lamps. The chorus usually consists of six men, led by the old man, who calls out the words a line ahead. The women and children can join in after the song is started. Both sexes have dances of their own, but occa-
35 sionally dance together, the woman being in the centre, the men dancing round her. There are inter-tribal competitions, like the *nith* contests of the Greenland Eskimo, each tribe putting forth its best actors.

On the first day there were Comic dances, and the tribe
40 won whose performers made the other laugh. On the second day there were Group dances, and on the third day the Totemic dances. In these last the actors went through the same motions as the ordinary dancers, but fitted their movements to the character presented, and the Eskimo believe that these performers are pos-
45 sessed by the spirits of the animals which they represent—another instance of our doctrine that the actor was originally a medium. These pantomimes began by a performance in which women appropriately costumed went through the household occupations, such as the curing of skins and the making of gar-
50 ments. Next an Unalaklit man wearing an elaborate walrus mask enacted the life of that animal, its chase, and death. Two young men with appropriate masks and fittings next gave the Red Fox dance, which in turn was followed by the White Fox dance, representing the stalking of a ptarmigan by that beast. Finally
55 came the famous Raven dance. The dancer came in cawing like that bird, wearing a Raven mask with an immense beak, bor-

dered with fur and feathers. Presently he disappeared and returned dragging a bashful woman similarly attired. They danced
for a short time together, the Raven continuing his amatory ca-
60   pers until, apparently tired of her, he again disappeared into the
crowd, and returned with another bride, evidently younger. The
three danced for some time. Then he returned to his first love,
who angrily repulsed him as he tried to embrace her, which
greatly pleased the audience. This concluded the dance proper.
65   The shaman now donned an *inua* (mask), and kept running round
the entrance with ever-lessening circles, until he collapsed in a
trance, while he was communing with the spirit guests, in the
fireplace below the Kazgi, as the Eskimo believe.

After a time he revived and told the hunters that the *inua*
70   had been pleased with the dances and promised a successful
hunting season. When appropriate offerings of meat, drink, and
tobacco had been made to them through the chinks in the floor,
the celebrations ended. After the feast is over, the masks used in
the dances are burned by the shaman.

From William Ridgeway, *The Dramas and Dramatic Dances of Non-European Races.*

31. The most important festival(s) for the Eskimo tribe is (are)

   A.   the Great Feast of the Dead.

   B.   the "Inviting-In" feast.

   C.   the Great Feast of the Dead and the "Inviting-In" feast.

   D.   the "Bladder feast" and the "Asking" festival.

32. The "Inviting-In" feast in St. Michael

   F.   is still an appeal to the spirits represented by the masks for future
        success in hunting.

   G.   maintains much of its religious character.

   H.   is an opportunity for trade between two friendly tribes.

   J.   has lost most of its social utility.

33. The narrator seems to be

   A.   indifferent to the tribes described.

   B.   concerned about depicting the history of the observances.

   C.   presenting the information from both a historical and a current point of
        view.

   D.   dismissive about superstitious beliefs and concerned only about pre-
        senting the factual information.

34. The narrator seems to be primarily concerned with the Eskimo tribes from

    F. a sociological perspective.

    G. the standpoint of a religious investigator—perhaps a missionary.

    H. a biological perspective, since so much attention is given to the rites associated with sex, death, and animals.

    J. the standpoint of one concerned with the fine arts, since so much attention is given to the songs, costumes, and dances.

35. The word "shaman" probably means

    A. one who is unable to commute with the spirit guests.

    B. a woman who would be given the lowly task of burning the used masks.

    C. an honored member of the tribe; a respected elder.

    D. a man who has shaved for the first time and is a very quiet, unknown member of the tribe who has no part in the ceremonies.

36. The writer does not make use of

    F. descriptions.   H. statistical research.

    G. interviews.   J. a secondary source.

37. To make an offering to the spirits, meat, drink, and tobacco

    A. are burned by the shaman.

    B. are not considered a necessary part of the ritual.

    C. are left upon an ice floe.

    D. are dropped through the chinks in the floor.

38. The writer can be best described as

    F. non-judgmental.

    G. judgmental in some respects.

    H. objective.

    J. reporting from a first-person point of view.

39. The Kazgi for the tribes might be best compared with

    A. a church in American society.

B.   a medical emergency room.

C.   a magistrate in our society.

D.   a town hall.

40. The feasts can best be described as:

I.   completely serious occasions.

II.   occasions in which everyone is equal in importance.

III. spontaneous affairs without rehearsals.

IV. occasions which involve some symbolism.

F.   I and IV only.   H.   III only.

G.   I and II only.   J.   IV only.

THIS IS THE END OF TEST 3.

Test 4: Science Reasoning

Time: 35 Minutes
40 Questions

DIRECTIONS: This test consists of seven passages, each followed by several questions. Once you have read a passage, answer each question. Then fill in the appropriate oval on your answer sheet.

Passage I

A chemist found an old bottle, containing a white powder, on the reagent shelf of her laboratory. The label on the bottle was partly worn away, leaving only the last three letters of the name of the contents of the bottle. These letters, "ose," suggested that the bottle might contain a sugar. In order to identify the white powder in the bottle, the chemist did several experiments.

Experiment 1

A solution was prepared by dissolving 1.500 g of the white powder in 10.00 g of water. The temperature of the system was recorded as the powder dissolved into the solution. A decrease in temperature was observed as the powder dissolved. Then, in order to dissolve the powder at constant temperature, heat must be added to the solution. The solution process is referred to as endothermic. The freezing point of the solution was measured to be $-1.90°C$, compared to the freezing point of water, $0.00°C$.

Experiment 2

Qualitative elemental analysis indicated that the white powder contained only carbon, hydrogen, and oxygen. The white powder melted with a sharp, well-defined melting point. In similar experiments, other pure compounds display sharp melting points, suggesting that the white powder is a pure compound.

Experiment 3

A 30.0 mg sample of the white powder was burned with excess oxygen in a combustion analysis apparatus. The carbon dioxide and water formed were collected and weighed. The mass of carbon dioxide obtained was 44.0 mg and that of water was 18.0 mg, which can be converted into one millimole of carbon dioxide and one millimole of water. One millimole of carbon dioxide contains one millimole of carbon and two millimoles of oxygen. Likewise, the one millimole of water contains two millimoles of hydrogen and one millimole of oxygen.

1. Which experiment(s) confirm that the white powder contains carbon, hydrogen, and oxygen?

   A. 3
   B. 2

   C. 2 and 3
   D. 1, 2, and 3

2. If a researcher burned 15.0 mg of the white powder in the combustion apparatus in Experiment 3, how many total millimoles of oxygen would be formed?

    F. 1.5

    G. 2.0

    H. 3.0

    J. 6.0

3. Do the results of the experiments definitely confirm the original hypothesis that the bottle contains a sugar?

    A. Yes, since the powder contains carbon, hydrogen, and oxygen.

    B. Yes, since the powder is a pure compound.

    C. No, since the exact ratio of carbon, hydrogen, and oxygen has not been determined.

    D. No, since the chemical composition of a known sugar compound has not been established.

4. What information would be most useful to a chemist in determining if the white powder were pure?

    F. Combustion analysis results only

    G. Both the melting point and freezing point

    H. The melting point only

    J. The elemental analysis only

5. Experiment 1 describes the dissolving of the white powder in water as an "endothermic process." What does this signify?

    A. Heat is given off as the temperature decreases.

    B. Heat is absorbed as the temperature decreases.

    C. Heat is absorbed as the temperature increases.

    D. Heat is neither absorbed nor given off as the temperature decreases.

6. In the combustion apparatus in Experiment 3, what is the function of using excess oxygen gas?

    F. To determine the amount of oxygen in the powder

    G. To dissolve the powder

    H. To cause the combustion reaction

    J. To support the combustion reaction

Passage II

Cosmology is the study of the structure of the Universe as the whole system of matter and energy in existence everywhere. There are two main theories in modern cosmology:

Theory 1: The Big Bang

Based on the observation that galaxies are receding away from each other, this theory states that there was a time when all of the matter in the Universe was close together. At the beginning, the Universe was extremely hot and very dense, from which it began to rapidly expand. Expansion from this configuration is known as the Big Bang, and it seeks to explain the Universe as we now see it. Recent evidence suggests that this event occurred around 14 ± 6 billion years ago. This theory predicts a certain abundance of light chemical elements such as deuterium (heavy hydrogen) and helium. It also predicts the existence of the microwave background radiation observed in 1965, which is a relic of the initial expansion. Most astronomers accept the Big Bang theory as the best available cosmological model of the Universe.

Theory 2: The Steady State

In this theory, the large scale structure of the Universe looks the same not only in each region of space, but also in different eras of time. Thus, in the Steady State cosmology there is no Big Bang, no beginning, and the Universe has looked about the same forever. According to this theory, new galaxies must constantly be forming in the spaces vacated as older galaxies recede, and this necessitates continuous creation of matter. Some scientists see this theory as a violation of the concept of conservation of mass, but defenders of the theory argue that it is hardly more outrageous than imagining all the mass of the whole Universe appearing at once, as in the Big Bang theory. A major argument against the Steady State theory, however, is its failure to predict the observed microwave background radiation.

7. It can be inferred from the passage that cosmology is

    A.   the study of the Universe's origin.

    B.   a study of the structure of the Universe as a single, orderly system.

    C.   the Big Bang theory.

    D.   the Steady State theory.

8. The Big Bang cosmology can be distinguished from the Steady State cosmology by the phrase

    F.   a static, non-evolving Universe.

    G.   continuous creation of matter.

H.   the galaxies receding away from each other.

J.   the Universe expanding from an extremely hot and very dense state.

9.   The Steady State cosmology essentially says

A.   the Universe is the same at all times.

B.   there should be microwave background radiation.

C.   galaxies are receding away from each other.

D.   the Universe began with a rapid expansion.

10. It is reported that quasars (distant bright galaxies known as quasi-stellar objects) are more numerous at great distances (hence, earlier times). This observation

F.   supports the Steady State theory.

G.   supports the idea of an initial explosion 14 billion years ago.

H.   supports the observation of the cosmic microwave background radiation.

J.   contradicts the predictions of the Steady State theory.

11. According to the Big Bang theory, the age of the Universe is at least

A.   14 billion years.   C.   20 billion years.

B.   8 billion years.   D.   6 billion years.

12. It can be inferred from the passage that most astronomers would

F.   support both theories.

G.   disapprove of the Big Bang theory.

H.   approve of the Steady State theory.

J.   agree with the Big Bang theory and disagree with the Steady State theory.

Passage III

As the moon revolves around the Earth, it moves between the Earth and the Sun forming a new Moon, when the Moon is not visible on Earth. When the Earth is between the Moon and the Sun, a full Moon is seen. At a new Moon or full Moon, the high tides are at their highest and the low tides are at their lowest. This event is called spring tides.

During the first and last quarter Moons, the Moon, Earth, and the Sun are at 90° or right angles. At this time, there is little difference between the high and low tides. These tides are called neap tides.

Tides for June 1994

Moon phase	Day	Tide
New	9	Spring
First quarter	16	Neap
Full	23	Spring
Last quarter	30	Neap

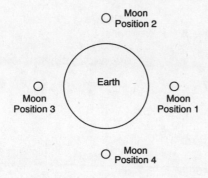 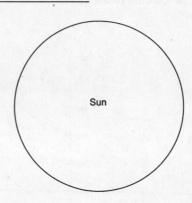

Figure 1

13. When the Moon is at position 3, more than likely

    A. spring tides are occurring.

    B. neap tides are occurring.

    C. no tides are occurring.

    D. there is not enough information to determine the type of tides.

14. On June 23, the Moon is probably

    F. at position 3.   H. at position 4.

    G. at position 2.   J. at position 2 or 4.

15. Spring tides occur about every

    A. day.   C. 7 days.

    B. spring.   D. 14 days.

16. Neap tides occur

    F. every quarter.   H. once a month.

    G. twice a month.   J. twice a year.

17. At position 2, the Moon is probably

    A. a full Moon.   C. a quarter Moon.

    B. a new Moon.   D. not seen.

Passage IV

We are investigating the pressure vs. temperature behavior of new materials for underwater applications. Below is a phase diagram obtained through measurements of the pressure vs. temperature.

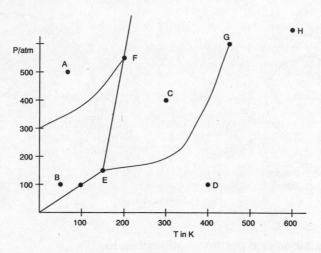

Figure 1

To assist in interpreting the phase diagram, the densities of certain points are recorded in Table 1. This material was shown to exist in two solid phases, one which was more stable than the other. The solid present at 100 K and 100 atm was soft and ductile; the other solid phase was hard and brittle.

Table 1

Point	Density, g/l
A	10.00
C	2.00
H	0.05
E	1.00

18. Which letter on the phase diagram indicates the pressure and temperature where the material exists in all three phases simultaneously?

    F. F

    G. G

    H. E

    J. H

19. Based on Table 1 and the phase diagram, which sequence shows the relationship of the densities among solids, liquids, and gases?

    A. solids > liquids > gases

    B. liquids > solids > gases

    C. gases > liquids > solids

    D. Depends on the pressure and temperature of the phase

20. How would a chemist adjust the temperature and pressure in order to liquefy the material at point D?

    F. At constant pressure, decrease the temperature.

    G. Increase the pressure while increasing the temperature.

    H. Decrease the pressure while decreasing the temperature.

    J. Increase the pressure at constant temperature.

21. At which combination of temperature and pressure will the material being studied exist in two phases at the same time?

    A. $T = 50$ K, $P = 100$ atm

    C. $T = 200$ K, $P = 550$ atm

    B. $T = 600$ K, $P > 600$ atm

    D. $T = 150$ K, $P = 150$ atm

22. At which point, A or B, is the material in a more stable phase?

    F. Point A is more stable because it is a solid.

    G. Point B is more stable because it is soft.

    H. Point A is more stable because it exists at a higher pressure.

    J. The stabilities cannot be compared based on the information given.

Passage V

The prediction of snow is often the most difficult forecast a meteorologist has to make. The threat of snow changing to sleet, rain, or freezing rain (rain freezing on contact with the surface due to a very shallow layer of cold air in the atmosphere) account for many false predictions. In addition, snowfall amounts are equally difficult to determine.

Experiment 1

Vertical temperature profiles are often used to assist in the attempt of issuing a prediction of snow. A vertical temperature profile shows how the temperature changes as the height of the atmosphere increases and is made based on weather observations. The greatest chance of snow is reflected by the vertical profile in Figure-A. The temperature is below freezing from 0 to 3000 meters in the atmosphere. The least chance for snow is in Figure-D. The temperatures are well above freezing from 0 to 1500 meters in the atmosphere.

Vertical Temperature Profiles

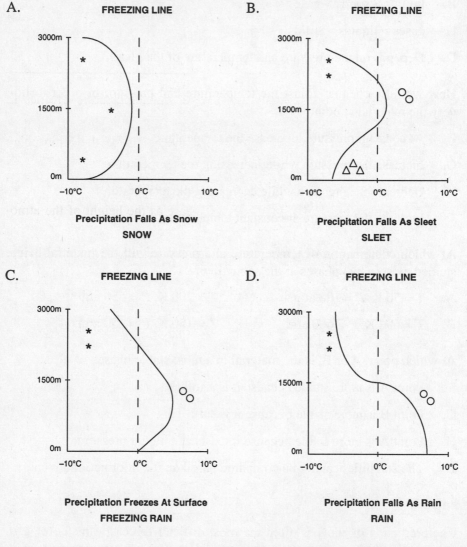

Figure 1

Experiment 2

The temperature often determines the amount of snow a location will receive and which type of snow crystal will fall to the ground. Each type of snow crystal is correlated to a specific ratio (Table 1) between measured snow on the ground and the liquid equivalent of the snow (snow melted down for measurement).

Table 1

Surface Temperature Range	Type of Crystal	Ratio
32 to 25 degrees F	Thin plates	8:1
25 to 14 degrees F	Columns	10:1
14 to 10 degrees F	Plates	12:1

23. What conclusion can be made about the vertical temperature profiles in Figure 1?

   A. The temperature always decreases as the height of the atmosphere increases.

   B. The temperature is always cold enough for snow at 1500 meters.

   C. The temperature does not always decrease as the height of the atmosphere increases.

   D. The temperature remains constant as the height of the atmosphere decreases.

24. Based on the passage, what conclusion can be made about how precipitation forms in the atmosphere?

   F. Precipitation usually forms as snow.

   G. Precipitation always begins as rain.

   H. Freezing rain forms at a height of 3000 meters in the atmosphere.

   J. Snow may change to rain but then usually reforms into snow.

Table 2

Height in the Atmosphere	Observed Temperature
3000 meters	–8 degrees Celsius
1500 meters	–5 degrees Celsius
0 meters (surface)	–2 degrees Celsius

25. Concord, NH took weather observations at 3 pm in the afternoon. The vertical temperature profile was recorded in Table 2. What would be the most probable form of precipitation to fall to the ground?

    A. Rain   C. Sleet

    B. Snow   D. Hail

26. If the surface temperature at observation time was 30°F and 1 inch of liquid equivalent snow fall was measured, how much snow would be expected to be on the ground at the time of observation?

    F. 1 inch   H. 14 inches

    G. 10 inches   J. 8 inches

27. If two locations, A and B, received the same amount of snow on the ground, and the amount of liquid equivalent snow was equal at both locations, what conclusion could be made?

    A. Both locations had similar vertical temperature profiles.

    B. Both locations had approximately the same surface temperature.

    C. The type of snow crystals that fell were different at the locations.

    D. Choices A and B are both correct.

28. What type of precipitation is most likely to fall if there is a very shallow layer of very cold air (below freezing) near the surface only?

    F. Rain   H. Snow

    G. Freezing rain   J. Sleet

Passage VI

Scientist 1

According to the theory of evolution, all species shared a common single-cell ancestor. Single-cell creatures evolved into multicellular organisms and later into the higher order species of mammals. This evolutionary theory was originally proposed by Darwin and others and was based upon comparisons of animal behavior and appearance, especially bone structure.

Molecular biology has provided additional evidence for the hypothesis that all creatures have evolved from a common single-cell ancestor. Comparisons of genetic material, mainly DNA and sometimes RNA, show that identical or very similar (homologous) sequences exist between humans and apes. That is, many human genes show a high homology with ape genes. In some cases, genetic homology is also seen between human, dog, mouse, bird, and even fly.

These comparisons allow scientists to construct an evolutionary tree. In many instances, this tree follows the same paths and structure as the one first created by the classical paleontologists in which all organisms evolve from a single root. Species with a greater degree of genetic homology are found close to each other, sometimes even on the same branch. Genetically more diverse organisms are placed farther apart.

Scientist 2

Recent advances in molecular biology provide evidence that all organisms did not evolve from a common ancestor, or progenote. Instead several ancestors may have existed. Living cells have previously been divided into two groups: prokaryotes and eukaryotes. Comparison of the ribosomal RNA of bacteria have led to the division of the prokaryotes into archaebacteria and the eubacteria. These two groups are as genetically distinct from each other as they are from the eukaryotes. Thus, living cells evolved from a minimum of three progenotes.

Additional evidence is provided by a study of the antigen HLA. HLA is found both in humans and monkeys. However, some chimpanzee molecules are closer to humans than some human antigens are to each other. This diversity is believed to have existed for at least a millennium. Computer simulations of human populations and their genes have shown that the one-ancestor hypothesis is impossible. Thus, the feasible explanation for genetic diversity is evolution from several ancestors.

29. Eukaryotes differ from eubacteria and archaebacteria. The eukaryotes have organelles, including a nucleus, so they are most likely to be the ancestors of present–day

    A. fungi.   C. animals.

    B. plants.   D. All of the above.

30. Scientist 1 suggests that all species share a common, single organism as an ancestor. By this he means

    F. evolution proceeds in a straight line, with the most highly developed beings, human beings, at the top.

    G. all living things share a high degree of genetic homology.

    H. Neither F nor G.

    J. Both F and G.

31. Scientist 2 presents the information about genetic diversity in humans to show that

    A. humans had prokaryotic ancestors.

    B. there was no single humanoid ancestor shared by all living humans.

C. chimpanzees are more closely related to humans than some humans are to other humans.

D. All of the above.

32. Scientist 1 mentions genetic homology between humans and birds to show that

F. genetic studies are not reliable.

G. if we trace the genetic tree back toward the root far enough, birds and humans had a common ancestor.

H. Darwin's comparisons of bone structure led to the wrong conclusions.

J. None of the above.

33. Neither archaebacteria nor eubacteria have nuclei, but eukaryotes do. Archaebacteria are anaerobes, and eubacteria are aerobes, and the two groups are genetically distinct. Scientist 1 would say that

A. Darwin's genetic tree doesn't apply to the lowest life forms.

B. genetic diversification began to occur in the earliest life forms, and differences among the descendants of a single ancestral prokaryote pre-disposed them to survive in different environments.

C. this supports evolution from several separate ancestors.

D. organisms descended from a common ancestor wouldn't have such different characteristics.

34. Neither archaebacteria nor eubacteria have nuclei, but eukaryotes do. Archaebacteria are anaerobes, and eubacteria are aerobes, and the two groups are genetically distinct. Scientist 2 would say that

F. the Darwinian genetic tree doesn't apply to the lowest life forms.

G. genetic diversification began to occur in the earliest life forms, and differences among the descendants of a single ancestral prokaryote predisposed them to survive in different environments.

H. this supports evolution from several separate ancestors.

J. different HLAs evolved from three separate progenotes.

35. The theory that eukaryotes (containing organelles, especially a nucleus) evolved from ancestral prokaryotes living in symbiosis with eubacteria is *disproved* by the evidence given by

A. Scientist 1.   C. both scientists.

B. Scientist 2.   D. neither scientist.

Passage VII

A new circuit company is investigating new multiple component circuits for use in leading edge equipment. They are examining a multiple capacitance circuit and a multiple resistor circuit shown below (Figures 1 and 2, respectively).

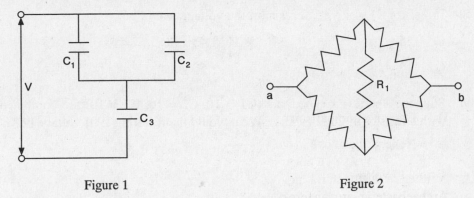

Figure 1   Figure 2

It is possible to vary a number of these components and observe interesting results.

If the individual capacitors and resistors are altered, the total voltage of each component is varied. Combinations of these components are tested to determine the most efficient configuration for specific industrial needs.

Table 1

Capacitors			voltage	Resistor	voltage
C1	C2	C3		R1	
10	10	20	100	10	50
20	20	20	133	20	50
10	10	10	67	5	50

36. Which of the following conclusions is supported by the data presented?

   F.   As resistance increases, voltage decreases.

   G.   As capacitance increases, voltage increases.

   H.   A resistor decreases the voltage of a series of capacitors.

   J.   A resistor has no effect on a series of capacitors.

37. The resulting voltage of the capacitors: C1 = 10, C2 = 20, C3 = 20 would be

    A.   67 volts.   C.   117 volts.

    B.   163 volts.   D.   100 volts.

38. If resistor R1 was a 15 Ω resistor, the voltage would be

    F.   25 volts.   H.   45 volts.

    G.   15 volts.   J.   50 volts.

39. Suppose a series of capacitors (C1 = 10, C2 = 10, C3 = 10) are combined with a resistor of 20 Ω (ohms). What would the resulting total voltage be?

    A.   17 volts   C.   87 volts

    B.   117 volts   D.   157 volts

40. Two resistors (R1 = 20, R2 = 10) were combined with one capacitor (20). The expected total voltage is

    F.   less than 50 volts.

    G.   more than 100 volts but less than 200 volts.

    H.   more than 50 volts but less than 100 volts.

    J.   more than 200 volts.

THIS IS THE END OF TEST 4.

DIAGNOSTIC TEST

ANSWER KEY

Question Number	Correct Answer	If You Answered this Question Incorrectly, Study Section on…

Test 1: English

1.	(C)	P. 155: The Sentence, P. 190: Misplaced Modifiers
2.	(J)	P. 157: The Comma
3.	(C)	P. 176: Subject-Verb Agreement
4.	(J)	P. 176: Subject-Verb Agreement, P. 157: The Comma
5.	(B)	P. 190: Misplaced Modifiers
6.	(F)	P. 197: Transitions
7.	(B)	P. 157: The Comma
8.	(J)	P. 178: Parallel Structure
9.	(D)	P. 197: Transitions
10.	(G)	P. 166: The Semicolon
11.	(B)	P. 200: Style
12.	(F)	P. 180: Comparisons
13.	(B)	P. 200: Style
14.	(F)	P. 157: The Comma
15.	(C)	P. 158: The Comma
16.	(J)	P. 174: Verbs
17.	(D)	P. 174: Verbs
18.	(H)	P. 170: The Apostrophe
19.	(B)	P. 176: Subject-Verb Agreement
20.	(G)	P. 198: Coherence/Unity

21.	(D)	P. 185: Subject Case of Pronoun
22.	(G)	P. 158: The Comma
23.	(D)	P. 200: Style
24.	(F)	P. 158: The Comma
25.	(B)	P. 158: The Comma
26.	(H)	P. 158: The Comma
27.	(C)	P. 174: Verbs
28.	(J)	P. 158: The Comma
29.	(B)	P. 200: Style
30.	(J)	P. 166: The Semicolon
31.	(C)	P. 198: Coherence/Unity
32.	(H)	P. 198: Coherence/Unity
33.	(B)	P. 197: Transitions
34.	(G)	P. 198: Coherence/Unity
35.	(A)	P. 198: Coherence/Unity
36.	(H)	P. 157: The Comma
37.	(C)	P. 198: Coherence/Unity
38.	(G)	P. 157: The Comma
39.	(C)	P. 198: Coherence/Unity
40.	(H)	P. 178: Parallel Structure
41.	(C)	P. 198: Coherence/Unity
42.	(F)	P. 157: The Comma
43.	(B)	P. 176: Subject-Verb Agreement
44.	(H)	P. 198: Coherence/Unity
45.	(C)	P. 198: Coherence/Unity
46.	(J)	P. 198: Coherence/Unity
47.	(C)	P. 158: The Comma
48.	(G)	P. 157: The Comma
49.	(B)	P. 197: Transitions
50.	(J)	P. 200: Style
51.	(D)	P. 158: The Comma
52.	(H)	P. 188: The Pronoun
53.	(B)	P. 155: The Sentence

54.	(H)	P. 184: The Relative Pronoun
55.	(B)	P. 180: Comparisons
56.	(F)	P. 158: The Comma
57.	(D)	P. 180: Comparisons
58.	(F)	P. 157: The Comma
59.	(B)	P. 200: Style
60.	(G)	P. 198: Coherence/Unity
61.	(A)	P. 198: Coherence/Unity
62.	(J)	P. 157: The Comma
63.	(C)	P. 200: Style
64.	(G)	P. 200: Style
65.	(A)	P. 178: Parallel Structure
66.	(J)	P. 176: Subject-Verb Agreement
67.	(C)	P. 200: Style
68.	(G)	P. 176: Subject-Verb Agreement
69.	(B)	P. 200: Style
70.	(J)	P. 198: Coherence/Unity
71.	(C)	P. 155: The Sentence
72.	(G)	P. 178: Parallel Structure
73.	(B)	P. 155: The Comma
74.	(H)	P. 198: Coherence/Unity
75.	(C)	P. 195: Strategy

Test 2: Mathematics

1.	(A)	P. 240: Radicals, P. 243: Exponents
2.	(F)	P. 267: Quadratic Equations
3.	(D)	P. 235: Percentages
4.	(G)	P. 254: Simplifying Algebraic Expressions
5.	(D)	P. 222: Fractions
6.	(G)	P. 258: Equations
7.	(D)	P. 240: Radicals
8.	(K)	P. 273: Absolute Value Equations

9.	(D)	P. 274: Inequalities
10.	(G)	P. 254: Simplifying Algebraic Expressions
11.	(B)	P. 222: Fractions, P. 258: Equations
12.	(G)	P. 258: Equations
13.	(B)	P. 278: Ratios and Proportions
14.	(G)	P. 258: Equations
15.	(C)	P. 254: Simplifying Algebraic Expressions
16.	(F)	P. 254: Simplifying Algebraic Expressions
17.	(B)	P. 267: Quadratic Equations
18.	(K)	P. 267: Quadratic Equations
19.	(C)	P. 258: Equations
20.	(K)	P. 222: Fractions
21.	(A)	P. 237: Converting a Percent to a Decimal
22.	(H)	P. 249: Operations with Polynomials
23.	(C)	P. 267: Quadratic Equations
24.	(H)	P. 249: Operations with Polynomials
25.	(C)	P. 274: Inequalities
26.	(G)	P. 254: Simplifying Algebraic Expressions
27.	(E)	P. 274: Inequalities
28.	(J)	P. 274: Inequalities
29.	(B)	P. 267: Quadratic Equations
30.	(K)	P. 262: Two Linear Equations
31.	(A)	P. 262: Two Linear Equations
32.	(F)	P. 249: Operations with Polynomials
33.	(B)	P. 258: Equations
34.	(G)	P. 309: Coordinate Geometry
35.	(D)	P. 309: Coordinate Geometry
36.	(G)	P. 309: Coordinate Geometry
37.	(E)	P. 274: Inequalities
38.	(G)	P. 305: Inscribed Angles
39.	(D)	P. 262: Two Linear Equations
40.	(H)	P. 309: Coordinate Geometry
41.	(C)	P. 246: Mean

42.	(J)	P. 260: Linear Equations
43.	(C)	P. 313: Angles and Trigonometric Functions
44.	(G)	P. 298: Quadrilaterals
45.	(C)	P. 313: Angles and Trigonometric Functions
46.	(J)	P. 298: Quadrilaterals
47.	(E)	P. 299: Rhombi
48.	(G)	P. 303: Circles, P. 298: Quadrilaterals
49.	(C)	P. 291: Triangles
50.	(G)	P. 291: Triangles, P. 303: Circles
51.	(B)	P. 284: Parallel Lines, P. 292: Triangles
52.	(H)	P. 288: Regular Polygons
53.	(B)	P. 298: Quadrilaterals
54.	(F)	P. 281: Types of Angles
55.	(D)	P. 291: Triangles
56.	(J)	P. 298: Quadrilaterals
57.	(C)	P. 313: Angles and Trigonometric Functions
58.	(K)	P. 316: Basic Identities
59.	(D)	P. 313: Angles and Trigonometric Functions
60.	(H)	P. 320: Graphs of Trigonometric Functions

Test 3: Reading

1.	(C)	P. 333: Explicit Statements and Inferences
2.	(J)	P. 336: Drawing Conclusions
3.	(A)	P. 337: Vocabulary
4.	(G)	P. 333: Explicit Statements and Inferences
5.	(A)	P. 333: Explicit Statements and Inferences
6.	(J)	P. 335: Supporting Details
7.	(C)	P. 333: Explicit Statements and Inferences
8.	(H)	P. 337: Vocabulary
9.	(B)	P. 335: Supporting Details
10.	(J)	P. 333: Explicit Statements and Inferences
11.	(B)	P. 335: Main Idea

12.	(G)	P. 336: Drawing Conclusions
13.	(B)	P. 336: Drawing Conclusions
14.	(F)	P. 336: Drawing Conclusions
15.	(C)	P. 335: Summarizing
16.	(H)	P. 336: Drawing Conclusions
17.	(D)	P. 336: Drawing Conclusions
18.	(J)	P. 336: Comparison/Contrast
19.	(C)	P. 336: Author's Tone/Attitude
20.	(J)	P. 335: Summarizing
21.	(B)	P. 333: Explicit Statements and Inferences
22.	(J)	P. 336: Drawing Conclusions
23.	(A)	P. 333: Explicit Statements and Inferences
24.	(G)	P. 333: Explicit Statements and Inferences
25.	(C)	P. 336: Relationship Between Ideas/Facts
26.	(F)	P. 336: Comparison/Contrast
27.	(B)	P. 333: Explicit Statements and Inferences
28.	(J)	P. 333: Explicit Statements and Inferences
29.	(D)	P. 336: Comparison/Contrast
30.	(H)	P. 336: Drawing Conclusions
31.	(C)	P. 333: Explicit Statements and Inferences
32.	(H)	P. 333: Explicit Statements and Inferences
33.	(C)	P. 336: Drawing Conclusions
34.	(F)	P. 336: Drawing Conclusions
35.	(C)	P. 337: Vocabulary
36.	(H)	P. 334: Fact/Opinion
37.	(D)	P. 334: Fact/Opinion
38.	(G)	P. 336: Author's Tone/Attitude
39.	(D)	P. 337: Vocabulary
40.	(J)	P. 336: Forming Generalizations

Test 4: Science Reasoning

1.	(B)	P. 401: Research Summaries
2.	(F)	P. 401: Research Summaries
3.	(D)	P. 401: Research Summaries
4.	(H)	P. 401: Research Summaries
5.	(B)	P. 401: Research Summaries
6.	(J)	P. 401: Research Summaries
7.	(B)	P. 415: Conflicting Viewpoints
8.	(J)	P. 415: Conflicting Viewpoints
9.	(A)	P. 415: Conflicting Viewpoints
10.	(J)	P. 415: Conflicting Viewpoints
11.	(B)	P. 415: Conflicting Viewpoints
12.	(J)	P. 415: Conflicting Viewpoints
13.	(A)	P. 385: Data Representation
14.	(F)	P. 385: Data Representation
15.	(D)	P. 385: Data Representation
16.	(G)	P. 385: Data Representation
17.	(C)	P. 385: Data Representation
18.	(H)	P. 385: Data Representation
19.	(A)	P. 385: Data Representation
20.	(J)	P. 385: Data Representation
21.	(C)	P. 385: Data Representation
22.	(J)	P. 385: Data Representation
23.	(C)	P. 401: Research Summaries
24.	(F)	P. 401: Research Summaries
25.	(B)	P. 401: Research Summaries
26.	(J)	P. 401: Research Summaries
27.	(B)	P. 401: Research Summaries
28.	(G)	P. 401: Research Summaries
29.	(D)	P. 415: Conflicting Viewpoints
30.	(H)	P. 415: Conflicting Viewpoints
31.	(B)	P. 415: Conflicting Viewpoints
32.	(G)	P. 415: Conflicting Viewpoints

33.	(B)	P. 415: Conflicting Viewpoints
34.	(H)	P. 415: Conflicting Viewpoints
35.	(D)	P. 415: Conflicting Viewpoints
36.	(G)	P. 385: Data Representation
37.	(C)	P. 385: Data Representation
38.	(J)	P. 385: Data Representation
39.	(B)	P. 385: Data Representation
40.	(G)	P. 385: Data Representation

DETAILED EXPLANATIONS OF ANSWERS

Test 1: English

1. **(C)** The correct choice is (C). The phrase "standing on the fire tower on Bear Swamp Hill" modifies the subject "One" and therefore cannot be separated from that sentence by a period, as (A) suggests. Beginning a new sentence with "While standing," as (B) is written, renders the second sentence incomplete. The semicolon separating "miles" and "while" indicates that the remainder of the sentence is an independent clause, which it is not, as it lacks a subject; therefore, choice (D) is also incorrect.

2. **(J)** (J) is the correct choice, as a comma is the appropriate mark of punctuation separating a short series of similar items. The semicolon is used to clarify groupings in a relatively long, complicated list of items; thus, both (F) and (G) are incorrect choices. (H) is incorrect, as it fails to capitalize "County." "County" must be capitalized as part of a proper name and to be in parallel form to "Washington Township."

3. **(C)** The correct choice is (C), as it employs, as does the rest of the paragraph, the third person form of "visitor," which agrees with the singular verb form "sees." (A) moves the pronoun to the second person form, "you," not in keeping with the rest of the text and uses the verb "sees," which does not agree with the subject "you." The plural third person use of "we" suggested in choice (B) does not agree with the singular third person set up in the rest of the paragraph, and (D) again incorrectly uses the second person form "you."

4. **(J)** Choice (J) is correct as the verb "stand" agrees with the subject "patches" and a comma separates the two adjectives "long" and "dark" which modify that subject. (G) is incorrect because the verb "stands" is not in agreement with "patches." (H) is incorrect because the comma separating the two modifying adjectives is missing, as it is missing, too, in choice (F).

5. **(B)** (B) is the correct choice as the participial phrase "Looking eastward" is separated from the pronoun "one" that it modifies. (B) is also correct because it *includes* the pronoun. The original sentence had no modifier. Choice (A) is incorrect as this participial phrase has no noun/pronoun to modify, making the phrase a dangling modifier. Choice (C) lacks the necessary comma separating the participial phrase from the modified word and further exhibits a subject-verb

agreement error between "one" and "perceive." (D), like (A), is in error because it is a dangling modifier lacking an object to be modified.

6. **(F)** Because it links the topic of the previous paragraph, the beauty of the Pine Barrens, with the topic of Paragraph 2, the transportation aspect, (F) is the best choice for transition and introduction. Choices (G) and (J) make no reference to the beauty of the area noted in paragraph 1, and choice (H) refers only to the industrial aspect of Paragraph 2; thus, none of these choices provides the necessary, logical link, or transition, between the passages.

7. **(B)** (B) is the correct choice as the phrase "called the Pine Barrens" is consistent in its punctuation, lacking commas at both its beginning and its end. Short appositive phrases must either be completely surrounded by commas or lack both surrounding commas entirely. Choices (A) and (C) are inconsistent as only one comma follows the phrase or precedes it. (D) is a poor choice as it is wordy, using the unnecessary phrase "by the name of."

8. **(J)** Parallel in structure to its counterpart direct object "sounds of industry," choice (J), "the smells of industry," is the best choice. (F) is not only unparallel, but is a cliché, inappropriate for fresh writing. Both (G) and (H) lack the parallelism of choice (J).

9. **(D)** The best answer is (D). The transitional term "Surprisingly" is a logical choice as one doesn't expect such a rural, East Coast area traversed by a seemingly small traffic corridor to cover such a large land area as 650,000 acres. Choice (B), "Therefore," implies a logical cause-and-effect relationship between the industrialization of the area and the size of the Barrens, which doesn't make sense, as industry doesn't cause the size of a space to increase or decrease. Choice (C), "On the contrary," suggests that Paragraph 3 takes an opposing stance to a point made in Paragraph 2, which is not the case.

10. **(G)** Choice (G) is correct as the semicolon joins two independent clauses. (F) is incorrect as a comma joining two independent clauses creates a comma splice error. Two independent clauses can be joined by a comma and a coordinating conjunction, such as "and." However, the semi-colon instead of the comma, as suggested in choice (H), is incorrect. (J), too, is incorrect as the second clause beginning with the subordinate conjunction "while" is dependent; the semicolon is used to join two independent clauses.

11. **(B)** Choice (B) is best in that it succinctly describes the town and is unrepetitive in its use of adjectives, whereas the other choices use the redundant adjectives "tiny" and "small."

12. **(F)**   The first choice, (F), is the correct one. The use of the term "as" is the only one which provides a logical means of comparing the present Pine Barrens to the past. (G) and (H) are incorrect in that the subordinating conjunctions "if" and "when" are not followed by a dependent clause (the subject "area" has no verb). "Then," used in choice (J), is an adverb telling when (not a conjunction) as is "than," which could be used to compare the past and present Pine Barrens.

13. **(B)**   Choice (B) is the best answer as it employs the most succinct wording to describe the location of the Barrens. Choices (A), (C), and (D) use unnecessary words which do nothing to improve the image provided by choice (B).

14. **(F)**   The original phrase is unmarred by unnecessary commas, and therefore, choice (F) is correct. Choice (G) inserts a comma between "Building" and "in" which would be grammatically correct only if a comma followed "City." A comma between "City" and "could" is correct only if a comma preceded "in," thus making choice (H) incorrect. Finally, choice (J) is incorrect because commas shouldn't separate auxiliary verbs from main verbs, as "could" and "see" are separated.

15. **(C)**   As a comma is the appropriate mark of punctuation separating an introductory dependent clause from the accompanying independent clause, choice (C) is correct. Choices (A) and (B) both incorrectly use the semicolon, reserved to join independent clauses. Choice (D)'s placement of a period incorrectly indicates that the dependent clause, "And...Richmond," is a complete sentence when it is not (the subordinate conjunction "if" which introduces the dependent clause cannot stand alone).

16. **(J)**   The correct choice is (J) as the subordinating conjunction "if" of the preceding clause indicates a *possible* state, thus necessitating the subjunctive verb form "would fall." (F) is incorrect as "fallen" lacks an auxiliary verb such as "had" and fails to conform to the needs of the "if" conjunction. (G) is simple past tense, not subjunctive, and (H) is not subjunctive either, lacking, as well, a necessary auxiliary verb such as "is."

17. **(D)**   Choice (D) is correct as its verb "has been" allows the bicycle to be viewed rather than the *bicycle* to do the viewing, which is illogical. Further, this choice provides the comma which accompanies the earlier one separating the clause "with...centuries." Choice (A) has the bicycle illogically doing the looking; choice (B) lacks the necessary comma to set off the clause and has the bicycle looking; and choice (C) also lacks the necessary comma.

18. **(H)**   (H) is the correct choice as the apostrophe is placed before the "s" in "child's," denoting singular possession of the following noun, "plaything."

Choice (F) lacks the necessary possessive apostrophe for "child's," while choice (G) lacks it for "children's." Choice (J) incorrectly places the possessive apostrophe for a singular noun "child" after the "s."

19. **(B)**   Because the singular subject "use" is again referred to in its singular form later in the sentence, choice (B)'s suggestion of the singular subject "use" agreeing with the singular verb "was" is correct. Further, this verb must be in past tense to agree with the consistent use of past tense throughout the passage. Choice (A) incorrectly places a plural verb "were" with a singular subject "use." Choice (C)'s present tense "are" is inconsistent with the passage's past tense usage, and choice (D) incorrectly employs the plural subject and the present tense verb, again resulting in inconsistency.

20. **(G)**   The most logical order for Paragraph 1 places Sentence 4 after Sentence 1, thus making choice (G) the best answer. Here the issues of children are logically placed together and in keeping with the progression of child to adult that the use of the bicycle suggests. Sentence 4 doesn't work well where it is now, as presented in choice (F), because it follows two sentences about adults and therefore seems out of order. Furthermore, it cannot be placed before Sentence 3, choice (H), as again it interrupts two sentences dealing with adult bicycle usage. Following Sentence 5 with Sentence 4 makes little sense, for we still have the great separation of the child references noted in Sentence 1. Therefore, choice (J) is incorrect.

21. **(D)**   Choice (D) is correct because it employs the subjective case pronoun "who," which serves as the subject of the following dependent clause "who...Paris." Choices (A) and (B) are incorrect as "whom" is in the objective case and thus cannot serve as the subject of a clause. Choice (C) does not make sense as "who's" is the contraction for "who is."

22. **(G)**   The correct choice is (G) as no mark of punctuation is necessary between the independent clause of the first half of the sentence and the following dependent clause beginning with "so." (F) incorrectly treats the subordinate clause, "So...steered," as a complete sentence, and (H) lacks the logical necessity of the connector "so" to join the independent and following dependent clauses. As (F) incorrectly treated the second clause as independent, so does choice (J), by setting it off with a semicolon, reserved for separating independent clauses, not one independent from one dependent.

23. **(D)**   The best answer here is choice (D) as it adheres to stylistic rules of concise, non-repetitive language. Choice (A) is far too wordy as "reverse," "change direction," and "go the other way" are redundant. Choices (B) and (C) unnecessarily include the words "one would find that it" which do nothing to further the basic meaning of the sentence.

24. **(F)** Choice (F) is the correct answer as a comma is necessary before "and" to separate the independent clauses ("In...velocifere" and "and...formed") and after "and" to enclose the intervening clause ("as...Paris,"). (G) is incorrect because it lacks the comma separating the independent clauses. (H) will not work because it lacks both the comma between the independent clauses and the comma to set off the intervening clause. The semicolon *with* the coordinating conjunction "and" is redundant and therefore unnecessary, so (J) is incorrect.

25. **(B)** In this case, (B) is the best choice as it treats the second clause, "when...steered," correctly as a dependent clause. Since "when...steered" is a dependent clause and therefore cannot stand alone, it should not be denoted as a complete sentence, as it suggested by choice (A), nor should it be preceded by a semicolon as in choice (C). Although choice (D) employs acceptable punctuation between the clauses, the word "however" illogically implies a contrast or difference of perspective between the idea presented in the first clause and that presented in the second clause. Baron von Drais' wheel of the second clause was the revolutionary improvement noted in the first clause. Thus, choice (D) is not the best answer.

26. **(H)** Correctly separating the introductory dependent clause from the following dependent clause by a comma, choice (H) is the right answer. (F) misuses the semicolon, while (G) fails to offer the necessary comma. Eliminating the comma between "Baden" and "von Drais," as does choice (J), is confusing as the phrase, "Grand Duke of Baden von Drais," seems to be one person's name, which a logical look at the entire sentence disproves.

27. **(C)** (C) is the only choice which provides the verb "gave" in the past tense, which is consistent with the rest of the passage. Further, choice (C) correctly uses the proper singular pronoun reference "it" for the singular antecedent "machine." Choice (A) is inconsistent in tense by using the present perfect form "has given," and choice (B) uses both the inconsistent past perfect "had given" and an incorrect plural pronoun reference, "them." (D) again is inconsistent in tense.

28. **(J)** Choice (J) is correct because it treats the clause beginning with "where" as dependent by not separating it from the previous independent clause with a period, as is done by choice (F), nor with a semicolon, as in choice (H). Further, (J) does not insert an unnecessary comma following the subordinating conjunction "where," as does choice (G).

29. **(B)** By using concise wording, choice (B) is the best answer. Choices (A), (C), and (D) all include unnecessary verbiage which does nothing to further the meaning of the more briefly and directly worded choice (B).

30. **(J)** Choice (J) correctly uses the semicolon to separate two independent clauses and is unambiguous in the use of "pastime" to refer to the sport of bicycle

riding. Choice (F) uses the vague and ambiguous pronoun "it," which has several possible antecedents in the previous clause; choice (G) incorrectly uses the comma to separate the independent clauses, and choice (H) again employs the vague and ambiguous pronoun "it."

31. **(C)**   The best answer is (C), as the passage deals with the steps of invention of the bicycle, a piece of equipment used for sport. Although the passage mentions French nobility, it doesn't deal with nobles' rise to power; therefore choice (A) is inappropriate. Certainly, bicycle riding is a hobby, but the passage deals with this hobby in the 1700s and the 1800s, thereby making choice (B) incorrect. Continental Europe is indeed the scene for some of the development of the bicycle, but garden paths have little to do with the passage; hence, choice (D) is not a logical choice.

32. **(H)**   Choice (H) is the best answer as it relates Paragraph 4's main point about the decline of the velocipede to the main point of Paragraph 1, the progress of the bicycle in America, thus uniting the passage as a whole. Choice (F) is limited in content to Europe and the demise of the bicycle, neither of which issues relate to Paragraph 1's point about the popularity of the bicycle in America. Choice (G) again centers on the demise of the velocipede but mentions nothing of America. Choice (J) does link the velocipede and America; however, its point about the lack of evidence of popularity in America is counter to the evident popularity of the American bicycle at the end of the 1800s.

33. **(B)**   Choice (B) is correct because "However" is used as a coordinating conjunction introducing a complete sentence and implies that that complete sentence will present an opposing perspective to the previous sentence. Sentence 1 focuses on Einstein's mystification; however, Sentence 2 focuses on his discovery in spite of that mystification. Choice (A) is incorrect because "since" is a subordinating conjunction used to introduce a dependent clause. Dependent clauses cannot stand alone as complete sentences. Choice (C) will not work for the same reason: "Inasmuch as" is a subordinate conjunctive phrase. The coordinate conjunction "Therefore" of choice (D) means "because," which doesn't work logically to link the opposing perspectives of Sentences 1 and 2.

34. **(G)**   "Of these concerned," choice (G), is the correct answer as it is consistent in its adjective usage of "these," as found in the previous sentence, and is direct and clear in its wording. Choice (F) is not as strong an answer because it is inconsistent in its use of "these." Choice (H) is problematic in that it is both inconsistent in its use of "those" and it is redundant in its use of "connections." Finally, choice (J), omitting the underlined portion, renders the sentence incomplete.

35. **(A)**   By giving the example of gravity having the ability to pass through any object or shield, which is an ability magnetism (another natural force) does not have, choice (A) supports the assertion of gravity's uniqueness and therefore is the correct answer. Choice (B) speaks of specific gravity but compares it to no other natural force. That Newton discovered gravity, choice (C), offers no consideration of gravity's traits nor of its comparison to other forces. Choice (D)'s focus on gravity as a part of our lives offers no proof of gravity being unique among other natural forces. Therefore, choices (B), (C), and (D) are incorrect.

36. **(H)**   Choice (H) is the best answer as it is uninterrupted by unnecessary commas, has a verb that agrees in number with its subject "we," and is not a cliché. (F) is incorrect as its verb "pays" does not agree in number with its subject "we." Because (G) has a comma incorrectly separating the subject "we" from the adverb "usually," this choice will not work. Nor will choice (J) work, as it uses a cliché (a well-worn set of words that, because of their overuse, fail to create a fresh image).

37. **(C)**   The correct answer is choice (C) because "think" is consistent with the present verb tense of the rest of the passage. Choices (A) and (B) are incorrect for two reasons: the preposition "of" illogically has been used instead of the necessary auxiliary verb "have," and the tense is not consistent with the passage. Although "of" has been corrected in choice (D), tense consistency is still a problem.

38. **(G)**   Choice (G) is the correct answer as no unnecessary marks of punctuation interrupt the two compound verb phrases. Choice (F) is incorrect as it places an unnecessary comma before "or." Usually a comma before a coordinating conjunction such as "or" is necessary only when three or more similar things are listed, when the conjunction separates two independent clauses, or when sentence misinterpretation would result. None of these situations is the case. Choice (H) incorrectly uses the semicolon, usually reserved for separating independent clauses or clarifying lists which include many commas. Choice (J) is incorrect for its use of an unnecessary comma.

39. **(C)**   The best choice is (C) as it logically links Paragraph 3's idea of competition and contests with Paragraph 4's concepts of cycles. Choice (A) gives no logical link to the ideas of the previous paragraph but rather focuses entirely on the concepts of Paragraph 4. The concept of the solar system mentioned in choice (B) has nothing to do with either Paragraph 3 or Paragraph 4. Finally, choice (D) represents the "workaday world" to the reader; yet, the ideas in both Paragraph 3 and 4 involve recreation and simple body movements, neither of which is expressly linked to the work day.

40. **(H)**   Choice (H) is the correct answer as it is parallel in construction to its counterparts in the sentence "climbing," "moving," and "lowering." Furthermore, "raising" is the transitive form of the verb "to raise." Transitive verbs require a direct object to act upon, as is provided with the direct object "things." Choice (G) is incorrect because it is not parallel with its counterparts, due to the insertion of "in," moreover, the verb "rising" is intransitive. Intransitive verbs do not act upon objects. (F) is also incorrect for this reason. (J) will not work because "raise" is not parallel to its counterparts which have the "ing" ending.

41.· **(C)**   The correct answer is choice (C), "our," as the voice throughout the passage has been in the first person plural, "we" or "our." Choice (A) is in first person singular; choice (B) is in the simple plural of the pronoun "one;" and choice (D) is not only in the wrong voice but is mispunctuated as a possessive (the apostrophe needs to precede the "s"). Therefore, choices (A), (B), and (D) are incorrect.

42. **(F)**   Choice (F), the original, is correct. Choice (G) unnecessarily places a comma before the coordinating conjunction "and," a comma that is usually reserved only to separate independent clauses or to precede the last item in a list of over three things. Choice (H), too, is incorrect as the semicolon is redundant with "and," and, further, should be used primarily to separate two independent clauses. "Give in to the gravity in the grave" is not an independent clause as it lacks a subject. Finally, choice (J) is incorrect for the same reason of a misused semicolon.

43. **(B)**   The correct choice here is (B). The singular verb "holds" agrees with the singular "adhesive." Choice (A) is incorrect due to the agreement error between "adhesives" and "holds." Choice (C) also has an agreement error between "adhesives" and "holds." Although agreement between "adhesive" and the verb phrase "has been holding" is not a problem in choice (D), the present perfect tense of the verb phrase is inconsistent with the simple present tense of the rest of the passage; therefore, choice (D) is incorrect.

44. **(H)**   (H) is the best choice as the human physique is the physical product of the human anatomy, and it is gravity's pull on the body which, in part, acts to shape that anatomy and physique. Choice (F) is incorrect as the first paragraph need not mention all vital information in the essay to follow. If it did, there would be no point to developing the rest of the essay! Paragraph 2 is, indeed, important as it proves that gravity is a tremendously strong albeit invisible force, and it is just that strength and invisibility that allow it to be almost forgotten in our daily lives yet at the same time such a shaper of our daily existence. Thus, Paragraph 2 is necessary to form a logical transition between the ideas of Paragraph 1 and Paragraph 3. Choice (G) is, then, incorrect. Finally, choice (J), too, is a poor answer as it fails to unite the ideas of Paragraph 5 and Paragraph 1. Paragraph 1 does not really deal with the human physique, as does the new material, but rather with the mysteries of gravity.

45. **(C)**   The best answer is (C) as it unites Paragraph 5's concept of the expanding Universe with Paragraph 1's concept of the puzzling mystery of gravity. Choice (A) focuses narrowly on a planet within the Universe and is unrelated entirely to Paragraph 1. Choice (B) relates well to Paragraph 5 in its focus on the stars and galaxies; however, it does not link to the puzzle of gravity as presented in Paragraph 1. Choice (D) is clearly linked to Albert Einstein, as mentioned in Paragraph 1; yet, it holds no strong relationship with Paragraph 5's topic of the Universe and gravity.

46. **(J)**   Choice (J) provides the best strategy, as it answers the need to compare various concepts. This need for comparison is indicated by the "est" ending on "profoundest," which demands at least two concepts with which to compare gravity. Citing mysteries in the process of gravity offers no other concepts with which to compare the process, so choice (F) is inappropriate. Explaining how philosophy originated does not offer concepts to compare with gravity; thus, choice (G) will not work, nor will choice (H), for it, too, lacks another concept of logic in natural philosophy with which to compare gravity.

47. **(C)**   Choice (C) is the correct answer as it surrounds the non-essential subordinate clause with commas. Choice (A) incorrectly places a comma only at the beginning of that same clause, while choice (B) fails to place the commas around it at all. Choice (D) is incorrect because it, like choice (A), only places a comma at one end of the non-essential clause, this time at the end.

48. **(G)**   As an appositive phrase, "the HMS *Eagle*" must be surrounded by commas or completely unencumbered by them. Thus, choice (G) is the correct answer as both commas are present. Choice (F) is incorrect as only the end comma is present, and choice (H) has only the beginning one, thus making it incorrect, as well. Finally, choice (J) does not work as the enclosing marks of punctuation, the comma and the dash, are inconsistent with each other.

49. **(B)**   Logically, choice (B) is the correct answer as the introductory word "Although" appropriately sets up the seemingly contrary action of removing the British vessels even though the American's attack was unsuccessful. Choice (A) implies expected results of the unsuccessful attack, and one usually wouldn't expect an unsuccessful attack to cause a fleet to retreat; therefore, choice (A) is incorrect. For the same reason, choices (C) and (D) are incorrect, as well.

50. **(J)**   The correct choice is answer (J) because of its clean and direct wording and its avoidance of the cliché, "out of harm's way." Choice (F) is guilty of using the aforementioned cliché, as are choices (G) and (H). Additionally, (G) and (H) are quite wordy.

51. **(D)** The correct choice (D) is punctuated with a comma, denoting that the following clause, begun with the subordinate conjunction "when," is dependent and cannot stand alone. Nor can this dependent clause follow a semicolon, as this mark of punctuation would denote incorrectly, as do choices (A) and (B), that it is an independent clause. Choice (C) presents a similar problem in that it treats this dependent clause as a complete sentence, which it is not as it depends on the preceding independent clause to make sense.

52. **(H)** Choice (H) is the correct answer as "its" is the possessive form of "it." The object of possession is "potential." (F) makes no sense as "it's" is the contraction for the words "it is." No such word exists as "its'," thereby eliminating (G) as a possible choice. The final choice (J), "there," doesn't work for two reasons. First, "there" refers to location, not to be confused with the plural possessive pronoun "their." Second, even if "their were a choice, it would be incorrect as the antecedent "Germany" is singular and requires the singular possessive form.

53. **(B)** Choice (B) is correct as no mark of punctuation is necessary between the adjective "German" and the modified noun "U-boats." By placing a period between these two words, as does choice (A), the newly created sentence beginning with "Wholesale" is rendered incomplete as it lacks a predicate; therefore, choice (A) is incorrect. Choice (C) adds an "s" to "German," making it "Germans," but fails to add a possessive apostrophe after the "s" to make the phrase grammatically sound. The semicolon placement between "German" and "U-boat," choice (D), indicates the words on either side of that mark are independent clauses; however, the first preceding words lack a predicate, and therefore cannot be considered a clause at all.

54. **(H)** Choice (H) is the correct answer as the relative pronoun "which" logically refers to the antecedent "Allied Submarine Devices Investigation Committee," a thing, rather than a person. The relative pronouns "who" and "whom" refer to antecedents which are persons, thus eliminating choices (F), (G), and (J) as possible choices.

55. **(B)** The correct choice is (B) as "more" clearly refers to the difficulty American subs had in finding German subs because of ineffective equipment prior to the closing months of World War I and the need for effective underwater detection equipment as the war came to an end. Choice (A) does not work because the adjective "real" is incorrectly employed as an adverb modifying "effective." Choice (C), too, is incorrect as is choice (D), for both are illogical. Certainly, America wouldn't seek less or least effective equipment.

56. **(F)** The original, choice (F), is correct as a comma precedes a concisely worded appositive phrase of moderate length renaming or defining the "trainable hydrophone." Choice (G) incorrectly uses a semi-colon; choice (H) uses the

unnecessary and wordy phrase "which was;" and choice (J) foregoes the necessary comma preceding the appositive.

57. **(D)** Because "than" is in the latter part of the sentence, it needs an earlier counterpart with which to complete the comparison. Choice (D) is the only answer which provides this counterpart so that the "more than" comparison is complete. Neither (A)'s "additional," (B)'s "extended," nor (C)'s "repeated" can grammatically work.

58. **(F)** The original choice (F) is the correct answer as a comma is necessary to separate items in a simple list. Choice (G) doesn't work as the semicolon is used in lists only if they are quite lengthy and include groupings of items in which commas are already present. Choice (H) lacks the required comma between items, while choice (J) incorrectly inserts a comma between an adjective, "additional," and the phrase it modifies, "battery capacity."

59. **(B)** "The modified snorkel," choice (B), is correct because of the accuracy and conciseness of language. Choices (A), (C), and (D) are all wordy and redundant and add neither clarification nor elaboration to the straightforward presentation of choice (B).

60. **(G)** Sentence 2 should be placed after Sentence 3, choice (G), because Sentence 3 elaborates on the means of converting the fleet-type submarine, the point of Sentence 1. Further, this correct placement now allows the closing phrase, "making the submarine a truly formidable craft," at the end of Sentence 2 to appear at the end of the paragraph, thus giving the paragraph unity. Therefore, (F) indicates incorrect placement within the paragraph. Placing Sentence 2 at the beginning of the paragraph, choice (H), comments on the success of the improvements before those improvements have even been explained, thus negating that answer as a correct choice. Choice (J)'s suggested placement of Sentence 2 at the end of the previous paragraph is illogical as it is not on the same topic as Paragraph 3 (the development of SONAR).

61. **(A)** Logic demands that the new sentences dealing with attack on British ironclads be placed in the paragraph already dealing with that topic, Paragraph 1. As no other paragraph concerns this issue, choice (A) is correct. (B) suggests placement in Paragraph 2 which discusses Allied battles; however, nothing in the new sentences deals with Allied ships. Thus, choice (B) is incorrect. Granted, in some cases, new, important information should stand alone as stated by choice (C), but the new sentences are an elaboration on an already established plan and need to go with that plan for clarification. Although choice (D) offers a valid suggestion for concluding paragraphs, placing the ironclad sentences at the end would put this chronologically arranged passage out of order.

62. **(J)**   Choice (J) is correct as it is succinctly worded and places no unnecessary comma between the introductory independent clause ending with "areas" and the following essential dependent clause beginning with "where." An intervening comma eliminates choice (F) as a possibility, as it does choice (G). Although choice (H) doesn't have the offending comma, the passage is wordy.

63. **(C)**   The best answer is choice (C), for it is both direct and economical in its wording. All other choices (A), (B), and (D) are unnecessarily wordy and redundant.

64. **(G)**   The correct choice here is (G). Again, economy of wording in addition to clarity of writing recommend this answer. Choice (F) is redundant in its use of cacti; (H) is convoluted in language and therefore unclear; and (J) introduces "latter" and "former," which slow the reader down as he/she seeks to remember which was which.

65. **(A)**   The original selection, choice (A), is the best answer. It is parallel in its construction of similar elements, concise in its wording, and the correct mark of punctuation, the comma, separates "surface" from "wiry or velvety hairs," elements in a simple list. The wordier choice (B) adds nothing to the more economical phrasing of choice (A), while both choices (C) and (D) incorrectly use a semicolon instead of a comma to separate items in a simple list.

66. **(J)**   Choice (J) is correct as it allows the subject "shape" to agree in number with the verb "provides." A common error is evident in choice (F). The subject has been misidentified as the plural "succulents," and the plural verb "provide" has been chosen to agree with it; however, a subject will never be found in a prepositional phrase, such as "of many succulents." Thus, choice (F) is incorrect. Choice (G) is incorrect as it suggests the present perfect verb form which is inconsistent with the simple present form of the rest of the passage. Choice (H) is also guilty of inconsistent verb tense as it suggests the progressive present and is therefore incorrect.

67. **(C)**   The best answer is choice (C), not only for its concise language but for its correct placement of the comma following the introductory participial phrase, "Possessed by cacti alone." Choice (A) is wordy, as is choice (B). Finally, choice (D) fails to place the necessary comma after the participial phrase.

68. **(G)**   Because the plural verb "arise" agrees in number with the plural subject, "spines, hairs (and the barbed hairs or spines of 'Opuntia')," choice (G) is correct. The original (F) is incorrect as the verb doesn't agree in number with the subject. One must be careful to check for subjects that follow the verb rather than precede it. Both choices (H) and (J) are inconsistent in verb tense with the

rest of the passage. (H) is in present perfect while (J) is in past; yet, the passage is in simple present.

69. **(B)** Freshness of language is the concern in this situation. The only answer which is not a cliché is choice (B), and therefore the only correct choice. Clichés are tired phrases which require little thought and no longer inspire images in the mind of the reader, which newly created phrases should do. Thus, clichés should be avoided.

70. **(J)** The focus of Paragraph 4 is the difficulty in differentiating some species of cacti from other succulents. Hence, the cost of travel to Madagascar is off the topic and should be eliminated from the passage, making (J) the correct choice. Because choices (F), (G), and (H) all deal with this same trip, they are incorrect choices.

71. **(C)** Choice (C) provides the correct answer here. It separates the first introductory independent clause by making it a complete sentence, thus clarifying what might be a rather confusing and lengthy sentence. Further, it begins the second sentence with the logical subordinating conjunction "although," which sets up the contrast between the ease of differentiating cacti and other succulents by their leaves and flowers and the difficulty of recognizing the areole. Choice (A) uses "Because" to introduce the new sentence, but there is no cause-and-effect relationship between identification by leaves and flowers and identification by areoles. Choice (B) correctly employs the semicolon; however, the subordinating conjunction "nevertheless" suggests that there is a disagreement or contrast between identification by leaves and flowers and some other method immediately stated earlier, which is not the case; therefore, choice (B), too, is wrong. Because of the lacking punctuation (a semicolon or a period) between "easy" and "although," choice (D) is incorrect, as well.

72. **(G)** Verb problems are the focus of this question. Choice (G) is the correct answer in that "are" is consistent with the present tense of the passage. Choice (F), the progressive present "are being," is inconsistent, as is choice (H), the future perfect "will have been," and choice (J), the progressive past "having been."

73. **(B)** Choice (B) is the correct answer in this case. It places a comma between the introductory independent clause and the non-essential dependent clause that follows, and it doesn't place an unnecessary comma after the word "provided." "Provided" is clearly connected to the subordinating conjunction "that," and to interrupt the two creates a jolt in sentence flow. Choice (A) treats the dependent clause as a complete sentence and is therefore incorrect. Choice (C) interjects the offending comma after "provided," and choice (D) fails to separate the non-essential clause by a comma and places, incorrectly, a comma after "provided."

74. **(H)**   Paragraph 3 should be placed after Paragraph 4, as choice (H) indicates, because it provides the descriptive means by which the areole can be identified, a demand set up in Paragraph 4. By leaving Paragraph 3 where it is now, as suggested by choice (F), one would present a specific description of a topic before that general topic was even introduced; therefore, (F) is not advisable. Placing Paragraph 3 after Paragraph 1 would interrupt the moisture storage sequence set up in Paragraphs 1 and 2, which would be a problem. Finally, placing Paragraph 3 after Paragraph 5 would interrupt the two paragraphs focusing on the need to describe the areole and that actual description; therefore, choice (J) is incorrect.

75. **(C)**   Comparing and contrasting cacti to succulents as a whole, choice (C), is the correct answer. The author states that both are excellent for ownership, thus negating choice (A) as a possibility. Choice (B)'s topic of the evolution of the succulents might be interesting, but it was not mentioned in this passage; thus, (B) is incorrect. So, too, is choice (D) incorrect, as indigenous North American flora are not a part of this essay.

Test 2: Mathematics

1.   **(A)**   We use the following approximate values:

$$\pi = 3.1416 \cong 3$$
$$\sqrt{2} = 1.414 \cong 1.5$$
$$2.17 \cong 2$$
$$(6.83)^2 \cong 7^2 = 49 \cong 50$$
$$(1.07)^2 \cong 1^2 = 1$$

Then,

$$A \cong \frac{3 \times 1.5 \times 2}{50 + 1} = \frac{9}{51} \cong \frac{10}{50} = 0.2.$$

2.   **(F)**   To find the other root of the quadratic equation, we must first solve for the coefficient a. Substituting 6 for x, we obtain:

$$x^2 - ax + 12 = 0$$
$$6^2 - a(6) + 12 = 0$$
$$36 + 12 = 6a$$
$$48 = 6a$$
$$8 = a$$

The quadratic equation that we obtain is:

$$x^2 - 8x + 12 = 0.$$

Factoring: $(x - 6)(x - 2) = 0$, $x = 6$ and $x = 2$.

Therefore, the roots are 6 and 2.

3. **(D)** The man originally buys the book for \$20. He wishes to make a 50% profit on the book. To do this, he must sell the book for:

$$20 + (50\%)(20) = \$30.$$

He would like the \$30 price to appear as if it is a mark down from an even higher price. We must find this phony price. Let this price be p. Then:

$$p - (40\%)(p) = 30$$
$$(.60)p = 30$$
$$p = \$50.$$

4. **(G)** $c = 12a + 54b$
$\qquad\qquad = 6(2a + 9b)$

Therefore, c must be divisible by 6 which is the greatest common divisor of 12 and 54.

5. **(D)**
$$\frac{a + \dfrac{a}{b}}{a - \dfrac{a}{b}} = \frac{4 + \dfrac{4}{7}}{4 - \dfrac{4}{7}}$$

$$= \frac{\dfrac{28}{7} + \dfrac{4}{7}}{\dfrac{28}{7} - \dfrac{4}{7}}$$

$$= \frac{\dfrac{32}{7}}{\dfrac{24}{7}}$$

$$= \frac{32}{7} \times \frac{7}{24}$$

$$= \frac{32}{24}$$

$$= \frac{4}{3}$$

6. **(G)** $\frac{7}{3}x = (a^4 + 1)^3$

Substituting $a = -1$, we obtain

$$\frac{7}{3}x = (1+1)^3 = 8.$$

Multiplying both sides by $\frac{3}{7}$, we solve the equation for x, i.e., $x = \frac{24}{7}$.

7. **(D)** $\sqrt{108} + 3\sqrt{12} - 7\sqrt{3} = \sqrt{(36)(3)} + 3\sqrt{(4)(3)} - 7\sqrt{3}$
$$= 6\sqrt{3} + 3(2\sqrt{3}) - 7\sqrt{3}$$
$$= 6\sqrt{3} + 6\sqrt{3} - 7\sqrt{3}$$
$$= 5\sqrt{3}$$

8. **(K)** $|3x - 2| = 7$

$3x - 2 = 7$ or	$3x - 2 = -7$
$3x = 9$	$3x = -5$
$x = 3$	$x = -\frac{5}{3}$

Therefore, the solution set is $\left\{3, -\frac{5}{3}\right\}$.

9. **(D)** $(7 - k)(18 - k) < 0$ (as both terms are non-zero and
           $7 < k < 18$ have opposite signs)

Therefore, the solution set is $\{8, 9, 10, 11, 12, 13, 14, 15, 16, 17\}$, and 17 is the biggest number from the solution set.

10. **(G)** $c = 18a + 24b = 6(3a + 4b)$

Therefore, c is a multiple of 6 and must be divisible by 6.

11. **(B)**   Let x = the number of days it would take the two men working together.

Then $\frac{x}{8}$ = the part of the job done by A and $\frac{x}{12}$ = the part of the job done by B.

The relationship used in setting up the equation is:

Part of job done by A + Part of job done by B = 1 job

$$\frac{x}{8} + \frac{x}{12} = 1.$$
$$3x + 2x = 24$$
$$5x = 24$$
$$x = 4.8$$

12. **(G)** The required set is the set of all x such that

$$\frac{2}{x+1} - 3 = \frac{4x+6}{x+1}$$

Multiplying each member by $(x + 1)$ to eliminate the fraction, we obtain

$$(x+1)\left(\frac{2}{x+1} - 3\right) = \left(\frac{4x+6}{x+1}\right)(x+1)$$

Distributing,

$$(x+1)\left(\frac{2}{x+1}\right) - (x+1)3 = 4x+6$$
$$2 - (3x+3) = 4x+6$$
$$-1 - 3x = 4x+6$$
$$-1 - 3x - 4x = 6$$
$$-7x = 7$$
$$x = -1$$

If we now substitute (-1) for x in our original equation,

$$\frac{2}{x+1} - 3 = \frac{4x+6}{x+1}$$
$$\frac{2}{-1+1} - 3 = \frac{4(-1)+6}{-1+1}$$
$$\frac{2}{0} - 3 = \frac{-4+6}{0}$$

Since division by zero is impossible, the above equation is not defined for $x = -1$. Hence, we conclude that the equation has no roots for $x = -1$.

$$\left\{ x \middle| \frac{2}{x+1} - 3 = \frac{4x+6}{x+1} \right\} = \phi,$$

where ϕ is the empty set.

13. **(B)**
$$\frac{a+3}{3a+5} = \frac{2}{3}$$
$$3(a+3) = 2(3a+5)$$
$$3a+9 = 6a+10$$
$$-1 = 3a$$
$$-\frac{1}{3} = a$$

14. **(G)**
$$x = (y+4)^2$$
$$x = (-7+4)^2 \qquad \text{(substituted } y = -7 \text{ into the equation)}$$
$$x = (-3)^2$$
$$x = 9$$

15. **(C)** Since the denominator of a fraction cannot equal zero, $2x \neq 0$ or, dividing by 2, we obtain the restriction $x \neq 0$.

Now we proceed to simplify the given expression, First, we note that $2x$ may be factored out of the numerator; thus

$$\frac{4x^3 + 6x^2}{2x} = \frac{2x(2x^2 + 3x)}{2x}$$
$$= \frac{2x}{2x} \times (2x^2 + 3x)$$
$$= 2x^2 + 3x$$

Thus, $\dfrac{4x^3 + 6x^2}{2x} = 2x^2 + 3x$, and $x \neq 0$.

16. **(F)**
$$\frac{6a^3bc^4}{18a^2b^3c^2} = \frac{a^3bc^4}{3a^2b^3c^2} = \frac{abc^4}{3b^3c^2} = \frac{ac^4}{3b^2c^2} = \frac{ac^2}{3b^2}$$

17. **(B)** The given equation is a quadratic equation of the form $ax^2 + bx + c = 0$. In the given equation, $a = 1$, $b = 2(k+2)$, and $c = 9k$. A quadratic equation has equal roots if the discriminant, $b^2 - 4ac$, is zero.

$$b^2 - 4ac = [2(k+2)]^2 - 4(1)(9k) = 0$$
$$4(k+2)^2 - 36k = 0$$
$$4(k+2)(k+2) - 36k = 0$$
$$4(k^2 + 4k + 4) - 36k = 0 \qquad \text{(distributed)}$$
$$4k^2 + 16k + 16 - 36k = 0$$
$$4k^2 - 20k + 16 = 0$$

Divide both sides of this equation by 4:

$$\frac{4k^2 - 20k + 16}{4} = \frac{0}{4}$$

or

$$k^2 - 5k + 4 = 0.$$

Factoring the left side of this equation into a product of two polynomials:

$$(k - 4)(k - 1) = 0.$$

When the product $ab = 0$, where a and b are any two numbers, either $a = 0$ or $b = 0$. Hence, in the case of this problem, either

$$k - 4 = 0 \text{ or } k - 1 = 0.$$

Therefore, $k = 4$ or $k = 1$.

18. **(K)**   If $(x - 1)$ is a factor, then $x = 1$ is a root, so it satisfies the equation

$$3x^2 - 2kx + 1 = 0.$$

Substituting $x = 1$, we get $3 - 2k + 1 = 0$. Hence, $k = 2$.

19. **(C)**   Given the expression:

$$\frac{3}{x + 4} + \frac{5}{x - 4} = \frac{8}{x^2 - 16}$$

factor the denominator of the right side:

$$\frac{3}{x + 4} + \frac{5}{x - 4} = \frac{8}{(x + 4)(x - 4)}$$

Multiply both sides by $(x + 4)(x - 4)$:

$$3(x - 4) + 5(x + 4) = 8.$$

Simplifying:

$$3x - 12 + 5x + 20 = 8$$
$$8x + 8 = 8$$
$$8x = 0$$
$$x = 0$$

20. **(K)**   Inserting the given values of a, b, and c:

$$p = \frac{[2-(-\frac{1}{2})][(2)(-\frac{1}{2})+(-3)]}{[(-3)(-\frac{1}{2})-2(2)]}$$

$$= \frac{[2+\frac{1}{2}][-1-3]}{[1\frac{1}{2}-4]}$$

$$= \frac{(2\frac{1}{2})(-4)}{-(2\frac{1}{2})}$$

The $2\frac{1}{2}$ in the numerator cancels the $2\frac{1}{2}$ in the denominator.

$$p = \frac{-4}{-1}$$

Multiplying the numerator and denominator by -1:

$$p = \frac{4}{1}$$
$$p = 4$$

21. **(A)**   To change a percent to a decimal, drop the percent sign and move the decimal point two place values to the left. The correct answer is 1.25937.

22. **(H)**   In order to eliminate the fractions in the numerator and denominator, we multiply the numerator and denominator by x.

$$\frac{1+\frac{1}{x}}{1-\frac{1}{x}} = \frac{x\left(1+\frac{1}{x}\right)}{x\left(1-\frac{1}{x}\right)} = \frac{x+\frac{x}{x}}{x-\frac{x}{x}} = \frac{x+1}{x-1}.$$

23. **(C)** $$x^2 - 5x + 6 = 0$$
$$(x-2)(x-3) = 0$$
$$x = 2 \text{ or } x = 3$$

24. **(H)** $$\frac{a}{b} = 5$$
$$a = 5b$$
$$a^2 - 25b^2 = (5b)^2 - 25b^2$$
$$= 25b^2 - 25b^2$$
$$= 0$$

25. **(C)**
$$4(2x - 6) - 10x \le -28$$
$$8x - 24 - 10x \le -28$$
$$-2x - 24 \le -28$$
$$-2x \le -4$$

or
$$\frac{-2x}{-2} \ge \frac{-4}{-2}$$

Hence,
$$x \ge 2$$

26. **(G)**
$$\frac{25\left(\frac{a}{b}\right)^3 \left(\frac{c}{a}\right)^4}{125\left(\frac{a}{c}\right)^7 \left(\frac{b}{c}\right)^{-2}} = \frac{\left(\frac{a}{b}\right)^3 \left(\frac{c}{a}\right)^4}{5\left(\frac{a}{c}\right)^7 \left(\frac{b}{c}\right)^{-2}}$$

$$= \frac{\dfrac{a^3}{b^3} \dfrac{c^4}{a^4}}{5\left(\dfrac{a^7}{c^7}\right)\left(\dfrac{b}{c}\right)^{-2}}$$

$$= \frac{\dfrac{c^4}{ab^3}}{5\left(\dfrac{a^7}{c^7}\right)\left(\dfrac{c}{b}\right)^2}$$

$$= \frac{\dfrac{c^4}{ab^3}}{5\dfrac{a^7}{c^7} \times \dfrac{c^2}{b^2}}$$

$$= \frac{\dfrac{c^4}{ab^3}}{5\dfrac{a^7}{b^2 c^5}}$$

$$= \frac{c^4}{ab^3} \times \frac{b^2 c^5}{5a^7}$$

$$= \frac{c^4}{ab} \times \frac{c^5}{5a^7}$$

$$= \frac{c^9}{5a^8 b}$$

27. **(E)**
$$x^2 - 3x - 4 < 0$$
$$(x + 1)(x - 4) < 0$$
$$-1 < x < 4$$

28. **(J)** The inequality $|2 - 5x| < 3$ may be rewritten as

$-3 < 2 - 5x < 3$.

Subtracting 2 from each side, we obtain

$-5 < -5x < 1$.

Dividing by -5 gives:

$$1 < x < -\frac{1}{5}$$

This is the interval over which all solutions lie. We are looking for an interval which does not contain any solutions to the inequality. The only interval given in the choices that satisfies this criterion is

$$-\frac{3}{5} < x < -\frac{1}{2}.$$

29. **(B)** If $(x - 2)$ is a factor, then 2 is a root so $f(2) = 0$. To obtain $f(2)$, we substitute 2 into the expression $x^3 - 7x^2 + kx - 12$, which results:

$$2^3 - 7(2)^2 + k(2) - 12 = 8 - 28 + 2k - 12$$

Since $f(2) = 0$, we obtain:

$$8 - 28 + 2k - 12 = 0$$
$$2k - 32 = 0$$
$$2k = 32$$
$$k = 16$$

30. **(K)** $2x + 3y = 6$

$$y - 2 = -\frac{2x}{3}$$

Multiplying the second equation by 3, we obtain:

$$3y - 6 = -2x.$$

Transposing, we obtain:

$$2x + 3y = 6.$$

Thus, both equations are equivalent and define one straight line. Since they intersect at every point, there are an infinite number of solutions.

31. **(A)** Substitute $x = 3$ and $y = 2$ into the given pair of equations, giving:

$$\begin{cases} 3k + 2m = 7 & (1) \\ 2k + 3m = 5 & (2) \end{cases}$$

Multiply Equation (1) by -2 and multiply Equation (2) by 3. You now have:

$$-6k - 4m = -14 \qquad (1)$$
$$6k + 9m = 15 \qquad (2)$$

To solve this for m, you must subtract Equation (1) from Equation (2), since Equation (1) is smaller, as follows:

$$\begin{array}{l} 6k + 9m = 15 \\ \underline{- 6k + 4m = 14} \qquad \text{(these signs all reverse when you subtract)} \\ 5m = 1 \end{array}$$

$$m = \frac{1}{5}$$

Substitute $m = \dfrac{1}{5}$ into Equation (2):

$$2k + \frac{3}{5} = 5$$

$$2k = \frac{25}{5} - \frac{3}{5}$$

$$2k = \frac{22}{5}$$

$$k = \frac{11}{5}$$

Therefore, $m = \dfrac{1}{5}$ and $k = \dfrac{11}{5}$.

32. **(F)** Add both fractions of the numerator together using the rule:

$\dfrac{a}{b} + \dfrac{c}{d} = \dfrac{ad + bc}{bd}$; and obtain $\dfrac{y - x}{xy}$. Similarly, for the denominator, obtain:

$\dfrac{y^2 - x^2}{x^2 y^2}$.

Now invert the fraction in the denominator and multiply by the numerator:

$$\frac{y-x}{xy} \times \frac{x^2y^2}{y^2-x^2} = \frac{(y-x)}{xy} \times \frac{(xy)(xy)}{(y-x)(y+x)}$$
$$= \frac{(y-x)(xy)(xy)}{xy(y-x)(y-x)}$$
$$= \frac{xy}{y+x}$$

33. **(B)** $\dfrac{2}{x} = \dfrac{\frac{1}{3}}{y}$ (cross multiply)

$$\frac{6}{y} = x$$

Substitute $x = \dfrac{6}{y}$ into the range of x:

$$1 < \frac{6}{y} < 10$$
$$\frac{1}{6} < \frac{1}{y} < \frac{5}{3}$$
$$6 > y > \frac{3}{5}$$

34. **(G)** $x = \dfrac{x_1 + x_2}{2}$

$$= \frac{-2+4}{2}$$
$$= 1$$
$$y = \frac{y_1 + y_2}{2}$$
$$= \frac{3+(-5)}{2}$$
$$= -1$$

The coordinates of the midpoint are $(x, y) = (1, -1)$.

35. **(D)**   Distance between two points

$$= \sqrt{(x_1 - x_2)^2 + (y_1 - y_2)^2}$$
$$= \sqrt{(0 - 7)^2 + (-2 - 0)^2}$$
$$= \sqrt{49 + 4}$$
$$= \sqrt{53}$$

36. **(G)**   slope $= \dfrac{y_2 - y_1}{x_2 - x_1} = \dfrac{3 - (-4)}{1 - (-2)}$

$$= \frac{7}{3}$$

37. **(E)**   Since the square of a real number is non-negative, $x^2 < -1$ and $x^2 < -4$ do not have solution sets on the real axis.

Consider a quadratic inequality of the form $ax^2 + bx + c > 0$:

If the discriminant $b^2 - 4ac$ is greater than or equal to zero, the inequality will have real roots; otherwise, the roots are complex.

Note $2^2 - 4(1)(2) = -4$

and $1^2 - 4(-3)(-1) = -11$.

Therefore, none of the choices are correct.

38. **(G)**   Let $m \angle A$ = the measure of angle A, arc $m(ABC)$ = the measure of arc ABC. Since $\angle CBD$ is formed by a tangent to circle O, $\overline{BD}$, and a chord, CB, intersecting at the point of tangency, B, it follows that,

$$m \angle DBC = \frac{1}{2} \text{arc } m(BEC)$$

$$70 = \frac{1}{2} \text{arc } m(BEC)$$

$$\text{arc } m(BEC) = (70)(2)$$

$$\text{arc } m(BEC) = 140$$

Since $\angle BAC$ is an inscribed angle in the arc BAC, and since arc BEC is intercepted by angle BAC, it follows that

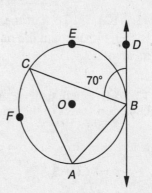

$$m \angle BAC = \frac{1}{2} \text{arc } m(BEC)$$

$$= \frac{1}{2}(140)$$

$$= 70°$$

39. **(D)** $y = f(x + 1) = 7(x + 1) + 3 = 7x + 10$

This is the slope-intercept form of an equation, and the y-intercept is given by the constant which is 10.

40   **(H)** $\begin{cases} 3x + 2y = 5 \\ x - 4y = 1 \end{cases}$ (1)
                                                                        (2)

Multiply Equation (1) by 2, and add the result to Equation (2), as follows:

$$6x + 4y = 10$$
$$\underline{x - 4y = 1}$$
$$= 11$$
$$x = \frac{11}{7}$$

Substitute $x = \frac{11}{7}$ into Equation (2):

$$\frac{11}{7} - 4y = 1$$
$$4y = \frac{4}{7}$$
$$y = \frac{1}{7}$$

41. **(C)**   To find the mean, first add the individual scores together. The sum is 133. Next, count the number of scores which is 19 and divide 19 into 133, for a mean of 7.

42. **(J)**   In general, a linear equation is represented by the form

$$y = mx + b$$

where m = slope and b = y-intercept (the point at which $x = 0$). Since

$$y = -6x + 3$$

is of the form $y = mx + b$, we see

$m = -6 = \text{slope}$

Answer choice (F) is incorrect because it reflects the equation

$$y = -\frac{1}{6x} + b$$

Answer choice (G) is incorrect because it reflects the equation

$y - 6x + b$

Answer choice (H) is incorrect because it reflects the equation

$y = 3x + b$

43. **(C)**

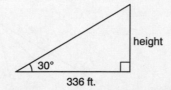

$$\tan 30° = \frac{\text{height}}{336}$$

$\text{height} = 336 \tan 30°$

$$\text{height} = 336 \times \frac{\sqrt{3}}{3}$$

$\text{height} = 112\sqrt{3}$

44. **(G)** The area of quadrilateral *ABCD* is the sum of the areas of $\triangle AOD$ and the trapezoid *OBCD*.

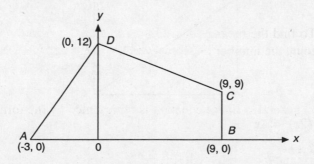

Area of triangle $= \frac{1}{2}bh = \frac{1}{2}(3)(12) = 18$

Area of trapezoid = $\frac{h}{2}(b + b')$, where b and b' are the bases, and h is the altitude. Therefore,

Area of $OBCD$ = $\frac{9}{2}(12 + 9) = \frac{9}{2}(21) = 94.5$

Total area = $18 + 94.5 = 112.5$

45. **(C)**   The situation is illustrated in the figure. Triangles APC and BPC are right triangles, so

$$\tan 45° = \frac{y}{x}, \qquad \tan 30° = \frac{y}{x + 50}$$

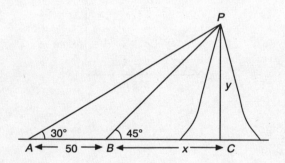

Since $\tan 45° = 1$ and $\tan 30° = \frac{1}{\sqrt{3}}$, these equations become

$$y = x,$$

and $x + 50 = \sqrt{3}y.$

When we solve these last two equations for y, we get:

$$y = \frac{50}{\sqrt{3} - 1}$$

46. **(J)**

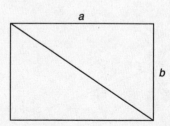

$$a^2 + b^2 = (2x)^2 = 4x^2$$

but $a = b$, so $a^2 = b^2$.

Therefore, $2a^2 = 4x^2$

$\qquad\qquad a^2 = 2x^2$

$\qquad\qquad a = \sqrt{2}x.$

Area of the second square = twice the area of the first square.

$\qquad$ Area of 1st square = $(\sqrt{2}x)(\sqrt{2}x) = 2x^2.$

Therefore, area of 2nd square = $4x^2$.

Since the area of the 2nd square = $4x^2$,

$\qquad$ length of each side = $\sqrt{4x^2} = 2x$

the second square = $4(2x) = 8x$.

47. **(E)**   Drawing a diagram will help clarify:

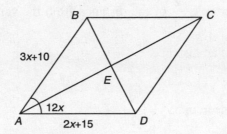

where $\angle BAD = 12x$, $\overline{BD}$ = the shorter diagonal, and $\overline{AC}$ = the longer diagonal.

Since all sides of a rhombus are equal:

$\qquad 3x + 10 = 2x + 15.$

Solving for x:

$\qquad x = 5.$

Substituting to find $\angle BAD$:

$\qquad \angle BAD = 12(5) = 60.$

In a rhombus, the diagonals bisect the angles they are drawn to, thus

$\qquad \angle EAD = \dfrac{1}{2}(\angle BAD) = \dfrac{1}{2}60 = 30.$

Side $\overline{AD} = 2x + 15 = 2(5) + 15 = 10 + 15 = 25.$

This is the hypotenuse of a 30-60 right triangle, *AED*. To get segment $\overline{ED}$, we use $\angle EAD$:

$\qquad \sin EAD = \dfrac{\overline{ED}}{\overline{AD}}.$

$$\overline{ED} = (\sin EAD)\overline{AD} = (\sin 30)25 = \frac{25}{2}.$$

Since the diagonals of a rhombus bisect each other, $\overline{ED} = \overline{BE}$. Thus,

$$\overline{BD} = \overline{ED} + \overline{BE} = \frac{25}{2} + \frac{25}{2} = 25.$$

48. **(G)**   One-fourth of each of the circles is contained in the square, so the total area is [the area of the 4 circles] + [area of the square] − [area of one circle] (since it was included twice) $= 4[\pi(6)^2] + (12)^2 - \pi(6)^2 = 4(36\pi) + 144 - 36\pi = 108\pi + 144$.

49. **(C)**   At the point where the medians of a triangle meet, the distance from the point to the vertex is $\frac{2}{3}$ of the distance from the vertex to the opposite side.

Thus, $\overline{GF}$ is $\frac{1}{3}$ of that distance.

Use Pythagorean theorem: $S^2 = \left(\frac{S}{2}\right)^2 + d^2$

$$d^2 = \frac{3S^2}{4}$$

$$d = \frac{\sqrt{3}}{2}S$$

Multiply by $\frac{1}{3}$ $\overline{GF} = \frac{\sqrt{3}}{6}S.$

50. **(G)**   From a theorem, the length of the radius of a circumscribed circle about an equilateral triangle is equal to $\frac{2}{3}$ the altitude of the triangle.

The altitude bisects the base. Therefore, a right triangle is formed and the Pythagorean Theorem is used:

$$S^2 = \left(\frac{S}{2}\right)^2 + (\text{Altitude})^2$$

$$\text{Altitude} = \frac{\sqrt{3}}{2}S$$

Multiplying by $\dfrac{2}{3}$ gives us the radius:

$$\dfrac{\sqrt{3}}{3}S$$

Multiplying by 2 gives us the diameter:

$$\dfrac{2\sqrt{3}}{3}S$$

51. **(B)** For two line segments to be parallel when cut by another segment, their opposite interior angles must be equal. These angles are listed in Statement II. The other criteria given are irrelevant to the problem.

52. **(H)** If a figure has exterior angles that are equal, then the figure is a form of a *regular polygon*.

From a theorem, the number of sides of a regular polygon can be found from the measure of an exterior angle. The relation is:

$$\text{ext. angle} = \dfrac{360°}{n},$$

where n is the number of sides. Solving for n:

$$n = \dfrac{360°}{\text{ext. angle}}$$

Substituting 72° for the ext. angle:

$$n = \dfrac{360°}{72°} = 5$$

A five-sided figure is a pentagon.

53. **(B)** $\text{Side} = \dfrac{\text{perimeter}}{4} = \dfrac{36}{4} = 9$

$\text{Area} = (9)^2 = 81$

54. **(F)** Two angles that are complementary must have measures that add up to $90°$.

Let the angle $= x$, its complement $= x - 40$.

These angles must add up to 90°. Therefore,

$$x + x - 40 = 90$$
$$2x = 130$$
$$x = 65°$$

Therefore, the angle is 65°.

55. **(D)** $\angle CDA = \angle CAD = 15°$. (Therefore, $\overline{AC} = \overline{CD}$)

$\angle CDB = \angle CBD = 15°$. (Therefore, $\overline{BC} = \overline{CD}$)

$\angle ADB = \angle CDA + \angle CDB$

$$= 15° + 15°$$

$$= 30°$$

Let $\angle CAB = \beta$.

$\angle CBA = \angle CAB = \beta$. (Therefore, $\overline{AC} = \overline{BC}$)

$\angle ADB + (\beta + 15°) + (\beta + 15°) = 180°$.

(Therefore, sum of interior $\angle$ s of $\triangle ADB$)

$$30° + 2\beta + 30° = 180°$$
$$2\beta = 120°$$
$$\beta = 60°.$$

$$\theta + \beta + \beta = 180° \qquad \text{(Therefore, sum of interior } \angle \text{ s of } \triangle ACB)$$
$$\theta = 180° - 120°$$
$$\theta = 60°$$

56. **(J)**   This problem is solved most easily by recognizing that the maximum rectangular area is contained by a square. We are given the perimeter:

$$P = 800$$

Since a square has 4 equal sides, each side is:

$$s = \frac{P}{4} = \frac{800}{4} = 200.$$

The area of a square is s^2.

Therefore, the maximum rectangular area is

$$s^2 = 200^2$$

$$= 40,000 \text{ ft}^2$$

57. **(C)**   Consider the trigonometric relationship:

$$\sin^2 x + \cos^2 x = 1$$

By dividing both sides by $\sin^2 x$, we obtain:

$$\frac{\sin^2 x}{\sin^2 x} + \frac{\cos^2 x}{\sin^2 x} = \frac{1}{\sin^2 x}$$
$$1 + \cot^2 x = \csc^2 x$$

58. **(K)**   To solve, we invoke the law of cosines:

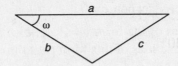

$$c^2 = a^2 + b^2 - 2ab\cos \text{ (included angle)}.$$

In the figure given, $a = 4$, $b = 7$, $c = 8$, and ω is then included angle.

We solve the law of cosines relation for $\cos\omega$:

$$c^2 = a^2 + b^2 - 2ab\cos\omega.$$

Transposing a^2 and b^2 and dividing through by $-2ab$, we obtain:

$$\frac{c^2 - a^2 - b^2}{-2ab} = \cos\omega$$

Substituting for a, b, and c, we obtain:

$$\cos\omega = \frac{8^2 - 4^2 - 7^2}{-2(4)(7)} = \frac{64 - 16 - 49}{-56} = \frac{-1}{-56} = \frac{1}{56}.$$

59. **(D)**   I. $\tan\theta = \dfrac{\text{opposite side}}{\text{adjacent side}} = \dfrac{a}{b}$

                II. $\tan\theta = \dfrac{\sin\theta}{\cos\theta}$ (trigonometric identity)

                III. $\tan\theta \ne \dfrac{a}{\sqrt{a^2 + b^2}}$

Therefore, (D) is the answer.

60. **(H)**   This problem may be solved using the following steps.

Step I

First decide whether the graph represents a sine function or a cosine function. Recall the following facts:

1)   cosine functions of the form $y = A \cos bx$ reach their maximum height when $x = 0$.

For instance,

$y = \cos x = 1$, when $x = 0$.

$y = A \cos x = A$, when $x = 0$.

$y = A \cos bx = A$, when $x = 0$.

2)   sine functions of the form $y = A \sin bx$ equal zero when $x = 0$ (that is, all sine functions of this form pass through the origin).

The given graph in the problem does not pass through the origin; instead it reaches a maximum at $x = 0$. Thus, the graph must represent a cosine function.

Step II

Write the cosine function in its general form,

$y = A \cos bx.$ (1)

To complete the problem, we must find A and b. Recall that

A = amplitude

    = maximum y-value

    = | minimum y-value | .

Looking at the graph, see that the maximum y - value is $y = 3$, and the minimum y - value is $y = -3$. Thus, the amplitude is $A = 3$. This function, so far, can be written as $y = 3 \cos bx$.

Step III

Now solve for b. Recall that

1)   For $y = \cos x$,   period $= 2\pi$.

2)   For $y = \cos bx$,   period $= \dfrac{2\pi}{b}$.

Thus we will solve for b in the equation

$$\text{period} = \frac{2\pi}{b}.$$ (2)

Remember that the period is the distance along the x - axis between any two adjacent peaks on the graph. We observe that the graph has a peak (a maximum y-value) at $x = \pi$ and an adjacent peak at $x = 2\pi$. Thus,

$$\text{period} = 2\pi - \pi.$$
$$= \pi.$$

Substituting this value for the period into Equation (2) gives

$$\pi = \frac{2\pi}{b}$$
$$b = \frac{2\pi}{\pi}$$
$$b = 2.$$

By substituting $A = 3$ and $b = 2$ into Equation (1), $y = A \cos bx$, we obtain the function in its final form:

$$y = 3 \cos 2x.$$

This is answer (H).

Test 3: Reading

1. **(C)** Alithea is the sister-in-law of Mr. Pinchwife, thus (C) is the correct answer. In the dialogue, the reader can infer this because Alithea and Mrs. Pinchwife call each other "sister." Additionally, Alithea refers to Mr. Pinchwife as "brother." Hence, answers (A), (B), and (D) are incorrect choices.

2. **(J)** Although Mrs. Pinchwife told Alithea that she did not enjoy the play she had seen, she wants to go again simply because her husband forbids her to, thus (J) is the correct answer. She voices no desire to add to her culture, so (F) is incorrect. When she had attended the play, her husband did not let her sit near the gentry and chances are he would never let her sit near them, so (G) is incorrect. Although (H) is a possible choice, Mrs. Pinchwife does not show much interest in spending time with her husband in the dialogue. Hence, the desire to spend time with him would be somewhat out of character for her.

3. **(A)** The husband enters in a bad mood reflected by his sour facial expression; (A) is the correct answer. The reader cannot infer from the dialogue that he has heard idle gossip (B) or that he wishes to be left alone (C); these answers should not be chosen. (D) should not be selected; again, the reader cannot infer that this is the cause of his bad mood.

4. **(G)** Mrs. Pinchwife, although longing to be more educated in the ways of the world, is naive at this point, so (G) is the best answer. She may be somewhat of a snob (F), but her naivete is the outstanding character trait; (F) is incorrect. There is no evidence in this passage that she is immoral and adulterous (H), or that she is the victim of idle gossip (J); these are both incorrect answer choices.

5. **(A)** When Mr. Pinchwife accuses Alithea of keeping the company of men of scandalous reputation, she replies, "Where? wou'd you not have me civil?" This reply admits that she has entertained men of dubious reputation, thus (A) is the correct answer. Although (B) and (C) are possible, there is no evidence in the passage to support these answers; therefore they are incorrect. (D) is a likely answer because Alithea is clearly protective of her reputation; however, the main point of the argument does not point to this answer, and it should not be chosen.

6. **(J)** Alithea has already taken Mrs. Pinchwife to the theater, and perhaps to more places, Statement I. In addition, Mr. Pinchwife leads his wife into more possibilities for misbehavior in his speech about the vices of naughty townswomen, which makes Statement II valid. Mrs. Pinchwife, innocent as she is at this time, is only too eager to have fun in the city, for she states that these vices he has mentioned make London "not so bad a place"; this supports Statement III. Mrs. Pinchwife's understatement, the exaggeration of her husband, combined with Alithea's protestations, create a humorous scene. Only (J) allows the reader to select all three elements of the scene. (F), (G), and (H) each only allow the reader to select part of the correct answer; they are all incorrect.

7. **(C)** (C) is the best choice because Mr. Pinchwife, in lines 79–80, immediately confirms that he has kept his wife "innocent." He does not openly express through his language intense jealousy at this point (although the reader can see that he is a jealous man); (A) is incorrect. He does not indicate that he does not trust her morals (B) or uncontrollable outrage (D); these are also incorrect.

8. **(H)** Because there is no indication that Mrs. Pinchwife is "past her prime" (F), unattractive (G), or "matronly" (J), these choices are all incorrect. Minx means "pert and saucy," therefore (H) is the correct answer.

9. **(B)** Mr. Pinchwife is obviously familiar with the pleasures of town life; however, (D) is an answer that cannot be determined by this passage. Of the remaining possibilities, all are somewhat likely and can be supported. Fine clothes and coaches cost a great deal of money (C), and all that time in entertainment would keep Mrs. Pinchwife away from home more than her husband would prefer (A). However, most of Mr. Pinchwife's conversation with his wife concerns her being attracted to the Player Men (B), making (B) the best answer selection.

10. **(J)** Mr. Pinchwife desires his wife to love him, as he states in line 88 (Statement III), to love none better, as he demands in line 85 (Statement IV), and to hate London, as he commands in line 95 (Statement II); only answer (J) includes all these correct options and, therefore, is correct. While (G) contains two-thirds of the correct answer, it does not contain the complete answer and is incorrect. (F) and (H) both contain Statement I which is opposite of what Mr. Pinchwife requires; consequently, both of these choices are incorrect.

11. **(B)** The appropriate selection is choice (B) because it is primarily about the differences between Shakespeare and the modern poets (here, the Romantics). Choices (A), (C), and (D) are incorrect because they each include an idea that was not addressed by the author at all in the passage.

12. **(G)** The author accuses the modern poets of being egotistical when he writes, "But to the men I speak of there is nothing interesting, nothing heroical, but themselves"; choice (G) is correct. Choices (F), (H), and (J) are incorrect because they are all grand emotions that the author thinks the modern poets lack in their poems.

13. **(B)** The correct selection is choice (B) because Shakespeare did understand nature and art, but with a "deeper," and by inference, "wider" understanding of human life. The passage does not address whether Shakespeare espoused the political conservatism of the modernists; choice (A) is incorrect. Choice (C) is inappropriate because Shakespeare did understand poetry in the same way as the modernists, on a different level. Although the author does believe that the modern age is one of egotism, that is not what this quote is addressing; choice (D) is also incorrect.

14. **(F)** Choice (F) is the correct selection because the modernists do not acknowledge that there are different stations in life and that is precisely what Classical Tragedy bases its tragedy on. Classical Tragedy is that a being of great or lofty station in life (read: "the fall of gods or of great men") is brought down to a much lower level. Because choices (G), (H), and (J) have nothing to do with the definition of a Classical Tragedy, they are incorrect choices.

15. **(C)** The second-to-last sentence in the first paragraph says, "the world repays their indifference with scorn," which in effect, is what choice (C) states, is the correct selection. The author does not address how the modernists feel about their reception, choice (A) is wrong. Choice (B) is incorrect because the author is certainly not indifferent to the modernists, he scorns them. Although the author does believe that there is nothing "heroical" in the modernist position, it is not what he addresses at the end of the first paragraph; choice (D) is incorrect.

16. **(H)** Choice (H) is correct because "girdle around the earth" is used in reference to how Shakespeare embraces and unites "opposite extremes." The author does not address Shakespeare's universal appeal; choice (F) is incorrect. Choice (G) is also not addressed in the passage, nor is choice (J). They are both incorrect selections.

17. **(D)** The author acknowledges that Shakespeare hurries through describing his subjects; choice (D) is correct. The author admires Shakespeare's almost

"plastic" conception of character (A), and doesn't criticize his bringing together dissimilar images (B); hence, these choices are incorrect. The author describes Shakespeare's description of character as such, "the stroke, like the lightning's, is sure as it is sudden." Something cannot be "sure" and "devious" at the same time, so choice (C) is also incorrect.

18. **(J)** Shakespeare, the author says, can easily bring together similar images "found in circumstances of the greatest dissimilitude." This is exactly what choice (J) states; it is correct. The ideas of choices (F), (G), and (H) are not addressed in the essay.

19. **(C)** Choice (C) is an appropriate selection. The writer is very favorable toward Shakespeare and his works; he is not highly critical so choice (A) is not the best option. The writer believes that Shakespeare and his power are still unexcelled in this day and age; choice (B) is inappropriate. The writer speaks with awe of Shakespeare's hieroglyphical writing which causes words to be translated into pictures; since he is not antagonistic, choice (D) is inappropriate.

20. **(J)** The writer does not believe that Shakespeare understands poetry; Statement I is incorrect. The author does not believe that Shakespeare translates nature for others; Statement II is invalid. The writer does not believe that Shakespeare tried to impose his mood upon those about him; Statement III is inaccurate. Only Statement IV is accurate since Shakespeare was able to recognize significant events and majesty in nature, according to the author. Answer choice (J) is correct, since it allows the reader to select the correct response.

21. **(B)** The author makes this clear in the sixth paragraph by emphasizing the words "mistakes," "error," and "falsifications." Proposing highly falsifiable theories is preferable to proposing nonfalsifiable ones, but, according the author's claims in this paragraph, we do not learn from either type of theory until it is falsified. Thus, (A) is incorrect. For the same reason, (D) and (C) are incorrect and, in addition, are too narrowly phrased. Science includes more than just theories of planetary motion.

22. **(J)** The author begins the second paragraph by stating he will illustrate the point he made in paragraph one. This point is: "A very good theory will be one that makes very wide-ranging claims about the world, and which is consequently highly falsifiable..." He then presents in this paragraph two theories of planetary motion, and explains in the third paragraph why the second theory is more falsifiable than the first. (F) and (G) are incorrect because the two theories are used only for purposes of illustration. The author does not particularly care about planetary orbits, except as an example of the falsifiability of two theories. (H) is incorrect because the author does not proceed to falsify either theory.

23. **(A)** The author defines this term in the sixth sentence of the third paragraph by telling us, "If we follow Popper and refer to those sets of observation statements that would serve to falsify a law or theory as potential falsifiers of that law or theory..." (B), (C), and (D) are all incorrect because potential falsifiers are not theories themselves, but statements that, if observed, would serve to falsify an existing theory.

24. **(G)** The author begins the passage by telling us what a good scientific theory does: it makes definite claims about the world. By inference, a bad scientific theory does not make definite claims about the world. (F) may in fact be true, but no information is given about theories which limit the advance of scientific knowledge. You may reason, that theories which do not make definite claims about the world are nonfalsifiable. Since it is the falsification of theories which leads to the striking achievements in science (sixth paragraph), you may conclude that theories which do not make definite claims about the world do limit the advance of scientific knowledge. Selecting (G), however, yields the same result more directly, and is, thus, the better answer. Although we are told in the fifth paragraph that falsified theories must be ruthlessly rejected, this does not make them bad scientific theories. Falsified theories have made enough definite claims about the world to be falsified, and thereby advance science. Thus, (H) is incorrect. (J) describes a theory which has not yet, but soon will be, falsified. It falls into the same category as (H), making (J) incorrect.

25. **(C)** The author's description of the theories of Kepler and Newton are intended to provide a second example of how one scientific theory can be superior to another. As we are told in the first paragraph and shown in the example in the second paragraph, theories which make broader claims are superior. The author explains in the fourth paragraph why Newton's law is considered broader, and therefore superior, to Kepler's. (A), (B), and (D) are all incorrect because the passage makes no mention of whether either of the theories have been falsified.

26. **(F)** This is the conclusion that should be reached after the author has presented his two examples to illustrate the point. (H) and (J) are incorrect because the fifth paragraph states that falsified theories "must be ruthlessly rejected." In the sixth paragraph, the author states that the value lies in what is learned by falsifying a theory, not the falsified theory itself.

27. **(B)** The author states this directly in the first paragraph, and again less directly in the fifth paragraph. Paragraph five also states why (III) is not part of a good scientific theory.

28. **(J)** The author makes this point directly in the sixth paragraph. (F) is incorrect because there is no mention in the passage of how a scientist learns to

propose broader theories. Although there is a preference for highly falsifiable theories, (H) is nevertheless incorrect because a theory is not learned from until it has been falsified.

29. **(D)**   In this question you are asked to determine which of the four options makes the broader claims about the world. From this problem it can be deduced which of the four options contains the largest set of decision makers. Although you may not know the size of the subsets Supreme Court justices, appellate judges, and judges, it should be clear that all the members of these three categories are people, but not all people are one type of judge or another. Thus, (D) has the largest set of decision makers and makes the broadest claims about the world. Based on the passage, this makes (D) the most falsifiable theory.

30. **(H)**   As described in the passage, Kepler's theory dealt exclusively with planetary motion. Since (H) is not an observation relating to planetary motion, it is not a potential falsifier of Kepler's theory (though it is of Newton's). (F), (G), and (J) are all statements suggesting the locations of various planets were not as predicted. These all relate to planetary motion and are, thus, potential falsifiers of Kepler's theory.

31. **(C)**   In the first paragraph, the author explains that the "Inviting-In" feast and the Great Feast of the Dead are equal in importance; since the two feasts are more important than the other two ceremonies mentioned, (C) is the best answer. Neither (A) nor (B) is correct since each is only one-half of the correct answer. While the "Bladder feast" and "Asking" festival are mentioned, the paragraph states that the "Inviting-In" feast and the Great Feast of the Dead are "...more important..."; accordingly, (D) is also incorrect.

32. **(H)**   The writer explains that the "Inviting-In" feast in St. Michael is primarily an opportunity for trade between two friendly tribes; (H) is the best answer. Although the feast was at one time an appeal to the spirits represented by the masks for future success in hunting, the feast is no longer for that purpose in St. Michael; (F) is not a good choice. In St. Michael the feast has lost most of its religious character; (G) is not an acceptable selection. Because the feast has not lost its social utility, answer (J) should not be chosen.

33. **(C)**   Since the narrator explains both the origins and current changes of the ceremonies and dances, the narrator does seek to give the significance of the historical events and to depict the ceremonies and dances as they exist today; (C) is the best answer. Rather than being indifferent to the tribes described, the narrator details their methods and purposes in holding each of the ceremonies and dances; (A) should not be chosen. The narrator is concerned about depicting the history of the observances, but this is not the only purpose that the narrator has;

(B), therefore, should not be selected. Since the narrator is neither dismissive about the superstitious beliefs nor concerned only with presenting the factual information, (D) should not be chosen.

34. **(F)**   The narrator seems to be primarily concerned with the Eskimo tribes from a sociological perspective; (F) is the best answer. (F) is the correct choice because most of the passage deals with "social utility" and "trade" in addition to hunting, rehearsing, food, and performing together in dances and choruses—all aspects of sociology or the science of social relations. While religion is mentioned in relation to the origins of the "Inviting-In" feast in St. Michael, the report is not necessarily a religious investigation; (G) should not be selected. The report is not one that can be described as primarily biological; (H) is not the best answer. Even though attention is given to the fine arts (J), that is not the only purpose of the passage. (J) should not be selected.

35. **(C)**   The word "shaman" refers to an honored member of the tribe—often a respected elder; (C) is the best answer. The shaman is able to commune with the spirits so (A), which suggests otherwise, should not be chosen. The shaman is not a woman since the narrator refers to the shaman as "he," or a man; (B) is a very poor choice. The word "shaman" has nothing to do with shaving and he occupies an important part in the ceremony; (D) should not be selected.

36. **(H)**   The writer describes the feasts; subsequently, (F) is not the proper choice. In the first paragraph, the writer mentions an old chief's remarks; the reader can assume that the narrator used interviews and that (G) is an incorrect choice. The writer begins the passage by referring to a secondary source—the works of Hawkes; (J) is an incorrect choice. Since the question asks for the item which does not apply, (H) should be chosen. No mention of a statistical study is mentioned in the passage.

37. **(D)**   To make an offering, the people drop the food, the drink, or the tobacco through a chink in the floor; (D) is the correct choice. The shaman does burn the masks but he does not burn the offerings; (A) should not be chosen. The offering is an important final part of the ritual; since (B) indicates that it is not, (B) is incorrect. No mention is made of putting the offering on an ice floe, so (C) should not be chosen.

38. **(G)**   The writer is not entirely objective. For instance, he judgmentally states, "There was nothing bad about their dances..."; (G) is the best answer. Since the writer does make judgments, (F), which states the opposite, cannot be selected. The writer is not entirely objective since he inserts some of his own beliefs and feelings in the piece; for instance, he refers to the doctrine of the actor as medium. (H), therefore, cannot be chosen. There is no use of the word "I" to indicate an entirely first-person point of view; (J) cannot be chosen.

39. **(D)** The Kazgi is a communal building where tribal meetings might be held. It might best be compared to a town hall where town meetings might be held; (D) is the best answer. The meeting place is not entirely for worship; (A) should not be selected; (A) refers to a place of worship or a church. A medical emergency room in no way resembles a Kazgi; (B) should be avoided. A Kazgi is a building, not a person; answer (C) which refers to a magistrate should not be accepted as a correct choice.

40. **(J)** Statement I is false because the first day of a feast consisted of comic dances designed to make other tribes laugh. Statement II is not true since only the shaman was considered important enough to burn the masks after the feasts. Statement III is untrue since the narrator describes the rehearsals. Using this information, it can be determined that choices (F), (G), and (H) are incorrect since each contains I, II, III, or some combination of these false statements. Statement IV indicates that some symbolism is involved in the occasions. Only answer (J) allows the reader to choose Statement IV, so (J) is the correct choice.

Test 4: Science Reasoning

1. **(B)** Because the powder in Experiment 3 was burned with oxygen, and it is not indicated whether the oxygen in the product originates from the powder and/or the excess oxygen, (A) is incorrect. (B) is the correct choice, because only Experiment 2 confirms the presence of carbon, hydrogen, and oxygen using qualitative elemental analysis. (C) is not the best choice since Experiment 3 gives no information to indicate that the excess oxygen does not combine with the powder. (D) is incorrect; Experiment 1 gives no data on the composition of the powder.

2. **(F)** The results from Experiment 3 indicate 30.0 mg of the powder is converted into 1 millimole of CO_2 which contains 2 millimoles of oxygen and 1 millimole of water which contains 1 millimole of oxygen for a total of 3.0 millimoles of oxygen. Thus, burning half the amount of the powder (15.0) will produce half the number of millimoles of oxygen, or 1.5 millimoles. (F) is, therefore, correct. Choice (G) is incorrect, since if 30.0 mg of the powder produces 3.0 millimoles of oxygen, half the amount of powder should produce half the number of millimoles of oxygen. Half of 3.0 is not 2.0. Choice (H), 3.0 millimoles, is incorrect, because burning a smaller amount of the powder must produce a smaller amount of oxygen. If the 3.0 millimoles of oxygen obtained from 30.0 mg of the powder is doubled, one gets 6.0 millimoles (J), which is not correct. Again, burning a smaller amount of powder must produce a smaller amount of oxygen.

3. **(D)** Since the passage does not explain what the properties nor the composition of a sugar are, (A) is incorrect. Choice (B) is false, because the

purity of the compound does not identify if the compound is indeed a sugar. The exact ratios of carbon to hydrogen to oxygen would give the chemical formula, but there is no comparison to a known sugar, hence choice (C) is not correct. (D) is the best choice since the passage and experiments do not reveal what the composition and properties of a sugar are.

4. **(H)** The combustion analysis only investigates the composition of the compound and not its identity; hence, (F) is not correct. In choice (G), while knowing the melting point would help, the freezing point for the compound was not discussed or determined in the experiments (only the freezing point for a water solution of the compound was determined). (H) is correct, because a distinct melting point indicates a pure compound, based on the results of Experiment 2. (J) is incorrect, because an elemental analysis reveals only the specific composition of the compound.

5. **(B)** According to Experiment 1, as the temperature is lowered, heat is absorbed or added. (A) is false. Choice (B) is the best response, because based on Experiment 1, as the temperature is lowered, heat is absorbed. (C) is incorrect since the temperature decreases not increases. Choice (D) is false, because as indicated in Experiment 1, as the temperature decreases some heat transfer must occur.

6. **(J)** There is no indication in Experiment 3 that the excess oxygen and oxygen in the powder are directly related, so (F) is incorrect. The dissolving of the powder is not stated in Experiment 3, and must thus be assumed to be irrelevant. Choice (G) is therefore incorrect. Choice (H) is not correct since the statement in Experiment 3 reads "burned in excess oxygen" which implies that the oxygen did not cause the burning. Choice (J) is the best answer, since the word "excess" would imply an exact quantity is not needed and that the continued burning is supported by oxygen.

7. **(B)** The correct answer can be taken directly from the passage; it is answer choice (B). Answer (A), the study of the Universe's origin, is known as cosmogony. Answers (C) and (D) are two possible theories in cosmology, and not the whole subject of cosmology.

8. **(J)** Big Bang cosmology can be distinguished from Steady State cosmology by the phrase "a Universe expanding from an extremely hot and very dense state" (J). This is the main point made by the Big Bang theory. (F) and (G) are statements made by proponents of the Steady State theory. (H) is a common statement to both theories and does not distinguish them.

9. **(A)** The correct answer is (A). This statement is the essence of the Steady State theory, as can be inferred from the first sentence of the paragraph

"Theory 2: The Steady State." (B) and (D) are statements proper to the Big Bang theory. (C) is a statement shared by both theories and is not the essence of the Steady State theory.

10. **(J)** The correct answer is (J), since the Steady State theory states that the Universe should look the same both in space and time, and hence there should be a homogenous distribution of quasars. Thus, (F) is wrong. (G) and (H) are two independent statements and are neither supported nor contradicted by the report on quasars.

11. **(B)** The correct answer, (B), can be inferred from the statement "...this moment occurred around 14 ± 6 billion years ago" which refers to the initial expansion giving birth to the Universe. One needs to obtain the minimum number consistent with 14 ± 6 and this minimum number is 14 − 6 = 8 billion years. The Universe is at least this old.

12. **(J)** The answer can be inferred from the last sentence in the paragraph on Theory 1, as well as from the last sentence in the paragraph on Theory 2. The answer is (J). Clearly, the author gives more arguments in favor of Theory 1 (the Hot Big Bang) and no arguments against it, and he gives one argument against Theory 2 (Steady State).

13. **(A)** Since the Moon, Earth, and Sun are lined up, there are spring tides occurring at position 3.

14. **(F)** On June 23, spring tides are occurring; therefore, the Sun, Earth and Moon must be in a straight line. At positions 2 and 4, the Earth, Moon, and Sun are at right angles; hence, answers (G), (H), and (J) are incorrect. Position 3 has the Sun, Moon, and Earth in a straight line, and is a spring tide. Therefore, (F) is the best answer.

15. **(D)** Spring tides occur on June 9 and June 23. There are 14 days between these dates; hence, (D) is correct.

16. **(G)** Neap tides occur on June 16 and June 30, which is twice a month. (G) is the correct answer.

17. **(C)** The Moon, Earth, and Sun form a right triangle at position 2. At that time a quarter Moon is seen. (C) is correct.

18. **(H)** Point F on the phase diagram lies on the boundary line separating solid and liquid phases, indicating that only two phases co-exist; (F) is incorrect.

Choice (G) is incorrect, because point G lies on the boundary line separating liquid and gas phases, indicating that only two phases co-exist. Choice (H) is correct. Point E lies on the intersection of three boundary lines separating solid, liquid, and gas phases, indicating the three phases co-existing. Point H lies in a region in which the material is in the gas phase, hence choice (J) is incorrect.

19. **(A)**   Based on the phase diagram, at point A the material is a solid, at point C the material is a liquid, and at point H the material is a gas. (A) is correct. Based on Table 1, a solid thus has a greater density than a liquid and a liquid has a greater density than a gas. Choice (B) is false, because a solid (point A) has a larger density than a liquid (point C). (C) is also false, the reverse sequence is true, because based on the phase diagram and Table 1, solids have the greatest densities followed by liquids, and then gases. (D) is incorrect, because no data is given which shows that changing the temperature and pressure of a phase changes the density.

20. **(J)**   Based on the phase diagram, decreasing the temperature at constant pressure would move point D directly left into the solid region; (F) is incorrect. Choice (G) is false, because increasing both pressure and temperature would keep point D in the gas phase (the upper right portion of the phase diagram). (H) is also incorrect. Decreasing both the pressure and temperature would move point D off of the diagram phase. Choice (J) is correct. Increasing the pressure at constant temperature will move point D straight up into the liquid phase portion of the diagram.

21. **(C)**   Choice (A) can be eliminated, because at point $T = 50$ K and $P = 100$ atm, the material is in the solid phase region of the diagram. Choice (B) is false, since $T = 600$ K and $P > 600$ is beyond the scope of the diagram and not accurately interpreted. Choice (C) is the correct response, because the point at $T = 200$ K and $P = 550$ atm is F, which lies on the boundary line separating two phases, solid and liquid. This indicates that the material co-exists as a solid and a liquid under these conditions. (D) is incorrect, because at $T = 150$ K and 150 atm, three boundary lines meet indicating that three phases co-exist.

22. **(J)**   The passage and the phase diagram indicate that both points A and B are in solid regions of the phase diagram, hence (F) is false. Choice (G) is incorrect, because the passage gives no data to indicate that a material's softness or hardness implies its stability or instability. Choice (H) is also false, for the reason that no data is shown which indicates that a higher pressure means greater stability. (J) is the best choice, because based on the information presented, one cannot compare the stabilities of the two solids.

23. **(C)**   The correct answer is (C). The temperature usually decreases as the height of the atmosphere increases, but there is usually a point in the atmosphere

where the temperature increases as the height increases. (A) is incorrect based on Figures A–C. (B) is incorrect based on Figures 1B–D. (D) is incorrect based on Figures 1A–D.

24. **(F)**   Precipitation does not always begin as rain and usually starts as snow, even in the warmer months; (F) is the best answer. (H) is incorrect because freezing rain occurs at the surface of the Earth. Snow that changes to rain will usually reform as sleet, thus (J) is incorrect.

25. **(B)**   Since the vertical temperature profile is below freezing for the entire height of the atmosphere, the precipitation will fall as snow. It cannot fall as rain (A) or sleet (C) because the temperature never got warm enough to melt the snow. The answer is (B). (D) is wrong because hail is formed during thunderstorms, begins as rain, and was never mentioned in the passage.

26. **(J)**   Using Table 1, with a temperature of 30° F, 1 inch of liquid equivalent snow would be about 8 inches of snow on the ground; (J) is correct. (F) is wrong because that is the amount of measured liquid equivalent snow. (G) and (H) are wrong because 10 and 14 inches would not correlate to a ratio of 8:1.

27. **(B)**   Although both locations may have similar temperature profiles, it cannot be determined by the information provided, thus (A) and (D) are incorrect. (C) is incorrect because if the amount of liquid equivalent snow and snow on the ground are equal, similar snow crystals would have to fall at both locations.

28. **(G)**   If there is a shallow layer of cold air, the precipitation will form as snow, melt at about 1500 meters, and refreeze on contact with the surface. This is freezing rain. It cannot fall as snow because the layer of cold air is too shallow to form snow. It cannot fall as sleet because the precipitation will not have enough time to refreeze before it reaches the surface. (G) is the correct answer. See Figure 1C.

29. **(D)**   The best answer is (D) because fungi, plants, and animals all have nuclei in their cells.

30. **(H)**   (H) is the best answer. Answer (F) is untrue: Scientist 1 says that the lines of evolution form a tree with many branches, not a straight line. (G) is untrue: He says that organisms on near-by branches show a high degree of genetic homology, but that there is much less homology between organisms on distant branches. Therefore, he means neither (F) nor (G), so (H) is true and (J) is false.

31. **(B)**   Scientist 2 says that computer simulations have shown that it is nearly impossible for all humans to have evolved from one ancestor only 1 to 2

million years ago (the recent past in the history of life on Earth). (B) is true. (A) is false: Although if we follow the evolutionary tree back far enough, humans had prokaryotic ancestors. Scientist 2 is not looking back that far with his comparison of human and monkey antigens. (C) is false: Scientist 2's statement was that the human leukocyte antigen of some humans was more closely related to that of monkeys than to that of some other humans. Since (A) and (C) are false, (D) is false.

32. **(G)**   Scientist 1 sees a common ancestor for all living things, including humans and birds. Answer (F) is incorrect: He believes in genetic research. Answer (H) is also incorrect: Darwin used gross comparisons such as bone structure, but his conclusions agreed with those reached by modern genetic methods. Since (G) is true, (J) is false.

33. **(B)**   The best choice is answer (B). Scientist 1 supports the ideas of Darwin's genetics: All organisms evolved from a single root. Answer (A) is not true: He supports Darwin's genetic tree theory. Answer (C) is false: He sees a single ancestor at the root of the genetic tree. Answer (D) is false: The distant progeny of a single ancestor can be expected to have different characteristics.

34. **(H)**   The best choice is (H). Scientist 2 sees a minimum of three separate progenotes. Answer (F) is incorrect: Scientist 2 does not discard Darwin's genetics. Answer (G) does not reflect Scientist 2's views: He does not believe that there was only a single ancestral prokaryote. Answer (J) is wrong: HLA appeared more recently in the genetic tree than the time of the appearance of the prokaryotes and the eukaryotes.

35. **(D)**   Neither scientist presents evidence that would disprove this theory; answer (D) is correct. Answer (A) is wrong, because his theory could be incorporated into the "common single-cell ancestor" view of Scientist 1. (B) is also wrong, because this theory could be incorporated into Scientist 2's "evolution from three progenotes" view. Therefore, choice (C) is also wrong.

36. **(G)**   By examining the data in Table 1, one can see that choice (G) is the correct answer. It is not shown that "as resistance increases, voltage decreases"; therefore, answer choice (A) is incorrect. There is no support for either choice (H) or (J) since the passage and table do not show an RC circuit, but rather show only individual resistor and capacitor circuitry.

37. **(C)**   This question solely relies on reasoning. A series of capacitors 10, 10, 20 gives a voltage of 100 volts. A series of 20, 20, 20 gives a voltage of 133 volts. If there is a series of 10, 20, 20, the voltage should be somewhere in the middle of the two. Therefore, (C) is the correct answer.

38. **(J)** According to Table 1, all the resistors give a voltage of 50 volts. Under this assumption, a resistor of 15 Ω would also provide 50 volts. (J) is the correct answer.

39. **(B)** The data from Table 1 provides the answer. The voltage of the series of capacitors is 67. The voltage of the 20 Ω resistor is 50. The combination, 67 + 50, yields an answer of 117; choice (B) is correct.

40. **(G)** Again, this is a reasoning question. The combination of the resistors alone gives 100 volts, so (F) and (H) are incorrect. However, the voltage of the single capacitor is unknown. One can estimate, though, that the voltage will be less than 200 volts because a series of capacitors 10, 10, 20 gives 100 volts. A single capacitor will only give a fraction of that. Therefore, the correct answer is (G).

CHAPTER 4

Attacking the
ACT English Test

Chapter 4

ATTACKING THE ACT ENGLISH TEST

DESCRIPTION OF THE ACT ENGLISH TEST

The ACT English Test is designed to measure your understanding of the rules of standard written English, as well as your knowledge of rhetorical skills. In other words, the test is a measure of your knowledge of grammar and English usage and your ability to distinguish good–that is, structured and logical–writing from poorly organized writing. The 45-minute English test contains 75 items within five prose passages. The questions are multiple-choice. Some questions refer to underlined portions of the text, while the rest refer to sections of the text or to the text as a whole. The ACT English Test reports three scores: a total score based on all 75 questions, a subscore based on 40 questions in Usage/Mechanics, and a subscore based on 35 items in Rhetorical Skills.

The Usage/Mechanics portion of the test assesses your knowledge of punctuation, grammar, and sentence structure. Punctuation is approximately 13 percent of the section and tests your knowledge of punctuation used in with and at the end of a sentence. Grammar questions comprise approximately 16 percent of this portion of the test and measure your knowledge of basic grammar and usage. Sentence structure questions total about 24 percent of the test and measure your knowledge of clause relationships, placement of modifiers, and shifts in construction.

The Rhetorical Skills portion of this test evaluates your knowledge of prose strategy, organization, and style. Strategy comprises about 16 percent of the English portion and tests your ability to choose language appropriate to the purpose of the passage as well as the audience it was designed to reach. In addition, this section tests your ability to recognize appropriate supporting material and to choose appropriate passage-related introductory, summary, concluding, and transitional sentences. Organization questions comprise about 15 percent of the test and measure your ability to organize ideas and maintain order, coherence, and unity within the context of the prose passage. Style, which comprises about 16 percent of the test, measures your ability to be precise and concise in your choice of words and images and tests your ability to avoid ambiguity in the use of modifiers.

ABOUT THE DIRECTIONS

Make sure to study and learn the directions to save yourself time during the actual test. You should simply skim them when beginning the section. The directions will read similar to the following:

DIRECTIONS: This test consists of five passages. In each passage, certain words and phrases have been underlined and numbered. The questions on each passage consist of alternatives for these underlined segments. Choose the alternative that follows standard written English, most accurately reflects the style and tone of the passage, or best relays the idea of the passage. Choose "NO CHANGE," if no change is necessary.

There are several important points for you to keep in mind about these instructions. First, although in the majority of the questions only a part of the sentence is underlined, you have to read the whole sentence very carefully. Very often, the problem with the sentence is in how the underlined part fits in with the rest of the sentence. Do not try to save time by reading only the underlined part. This will only hurt your score.

Second, in giving you the choice to select the original as the best version of the sentence, the testmakers imply that not all of the sentences contain mistakes. In fact, choice (A) will be the correct answer as frequently as any of the other choices. Do not assume that something must be wrong with the original. Check for mistakes; if you do not find any, choose (A) and move on.

Finally, since choice (A) repeats the underlined part of the original sentence, there is no reason to read (A) when you are considering answer choices.

Your answer choice should be the one that "best expresses the idea, makes the statement appropriate for standard written English, or is worded most consistently with the style and tone of the passage as a whole." Thus, while in some questions the original sentence is not wrong, it is written poorly; and one of the answer choices presents a better version of "standard written English." Here, the testmakers are defining what standards they use for judging sentences. These standards comprise a way of writing that rigidly adheres to the rules of grammar and to conventions for choosing words and constructing sentences. Standard written English on the ACT is more formal than the way most of us write and is much more formal than the way we speak. It is the style of writing found in most textbooks.

In selecting an answer, you have to make sure you do not change the meaning of the original sentence. A choice that alters the meaning of the sentence even slightly is not acceptable. To safeguard against making such a mistake, reread the whole sentence, keeping in mind its relation to the whole passage, and then substitute the version you think is correct for the original. In fact, this technique will help you make sure that the new version works with the whole sentence and does not introduce new errors.

The questions that are identified by a number or numbers in a box are questions that refer to the section of the passage or the entire passage. Some of these questions are designed to test your ability to recognize the author's purpose and intended audience. In addition, the questions may test your knowledge of effective organization, which includes the unity, focus, and development of the passage. In order to analyze a passage for purpose and audience, you will need to read the whole passage through, looking for key words and phrases used by the author to establish the overall purpose and the intended audience.

Questions that test organization require you to look for the main idea of the passage as a whole, as well as the main idea of each paragraph. The main idea of the passage may be found within the first few sentences of the passage. The main idea of the paragraph may be in either the first or last sentence of each paragraph. Skim over the detailed points of the passage, while making sure to circle key words and phrases. These are words or phrases such as: but, on the other hand, although, however, yet, and except. These words and phrases give you an indication of the author's reasoning and logic. If a question requires you to change a numbered section and you cannot determine the answer, try plugging in the answer choices to see which works.

STRATEGIES FOR THE ENGLISH SECTION

Before the test, this is your plan of attack:

| STEP 1 | Study our review to build your English skills. |
| STEP 2 | Study and learn the directions to ensure that you know how to approach the questions in this section. |

You should follow this plan of attack *when answering English Section questions*.

| STEP 1 | Read the whole passage, and look at the underlined part in relation to the rest of the passage. Do not pay attention simply to the underlined words. The words that are not underlined can determine whether or not the underlined words are correct. |
| STEP 2 | Try to determine what, if anything, is wrong with the sentence before looking at the answer choices. Do not be afraid to choose |

(A) if you think the original is the best version. Do not read choice (A) since it merely repeats the question.

| STEP 3 | Examine the choices carefully and eliminate the obviously incorrect. Remember that this is a test of STANDARD WRITTEN ENGLISH. Look for choices that reflect the language of formal writing you would find in a textbook. |

A.   Is the sentence complete? Find the subject and the predicate.

B.   In compound sentences, are clauses connected to avoid run-ons?

C.   Make sure subject and predicate verb agree in number and in person.

D.   Check verb tense. Is the sequence of events properly expressed?

E.   Are there misplaced modifiers? Is there ambiguity in the sentence?

F.   Check the pronouns. Does each pronoun have one clear antecedent? Do they agree with their antecedents in number, person, and gender?

G.   Check for problems with parallel structures or comparisons.

H.   Is the active voice used? Is the sentence too wordy or redundant?

| STEP 4 | Choose the best answer. In deciding between two choices, select the one that is more concise and effective. If you are unsure, take a guess. Sometimes it helps to say the sentence to yourself. This enables you to determine if the pauses reflected by the punctuation are correct. |

| STEP 5 | Reread the passage with your answer to see if it makes sense. |

| STEP 6 | The questions that do not refer to underlined sections test your rhetorical skills. |

A.   Is language appropriate to author's purpose and intended audience?

B.   Make sure the sentences within paragraphs share a main idea.

C.   Transitional sentences should be logically arranged within the context of the text.

D.   A text should be organized in the following sequence: an introductory paragraph, at least one paragraph that develops the idea(s), and a concluding paragraph.

E.   Do not create a one-sentence paragraph. Most paragraphs are composed of at least two to three sentences.

SKILLS TESTED

In the ACT English test you will be required to draw on your knowledge of the elements of standard written English in order to answer the test questions correctly. The test will cover both the mechanics and usage of proper grammar and rhetorical skills. A specific breakdown of these skills follows.

Punctuation

You will be evaluated on your ability to recognize and use both internal and end-of-sentence punctuation. There is an emphasis on the use of punctuation to clarify the meaning of a sentence.

Basic Grammar and Usage

You will be tested on your understanding of agreement between subject and verb, pronoun and antecedent, and modifiers and the word modified. You will also be required to know verb formation, pronoun cases, the use of adjectives and adverbs in the comparative and superlative cases; and correct usage of idiomatic expressions.

Sentence Structure

The relationship between and among clauses, the proper placement of modifiers, and shifts in sentence construction will be the focus of these test items.

Strategy

In order to answer questions in this area correctly, you should be able to choose expression appropriate to the purpose and audience of a particular essay. You will also be tested on your ability to strengthen an essay with supporting material, and the ability to select introductory, summary, concluding, and transitional sentences that are appropriate for a piece of writing.

Organization

These items will test your ability to organize ideas. You will also be asked to evaluate the relevance of statements in context.

Style

Your ability to select the most appropriate words and images, manage the elements of a sentence, avoid ambiguity, and write economically will be evaluated in these items.

I. STANDARD WRITTEN ENGLISH REVIEW

GRAMMAR/USAGE MECHANICS

This review is designed to familiarize you with the rules of English grammar and usage. At the conclusion of each section are questions designed to test your understanding of that particular rule.

The Sentence

A sentence is a group of words that communicates a complete thought.

NO: The dogs in my neighborhood.

YES: The dogs in my neighborhood bark all night.

The first example is not a sentence because it does not present a complete thought. The second example completes the thought and is a sentence.

To be a sentence—to communicate a complete thought—a group of words must have both a subject and a predicate. The subject is a word (or combination of words) that represents the person or thing that the sentence is about. The predicate is a word (or group of words) that states what the subject is doing, or what is being done to the subject. The predicate is the part of the sentence that contains the verb.

My dog   does not bark.
subject   predicate

There are two types of common sentence errors: (1) sentence fragments and (2) run-on sentences.

Sentence Fragments

NO: A tree as old as your father.

      A sentence fragment does not have enough in it to make a complete thought. It is usually missing a subject or verb.

YES: The tree is as old as your father.

Run-On Sentences

NO: It was a pleasant drive the sun was shining.

      A run-on sentence is a sentence with too much in it. It usually contains two complete sentences separated by a comma, or two complete sentences merged together.

YES: It was a pleasant drive because the sun was shining.

NO: Talk softly, someone is listening.

Sometimes the writer will try to correct a run-on sentence by inserting a comma between the clauses, but this creates another error, a comma splice. The following examples illustrate various ways to correct the comma splice.

YES: Talk softly; someone is listening.

or

Talk softly, because someone is listening.

☞ Drill: The Sentence, Sentence Fragments, and Run-On Sentences

> **DIRECTIONS:** The following sentences may be either run-on sentences or sentence fragments. Make any necessary corrections.

1. After the rain stopped.

2. Mow the lawn, it is much too long.

3. The settlement you reached it seems fair.

4. When I read, especially at night. My eyes get tired.

5. It was impossible to get through on the phone, the lines went down because of the storm.

6. Is this the only problem? The leaky pipe?

7. Everyone saw the crime, no one is willing to come forth.

8. The weather was bad, she played in the rain.

9. Ellen paced the floor. Worrying about her economics final.

10. Their season was over, the team had lost the playoffs.

The Comma

Of all the marks of punctuation, the comma (,) has the most uses. Before you tackle the main principles that guide its usage, be sure you read the section entitled THE SENTENCE. There are actually only a few rules and conventions to follow when using commas; the rest is common sense. The worst abuse of commas comes from overusing them—or placing them illogically. If you are ever in doubt as to whether or not to use a comma, do not use it.

In a Series

When more than one adjective (an adjective series) describes a noun, use a comma to separate and emphasize each adjective.

> the long, dark passageway
>
> another confusing, sleepless night
>
> the beautiful, starry night
>
> the haunting, melodic sound
>
> the old, grey, crumpled hat

In these instances, the comma takes the place of "and." To test if the comma is needed, try inserting "and" between the adjectives in question. If it is logical, you should use a comma. The following are examples of adjectives that describe an adjective-noun combination that has come to be thought of as almost one word. In such cases, the adjective in front of the adjective-noun combination needs no comma.

> a stately oak tree   my worst report card
>
> an exceptional wine glass   a borrowed record player
>
> a successful garage sale   a porcelain dinner plate

If you insert "and" between the adjectives in the above examples, it will not make sense.

The comma is also used to separate words, phrases, and whole ideas (clauses); it still takes the place of "and" when used this way.

> an apple, a pear, a fig, and a banana
>
> a lovely lady, an indecent dress, and many admirers
>
> She lowered the shade, closed the curtain, turned off the light, and went to bed.
>
> John, Frank, and my Uncle Harry all thought it was a questionable theory.

The only question that exists about the use of commas in a series is whether or not one should be used before the final item. Usually "and" or "or" precedes the final item, and many writers do not include the comma before the final "and" or "or." When first learning, however, it is advisable to use the comma because often its omission can be confusing; in such cases as these for instance:

NO: Would you like to shop at Sak's, Lord and Taylor's and Bloomingdales?

NO: He got on his horse, tracked a rabbit and a deer and rode on to Canton.

NO: We planned the trip with Mary and Harold, Susan, Dick and Joan, Gregory and Jean and Charles. (Is it Gregory and Jean, or Jean and Charles, or Gregory and Jean and Charles?)

With A Long Introductory Phrase

Usually if a phrase of more than five or six words precedes the subject at the beginning of a sentence, a comma is used to set it off.

> After last night's fiasco at the disco, she couldn't bear the thought of looking at him again.

> Whenever I try to talk about politics, my husband leaves the room.

> When it comes to actual facts, every generation makes the same mistakes as the preceding one.

> Provided you have said nothing, they will never guess who you are.

It is not necessary to use a comma with a short sentence.

> In January she will go to Switzerland.

> After I rest I'll feel better.

> At Grandma's we had a big dinner.

> During the day no one is home.

If an introductory phrase includes a verb form that is being used as another part of speech (a "verbal"), it must be followed by a comma. Try to make sense of the following sentences without commas.

NO: When eating Mary never looked up from her plate.

YES: When eating, Mary never looked up from her plate.

NO: Because of her desire to follow her faith in James wavered.

YES: Because of her desire to follow, her faith in James wavered.

NO: Having decided to leave Mary James wrote her a letter.

YES: Having decided to leave Mary, James wrote her a letter.

Above all, common sense is the best guideline when trying to decide whether or not to use a comma after an introductory phrase. Does the comma make the meaning clearer? If it does, use it; if not, do not insert it.

To Separate Sentences With Two Main Ideas (Compound Sentences)

When a sentence contains more than two subjects and verbs (clauses) and the two clauses are joined by a connecting word (and, but, or, yet, for, nor), use a comma before the connecting word to show that another clause is coming.

> I thought I knew the poem by heart, but he showed me three lines I had forgotten.

> Are we really interested in helping the children, or are we more concerned with protecting our good names?

> He is supposed to leave tomorrow, but who knows if he will be ready to go.

> Jim knows you are disappointed, and he has known it for a long time.

If the two parts of the sentence are short and closely related, it is not necessary to use a comma.

> He threw the ball and the dog ran after it.

> Jane played the piano and Charles danced.

Be careful not to confuse a sentence that has a compound verb and a single subject with a compound sentence. If the subject is the same for both verbs, there is no need for a comma.

> NO: Charles sent some flowers, and wrote a long letter explaining why he had not been able to come.

> NO: Last Thursday we went to the concert with Julia, and afterwards dined at an old Italian restaurant.

> NO: For the third time, the teacher explained that the literary level of high school students was much lower than it had been in previous years, and, this time, wrote the statistics on the board for everyone to see.

To Set Off Interrupting Material

There are so many different kinds of interruptions that can occur in a sentence that a list of them all would be quite lengthy. In general, words and phrases that stop the flow of the sentence or are unnecessary for the main idea are set off by commas. Some examples are:

> Abbreviations after names

> Did you invite John Paul, Jr., and his sister?

> Martha Harris, Ph.D., will be the speaker tonight.

Interjections: An exclamation added without grammatical connection

Oh, I'm so glad to see you.

I tried so hard, alas, to do it.

Hey, let me out of here.

No, I will not let you out.

Direct Address

Roy, won't you open the door for the dog?

I can't understand, mother, what you are trying to say.

May I ask, Mr. President, why you called us together?

Hey, lady, watch out for the car!

Tag questions: A question that repeats the helping verb in a negative phrase.

I'm really hungry, aren't you?

Jerry looks like his father, doesn't he?

You'll come early, won't you?

We are expected at nine, aren't we?

Mr. Jones can chair the meeting, can't he?

Geographical names and addresses

The concert will be held in Chicago, Illinois, on August 12.

They visited Tours, France, last summer.

The letter was addressed to Ms. Marion Heartwell, 1881 Pine Lake, Palo Alto, California 95824. (No comma is needed before the zip code because it is already clearly set off from the state name.)

Transitional words and phrases

On the other hand, I hope he gets better.

In addition, the phone rang six times this afternoon.

I'm, nevertheless, going to the beach on Sunday.

You'll find, therefore, no one is more loyal to me than you.

To tell the truth, I don't know what to believe.

Parenthetical words and phrases

You will become, I believe, a great statesman.

We know, of course, that this is the only thing to do.

In fact, I planted corn last summer.

The Mannes affair was, to put it mildly, a surprise.

Bathing suits, generally speaking, are getting smaller.

Unusual word order

The dress, new and crisp, hung in the closet. (Normal word order: The new, crisp dress hung in the closet.)

Intently, she stared out the window. (Normal word order: She stared intently out the window.)

Nonrestrictive Elements (Not Essential To Meaning)

Parts of a sentence that modify other parts are sometimes essential to the meaning of the sentence and sometimes not. When a modifying word or group of words is not vital to the meaning of the sentence, it is set off by commas. Since it does not restrict the meaning of the words it modifies, it is called "nonrestrictive." Modifiers that are essential to the meaning of the sentence are called "restrictive" and are not set off by commas. Compare the following pairs of sentences:

The girl who wrote the story is my sister. (essential)

My sister, the girl who wrote the story, has always been drawn to adventure. (nonessential)

John Milton's famous poem "Paradise Lost" tells a remarkable story. (essential - Milton has written other poems)

Dante's great work, "The Divine Comedy," marked the beginning of the Renaissance and the end of the Dark Ages. (nonessential - Dante wrote only one great work)

The cup that is on the piano is the one I want. (essential)

The cup, which my brother gave me last year, is on the piano. (nonessential)

My parakeet Simian has an extensive vocabulary. (essential - because there are no commas, the writer must have more than one parakeet)

My parakeet, Simian, has an extensive vocabulary. (nonessential - the writer must have only one parakeet whose name is Simian)

The people who arrived late were not seated. (essential)

George, who arrived late, was not seated. (nonessential)

To Set Off Direct Quotations

Most direct quotes or quoted materials are set off from the rest of the sentence by commas.

"Please try to be on time," said her mother.

"I won't know what to do," said Michael, "if you leave me now."

The teacher said sternly, "I will not dismiss this class until I have silence."

Mark looked up from his work, smiled, and said, "I'll be right with you."

Be careful not to set off indirect quotations or quotes that are used as subjects or complements.

"To be or not to be" is the famous beginning of a soliloquy in Shakespeare's Hamlet. (subject)

Back then my favorite song was "A Summer's Place." (complement)

Jaclyn said she would be back later. (indirect quote)

"Put the cake in the oven" were the chef's first words to his apprentice. (subject)

To Set Off Contrasting Elements

Her intelligence, not her beauty, got her the job.

Your plan will take you further from, rather than closer to, your destination.

He wanted glory, but found happiness instead.

James wanted an active, not a passive, partner.

In Dates

Both forms of the date are acceptable.

She will arrive on April 6, 1981.

She will arrive on 6 April 1981.

In January, 1967, he handed in his resignation.

In January 1967 he handed in his resignation.

☞ Drill: The Comma

DIRECTIONS: In the following sentences insert commas wherever necessary. You may also want to note the reason for your choice.

1. However I am willing to reconsider.

2. She descended the long winding staircase.

3. Whenever I practice the violin my family closes the windows.

4. While driving Francis never took his eyes off the road.

5. The car which I bought last year is in the garage.

6. "Answer the door" said his mother loudly.

7. Miss can I ask you for the time?

8. He was after all an ex-convict.

9. I'm so bored aren't you?

10. The old tall shady tree is wonderful during the summer.

11. George Gary and Bill were on line early this morning. They bought their tickets read the newspaper and spoke for awhile.

12. The author James Grey was awarded the prize.

13. She attended school in London England last year.

14. They said they would do the job.

15. His weight not his height prevented him from competing in the race.

16. The family who won the lottery lives in New Jersey.

17. She got in the car turned on the ignition and left the curb.

18. Incidentally he called last night.

19. The kitten small and cute was adopted by the Brown family.

20. Mary did you see James Jr. at the party last night?

21. Lisa saw the mailman and gave him the letter.

22. Last night I finished my essay and started on my next assignment.

23. Really I can't believe that is the truth.

24. We thought it was time to leave but we arrived early.

25. Monday she will leave for Boston.

26. After he got home he read a magazine ate dinner and left for the movies.

27. If you pass the test you will graduate.

28. When she decided to leave everyone was disappointed.

29. Hey John it's time to go.

30. He seemed wrong for the part yet he turned out to be the best actor in the production.

The Colon

The colon (:) is the sign of a pause about midway in length between the semicolon and the period. It can often be replaced by a comma and sometimes by a period. Although used less frequently now than it was 50 to 75 years ago, the colon has a definite purpose, for it signals to the reader that more information is to come on the subject. The colon can also create a slight dramatic tension.

It is used to introduce a word, phrase, or complete statement (clause) that emphasizes, illustrates, or exemplifies what has already been stated.

He had only one desire in life: to play baseball.

The weather that day was the most unusual I'd ever seen: It snowed and rained while the sun was still shining.

In his speech, the president surprised us by his final point: The conventional grading system would be replaced next year.

Jean thought of only two things the last half hour of the hike home: a bath and her bed.

Notice that the word following the colon can start with either a capital or a small letter. Use a capital letter if the word following the colon begins another complete sentence. But when the words following the colon are part of the sentence preceding the colon, use a small letter.

> May I offer you a suggestion: Don't drive without your seatbelt fastened.

> The thought continued to perplex him: Where will I go next?

When introducing a series that illustrates or emphasizes what has already been stated, use the colon.

> Only a few of the graduates were able to be there: Jamison, Henek, Zand, and Cohen.

> For Omar Khayyam, a Persian poet, three things are necessary for a paradise on earth: a loaf of bread, a jug of wine, and his beloved.

> In the basement he kept some equipment for his experiments: the test tubes, some chemical agents, three sunlamps, and the drill.

Long quotes set off from the rest of the text by indentation, rather than quotation marks, are generally introduced with a colon.

> The first line of Lincoln's Gettysburg address is familiar to most Americans:

>> Fourscore and seven years ago our fathers brought forth on this continent a new nation, conceived in liberty and dedicated to the proposition that all men are created equal.

> I quote from Shakespeare's Sonnets:

>> When I do count the clock that tells the time,
>> And see the brave day sunk in hideous night;
>> When I behold the violet past prime,
>> And sable curls all silver'd o'er with white...

It is also customary to begin a business letter with a colon.

> Dear Senator Jordan:

> To Whom It May Concern:

> Gentlemen:

> Dear Sir or Madam:

But in informal letters, use a comma.

> Dear Carly,

> Dear Arthur,

The colon is also used in introducing a list.

Please send the following:

1. 50 index cards,

2. 4 typewriter ribbons,

and

3. 8 erasers.

Prepare the recipe as follows:

1. Slice the oranges thinly.

2. Arrange them in a circle around the strawberries.

3. Pour the liqueur over both fruits.

At least three ladies will have to be there to help:

1. Joan, who will greet the guests;

2. Ilene, who will serve the lunch;

and

3. Suzanne, who will do whatever else needs to be done.

Finally, the colon is used between numbers when writing the time, between the volume and number or volume and page number of a journal, and also between the chapter and verse in the Bible.

4:30 P.M.
The Nation, 34:8
Genesis 5:18

The Semicolon

Semicolons (;) are sometimes called mild periods. They indicate a pause midway in length between the comma and the colon. Writing that contains many semicolons is usually in a dignified, formal style. To use them correctly, it is necessary to be able to recognize main clauses—complete ideas. When two main clauses occur in a single sentence without a connecting word (and, but, or, nor, for), the appropriate mark of punctuation is the semicolon.

It is not a good idea for you to leave the country right now; you should actually try to stay longer.

Music lightens life; literature deepens it.

In the past, boy babies were dressed in blue; girls in pink. ("were dressed" is understood in the second part of the sentence.)

Can't you see it's no good to go on alone; we'll starve to death if we keep traveling this way much longer.

Burgundy and maroon are very similar colors; scarlet is altogether different.

Notice how using either the comma, period, or semicolon gives a sentence a slightly different shade of meaning.

Music lightens life; but, literature deepens it.

Just as music lightens life, literature deepens it.

Music lightens life. Literature deepens it.

The semicolon lends a certain balance to writing that would otherwise be difficult to achieve. Nonetheless, you should be careful not to overuse it. A comma can just as well join parts of a sentence with two main ideas; the semicolon is particularly appropriate if there is a striking contrast in the two ideas expressed.

Ask not what your country can do for you; ask what you can do for your country.

It started out as an ordinary day; it ended being the most extraordinary of her life.

Our power to apprehend truth is limited; to seek it, limitless.

If any one of the following words or phrases are used to join together compound sentences, they are generally preceded by a semicolon:

then	however	thus	furthermore
hence	indeed	so	consequently
also	that is	yet	nevertheless
anyhow	in addition	in fact	on the other hand
likewise	moreover	still	meanwhile
instead	besides	otherwise	in other words
henceforth	for example	therefore	at the same time
even now			

For a long time, people thought that women were inferior to men; even now, it is not an easy attitude to overcome.

Because he was clever and cynical, he succeeded in becoming president of the company; meanwhile, his wife left him.

Some say Bach was the greatest composer of all time; yet he still managed to have an ordinary life in other ways: he and his wife had 20 children.

We left wishing we could have stayed longer; in other words, we had a good time.

When a series of complicated items are listed, or if there is internal punctuation in a series, the semicolon is sometimes used to make the meaning more clear.

> You can use your new car for many things: to drive to town or to the country; to impress your friends and neighbors; to protect yourself from rain on a trip away from home; and to borrow against should you need money right away.

> The scores from yesterday's games came in late last night: Pirates - 6, Zoomers - 3; Caterpillars - 12, Steelys - 8; Crashers - 9, Links - 8; and Greens 15, Uptowns - 4.

> In October, a bag of potatoes cost 69 cents; in December, 99 cents; in February, $1.09; in April, $1.39. I wonder if this inflation will ever stop.

The semicolon is placed outside quotation marks or parentheses, unless it is part of the material enclosed in those marks.

> I used to call him "my lord and master"; it made him laugh every time.

> The weather was cold for that time of year (I was shivering wherever I went); nevertheless, we set out to hike to the top of that mountain.

☞ Drill: The Colon and the Semicolon

DIRECTIONS: Correctly place the colon and/or the semicolon in the following sentences.

1. I have only one thing to say don't do it.

2. They seemed compatible yet they did not get along.

3. She had only one goal in life to be a famous pianist.

4. He thought the problem was solved instead his solution proved to be entirely wrong.

5. By the end of the day there were only two things on her mind rest and relaxation.

6. Only a few members were able to attend the convention Henry, Karen, David, Mark, and Susan.

7. They were willing to accept the proposal he was not.

8. The art students were expected to supply the following brushes, paints, pallets, and pads.

9. The time is now the time is right.

10. The highest scores on the final exam are as follows Linda Jones 96 John Smith 94 Susan Green 90. These grades are unusually high they must have studied well.

The Apostrophe

Use the apostrophe to form contractions: to indicate that letters or figures have been omitted.

can't (cannot)	o'clock (of the clock)
I'll (I will)	it's (it is)
memories of '68 (1968)	won't (will not)
you've (you have)	they're (they are)

Notice that the apostrophe is always placed where a letter or letters have been omitted. Avoid such careless errors as writing wo'nt instead of won't, for example. Contractions are generally not used in formal writing. They are found primarily in speech and informal writing.

An apostrophe is also used to indicate the plural form of letters, figures, and words that normally do not take a plural form. In such cases, it would be confusing to add only an "s."

He quickly learned his r's and s's.

Children have difficulty in remembering to dot their i's and cross their t's.

Most of the Ph.D.'s and M.D.'s understand the new technology they are using for anticancer drugs.

Her 2's always looked like her 4's.

Marion used too many the's and and's in her last paper for English literature.

Whenever possible, try to form plurals of numbers and of single or multiple letters used as words by adding only "s."

the ABCs	the 1960s
in threes and fours	three Rs

Placement of the Apostrophe to Indicate Possession

In spoken English, the same pronunciation is used for the plural, singular possessive, and plural possessive of most nouns. It is only by the context that the listener is able to tell the difference in the words used by the speaker. In written English, the spelling as well as the context tells the reader the meaning of the noun the writer is using. The writer has only to master the placement of the apostrophe so that the meaning is clearly conveyed to the reader. These words are pronounced alike but have different meanings.

Plural	*Singular Possessive*	*Plural Possessive*
neighbors	neighbor's	neighbors'
weeks	week's	weeks'
sopranos	soprano's	sopranos'
civilizations	civilization's	civilizations'

If you are not sure of the apostrophe's placement, you can determine it accurately by this simple test: change the possessive phrase into "belonging to" or an "of" phrase to discover the basic noun. You will find this a particularly useful trick for some of the more confusing possessive forms such as those on words that end in "s" or "es."

> Keats' poem: The poem belonging to Keats. Base noun is Keats; possessive is Keats' or Keats's, not Keat's or Keat'es.

> Four months' pay: The pay of four months. Months is base noun; possessive is months', not month's.

> In two hours' time: In the time of two hours. Hours is the base; possessive is hours', not hour's.

> It is anybody's guess: The guess of anybody. Anybody is the base noun; possessive is anybody's, not anybodys' or anybodies'.

☞ Drill: The Apostrophe

> **DIRECTIONS:** Write the contractions for the following words.

1. she will

2. will not

3. Class of 1994

4. does not

5. they have

> **DIRECTIONS:** In the following sentences, make the necessary corrections.

6. This boat isnt yours. We sold our's last year to Roberts parents.

7. At 10 oclock theyll meet us at Macys department store.

8. In Ms. Greens first grade class, she had difficulty writing x's and learning her ABC's.

9. Wordsworths poem "the Solitary Reaper" was published in J. Mahoneys edition of *The Romantic Poet's*.

> **DIRECTIONS:** Write the possessive singular and the plural possessive of each of the following words.

10. lady

11. child

12. cashier

13. Filipino

Titles — Quotation Marks and Underlines

To set off titles of radio and TV shows, poems, stories, and book chapters in sentences, use quotation marks.

My favorite essay by Montaigne is "On Silence."

Ron Howard starred in "Happy Days."

The teacher assigned the students to read chapter 18 entitled "Childhood Development."

To set off titles of books, motion pictures, plays, newspapers, and magazines in sentences, use an underline.

William Shakespeare wrote <u>Romeo and Juliet</u>.

A famous Charles Dickens' book is <u>A Tale of Two Cities</u>.

Tom Hanks starred in <u>Apollo 13</u>.

Shelly read an article in <u>The New York Times</u> on the problems drugs in the United States.

A special note should be made about the style of presenting titles of books, motion pictures, plays, newspapers, and magazines. While it is correct to either italicize or underline these titles, it is preferred to underline them because some computer printers have indistinct italics characters, or none at all.

☞ Drill: Titles—Quotation Marks and Underlines

DIRECTIONS: In the following sentences insert quotation marks and underlines wherever necessary.

1. Chapter 13 of Modern Biological Principles is called Plant Reproduction.

2. The teacher told the students to read chapter 2, The Market-Place, in Nathaniel Hawthorne's The Scarlet Letter.

3. John Travolta starred in the movie Grease.

4. Last night, Michele watched Seinfeld on television.

5. You will find Keats' Ode on a Grecian Urn in chapter 3, The Romantic Era, in Lastly's Selections from Great English Poets.

Interjections

An interjection is a word or group of words used as an exclamation to express emotion. It need not be followed by an exclamation point. Often an interjection is followed by a comma if it is not very intense. Technically, the interjection has no grammatical relation to other words in the sentence; yet it is still considered a part of speech.

Examples:

Oh dear, I forgot my keys again.

Ah! Now do you understand?

Ouch! I didn't realize that the stove was hot.

Dashes

Use the dash to indicate a sudden or unexpected break in the normal flow of the sentence. It can also be used in the place of parentheses or of commas if the meaning is clarified. Usually the dash gives the material it sets off special emphasis.

Could you—I hate to ask!—help me with these boxes?

She said—we all heard it—"The safe is not locked."

That day was the longest in her life—or so it seemed to her.

A dash is often used to summarize a series of ideas that have already been expressed.

Freedom of speech, freedom to vote, and freedom of assembly—these are the cornerstones of democracy.

Carbohydrates, fats, and proteins—these are the basic kinds of food we need.

Parentheses

To set off material that is only loosely connected to the central meaning of the sentence, use parentheses [()].

Most men (at least most that I know) like wine, women, and song.

Last year at Sunday River (we go there every year), the skiing was the best I've ever seen.

Watch out for punctuation when you use parentheses. Punctuation that refers to the material enclosed in the parentheses occurs inside the marks. Punctuation belonging to the rest of the sentence comes outside the parentheses.

I thought I knew the poem by heart (boy was I wrong!).

We must always strive to tell the truth. (Are we even sure we know what truth is?)

☞ Drill: Interjections, Dashes, and Parentheses

DIRECTIONS: Read the following sentences. What effect does the dash have on the writing, especially the mood and tone?

1. Can you?—I would be ever so grateful—I'm having so much difficulty.

2. Could it be—no it can't be—not after all these years.

3. Time and patience—two simple words—yet why are they so hard for me to remember?

4. Most of the paintings in the gallery—in fact all but one—were done in the 19th century.

5. According to John Locke, these are man's inalienable rights—life, liberty, and property.

> **DIRECTIONS:** Read the following sentences. What effect does the use of parentheses have on the writing? Also, make any necessary corrections.

6. The choice (in my opinion,) was a good one.

7. Linda's comment ("Where did you get that dress")? wasn't intended to be sarcastic.

8. After today (and what a day it was!) I will begin to work harder.

9. Last summer in Cape Cod (this is the first year we went there,) we did a lot of sightseeing.

10. The first time I went driving (do you remember that day)?, I was so scared.

Verbs

The verb is the most important part of any sentence. It tells us what is happening to the subject or what the subject is doing. Furthermore, the verb lets us know the time of the action. Many questions on the ACT test your knowledge of verb tenses and verb forms.

Tenses

Tenses are unique to verbs. They indicate the time of the action. There are three simple tenses and three perfect tenses.

>   Present: I see the dog.

The present tense is used when the action in the sentence is taking place in the present.

>   Past: I saw the dog.

The past tense is used when the action took place in the past.

>   Future: I shall (will) see the dog.

The future tense is used when the action will take place in the future.

>   Present Perfect: I have seen the dog.

The present perfect tense is used when the action is completed at the time of writing. It can also be used to indicate that the action is continuing into the present.

The past perfect tense is used when the action in the sentence was completed at a definite point in time.

Past Perfect: I had seen the dog.

Future Perfect: I shall (will) have seen the dog.

The future perfect tense is used when the action will be completed at some definite time in the future.

Each of the six tenses also has a progressive form. Progressive forms are used when the action is continuing at the time indicated by the tense.

Progressive:

Present	You are reading.
Past	You were reading.
Future	You will (shall) be reading.
Present Perfect	You have been reading.
Past Perfect	You had been reading.
Future Perfect	You will (shall) have been reading.

If two events happen at the same time, the same tense must be used.

NO: Mary fell asleep just as the movie starts.

YES: Mary fell asleep just as the movie started.

If events happen at different times, the tenses must reflect the difference. This is easy to do with the simple tenses.

Bob and I ate lunch together, and now I am going to meet with Bob.

If events happened at different times in the past, the past perfect must be used for the event that happened first, and the past tense for the event that happened later.

NO: The dinosaurs died out before the mammals came to dominate the Earth.

YES: The dinosaurs had died out before the mammals came to dominate the Earth.

Similarly, if events take place at different times in the future, the future perfect must be used for the event that will happen first, and the future tense for the event that will happen later.

NO: I will play tennis tomorrow, when the rain will pass.

YES: I will play tennis tomorrow, when the rain will have passed.

Mood

In addition to tenses, verbs also change to reflect mood. The mood indicates the author's attitude toward the action. There are three moods in English. The indicative is used for factual statements. The imperative is used to command. And the subjunctive is used to communicate doubts, wishes, and requirements.

The two most important characteristics of the subjunctive are: The subjunctive form of "to be" in the past tense is "were" in the first, second, and third persons, singular or plural.

I wish I were a baseball star.

If he were taller, he could reach the top shelf.

For all other verbs in the present tense, third person, singular, the "s" is omitted.

If the generator should fail, we will need candles.

The doctor suggested that Lillian take a trip.

☞ Drill: Verbs

DIRECTIONS: Correct the verb errors in the following sentences.

1. If it snows tomorrow, the children stay home from school.

2. Whenever the doorbell rings, the dog jump up and bark.

3. He promises many things if we elected him to office.

4. If he had more money, he can go on the trip.

5. What do you do if he asks you to the dance?

Subject-Verb Agreement

A verb and its subject must agree in number and person. If the subject is singular, the verb must be singular. If the subject is plural, the verb must be plural.

NO: The girls (plural) stands (singular) in the rain.

YES: The girls stand in the rain.

Similarly, if the subject is in the first person, (I, we) second person (you), or third person (he, she, it, they), the verb must agree.

NO: My parrot do not speak.

YES: My parrot does not speak.

Intervening Phrases

Often the subject and the verb in a sentence are separated by a group of words. The intervening phrase might be a parenthetical comment, a description, and so on. The intervening phrase might be very short or might be quite long. The point is that no matter how many words come between the verb and its subject, the two must agree.

NO: The passengers, who had watched in amazement as the train sped through the station, was told that another would arrive within the hour.

YES: The passengers, who had watched in amazement as the train sped through the station, were told that another train would arrive within the hour.

Compound Subjects

Compound subjects are formed when two or more simple subjects are joined by connecting words, such as "and, or, nor, either...or, and neither...nor."

Mary and John are in the same class.

If the subject is a compound formed by two singular subjects joined by "or, nor, either...or, or neither...nor" the verb is always singular.

Dave or Sam has to mow the lawn.

Neither the fifth nor sixth grade is going to the carnival.

If the subject is a compound formed by a singular and a plural subject joined by "or, nor, either...or, or neither...nor" the verb must agree with the subject closest to it. If both subjects are plural, however, the verb must also be plural.

Neither soothing words nor a hug was enough to console the crying child.

Either apples or oranges were always served after dinner.

Collective Nouns

Words such as group, committee, crowd, and so on, are called collective nouns because they represent a number of people or objects considered as a unit. When the subject of a sentence is a collective noun that is singular in meaning, the verb must be singular.

The theater group was thrilled by the critics' enthusiastic reviews.

☞ Drill: Subject-Verb Agreement

DIRECTIONS: Correct the errors in the following sentences.

---

1. The class are going to the playground.

2. Ice cream and candy ruins the teeth.

3. Either skating or skiing are good winter sports.

4. Sam, who had just applied for a driver's license, were told she needed her parents' approval.

5. Mr. Jones or Mr. Brown are accompanying Mr. Elon on the trip.

6. The Senate committee are in session for many weeks.

7. The girl, who had just left the library, have to go back to check out another book.

8. Dogs, cats, and birds is the most frequently cited types of pets preferred by people.

9. Neither the extra notes nor the cram course are a substitute for studying early enough for the test.

10. The crowd, reacting to the presence of news cameras and reporters, were going to continue its protest.

Parallel Structure

When similar ideas are expressed in one sentence, they should be in similar grammatical form. This is true of items in a list, elements of a compound subject or predicate, compared ideas, and parallel clauses of a compound sentence.

The following are illustrations of several common parallelism errors.

Lists

NO: Last summer, Mark traveled to New Mexico, Texas, and to Colorado.

YES: Last summer, Mark traveled to New Mexico, Texas, and Colorado.

Last summer, Mark traveled to New Mexico, to Texas, and to Colorado.

NO: Doris wanted to study French, Italian, or learn Spanish.

YES: Doris wanted to study French, Italian, or Spanish.

Compounds

NO: Industrial pollutants, car emissions, and the use of aerosols contribute to global warming.

YES: Industrial pollutants, car emissions, and aerosols contribute to global warming.

NO: The astronauts had orbited the Earth, deployed a satellite, and had conducted several biological experiments.

YES: The astronauts had orbited the Earth, deployed a satellite, and conducted several biological experiments.

Correlative Conjunctions

NO: Mary not only enjoyed camping but also fishing.

YES: Mary enjoyed not only camping but also fishing.

Compared Ideas

NO: Drinking alcohol can be as dangerous to your health as to smoke cigarettes.

YES: Drinking alcohol can be as dangerous to your health as smoking cigarettes.

To drink alcohol can be as dangerous to your health as to smoke cigarettes.

☞ Drill: Parallel Structure

> **DIRECTIONS:** The following group of sentences may contain errors in parallel structure. Make the necessary corrections.

1. In the summer, I usually like swimming and to water-ski.

2. The professor explained the cause, effect, and the results.

3. Mary read the book, studied the examples, and takes the test.

4. Mark watched the way Matthew started the car, and how he left the curb.

5. They bought the house because of location and its affordability.

6. The movie was interesting and had a lot of excitement.

7. Shakespeare both wrote beautiful sonnets and complex plays.

8. The painting is done either in watercolors or with oils.

9. The lecturer spoke with seriousness and in a concerned tone.

10. Either we forget those plans, or accept their proposal.

Comparisons

For a sentence that makes a comparison to be correct, there must be no ambiguity about what is being compared. In addition, the comparison must be logical. In other words, you cannot compare people with objects, groups with individuals, and so on.

NO: Jim enjoyed the play more than Sally.

YES: Jim enjoyed the play more than Sally did.

NO: Many doctors claim that the benefits of walking are greater than running.

YES: Many doctors claim that the benefits of walking are greater than those of running.

☞ Drill: Comparisons

DIRECTIONS: Correct the errors in the following sentences.

1. Key West is farther south than any town in the continental United States.

2. It is thought that bananas have more nutritional value than peaches.

3. Andrew enjoyed the movie more than Mike.

4. Some people prefer jogging to other exercise.

5. People who live in insulated homes pay less for their heating than homes that do not.

Comparison of Adjectives

NO: That was the most bravest thing he ever did.

Do not combine two superlatives.

YES: That was the bravest thing he ever did.

NO: Mary was more friendlier than Susan.

Do not combine two comparatives.

YES: Mary was friendlier than Susan.

NO: I can buy either the shirt or the scarf. The shirt is most expensive.

The comparative should be used when only two things are being compared.

YES: I can buy either the shirt or the scarf. The shirt is more expensive.

☞ Drill: Comparison of Adjectives

> **DIRECTIONS:** In the following sentences, make the changes indicated in the parentheses.

1. He was sad to leave. (superlative)

2. She ran as fast as the others on the team. (comparative)

3. Throughout school, they were good in math. (superlative)

4. This class is as interesting as the European history class. (comparative)

5. He arrived as soon as I did. (comparative)

6. The test was as hard as we expected. (superlative)

7. He responded to the interviewer as candidly as Tom. (comparative)

8. The beggar had less possessions than she. (superlative)

9. That answer is perfectly correct. (superlative)

10. She read the part best. (comparative)

Pronouns

A pronoun is a word that stands in for a noun or another pronoun. There are five classes of pronouns in English: personal, interrogative, demonstrative, indefinite, and relative. For the purpose of preparing for the ACT, you only need to concern yourself with personal, indefinite, and relative pronouns. Study the examples of these three classes of pronouns.

> Personal Pronouns
>
>> I, you, he, she, we, they, it
>
> Indefinite Pronouns
>
>> one, anybody, everything, each
>
> Relative Pronouns
>
>> who, whom, whose, which, that, what

Reference

Since the role of the pronoun is to stand in for another word, there must be no confusion as to which word the pronoun is replacing. The pronoun must clearly refer to one antecedent.

> NO: Barry asked Jon to be on the softball team because he is a good hitter.

> YES: Because Jon is a good hitter, Barry asked him to be on the softball team.

In the first sentence, the pronoun "he" can refer to either Barry or Jon. Therefore, the sentence is confusing. In the second sentence, however, the pronoun "him" clearly refers to Jon.

Another reference error to watch out for involves a pronoun that refers to an unspecified antecedent. This is particularly common with the pronoun "they."

> NO: They expect rain this evening.

> YES: Rain is expected this evening.

An exception to this rule is the pronoun "it," which can be used to refer to an indefinite antecedent.

> It might rain this evening.

Agreement

As is the case with verbs and their subjects, pronouns must agree with their antecedents in number and person.

> NO: The houses on our block are smaller than that on the next block.

YES: The houses on our block are smaller than those on the next block.

Some pronouns are always singular. A pronoun that refers to one of these indefinite pronouns must also be singular.

Neither of the candidates had met his opponent.

Below is a list of indefinite pronouns that are always singular.

anybody	somebody	everybody	nobody
anyone	someone	everyone	no one
one	each	either	neither
other			

Conversely, some pronouns are always plural. Pronouns that refer to them must always be plural.

Few imagined the greatness their futures held.

The following pronouns are always plural.

both	few	many	others	several

Pronouns that refer to compound antecedents follow the same rules as verbs that refer to compound subjects. If the parts of the compound antecedent are joined by "and," the pronoun must be plural. If the parts are joined by "either...or" or "neither...nor" and are both singular, the pronoun must be singular. If the parts are plural, the pronoun must be plural. And if the parts of the antecedent are different in number, the pronoun must agree with the one closest to it.

The dog and the cat have marked their territories.

Either Greg or Mark left his mitt on the field.

Neither the men nor the women left their chairs.

Neither Dave nor his brothers own their own tuxedos.

Pronouns that refer to collective nouns, such as "group, band, etc.," must be singular. Although there are exceptions to this rule, you do not have to concern yourself with these for the ACT.

The party nominated its candidate at the convention.

As we have said, pronouns must agree with their antecedents in person. A very common mistake in English of which you should be aware is to start a sentence in the third person and then use a second person pronoun to refer to the antecedent. This is especially true when "one" and "you" are used. "One" is the third person. "You" is the second person. These pronouns must not be mixed in one sentence.

NO: When one studies, you do better on exams.

YES: When one studies, one does better on exams.

When you study, you do better on exams.

In addition to number and person, pronouns must agree with their antecedents in gender. In grammar, gender means the classification of nouns and pronouns according to sex. There are four genders in English.

Masculine: he, him, uncle, actor

Feminine: she, her, aunt, actress

Common: parent, cousin, friend

Neuter: it, candle, chair

The pronoun must be the same gender as its antecedent. Such agreement rarely presents problems except in the cases of common gender and indefinite pronouns.

If the antecedent of a pronoun is common gender, the pronoun can be either masculine or feminine. However, if the sentence clearly indicates that the antecedent refers to a specific gender, the pronoun of that gender must be used.

NO: My uncle took her children to Florida.

YES: My uncle took his children to Florida.

My uncle took Amanda's children to Florida.

In cases where the antecedent of a pronoun is an indefinite pronoun, the masculine pronoun has been traditionally used. Many authors now use "his or her" in such cases.

Everyone is entitled to his opinion.

Everyone is entitled to his or her opinion.

Furthermore, if a sentence indicates clearly that the indefinite pronoun refers to members of one sex, the pronoun of the appropriate gender should be used.

Anyone in the Boys' Choir could invite his family and friends to the performance.

Relative Pronouns

The relative pronouns are "who," "whom," "whose," "which," "that," and "what." "Who" is used when the antecedent is a person. "That" is used for persons or things. And "which" is used when the antecedent is anything other than a person.

Relative pronouns play the part of the subject or object in sentences within sentences (clauses). They often refer to nouns that have preceded them, making the sentence more compact.

NO: The flower—the flower was yellow—made her smile.

YES: The flower, which was yellow, made her smile.

NO: The girl—the girl lived down the block—loved him.

YES: The girl who lived down the block loved him.

Sometimes their reference is indefinite.

I wonder what happened. (The event that occurred is uncertain.)

I'll call whomever you want. (The people to be called are unknown.)

"Who" (for persons), "that" (for persons and things), and "which" (for things) are the most common pronouns of this type.

Case - The Function of the Pronoun in a Sentence

By far the pronouns with which we are apt to make the most mistakes are those that change form when they play different parts in a sentence—the personal pronouns and the relative pronoun "who." A careful study of the peculiarities of these changes is necessary to avoid the mistakes associated with their use. "Who" can cause problems because it changes form depending on the part it plays in the interior sentence (clause).

Subject	Object	Possessive
who	whom	whose

Mr. Jackson, who is my friend, called yesterday. (subject)

Mr. Jackson, whom I know well, called yesterday. (object)

Mr. Jackson, whose friendship is important to me, called yesterday. (possessive)

Subject Case (used mainly when the pronoun is a subject)

Use the subject case (I, we, you, he, she, it, they, who, and whoever) for the following purposes:

1.   As a subject or a repeated subject:

NO: Mrs. Jones and me left early yesterday.

YES: Mrs. Jones and I left early yesterday.

NO: I know whom that is.

YES: I know who that is. (subject of "is")

NO: Us girls always go out together.

YES: We girls always go out together. ("girls" is the subject; "we" repeats it)

Watch out for a parenthetical expression (an expression that is not central to the meaning of the sentence). It looks like a subject and verb when actually it is the pronoun that is the subject.

NO: Larry is the one whom we know will do the job best.

YES: Larry is the one who we know will do the best job. (Do not be misled by "we know"; "who" is the subject of the verb "will do.")

2.   Following the verb "to be" when it has a subject:

This is part of the language that appears to be changing. It is a good example of how the grammar of a language follows speech and not the other way around. The traditional guideline has been that a pronoun following a form of "be" must be in the same case as the word before the verb.

It is I. ("It" is the subject.)

I thought it was she. ("it" is the subject)

Was it they who arrived late? ("it" is the subject)

Our ear tells us that in informal conversation "It is I" would sound too formal, so instead we tend to say:

It is me. (in conversation)

I thought it was her. (in conversation)

Was it them who arrived late? (in conversation)

In written English, however, it is best to follow the standard of using the subject case after the verb "be" when "be" is preceded by a word in the subject case, even though the pronoun is in the position of an object.

NO: Last week, the best students were you and me.

YES: Last week, the best students were you and I. (refers to "students," subject of "were")

NO: Whenever I hear that knock, I know it must be him.

YES: Whenever I hear that knock, I know it must be he. (refers to "it," subject of "must be")

NO: The leaders of the parade were John, Susan, and me.

YES: The leaders of the parade were John, Susan, and I. (refers to "leaders," subject of "were")

3.   As a subject when the verb is omitted (often after "than" or "as"):

I have known her longer than he. ("has known her" is understood)

She sings as well as I. ("sing" is understood)

We do just as well in Algebra as they. ("do" is understood)

To test whether the subject or the object form is correct, complete the phrase in your mind and it will be obvious.

Object Case (used mainly when the pronoun is an object)

Use the object case (me, us, him, her, it, you, them, whom, whomever) as follows:

1. As the direct or indirect object, object of a preposition, or repeated object:

    The postman gave me the letter. (indirect object)

    Mr. Boone appointed him and me to clean the room. ("him and me" is the object of "appointed")

    They told us managers to rewrite the first report. ("managers" is the indirect object of "told"; "us" repeats)

    My attorney gave me a letter giving her power of attorney. ("me" is the indirect object of "gave"; "her" is the indirect object of "giving")

    The package is from me. (object of "from")

    Between you and me, I'm voting Republican. (object of "between")

    Whom were you thinking about? (object of "about")

    I know whom you asked. (object of "asked")

    My teacher gave both of us, June and me, an "A." ("us" is the object of "of"; June and me" repeats the object)

2. As the subject of an infinitive verb:

    I wanted her to come.

    Janet invited him and me to attend the conference.

    He asked her to duplicate the report for the class.

    Whom will we ask to lead the group? ("Whom" is the subject of "to lead")

3. As an object when the verb or preposition is omitted:

    Father told my sister June more about it than (he told) me.

    The telephone calls were more often for Marilyn than (they were for) him.

    Did they send them as much candy as (they sent) us?

    He always gave Susan more than (he gave) me.

4. Following "to be":

In point number 2, you learned that the subject of an infinitive verb form must be in the object case. The infinitive "to be" is an exception to this rule. Forms of "to be" must have the same case before and after the verb. If the word preceding the verb is in the subject case, the pronoun following must be in the subject case also. (For example, It is I.) If the word before the verb is an object, the pronoun following must be objective as well.

> We thought the author of the note to be her.
>
> You expected the winner to be me.
>
> Mother did not guess it to be Julie and me at the door.
>
> Had you assumed the experts to be us?

5. Subject of a progressive verb form that functions as an adjective (participle—"ing" ending):

Two kinds of words commonly end in "ing": a participle, or a word that looks like a verb but acts like an adjective, and a gerund, a word that looks like a verb but acts like a noun. When an "ing" word acts like an adjective, its subject is in the object case.

> For example:
> Can you imagine him acting that way? ("Acting" refers to the pronoun and is therefore a participle which takes a subject in the object case, "him.")
>
> They watched me smiling at all the visitors. ("smiling" refers to the pronoun, which must be objective, "me")
>
> Compare:
> Can you imagine his acting in that part? (Here the emphasis is on "acting"; "his" refers to "acting," which is functioning as a noun [it is a gerund] and takes the possessive case.)
>
> It was my smiling that won the contest. (Emphasis is on "smiling"—it is playing the part of a noun and so takes a possessive case pronoun, "my.")

Possessive Case

Use the possessive adjective case (my, our, your, her, his, its, their, whose) in the following situations:

1. To indicate possession, classification of something, or connection. Possession is the most common.

> I borrowed her car. (The car belongs to her.)
>
> Come over to our house. (The house belongs to us.)
>
> That is Jane's and my report. (The report belongs to us.)

It is anyone's guess.

Whose coat is this?

The plant needs water; its leaves are fading.

2. Preceding a verb acting as a noun (gerund):

    Our leaving early helped end the party.

    Whose testifying will you believe?

    His reading was excessive.

Since there are no possessive forms for the demonstrative pronouns "that," "this," "these," and "those," they do not change form before a gerund.

NO: What are the chances of that's being painted today?

YES: What are the chances of that being painted today?

Use the possessive case (mine, ours, yours, hers, his, its, theirs, whose) in the following situations:

In any role a noun might play—a subject, object, or complement with a possessive meaning.

Hers was an exciting career. ("Hers" is the subject of "was")

Can you tell me whose this is? ("whose" is the complement of "is")

We borrowed theirs last week; it is only right that they should use ours this week. ("theirs" is the object of the verb "borrowed"; "ours" is the object of the verb "use")

I thought that was Mary's and his. ("Mary's and his" is the complement of the verb "was")

☞ Drill: Pronouns

> **DIRECTIONS:** In the following sentences, make the necessary corrections.

1. Roy wanted Joe to take vitamins so he would be healthy.

2. The candidate was sure that if his opponent did not propose an economic plan, he would win the election.

3. It's Marcia from who I received the assignment.

4. The dress, what I borrowed from Jane, was lost in the cleaners.

5. I am older than her.

6. Boys like they could never make the football team.

7. We joining in to help made cleaning up easier and faster.

8. They selected we musicians.

9. They missed the train because of he.

10. What are the chances of you being finished tomorrow?

Misplaced Modifiers

An element in a sentence that describes another element of that sentence is called a modifier. Adjectives and adverbs are modifiers. Adjectives describe nouns, and adverbs describe verbs. Phrases and even relative clauses can be modifiers. For example, in the sentence "Jim, who is a very fast runner, won the race," the relative clause "who is a very fast runner" modifies the subject, "Jim."

Because English depends primarily on word order for the meaning of sentences, modifiers have to come immediately before or after the elements they modify. Misplaced modifiers—modifiers that are placed away from their antecedents (the things they modify)—cause a lot of confusion.

> Frustrated with the two party system, the independent candidate was favored by many voters.

In the above example, "Frustrated with the two party system" is a modifier, and "candidate" is its antecedent. The sentence does not make a lot of sense, however. The author means that the voters are frustrated. The modifier is in the wrong place, and the meaning is confused.

We can correct the mistake in three different ways.

> Frustrated with the two party system, many voters favored the independent candidate.

> Many voters, frustrated with the two party system, favored the independent candidate.

> The independent candidate was favored by many voters who were frustrated with the two party system.

Notice that all of the rewritten sentences place the modifier right next to "voters." That is the key to correcting modification errors. The closer the modifier is to its antecedent, the less likely the sentence is to be confusing.

> Cold, numb Ellen took off her shoes and rested her feet near the fire-place.

In this example you have to decide what the author meant to say. This is often the case with sentences that have modification problems. The sentence would make the most sense if the adjectives "cold" and "numb" modified "feet." Ellen's feet are cold and numb, therefore, she takes off her shoes and rests her feet near the fireplace.

> Ellen took off her shoes and rested her cold, numb feet near the fire-place.

☞ Drill: Misplaced Modifiers

> **DIRECTIONS:** In the following sentences, make all the necessary changes.

1. I saw a stray dog riding the bus this afternoon.

2. The clothing was given to the poor in large packages.

3. I found five dollars eating lunch in the park.

4. We saw two girls riding bicycles from our car.

5. Reading my book quietly, I jumped up when the car crashed.

6. He ran the mile with a sprained ankle.

7. The history majors only were affected by the new requirements.

8. Running quickly to catch the bus, Susan's packages fell out of her arms onto the ground.

9. He just asked the man directions to make sure.

10. He discovered a new route driving home.

Words and Idioms Commonly Misused

Some questions on the ACT will test your ability to recognize diction and idiomatic errors. A diction error is the use of a word in an inappropriate context. An idiomatic error is the incorrect use of a commonly accepted expression.

Below is a list of some words and idioms that are commonly misused.

Affect, Effect

"Affect" is a verb which means "to influence." "Effect" is usually used as a noun which means "result." As a verb, "effect" means "to bring about."

> The rain did not affect our outing.

> The rain had no effect on our outing.

Among, Between

"Among" is used when more than two people or things are involved. "Between" is used when two people or things are involved, or if more than two are involved but each is considered individually.

> I could not choose between the cake and the pie.

> The candy was divided among all the children.

Amount, Number

"Amount" is used to refer to a collective. "Number" is used to refer to a quantity that can be counted.

> The amount of money I have is rather small.

> I have a rather small number of bills in my wallet.

As good as, or better than

The correct idiom is "as good as." Therefore, the expression should be "as good as, or better."

> NO: My dog is as strong or stronger than yours.

> YES: My dog is as strong as your dog, or stronger.

Compare to, Compare with

To "compare to" is to point out a resemblance between essentially different things. To "compare with" is to point out a difference between essentially similar things.

> Writing has sometimes been compared to boxing.

> New York has often been compared with London.

Different from

Since one thing differs from another, the expression is "different from."

> NO: Huskies are different than Labradors.

> YES: Huskies are different from Labradors.

Each other, One another

"Each other" is used to refer to two things. "One another" is used to refer to three or more things.

> Dolly and John really like each other.

> The members of the group got along with one another.

Fewer, Less

"Fewer" is used to refer to number. "Less" refers to quantity.

> Fewer people are interested in soccer than in baseball.

> People now have less time to relax.

Hopefully

This is an adverb meaning "with hope." It is wrong to use it to mean "I hope" or "it is to be hoped."

> NO: Hopefully, you will be accepted by the school of your choice.

> YES: I hope you will be accepted by the school of your choice.

Lay, Lie

"Lay" means to put something down. The verb "lie" means to recline, to rest, or to remain in a reclining position.

> I lay my hat on the table.

> My hat lies on the table.

Like, As

"Like" should be followed by a noun or a pronoun. "As" introduces phrases and clauses.

> My dog looks like a German shepherd.

> That dog looks as if he is going to attack.

Not only...but also

"Not only" must always be used with "but also."

> NO: Ted not only dances and sings.

> YES: Ted not only dances but also sings.

Regard...as

The correct idiom is "regard as."

> NO: I regard Chaucer to be the greatest poet.

> YES: I regard Chaucer as the greatest poet.

That, Which

"That" is the restrictive pronoun. A phrase or subordinate clause introduced by "that" limits the meaning of the word it modifies. A restrictive phrase or clause is essential to the meaning of the sentence and is not set off by commas. "Which" is nonrestrictive.

> The bus that stops near my house just left.

> The bus, which stops near my house, just left.

☞ Drill: Words and Idioms Commonly Misused

> **DIRECTIONS:** Correct the errors in the following sentences.

1. You'd be amazed at how much weather actually effects the moods of people.

2. I like both equally well. It's hard to make a decision among them.

3. Mike and Jackie have gotten along with one another since they were babies.

4. Jane said she was so nervous that it effected her test score.

5. Will that number of paper in your notebook be enough?

6. The dog which always begs for treats is at our door.

7. Our new gardener not only mows the grass but also weeds the lawn.

8. Ever since he won that contest I regard his to be the smartest.

9. Even though they wear the same style of glasses, the twins look different than one another.

10. Jay Leno has often been compared to David Letterman.

II. RHETORICAL SKILLS REVIEW

STRATEGY

Rhetorical Skills questions on the ACT English Test are those that evaluate your ability to determine the author's use of strategy (audience, purpose); organization (transitions, ordering ideas, coherence and unity); and style (short sentences/wordiness) in his/her writing. Most people wrongly think that writers just sit down and churn out wonderful essays or poems in one sitting. This is not true! Writers use the writing process from start to finish to help them develop a well-composed document.

The writer's responsibility is to write clearly, honestly, and cleanly for the reader's sake. Essays would be pointless without an audience. Why write an essay if no one wants or needs to read it? Why add evidence, organize your ideas, or correct bad grammar? The reason to do any of these things is because someone out there needs to understand what you mean or say.

If you ask a series of questions about a given passage, you can determine the nature of the audience. As you read, keep in mind the writer's purpose as you understand it. Using the questions below, develop through your answers a mental picture of the audience (besides yourself) reading this passage.

1. What does the writer intend the readers of this passage to take away with them? The writer's point of view? Information?

2. How old are the readers?

3. What is their level of education?

4. What attitudes, prejudices, opinions, fears, experience, and concerns might the audience for this passage have?

Consideration of audience will directly affect the tone of a passage, and thus determine what level of usage or meaning is appropriate in a given paragraph or section of an essay. For example, if I am writing to a 13-year-old, should I write: "Please peruse with comprehension the tome offered," or "Please be sure to read and study what is in this book." The latter sentence, with its simple vocabulary, is the appropriate choice.

☞ Drill: Strategy

> **DIRECTIONS:** Read the following passage, and answer the questions that follow.

Immigration

The influx of immigrants that America had been experiencing slowed during the conflicts with France and England, but the flow increased between 1815 and 1837, when an economic downturn sharply reduced their numbers. Thus, the overall rise in population during these years was due more to incoming foreigners than to natural increase. Most of the newcomers were from Britain, Germany, and southern Ireland. The Germans usually fared best, since they brought more money and more skills. Discrimination was common in the job market, primarily directed against the Catholics. "Irish Need Not Apply" signs were common. However, the persistent labor shortage prevented the natives from totally excluding the foreign elements. These newcomers huddled in ethnic neighborhoods in the cities, or those who could, moved on west to try their hand at farming.

In 1790, 5 percent of the U.S. population lived in cities of 2,500 or more. By 1860, that figure had risen to 25 percent. This rapid urbanization created an array of problems.

The rapid growth in urban areas was not matched by the growth of service. Clean water, trash removal, housing, and public transportation all lagged behind, and the wealthy got them first. Bad water and poor sanitation produced poor health, and epidemics of typhoid fever, typhus, and cholera were common. Police and fire protection were usually inadequate and the development of professional forces was resisted because of the cost and the potential for political patronage and corruption.

Rapid growth helped to produce a wave of violence in the cities. In New York City in 1834, the Democrats fought the Whigs with such vigor that the state militia had to be called in. New York and Philadelphia witnessed race riots in the mid-1830s, and a New York mob *sacked* a Catholic convent in 1834. In the 1830s, 115 major incidents of mob violence were recorded. Street crime was common in all the major cities.

1.   What is the author's purpose for writing this essay?

2.   What type of audience is addressed in this essay?

TRANSITIONS

It is very important to have an organized essay so that the reader can follow the flow of ideas in a logical way. One way of doing this is through the use of transitions. Transitional words are used to show connections and unify the ideas in an essay. You may use transitions either at the beginnings of paragraphs, or you may use them to show the connections among the ideas within a single paragraph.

Here are some typical transitional words and phrases.

Links similar ideas

again	for example	likewise
also	for instance	moreover
and	further	nor
another	furthermore	of course
besides	in addition	similarly
equally important	in like manner	too

Links dissimilar/contradictory ideas

although	however	otherwise
and yet	in spite of	provided that
as if	instead	still
but	nevertheless	yet
conversely	on the contrary	
even if	on the other hand	

Indicates cause, purpose, or result

as	for	so
as a result	for this reason	then
because	hence	therefore
consequently	since	thus

Indicates time or position

above	before	meanwhile
across	beyond	next
afterward	eventually	presently
around	finally	second
at once	first	thereafter
at the present time	here	thereupon

Indicates an example or summary

as a result	in any event	in short
as I have said	in brief	on the whole
for example	in conclusion	to sum up
for instance	in fact	
in any case	in other words	

☞ Drill: Transitions

DIRECTIONS: Each of the following sentences contains problems with the use of transitions. Correct them so that the ideas are expressed clearly.

1.   She enjoys all winter sports; nevertheless, she particularly enjoys skiing.

2.   We are now at the end of a particularly long lecture. So eventually, let me say that computer science is the subject all students should be studying.

3.   Barbara missed many classes, didn't study for any tests, and in conclusion, failed the course.

4.   Elon is first, Mitchell is second, and beyond that we have Jaclyn.

5.   You will be graded on your knowledge of the subject; consequently, all information in your textbook and outside readings.

ORDERING IDEAS

All sentences and paragraphs in an essay should be logically constructed. Within a paragraph, all sentences should expand on one main idea; and within an essay, all paragraphs should be organized so that the ideas flow in the following sequence: introduction, development of idea, and then the conclusion. Your introduction should contain sentences that foreshadow your topic. The developmental paragraphs contain ideas which develop the topic or theme of the text. Most topic ideas can be expanded clearly through the use of examples or illustrations. Each paragraph is composed of sentences supporting one main idea. The conclusion of a text should be based on a logical set of premises that have been stated within the preceding paragraphs.

COHERENCE/UNITY

Cohesion within a written text is determined by the lexical and grammatical relationships that exist between sentences and between paragraphs. In other words, sentences and paragraphs within a text contain words and grammatical elements which are interrelated. One sentence (or paragraph) is dependent on another sentence (or paragraph). Native speakers of a language seem to know intuitively when a text is cohesive or not. For example:

NO: The boy ate his dinner. I'm not sure I want to go. The flowers will die if the weather does not improve.

YES: Carly and Uriel will be spending a few days in Chicago. I enjoy having them visit. Last time they were here we all went to Michigan Avenue and bought new toys. Carly picked out a doll house, and Uriel a train set.

In the first example, sentences are lexically unrelated; and, as a result, this is not a cohesive text. In the second example, the sentences are related and the text is cohesive.

☞ Drill: Ordering Ideas and Coherence/Unity

> **DIRECTIONS:** The following text is poorly written. Each of the sentences and paragraphs are randomly ordered. Rewrite the following text so that the sentences within each paragraph are logically related to each other. Also, rearrange the paragraphs so that they follow the sequence of: introduction, development of idea, and conclusion.

Consequently, stress and strain are placed on the wrists and hands, which can result in CTS. For example, the meatpacking industry is considered one of the most hazardous industries in the United States because workers can make as many as 10,000 repetitive motions per day in assembly line processes, such as deboning meats, with no variation in motion. CTS develops in the hands and wrists from repetitive and/or forceful manual tasks performed over a period of time.

(Other garment workers, who are required to push large amounts of materials through machinery, often sustain disabling wrist, back, and leg injuries.) Today, more than half of all U.S. workers are susceptible to developing CTS. Anyone whose job demands a lot of repetitive wrist, hand, and arm motion, which need not always be forceful or strenuous, might be a potential victim of CTS. In manufacturing, garment makers, who often perform fast-paced piece-work operations involving excessive repetitive tasks, increase their risk of developing CTS.

As a result, the number of penalties issued against companies for these types of ergonomics-related safety and health violations has increased. In recent years, there has been a dramatic increase in the occurrence of cumulative trauma disorders (CTDs) or repetitive motion disorders, and other work-related injuries and illnesses due to ergonomic hazards.

STYLE

Although grammar is the focus of the majority of questions on the English test, some questions do measure your sense of effective style. The three types of stylistic problems that most often appear are

(1) passive-voice constructions,

(2) redundancy, and

(3) wordiness.

In active-voice constructions, the subject of the sentence is doing the action.

I shall always remember this trip to Alaska.

In passive-voice constructions, the subject of the sentence is the receiver of the action expressed by the verb.

This trip to Alaska will always be remembered by me.

The active voice is always more direct and crisp, and is usually preferred to the passive.

Redundancy is the use of words or phrases that are identical in meaning in the same sentence.

NO: The international buffet featured foods from many countries.

YES: The buffet featured foods from many countries.

NO: He wrote his own autobiography.

YES: He wrote his autobiography.

Effective writing means concise writing. Wordiness, on the other hand, decreases the clarity of expression by cluttering sentences with unnecessary words. Of course, all short sentences are not better than long ones simply because they are brief. As long as a word serves a function, it should remain in the sentence. However, repetition of words, sounds, and phrases should be used only for emphasis or other stylistic reasons. Editing your writing will reduce its bulk.

NO: The medical exam that he gave me was entirely complete.

YES: The medical exam he gave me was complete.

NO: Arthur asked his friend Ed, who was a good, old friend, if he would join him and go along with him to see the new movie made by Spielberg.

YES: Arthur asked his good, old friend Ed if he would join him in seeing the new Spielberg movie.

NO: They went to Florida by means of an airplane.

YES: They went to Florida by airplane. *or* They flew to Florida.

NO: It will be our aim to ensure proper health care for each and every one of the people in the United States.

YES: Our aim will be to ensure proper health care for all Americans.

☞ Drill: Style

> **DIRECTIONS:** Rewrite the following sentences so they are less wordy. Remember to keep the main idea intact.

1. He graduated college. In no time he found a job. Soon after he rented an apartment. He was very happy.

2. The book that she lent me was lengthy. It was boring. I wouldn't recommend it to anyone. There was nothing about the book that I enjoyed.

3. It was raining. We expected to go on a picnic. Now our plans are ruined. We have nothing to do.

4. Whenever anyone telephoned her to ask her for help with his/her homework she always obliged right away.

5. She liked to paint. She was quite good. Materials are expensive. She can't afford them.

6. Jane is just one of those people who you can't really describe with words.

7. It was time to leave. They hoped they packed everything. There was no time to think. The taxi was outside. It was waiting.

8. The candidate promised he would do what was necessary to lengthen prison terms. This was his major issue. He hoped he was elected.

9. "Long Day's Journey Into Night" is a play. It is a dramatic play. Eugene O'Neill wrote it. The play is also autobiographical.

10. He could have still asked her for her approval.

ANSWER KEY

STANDARD WRITTEN ENGLISH

Drill: The Sentence, Sentence Fragments, and Run-On Sentences

1. Fragment: We went out after the rain stopped.

2. Run-on: Mow the lawn. It is much too long.

3. Run-on: The settlement you reached seems fair.

4. Fragment: My eyes get tired when I read, especially at night.

5. Run-on: It was impossible to get through on the phone, since the lines were down because of the storm.

6. Fragment: Is the leaky pipe the only problem?

7. Run-on: Everyone saw the crime, but no one is willing to come forth.

8. Run-on: The weather was bad. She played in the rain.

9. Fragment: Ellen paced the floor and worried about her economics final.

10. Run-on: The team had lost the playoffs; their season was over.

Drill: The Comma

1. However, I am willing to reconsider. Reason: "However" is a transitional word and requires a comma after it.

2. She descended the long, winding staircase. Reason: A comma is used in a series to emphasize each adjective.

3. Whenever I practice my violin, my family closes the window. Reason: Use a comma after a long introductory phrase.

4. While driving, Francis never took his eyes off the road. Reason: When the introductory phrase includes a "verbal," a comma is necessary.

5. The car, which I bought last year, is in the garage. Reason: The modifying group of words ("which I bought last year") is not vital to the meaning of the sentence and, therefore, is set off by commas.

6. "Answer the door," his mother said loudly. Reason: Use a comma to set off direct quotations.

7. Miss, can I ask you for the time? Reason: Use a comma to set off direct address.

8. He was, after all, an ex-convict. Reason: Use commas to set off parenthetical words and phrasing.

9. I'm so bored, aren't you? Reason: Use a comma to set off tag questions.

10. The old, tall, shady tree is wonderful during the summer. Reason: When an adjective series describes a noun, use a comma to separate and emphasize each adjective.

11. George, Gary, and Bill were on line early this morning. They bought their tickets, read the newspaper, and spoke for a while. Reason: For both sentences use a comma to separate words, phrases, and whole ideas (clauses).

12. The author, James Grey, was awarded the prize. Reason: Use commas to set off nonrestrictive words.

13. She attended school in London, England, last year. Reason: Use commas to set off geographical names.

14. No correction necessary.

15. His weight, not his height, prevented him from competing in the race. Reason: Use commas to set off contrasting elements.

16. No correction necessary.

17. She got in the car, turned on the ignition, and left the curb. Reason: A comma is used to separate words, phrases, and whole ideas.

18. Incidentally, he called last night. Reason: Use a comma to set off parenthetical words and phrases.

19. The kitten, small and cute, was adopted by the Brown family. Reason: Use commas to set off nonrestrictive elements.

20. Mary, did you see James, Jr., at the party last night? Reason: 1. Use a comma to set off direct address. 2. Use a comma to set off abbreviations after names.

21. No change necessary.

22. No change necessary.

23. Really, I can't believe that is the truth. Reason: Use a comma to set off an interjection.

24. We thought it was time to leave, but we arrived early. Reason: Use a comma to set off sentences with two main ideas.

25. Monday, she will leave for Boston. Reason: Use a comma to set off parenthetical words and phrases.

26. After he got home he read a magazine, ate dinner, and left for the movies. Reason: The comma is used to separate words, phrases, and clauses.

27. No correction necessary.

28. When she decided to leave, everyone was disappointed. Reason: Use a comma to set off a long introductory phrase.

29. Hey, John, it's time to go. Reason: Use commas to set off direct address.

30. He seemed wrong for the part, yet he turned out to be the best actor in the production. Reason: Use a comma to separate sentences with two main ideas.

Drill: The Colon and the Semicolon

1. I have only one thing to say: don't do it.

2. They seemed compatible; yet they did not get along.

3. She had only one goal in life: to be a famous pianist.

4. He thought the problem was solved; instead, his solution proved to be entirely wrong.

5. By the end of the day there were only two things on her mind: rest and relaxation.

6. Only a few members were able to attend the convention: Henry, Karen, David, Mark, and Susan.

7. They were willing to accept the proposal; he was not.

8. The art students were expected to supply the following: brushes, paints, pallets, and pads.

9. The time is now: the time is right.

10. The highest scores on the final exam are as follows: Linda Jones, 96; John Smith, 94; Susan Green, 90. These grades are unusually high: they must have studied well.

Drill: The Apostrophe

1. she'll
2. won't
3. Class of '94

4. doesn't
5. they've

6. This boat isn't yours. We sold ours last year to Robert's parents.

7. At 10 o'clock they'll meet us at Macy's department store.

8. In Ms. Green's first grade class, she had difficulty writing x's and learning her ABCs.

9. Wordsworth's poem "The Solitary Reaper" was published in J. Mahnoey's edition of *The Romantic Poets*.

10. lady's, ladies'

11. child's, children's

12. cashier's, cashiers'

13. Filipino's, Filipinos'

Drill: Interjections, Dashes, and Parentheses

1. Chapter 13 of <u>Modern Biological Principles</u> is called "Plant Reproduction."

2. The teacher told the students to read chapter 2, "The Market-Place," in Nathaniel Hawthorne's <u>The Scarlet Letter</u>.

3. John Travolta starred in the movie <u>Grease</u>.

4. Last night, Michele watched "Seinfeld" on television.

5. You will find Keats' "Ode on a Grecian Urn" in chapter 3, "The Romantic Era," in Lastly's <u>Selections from Great English Poets</u>.

Drill: Interjections, Dashes, and Parentheses

1. The use of the dashes makes the sentence more urgent.

2. The use of the dash helps convey a feeling of disbelief.

3. The use of the dash emphasizes and modifies the key words "time" and "patience."

4. The dashes emphasize how many is "most."

5. The dashes are used to set off the specific rights.

6. The choice (in my opinion) was a good one. The comma is unnecessary.

7. Linda's comment ("Where did you get that dress?") wasn't intended to be sarcastic. The parentheses are a clear method for containing a quote.

8. The parentheses properly set off material that is loosely connected to the central meaning of the sentence.

9. Last summer in Cape Cod (that was the first year we went there) we did a lot of sightseeing. The parentheses effectively contain the additional information.

10. The first time I went driving (do you remember that day?) I was so scared. The parentheses smoothly incorporate an important aside from the speaker.

Drill: Verbs

1. If it snows tomorrow, the children will have to stay home from school.

2. Whenever the doorbell rings, the dog jumps up and barks.

3. He promises many things if we elect him to office.

4. If he had more money, he could go on a trip.

5. What will you do if he asks you to the dance?

Drill: Subject-Verb Agreement

1. The class is going to the playground.

2. Ice cream and candy ruin the teeth.

3. Either skating or skiing is a good winter sport.

4. Sam, who had just applied for a driver's license, was told she needed her parents' approval.

5. Mr. Jones or Mr. Brown is accompanying Mr. Elon on the trip.

6. The Senate committee is in session for many weeks.

7. The girl, who had just left the library, has to go back to check out another book.

8. Dogs, cats, and birds are the most frequently cited types of pets preferred by people.

9. Neither the extra notes nor the cram course is a substitute for studying early enough for the test.

10. The crowd, reacting to the presence of news cameras and reporters, was going to continue its protest.

Drill: Parallel Structure

1. In the summer I usually like to swim and water-ski.

2. The professor explained the cause, the effect, and the results.

3. Mary read the book, studied the examples, and took the test.

4. Mark watched the way Matthew started the car and the way he left the curb.

5. They bought the house because of its location and its affordability.

6. The movie was both interesting and exciting.

7. Shakespeare wrote both beautiful sonnets and complex plays.

8. The painting is done with either watercolor or oils.

9. The lecturer spoke in a serious, concerned tone.

10. Either we forget those plans, or we accept their proposal.

Drill: Comparisons

1. Key West is farther south than any other town in the continental United States.

2. It is thought that bananas have more nutritional value than that of peaches.

3. Andrew enjoyed the movie more than Mike did.

4. Some people prefer jogging to other forms of exercise.

5. People who live in insulated homes pay less than people who do not live in insulated homes.

Drill: Comparison of Adjectives

1. He was saddest to leave.

2. She ran faster than the others on the team.

3. Throughout school, they were the best in math.

4. This class is more interesting than European history class.

5. He arrived sooner than I did.

6. The test was the hardest we expected.

7. He responded to the interviewer more candidly than Tom.

8. This sentence (referring to "she") cannot be put in the superlative form.

9. That answer is most perfectly correct.

10. She read the part better.

Drill: Pronouns

1. Because Roy wanted Joe to be healthy, he asked him to take vitamins.

2. The candidate was sure that he would win the election if his opponent did not propose an economic plan.

3. It's Marcia from whom I received the assignment.

4. The dress, which I borrowed from Jane, was lost in the cleaners.

5. I am older than she.

6. Boys like them could never make the football team.

7. Our joining in to help made cleaning up easier and faster.

8. They selected us musicians.

9. They missed the train because of him.

10. What are the chances of your being finished tomorrow?

Drill: Misplaced Modifiers

1. I saw a stray dog while I was riding the bus this afternoon.

2. The clothing was given in large packages to the poor.

3. I found five dollars while I was eating lunch in the park.

4. While we were in our car, we saw two girls riding bicycles.

5. When the car crashed, I jumped up from quietly reading my book.

6. He ran the mile although his ankle was sprained.

7. Only the history majors were affected by the new requirements.

8. Susan's packages fell out of her arms onto the ground as she was running quickly for the bus.

9. He asked the man the directions just to make sure.

10. While driving home, he discovered a new route.

Drill: Words and Idioms Commonly Misused

1. You'd be amazed at how much the weather actually effects the moods of people.

2. I like both equally well. It's hard to make a decision between them.

3. Mike and Jackie have gotten along with each other since they were babies.

4. Jane said she was so nervous that it affected her test score.

5. Will that amount of paper in your notebook be enough?

6. The dog, which always begs for treats, is at our door.

7. Our new gardener not only mows the grass, but also weeds the lawn.

8. Ever since he won that contest, I regard him as the smartest.

9. Even though they wear the same style of glasses, the twins look different from each other.

10. Jay Leno has often been compared with David Letterman.

RHETORICAL SKILLS

Drill: Strategy

1. The author's purpose in writing this essay is to present his/her thesis that the wave of immigration between 1815 and 1837 caused the rapid urbaniza-

tion of American cities during the first half of the nineteenth century. The author also mentions a variety of problems caused by this urbanization.

2. The audience for this essay is assumed by the author to be supportive--the author is not writing in an argumentative style. The writing and ideas presented are not complex, which would indicate that the audience is not highly knowledgeable about the time period and events discussed.

Drill: Transitions

1. She enjoys all winter sports; moreover, she particularly enjoys skiing.

2. We are now at the end of a particularly long lecture. In conclusion, let me say that computer science is the subject all students should be studying.

3. Barbara missed many classes, didn't study for any tests, and therefore, failed the course.

4. Elon is first, Mitchell is second, and finally we have Jaclyn. or Elon is first, Mitchell is second, and Jaclyn is third.

5. You will be graded on your knowledge of the subject; in other words, all information in your textbook and outside readings.

Drill: Ordering Ideas and Coherence/Unity

In recent years, there has been a dramatic increase in the occurrence of cumulative trauma disorders (CTDs) or repetitive motion disorders, and other work-related injuries and illnesses due to ergonomic hazards. As a result, the number of penalties issued against companies for these types of ergonomics-related safety and health violations has increased.

CTS develops in the hands and wrists from repetitive and/or forceful manual tasks performed over a period of time. For example, the meat-packing industry is considered one of the most hazardous industries in the United States because workers can make as many as 10,000 repetitive motions per day in assembly line processes, such as deboning meats, with no variation in motion. Consequently, stress and strain are placed on the wrists and hands which can result in CTS.

In manufacturing, garment makers, who often perform fast-paced piece-work operations, involving excessive repetitive tasks, increase their risk of developing CTS. (Other garment workers, who are required to push large amounts of materials through machinery, often sustain disabling wrist, back, and leg injuries.) Today, more than half of all U.S. workers are susceptible to developing CTS. Anyone whose job demands a lot of repetitive wrist, hand, and arm motion, which need not be forceful or strenuous, might be a potential victim of CTS.

Drill: Style

1. He graduated from college and, in no time, found a job and rented an apartment. He was happy.

2. The book she lent me was lengthy, boring, and unenjoyable. I wouldn't recommend it to anyone.

3. We have nothing to do because our plans to go on a picnic have been ruined by the rain.

4. She immediately obliged anyone who telephoned for help with his/her homework.

5. She liked to paint and was quite good; unfortunately, she couldn't afford the expensive materials.

6. Jane is an indescribable person.

7. It was time to leave; the taxi was waiting. There was no time to think; they hoped everything was packed.

8. The campaigning candidate's major issue was his promise to lengthen prison terms.

9. "Long Days Journey Into Night" is a dramatic and autobiographical play by Eugene O'Neill.

10. He still could have asked for her approval.

CHAPTER 5

Attacking the ACT Mathematics Test

Chapter 5

ATTACKING THE ACT MATHEMATICS TEST

DESCRIPTION OF THE ACT MATHEMATICS TEST

The mathematics section of the ACT test is designed to measure the mathematics knowledge and skills that you have acquired through grade 12. The main emphasis on the test is on your ability to reason with numbers, algebraic variables, formulas, and geometric figures.

The questions in the ACT Mathematics test can be divided into three categories. The *basic* category tests recognition of concepts, the *application* category requires that problems be solved by applying one or two of these concepts, and the *analysis* category requires that problems be solved by reasoning with several concepts simultaneously.

The test consists of 60 multiple-choice mathematics questions, each with five possible answer choices. There are 24 basic algebra questions, 18 intermediate algebra and coordinate plane questions, 14 plane geometry questions, and 4 trigonometry questions. Only basic formulas and concepts, as well as simple computations, are included in the test; long, complex, or extensive ones are not.

The ACT Mathematics test is only 60 minutes in length, which means that you have to complete, on average, one question per minute. As a result, it is important not only to know and understand the material covered on the exam, but also to be able to solve the problems correctly and quickly. Even if you are sure you know the fundamental mathematics concepts presented here, the drill sections of this review will help to warm you up so that you can go into the test with quick, sharp math skills.

ABOUT THE DIRECTIONS

Make sure to study and learn the directions to save yourself time during the actual test. You should simply skim them when beginning the section. The directions will read similar to the following:

DIRECTIONS: Solve the following problems, and fill in the appropriate ovals on your answer sheet. Do not use a calculator.

Unless otherwise indicated:

1. Figures may not have been drawn to scale.

2. All geometric figures lie in a plane.

3. "Line" refers to a straight line.

4. "Average" refers to arithmetic mean.

STRATEGIES FOR THE MATHEMATICS SECTION

You should follow this plan of attack when answering Mathematics Section questions.

Before the test, this is your plan of attack:

| STEP 1 | Study our review to build your mathematics skills. |

| STEP 2 | Make sure to study and learn the directions to save yourself time during the actual test. You should simply skim them when beginning the section. |

When solving the problems, this is your strategy:

| STEP 1 | Avoid doing extensive computations. If that happens, it is possible that you have taken a wrong route in solving the problem, because the ACT Mathematics test does not contain those kind of questions. |

| STEP 2 | Set a limit to the amount of time you spend on each question, for example, 1.5 minutes. If you find that you are spending more time, move on to the next problem. That is, answer the easy questions first before attempting the more difficult ones. |

| STEP 3 | Read all the answer choices. Just because you think you have found the correct response does not necessarily mean that you have. |

| STEP 4 | Eliminate answer choices that are obviously wrong. Cross them out right away. This will save time. |

For questions that cannot be solved right away, use the following strategies:

STEP 1	Put the answer choices into the question and see how they fit. For simple numbers and easy calculations, this strategy can sometimes give the answer easily.
STEP 2	Make the best possible guess based on a comparison of the answer choices to the questions. Sometimes it is easy to see an obviously correct or obviously incorrect answer. Use this strategy when time is extremely tight.
STEP 3	Make an educated guess if everything else fails. Don't leave any question unanswered, there is still a chance of your answer being correct.

➤ Additional Tip

Like all standardized tests, the ACT Mathematics test is composed of the *same type* of problems year after year. The problems in each test may *look* different, but the format, or *type*, of these problems remains the same. After you have done enough practice problems, it will become easier to determine what any ACT problem is about by just one look. The next step is to put each problem you have completed into one particular category. If this is done for each problem, you will soon discover that there are only a limited number of categories. Before going to the test, review these categories.

SKILLS TESTED

The ACT Mathematics test can be divided into five areas of study. They are as follows:

Pre-Algebra

This topic makes up 23 percent of the exam and involves computations using whole numbers, integers, decimals, and fractions.

Elementary Algebra

This topic makes up 17 percent of the exam, and covers quadratic equations and other operations with algebraic expressions.

Intermediate Algebra and Coordinate Geometry

Making up 30 percent of the test, this topic includes coordinate planes, graphing, operations with integers, radicals, rational numbers, quadratic equations, and linear graphs.

Plane Geometry

This topic makes up 23 percent of the exam and deals with lines, circles, and polygons, and the properties associated with figures.

Trigonometry

Making up 7 percent of the exam, this section involves graphing, right angle trigonometry, and basic trigonometric functions.

I. ARITHMETIC REVIEW

INTEGERS AND REAL NUMBERS

Most of the numbers used in algebra belong to a set called the **real numbers** or **reals**. This set can be represented graphically by the real number line.

Given the number line below, we arbitrarily fix a point and label it with the number 0. In a similar manner, we can label any point on the line with one of the real numbers, depending on its position relative to 0. Numbers to the right of 0 are positive, while those to the left are negative. Value increases from left to right, so that if *a* is to the right of *b*, it is said to be greater than *b*.

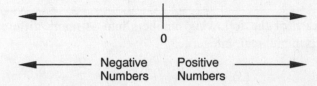

If we now divide the number line into equal segments, we can label the points on this line with real numbers. For example, the point 2 lengths to the left of 0 is − 2, while the point 3 lengths to the right of 0 is + 3 (the + sign is usually assumed, so + 3 is written simply as 3). The number line now looks like this:

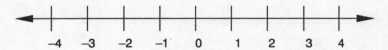

These boundary points represent the subset of the reals known as the **integers**. The set of integers is made up of both the positive and negative whole numbers:

$$\{..., -4, -3, -2, -1, 0, 1, 2, 3, 4, ...\}.$$

Some subsets of integers are:

Natural Numbers or Positive Integers—the set of integers starting with 1 and increasing:

$$\mathcal{N} = \{1, 2, 3, 4, ...\}.$$

Whole Numbers—the set of integers starting with 0 and increasing:

$$\mathcal{W} = \{0, 1, 2, 3, ...\}.$$

Negative Integers—the set of integers starting with − 1 and decreasing:

$$\mathcal{Z} = \{-1, -2, -3, ...\}.$$

Even Integers—the set of integers divisible by 2:

$\{..., -4, -2, 0, 2, 4, 6, ...\}.$

Odd Integers—the set of integers not divisible by 2:

$\{..., -3, -1, 1, 3, 5, 7, ...\}.$

Consecutive Integers—the set of integers that differ by 1:

$\{n, n+1, n+2, ...\}$ (n = an integer).

Prime Numbers—the set of positive integers greater than 1 that are divisible only by 1 and themselves:

$\{2, 3, 5, 7, 11, ...\}.$

PROBLEM

Classify each of the following numbers into as many different sets as possible. Example: real, integer ...

(1) 0 (3) $\sqrt{6}$ (5) $\frac{2}{3}$ (7) 11

(2) 9 (4) $\frac{1}{2}$ (6) 1.5

SOLUTION

(1) 0 is a real number, an integer, and a whole number.

(2) 9 is a real number, an odd number, and a natural number.

(3) $\sqrt{6}$ is a real number.

(4) $\frac{1}{2}$ is a real number.

(5) $\frac{2}{3}$ is a real number.

(6) 1.5 is a real number and a decimal.

(7) 11 is a prime number, an odd number, a real number, and a natural number.

Absolute Value

The **absolute value** of a number is represented by two vertical lines around the number, and is equal to the given number, regardless of sign.

The absolute value of a real number A is defined as follows:

$$|A| = \begin{cases} A \text{ if } A \geq 0 \\ -A \text{ if } A < 0 \end{cases}$$

EXAMPLES

$|5| = 5, |-8| = -(-8) = 8$

Absolute values follow the given rules:

(A) $|-A| = |A|$

(B) $|A| \geq 0$, equality holding only if $A = 0$

(C) $\left|\dfrac{A}{B}\right| = \dfrac{|A|}{|B|}, B \neq 0$

(D) $|AB| = |A| \times |B|$

(E) $|A|^2 = A^2$

PROBLEM

Calculate the value of each of the following expressions:

(1) $||2 - 5| + 6 - 14|$

(2) $|-5| \times |4| + \dfrac{|-12|}{4}$

SOLUTION

Before solving this problem, one must remember the order of operations: parenthesis, multiplication and division, addition and subtraction.

(1) $||-3| + 6 - 14| = |3 + 6 - 14| = |9 - 14| = |-5| = 5$

(2) $(5 \times 4) + {}^{12}/_4 = 20 + 3 = 23$

Positive and Negative Numbers

A) **To add two numbers with like signs,** add their absolute values and write the sum with the common sign. So,

$6 + 2 = 8, (-6) + (-2) = -8$

B) **To add two numbers with unlike signs,** find the difference between their absolute values, and write the result with the sign of the number with the greater absolute value. So,

$(-4) + 6 = 2, 15 + (-19) = -4$

C) **To subtract a number *b* from another number *a*,** change the sign of *b* and add to *a*. Examples:

$$10 - (3) = 10 + (-3) = 7 \tag{1}$$

$$2 - (-6) = 2 + 6 = 8 \tag{2}$$

$$(-5) - (-2) = -5 + 2 = -3 \tag{3}$$

D) **To multiply (or divide) two numbers having like signs,** multiply (or divide) their absolute values and write the result with a positive sign. Examples:

$$(5)(3) = 15 \tag{1}$$

$$(-6) \div (-3) = 2 \tag{2}$$

E) **To multiply (or divide) two numbers having unlike signs,** multiply (or divide) their absolute values and write the result with a negative sign. Examples:

$$(-2)(8) = -16 \tag{1}$$

$$9 \div (-3) = -3 \tag{2}$$

According to the law of signs for real numbers, the square of a positive or negative number is always positive. This means that it is impossible to take the square root of a negative number in the real number system.

PROBLEM

Calculate the value of each of the following expressions:

(1) $||2 - 5| + 6 - 14|$ (2) $|-8| \times 2 + \dfrac{|-12|}{4}$

SOLUTION

Before solving this problem, one must use the rules for the **order of operations.** Always work within the parentheses or with absolute values first while keeping in mind that multiplication and division are carried out before addition and subtraction.

(1) $||-3| + 6 - 14| = |3 + 6 - 14|$

$$= |9 - 14|$$

$$= |-5|$$

$$= 5$$

(2) $(8 \times 2) + \dfrac{12}{4} = 16 + 3$

$$= 19$$

Odd and Even Numbers

When dealing with odd and even numbers keep in mind the following:

Adding:

> even + even = even
>
> odd + odd = even
>
> even + odd = odd

Multiplying:

> even × even = even
>
> even × odd = odd
>
> odd × odd = even

☞ Drill: Integers and Real Numbers

Addition

1. Simplify $4 + (-7) + 2 + (-5)$.

(A) -6 (B) -4 (C) 0   (D) 6   (E) 18

2. Simplify $144 + (-317) + 213$.

(A) -357 (B) -40 (C) 40   (D) 357   (E) 674

Subtraction

3. Simplify $319 - 428$.

(A) -111 (B) -109 (C) -99 (D) 109   (E) 747

4. Simplify $91,203 - 37,904 + 1,073$.

(A) 54,372   (B) 64,701   (C) 128,034   (D) 129,107   (E) 130,180

Multiplication

5. Simplify $(-3) \times (-18) \times (-1)$.

(A) -108 (B) -54 (C) -48 (D) 48   (E) 54

6. Simplify $|-42| \times |-7|$.

(A) -294 (B) -49 (C) -35 (D) 284   (E) 294

Division

7. Simplify $(-24) \div 8$.

(A) -4 (B) -3 (C) -2 (D) 3 (E) 4

8. Simplify $(-180) \div (-12)$.

(A) -30 (B) -15 (C) 1.5 (D) 15 (E) 216

Order of Operations

9. Simplify $\dfrac{4 + 8 \times 2}{5 - 1}$.

(A) 4 (B) 5 (C) 6 (D) 8 (E) 12

10. $96 \div 3 \div 4 \div 2 =$

(A) 65 (B) 64 (C) 16 (D) 8 (E) 4

11. $3 + 4 \times 2 - 6 \div 3 =$

(A) -1 (B) $\dfrac{5}{3}$ (C) $\dfrac{8}{3}$ (D) 9 (E) 12

12. $[(4 + 8) \times 3] \div 9 =$

(A) 4 (B) 8 (C) 12 (D) 24 (E) 36

13. $18 + 3 \times 4 \div 3 =$

(A) 3 (B) 5 (C) 10 (D) 22 (E) 28

FRACTIONS

The fraction, a/b, where the **numerator** is a and the **denominator** is b, implies that a is being divided by b. The denominator of a fraction can never be zero since a number divided by zero is not defined. If the numerator is greater than the denominator, the fraction is called an **improper fraction**. A **mixed number** is the sum of a whole number and a fraction, i.e.,

$$4\frac{3}{8} = 4 + \frac{3}{8}.$$

Operations with Fractions

A) **To change a mixed number to an improper fraction**, simply multiply the whole number by the denominator of the fraction and add the numerator. This product becomes the numerator of the result and the denominator remains the same, e.g.,

$$5\frac{2}{3} = \frac{(5 \times 3) + 2}{3} = \frac{15 + 2}{3} = \frac{17}{3}$$

To change an improper fraction to a mixed number, simply divide the numerator by the denominator. The remainder becomes the numerator of the fractional part of the mixed number, and the denominator remains the same, e.g.,

$$\frac{35}{4} = 35 \div 4 = 8\frac{3}{4}$$

To check your work, change your result back to an improper fraction to see if it matches the original fraction.

B) **To find the sum of fractions having a common denominator**, simply add together the numerators of the given fractions and put this sum over the common denominator.

$$\frac{11}{3} + \frac{5}{3} = \frac{11 + 5}{3} = \frac{16}{3}$$

Similarly for subtraction,

$$\frac{11}{3} - \frac{5}{3} = \frac{11 - 5}{3} = \frac{6}{3} = 2$$

C) **To find the sum of two fractions having different denominators**, it is necessary to find the **lowest common denominator (LCD)** of the different denominators using a process called **factoring**.

To **factor** a number means to find numbers that when multiplied together have a product equal to the original number. These numbers are then said to be **factors** of the original number; e.g., the factors of 6 are

(1)   1 and 6 since $1 \times 6 = 6$.

(2)   2 and 3 since $2 \times 3 = 6$.

Every number is the product of itself and 1. A **prime factor** is a number that does not have any factors besides itself and 1. This is important when finding the LCD of two fractions having different denominators.

To find the LCD of $^{11}/_6$ and $^5/_{16}$, we must first find the prime factors of each of the two denominators.

$$6 = 2 \times 3$$

$$16 = 2 \times 2 \times 2 \times 2$$

$$\text{LCD} = 2 \times 2 \times 2 \times 2 \times 3 = 48$$

Note that we do not need to repeat the 2 that appears in both the factors of 6 and 16.

Once we have determined the LCD of the denominators, each of the fractions must be converted into equivalent fractions having the LCD as a denominator.

Rewrite $^{11}/_6$ and $^5/_{16}$ to have 48 as their denominators.

$$6 \times ? = 48 \qquad\qquad 16 \times ? = 48$$

$$6 \times 8 = 48 \qquad\qquad 16 \times 3 = 48$$

If the numerator and denominator of each fraction is multiplied (or divided) by the same number, the value of the fraction will not change. This is because a fraction b/b, b being any number, is equal to the multiplicative identity, 1.

Therefore,

$$\frac{11}{6} \times \frac{8}{8} = \frac{88}{48} \qquad \frac{5}{16} \times \frac{3}{3} = \frac{15}{48}$$

We may now find

$$\frac{11}{6} - \frac{5}{16} = \frac{88}{48} + \frac{15}{48} = \frac{73}{48}$$

Similarly for subtraction,

$$\frac{11}{6} - \frac{5}{16} = \frac{88}{48} - \frac{15}{48} = \frac{73}{48}$$

D) **To find the product of two or more fractions,** simply multiply the numerators of the given fractions to find the numerator of the product and multiply the denominators of the given fractions to find the denominator of the product, e.g.,

$$\frac{2}{3} \times \frac{1}{5} \times \frac{4}{7} = \frac{2 \times 1 \times 4}{3 \times 5 \times 7} = \frac{8}{105}$$

E) **To find the quotient of two fractions,** simply invert (or flip-over) the divisor and multiply, e.g.,

$$\frac{8}{9} \div \frac{1}{3} = \frac{8}{8} \times \frac{3}{1} = \frac{24}{9} = \frac{8}{3}$$

F) **To simplify a fraction** is to convert it into a form in which the numerator and denominator have no common factor other than 1, e.g.,

$$\frac{12}{18} = \frac{12 \div 6}{18 \div 6} = \frac{2}{3}$$

G) A **complex fraction** is a fraction whose numerator and/or denominator is made up of fractions. To simplify the fraction, find the LCD of all the fractions. Multiply both the numerator and denominator by this number and simplify.

PROBLEM

If $a = 4$ and $b = 7$, find the value of $\dfrac{a + \frac{a}{b}}{a - \frac{a}{b}}$.

SOLUTION

By substitution,

$$\frac{a + \frac{a}{b}}{a - \frac{a}{b}} = \frac{4 + \frac{4}{7}}{4 - \frac{4}{7}}$$

In order to combine the terms, we must find the LCD of 1 and 7. Since both are prime factors, the LCD = $1 \times 7 = 7$.

Multiplying both the numerator and denominator by 7, we get

$$\frac{7\left(4 + \frac{4}{7}\right)}{7\left(4 - \frac{4}{7}\right)} = \frac{28 + 4}{28 - 4} = \frac{32}{24}$$

By dividing both the numerator and denominator by 8, $\frac{32}{24}$ can be reduced to $\frac{4}{3}$.

☞ Drill: Fractions

Changing an Improper Fraction to a Mixed Number

DIRECTIONS: Write each improper fraction as a mixed number in simplest form.

1. $\dfrac{50}{4}$

(A) $10\dfrac{1}{4}$ (B) $11\dfrac{1}{2}$ (C) $12\dfrac{1}{4}$ (D) $12\dfrac{1}{2}$ (E) 25

2. $\dfrac{17}{5}$

(A) $3\dfrac{2}{5}$ (B) $3\dfrac{3}{5}$ (C) $3\dfrac{4}{5}$ (D) $4\dfrac{1}{5}$ (E) $4\dfrac{2}{5}$

3. $\dfrac{42}{3}$

(A) $10\dfrac{2}{3}$ (B) 12   (C) $13\dfrac{1}{3}$ (D) 14   (E) $21\dfrac{1}{3}$

Changing a Mixed Number to an Improper Fraction

DIRECTIONS: Change each mixed number to an improper fraction in simplest form.

4. $2\dfrac{3}{5}$

(A) $\dfrac{4}{5}$ (B) $\dfrac{6}{5}$ (C) $\dfrac{11}{5}$ (D) $\dfrac{13}{5}$ (E) $\dfrac{17}{5}$

5. $4\dfrac{3}{4}$

(A) $\dfrac{7}{4}$ (B) $\dfrac{13}{4}$ (C) $\dfrac{16}{3}$ (D) $\dfrac{19}{4}$ (E) $\dfrac{21}{4}$

6. $6\dfrac{7}{6}$

(A) $\dfrac{13}{6}$ (B) $\dfrac{43}{6}$ (C) $\dfrac{19}{36}$ (D) $\dfrac{42}{36}$ (E) $\dfrac{48}{6}$

Adding Fractions with the Same Denominator

DIRECTIONS: Add and write the answer in simplest form.

7. $\dfrac{5}{12} + \dfrac{3}{12} =$

(A) $\dfrac{5}{24}$ (B) $\dfrac{1}{3}$ (C) $\dfrac{8}{12}$ (D) $\dfrac{2}{3}$ (E) $1\dfrac{1}{3}$

8. $\frac{5}{8} + \frac{7}{8} + \frac{3}{8} =$

(A) $\frac{15}{24}$ (B) $\frac{3}{4}$ (C) $\frac{5}{6}$ (D) $\frac{7}{8}$ (E) $1\frac{7}{8}$

Subtracting Fractions with the Same Denominator

DIRECTIONS: Subtract and write the answer in simplest form.

9. $4\frac{7}{8} - 3\frac{1}{8} =$

(A) $1\frac{1}{4}$ (B) $1\frac{3}{4}$ (C) $1\frac{12}{16}$ (D) $1\frac{7}{8}$ (E) 2

10. $132\frac{5}{12} - 37\frac{3}{12} =$

(A) $94\frac{1}{6}$ (B) $95\frac{1}{12}$ (C) $95\frac{1}{6}$ (D) $105\frac{1}{6}$ (E) $169\frac{2}{3}$

Finding the LCD

DIRECTIONS: Find the lowest common denominator of each group of fractions.

11. $\frac{2}{3}, \frac{5}{9}$, and $\frac{1}{6}$

(A) 9   (B) 18   (C) 27   (D) 54   (E) 162

12. $\frac{1}{2}, \frac{5}{6}$, and $\frac{3}{4}$

(A) 2   (B) 4   (C) 6   (D) 12   (E) 48

13. $\frac{7}{16}, \frac{5}{6}$, and $\frac{2}{3}$

(A) 3   (B) 6   (C) 12   (D) 24   (E) 48

14. $\frac{8}{15}, \frac{2}{5}$, and $\frac{12}{25}$

(A) 5   (B) 15   (C) 25   (D) 75   (E) 375

15. $\frac{2}{3}, \frac{1}{5}$, and $\frac{5}{6}$

(A) 15   (B) 30   (C) 48   (D) 90   (E) 120

Adding Fractions with Different Denominators

DIRECTIONS: Add and write the answer in simplest form.

16. $\frac{1}{3} + \frac{5}{12} =$

(A) $\frac{2}{5}$ (B) $\frac{1}{2}$ (C) $\frac{9}{12}$ (D) $\frac{3}{4}$ (E) $1\frac{1}{3}$

17. $3\frac{5}{9} + 2\frac{1}{3} =$

(A) $5\frac{1}{2}$ (B) $5\frac{2}{3}$ (C) $5\frac{8}{9}$ (D) $6\frac{1}{9}$ (E) $6\frac{2}{3}$

18. $12\frac{9}{16} + 17\frac{3}{4} + 8\frac{1}{8} =$

(A) $37\frac{7}{16}$ (B) $38\frac{7}{16}$ (C) $38\frac{1}{2}$ (D) $38\frac{2}{3}$ (E) $39\frac{3}{16}$

Subtracting Fractions with Different Denominators

DIRECTIONS: Subtract and write the answer in simplest form.

19. $8\frac{9}{12} - 2\frac{2}{3} =$

(A) $6\frac{1}{12}$ (B) $6\frac{1}{6}$ (C) $6\frac{1}{3}$ (D) $6\frac{7}{12}$ (E) $6\frac{2}{3}$

20. $185\frac{11}{15} - 107\frac{2}{5} =$

(A) $77\frac{2}{15}$ (B) $78\frac{1}{5}$ (C) $78\frac{3}{10}$ (D) $78\frac{1}{3}$ (E) $78\frac{9}{15}$

21. $34\frac{2}{3} - 16\frac{5}{6} =$

(A) 16   (B) $16\frac{1}{3}$ (C) $17\frac{1}{2}$ (D) 17   (E) $17\frac{5}{6}$

Multiplying Fractions

> **DIRECTIONS**: Multiply and reduce the answer.

22. $\frac{2}{3} \times \frac{4}{5} =$

(A) $\frac{6}{8}$ (B) $\frac{3}{4}$ (C) $\frac{8}{15}$ (D) $\frac{10}{12}$ (E) $\frac{6}{5}$

23. $\frac{7}{10} \times \frac{4}{21} =$

(A) $\frac{2}{15}$ (B) $\frac{11}{31}$ (C) $\frac{28}{210}$ (D) $\frac{1}{6}$ (E) $\frac{4}{15}$

24. $5\frac{1}{3} \times \frac{3}{8} =$

(A) $\frac{4}{11}$ (B) 2   (C) $\frac{8}{5}$ (D) $5\frac{1}{8}$ (E) $5\frac{17}{24}$

Dividing Fractions

> **DIRECTIONS**: Divide and reduce the answer.

25. $\frac{3}{16} \div \frac{3}{4} =$

(A) $\frac{9}{64}$ (B) $\frac{1}{4}$ (C) $\frac{6}{16}$ (D) $\frac{9}{16}$ (E) $\frac{3}{4}$

26. $\frac{4}{9} \div \frac{2}{3} =$

(A) $\frac{1}{3}$ (B) $\frac{1}{2}$ (C) $\frac{2}{3}$ (D) $\frac{7}{11}$ (E) $\frac{8}{9}$

27. $5\dfrac{1}{4} \div \dfrac{7}{10} =$

(A) $2\dfrac{4}{7}$ (B) $3\dfrac{27}{40}$ (C) $5\dfrac{19}{20}$ (D) $7\dfrac{1}{2}$ (E) $8\dfrac{1}{4}$

DECIMALS

When we divide the denominator of a fraction into its numerator, the result is a **decimal**. The decimal is based upon a fraction with a denominator of 10, 100, 1,000, ... and is written with a **decimal point**. Whole numbers are placed to the left of the decimal point where the first place to the left is the units place; the second to the left is the tens; the third to the left is the hundreds, etc. The fractions are placed on the right where the first place to the right is the tenths; the second to the right is the hundredths, etc.

EXAMPLES

$$12\dfrac{3}{10} = 12.3 \qquad 4\dfrac{17}{100} = 4.17 \qquad \dfrac{3}{100} = .03$$

Since a **rational number** is of the form a/b, $b \neq 0$, then all rational numbers can be expressed as decimals by dividing b into a. The result is either a **terminating decimal**, meaning that b divides a with a remainder of 0 after a certain point; or **repeating decimal**, meaning that b continues to divide a so that the decimal has a repeating pattern of integers.

EXAMPLES

(A) $\dfrac{1}{5} = .2$

(B) $\dfrac{1}{3} = .333...$

(C) $\dfrac{11}{16} = .6875$

(D) $\dfrac{4}{7} = .5714285714...$

(A) and (C) are terminating decimals; (B) and (D) are repeating decimals. This explanation allows us to define **irrational numbers** as numbers whose decimal form is non-terminating and non-repeating, e.g.,

$$\sqrt{2} = 1.414...$$
$$\sqrt{3} = 1.732...$$

PROBLEM

Write $\dfrac{2}{7}$ as a repeating decimal.

SOLUTION

To write a fraction as a repeating decimal divide the numerator by the denominator until a pattern of repeated digits appears.

$2 \div 7 = .285714285714\ldots$

Identify the entire portion of the decimal which is repeated. The repeating decimal can then be written in the shortened form:

$\dfrac{2}{7} = .\overline{285714}$

Operations with Decimals

A) **To add numbers containing decimals,** write the numbers in a column making sure the decimal points are lined up, one beneath the other. Add the numbers as usual, placing the decimal point in the sum so that it is still in line with the others.

EXAMPLES

$2.558 + 6.391$

$$\begin{array}{r} 2.558 \\ +\ 6.391 \\ \hline 8.949 \end{array}$$

$57.51 + 6.2$

$$\begin{array}{r} 57.51 \\ +\ \ 6.20 \\ \hline 63.71 \end{array}$$

Similarly with subtraction,

$78.54 - 21.33$

$$\begin{array}{r} 78.54 \\ -\ 21.33 \\ \hline 57.21 \end{array}$$

$7.11 - 4.2$

$$\begin{array}{r} 7.11 \\ -\ 4.20 \\ \hline 2.91 \end{array}$$

Note that if two numbers differ according to the number of digits to the right of the decimal point, zeros must be added.

$.63 - .214$

$$\begin{array}{r} .630 \\ -\ .214 \\ \hline .416 \end{array}$$

$15.224 - 3.6891$

$$\begin{array}{r} 15.2240 \\ -\ \ 3.6891 \\ \hline 11.5349 \end{array}$$

B) **To multiply numbers with decimals,** simply multiply as usual. Then, to figure out the number of decimal places that belong in the product, find the total number of decimal places in the numbers being multiplied.

EXAMPLES

$$
\begin{array}{rl}
6.555 & \text{(3 decimal places)} \\
\times \quad 4.5 & \text{(1 decimal place)} \\
\hline
32775 \quad 2128 & \\
26220 & \\
\hline
29.4975 & \text{(4 decimal places)}
\end{array}
$$

$$
\begin{array}{rl}
5.32 & \text{(2 decimal places)} \\
\times \quad .04 & \text{(2 decimal places)} \\
\hline
000 & \\
\hline
.2128 & \text{(4 decimal places)}
\end{array}
$$

C) **To divide numbers with decimals,** you must first make the divisor a whole number by moving the decimal point the appropriate number of places to the right. The decimal point of the dividend should also be moved the same number of places. Place a decimal point in the quotient directly in line with the decimal point in the dividend.

EXAMPLES

$$12.92 \div 3.4$$

$$
\begin{array}{r}
3.8 \\
3.4, \overline{)12.9,2} \\
-102 \\
\hline
272 \\
-272 \\
\hline
0
\end{array}
$$

$$40.376 \div 7.21$$

$$
\begin{array}{r}
5.6 \\
7.21, \overline{)40.37,6} \\
-3605 \\
\hline
4326 \\
-4326 \\
\hline
0
\end{array}
$$

If the question asks you to find the correct answer to two decimal places, simply divide until you have three decimal places and then round off. If the third decimal place is a 5 or larger, the number in the second decimal place is increased by 1. If the third decimal place is less than 5, that number is simply dropped.

PROBLEM

Find the answer to the following to two decimal places:

(1) $44.3 \div 3$

(2) $56.99 \div 6$

SOLUTION

(1)
$$
\begin{array}{r}
14.766 \\
3\overline{)44.300} \\
\underline{-3} \\
14 \\
\underline{-12} \\
23 \\
\underline{-21} \\
20 \\
\underline{-18} \\
20 \\
\underline{-18} \\
2
\end{array}
$$

(2)
$$
\begin{array}{r}
9.498 \\
6\overline{)56.990} \\
\underline{-54} \\
29 \\
\underline{-24} \\
59 \\
\underline{-54} \\
50 \\
\underline{-48} \\
2
\end{array}
$$

14.766 can be rounded off to 14.77.

9.498 can be rounded off to 9.50.

D) **When comparing two numbers which begin with a decimal point to see which is the larger,** first look at the tenths place. The larger digit in this place represents the larger number. If the two digits are the same, however, take a look at the digits in the hundredths place, and so on.

EXAMPLES

.518 and .216

5 is larger than 2, therefore, .518 is larger than .216.

.723 and .726

6 is larger than 3, therefore, .726 is larger than .723.

☞ Drill: Decimals

Addition and Subtraction

DIRECTIONS: Solve the following equations.

1. $1.032 + 0.987 + 3.07 =$

(A) 4.089 (B) 5.089 (C) 5.189 (D) 6.189 (E) 13.972

2. $132.03 + 97.1483 =$

(A) 98.4686 (B) 110.3513 (C) 209.1783

(D) 229.1486 (E) 229.1783

3.   7.1 + 0.62 + 4.03827 + 5.183 =

(A) 0.2315127   (B) 16.45433   (C) 16.94127

(D) 18.561   (E) 40.4543

4.   3.972 − 2.04 =

(A) 1.932   (B) 1.942   (C) 1.976   (D) 2.013   (E) 2.113

5.   16.047 − 13.06 =

(A) 2.887   (B) 2.987   (C) 3.041   (D) 3.141   (E) 4.741

Multiplication and Division

DIRECTIONS: Solve the following equations.

6.   1.03 × 2.6 =

(A) 2.18   (B) 2.678   (C) 2.78   (D) 3.38   (E) 3.63

7.   93 × 4.2 =

(A) 39.06   (B) 97.2   (C) 223.2   (D) 390.6   (E) 3,906

8.   123.39 ÷ 3 =

(A) 31.12   (B) 41.13   (C) 401.13   (D) 411.3   (E) 4,113

9.   1,428.6 ÷ 6 =

(A) 0.2381   (B) 2.381   (C) 23.81   (D) 238.1   (E) 2,381

10. 25.2 ÷ 0.3 =

(A) 0.84   (B) 8.04   (C) 8.4   (D) 84   (E) 840

Comparing

DIRECTIONS: Solve the following equations.

11. Which is the **largest** number in this set—{0.8, 0.823, 0.089, 0.807, 0.852}?

(A) 0.8   (B) 0.823   (C) 0.089   (D) 0.807   (E) 0.852

12. Which is the **smallest** number in this set—{32.98, 32.099, 32.047, 32.5, 32.304}?

(A) 32.98   (B) 32.099   (C) 32.047   (D) 32.5   (E) 32.304

13. In which set below are the numbers arranged correctly from smallest to largest?

    (A) {0.98, 0.9, 0.993}   (B) {0.113, 0.3, 0.31}

    (C) {7.04, 7.26, 7.2}   (D) {0.006, 0.061, 0.06}

    (E) {12.84, 12.801, 12.6}

Changing a Fraction to a Decimal

DIRECTIONS: Solve the following equations.

14. What is $\dfrac{1}{4}$ written as a decimal?

(A) 1.4   (B) 0.14   (C) 0.2   (D) 0.25   (E) 0.3

15. What is $\dfrac{3}{5}$ written as a decimal?

(A) 0.3   (B) 0.35   (C) 0.6   (D) 0.65   (E) 0.8

PERCENTAGES

A **percent** is a way of expressing the relationship between part and whole, where whole is defined as 100%. A percent can be defined by a fraction with a denominator of 100. Decimals can also represent a percent. For instance,

$$56\% = 0.56 = \frac{56}{100}$$

PROBLEM

Compute the value of

(1)   90% of 400   (2)   180% of 400

SOLUTION

The symbol % means per hundred, therefore, $5\% = {}^{5}\!/_{100}$.

(1) 90% of 400 = 90 ÷ 100 × 400 = 90 × 4 = 360

(2) 180% of 400 = 180 ÷ 100 × 400 = 180 × 4 = 720

PROBLEM

What percent of

(1)   100 is 99.5   (2)   200 is 4

SOLUTION

(1) $99.5 = x \times 100$

$99.5 = 100x$

$.995 = x$; but this is the value of x per hundred. Therefore,

$99.5\% = x$

(2) $4 = x \times 200$

$4 = 200x$

$.02 = x$. Again, this must be changed to percent, so

$2\% = x$

Equivalent Forms of a Number

Some problems may call for converting numbers into an equivalent or simplified form in order to make the solution more convenient.

A) **Converting a fraction to a decimal:**

$\dfrac{1}{2} = 0.50$

Divide the numerator by the denominator:

$$\begin{array}{r} .50 \\ 2\overline{\smash{\big)}\,1.00} \\ \underline{-10} \\ 00 \end{array}$$

B) **Converting a number to a percent:**

$0.50 = 50\%$

Multiply by 100:

$0.50 = (0.50 \times 100)\% = 50\%$

C) **Converting a percent to a decimal:**

   30% = 0.30

Divide by 100:

   30% = 30 ÷ 100 = 0.30

D) **Converting a decimal to a fraction:**

   $0.500 = \dfrac{1}{2}$

Convert .500 to $^{500}/_{1000}$ and then simplify the fraction by dividing the numerator and denominator by common factors:

$$\frac{\cancel{2} \times \cancel{2} \times \cancel{5} \times \cancel{5} \times \cancel{5}}{\cancel{2} \times \cancel{2} \times 2 \times \cancel{5} \times \cancel{5} \times \cancel{5}}$$

and then cancel out the common numbers to get ½.

PROBLEM

Express

(1)   1.65 as a percent   (2)   0.7 as a fraction

(3) $-\dfrac{10}{20}$ as a decimal   (4) $\dfrac{4}{2}$ as an integer

---

SOLUTION

(1)   1.65 × 100 = 165%

(2) $0.7 = \dfrac{7}{10}$

(3) $-\dfrac{10}{20} = -0.5$

(4) $\dfrac{4}{2} = 2$

☞ Drill: Percentages

Finding Percents

> **DIRECTIONS**: Solve to find the correct percentages.

1. Find 3% of 80.

(A) 0.24   (B) 2.4   (C) 24   (D) 240   (E) 2,400

2. Find 50% of 182.

(A) 9   (B) 90   (C) 91   (D) 910   (E) 9,100

3. Find 83% of 166.

(A) 0.137   (B) 1.377   (C) 13.778   (D) 137   (E) 137.78

4. Find 125% of 400.

(A) 425   (B) 500   (C) 525   (D) 600   (E) 825

5. Find 300% of 4.

(A) 12   (B) 120   (C) 1,200   (D) 12,000   (E) 120,000

Changing Percents to Fractions

> **DIRECTIONS**: Solve to find the correct fractions.

6. What is 25% written as a fraction?

(A) $\dfrac{1}{25}$ (B) $\dfrac{1}{5}$ (C) $\dfrac{1}{4}$ (D) $\dfrac{1}{3}$ (E) $\dfrac{1}{2}$

7. What is $33\dfrac{1}{3}$% written as a fraction?

(A) $\dfrac{1}{4}$ (B) $\dfrac{1}{3}$ (C) $\dfrac{1}{2}$ (D) $\dfrac{2}{3}$ (E) $\dfrac{5}{9}$

8. What is 200% written as a fraction?

(A) $\dfrac{1}{2}$ (B) $\dfrac{2}{1}$ (C) $\dfrac{20}{1}$ (D) $\dfrac{200}{1}$ (E) $\dfrac{2,000}{1}$

Changing Fractions to Percents

DIRECTIONS: Solve to find the following percentages.

9. What is $\frac{2}{3}$ written as a percent?

(A) 23%　　(B) 32%　　(C) $33\frac{1}{3}\%$　　(D) $57\frac{1}{3}\%$　　(E) $66\frac{2}{3}\%$

10. What is $\frac{3}{5}$ written as a percent?

(A) 30%　　(B) 35%　　(C) 53%　　(D) 60%　　(E) 65%

Changing Percents to Decimals

DIRECTIONS: Convert the percentages to decimals.

11. What is 42% written as a decimal?

(A) 0.42　　(B) 4.2　　(C) 42　　(D) 420　　(E) 422

12. What is 0.3% written as a decimal?

(A) 0.0003　　(B) 0.003　　(C) 0.03　　(D) 0.3　　(E) 3

13. What is 8% written as a decimal?

(A) 0.0008　　(B) 0.008　　(C) 0.08　　(D) 0.80　　(E) 8

Changing Decimals to Percents

DIRECTIONS: Convert the following decimals to percents.

14. What is 0.43 written as a percent?

(A) 0.0043%　(B) 0.043%　(C) 4.3%　　(D) 43%　　(E) 430%

15. What is 1 written as a percent?

(A) 1%　　(B) 10%　　(C) 100%　　(D) 111%　　(E) 150%

RADICALS

The **square root** of a number is a number that when multiplied by itself results in the original number. Thus, the square root of 81 is 9 since 9 × 9 = 81. However, − 9 is also a root of 81 since (− 9) (− 9) = 81. Every positive number will have two roots. The principal root is the positive one. Zero has only one square root, while negative numbers do not have real numbers as their roots.

A **radical sign** indicates that the root of a number or expression will be taken. The **radicand** is the number of which the root will be taken. The **index** tells how many times the root needs to be multiplied by itself to equal the radicand, e.g.,

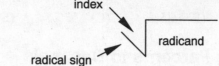

(1) $\sqrt[3]{64}$;

    3 is the index and 64 is the radicand. Since 4 × 4 × 4 = 64, then $\sqrt[3]{64}$ = 4.

(2) $\sqrt[5]{32}$;

    5 is the index and 32 is the radicand. Since 2 × 2 × 2 × 2 × 2 = 32, then $\sqrt[5]{32}$ = 2.

Operations with Radicals

A) **To multiply two or more radicals**, we utilize the law that states

$$\sqrt{a} \times \sqrt{b} = \sqrt{ab}.$$

Simply multiply the whole numbers as usual. Then, multiply the radicands and put the product under the radical sign and simplify, e.g.,

    (1) $\sqrt{12} \times \sqrt{5} = \sqrt{60} = 2\sqrt{15}$

    (2) $3\sqrt{2} \times 4\sqrt{8} = 12\sqrt{16} = 48$

    (3) $2\sqrt{10} \times 6\sqrt{5} = 12\sqrt{50} = 60\sqrt{2}$

B) **To divide radicals**, simplify both the numerator and the denominator. By multiplying the radical in the denominator by itself, you can make the denominator a rational number. The numerator, however, must also be multiplied by this radical so that the value of the expression does not change. You must choose as many factors as necessary to rationalize the denominator, e.g.,

(1) $\dfrac{\sqrt{128}}{\sqrt{2}} = \dfrac{\sqrt{64} \times \sqrt{2}}{\sqrt{2}} = \dfrac{8\sqrt{2}}{\sqrt{2}} = 8$

(2) $\dfrac{\sqrt{10}}{\sqrt{3}} = \dfrac{\sqrt{10} \times \sqrt{3}}{\sqrt{3} \times \sqrt{3}} = \dfrac{\sqrt{30}}{3}$

(3) $\dfrac{\sqrt{8}}{2\sqrt{3}} = \dfrac{\sqrt{8} \times \sqrt{3}}{2\sqrt{3} \times \sqrt{3}} = \dfrac{\sqrt{24}}{2 \times 3} = \dfrac{2\sqrt{6}}{6} = \dfrac{\sqrt{6}}{3}$

C) **To add two or more radicals**, the radicals must have the same index and the same radicand. Only where the radicals are simplified can these similarities be determined.

EXAMPLES

(1) $6\sqrt{2} + 2\sqrt{2} = (6+2)\sqrt{2} = 8\sqrt{2}$

(2) $\sqrt{27} + 5\sqrt{3} = \sqrt{9}\sqrt{3} + 5\sqrt{3} = 3\sqrt{3} + 5\sqrt{3} = 8\sqrt{3}$

(3) $7\sqrt{3} + 8\sqrt{2} = 5\sqrt{3} = 12\sqrt{3} + 8\sqrt{2}$

Similarly, to subtract,

(1) $12\sqrt{3} - 7\sqrt{3} = (12-7)\sqrt{3} = 5\sqrt{3}$

(2) $\sqrt{80} - \sqrt{20} = \sqrt{16}\sqrt{5} - \sqrt{4}\sqrt{5} = 4\sqrt{5} - 2\sqrt{5} = 2\sqrt{5}$

(3) $\sqrt{50} - \sqrt{3} = 5\sqrt{2} - \sqrt{3}$

☞ Drill: Radicals

Multiplication

DIRECTIONS: Multiply and simplify each answer.

1. $\sqrt{6} \times \sqrt{5} =$

(A) $\sqrt{11}$ (B) $\sqrt{30}$ (C) $2\sqrt{5}$ (D) $3\sqrt{10}$ (E) $2\sqrt{3}$

2. $\sqrt{3} \times \sqrt{12} =$

(A) 3   (B) $\sqrt{15}$ (C) $\sqrt{36}$ (D) 6   (E) 8

3. $\sqrt{7} \times \sqrt{7} =$

(A) 7   (B) 49   (C) $\sqrt{14}$ (D) $2\sqrt{7}$ (E) $2\sqrt{14}$

Division

> **DIRECTIONS**: Divide and simplify the answer.

4. $\sqrt{10} \div \sqrt{2} =$

(A) $\sqrt{8}$ (B) $2\sqrt{2}$ (C) $\sqrt{5}$ (D) $2\sqrt{5}$ (E) $2\sqrt{3}$

5. $\sqrt{30} \div \sqrt{15} =$

(A) $\sqrt{2}$ (B) $\sqrt{45}$ (C) $3\sqrt{5}$ (D) $\sqrt{15}$ (E) $5\sqrt{3}$

6. $\sqrt{100} \div \sqrt{25} =$

(A) $\sqrt{4}$ (B) $5\sqrt{5}$ (C) $5\sqrt{3}$ (D) 2   (E) 4

Addition

> **DIRECTIONS**: Simplify each radical and add.

7. $\sqrt{7} + 3\sqrt{7} =$

(A) $3\sqrt{7}$ (B) $4\sqrt{7}$ (C) $3\sqrt{14}$ (D) $4\sqrt{14}$ (E) $3\sqrt{21}$

8. $\sqrt{5} + 6\sqrt{5} + 3\sqrt{5} =$

(A) $9\sqrt{5}$ (B) $9\sqrt{15}$ (C) $5\sqrt{10}$ (D) $10\sqrt{5}$ (E) $18\sqrt{15}$

9. $3\sqrt{32} + 2\sqrt{2} =$

(A) $5\sqrt{2}$ (B) $\sqrt{34}$ (C) $14\sqrt{2}$ (D) $5\sqrt{34}$ (E) $6\sqrt{64}$

Subtraction

> **DIRECTIONS**: Simplify each radical and subtract.

10. $8\sqrt{5} - 6\sqrt{5} =$

(A) $2\sqrt{5}$ (B) $3\sqrt{5}$ (C) $4\sqrt{5}$ (D) $14\sqrt{5}$ (E) $48\sqrt{5}$

11. $16\sqrt{33} - 5\sqrt{33} =$

(A) $3\sqrt{33}$ (B) $33\sqrt{11}$ (C) $11\sqrt{33}$ (D) $11\sqrt{0}$ (E) $\sqrt{33}$

EXPONENTS

When a number is multiplied by itself a specific number of times, it is said to be **raised to a power**. The way this is written is $a^n = b$ where a is the number or **base**, n is the **exponent** or **power** that indicates the number of times the base is to be multiplied by itself, and b is the product of this multiplication.

In the expression 3^2, 3 is the base and 2 is the exponent. This means that 3 is multiplied by itself 2 times and the product is 9.

An exponent can be either positive or negative. A negative exponent implies a fraction such that if n is a negative integer

$$a^{-n} = \frac{1}{a^n}, a \neq 0. \quad \text{So, } 2^{-4} = \frac{1}{2^4} = \frac{1}{16}.$$

An exponent that is 0 gives a result of 1, assuming that the base is not equal to 0.

$a^0 = 1, a \neq 0.$

An exponent can also be a fraction. If m and n are positive integers,

$$a^{\frac{m}{n}} = \sqrt[n]{a^m}$$

The numerator remains the exponent of a, but the denominator tells what root to take. For example,

(1) $4^{\frac{3}{2}} = \sqrt[2]{4^3} = \sqrt{64} = 8$ (2) $3^{\frac{4}{2}} = \sqrt[2]{3^4} = \sqrt{81} = 9$

If a fractional exponent were negative, the same operation would take place, but the result would be a fraction. For example,

(1) $27^{-\frac{3}{2}} = \frac{1}{27^{2/3}} = \frac{1}{\sqrt[3]{27^2}} = \frac{1}{\sqrt[3]{729}} = \frac{1}{9}$

PROBLEM

Simplify the following expressions:

(1) -3^{-2} (3) $\dfrac{-3}{4^{-1}}$

(2) $(-3)^{-2}$

SOLUTION

(1) Here the exponent applies only to 3. Since

$$x^{-y} = \frac{1}{x^y}, \quad -3^{-2} = -(3)^{-2} = -\left(\frac{1}{3^2}\right) = -\frac{1}{9}$$

(2) In this case the exponent applies to the negative base. Thus,

$$(-3)^{-2} = \frac{1}{(-3)^2} = \frac{1}{(-3)(-3)} = \frac{1}{9}$$

(3) $\quad \dfrac{-3}{4^{-1}} = \dfrac{-3}{\left(\dfrac{1}{4}\right)^1} = \dfrac{-3}{\dfrac{1^1}{4^1}} = \dfrac{-3}{\dfrac{1}{4}}$

Division by a fraction is equivalent to multiplication by that fraction's reciprocal, thus

$$\frac{-3}{\dfrac{1}{4}} = 3 \times \frac{4}{1} = -12 \quad \text{and} \quad \frac{-3}{4^{-1}} = -12$$

General Laws of Exponents

A) $\quad a^p a^q = a^{p+q}$

$\quad 4^2 4^3 = 4^{2+3} = 1{,}024$

B) $\quad (a^p)^q = a^{pq}$

$\quad (2^3)^2 = 2^6 = 64$

C) $\quad \dfrac{a^p}{a^q} = a^{p-q}$

$\quad \dfrac{3^6}{3^2} = 3^4 = 81$

D) $\quad (ab)^p = a^p b^p$

$\quad (3 \times 2)^2 = 3^2 \times 2^2 = (9)(4) = 36$

E) $\quad \left(\dfrac{a}{b}\right)^p = \dfrac{a^p}{b^p}, \ b \neq 0$

$\quad \left(\dfrac{4}{5}\right)^2 = \dfrac{4^2}{5^2} = \dfrac{16}{25}$

☞ Drill: Exponents

Multiplication and Division

> **DIRECTIONS:** Simplify.

1. $4^6 \times 4^2 =$

(A) 4^4 (B) 4^8 (C) 4^{12} (D) 16^8 (E) 16^{12}

2. $2^2 \times 2^5 \times 2^3 =$

(A) 2^{10} (B) 4^{10} (C) 8^{10} (D) 2^{30} (E) 8^{30}

3. $6^6 \times 6^2 \times 6^4 =$

(A) 18^8 (B) 18^{12} (C) 6^{12} (D) 6^{48} (E) 18^{48}

4. $6^5 \div 6^3 =$

(A) 0 (B) 1 (C) 6 (D) 12 (E) 36

5. $11^8 \div 11^5 =$

(A) 1^3 (B) 11^3 (C) 11^{13} (D) 11^{40} (E) 88^5

Power to a Power

> **DIRECTIONS:** Simplify.

6. $(3^6)^2 =$

(A) 3^4 (B) 3^8 (C) 3^{12} (D) 9^6 (E) 9^8

7. $(4^3)^5 =$

(A) 4^2 (B) 2^{15} (C) 4^8 (D) 20^3 (E) 4^{15}

8. $(a^4b^3)^2 =$

(A) $(ab)^9$ (B) a^8b^6 (C) $(ab)^{24}$ (D) a^6b^5 (E) $2a^4b^3$

AVERAGES

Mean

The mean is the arithmetic average. It is the sum of the variables divided by the total number of variables. For example, the mean of 4, 3, and 8 is

$$\frac{4+3+8}{3} = \frac{15}{3} = 5$$

PROBLEM

Find the mean salary for four company employees who make $5/hr., $8/hr., $12/hr., and $15/hr.

SOLUTION

The mean salary is the average.

$$\frac{\$5 + \$8 + \$12 + \$15}{4} = \frac{\$40}{4} = \$10/hr$$

Median

The median is the middle value in a set when there is an odd number of values. There is an equal number of values larger and smaller than the median. When the set is an even number of values, the average of the two middle values is the median. For example:

The median of (2, 3, 5, 8, 9) is 5.

The median of (2, 3, 5, 9, 10, 11) is $\frac{5+9}{2} = 7$.

Mode

The mode is the most frequently occurring value in the set of values. For example, the mode of 4, 5, 8, 3, 8, 2 would be 8, since it occurs twice while the other values occur only once.

PROBLEM

For this series of observations, find the mean, median, and mode.

500, 600, 800, 800, 900, 900, 900, 900, 900, 1,000, 1,100

SOLUTION

The mean is the value obtained by adding all the measurements and dividing by the number of measurements.

$$\frac{500+600+800+900+900+900+900+900+1,000+1,100}{11}$$

$$=\frac{9,300}{11}=845.45$$

The median is the value appearing in the middle. We have 11 values, so here the sixth, 900, is the median.

The mode is the value that appears most frequently. That is also 900, which has five appearances.

All three of these numbers are measures of central tendency. They describe the "middle" or "center" of the data.

☞ Drill: Averages

Mean

> **DIRECTIONS**: Find the mean of each set of numbers.

1. 18, 25, and 32

(A) 3　　　(B) 25　　　(C) 50　　　(D) 75　　　(E) 150

2. $\frac{4}{9}, \frac{2}{3},$ and $\frac{5}{6}$

(A) $\frac{11}{18}$　　(B) $\frac{35}{54}$　　(C) $\frac{41}{54}$　　(D) $\frac{35}{18}$　　(E) $\frac{54}{18}$

3. 97, 102, 116, and 137

(A) 40　　　(B) 102　　　(C) 109　　　(D) 113　　　(E) 116

Median

> **DIRECTIONS**: Find the median value of each set of numbers.

4. 3, 8, and 6

(A) 3　　　(B) 6　　　(C) 8　　　(D) 17　　　(E) 20

5. 19, 15, 21, 27, and 12

(A) 19   (B) 15   (C) 21   (D) 27   (E) 94

6. $1\frac{2}{3}, 1\frac{7}{8}, 1\frac{3}{4}$, and $1\frac{5}{6}$

(A) $1\frac{30}{48}$ (B) $1\frac{2}{3}$ (C) $1\frac{3}{4}$ (D) $1\frac{19}{24}$ (E) $1\frac{21}{24}$

Mode

> **DIRECTIONS**: Find the mode(s) of each set of numbers.

7. 1, 3, 7, 4, 3, and 8

(A) 1   (B) 3   (C) 7   (D) 4   (E) None

8. 12, 19, 25, and 42

(A) 12   (B) 19   (C) 25   (D) 42   (E) None

9. 16, 14, 12, 16, 30, and 28

(A) 6   (B) 14   (C) 16   (D) $19.\overline{3}$ (E) None

II. ALGEBRA REVIEW

In algebra, letters or variables are used to represent numbers. A **variable** is defined as a placeholder, which can take on any of several values at a given time. A **constant**, on the other hand, is a symbol which takes on only one value at a given time. A **term** is a constant, a variable, or a combination of constants and variables. For example: 7.76, $3x$, xyz, $5z/_x$, $(0.99)x^2$ are terms. If a term is a combination of constants and variables, the constant part of the term is referred to as the **coefficient** of the variable. If a variable is written without a coefficient, the coefficient is assumed to be 1.

EXAMPLES

$3x^2$ y^3

coefficient: 3   coefficient: 1

variable: x variable: y

An **expression** is a collection of one or more terms. If the number of terms is greater than 1, the expression is said to be the sum of the terms.

EXAMPLES

$$9, 9xy, 6x + \frac{x}{3}, 8yz - 2x$$

An algebraic expression consisting of only one term is called a **monomial**; of two terms is called a **binomial**; of three terms is called a **trinomial**. In general, an algebraic expression consisting of two or more terms is called a **polynomial**.

OPERATIONS WITH POLYNOMIALS

A)   **Addition of polynomials** is achieved by combining like terms, terms which differ only in their numerical coefficients, e.g.,

$$P(x) = (x^2 - 3x + 5) + (4x^2 + 6x - 3)$$

Note that the parentheses are used to distinguish the polynomials.

By using the commutative and associative laws, we can rewrite $P(x)$ as:

$$P(x) = (x^2 + 4x^2) + (6x - 3x) + (5 - 3)$$

Using the distributive law, $ab + ac = a(b + c)$, yields:

$$(1 + 4)x^2 + (6 - 3)x + (5 - 3)$$

$$= 5x^2 + 3x + 2$$

B) **Subtraction of two polynomials** is achieved by first changing the sign of all terms in the expression which are being subtracted and then adding this result to the other expression, e.g.,

$(5x^2 + 4y^2 + 3z^2) - (4xy + 7y^2 - 3z^2 + 1)$

$= 5x^2 + 4y^2 + 3z^2 - 4xy - 7y^2 + 3z^2 - 1$

$= 5x^2 + (4y^2 - 7y^2) + (3z^2 + 3z^2) - 4xy - 1$

$= 5x^2 + (-3y^2) + 6z^2 - 4xy - 1$

C) **Multiplication of two or more polynomials** is achieved by using the laws of exponents, the rules of signs, and the commutative and associative laws of multiplication. Begin by multiplying the coefficients and then multiply the variables according to the laws of exponents, e.g.,

$(y^2) (5) (6y^2) (yz) (2z^2)$

$= (1) (5) (6) (1) (2) (y^2) (y^2) (yz) (z^2)$

$= 60[(y^2) (y^2) (y)] [(z) (z^2)]$

$= 60(y^5) (z^3)$

$= 60y^5z^3$

D) **Multiplication of a polynomial by a monomial** is achieved by multiplying each term of the polynomial by the monomial and combining the results, e.g.,

$(4x^2 + 3y) (6xz^2)$

$= (4x^2) (6xz^2) + (3y) (6xz^2)$

$= 24x^3z^2 + 18xyz^2$

E) **Multiplication of a polynomial by a polynomial** is achieved by multiplying each of the terms of one polynomial by each of the terms of the other polynomial and combining the result, e.g.,

$(5y + z + 1) (y^2 + 2y)$

$[(5y) (y^2) + (5y) (2y)] + [(z) (y^2) + (z) (2y)] + [(1) (y^2) + (1) (2y)]$

$= (5y^3 + 10y^2) + (y^2z + 2yz) + (y^2 + 2y)$

$= (5y^3) + (10y^2 + y^2) + (y^2z) + (2yz) + (2y)$

$= 5y^3 + 11y^2 + y^2z + 2yz + 2y$

F) **Division of a monomial by a monomial** is achieved by first dividing the constant coefficients and the variable factors separately, and then multiplying these quotients, e.g.,

$$6xyz^2 \div 2y^2z$$

$$= \left(\frac{6}{2}\right)\left(\frac{x}{1}\right)\left(\frac{y}{y^2}\right)\left(\frac{z^2}{z}\right)$$

$$= 3xy^{-1}z$$

$$= \frac{3xz}{y}$$

G) **Division of a polynomial by a polynomial** is achieved by following the given procedure, called long division.

Step 1: The terms of both the polynomials are arranged in order of ascending or descending powers of one variable.

Step 2: The first term of the dividend is divided by the first term of the divisor which gives the first term of the quotient.

Step 3: This first term of the quotient is multiplied by the entire divisor and the result is subtracted from the dividend.

Step 4: Using the remainder obtained from Step 3 as the new dividend, Steps 2 and 3 are repeated until the remainder is zero or the degree of the remainder is less than the degree of the divisor.

Step 5: The result is written as follows:

$$\frac{\text{dividend}}{\text{divisor}} = \text{quotient} + \frac{\text{remainder}}{\text{divisor}}$$

$\text{divisor} \neq 0$

e.g. $(2x^2 + x + 6) \div (x + 1)$

$$
\require{enclose}
\begin{array}{r}
2x - 1 \\
(x+1) \enclose{longdiv}{2x^2 + x + 6} \\
\underline{-(2x^2 + 2x)} \\
-x + 6 \\
\underline{-(-x-1)} \\
7
\end{array}
$$

The result is $(2x^2 + x + 6) \div (x + 1) = 2x - 1 + \dfrac{7}{x+1}$.

☞ Drill: Operations with Polynomials

Addition

DIRECTIONS: Add the following polynomials.

1. $9a^2b + 3c + 2a^2b + 5c =$

(A) $19a^2bc$ (B) $11a^2b + 8c$ (C) $11a^4b^2 + 8c^2$

(D) $19a^4b^2c^2$ (E) $12a^2b + 8c^2$

2. $14m^2n^3 + 6m^2n^3 + 3m^2n^3 =$

(A) $20m^2n^3$ (B) $23m^6n^9$ (C) $23m^2n^3$

(D) $32m^6n^9$ (E) $23m^8n^{27}$

3. $3x + 2y + 16x + 3z + 6y =$

(A) $19x + 8y$ (B) $19x + 11yz$ (C) $19x + 8y + 3z$

(D) $11xy + 19xz$ (E) $30xyz$

4. $(4d^2 + 7e^3 + 12f) + (3d^2 + 6e^3 + 2f) =$

(A) $23d^2e^3f$ (B) $33d^2e^2f$ (C) $33d^4e^6f^2$

(D) $7d^2 + 13e^3 + 14f$ (E) $23d^2 + 11e^3f$

5. $3ac^2 + 2b^2c + 7ac^2 + 2ac^2 + b^2c =$

(A) $12ac^2 + 3b^2c$ (B) $14ab^2c^2$ (C) $11ac^2 + 4ab^2c$

(D) $15ab^2c^2$ (E) $15a^2b^4c^4$

Subtraction

DIRECTIONS: Subtract the following polynomials.

6. $14m^2n - 6m^2n =$

(A) $20m^2n$ (B) $8m^2n$ (C) $8m$ (D) 8 (E) $8m^4n^2$

7. $3x^3y^2 - 4xz - 6x^3y^2 =$

(A) $-7x^2y^2z$ (B) $3x^3y^2 - 10x^4y^2z$ (C) $-3x^3y^2 - 4xz$

(D) $-x^2y^2z - 6x^3y^2$ (E) $-7xyz$

8. $9g^2 + 6h - 2g^2 - 5h =$

(A) $15g^2h - 7g^2h$ (B) $7g^4h^2$ (C) $11g^2 + 7h$

(D) $11g^2 - 7h^2$ (E) $7g^2 + h$

9. $7b^3 - 4c^2 - 6b^3 + 3c^2 =$

(A) $b^3 - c^2$ (B) $-11b^2 - 3c^2$ (C) $13b^3 - c$

(D) $7b - c$ (E) 0

10. $11q^2r - 4q^2r - 8q^2r =$

(A) $22q^2r$ (B) q^2r (C) $-2q^2r$

(D) $-q^2r$ (E) $2q^2r$

Multiplication

DIRECTIONS: Multiply the following polynomials.

11. $5p^2t \times 3p^2t =$

(A) $15p^2t$ (B) $15p^4t$ (C) $15p^4t^2$

(D) $8p^2t$ (E) $8p^4t^2$

12. $(2r + s)\,14r =$

(A) $28rs$ (B) $28r^2 + 14sr$ (C) $16r^2 + 14rs$

(D) $28r + 14sr$ (E) $17r^2s$

13. $(4m + p)\,(3m - 2p) =$

(A) $12m^2 + 5mp + 2p^2$ (B) $12m^2 - 2mp + 2p^2$ (C) $7m - p$

(D) $12m - 2p$ (E) $12m^2 - 5mp - 2p^2$

14. $(2a + b)\,(3a^2 + ab + b^2) =$

    (A) $6a^3 + 5a^2b + 3ab^2 + b^3$ (D) $3a^2 + 2a + ab + b + b^2$

    (B) $5a^3 + 3ab + b^3$ (E) $6a^3 + 3a^2b + 5ab^2 + b^3$

    (C) $6a^3 + 2a^2b + 2ab^2$

15. $(6t^2 + 2t + 1)\,3t =$

(A) $9t^2 + 5t + 3$ (B) $18t^2 + 6t + 3$ (C) $9t^3 + 6t^2 + 3t$

(D) $18t^3 + 6t^2 + 3t$ (E) $12t^3 + 6t^2 + 3t$

Division

DIRECTIONS: Divide the following polynomials.

16. $(x^2 + x - 6) \div (x - 2) =$

(A) $x - 3$　　(B) $x + 2$　　(C) $x + 3$　　(D) $x - 2$　　(E) $2x + 2$

17. $24b^4c^3 \div 6b^2c =$

(A) $3b^2c^2$　　(B) $4b^4c^3$　　(C) $4b^3c^2$　　(D) $4b^2c^2$　　(E) $3b^4c^3$

18. $(3p^2 + pq - 2q^2) \div (p + q) =$

(A) $3p + 2q$　　　　　(B) $2q - 3p$　　　　　(C) $3p - q$

(D) $2q + 3p$　　　　　(E) $3p - 2q$

19. $(y^3 - 2y^2 - y + 2) \div (y - 2) =$

(A) $(y - 1)^2$　　　　　(B) $y^2 - 1$　　　　　(C) $(y + 2)(y - 1)$

(D) $(y + 1)^2$　　　　　(E) $(y + 1)(y - 2)$

20. $(m^2 + m - 14) \div (m + 4) =$

(A) $m - 2$　　　　　(B) $m - 3 + \dfrac{-2}{m + 4}$　　　　　(C) $m - 3 + \dfrac{4}{m + 4}$

(D) $m - 3$　　　　　(E) $m - 2 + \dfrac{-3}{m + 4}$

SIMPLIFYING ALGEBRAIC EXPRESSIONS

To factor a polynomial completely is to find the prime factors of the polynomial with respect to a specified set of numbers.

The following concepts are important while factoring or simplifying expressions.

A) The factors of an algebraic expression consist of two or more algebraic expressions which, when multiplied together, produce the given algebraic expression.

B) A **prime factor** is a polynomial with no factors other than itself and 1. The **least common multiple (LCM)** for a set of numbers is the smallest quantity divisible by every number of the set. For algebraic expressions, the least common numerical coefficients for each of the given expressions will be a factor.

C)   The **greatest common factor (GCF)** for a set of numbers is the largest factor that is common to all members of the set.

D)   For algebraic expressions, the greatest common factor is the polynomial of highest degree and the largest numerical coefficient which is a factor of all the given expressions.

Some important formulas, useful for the factoring of polynomials, are listed below.

$$a(c + d) = ac + ad$$

$$(a + b)(a - b) = a^2 - b^2$$

$$(a + b)(a + b) = (a + b)^2 = a^2 + 2ab + b^2$$

$$(a - b)(a - b) = (a - b)^2 = a^2 - 2ab + b^2$$

$$(x + a)(x + b) = x^2 + (a + b)x + ab$$

$$(ax + b)(cx + d) = acx^2 + (ad + bc)x + bd$$

$$(a + b)(c + d) = ac + bc + ad + bd$$

$$(a + b)(a + b)(a + b) = (a + b)^3 = a^3 + 3a^2b + 3ab^2 + b^3$$

$$(a - b)(a - b)(a - b) = (a - b)^3 = a^3 - 3a^2b + 3ab^2 - b^3$$

$$(a - b)(a^2 + ab + b^2) = a^3 - b^3$$

$$(a + b)(a^2 - ab + b^2) = a^3 + b^3$$

$$(a + b + c)^2 = a^2 + b^2 + c^2 + 2ab + 2ac + 2bc$$

$$(a - b)(a^3 + a^2b + ab^2 + b^3) = a^4 - b^4$$

$$(a - b)(a^4 + a^3b + a^2b^2 + ab^3 + b^4) = a^5 - b^5$$

$$(a - b)(a^5 + a^4b + a^3b^2 + a^2b^3 + ab^4 + b^5) = a^6 - b^6$$

$$(a - b)(a^{n-1} + a^{n-2}b + a^{n-3}b^2 + \ldots + ab^{n-2} + b^{n-1}) = a^n - b^n$$

where n is any positive integer (1, 2, 3, 4, ...).

$$(a + b)(a^{n-1} - a^{n-2}b + a^{n-3}b^2 - \ldots - ab^{n-2} + b^{n-1}) = a^n + b^n$$

where n is any positive odd integer (1, 3, 5, 7, ...).

The procedure for factoring an algebraic expression completely is as follows:

Step 1: First find the greatest common factor if there is any. Then examine each factor remaining for greatest common factors.

Step 2: Continue factoring the factors obtained in Step 1 until all factors other than monomial factors are prime.

EXAMPLE

Factoring $4 - 16x^2$,

$$4 - 16x^2 = 4(1 - 4x^2) = 4(1 + 2x)(1 - 2x)$$

PROBLEM

Express each of the following as a single term.

(1) $3x^2 + 2x^2 - 4x^2$ (2) $5axy^2 - 7axy^2 - 3xy^2$

SOLUTION

(1) Factor x^2 in the expression.

$$3x^2 + 2x^2 - 4x^2 = (3 + 2 - 4)x^2 = 1x^2 = x^2$$

(2) Factor xy^2 in the expression and then factor a.

$$5axy^2 - 7axy^2 - 3xy^2 = (5a - 7a - 3)xy^2$$
$$= [(5 - 7)a - 3]xy^2$$
$$= (-2a - 3)xy^2$$

PROBLEM

Simplify $\dfrac{\dfrac{1}{x-1} - \dfrac{1}{x-2}}{\dfrac{1}{x-2} - \dfrac{1}{x-3}}$.

SOLUTION

Simplify the expression in the numerator by using the addition rule:

$$\frac{a}{b} + \frac{c}{d} = \frac{ad + bc}{bd}$$

Notice bd is the Least Common Denominator, LCD. We obtain

$$\frac{x - 2 - (x - 1)}{(x - 1)(x - 2)} = \frac{-1}{(x - 1)(x - 2)}$$

in the numerator.

Repeat this procedure for the expression in the denominator:

$$\frac{x-3-(x-2)}{(x-2)(x-3)} = \frac{-1}{(x-2)(x-3)}$$

We now have

$$\frac{\dfrac{-1}{(x-1)(x-2)}}{\dfrac{-1}{(x-2)(x-3)}}$$

which is simplified by inverting the fraction in the denominator and multiplying it by the numerator and cancelling like terms

$$\frac{-1}{(x-1)(x-2)} \times \frac{(x-2)(x-3)}{-1} = \frac{x-3}{x-1}.$$

☞ Drill: Simplifying Algebraic Expressions

> **DIRECTIONS**: Simplify the following expressions.

1. $16b^2 - 25z^2 =$

(A) $(4b - 5z)^2$ (B) $(4b + 5z)^2$ (C) $(4b - 5z)(4b + 5z)$

(D) $(16b - 25z)^2$ (E) $(5z - 4b)(5z + 4b)$

2. $x^2 - 2x - 8 =$

(A) $(x - 4)^2$ (B) $(x - 6)(x - 2)$ (C) $(x + 4)(x - 2)$

(D) $(x - 4)(x + 2)$ (E) $(x - 4)(x - 2)$

3. $2c^2 + 5cd - 3d^2 =$

(A) $(c - 3d)(c + 2d)$ (B) $(2c - d)(c + 3d)$ (C) $(c - d)(2c + 3d)$

(D) $(2c + d)(c + 3d)$ (E) $(2d + c)(c + 3d)$

4. $4t^3 - 20t =$

(A) $4t(t^2 - 5)$ (B) $4t^2(t - 20)$ (C) $4t(t + 4)(t - 5)$

(D) $2t(2t^2 - 10)$ (E) $12t(t - 20)$

5. $x^2 + xy - 2y^2 =$

(A) $(x - 2y)(x + y)$ (B) $(x - 2y)(x - y)$ (C) $(x + 2y)(x + y)$

(D) $(x + 2y)(x - y)$ (E) $(x - y)(2y - x)$

EQUATIONS

An **equation** is defined as a statement that two separate expressions are equal. A **solution** to an equation containing a single variable is a number that makes the equation true when it is substituted for the variable. For example, in the equation $3x = 18$, 6 is the solution since $3(6) = 18$. Depending on the equation, there can be more than one solution. Equations with the same solutions are said to be **equivalent equations**. An equation without a solution is said to have a solution set that is the **empty** or **null** set and is represented by ϕ.

Replacing an expression within an equation by an equivalent expression will result in a new equation with solutions equivalent to the original equation. Suppose we are given the equation

$$3x + y + x + 2y = 15.$$

By combining like terms we get

$$3x + y + x + 2y = 4x + 3y.$$

Since these two expressions are equivalent, we can substitute the simpler form into the equation to get

$$4x + 3y = 15$$

Performing the same operation to both sides of an equation by the same expression will result in a new equation that is equivalent to the original equation.

A) **Addition or subtraction**

$$y + 6 = 10$$

We can add (-6) to both sides

$$y + 6 + (-6) = 10 + (-6)$$

to get $y + 0 = 10 - 6 \rightarrow y = 4$

B) **Multiplication or division**

$$3x = 6$$
$$\frac{3x}{3} = \frac{6}{3}$$
$$x = 2$$

$3x = 6$ is equivalent to $x = 2$.

C) **Raising to a power**

$$a = x^2 y$$
$$a^2 = (x^2 y)^2$$
$$a^2 = 4^4 y^2$$

This can be applied to negative and fractional powers as well, e.g.,

$$x^2 = 3y^4$$

If we raise both sides to the -2 power, we get

$$(x^2)^{-2} = (3y^4)^{-2}$$
$$\frac{1}{(x^2)^2} = \frac{1}{(3y^4)^2}$$
$$\frac{1}{x^4} = \frac{1}{9y^8}$$

If we raise both sides to the $^1/_2$ power, which is the same as taking the square root, we get

$$(x^2)^{1/2} = (3y^4)^{1/2}$$
$$x = \pm\sqrt{3}y^2$$

D) The **reciprocal** of both sides of an equation are equivalent to the original equation. Note: The reciprocal of zero is undefined.

$$\frac{2x+y}{z} = \frac{5}{2} \qquad \frac{z}{2x+y} = \frac{2}{5}$$

PROBLEM

Solve for x, justifying each step.

$$3x - 8 = 7x + 8$$

SOLUTION

$$3x - 8 = 7x + 8$$

Add 8 to both sides: $\qquad 3x - 8 + 8 = 7x + 8 + 8$

Additive inverse property: $\qquad 3x + 0 = 7x + 16$

Additive identity property: $\qquad 3x = 7x + 16$

Add $(-7x)$ to both sides: $\qquad 3x - 7x = 7x + 16 - 7x$

Commute: $-4x$ $= 7x - 7x + 16$

Additive inverse property: $-4x = 0 + 16$

Additive identity property: $-4x = 16$

Divide both sides by -4: $x = {}^{16}\!/_{-4}$

$x = -4$

Check: Replacing x with -4 in the original equation:

$$3x - 8 = 7x + 8$$

$$3(-4) - 8 = 7(-4) + 8$$

$$-12 - 8 = -28 + 8$$

$$-20 = -20$$

Linear Equations

A linear equation with one unknown is one that can be put into the form $ax + b = 0$, where a and b are constants, $a \neq 0$.

To solve a linear equation means to transform it in the form $x = {}^{-b}\!/_{a}$.

A)   If the equation has unknowns on both sides of the equality, it is convenient to put similar terms on the same sides. Refer to the following example.

$$4x + 3 = 2x + 9$$

$$4x + 3 - 2x = 2x + 9 - 2x$$

$$(4x - 2x) + 3 = (2x - 2x) + 9$$

$$2x + 3 = 0 + 9$$

$$2x + 3 - 3 = 0 + 9 - 3$$

$$2x = 6$$

$$\frac{2x}{2} = \frac{6}{2}$$

$$x = 3$$

B)   If the equation appears in fractional form, it is necessary to transform it, using cross-multiplication, and then repeat the same procedure as in A). We obtain:

$$\frac{3x + 4}{3} \diagdown\!\!\!\!\diagup \frac{7x + 2}{5}$$

By using cross-multiplication we would obtain:

$$3(7x + 2) = 5(3x + 4).$$

This is equivalent to:

$$21x + 6 = 15x + 20,$$

which can be solved as in A).

$$21x + 6 = 15x + 20$$
$$21x - 15x + 6 = 15x - 15x + 20$$
$$6x + 6 - 6 = 20 - 6$$
$$6x = 14$$
$$x = \frac{14}{6}$$
$$x = \frac{7}{3}$$

C) If there are radicals in the equation, it is necessary to square both sides and then apply A).

$$\sqrt{3x + 1} = 5$$
$$(\sqrt{3x + 1})^2 = 5^2$$
$$3x + 1 = 25$$
$$3x + 1 - 1 = 25 - 1$$
$$3x = 24$$
$$x = \frac{24}{3}$$
$$x = 8$$

☞ Drill: Equations

DIRECTIONS: Solve for x.

1. $4x - 2 = 10$

(A) – 1   (B) 2   (C) 3   (D) 4   (E) 6

2. $7z + 1 - z = 2z - 7$

(A) – 2   (B) 0   (C) 1   (D) 2   (E) 3

3. $\frac{1}{3}b + 3 = \frac{1}{2}b$

(A) $\frac{1}{2}$ (B) 2 (C) $3\frac{3}{5}$ (D) 6 (E) 18

4. $0.4p + 1 = 0.7p - 2$

(A) 0.1 (B) 2 (C) 5 (D) 10 (E) 12

5. $4(3x + 2) - 11 = 3(3x - 2)$

(A) -3 (B) -1 (C) 2 (D) 3 (E) 7

TWO LINEAR EQUATIONS

Equations of the form $ax + by = c$, where a, b, c are constants and a, $b \neq 0$ are called **linear equations** with two unknown variables.

There are several ways to solve systems of linear equations with two variables.

Method 1: **Addition or subtraction**—If necessary, multiply the equations by numbers that will make the coefficients of one unknown in the resulting equations numerically equal. If the signs of equal coefficients are the same, subtract the equation, otherwise add.

The result is one equation with one unknown; we solve it and substitute the value into the other equations to find the unknown that we first eliminated.

Method 2: **Substitution**—Find the value of one unknown in terms of the other. Substitute this value in the other equation and solve.

Method 3: **Graph**—Graph both equations. The point of intersection of the drawn lines is a simultaneous solution for the equations, and its coordinates correspond to the answer that would be found analytically.

If the lines are parallel they have no simultaneous solution.

Dependent equations are equations that represent the same line; therefore, every point on the line of a dependent equation represents a solution. Since there is an infinite number of points on a line, there is an infinite number of simultaneous solutions, for example,

$$\begin{cases} 2x + y = 8 \\ 4x + 2y = 16 \end{cases}$$

These equations are dependent. Since they represent the same line, all points that satisfy either of the equations are solutions of the system.

A system of linear equations is consistent if there is only one solution for the system.

A system of linear equations is inconsistent if it does not have any solutions.

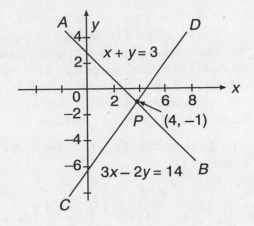

EXAMPLE

Find the point of intersection of the graphs of the equations as shown in the previous figure.

$$x + y = 3$$

$$3x - 2y = 14$$

To solve these linear equations, solve for y in terms of x. The equations will be in the form $y = mx + b$, where m is the slope and b is the intercept on the y-axis.

$$x + y = 3$$

Subtract x from both sides: $y = 3 - x$

Subtract $3x$ from both sides: $3x - 2y = 14$

Divide by -2: $-2y = 14 - 3x$

$$y = -7 + \frac{3}{2}x$$

The graphs of the linear functions, $y = 3 - x$ and $y = 7 + {}^3/_2 x$ can be determined by plotting only two points. For example, for $y = 3 - x$, let $x = 0$, then $y = 3$. Let $x = 1$, then $y = 2$. The two points on this first line are $(0, 3)$ and $(1, 2)$. For $y = -7 + {}^3/_2 x$, let $x = 0$, then $y = -7$. Let $x = 1$, then $y = -5^1/_2$. The two points on this second line are $(0, -7)$ and $(1, -5^1/_2)$.

To find the point of intersection P of

$$x + y = 3 \quad \text{and} \quad 3x - 2y = 14,$$

solve them algebraically. Multiply the first equation by 2. Add these two equations to eliminate the variable y.

$$
\begin{array}{r}
2x + 2y = 6 \\
3x - 2y = 14 \\
\hline
5x = 20
\end{array}
$$

Solve for x to obtain $x = 4$. Substitute this into $y = 3 - x$ to get $y = 3 - 4 = -1$. P is $(4, -1)$. AB is the graph of the first equation, and CD is the graph of the second equation. The point of intersection P of the two graphs is the only point on both lines. The coordinates of P satisfy both equations and represent the desired solution of the problem. From the graph, P seems to be the point $(4, -1)$. These coordinates satisfy both equations, and hence are the exact coordinates of the point of intersection of the two lines.

To show that $(4, -1)$ satisfies both equations, substitute this point into both equations.

$$x + y = 3 \qquad\qquad 3x - 2y = 14$$
$$4 + (-1) = 3 \qquad\qquad 3(4) - 2(-1) = 14$$
$$4 - 1 = 3 \qquad\qquad 12 + 2 = 14$$
$$3 = 3 \qquad\qquad 14 = 14$$

EXAMPLE

Solve the equations $2x + 3y = 6$ and $4x + 6y = 7$ simultaneously.

We have two equations and two unknowns,

$$2x + 3y = 6 \qquad (1)$$

and

$$4x + 6y = 7 \qquad (2)$$

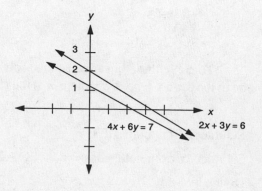

There are several methods to solve this problem. We have chosen to multiply each equation by a different number so that when the two equations are added, one of the variables drops out. Thus,

Multiply equation (1) by 2: $\qquad 4x + 6y = 12 \qquad\qquad\qquad (3)$

Multiply equation (2) by -1: $\qquad \underline{-4x - 6y = -7} \qquad\qquad\quad (4)$

Add equations (3) and (4): $\qquad\qquad 0 = 5$

We obtain a peculiar result!

Actually, what we have shown in this case is that if there were a simultaneous solution to the given equations, then 0 would equal 5. But the conclusion is impossible; therefore, there can be no simultaneous solution to these two equations, hence no point satisfying both.

The straight lines which are the graphs of these equations must be parallel if they never intersect, but not identical, which can be seen from the graph of these equations (see the accompanying diagram).

EXAMPLE

Solve the equations $2x + 3y = 6$ and $y = -({}^{2x}\!/_3) + 2$ simultaneously.

We have two equations and two unknowns.

$$2x + 3y = 6 \tag{1}$$

and

$$y = -\left(\frac{2x}{3}\right) + 2 \tag{2}$$

There are several methods of solution for this problem. Since equation (2) already gives us an expression for y, we use the method of substitution. Substitute $-({}^{2x}\!/_3) + 2$ for y in the first equation:

$$2x + 3(-\frac{2x}{3} + 2) = 6$$

Distribute: $\qquad\qquad\qquad 2x - 2x + 6 = 6$

$$6 = 6$$

The result $6 = 6$ is true, but indicates no solution. Actually, our work shows that no matter what real number x is, if y is determined by the second equation, then the first equation will always be satisfied.

The reason for this peculiarity may be seen if we take a closer look at the equation $y = -({}^{2x}\!/_3) + 2$. It is equivalent to $3y = -2x + 6$, or $2x + 3y = 6$.

In other words, the two equations are equivalent. Any pair of values of x and y which satisfies one satisfies the other.

It is hardly necessary to verify that in this case the graphs of the given equations are identical lines, and that there are an infinite number of simultaneous solutions of these equations.

A system of three linear equations in three unknowns is solved by eliminating one unknown from any two of the three equations and solving them. After finding two unknowns substitute them in any of the equations to find the third unknown.

PROBLEM

Solve the system

$$2x + 3y - 4z = -8 \tag{1}$$

$$x + y - 2z = -5 \tag{2}$$

$$7x - 2y + 5z = 4 \tag{3}$$

SOLUTION

We cannot eliminate any variable from two pairs of equations by a single multiplication. However, both x and z may be eliminated from equations (1) and (2) by multiplying equation (2) by -2. Then

$$2x + 3y - 4z = -8 \tag{1}$$

$$-2x - 2y + 4z = 10 \tag{4}$$

By addition, we have $y = 2$. Although we may now eliminate either x or z from another pair of equations, we can more conveniently substitute $y = 2$ in equations (2) and (3) to get two equations in two variables. Thus, making the substitution $y = 2$ in equations (2) and (3), we have

$$x - 2z = -7 \tag{5}$$

$$7x + 5z = 8 \tag{6}$$

Multiply equation (5) by 5 and multiply (6) by 2. Then add the two new equations. Then $x = -1$. Substitute x in either equation (5) or (6) to find z.

The solution of the system is $x = -1$, $y = 2$, and $z = 3$. Check by substitution.

A system of equations, as shown below, that has all constant terms b_1, b_2, ..., b_n equal to zero is said to be a homogeneous system.

$$\begin{cases} a_{11}x_1 + a_{12}x_2 + \ldots + a_{1n}x_m = b_1 \\ a_{21}x_1 + a_{22}x_2 + \ldots + a_{2n}x_m = b_2 \\ \vdots \quad\quad \vdots \quad\quad\quad \vdots \quad\quad \vdots \\ a_{n1}x_1 + a_{n2}x_2 + \ldots + a_{nn}x_m = b_n \end{cases}$$

A homogeneous system (one in which each variable can be replaced by a constant and the constant can be factored out) always has at least one solution which is called the trivial solution that is $x_1 = 0$, $x_2 = 0$, ..., $x_m = 0$.

For any given homogeneous system of equations, in which the number of variables is greater than or equal to the number of equations, there are non-trivial solutions.

Two systems of linear equations are said to be equivalent if and only if they have the same solution set.

☞ Drill: Two Linear Equations

> **DIRECTIONS**: Find the solution set for each pair of equations.

1. $3x + 4y = -2$
   $x - 6y = -8$

(A) $(2, -1)$ (B) $(1, -2)$ (C) $(-2, -1)$

(D) $(1, 2)$ (E) $(-2, 1)$

2. $2x + y = -10$
   $-2x - 4y = 4$

(A) $(6, -2)$ (B) $(-6, 2)$ (C) $(-2, 6)$

(D) $(2, 6)$ (E) $(-6, -2)$

3. $6x + 5y = -4$
   $3x - 3y = 9$

(A) $(1, -2)$ (B) $(1, 2)$ (C) $(2, -1)$

(D) $(-2, 1)$ (E) $(-1, 2)$

4. $4x + 3y = 9$
   $2x - 2y = 8$

(A) $(-3, 1)$ (B) $(1, -3)$ (C) $(3, 1)$

(D) $(3, -1)$ (E) $(-1, 3)$

5. $x + y = 7$
   $x = y - 3$

(A) $(5, 2)$ (B) $(-5, 2)$ (C) $(2, 5)$

(D) $(-2, 5)$ (E) $(2, -5)$

QUADRATIC EQUATIONS

A second degree equation in x of the type $ax^2 + bx + c = 0$, $a \neq 0$, a, b, and c are real numbers, is called a **quadratic equation.**

To solve a quadratic equation is to find values of x which satisfy $ax^2 + bx + c = 0$. These values of x are called **solutions,** or **roots,** of the equation.

A quadratic equation has a maximum of two roots. Methods of solving quadratic equations:

A) **Direct solution**: Given $x^2 - 9 = 0$.

   We can solve directly by isolating the variable x.

   $$x^2 = 9$$

   $$x = \pm 3$$

B) **Factoring**: Given a quadratic equation $ax^2 + bx + c = 0$, a, b, $c \neq 0$, to factor means to express it as the product $a(x - r_1)(x - r_2) = 0$, where r_1 and r_2 are the two roots.

   Some helpful hints to remember are:

   a) $r_1 + r_2 = -\dfrac{b}{a}$.

   b) $r_1 r_2 = \dfrac{c}{a}$.

   Given $x^2 - 5x + 4 = 0$.

   Since

   $$r_1 + r_2 = -\frac{b}{a} = -\frac{(-5)}{1} = 5,$$

   the possible solutions are $(3, 2)$, $(4, 1)$, and $(5, 0)$. Also

   $$r_1 r_2 = \frac{c}{a} = \frac{4}{1} = 4;$$

   this equation is satisfied only by the second pair, so $r_1 = 4$, $r_2 = 1$, and the factored form is $(x - 4)(x - 1) = 0$.

   If the coefficient of x^2 is not 1, it is necessary to divide the equation by this coefficient and then factor.

   Given $2x^2 - 12x + 16 = 0$.

   Dividing by 2, we obtain

   $$x^2 - 6x + 8 = 0.$$

   Since

   $$r_1 + r_2 = -\frac{b}{a} = 6,$$

   the possible solutions are $(6, 0)$, $(5, 1)$, $(4, 2)$, and $(3, 3)$. Also $r_1 r_2 = 8$, so the only possible answer is $(4, 2)$ and the expression $x^2 - 6x + 8 = 0$ can be factored as $(x - 4)(x - 2)$.

C) **Completing the square**: If it is difficult to factor the quadratic equation using the previous method, we can complete the square.

Given $x^2 - 12x + 8 = 0$.

We know that the two roots added up should be 12 because

$$r_1 + r_2 = -\frac{b}{a} = \frac{-(-12)}{1} = 12.$$

The possible roots are $(12, 0)$, $(11, 1)$, $(10, 2)$, $(9, 3)$, $(8, 4)$, $(7, 5)$, and $(6, 6)$.

But none of these satisfy $r_1 r_2 = 8$, so we cannot use (B).

To complete the square, it is necessary to isolate the constant term,

$$x^2 - 12x = -8.$$

Then take $^1/_2$ of the coefficient of x, square it and add to both sides.

$$x^2 - 12x + \left(\frac{-12}{2}\right)^2 = -8 + \left(\frac{-12}{2}\right)^2$$

$$x^2 - 12x + 36 = -8 + 36 = 28$$

Now we can use the previous method to factor the left side.

$$r_1 + r_2 = 12, r_1 r_2 = 36$$

is satisfied by the pair $(6, 6)$, so we have

$$(x - 6)^2 = 28.$$

Now extract the root of both sides and solve for x.

$$(x - 6) = \pm\sqrt{28} = \pm 2\sqrt{7}$$

$$x = \pm 2\sqrt{7} + 6$$

So the roots are

$$x = 2\sqrt{7} + 6, \ x = -2\sqrt{7} + 6.$$

PROBLEM

Solve the equation $x^2 + 8x + 15 = 0$.

SOLUTION

Since

$$(x + a)(x + b) = x^2 + bx + ax + ab$$

$$= x^2 + (a + b)x + ab,$$

we may factor the given equation,

$$0 = x^2 + 8x + 15,$$

replacing $a + b$ by 8 and ab by 15. Thus,

$$a + b = 8, \quad \text{and} \quad ab = 15.$$

We want the two numbers a and b whose sum is 8 and whose product is 15. We check all pairs of numbers whose product is 15.

(a) $1 \times 15 = 15$; thus, $a = 1$, $b = 15$, and $ab = 15$.

$1 + 15 = 16$; therefore, we reject these values because $a + b \neq 8$.

(b) $3 \times 5 = 15$; thus, $a = 3$, $b = 5$, and $ab = 15$.

$3 + 5 = 8$; therefore, $a + b = 8$, and we accept these values.

Hence, $x^2 + 8x + 15 = 0$ is equivalent to

$$0 = x^2 + (3 + 5)x + 3 \times 5 = (x + 3)(x + 5)$$

Hence, $x + 5 = 0$ or $x + 3 = 0$.

Since the product of these two numbers is zero, one of the numbers must be zero. Hence, $x = -5$, or $x = -3$, and the solution set is $x = \{-5, -3\}$.

Note that $x = -5$ or $x = -3$. We are certainly not making the statement that $x = -5$ and $x = -3$. Also, check that both these numbers do actually satisfy the given equations and hence are solutions.

Check: Replacing x by (-5) in the original equation:

$$x^2 + 8x + 15 = 0$$

$$(-5)^2 + 8(-5) + 15 = 0$$

$$25 - 40 + 15 = 0$$

$$-15 + 15 = 0$$

$$0 = 0$$

Replacing x by (-3) in the original equation:

$$x^2 + 8x + 15 = 0$$

$$(-3)^2 + 8(-3) + 15 = 0$$

$$9 - 24 + 15 = 0$$

$$-15 + 15 = 0$$

$$0 = 0$$

PROBLEM

> Solve the following equations by factoring.
>
> (1) $2x^2 + 3x = 0$ (2) $y^2 - 2y - 3 = y - 3$
>
> (3) $z^2 - 2z - 3 = 0$ (4) $2m^2 - 11m - 6 = 0$

SOLUTION

(1) $2x^2 + 3x = 0$. Factor out the common factor of x from the left side of the given equation.

$$x(2x + 3) = 0$$

Whenever a product $ab = 0$, where a and b are any two numbers, either $a = 0$ or $b = 0$. Then, either

$$x = 0 \quad \text{or} \quad 2x + 3 = 0$$
$$2x = -3$$
$$x = -\frac{3}{2}$$

Hence, the solution set to the original equation $2x^2 + 3x = 0$ is: $\{-3/2, 0\}$.

(2) $y^2 - 2y - 3 = y - 3$. Subtract $(y - 3)$ from both sides of the given equation.

$$y^2 - 2y - 3 - (y - 3) = y - 3 - (y - 3)$$
$$y^2 - 2y - 3 - y + 3 = y - 3 - y + 3$$
$$y^2 - 2y \cancel{-3} - y \cancel{+3} = \cancel{y} \cancel{-3} \cancel{-y} \cancel{+3}$$
$$y^2 - 3y = 0$$

Factor out a common factor of y from the left side of this equation:

$$y(y - 3) = 0$$

Thus, $y = 0$ or $y - 3 = 0$, $y = 3$.

Therefore, the solution set to the original equation $y^2 - 2y - 3 = y - 3$ is $\{0, 3\}$.

(3) $z^2 - 2z - 3 = 0$. Factor the original equation into a product of two polynomials.

$$z^2 - 2z - 3 = (z - 3)(z + 1) = 0$$

Hence,

$$(z - 3)(z + 1) = 0; \text{ and} \quad z - 3 = 0 \quad \text{or } z + 1 = 0$$
$$z = 3 \qquad\qquad z = -1$$

Therefore, the solution set to the original equation $z^2 - 2z - 3 = 0$ is $\{-1, 3\}$.

(4) $2m^2 - 11m - 6 = 0$. Factor the original equation into a product of two polynomials.

$$2m^2 - 11m - 6 = (2m + 1)(m - 6) = 0$$

Thus,

$$2m + 1 = 0 \quad \text{or} \quad m - 6 = 0$$

$$2m = -1 \qquad\qquad m = 6$$

$$m = -\frac{1}{2}$$

Therefore, the solution set to the original equation $2m^2 - 11m - 6 = 0$ is $\{-^1/_2, 6\}$.

☞ Drill: Quadratic Equations

DIRECTIONS: Solve for all values of *x*.

1. $x^2 - 2x - 8 = 0$

(A) 4 and −2   (B) 4 and 8   (C) 4

(D) −2 and 8   (E) −2

2. $x^2 + 2x - 3 = 0$

(A) −3 and 2   (B) 2 and 1   (C) 3 and 1

(D) −3 and 1   (E) −3

3. $x^2 - 7x = -10$

(A) −3 and 5   (B) 2 and 5   (C) 2

(D) −2 and −5   (E) 5

4. $x^2 - 8x + 16 = 0$

(A) 8 and 2   (B) 1 and 16   (C) 4

(D) −2 and 4   (E) 4 and −4

5. $3x^2 + 3x = 6$

(A) 3 and −6   (B) 2 and 3   (C) −3 and 2

(D) 1 and −3   (E) 1 and −2

ABSOLUTE VALUE EQUATIONS

The absolute value of a, $|a|$, is defined as

$|a| = a$ when $a > 0$,

$|a| = -a$ when $a < 0$,

$|a| = 0$ when $a = 0$.

When the definition of absolute value is applied to an equation, the quantity within the absolute value symbol is considered to have two values. This value can be either positive or negative before the absolute value is taken. As a result, each absolute value equation actually contains two separate equations.

When evaluating equations containing absolute values, proceed as follows:

EXAMPLE

$|5 - 3x| = 7$ is valid if either

$$5 - 3x = 7 \qquad \text{or} \qquad 5 - 3x = -7$$

$$-3x = 2 \qquad\qquad\qquad -3x = -12$$

$$x = -\frac{2}{3} \qquad\qquad\qquad x = 4$$

The solution set is therefore $x = (-^2/_3, 4)$.

Remember, the absolute value of a number cannot be negative. So, for the equation $|5x + 4| = -3$, there would be no solution.

☞ Drill: Absolute Value Equations

DIRECTIONS: Find the appropriate solutions.

1. $|4x - 2| = 6$

(A) -2 and -1 (B) -1 and 2 (C) 2

(D) $\dfrac{1}{2}$ and -2 (E) No solution

2. $\left| 3 - \dfrac{1}{2}y \right| = -7$

(A) -8 and 20 (B) 8 and -20 (C) 2 and -5

(D) 4 and -2 (E) No solution

3. $2|x+7|=12$

(A) -13 and -1 (B) -6 and 6 (C) -1 and 13

(D) 6 and -13 (E) No solution

4. $|5x|-7=3$

(A) 2 and 4 (B) $\dfrac{4}{5}$ and 3 (C) -2 and 2

(D) 2 (E) No solution

5. $\left|\dfrac{3}{4}m\right|=9$

(A) 24 and -16 (B) $\dfrac{4}{27}$ and $-\dfrac{4}{3}$ (C) $\dfrac{4}{3}$ and 12

(D) -12 and 12 (E) No solution

INEQUALITIES

An inequality is a statement where the value of one quantity or expression is greater than (>), less than (<), greater than or equal to (≥), less than or equal to (≤), or not equal to (≠) that of another.

EXAMPLE

$5 > 4$

The expression above means that the value of 5 is greater than the value of 4.

A **conditional inequality** is an inequality whose validity depends on the values of the variables in the sentence. That is, certain values of the variables will make the sentence true, and others will make it false.

$3 - y > 3 + y$

is a conditional inequality for the set of real numbers, since it is true for any replacement less than zero and false for all others.

$x + 5 > x + 2$

is an **absolute inequality** for the set of real numbers, meaning that for any real value x, the expression on the left is greater than the expression on the right.

$5y < 2y + y$

is inconsistent for the set of non-negative real numbers. For any y greater than 0 the sentence is always false. A sentence is inconsistent if it is always false when its variables assume allowable values.

The solution of a given inequality in one variable x consists of all values of x for which the inequality is true.

The graph of an inequality in one variable is represented by either a ray or a line segment on the real number line.

The endpoint is not a solution if the variable is strictly less than or greater than a particular value.

EXAMPLE

$x > 2$

2 is not a solution and should be represented as shown.

The endpoint is a solution if the variable is either (1) less than or equal to or (2) greater than or equal to a particular value.

EXAMPLE

$5 > x \geq 2$

In this case 2 is the solution and should be represented as shown.

Properties of Inequalities

If x and y are real numbers, then one and only one of the following statements is true.

$x > y, x = y,$ or $x < y.$

This is the order property of real numbers.

If a, b, and c are real numbers, the following are true:

A)   If $a < b$ and $b < c$ then $a < c$.

B)   If $a > b$ and $b > c$ then $a > c$.

This is the transitive property of inequalities.

If a, b, and c are real numbers and $a > b$, then $a + c > b + c$ and $a - c > b - c$. This is the **addition property of inequality**.

Two inequalities are said to have the same **sense** if their signs of inequality point in the same direction.

The sense of an inequality remains the same if both sides are multiplied or divided by the same positive real number.

EXAMPLE

$4 > 3$

If we multiply both sides by 5, we will obtain

$4 \times 5 > 3 \times 5$

$20 > 15$

The sense of the inequality does not change.

The sense of an inequality becomes opposite if each side is multiplied or divided by the same negative real number.

EXAMPLE

$4 > 3$

If we multiply both sides by -5, we would obtain

$4 \times -5 < 3 \times -5$

$-20 < -15$

The sense of the inequality becomes opposite.

If $a > b$ and a, b, and n are positive real numbers, then

$a^n > b^n$ and $a^{-n} < b^{-n}$

If $x > y$ and $q > p$, then $x + q > y + p$.

If $x > y > 0$ and $q > p > 0$, then $xq > yp$.

Inequalities that have the same solution set are called **equivalent inequalities**.

PROBLEM

Solve the inequality $2x + 5 > 9$.

SOLUTION

Add -5 to both sides: $\qquad 2x + 5 + (-5) > 9 + (-5)$

Additive inverse property: $\qquad 2x + 0 > 9 + (-5)$

Additive identity property: $\qquad 2x > 9 + (-5)$

Combine terms: $\qquad 2x > 4$

Multiply both sides by $\dfrac{1}{2}$: $\qquad \dfrac{1}{2}(2x) > \dfrac{1}{2} \times 4$

$$x > 2$$

The solution set is

$$X = \{x \mid 2x + 5 > 9\}$$
$$= \{x \mid x > 2\}$$

(that is all x, such that x is greater than 2).

☞ Drill: Inequalities

DIRECTIONS: Find the solution set for each inequality.

1. $3m + 2 < 7$

(A) $m \geq \dfrac{5}{3}$ (B) $m > 2$ (C) $m < 2$ (D) $m > 2$ (E) $m < \dfrac{5}{3}$

2. $\dfrac{1}{2}x - 3 \leq 1$

(A) $-4 \leq x \leq 8$ (B) $x \geq -8$ (C) $x \leq 8$

(D) $2 \leq x \leq 8$ (E) $x \geq 8$

3. $-3p + 1 \geq 16$

(A) $p \geq -5$ (B) $p \geq \dfrac{-17}{3}$ (C) $p \leq \dfrac{-17}{3}$

(D) $p \leq -5$ (E) $p \geq 5$

4. $-6 < \dfrac{2}{3}r + 6 \leq 2$

(A) $-6 < r \leq -3$ (B) $-18 < r \leq -6$ (C) $r \geq -6$

(D) $-2 < r \leq -\dfrac{4}{3}$ (E) $r \leq -6$

5. $0 < 2 - y < 6$

(A) $-4 < y < 2$ (B) $-4 < y < 0$ (C) $-4 < y < -2$

(D) $-2 < y < 4$ (E) $0 < y < 4$

RATIOS AND PROPORTIONS

The ratio of two numbers x and y written $x : y$ is the fraction x/y where $y \neq 0$. A ratio compares x to y by dividing one by the other. Therefore, in order to compare ratios, simply compare the fractions.

A proportion is an equality of two ratios. The laws of proportion are listed below.

If $\dfrac{a}{b} = \dfrac{c}{d}$, then

- (A) $ad = bc$

- (B) $\dfrac{b}{a} = \dfrac{d}{c}$

- (C) $\dfrac{a}{c} = \dfrac{b}{d}$

- (D) $\dfrac{a+b}{b} = \dfrac{c+d}{d}$

- (E) $\dfrac{a-b}{b} = \dfrac{c-d}{d}$

Given a proportion $a : b = c : d$, then a and d are called **extremes**, b and c are called the **means**, and d is called the fourth proportion to a, b, and c.

PROBLEM

Solve the proportion $\dfrac{x+1}{4} = \dfrac{15}{12}$.

SOLUTION

Cross-multiply to determine x; that is, multiply the numerator of the first fraction by the denominator of the second, and equate this to the product of the numerator of the second and the denominator of the first.

$$(x + 1)\, 12 = 4 \times 15$$

$$12x + 12 = 60$$

$$x = 4$$

☞ Drill: Ratios and Proportions

DIRECTIONS: Find the appropriate solutions.

1. Solve for *n*: $\dfrac{4}{n} = \dfrac{8}{5}$.

(A) 10   (B) 8   (C) 6   (D) 2.5   (E) 2

2. Solve for *n*: $\dfrac{2}{3} = \dfrac{n}{72}$.

(A) 12   (B) 48   (C) 64   (D) 56   (E) 24

3. Solve for *n*: $n : 12 = 3 : 4$.

(A) 8   (B) 1   (C) 9   (D) 4   (E) 10

4. Four out of every five students at West High take a mathematics course. If the enrollment at West is 785, how many students take mathematics?

(A) 628   (B) 157   (C) 705   (D) 655   (E) 247

5. At a factory, three out of every 1,000 parts produced are defective. In a day, the factory can produce 25,000 parts. How many of these parts would be defective?

(A) 7   (B) 75   (C) 750   (D) 7,500   (E) 75,000

6. A summer league softball team won 28 out of the 32 games they played. What is the ratio of games won to games played?

(A) 4 : 5   (B) 3 : 4   (C) 7 : 8   (D) 2 : 3   (E) 1 : 8

III. GEOMETRY AND TRIGONOMETRY REVIEW

POINTS, LINES, AND ANGLES

Geometry is built upon a series of undefined terms. These terms are those which we accept as known in order to define other undefined terms.

A) **Point**: Although we represent points on paper with small dots, a point has no size, thickness, or width.

B) **Line**: A line is a series of adjacent points which extends indefinitely. A line can be either curved or straight; however, unless otherwise stated, the term "line" refers to a straight line.

C) **Plane**: A plane is a collection of points lying on a flat surface, which extends indefinitely in all directions.

If A and B are two points on a line, then the **line segment** $\overline{AB}$ is the set of points on that line between A and B and including A and B, which are endpoints. The line segment is referred to as $\overline{AB}$.

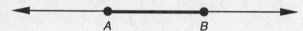

A **ray** is a series of points that lie to one side of a single endpoint.

PROBLEM

How many lines can be found that contain (a) one given point, (b) two given points, (c) three given points?

(a)

(b)

(c)

SOLUTION

(a)   *Given one point A*, there are an infinite number of distinct lines that contain the given point. To see this, consider line l_1 passing through point A. By rotating l_1 around A like the hands of a clock, we obtain different lines l_2, l_3, etc. Since we can rotate l_1 an infinite amount of ways, there are an infinite amount of lines containing A.

(b)   *Given two distinct points B and C*, there is one and only one straight line passing through both. To see this, consider all the lines containing point B: l_5, l_6, l_7, and l_8. Only l_5 contains both points B and C. Thus, there is only one line containing both points B and C. Since there is always at least one line containing two distinct points and never more than one, the line passing through the two points is said to be determined by the two points.

(c)   *Given three distinct points*, there may be one line or none. If a line exists that contains the three points, such as D, E, and F, then the points are said to be **colinear**. If no such line exists (as in the case of points G, H, and I), then the points are said to be **noncolinear**.

Intersection Lines and Angles

An **angle** is a collection of points which is the union of two rays having the same endpoint. An angle such as the one illustrated below can be referred to in any of the following ways:

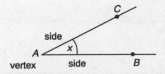

A)   by a capital letter which names its vertex, i.e., $\angle A$;

B)   by a lowercase letter or number placed inside the angle, i.e., $\angle x$;

C)   by three capital letters, where the middle letter is the vertex and the other two letters are not on the same ray, i.e., $\angle CAB$ or $\angle BAC$, both of which represent the angle illustrated in the figure.

Types of Angles

A)   **Vertical angles** are formed when two lines intersect. These angles are equal.

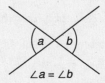

281

B) **Adjacent angles** are two angles with a common vertex and a common side, but no common interior points. In the following figure, ∠ *DAC* and ∠ *BAC* are adjacent angles. ∠ *DAB* and ∠ *BAC* are not.

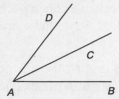

C) A **right angle** is an angle whose measure is 90°.

D) An **acute angle** is an angle whose measure is larger than 0° but less than 90°.

E) An **obtuse angle** is an angle whose measure is larger than 90° but less than 180°.

F) A **straight angle** is an angle whose measure is 180°. Such an angle is, in fact, a straight line.

G) A **reflex angle** is an angle whose measure is greater than 180° but less than 360°.

H) **Complimentary angles** are two angles whose measures total 90°.

I) **Supplementary angles** are two angles whose measures total 180°.

J) **Congruent angles** are angles of equal measure.

PROBLEM

In the figure, we are given $\overline{AB}$ and triangle *ABC*. We are told that the measure of ∠ 1 is five times the measure of ∠ 2. Determine the measures of ∠ 1 and ∠ 2.

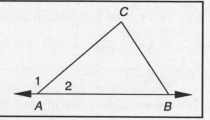

SOLUTION

Since ∠ 1 and ∠ 2 are adjacent angles whose non-common sides lie on a straight line, they are, by definition, supplementary. As supplements, their measures must total 180°.

If we let x = the measure of ∠ 2, then $5x$ = the measure of ∠ 1.

To determine the respective angle measures, set $x + 5x = 180$ and solve for x. $6x = 180$. Therefore, $x = 30$ and $5x = 150$.

Therefore, the measure of ∠ 1 = 150 and the measure of ∠ 2 = 30.

PERPENDICULAR LINES

Two lines are said to be **perpendicular** if they intersect and form right angles. The symbol for perpendicular (or, is therefore perpendicular to) is ⊥; $\overline{AB}$ is perpendicular to $\overline{CD}$ is written $\overline{AB} \perp \overline{CD}$.

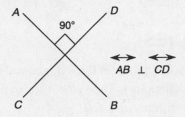

PROBLEM

We are given straight lines $\overline{AB}$ and $\overline{CD}$ intersecting at point P. $\overline{PR} \perp \overline{AB}$ and the measure of ∠ APD is 170°. Find the measures of ∠ 1, ∠ 2, ∠ 3, and ∠ 4.

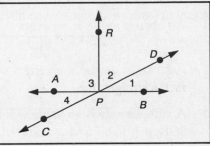

SOLUTION

This problem will involve making use of several of the properties of supplementary and vertical angles, as well as perpendicular lines.

∠ APD and ∠ 1 are adjacent angles whose non-common sides lie on a straight line, $\overline{AB}$. Therefore, they are supplements and their measures total 180°.

$$m \angle APD + m \angle 1 = 180°.$$

We know $m \angle APD = 170°$. Therefore, by substitution, $170° + m \angle 1 = 180°$. This implies $m \angle 1 = 10°$.

∠ 1 and ∠ 4 are vertical angles because they are formed by the intersection of two straight lines, $\overline{CD}$ and $\overline{AB}$, and their sides form two pairs of opposite rays. As vertical angles, they are, by theorem, of equal measure. Since $m \angle 1 = 10°$, then $m \angle 4 = 10°$.

Since $\overline{PR} \perp \overline{CD}$, at their intersection the angles formed must be right angles. Therefore, ∠ 3 is a right angle and its measure is 90°. $m \angle 3 = 90°$.

The figure shows us that ∠ APD is composed of ∠ 3 and ∠ 2. Since the measure of the whole must be equal to the sum of the measures of its parts, $m \angle APD = m \angle 3 + m \angle 2$. We know the $m \angle APD = 170°$ and $m \angle 3 = 90°$, therefore, by substitution, we can solve for $m \angle 2$, our last unknown.

$$170° = 90° + m \angle 2$$

$$80° = m \angle 2$$

Therefore,　　$m \angle 1 = 10°$,　　　　$m \angle 2 = 80°$,

　　　　　　$m \angle 3 = 90°$,　　　　$m \angle 4 = 10°$.

PARALLEL LINES

Two lines are called **parallel lines** if, and only if, they are in the same plane (coplanar) and do not intersect. The symbol for parallel, or is parallel to, is $\parallel$; $\overline{AB}$ is parallel to $\overline{CD}$ is written $\overline{AB} \parallel \overline{CD}$.

The distance between two parallel lines is the length of the perpendicular segment from any point on one line to the other line.

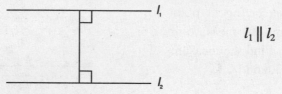

$l_1 \parallel l_2$

Given a line l and a point P not on line l, there is one and only one line through point P that is parallel to line l.

Two coplanar lines are either intersecting lines or parallel lines.

If two (or more) lines are perpendicular to the same line, then they are parallel to each other.

If $l_1 \perp l_0$ and $l_2 \perp l_0$, then $l_1 \parallel l_2$.

If two lines are cut by a transversal (a line intersecting two or more other lines) so that alternate interior angles are equal, the lines are parallel.

If $\angle \alpha = \angle \beta$, then $l_1 \parallel l_2$.

If two lines are parallel to the same line, then they are parallel to each other.

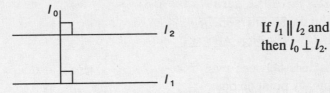

If $l_1 \parallel l_0$ and $l_2 \parallel l_0$, then $l_1 \parallel l_2$.

If a line is perpendicular to one of two parallel lines, then it is perpendicular to the other line, too.

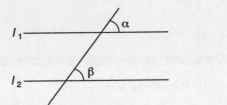

If $l_1 \parallel l_2$ and $l_1 \perp l_0$, then $l_0 \perp l_2$.

If two lines being cut by a transversal form congruent corresponding angles, then the two lines are parallel.

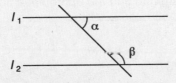

If $\angle \alpha = \angle \beta$, then $l_1 \parallel l_2$.

If two lines being cut by a transversal form interior angles on the same side of the transversal that are supplementary, then the two lines are parallel.

If $m \angle \alpha + m \angle \beta = 180°$, then $l_1 \parallel l_2$.

If a line is parallel to one of two parallel lines, it is also parallel to the other line.

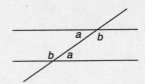

If $l_1 \parallel l_2$ and $l_0 \parallel l_1$, then $l_0 \parallel l_2$.

If two parallel lines are cut by a transversal, then:

A)   The alternate interior angles are congruent.

B) The corresponding angles are congruent.

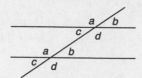

C) The consecutive interior angles are supplementary.

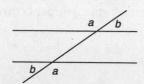

D) The alternate exterior angles are congruent.

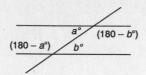

☞ Drill: Points, Lines, and Angles

Intersecting Lines

DIRECTIONS: Refer to the diagram and find the appropriate solution.

1. Find a.

(A) 38°   (B) 68°   (C) 782°

(D) 90°   (E) 112°

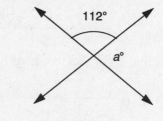

2. Find x.

(A) 8   (B) 11.75   (C) 21

(D) 22   (E) 32

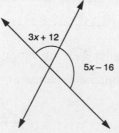

3. Find z.

    (A) 29°   (B) 54°   (C) 61°

    (D) 88°   (E) 92°

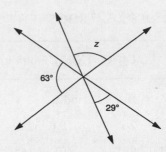

Perpendicular Lines

DIRECTIONS: Refer to the diagram and find the appropriate solution.

4. $\overrightarrow{BA} \perp \overrightarrow{BC}$ and $m \angle DBC = 53°$. Find $m \angle ABD$.

    (A) 27°   (B) 33°   (C) 37°

    (D) 53°   (E) 90°

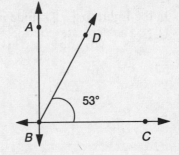

5. $m \angle 1 = 90°$. Find $m \angle 2$.

    (A) 80°   (B) 90°   (C) 100°

    (D) 135°   (E) 180°

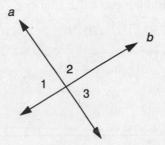

6. $\overline{CD} \perp \overline{EF}$. If $m \angle 1 = 2x$, $m \angle 2 = 30°$, and $m \angle 3 = x$, find x.

    (A) 5°   (B) 10°   (C) 12°

    (D) 20°   (E) 25°

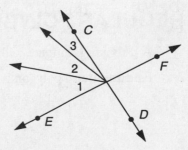

Parallel Lines

DIRECTIONS: Refer to the diagram and find the appropriate solution.

---

7. If $a \parallel b$, find z.

(A) 26°   (B) 32°   (C) 64°

(D) 86°   (E) 116°

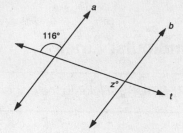

8. In the figure, $p \parallel q \parallel r$. Find $m \angle 7$.

(A) 27°   (B) 33°   (C) 47°

(D) 57°   (E) 64°

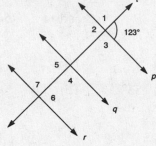

9. If $a \parallel b$ and $c \parallel d$, find $m \angle 5$.

(A) 55°   (B) 65°   (C) 75°

(D) 95°   (E) 125°

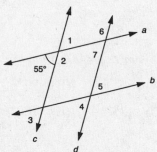

REGULAR POLYGONS (CONVEX)

A **polygon** is a figure with the same number of sides as angles.

An **equilateral polygon** is a polygon all of whose sides are of equal measure.

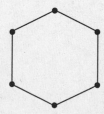

An **equiangular polygon** is a polygon all of whose angles are of equal measure.

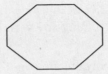

A **regular polygon** is a polygon that is both equilateral and equiangular.

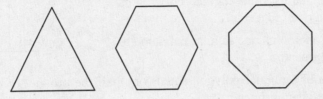

PROBLEM

Each interior angle of a regular polygon contains 120°. How many sides does the polygon have?

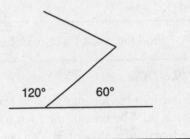

SOLUTION

At each vertex of a polygon, the exterior angle is supplementary to the interior angle, as shown in the diagram.

Since we are told that the interior angles measure 120°, we can deduce that the exterior angle measures 60°.

Each exterior angle of a regular polygon of n sides measure $\frac{360°}{n}$ degrees. We know that each exterior angle measures 60°, and, therefore, by setting $\frac{360°}{n}$ equal to 60°, we can determine the number of sides in the polygon. The calculation is as follows:

$$\frac{360°}{n} = 60°$$

$$60°n = 360°$$

$$n = 6$$

Therefore, the regular polygon, with interior angles of 120°, has six sides and is called a hexagon.

The area of a regular polygon can be determined by using the **apothem** and **radius** of the polygon. The apothem (a) of a regular polygon is the segment from the center of the polygon perpendicular to a side of the polygon. The radius (r) of a regular polygon is the segment joining any vertex of a regular polygon with the center of that polygon.

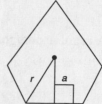

(1) All radii of a regular polygon are congruent.

(2) The radius of a regular polygon is congruent to a side.

(3) All apothems of a regular polygon are congruent.

The **area** of a regular polygon equals one-half the product of the length of the apothem and the perimeter.

$$\text{Area} = \frac{1}{2}\, a \times p$$

PROBLEM

Find the area of a regular hexagon if one side has length 6.

SOLUTION

Since the length of a side equals 6, the radius also equals 6 and the perimeter equals 36. The base of the right triangle, formed by the radius and apothem, is half the length of a side, or 3. You can find the length of the apothem by using what is known as the Pythagorean Theorem (discussed further in the next section).

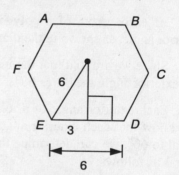

$$a^2 + b^2 = c^2$$
$$a^2 + (3)^2 = (6)^2$$
$$a^2 = 36 - 9$$
$$a^2 = 27$$
$$a = 3\sqrt{3}$$

The apothem equals $3\sqrt{3}$. Therefore, the area of the hexagon

$$= \frac{1}{2}\, a \times p$$
$$= \frac{1}{2}\, (3\sqrt{3})\,(36)$$
$$= 54\sqrt{3}$$

☞ Drill: Regular Polygons

Angle Measures

> **DIRECTIONS**: Find the appropriate solution.

1. Find the measure of an interior angle of a regular pentagon.

(A) 55°   (B) 72°   (C) 90°   (D) 108°   (E) 540°

2. Find the sum of the measures of the exterior angles of a regular triangle.

(A) 90°   (B) 115°   (C) 180°   (D) 250°   (E) 360°

Area(s) and Perimeter(s)

> **DIRECTIONS**: Find the appropriate solution.

3. A regular triangle has sides of 24 mm. If the apothem is $4\sqrt{3}$ mm, find the area of the triangle.

(A) 72 mm^2 (B) $96\sqrt{3}$ mm^2 (C) 144 mm^2

(D) $144\sqrt{3}$ mm^2 (E) 576 mm^2

4. Find the area of a regular hexagon with sides of 4 cm.

(A) $12\sqrt{3}$ cm^2 (B) 24 cm^2 (C) $24\sqrt{3}$ cm^2

(D) 48 cm^2 (E) $48\sqrt{3}$ cm^2

5. Find the area of a regular decagon with sides of length 6 cm and an apothem of length 9.2 cm.

(A) 55.2 cm^2 (B) 60 cm^2 (C) 138 cm^2

(D) 138.3 cm^2 (E) 276 cm^2

TRIANGLES

A closed three-sided geometric figure is called a **triangle**. The points of the intersection of the sides of a triangle are called the **vertices** of the triangle.

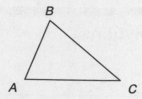

The **perimeter** of a triangle is the sum of the measures of the sides of the triangle.

A triangle with no equal sides is called a **scalene triangle**.

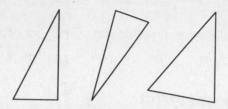

A triangle having at least two equal sides is called an **isosceles triangle**. The third side is called the **base** of the triangle.

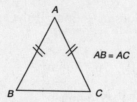

A side of a triangle is a line segment whose endpoints are the vertices of two angles of the triangle.

An **interior angle** of a triangle is an angle formed by two sides and includes the third side within its collection of points.

An **equilateral triangle** is a triangle having three equal sides. $\overline{AB} = \overline{AC} = \overline{BC}$.

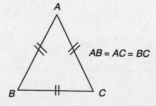

The sum of the measures of the interior angles of a triangle is 180°.

A triangle with one obtuse angle greater than 90° is called an **obtuse triangle**.

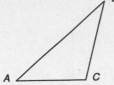

An **acute triangle** is a triangle with three acute angles (less than 90°).

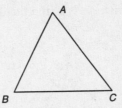

A triangle with a right angle is called a **right triangle**. The side opposite the right angle in a right triangle is called the hypotenuse of the right triangle. The other two sides are called arms or legs of the right triangle.

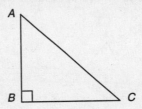

An **altitude** of a triangle is a line segment from a vertex of the triangle perpendicular to the opposite side.

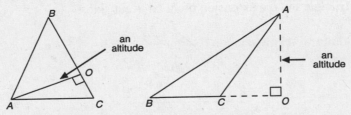

A line segment connecting a vertex of a triangle and the midpoint of the opposite side is called a **median** of the triangle.

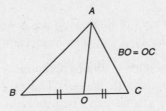

A line that bisects and is perpendicular to a side of a triangle is called a **perpendicular bisector** of that side.

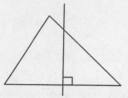

An **angle bisector** of a triangle is a line that bisects an angle and extends to the opposite side of the triangle.

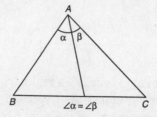

The line segment that joins the midpoints of two sides of a triangle is called a **midline** of the triangle.

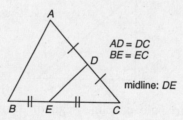

An **exterior angle** of a triangle is an angle formed outside a triangle by one side of the triangle and the extension of an adjacent side.

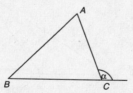

A triangle whose three interior angles have equal measure (60° each) is said to be **equiangular**.

Three or more lines (or rays or segments) are concurrent if there exists one point common to all of them, that is, if they all intersect at the same point.

In a right triangle, the square of the hypotenuse (c) is equal to the sum of the squares of the other two sides (a and b). This is commonly known as the theorem of Pythagoras or the Pythagorean Theorem: $a^2 + b^2 = c^2$.

PROBLEM

The measure of the vertex angle of an isosceles triangle exceeds the measurement of each base angle by 30°. Find the value of each angle of the triangle.

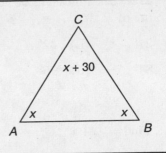

SOLUTION

We know that the sum of the values of the angles of a triangle is 180°. In an isosceles triangle, the angles opposite the congruent sides (the base angles) are, themselves, congruent and of equal value.

Therefore,

(1) Let x = the measure of each base angle.

(2) Then $x + 30$ = the measure of the vertex angle.

We can solve for x algebraically by keeping in mind the sum of all the measures will be 180°.

$$x + x + (x + 30) = 180$$
$$3x + 30 = 180$$
$$3x = 150$$
$$x = 50$$

Therefore, the base angles each measure 50°, and the vertex angle measures 80°.

☞ Drill: Triangles

Angle Measures

DIRECTIONS: Refer to the diagram and find the appropriate solution.

1. In $\triangle PQR$, $\angle Q$ is a right angle. Find $m \angle R$.

(A) 27°   (B) 33°   (C) 54°

(D) 67°   (E) 157°

2. Δ *MNO* is isosceles. If the vertex angle, $\angle N$, has a measure of 96°, find the measure of $\angle M$.

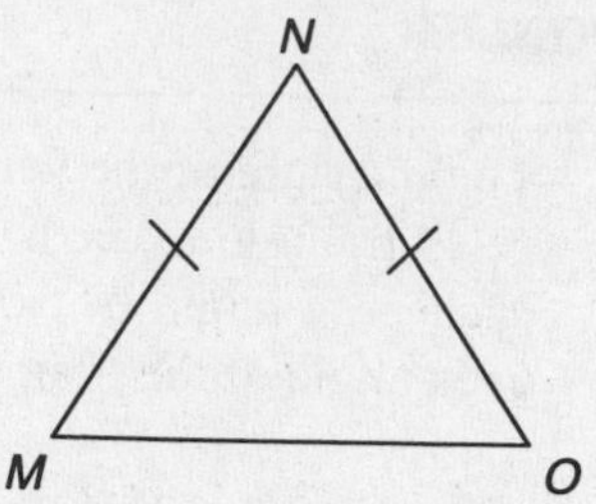

(A) 21° (B) 42° (C) 64°

(D) 84° (E) 96°

3. Find x.

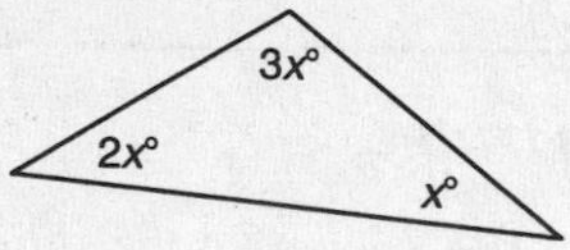

(A) 15° (B) 25° (C) 30°

(D) 45° (E) 90°

Similar Triangles

DIRECTIONS: Refer to the diagram and find the appropriate solution.

4. The two triangles shown are similar. Find b.

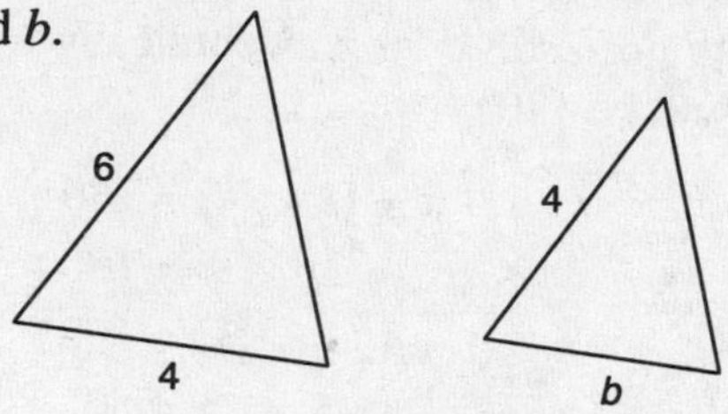

(A) $2\frac{2}{3}$ (B) 3 (C) 4

(D) 16 (E) 24

5. The two triangles shown are similar. Find a and b.

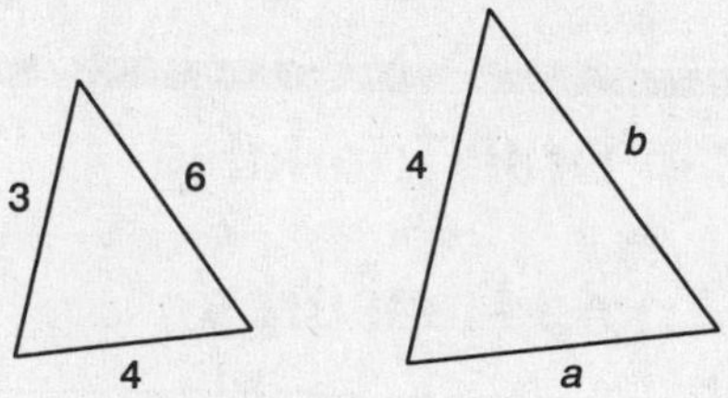

(A) 5 and 10 (B) 4 and 8

(C) $4\frac{2}{3}$ and $7\frac{1}{3}$ (D) 5 and 8

(E) $5\frac{1}{3}$ and 8

Area

DIRECTIONS: Refer to the diagram and find the appropriate solution.

---

6. Find the area of △ *MNO*.

(A) 22   (B) 49   (C) 56

(D) 84   (E) 112

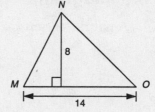

7. Find the area of △ *PQR*.

(A) 31.5   (B) 38.5   (C) 53

(D) 77   (E) 82.5

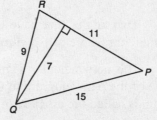

8. Find the area of △ *STU*.

(A) $4\sqrt{2}$ (C) $12\sqrt{2}$ (E) $32\sqrt{2}$

(B) $8\sqrt{2}$ (D) $16\sqrt{2}$

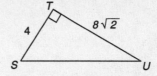

9. Find the area of △ *ABC*.

(A) 54 cm²   (B) 81 cm²   (C) 108 cm²

(D) 135 cm²   (E) 180 cm²

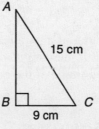

10. Find the area of △ *XYZ*.

(A) 20 cm²   (B) 50 cm²

(C) $50\sqrt{2}$ cm²   (D) 100 cm²

(E) 200 cm²

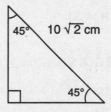

QUADRILATERALS

A **quadrilateral** is a polygon with four sides.

Parallelograms

A **parallelogram** is a quadrilateral whose opposite sides are parallel.

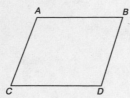

Two angles that have their vertices at the endpoints of the same side of a parallelogram are called **consecutive angles**.

The perpendicular segment connecting any point of a line containing one side of the parallelogram to the line containing the opposite side of the parallelogram is called the **altitude** of the parallelogram.

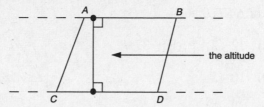

A diagonal of a polygon is a line segment joining any two non-consecutive vertices.

The area of a parallelogram is given by the formula $A = bh$, where b is the base and h is the height drawn perpendicular to that base. Note that the height equals the altitude of the parallelogram.

$A = bh$

$A = (10)(3)$

$A = 30$

Rectangles

A **rectangle** is a parallelogram with right angles.

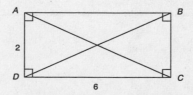

The diagonals of a rectangle are equal.

If the diagonals of a parallelogram are equal, the parallelogram is a rectangle.

If a quadrilateral has four right angles, then it is a rectangle.

The area of a rectangle is given by the formula $A = lw$, where l is the length and w is the width.

$A = lw$

$A = (3)(10)$

$A = 30$

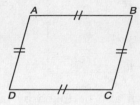

3

10

Rhombi

A **rhombus** is a parallelogram which has two adjacent sides that are equal.

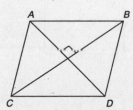

All sides of a rhombus are equal.

The diagonals of a rhombus are perpendicular to each other.

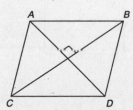

The diagonals of a rhombus bisect the angles of the rhombus.

If the diagonals of a parallelogram are perpendicular, the parallelogram is a rhombus.

If a quadrilateral has four equal sides, then it is a rhombus.

A parallelogram is a rhombus if either diagonal of the parallelogram bisects the angles of the vertices it joins.

Squares

A **square** is a rhombus with a right angle.

A square is an equilateral quadrilateral.

A square has all the properties of parallelograms and rectangles.

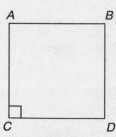

A rhombus is a square if one of its interior angles is a right angle.

In a square, the measure of either diagonal can be calculated by multiplying the length of any side by the square root of 2.

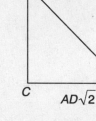

The area of a square is given by the formula $A = s^2$, where s is the side of the square. Since all sides of a square are equal, it does not matter which side is used.

$A = s^2$

$A = 6^2$

$A = 36$

6

The area of a square can also be found by taking $1/2$ the product of the length of the diagonal squared.

$A = \dfrac{1}{2}d^2$

$A = \dfrac{1}{2}(8)^2$

$A = 32$

8

Trapezoids

A **trapezoid** is a quadrilateral with two and only two sides parallel. The parallel sides of a trapezoid are called **bases**.

The **median** of a trapezoid is the line joining the midpoints of the non-parallel sides.

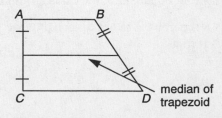

median of trapezoid

The perpendicular segment connecting any point in the line containing one base of the trapezoid to the line containing the other base is the **altitude** of the trapezoid.

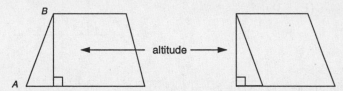

An **isosceles trapezoid** is a trapezoid whose non-parallel sides are equal. A pair of angles including only one of the parallel sides is called **a pair of base angles**.

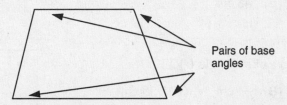

Pairs of base angles

The median of a trapezoid is parallel to the bases and equal to one-half their sum.

The base angles of an isosceles trapezoid are equal.

The diagonals of an isosceles trapezoid are equal.

The opposite angles of an isosceles trapezoid are supplementary.

☞ Drill: Quadrilaterals

Parallelograms, Rectangles, Rhombi, Squares, Trapezoids

> **DIRECTIONS**: Refer to the diagram and find the appropriate solution.

1. Quadrilateral *ABCD* is a parallelogram. If $m \angle B = 6x + 2$ and $m \angle D = 98$, find x.

   (A) 12 (B) 16 (C) $16\frac{2}{3}$

   (D) 18 (E) 20

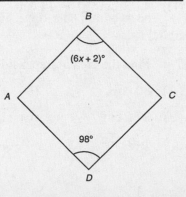

2. Find the area of parallelogram *STUV*.

    (A) 56   (B) 90   (C) 108

    (D) 162   (E) 180

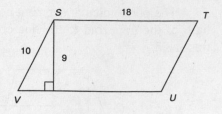

3. In rectangle *ABCD*, $\overline{AD}$ = 6 cm and $\overline{DC}$ = 8 cm. Find the length of the diagonal $\overline{AC}$.

    (A) 10 cm   (B) 12 cm   (C) 20 cm

    (D) 28 cm   (E) 48 cm

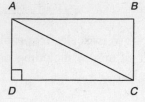

4. Find the area of rectangle *UVXY*.

    (A) 17 cm^2 (B) 34 cm^2 (C) 35 cm^2

    (D) 70 cm^2 (E) 140 cm^2

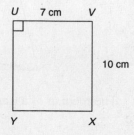

5. Find the length of $\overline{BO}$ in rectangle *BCDE* if the diagonal $\overline{EC}$ is 17 mm.

    (A) 6.55 mm   (B) 8 mm   (C) 8.5 mm

    (D) 17 mm   (E) 34 mm

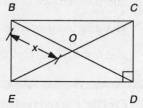

6. In rhombus *GHIJ*, $\overline{GI}$ = 6 cm and $\overline{HJ}$ = 8 cm. Find the length of $\overline{GH}$.

    (A) 3 cm   (B) 4 cm   (C) 5 cm

    (D) $4\sqrt{3}$ cm   (E) 14 cm

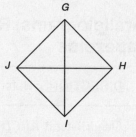

7. Find the area of trapezoid *RSTU*.

    (A) 80 cm^2 (D) 147.5 cm^2

    (B) 87.5 cm^2 (E) 175 cm^2

    (C) 140 cm^2

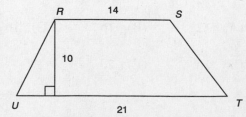

8. *ABCD* is an isosceles trapezoid. Find the perimeter.

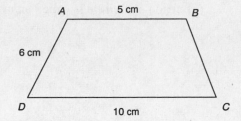

(A) 21 cm

(B) 27 cm

(C) 30 cm

(D) 50 cm

(E) 54 cm

9. Find the area of trapezoid *MNOP*.

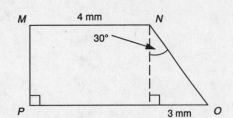

(A) $(17 + 3\sqrt{3})$ mm^2

(B) $\dfrac{33}{2}$ mm^2

(C) $\dfrac{33\sqrt{2}}{2}$ mm^2

(D) 33 mm^2

(E) $33\sqrt{3}$ mm^2

10. Trapezoid *XYZW* is isosceles. If $m \angle W = 58°$ and $m \angle Z = (4x - 6)$, find $x°$.

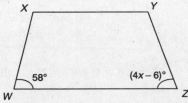

(A) 8°

(B) 12°

(C) 13°

(D) 16°

(E) 58°

CIRCLES

A **circle** is a set of points in the same plane equidistant from a fixed point, called its center.

A **radius** of a circle is a line segment drawn from the center of the circle to any point on the circle.

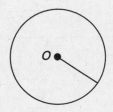

A portion of a circle is called an **arc** of the circle.

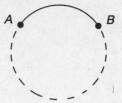

A line that intersects a circle in two points is called a **secant.**

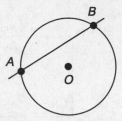

A line segment joining two points on a circle is called a **chord** of the circle.

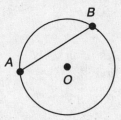

A chord that passes through the center of the circle is called a **diameter** of the circle.

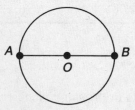

The line passing through the centers of two (or more) circles is called the **line of centers.**

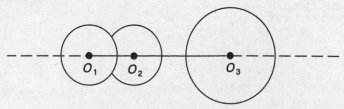

An angle whose vertex is on the circle and whose sides are chords of the circle is called an **inscribed angle**.

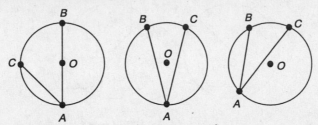

An angle whose vertex is at the center of a circle and whose sides are radii is called a **central angle.**

The measure of a minor arc is the measure of the central angle that intercepts that arc.

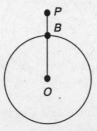

$$m \stackrel{\frown}{AB} = \alpha = m \angle AOB$$

The distance from a point P to a given circle is the distance from that point to the point where the circle intersects with a line segment with endpoints at the center of the circle and point P.

The distance of point P to the diagrammed circle with center O is the line segment $\overline{PB}$ of line segment $\overline{PO}$.

A line that has one and only one point of intersection with a circle is called a tangent to that circle, while their common point is called a **point of tangency**.

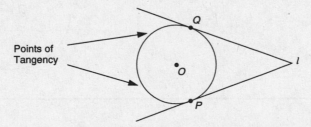

Congruent circles are circles whose radii are congruent.

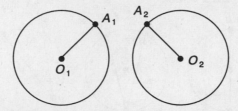

If $O_1A_1 \cong O_2A_2$, then $O_1 \cong O_2$.

The measure of a semicircle is 180°.

A **circumscribed circle** is a circle passing through all the vertices of a polygon.

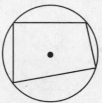

Circles that have the same center and unequal radii are called **concentric circles**.

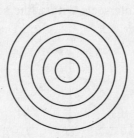

Concentric Circles

PROBLEM

A and B are points on circle Q such that Δ AQB is equilateral. If the length of side $\overline{AB} = 12$, find the length of arc AB.

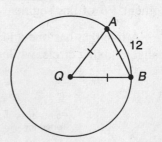

SOLUTION

To find the arc length of arc AB, we must find the measure of the central angle $\angle AQB$ and the measure of the radius $\overline{QA}$. $\angle AQB$ is an interior angle of the equilateral triangle $\triangle AQB$. Therefore,

$$m \angle AQB = 60°.$$

Similarly, in the equilateral $\triangle AQB$,

$$\overline{AQ} = \overline{AB} = \overline{QB} = 12.$$

Given the radius, r, and the central angle, n, the arc length is given by

$$\frac{n}{360} \times 2\pi r.$$

Therefore, by substitution,

$$\angle AQB = \frac{60}{360} \times 2\pi \times 12 = \frac{1}{6} \times 2\pi \times 12 = 4\pi.$$

Therefore, the length of arc $AB = 4\pi$.

☞ Drill: Circles

Circumference, Area, Concentric Circles

> **DIRECTIONS**: Determine the accurate measure.

1. Find the circumference of circle A if its radius is 3 mm.

(A) 3π mm   (B) 6π mm   (C) 9π mm   (D) 12π mm   (E) 15π mm

2. Find the area of circle I.

(A) 22 mm²   (D) 132 mm²

(B) 121 mm²   (E) 132π mm²

(C) 121π mm²

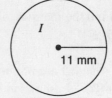

3. The diameter of circle Z is 27 mm. Find the area of the circle.

(A) 91.125 mm²   (D) 182.25π mm²

(B) 182.25 mm²   (E) 729 mm²

(C) 191.5π mm²

4. The area of circle B is 225π cm^2. Find the length of the diameter of the circle.

(A) 15 cm   (B) 20 cm   (C) 30 cm   (D) 20π cm   (E) 25π cm

5. The area of circle X is 144π mm^2 while the area of circle Y is 81π mm^2. Write the ratio of the radius of circle X to that of circle Y.

(A) 3 : 4   (B) 4 : 3   (C) 9 : 12   (D) 27 : 12   (E) 18 : 24

6. The radius of the smaller of two concentric circles is 5 cm while the radius of the larger circle is 7 cm. Determine the area of the shaded region.

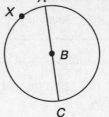

(A) 7π cm^2 (D) 36π cm^2

(B) 24π cm^2 (E) 49π cm^2

(C) 25π cm^2

7. Find the measure of arc MN if $m \angle MON = 62°$.

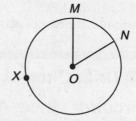

(A) 16°   (D) 62°

(B) 32°   (E) 124°

(C) 59°

8. Find the measure of arc AXC.

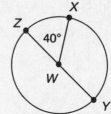

(A) 150°   (D) 270°

(B) 160°   (E) 360°

(C) 180°

9. Find the measure of arc XY in circle W.

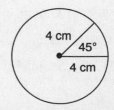

(A) 40°   (D) 180°

(B) 120°   (E) 220°

(C) 140°

10. Find the area of the sector shown.

(A) 4 cm^2 (D) 8π cm^2

(B) 2π cm^2 (E) 16π cm^2

(C) 16 cm^2

COORDINATE GEOMETRY

Coordinate geometry refers to the study of geometric figures using algebraic principles.

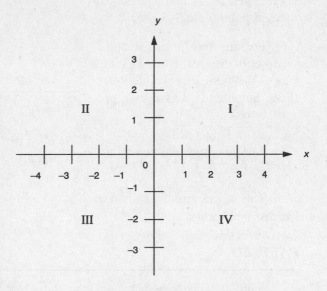

The graph shown is called the Cartesian coordinate plane. The graph consists of a pair of perpendicular lines called **coordinate axes**. The **vertical axis** is the *y*-axis and the **horizontal axis** is the *x*-axis. The point of intersection of these two axes is called the **origin**; it is the zero point of both axes. Furthermore, points to the right of the origin on the *x*-axis and above the origin on the *y*-axis represent positive real numbers. Points to the left of the origin on the *x*-axis or below the origin on the *y*-axis represent negative real numbers.

The four regions cut off by the coordinate axes are, in counterclockwise direction from the top right, called the first, second, third, and fourth quadrant, respectively. The first quadrant contains all points with two positive coordinates.

In the graph shown, two points are identified by the ordered pair, (*x*, *y*) of numbers. The *x*-coordinate is the first number and the *y*-coordinate is the second number.

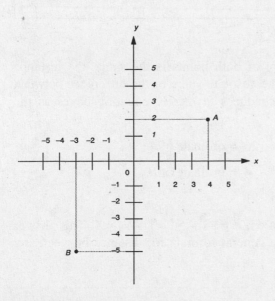

To plot a point on the graph when given the coordinates, draw perpendicular lines from the number-line coordinates to the point where the two lines intersect.

To find the coordinates of a given point on the graph, draw perpendicular lines from the point to the coordinates on the number line. The *x*-coordinate is written before the *y*-coordinate and a comma is used to separate the two.

In this case, point A has the coordinates $(4, 2)$ and the coordinates of point B are $(-3, -5)$.

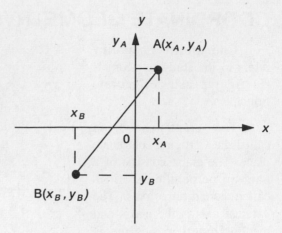

For any two points A and B with coordinates (X_A, Y_A) and (X_B, Y_B), respectively, the distance between A and B is represented by:

$$AB = \sqrt{(X_A - X_B)^2 + (Y_A - Y_B)^2}$$

This is commonly known as the distance formula.

PROBLEM

Find the distance between the point $A(1, 3)$ and $B(5, 3)$.

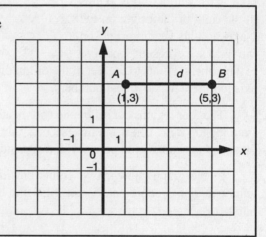

SOLUTION

In this case, where the ordinate of both points is the same, the distance between the two points is given by the absolute value of the difference between the two abscissas. In fact, this case reduces to merely counting boxes as the figure shows.

Let, x_1 = abscissa of A y_1 = ordinate of A

x_2 = abscissa of B y_2 = ordinate of B

d = the distance

Therefore, $d = |x_1 - x_2|$. By substitution, $d = |1 - 5| = |-4| = 4$. This answer can also be obtained by applying the general formula for distance between any two points.

$$d = \sqrt{(x_1 - x_2)^2 + (y_1 - y_2)^2}$$

By substitution,

$$d = \sqrt{(1-5)^2 + (3-3)^2}$$
$$= \sqrt{(-4)^2 + (0)^2}$$
$$= \sqrt{16}$$
$$= 4$$

The distance is 4.

To find the midpoint of a segment between the two given endpoints, use the formula

$$MP = \left(\frac{x_1 + x_2}{2}, \frac{y_1 + y_2}{2} \right)$$

where x_1 and y_1 are the coordinates of one point; x_2 and y_2 are the coordinates of the other point.

☞ Drill: Coordinate Geometry

Coordinates

> **DIRECTIONS**: Refer to the diagram and find the appropriate solution.

1. Which point shown has the coordinates $(-3, 2)$?

    (A) A

    (B) B

    (C) C

    (D) D

    (E) E

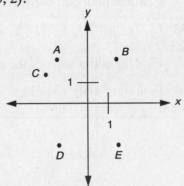

2. The correct *y*-coordinate for point *R* is what number?

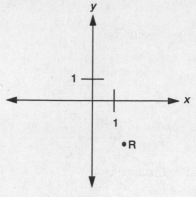

(A) –7   (C) – 2   (E) 8

(B) 2   (D) 7

Distance

> **DIRECTIONS**: Determine the distance or value as appropriate.

3. Find the distance between $(4, -7)$ and $(-2, -7)$.

(A) 4   (B) 6   (C) 7   (D) 14   (E) 15

4. Find the distance between $(3, 8)$ and $(5, 11)$.

(A) 2   (B) 3   (C) $\sqrt{13}$ (D) $\sqrt{15}$ (E) $3\sqrt{3}$

Midpoints and Endpoints

> **DIRECTIONS**: Determine the coordinates or value as appropriate.

5. Find the midpoint between the points $(-2, 6)$ and $(4, 8)$.

(A) $(3, 7)$ (B) $(1, 7)$ (C) $(3, 1)$ (D) $(1, 1)$ (E) $(-3, 7)$

6. Find the coordinates of the midpoint between the points $(-5, 7)$ and $(3, -1)$.

(A) $(-4, 4)$ (B) $(3, -1)$ (C) $(1, -3)$ (D) $(-1, 3)$ (E) $(4, -4)$

TRIGONOMETRY

Angles and Trigonometric Functions

Given a right triangle $\triangle ABC$ as shown in the figure below:

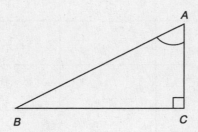

Definition 1: $\sin \angle A = \dfrac{BC}{AB}$

$= \dfrac{\text{measure of side opposite } \angle A}{\text{measure of hypotenuse}}$

Definition 2: $\cos \angle A = \dfrac{AC}{AB}$

$= \dfrac{\text{measure of side adjacent to } \angle A}{\text{measure of hypotenuse}}$

Definition 3: $\tan \angle A = \dfrac{BC}{AC}$

$= \dfrac{\text{measure of side opposite } \angle A}{\text{measure of side adjacent to } \angle A}$

Definition 4: $\cot \angle A = \dfrac{AC}{BC}$

$= \dfrac{\text{measure of side adjacent to } \angle A}{\text{measure of side opposite } \angle A}$

$\sec \angle A = \dfrac{AB}{AC}$

$= \dfrac{\text{measure of hypotenuse}}{\text{measure of side adjacent to } \angle A}$

$\csc \angle A = \dfrac{AB}{BC}$

$= \dfrac{\text{measure of hypotenuse}}{\text{measure of side opposite } \angle A}$

The following table gives the values of sine, cosine, tangent, and cotangent for some special angles. The angles are given in radians and in degrees.

α	Sin α	Cos α	Tan α	Cot α
0°	0	1	0	∞
$\frac{\pi}{6} = 30°$	$\frac{1}{2}$	$\frac{\sqrt{3}}{2}$	$\frac{1}{\sqrt{3}}$	$\sqrt{3}$
$\frac{\pi}{4} = 45°$	$\frac{1}{\sqrt{2}}$	$\frac{1}{\sqrt{2}}$	1	1
$\frac{\pi}{3} = 60°$	$\frac{\sqrt{3}}{2}$	$\frac{1}{2}$	$\sqrt{3}$	$\frac{1}{\sqrt{3}}$
$\frac{\pi}{2} = 90°$	1	0	∞	0

A circle with center located at the origin of the rectangular coordinate axes and radius equal to one unit length is called a unit circle.

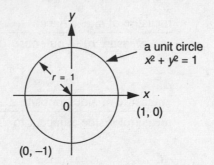

An angle whose vertex is at the origin of a rectangular coordinate system and whose initial side coincides with the positive x-axis is said to be in standard position with respect to the coordinate system.

An angle in standard position with respect to a Cartesian coordinate system whose terminal side lies in the first (or second or third or fourth) quadrant is called a first (or second or third or fourth) quadrant angle.

A quadrant angle is an angle in standard position whose terminal side lies on one of the axes of a Cartesian coordinate system.

If θ is a non-quadrantal angle in standard position and $P(x, y)$ is any point, distinct from the origin, on the terminal side of θ, then the six trigonometric functions of θ are defined in terms of the abscissa (x-coordinate), ordinate (y-coordinate), and distance $\overline{OP}$ as follows:

$$\text{sine } \theta = \sin \theta = \frac{\text{ordinate}}{\text{distance}} = \frac{y}{r}$$

$$\text{cosine } \theta = \cos \theta = \frac{\text{abscissa}}{\text{distance}} = \frac{x}{r}$$

$$\text{tangent } \theta = \tan \theta = \frac{\text{ordinate}}{\text{abscissa}} = \frac{y}{x}$$

$$\text{cotangent } \theta = \cot \theta = \frac{\text{abscissa}}{\text{ordinate}} = \frac{x}{y}$$

$$\text{secant } \theta = \sec \theta = \frac{\text{distance}}{\text{abscissa}} = \frac{r}{x}$$

$$\text{cosecant } \theta = \csc \theta = \frac{\text{distance}}{\text{ordinate}} = \frac{r}{y}$$

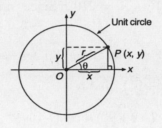

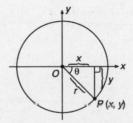

The value of trigonometric functions of quadrantal angles are given in the table below.

θ	$\sin \theta$	$\cos \theta$	$\tan \theta$	$\cot \theta$	$\sec \theta$	$\csc \theta$
0°	0	1	0	$\pm\infty$	1	$\pm\infty$
90°	1	0	$\pm\infty$	0	$\pm\infty$	1
180°	0	−1	0	$\pm\infty$	−1	$\pm\infty$
270°	−1	0	$\pm\infty$	0	$\pm\infty$	−1

EXAMPLES:

1. Find sin θ given $A = 30°$.

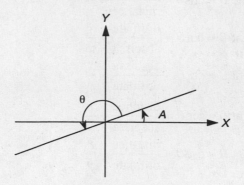

Obviously, $\theta = 180° + A = 210°$. Since sine is negative in the third quadrant, we have

$$\sin\theta = \sin 210° = -\left|\sin(210° - 180°)\right| = -\sin 30° = -\frac{1}{2}.$$

2. If $\sin 2x = -\cos(-x + 9°)$, find x.

$$\sin 2x = -\cos(-x + 9°) = \cos(-x + 9° + 180°).$$

$$\text{But } 2x + x + 9° + 180° = 90°$$

$$x = -99°$$

Basic Identities

$$\sin^2\alpha + \cos^2\alpha = 1$$

$$\tan\alpha = \frac{\sin\alpha}{\cos\alpha}$$

$$\cot\alpha = \frac{\cos\alpha}{\sin\alpha} = \frac{1}{\tan\alpha}$$

$$\csc\alpha = \frac{1}{\sin\alpha}$$

$$\sec\alpha = \frac{1}{\cos\alpha}$$

$$1 + \tan^2\alpha = \sec^2\alpha$$

$$1 + \cot^2\alpha = \csc^2\alpha$$

One can find all the trigonometric functions of an acute angle when the value of any one of them is known.

EXAMPLE

Given α is an acute angle and $\csc \alpha = 2$, then

$$\sin \alpha = \frac{1}{\csc \alpha} = \frac{1}{2}$$

$$\cos^2 \alpha + \sin^2 \alpha = 1, \quad \cos \alpha = \sqrt{1 - \sin^2 \alpha}$$

$$= \sqrt{1 - \left(\tfrac{1}{2}\right)^2}$$
$$= \sqrt{1 - \tfrac{1}{4}}$$
$$= \frac{\sqrt{3}}{2}$$

$$\tan \alpha = \frac{\sin \alpha}{\cos \alpha} = \frac{\frac{1}{2}}{\frac{\sqrt{3}}{2}} = \frac{1}{\sqrt{3}} = \frac{\sqrt{3}}{3}$$

$$\cot \alpha = \frac{1}{\tan \alpha} = \sqrt{3}$$

$$\sec \alpha = \frac{1}{\cos \alpha} = \frac{1}{\frac{\sqrt{3}}{2}} = \frac{2}{\sqrt{3}} = \frac{2\sqrt{3}}{3}$$

i)   If θ is a first quadrant angle, then

   a) $\sin \theta \ = \ \sin \phi$
   b) $\cos \theta \ = \ \cos \psi$
   c) $\tan \theta \ = \ \tan \phi$
   d) $\cot \theta \ = \ \cot \phi$
   e) $\sec \theta \ = \ \sec \phi$
   f) $\csc \theta \ = \ \csc \phi$

ii) If θ is a second quadrant angle:

   a) $\sin \theta \ = \ \sin \phi$
   b) $\cos \theta \ = \ -\cos \phi$
   c) $\tan \theta \ = \ -\tan \phi$
   d) $\cot \theta \ = \ -\cot \phi$
   e) $\sec \theta \ = \ -\sec \phi$
   f) $\csc \theta \ = \ \csc \phi$

iii) If θ is a third quadrant angle, then

    a) $\sin\theta = -\sin\phi$

    b) $\cos\theta = -\cos\phi$

    c) $\tan\theta = \tan\phi$

    d) $\cot\theta = \cot\phi$

    e) $\sec\theta = -\sec\phi$

    f) $\csc\theta = -\csc\phi$

iv) If θ is a fourth quadrant angle, then

    a) $\sin\theta = -\sin\phi$

    b) $\cos\theta = \cos\phi$

    c) $\tan\theta = -\tan\phi$

    d) $\cot\theta = -\cot\phi$

    e) $\sec\theta = \sec\phi$

    f) $\csc\theta = -\csc\phi$

Addition and Subtraction Formulas

$$\sin(A \pm B) = \sin A \cos B \pm \cos A \sin B$$
$$\cos(A \pm B) = \cos A \cos B \mp \sin A \sin B$$
$$\tan(A \pm B) = \frac{\tan A \pm \tan B}{1 \mp \tan A \tan B}$$
$$\cot(A \pm B) = \frac{\cot A \cot B \mp 1}{\cot B \pm \cot A}$$

Double-angle Formulas

$$\sin 2A = 2\sin A \cos A$$
$$\cos 2A = \cos^2 A - 1$$
$$= 1 - 2\sin^2 A$$
$$= \cos^2 A - \sin^2 A$$
$$\tan 2A = \frac{2\tan A}{1 - \tan^2 A}$$

Half-Angle Formulas

$$\sin\frac{A}{2} = \pm\frac{\sqrt{1-\cos A}}{2}$$

$$\cos\frac{A}{2} = \pm\frac{\sqrt{1+\cos A}}{2}$$

$$\tan\frac{A}{2} = \pm\frac{\sqrt{1-\cos A}}{1+\cos A}$$

$$= \frac{1-\cos A}{\sin A}$$

$$= \frac{\sin A}{1+\cos A}$$

$$\cot\frac{A}{2} = \pm\frac{\sqrt{1+\cos A}}{1-\cos A} = \frac{1+\cos A}{\sin A} = \frac{\sin A}{1-\cos A}$$

Sum and Difference Formulas

$$\sin\alpha + \sin\beta = 2\sin\left(\frac{\alpha+\beta}{2}\right)\cos\left(\frac{\alpha-\beta}{2}\right)$$

$$\sin\alpha - \sin\beta = 2\cos\left(\frac{\alpha+\beta}{2}\right)\sin\left(\frac{\alpha-\beta}{2}\right)$$

$$\cos\alpha + \cos\beta = 2\cos\left(\frac{\alpha+\beta}{2}\right)\cos\left(\frac{\alpha-\beta}{2}\right)$$

$$\cos\alpha - \cos\beta = -2\sin\left(\frac{\alpha+\beta}{2}\right)\sin\left(\frac{\alpha-\beta}{2}\right)$$

$$\cos\alpha - \cos\beta = -2\sin\left(\frac{\alpha+\beta}{2}\right)\sin\left(\frac{\alpha-\beta}{2}\right)$$

$$\tan\alpha + \tan\beta = \frac{\sin(\alpha+\beta)}{\cos\alpha\cos\beta}$$

$$\tan\alpha \times \tan\beta = \frac{\sin(\alpha-\beta)}{\cos\alpha\cos\beta}$$

Product Formulas of Sines and Cosines

$$\sin A \sin B = \tfrac{1}{2}[\cos(A - B) - \cos(A + B)]$$

$$\cos A \cos B = \tfrac{1}{2}[\cos(A + B) + \cos(A - B)]$$

$$\sin A \cos B = \tfrac{1}{2}[\sin(A + B) + \sin(A - B)]$$

$$\cos A \sin B = \tfrac{1}{2}[\sin(A + B) - \sin(A - B)]$$

EXAMPLE

If $\sin \alpha = \dfrac{3}{5}$ and $\cos \beta = \dfrac{3}{5}$, find $\cos(\alpha + \beta)$.

Since $\cos(\alpha + \beta) = \cos\alpha\cos\beta - \sin\alpha\sin\beta$, we need to find $\cos\alpha$ and $\sin\beta$. But,

$$\cos\alpha = \sqrt{1 - \sin^2\alpha} = \sqrt{1 - \tfrac{9}{25}} = \sqrt{\tfrac{16}{25}} = \tfrac{4}{5}$$

$$\sin\beta = \sqrt{1 - \cos^2\beta} = \sqrt{1 - \tfrac{9}{25}} = \sqrt{\tfrac{16}{25}} = \tfrac{4}{5}$$

So,

$$\cos(\alpha + \beta) = \frac{4}{5} \times \frac{3}{5} - \frac{3}{5} \times \frac{4}{5} = 0$$

Properties and Graphs of Trigonometric Functions

The **sine function** is the graph of $y = \sin x$. Other trigonometric functions are defined similarly.

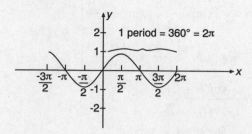

Sine Function

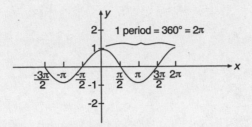

Cosine Function

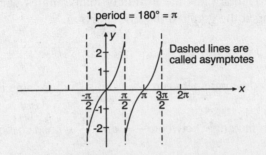

Tangent Function

EXAMPLE

Draw one period of the graph for the function $y = 0.5 \sin(4x + \frac{\pi}{6})$ and indicate its amplitude, period, and phase shift.

$$x = 0, \ y = 0.5\sin\frac{\pi}{6}$$

$$x = \frac{\pi}{4}, \ y = 0.5\sin(\pi + \frac{\pi}{6}) = -0.5\sin\frac{\pi}{6}$$

$$x = \frac{\pi}{2}, \ y = 0.5\sin(2\pi + \frac{\pi}{6}) = 0.5\sin\frac{\pi}{6}$$

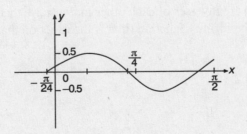

So, amplitude $= \dfrac{1}{2}$

period $= \dfrac{\pi}{2}$

phase shift $= -\dfrac{\pi}{24}$

Inverse Trigonometric Functions

If $-1 < x < 1$, then there are infinitely many angles whose sine is x, as we can see by looking at the graph of the sine function.

Definition:

arcsin $x =$ the angle between $-\dfrac{\pi}{2}$ and $\dfrac{\pi}{2}$ whose sine is x.

arccsc $x =$ the angle between $-\dfrac{\pi}{2}$ and $\dfrac{\pi}{2}$ whose cosecant is x.

arctan $x =$ the angle between $-\dfrac{\pi}{2}$ and $\dfrac{\pi}{2}$ whose cotangent is x.

arccos $x =$ the angle between θ and π whose cosine is x.

arcsec $x =$ the angle between θ and π whose secant is x.

arctan $x =$ the angle between θ and π whose tangent is x.

EXAMPLE

Evaluate arcsin $\dfrac{1}{2}$.

SOLUTION

Since $\sin\dfrac{\pi}{6} = \dfrac{1}{2}$, arcsin$\dfrac{1}{2} = \dfrac{\pi}{6}$. The sine function and the arcsine function (abbreviated arcsin or $\sin^{-1}$) are inverses of each other in the sense that the composition of the two functions is the identity function (that is the function that takes x back to x).

sin(arcsin x) $= x$

arcsin (sin x) $= x$

PERIODICITY

The **period** of a (repeating) function, f, is the smallest positive number p such that $f(x) = f(x + p)$ for all x.

The period of the tangent and cotangent function is π. This fact is clear from the graphs of the tangent and cotangent functions. Pick any angle, x, on the x-axis, and notice $x + \pi$ has the same tangent as x. The period of the other trigonometric functions is 2π.

If the period of a function f is p, and $g(x) = f(nx)$, then the period of g is p/n.

EXAMPLE

What is the period of $\sin 3x$?

SOLUTION

Since the period of $\sin x$ is 2π, the period of $\sin 3x$ is $\dfrac{2\pi}{3}$.

☞ Drill: Trigonometry

1. $\tan^{-1}(-\sqrt{3}) =$

(A) $-60°$ (B) $60°$ (C) $30°$ (D) $-30°$ (E) $-120°$

2. Calculate $\dfrac{\sin^{-1}\frac{1}{2}}{\tan^{-1}1}$.

(A) $\dfrac{1}{2}$ (B) $30°$ (C) $45°$ (D) $\dfrac{3}{2}$ (E) $\dfrac{2}{3}$

3. Find $\cos[\arcsin(-1)]$.

(A) $\dfrac{1}{2}$ (B) $\dfrac{\sqrt{3}}{2}$ (C) 0 (D) $-\dfrac{\sqrt{3}}{2}$ (E) $-\dfrac{1}{2}$

4. If x is inside $[0, \pi]$, one solution for the equation $\sqrt{1 + \sin^2 x} = \sqrt{2}\sin x$ is

(A) $\dfrac{5}{2}\pi$.   (B) $\dfrac{\pi}{6}$.   (C) $\dfrac{3}{2}\pi$.   (D) $\dfrac{\pi}{2}$.   (E) $\dfrac{\pi}{4}$.

5. $\sec^2 \theta - \tan^2 \theta =$

(A) $\dfrac{4}{5}$　　(B) $\dfrac{1}{2}$　　(C) -1　　(D) 1　　(E) $-\dfrac{1}{2}$

6. $\dfrac{\sin(45° + x) + \sin(45° - x)}{\cos x} =$

(A) $\sqrt{2}$　　(B) $\tan x$　　(C) $\dfrac{\sqrt{2}}{2}$　　(D) $\dfrac{\sqrt{2}}{2}\cos x$ (E) 1

7. The amplitude of $y = \dfrac{\sqrt{3}}{3}\sin x + \cos x$ is

(A) $\dfrac{\sqrt{3}}{2}.$　　(B) $\dfrac{\sqrt{2}}{2}.$　　(C) $\dfrac{\sqrt{3}}{4}.$　　(D) $\dfrac{2}{\sqrt{3}}.$　　(E) $\dfrac{1}{\sqrt{3}}.$

8. $\dfrac{\csc x}{2\cos x} =$

(A) $\cos 3x$　　(B) $\tan 2x$　　(C) $\sin 2x$　　(D) $\csc \dfrac{x}{2}$　　(E) $\csc 2x$

ANSWER KEY

ARITHMETIC

Drill: Integers and Real Numbers

1. (A)	5. (B)	8. (D)	11. (D)
2. (C)	6. (E)	9. (B)	12. (A)
3. (B)	7. (B)	10. (E)	13. (D)
4. (A)			

Drill: Fractions

1. (D)	8. (E)	15. (B)	22. (C)
2. (A)	9. (B)	16. (D)	23. (A)
3. (D)	10. (C)	17. (C)	24. (B)
4. (D)	11. (B)	18. (B)	25. (B)
5. (D)	12. (D)	19. (A)	26. (C)
6. (B)	13. (E)	20. (D)	27. (D)
7. (D)	14. (D)	21. (E)	

Drill: Decimals

1. (B)	5. (B)	9. (D)	13. (B)
2. (E)	6. (B)	10. (D)	14. (D)
3. (C)	7. (D)	11. (E)	15. (D)
4. (A)	8. (B)	12. (C)	

Drill: Percentages

1. (B)	5. (A)	9. (E)	13. (C)
2. (C)	6. (C)	10. (D)	14. (D)
3. (E)	7. (B)	11. (A)	15. (C)
4. (B)	8. (B)	12. (B)	

Drill: Radicals

1.	(B)	4.	(C)	7.	(B)	10.	(A)
2.	(D)	5.	(A)	8.	(D)	11.	(C)
3.	(A)	6.	(D)	9.	(C)		

Drill: Exponents

1.	(B)	3.	(C)	5.	(B)	7.	(E)
2.	(A)	4.	(E)	6.	(C)	8.	(B)

Drill: Averages

1.	(B)	4.	(B)	6.	(D)	8.	(C)
2.	(B)	5.	(A)	7.	(3)	9.	(C)
3.	(D)						

ALGEBRA

Drill: Operations with Polynomials

1.	(B)	6.	(B)	11.	(C)	16.	(C)
2.	(C)	7.	(C)	12.	(B)	17.	(D)
3.	(C)	8.	(E)	13.	(E)	18.	(E)
4.	(D)	9.	(A)	14.	(A)	19.	(B)
5.	(A)	10.	(D)	15.	(D)	20.	(B)

Drill: Simplifying Algebraic Expressions

1.	(C)	3.	(B)	4.	(A)	5.	(D)
2.	(D)						

Drill: Equations

1.	(C)	3.	(E)	4.	(D)	5.	(B)
2.	(A)						

Drill: Two Linear Equations

1.	(E)	3.	(A)	4.	(D)	5.	(C)
2.	(B)						

Drill: Quadratic Equations

| 1. | (A) | 3. | (B) | 4. | (C) | 5. | (E) |
| 2. | (D) | | | | | | |

Drill: Absolute Value Equations

| 1. | (B) | 3. | (A) | 4. | (C) | 5. | (D) |
| 2. | (E) | | | | | | |

Drill: Inequalities

| 1. | (E) | 3. | (D) | 4. | (B) | 5. | (A) |
| 2. | (C) | | | | | | |

Drill: Ratios and Proportions

| 1. | (D) | 3. | (C) | 5. | (B) | 6. | (C) |
| 2. | (B) | 4. | (A) | | | | |

GEOMETRY AND TRIGONOMETRY

Drill: Points, Lines, and Angles

1.	(B)	4.	(C)	6.	(D)	8.	(D)
2.	(D)	5.	(B)	7.	(C)	9.	(A)
3.	(D)						

Drill: Regular Polygons

| 1. | (D) | 3. | (D) | 4. | (C) | 5. | (E) |
| 2. | (E) | | | | | | |

Drill: Triangles

1.	(D)	4.	(A)	7.	(B)	9.	(A)
2.	(B)	5.	(E)	8.	(D)	10.	(B)
3.	(C)	6.	(C)				

Drill: Quadrilaterals

1.	(B)	4.	(D)	7.	(E)	9.	(C)
2.	(D)	5.	(C)	8.	(B)	10.	(D)
3.	(A)	6.	(C)				

Drill: Circles

1.	(B)	4.	(C)	7.	(D)	9.	(C)
2.	(C)	5.	(B)	8.	(C)	10.	(B)
3.	(D)	6.	(B)				

Drill: Coordinate Geometry

1.	(C)	3.	(B)	5.	(B)	6.	(D)
2.	(A)	4.	(C)				

Drill: Trigonometry

1.	(A)	3.	(C)	5.	(D)	7.	(D)
2.	(E)	4.	(D)	6.	(A)	8.	(E)

ASSESSMENT

CHAPTER 6

Attacking the ACT Reading Test

Chapter 6

ATTACKING THE ACT READING TEST

DESCRIPTION OF THE ACT READING TEST

The reading section of the ACT test measures your ability to read and understand the kind of material required in college coursework. Considering the large volume of reading in store for you when you enter college, your success as a student will be determined by your ability to pace your reading and comprehend the meanings inherent in the text. The ACT test questions will ask you to acquire meaning from reading passages by referring to content that is explicitly stated and to find the implicit meanings in the passage by reasoning. To interpret the passage, you will be asked to use your reasoning skills to draw conclusions or inferences and make generalizations.

The ACT Reading Test contains four prose passages representative of text normally found in college freshman curricula.

1. Social Studies — approximately 775 words (e.g., history, economics, political science, etc.)

2. Natural Science — approximately 545 words (e.g., biology, chemistry, physics, meteorology, etc.)

3. Prose Fiction — approximately 885 words (e.g., Cather, Dickens, Twain, etc.)

4. Humanities — 600 words (e.g., philosophy, fine arts, etc.)

Each passage is followed by a set of 10 multiple-choice questions. The test is comprised of 40 questions in all with a time limit of 35 minutes. There are approximately 20 questions that refer to what the passage states explicitly and 20 questions that require reasoning to determine implicit meanings. To find implicit meanings, you must use your reasoning skills to make judgments about what the writer implies or infers.

The test contains four multiple-choice options for each question. It does not test isolated vocabulary terms, rules of formal logic, the recall of facts that would require previous knowledge of the contents of the passage. In answering the questions, all you need to know is within the passage. Through this review, you will learn to distinguish between questions that refer to explicit statements within the passage and those that require reasoning to determine implicit meanings.

ABOUT THE DIRECTIONS

Make sure to study and learn the directions to save yourself time during the actual test. You should simply skim them when beginning the section. The directions will read similar to the following:

DIRECTIONS: This test consists of four passages, each followed by ten questions. Once you have read a passage, answer each question, and fill in the appropriate oval on your answer sheet.

STRATEGIES FOR THE READING SECTION

You should follow this plan of attack when answering Reading questions.

Before the test, this is your plan of attack:

| STEP 1 | Study the review to build your reading skills. |
| STEP 2 | Study and learn the directions to ensure that you know how to approach the questions in this section. |

When reading the passage, this is your plan of attack:

STEP 1	Read quickly while keeping in mind that questions will follow.
STEP 2	Uncover the main idea or theme of the passage. Many times it is contained within the first few lines of the passage.
STEP 3	Uncover the main idea of each paragraph. Usually it is contained in either the first or last sentence of the paragraph.
STEP 4	Skim over the detailed points of the passage while circling key words or phrases. These are words or phrases such as *but, on the other hand, although, however, yet,* and *except.*

When answering the questions, this is your plan of attack:

| STEP 1 | Attack one question at a time. Read the question carefully. |

| STEP 2 | If the question is asking for a general answer, such as the main idea or the purpose of the passage, answer it immediately. |

| STEP 3 | If the question is asking for an answer that can only be found in a specific place in the passage, save it for last since this type of question requires you to go back to the passage and, therefore, takes more of your time. |

| STEP 4 | For the detail-oriented questions, try to eliminate or narrow down your choices before looking for the answer in the passage. |

| STEP 5 | Go back into the passage, utilizing the key words you circled, to find the answer. |

| STEP 6 | Any time you cannot find the answer, use the process of elimination to the greatest extent and then guess. |

➤ Additional Tips

- Look over all the passages first and then attack the passages that seem easiest and most interesting.

- Identify and underline what sentences are the main ideas of each paragraph.

- Identify what sentences are example sentences and label them with an "E." Determine whether the writer is using facts or opinions.

- Circle key transitions and identify dominant patterns of organization.

- Use the context of the sentence to figure out the meaning of an unfamiliar word.

- When a question asks you to draw inferences, your answer should reflect what is implied in the passage, rather than what is directly stated.

- To answer questions dealing with specific details, locate the detail in the passage and reread it in context. Many questions on the ACT provide line references; do not get trapped into reading only the lines specified.

- Do not make assumptions. Use only the information provided, explicitly or implicitly, in the passage to answer the questions.

- Scratch off wrong answer choices on the test booklet as you read them.

- If you cannot decide which choice is correct, eliminate all wrong choices and guess. **Do not guess unless you can eliminate at least**

two choices. (Since the ACT does not penalize for incorrect answers, it would be wise to answer the questions that you are confident about, and then return to those that you were less sure of.)

- Make your final choice and move on. Do not dawdle or get frustrated by the really troubling passages. If you have not gotten answers after two attempts, answer the best you can and move on.

- If you have time at the end, go back to the passages that were difficult and review them again.

- Do not second guess yourself. Be confident.

- Do not scan the passage for facts when the question calls for reasoning to determine implicit meanings. By the same token, do not look for implicit meanings when the question asks for the recall of facts.

- Avoid answer choices that do not fully and precisely provide all the information required, or choices that are partially correct but contain some wrong or contradictory information. Also, avoid choices that are too broad, containing too much information, and are, therefore, incorrect.

- Attack a question objectively. Do not let your own personal experience or opinion influence your answer choice. Remember, all you need to know about the subject is given within the passage.

SKILLS TESTED

Explicit Statements and Inferences

In the ACT Reading Test, you will be asked to distinguish between what is stated explicitly in the reading passage and what is inferred. In questions that call for explicit facts from the passage, you will need to recall the answer or refer back to the passage for what is explicitly stated. Inference questions, on the other hand, will require you to use your reasoning skills to draw a conclusion or make a deduction based on the facts or indications in the reading passage.

The following are examples of key phrases in the ACT question stems that refer to what is explicitly stated:

"the passage clearly indicates…"

"according to the passage…"

"the passage states…"

The following are examples of key phrases in the ACT question stems that require reasoning to determine implicit meanings or inferences about the passage:

"the main point…"

"the passage suggests..."

"the author implies that..."

"the main idea is..."

"the primary purpose of this passage..."

"the author infers..."

The reading questions will test your skill in drawing inferences or making determinations based on what you have read in the passage. The questions will ask you to

1. know the difference between fact (recall) and opinion (inference) in the reading passage.

2. determine which fact best supports the writer's main idea.

3. identify the implications of the supporting details in the passage.

4. determine which of the answer choices best summarizes the information presented in the passage.

5. determine the implications of the author's general tone or attitude.

6. identify the author's use of comparison and contrast for the purpose of analysis.

7. draw a conclusion based on your reading of the passage.

8. determine the author's idea through generalization of the facts.

9. determine the relationship between fact and idea.

10. analyze cause-and-effect relationships based on information in the passage.

11. sequence the events in the passage.

12. identify multiple meanings of a word and determine its definition with the use of context clues from the passage.

Fact/Opinion

You will be tested on your ability to identify the difference between statements of fact presented in the passage and statements of the writer's opinion. In the following examples, ask yourself: which one is a fact and which one is an opinion?

1. Some birds nest in trees.

2. The singing of birds is always relaxing.

3. Birds are noisy and bothersome in the morning.

4. Birds are beautiful winged creatures.

Number 1 is a fact. There are, however, birds who do not nest in trees but some birds do. Meadowlarks nest on the ground, but robins, sparrows, and blackbirds nest in trees. Therefore, some birds nest in trees.

Number 2 is an opinion. The singing of birds relaxes some people, but not all of them. It might also be relaxing at one time, but not at another; so it is not always relaxing.

Number 3 is an opinion. What is noise to some, is music to others. If it is noise, it is, of course, bothersome. The two go hand in hand. For someone who wishes to sleep, the sound of birds could be noisy and bothersome. For another, it could be sweet music by which to awaken. It is a matter of opinion.

Number 4 is an opinion. Beauty is an abstract quality, and, therefore, what is beautiful to some people may not be so to others.

Main Idea

It is important for your understanding of the passage that you grasp the main idea the author presents. From the central idea, the supporting information and the logic of the argument will follow. The main idea and the supporting evidence must be considered together if you are to understand the author's purpose in writing the passage. The main idea, usually found in the first paragraph of the passage, might be expressing an opinion, setting forth a recent hypothesis, explaining a new theory, criticizing someone's view, or defending a viewpoint. You can determine the main idea by asking yourself why the author is writing the passage. What is the author's purpose?

Supporting Details

The reading test will require you to analyze supporting details from the passage. When you have established the main idea, you should scan the passage to determine the significant details that support or back up that idea. These details may be in the form of examples, illustrations, research, etc. As was stated above, the author usually sets forth the main idea in the first paragraph. The supporting details are generally found in each succeeding paragraph. You might, in fact, find them in the first line of the paragraph. Recognizing the details that support the main idea will enhance your understanding of the total structure of the passage and the author's primary purpose or intent.

Summarizing

You will be tested on your ability to summarize what you have read in the passage. An accurate summary condenses what the author has demonstrated, based on the implied thesis. In the summary, you will find only information that is stated or implied in the passage. A good understanding of the way in which the author structures the main idea and supporting details will help you focus your comprehension skills on a clear summarization. To master the skill of summarizing, read the passage carefully and methodically with an ever-present eye on the structure of the passage.

Author's Tone/Attitude

Some questions may ask you to decide what the passage implies about the author's tone or attitude. The author's tone is usually revealed in the first paragraph of the passage. You can establish the author's attitude or feeling toward his/her subject by determining whether the tone is negative, positive, or neutral. A solid understanding of the tone will improve your comprehension of the passage.

Comparison/Contrast

Comparison and contrast questions often involve judgments about the way one idea in the essay relates to another idea or to the essay as a whole. The question might ask you to compare two different aspects of the passage to determine how they are alike, or contrast two ideas to determine their differences. What is the author trying to express through the use of either of similar or contrasting ideas? Is one superior to the other? What point is he/she trying to make?

Drawing Conclusions

Some questions on the ACT Reading Test will ask you to draw conclusions based on your reading of the passage. The answer will not be stated directly; so, using whatever facts you have at hand within the passage, you will need to use your reasoning skills to draw a conclusion. For example, the passage might state that a man moved to another city. You also know his long commute to work has been shortened. You may safely conclude that he moved so he could be closer to his job. The information is not explicitly stated but is strongly implied.

Forming Generalizations

Some ACT reading questions ask you to make a judgment based on what the author means but does not actually state. Does the author use generalizations to prove a point? If so, the question might refer to a general group of people who are typical of a certain behavior. In answering the question, ask yourself what general traits or characteristics this group typifies. You will need to make an implied generalization based on specific details stated in the passage.

Relationships Between Ideas/Facts

The ACT reading questions will require you to identify the relationship between ideas and facts in the passage. This is similar to main idea/detail where the author proposes an idea or thesis and then sets out to support or prove it with facts. To prove that the idea is sound, the author uses facts such as examples, illustrations, or research. In answering the question, you need to examine all the facts to determine the author's purpose. Ask yourself whether he/she has proven the idea.

Cause/Effect

A cause-and-effect question requires you to analyze a situation stating that one thing caused something else. For example, there was a hailstorm and your car was damaged. Before the storm, the car's paint job looked fine. After the storm, the paint was pitted. It follows that the hailstorm caused the damage to the car (cause – hailstorm/effect – damaged car). To determine cause-and-effect questions, look for key phrases like "the result of" or "the cause of" in the question stem.

Sequencing Events

Authors often use stylistic patterns of writing, such as the sequencing of events in history or the progression of events in a story. Usually this systematic move forward in time reflects not only the author's style but the meaning as well. You need to ask yourself what the author is saying. Is he/she trying to convince you of something? Is he/she establishing an idea or theme in a prose fiction passage?

Vocabulary: Multiple Meanings/Context Clues

In the ACT reading passages you will encounter vocabulary you have not seen before or of which you do not know the meaning. To determine the meaning of an unfamiliar word, pay close attention to the words and phrases that surround it. These should give you some clues. Examples that appear in the passage may also give you some hints. There may be words that you would normally understand, but that you cannot grasp in the context of this particular passage. Many words in our language contain multiple meanings depending on the way they are used and in what context. The author's intent will give you another clue. What is he/she trying to say? If context does not provide a clue, look at the word itself. Perhaps the root of the word or the suffix will help you find the answer.

READING REVIEW

The following sample passages and subsequent questions based on the text are representative of those on the ACT Reading Test. Read the passages carefully and then answer the questions using the skills that have been identified in this review.

PROSE FICTION

The prose fiction passage contains dialogue and narration taken from short stories or novels. In this excerpt from Hawthorne's *The Scarlet Letter*, Hester Prynne is meeting with the Governor and several men of the church concerning her daughter Pearl.

"God gave me the child!" cried she. "He gave her in requital of all things else, which he had taken from me. She is my
happiness!—she is my torture, none the less! Pearl keeps me
here in life! Pearl punishes me too! See ye not, she is the scarlet
5   letter, only capable of being loved, and so endowed with a
millionfold the power of retribution for my sin? Ye shall not take
her! I will die first!"

"My poor woman," said the not unkind old minister, "the
child shall be well cared for!—far better than thou canst do it."

10   "God gave her into my keeping," repeated Hester Prynne,
raising her voice almost to a shriek. "I will not give her up!"—
And here, by a sudden impulse, she turned to the young clergy-
man, Mr. Dimmesdale, at whom, up to this moment, she had
seemed hardly so much as once to direct her eyes.—"Speak thou

15   for me!" cried she. "Thou wast my pastor, and hadst charge of
my soul, and knowest me better than these men can. I will not
lose the child! Speak for me! Thou knowest,—for thou hast sympathies which these men lack!—thou knowest what is in my
heart, and what are a mother's rights, and how much the stronger

20   they are, when that mother has but her child and the scarlet
letter! Look thou to it! I will not lose the child! Look to it!"

At this wild and singular appeal, which indicated that Hester
Prynne's situation had provoked her to little less than madness, the
young minister at once came forward, pale, and holding his hand

25   over his heart, as was his custom whenever his peculiarly nervous
temperament was thrown into agitation. He looked now more
careworn and emaciated than as we described him at the scene of
Hester's public ignominy; and whether it were his failing health,
or whatever the cause might be, his large dark eyes had a world of

30   pain in their troubled and melancholy depth.

"There is truth in what she says," began the minister, with a voice sweet, tremulous, but powerful, insomuch that the hall reechoed, and the hollow armor rang with it,—"truth in what Hester says, and in the feeling which inspires her! God gave her
35   the child, and gave her, too, an instinctive knowledge of its nature and requirements,—both seemingly so peculiar,—which no other mortal being can possess. And, moreover, is there not a quality of awful sacredness in the relation between this mother and this child?"
40   "Ay!—how is that, good Master Dimmesdale?" interrupted the Governor. "Make that plain, I pray you."

"It must be even so," resumed the minister. "For, if we deem it otherwise, do we not thereby say that the Heavenly Father, the Creator of all flesh, hath lightly recognized a deed of
45   sin, and made of no account the distinction between unhallowed lust and holy love? This child of its father's guilt and its mother's shame hath come from the hand of God, to work in many ways upon her heart, who pleads so earnestly, and with such bitterness of spirit, the right to keep her. It was meant for a
50   blessing; for the one blessing of her life! It was meant, doubtless, as the mother herself hath told us, for a retribution too; a torture to be felt at many an unthought of moment; a pang, a sting, an ever-recurring agony, in the midst of a troubled joy! Hath she not expressed this thought in the garb of the poor child, so forcibly
55   reminding us of that red symbol which sears her bosom?"

"Well said, again!" cried good Mr. Wilson. "I feared the woman had no better thought than to make a mountebank of her child!"

"O, not so!—not so!" continued Mr. Dimmesdale. "She
60   recognizes, believe me, the solemn miracle which God hath wrought, in the existence of that child. And may she feel, too,— what, methinks, is the very truth,—that this boon was meant, above all things else, to keep the mother's soul alive, and to preserve her from blacker depths of sin into which Satan might
65   else have sought to plunge her! Therefore it is good for this poor, sinful woman that she hath an infant immortality, a being capable of eternal joy or sorrow, confided to her care,—to be trained up by her to righteousness,—to remind her, at every moment, of her fall,—but yet to teach her, as it were by the
70   Creator's sacred pledge, that, if she bring the child to heaven, the child also will bring its parent thither! Herein is the sinful mother happier than the sinful father. For Hester Prynne's sake, then, and no less for the poor child's sake, let us leave them as Providence hath seen fit to place them!"
75   "You speak, my friend, with a strange earnestness," said

old Roger Chillingworth, smiling at him.

"And there is a weighty import in what my young brother hath spoken," added the Reverend Mr. Wilson. "What say you, worshipful Master Bellingham? Hath he not pleaded well for the
80   poor woman?"

"Indeed hath he," answered the magistrate, "and hath adduced such arguments, that we will even leave the matter as it now stands; so long, at least, as there shall be no further scandal in the woman. Care must be had, nevertheless, to put the child to
85   due and stated examination in the catechism, at thy hands or Master Dimmesdale's. Moreover, at a proper season, the tithing-men must take heed that she go both to school and to meeting."

1.   According to the passage, Hester feels

    (A)   Pearl has brought nothing but sadness into her life.

    (B)   angry at Pearl for causing her pain.

    (C)   Pearl was given to her in requital for things that had been taken from her.

    (D)   Reverend Wilson's unkindness directed toward her.

The key phrase "according to the passage" is your clue to refer back to the passage for the answer to the question. The answer in this case is stated explicitly in the passage.

Choice (C) is correct because "he (God) gave her in requital of all things...taken from me" is stated directly in the passage. Hester feels that God gave her the child in return for all her loneliness and pain. Choice (A) is not correct because even though the passage indicates that Pearl brings her "torture," she also brings her happiness. Choice (B) is not correct because nowhere in the passage does it state or imply that she is angry at Pearl for causing her pain. Choice (D) is incorrect because the passage clearly states that the Reverend Wilson is "not unkind."

2.   What is the author's overall attitude toward Hester Prynne's custody of her own child?

    (A)   She will be better cared for by someone else.

    (B)   Because Pearl represents the scarlet letter, Hester should give her up.

    (C)   Hester should be allowed to keep her child.

    (D)   Hester should listen to Reverend Wilson, the wise minister.

The phrase "author's overall attitude" should immediately alert you to the fact that you will need to use your **inferencing** skills to find the tone of the passage.

Answer choice (C) is correct. The tone of the passage brings out the love Hester feels for her child. It is reasonable that a mother who would die before she would give up her child ("I will die first") should be allowed to keep her; for it would be in the best interest of the child. Choice (A) is incorrect. The "shriek" in Hester's voice, when told that someone else could care for Pearl better than she could, shows the author's attitude. Choice (B) is incorrect because Hester's love for her child convinces us that even though Pearl symbolizes the scarlet letter, she also symbolizes love. Choice (D) is not correct because of the way in which Hester reacts when Reverend Wilson tells her the child will be well cared for by someone else.

3. In this passage the word "ignominy" (line 28) means

    (A) happiness.

    (B) fear.

    (C) disgrace.

    (D) pride.

The question obviously tests **vocabulary-in-context**. Your strategy should be to look at the words surrounding it. In this case, "public" would necessarily precede your choice, since it is given in the passage. The author's intent is another clue.

Choice (C) is the correct response since it was Hester's public disgrace. The scarlet letter has already been referred to as Hester's sin. Since Hester comments earlier that "all things else, which he (God) had taken from me," we can assume she has been publicly disgraced and left without friends or companionship. Choice (A) is incorrect because the author's tone of the language surrounding ignominy does not suggest happiness. Such words as "careworn," "emaciated," "and failing health" suggest a morbid tone as Dimmesdale refers to "Hester's public ignominy." Later, the passage alludes to the child as the product of "unhallowed lust" and "its mother's shame," indicating that Hester's situation is not one of happiness. Choice (B) is not fitting in the context of the sentence because public fear would not be suggestive of a public scene. Choice (D) is not correct. The passage states that "Hester Prynne's situation had provoked her to little less than madness." A situation provoking her to madness would not be one of public pride.

4. In what way is Pearl like the scarlet letter?

    (A) Both are representative of love.

    (B) They both keep Hester here in life.

    (C) They both give Hester joy.

    (D) Both are reminders of Hester's punishment and sin.

You will immediately recognize the word "like" in the question stem indicating that a comparison is being made. The simile calls for an interpretation based on **inference**.

Choice (D) is correct. The passage states that "she (Pearl) is the scarlet letter." We can infer that both Pearl and the scarlet letter are constant reminders of Hester's punishment and sin. In this way, Pearl is like the scarlet letter. Choice (A) is incorrect. Although Pearl represents love, the scarlet letter is a curse upon Hester. Choice (B) is not correct because the scarlet letter is symbolic of Hester's sin and shame, but Pearl "keeps her in life" or, in other words, endows Hester with Pearl's vitality and zest for life. Choice (C) is incorrect because the scarlet letter is a mark of shame and does not give Hester joy.

5. What does the author imply when he writes in lines 54–55 "the garb of the poor child, so forcibly reminding us of that red symbol which sears her (Hester's) bosom"?

    (A) Hester dresses Pearl in red.

    (B) Hester is too poor to dress Pearl properly.

    (C) Hester dresses Pearl to please the Puritans.

    (D) Pearl's clothes give the appearance of a neglected child.

As you read the question stem, the word "imply" will suggest that you will need to imply or **infer** what is not explicitly stated in the text.

Answer choice (A) is correct. Hester dresses Pearl in the same color of the "red symbol" or "the scarlet letter" that she is forced to wear on her bosom. Choice (B) is incorrect. The issue of money to support Hester's child does not appear anywhere in the passage. Choice (C) is not correct. The Puritan children wore nothing but black and although this is not stated anywhere in the passage, we can assume that Pearl's attire was not like other children's or else it would not have been an issue. Choice (D) is incorrect. Nowhere in the passage do we get the message that Pearl is a neglected child. Since Hester has only Pearl, she focuses all her attention on her.

6. What is the meaning of "mountebank" (line 57)?

    (A) Child prodigy

    (B) Imposter

    (C) Blessing

    (D) Church member

This is another **vocabulary-in-context** question. This word is most likely unfamiliar. Again, look at the context of the word in the passage. Since mountebank has a negative connotation within the context of the sentence, it gives you a strong clue.

Choice (B) is correct. We have just been told by Dimmesdale that Pearl's dress is a symbol of the scarlet letter. It is negatively construed by Mr. Wilson that Hester is making an imposter of her child in this way. We also know the word is negative because Mr. Dimmesdale immediately comes to Hester's defense and denies it. Choice (A) is incorrect because, within the context of the passage, the word is an insult. Child prodigy is the opposite. Choice (C) is incorrect. Although Pearl is a blessing to Hester, the word does not fit into the context of the passage. She would not be accused of making a blessing of her child. Choice (D) is incorrect. If Hester would want to make a church member of her child, Mr. Wilson would obviously be pleased, not disappointed.

7. The main point of Mr. Dimmesdale's argument is

   (A) that the child is torturing the mother.

   (B) that the child would benefit from another home where she would not have her father's guilt and her mother's shame upon her.

   (C) that Hester Prynne is a fit mother and should be given the custody of her child.

   (D) that the child should be made to dress like other children.

The question asks you to pick out the **main idea** in the passage. You will need to ask yourself what is central to Mr. Dimmesdale's argument.

Answer choice (C) is the correct response. Dimmesdale argues that for the sake of the mother and the child, it would be best to leave things as they are. She is a fit mother because she recognizes that the child came from "the hand of God." Choice (A) is incorrect because Dimmesdale argues that although the child is a reminder of Hester's sin, she is, at the same time, a blessing to her. Choice (B) is incorrect. Dimmesdale argues that Hester recognizes that the child who came from her "father's guilt" and her "mother's shame" also came from God. Dimmesdale does not advocate another home for Pearl. Choice (D) is incorrect. Nowhere in the passage does Dimmesdale argue that Pearl's clothes should be like other children's clothes.

8. What is Mr. Dimmesdale's occupation?

   (A) Pastor

   (B) Philosopher

   (C) Farmer

   (D) Deacon

The answer to the question will be explicitly stated in the passage. Skim the passage for the correct answer. Look for words that correspond to the answer choices.

Choice (A) is correct. Hester refers to Dimmesdale as her pastor. She asks him to speak for her since he knows what is in her heart. Choice (B) is incorrect. Nowhere in the passage is it stated or implied that he is a philosopher by occupation. Choice (C) is incorrect. Nowhere in the passage is it stated or implied that he is a farmer. Choice (D) is incorrect. He could not be a pastor and a deacon at the same time. The passage does not refer to him as a deacon.

9. The passage suggests that Dimmesdale's relationship with his colleagues can best be described by the following statement:

   (A) They tolerate Dimmesdale's arguments, but then make their own decisions.

   (B) They have a deep respect for Dimmesdale and honor his judgment.

   (C) They realize Dimmesdale is younger than they are and, therefore, more idealistic.

   (D) They are suspicious of Dimmesdale's concern for Hester.

The word "suggest" in the question stem identifies it as an **inference** question. To answer the question, scan the passage and draw your conclusion based on the way in which Dimmesdale's colleagues react to him. Are they positive? Negative?

Choice (B) is the correct answer. Scanning the passage will reveal comments such as "Well said…" and "Hath he not pleaded well?" by the Governor and Reverend Wilson. They listen to him and respect his opinion. Choice (A) is incorrect. They encourage him to go on with his argument. At the end, they allow Hester to keep her child based on Dimmesdale's arguments. Choice (C) is incorrect. Nowhere in the passage do we find evidence that they think he is idealistic because he is young. Choice (D) is not correct. There is no indication in the passage of their suspicion of Dimmesdale's concern for Hester.

10. According to the passage, Hester is granted custody of her child with the understanding that Hester

   (A) allow Pearl to take catechism and later attend school and church.

   (B) allow the Governor to test Pearl in the catechism.

   (C) must dress Pearl like other Puritan children.

   (D) allow Roger Chillingworth to tutor Pearl.

This is a **detail** question and must be answered by referring back to the passage. To answer the question, scan the passage for key words from the answer choices.

Answer choice (A) is correct. The passage states explicitly that Hester must make sure Pearl take "catechism" and "go both to school and to meeting." Choice (B) is incorrect. The passage suggests that Master Dimmesdale, not the Governor, might test her "in the catechism." Choice (C) is incorrect. Nowhere in the passage is this a directive for Hester. Choice (D) is incorrect. This answer cannot be found anywhere in the passage.

NATURAL SCIENCE

The natural science passage contains information taken from the study of biology, geology, astronomy, chemistry, or physics. The following is an example of a passage from one of these disciplines.

The scientific naming and classification of all organisms is known as taxonomy. Both extant (living) and extinct (no longer existing) organisms are taxonomically classified into specific and carefully defined categories. A single category is called a
5   taxon; multiple categories are taxa.

There have been several classification schemes throughout history. Aristotle devised a system of categorizing plants and animals that was used for almost 2,000 years. With the exploration of the New World and the invention of the microscope,
10   more and more organisms were discovered. A universal, comprehensive classification system was needed: one that could be used by all biologists, regardless of language.

The founder of the modern scheme of taxonomy was the Swedish naturalist Carl von Linne (1707 – 1778), whose interest
15   in plants began in medical school where he took care of a botanical garden and started an insect collection. He took meticulous notes on all the plants, and these were later used in the books he wrote. In 1732, the Royal Society of Science funded his trip to Lapland, where he walked many miles gathering plants for his
20   collection. His book *Species Plantarum*, covering plant classification, was published in 1753. He had published his *Systema Naturae* (Systems of Nature) in 1735. The tenth edition, which was the basis for animal classification, was published in 1758. It is still used as the authoritative taxonomical source today.
25   Linne's system is hierarchical. It begins with a large, inclusive taxon called a kingdom, followed by a phylum or a division (for plants), class, order, family, genus, species, and, in some cases, subspecies. Each level becomes more specific, until the lowest level describes only one type of organism.
30   Linne defined two kingdoms, one for plants and one for animals. In 1969, Robert Whittaker developed a new classification system using five kingdoms. This revision reduced, but did

not completely eradicate, the confusion faced by biologists at-
tempting to classify organisms, such as fungi, that do not fit into
35 either the plant or animal category.

There is still some debate about the categorization, but a
species is generally recognized as a group of organisms that
share the same morphological, ecological, and genetic characteristics, and whose members can interbreed and produce fertile
40 offspring.

The current classification system tries to take into account
not only how various taxa are related because of shared characteristics, such as all members of Class Aves (birds) have feathers, but also how they are related through evolution.

45 Linne used Latin, the universal scientific language for centuries, and taxonomy still uses Latin names for all classes of
taxa. The complete taxonomical classification of the California
grizzly bear, for example, is Kingdom Animalia, Phylum
Chordata, Class Mammalia, Order Carnivora, Family Ursidae,
50 Genus Ursus, Species horribilis.

The genus and species make up the organism's scientific
name, in this case, *Ursus horribilis*. This is known as the binomial system of nomenclature, also developed by Linne. The genus is always capitalized and italicized, and the species is always
55 lowercase and italicized.

Given any particular species of plant, animal, or other organism that has been discovered and classified, and with sufficient information about its appearance, biochemistry, reproductive habits, and so on, a biologist can determine its taxonomy.
60 When linked with the technology of DNA studies, taxonomy can
be a valuable tool to help scientists unlock the evolutionary se-
crets of all organisms.

11. What is the main idea of the passage?

   (A) The contributions of Carl von Linne

   (B) Taxonomy and modern biological categorization

   (C) The new classification system of Robert Whittaker

   (D) A brief history of taxonomy

You must interpret the passage and the author's **main idea** by asking yourself what idea the author is setting forth to accomplish his/her purpose. Is the
author expressing an opinion? Explaining a theory? For what purpose? The main
idea is usually stated or implied in the first paragraph of the passage.

Choice (B) is correct. It is broad enough to be an appropriate choice. The
passage does give a brief history of taxonomy and discusses the modern categori-

zation of organisms by biologists. Choice (A) is incorrect. The passage does discuss the contributions of Carl von Linne quite extensively, but other scientists and their contributions are discussed also. Choice (C) is incorrect. Robert Whittaker's new classification system is discussed, but his contribution is not the only one. Choice (D) is incorrect. Although the history of taxonomy is discussed, the passage is not limited to the history.

12. Based on the information presented in the passage, which of the following statements are true?

   I.   The scientific name for an organism is made up of the genus and species names.

   II. There are two kingdoms used to classify all living and extinct organisms.

   III. The family taxon is more specific than the phylum, but less specific than the genus.

   (A) I only.   (C) III only.

   (B) II only.   (D) I and III only.

The question stem asks you to refer directly to the passage to find the answer. "Based on the information presented in the passage," the **key phrase**, is your clue that the answer will be explicitly stated in the text.

Choice (D) is the correct answer. Paragraph eight states that the scientific name of an organism is made up of the genus and species name; (I) is the binomial system of nomenclature. Paragraph three gives the ranking of the hierarchy used for taxonomy. It is evident from this listing that the phylum is the second-highest (most general) tier, and that the genus is the second-lowest (most specific) tier. The family taxon lies in between genus and phylum; III is a true statement. While Linne's system of classification used only two kingdoms, paragraph four states that in 1969 Robert Whittaker devised a system based on five kingdoms to allow for the classification of the organisms that are neither plants nor animals. II is not a true statement. Therefore, (D), I and III only, is the correct answer.

13. The author would be most likely to agree with which of the following statements?

   (A) Taxonomy is necessary to classify different species of organisms, but the current system is too complex and should be simplified.

   (B) Taxonomy is a useful method of classifying different species, but soon new methods will be necessary to distinguish between the new types of organisms being discovered by DNA research.

(C) The system of taxonomy developed by Linne is the best method devised for categorizing different species, and Whittaker's more recent five-kingdom scheme is an unnecessary complication.

(D) Taxonomy is a useful method of categorizing species, and when combined with new techniques in DNA tracing, it can help scientists trace the evolution of various species.

The key phrase in the question stem is "most likely." This is your clue that you will need to **infer** the author's meaning. Inference questions test your ability to recognize information that is not explicitly stated but is strongly implied.

Choice (D) is correct. In the last paragraph of the passage, the author states that utilizing taxonomic methods with DNA research can provide a valuable tool to scientists studying the evolution of all organisms. The author would be most likely to agree with (D). Choice (A) is incorrect. The author never describes the current method of taxonomy as complex and never mentions simplification. Choice (B) is incorrect. The author does not claim that DNA research has discovered any new organisms, or that new methods of classification will soon be necessary. Choice (C) is not correct. The author states that Whittaker's five-kingdom scheme has made it less difficult for biologists to categorize organisms, such as fungi, that do not fit into the two kingdoms used by Linne.

14. According to the information given in the passage, what is the binomial system of nomenclature?

(A) The two-kingdom system of classifying all organisms developed by Carl von Linne

(B) The five-kingdom system of classifying all organisms developed by Robert Whittaker

(C) The formation of the scientific name of an organism from the genus and species names of that organism

(D) The Aristotelian method of taxonomic classification that was superseded by Linne's method

The question stem gives you the clue to refer to the passage for the answer. Scan the passage for the "binomial system of nomenclature."

The correct answer is (C). Paragraph eight clearly defines the binomial system of nomenclature as the practice of using the genus and species names of an organism to form the scientific name for that organism. Choice (A) is incorrect. The passage states that the binomial system of nomenclature is a system of scientific naming of organisms rather than classifying of organisms. Choice (B) is incorrect. Again, the question is referring to the naming rather than the classifying of organisms. The Aristotelian method did not use the genus and species names for an organism. Therefore, choice (D) is incorrect.

15. All of the following statements about taxonomy are true EXCEPT

(A) a species is usually defined as a group of organisms possessing the same morphological, ecological, and genetic characteristics whose members can interbreed and produce fertile offspring.

(B) taxonomy takes evolutionary relationships between organisms into account, as well as the shared characteristics of related taxa.

(C) the hierarchical system developed by Linne moves from the top, specific level down to the lower, more general level.

(D) there are many organisms that are neither plant nor animal; these organisms could not be classified under Linne's system but can be classified using Whittaker's five-kingdom system.

The question calls for answers that are clearly stated in the passage. Scan the passage for words and phrases used in the answer choices (morphological, ecological, evolutionary relationships, related taxa, Whittaker, etc.).

Choice (C) is a false statement and is, therefore, the correct answer choice. Paragraph three clearly states that Linne's hierarchy begins with a large, inclusive (general) taxon, and that each subsequent level becomes more specific, until the bottom level describes a single type of organism. Choices (A), (B), and (D) are all true and are explicitly stated in the passage.

16. According to the passage, taxonomy involves

(A) the classification of all organisms, extant and extinct, into distinct taxa.

(B) the scientific naming of all organisms, extant and extinct.

(C) the categorization of living organisms into distinct taxa.

(D) the scientific naming of all organisms and their classification into distinct taxa.

The phrase "according to the passage" in the question stem is your clue to refer to the passage for the answer which is stated explicitly in the text.

Answer choice (D) is correct. Taxonomy is defined in paragraph one as the scientific naming and classification of all organisms. The paragraph makes it clear that all organisms, living or extinct, are taxonomically classified into specific taxa. Choice (C) is incorrect because it specifies only living organisms. Choice (A) is incorrect because it omits the scientific naming of organisms. Choice (B) is incorrect because it omits the classification of organisms into distinct taxa.

17. Which of the following best describes the relationship between the first paragraph and the rest of the passage?

(A) The first paragraph presents a brief history of taxonomy, and the rest of the passage details how to classify an organism according to the scheme devised by Carl von Linne.

(B) The first paragraph gives a definition of taxonomy, and the rest of the passage is a synopsis of the history of taxonomy, focusing on the contributions made by Carl von Linne and Robert Whittaker.

(C) The first paragraph provides a definition of taxonomy, and the rest of the passage describes the inadequacies of the current method and suggests modifications.

(D) The first paragraph presents a definition of taxonomy, and the rest of the passage includes a brief history of the development of the modern system and an example of how it is used to classify organisms.

This question asks you to determine the relationship between the **main idea** and the **facts** that support it. In this case, you will need to look for examples or research to verify the facts.

Choice (D) is correct. The first paragraph presents a definition of taxonomy. The remainder of the passage includes a brief history of taxonomic methods and provides an example of the taxonomic classification of the California grizzly bear. Choice (A) is incorrect. The first paragraph does not present a brief history of taxonomy. Choice (B) is incorrect because the remainder of the passage is not a synopsis of the history of taxonomy. Choice (C) is incorrect because the remainder of the passage does not describe the inadequacies of the current taxonomic method.

18. Aristotle's system of categorizing plants and animals became obsolete as a result of

(A) the need for a universal classification system brought about by the invention of the microscope and the discovery of many new organisms.

(B) a flaw in Aristotle's classification and categorization system.

(C) the confusion biologists faced regarding the classification of fungi.

(D) Carl von Linne's classification system which was translated into English, the universal language.

You can immediately identify the question type by the phrase "as a result of" in the question stem. This identifies it as a **cause-and-effect** question. You will need to use your inferencing skills to determine the cause of the problem.

Choice (A) is correct. Aristotle's system became obsolete because with the invention of the microscope the task of identifying and naming all the new organisms became unmanageable. A new system needed to be devised. Choice

(B) is incorrect. Aristotle's system of classification was used for 2,000 years. It stands to reason that it was a sound system. Choice (C) is not correct. The passage clearly states that Whittaker's new system "reduced" the confusion. Choice (D) is incorrect. Carl von Linne's classification system was translated into Latin.

19. According to the passage, the genus and species making up the scientific name for the California grizzly bear is

   (A) *Phylum Chordata.*

   (B) *Ursus horribilis.*

   (C) *Order Carnivora.*

   (D) *Animalia Mammalia.*

The answer to this question is explicitly stated in the passage. Refer to the text for **key words**.

Choice (B) is correct. Although the complete scientific classification for the California grizzly bear includes kingdom, phylum, class, order, family, genus and species, it is named by genus and species only. In this case, that is *Ursus horribilis*. Choice (A) is incorrect. Chordata is the phylum or division, not the genus and species. Choice (C) is incorrect. Carnivora is the order. Choice (D) is not correct. Animalia is a kingdom and Mammalia is a class.

20. Paragraph five states that a species is a group that shares the same morphological characteristics. The best definition of "morphological characteristics" is

   (A) the appearance of the group of organisms.

   (B) the reproductive habits of the group of organisms.

   (C) the structure and form of the organisms.

   (D) the size and color of the organisms.

This is a **vocabulary-in-context** question. Remember to look at the words surrounding it. Also, consider the meaning of the word as it applies to the passage as a whole. Consider other familiar words containing the root of the word. Analyze the suffix "ology" which means the study of something. The analysis of the structure of the word should also give you a clue.

Choice (C) is the correct answer. Metamorphosis is a familiar word containing the root "morph" and involving change in form. Morphology is, therefore, the structure and form of an object. Thus, the morphological characteristics of an organism are those pertaining to the structure and form of the organism. Choice (A) is incorrect. Although structure and form include appearance, they also include internal characteristics. Choice (B) is incorrect. The reproductive habits of the organism are not morphological characteristics. Structure and form of an organism by its very definition excludes its functions. Choice (D) is not correct. Structure and form include size and color but also include internal characteristics.

HUMANITIES

The humanities passage includes the study of philosophy, art, music, theater, dance, and literature. This passage is a discussion of tragedy and comedy as it relates to the theater or to literature as a whole.

In Aristotle's *Poetics* he originated the definition of tragedy, stating that tragedy should be an imitation of complex actions which should arouse an emotional response combining fear and pity. Comedy shows a progression from adversity to pros-
5   perity. Tragedy shows the reverse. He states that this progression must be experienced by a certain kind of character whom we can designate as the tragic hero. This central figure must be basically good and noble: "good" because we will not be aroused to fear and pity over the misfortunes of a villain, and "noble" both by
10   social position and moral stature because the fall to misfortune would not otherwise be great enough for tragic impact. These virtues do not make the tragic hero perfect, however, for he must also possess hamartia—a tragic flaw—the weakness which leads him to make an error in judgment which initiates the reversal in
15   his fortunes, causing his death or the death of others or both. These dire consequences become the hero's catastrophe. The most common tragic flaw is Hubris, an excessive pride that adversely influences the protagonist's judgment.

Often the catastrophic consequences involve an entire na-
20   tion because the tragic hero's social rank carries great responsibilities. Witnessing these events produces the emotional reaction Aristotle believed the audience should experience, the catharsis. Although tragedy must arouse our pity for the tragic hero as he endures his catastrophe and must frighten us as we witness the
25   consequences of a flawed behavior which anyone could exhibit, there must also be a purgation, "a cleansing," of these emotions which should leave the audience feeling not depressed but relieved and almost elated. The assumption is that while the tragic hero endures a crushing reversal, somehow he is not thoroughly
30   defeated as he gains new stature through suffering and the knowledge that comes with suffering. Classical tragedy insists that the universe is ordered. If truth or universal law is ignored, the results are devastating, causing the audience to react emotionally; simultaneously, the tragic results prove the existence of
35   truth, thereby reassuring our faith that existence is sensible.

In comparison to tragedy, comedy is a lighter form of drama which aims to amuse and please the audience and which ends happily rather than tragically. Comedies can vary according to the attitudes they project. In general the comic effect is
40 achieved through some incongruity either in speech, in the action of the drama, or in the characterization of the actors. If the incongruity is verbal, it might take the form of a play on words or verbal exaggeration. It might also be revealed in the physical action of the drama. For example, when a person who is tone
45 deaf tries to sing opera, a comic effect is achieved.

Comedy can be broadly identified as "high comedy" or "low comedy" which can, in fact, be further apart in nature than tragedy is to some forms of weighty or serious comedy. Satire is a high comic form implying that humanity and human institu-
50 tions are in need of reform. In Neo-Classic times, high comedy had a sense of decorum and appealed only to a higher social class. The incongruities of conventional life were often ridiculed and appealed to the intellectual playgoer. Shakespeare's *As You Like It* offers an example of this type of comedy.

55 Low comedy lacks subtlety and has very little intellectual appeal. Shakespeare often used low comedy for dramatic purposes such as comic relief or marking time in the drama. Low comedy depends less on plot and character than on gross absurdities. The "higher" a comedy goes, the more natural the charac-
60 ters seem and the less boisterous their behavior.

21. The author introduces Aristotle as a leading source for the definition of tragedy. He does this

(A) to emphasize how outdated the tragedy is for the modern audience.

(B) because Greek philosophy is the only way to truly understand the world of the theater.

(C) because Aristotle was one of Greece's greatest actors.

(D) because Aristotle instituted the definition of tragedy still used widely today.

The answer to the question is explicitly stated in the passage. The phrase "definition of tragedy" is your clue to the answer. Scan the passage for the phrase.

Answer choice (D) is correct. The first paragraph of the passage clearly names Aristotle as the one who defined tragedy. Choice (A) is incorrect. The passage does not state that the classical concept of tragedy is outdated. Choice (B) is incorrect. The passage does not mention Greek philosophy. Choice (C) is not correct. Nowhere in the passage does it say that Aristotle was a Greek actor.

22. In the first paragraph of the passage, "noble" most nearly means

    (A) a high degree and superior virtue.

    (B) of great wealth and self-esteem.

    (C) of quick wit and high intelligence.

    (D) of manly courage and great strength.

You will immediately recognize the **vocabulary-in-context** question. Look at the context of the word in the passage. The words surrounding it are "good," and later "social position and moral stature." These should give you a clue.

Choice (A) is correct. "High degree" and "superior virtue" match the positive language in the context of the passage. Choice (B) is not correct. Wealth and self-esteem are not stated nor implied in the passage. Choice (C) is incorrect. Although wit and intelligence could be virtues of the tragic hero, they are not mentioned in the passage. Choice (D) is incorrect. The passage also does not mention courage and strength as attributes of the tragic hero, although these could be some of his attributes.

23. Which of the following is an example of harmatia in the first paragraph?

    (A) Courtesy to the lower class

    (B) The ability to communicate freely with others

    (C) Excessive suspicion about a spouse's possible unfaithfulness

    (D) A weak, miserly peasant

"Harmatia" is defined in the passage. You will need to draw a conclusion about the implied example of harmatia in the answer choices. There are no examples given in the passage.

Choice (C) is correct. The passage states that harmatia is the protagonist's "tragic flaw" that clouds his judgment. Excessive suspicion is an example of harmatia. Choice (A) is incorrect. Courtesy to the lower class is not a flaw in a character. It is the opposite. Choice (B) is not correct. A person's ability to communicate freely is not a flaw. Choice (D) is incorrect. The passage states that the tragic hero must have "social position" which would be the opposite of a "weak, miserly peasant."

24. Which of the following best summarizes the idea of catharsis?

    (A) All of the tragic consequences are reversed at the last moment; the hero is rescued from certain doom and is allowed to live happily for the rest of his life.

    (B) The audience gains a perverse pleasure from watching another's suffering.

(C) When the play ends, the audience is happy to escape the drudgery of the tragedy's depressing conclusion.

(D) The audience lifts itself from a state of fear and pity for the tragic hero to a sense of renewal and absolution for the hero's endurance of great suffering.

The word "summarizes" in the question stem is your clue to condense what the author has set forth about the whole idea of tragedy.

Choice (D) is correct. The passage clearly states that the audience should experience a "catharsis" and it should bring about a "cleansing" or renewal. Choice (A) is incorrect. The passage does not state or imply that the hero is "rescued from certain doom." Choice (B) is incorrect. Nowhere in the passage does the author state or imply that the audience "gains a perverse pleasure from watching another's suffering." The audience does, in fact, feel pity instead. Choice (C) is incorrect. The passage clearly states that "the audience does not feel depressed."

25. Unlike comedy, tragedy is

(A) a higher form of drama.

(B) on the decline in modern society.

(C) a cleansing of human emotions for the audience.

(D) satiric about the reform of institutions.

The word "unlike" in the question stem is your clue that this is a contrast question. You will need to use your inferencing skills to determine the way in which tragedy differs from comedy.

Answer choice (C) is correct. Only in tragedy is the catharsis a cleansing of human emotions. Choice (A) is incorrect. The superiority of comedy to tragedy is not stated or implied anywhere in the passage. Choice (B) is incorrect. The passage does not state or imply that tragedy is on the decline in modern society. Choice (D) is not correct. It is comedy that is satiric, not tragedy.

26. In paragraph three what does "incongruity" mean?

(A) Inappropriate

(B) Inadequate

(C) Effortless

(D) Unintellectual

This is a **vocabulary-in-context** question. Look at the context of the word in the passage. The word is used several times in the passage. Refer to each of those for a clue. Also, refer to the example of the incongruity of a tone-deaf person who tries to sing opera. The comic effect of this should give you a clue to the meaning of incongruity.

Choice (A) is the correct answer. The passage gives the example of incongruity as a tone-deaf person singing opera. This is inappropriate and, therefore, comical. Inadequate, effortless, and unintellectual do not fit the passage. Choices (B), (C), and (D) are incorrect answers.

27. According to the passage, which of the following statements are true?

   I.   Shakespeare used low comedy for dramatic purposes such as comic relief.

   II. Shakespeare used high comedy for dramatic purposes such as marking the passage of time in the drama.

   III. Shakespeare used both low and high comedy in the drama.

   (A) I only   (C) III only

   (B) II only   (D) I and III only

"According to the passage" is your clue to refer directly to the passage to find the answer. Scan the passage for key words such as "Shakespeare," "high comedy," and "low comedy."

Choice (D) is the correct answer. Paragraph four states that Shakespeare's comedy *As You Like It* is an example of high comedy with a sense of decorum. Paragraph five gives the reasons for Shakespeare's occasional use of low comedy in his plays. He used low comedy for "comic relief" from the intensity of serious drama such as his tragedies (I). While Shakespeare used high comedy, paragraph five states he used low comedy for marking time in the drama. II is not a true statement. Therefore, (D), I and III only is the correct answer.

28. The author implies that high comedy can be

   (A) further from tragedy than it is from low comedy.

   (B) more closely identified with tragedy than with low comedy.

   (C) erroneously associated with tragedy.

   (D) a form of low comedy.

The word "implies" in the question stem is your clue that the answer is not explicitly stated in the passage. You will need to **infer** the answer to the question based on what you have read in the passage.

Answer choice (B) is correct. The author implies that high comedy is serious in tone and in this respect is more akin to tragedy than to low comedy. A further implication is that high comedy does not necessarily provoke laughter, coming close to the nature of tragedy. Choice (A) is incorrect. The opposite is true. High comedy is closer to tragedy than it is to low comedy. Choice (C) is incorrect. The idea that high comedy is associated with tragedy is not erroneous. Choice (D) is incorrect. High comedy is not a form of low comedy.

29. According to the passage, a comic effect is achieved through

 (A) a character's incongruity in speech.

 (B) the incongruity of high comedy and low comedy.

 (C) an incongruous situation involving the audience.

 (D) the incongruity of the stage lighting and the actor's costuming.

The answer to the question is explicitly stated in the passage. You will need to search the passage for clues. Look for **key words** in the passage such as "speech," "audience," and "high and low comedy."

Choice (A) is the correct answer. Paragraph three states explicitly that "the comic effect is achieved through some incongruity in speech...or in the characterization." Choice (B) is incorrect. The incongruity of high and low comedy could be applicable, but it is not stated nor implied anywhere in the passage. Choice (C) is incorrect. The audience is not pictured in an incongruous situation in the passage. Choice (D) is incorrect. Stage lighting and costuming could possibly lend a comic atmosphere, but it is not touched upon in the text.

30. All of the following statements are true EXCEPT

 (A) a lack of subtlety and intellectual sophistication are marks of low comedy.

 (B) a high sense of decorum is indicative of low comedy.

 (C) satire is a form of high comedy.

 (D) gross absurdities are a mark of low comedy.

The answer to the question is explicitly stated in the passage. Scan the passage for **key words** (decorum, satire, gross absurdities). Notice the word "EXCEPT." This means the wrong answer will be the correct one.

Choice (B) is the right answer. The passage clearly states that a sense of decorum is associated with high, not low comedy. Choice (A) is a true statement. The passage makes it clear that a lack of subtlety and intellectual appeal are associated with low comedy. Choice (C) is a true statement. According to the passage "satire is a form of high comedy." Choice (D) is a true statement. Low comedy depends on "gross absurdities." Therefore, (B) is the correct answer.

SOCIAL SCIENCE

A social science passage may discuss such topics as psychology, archaeology, anthropology, economics, political science, sociology, and history. The following is an example of a passage from one of these disciplines.

Juan Ponce de Leon was the first Spaniard to touch the shores of the present United States. As Columbus had not remotely realized the extent of his momentous discovery, so de Leon never dreamed that his "island" of Florida was a peninsular
5 extension of the vast North American continent. After coming to the New World with Columbus in 1493, he had led the occupation of Puerto Rico in 1508 and governed it from 1509 to 1512. In 1509, he started a colony at Caparra, later abandoned in favor of San Juan. He was one of the first of the *adelantados*—men
10 who "advanced" the Spanish Empire by conquest, subjugation of the Indians, and establishment of a quasi-military government.

In 1513, the aging King Ferdinand awarded de Leon a patent to conquer and govern the Bimini Islands in the Bahamas of which the Spaniards had heard but not yet seen. According to
15 a persistent legend, there de Leon would find the marvelous spring whose waters would restore lost youth and vigor. The famed legend, rumored by tribes of Indians in Central America, was as well known in Europe as in America. The legend had come from Europe originally, and the Indians were only repeat-
20 ing what they had heard from white settlers. According to European Medieval Lore the fountain was in the Garden of Eden, reportedly in the Far East. The early Spaniards who settled America thought they were in the Far East. So many wonders had the Spaniards already encountered in the New World that
25 only a cynic would have doubted the existence of such a spring.

In March 1513, de Leon sailed off confidently from Puerto Rico for the Bahamas. Landing briefly at San Salvador, Bahamas, he wound through uncharted islands until he sighted an extensive coastline. He had no reason to suspect that it was any-
30 thing more than an island, but he followed the coast for a day without rounding its end or finding a suitable landing place. He named the "island" *La Florida*, probably because of the season—*Pascua Florida*, or the Easter festival of flowers. The name came to be applied by the Spanish to the entire present
35 Southeastern United States and beyond.

Then, near the 30th parallel, not far from the site of St. Augustine, de Leon landed at the mouth of the St. Johns River. Determined to be the first to circumnavigate the "island," he turned south, traced the coast around the tip of the peninsula, and

40 passed through the treacherous waters of the Florida Keys. These
    small islands or coral reefs stretched for 200 miles in a curved
    line from the present-day Biscayne Bay to the Gulf of Mexico.
    He then moved up the western coast, perhaps reaching Tampa
    Bay. After seven weeks, he gave up hope of circling the northern
45 tip of his "island"; it was incredibly large—bigger even than
    Cuba—and he may have suspected that he had discovered the
    long sought mainland. If so, it all belonged to his king, for he
    had earlier planted the Spanish flag and claimed Florida and all
    lands contiguous to it for Ferdinand.
50   Of gold and restorative waters, de Leon had seen nothing;
    of hostile Indians, predecessors of the Seminoles, he had seen
    too much. Returning to Puerto Rico in September 1513, he
    reprovisioned and then spent the next six weeks back in the
    Bahamas fruitlessly searching for the Fountain of Youth. He
55 drank the water of every spring he came to in Florida in the ever-
    present hope that he would one day come across the legendary
    fountain. Before the year was out, he sailed for Spain empty-
    handed. Ferdinand rewarded him, however, with new patents to
    the "islands" of Bimini and Florida, but he was to bear the ex-
60 pense of conquest.
         Not until 1521 was de Leon able to return to take posses-
    sion of his grant. By that time, his search for the Fountain of
    Youth took on a more immediate importance for he was 61 years
    of age. At large cost he equipped two ships, enlisted 200 men,
65 and set out to found a permanent base from which an exhaustive
    search could be conducted for the fabled fountain. Not only did
    he fail to find the fountain, but he also lost his life. Almost as
    soon as he landed on the western shore of Florida, probably near
    Tampa Bay, Indians attacked, killed scores of men, and mortally
70 wounded de Leon himself. The expedition hastily retreated to
    Cuba, where the "Valiant Lion," as his epitaph was to read, died.

31. Which of the following best describes the relationship between the first
    paragraph and the rest of the passage?

    (A) The first paragraph discusses the early years of Ponce de Leon's ca-
        reer, and the rest of the passage describes the later years.

    (B) The first paragraph describes how Ponce de Leon heard of the Foun-
        tain of Youth, and the rest of the passage details his search for it.

    (C) The first paragraph discusses Ponce de Leon's motives for becoming
        an *adelantado*, and the rest of the passage describes his career as an
        explorer.

(D) The first paragraph describes Ponce de Leon's first voyage with Columbus, and the rest of the passage details his attempts to circumnavigate Florida.

This question deals with the **sequencing of events** in the passage. You will need to check the text for details and the way in which they move forward in time. What is the author's purpose in structuring the passage in this way?

Answer choice (A) is correct. The first paragraph discusses the early years of Ponce de Leon's career, and the rest of the passage details the later years. Choice (B) is incorrect. The first paragraph does not describe how Ponce de Leon heard about the Fountain of Youth. Choice (C) is incorrect. While the first paragraph does mention that Ponce de Leon was one of the first *adelantados*, it does not discuss his motives for becoming one. Choice (D) is incorrect. The first paragraph does mention Ponce de Leon's voyage with Columbus, but the rest of the passage does more than detail Ponce de Leon's attempt to circumnavigate Florida.

32. Although Ponce de Leon was an explorer, the passage suggests that his main goal was to

(A) conquer and govern the Bimini Islands.

(B) locate the Fountain of Youth.

(C) circumnavigate Florida.

(D) subdue the Seminole Indians.

The word "suggests" in the question stem is your clue that you will need to utilize your reasoning skills in drawing conclusions. To answer this question you will need to reach a conclusion about Ponce de Leon's main goal, based on the information given in the passage.

Answer choice (B) is correct. Paragraph five refers to de Leon fruitlessly searching for the Fountain of Youth. Choice (A) is incorrect. Paragraph two states that de Leon received "a patent to conquer and govern the Bimini Islands," but the passage suggests that the islands' attraction to de Leon was the restorative powers of the legendary spring. Choice (C) is incorrect. Although paragraph four states that de Leon was "determined to be the first to circumnavigate the 'island' (Florida)" the passage also states that after seven weeks he gave up hope of circling the northern tip. According to the passage, he searched for the Fountain of Youth until he died. Choice (D) is not correct. Paragraph five states that de Leon had seen too much of the hostile Indians.

33. Ponce de Leon was classified as an *adelantado* (line 9) because he

(A) was a great explorer.

(B) was the first Spaniard to see the shores of the United States.

(C) was awarded patents by the king for the Bahamas and Florida.

(D) conquered and ruled by military force.

The answer to this question is stated explicitly in the passage. Scan the text for the definition of *adelantado*.

Answer choice (D) is the correct one. Paragraph one states that de Leon was an *adelantado* because he "'advanced' the Spanish Empire by conquest, subjugation of the Indians and establishment of quasi-military government." Choices (A), (B), and (C) are all true statements, but none of them gives a full description of an *adelantado*.

34. According to the information given in the passage, which of the following statements are true?

I. Ponce de Leon received royal funding for the conquest of Florida.

II. Belief in the existence of a "Fountain of Youth" was widespread among the Spanish explorers.

III. Ponce de Leon claimed Florida for Spain, and was rewarded with a royal patent to Florida and Bimini.

(A) I only   (C) I and II only

(B) II only   (D) II and III only

You should refer to the passage for the answer to the question. The correct answer is explicitly stated in the text.

Choice (D) is correct. Only II and III are true. Paragraph two states that the Spanish had already seen so many wonders in the New World that "only a cynic would have doubted the existence" of the Fountain of Youth (II). In paragraph four, the passage states that Ponce de Leon had "claimed Florida and all lands contiguous to it" for the Spanish crown, and paragraph five states that the king rewarded Ponce de Leon with "new patents" to Florida and Bimini (III). The same paragraph also states that Ponce de Leon had "to bear the expense of conquest" for his new lands, so I is false.

35. All of the following are true EXCEPT

(A) Ponce de Leon was motivated by a desire to discover the Fountain of Youth.

(B) legend held that the Fountain of Youth was in Florida.

(C) hostile natives mortally wounded Ponce de Leon.

(D) Ponce de Leon was one of the first *adelantados*.

Here again, look for explicit answers given in the passage.

Only (B) is false; paragraph two states that the Spanish had heard of the Bahamas, where legend held there was a "marvelous spring whose waters would restore lost youth." Choice (A) is true. Ponce de Leon was motivated by a desire to discover the Fountain of Youth, and he discovered Florida during his search for the mythical spring. Choice (C) is true. When Ponce de Leon returned to Florida to carry out his patent, he was mortally wounded by Seminoles trying to prevent the Spanish seizure of their land. Choice (D) is true. Ponce de Leon came to the New World as one of the first *adelantados*. (B) is the only false statement, and, therefore, it is the correct answer.

36. The main point of the author's presentation is

    (A) the Spanish attempts to discover the Fountain of Youth.

    (B) the Spanish discovery of Florida.

    (C) the career of Juan Ponce de Leon.

    (D) the Spanish treatment of New World natives.

This question asks you to identify the **main idea** of the passage. You will need to think in broad terms. A narrow focus might cover one detail, but the main idea incorporates each supporting detail.

Answer choice (C) is correct. Although all of the answer choices are stated in the passage, only the career of Ponce de Leon covers the entire passage. The answer choice is broad enough to cover all of the other choices and is, therefore, the main idea of the passage. Choice (A) is incorrect. The author's presentation covers more than the fruitless search to locate the Fountain of Youth. Choice (B) is incorrect. The passage covers more than the discovery of Florida. Choice (D) is not correct. There is no discussion of the Spanish treatment of the native peoples of the New World.

37. Ponce de Leon advanced the Spanish Empire by conquests, subjugation of the original inhabitants, and military rule. The passage suggests

    (A) Ponce de Leon had no idea the northern tip of Florida was attached to the mainland.

    (B) Ponce de Leon lacked the funds to return to Bimini and Florida immediately to claim his grant.

    (C) Ponce de Leon was subject to no man although he claimed all discovered lands for his king.

    (D) Ponce de Leon was determined to locate the Fountain of Youth for his aging king.

The word "suggests" in the question stem is your clue that you will need to **draw conclusions** from the facts you have at hand in the passage.

Answer choice (B) is correct. The passage states that Ponce de Leon "was to bear the expense of the conquest." He was not able to return to take possession of his grant for several years. It follows that de Leon's lack of funds kept him from returning to Bimini and Florida. Choice (A) is incorrect. The passage clearly states that de Leon "may have suspected that he had discovered the long sought mainland." Choice (C) is a false statement. The passage clearly states that Ferdinand rewarded de Leon with "patents" to Bimini and Florida. Choice (D) is incorrect. The passage implies that Ponce de Leon was searching for the Fountain of Youth for himself since he was already 61 years old.

38. Which of the following best describes an opinion expressed by the author rather than a fact?

    (A) Ponce de Leon "may have suspected that he had discovered the long sought mainland."

    (B) "According to a persistent legend, there de Leon would find the marvelous spring whose waters would restore lost youth and vigor."

    (C) Ponce de Leon "named the 'island' *La Florida*, probably because of the season—*Pascua Florida*, or the Easter festival of flowers."

    (D) "Before the year was out, he sailed for Spain empty-handed."

You can tell immediately that this is a **fact vs. opinion** question. Given the knowledge that an opinion is a statement for which the absolute evidence has yet to be proven, it is important to weigh the evidence against a well-established fact.

Answer choice (A) is correct. There is no evidence to support the author's opinion that Ponce de Leon "suspected that he had discovered the long sought mainland." Choice (B) is incorrect. According to the passage, the existence of the legend was a fact. It is not the author's opinion. Choice (C) is not correct. According to the passage, we can infer that Ponce de Leon's naming of Florida is a well-documented fact. Choice (D) is incorrect. It is simply a factual statement in the passage.

39. Based on the passage, what would most likely be the major cause of Ponce de Leon's failure to settle Florida?

    (A) He knew the king would claim Florida in the end.

    (B) He spent time and a great deal of money trying to find the Fountain of Youth.

    (C) He gave up his hope of circumnavigating the whole "island" of Florida.

    (D) Ferdinand was not supportive of Ponce de Leon's conquests.

This question asks you to determine a **cause-and-effect** relationship. Your task is to determine the cause. The effect is "Ponce de Leon's failure to settle Florida."

Answer choice (B) is correct. The passage suggests that Ponce de Leon concentrated much of his effort and money, "two ships and 200 men," in an exhaustive search for the legendary fountain rather than concentrating his efforts on conquering the new territory. Choice (A) is not correct. The passage clearly states that Ferdinand rewarded him "with new patents to the 'islands' of Bimini and Florida." He took possession in 1521. Choice (C) is incorrect. Giving up hope of circumnavigating Florida is an effect rather than a cause of his failure. Choice (D) is not correct. The opposite is true.

40. In the context of the passage, "cynic" might be most nearly defined as

    (A) a hopeless romantic.

    (B) a person who is trustful of others.

    (C) a gullible person.

    (D) a person who is scornful of others.

This is clearly a **vocabulary-in-context** question. Since "cynic" has no prefixes or suffixes, you will need to depend completely on its meaning in the context of the passage.

Choice (D) is the best answer. It stands to reason that the author is making the point that the wonders encountered by the Spaniards in the New World could be counteracted or doubted only by a scornful or cynical person. Choice (A) is incorrect. The word does not fit into the context of the sentence. A hopeless romantic would not doubt the existence of the fountain. He/she would, in fact, do the opposite. Choice (B) is incorrect. A "trustful" person would not "doubt." Choice (C) is incorrect. A gullible person would believe, not doubt.

☞ Drill: Reading

DIRECTIONS: This test consists of four passages, each followed by ten questions. Once you have read a passage, answer each question, and fill in the appropriate oval on your answer sheet.

Passage I

One January day, thirty years ago, the little town of Hanover, anchored on a windy Nebraska tableland, was trying not to be blown away. A mist of fine snowflakes was curling and eddying about the cluster of low drab buildings huddled on the

5 gray prairie, under a gray sky. The dwelling-houses were set about haphazard on the tough prairie sod; some of them looked as if they had been moved in overnight, and others as if they were straying off by themselves, headed straight for the open plain. None of them had any appearance of permanence, and the
10 howling wind blew under them as well as over them. The main street was a deeply rutted road, now frozen hard, which ran from the squat red railway station and the grain "elevator" at the north end of the town to the lumber yard and the horse pond at the south end. On either side of this road straggled two uneven rows
15 of wooden buildings; the general merchandise stores, the two banks, the drug store, the feed store, the saloon, the post-office. The board sidewalks were gray with trampled snow, but at two o'clock in the afternoon the shopkeepers, having come back from dinner, were keeping well behind their frosty windows. The
20 children were all in school, and there was nobody abroad in the streets but a few rough-looking countrymen in coarse overcoats, with their long caps pulled down to their noses. Some of them had brought their wives to town, and now and then a red or a plaid shawl flashed out of one store into the shelter of another.
25 At the hitch-bars along the street a few heavy work-horses, harnessed to farm wagons, shivered under their blankets. About the station everything was quiet, for there would not be another train in until night.

On the sidewalk in front of one of the stores sat a little
30 Swede boy, crying bitterly. He was about five years old. His black cloth coat was much too big for him and made him look like a little old man. His shrunken brown flannel dress had been washed many times and left a long stretch of stocking between the hem of his skirt and the tops of his clumsy, copper-toed
35 shoes. His cap was pulled down over his ears; his nose and his chubby cheeks were chapped and red with cold. He cried quietly, and the few people who hurried by did not notice him. He was afraid to stop anyone, afraid to go into the store and ask for help, so he sat wringing his long sleeves and looking up a telegraph
40 pole beside him, whimpering, "My kitten, oh, my kitten! Her will fweeze!" At the top of the pole crouched a shivering gray kitten, mewing faintly and clinging desperately to the wood with her claws. The boy had been left at the store while his sister went to the doctor's office, and in her absence a dog had chased his
45 kitten up the pole. The little creature had never been so high before, and she was too frightened to move. Her master was sunk in despair. He was a little country boy, and this village was to him a very strange and perplexing place, where people wore fine clothes and had hard hearts. He always felt shy and awkward

50 here, and wanted to hide behind things for fear someone might laugh at him. Just now, he was too unhappy to care who laughed. At last he seemed to see a ray of hope: his sister was coming, and he got up and ran toward her in his heavy shoes.

His sister was a tall, strong girl, and she walked rapidly and 55 resolutely, as if she knew exactly where she was going and what she was going to do next. She wore a man's long ulster (not as if it were an affliction, but as if it were very comfortable and belonged to her; carried it like a young soldier), and a round plush cap, tied down with a thick veil. She had a serious, thoughtful 60 face, and her clear, deep blue eyes were fixed intently on the distance, without seeming to see anything, as if she were in trouble. She did not notice the little boy until he pulled her by the coat. Then she stopped short and stooped down to wipe his wet face.

65 "Why, Emil! I told you to stay in the store and not to come out. What is the matter with you?"

"My kitten, sister, my kitten! A man put her out, and a dog chased her up there." His forefinger, projecting from the sleeve of his coat, pointed up to the wretched little creature on the pole.

70 "Oh, Emil! Didn't I tell you she'd get us into trouble of some kind, if you brought her? What made you tease me so? But there, I ought to have known better myself." She went to the foot of the pole and held out her arms, crying, "Kitty, kitty, kitty," but the kitten only mewed and faintly waved its tail. Alexandra 75 turned away decidedly. "No, she won't come down. Sombody will have to go up after her. I saw the Linstrums' wagon in town. I'll go and see if I can find Carl. Maybe he can do something."

1. According to the passage, the town of Hanover

   (A) was the only bright spot on the cold, windblown prairie landscape.

   (B) was populated by people who lived in drafty houses that had a temporary look about them.

   (C) had a main street that was deeply rutted and flanked with sod houses on either side.

   (D) had no public school because the children were tutored by their mothers in their own homes.

2. The statement that the houses looked "as if they were straying off by themselves" (lines 7 – 8) most likely means

   (A) that the villagers were moving the houses down the road to a different location.

(B) they looked as if they were being blown away by the strong wind.

(C) that their staggered appearance on the barren prairie landscape made them look as if they had taken legs and were wandering off.

(D) that the houses had been built along a crooked prairie road.

3. The passage suggests that the shopkeepers "were keeping well behind their frosty windows" (lines 18–19) because

(A) it was very cold outside, and they were too poor to buy adequate clothing for the cold weather.

(B) it was cold outside, and they were careful not to disturb the school children.

(C) it was a cold, snowy, gray day and not fit for humans to be out.

(D) it was dangerously cold for their horses to be out in the snowy weather.

4. According to the passage, the little boy was

(A) about ten years old.

(B) about eight years old.

(C) about three years old.

(D) about five years old.

5. The little boy (Emil) in the passage would most likely agree with the following statement:

(A) The town of Hanover was an exciting change from his dull life in the country.

(B) Hanover was an uncomfortable place to be because he felt like a duck out of water there.

(C) He liked going to the town of Hanover because his sister would buy him candy in the general store.

(D) Hanover was a good place for his kitten since he could buy cat food for her in the store.

6. The little boy's kitten was stranded at the top of a telegraph pole as a result of

(A) an encounter with a frightening dog.

(B) an encounter with a rabid dog.

(C) the kitten's insatiable curiosity.

(D) an encounter with the storekeeper who chased her up the pole.

7. The narrator's attitude toward the villagers can best be described as

(A) fearful for the safety of Emil.

(B) complimentary of them because they dressed well.

(C) indifferent to their strange coldness.

(D) judgmental for their cold treatment of Emil's situation with his stranded kitten.

8. The narrator's comment that Emil's "sister was a tall, strong girl, and she walked rapidly and resolutely" (lines 54 – 55) suggests that

(A) she walked very fast because she was in a hurry to get home.

(B) she had a firm control of her life, and she walked with determination and purpose.

(C) she was angry at the doctor and knew what she must do about it.

(D) she was angry at Emil for bringing his kitten.

9. What is the meaning of "ulster" (line 56)?

(A) A pair of man's overalls

(B) Men's snowshoes

(C) A man's long overcoat

(D) A man's scarf wrapped around the neck

10. The passage clearly indicates that

(A) Alexandra realizes she should have used better judgment in allowing Emil to bring the kitten.

(B) Emil wanted to bring the kitten to show to his friends.

(C) Alexandra refuses to do anything about the kitten because she cannot climb the pole.

(D) Alexandra realizes she must try to climb the pole to retrieve the kitten.

Passage II

A cave or cavern is an opening in the side of a mountain or underneath the surface of the earth, usually formed by some natural action such as water trickling through the cracks or flowing in underground streams. Caves are often formed in limestone
5 or some other soft rock when the water drips and wears away the stone. If the water carries the mineral called calcite, or calcium carbonate, it produces a phenomena of nature in the form of colorful rock formations inside the caves. These decorative dripstone features are called **speleothems** (from the Greek **spelaion**
10 for cave and **thema** for deposit). When these structures are highlighted by lanterns or electric lights, they transform a cave into a natural wonderland.

The most familiar speleothems are **stalactites** and **stalagmites**. Stalactites hang downward from the ceiling and are
15 formed as drop after drop of water slowly trickles through cracks in the cave roof. As each drop of water hangs from the ceiling, it loses carbon dioxide and deposits a film of calcite. Successive drops add ring below ring, the water dripping through the hollow center of the rings, until a pendant cylinder forms. Tubular or
20 "soda straw" stalactites grow in this way; most are fragile and have the diameter of a drop of water, but some reach a length of perhaps a yard or more. The large cone-shaped stalactites begin as these fragile tubes and then enlarge to cones when enough water accumulates to flow along the outside of the soda straws.
25 Deposition of calcite on the outside of the tubes, most of which are near the ceiling and taper downward, results in the familiar cone shapes.

Stalagmites grow upward from the floor of the cave generally as a result of water dripping from overhanging stalactites. A
30 "column" forms when a stalactite and a stalagmite grow until they join. A "curtain" or "drapery" begins to form on an inclined ceiling when the drops of water trickle along a slope. Gradually a thin sheet of calcite grows downward from the ceiling and hangs in decorative folds like a drape. Sheets of calcite that are depos-
35 ited on the walls or floor by flowing water are called **flowstone**. **Rimstone dams** are raised fencelike deposits of calcite on the cave floor that form around pools of water.

Helictites are curious twisted or spiraling cylinders or needles. They apparently develop when water seeps through the
40 ceiling so slowly that slight chemical or physical changes can cause reorientation of the crystal structure of the calcite or gypsum. **Cave corals**, also formed by slowly seeping water, are small clusters of individual knobs.

Most cave passages contain deposits of material that have
45 been washed into the cave. This material, known as cave **fill**,
varies from sand and clay to stratified gravel. The pebbles in
these deposits often are highly polished or frosted and sometimes
are as large as six inches in diameter. Cave fills are particularly
noteworthy because they contain materials that reflect a geologic
50 history and a record of past climates of the surrounding area.

Rock material produced by the collapse of the ceiling or
walls of a cave is called **breakdown** and may range in size
from plates and chips to massive blocks. Most breakdown
present in caves today appears to have occurred thousands of
55 years ago. It is generally associated with the early history of
cave development.

11. The primary purpose of the passage is to

    (A) analyze a situation.

    (B) define phenomena.

    (C) propose a theory.

    (D) describe a specific place.

12. The information in the passage is most relevant to which field of study?

    (A) Geography   (C) Archaeology

    (B) Physics   (D) Geology

13. Which of the following statements best summarizes the details of the passage?

    (A) All six paragraphs discuss various kinds of cave features, from dripstone to breakdown.

    (B) Paragraphs one through four describe speleothems, while five and six discuss external matter brought into caves from the outside.

    (C) Paragraphs one through four describe phenomena caused by water, whereas five and six describe phenomena caused by other means.

    (D) The first three paragraphs discuss typical cave features, and the last three discuss atypical ones.

14. According to the passage, all of the following are caused by dripping water EXCEPT

    (A) stalactites.   (C) curtains.

    (B) stalagmites.   (D) rimstones.

15. According to the passage, all of the following are formed when water loses carbon dioxide and deposits calcite EXCEPT

    (A) drapery.   (C) helicites.

    (B) columns.   (D) stalagmites.

16. The passage provides information that answers which of the following questions?

    I.   Do cone-shaped stalactites begin as tubular stalactites?

    II. Are stalactites or stalagmites longer when they join to form columns?

    III. Do stalagmites, stalactites, and flowstone contain calcite?

    (A) I only   (C) I and III only

    (B) I and II only   (D) II and III only

17. It can be inferred from the passage that which of the following is the most geologically useful?

    (A) Breakdown   (C) Stalactites

    (B) Fill   (D) Helicites

18. It can be inferred from the passage that which of the following is LEAST likely to contain calcite?

    (A) Columns   (C) Helicites

    (B) Curtains   (D) Fill

19. According to information in the passage, the following is a definition of stalagmites:

    (A) They are formed when water drips from cracks in the roof of the cave and deposits a film of calcite hanging from the ceiling.

    (B) They are formed when water drips from cracks in the roof to form deposits growing upward from the floor of the cave.

    (C) They are formed when the crystal structure is reoriented into a spiral form.

    (D) They are formed as deposits of calcite around pools of water in a cave.

20. According to the passage, which of the following is an example of a speleothem?

    (A) Stalactites   (C) Rimstone dams

    (B) Stalagmites   (D) All of the above.

Passage III

The ancient philosopher Socrates was put on trial in Athens in 400 B.C. on charges of corrupting the youth and demonstrating impious behavior. As recorded in Plato's *The Apology*, Socrates began his defense by saying he was going to "speak plainly and honestly" unlike the eloquent sophists the Athenian jury was accustomed to hearing. His appeal to unadorned language offended the jurors who were expecting to be entertained.

The philosopher addressed the charges leveled against him, dismissing them as mere ploys to gain advantage in a deeper attack against his philosophical activity. That activity had given rise to Socrates' motto, "The unexamined life is not worth living," and to the "Socratic Method" which is still employed in many law schools today. This critical questioning of leading Athenians had made Socrates very unpopular with those in power and, he insisted, was what led to his trial. This challenge to the legitimacy of the legal system itself further alienated his judges.

Socrates tried to explain that his philosophical life had come about by accident. He had been content to be a humble stone mason until the day that a friend informed him that the Oracle of Delphi had said that "Socrates is the wisest man in Greece." Socrates had set about disproving it by talking to the reputed wise men of Athens. Unfortunately, those citizens (politicians, businessmen, artists) turned out to be anything but wise. Of these, Socrates had to admit, "I am wiser because although all of us have little knowledge, I am aware of my ignorance, while they are not." Revealing the ignorance as well as the arrogance of the prominent citizens did not earn Socrates their affection, especially when the bright young men of Athens began following him around and delighted in disgracing their elders. Hence, in his view, the formal charges by the citizens of Athens that he had "corrupted their youth" and "demonstrated impious behavior" were only a pretext on their part. Their real concern was his offense of challenging the pretensions of the establishment.

Although Socrates viewed the whole trial as a sham, he cleverly refuted the charges by using the same method of questioning that got him into trouble in the first place. Against the charges of corrupting the youth, Socrates asked his chief accuser, Meletus, whether anyone would want to harm himself, to which Meletus answered, "no." Then, Socrates asked if one's associates would have an effect on one: good people for good, and evil people for evil, to which Meletus answered, "yes." Next, Socrates asked whether corrupting one's companions would

make them better or worse, to which Meletus responded,
45 "worse." Finally Socrates set the trap by asking Meletus if
Socrates had corrupted the youth intentionally or unintentionally.
Meletus, wanting to make the charges as bad as possible, answered, "intentionally." Socrates showed the contradictory nature of the charge, since by intentionally corrupting his compan-
50 ions he made them worse, thereby bringing harm on himself. He
also refuted the second charge of demonstrating impiety by
showing that its two components (teaching about strange gods
and atheism) were inconsistent.

   Although Socrates had logically refuted the charges against
55 him, the Athenian jury found him guilty, and Meletus proposed
the death penalty. Socrates was allowed to propose an alternative
penalty, and he proposed a state pension so he could continue his
philosophical activity to the benefit of Athens. He stated that this
is what he deserved. The Athenian jury, furious over his pre-
60 sumption, voted the death penalty, and, thus, one of the greatest
philosophers of our Western heritage was executed.

21. According to the passage, Socrates' defense at his own trial

   (A) was written by Socrates himself in *The Apology*.

   (B) was recorded by the eloquent sophists of the Athenian jury.

   (C) was recorded in Socrates' unadorned language by the Athenian jury.

   (D) is recorded in Plato's *The Apology*.

22. What does the author imply when he/she writes that the philosopher felt the charges against him were "mere ploys to gain advantage in a deeper attack against his philosophical activity"?

   (A) The charges the Athenians leveled against Socrates were deeper than those against his philosophical activity.

   (B) Socrates felt that the charges of corrupting the youth and demonstrating impiety were only a deceptive strategy to attack their real objection to him, which was his philosophical activities.

   (C) The charges against Socrates were designed to give him advantages in his philosophical activities.

   (D) The charges against Socrates were "mere ploys" and, therefore, taken lightly by the Athenian jury.

23. The main point of Socrates' argument at the trial was

   (A) that the only wise people are those who are aware of their own ignorance.

(B) that the prominent citizens could never be wise as long as they be-longed to the establishment.

(C) that the wisdom of the young is usually superior to that of their par-ents.

(D) that wisdom comes with age and maturity.

24. According to the passage, who identified Socrates as "the wisest man in Greece"?

(A) The young men of Athens

(B) Plato

(C) The Oracle of Delphi

(D) Meletus

25. The author would be most likely to agree with which of the following statements?

(A) Socrates contradicted himself when Meletus questioned him and this mistake awarded him the death penalty.

(B) Socrates, a born philosopher, had spent his whole life earning the reputation as "the wisest man in Greece."

(C) Socrates was not an eloquent speaker, but he had the truth on his side.

(D) Socrates viewed the trial as a stain on his reputation.

26. All of the following can be found in the passage EXCEPT

(A) Socrates corrupted the youth of Athens to spite Meletus.

(B) Meletus agreed with Socrates that corrupting one's companions would make them worse.

(C) Meletus charged Socrates with corrupting the youth intentionally.

(D) Meletus agreed that nobody would want to bring harm upon himself.

27. Judging from the passage "Socratic Method" means

(A) the unexamined life.

(B) law school examinations.

(C) a plain and honest way of speaking.

(D) logical repetition of questions to elicit the truth.

28. According to the passage, Socrates was a

    (A) politician.   (C) poet.

    (B) philosopher.   (D) businessman.

29. Which one of the following statements is the author's opinion instead of a historical fact?

    (A) The philosopher Socrates was put on trial on charges of corrupting the youth and demonstrating impious behavior.

    (B) One of the greatest philosophers of our Western heritage was executed.

    (C) The Athenian jury found him guilty, and Meletus proposed the death penalty.

    (D) He also refuted the second charge of demonstrating impiety by showing that its two components (teaching about strange gods and atheism) were inconsistent.

30. The Athenian jury voted the death penalty for Socrates as a result of

    (A) Meletus' alternative penalty.

    (B) Socrates' refusal to propose an alternative penalty.

    (C) Socrates' alternative proposal which angered them.

    (D) the contradictory nature of the charge.

Passage IV

Pennsylvania was the most successful of the proprietary colonies. Admiral Sir William Penn was a wealthy and respected friend of Charles II. Penn's son William was an associate of George Fox, founder of the Society of Friends (Quakers). In
5   1670, when the senior Penn died, his Quaker son inherited not only the friendship of the crown but also an outstanding unpaid debt of some magnitude owed to his father by the king. As settlement, in 1681, he received a grant of land in America called Pennsylvania (Penn's woods) which he decided to use as a ref-
10   uge for his persecuted coreligionists. It was a princely domain extending along the Delaware River from the 40th to the 43rd parallel. As proprieter, Penn was both ruler and landlord. The restrictions on the grant were essentially the same as those imposed on the second Lord Baltimore. Colonial laws had to be in
15   harmony with those of England and had to be assented to by a representative assembly.

Penn lost little time in advertising his grant and the terms on which he offered settlement. He promised religious freedom and virtually total self-government. More than 1,000 colonists
20 arrived the first year, most of whom were Mennonites and Quakers. Many came from the lower Rhine River area of Germany to escape persecution. Penn himself arrived in 1682 at New Castle and spent the winter at Upland, a Swedish settlement on the Delaware that the English had taken over. He renamed it
25 Chester. He founded the capital city a few miles upstream and named it Philadelphia, the City of Brotherly Love. Well-situated and well-planned, it grew rapidly. Within two years it had more than 600 houses, many of them handsome brick residences surrounded by lawns and gardens.
30 Sharing the same principles of peace and nonviolence, Quakers and Mennonites also came from Crefeld in Germany in 1683 to settle in Germantown, Pennsylvania, now incorporated as part of Philadelphia. These Dutch-speaking Mennonites, under the leadership of Francis Daniel Pastorius, were weavers and
35 millers who were accustomed to living simply. Legend has it that William Penn personally invited the Mennonites in Germany to come to Pennsylvania, though there is no written evidence of his alleged invitation in any of Penn's publications nor of his rumored personal visits to Mennonites in Germany encouraging
40 them to come to his new colony.
The persecuted people of many countries found refuge in Penn's new colony. Shiploads of Quakers poured into the colony. By the summer of 1683, more than 3,000 settlers had arrived. Though the Quakers surpassed the others in sheer num-
45 bers, the Welsh, Germans, Scotch-Irish, Mennonites, Jews, and Baptists all mingled in a New World Utopia. Not even the great Puritan migration had populated a colony so fast. Pennsylvania soon rivaled Massachusetts, New York, and Virginia. In part, its prosperity was attributable to its splendid location and fertile
50 soils but even more to the proprietor's felicitous administration. In a series of laws—the Great Law and the First and Second Frames of Government—Penn created one of the most humane and progressive governments then in existence. It was characterized by broad principles of religious toleration, a well-organized
55 bicameral legislature, and a forward-looking penal code. Complete religious freedom was probably the most important concession since it empowered the settlers with individual rights far above those of any other colony in the New World. Penn instituted the death penalty only for treason and murder. The long list
60 of lesser crimes awarded the same sentence in other colonies was

a sharp contrast. He also allowed all Christians to vote and hold office as long as they owned a certain amount of property.

65 Another reason for the colony's growth was that, unlike the other colonies, it was not troubled by the Indians. Penn had bought their lands and made a series of peace treaties that were scrupulously fair and rigidly adhered to. Upon his arrival in Upland in 1683, Penn immediately made his "Great Treaty" with the Indians. He agreed to pay them well for their land. Penn's conscientiousness reduced hostilities between the Indians and the

70 new settlers. For more than half a century, Indians and whites lived in Pennsylvania in peace. Quaker and Mennonite farmers were never armed, and their satisfaction with the liberal and free government of the colony provided a peaceful and prosperous atmosphere. In 1750, after Penn's death, the French and Indian

75 Wars broke in harshly upon that peaceful prosperity.

By any measure, Penn's "Holy Experiment" was a magnificent success. Penn proved that a state could function smoothly on Quaker principles, without oaths, arms, or priests, and that these principles encouraged individual morality and freedom of

80 conscience. Furthermore, ever a good businessman, he made a personal fortune while treating his subjects with unbending fairness and honesty.

31. Which of the following statements would the author most likely agree with?

(A) The King of England imposed severe restrictions on Penn's land grant.

(B) Penn was an opportunistic businessman.

(C) Penn was too friendly with the King of England.

(D) Indians didn't bother the settlers because they were permitted to practice their own religion.

32. According to the passage, the "Holy Experiment" is an example of

(A) English-Colonial collaboration.

(B) an early bicameral.

(C) a treaty with Indians.

(D) religious toleration.

33. Which of the following was NOT true of Pennsylvania's colony?

(A) Rapid settlement

(B) Refuge for religious nonconformists

(C) Tolerant state religion

(D) Laws in harmony with those of England

34. It can be inferred from the selection that

(A) all other colonies would have grown more rapidly if they had been organized in a manner similar to Pennsylvania.

(B) all colonies should have been in harmony with the laws of England and had a representative assembly.

(C) those colonies that were awards for service from the crown were better administered.

(D) life with the Indians would have been much easier in other colonies if land had been purchased and treaties adhered to.

35. According to the passage, "the Great Law and the First and Second Frames of Government"

(A) established Penn's political reputation.

(B) created treaties with the Indians.

(C) became the basis of a progressive republic form of government.

(D) placed restrictions on immigration.

36. After the summer of 1683 the Pennsylvania Colony could be referred to as

(A) a "melting-pot" colony.

(B) a Quaker colony.

(C) the largest American colony.

(D) the first "democratic" colony.

37. According to the selection, as religious freedom was guaranteed, all of the following religious sects were mentioned as settlers in Pennsylvania EX-CEPT

(A) Catholics. (C) Mennonites.

(B) Jews. (D) Quakers.

38. The author uses which of the following writing techniques?

(A) Development of an analogy

(B) Literary allusion

(C)   Direct quotation

(D)   Supporting details

39.   According to the passage, the rapid growth of the colony of Pennsylvania could be attributed to all of the following EXCEPT

(A)   the proprietor's felicitous administration.

(B)   the splendid location and fertile soil of the farmland.

(C)   freedom from English rule.

(D)   the offer of religious freedom.

40.   The main idea of the passage is

(A)   the peace and nonviolence of Quakers and Mennonites.

(B)   the success of the Pennsylvania colony.

(C)   William Penn's success with the Indians.

(D)   England's oppressive treatment of the Pennsylvania colonists.

ANSWER KEY

Drill: Reading

1. (B)	11. (B)	21. (D)	31. (B)
2. (C)	12. (D)	22. (B)	32. (D)
3. (C)	13. (A)	23. (A)	33. (C)
4. (D)	14. (D)	24. (C)	34. (D)
5. (B)	15. (C)	25. (C)	35. (C)
6. (A)	16. (C)	26. (A)	36. (A)
7. (D)	17. (B)	27. (D)	37. (A)
8. (B)	18. (D)	28. (B)	38. (D)
9. (C)	19. (B)	29. (B)	39. (C)
10. (A)	20. (D)	30. (C)	40. (B)

CHAPTER 7

Attacking the ACT Science Reasoning Test

Chapter 7

ATTACKING THE ACT SCIENCE REASONING TEST

DESCRIPTION OF THE ACT SCIENCE REASONING TEST

The ACT Science Reasoning Test is designed to evaluate your ability to reason through a scientific problem. This part of the exam consists of seven passages. Each passage is followed by five or six multiple-choice questions, for a total of 40 questions. Your score will be based upon the total of 40 questions. You should answer all the questions, even if you must guess. You will be given one credit for each correct answer, and you will not lose credit for any wrong answers. You will have 35 minutes to finish this part of the exam. Each passage is rather short and can be read in about two minutes, and then you will have about 30 seconds to answer each question. If you can spend less time on the passages and questions which you find easy, you will have more time to work through the more difficult ones. Any extra time should be used to review your work.

The Science Reasoning portion of the ACT tests your skills of interpreting scientific data and experiments and making conclusions based upon that data. It will measure how well you understand, analyze, and then finally summarize the results. While you should have a basic background of science knowledge, the test will not require that you know or recall specific facts. For example, you should remember that RNA and DNA are involved in cell division, but you do not have to recognize their chemical structures.

It is also important to note that some Science Reasoning questions will require you to call on your background in more than one area of science. A question based on an experiment with the cell may require you to consider what you know about the cell from your study of both biology and chemistry. This is another way in which your ability to reason scientifically will be tested.

This test will cover all the areas of high school science. Most passages and their following questions will be taken from earth science, biology, chemistry, and physics. However, sometimes the areas of geology, astronomy, and meteorology are included. In each passage, a set of experiments or scientific viewpoints will be presented. The questions for each passage will evaluate your ability to interpret the problem, analyze the data, reason through the possible conclusions, and finally determine the one that is best supported by the data. Simply, this test determines your ability to think critically.

The first question(s) after the passage will require you to understand the passage. They may ask you the main idea behind the experiments. Or they may ask you to find a specific fact or definition in the passage. The next questions ask you to interpret the data: either by reading graphs or tables, or following a figure or flow sheet. These questions may also ask you to compare two figures or a figure and a table. The last questions involve making conclusions about the information that has been presented. You may be asked to describe the meaning of a graph, or summarize the results and explain how they fit in with the rest of the data, whether they confirm or contradict it. Your decision should be based solely on the information in the passage. These last questions may be the hardest for you to answer.

The information in the passages is presented in three different formats: data representations, research summaries, and conflicting viewpoints. Data representation may include graphs, tables, and schematic diagrams. Research summaries describe experiments and their outcomes. Finally, in the conflicting viewpoints passage, two scientists give opposing sides of a posed hypothesis, and each scientist states the data supporting his side. An example may be evolution theory versus the creation theory to explain the existence of man.

ABOUT THE DIRECTIONS

Make sure to study and learn the directions to save yourself time during the actual test. You should simply skim them when beginning the section. The directions will read similar to the following:

DIRECTIONS: This test consists of seven passages, each followed by several questions. Once you have read a passage, answer each question. Then fill in the appropriate oval on your answer sheet.

STRATEGIES FOR THE SCIENCE REASONING SECTION

You should follow this plan of attack when answering Science Reasoning Section questions:

Before the test, this is your plan of attack:

| STEP 1 | Study our review to build your science reasoning skills, and study our subject reviews to refresh yourself on the various subjects. |

| STEP 2 | Make sure to study and learn the directions to save yourself time during the actual test. You should simply skim them when beginning the section. |

When reading the passages, this is your plan of attack:

| STEP 1 | Review the questions. This should only take a few seconds. Ask yourself: what exactly is each question asking? Identify the words that are new to you and later look for them in the passage. How are they related to each other? Pay special attention to questions that ask the negative question, i.e., What conclusion is **not** supported by the data in Table 1? This question is sometimes used to confuse the student by asking the opposite of what is expected. By reviewing the questions first, you will be able to read the passage and specifically look for the information to answer the questions, and hence filter out the unnecessary details. |

| STEP 2 | Read the passage and figures or tables. What is the main point or the object of this study? What has been done? Many times the first sentence will tell the main idea of the passage. In these passages, each experiment is usually plainly and clearly stated: i.e., "…in the first experiment,…, the second experiment was done to show…" These sentences set up the problem and tell you exactly what was done. The supporting figures and tables, when present, provide the results, else the results are stated in the text. |

| STEP 3 | Fully read each question and the four possible answers. Estimate any numerical answers. Calculations by hand can be very time consuming; only do them if you have extra time after you have completed the entire science reasoning test. If you can immediately answer the question, then do so. Eliminate any answer choices that you can. Then go back to the passage and figures and look for the remaining choices. If you are still unsure of the answer, then guess wisely. If you have time later, you can come back to the difficult questions and work on them some more. |

SKILLS TESTED

Data Representation

The data representation passages and questions involve both text and figures, and in many cases the data is numerical. You may expect that only one experiment is involved. You will be required to interpret, analyze, and compare the data. First, a review of the graphs and tables will be given. Graphs and figures may include line graphs, bar and pie charts, lineage charts, and surface maps.

You are probably most familiar with line and scatter diagrams. An example of a line graph is shown in Figure 1. In scatter diagrams the points are not connected together.

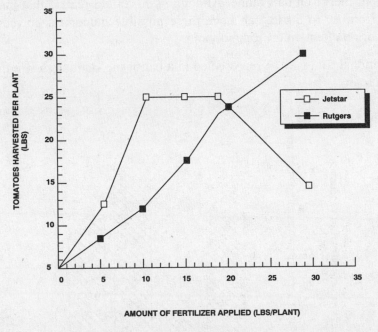

Figure 1

When examining the graph, first determine the variables. These are found in the axes and in the legend. This figure shows how fertilizer affects the production of tomatoes. From the legend, you can see that two types of tomatoes are shown: Jetstar and Rutgers. Next notice the units of each variable. Then read the data. In this case, you can directly read the graph: 10 lb. of fertilizer yielded 12 lb. of Rutgers tomatoes and 25 lb. of Jetstar tomatoes. Also, you can use the lines to estimate values. For example: if you applied 17 lb. of fertilizer, how many lb. of Rutgers tomatoes would be produced? Approximately 20-21 lb. Another question may be in order to get 20 lb. of Jetstar tomatoes, how much fertilizer would you need? You can estimate it to be 7 lb.

Finally, examine any trends in the data. For the Jetstar tomatoes, increasing the fertilizer from 0 to 5 lb. or 5 to 10 lb. increased production, but increases from 10 to 20 lb. had no effect on production, and finally increasing from 20 to 30 lb. actually decreased production. Then in this case, for optimum yield, 10 lb. of fertilizer should be used, as greater amounts do not increase production. For the Rutgers tomatoes, an increase in fertilizer always increased the tomato yield. From this data the optimal tomato yield needed 30 lb. of fertilizer.

If Rutgers tomatoes were grown with 50 lb. of fertilizer, what would the yield be? While you may be tempted to estimate a yield greater than 30 lb., this is incorrect. The graph shows data for the range of 0 to 30 lb. of fertilizer. There is no data shown for 50 lb., and therefore the question cannot be answered from the given data alone. Although you should realize that increasing fertilizer from 30 to 50 lb. can have three possible outcomes: an increase, a decrease, or no effect on the tomato yield.

Additional data may be represented in a bar or pie chart as shown in Figure 2 and Figure 3.

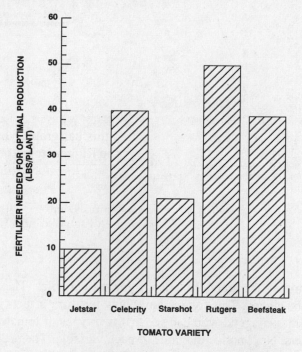

Figure 2

SIZES OF TOMATOES

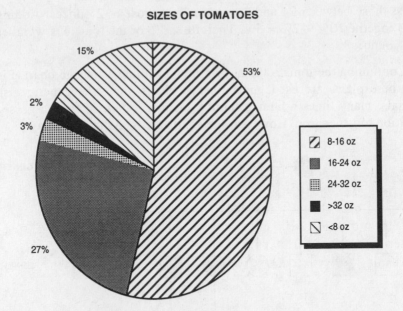

**100 BEEFSTEAK TOMATOES WERE HARVESTED,
WEIGHED AND GROUPED INTO 5 CLASSES**

Figure 3

The variables in Figure 2 are the tomato variety and the fertilizer needed for optimal production. There are no units for tomato variety; they are distinct types. The fertilizer is given in lb./plant. From this bar graph, you can see that the Celebrity variety needs 40 lb./plant, while the Rutgers tomatoes need 50 lb./plant. Again you are asked the question: if Rutgers tomatoes were grown with 50 lb./plant of fertilizer, what would the yield be? This can be deduced by combining information from Figure 1 and Figure 2. You can assume that the optimum may be greater than the 30 lb. shown in Figure 1, and Figure 2 shows the optimum to be 50 lb./plant. However, Figure 2 does not show what the actual yield was. Thus, the correct answer will be >30 lb. of tomatoes. In this bar graph you can also see that there is no correlation or trend between the optimal fertilizer needed for the optimal yield and the tomato variety. Trends do not always occur, so while you should look for them, you may sometimes conclude that none exists.

Pie charts, like the one shown in Figure 3, are used to represent data as a fraction of the whole group. Here the tomato weight is shown with respect to a group of tomatoes. As the figure legend states, 100 tomatoes were grouped according to weight, so the variables are the number of tomatoes and weight. The unit used for the weight is ounces. What fraction of the tomatoes weighed more than 32 ounces? The correct answer is 2%. What fraction weighed more than 24 ounces? In this case, two groups of tomatoes weighed more than 24 ounces: those between 24 and 32 ounces and those >32 ounces. Adding these groups together: 3% + 2% = 5%. Therefore, 5% of the tomatoes weighed more that 24 ounces.

Continuing the tomato theme, we now examine a lineage chart, Figure 4. While here plants are used, most lineage charts show the genetic history of mammals, many times a human family, or how a genetic trait is passed from generation to generation. However, the charts are read the same way.

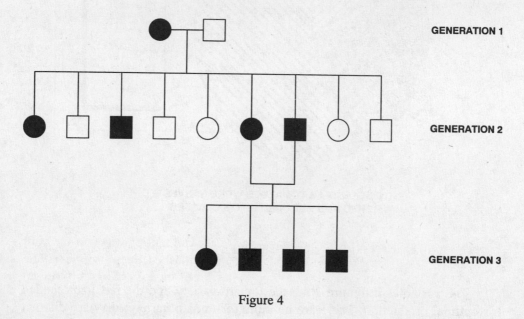

Figure 4

In these diagrams, circles represent females and the squares are the males. In this chart, the open symbols represent tomato plants with long leaves and normal sized fruit. The colored (black) symbols are plants with short leaves and very large fruit, greater than twice normal. The colored symbols also are more susceptible to the tobacco mosaic virus (TMV) which can kill the plant. In Figure 4, two plants were cross-pollinated and their seeds were planted. A sample of these plants are shown in Generation 2. Some of these plants do have short leaves and larger fruit. Thus, the gene was passed on from a female plant to both male and female plants. When two short-leafed plants were cross-pollinated (Generation 3), their seeds produced all short-leafed plants. From this lineage chart one can see that the gene is recessive and is not sex-linked. (Both male and female plants were produced with the gene.) If the gene were dominant, all of the Generation 2 would have the short-leaf gene.

Figure 5 shows the plot of land where tomatoes are grown. This is a surface map. It shows the elevation of the soil and its moisture level.

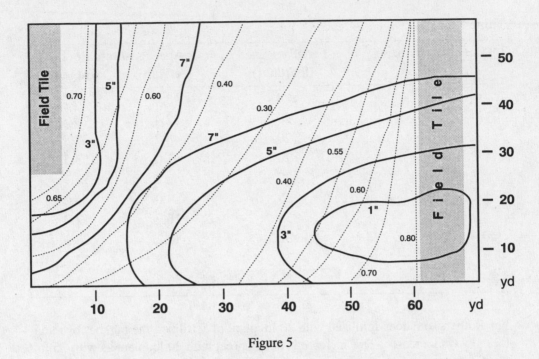

Figure 5

The variables are areas in the field, in yd., and the amount of water in the soil, given as lb. water/lb. soil. These are shown by the dashed lines (isolines). The enclosed areas, or contour lines show the areas of constant elevation, connected by solid lines. You may have seen these on other maps showing mountains and valleys. The elevation in the field is shown in inches by the solid lines. Also notice that two areas of the field contain field tiles, and that the soil near these field tiles has more water in it. The lines show areas of equal moisture content. Therefore, this graph shows two sets of information: the elevation of the soil and the moisture content. From this data, the moisture content of the soil appears to be affected by the position of the field tiles, but not by the soil elevation. Finally, what is the elevation at the location of 30 yd. E and 20 yd. N? The moisture content? The elevation is between 3" and 5" and the moisture content is between 0.40 and 0.30 lb. water/lb. soil. At 43 E and 5 N, the elevation is 1" and the moisture content is between 0.60 and 0.70 lb. water/lb. soil.

Sometimes data is represented in table form. These are the easiest to read because you do not have to estimate from a line or read isolines or contours. An example is shown in Table 1. Again you should first identify the variables and units. In Table 1, the variables are time after planting (in days), amount of fertilizer used (in lb./plants), and average number of tomatoes per plant for either Jetstar or Rutgers tomatoes. Determine if any variables are being compared; here Jetstar tomatoes are compared to Rutgers. Also look for trends among the numbers. The Jetstar tomatoes, when fertilized with 20 lb./plant, increase the number of tomatoes after 30 to 90 days of growing. After 90 days, the number of tomatoes decreases.

Table 1

Time after planting (days)	Fertilizer used (lb./plant)	Average # tomatoes	
		Jetstar	Rutgers
30	20	3.6	5.7
60	20	22.4	15.3
75	20	48.2	37.8
90	20	61.0	53.5
100	20	42.2	72.7
30	35	4.0	6.2
60	35	16.7	12.0
75	35	18.2	28.3
90	35	31.3	32.4
100	35	36.5	43.8

For Rutgers tomatoes fertilized with 20 lb./plant of fertilizer, the number of tomatoes always increased. This increase is not as great with 20 lb./plant as with 35 lb./plant. Compare 5.7 to 72.7 (with 20 lb./plant) to 6.2 to 43.8 with 35 lb./plant.

Finally, data may be represented in figures in non-numeric form. These figures may include flow diagrams, geology charts, or process diagrams. All represent data in a qualitative form. A flow diagram shows how a substrate is transformed. Figure 6 shows how glucose is metabolized by the mitochondria. Pay special attention to the order of events. From the diagram, sugar diphosphate with 6 carbons is needed to make 2 molecules of PGAL with 3 carbons atoms each. Sometimes more than one action can occur, leading to a branch in the flow diagram. For example, in the absence of oxygen, pyruvic acid becomes lactic acid. But if oxygen is present, then ethyl alcohol is produced (Figure 7).

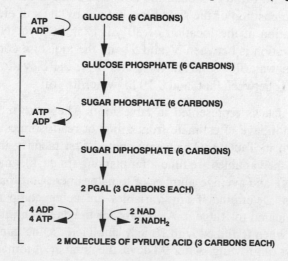

Figure 6

The steps are summarized as follows:

– Activation of glucose

– Formation of sugar diphosphate

– Formation and oxidation of PGAL, phosphoglyceraldehyde

– Formation of pyruvic acid ($C_3H_4O_3$). Net gain of two ATP molecules

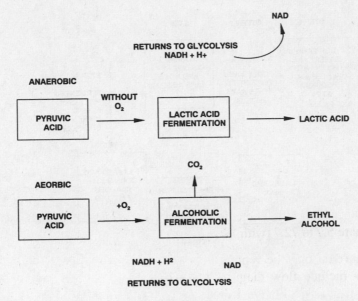

Figure 7

Geology diagrams usually display the depth of cross-sections of the earth. In Figure 8, the layers of an artesian well are shown. Notice the different layers of rock and the locations of the wells. Well 1 and Well 2 reach to the permeable rock layer and the artesian water table. In contrast, Well 3 reaches the local water table, and Well 4 reaches into the impermeable rock layer. Thus, Well 4 probably does not have much water, and the water from Well 3 will require pumping. The water from Well 3 will be affected by changes in local rainfall and weather conditions.

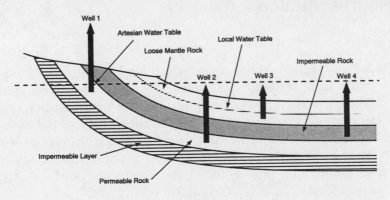

Figure 8

A series of chemical or physical changes can be displayed by a process diagram. One example of fermenting beer is shown in Figure 9. This is an open process. During each step new ingredients are added. The temperature and time of each step also are varied. Note that ethanol is made during Step 4 and that carbonation occurs during step 6. The steps must be followed in the proper order to achieve the desired outcome.

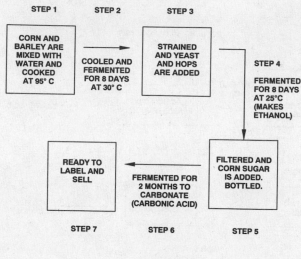

Figure 9

You may encounter other types of figures and charts. For each one, identify the variables. Determine whether the data is numeric or not. What is being compared? Are there any trends in the data? What units are used? Finally, determine how the figure corresponds to the accompanying text or other figures. Following are three sample passages and questions to practice your data interpretation skills.

SAMPLE PASSAGES AND QUESTIONS

Data Representation

Passage I

An automobile manufacturing company is testing new designs for car hoods. The shape of the hood can aid in the overall speed of the car, either increase or decrease it. These effects are due to the air flow over the hood. The air passing over the hood can exert a force on the hood. The location of where the force acts is shown in Figure 10. The angles of curvature of the hoods are also shown in the figure. The hood is mounted on a cart for testing. The cart is accelerated to a given constant speed and then the force of the air passing over the hood is measured. In addition, the time for the cart to come to a full stop is recorded.

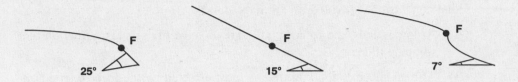

Figure 10

Table 2

Hood type	Speed (mph)	Time to stop (sec) ±0.5	Downward force (N)
A	10	7.50	+6.4
B	10	7.78	+2.5
C	10	7.95	−0.5
A	30	31.4	+12.6
B	30	42.4	+2.5
C	30	51.7	−3.7

1. According to the data, what hood design (type) exhibits the greatest downward force at either speed?

    (A) Hood B at 10 mph   (C) Hood C at 30 mph

    (B) Hood C at 10 mph   (D) Hood A at 30 mph

1   **(D)**   The greatest force downwards is the largest positive number. Thus: hood A at 30 mph has a force of +12.6N, followed by hood A at 10 mph (+6.4N), hood B at 10 mph (+2.5N), and hood C at 30 mph (−3.7N).

2. What hood type requires the longest time to stop at either speed?

    (A) Hood A

    (B) Hood B

    (C) Hood C

    (D) They all stop at the same time.

2. **(C)**   The longest stopping time was 51.7 sec by hood C at 30 mph so choice (C) is correct.

3. What conclusion can you draw from the data?

(A) At low speeds, the forces on the hoods have the greatest effect on the stopping times.

(B) At high speeds, stopping time is most affected by the force exerted on the hood.

(C) Force exerted on the hood does not affect the stopping time.

(D) Force exerted on the hood affects stopping time at high speeds but not at low speeds.

3. **(D)** At both speeds, a decrease in the force exerted on the hood increases the stopping time, however, at the low speed, 10 mph, the stopping time increase is very little and can be considered insignificant as these values fall within the standard deviation of ±0.5 sec.

4. The angle of the hood shape has what effect on the stopping time?

(A) No effect at low speeds, but increasing the angle decreases the stopping time at higher speeds.

(B) Increasing the angle increases the stopping time at low speeds.

(C) Decreasing the angle increases stopping times at low speeds, but the angle has no effect at high speeds.

(D) Decreasing the angle decreases the stopping times at high speeds.

4. **(A)** By comparing the angles in Figure 10 and the stopping times in Table 2, choice (A) best describes the results. The angles decrease from hood A to hood B to hood C. The stopping times at low speed, 10 mph, are not significantly different. However, at the higher speed, 30 mph, the stopping times increase from hood A to hood B to hood C.

5. The car manufacturer wants the hood design to add "the greatest drag" to the car, thus slightly pushing the car towards the ground. Which hood should be used?

(A) Hood A

(B) Hood B

(C) Hood C

(D) Any of the hoods can be used.

5. **(A)** The force that pushes the car towards the ground is a downward force. Hood A has the greatest downward force at +6.4N at 10 mph and +12.6N at 30 mph, therefore, choice (A) is correct.

Passage II

A study was done to evaluate immunization methods in both the industrialized Western nations (First World) and in the poorer non-industrialized nations (Third World). The cost and effectiveness of vaccines were two parameters that were examined. Cost is a very important public health consideration. In the Western World, most of the population can afford to have their children immunized. Those who cannot can receive free immunizations at public clinics. In the Third World, very few people can afford immunizations. While some clinics do exist, most of the population does not utilize them. The distance that each family must travel to reach the clinic may be a factor. How the cost of a vaccine and distance from the clinic affect the number of immunizations administered per 1,000 children is shown in Table 3.

Many vaccines are heat-labile; they need to be stored refrigerated or frozen, or they become inactive. Refrigeration is not always available in the Third World, and many times the vaccines are stored at room temperature. In this study, two vaccines for measles were used to vaccinate 100 children in three Third World countries. The number of cases of measles in each country were recorded 1, 5, and 10 yr. after immunization. This data is shown in Table 4.

Table 3

Vaccine	Cost/shot	First World Children		Third World Children	
		Percent immunized	Distance	Percent immunized	Distance
I	$40.00	82.3	21.7 miles	0.6	93.6 miles
II	$ 2.25	12.7	21.7 miles	2.9	93.6 miles
III	$ 0.37	not used		7.2	76.9 miles

Table 4

Vaccine Used	Room Temp.	Days Stored	Cases of Measles After		
			1 year	5 years	10 years
II	75°F	0	2	5	7
		1	21	27	32
		7	50	57	63
II	99°F	0	2	5	8
		1	25	32	38
		7	27	33	39
III	75°F	0	1	2	12
		1	7	18	40
		7	6	21	33
III	99°F	0	2	3	10
		1	62	71	85
		7	89	94	97

1. Which vaccine is used most in the Western World?

   (A) Vaccine I

   (B) Vaccine II

   (C) Vaccine III

   (D) All are used equally.

1. **(A)**   (A) is the correct answer choice. From Table 3, Vaccine I is used in 82.3% of the immunizations in the Western World. Vaccine II is used in only 12.7% of the immunizations. Vaccine III is not used at all.

2. Which vaccine was most effective in preventing measles for up to five years after immunization?

   (A) II stored at 75°F for 7 days

   (B) II stored at 99°F for 0 days

   (C) III stored at 75°F for 7 days

   (D) III stored at 99°F for 1 day

2. **(B)**   Vaccine II at 99°F stored for 0 days only had 5 cases of measles. All the other choices had more cases and thus were less effective. Vaccine II at 75°F for 7 days had 57 measles cases. Vaccine III stored at 75°F for 7 days had 21 measles cases. Finally, Vaccine III stored at 99°F for 1 day resulted in 71 cases.

3. Why was Vaccine I omitted from the study of children in the Third World?

   (A) Vaccine I does not prevent measles in the Third World.

(B)   Vaccine II is usually used in the Third World.

(C)   Vaccine I was too expensive to use in the Third World.

(D)   Vaccine III is not available in the First World.

3.   **(C)**   Choice (A), that the first vaccine does not work in the Third World, is not supported by any of the data. Choices (B) and (D) also are not supported by the data. The cost of Vaccine I is the greatest. Also the text states that very few people in the Third World can afford to immunize children and that cost is an important factor, which supports the best choice, (C).

4.   If a vaccine is to be used in a tropical country (80–100°F) where the children can be immunized only once every five years, which will be the most effective?

(A)   Vaccine I   (C)   Vaccine III

(B)   Vaccine II   (D)   All are equally effective.

4.   **(B)**   Vaccine I was not used in the study and thus has no data to support any conclusion. Vaccine II, stored at 99°F, has fewer cases of measles than Vaccine III stored at 99°F. Thus, Vaccine II is more effective. Choice (B) is correct.

5.   What conclusion regarding the effectiveness of a vaccine and storage temperature CANNOT be drawn from Table 4?

(A)   Vaccine II is more effective in a 75°F climate after 0 days of storage than Vaccine III after 1 day.

(B)   Vaccine III stored at 99°F for 7 days is more effective than Vaccine II.

(C)   Vaccine II stored at 75°F for 7 days is more effective than Vaccine III stored at 99°F for 1 day.

(D)   Vaccine II stored at 99°F for 1 day is as effective after 5 years as Vaccine III stored at 99°F for 7 days is after 1 year.

5.   **(B)**   Choices (A), (C), and (D) are supported by the data. At 75°F after 0 days of storage, Vaccine II had less cases of measles (2, 5, and 7) than Vaccine III after 1 day (7, 18, and 40). Vaccine II (75°F for 7 days) had fewer cases of measles (50, 57, and 63) than Vaccine III (99°F for 1 day at 62, 71, and 85). Vaccine II (99°F for 1 day) 5 years after immunization resulted in 32 cases of measles, while Vaccine III (99°F for 7 days) produced 89 cases of measles after only 1 year. However, Vaccine III at 99°F for 7 days produced 89, 93, and 97 measles cases while Vaccine II at 99°F for 7 days produced 27, 33, and 39 cases. Thus, Vaccine III is not more effective than Vaccine II in this case, and choice (B) is the only conclusion that is not supported by the data.

Passage III

Several years after a volcanic eruption, scientists are tracking the development of new plant and animal life and growth. They have compared the temperature profile just after the eruption (Figure 11) to the presence of new plants and animals. This map also shows elevations after the eruption. The relative differences in elevations between sites did not change before and after the eruption. As a lake had previously existed quite near the site, new aquatic life has also been examined (See Table 5 and Table 6). The scientists hoped to use this information to study the regrowth of life forms after other forms of destruction, especially those which greatly increase the surface temperatures of the soil and water.

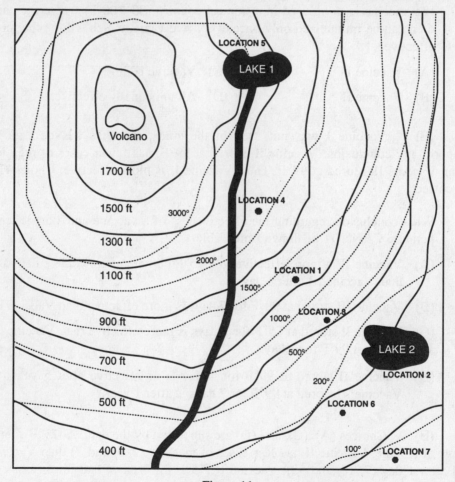

Figure 11

Table 5—Plant Life

Location	Before Eruption	After Eruption
1	pines, brush	brush, grass
2	tall water grasses	small water grasses
3	grasses/deciduous trees/pines	grasses
4	mosses/lichens	mosses/lichens
5	small water grasses/mosses	algae
6	pines/brush	mosses
7	deciduous trees	young deciduous trees/pines

Table 6—Animal Life*

Location	Before Eruption	After Eruption
1	2/27/52,000	0/0/28,000
2	614/242,000	450/350,000
3	1/14/63,000	0/0/30,000
4	0/10/13,800	0/0/30,000
5	514/152,000	14/250,000
6	4/65/65,000	0/2/37,000
7	7/127/75,400	1/15/150,000

*either given as the # large mammals/# small mammals/# insects for land areas or as # fish/# insects for aquatic locations (2 and 5) per 1,000 ft area

1.   Which location had the highest surface temperature?

  (A) 2   (C) 4

  (B) 5   (D) 1

1.   **(B)**   (B) is the correct choice. From the surface temperature, location 5 is at 3,000°F, location 2 at 100°F, location 4 at 2,000°F and location 1 at 1,000°F.

2. What is the elevation of the lake in location 2?

(A) 100 ft   (C) 2,000 ft

(B) 5,00 ft   (D) 400 ft

2. **(D)** Choice (D) is correct. The lake is at 400 ft because it is enclosed by the 400 ft contour line. The lake is outside of the 500 ft contour. The temperature of the lake is 100°F.

3. In location 6, what changes were seen among plant and animal life?

(A) Deciduous trees were replaced by pine trees, and small mammals declined.

(B) Grasses and mosses were replaced by mosses and lichens, and large mammals declined.

(C) Pines were replaced by mosses, and small and large mammals declined.

(D) Tall water grasses were replaced by algae, and insects increased.

3. **(C)** From Table 5, before the eruption, location 6 had pine trees and brush, afterward it had mosses. Also, the large mammals decreased from 4 to 0, small mammals decreased from 65 to 2, and insects decreased from 65,000 to 37,000. Thus (C) is the correct choice.

4. Locations 1 and 3 had very different plant and animal life before the eruption, however their profiles after the eruption were quite similar. Why?

(A) Before the blast, locations 1 and 3 were at different elevations, but at the same elevation after the eruption.

(B) The surface temperatures were different before the eruption, but the same afterwards.

(C) Elevations before the eruptions were different, but temperatures of the soil afterwards were the same.

(D) Elevations were different before the eruptions, surface temperatures after the eruption were different, but high enough to destroy all life forms, and thus each location had the same "starting point".

4. **(D)** The elevations of locations 1 and 3 are 700 and 500 ft, respectively. The elevations did not change after the eruption, thus choice (A) is incorrect. The surface temperatures after the eruption were 1,000°F for location 1 and 500°F for location 3. Thus choices (B) and (C) are incorrect. Choice (D) is correct, elevations and temperatures are different. However, examining Table 6, both locations

and location 4 all have the same animal life, leading to the conclusion that in all cases all life was destroyed and later reappeared in the same time frame.

5.   What conclusion can you draw from this data?

(A)   Insects reappear before small mammals and fish.

(B)   After the eruption, deciduous trees and pines are replaced by mosses and lichens.

(C)   Elevation does not affect the reappearance of new life forms.

(D)   After the eruption, small mammals reappear before the insects.

5.   **(A)**   From Table 6, insects appear before small mammals and fish. Greater numbers of insects were found than of the small mammals or fish. Thus, choice (A) is the correct answer. From Table 5, deciduous trees were replaced by pines and brushes, not mosses and lichens, thus (B) is incorrect. The plant life was affected by elevations, i.e., Location 4 had mosses while 3 had grasses, thus (C) is incorrect. From Table 6, small mammals appear after insects. Insects appear first, thus choice (D) is incorrect.

Research Summaries

The research summaries present a series of experiments, two or three, with the resulting data. Sometimes the data is shown in a figure or a table, or else it is reported in the text. You should review each experiment and understand what the scientist is trying to test or show. What question is being asked? Try to visualize the experiment. Sometimes a figure is used to explain the design of the experiment. After you understand the experiment, you can then examine the data. How is the data presented? Like in the data representation passages, you should determine what variables were used. How were they measured? What are the units? What is the relationship between the first experiment and the second, and possibly the third?

All experiments must have controls. A control ensures that the observed outcome was caused by the change of variable, or condition of interest, and not by a change in the background or other supposedly constant variables. A negative control is designed to give no effect or only background. For example, you are testing for the sugar content of a variety of sodas, and the reaction is calorimetric (produces a color change, say from yellow to dark blue). For the negative control you may use seltzer water, which has no sugar in it, and thus will produce a yellow color. The positive control is designed to definitely give you the desired outcome. In the soda example, you may add several teaspoons of sugar to the seltzer and then test it and obtain a dark blue color. Any other soda will give you colors between the yellow (seltzer, no sugar) and dark blue (seltzer with a known amount of sugar). The results may be shades of green. Positive and negative controls are used to make sure that your testing technique (or assay) is working properly.

Once you understand the experiment in the passages and have reviewed the results, you should try to make conclusions. What have the experiments shown? Did they support or contradict the hypothesis? Were there any flaws in the experiments? What were they? How did they affect the results and the conclusions?

A few sample passages and questions follow. Read the passages and try to understand the experiments. Answer the questions. Explanations of the correct answers follow each passage.

Passage IV

Neurons communicate with one another by synapses. Chemicals are released by one neuron into the synaptic cleft, then the chemical or neurotransmitters cross the synapse and reach the second neuron. The neurotransmitter binds to receptors on the second neuron, hence the message has been sent. One of these neurotransmitters is γ^- aminobutyric acid (GABA) which is dependent upon ATP for its uptake. Several experiments were done to study the uptake of GABA.

Experiment 1

Rat brain synaptic vesicles were purified. GABA uptake is thought to be dependent upon two factors: the membrane potential of the cell ($\Delta\psi$) and the pH gradient which occurs across the cell membrane (ApH). The synaptic vesicles maintained both of these gradients. To examine the uptake of GABA, radio labeled GABA, [3H]GABA, was added to the buffer solution. At each time point, vesicles were collected, fractionated, and assayed in a solution containing 2 mM Mg-ATP for the amount of GABA inside (i.e., how much had been taken in). These results are shown in Table 7. The compound FCCP is known to reduce uptake. Its effect is also reported.

Table 7

Time (min)	GABA uptake (pmol/mg protein)	
	2 mM Mg-ATP	2 mM Mg-ATP+ 40 µM FCCP
1	20	70
2	100	110
5	270	85
10	330	190
15	380	65

Experiment 2

The vesicles also contained transporters for glutamate and dopamine. The uptake of these molecules was also evaluated. In all cases several pharmacological inhibitors were added. The compound FCCP is known to uncouple the proton pump from the GABA transporter, and thus eliminate the pH gradient.

Table 8

Compound added	Uptake (pmol/mg protein)		
	GABA	**Glutamate**	**Dopamine**
Control (ATP)	213 ± 72	862 ± 230	18.4 ± 3.1
FCCP (20 μM)	152 ± 45	95 ± 42	2.5 ± 0.9
Gramicidin D	168 ± 19	85 ± 27	ND
(40 μM)			
Reserpine	ND	ND	3.1 ± 0.7
Reserpine + FCCP	ND	ND	2.7 ± 0.5
(20 μM)			
Water	150 ± 85	90 ± 51	1.3 ± 0.2

ND = experiment was not performed

1. Based on the experimental results, which factor will not affect GABA uptake?

   (A) Amount of dopamine present

   (B) Membrane potential

   (C) Amount of FCCP present

   (D) pH gradient

1. **(A)** The text states that GABA uptake is dependent upon the membrane potential and the pH gradient, so choices (B) and (D) both will affect uptake. From Table 7 and Table 8, FCCP is shown to reduce GABA uptake. Neither the data nor the text link dopamine presence and GABA uptake. Thus dopamine does not affect GABA uptake. Choice (A) is correct.

2. Why did 40 μM of FCCP reduce the GABA uptake in Table 7?

   (A) FCCP competed with GABA for the active site on the transporter

(B) FCCP inhibited glutamate uptake

(C) FCCP uncoupled the proton pump

(D) FCCP changed the membrane potential

2. **(C)** From Table 7, GABA uptake is initially greater in the presence of FCCP, at 1 and 2 minutes. At 5 minutes and longer times, the GABA uptake was decreased in the presence of FCCP. Therefore, choice (C) is correct.

3. What compound was used as the negative control for dopamine uptake?

(A) Gramicidin D   (C) Reserpine

(B) Water   (D) FCCP

3. **(C)** (C) is the correct answer. From the text of experiment 2, FCCP was stated to uncouple the proton pump and thus eliminate the pH gradient. The GABA uptake is dependent upon the pH gradient. The other choices are not supported by the data or the text.

4. How was GABA uptake affected by FCCP?

(A) Uptake was always less than control.

(B) Uptake was initially less than control, then it was the same.

(C) Uptake was initially greater than control and then less.

(D) Uptake was always greater than control.

4. **(B)** The correct answer is (B). Table 8 shows the effects of different drugs: FCCP, Gramicidin D, and reserpine on dopamine uptake. The control (ATP) is the positive control in this experiment. The negative control was the water, the measurement obtained without the addition of the ATP, drugs, or synaptic vesicles. The water is the background of the assay.

5. What conclusions can be drawn about the synaptic vesicles and their transporters?

(A) They contain GABA and dopamine transporters, but not glutamate transporters.

(B) Gramicidin D can inhibit the uptake of both glutamate and GABA.

(C) Dopamine uptake is reduced with Gramicidin, but the dopamine transporter can also transport glutamate.

(D) GABA uptake is dependent upon the glutamate concentration.

5.   **(B)**   From Table 8, all three transporters exhibited uptake. Hence the vesicles contained all three transporters and choice (A) is incorrect. Choice (C) is incorrect because the effect of Gramicidin on the dopamine transporter was not reported. Also no evidence suggests that the dopamine transporter can transport glutamate. Choice (D) is incorrect as again there is no evidence linking glutamate concentration to GABA uptake. The table does show that Gramicidin D inhibited the uptake of both GABA and glutamate. The correct choice is (B).

Passage V

The HIV virus contains RNA inside of a protein coat (or shell). The protein coat is used to carry the virus from cell to cell and to infect cells. Part of the protein coat, the docking region, functions solely to recognize the appropriate receptor, bind to the receptor, and then inject the RNA into the cell. The RNA then incorporates itself into the cell's replication process and alters the process to make multiple copies of itself. The viral RNA also programs the cell to produce multiple copies of the protein coat. The new viruses then infect other cells. This virus is also known to change its protein coat, thus several strains of the virus can exist.

A chemist is purifying a new protein which may prevent the binding of the AIDS virus to its receptor, the CD3 receptor on T cells. This new molecule is thought to be released by the cell into the extracellular fluid. The molecule must then pass through the cell membrane before it is excreted. Once in the extracellular fluid, the molecule is hypothesized to bind to the protein coat of the HIV virus such that the virus cannot bind to the CD3 receptor. Thus the virus cannot infect the T cell.

This new molecule was purified and evaluated in the following series of experiments.

Experiment 1
Since the molecule was believed to be excreted, cell media was collected and concentrated. Then, cultured T cells were grown with the HIV virus and different amounts, 50, 100, 500, and 1,000 ul, of the concentrated media. From this it was determined that the HIV infection was prevented when 500 ul and 1,000 ul of concentrated media was added.

Experiment 2
Cell media was then separated by column chromatography and the fractions were assayed. Five fractions containing large amounts of protein and two fractions containing no protein were used. Two of the protein fractions prevented HIV infection. The two non-protein fractions had no effect on the HIV virus. Gel electrophoresis showed the protein fractions to have molecular weights of 23 and 46 kiloDaltons (kD).

Experiment 3

The two fractions were further purified and binding assay was performed. It was determined that the 46 kD protein binds in a 1:1 ratio with the HIV virus and the 23 kD protein binds in a 2:1 ratio.

1. Why was the protein initially purified from the cell media?

    (A) It was membrane bound and portions of the membrane were left in the media.

    (B) The cell excreted the protein into the media.

    (C) The protein was inactive inside the cell but became activated after excretion into the media.

    (D) The media was the easiest fraction to purify.

1. **(B)**   The protein was believed to be excreted into the media. In experiment 1, cell media prevented the HIV infection, thus the molecule had been excreted into the media. Choice (A) is incorrect because the text did not discuss cell lysis or membrane portions in the media, it only stated that the molecule must first pass through the membrane. Choice (C) is incorrect because protein activation or inactivation was never discussed. For choice (D), while the media may have been the easiest to purify, no mention was made for other sources of the protein.

2. What was the motivation for experiment 1?

    (A) To determine if HIV virus was in the media

    (B) To determine if T cells could be infected with rhinovirus

    (C) To determine if the protein excreted in the media could prevent HIV infection

    (D) To determine the concentration of the protein in the media

2. **(C)**   Experiment 1 confirmed the hypothesis that the molecule was excreted into the media thus, choice (C) is correct. This excreted molecule could prevent the HIV infection. Therefore the cell media was a source of the molecule.

3. Why were different volumes of concentrated media used in Experiment 1?

    (A) To approximate the effectiveness of the concentrate

    (B) To determine the amount of HIV virus

    (C) To determine the number of cells needed for HIV infection

    (D) To determine the protein concentration of the media

3. **(A)**   The different volumes were used to approximate the effectiveness and to determine how concentrated the media must be to be effective. Choice (B) is incorrect because the concentration of the HIV virus was not determined. Neither the number of cells nor the protein concentrations were determined, thus choices (C) and (D) are incorrect. (A) is the only choice supported by the text, and therefore is correct.

4.   Why did the scientist separate the cell media into different fractions and assay the fractions individually?

(A)   Small amounts of cell media were needed to prevent HIV infection.

(B)   Chromatography increased the effectiveness of the molecule.

(C)   Only molecules of specific molecular weights could be assayed.

(D)   Isolation of the exact molecule for the cell media allowed it to be identified and studied individually.

4. **(D)**   The scientist was trying to isolate the molecule which prevented infection to later study it, therefore, (D) is the correct choice. The amount of cell media needed to prevent infection does not help in isolating the molecule. Chromatography was one of the tools used. The molecular weights were determined after the fractions were separated, and no previous data support the limitations of only assaying molecules of a particular weight.

5.   Which conclusion can be drawn from Experiment 3?

(A)   The 46 kD molecules may contain two subunits molecules of 23 kD each which bind to HIV.

(B)   Non-protein molecules are as effective as the 46 kD molecules in preventing HIV infection.

(C)   Binding assays are not effective in determining the ratios of proteins needed to prevent HIV infection.

(D)   Gel electrophoresis can be used to separate protein fractions.

5. **(A)**   Since twice as much of the 23 kD protein than 46 kD was needed to bind the virus, one might expect the 46 kD molecule to have 2 -23 kD subunits. Non-protein molecules did not prevent HIV infections to any extent. The binding assays were effective in determining the ratios. Finally, while the gel electrophoresis was used to separate the fractions, this was done in experiment 2. Choice (A) is correct.

Passage VI

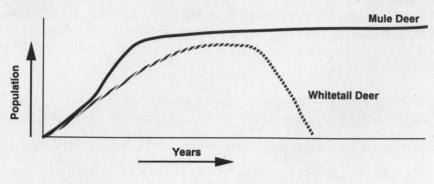

Figure 12

An ecologist has been studying the deer population in a national forest. Over the last several years the population of whitetail deer has fallen as shown in Figure 12. The ecologist then went on to investigate some possible causes for the change in deer population. He first examined the population growth in the surrounding area. Several changes have occurred in the last 40 years, the period covered in Figure 12. Three small factories have moved out of the area and one large factory has been built. The small factories produced paper pulp and paper. One also was a textile mill. The new factory is a plastics manufacturer. A new reservoir was built to supply the new factory with water for cooling. This reservoir is close to the national park where the deer live. Table 9 shows the changes in population and consumption of electricity and water during the last 40 yrs. All values have been normalized to year 0 values.

Table 9

| Time | Pop. density | Per capita consumption | | | |
		Wood	Natural Gas	Electric	Water
0	1	1	1	1	1
10	2.3	2	1.5	1.3	2.3
20	4.5	2.7	5.0	3.4	5.6
30	5.7	3.0	8.5	5.7	8.3
40	8.2	3.1	13.2	10.2	12.7

Secondly, the ecologist examined the quality of the water and how the water chemistry had changed during the time period covered in the study. The change in water chemistry (or pH) can also cause changes in the types of plants and grasses that can grow. These results are shown in Table 10.

Table 10

Time	Water pH	Toxin conc.	Plant life near streams and lakes
0	7.82	2 ppb	long grasses and trees
10	7.34	10 ppb	long grasses
20	7.02	10 ppm	long grasses, some short grasses
30	6.50	20 ppm	short grasses, algae
40	6.16	150 ppm	algae, very little short grasses

ppb = parts per billion
ppm = parts per million

1. According to Figure 12, two species with the same living requirements cannot live long together in the same environment. Competition will eliminate one of the two.

   (A) This conclusion is supported by the data.

   (B) This conclusion is not supported by the data.

   (C) This conclusion includes the effect of hunting and is supported by the data.

   (D) This conclusion includes the effect caused by a drought and is supported by the data.

1. **(A)** (A) is the correct answer since the gray line representing the whitetail deer population drops over a period of time, and the mule deer (black line) stays the same or shows an increase in population. Choice (B) cannot be the correct answer since one can determine that there were fewer whitetail deer over a period of time. Choice (C) cannot be the correct answer since no mention was made that hunting was allowed or had an effect. Choice (D) is wrong because no drought was mentioned in the text.

2. The changes in industry of the area altered the environment and thus the deer population. What evidence can be used to support this idea?

   (A) A change in industry resulted in an increase in radioactive material present in the drinking water.

   (B) Overall wood use increased by nearly ten times.

   (C) An increase in toxic organic compounds was seen in the water, followed by a decrease in plant life.

   (D) The pulp and paper companies cut down all the trees in the forest.

2.   **(C)**   Deer population is part of the overall wildlife. The water chemistry changed with changes in local industry. As the water changed so did the plant life. As deer are herbivores, their food source has been altered. Choice (A) is wrong as no mention of radioactivity has been made. Choice (B) is false, wood consumption only increased by three times. Choice (D) is incorrect as no mention of this fact was made. Choice (C) is correct.

3.   From Table 9, which item of per capita consumption was increased the least?

   (A)   Wood   (C)   Electricity

   (B)   Natural Gas   (D)   Water

3.   **(A)**   Per capita consumption of wood increased 3.1 times, gas increased 13.2 times, electricity 10.2 times, and water 12.7 times. Wood is the lowest; choice (A) is correct.

4.   If the projected population density for 50 years is an increase of 20% over 40 years, what is the projected effect on the mule deer?

   (A)   Increase by 20%   (C)   No effect

   (B)   Decrease by 20%   (D)   Decrease by 10%

4.   **(C)**   Choice (C) is correct. By examining Figure 12, mule deer population is projected to maintain the same level. Then no effect is expected.

5.   What is the most probable reason for the decline of the whitetail deer?

   (A)   The new factory released radioactive waste into the water and poisoned the deer.

   (B)   The increase in population led to an increase in deer hunting, and whitetail deer are the preferred deer for meat, thus their population decreased.

   (C)   An increase in the use of electricity reduced the water available to the deer.

   (D)   The new factory dumped toxic wastes into the water which lowered the pH and destroyed the plant life, which was the main food source for the deer.

5.   **(D)**   An increase of toxic waste was shown in the water, followed by a decrease in the plant life. As deer are herbivores, their food supply may have decreased. (D) is the best choice. The whitetail deer eat a different diet than mule deer. The mule deer food source was not affected. Choice (A) is wrong

because radioactive waste was not considered. (B) is incorrect as hunting was not allowed in the national forest, and (C) is incorrect because no correlation was made between water and electricity.

Passage VII

A chemist is investigating the possible use of catalysts to increase the rate of a reaction. A polymerization reaction is used to make a polyacetal compound which is used in medical prosthetics. Currently the reaction is done in a solution with an acid solvent. But the reaction is very slow and the product output is low. About 1 mg of polyacetal is produced from every 25 mg of acetal monomer. The remaining 24 mg contain unreacted monomers, dimers, (two acetal monomers linked together), and trimers. The desired chain length for the polyacetal is at least 7 monomers linked together. A chain length of 10 is most desired. The current reaction produces 10% of the 10 length, 15% of 8 length, and 60% of 7 units.

Experiment 1

The reaction is performed in the presence of a solid nickel catalyst. The polymer is then separated from the nickel beads, and the distribution of chain lengths of monomers is tested. For every 25 mg of monomer used 2.5 mg of polyacetal with chain lengths greater than 7 is produced. The chain distribution is 20% greater than 10, 25% of 9 lengths, 20% of 8 lengths, and 3% of 7 lengths. The remaining 20 mg of monomers have either been converted to dimers, trimers, or unreacted monomers.

Experiment 2

The solvent in which the reaction is performed was changed. Now the reaction was done in a combination of acetic acid and acetone with the nickel catalyst. The yield increased to 7.5 mg of polyacetal for every 25 mg of monomer. The distribution of polymer sizes was the same as with the nickel catalyst and the acid solvent.

Experiment 3

The catalyst was then changed to a cadmium sheet. The reaction was still in the acetic acid and acetone solvent. The results were 5.0 mg of product for every 25 mg of monomer used. However of the 5.0 mg, 80% had lengths of 10 or greater, and the remaining 20% had lengths of 8 or more. The remaining 20 mg contained mostly trimers.

1. What is the order of experimental conditions of solvent and catalyst which gives the highest to lowest yields of product?

    (A) Acid solvent > acid solvent + nickel > acid/acetone solvent + nickel > acid/acetone + cadmium

(B) Acid solvent + nickel > acetone/acid solvent + nickel > acid solvent > acid/acetone solvent + cadmium

(C) Acid/acetone solvent + cadmium > acid/acetone solvent + nickel > acid solvent + nickel > acid solvent

(D) Acid/acetone solvent + nickel > acid solvent + nickel > acid/acetone solvent + cadmium > acid solvent

1. **(D)** (D) is correct. The highest yield was obtained with the acid/acetone solvent and the nickel catalyst (7.5 mg). The other conditions produced the following yields: acid/acetone + cadmium 5.0 mg, acid solvent + nickel 2.5 mg, acid solvent 1.0 mg.

2. Which conditions produced the highest number of polymers of length 10 or greater?

(A) Acid solvent

(B) Acid solvent + nickel

(C) Acid/acetone solvent + nickel

(D) Acid/acetone solvent + cadmium

2. **(D)** The number of polymer of length 10 or greater can be calculated by multiplying the % by the weight produced. Thus:

acid solvent	$10\% \times 1 \text{ mg} = 0.1 \text{ mg}$
acid solvent + nickel	$20\% \times 2.5 \text{ mg} = 0.5 \text{ mg}$
acid/acetone solvent + nickel	$20\% \times 7.5 \text{ mg} = 1.5 \text{ mg}$
acid/acetone solvent + cadmium	$80\% \times 5.0 \text{ mg} = 4.0 \text{ mg}$

The acid/acetone solvent with the cadmium produced the most polymers of length 10 or more. Choice (D) is correct.

3. In comparison to the other yields, what yield would you predict under the condition of acid solvent + cadmium?

(A) Between 1 mg and 2.5 mg

(B) Between 2.5 mg and 5.0 mg

(C) Between 5.0 mg and 7.5 mg

(D) Greater than 7.5 mg

3. **(B)** The cadmium catalyst in the acid/acetone solvent (5 mg) produced less polyacetal than the nickel (7.5 mg) catalyst with the acid/acetone solvent. The nickel catalyst in the acid solvent (2.5 mg) produced more polyacetal than the acid solvent alone (1 mg). Therefore, you may conclude that the cadmium catalyst in the acid solvent would produce more than the acid solvent alone (greater than 1 mg) but less than the nickel catalyst with the acid solvent (less than 2.5 mg). The correct choice is (B).

4. The surface area of the nickel beads was 10 times greater than the surface area of the cadmium sheet. If the surface area of the catalyst was found to be important in determining the reaction rate and product outcome, then what statement is most likely to be true?

(A) Using cadmium beads would increase the productions of polyacetal.

(B) Using a nickel sheet would increase the production of polyacetal.

(C) Using cadmium beads would decrease the production of polyacetal.

(D) Using a zinc sheet would decrease the production of polyacetal.

4. **(A)** (A) is the best answer. The surface of the nickel was greater than the cadmium. The nickel (7.5 mg) produced a greater yield than the cadmium (5.0). Cadmium beads would increase the surface area by 10 times, and increase the yield by 10 times (5 mg)(10) = 50 mg. A nickel sheet would decrease the nickel surface area by 10 times, and thus yield (7.5)/10 = 0.75 mg. Zinc is not used in these experiments and thus no data is given to support choice (D).

5. Compare the effects of the overall use of the catalyst and solvent changes on the production of polyacetal polymers.

(A) The solvent change increased production, but the catalyst decreased it.

(B) The solvent change decreased production, but the catalyst increased it.

(C) The solvent change and catalyst both increased production.

(D) The solvent change and catalyst both decreased production.

5. **(C)** Compared to the acid solvent alone (1 mg), the addition of the nickel catalyst increased the production of polyacetal (2.5 mg). In addition, the change in solvent from acid to acid/acetone (both in the presence of nickel) increased the production from 2.5 mg to 7.5 mg. Thus both the solvent change and the catalyst increased the production and choice (C) is correct.

Conflicting Viewpoints

The conflicting viewpoints passages present two arguments for opposing sides of a hypothesis or theory. The scientist may be asked to answer a question. Each scientist will cite facts or experiments to support his argument. You will not be asked to decide which opinion is correct. Instead you will need to analyze each viewpoint and understand the passage. Identify how each piece of evidence is used and understand how it is used to support the scientist's side of the debate.

Read each question or hypothesis carefully. Then read each scientist's view. Pay special attention to the evidence presented. Sometimes the same evidence will be used to support each side. Note any criticisms of each scientist. After you have read the passages, re-read the question again. Has each scientist addressed the question or hypothesis? Keep the question in mind when you answer the questions following the passage. Refer back to the passage as necessary in order to answer the questions.

Passage VIII

Do humans need to eat meat to have proper nutrition?

Nutritionist 1
Humans are designed to need at least a small amount of meat or fish incorporated into their diets. Meat contains essential amino acids which are not present in other food products. These amino acids cannot be manufactured by the human body. Without these amino acids, malnutrition may result. The body becomes protein deficient. Long term deprivation of total protein, or a complete supply of the amino acids, can cause other medical problems such as some forms of liver disease or muscle wasting.

While plants, including grains and legumes, do contain some amino acids, none of these foods contain all of them. Even when grains and legumes are eaten together these amino acids are not present in the proper proportions needed. Also, milk and dairy products do contain protein. However these are high in fat, much higher than the average portion of meat, chicken, or fish.

Meat and fish also provide the body with iron and vitamins. They have more iron per serving than any plant food. The fat soluble vitamins, especially the B vitamins and vitamin K, are found in meats in high concentrations. Since most plants have almost no fat, they do not contain these essential fat soluble vitamins. To ensure proper nutrition, man should include meat and fish in his diet.

Nutritionist 2
Humans do not need to include animals and animal products in their diets to obtain complete nutrition. By eating both grains and legumes the entire set of 20 essential amino acids are consumed. The amino acids do not need to be included in the same food or even at the same meal to be effective. The human body uses

these amino acids as needed, so any additional amino acids are stored as fat. Foods such as meat contain unnecessary fat, and if excess protein is consumed, it too will be stored as fat.

While meat does contain iron and fat soluble vitamins, these nutrients can be obtained from plants. Iron is found in high concentrations in dark green leafy vegetables, such as spinach. The vitamins, K and B's, are found in avocados, grains, and especially nuts. Since all the essential nutrients can be obtained by eating solely plant products, meat is not necessary for proper nutrition.

1.   Which person uses the fact that humans need amino acids for his arguments?

   (A) Nutritionist 1   (C) Both nutritionists

   (B) Nutritionist 2   (D) Neither nutritionist

1.   **(C)**   Both nutritionists cite the need for all the amino acids for proper nutrition; (C) is the correct answer.

2.   What argument is NOT used by Nutritionist 1?

   (A) Deprivation of total protein can lead to malnutrition.

   (B) All amino acids can be provided by plant foods.

   (C) Meat contains iron and vitamins.

   (D) Plant foods contain very little fat, and thus they cannot contain fat soluble vitamins.

2.   **(B)**   Nutritionist 1 states that protein deprivation can lead to malnutrition. Nutritionist 1 also used the facts that meat contains iron and vitamins and that plant foods do not. However, Nutritionist 2, choice (B) stated that all amino acids can be provided by plant food. Thus Nutritionist 1 did not use argument (B).

3.   Which argument is used by Nutritionist 2?

   (A) Amino acids do not need to be eaten at the same time to be effective.

   (B) Deprivation of total protein can lead to malnutrition.

   (C) Meat products are the best source of iron.

   (D) Dairy products do contain protein.

3.   **(A)**   Answer choice (A) is correct, since Nutritionist 2 stated that the amino acids did not need to be eaten at the same time. Choices (B) and (D) were used by Nutritionist 1. Neither nutritionist used choice (C).

4. Which statement would greatly weaken Nutritionist 2's argument?

   (A) Less than 1% of the population eats nuts or avocados.

   (B) Fish is more expensive than grain products.

   (C) Soy products, made from the soybean, do have complete protein.

   (D) The human body can manufacture the B vitamins.

4. **(A)** Since Nutritionist 2 cites plants sources for vitamins, if these foods are not available, then they cannot be used as meat substitutes. Choice (A) is the only statement that would weaken the argument. Choices (B), (C), and (D) will strengthen the arguments of Nutritionist 2.

5. Which statement would greatly weaken Nutritionist 1's argument?

   (A) Meat and fish, per serving, are less expensive than soy products.

   (B) Less than 1% of the population eats nuts or grains high in protein.

   (C) Soy products have complete protein.

   (D) Humans cannot manufacture vitamin K.

5. **(C)** If soy products, a plant food, contain complete protein, then a meat substitute does exist, unlike the statements of Nutritionist 1. Then choice (C) will greatly weaken the argument of Nutritionist 1. Choice (A) would make meat and fish more accessible than soy products, and choice (B) would also make meat a better alternative. Therefore, arguments (A) and (B) support Nutritionist 1's arguments. Choice (D) would also support Nutritionist 1.

Passage IX

How economically and environmentally efficient are battery-powered (electric) automobiles?

Scientist 1

Considering the increasing cost of crude oil, an electric or battery-powered automobile is a better economic choice. With new regulations on the refineries, petroleum products will increase in cost even more. The drivers of petroleum-powered vehicles will also have to pay more for catalytic converters and other pollution control devices. Battery-powered automobiles will not be affected by the increasing cost of petroleum. The battery-powered cars will also be cleaner to operate.

These cars do not emit toxic gases such as unburned fuel or carbon monoxide into the atmosphere. The batteries are rechargeable, so they will be recycled and cause very little waste. Since these vehicles do not use gasoline, overall petroleum use will decrease. Therefore the refineries will not produce toxic fumes and release organic compounds into the atmosphere. Thus, overall environmental stress will be reduced.

Scientist 2

While on the surface, battery-powered cars appear to be more efficient than their gas-powered counterparts, they have many hidden costs. These costs are both financial and environmental. With current technology, the operating costs of an electric car are in excess of twice that of a gas-powered vehicle. The replacement of the battery also causes other inconveniences. Very few sites can recharge and/or replace the battery. The battery needs at least 12 hours to recharge. An adapter may be purchased for home use, but at a cost of a few thousand dollars. If the battery is drained and no replacement station is nearby, the car must be towed, inflicting more cost. These battery-powered vehicles also do not travel as fast as their gas counterparts. Thus time is lost during travel.

The battery powered car has many harmful ecological effects. The battery contains many concentrated acids and lead products. The manufacturing process of the batteries produces large quantities of waste. While the batteries can be recharged, this is only possible for a finite number of times. Afterwards the batteries must be disposed of, in most cases they will find their way to a local landfill. Thus the battery-powered cars have their own problems, and they are not as economical as the gas-powered vehicles.

1.   Which evidence is used to support Scientist 1?

(A)   High cost of gasoline

(B)   High cost of battery replacement

(C)   Low speed of electric cars

(D)   High operating costs of battery-powered automobiles

1.   **(A)**   Choice (A) is correct. Scientist 1 argues that the battery powered cars are more inexpensive than gas powered ones. Choices (B), (C), and (D) demonstrate the higher costs of battery-powered cars.

2.   What is the opinion of Scientist 1 with respect to battery replacement?

(A)   It is expensive.

(B)   It is inconvenient.

(C)   It can lead to an increase in toxic waste.

(D)   Scientist 1 does not state an opinion about battery replacement.

2. **(D)** Scientist 2 used choices (A), (B), and (C) to support his argument. Scientist 1 does not use the cost of battery replacement in his argument. (D) is the correct choice.

3. According to Scientist 2, what is a disadvantage of the battery-powered automobile?

(A) Replacing the battery on the road is a simple and convenient process.

(B) It travels much slower than gas-powered vehicles.

(C) Recharging at home is inexpensive and simple.

(D) They are cost efficient.

3. **(B)** Scientist 2 argues that recharging and replacing are expensive, long processes away or at home. Therefore, choices (A) and (C) are incorrect. The main argument by Scientist 2 is that the cars are inefficient. Therefore, choice (B) is correct.

4. Which statement would greatly weaken Scientist 2's argument?

(A) Petroleum refinery costs are decreasing.

(B) Home recharging systems require at least 24 hours to fully recharge the battery.

(C) New technology has decreased the cost of batteries by nearly 70%.

(D) Gas-powered vehicles can release ozone which further degrades the atmosphere.

4. **(C)** Scientist 2 cites the cost of the battery as one of the major disadvantages. Therefore, a decrease in the cost would weaken the argument. Choice (C) is correct.

5. Which statement would strengthen Scientist 1's argument?

(A) Petroleum refinery costs are decreasing.

(B) Home recharging systems require at least 24 hours to fully recharge the battery.

(C) New technology has decreased the cost of batteries by nearly 70%.

(D) New catalytic converters reduce gas emissions by nearly 70%.

5. **(C)** (C) is the correct choice. The fact, which weakens Scientist 2's argument in question 4, will strengthen Scientist 1's arguments. Choice (D) would weaken Scientist 1's argument.

COMMON TERMS

Below is a list of common terms that you should know. These terms are all found in boldface type in the following review sections.

absorption
acceleration
acid
activation energy
adenoid
aerobic
allele
allergy
alveoli
amino acid
anaerobic
anaphase
anatomy
Animalia kingdom
Archimedes' Principle
assimilation
asteroid
astronomy
atmosphere
atom
atomic number
ATP
axosphere
bacteriology
basal body
base
behavior
binomial nomenclature
biology
biosphere
boiling point
botany
carbon cycle
cardiac muscle
cell

cell membrane
cell wall
Cenozoic era
centriole
chemical equation
chemical kinetics
chemical property
chemistry
chloroplast
chromosome
circulatory system
classification
climate
colloid
comet
compound
conductor
conservation
constellation
continental drift
continental shelf
corrosion
covalent bond
cytology
cytoplasm
density
dermis
digestion
digestive system
diurnal tide
DNA
earthquake
ecology
eddy
electrical circuit

electrical current

electricity

electrolytic reaction

electron

element

embryology

endothermic reaction

energy

energy cycle

enzyme

epidermis

equilibrium

erosion

eukaryote

excretion

exothermic reaction

flooding

fog

force

formula

freezing point

frequency

friction

Fungi kingdom

galaxy

gas

gene

genetics

genotype

genus

Golgi apparatus

gravity

habitat

Hardy-Weinberg Law

heat

heterozygous trait

high water

histology

homeostasis

homologous chromosome

homozygous trait

hormone

Hot Big Bang Theory

hot spring

hurricane

hybrid

hypothesis

igneous rock

illumination

inertia

ingestion

insulator

interphase

ionic bond

ionosphere

irritability

kinetic energy

kingdom

laser

Law of Conservation of Matter and Energy

Law of Conservation of Momentum

Law of Constant Acceleration

Law of Dominance

Law of Independent Assortment

Law of Inertia

Law of Reflection

Law of Refraction

Law of Segregation and Recombination

Lenz's Law

lethal

light

liquid

low water

lysosome

machine

magnetic field

magnetism

mass

matter
meiosis
Mendel's Law of Genetics
mesosphere
Mesozoic era
messenger RNA
metallic bond
metamorphic rock
metaphase
meteoroid
migration
mineral
mitochondria
mitosis
mixture
molecule
momentum
Monera kingdom
Moon
motion
movement
muscular system
mutation
neuron
nucleolus
nucleus
ocean
Ohm's Law
oogenesis
ore
organic chemistry
osmosis
oxidation
oxidation number
Periodic Table
peroxisome
pH
phenotype

photosynthesis
physical property
physics
physiology
planet
Plantae kingdom
plasma
plastid
polarization
polyploidy
potential energy
power
Precambrian era
pressure
prokaryote
protein
Protista kingdom
Punnett Square
quantum
rate of reaction
reaction
reflection
refraction
regulation
reproduction
respiration
ribosomal RNA
RNA
rough endoplasmic reticulum
secretion
sedimentary rock
semidiurnal tide
skeletal muscle
skeletal system
smooth endoplasmic reticulum
smooth muscle
solar system
solid

solute

solution

solvent

sound

species

speed

static electricity

stratosphere

substance

suspension

Sutton Law

synthesis

telophase

temperature

Theory of Evolution

Theory of Natural Selection

Theory of Relativity

thymus

tide

tonsil

transfer RNA

transportation

transverse

troposphere

typhoon

vacuole

velocity

volcano

volume

water cycle

wave

weathering

weight

work

x-rays

zoology

I. BIOLOGY REVIEW

THEMES AND GENERAL VOCABULARY

Biology is an independent set of explanatory concepts. Thus, we describe biology as the study of living organisms/things.

A **hypothesis** is very tentative and is something to be proven; it is only tentatively held and must be checked out fully and possibly proven. A hypothesis is an educated guess.

There are many fields of study in the biological sciences. **Zoology**, for example, is the study of animal life. **Botany** is the study of plant life; **ecology** is the study of the relationship of living things to their environment; **embryology** is the study of embryos; **anatomy** is the study of structures of the body; **physiology** is the study of the function of the body; **genetics** is the study of heredity; **cytology** is the study of the cell; **histology** is the study of tissues; and **bacteriology** is the study of bacteria and/or one-celled plant life.

THE CELL

The **cell** is the basic structure of all living things. This is the foundation of the cell theory. Some cells are total living organisms while other cells are the basic units of structure of other living things. All cells reproduce from identical cells by reproduction. Sex cells reproduce by meiosis while somatic cells (autosomes or body cells) reproduce by mitosis.

Cells are of two types: **prokaryotic** or **eukaryotic**. Prokaryotes are cells that do not have a nuclear membrane or a membrane surrounding its organelles. Bacteria and blue-green bacteria are examples of prokaryotes. Eukaryote refers to most cells making up all other living organisms.

A generalized cell will contain:

1. a **cell membrane** which is a double layer of lipids that surrounds the cell, thus acting as a "gatekeeper," controlling what moves into and out of the cell.

2. a **nucleus** which is separated from the cytoplasm by a thickened membrane that is more selective than the cell membrane.

3. **cytoplasm**, the gel-like material that surrounds and protects by cushioning the organelles. It also contains all the chemicals for that particular cell to carry out its living activities.

Depending upon the kind of cell and the function of the cell, any cell can contain any number of the following organelles:

1. **Mitochondria:** the powerhouse of the cell. It is the site where energy is obtained from food consumed and made available for the cell's use.

2. **Chloroplast:** the site of photosynthesis.

3. **Plastids:** store chlorophyll for use by the chloroplasts.

4. **Lysosomes:** carry out digestive functions and store digestive enzymes as needed by the cell.

5. **Smooth endoplasmic reticulum:** does not have ribosomes attached and is the transportation system of the cell.

6. **Rough endoplasmic reticulum:** has ribosomes attached and also carries out cell transportation but mainly of necessary protein materials needed by the cell.

7. **Golgi apparatus:** manufacture, synthesize, store, and distribute hormone and enzyme materials needed by the cell.

8. **Peroxisomes:** manufacture, store and secrete oxidation enzymes needed by the cell.

9. **Vacuoles:** spaces that act as a vacuum cleaner to rid the cell of wastes and water. Also, when not cleaning the cell, the vacuole will act as a storehouse for chemicals and compounds needed by the cell.

10. **Basal bodies:** structures that clean the cell.

11. **Cell wall:** a tough outer membrane that supports and protects the plant cell.

12. **Centrioles:** rod-shaped structures responsible for animal cell reproduction.

13. **Nucleolus:** the center of the nucleus that resembles a golf ball and houses the genes, chromosomes, and their needed materials.

14. **Chromosomes:** hereditary structures that contain the genes which determine the hereditary information contained in the cell.

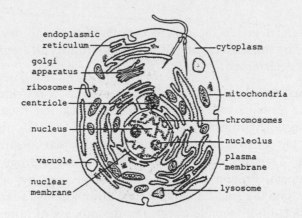

Typical Animal Cell

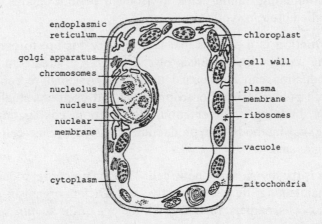

Typical Plant Cell

Cells maintain a balance or working equilibrium that is optimum for their needs. This balance, obtained by this internal control, is called **homeostasis**. This accounts for all movement into and out of the cell. Though the cell can adjust to a wide range of environmental needs and amounts, there is a limit to how much and how often it can adjust.

To understand homeostasis, one must understand how molecules move by osmosis and diffusion. When molecular movement has met needed concentrations of materials on either side of the cell membrane, the state of equilibrium exists. It is in this state that the cell operates most efficiently.

Materials move into and out of the cell either by active transport, passive transport, endocytosis, phagocytosis, or exocytosis. The exact method used depends on the type, function, and environment of the cell. A cell exists in a constantly changing environment and has constantly changing needs which must be met in order to stay alive and function. All transport occurs over a semipermeable membrane. Turgor pressure is necessary for the cell to adjust to its needs and environment. This pressure determines the amount of water maintained inside the cell to counterbalance the environment outside the cell. It is by the maintaining of this pressure that all transportation needed in the cell is determined.

Proteins are used by the cell or organism to provide energy, general maintenance, growth, and reproduction functions. All living material needs carbon, nitrogen, hydrogen, and oxygen to survive. Also, these elements are essential for the construction of organic molecules that constitute what it means to be "living." Only protein will supply the necessary nitrogen for life within a cell or organism. Protein degradation is the process by which proteins are broken down into the smallest units, called **amino acids**. Then, the amino acids are reconstructed into peptide chains (by the process of protein synthesis) that can be used by cell organelles or other materials as needed by the cell. This process of combining amino acids to produce peptide chains to reconstruct proteins is called protein synthesis.

Reproduction is a process that is necessary for life to continue. Reproduction is the process the organism or cell utilizes to create an offspring like itself. Reproduction can be asexual or sexual. Asexual reproduction occurs when one split produces a carbon-copy of the cell itself. Asexual processes are called fission, budding, fragmentation, regeneration, conjugation, or sporulation. The asexual methods of reproduction are used by one-cell organisms or lower life organisms.

Mitosis is the division of a body cell. The division or reproduction is for the purpose of maintaining life as a productive and efficient organism. **Meiosis** is the division of sex cells, namely, production of the egg or the sperm.

Cell Division

Mitosis

Mitosis is a form of cell division whereby each of two daughter nuclei receives the same chromosome complement as the parent nucleus. All kinds of asexual reproduction are carried out by mitosis; it is also responsible for growth, regeneration, and cell replacement in multicellular organisms.

Interphase – Interphase is no longer called the resting phase because a great deal of activity occurs during this phase. In the cytoplasm, oxidation and synthesis reactions take place. In the nucleus, DNA replicates itself and forms messenger RNA, transfer RNA, and ribosomal RNA.

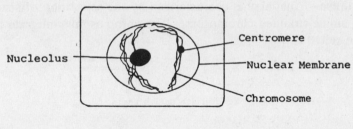

Interphase

Prophase – Chromatids shorten and thicken during this stage of mitosis. The nucleoli disappear and the nuclear membrane breaks down and disappears as well. Spindle fibers begin to form. In an animal cell, there is also division of the centrosome and centrioles.

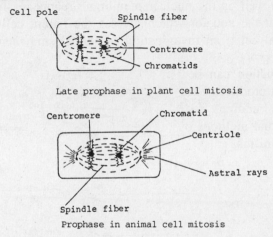

Late prophase in plant cell mitosis

Prophase in animal cell mitosis

Metaphase – During this phase, each chromosome moves to the equator, or middle of the spindle. The paired chromosomes attach to the spindle at the centromere.

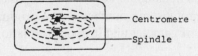

Metaphase in plant cell mitosis

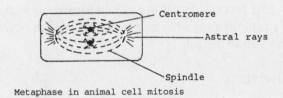

Metaphase in animal cell mitosis

Anaphase – Anaphase is characterized by the separation of sister chromatids into a single-stranded chromosome. The chromosomes migrate to opposite poles of the cell.

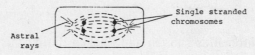

Anaphase in plant cell mitosis

Single stranded chromosomes

Single stranded chromosomes

Astral rays

Anaphase in animal cell mitosis

Telophase – During the telophase, the chromosomes begin to uncoil and the nucleoli as well as the nuclear membrane reappear. In plant cells, a cell plate appears at the equator which divides the parent cell into two daughter cells. In animal cells, an invagination of the plasma membrane divides the parent cell.

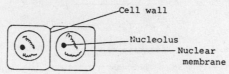

Cell wall

Nucleolus

Nuclear membrane

Late telophase in animal cell

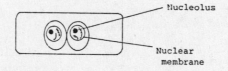

Nucleolus

Nuclear membrane

Late telophase in plant cell

Meiosis

Meiosis consists of two successive cell divisions with only one duplication of chromosomes. This results in daughter cells with a haploid number of chromosomes or one-half of the chromosome number in the original cell. This process occurs during the formation of gametes and in spore formation in plants.

Spermatogenesis – This process results in sperm cell formation with four immature sperm cells with a haploid number of chromosomes.

Oogenesis – This process results in egg cell formation with only one immature egg cell with a haploid number of chromosomes, which becomes mature and larger as yolk forms within the cell.

First Meiotic Division

Interphase I – Chromosome duplication begins to occur during this phase.

Prophase I – During this phase, the chromosomes shorten and thicken and synapsis occurs with pairing of homologous chromosomes. Crossing-over between non-sister chromatids will also occur. The centrioles will migrate to opposite poles and the nucleolus and nuclear membrane begin to dissolve.

Metaphase I – The tetrads, composed of two doubled homologous chromosomes, migrate to the equatorial plane during Metaphase I.

Anaphase I – During this stage, the paired homologous chromosomes separate and move to opposite poles of the cell. Thus, the number of chromosome types in each resultant cell is reduced to the haploid number.

Telophase I – Cytoplasmic division occurs during telophase I. The formation of two new nuclei with half the chromosomes of the original cell occurs.

Prophase II – The centrioles that had migrated to each pole of the parental cell, now incorporated in each haploid daughter cell, divide, and a new spindle forms in each cell. The chromosomes move to the equator.

Metaphase II – The chromosomes are lined up at the equator of the new spindle, which is at right angles to the old spindle.

Anaphase II – The centromeres divide and the daughter chromatids, now chromosomes, separate and move to opposite poles.

Telophase II – Cytoplasmic division occurs. The chromosomes gradually return to the dispersed form and a nuclear membrane forms.

A living organism could be called a chemical factory. More chemical activity is carried on inside the cell or inside the living organism than any other place. Chemical bonds are broken, constructed and reconstructed in a continuous operation. Chemical reactions occur simultaneously throughout the organism so that life will be an ongoing process. Carbohydrates, starches, lipids, proteins, water, and nucleic acids are the chemicals (organic molecules) and compounds that are basic to all life.

DNA was discovered in 1869. It was not until the development of the electron microscope in the mid-1940s that scientists gained a true realization of the functioning of DNA.

DNA (deoxyribonucleic acid) is the basic chemical of life. It is a giant molecule made of four different nitrogenous bases (adenine, guanine, cytosine, thymine), phosphate groups, and 5-carbon sugars that collectively are called a nucleotide. It is a self-duplicating molecule that is in a double helix (spiral staircase appearance). It is found inside the nucleus of the cell. It contains the directions, or "blueprints," for the making of all the proteins that a cell needs. Proteins play a major role in cell metabolism and are the basic building blocks of a cell. DNA is the controller of heredity and all life activities of the cell. Its function is linked to the functioning of a companion chemical called **RNA** (ribonucleic acid).

The Chemical Composition of DNA

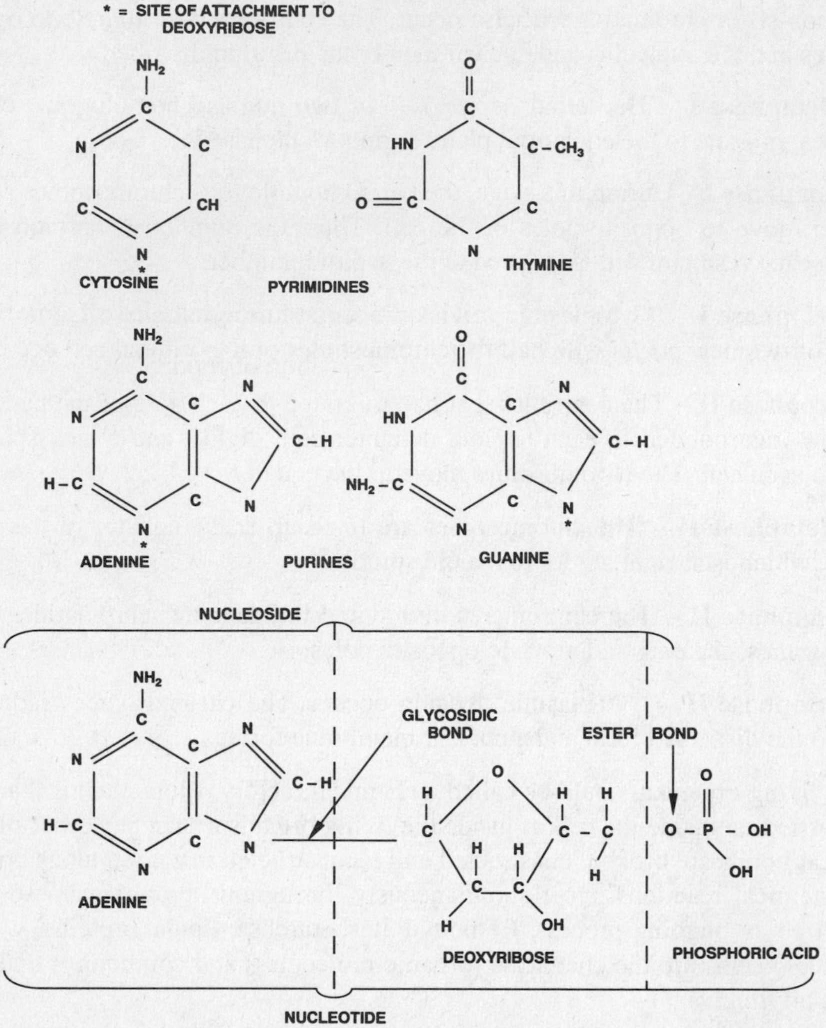

STRUCTURAL FORMULAS OF PURINES (ADENINE AND QUANINE), PYRIMIDINES (THYMINE AND CYTOSINE), AND A NUCLEOTIDE

Ribonucleic acid differs from DNA in that uracil replaces thymine as nitrogenous base, and the sugar bond used by RNA has one less oxygen present. Also, RNA is a straight chain. The genetic information in DNA is carried out of the nucleus by what is called **messenger RNA** (mRNA). Protein synthesis is carried out in the cytoplasm of the cell by **transfer RNA** (tRNA) using ribosomes comprised of **ribosomal RNA** and proteins.

The DNA acts as an interpreter or decoder for the many chemical messages that are carried through the cell as a part of the life activities. The DNA cannot leave the nucleus and, therefore, must have a messenger and translator working directly with it. In addition, the **tRNA** picks up and delivers necessary amino acids to complete the needed activity. This process enables the cell to carry out digestion, oxidation, assimilation, synthesis, and other necessary cell activities.

The basic functions of life comprising total cell metabolism are:

1. **Ingestion:** taking in of food.

2. **Digestion:** breaking down of food by enzymes to simpler, soluble forms.

3. **Secretion:** formation of useful substances.

4. **Absorption:** diffusion of dissolved material through cell membranes.

5. **Respiration:** release of energy by oxidation of food.

6. **Excretion:** getting rid of wastes of the cells.

7. **Transportation:** circulation of materials throughout the organism.

8. **Assimilation:** formation of more protoplasm, resulting in growth and repair.

9. **Regulation:** maintaining stability of organism's chemical makeup under constantly changing internal and external environment (homeostasis).

10. **Synthesis:** building up of complex molecules from simple compounds.

11. **Reproduction:** production of more living individuals.

12. **Irritability:** response to stimuli.

13. **Movement:** the ability to change position. In some rare cases, as in plants, movement is coupled with irritability.

14. **Bioluminescence:** production of internal light within some organisms.

Photosynthesis is a process that occurs within all plant cells which supply all of the carbohydrates used by both plants and animals. Not only are essential organic compounds formed, but needed water and oxygen are given off as by-products in this autotrophic nutrition process.

Chloroplasts absorb light energy from the sun. Carbon dioxide and water are present as raw materials at the chloroplast manufacturing site.

An overall chemical description of photosynthesis is the equation

$$6\,CO_2 + 6\,H_2O \xrightarrow[\text{CHLOROPHYLL}]{\text{LIGHT}} C_6H_{12}O_6 + 6\,O_2$$

Photosynthesis is a two-step process involving light reactions and dark reactions. In the light reaction process, light must be present along with chlorophyll to start the chemical reaction. Carbon dioxide and water are broken down into free atoms. Then the dark reaction can happen. Light is not necessary for this chemical reaction to occur. Carbon, acting as a centerpiece, joins with oxygen and hydrogen to form carbohydrates. Water and unused oxygen are given off as waste products.

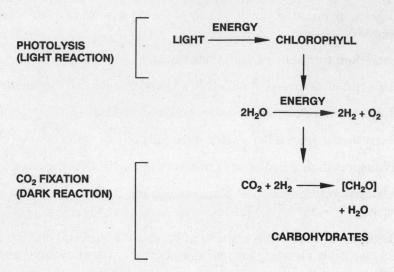

PHOTOLYSIS AND CO_2 FIXATION

Cellular respiration is the process by which the cell or organism gets energy for all of its activities. It is through this respiration process that chemical energy is released. This process occurs in the mitochondria through a series of steps.

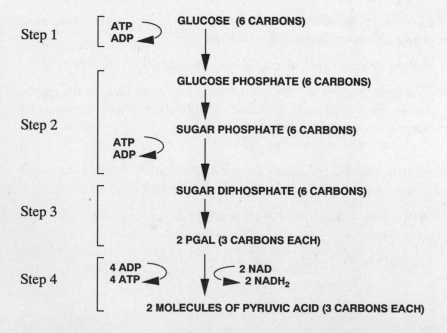

The steps are summarized as follows:

Step 1 – Activation of glucose

Step 2 – Formation of sugar diphosphate

Step 3 – Formation and oxidation of PGAL, phosphoglyceraldehyde

Step 4 – Formation of pyruvic acid ($C_3H_4O_3$). Net gain of two ATP molecules

Cellular respiration can be either **aerobic** or **anaerobic**. In aerobic respiration, release of energy from organic compounds occurs in the presence of oxygen. The **oxidation**, or process of breaking down and releasing energy, is stimulated by enzymes and acids present in and around the mitochondria. In anaerobic respiration, there is no oxygen present, and it must occur by a fermentation process. Lactic acid is produced as a by-product of this process. Lactic acid in muscles results in muscle fatigue and soreness.

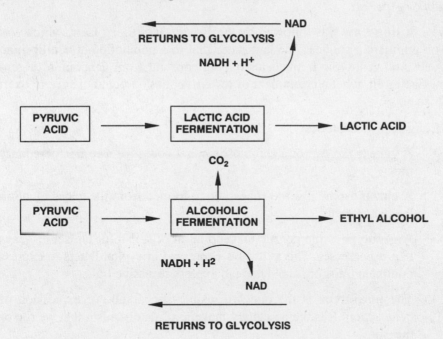

Usually, offspring will resemble their parents. Yet, the offspring may have traits that are not present in either parent. In 1857, Gregor Mendel developed his Laws of Genetics after seven years of studying the garden green pea. **Mendel's Laws of Genetics** are:

1. **Law of Dominance:** Every organism receives a trait from the mother and a trait from the father. One trait may have dominance over the other and mask the recessive trait to keep it from showing in the offspring. Dominant traits are normally the darker, heavier, or larger of the two traits.

2. **Law of Segregation and Recombinant:** Genes separate into single units at the time the egg and sperm unite. Each character links with a like character to form a gene. It is segregation that assures each parent contributes equally to the offspring.

3. **Law of Independent Assortment:** Each unit or character for a trait is independently distributed to link with a like gene to form another pair. There is no pattern to their separation and rejoining to form the genes for the potential offspring. Genes on separate chromosomes are inherited independently.

In 1900, Walter Sutton began further studies based on Mendel's studies. Sutton compared the behavior of the chromosomes to the principles of inheritance. He confirmed all that Gregor Mendel had formulated. Sutton learned that the "factors" Mendel referred to were units located in the **chromosomes**. Sutton named these factors "genes." The chromosomal theory of inheritance, established by Sutton, states that genes are located on chromosomes and forms the basis for the study of genetics.

The **Sutton Law** was followed by the **Hardy-Weinberg Law**, which was based on population studies. The law states that in a population at equilibrium, both genes and genotypic frequencies remain constant from generation to generation. Each trait, whether dominant or recessive, has an equal chance to exert its influence.

Basic Language of Genetics:

1. A **gene** is the part of a chromosome that codes for a certain hereditary trait.

2. A **chromosome** is a rod-shaped body formed from the genes found in the cell nucleus.

3. A **genotype** is the genetic makeup of an organism or the set of genes that it possesses. This is always expressed in capital letters to express dominant traits or small letters to express recessive traits.

4. The **phenotype** is the outward visible appearance or expression of gene action. It is the hereditary makeup of an organism that we see or measure.

5. **Homologous chromosomes** are chromosomes bearing genes for the same characters.

6. A **homozygous trait** is an identical pair of alleles on homologous chromosomes for any given trait.

7. A **heterozygous trait** is a mixed pair of alleles on homologous chromosomes for any given trait.

8. **Hybrid** refers to an organism carrying unlike genes for certain traits. This is a preferred trait when breeding for the "best of both" traits.

9. **Mutation** is a sudden appearance of a new trait or variation which is inherited.

10. **Lethal** means deadly. This trait will cause death of the organism.

Each gene has a particular location on a chromosome (**allele**). Genes carried on the X chromosome are called sex-linked genes. Males carrying a recessive allele on their single X chromosome express a recessive phenotype. Females must carry recessive alleles on both X chromosomes to express a recessive phenotype.

Mutations can affect other chromosomes or individual genes. Chromosomal aberrations like mutations occur in reproductive cells and may be passed on to the offspring. Nondisjunction of the chromosomes results in gametes that have too few or too many chromosomes. In **polyploidy**, organisms have an extra set of chromosomes. In the disease called trisomy 21 or Down's Syndrome, a person has an extra twenty-first chromosome. Gene mutations occur due to a change in the DNA sequence for that particular gene at that particular time. A mutated gene does not give correct directions for protein synthesis and normally harms the organism. There are a few mutations that have proven to be beneficial, however.

The **Punnett Square** is a method used to predict the probable outcome of a particular genetic cross. This testcross will help determine information about an organism or potential organism. Study the basis crosses worked out below.

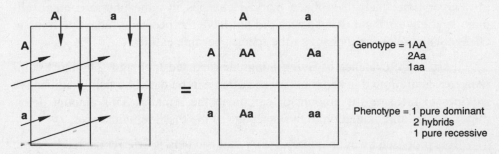

BREAKING THE CODE OF LIFE

More is being learned about the code of life that is locked into the DNA of every cell. Every living organism has its own unique pattern of DNA that accounts for the individualism in each organism. This is why DNA replication must occur prior to mitosis or meiosis in order for organisms to grow, develop, and reproduce. In this process, DNA unspirals, unzips, and separates, and new strands of DNA are constructed from nucleotides present in the nucleus. Then the process of cell division may occur. This occurrence is what holds the code of life. Never is the code altered in any replication that totally alters the organism. Although this may be the key to answering questions about cancer and other life-threatening diseases that affect certain organisms, much research still needs to be done.

EVOLUTION OF ORGANISMS

Several theories have been formulated on how life evolves. One such theory was proposed by Jean Lamarck in 1809 when he proposed that an organism evolves in response to its environment by acquiring a trait which would adapt it to life in its changing environment. For instance, if a giraffe's neck were too short, by the constant stretching during the parent's life, offspring would be born with longer necks.

In 1859, Darwin formulated his theory in his book called *The Origin of Species*. The book supported the **theory of evolution** but gave a completely different twist to the evolution idea. After studying many plants and animals, Darwin concluded that no two organisms are exactly alike, but instead differ in size, shape, color, etc., and that these traits are inherited from the parents to the offspring and not acquired. Individuals who inherit adaptive traits have a greater chance for survival thus, Darwin's **theory of natural selection**.

Evidence that supports evolutionary theories includes adaptation to the environment, homologous organs, vestigial organs, similarity of embryonic development, similarity of nucleic acids, and similar protein structure. With the groundwork laid by Lamarck and Darwin, modern evolutionists include speciation, adaptive radiation, convergent evolution, divergent evolution, and population genetics as phenomena that support evolutionary theory.

Over time, there have been marked changes in atmospheric content, climate, and environment. If a species did not have the necessary adaptive traits to change with the external changes, the species became extinct.

Fossils are evidence of living things that existed long ago. The most common fossils are found in sedimentary rock that can be dated by using radioactive isotopes to measure the amount of carbon in the remains. This amount determines a close approximation to the exact age of the fossil remains.

It is proposed by evolutionary theory that each era is briefly marked by rapid adaptive radiation normally followed by mass extinction that ended each era. Stanley Miller provided evidence that life-supporting molecules arose under abiotic conditions. He produced the exact atmosphere that was thought to have first existed and showed how heterotrophs used the available organic substances for food.

Geological evolution is as follows:

Precambrian Era	unicellular organisms originated
Paleozoic Era	multicellular animals and fern-like plants originated
Mesozoic Era	birds, mammals, reptiles, and flowering plants originated
Cenozoic Era	radiation of birds, mammals, reptiles, and flowering plants occurred

CLASSIFICATION

Classification is a method of organizing information based on similarities. Aristotle was the first scientist to attempt to classify living things by grouping them into two major groups—plants or animals. Then they were divided into three major sub-groups as to their habitat—land, water, or air. Since Aristotle's first attempt at classification, man has used various systems of classifying living things in an effort to identify them. With so many languages and word meanings, a standard language had to be developed so that the use of common names in each language could be avoided. Thus, scientists began to use the genus and species names as this would be a consistent language in any nation. This classification system is called **binomial nomenclature**.

The levels of classification from largest to smallest are kingdom, phylum class, order, family, genus, and species. All living organisms are classified into one of five **kingdoms** to start the identifying procedure. Then the organism will be studied, compared to specific requirements, and placed in an appropriate level until a species is finally established. The biological name would be the **genus** and **species**.

A classification key can be used as an aid to identify organisms. It uses an organism's general characteristics and special features to find its appropriate placement. (Study the following mini-key.)

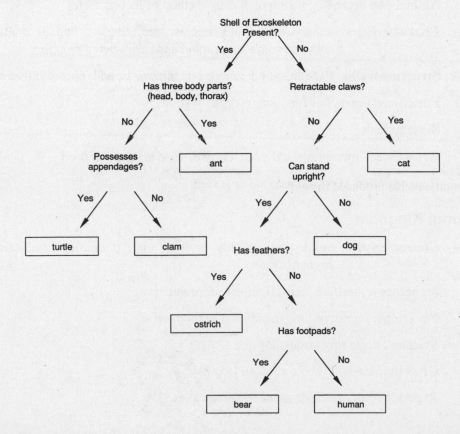

Often, as seen throughout time, organisms change in order to survive. Natural selection causes all species to adapt to changing environmental conditions. This change is called adaptation. The organisms change to adapt to their new environments and through time they evolve into entirely different organisms. This is called speciation.

Monera Kingdom

Bacteria and blue-green bacteria

Characteristics: prokaryotes, microscopic, lives as a single cell or in colonies in water, autotrophic, few heterotrophic

Structures: flagella capsules

Functions: food getting, respiration, reproduction

Systems: none

Growth: cell membrane and availability of food set growth limit

Reproduction Method: binary fission

Protista Kingdom

Animal-like organism, distinguished by method of locomotion

Characteristics: eukaryotes, mainly microscopic, single-celled or multicellular; some autotrophic and many heterotrophic

Structures: cilia, flagella, cell organelles membrane bound, photosynthetic

Functions: organelles function as organ systems

Systems: none

Growth: cell membrane and availability of food set growth limit

Reproduction Method: asexual or sexual

Fungi Kingdom

Characteristics: eukaryotes, mainly multicellular, parasitic, symbiotic, mycorrhizae

Structures: root-like, caps, filaments, reproductive

Functions: digestive-like, respiration, reproductive

Systems: beginning to develop

Growth: based on food source and availability

Reproduction Method: asexual, sexual

Plantae Kingdom

Characteristics: eukaryotes, multicellular, nonmotile, autotrophic

Structures: cellulose cell walls

Functions: based on cell and tissue chemistry

Systems: all present and functioning

Growth: based on hormone action

Reproduction Method: asexual, sexual by spores, seeds, flowers, and cones

Animalia Kingdom

Characteristics: eukaryotes, multicellular, heterotrophic, most are motile at some point in lifetime

Structures: all present and unique to organism

Functions: based on nutrition, cell and tissue chemistry, and individual demands

Systems: all present and functioning

Growth: based on hormone action and nutrition

Reproduction Method: asexual, sexual

HUMAN SYSTEMS BIOLOGY

Digestive System

The digestive system is responsible for both mechanical and chemical digestion that break down food into molecules so they can move into the cell and be used for the living process. The mouth, teeth, and tongue begin the chemical digestion by mechanically breaking down the food through the chewing process and the addition of saliva. The enzyme amylase breaks down carbohydrates and starts the breakdown of starches. Food moves from the mouth to the stomach by way of the esophagus. In the stomach, other digestive enzymes and hydrochloric acid begin the breakdown of proteins. The stomach churns and mixes the food. Food, now in a liquid-like state, moves from the stomach into the small intestine, where it is absorbed through the villa into the bloodstream where it is delivered and assimilated by the cells of the body. Waste materials and used food are carried back to the large intestine where they mix with roughage and water. The undigested materials are excreted from the body.

Circulatory System

The circulatory system is composed of the heart, arteries, veins, red blood cells, white blood cells, antibodies, thrombin, water, and plasma. A four-chambered heart, controlled by the pacemaker, rhythmically controls the pumping action by alternating contractions of the atria and ventricles. Blood circulates through the body in two loops—arteries carrying oxygenated blood away from the heart to all parts of the body, and veins returning deoxygenated blood to the heart and lungs to be reoxygenated. An auxiliary portion is the lymphatic system, which drains excess tissue fluids back into the circulatory system along with white blood cells that destroy harmful microorganisms.

Skeletal System

The skeleton is the basic framework of the human body and is made of connective tissue—bones and cartilage. Bone is living tissue with vitamins, collagen, and minerals to give it strength and hardness. The process by which the bones harden is called ossification. Bones are joined by cartilage at joints. Joints are classified as to the amount of movement they allow: stationary (skull), hinge (elbow), or ball and socket (hip).

Muscular System

Three human muscle types are **skeletal**, **cardiac**, and **smooth**. All muscle tissue exerts force when it contracts; therefore, muscles are responsible for all movement of the body, voluntary or involuntary. Energy for all movement is derived from an ample supply of mitochondria in the muscle cell. **ATP**, a high level energy carrier, is produced by the mitochondria for use by other cells and tissue parts during movement or exercise. Muscles are paired to accomplish full movement. Each contracting muscle will be paired with an antagonistic muscle, and tendons attach paired muscle groups to bones to complete the movement action. The skeletal muscles make up this grouping of muscles and are mainly voluntary.

Cardiac muscle is found only in the heart. The heart is the strongest muscle of the body. It is responsible for keeping the blood flowing through the circulatory system at a given pressure. The cardiac muscle is an involuntary muscle.

Smooth muscles are found in the linings of the body such as the digestive system and internal organs. They are generally involuntary muscles.

Nervous System

The basic unit of the nervous system is the **neuron** (nerve cell). Its structure allows electrochemical signals to travel across synapses to activate muscles, glands, or organ tissue. The nervous system is divided into two parts. One part, the central nervous system, includes the brain, spinal cord, and the peripheral nervous system, which is a vast network of nerves that totally connect all parts of the body. Receptors located in sense organs and in the skin send information along the sensory neurons to the spinal cord and then to the brain where the information is chemically interpreted, causing a motor response.

Respiratory System

Respiration involves actions started by nerves stimulating muscles and bones to mechanically enlarge the respiratory cavity of the body. The breathing rate is controlled by nerves originating in the brain based on carbon dioxide content. The human nasal passages are adapted to clean, moisten, and warm the air before it enters the lungs by way of the trachea and bronchi. The lungs are made up of many tiny air sacs called alveoli that are found at the end of the bronchiole in clusters. The exchange of gases between the lungs and circulatory system occurs in the **alveoli**.

Excretory System

The excretory system is made up of the kidney, bladder, connecting tubes, and capillaries joined to the kidney. Urine is collected by structures in the kidney called nephrons. From the nephrons, the liquid wastes are collected and stored in the bladder. Urine leaves the body through the urethra.

Endocrine System

The endocrine system produces **hormones** which travel by way of the bloodstream to specific target cells. The manner in which the hormone acts on the target cells depends on whether it is a protein or steroid. Each will cause a feedback, which is one way to regulate hormones secreted into the body. Homeostasis depends on the actions of the nervous and endocrine systems. Organs, like the kidney, function based on endocrine stimulation.

Integumentary System

The integumentary covering of the body is called the skin. Skin consists of two layers, the **epidermis** and the **dermis**. Skin protects the body, rids the body of mineral salts and wastes, regulates body temperature, and picks up environmental signals. The skin is the bonding or holding agent that keeps the body intact and functioning. Also part of the integumentary system are the hair and nails.

Immunity and Diseases

IMPORTANT LYMPHATIC ORGANS—A defense against pathogens

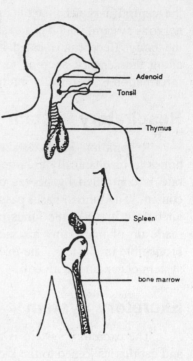

Adenoids and Tonsils – Organs that filter out antigens (substances, such as viruses, which stimulate antibody synthesis) that enter the body via the upper-respiratory and gastrointestinal tracts.

Thymus – Produces cells that eventually become what are called peripheral T cells, which possess surface receptors for antigens.

Bone Marrow – Produces blood-forming stem cells.

Spleen – Has three functions:

(1) Can mount an immune response to antigens in the blood stream.

(2) Scavenges old red blood cells.

(3) Reserve site for making blood forming stem cells.

DISORDERS OF THE IMMUNE SYSTEM

Lupus – People develop immune reactions to their own nucleic acids.

Allergies – People become hypersensitive to environmental substances, called allergens.

AIDS (Acquired Immune Deficiency Syndrome) –

(1) People have reduced numbers of helper T cells.

(2) People may not be able to form antibodies against diseases like pneumonia.

ECOLOGY

Ecology can be defined as the study of interactions between groups of organisms and their environment. Groups are referred to as populations. Ecology is the basis of all life and all support systems of life. It is made up of chains—the food chain, carbon/oxygen chain, energy chain, and water chain. It is through the linking of the chains that life continues. Each organism has a specific **habitat** in an ecosystem carrying out a specific role (niche).

Ecology and **behavior** are closely linked. It is because of learned and innate behaviors that organisms are equipped to meet the ever-changing environmental demands and the interactions with other living organisms.

Life on earth exists in a thin layer known as the **biosphere**. The land, air, and water that make up the biosphere each have their own areas where life exists. The land, or terrestrial, biomes are determined mainly by climate. Water, or aquatic, biomes are classified as freshwater or marine, depending upon the amount of salt (salinity) in the water. Marine life occurs in various zones depending on depth, temperature, and light intensity. Freshwater abiotic factors are depth, turbidity, temperature, and light intensity. Estuaries are mixtures of salt and fresh water. They are more protected than the ocean, but more nutrient-rich than rivers and support a wide variety of species.

The size of a population at a given time is determined by its growth rate. Growth rate is determined by the factors of birth rate, immigration, death rate, and emigration. Other factors like natural disasters, availability of food, and disease also independently affect population. Environmental resistance to increased population often depends on population density. Crowding of organisms can reduce nutrients, spread disease, and interfere with reproduction. Competition for an environment's limited resources occurs between members of a population (intraspecific competition) and between different species in an area (interspecific competition). Competition also limits population size.

Humans are unique in their ability to modify the carrying capacity of their environment to be favorable for population growth. Most scientists agree that it is only a matter of time before humans will be unable to increase the earth's carrying capacity any further. At that time, the birth rate must decrease and the death rate must increase to balance population growth.

Natural resources are necessary for human survival and the making of necessary products. The natural resources are water, soil, air, wildlife, and forests. Problems that are now being faced are related to erosion, soil depletion, species extinction, deforestation, desertification, and water shortages. Efforts to reverse these problems and their environmental damages are found in the planned programs of reforestation, captive breeding, biological harvesting, or planned farming through efficient plowing and planting procedures.

Pollution is damaging both the ecosystems and living organisms. Air, water, soil, and food resources are being affected by pollution. Pollutants include automobile exhaust, fertilizers, pesticides, industrial wastes, radioactive wastes, and most of all, household wastes. The growing population and modern conveniences greatly contribute to this insurmountable problem. Government regulations, community efforts, and changes in the habits of industries and individuals are necessary to solve pollution problems.

☞ Drill: Biology

1. A hypothesis explains and relates

    (A) conclusions.   (C) theories.

    (B) facts.   (D) guesses.

2. How do body cells, such as muscle or bone cells, reproduce?

    (A) Osmosis   (C) Diffusion

    (B) Mitosis   (D) Meiosis

3. According to the cell theory,

    (A) all living things are composed of cells.

    (B) the number of cells in an organism is set before birth.

    (C) cell activity is controlled by the nucleus.

    (D) eukaryotic cells have a cell wall for protection.

4. Which cellular component is responsible for the regulation of exchanges of substances between a cell and its environment?

    (A) The endoplasmic reticulum

    (B) The cell nucleus

    (C) The cytoplasm

    (D) The cell membrane

5. Maintaining a balanced internal control is called

    (A) homeostasis.   (C) diffusion.

    (B) osmosis.   (D) pump balance.

6. An organic molecule is any molecule

    (A) containing carbon.   (C) found in dead organisms.

    (B) containing phosphorus.   (D) that is naturally grown.

7. Mitosis results in

    (A) offspring cells exactly like the parent cell.

    (B) offspring cells different from the parent cell.

(C) new combinations of mother cells.

(D) a smaller number of cells.

8. Meiosis produces

(A) gametes
(B) body cells.
(C) sex cells.
(D) Both (A) and (C).

9. The RNA molecule that transcribes (receives information) from DNA and carries the information to code for a particular protein chain is called

(A) snRNA.
(B) mRNA.
(C) tRNA.
(D) rRNA.

10. The structural unit of photosynthesis is the

(A) chloroplast.
(B) stroma.
(C) cristae.
(D) mitochondrion.

11. The phenotype of an organism

(A) represents its genetic composition.

(B) is all the traits that are actually expressed.

(C) cannot be observed.

(D) is equivalent to the genotype.

12. The process by which DNA copies itself is called

(A) transcription.
(B) replication.
(C) nucleotide.
(D) translation.

13. The type of evolution that explains the polar bear and the brown bear is called

(A) divergent evolution.
(B) convergent evolution.
(C) directional evolution.
(D) disruptive evolution.

14. Monerans do not have a true nucleus or membrane-bound organelles; therefore they are called

(A) eukaryotes.
(B) cokaryotes.
(C) prokaryotes.
(D) nokaryotes.

15. An example of a fungus is

    (A) mushroom.

    (B) bread mold.

    (C) penicillum.

    (D) All of the above.

16. The circulatory system is responsible for all of the following except

    (A) the distribution of oxygen.

    (B) carrying nutrients.

    (C) removing urea from the body.

    (D) stopping the flow of blood after an injury.

17. The type of muscle tissue found in the walls of many internal organs is identified as

    (A) striated.

    (B) smooth.

    (C) skeletal.

    (D) cardiac.

18. The junction where an impulse travels from one neuron to another is called the

    (A) synapse.

    (B) stimuli.

    (C) nerve message.

    (D) affector node.

19. Infectious diseases are caused by

    (A) bacteria, fungi, and protozoans.

    (B) bacteria only.

    (C) fungi only.

    (D) protozoans only.

20. The biotic potential of a population is

    (A) the rate at which a population would reproduce if every individual lived.

    (B) the rate at which a population would die.

    (C) the rate at which a population would over-populate.

    (D) All of the above.

II. CHEMISTRY REVIEW

INTRODUCTION TO CHEMISTRY

Chemistry is one of the oldest branches of science. The study of chemistry can be traced back as far as the Babylonian period. The field of chemistry seeks to transform one molecule into another to tailor or refine such chemicals as plastics, drugs, food technology, fuels, and dyes. Out of these raw materials, countless products required to meet our needs of daily living can be manufactured. Chemistry is defined as the study of the composition and behavior of elements in combination with each other.

Chemistry began to grow as knowledge spread about the atomic theory proposed by Thomas Dalton about 1807. He advocated that all matter is composed of small indivisible particles which he named "**atoms**" and described as little round balls. He believed these particles could combine with one another in many forms to produce all possible substances. It was remarkable how close his theory was to being correct considering the lack of experimental techniques available at that time. He was correct in stating that atoms join together to form complex substances. Dalton was incorrect in his assumption that all atoms are alike.

A great growth was experienced in the field of chemistry after the discovery of the group-forming pattern by D. L. Mendeleev in 1896. With the newly acquired information, a listing of all of the known chemical elements was placed on a chart in the order of their increasing atomic weights and number of energy levels. This charted information was the first periodic table.

As information in the field of chemistry grew, studies branched into the areas of organic chemistry and inorganic chemistry. **Organic chemistry** deals with the carbon compounds while inorganic chemistry deals with all the other elements and compounds.

The field of chemistry has vastly expanded based on the study of the atomic structure of **elements** and their behavior. Atomic structure is related to the properties and arrangement of elements in the periodic chart. The elements are classified into groups, periods, and families. It is from these groupings that matter is classified and its behavior is studied based on the ability of an element to combine or react with other elements. The study of the behavior of matter is based on properties of the elements and their ability to combine through the transfer and sharing of **electrons** to form compounds and other matter. This is commonly referred to as the process of bonding.

Every element has its own letter symbol. With these letter symbols and atomic numbers used together correctly, one can construct a formula. The formulas can be combined to show the composition of compounds, reactions between elements, chemical equilibrium, and oxidation and reaction rates. This is accomplished by the process of balancing equations.

It is necessary that everyone understands the basics of chemistry since our lives are centered around this subject. Also, how far we can progress is based on our ability to understand chemical concepts and apply them to our everyday life.

STRUCTURE OF MATTER

Matter is anything that occupies space and has mass. Matter resists changes in motion. It takes force to accelerate matter. There are four states of matter — **solid, liquid, gas**, and a fourth state called the **plasma** state. This state only exists at extremely high temperatures, such as those found on the sun. Plasma consists of high-energy, electrically charged particles. Plasma is created when a fluorescent lamp is turned on. Most of the matter in the universe is in the plasma state.

The structure of matter depends on the number and types of atoms that combine or react to form the matter. Matter is measured by the force with which gravity pulls on the mass toward the center of the earth. Matter can also be measured by its capacity for doing work, or the energy that it contains. This energy can be either activation, potential, or (**kinetic energy**.) **Activation energy** is that energy necessary to start a reaction. **Potential energy** is stored energy, while **kinetic energy** is the energy that matter possesses due to motion.

It can be shown experimentally that potential energy can be transformed into kinetic energy without any energy loss. This is an illustration of the **Law of Conservation of Matter or Energy** which states that under ordinary conditions, matter or energy can neither be created nor destroyed but can be converted from one form to another.

One method of classifying matter is to find out if it is a substance or a **mixture** of substances. If a substance is composed of only one kind of atom, it is an element. If the substance is composed of two or more kinds of atoms, the matter can be a mixture or a compound, depending on how the atoms are joined and react to each other under normal conditions.

Mixtures do not follow the law of definite proportions, which means that the two substances can be mixed in almost any proportion. Thus, the properties of a mixture vary with composition. If the substances in a mixture are spread out evenly, it is considered to be a homogeneous mixture. If the substances in a mixture are not spread out evenly, it is considered to be a heterogeneous mixture. Vinegar is a homogeneous mixture as the substances are spread evenly throughout. A homogenous mixture can be called a **solution**. Other solutions include seawater, soft drinks, tea, or milk.

A **suspension** is a heterogeneous mixture in which the particles are large enough to be seen by a microscope or the eye. These particles are affected by gravity and may settle out of the mixture. The particles can be temporarily suspended again by shaking. The mixing of water and pepper is an example of a suspension. Stirring up the bottom of a river will produce a suspension. With time, the action of gravity on the sand and soil will cause the particles to settle back to the bottom of the river.

If particles of a mixture are larger than those found in a solution, yet smaller than particles found in a suspension, the mixture is referred to as a **colloid**. Colloidal particles appear to be evenly distributed, and they will not settle out. The small size of the particles causes gravity to have less of an effect. Thus, there is less possibility of settling out caused by gravity.

All matter can be identified as having either **physical** or **chemical properties**. A **physical property** is a characteristic of matter that can be observed without changing the makeup of the substance. Boiling points and freezing points are examples of physical properties. Other physical properties are color, odor, hardness, density, and the ability to conduct heat or electricity. Physical properties can be used to separate mixtures. A mixture of iron and sand can be separated by a magnet. Iron is magnetic; sand is not. Thus they can be separated with ease.

A physical change occurs when matter changes in size, shape, color, or state. A physical change does not change the chemical composition of a substance. When a glass breaks, the size and shape of the glass change, but the chemical makeup remains the same no matter in how many pieces the glass might exist.

A **chemical property** is a characteristic that determines how a substance reacts to form other substances. Chemical properties are determined by chemical changes. When a chemical change occurs, the substance seldom will, if ever, return to its original state. For example, iron will rust in the presence of water and oxygen. Rusting is an example of the chemical property known as corrosion. **Corrosion** occurs when metals are destroyed as they combine chemically with other substances.

In a chemical change, a substance is changed to a new substance which has different properties. Chemical changes may release thermal energy, light, or electricity. Some chemical changes need energy. All changes, chemical and physical, involve an energy change of some kind. Many compounds are formed from elements by chemical changes. In the same respect, many compounds are broken down by a chemical change.

When wood burns, heat is given off and a small amount of ashes is left. The substance of the wood has changed. Wood is made of carbon, hydrogen, and oxygen. When wood burns, the elements unite with atmospheric oxygen resulting in the formation of carbon dioxide and water. Also, carbon is the element of the ash substance that remains. This is a chemical change as energy is used to bring about the change and heat (an energy form) is given off; other compounds have been formed and the elements can never return to the state of wood (unless they again become integrated into the growth of a tree).

SIMPLE EQUATIONS SHOWING STRUCTURE OF MATTER

Matter can be identified not only by name, but by the way the element fits together with other elements to form matter. It is important for one to know if the proposed combination actually exists. For example, no chemist has ever been able to prepare hydrogen nitrate. Additionally, in making combinations, one must have a positive and a negative component. Generally speaking, metals are positive components, while nonmetals are negative components (with the exception of ammonia and radicals). When elements combine in varying proportions, prefixes are used for the naming of the compound and for formula writing. Mono- means one, bi- or di- means two, tri- means three, tetra- means four, pent- means five, and so on. Common suffixes and meanings are -ide (for naming monatomic anions), -ous (for the ion with the lower charge), and -ic (for the ion with the higher charge).

PERIODICITY OF ELEMENTS

The latter half of the 19th century brought about the updating of the **Periodic Law**: the properties of the elements are periodic functions of their atomic numbers. **Atomic numbers** represent the number of protons and also the number of electrons in a neutral atom. The electron structures of the atoms provide information showing the properties of the elements. Vertical columns represent the chemical families while horizontal columns represent the period or row. Proceeding across a row, the ability to hold electrons decreases. For example, lithium is the most metallic while fluorine is the least metallic. Study the **Periodic Table** which appears in the appendix of this book.

Some atoms tend to join with other atoms, while others will show no tendency to join with like atoms or like elements. The results of this tendency or attraction of the atoms involved in joining is called a chemical bond. When atoms combine to form new molecules, there is a shifting or transfer of valence electrons found in the outer shell of each atom. This usually results in the completing of outer shells by each atom. A more stable compound or form is achieved by the gaining, losing, or sharing of pairs of electrons. In forming chemical bonds, there is a release of energy or an absorption of energy. The bonds can be **ionic, covalent,** or **metallic.**

The kinetic model explains the forces between molecules and the energy they possess in three basic assumptions:

1. All matter is composed of extremely small particles.

2. The particles making up all matter are in constant motion.

3. When these particles collide with each other or with the walls of the container, there is no loss of energy.

BEHAVIOR OF MATTER

The behavior and classification of matter is dependent upon the electron attraction and interaction of electrons forming the matter. When atoms react with one another, it is the electrons that are involved in bonding, whether it be ionic or covalent.

All **reactions** need to receive a certain amount of energy before they can start. The amount of energy needed or received to start the chemical reaction is called activation energy. Some reactions require so little energy that it can be absorbed from the surroundings. This is called a spontaneous reaction which takes place with so little energy that it seems as if no energy was needed. A reaction that gives off energy is called an **exothermic reaction**. A reaction that absorbs energy is called an **endothermic reaction**. Combustion is a decomposition reaction. A catalyst can be added to a chemical reaction to control the reaction rate.

Acids

Acid properties are:

1. Water solutions of acids conduct electricity.

2. Acids will react actively with metals.

3. Acids will change blue litmus to pink.

4. Acids will react with bases resulting in both a loss of water and leaving a salt (neutralization).

5. Weak acid solutions taste sour.

6. Acids react with carbonates to release carbon dioxide.

Bases

Base properties are:

1. Bases are conductors of electricity in strong solutions.

2. Bases change red litmus paper blue.

3. Bases react with acids to neutralize each other and to form a salt and water.

4. Bases react with fats to form a class of compounds called soaps.

5. Bases feel slippery and strong solutions are caustic to the skin.

Salts

A salt is an ionic compound containing positive ions other than hydrogen and a negative ion other than hydroxide ions. It is usually formed by neutralization when certain acids and bases are combined and form water and salt as the products.

A **formula** is a sort of road map, or a detailed description, of how something is organized or produced. A formula will not reveal the hidden structures of substances. In some reactions, no product is formed at completion, or reactants and products may react both ways. The reaction is said to have reached **equilibrium** when the rate of the forward reaction is equal to the rate of the reverse reaction. Factors that affect chemical equilibrium are changing concentration, temperature, and pressure.

Reactions that do not occur spontaneously can be forced by an external supply of energy. This is called an **electrolytic reaction**. Many chemicals and useful products are produced in this manner. Electroplating, electrolysis of water or salts, and the cathode functioning of a battery all are examples of electro-chemistry.

Simple electrochemical cells, in which electrons produced by the oxidation of zinc atoms are transferred through an external circuit into a copper solution, are called galvanic cells or voltaic cells. All electrochemical cells have the same general components: an oxidation half-cell, a reduction half-cell, and a means of separation so that the electrons produced by the oxidation reaction can be supplied through an external circuit into the reduction reaction. The voltage of the cell is the net voltage or potential voltage of two half-cell reactions. Lead storage cells contain a series of lead grids separated by an insulating material. The grids are alternately filled with spongy lead and lead dioxide that compose what are called dry cells. As long as the grids remain intact, the cell will deliver about two volts of electric current.

SOLUTIONS

Forces of attraction between particles produce a solution. One must mix a **solute** and a **solvent** to produce a solution. The particles making up each have certain forces of attraction that produce bonds. The bonds produced by these forces of attraction will determine the solubility of the solute. **Temperature** also affects the solubility of a solution. If the solution is made of gases, the solubility will be affected by **pressure**. Pressure does not affect the solubility of solids and liquids. If no more solute can be dissolved in the solvent, the solution is said to be saturated. In an unsaturated solution, more solute can be added to the solvent, while in a supersaturated solution, the solution is holding more dissolved solute than normal at that given temperature.

Matter exists as a substance or a mixture. If a substance is made of only one kind of atom, it is an element. If it is made of two or more kinds of atoms in a definite grouping, it a compound. A compound always occurs in a definite composition based on the **Law of Definite Composition**, which states, "A compound is composed of two or more elements chemically combined in a definite ratio by weight." Compounds always have a fixed composition and will be classified as ionic or covalent depending on the type of bonding that occurs when the atoms are combined. The ability to combine is dependent upon the valence of the atom or element. An ionic compound contains ionic bonds— a force of attraction between oppositely charged ions. A covalent compound is a compound that is composed of covalent bonds—a bond in which the electrons are shared between atoms. When a compound is formed, the elements or atoms making up the compound lose their properties and take on the properties of the compound formed.

It is important to remember that the gain of electrons is reduction, and the loss of electrons is oxidation. The **oxidation number** of a bonded atom is the number of electrons gained, lost, or shared in a chemical reaction. The metal elements that lose electrons easily and become positive ions are placed high in the electromotive series.

The metal elements that lose electrons with greater difficulty are placed lower on the periodic chart. The energy required to remove electrons from metallic atoms can be assigned numeric values called electrode potentials. Binary compounds are named by changing the name of the element that has the negative oxidation number to end in "ide".

The **rate of the reaction** is defined as the quantity of product formed in some stated interval or the rate at which the reaction will take place. The rate of the chemical reaction can be defined in terms of the change in concentration of any species in the reaction with respect to time. The rate of the reaction can be determined by measuring how fast the product is formed after the reactants are mixed, or how many moles are formed per second. Also, increase in temperature will increase frequency of molecular collision and increase rate of reaction. Activation energy is necessary to produce enough energy to break or weaken bonds before new bonds can be formed. Some reactions produce energy in the formation of new compounds or the products have more energy than the reactants (exothermic reactions) while other reactants need a greater amount of energy than the activation energy (endothermic reactions). The study of reaction rate factors is called **chemical kinetics**.

☞ Drill: Chemistry

1. The atomic theory states that all matter is composed of

    (A) carbon. (C) molecules.

    (B) atoms. (D) compounds.

2. An element near the bottom of the periodic table would have

    (A) electrons in low energy levels only and low atomic weight.

(B) electrons in high energy levels and low atomic weight.

(C) electrons in high energy levels and high atomic weight.

(D) one energy level and high atomic weight.

3. The sharing of electrons or transfer of electrons is called

(A) bonding.   (C) boiling.

(B) transference.   (D) kinetic flow.

4. Equilibrium can be expressed as the point at which

(A) all the chemicals present stop reacting.

(B) the chemical reactants are used up.

(C) the products react together at the same rate as the reactants.

(D) the reactants are chemically reacting at maximum velocity.

5. Mendeleev discovered there was a pattern when one started to arrange elements based on their

(A) name.   (C) particulate composition.

(B) atomic weights.   (D) melting point.

6. Activation energy is

(A) the energy necessary to cause motion.

(B) the energy that measures an activity.

(C) the energy necessary to start a reaction.

(D) the energy needed to keep a reaction under control.

7. The Law of Conservation of Energy states

(A) that either energy or mass may be destroyed.

(B) energy may neither be created nor destroyed.

(C) energy can be converted to only one form.

(D) energy may either be created or destroyed.

8. Chemical action may involve all of the following except

(A) combining of atoms of the elements to form a molecule.

(B) separation of the molecules in a mixture.

(C) breaking down compounds into elements.

(D) reacting a compound and an element to form an element and a new compound.

9. All chemical changes involve

(A) a decreased stability in a solution.

(B) an increased stability in a solution.

(C) breaking of bonds and forming new ones.

(D) formation of ion reactants.

10. Which of the following involves a chemical change?

(A) The rusting of iron

(B) The evaporation of water

(C) The melting of ice

(D) An ice cube floating in a glass of water

11. According to the kinetic model, matter is NOT made of

(A) atoms.

(B) atoms in constant motion.

(C) particles moving without collisions.

(D) atoms that do not lose energy during rebounding.

12. Under Ideal gas circumstances, when atoms collide together

(A) there is no energy loss.

(B) there is an energy gain.

(C) there is energy exchanged.

(D) there is no source of comparison.

13. In a(n) _____ reaction, the products are lower in energy than the reactants.

(A) exothermic   (C) isothermic

(B) endothermic   (D) chemothermic

14. Combustion is a(n)

    (A) reaction where things are broken down to products with less potential energy.

    (B) reaction where things are combined together to form a more complex product.

    (C) endothermic reaction.

    (D) exothermic reaction.

15. A formula will

    (A) describe the organization and composition of a substance.

    (B) tell the rate of the chemical reaction.

    (C) show when equilibrium is reached.

    (D) describe the physical properties of each element involved.

16. In a chemical reaction at equilibrium, which of the following changes would always increase the concentration of the product?

    (A) Add a catalyst

    (B) Increase pressure

    (C) Increase temperature

    (D) Increase concentration of reactant

17. Which one of the following metals does not undergo corrosion and thus does not need to be electroplated?

    (A) Iron   (C) Nickel

    (B) Copper   (D) Gold

18. A galvanic cell has a porous barrier between the half-cell on the left and the half-cell on the right in order to

    (A) halt the movement of ions.

    (B) preserve the strong acid nature of the solutions.

    (C) allow movement of ions for preserving neutrality.

    (D) measure the quantity of current.

19. The Law of Definite Composition is based on definite composition by

    (A) volume.   (C) specific weight.

    (B) density.   (D) temperature.

20. Chemical action may involve all of the following EXCEPT

    (A) combining of atoms of elements to form a molecule.

    (B) separation of the molecules in a mixture.

    (C) reacting a compound and an element to form a new compound and a new element.

    (D) combusting a compound to form a new substance.

III. PHYSICS REVIEW

BASIC CONCEPTS OF PHYSICS

Physics is the study of matter, energy, and the relationships between the two phenomenal areas of study. Relationships between matter and energy have existed as long as the universe has existed, though man has not totally understood all relationships. Every time you lift a baby, push a wheelbarrow, or physically work out you are demonstrating or applying the principles of physics. Basic principles or concepts of physics may be divided into eight general areas: **mechanics** (motion and force), **energy**, **magnetism**, **sound**, **light**, **heat**, **waves**, and **electricity**.

A scientific law is usually constructed after a limited number of experiments or observations have been tried. It summarizes the order that is believed to exist within certain prescribed conditions and can only occasionally be modified or extended to fit new situations. A scientific law is a statement that (1) fits new facts, (2) uses inductive and deductive reasoning, and (3) successfully predicts what is found in nature.

Law of Acceleration

The amount of **acceleration** is directly proportional to the acting force and inversely proportional to mass:

$$F = ma$$

Drop a rock and it falls to the ground. The rock starts its fall from a resting position and gains speed as it falls. This gain in speed indicates the acceleration of the rock as it falls. **Gravity** (acting force) causes the rock to fall downward once it moves from its resting position. Remember, acceleration is equal to the change in speed divided by the time interval.

Archimedes' Law of Buoyancy or Archimedes' Principle

The relationship between buoyancy and displaced liquid was discovered in ancient times by the Greek philosopher Archimedes in the third century B.C. It states that "an immersed object is pushed up by a force equal to the weight of the fluid it displaces." When an object is suspended in water, the pressures on opposite sides cancel each other. The pressure increases with depth, and the upward force on the bottom of the object will be greater than the downward forces on the top. Thus, an object is lighter in water than in air. This relationship, called **Archimedes' Principle**, is found to be true of both liquids and gases.

Bernoulli's Law

"A moving stream of gas or liquid appears to exert less sideways pressure than if it were at rest." Bernoulli studied the relationship of fluid speed and pressure, and wondered how the fluid got the energy for extra speed. He discovered that the pressure in a fluid decreases as the speed of the fluid increases. This principle is a consequence of the conservation of energy and supports the concept of steady flow. If the flow speed is too great, then it becomes turbulent and follows changing, curling paths known as **eddies**. Also, this same principle application accounts for the flight of birds and aircraft abilities.

Boyle's Law

If the temperature of a gas remains constant,

$$V = P$$

where P and V are the pressure and volume, respectively. When the density of the gas increases in a given space, the pressure is increased. The density of the gas also can be doubled by simply compressing the air to half its volume. This law is applied when one inflates a tire, balloon, or any other such object.

Charles' Law

"The volume of gas increases as its temperature increases if the pressure stays the same." Charles' measurements suggested that the volume of a gas would become zero at a temperature of $-273°C$. Thus, this temperature is called absolute zero. This law applies only to gases. Scientists have found all gases become liquids or solids before they are cooled to the temperature of $-273°C$. Charles' Law is used to explain the kinetic theory as four factors are needed to describe a gas—the mass, the volume, the pressure, and the temperature. Charles' Law explains the increase in volume within tires after traveling long distances or traveling on hot days.

Hooke's Law

The amount of stretch or compression, x, is directly proportional to the applied force F:

$$(x = F)$$

This law is used to explain the property of elasticity. Elasticity is the ability of a body to change shapes when a force is applied and then return to its original shape when that force is removed. Steel is an example of an elastic material. It can be stretched and it can be compressed. Because of its strength and elastic properties, it is used to make springs for construction girders. Also, spring construction and functioning is based on Hooke's Law.

Newton's Laws

Sir Isaac Newton's laws describe how forces change the motion of an object and are stated in the Three Laws of Motion.

The First Law (Law of Inertia) states that every body remains in a state of rest or uniform motion unless acted upon by forces from the outside.

The Second Law (Law of Constant Acceleration) states that the acceleration of an object increases as the amount of net force applied from outside the object increases. The formula of this law is

Force = mass × acceleration

Force = mass × meter divided by seconds squared $\left(\dfrac{m}{s^2}\right)\dfrac{kg \times m}{s^2}$

Therefore, applying the formula to determine one newton is the force needed to give a mass of one kilogram an acceleration of one meter per second squared, or:

Force (1 newton) = mass 1(kg) × acceleration $\left(\dfrac{1m}{s^2}\right) 1\,N = 1\,kg \times 1\dfrac{m}{s^2}$

Newton's Third Law (Law of Conservation of Momentum) states that forces always come in pairs: to every action there is an equal and opposite reaction. When one object exerts a force on a second object, the second object exerts a force that would be equal to and opposite the force of the first object. Mass is a measure of the amount of inertia of a body. The product of mass and velocity is the amount of momentum an object possesses. A quantity that is not changed is said to be conserved. In a collision the total momentum of the colliding bodies is not changed. This is the Law of Conservation of Momentum or Newton's Third Law. Momentum is conserved provided there are no outside forces acting on a set of objects.

Law of Conservation of Energy

Energy cannot be created or destroyed; it changes forms but does not cease to exist. This law explains how energy can change from one form to another. As energy can never be created or destroyed, the total energy of the universe remains the same.

Law of Conservation of Mechanical Energy

In the absence of friction, energy stored in a machine remains constant and work done by the machine is equal to the work done on it. The energy of an object enables it to do work. Mechanical energy is due to the position of something (potential energy) or the movement of something (kinetic energy).

Mechanical energy is produced by a machine that is a device for multiplying forces or changing the directions of forces.

Law of Gravitation

Any two bodies in the universe attract each other with a force that is directly proportional to their masses and inversely proportional to the square of their distance apart:

$$F = Gm\frac{m}{d}$$

Forces are always applied at several different places under normal circumstances, not just at one point. This force on objects found on the Earth is what we call gravity.

Lenz's Law

The direction of an induced current is always such that its magnetic field opposes the operation that causes it. This law is the basis for the design of a generator and its ability to function by converting mechanical energy into electrical energy. A changing magnetic field induces an electric field. A generator uses the electromagnetic induction to convert mechanical energy into electrical energy.

Ohm's Law

The current in a wire is proportional to the potential difference between the ends of the wire:

$$V \text{ (voltage)} = I \text{ (current)} \times R \text{ (resistance)}$$

Ohm's Law determines the strength of the current that flows into the circuit and the basis for the concept of electrical current. Any path along which electrons can flow is a circuit. A complete circuit is needed to maintain a continuous electron flow.

Law of Reflection

The angle of the incidence equals the angle of reflection. This law explains how a wave changes its direction or how it is reflected back. When light is reflected from a flat surface or plane such as a mirror, the incoming light ray (incident ray) and the reflected ray of light (reflected ray) are measured with respect to a line perpendicular to the flat surface. When a light ray strikes a flat surface, the angle of incidence always equals the angle of reflection. Sunlight is an example showing this law.

Law of Refraction

Light rays passing through a transparent substance are bent, or refracted; the thicker the substance is, the farther apart its actual and apparent locations will be. The law also states that the incident ray and the refracted ray both lie on one plane.

A theory applies to a broad range of phenomena and is applied to a small aspect of nature. A theory attempts to explain the "how's" and "why's" of science. It is in the establishing and testing of theories that discoveries are made. The primary purpose of a theory is to enable us to see a natural phenomenon as a part of a simple, unified whole as it

1. correlates many facts in a single concept or reasonable assumption;

2. suggests or accommodates new ideas;

3. stimulates research;

4. is useful in solving long-range problems; and

5. makes predictions.

Albert Einstein developed the **Theory of Relativity**, which is often referred to as Einstein's Theory. The relativity theory is based on mathematical formulas and calculations dealing with gravitation, mass, motion, space, and time. Basic principles of this theory are:

1. Motion in a straight line will have constant velocity. All other motion is judged from this frame of reference.

2. The speed of light in empty space will always have the same value regardless of the motion of the source or the motion of the observer.

Before a hypothesis can be scientific, it must conform to the scientific rule of being testable. Then, one must test by following the scientific method:

1. recognize the problem;

2. formulate your hypothesis;

3. complete related research;

4. perform test-to-test prediction;

5. collect data while performing the test;

6. summarize research and test results in an orderly manner; and

7. draw conclusions.

MATTER, MASS, AND DENSITY

Matter is found in everything. Everything is made of atoms. All matter, living or nonliving, is a combination of elements (atoms). Matter is anything that has mass and occupies space. Matter can exist in four states dependent upon its

Brownian Motion: (1) solid, (2) liquid, (3) gas, or (4) plasma, which makes up the greatest quantity of matter.

Mass is the quantity of matter in a body that exhibits a response to any effort (energy or movement) made to start it, stop it, or change in any way its state of motion. Mass is measured by the amount of inertia an object has. The greater the mass, the greater the force necessary to change its state of motion. Mass is often confused with weight. Weight is a specific numerical measurement or unit, while mass is anything that takes up space and has weight.

Density is the measure of compactness of a material. It being as light as a feather or heavy as a rock is dependent upon its density. Density is not mass nor is it volume. Density cannot be equated to size in all cases; rather, it is the compactness of the mass per unit of volume. Both the mass of the atoms making up the substance or material and the spacing between the atoms determine the density of materials or state of materials.

MOTION

Motion is all around us. Our bodies, no matter how still we think we are, are in a constant state of motion. Motion is easy to see but almost impossible to describe or define. Therefore, when speaking of motion, one must address it as relative to an object rate.

Velocity

Velocity is the speed in a given direction. Speed and velocity can be used interchangeably if the description is asking for how fast a movement occurs in a certain direction. Velocity can be described as constant or changing. A constant velocity requires that both the speed stay the same and direction not be changed or altered. Motion at constant velocity is motion in a straight line at a constant speed. A body may be moving at a constant speed along a curved path or the speed may vary along a constant path. The latter is referred to as changing velocity.

Acceleration

Acceleration is a rate that applies to a decreasing speed (deceleration) as well as an increasing speed (acceleration). Acceleration applies to a change in direction as well as the change in speed. Pressing the gas pedal of a car will accelerate the speed of the car; pressing the brakes will retard the speed, or decelerate the car. Like velocity, acceleration is directional.

Momentum

Momentum is the mass of an object multiplied by its velocity

$$momentum = mass \times velocity - m = m \times v.$$

If the momentum of an object changes, either the mass or the velocity or both change. Thus, acceleration occurs.

Gravity causes a rock to fall downward once it has been dropped. This action on movement is referred to as gravitational motion. If there were no gravitational action, the motion would be called free fall. The time that it takes an object to fall from the beginning of the fall to the point of rest is called elapsed time. The concept of gravity effects was first credited to Isaac Newton after he was hit on the head with an apple that fell from a tree he was sitting beneath.

Speed

Speed is a measure of how fast something is moving or the rate at which a distance is being covered. Speed is calculated as the distance covered divided by the unit of time. Speed is the rate of change of the position of an object. The average speed describes the motion of objects even if they are not moving at a constant speed. This average speed can be calculated by the total distance traveled divided by the total time taken for travel.

Inertia

Inertia is the resistance an object has to a change in its state of motion. Inertia can be measured by its mass depending upon the amount and type of matter in it. The idea of inertia while in motion is called momentum in reference to moving objects.

Force

Force is the push or pull one body exerts on another body. "For every action, there is an equal and opposite reaction" is another way of describing force. Force is the product of acceleration. The combination of all the forces that act on an object is called the net force. When a body is at rest, a force is at work. The fact that the body is at rest rather than accelerating shows another force at work. Force is necessary to maintain balance and reach net force zero. For a book to be at rest on a table, the sum of the forces acting upon the book must equal zero.

The process of determining the components of a vector is called resolution. A person pushes a lawn mower. This in turn applies force against the ground causing the lawn mower to roll forward. In this example, the vector is a combination of two components. Any vector can be represented by a pair of components that are at right angles to each other.

Friction is the name given to the force that acts between materials that are moving past each other. Friction is a result that arises from irregularities in the surfaces of sliding objects. If no friction were present, a moving object would need no force whatever for its motion to continue. Even for a surface that appears to be smooth, there are microscopic irregularities causing friction to occur.

Parallel

When the forces on two opposite sides are equal, this is said to be a parallel force. Thus, this produces, considering all forces are equal, an action-reaction situation.

ENERGY

Energy is the ability of an object to cause change; energy is the ability to do work. Energy is produced when forces are at work. Objects in motion cause change. The greater the speed, the greater the change that occurs. If you experience an energy surge, then you can work more or move faster. Objects as well as people can have energy. Energy can exist in various forms and can change from one form to another form. This energy and its changes can be measured. The unit of measurement of energy is called a joule.

Energy exists in three states: potential, kinetic, and activation energies. An object possessing energy because of its motion has kinetic energy. The energy that an object has as the result of its position or condition is called potential energy. The energy necessary to transfer or convert potential energy into kinetic energy is called activation energy.

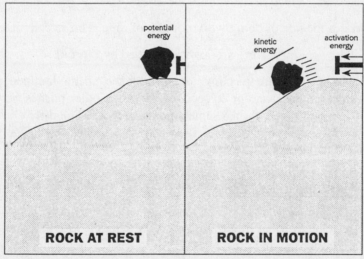

Study the diagram to see that a rock at rest is considered to be potential energy. If a force is used to set that rock in motion, that force would be the activation energy. The rock rolling down the hill until it reaches a point of rest (potential energy) is considered kinetic energy.

Other forms of energy are a result of conditions or combinations of the states of energy. When kinetic and potential energy of lifting, bending, and stretching are grouped together, they are called mechanical energy. The total energy of the particles that make up an object or body is thermal energy. A raised weight possesses potential energy called gravitational potential energy. When it is released, it will return to its former level. This is the principle applied to the functioning of a spring or stretching an object.

Work is the transfer of energy as the result of motion. Most people think of work as an amount of effort exerted. However, if you attempted to move a boulder without any success, you expended energy but no work was accomplished. Work is a derived unit; it may be expressed as any force unit times any distance unit. The only thing that matters in calculating work is the distance moved in the direction of the force.

A **machine** is any device by which energy can be transferred from one place to another or one form to another. Think back to the diagram of the rock rolling down the hill. This is an example of a machine. Often, when we think of a machine or using a machine, some outside agent—a motor, a battery, your muscles—does the work on the machine. The machine then delivers work to something on which it acts.

The principle of conservation of mechanical energy deals with the functioning of a machine. This principle dictates how two kinds of work are related. "In the absence of other forces that dissipate energy, the total mechanical energy of a system remains constant." So long as any energy that is stored within a machine remains constant, and in the absence of friction, the work done by the machine is exactly equal to the work done on it.

Power is the rate of doing work per unit of time. This is calculated by:

P (power) = W (work) divided by t (time).

Suppose two workers are pushing identical boxes up an inclined plane. One pushes his box up the plane in 20 seconds while the other pushes his box up the plane in 40 seconds. Both do the same amount of work. The difference is the rate of time in which the work is done. The unit for power is watt. One watt is one joule of work per second.

HEAT

Heat is a necessity of life. It is also a very valuable tool that cooks our food, frees metals from ores, and creates usable products (to mention a few of its uses). Heat is a form of energy and that energy is created by the motion of the molecules making up an object. Heat is the transfer of energy from an object of high temperature to one of lower temperature.

Heat has several properties: it is a conductor, it can be measured, it can be transferred or radiated, and it can travel by convection. Nearly all materials will either expand or contract when heat is added or taken away. When the amount of heat within an object or around an object varies, that object will vary. There is an exact point at which the variation will occur. We call this the specific heat. The specific heat of any substance is defined as the quantity of heat required to raise the temperature of a unit of mass of that substance by one degree. For instance, a gram of water requires one calorie of energy to raise the temperature 1°C.

Heat is commonly measured in calories or kilocalories, although scientifically the SI or joule is preferred. SI is the abbreviation of Le Système International d'Unites (French), which is the international system of measurement. The term applied here would be the degree. The degree is a measure of temperature. Temperature is a measure of the average kinetic energy of the particles in a body. The degree might be stated in terms of Fahrenheit (F), Kelvin (K), or Celsius (C).

Fahrenheit is based on the freezing temperature of a body or substance being 0 degrees. To totally remove all possible internal heat within a body or substance, one must reduce the temperature to –273 degrees. This point is considered to be 0 on the Kelvin scale and is called absolute zero. The Fahrenheit scale measures the freezing point at 32°F. To convert from the Fahrenheit scale to the Celsius scale use the formula:

$$\text{(degrees) } F = 9/5 \text{ (degrees) } C + 32$$

unless the temperature is below zero on either scale. In that case, you must place a minus sign in front of its number in the equation.

Heat and work are similar when discussing the transfer of energy. Heat is transferred by convection, conduction, or radiation. As work is accomplished, heat is transferred. One way that heat passes from one object to another is by conduction. Not all objects will conduct heat at the same rate; therefore, they are considered poor heat conductors. A very poor conductor of heat is called an **insulator**.

Most gases and liquids are poor **conductors**. They can transfer heat by convection, the mass movement of the heated gas or liquid. This is accomplished by spurring, or sporadic movement of molecules in the mass that pass heat when they bump together. Another method of heat transfer is called radiation. Unlike conduction and convection, radiation does not require direct contact between bodies or masses. Almost all of the energy that comes to Earth is by radiation from the sun. The amount of heat that a body can radiate depends not only on its temperature but on the nature of its surface. Dark, rough surfaces tend to send out more heat than smooth, light-colored surfaces.

WAVES

A British physicist, Edward Victor Appleton, received a Nobel Prize in 1947 for his work dealing with waves. His discoveries led to defining an important region of the atmosphere called the "**ionosphere**." It was established that there were definite layers that would reflect and absorb various radio waves, and thus, the Appleton layers were established. These layers reflect and absorb only the long radio waves used in ordinary radio broadcasts. The shorter waves, used for television broadcasting, pass through, and that is why televisions have a limited range and must use satellite relay stations. The ionosphere is the strongest at the end of the day, after the day long effect of the sun's radiation, and weakens by dawn because many ions and electrons have recombined. Storms on the sun, intensifying the streams of particles and high-energy radiation sent to the Earth, cause the ionized layers to strengthen and thicken. The regions above the ionosphere also flare up into aurora displays.

A **wave** is a wiggle in space and time that can extend from one place to another. Light and sound are both forms of energy that move through space as waves. If this wiggle only occurs in time, it is called a vibration. A wave is measured in wavelengths. The high points are called the crests, the low points the troughs, and the distance from the midpoint to the crest is the amplitude. How frequently a vibration occurs is described by its frequency. The time necessary for the wave to complete one cycle is called a period.

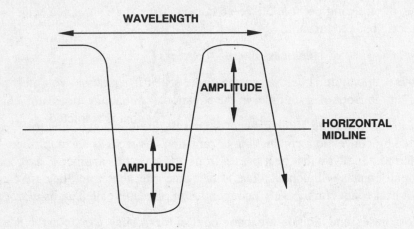

Microwaves

Microwaves, having wavelengths shorter than radio waves, are used in communications and to cook food.

LIGHT

The only thing that we can really see is light. Most objects are made visible by the light they reflect from such light sources. Scientists agree that light has a dual nature—part particle and the other part wave. The particles may be measured as photons. The waves are measured by the distance the light travels in one year. This is called a light year. Light is defined as the only visible portion of the electromagnetic spectrum. Light is produced by vibrating electrically charged atoms that have the ability to absorb energy and emit it as light. The transfer of energy by electromagnetic waves is called radiation.

Properties

The properties of light are reflection, refraction, diffraction, and interference. The amount of the property being demonstrated depends on the amount of light, angle of the light ray, object composition, and density. Material that allows all the light to pass through is called transparent. Material that blocks the light is called opaque.

Quantum is an elemental unit that describes the smallest amount of anything. One quantum of light energy is called a photon. In the micro-world, one quantum of anything is an atom. The Quantum Theory is the study of the behavior of the basic elemental form of anything. This can be adapted to all branches of science to explain behavior of matter.

Reflection occurs when a wave bounces off an object. Waves that strike the object are called incident waves, while waves that bounce off are called reflected waves. The angle between the reflected wave and the normal is called the angle of reflection. When the waves are reflected from a surface, the angle of incidence always equals the angle of reflection.

Refraction is the bending of waves toward the direction of slower wave velocity. When wavelengths become shorter, the frequency does not change. Thus, the material will determine the amount of light that is refracted.

Diffraction

The bending of light around the edge of the object blocking its path is called diffraction. The effects of diffraction occur when waves pass either through an opening or around an object that blocks their path.

Light travels in waves that are **transverse**. This is called **polarization**. Other waves are longitudinal as they travel. Polarized light waves are waves that travel on one plane. Light vibrating parallel to a molecule is absorbed. The light vibrating at right angles to the rows pass through. This concept is used in the sunglass industry—sunglass lenses are designed to reduce glare.

Illumination is the process of making an object bright by increasing the amount of light per unit of area of a surface.

X-rays are electromagnetic waves with the shortest wavelength and the highest amount of energy. Electrically charged particles are filled with kinetic energy that is changed to radiation when these rays crash into other matter.

Lasers are a source of light that produces a bright and narrow beam of light of one color length and is coherent. Coherent light has the troughs and crests of the light lined up together. Lasers convert one form of energy into light energy. The laser is very bright but extremely inefficient as a light source. They are used extensively by surveyors, welders, surgeons, and by code interpreters for barcoding, as a method of ringing up sales at the supermarket.

SOUND

Sound travels about four and one-half times faster in seawater than in air. Its speed is affected by temperature, salinity, and pressure; an increase in any of these results in an increase in the speed of sound.

Sound energy does not travel in straight lines in the ocean because of density differences in water. It is refracted, or bent, by variations in sound speed of the water, scattered by suspended material or marine organisms, reflected and scattered by the surface and bottom, and attenuated by the water through which it travels.

Ambient noise refers to any noise or sound produced by the environment or living creatures or organisms.

There are many varieties of sounds that are produced to be captured by the ear and interpreted by the brain. The brain easily distinguishes one sound from another, yet sound is only a longitudinal wave, a rhythmic disturbance of the air that carries energy. Sound waves are compression waves produced by vibrating matter. Ultrasound is used extensively in medical treatment. One way is through picturing a fetus in the womb without any danger to the fetus or the mother.

When any **frequency** of forced vibrations on an object matches the natural frequency of the object, the measure of the sound increases. The use of tuning forks adjusted to the same frequency and spaced a meter apart is the most common way to demonstrate resonance.

ELECTRICITY

An electrical charge resting on an object is called **static electricity**. If this static electricity is placed in motion, it becomes an **electrical current**. It is the electrical current that we use in most electrical appliances. This same static electricity can be produced by rubbing a hard rubber rod or sealing wax with a piece of fur or flannel. Also, the same result can be accomplished by rubbing a glass rod with a piece of silk.

Electricity can be carried by matter that is a conductor. Sometimes this is accomplished by a spark, which is a static discharge, or a transfer of static electricity. Materials that are poor conductors, such as wood, plastic, rubber, or glass, are used as insulators or grounds which allow an object to lose its charge in a given direction.

A flow of electrons or charged particles through a conductor is called an electric current. This is demonstrated by use of an electroscope.

Electrical circuits function very efficiently within homes. Most circuits are either alternating current (AC) or direct current (DC). Electricity can be supplied to a water heater to heat water, or through wiring and a bulb to produce artificial light. The energy is carried by means of electrical current from a power plant. One common **electrical circuit** is the series circuit. A path is formed by electric conductors in the form of wire to carry the current. The series circuit has only one path for the current so the current will be the same through every part.

Another circuit is the parallel circuit, in which there are two or more separate branches for the current to flow. This is the type of circuit used in string lights for a Christmas tree such that when one light goes out, the rest of the lights will stay on. Also, this type of wiring pattern is used for the outlets in our homes. It is not necessary for all the outlets to be in use at all times for electricity to be available at the flip of a switch.

One electronic device that is commonly used is the battery. A battery acts like a pump forcing electrons through a conductor. There are two types of batteries: wet cell battery and dry cell battery. A wet cell battery contains two different metals in a solution containing an electrode. The car battery is an example of the wet cell battery. The dry cell battery contains a carbon rod set in the middle of a zinc holder. A moist paste sets up a chemical reaction that causes electrons to be released.

MAGNETISM

Magnetism is the ability to attract iron and certain other metals that have a molecular structure similar to iron. Magnetism is related to electricity in that it travels in currents. Magnets exert a force on another magnet just like an electrical charge. They can attract or repel each other without touching because of their electrical charges. The strength of their interaction depends on the distance of separation of the two magnets.

Magnetism was explained by Albert Einstein in 1905 in his theory of special relativity when he showed that a magnetic field is a by-product of the electric field. Charges in motion have associated with them both an electric and a magnetic field. A **magnetic field** is produced by the motion of the electric charge.

A **voltmeter** is a calibrated device used to measure the electric potential. This electrical current produces a magnetic field. The same principal construction is used in the making of an electric motor. The principal difference is that the current is made to change direction every time the coil makes a half revolution.

Speakers used in car radios, home stereos, and loudspeaker systems belong in the grouping of electromagnets. A speaker consists of a coil of thin wire that goes between the poles of a magnet. The coil is attached to a cone-shaped piece of stiff paper that converts the electrical current into sound.

☞ Drill: Physics

1. Acceleration is defined as the

    (A) change in position divided by the time needed to make that change.

    (B) change in velocity divided by the time needed to make that change.

    (C) time it takes to move from one speed to another speed.

    (D) time it takes to move from one place to another place.

2. Archimedes' Principle says that an object is buoyed up by a force that is equal to

    (A) the weight of the fluid displaced.

    (B) the volume of the fluid displaced.

    (C) the mass of the fluid displaced.

    (D) the mass of the object.

3. Bernoulli's Principle states that

    (A) internal fluid pressure decreases as fluid speed increases.

    (B) as the volume of a gas increases at constant temperature, the pressure decreases.

    (C) an object in air is buoyed up by a force equal to the weight of the air displaced.

    (D) internal fluid pressure increases as fluid speed increases.

4. The ability of a body to change shapes when a force is applied and then return to its original shape when that force is removed is

    (A) elasticity.   (C) springforce.

    (B) compression.   (D) girders.

5. Energy can

    (A) not be created.   (C) be changed in form.

    (B) not be destroyed.   (D) All of the above.

6. Friction acts parallel to the surfaces which are sliding over one another and in the

    (A) same direction as the motion.

    (B) opposite direction of the motion.

(C) contact line and circular motion.

(D) direction of the sliding force.

7. When refraction occurs, part of a wave

(A) is bent more than another part.

(B) slows down before another part.

(C) is pushed to one side.

(D) is closer together than it appears.

8. When light is refracted,

(A) the rays all lie on different planes.

(B) the rays lie on one plane.

(C) the rays lie on one thickness.

(D) the rays lie behind the plane.

9. The greater the mass of an object, the greater the force necessary

(A) to change its position.

(B) to change its force.

(C) to change its state of motion.

(D) to change its shape.

10. The idea of inertia while in motion is called

(A) momentum in reference to moving objects.

(B) inertia frame of reference.

(C) measurement of momentum.

(D) momentum in reference to nonmoving objects.

11. The idea of parallel force can be applied to circuits. A parallel circuit would

(A) have equal currents.

(B) have action-reaction forces producing static electricity.

(C) have a constant supply of electricity.

(D) have an on-off supply of electricity depending on all forces being constant.

12. The two factors which determine the amount of work done are

    (A) magnitude of the force exerted and the weight of the object moved.

    (B) the distance of the object moved in the time required.

    (C) the displacement of the object and the magnitude of the force in the direction of the displacement.

    (D) the magnitude of the force in the direction of the displacement and the time required.

13. Machines may be used

    (A) to divide the force.

    (B) to multiply speed.

    (C) to divide force and speed simultaneously.

    (D) to keep the direction of the force constant.

14. The principle of conservation of mechanical energy dictates how two kinds of work are related. They are

    (A) friction and mechanical energy.

    (B) absence of friction and work by a machine.

    (C) speed and type of machine.

    (D) mass and speed of machine.

15. Heat transfer occurs

    (A) from an object of a lower temperature to one of higher temperature.

    (B) from an object of a higher temperature to one of lower temperature.

    (C) when electrons bump into each other.

    (D) when the temperature rises.

16. Specific heat is related to the amount of heat

    (A) a specific object has.

    (B) one molecule contains.

    (C) transferred by one molecule.

    (D) needed to change the temperature of one gram of a substance by one degree Celsius.

17. The wiggle formed by a wave in time is called the

    (A) amplitude.   (C) vibration.

    (B) frequency   (D) interference.

18. Diffraction

    (A) occurs only for radio waves.

    (B) occurs only for light.

    (C) occurs only for X-rays.

    (D) can occur for any wave.

19. Light traveling in waves that are transverse and travel on one plane is called

    (A) diffracted light.   (C) polarized light.

    (B) refracted light.   (D) distracting light.

20. The use of the tuning forks demonstrates

    (A) amplitude.   (C) resonance.

    (B) frequency.   (D) pitch.

IV. EARTH SCIENCE REVIEW

ASPECTS OF EARTH SCIENCE

An understanding of the beginnings of the **solar system** and the Earth's development within it is essential to environmental survival. This understanding is filled with curiosity, and may be the price of environmental survival. A lack of curiosity and understanding may signal the environment's demise.

Hipparchus, in 150 B.C., determined the distance of the moon, based on his calculations of the Earth's diameter. The Greeks added to the study of **astronomy** by determining that an eclipse was caused by the Earth passing between the sun and the moon, and, the sun was at the center of the solar system. These and other basic studies concerning the sun, moon, planets, galaxies, and solar system have led to questions like, "Does the universe go on forever? Where does it all end? Is space infinite?" It is because of such challenging questions that astronomy has developed into an exact science.

Theories

The theory developed by Sir Isaac Newton is in direct opposition to the theory developed by Albert Einstein. Newton stated that a planet moves around the sun because of the gravitational force exerted by the sun. This theory holds true if one is studying the velocities of small objects compared to light. Einstein's theory of relativity states that the planet chooses the shortest possible path throughout the four-dimensional world which is defined by the presence of the sun. According to this theory, if you left home and walked in a straight line, you would eventually return home. Both these theories were inventions by human minds and have been used to create many of our scientific explanations (theories). New theories will show weaknesses and limitations to each theory.

Most scientists tend to believe the theory stating the solar system probably developed as a nebula (cloud of gas and dust) that once swirled around the sun and slowly flattened out. Sections of the cloud began to spin like eddies in a stream, collecting gases and dust and causing the sections to grow and form planets. They slowly developed into spinning planets that now travel around the sun.

How did the Earth and the life on it come into existence? The most widely held scenario on this is known as the **Big Bang Theory**, which states that it was from a colossal explosion 10 to 14 billion years ago that a highly concentrated mass of gaseous matter formed and then radiated outward, creating the universe. It is widely believed that the life on Earth is a natural consequence of the events set in motion by the Big Bang. It is also generally thought that the universe continues to expand today. The Big Bang, however, is not universally accepted. Among the things that cause it to be called into question are observations (a) that some globular clusters appear to be older than the universe itself and (b) that galaxies exist in superclumps, with enormous voids between them.

In the early 1700s, Abraham Werner presented his theory that an ocean once covered the Earth. The chemicals in the water slowly settled to the bottom of the water where they formed granite and other forms of rock layers. The Earth was completely formed with the settling of the water and no other changes occurred. All life, according to Werner, began with the settling of the water and the formation of the Earth.

The **Hutton Theory** of 1785 claimed that the Earth was gradually changing and would continue to change in the same ways. According to Hutton, these changes could be used to explain the past. He died before he could get other scientists to accept his ideas, yet after his death and publication of his ideas, they became a leading guide for the geological thinkers.

The **Creation Theory** with which we are most familiar is that given in the first chapters of Genesis. Various attempts have been made to work out the date of the creation on the basis of the data given in the Bible and the date of creation has been set at 3760 B.C. The creation, as explained in Genesis, is accepted by some people as the formation of the Earth and the origin of life.

Battle lines have been drawn. One theorist will research and develop a possible strategy for solving the age-old question, only for another theorist to come along and find a flaw in that research and then develop a new theory. Thus new theories are constantly developed. Each theory developed is viewed in a manner to gain an understanding of the information presented pertaining to the Earth's formation for the purpose of survival and prosperity of the universe.

Solar System

The solar system includes the sun, nine planets with their **moons**, asteroids, meteoroids, comets, interplanetary dust, and interplanetary plasma that is circular in shape. The sun is the center of the solar system with a mass 750 times greater than that of all of the planets combined. The **planets** rotate around the sun with Mercury being the closest to and Pluto being the farthest from the sun. The terrestrial (earth-like) planets—Mercury, Venus, Mars, and Earth—are composed chiefly of iron and rock. These planets are smallest in comparison to the four largest planets, Jupiter, Saturn, Uranus, and Neptune, which are called the Major planets. They are composed chiefly of hydrogen, helium, ammonia, and methane. Pluto is believed to be less than one-fifth the size of Earth, which makes it smaller than our moon.

Asteroids, or planetoids, are small, irregularly-shaped objects orbiting between Jupiter and Mars. **Meteoroids** are chunks of iron resulting from collisions between asteroids. **Comets** are round heads consisting of dust particles mixed with frozen water, frozen methane, and frozen ammonia, and a tail made of dust and gases escaping from the head.

Meteors and Meteorites

A **meteor** is a metallic or stony mass belonging to the solar system that is hurtled into the Earth's atmosphere. The meteor cannot be seen until it enters the atmosphere, at which time the friction with the air makes it glow and shine for only a few seconds as it falls to the Earth. Thus, it is called a falling, or shooting, star.

Meteorites seldom do damage, yet they have devastating potential. Meteorites are pieces of extraterrestrial matter that are studied to determine the origins of the universe and the solar system. Meteorites make up only a tiny fraction of the matter falling into the Earth's atmosphere from space. They sometimes explode into fragments with a noise that can be heard for many miles when they strike the surface of the Earth.

Stars

When you look at the sky, you see only a tiny part of the universe consisting mainly of stars, clouds of dust, and the solar system. Astronomers study the brightness and color of the stars. Brightness indicates the mass of the stars, while the color indicates the temperature of the star's surface. The distance is difficult to determine as most stars are so far away. Stars have been studied as early as 3000 B.C.; yet, they still remain a mystery.

Stars and star groupings (**constellations**) are used as compasses at night, as a navigational aid, as a basis for astrology, for study, and for viewing at the planetarium. What appears as movement of the stars and the nearly 80 constellations is actually the spinning and placement of the Earth. Seasonally and yearly, the constellations that can be seen will differ, causing the sky to appear to move west during the year.

Galaxies

Galaxies are groups or systems of stars located millions to billions of light-years from Earth. Sometimes called stellar universes, galaxies include billions of stars, and are classified as to their appearance. Irregular systems have no special form or symmetry. The spiral system resembles a large pinwheel with arms extending from the dense central core. Elliptical systems appear round without the spiral arms.

Our solar system is in the Milky Way Galaxy. The Milky Way is a spiral galaxy and is held together by gravity. It slowly rotates, with its spiral arms turning once in about 200 million years. The Milky Way contains clouds of gas, dust, and millions or billions of star clusters which form their own distinct patterns. Bands of stars making up the spiral arms of our galaxy can be seen in the night sky. The Andromeda Nebula Galaxy, first studied in 1612, resembles the Milky Way. It is the nearest galaxy that northern hemisphere observers can see.

In the past few decades, radio astronomy has played a great role in studying celestial objects. In 1959, the first quasar was discovered. It was noticed that some sources of celestial radio waves appeared to be point-like—"quasi-stellar"—instead of looking like radio waves emitted by galaxies. These "quasi-stellar radio sources," or quasars as they are known, give off radio waves and light at a rate over 100,000 billion times as fast as the sun. **Quasars** appear to be far smaller than ordinary galaxies, and are believed by some astronomers to be the core of violently exploding galaxies. Quasars appear to be among the most distant objects in the universe. Today, astronomers have identified over 1,000 quasars.

PHYSICS AND CHEMISTRY OF THE EARTH

Physical Properties

The Earth has three motions: it spins like a top, moves in the spinning motion around the sun, while moving through the Milky Way with the rest of the solar system. The Earth spins around on its axis, an imaginary line that connects the north and south poles at either end of the planet. The spinning motion has a path it follows around the sun (orbit), making the sun seem to move from east to west and causing the occurrences of day and night.

The Earth has only one moon. The Sun's gravity acts on both the Earth and the Moon, causing the moon to travel in an oval-like orbit around the Earth. Because of this movement, we have the seasons of spring, summer, fall, and winter. The seasons are a result of the tilting of the Earth on its axis, movement, and position of the moon in relation to the sun.

Chemical Composition

The Earth's surface is about 70 percent water, with most of the water being oceans with depths extending to 12,450 feet. The land surface makes up the remaining 30 percent and extends an average of 2,757 feet above the division of land and water. The highest peak is Mount Everest in Asia at 29,028 feet above sea level. Oceans, lakes, rivers, and all other bodies of water and ice make up a part of the Earth called the hydrosphere. Land bodies surrounded by water make up the continents. Together, land and water surfaces that support life are called the biosphere.

The chemical composition of the Earth is 46.6 percent oxygen, 27.72 percent silicon, 8.13 percent aluminum, 5.0 percent iron, 3.60 percent calcium, 2.83 percent sodium, 2.59 percent potassium, 2.09 percent magnesium, 0.44 percent titanium, and all other elements total 1.0 percent. A geologist is a person who studies the Earth and its contents. It is through the work of geologists that the chemical composition of the Earth has been established.

Rocks

The hard, solid part of the Earth's surface is called **rock**. Rock may be exposed from its soil cover when highways are cut through hillsides or mountain regions. River channels or shorelines frequently cut through rock beds. Some mountain chains expose rock beds when weathering exposes the rock base. Rocks are useful in many ways as granite (**igneous**), marble (**metamorphic**), or limestone (**sedimentary**) can be used in buildings, dams, highways, or the making of cement. Metals like aluminum, iron, lead, and tin are removed from rock that is called ore.

Minerals

Minerals are the most common form of solid material found in the Earth's crust. Even soil contains bits of minerals that have broken away from its rock source. Minerals are dug from the Earth and are used to make a variety of products. To be considered a mineral, the element must be found in nature and never have been a part of any living organism. Atoms making up the element or substance must be arranged in regular patterns to form crystals and must have the same chemical makeup as the area where it is found.

Ores

Ores are deposits high enough in an element content that it would be economically feasible to be mined and sold for a profit. Ore deposits are located from geological knowledge about crustal movements and ore formations along with sophisticated instruments and a lot of luck. Once the ore has been located, the mining process is based on the most economical method to remove the highest amount of the mineral from the rock with the least amount of environmental damage. Processes include leaching or separating the mineral from the rock by heat, brine solutions, evaporation of seawater, or chemically removing the metal from the ore.

Earth's Magnetism

Imaginary lines curve from the north pole to the south pole, making up the Earth's **magnetic field**. The Earth acts as though its center is a large magnet. These imaginary lines aid the compass needle to determine directions based on the Earth's natural magnetic field. Scientists are not sure what produces the enormous currents that are deep within the Earth and responsible for the Earth's magnetic fields.

EVOLUTION AND CRUSTAL PROCESS

Changing of the Earth

The Moon's gravitational pull produces tides both in the ocean and in the Earth's solid crust. Throughout time, slow evolutionary changes have taken place and continue to take place. As shorelines are inched away in one location, mud and silt build up in other areas, adding to the land surface. With all these changes occurring slowly over long periods of time, little difference can be recorded as to variations in land or water surfaces of the Earth.

Continental Drifts

The **continental shelves** are zones of relatively shallow portions of the continent extending out under the oceans. The continental shelves, or edges, are a part of the continent they adjoin, and the edge of the shelf is the true boundary of the continent. The continental shelf is not small. In some areas, it may contain the same area as the size of the Soviet Union under the waters of the ocean. The shelves were formed eighteen to twenty thousand years ago due to the melting of the glaciers, along with time, wave-cutting terraces, erosion, and sedimentation all part of the formation explanation. At the edge of the shelf, the continental slope leads downward to the deep ocean. At the bottom of the slope, an area of deposition called the continental rise may form a gentler slope. Other features included in the continental margin are trenches, ridges, and submarine canyons. A reef is a rocky or coral elevation dangerous to surface navigation which may or may not be uncovered by water. A rocky reef is always detached from shore; a coral reef may or may not be connected to the shoreline.

Nature's Recycling

Nature's method of recycling is evident through many processes. Some processes are the water cycle, carbon cycle, oxygen cycle, and energy cycle as demonstrated by prey and predators. These concepts are explained through the following drawings.

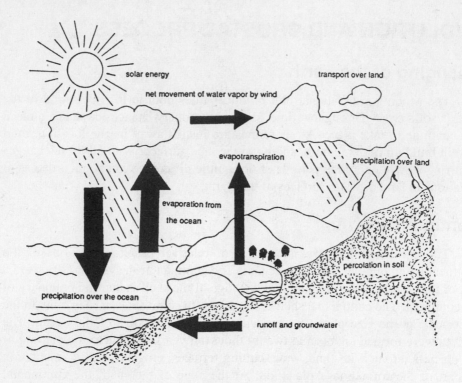

The Hydrologic (Water) Cycle

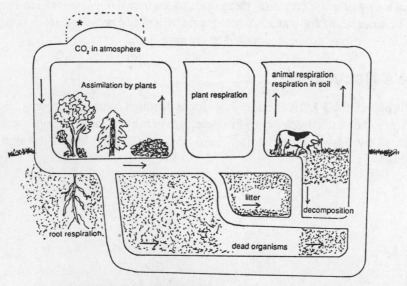

* A seasonal change in atmospheric CO_2 levels is caused by variations in the distribution of vegetation on the earth.

Carbon Cycle

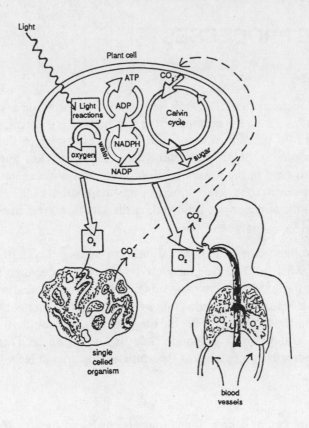

Oxygen Cycle

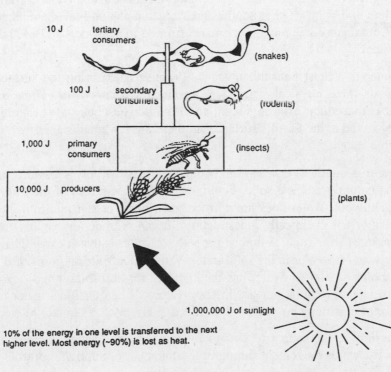

10% of the energy in one level is transferred to the next higher level. Most energy (~90%) is lost as heat.

Energy Cycle

SURFACE PROCESSES

Atmosphere

Air, an odorless and colorless gas, surrounds the Earth and extends approximately 1,000 miles above the surface of the Earth. This is called the atmosphere. It is made up of 78 percent nitrogen and 21 percent oxygen; the remaining 1 percent consists mainly of argon, water vapor, dust particles, and other gases. Cloud formations float in the lowest portion of the **atmosphere** called the troposphere. Weather occurrences are formed in the **troposphere**. It is also the more dense portion of the atmosphere, followed by the **stratosphere**, **mesosphere**, and **exosphere**.

The **ionosphere** is a belt of radiation surrounding the Earth. Outside the atmosphere, in what used to be considered "empty" space, man's satellites in 1958 disclosed the existence of magnetism. The aurora borealis or "northern dawn/lights" is a beautiful display of moving, colored streamers or folds of light. Its counterpart in the Antarctic is the aurora australis, or "southern dawn/lights," both connected to the Earth's magnetic field or lines of force. During magnetic storms, aurora borealis can be seen as far south as Boston and New York.

Water

The most important source of sediment is earth and rock material carried to the sea by rivers and streams; the same materials may also have been transported by glaciers and winds. Other sources are volcanic ash and lava, shells and skeletons of organisms, chemical precipitates formed in seawater, and particles from outer space.

Water is a most unusual substance because it exists on the surface of the Earth in its three physical states: ice, water, and water vapor. There are other substances that might exist in a solid and liquid or gaseous state at temperatures normally found at the Earth's surface, but there are fewer substances which occur in all three states.

Water is odorless, tasteless, and colorless. It is the only substance known to exist in a natural state as a solid, liquid, or gas on the surface of the Earth. It is a universal solvent. Water does not corrode, rust, burn, or separate into its components easily. It is chemically indestructible. It can corrode almost any metal and erode the most solid rock. A unique property of water is that it expands and floats on water when frozen or in the solid state. Water has a **freezing point** of 0°C and a **boiling point** of 100°C. Water has the capacity for absorbing great quantities of heat with relatively little increase in temperature. When distilled, water is a poor conductor of electricity but when salt is added, it is a good conductor of electricity.

Sunlight is the source of energy for temperature change, evaporation, and currents for water movement through the atmosphere. Sunlight controls the rate of photosynthesis for all marine plants, which are directly or indirectly the source of food for all marine animals. Migration, breeding, and other behaviors of marine animals are affected by light.

Water, as the ocean or sea, is blue because of the molecular scattering of the sunlight. Blue light, being of short wavelength, is scattered more effectively than light of longer wave lengths. Variations in color may be caused by particles suspended in the water, water depth, cloud cover, temperature, and other variable factors. Heavy concentrations of dissolved materials cause a yellowish hue, while algae will cause the water to look green. Heavy populations of plant and animal materials will cause the water to look brown.

Weathering

Weathering is the natural wearing away of rock or soil due to chemical or physical actions on these Earth surfaces. This occurs very slowly over a long period of time. Through chemical weathering, rocks break down as oxygen, carbon dioxide, and water vapor react with rock until it is finally changed into soil. Physical weathering occurs in dry regions by the wind action constantly wearing away the surface of the rock.

Erosion

The first concept of erosion was that natural weathering that we call erosion led to the formation of mountains and mountain chains. The main causes of erosion are air and/or water movement across rock or soil, changes in the temperature, or any combination of these factors. Chemical erosion can occur as carbon dioxide and water vapor are removed from dead organic matter. These are all natural forms of erosion. Man can cause erosion with poor crop-planting procedures, lack of crop rotation, and the cutting of trees without planning or replacement.

Temperature

Temperature is controlled by the position of the earth on its axis and its distance from the sun at rotation. At the equator, the air would be warmest and always pushing upward while cold air would be flowing in to be warmed. The constant changing of air will cause changes in the temperature.

Pressure

Air pressure also plays an important role in the movement of air and the changing of air temperatures and weather changes. Next to the equator, a low pressure cell is formed because the air is warmer, lighter, and moving upward. The low pressure is a result of the molecules of air being further apart. The colder air has closer air molecules; thus, a high pressure cell is formed. Extreme weather conditions, such as flooding, may result when both low cells and high cells occupy the same air space.

Climate

Climate is the usual weather that occurs in a general area over a period of time. The study of climate is called climatology. When referring to climate, one takes into consideration air temperature, wind speed, sunshine, humidity, amount of precipitation, air pressure, and general geographic conditions. Climate has a direct effect upon living organisms and the type(s) of life that can exist in the region being considered. Climate also affects our method of transportation, outdoor activities, choices for employment, type of clothing, type of housing, and food naturally available or that can be grown.

Alternate Energy Forms

About 90 percent of today's energy is supplied from fossil fuels as crude oil, natural gas, and coal. These materials are a result of nature providing such supplies for man's use. Thus, these are considered nonrenewable resources as they cannot be replaced after they have been used. With conservation and suitable alternate energy sources, natural resources will last longer and these fossil fuels can be usable for many more years. Alternate energy sources include methanol, ethanol, wood and wood wastes, garbage and plant material, corn, other grains, solar energy, photovoltaic cells, hydroelectricity, nuclear power, wind energy (windmills), tidal energy, geothermal energy (geysers), and fusion using nuclear waste materials.

EARTH'S HAZARDS AND RESOURCES

Earthquakes

Earthquakes are vibrations due to the movements within and beneath the Earth's crust. They occur as a result of faulting or other structural processes happening as a result of a strain on the rocks at the edge of the crust. A long series of quakes with none being greater than the others is called an **Earth swarm** and occurs near volcanic regions. Imperial Valley, California, is known for having Earth swarms. Earth tremors are vibrations of low intensity and can be felt only by those located directly over the affected area.

Earthquake intensity is measured on a scale from 0 to 9, where each number represents an energy release ten times that of the number. This energy release is measured by the "Richter Scale" as it was introduced by Charles F. Richter in 1935. Richter was an American seismologist. About 80 percent of earthquake energy is released in the areas bordering the vast Pacific Ocean, with 15 percent released in an east-west band across the Mediterranean. The remaining 5 percent occur sporadically throughout the remaining parts of the world bordering large bodies of water.

Volcanoes

Volcanoes are a natural phenomenon with their effects confined to a small area. About 500 volcanoes are known to have been active, with two-thirds of them in the Pacific Ocean area. Modern research into volcanoes and their role in forming much of the Earth's crust began with the French geologist Jean Etienne Guettard in the mid-eighteenth century.

Volcanoes discharge a large amount of carbon dioxide into the air; the weathering of rocks utilizes carbon dioxide. This presents a pair of mechanisms for possible long-term climatic changes. A period of greater than normal volcanic action might initiate a warming of the Earth. The mountains built by the volcanic ash might expose large areas of new and unweathered rock to the air, which will lower the carbon dioxide levels, thus reducing the atmospheric temperature.

Oceans

It is estimated the world's oceans extend over 328 million cubic miles with the greatest depth being 36,198 feet off the coast of Guam. The deepest of all oceans is the Pacific Ocean, averaging 14,048 feet, and the most shallow is the Baltic Sea at 180.4 feet deep. Sedimentary rock at the bottom of the oceans has been dated at 3 billion years old with the water dated at 4 billion years old.

The oceans supply man with a means of transportation, habitat for aquatic life that is used for food, a source of minerals, and a means of weather control. Also, the ocean offers various sources of energy for consumption and use in the future. Currently, oil and gas are being derived from the ocean as sources of energy. Research is being conducted as to the feasibility of waves or water of the ocean being used to produce power. Also, the ocean is used to stimulate islands of lush plant growth to increase the photosynthesis process as a possible way to reduce the depletion of the ozone layer.

Hot Springs

Hot springs are naturally occurring bodies of water that are warmer than surrounding air. Hot springs (thermal springs) occur in regions of faulted or folded rock due to volcanic action. The water that comes from underground where the rocks are hot will produce hot water that rises to the Earth's surface in the form of a spring. Not all hot springs are a direct result of volcanoes, some are produced by geysers.

Migration

Migration is the movement of people or animals from one area to another area. Migration occurs because of seasonal changes, wars, famines, floods, volcanic eruptions, weather, and other natural disasters for the purpose of survival. Migration practices began with prehistoric man. Little is known about the pattern of movement or why migrations took place. It is believed the first migrations were to escape the spread of the great glaciers and ice sheets. The most common application of migration is that of birds and other animals moving to survive winters or for the purpose of reproduction as illustrated by the salmon moving into the colder waters.

Flooding

Flooding is the natural occurrence of an extremely large amount of water flowing into a given area faster than it can leave the area. As a result, the stream, lake, or river will overflow its natural level. Estuary zones and sand dunes are natural flood control devices. Man-made devices include dams and sandbags to control flood waters. The control of flood waters is important to the survival of coastal habitats for wading marsh birds, birds of prey, migratory birds, water fowl, and other aquatic life, as well as man.

Water Based Formations

The commonly seen waves on the surface of water are caused principally by wind. When a breeze blows over calm water, it forms small ripples or capillary waves. As the wind speed increases, larger, more visible gravity waves are formed. When the wind reaches high speeds, whitecaps are formed. However, submarine earthquakes, volcanic eruptions, and tides also cause waves. Waves will always break parallel to the shoreline.

The **tide** is the continuous cycle of alternating rise and fall of the sea level observed along the coastlines and bodies of water connected to the sea. On most coastlines, the cycle occurs about every 12 hours. Along the gulf coastline, a tidal cycle can occur about every 24-25 hours. The rise and fall of sea level observed along coastlines is produced by waves of extreme length; high water is the crest of the wave; low water is the trough. Tides can be predicted once observations have been mathematically related to the positions of Earth, moon, and sun. Tides are caused by the gravitational interaction between the sun, moon, and Earth. The moon exercises the greatest influence on our tide; although its mass is much less than the sun's, it is closer to the earth and its tide-producing effect is more than twice as great.

The maximum height reached by a rising tide is called **high water**. This is due solely to the periodic tidal force, but at times, the meteorological effects of severe storms or strong winds may be superimposed on the normal tide to produce high water.

Low water is the minimum height reached by a falling tide. Often, this is due solely to the influence of a periodic tidal force, but sometimes the influence of severe storms or strong winds may be superimposed on the normal tide to produce low water.

Tides are classified as **semidiurnal, diurnal,** and **mixed**. Areas having semidiurnal tides have two high waters and two low waters each day; this is the most common type. Diurnal tides consist of one high water and one low water each day. Tides are classified as mixed when they are diurnal on some days and semidiurnal on others.

Hurricanes occur when the atmospheric conditions, tail movements, winds, and pressure change severely. Hurricanes begin with winds moving in a circular motion over bodies of water, picking up both speed and rainy weather conditions. When a hurricane approaches a coastline, the sea level will go 20 feet above normal tide level. The months of June through November are considered hurricane season. August, September, and October normally have more hurricanes documented than any other months with September having the greatest number of hurricanes. May and December, on rare occasions, have logged hurricanes. Hurricanes can cause both property damage and personal damage when they move from the water to land surfaces with a tornado resulting from its wind force as it moves further inland.

A **typhoon** is a severe storm over the oceans that is made of rain, wind, and water and will affect tidal movements of shorelines of islands near their occurrences.

Currents are water movements in horizontal or vertical flow occurring at differing depths of the water. Currents stabilize the climate of adjacent land areas, preventing extremes of temperatures. Currents are also influenced/affected by the moon and its position relative to the equator.

Density differences may produce both horizontal and vertical movement of water, causing modifications to the wind-driven surface currents. Water tends to flow from an area of low density to an area of high density. Water may tend to become of greater density as the temperature decreases.

Fog is a hydrometer which consists of a visible collection of minute water droplets suspended in the atmosphere near the earth's surface. It will interfere with the ability to see at a distance over the area that it covers. It is caused by atmospheric humidity and a warm temperature layer being transported over a cold body of water or land surface.

Economics of Earth's Resources

Conservation is the protection and wise management of Earth's resources or natural resources, for the benefit of not only man, but all living things. Without wise practices of conservation and concern for the quality of the environment, all natural resources necessary for life, such as air, animals, energy, minerals, plants, soil, water, and other elemental forms would be damaged, wasted, or destroyed. With greater conservation enforcement, the cost of living will be lower for everyone and more ideal surroundings will be present. The Earth not only has limited resources, but the demands are greater as populations increase, which means there must be a wiser use of Earth's resources if they are to last as long as man, or if man is to survive. The cost of man's poor resource management can be life itself.

☞ Drill: Earth Science

1. When the Earth passes between the sun and the moon, this causes the occurrence of a(n)

   (A) phase.   (C) darkness.

   (B) ellipse.   (D) eclipse.

2. The factors that dispel the collision theory are

   (A) escape of dust and gases.

   (B) the study of gravity and speed the planets are traveling.

   (C) temperature and gaseous mass.

   (D) temperature and Earth's atmosphere.

3. Hutton's theory stated

   (A) how the sun and moon were the same.

   (B) how the Earth was gradually changing and would cease the gradual changing.

   (C) how the Earth was gradually changing and would continue to change in the same ways.

   (D) that the Earth is not changing.

4. Which planet is the closest to the sun?

   (A) Earth   (C) Mercury

   (B) Mars   (D) Pluto

5. Meteoroids are chunks of iron resulting from collisions between

   (A) asteroids.   (C) stars.

   (B) planetoids.   (D) meteorites.

6.   An axis is

  (A) a connecting line at the equator.

  (B) a connecting line between the poles.

  (C) a connecting line between orbits.

  (D) a pole.

7.   The percentage of the Earth's surface that is water is

  (A) 30 percent.   (C) 70 percent.

  (B) 50 percent.   (D) 90 percent.

8.   Igneous rock forms are commonly called

  (A) marble.   (C) granite.

  (B) limestone.   (D) cement.

9.   To be considered a mineral, the substance must never have been a part of a living organism and must be found in

  (A) rock.   (C) nature.

  (B) ore.   (D) sand.

10. The cause of the Earth's magnetic field is

  (A) enormous currents.   (C) a lost secret.

  (B) space satellites.   (D) in the Earth's crust.

11. An odorless, colorless gas that surrounds the Earth is commonly called

  (A) nitrogen.   (C) air.

  (B) oxygen.   (D) carbon dioxide.

12. The source of evaporation is the

  (A) movement of air.   (C) sunlight.

  (B) atmosphere.   (D) currents.

13. Warmer air has molecules of air that are far apart. Therefore, it produces

  (A) a low pressure cell.   (C) rainy weather.

  (B) a high pressure cell. (D) dry conditions.

14. Crude oil, natural gas, and coal are called

    (A) nuclear energy sources.

    (B) alternate energy sources.

    (C) natural sources.

    (E) None of the above.

15. The Richter Scale was introduced in

    (A) 1934.   (C) 1935.

    (B) 1844.   (D) 1955.

16. Two-thirds of all known active volcanoes have occurred in the

    (A) Atlantic Ocean.   (C) Gulf of Mexico.

    (B) Pacific Ocean.   (D) Baltic Sea.

17. Migration occurs because of

    (A) famines.

    (B) the need for cold weather.

    (C) the need to develop a pattern of movement to be studied.

    (D) the need to escape floods.

18. The continuous cycle of alternating rise and fall of the sea level observed along the coastlines and bodies of water connected to the sea is called

    (A) the tide.   (C) sun exercises.

    (B) moon exercises.   (D) a tidal wave.

19. Hurricanes occur over

    (A) land.   (C) land during the day.

    (B) water.   (D) water and land.

20. Fog is

    (A) the same as smog.

    (B) caused when cold air moves over warm air.

    (C) a collection of minute water droplets.

    (D) associated with a tornado.

V. GEOLOGY REVIEW

Geology is the study of the earth. Several different aspects of geology exist: nature appreciation, environmental protection, hazard reduction, material resources, and scientific research. Geologists study from the history of the earth and its continents, rivers, and oceans, and the impacts of man on the planet. Geologists are also involved in the study of the planets, or **planetology**.

HISTORY OF THE EARTH

Several theories of creation have been proposed over the centuries. The **nebular hypothesis** was proposed by Immanuel Kant, and it states that the earth evolved from a rotating cloud of gases, or **nebula**. The **collision hypothesis** says that giant pieces of material broke away from the sun and became the planets. The recent theories involve the collapse of a nebula to form the sun and the planets, triggered by a **supernova**.

The earth was extremely hot, at temperatures high enough to melt iron. The composition was probably uniform, or homogeneous, throughout. As the earth cooled, an early ocean of molten rock, the **magma ocean**, was lighter than the solid material and floated to the surface, forming the earth's **crust**. This formation of the crust was the first step in the **differentiation** process. Gases may then have escaped from the interior and formed the atmosphere. As the earth continued to cool and further evolve, several layers formed. These are shown in the figure below.

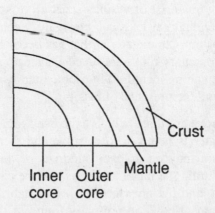

ROCKS

Geologists can determine the history of the earth's events by examining the rocks in the crust. Rock and soil particles settle and form layers. These layers are known as **stratification**, and are the basis for the **stratographic time scale** which is used as the first measure of the time and date of events. These time scales can cover thousands, even millions, of years. The next method for determining time is to examine **fossils**. Fossils are the remains of ancient plants and animals which have been preserved in the rocks. Sedimentary rocks such as limestone, shale, and sandstone are all good sources of fossils. A fossil's age can be determined by the layer of rock in which it was found. Another dating technique is to look at the amount of radioactive decay of the carbon-14 isotope found in the sample. Carbon-14 dating is used for samples 80,000 years old or younger.

Rocks are classified into three major groups: igneous, metamorphic, and sedimentary. **Igneous rocks** were solidified or hardened from the cooling of molten material, either magma or lava. Magma is molten rock plus dissolved gases and is found underground. Lava is just molten rock, and flows above the earth's surface. **Volcanic** rocks are fine-grained, and coarse-grained ones are called **plutonic** after the Greek god Pluto. Igneous rocks are further classified by texture: **phaneritic** or **aphanitic**. Some examples of igneous rocks are granite, rhyolite, pumice, obsidian, gabbro, basalt, scoria, and diorite.

Sedimentary rocks are formed at normal earth temperatures and pressure from the accumulation (or sedimentation) of weathered debris. This debris is the silt and small rock and soil particles found at the bottom of rivers, lakes, and oceans. These rocks are composed of clay (as found in shale), silica (sandstone), or calcium carbonate (limestone), or a combination of any three. **Clastic** rock is composed of particulate material of various sizes, from sand grains to boulders. In clastic rock the individual particles can be easily seen. **Non-clastic** rocks are composed of organic or inorganic material that has been chemically precipitated. Some examples of sedimentary rocks are breccia, sandstone, siltstone, shale, and limestone. These rocks can be identified by ripple marks, stratification (or layering), graded bedding, and the presence of fossils.

Metamorphic rocks are those which have been transformed by heat, pressure, or chemicals. Water is believed to dissolve and then transport the chemicals. The transformation may occur over hundreds or thousands of years. The alterations that occur during the metamorphosis may be categorized into reorientation, recrystallization, and the growth of new and stable minerals. **Reorientation** changes the random orientation normally found in the rock to a preferred orientation. Many times the rock will contain flat and elongated regions. **Recrystallization** occurs under high pressure. The rock's original grains lose their individual identity and the pores will appear smaller than the original rock. Under high heat and pressure, the chemical and physical properties of the rock can be altered to yield new minerals. Examples of minerals that are formed by the new and stable growth are garnet, graphite, tourmaline, and serpentine. Other common metamorphic rocks are marble from transformed limestone, slate from shale, gneiss from granite, and anthracite coal from bituminous coal.

MINERALS

To further understand rocks, which are defined as aggregates or collections of **minerals**, the structure of minerals will be outlined. Minerals exist in solid form, as opposed to liquids or gases, the other states of matter. Solids are found in one of three states: crystal, crystalline, or amorphous substances. A **crystal** has an orderly arrangement of atoms known as a **lattice**. Lattices are three-dimensional arrays which have length, width, and depth. The lattices may not be perfect, but may have defects which include missing ions, displaced ions, ordered substitutions, random substitutions, and interstitial substitutions. These defects ultimately affect the density of the crystal. The crystal lattice results in a regular external geometric form, or **symmetry**. Some shapes that crystals occur in are cubes, prisms, and pyramids among others. A **crystalline substance** also has an orderly arrangement of atoms, but it does not possess the external geometric form. Thus it does not have symmetry. Most everyday substances are crystalline. The last type of substance, **amorphous**, does not have an orderly arrangement of atoms; nor does it have an external geometric form. The atoms are arranged randomly. Sometimes minerals are found in two or three forms but still maintain the same chemical composition; this is known as **polymorphism**. The polymorphism of carbon are diamond, oil, and graphite. Another example of polymorphism is quartz.

Minerals are often identified by their **physical properties**. The simplest property is its color. However, the color may not always be accurate since some colors may be due to impurities or lattice defects, as opposed to the true chemical composition. The next physical property is **luster**, or the way a mineral reflects light off of its surface. **Metallic** and **non-metallic** are the two major types of luster. Metallic luster is shiny like the surface of metals. Some types of non-metallic luster include: vitreous—glassy in appearance; pearly—looking like a pearl; earthy—dull and looking like clay; and finally adamantine—brilliant like a diamond. A mineral may cleave in one or more directions; this is referred to as **cleavage**. Cleavage is dependent upon the crystal structure of the mineral. **Fracture** is the random or haphazard breakage which occurs under one of two conditions. The atom structure may be too complex to give an even break (or cleave). The lattice may also have been poorly developed, with many defects, or bordering on amorphous. Some types of fracture are **concoidal**—the breaks are with smooth curved surfaces (an example is glass); **splintering**—which shows fibers and long slices (asbestos); and **hackly**—which has a rough surface and many sharp points (metals). The mineral may be tested for its ability to resist scratching. This is known as a **hardness** test. The hardness scale is a relative scale that ranges from 1 for talc, the softest mineral, to 10 for diamond, the hardest naturally occurring mineral. The final physical property used for identification is streak. **Streak** is the color of the powdered mineral. The streak will always be the same for the same mineral, regardless of the crystal structure previous to pulverizing, and streak is thus a more accurate measure than the simple color. Other minor physical properties are sometimes used on select minerals. Examples are magnetism, taste, odor, feel, the ability to transmit light, and double refraction.

ROCK DEFORMATION

The two common ways that rocks deform are by folding and fracturing. Rocks can be either brittle or ductile. **Brittle** rocks break suddenly when forced beyond a critical limit. **Ductile** rocks will deform in a smooth, continuous way before they break. **Basement** rocks, sometimes called the bedrock, are found underneath the soil layer in the earth's crust. Basement rocks are crystalline and are usually more brittle than the sedimentary rocks that cover them. **Folded** rock was originally planar, or flat like a sheet. Folds are the result of either horizontal or vertical forces. The folds are often found in young mountains. The folds can be gentle slopes or steep breaks. They are classified as either asymmetrical shapes, overturned, or recumbent folds. Domes and basins are the results of folds.

Fractures are breaks in the rocks and are found in brittle rocks, whereas folds are usually in the more ductile rocks. Fractures are divided into two categories: joints and faults. A **joint** is a crack along a rock where no movement has occurred. If the rocks on both sides of the fracture have moved, then it is called a **fault**. If the movement is only vertical, then a **dip-slip fault** has been made. Horizontal movement leads to a **strike-slip fault**. If both horizontal and vertical movement has occurred, then the fault is classified as an **oblique-slip fault**. When two breaks result in the formation of a valley or trough, it is called a **graben**. Conversely, if a ridge is formed, it is a **horst**. When the folding and faulting happen, the igneous rocks in the structures are subjected to different forces and sometimes high pressure leading to metamorphism. The metamorphic rocks found in the folds and faults are used by geologists to understand the history of the rock deformation.

WEATHERING OF ROCK

Weathering is the wearing away of the rocks. It is a twofold process which is a combination of both **mechanical forces**, or fragmentation of the rock, and **chemical processes**, or decay. The weathering process results in the formation of sands and soils. Three major soils groups exist. The first is the **pedalfer** group which are high in aluminum and iron and cover the eastern half of the United States. Pedalfers are the result of the silicates in the soil being transformed to clays by the humid climate. The drier western half of the United States has soils that are high in calcium carbonate pellets and that contain less clay and more unaltered silicates. These soils are **pedocals**. The third type of soil is the **laterite** or the deep red soil found in the tropics. This soil has aluminum and iron oxides which give it its red color. All of the silicates have been chemically altered, and the calcium carbonate has been leached from it. The process of soil formation can occur very quickly within a few years or very slowly over thousands of years.

The chemical reactions of weathering, the oxidation of iron to rust or the decay of organic material, will vary with the climate and composition of the rock. Chemical weathering is most active in warm and humid climates and least active in cold and dry ones. In different climates different types of clays—kaolinite, smectite, and illite—are formed. Physical weathering results in the formation of rock fragments from pebbles to boulders. The size of the fragment is largely due to the crystalline structure of the original rock.

EROSION AND LANDSCAPE

The **landscape** is the result of a combination of rock being uplifted from the earth's surface and the erosion of this rock. Mass movements are rock fall, landslides, and soil creep which are all induced by gravity. They occur when the slope of the land has been steepened by erosion. The study of the earth's surface and its heights and depths is called **topography**. All heights are compared to the reference height of the **mean sea level**. Vertical distances are called **altitudes** or **elevations**. On maps, lines that connect points of equal elevation are **contour lines**.

The landscape of the Grand Canyon was developed by erosion of the series of flat sediments. These sediments are seen as layers in the canyon's walls. The valley of the Grand Canyon is referred to as **V-shaped**. Another landscape, the Ozark Mountains, have much gentler shapes. Granite was initially uplifted and then eroded for a long time. Mountains, especially high and steep mountains, are eroded most quickly. On the other hand, low and flat areas usually are eroded the slowest. Similar to weathering, erosion is also dependent upon the climate of the region. The different chemical compositions of the rock also contribute to the erosion patterns.

MAPS AND TOPOGRAPHY

The geologist uses maps constantly for his work. A **map** is a graphic representation of the earth's surface. **Location** on a map is designated by the longitude and latitude. **Longitude** lines runs from the North Pole to the South Pole, and they are used to measure the distances west or east of a reference. The reference point (or line) for longitude is the **Prime Meridian**. The **latitude** lines are used to measure distance north or south. The **equator** is used as the point of reference for the latitude lines.

Since a map is a portrayal of an area, the total area must be scaled to the sheet of paper that has the map. A **scale** is the proportion or ratio of distance on the map to the distance in reality, i.e., 1 inch = 10 miles. Sometimes a bar scale is used. Directions on a map are usually from **true north** (TN). This is sometimes called the **geographic north**. This north is different from the **magnetic north** to which compasses point. The true north and magnetic north are not the same; the magnetic north is located 900 miles south of the geographic north pole. The angle between the true north and magnetic north is called **declination**. The **Agonic line** is the location where the two poles appear to be in the same line. This line is where the declination is zero. **Elevations** are measured from the **mean sea level**. Elevations are shown on maps in many different ways: sometimes different colors are used, sometimes different designs. As mentioned before, in contour maps, the areas of equal elevation are connected by contour lines. The spacing of the contour lines indicate the steepness of the slope that is being presented. Occasionally, a **depression**, or decrease in elevation such as a sinkhole or volcanic crater, must be shown. The depression contours often have small tick marks or little hashures around the inside of the lines.

GROUNDWATER

Groundwater is the water that is found underground in the cracks and openings in rocks and sometimes in glaciated sands. It is a renewable resource. The branch of geology that studies groundwater is known as **hydrogeology**. The groundwater is surface water that has seeped downwards into the bedrock, which is also porous. Eventually, the rock is non-porous and the water can no longer migrate downward, but instead it collects in the underground spaces. The water will start to fill all spaces and completely saturate the rock. The region of rock which is completely saturated is known as the **zone of saturation**. Rock that is only partially filled with water is known as the **capillary fringe**. The top of the zone of saturation is defined as the **groundwater table**. The water in the zone of saturation, like the surface water, is always in motion. In most cases they both move in the same direction. The **porosity** of the rock is the amount of empty space in the rock which can be filled with water. **Permeability** is the measure of how the pores are interconnected and thus how well the water can move through the rock. The flow rate of water through the rock is dependent upon the permeability.

The major effect of groundwater movement is the dissolving of certain minerals and rocks. Limestone can be dissolved by acidic rain water into calcium and bicarbonate ions. The dissolved limestone will eventually be precipitated at another location. This is how **stalactites** and **stalagmites** are formed. Groundwater can also physically erode underground surfaces increasing the likelihood of landslides. Groundwater has many useful purposes. It is used for drinking, irrigating crops, and watering livestock. It can come out of the ground naturally or be pumped out with a well. When a well is drilled, the water table is affected, and the water table around the well is changed into the shape of a cone called the **cone of depression**.

RIVERS

Water flow can be classified as either laminar or turbulent. In **laminar flow**, particles move in parallel layers and do not mix with one another. In **turbulent flow**, which is faster, water flows in confused patterns and particles are mixed. When a fast moving turbulent stream suddenly steepens and starts to move even faster, the water may appear to flow in a very smooth straight pattern. The flow is so fast that it is called **shooting flow**. Turbulent flow at slower velocities is referred to as **streaming flow**.

Particles can be moved in all of these flows. Laminar flows are the gentlest and carry only the smallest particles. Turbulent flows can carry much larger particles, up to the sizes of pebbles, thus eroding the streams and rivers. This debris is eventually deposited as sediment, or **alluvium**. The current in rivers can erode both the soil material and the hard rock, although the hard rock is eroded at a much slower rate.

Rivers are dynamic systems. Input to the river is all the water that reaches it from surface run-off, groundwater, plus the erosional debris from the entire area drained by the river. The output is the water and sediment that are carried to the ocean. Changes in the river occur when an imbalance exists between the output and input. **Floods** are an example of an imbalance when the river is not able to carry away extra water and sediment. Instead, the river overflows and invents new channels to carry the water.

The **continental divide** is located near Denver. It is a crest more than 11,000 feet above the sea level. This structure divides the water flow patterns in the United States. All water west of the continental divide eventually flows into the Pacific Ocean, and all water east flows into the Atlantic Ocean. **Drainage basins** are areas which funnel all their water into streams. These drainage networks show patterns in their branches—dendritic, rectangular, trellis, or radial. The patterns depend upon the topography, rock type, and structure of the area.

☞ Drill: Geology

1. One accepted theory for the formation of our solar system from a rotating cloud of gas and dust

    (A) has been proven to be true.

    (B) was proposed by many scientists, including Immanuel Kant.

    (C) is called the Nebular Hypothesis.

    (D) Both (B) and (C).

2. The names for the layers of the earth include all of the following EXCEPT

    (A) asthenosphere.   (C) differentiation.

    (B) lithosphere.   (D) solid iron core.

3. Which is the best term to describe the remains of ancient plants and animals that have been preserved in solid rock?

    (A) Stratification   (C) Coproliths

    (B) Fossils   (D) None of the above.

4. Sedimentary rocks are formed from the accumulation of silt, rock, and soil particles on the surface of Earth. Of the following, which is NOT identified as a sedimentary rock type?

    (A) Limestone   (C) Shale

    (B) Diorite   (D) Both (B) and (C).

5. Rocks are classified into three main groups. Which major rock classification consists of rock that forms from molten material that has solidified?

    (A) Igneous   (C) Volcanic

    (B) Sedimentary   (D) Metamorphic

6. Which of the following are characteristic of metamorphic rocks?

    (A) Shows evidence of recrystallization

    (B) Evidence of fossils of animals and plants

    (C) Reorientation of crystals within rock

    (D) Both (A) and (C).

7. The crust of the earth is composed of a thin layer of rocks covering the surface. Rocks are defined as aggregates or collections of

    (A) symmetry.   (C) minerals.

    (B) fossils.   (D) clastics.

8. Of the following, which types of fracture are associated with faults and earthquakes?

    (A) Horsts   (C) Grabens

    (B) Oblique-slip   (D) All of the above.

9. As a study of the surface of the earth, topography consists of an understanding of

   (A) altitudes.   (C) mean sea level.

   (B) elevations.   (D) All of the above.

10. Weathering is the wearing away of rocks, and is a never ending process. Chemical weathering, which is more active in warm and humid climates, consists of

    (A) the oxidation of iron in the rocks.

    (B) decay, alteration, and leaching.

    (C) the faulting and fracture of rocks.

    (D) Both (A) and (B).

11. Many geologists use maps as model representations of the surface of the earth. These maps consist of

    (A) latitude and longitude.   (C) All of the above.

    (B) declination and hashures.   (D) None of the above.

12. The proportion or ratio of distance on a map to the distance in reality is called

    (A) meridian.   (C) scale.

    (B) topography.   (D) agonic line.

13. Of the following, which is NOT a term that would directly be associated with hydrogeology?

    (A) Zone of saturation   (C) Groundwater table

    (B) Capillary fringe   (D) Aphanitic plutons

14. Laminar and turbulent water flow are SIMILAR in that

    (A) both have parallel layers that do mix.

    (B) both have parallel layers that do not mix.

    (C) both can carry large particles within their water flow.

    (D) None of the above.

15. Laminar and turbulent water flow are DIFFERENT in that

    (A) laminar water flow mixes, turbulent does not.

(B) laminar water flows parallel, turbulent does not.

(C) Both (A) and (B).

(D) Neither (A) or (B).

16. Input into a river drainage system consists of all of the following EXCEPT

(A) groundwater.   (C) floods.

(B) surface run-off.   (D) rain.

17. Drainage basins funnel all water input into streams within the basin. The streams show patterns that form dependent upon topography, rock type, and geologic structure. All of the following are examples of drainage patterns EXCEPT

(A) trellis.   (C) dendritic.

(B) continental.   (D) radial.

18. Minerals can be found in two or more forms while still maintaining the same chemical composition. This property is called polymorphism. Examples of this property include

(A) quartz.   (C) carbon.

(B) conchoidal.   (D) Both (A) and (C).

19. Sedimentary rocks include samples that include non-clastic and clastic properties. Which of the following properties will NOT be found in sedimentary rocks?

(A) Graded bedding   (C) Recrystallization

(B) Stratification   (D) Ripple marks

20. Which is a type of fracture that is associated with mineral identification?

(A) Streak   (C) Cleavage

(B) Hackly   (D) Metallic

VI. ASTRONOMY REVIEW

THE CELESTIAL SPHERE

Astronomy is the scientific study of the Universe and its contents beyond Earth's atmosphere. Earth is swimming in extraterrestrial space which can be thought of as a **celestial sphere**.

The celestial sphere is an imaginary sphere centered on and surrounding Earth, and upon which the background stars are projected. The Sun, Moon, planets, and other celestial bodies appear to move against this backdrop of fixed stars. In reality, the stars are at varying distances from Earth, and the celestial sphere is simply a model used in describing positions and motions of astronomical bodies. Earth's eastward rotation makes the celestial sphere appear to rotate westward. The projection of Earth's equator onto the celestial sphere is known as the **celestial equator**, and the **north** and **south celestial poles** are extensions of Earth's **north** and **south geographic poles**.

The apparent annual path of the Sun along the celestial sphere defines the **ecliptic**, and eclipses can only occur when the Moon's orbit crosses the ecliptic. A **solar eclipse** occurs when the new moon lies between the Sun and the Earth. A **lunar eclipse** occurs when the Earth lies between the Sun and the full moon.

There are two opposite points on the celestial sphere where the ecliptic crosses the celestial equator; they are called the **spring** and **autumnal equinoxes**. Similarly, there are two opposite points where the Sun reaches its highest declination north (+23.5°) or south (−23.5°) of the celestial equator, and these are known as the **summer** and **winter solstices**, respectively. Along the celestial sphere, distances between objects are measured in angular units of degrees, minutes, and seconds.

It is possible to define an ecliptic coordinate system to specify positions of celestial objects in the sky using angular coordinates called **celestial longitude** and **celestial latitude**. Celestial longitude is measured eastward along the ecliptic (from 0° to 360°) starting at the vernal equinox. Celestial latitude measures positions in degrees north (+) and south (−) from the ecliptic (at 0°) to the ecliptic poles (at + and − 90°).

Another widely used system is the **equatorial coordinate** system. This system specifies positions in the sky using time and angular coordinates called **right ascension** and **declination**. Right ascension measures angular direction in units of time (0 to 24 hours) eastward along the celestial equator from the vernal equinox. It is convenient to use time because it relates the position of a star to its apparent motion across the sky. Declination measures angular direction in degrees north (+) and south (−) from the celestial equator (0°) to the celestial poles (+ and −90°).

Another important element in the celestial sphere is the **celestial meridian**. This is an imaginary half-great circle that connects the north and south points on your horizon while passing through your **zenith** (point directly overhead). An hour angle is the angular measurement in units of time of how far westward an object is from your celestial meridian. One hour corresponds to 15° of arc.

MEASURING DISTANCES FROM EARTH

In order to measure distances from Earth to objects in the real sky, astronomers use the following units: The **astronomical unit** (AU); this is the average distance between Earth and the Sun—approximately 93 million miles. The **light year** (LY), which is the distance light travels through a vacuum in one year—approximately six trillion miles. The **parsec** (pc) is the distance at which an object would have a parallax of one arcsecond and is equal to 3.26 LY.

Stellar trigonometric parallax is the apparent displacement of a nearby star, relative to a background of far more distant stars, which results from the motion of the Earth around the Sun in half a year. The distance in parsecs equals the inverse of the parallax in arcseconds.

THE SOLAR SYSTEM

The nearest star is the Sun, and it is at the center of our solar system, which is comprised of nine major planets, natural planetary satellites, asteroids, meteoroids, comets, and the interplanetary medium. The Sun holds all members of the solar system captive within its gravitational field, and they orbit around it at various speeds and distances. The Sun is a hot glowing body of ionized gas (**plasma**). It is a star of medium size and brightness in comparison to other stars in our galaxy. It generates energy by nuclear fusion. The Sun's surface, known as the **photosphere**, is responsible for emitting the sunlight that we see and exhibits other activities such as sunspots and solar flares.

Planets are astronomical bodies which orbit a star (such as the Sun) and cannot produce their own light. Therefore they shine by reflecting starlight. In the solar system, planets that orbit closer to the Sun than Earth are called "inferior" planets—these are Mercury and Venus. Those that orbit farther away than Earth are called "superior" planets—Mars, Jupiter, Saturn, Uranus, Neptune, and Pluto.

The distances and speeds at which planets orbit the Sun are not arbitrary; they are governed by three fundamental laws known as **Kepler's Laws of Planetary Motion**. Kepler's First Law states that all planets revolve along closed orbits called **ellipses**. The Second Law states that the rotating vector connecting the Sun to the planet moves across equal areas of its orbit in equal intervals of time. The Third Law states that the square of a planet's orbital period is directly proportional to the cube of its semi-major axis.

With respect to their increasing distance from the Sun; Mercury, Venus, Earth, and Mars are the innermost planets of the Solar System and are known as the **terrestrial planets**. All are rocky in nature and have a similar fundamental structure. Jupiter, Saturn, Uranus, and Neptune represent four of the five outermost planets and are known as the **Jovian planets**. They are gaseous giants with ring systems. Pluto is normally the farthest planet from the Sun, but its highly eccentric orbit causes it to pass inside of Neptune's orbit for 20 years of Pluto's 248-year orbit around the Sun. It is much smaller than the Jovian planets and is much like the terrestrial planets.

Except for Mercury and Venus, all planets have natural satellites. The Moon is Earth's natural satellite; it exhibits different phases depending on where it is in its orbit around the Earth, and it, along with the Sun, is responsible for ocean tides. The Jovian planets have 8 or more natural satellites each, and also have ring systems. Other constituents of the solar system are **asteroids, meteoroids**, and **comets**. Asteroids can be thought of as minor planets, and they are concentrated in an orbital region between Mars and Jupiter known as the asteroid belt. Meteoroids are small celestial objects which pass through Earth's atmosphere, heat up, and glow (**meteors**). A **meteorite** is a meteor that actually falls on Earth. Comets are icy bodies a few kilometers across normally orbiting in the outer Solar System. They partially vaporize and form a diffuse envelope of gas around the nucleus (**coma**). The passage of Earth through the debris of comets is what causes **meteor showers**.

STARS

The most obvious feature of the night sky is the presence of **stars**. All of the stars seen with the unaided eye are part of our galaxy, the Milky Way. They are always in the sky, but the brightness of the Sun during the day makes it impossible to see them. They appear to rise and set as the Earth rotates eastward, and their twinkling is due to turbulence in the Earth's atmosphere. We obtain information about stars by analyzing their light using a method called **spectroscopy**. Starlight is passed through a spectroscope and the resulting spectrum reveals information that includes temperature, composition, and relative motion. It is found that stars vary widely in mass, diameter, brightness, temperature, and spectral properties.

The brightness of stars and all other celestial objects is measured in **magnitudes**. Magnitudes follow a reverse logarithmic scale where a decrease of one unit corresponds to an increase of brightness by a factor of 2.5. On this scale, the lowest numbers correspond to the brightest objects. The Sun at magnitude –27 is the brightest star in the entire sky, while Sirius (the "dog" star) at magnitude 1.5 is the brightest in the night sky. The faintest magnitude detectable by the unaided human eye is +6. Note that these magnitudes refer to apparent brightness as seen from Earth, which depends on how distant the object is from us. **Apparent magnitude** increases as the distance to the object increases, resulting in the object appearing fainter. The **absolute magnitude** of an object, which is a measure of its intrinsic brightness or **luminosity**, is defined as its apparent magnitude as measured from a reference distance of 10 parsecs. In order to determine the absolute magnitude of a star from its apparent magnitude, you must know its distance. Trigonometric parallax is the only direct method of determining distance to stars, but this method only works for those stars that are nearby. Since the vast majority of stars are too distant to have their parallaxes measured, indirect or statistical methods are used.

A striking feature in the classification of stars appears when we plot their absolute magnitude versus their temperature. On this diagram, known as the **Hertzsprung-Russell (H-R) diagram**, approximately 90 percent of all stars (the Sun included) fall within a narrow region called the **main sequence**. Since absolute magnitude is a measure of a star's luminosity, and its temperature is a measure of its spectral type, the H-R diagram is also referred to as the luminosity-temperature diagram.

An example of an indirect method of determining a star's distance is the use of its known temperature or spectral type to determine its absolute magnitude (if it is a main sequence star), which is then combined with its apparent magnitude to give the distance.

Besides their apparent westward motion due to Earth's rotation, stars undergo their own true motion in space. The apparent angular shift of a star across the sky over a period of time is known as its **proper motion**. The motion of a star in a direction across the line-of-sight is known as its **radial motion**. Its radial velocity can be determined from a shift in its spectral lines known as the **Doppler shift**; it is positive if the star is moving away from the Sun, and negative if it is approaching.

Stars have lives of their own and are not eternal. They are born from huge interstellar clouds of gas and dust known as star-forming regions, or **nebulae**. A star's life expectancy depends on how massive it is. The more massive the star, the shorter its lifetime and the more violent its death. The Sun will spend 10 billion years of its life on the main sequence, and then will expand and cool down to become a **red giant**. Finally, it will contract to a very dense Earth-size star called a **white dwarf** and then ultimately dim out to become a **black dwarf**. More massive stars live out their lives in more extreme states such as a **neutron star** or a **black hole**.

Another important feature of the night sky is the presence of **constellations**, which are star groupings that appear to connect stars in a certain pattern. Examples are Ursa Major (Big Bear) in the northern hemisphere; and the Southern Cross, seen from the southern hemisphere. These constellations are imaginary star patterns, and the stars in them are at varying distances from the Sun.

GALAXIES

Perhaps the most striking feature of the night sky is a band of diffuse light that stretches across the celestial sphere on a clear and moonless night. This is understood to be the giant disk of the Milky Way. It measures 100,000 LY across and is composed of 100 billion stars and their unseen planets, and interstellar gas and dust, as well as a central bulge of about 10,000 LY in diameter made up of densely packed older stars. The total mass of our galaxy, including the disk and the bulge is estimated at 200 billion solar masses. The disk and bulge are surrounded by a halo of matter on each side of the galaxy's central plane, perhaps adding 10 times as much mass of unseen dark matter.

This system is arranged in a pinwheel pattern of spiral arms that revolve around the galactic center. Speeding along at about 200 kilometers per second, the Sun takes 230 million years to circle the galaxy once in a galactic year.

In addition, white spots with a cloudlike appearance, called nebulae, are visible in certain parts of the sky. Some of these bodies were proven to be so distant as to be far outside the Milky Way and were then resolved into galaxies in their own right. An example is the Andromeda Galaxy, which is two million light years away. Galaxies come in three basic shapes: **disk spiral**, **elliptical**, and **irregular**. An example of the latter is the Magellanic Clouds seen in the southern hemisphere. Distant galaxies appear to be receding from Earth at speeds increasing in proportion to their distance from Earth. This is observed as a Doppler red shift in their light spectra. Certain celestial objects resembling stars can be observed at distances greater than that of the farthest galaxy, yet are identifiable and seem to emit more energy than our own galaxy. They're characterized by a large red shift and are called **quasars** because of their quasi-stellar appearance.

The observable universe appears to be expanding as a result of the other galaxies receding away. This expansion is the basis of the theory that the universe originated in a "Big Bang," occurring between 8 and 20 billion years ago. Additional support for this theory is provided by the cosmic microwave background radiation and the abundance of light chemical elements in the observable universe.

☞ Drill: Astronomy

1. This review treats astronomy as

    (A) a set of observations.

    (B) a systematic and scientific way of exploring and understanding what is observed in the sky.

    (C) the casting of horoscopes.

    (D) the study of the solar system.

2. The projection of the Earth's axis on the sky is the

   (A) celestial equator.   (C) celestial poles.

   (B) zenith.   (D) ecliptic.

3. The path of the Sun across the celestial sphere is called the

   (A) ecliptic.   (C) equinox.

   (B) celestial equator.   (D) solstice.

4. The Sun crosses the celestial equator going north on March 21. This is known as the

   (A) solstice.   (C) solar eclipse.

   (B) lunar eclipse.   (D) spring equinox.

5. If the Moon completely covers the Sun as seen by an earthbound observer, there is a

   (A) total lunar eclipse.   (C) partial lunar eclipse.

   (B) total solar eclipse.   (D) partial solar eclipse.

6. Declination is from what coordinate system?

   (A) Ecliptic   (C) Equatorial

   (B) Galactic   (D) Metric

7. The coordinate right ascension is usually measured in

   (A) degrees, minutes, and seconds.

   (B) radians.

   (C) meters.

   (D) hours, minutes, and seconds.

8. The parallax of a star is

   (A) its temperature divided by its mass.

   (B) its mass divided by its temperature.

   (C) the angle through which the star appears to move in the course of half a year.

   (D) the angle through which the star appears to move in the course of a year.

9. If a star has a parallax of 0.1 second of arc, its distance is how many parsecs?

   (A) 2   (C) ½

   (B) 1   (D) 10

10. Astronomers call the visible surface of the sun the

    (A) photosphere.   (C) sunspot.

    (B) plasma.   (D) flare.

11. Which of the following planets is closer to the Sun than Earth is?

    (A) Mars   (C) Venus

    (B) Saturn   (D) Jupiter

12. The AU is

    (A) the radius of the Moon.

    (B) the average distance of the earth from the Sun.

    (C) the force that the Sun exerts on a planet.

    (D) a recently discovered satellite of Jupiter.

13. Kepler's Second Law says, essentially, that

    (A) force equals mass times acceleration.

    (B) the square of the period is proportional to the cube of the semi-major axis.

    (C) the orbits of the planets are ellipses with the Sun at one focus.

    (D) the line from the Sun to a planet sweeps equal areas in equal times.

14. In order of increasing distance from the Sun, the terrestrial planets are

    (A) Mars, Venus, Earth, and Mercury.

    (B) Mercury, Venus, Earth, and Mars.

    (C) Jupiter, Saturn, Uranus, Neptune, and Pluto.

    (D) Mercury, Venus, Mars, and Earth.

15. Which of the following planets has no natural satellites?

    (A) Mars   (C) Jupiter

    (B) Earth   (D) Venus

16. Icy worlds with a size of a few kilometers across are

    (A) meteoroids.

    (B) meteors.

    (C) comets.

    (D) asteroids.

17. If Star X appears to be 2.5 times as bright as Star Y, then the two stars differ in magnitude by

    (A) 0.

    (B) 1.

    (C) 2.5.

    (D) 0.5.

18. We can get the temperature for a star by

    (A) measuring its spectrum.

    (B) the Doppler shift of its spectral lines.

    (C) measuring its distance and apparent magnitude.

    (D) obtaining its chemical composition.

19. The Sun's galactic motion in the Milky Way can be described as

    (A) radial motion towards the center of the galaxy.

    (B) radial motion away from the center of the galaxy.

    (C) motion along a very elongated ellipse.

    (D) motion in a circular orbit.

20. The theory of an expanding universe is supported by which one of the following observations?

    (A) A cosmic explosion known as the Big Bang occurred 15 billion years ago.

    (B) The Doppler red shift of distant galaxies

    (C) The cosmic microwave background radiation

    (D) The observed abundances of light chemical elements

VII. METEOROLOGY REVIEW

THE ATMOSPHERE

Our **atmosphere** is composed of several distinct layers which contain the necessary gases to support biological life on earth. By volume, the atmosphere is 78.08 percent nitrogen and 20.95 percent oxygen. Other trace gases constitute the remaining 0.97 percent. Two of the most important trace gases vary in amount throughout the atmosphere. Carbon dioxide usually occupies 0.03 percent and water vapor takes up anywhere from near 0 percent to as much as 4 percent of the atmosphere. Gravitational compression of the gases creates a higher concentration of matter near the surface with decreasing amounts at higher elevations. Because of this, both air pressure and density decrease with height.

The atmosphere is divided into four primary layers. In ascending order, they are the **troposphere**, **stratosphere**, **mesosphere**, and the **thermosphere**. Each layer has different characteristics from any adjacent layer which makes layer identification possible. The troposphere is sometimes referred to as the "weather sphere" because it is in this layer where all significant weather phenomena take place. This layer contains nearly all of the water vapor and carbon dioxide found in the atmosphere and has a decrease in temperature with height. The stratosphere has a high concentration of ozone which is often referred to as the ozone layer. Because ozone is a strong absorber of the suns ultraviolet rays, temperatures increase with height throughout the stratosphere (this is known as a temperature inversion). Though important in their own right, the mesosphere and thermosphere have only an indirect impact on daily weather events.

As radiant energy from the sun travels through the atmosphere, it is scattered, transmitted, reflected, and absorbed by all matter it comes into contact with. The energy left over is available to heat the surface of the earth. Due to the 23.5° tilt of the earth's rotational axis, equatorial regions annually receive more solar energy than they radiate back to space. Conversely, polar regions lose more energy than they receive. This is why the poles are ice-capped while lush rainforests can thrive in the tropics. However, without a mechanism to distribute the earth's heat more evenly, the poles would grow colder every year while tropical areas got warmer. This redistribution of heat is the responsibility of global air's circulation and large scale storm systems.

THE SEASONS

The combination of Earth's tilted axis and its orbit around the Sun give temperate zones four seasons: winter, spring, summer, and fall. Winter begins in the northern hemisphere on December 22nd (June 22nd in the southern hemisphere), the time of the **winter solstice**. On this date, the northern half of the earth is tilted furthest from the Sun. Minimum winter temperatures are normally reached sometime after this date because of the time it takes for the mass of the earth to radiate its stored heat. Summer begins on June 22nd in the northern hemisphere (December 22nd in the southern hemisphere), the time of the **summer solstice**. Now the northern half of the earth is tilted closest to the Sun. Maximum summer temperatures occur at a later date due to the lag involved in heating large quantities of mass.

March 21st and September 23rd are the dates of the **vernal** (spring) and **autumnal** (fall) **equinoxes**, respectively. The dates are reversed for the southern hemisphere. At these times, the tilt of the earth is perpendicular to the plane of the Earth and Sun. This puts the earth at a neutral tilt relative to the sun and gives all locations in both hemispheres equal amounts of daylight and darkness. This is in contrast to summer and winter when the respective poles experience either 24 hours of daylight or 24 hours of darkness.

WEATHER TYPES

The amount of heat energy available to the earth and atmosphere is also important on a daily basis. It is possible to estimate this amount of energy by using **radiosondes** to measure temperature, pressure, water vapor, and wind velocity vertically through the atmosphere. This estimate is represented in the concept of stability. Since hot air is less dense than cold air, isolated pockets of hot air that form near the surface will begin to rise. If the atmosphere is unstable, these isolated pockets of hot air, or **parcels**, will continue to rise without any additional forcing from below. The more energy available to the parcel, the faster it will rise. A stable atmosphere will act to force a rising parcel back to the surface and is thought of as having less energy available to the parcel. When a condition of neutral stability exists, a parcel will rise as long as it encounters an upward force. Once the force is removed and the parcel comes to rest, it will remain where it stops. Upward motion imparted to a parcel of air due to differential heating of the earth's initiates is called convection.

By plotting data from a radiosonde on a skew-t diagram, a meteorologist can calculate how fast the temperature changes with height. This is called the **lapse rate** of the atmosphere. Since both pressure and density decrease with height in the troposphere, we know from the equation of state that a rising parcel will expand and therefore cool. A process which results in cooling or warming due to expansion or compression with no loss or gain of heat is called an **adiabatic process**. A standard atmosphere has been established for use in comparing daily values of meteorological parameters. Its dry adiabatic lapse rate has been set at 5.5°F per 1,000 feet (i.e., for every 1,000 ft of elevation, the air will expand and cool 5.5°F). Saturation of a parcel complicates lapse rate computation and necessitates a second lapse rate for the standard atmosphere. Thus, its moist adiabatic lapse rate has been determined to be 3.3°F per 1,000 feet. It should now be obvious that stability computations can get quite involved. The main point is that if a parcel cools slower as it rises than the surrounding atmosphere, it will stay warmer and continue to rise.

Upward motion is very important to the production of precipitation. Convection, as well as **orographic lift**, **frontal lift**, and **convergence** all result in rising motion in the atmosphere. Orographic lift refers to air that is being forced up and over terrain features such as mountains. Frontal lift is created by warm and cold fronts. Since a cold front normally has a steep frontal surface with cold, dense air behind it, it forces the warmer and less dense air ahead of the front abruptly upward, resulting in convective-type weather. A warm front is normally not as steep and has warm air behind it. This less dense warm air will overrun the colder, denser air ahead of the front and cause **stratiform-type** weather. **Convergence** refers to air which flows together as in toward the center of a surface low pressure circulation. When the air converges at the center, it must either go up or down. The ground prohibits downward motion so the air is forced upward.

The two previously mentioned weather types, convective and stratiform, both originate from upward motion yet produce distinctly different weather. The rapidly rising air involved with convection produces cumuliform clouds which make up the group of clouds with vertical development. When these clouds are short, they are called cumulus (when very short, "fair-weather" cumulus may be used), and may resemble stalks of cauliflower. When these clouds grow to extreme heights and develop ice crystals at their tops, they are called cumulonimbus. Extensive convective activity will usually produce rainshowers and thunderstorms. Cumulonimbus clouds, or cells, are sometimes called "thunderheads" and can produce lightning, heavy rain, and possibly hail. When the top of the cumulonimbus encounters stable air and strong winds aloft, the ice crystals spread out and get blown into the familiar anvil shape associated with thunderstorms.

A thunderstorm actually goes through a three-stage life cycle: the **cumulus stage**, the **mature stage**, and the **dissipating stage**. During the cumulus stage, the cell is composed only of rising air which is called the **updraft**. At this stage, the initial cumulus cloud forms and begins to tower skyward. A general rule of thumb is that the tallest thunderstorms are usually the strongest. As droplets within the cloud grow by the process of collision and coalescence, they eventually become too heavy to be supported by the updraft and fall out of the cloud as precipitation. Once precipitation begins, friction caused by precipitation drag will pull surrounding air down with it. This creates the **downdraft** and marks the start of the mature stage. As the downdraft descends, drier air from the surrounding atmosphere may mix in, causing evaporative cooling. Since cold air is more dense than warm air, this cooling strengthens the downdraft by allowing it to descend faster. Very strong downdrafts can cause damaging straight-line winds as they hit the ground and spread out radially.

After some time, the descending air will choke off the updraft producing downdraft throughout the cell. This begins the dissipating stage. With no more rising motion available, precipitation comes to an end and the cloud begins to evaporate. This entire life cycle can be completed in less than one hour. However, when atmospheric conditions are right, a supercell thunderstorm can develop. In a supercell, once the initial updraft is extinguished, a new updraft will form allowing the storm to sustain itself for several hours. Storms such as these produce severe weather such as large hail, damaging winds, flash floods, and tornadoes during their mature stage.

Stratiform weather is caused by a more gradual ascent of air and produces clouds of great horizontal extent. These clouds do not grow very tall and usually exhibit flat tops. The clouds often appear as a continuous layer which can stretch from horizon to horizon. Stratiform clouds are found in the low, middle, and high cloud groups. Stratiform weather is generally characterized by persistent light rain, drizzle, and fog. Fog, by definition, is a stratus cloud with its base at the surface.

It should be noted that these weather types are not mutually exclusive. It is not uncommon for stratiform areas to contain embedded convective cells. Likewise, it is not uncommon for cumulus clouds to spread out, merge bases, and form an extensive stratocumulus cloud deck. Some of the most challenging forecasts meteorologists face are caused by just such interactive situations.

Wind is the mechanism responsible for transporting weather phenomena around the world to balance the global energy budget. The pressure gradient force is what moves the air in a direction from higher pressure to lower pressure. On a weather map, wind speeds will be greatest where the isobars (lines connecting points of equal pressure) are packed closest together. An area such as this is said to have a steep pressure gradient. However, careful observation shows that the wind does not blow directly across the isobars. Further inspection reveals that wind is the vector sum of several forces acting on the air simultaneously.

THE CORIOLIS EFFECT

The **Coriolis force** is caused by the rotation of the earth. It is strongest near the poles and weakest near the equator. Its strength is also related to wind velocity since stronger winds produce a stronger Coriolis force. Relative to the direction of wind flow, the Coriolis force acts to deflect the wind to the right in the northern hemisphere and to the left in the southern hemisphere. Thus, strong winds at high latitudes experience the greatest amount of deflection. The Coriolis force and pressure gradient force are equal and opposite for parallel isobaric fields in the upper atmosphere. Together, their net force causes the air to flow parallel to the isobars. However, if the isobaric field curves, centripetal acceleration causes an imbalance between the Coriolis and pressure gradient forces. The net force is now in the direction of the pressure gradient force and allows the wind to parallel a curved isobaric field.

Closer to the ground, air encounters friction due to the roughness of the earth's surface. This slows the wind speed and causes a decrease in the Coriolis force. The result is an imbalance which leaves the net force in the direction of the pressure gradient force. This causes the wind to cross the isobars at an angle. The angle of crossing is dependent upon the amount of friction, and hence upon the roughness of the surface. Over the entire surface of the earth, this angle averages about 30°. Putting all of this together, we can now see that in the northern hemisphere, wind will flow counter-clockwise around a low pressure circulation and converge to its center but will flow clockwise around a high pressure circulation and diverge from its center.

☞ Drill: Meteorology

1. Why is stratospheric ozone depletion (destruction of the ozone layer) a serious concern?

    (A) It is a major cause of the "greenhouse effect".

    (B) It will increase the amount of ultraviolet radiation reaching the ground.

    (C) It causes acid rain.

    (D) It is really nothing to worry about.

2. Land and sea (or lake) breezes form because of

    (A) uneven heating of coastal environments.

    (B) the pressure gradient force.

    (C) the difference in temperature between land and water surfaces.

    (D) All of the above.

3. Mountain and valley breezes form because of

    (A) gravity and the pressure gradient force.

    (B) the pressure gradient force and heating.

    (C) gravity and heating.

    (D) the pressure gradient force and the Coriolis force.

4. Which of the following pictures represents a possible aerial view of tree damage caused by thunderstorm downdraft winds? (The arrows represent the trees with the arrow head being the top of the tree.)

(A)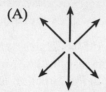

(C)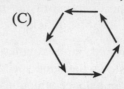

(B)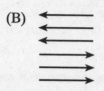

(D)

5. How is the relative strength of a thunderstorm updraft estimated?

   (A) By the intensity of the lightning

   (B) By the height of the cloud base

   (C) By the speed of the wind gusts measured at the surface

   (D) By the size of the precipitation particles (raindrops or hailstones)

6. Why does saturation of a rising parcel lead to a slower adiabatic lapse rate?

   (A) Because of the release of latent heat by condensing water vapor

   (B) Because of the release of latent heat by evaporating water droplets

   (C) Because cloud droplets add frictional drag to the rising parcel and slow it down

   (D) Because temperature decreases with height

7. What happens to descending air?

   (A) It becomes more humid.

   (B) It expands.

   (C) It warms.

   (D) It becomes less dense.

8. Mt. Adiabatic a three thousand ft. mountain, separates towns A and B. Air is being forced up on the side facing town A but downslope on the side facing town B. Town A has launched a weather balloon and found that the rising air will be 100% saturated at 1,000 ft. (the lifting condensation level). Assuming town A has an air temperature of 70° F, what will be the temperature of the air when it reaches town B?

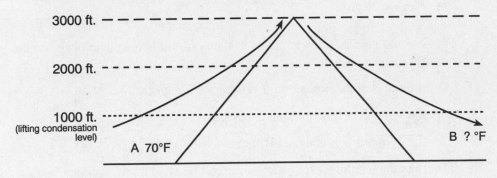

    (A) 70.0°F   (C) 74.4° F

    (B) 67.8° F   (D) 70.2° F

9. An inversion is

    (A) unstable.   (C) neutrally stable.

    (B) stable.   (D) None of the above.

10. Why do we see lightning before we hear thunder?

    (A) Because the lightning occurred closer than the thunder

    (B) Because lightning is composed of multiple strokes

    (C) Because thunder occurs higher in the cloud

    (D) Because of the difference between the speeds of light and sound

11. Why is radiation the only method of heat transfer capable of bringing the sun's energy to the earth?

    (A) Because space is a vacuum

    (B) Because other methods are too slow and lose too much energy by the time they reach earth

    (C) Because blockage by stellar debris inhibits other methods

    (D) Because solar convection is propelled away from the earth

12. Why does evaporation lead to cooling?

    (A) Because of the change in state involved as water evaporates

    (B) Because of the absorption of latent heat by water droplets

    (C) Because of the release of latent heat by water droplets

    (D) (A) and (B) only.

13. The warmest summer temperatures in the northern hemisphere occur on the summer solstice because

    (A) the sun is at its closest to the northern hemisphere.

    (B) the sun reaches its maximum azimuth.

    (C) the northern hemisphere is tilted toward the sun.

    (D) maximum summer temperatures aren't reached on the solstice.

14. The sky is blue because

    (A) outer space is blue.

    (B) it is a reflection of the blue bodies of water at the surface.

    (C) sunlight is scattered by the atmosphere before it reaches the earth.

    (D) the sun emits most of its light in the blue portion of the spectrum.

15. Assume that the earth does not rotate, has a homogeneous surface, and that the sun always shines on the equator. Which sort of global circulation pattern would you expect?

    (A) 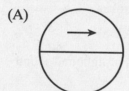   (C)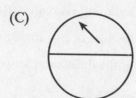

    (B) 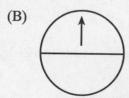   (D)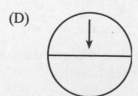

16. You would expect higher surface pressure over land masses with lower surface pressure over bodies of water during

    (A) winter.   (C) summer.

    (B) spring.   (D) fall.

17. It can rain when the temperature is

    (A) 32°F.   (C) 33°F.

    (B) 25°F.   (D) All of the above.

18. Water can remain a liquid at

    (A) 60°F.   (C) 0°F.

    (B) 40°F.   (D) All of the above.

19. Why does your body perspire when you get hot?

    (A) Water vapor condenses on your skin.

    (B) It is your body's biological method to cool itself.

    (C) Your body temperature slowly increases and approaches the dew point of the surrounding air.

    (D) None of the above.

20. It is possible for snow to fall in tropical regions because

    (A) hurricanes can be very cold.

    (B) of elevation considerations.

    (C) the land cools significantly at night.

    (D) All of the above.

ANSWER KEY

Drill: Biology

1.	(D)	6.	(A)	11.	(B)	16.	(C)
2.	(B)	7.	(A)	12.	(B)	17.	(B)
3.	(A)	8.	(D)	13.	(A)	18.	(A)
4.	(D)	9.	(B)	14.	(C)	19.	(A)
5.	(A)	10.	(A)	15.	(D)	20.	(A)

Drill: Chemistry

1.	(B)	6.	(C)	11.	(C)	16.	(D)
2.	(C)	7.	(B)	12.	(A)	17.	(D)
3.	(A)	8.	(B)	13.	(A)	18.	(C)
4.	(C)	9.	(C)	14.	(A)	19.	(C)
5.	(B)	10.	(A)	15.	(A)	20.	(B)

Drill: Physics

1.	(B)	6.	(B)	11.	(C)	16.	(D)
2.	(A)	7.	(B)	12.	(C)	17.	(C)
3.	(A)	8.	(B)	13.	(B)	18.	(D)
4.	(A)	9.	(C)	14.	(B)	19.	(C)
5.	(D)	10.	(A)	15.	(B)	20.	(C)

Drill: Earth Science

1.	(D)	6.	(B)	11.	(C)	16.	(B)
2.	(D)	7.	(C)	12.	(C)	17.	(A)
3.	(C)	8.	(C)	13.	(A)	18.	(A)
4.	(C)	9.	(C)	14.	(D)	19.	(D)
5.	(A)	10.	(C)	15.	(C)	20.	(C)

Geology, Astronomy, and Meteorology make up a small portion of the ACT Science Test. The reviews for these sections reflect this. For extra preparation, we are providing detailed explanations to the drills in these reviews.

Drill: Geology

1. **(D)**   (D) is the best answer, the name of this theory is the nebular hypothesis (C), and was proposed by Kant (B) as a possible explanation. At this time, not proven to be true (A) does seem to fit the observations and evidence set forth by science.

2. **(C)**   The process of differentiation (C) is not recognized as a layer of the earth, but is a step in the separation of the internal layers of earth. Choices (A), (B), and (D) do fit as recognized layers of the earth but are NOT correct answers for this question as the exception is the answer requested.

3. **(B)**   Fossils are the remains of plants and animals found in rock, hence (B) is correct. Stratification (A) is the layering of sedimentary rock but does not refer directly to fossils. (C) is incorrect. Coproliths are the fossilized remains of animal droppings or feces, and are considered animal trace fossils and not plant fossils. Choice (D) is incorrect because there is an acceptable answer for this question in (B).

4. **(B)**   Diorite (B) is recognized and accepted as igneous in origin. Limestone (A) and shale (C) are both sedimentary in origin and thus do not fit the criteria of the question. (D) is not correct since choice (C) is sedimentary and the question is directed to point out the non-sedimentary selection (B).

5. **(A)**   Underground magma or above ground lava will cool and solidify to form igneous rocks (A) from molten material. Sedimentary rock (B) does not form directly from molten material. Volcanic (C) rock would seem to be an acceptable answer but both magma and lava are considered to be igneous, thus, (A) is the best possible answer, and the word volcanic is at best a partial answer. Metamorphic rock (D) is rock that has been pressurized and heated to create change, but has not been melted to create metamorphic changes.

6. **(D)**   (D) is the best possible answer since both recrystallization (A) and crystal reorientation (C) are recognized traits of metamorphic rocks. Due to the destructive nature of metamorphic change, fossils (B) are very rare in this rock group, thus, are not characteristic of metamorphic rocks.

7. **(C)**   All rocks are made up of minerals (C), which are the building blocks of the crust of the earth. Symmetry (A) is the geometric shape of the

crystal lattice of a mineral. (B) and (D) do not apply as they are terms associated with sedimentary rock and do not universally apply to all types of rock.

8. **(D)** (D) is the best possible answer because (A), (B), and (C) are all tectonic features associated with ground movement. Horsts are blocks of earth that are forced upward due to compressional forces. Grabens are down-faulted blocks caused by tension; they create valley like structures. Oblique-slip faults are caused by sheafing forces.

9. **(D)** (D) is the best possible answer because (A), (B), and (C) are some of the many topographic features that need to be studied and understood in order to have a complete grasp of landforms, their formation, and the topography of Earth.

10. **(D)** Chemical weathering is a complex process consisting of many factors. Choice (D) is most inclusive of the various parts (A) and (B), of the chemical weathering process. Faulting and fracturing (C) are mechanical forms of weathering, and though they may assist in speeding up the chemical cycle, they are still grouped in the mechanical process.

11. **(C)** (C) is the best selection for this question as latitude and longitude (A), as well as declination and hashures (B), are important aspects of map interpretation and understanding. (D) is an incorrect response as several selections are correct.

12. **(C)** The best answer is (C). Scale is defined as the ratio of distance on a map to the distance in the real world. Meridians (A) are lines of longitude. Topography (B) is a description of the structure of the landscape of a given area. Agonic line (D) is an indication of zero magnetic declination with reference to magnetic north.

13. **(D)** The excluded term for this question is (D) because aphanitic plutons are igneous rock masses. Choices (A) zone of saturation, (B) capillary fringe, and (C) groundwater table, are all terms that a person researching hydrogeology would need to understand and would also use often.

14. **(D)** (D) is the best possible answer. Choices (A), (B), and (C), do not represent combinations of laminar and turbulent water flow that are correct in their description. If it were assumed that BOTH had (A) parallel/mix, (B) parallel/not mix, or (C) carry large particles, then they may be similar enough in characteristics to be classified under the same name.

15. **(B)**   (B) is the choice that points out the difference in the types of water flow that is characteristic of laminar and turbulent. (A) is incorrect because turbulent water is described as water that swirls and mixes, and laminar flow is calm and non-mixed. Selections (C) and (D) are incorrect in that they request the selection or exclusion of items that will not correctly help answer the question.

16. **(C)**   The exception choice in this case is (C) floods. River floods are an output of overflow that occur when drainage systems cannot handle the input of water. Choices (A), (B), and (D) are all considered to be standard drainage input and thus are not correct selections for this question.

17. **(B)**   Continental drainage (B) may be confused with a drainage pattern but in the case of a continental divide a drainage area is described, not a pattern to be identified in a geologic area. Thus, continental is not a type of stream drainage pattern. Choices: (A) trellis, (C) dendritic, and (D) radial are all types of river drainage that help to identify the underlying geology of an area.

18. **(D)**   (D) is the best possible answer because it is inclusive of quartz (A) and carbon (C) which are well known polymorphs. Quartz can be found in nature in many various colors and can take on several natural shapes though the basic chemical composition is the same. The same can be said for carbon in the form of graphite and diamond. Conchoidal (B) is a specific property of minerals that refers to a type of fracture or breaking in the silicates and thus is not a correct selection.

19. **(C)**   Recrystallization (C) is a process that occurs in igneous and metamorphic rocks and will not be found in true sedimentary layers. Graded beds (A) and stratification (B) are the result of sediment precipitation in water and are very common in sedimentary rock. Ripple marks (D) are also found in sedimentary rock that forms in shallow to medium depth water.

20. **(B)**   Hackly (B) is the best answer for this question. It is a type of fracture used to identify metallic minerals. (A) streak is the color of powder that a mineral makes when crushed and is used to identify minerals. (C) cleavage is described as the way a mineral splits according to its internal crystal structure. Each mineral will cleave in very specific patterns governed by the chemical composition of the mineral. (D) metallic is described as a luster or shine that a mineral has.

Drill: Astronomy

1. **(B)**   (B) is the correct answer. Astronomy is more than just a set of observations (A), but also an interpretation of these observations and their systematic organization in a system of inquiry and understanding of all phenomena in the sky, and not just the solar system (D). Astrology (C) is not really a science.

2. **(C)**   The correct answer is celestial poles (C). The text states that "the north and south celestial poles are extensions of Earth's north and south geographic poles." Earth's rotation axis is the line that joins the geographic poles. Answer choice (A) identifies the projection of the Earth's equator. The zenith (B) is the point directly overhead an observer. The ecliptic (D) is the line that describes the Sun's orbit across the celestial sphere.

3. **(A)**   (A) is the correct response. The ecliptic is the apparent annual path among the stars.

4. **(D)**   (D) is the correct answer. The text describes equinoxes as the two points on the celestial sphere where the ecliptic crosses the celestial equator, and since this crossing occurs on March 21, it is the spring equinox. (A) is incorrect because solstices occur in the summer and winter, and correspond to the ecliptic being farthest from the celestial equator. (B) and (C) should not be chosen because in general when this crossing occurs on March 21 the Moon is not necessarily aligned with the Earth and the Sun.

5. **(B)**   The correct answer choice is (B), because the question describes an eclipse, and the eclipse must be a solar eclipse because the Moon is between the Earth and the Sun. (A) and (C) are wrong choices, since they do not refer to an eclipse. (D) is incorrect; the solar eclipse is total because the Moon's disk covers the sun from our view completely.

6. **(C)**   In the text, it is stated that "declination measures angular direction in degrees north (+) and south (–) from the celestial equator." Choices (A) and (D) are incorrect since neither is a coordinate system. (B) should not be chosen, since it is not discussed in the text.

7. **(D)**   The coordinate right ascension is usually measured in hours, minutes, and seconds; (D) is the correct answer. The coordinate is not measured in radians (B) or (C) meters. Choice (A) mixes units of measure, and should not be chosen.

8. **(C)**   Choices (A) and (B) have no relevance to the concept of parallax. (D) should not be chosen, since it does not refer to the proper time-frame. Therefore, the correct answer is (C), the angle through which a star appears to move in one half a year.

9. **(D)**   The distance in parsecs is equal to the inverse of a star's parallax in arcseconds, therefore, (D) is correct. Choices (A), (B), and (C) all refer to the wrong distance.

10. **(A)** The correct answer is (A). The photosphere is what we observe of the Sun's surface. Plasma (B) is the state of the Sun's interior. Choices (C) and (D) are local phenomena on the Sun's surface, but not the whole surface; they should not be chosen.

11. **(C)** In the text, it is stated that Mercury and Venus are closer to the Sun than Earth, and are inferior planets. Therefore, (C) is the only correct answer out of the four choices. Choices (A), (B) and (D), all refer to superior planets, and are incorrect.

12. **(B)** The AU is defined in the text as the average distance of the earth from the Sun. Answer choices (A), (C), and (D) have no support in the text, and are therefore incorrect.

13. **(D)** Kepler's Second Law states that the line from the Sun to a planet sweeps equal areas in equal lines (D). Choice (A) is Newton's second law, (B) is Kepler's Third Law, and (C) is Kepler's First Law. All of those are incorrect choices.

14. **(B)** (B) is the correct choice. Choice (A) is wrong because it transposes the order of Mercury and Mars. (C) incorrectly lists the Jovian planets. (D) transposes the order of Mars and Earth, and should not be selected.

15. **(D)** It is stated in the text that "except for Mercury and Venus, all planets have natural satellites," therefore, answer choice (D) should be selected. Mars (A), Earth (B), and Jupiter (C), are all incorrect choices.

16. **(C)** The correct choice is (C) comets. Meteoroids (A) and meteors (B) are generally smaller and not icy, and asteroids (D) are generally larger and rocky.

17. **(B)** It is stated in the text that "a decrease of one unit corresponds to an increase of brightness by a factor of 2.5." You can determine from that statement that the magnitude of the two stars differ by 1 (B). Choices (A), (C), and (D) are all incorrect.

18. **(A)** The temperature of a star is determined from measuring its spectrum, therefore choice (A) is correct. The text states the spectrum reveals information about the temperature, composition (D), and relative motion (B). Choice (C) is incorrect because it refers to absolute magnitude (intrinsic brightness), which is another property of the star and not directly related to its temperature.

19. **(D)**   The correct choice is (D), since the Sun's orbit in the Milky Way galaxy is nearly circular. This can be inferred from the statement that "the Sun takes 230 million years to circle the galaxy once in a galactic year." The choices referring to radial motion towards the center of the galaxy (A) and radial motion away from the center of the galaxy (B) describe linear motion and are incorrect. Choice (C) refers to an extreme type of orbit which doesn't really agree with the statement given in the text.

20. **(B)**   The Doppler red shift of distant galaxies (B), which is interpreted as recessional motion of the galaxies, and therefore an expansion of the universe, is the correct answer. Choice (A) is not an observation but rather a hypothesis drawn from (B), (C), and (D). (C) and (D) directly support (A), but do not imply an expanding universe.

Drill: Meteorology

1. **(B)**   The "greenhouse effect" is caused mainly by other atmospheric gases such as water vapor and carbon dioxide, so choice (A) is incorrect. Acid rain is caused by oxides of sulfur and nitrogen, so choice (C) is incorrect. Photochemical reactions involving oxides of nitrogen and chlorofluorocarbons play a major role in ozone destruction. These chemicals react with ozone and lead to a net decrease in ozone concentration in the stratosphere. Since ozone is a strong absorber of incoming ultraviolet (uv) radiation, any decrease in ozone concentration will increase the amount of uv radiation reaching the surface. This will increase the risk of skin cancer from contact with the sun significantly. With this in mind, it is easy to see that (D) is incorrect, leaving (B) as the correct answer.

2. **(D)**   Due to the high specific heat capacity of water, land surfaces will heat up more rapidly than water surfaces. Since warmer air is less dense than cooler air, this uneven heating along coastal areas causes vertical expansion of the isobaric field over the land and compression of the field over the water. This forms an elevated area of high pressure over the land and an elevated area of low pressure over the water. The pressure gradient force acts on the air and moves it from higher pressure to lower pressure. The net movement of air toward the low pressure aloft induces an area of high pressure on the water surface while the net movement of air away from the high pressure aloft induces an area of low pressure on the land surface. The pressure gradient force now begins to move the surface air from the higher pressure on the water surface towards the lower pressure on the land surface. It is this surface flow of air which is the sea (or lake) breeze. The greater the contrast between water temperature and land temperature, the stronger the breeze. At night, the land will cool faster than the adjacent water, reversing the process and forming a land breeze from the land towards the water.

3. **(C)** The pressure gradient force plays no significant role in vertical air circulations. This fact effectively eliminates (A), (B), and (D) leaving (C) as the correct answer. Since temperature decreases with height, as the valley air warms during the day, it becomes less dense than the air along the adjacent hillsides and begins to flow up the surrounding slopes. At night, air in the hills cools faster than the air in the valleys. Gravity pulls the cooler, more dense air down the hillsides and into the valleys.

4. **(A)** Since a downdraft spreads out radially along the ground, any pattern showing divergence (i.e., resembling spokes on a wagon wheel) is correct. Choice (B) requires winds from two different directions to occur which would not normally happen during a downdraft. Choice (C) implies a rotating wind which is also not associated with downdrafts. Selection (D) would need several different wind directions. Of the sketches given, only (A) shows the necessary divergent pattern often associated with downdrafts. In this sketch, the downdraft would have impacted the ground at the center and spread out from there.

5. **(D)** The intensity of the lightning is determined by complex processes which electrify the cloud. The updraft is only indirectly associated with this, so (A) is not a good answer. The height of the cloud base is determined by the vertical temperature and dew point lapse rates in the atmosphere. This height can be estimated well before a thunderstorm ever forms and is not dependent on the updraft. This eliminates choice (B). Wind gusts at the surface are mainly caused by the downdraft, so (C) is also incorrect. (D) is the correct answer. It is the strength of the updraft which determines how large individual precipitation elements will grow before they can no longer remain suspended in the cloud. Thus, stronger updrafts produce larger raindrops (or hailstones) than do weaker ones.

6. **(A)** Evaporation is an endothermic process which requires the input of additional energy to take place. When this energy is taken from the environment, evaporative cooling takes place. This would ultimately lead to an increase in the lapse rate, so (B) is incorrect. (C) is a physical process which does not apply in any way to lapse rates because they involve thermodynamic processes. Thus, (C) is incorrect. Although (D) is correct, it offers no explanation as to why the lapse rate slows after parcel saturation. This eliminates choice (D), leaving (A) as the correct answer. As a parcel rises, it expands and cools. Eventually, it cools to its dew point temperature—the temperature at which the parcel is 100% saturated. Any further cooling will lead to condensation. Since condensation is an exothermic process, it releases the latent heat of condensation stored in the water vapor. This latent heat partially offsets the adiabatic cooling of a rising parcel.

7. **(C)** Descending air will compress, warm, become more dense, and dry out. This eliminates all choices except (C). The drying out refers to a decrease in relative humidity. Since warmer air can hold more water vapor than cooler air, an increase in temperature with no change in water vapor content will

create drier air. This process is what causes the "rainshadow" on the leeward side of many mountains.

8.   **(C)**   Since the air is not saturated until it reaches 1,000 ft., we can use the dry adiabatic lapse rate of 5.5°F per 1,000 ft. from the surface up to 1,000 ft. At 1,000 ft., the air temperature is 64.5°F. From here to the top of the mountain, the air will be 100 percent saturated and cool at the moist adiabatic lapse rate of 3.3°F per 1,000 ft. So after rising the next 2,000 ft, the air is 57.9°F at the peak. Once the air begins to descend and warm, it will no longer be 100 percent saturated. This means it will warm at the dry adiabatic lapse rate of 5.5°F per 1,000 ft. This gives us an air temperature at Town B of 74.4°F.

9.   **(B)**   Since temperature will increase with height through an inversion, any rising air will be cooler than its surroundings and be forced back down. This represents stability. Instability (the condition where a parcel cools slower than its environment) and neutral stability (the condition where a parcel cools slower than its environment only after it is saturated) are never found in an inversion.

10.   **(D)**   Lightning heats the air to several thousand degrees in only a fraction of a second. This causes the air to expand rapidly. Surrounding air rushes in to fill the space left by the expanding heated air. It is the air rushing in which creates the sonic boom we know as thunder. By now, it should be evident that lightning and thunder originate at essentially the same location, making choices (A) and (C) incorrect. (B) is also incorrect but can explain why some thunder rumbles for a very long time. We see the lightning before we hear the thunder because the speed of light is much faster than the speed of sound, choice (D). Since sound travels approximately one mile in five seconds, if we saw lightning and heard the thunder ten seconds later, the lightning struck two miles away.

11.   **(A)**   While other methods can be somewhat slower than radiation and may lose some energy in molecular transfer, this is not why they cannot function in space. Stellar debris is present in such small quantities, it has little effect on anything. And since the sun emits energy in essentially every direction, we have eliminated choices (B), (C), and (D), leaving (A) as the correct answer. Conduction relies on molecular contact to transfer heat. Since space is nearly a perfect vacuum, not enough molecules are present to allow conduction to take place. Meteorologists refer to convection as the vertical component of heat transfer by mass movement of a fluid and advection as the horizontal component. Both methods require the presence of a fluid and cannot function in space for the same reason as conduction. Radiation transfers energy via electromagnetic waves which do not require a medium to propagate. This property makes radiation the only means possible to transfer energy through space.

12.   **(D)**   The change in state from liquid water to water vapor is an endothermic process which requires the addition of additional heat energy to take place.

This heat is taken from the surrounding air, causing the air to cool. The amount of energy needed is called the latent heat of vaporization. Since choice (C) represents an exothermic process, (C) is incorrect. Thus, (B) is correct because it is endothermic and (A) is correct because it is directly related to (B). This makes the best choice (D).

13. **(D)** Choices (A), (B), and (C) are all generally correct statements but none of them lead to maximum summer temperatures on the date of the summer solstice. Warmest summer temperatures occur somewhat after the summer solstice due to the temperature lag associated with heating the mass of the earth. This leaves (D) as the correct answer.

14. **(C)** The sun emits energy throughout the entire electromagnetic spectrum, including all wavelengths of visible light. This eliminates choice (D). Bodies of water only appear to be reflected by the sky under certain conditions when a mirage forms. Since not every day meets these conditions but the sky is usually blue, choice (B) can be eliminated. And since very little light reaches our eyes from stars other than our sun, outer space appears black. This eliminates (A) and leaves (C) as the correct answer. Air molecules scatter the sun's light in all directions. However, air is a selective scatterer which scatters shorter wavelengths much more than longer ones. This causes more light from the shorter wavelength of the blue portion of the spectrum to be scattered to the earth. This gives the sky its bluish appearance. At sunrise and sunset though, the light must travel through much more of the atmosphere due to its low angle of elevation. This causes most of the shorter wavelength blue portion of the spectrum to be scattered out before reaching the earth, leaving the longer wavelength red portion to be seen. This is what gives both sunrise and sunset a reddish appearance.

15. **(B)** Since we assume the earth is not rotating, airflow will be dictated by differential heating of the earth. Heating at the equator will cause rising motion and form an area of surface low pressure. Cooling at the poles will cause sinking motion and form a surface area of high pressure. The pressure gradient force will now drive the air from the poles towards the equator, causing a return flow aloft from the equator towards the poles. No Coriolis force is available to deflect the winds so (A) and (C) are incorrect. Knowing that the poles are cooler than the equator, (D) is obviously wrong. This leaves (B) as the correct choice. This circulation would help even out the global heat distribution. The theoretical circulation is called the Hadley cell and would be the same for both northern and southern hemispheres. Since the earth does rotate, the Coriolis force breaks the circulation into three different cells per hemisphere. Surface convergence and divergence leads to the formation of surface high pressure and low pressure areas as shown in the diagram. The airflow around these surface pressure systems creates prevailing wind patterns such as the trade winds found in the tropics. (B) is illustrated on the following page.

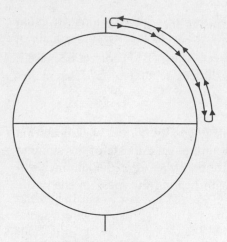

Hadley Cell: Non-rotating Earth

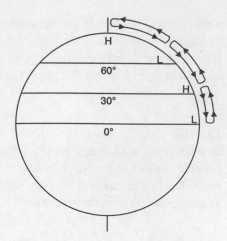

Three Cells: Rotating Earth

16. **(A)**   In winter, the continents are cooler than the oceans, creating rising motion over the water and sinking motion over the land. This leads to surface high pressure over the land and surface low pressure over the water, so the correct answer is (A). The situation is reversed for summer with surface high pressure over the water and surface low pressure over the land. Spring and fall are transition seasons which typically find widely varied surface pressure patterns.

17. **(D)**   If a layer of cold air at the surface is shallow, rain will not have time to freeze before it reaches the ground. However, once it does hit the cold ground, it will freeze quickly. This is known as freezing rain. When large ice accumulations are observed, this type of event is often referred to as an ice storm. If the layer of cold air at the surface is thick, the rain may freeze before reaching the ground and fall as sleet (ice pellets). Although both are formed of ice, sleet (ice pellets) are not the same as hail. Hail only forms by a complex cyclical process high within a thunderstorm.

18. **(D)**   Very pure, very small water droplets can remain liquid at temperatures approaching –40°F! At these temperatures, the droplets are said to be super-cooled.

19. **(B)**   Perspiration is the biological method of cooling your body. As the perspiration evaporates, you are cooled by evaporative cooling. The process is slowed by humid air, which makes it difficult to keep cool on hot and humid summer days. Choices (A) and (C) are related, but are both incorrect. In order for water vapor to condense on your skin, it would have to approach the dew point of the surrounding air. However, this would involve a decrease in your body temperature as opposed to an increase. Meteorologists use something called the heat index to warn you of conditions which inhibit evaporative cooling and can lead

to heat stroke if your body overheats. In the winter, strong, cold winds can cause high rates of evaporative cooling, causing your body to lose large amounts of heat quickly. Prolonged exposure to these conditions may lead to hypothermia. Meteorologists can warn of these conditions by monitoring the wind chill factor—the temperature you perceive due to evaporative cooling.

20. **(B)**   Hurricanes are born over warm tropical waters and would quickly dissipate in air temperatures cold enough for snow. This eliminates choice (A). Tropical regions do not experience large diurnal temperature changes due to the dense vegetation cover and high moisture content of the tropical atmosphere. This eliminates choice (C). The fact that temperature decreases with height has profound effects on climate zones on a mountain. It is possible for lush vegetation to thrive at the base of a tall mountain while snow and ice cap its peak. This allows high mountains in the tropics to routinely experience snowfall at their higher elevations.

PRACTICE
EXAM I

ACT ASSESSMENT PRACTICE EXAM I

(An answer sheet for this test appears in the back of this book.)

Test 1: English

TIME: 45 Minutes
75 Questions

DIRECTIONS: This test consists of five passages. In each passage, certain words and phrases have been underlined and numbered. The questions on each passage consist of alternatives for these underlined segments. Choose the alternative that follows standard written English, most accurately reflects the style and tone of the passage, or best relays the idea of the passage. Choose "NO CHANGE," if no change is necessary.

In addition, you will also encounter questions about part of the passage, or the passage as a whole. These questions are indicated by a number in a box at the end of the section, rather than an underlined portion.

Once you have selected the best answer, fill in the appropriate oval on the answer sheet for the correct choice.

Passage I

[1]

The first architect of the Capitol was appointed in 1793 by the President of the United States. During the period of the construction of the Capitol (1793-1865), several appointments such as <u>this was</u> made to the position of architect at
1
such times and for such periods as the various stages of the construction of the work required. The office of architect <u>has; however, been</u> continuous from 1851
2
to the present.

[2]

The <u>office's functions</u> have <u>change</u> materially through the years in accor-
  3   4
dance with the increased activities imposed on it by Congress, due principally to
the addition of new buildings and grounds. Originally, the duties of the Architect
of the Capitol <u>was</u> to plan and construct the Capitol <u>Building; yet,</u> later they
                5   6
included the requirement to supervise its care and maintenance.

[3]

Permanent <u>authority, for the care and maintenance of the Capitol Building,</u>
                                      7
is provided by an act of August 15, 1876. This <u>act has been amended from time</u>
                                                                8
<u>to time to provide</u> for the care and maintenance of the additional buildings and
        8
grounds placed under the jurisdiction of the Architect of the Capitol by Congress
in subsequent years. ┌─┐
                     │9│
                     └─┘

[4]

The Architect of the Capitol is <u>much more</u> in charge of the structural and
                                     10
mechanical care of the United States Capitol Building and making arrangements
with <u>the authorized authorities in charge</u> for ceremonies held in the building and
                    11
on the grounds; is responsible for the care, <u>maintenance, and sprucing up</u> of the
                                                          12
Capitol grounds, comprising approximately 208.7 acres of landscaping, parks,
streets, and parking; is responsible for the structural and mechanical care of the
Library of Congress Buildings and the United States Supreme Court; and under
the direction of the Senate Committee on Rules Land Administration and the
Committee on House Administration, respectively, is charged with the operation
of the United States Senate and House restaurants.

[5]

The Architect of the Capitol also <u>is charged with the perk of</u> planning and
13
constructing of such <u>buildings as</u> may be assigned by Congress from time to
14
time. Current projects include extension, reconstruction, alteration, and improvements under the additional House Office Building projects; and expansion, modification, and enlargement of the facilities of the Capitol Power Plant. 15

1. A. NO CHANGE   C. these are
   B. these was   D. this were

2. F. NO CHANGE   H. has however; been
   G. has, however, been   J. has, however been

3. A. NO CHANGE   C. function of the office's
   B. offices'   D. function of the offices'

4. F. NO CHANGE   H. changes
   G. changed   J. been change

5. A. NO CHANGE   C. will have been
   B. were   D. OMIT the underlined portion.

6. F. NO CHANGE   H. Building, hence,
   G. Building, however;   J. Building yet;

7. A. NO CHANGE
   B. authority for the care and maintenance of the Capitol Building,
   C. authority, for the care and maintenance of the Capitol Building
   D. authority for the care and maintenance of the Capitol Building

8. F. NO CHANGE
   G. act, amended occasionally, provides

H.   act, which has been amended on occasion to provide

J.   act, amended from time to time provides,

9.   Which of the suggested sentences makes the best introduction to Paragraph 4 and the best transition from Paragraph 3?

A.   NO CHANGE

B.   The care of restaurants and streets is certainly a burden for the Architect of the Capitol.

C.   Because it was established in the last century, this act has been met with continual debate due to the progress of the twentieth century.

D.   Granted by the act of 1876, the Architect's authority to care for and maintain United States buildings and grounds encompasses a varied set of duties.

10. F.   NO CHANGE   H.   quite a good deal more

     G.   more than   J.   OMIT the underlined portion.

11. A.   NO CHANGE   C.   those

     B.   the proper authorities   D.   the authorities in charge,

12. F.   NO CHANGE

     G.   maintenance, nor improvements

     H.   maintenance, and improvements

     J.   maintenance and, sprucing up

13. A.   NO CHANGE

     B.   is charged with

     C.   is charged with the "perk" of

     D.   is burdened with the responsibility of

14. F.   NO CHANGE   H.   buildings; as

     G.   buildings, that   J.   buildings. As

15. For the sake of paragraph unity, which sentence would best close Paragraph 5?

     A.   The sentence which currently ends the paragraph

B.   Although the current projects are extensive, they do not preclude the Architect's integral involvement in the future Congressionally approved planning and constructing of buildings.

C.   For example, the extension of the United States Supreme Court has been in progress for five years to date.

D.   Issues of landscaping, park appropriation, and street improvement can be dealt with by the Committee on House Administration.

Passage II

[1]

Life in the American colonial era was <u>harsh, the refinement</u> of the mother
16
country was ordinarily lacking. The colonists, however, soon began <u>to mold it</u> to
17
the fresh environment of a new land. The influence of religion permeated the
entire way of life. In most Southern colonies, the Anglican Church was the
legally established church. In New England, the <u>Puritans were the big guns;</u> and
18
in Pennsylvania, the Quakers. Especially in the New England <u>colonies. The</u> local
19
or village church was the hub of community life; the authorities strictly enforced
the Sabbath.

[2]

Unfortunately, the same sort of religious intolerance, bigotry, and superstition <u>as that of the European Reformation</u> prevailed in some of the colonies,
20
though on a lesser scale. In the last half of the seventeenth century, fanaticism
and hysteria grew under Massachusetts and Connecticut authority. <u>Neither one,</u>
21
<u>nor the other perceived</u> the benefits in diverse religious views. Nonbelievers,
21
dissenters, and those who didn't fit in were sometimes banished or otherwise
punished. As the decades passed, however, religious toleration developed in the
colonies.

[3]

Because of the strong religious influence in the colonies, especially in New England; religious instruction and Bible reading played an important part in
<u>22</u>
education. In Massachusetts, for example, a law of 1645 required each community with 50 households to establish an elementary school. Two years later the same colony <u>past</u> the "Deluder Satan" law which required each town of 100
<u>23</u>
families to maintain a grammar <u>school for the purpose of providing</u> religious, as
<u>24</u>
well as general, instruction. | 25 |

[4]

In the Southern colonies, only a few privately endowed free schools existed. Private tutors instructed the sons of well-to-do <u>planters, they</u> completed their
<u>26</u>
educations at English universities. Young males in poor families throughout the colonies were ordinarily apprenticed for vocational education.

[5]

By 1700, two colleges had been <u>founded, one was Harvard established</u> by the
<u>27</u>
Massachusetts Legislature in 1636, and the other, Virginia's William and <u>Mary</u>
<u>28</u>
<u>University. Which</u> originated in 1693 under a royal charter. Other cultural activi-
<u>28</u>
ties before 1700 were limited. The few literary products of the colonists, mostly <u>historical narratives, daily journals, fiery sermons, and religious poetry,</u> were
<u>29</u>
printed in England. The *Bay Psalm Book* (1640) was the first book printed in the colonies. Artists and composers, who were few, produced an output of relatively simple character.

16. F.   NO CHANGE
    G.   harsh, refinement

    H.   , for the refinement
    J.   , however

17. A.   NO CHANGE
    B.   the molding of it

    C.   to mold their life
    D.   to shape it

18. F.   NO CHANGE
    G.   Puritans were the big guns.
    H.   Puritans dominated,
    J.   Puritans authorized;

19. A.   NO CHANGE
    B.   colonies, the

    C.   colonies, where the
    D.   colonies' the

20. F.   NO CHANGE
    G.   associated with the Age of the Reformation in Europe
    H.   which marked Europe's era of Reformation
    J.   which we associate with the European period of Reformation

21. A.   NO CHANGE
    B.   Neither perceived
    C.   Neither one nor the other perceive
    D.   Not one nor both perceives

22. F.   NO CHANGE
    G.   England religious

    H.   England; yet, religious
    J.   England, religious

23. A.   NO CHANGE
    B.   went past

    C.   have passed
    D.   passed

24. F.   NO CHANGE
    G.   school, for the purpose of providing
    H.   school which would provide
    J.   school to provide

25. Which of the suggested sentences makes the best introduction to Paragraph 4 and the best transition from Paragraph 3?

    A.   Yet it was obvious that the legal precedents set in Massachusetts were also to be enacted in the South.

    B.   Although religion and education were inseparable in the North, more secular instruction took place in the South.

    C.   The "Deluder Satan" law harkened back to the religious intolerance of early Massachusetts and Connecticut.

    D.   Private and individualized education characterized the Southern colonies' schools.

26. F.   NO CHANGE   H.   planter, among whom they

      G.   planters; who   J.   planters, who

27. A.   NO CHANGE

      B.   founded; one was Harvard established

      C.   founded. One was Harvard, established

      D.   founded, one was Harvard, established

28. F.   NO CHANGE   H.   Mary, who

      G.   Mary it   J.   Mary, which

29. A.   NO CHANGE

      B.   narratives involving history, daily journals, a few sermons of a fiery nature, and some poetry,

      C.   historical-narratives, journals-daily, sermons-fiery; and religious poetry,

      D.   narratives of history; daily journals; sermons of fire and brimstone; and nonsecular poems,

---

Items 30 and 31 pose questions about Passage II as a whole.

---

30. Suppose the writer wished to add the following sentences to the passage:

> Colonists tried and hanged a few women as "witches." Early in the seventeenth century, some other witchcraft persecution occurred in Virginia, North Carolina, and Rhode Island, as well.

The new sentences would most logically be placed in which of the following paragraphs?

F. Paragraph 1, because witchcraft is surely to draw the immediate interest of the reader

G. Paragraph 2, because the persecution of witches clearly indicates religious intolerance

H. In a separate paragraph, because interesting information needs to stand out on its own

J. Paragraph 5, because the reader must be left with an important image to remember

31. If you were putting together a collection of essays for high school seniors, it would be most appropriate to include this passage in a section containing essays on

A. systems of punishment in American society.

B. biographies of famous American colonists.

C. colonial religion's impact on American society.

D. the importance of the printing press in colonial America.

Passage III

[1]

The words "organic," "chemicals," "natural," and "health" are among the most misunderstood, misused, and maligned in our vocabulary, especially when they are applied to food. All organic materials <u>is a complex combination</u> of
32
chemicals and contain one chemical element in common. That element is carbon. But not all chemicals occur in the form of organic material. All of our usual food is in organic <u>form; because</u> it has come from animal or plant sources, and,
33
interestingly enough, most man-made foods are also in organic form.

[2]

Today our chief concern about <u>them</u> relates to how foods are grown and
34

processed. There are no precise, official definitions for <u>these but some</u> have been
35
proposed for legal use and can be useful for the consumer, as well. The term
"organically grown food" means food which has not been subjected to pesticides
or artificial fertilizers and which has been grown in soil <u>whose</u> humus content has
36
been increased by the addition of organic matter. The term "organically processed food" means organically grown food which in its processing has not been
treated with preservatives, hormones, antibiotics, or synthetic additives of any
kind.

[3]

Organic material or humus used in growing the plants which we eat directly, or which are fed to the animals that furnish <u>ones</u> meat, includes manures,
37
plant composts, and other plant residues such as peat moss and aged sawdust.
Inorganic or <u>store-bought</u> fertilizers contain the same chemical nutrients but in
38
simpler forms and not always in combination with carbon. It is <u>neither accurate</u>
39
<u>nor exact</u> to refer to inorganic fertilizers as "artificial" just because they have not
39
been made by living cells. ⬚40⬚

[4]

A plant is not aware of the type of fertilizer, organic or inorganic, that is
furnishing the chemicals <u>more</u> for its <u>growth. When it does</u> demand
41   42
that these building blocks for its nutrients be in inorganic form. <u>Cells of the plant</u>
43
<u>themselves</u> synthesize the complex materials needed for growth rather than ab-
43
sorbing them ready-made from the soil.

32. F.   NO CHANGE
    G.   are being a complex combination
    H.   is complex combinations
    J.   are a complex combination

33. A.   NO CHANGE
    B.   form because
    C.   form; Because
    D.   form; yet, because

34. F.   NO CHANGE
    G.   it
    H.   these
    J.   organic and chemical labels

35. A.   NO CHANGE
    B.   these, however, some
    C.   these, but some
    D.   these; because some

36. F.   NO CHANGE
    G.   who's
    H.   whos
    J.   in which the

37. A.   NO CHANGE
    B.   one's
    C.   its
    D.   our

38. F.   NO CHANGE
    G.   commercial
    H.   over-the-counter
    J.   customer-ready

39. A.   NO CHANGE
    B.   neither accurate, nor exact
    C.   not accurate nor exact
    D.   inaccurate

40. Which of the suggested sentences makes the best introduction to Paragraph 3 and the best transition from Paragraph 2?

    F.   For these definitions to make sense, we must understand exactly what constitutes organic and inorganic material for food growth.

    G.   Definitions of organically grown and processed foods are vital for the food processing industry.

H. Inorganic and organic issues with respect to edible plants and meat must be addressed by today's businessmen and businesswomen.

J. Humus in its various forms is essential to the growth of organically labeled plants.

41. A. NO CHANGE
    B. much more
    C. inasmuch
    D. OMIT the underlined portion.

42. F. NO CHANGE
    G. growth; when it does
    H. growth. However they do
    J. growth; yet, it does

43. A. NO CHANGE
    B. The plant's cells
    C. Cells themselves of the plant
    D. The cells' plants

Items 44–46 pose questions about Passage III as a whole.

---

44. Which of the following sentences, if added to the end of Paragraph 4, would best relate Paragraph 4 to Paragraph 1, unifying the passage as a whole?

    F. Plants seem to have figured out their answer to the organic-inorganic labeling quandry; the question is, can humans?

    G. Indeed, the plant is not too discerning; however, it has the ability to adapt to whatever form of nutrient it receives.

    H. Terminology is indeed an issue in the food industry; for labeling can determine if a product sells or remains standing on the grocer's shelf.

    J. Animals nourished on a diet of organically fortified feed yield a meat product essentially no different from those animals nourished by chemically fertilized feed.

45. If the writer wanted to strengthen the aspect of the passage relating to the trends in American consumer buying of foods labeled as "natural" or "chemically treated," it would be most logical to put this new material in

    A. Paragraph 2, because that paragraph is too technical and needs some simpler material.

B. Paragraph 3's place, because that paragraph contains definitions all readers already know and therefore is unnecessary.

C. a separate paragraph, because it would be the only one devoted solely to labeling's effect on American buyers.

D. Paragraph 4, because it sums up the points made earlier.

46. Suppose the writer wanted to add the following sentences to the passage:

> Those organic foods given to meat-producing animals include sorghum, maize, a variety of grasses, and commercially developed livestock feeds. Yes, even these latter nutrients are categorized as organic.

The new sentences would be most logically placed in which of the following paragraphs?

F. Paragraph 1, because all important information has to be introduced immediately

G. A separate paragraph following Paragraph 1, because important new material must be placed alone so it stands out

H. Paragraph 3, because it discusses specific organic materials used as nutrients for edible plants and animals

J. Paragraph 4, because every essay should have an important ending

Passage IV

[1]

Because they engage the feelings and not the mind, horror movies, which have always had a special place in the lives of theater-goers, have enjoyed a recent <u>revival. Because when</u> we examine the makeup of this kind of film, we
                        47
<u>find, just</u> beneath the surface assumptions about science. First, the major horror
   48
types in question here are the Interplanetary Monster, the Atomic Beast, and the

Mad Doctor.

[2]

[1] Probably the <u>older of the three</u> would be the Mad Doctor. [2] Rooted in
                        49
European folklore, the figure sprang from Balkan legends about vampires and

werewolves. [3] The Frankenstein monster, typical of this figure of the Mad

Doctor, can be traced back to <u>Golem; a figure</u> that the Jews created from clay to
                                    50
lead them from oppression. [4] However, these religious and superstitious tones

now exist in theaters in the area of science—at least science that has been dis-

torted somewhat. [5] The combination of crude religious overtones and supersti-

tions gives these stories a medieval flavor. [6] Where old horror movies would

convert humans into perverted lower forms of life, newer horror movies have

now converted them to mad scientists. [7] Whereas Dr. Faustus, that figure in

Christopher Marlowe's play about black magic, was a church scholar, his later

counterpart, Dr. <u>Frankenstein, will have been</u> the research physician. [8] The
                            51
black arts that call up evil and demonic <u>spirits. Now</u> give way to test tubes and
                                            52
electrical equipment. $\boxed{53}$

[3]

In Marlowe's play and in movies patterned after <u>them, Dr.</u> Faustus <u>stepped</u>
                                                    54   55
<u>beyond natural bounds</u> by conjuring up demonic spirits. Frankenstein <u>as well</u>
    55   56
steps too far by exploring taboo areas for humans. Dr. Frankenstein resumes the

role of the villain absorbed in his work among the network of complex machin-

ery in his laboratory; he becomes the picture of an immortal being whose com-

plete madness is commensurate with his great intellect.

[4]

Essentially, Dr. Frankenstein represents the victory of his intellect over the conscience of <u>those who oppose him.</u> And as he becomes increasingly aware of
57
the refusal of his neighbors to accept the validity of his work, he becomes set on

<u>revenge, he victimizes</u> the surrounding countryside in a mad rage of violence.
58
Ultimately, the <u>more the</u> rage turns on the scientist and destroys him. And as the
59
movie-goers view the superior intellect self-destruct on film, they <u>are able to</u>
60
<u>fully comfort themselves</u> that even though they themselves are not as intelligent
60
as Dr. Frankenstein they are still loved by God.

47. A. NO CHANGE

    B. revival, when

    C. revival; yet, when

    D. revival and

48. F. NO CHANGE

    G. find just

    H. find—just

    J. find. Just

49. A. NO CHANGE

    B. oldest of the three

    C. older

    D. older, of the three

50. F. NO CHANGE

    G. Golem, a figure

    H. Golem who was a figure

    J. Golem, who was a figure

51. A. NO CHANGE

    B. Frankenstein, would have been

    C. Frankenstein is

    D. Frankenstein, was

52. F. NO CHANGE

    G. spirits, now

    H. spirits now

    J. spirits; now

53. For the sake of unity and coherence, Sentence 5 should be placed

    A. where it is now.

    B. after Sentence 3.

    C. after Sentence 6.

    D. after Sentence 7.

54. F. NO CHANGE   H. those, Dr.
    G. them Dr.   J. it, Dr.

55. A. NO CHANGE   C. went out on a limb
    B. stuck his neck out   D. went overboard

56. F. NO CHANGE   H. , similarly
    G. as well,   J. similarly,

57. A. NO CHANGE   C. those who stand in opposition.
    B. his opposition.   D. those whom oppose.

58. F. NO CHANGE
    G. revenge; and he victimizes
    H. revenge, victimizes
    J. revenge, victimizing

59. A. NO CHANGE   C. the most
    B. the greater   D. OMIT the underlined portion.

60. F. NO CHANGE   H. are able to lay themselves at rest
    G. are comforted to know   J. lay in the comfort

Item 61 poses a question about Passage IV as a whole.

---

61. The writer wants to support the assertion in Paragraph 3 that Dr. Frankenstein is a villain. Which of the following strategies would best accomplish that goal?

    A. Comparing Frankenstein's readers with Dracula's readers

    B. Describing the physical characteristics of Dr. Frankenstein's detractors

    C. Citing examples of instances when Frankenstein sacrificed the human needs of his community for the success of his experiment

    D. Explaining how Frankenstein is more humane than Golem

Passage V

[1]

You can take it from Julius Caesar: <u>you've got</u> to watch people. I've
                                    62

watched them for a long time, and it's not a pretty sight. I shake at lean men

around me. You find all sorts of these "leanies" <u>about if one looks</u> long enough:
                                                  63

the condescending lean man, the "he has it all together" lean man, the efficiency

expert lean man—all lean, all a social nuisance.

[2]

<u>Leanies were funless. They don't</u> mess around in the fat way. Their messing
                    64

leads somewhere, amounts to something, proves constructive in some way. Five

minutes with nothing to do but drink coffee will get you an empty cup, cleaned

and washed and put back on the rack. Full of industry, the leanies say things like,

"I need a twenty-five-hour day to get everything done." Fat people consider the

day too confounded <u>long while</u> it is.
                    65

[3]

Also, leanies are tiringly <u>energetic to the point of being unhealthy.</u> There's
                            66

always that executive briskness in their walk, as if they are headed on their way

to an important meeting with the <u>board when</u> all they're really headed for is the
                                 67

bathroom. But fat people say, "Give me your sluggish, your inert, your 'give me

a minute, will ya!' <u>people who</u> intelligently conclude: mop it today, they just
                     68

track it up tomorrow."

[4]

And leanies are stupidly <u>logical. That</u> condescending shake of the head

69

before they start to tell you how stupid you are. They know the TV schedule—

those that even watch TV—when it comes <u>to news programs, educational pro-</u>

70

<u>grams, and exercise shows.</u> They know about cholesterol, smoking, and body

70

fats. And always, always they are financially responsible and sound. <u>Tall people</u>

71

<u>never, but never read the paper.</u>

71

[5]

Fat people, on the other hand, are comfortably illogical—not stupid, you

understand. But we tend to see the other side of "smart" and "with it." We don't

know the TV schedule because we don't have a TV schedule. Not only that, but

having a TV <u>schedule implied</u> planning ahead. Planning ahead to watch a show

72

you watch each week whether you plan to or not somehow takes the fun out of it;

it removes the spontaneity of life. And while fat people aren't into keeping up

with their cholesterol or triglycerides, they are aware that chances are you'll die

in a car accident before <u>you're</u> arteries kill you.

73

62. F. NO CHANGE

    G. you have got

    H. you have

    J. we've got

63. A. NO CHANGE

    B. about if you look

    C. about; if one looks

    D. about, if we look

64. F. NO CHANGE

    G. These lean pests are neither fun, nor do they

    H. Funless and efficient, leanies don't

    J. Leanies, these funless and efficient social pests, don't

65. A. NO CHANGE   C. long as

    B. long, while   D. long when

66. F. NO CHANGE

    G. and unhealthily energetic.

    H. so energetic that they seem almost to be unhealthy.

    J. and unhealthy.

67. A. NO CHANGE   C. board, when,

    B. board. When   D. board; yet when

68. F. NO CHANGE   H. people. Who

    G. people which   J. people whom

69. A. NO CHANGE   C. logical. There's that

    B. logical; theres that   D. logical, that

70. F. NO CHANGE

    G. news, educational, and exercise programs.

    H. news reports, programs on education, and exercising.

    J. coverage of the news, educational documentaries, and programs involving exercise.

71. A. NO CHANGE

    B. Tall people never read the newspaper.

    C. Never, but never, do tall people read the newspaper.

    D. OMIT the underlined portion.

72. F. NO CHANGE   H. schedule implies

    G. scheduling implied   J. schedule has implied

73. A. NO CHANGE   C. your

    B. your'e   D. one's

Items 74 and 75 pose questions about Passage V as a whole.

---

74. Considering the tone and subject matter of the essay, is the writer's use of the pronoun "you" appropriate?

    F.   No, because the writer does not personally know the reader.

    G.   No, because the rules of grammar dictate that one should avoid "you" in personal writing.

    H.   Yes, because the rules of grammar require a writer to use "you" whenever writing about anything he or she has personally experienced.

    J.   Yes, because this is a personal narrative with a tone of informality, and using "you" gives it a sense of camaraderie.

75. The tone the writer employs in her depiction of lean and fat people is

    A.   one of hopefulness, because she notes she would like to be as constructive and energetic as the leanies are.

    B.   one of anger, because she notes logical leanies are smarter than fat people.

    C.   one of humor, because she pokes fun at herself for being comfortably illogical about floor mopping and spontaneous about her selection of television programs to watch.

    D.   one of sadness, because she lists the many hardships of being overweight.

THIS IS THE END OF TEST 1.

Test 2: Mathematics

TIME: 60 Minutes
60 Questions

DIRECTIONS: Solve the following problems, and fill in the appropriate ovals on your answer sheet.

Unless otherwise indicated:

1. Figures may not have been drawn to scale.

2. All geometric figures lie in a plane.

3. "Line" refers to a straight line.

4. "Average" refers to arithmetic mean.

---

1. Evaluate $2 - \{5 + (2 - 3) + [2 - (3 - 4)]\}$.

   A. 5
   B. −5
   C. −3

   D. 1
   E. 2

2. If x is an odd integer and y is even, then which of the following must be an even integer?

   I. $2x + 3y$

   II. xy

   III. $x + y - 1$

   F. I only.
   G. II only.
   H. I and II only.

   J. II and III only.
   K. I, II, and III.

3. If $x^{-2} - 9 = 0$, solve for x.

   A. 3
   B. $-\dfrac{1}{3}$
   C. $\dfrac{1}{3}$

   D. ±3
   E. $\pm\dfrac{1}{3}$

4. If a and b are odd integers, which of the following must be an even integer?

I. $\dfrac{a+b}{2}$

II. $ab - 1$

III. $\dfrac{ab+1}{2}$

F. I only.   J. II and III only.

G. II only.   K. I, II, and III.

H. I and II only.

5. If $\dfrac{1}{\dfrac{b}{3}} = \dfrac{1}{4}$, then $b =$

A. $\dfrac{1}{4}$.   D. $\dfrac{4}{3}$.

B. $\dfrac{3}{4}$.   E. 12.

C. $\dfrac{13}{4}$.

6. If the cost of a box of 12 pens is $7.20 and a box of 16 pencils costs $4.00, what is the cost of 3 pens and 3 pencils?

F. $1.30   J. $3.50

G. $2.55   K. $9.20

H. $2.65

7. If $\dfrac{2}{\dfrac{x}{3}} = \dfrac{3}{7}$, then $x =$

A. 6.   D. 14.

B. 7.   E. 16.

C. 9.

8. What value must x take on in order for the following equation to be true:

$$\frac{7}{x+3} = \frac{8}{x+5}?$$

F.   3

G.   5

H.   7

J.   8

K.   11

9. Two statements, p and q, are defined as follows:

$p: a + b < c + d$

$q: a < c, b < d$

Which of the following is true?

A. p implies q.

B. p and q imply each other.

C. q implies p.

D. q is the contrapositive of p.

E.   Neither q nor p implies the other.

10. If $\frac{2}{3}x = 1$, then $\frac{3}{4} + x =$

F. $\frac{9}{4}$.

G.   2.

H. $\frac{7}{4}$.

J.   1.

K. $\frac{3}{4}$.

11. If $x = 3$ and $y = -2$, then $\frac{1}{2x} + \frac{1}{3y} - \frac{2xy}{3x+2y} =$

A. $\frac{7}{5}$.

B. $\frac{8}{5}$.

C. $\frac{9}{5}$.

D. $\frac{11}{5}$.

E. $\frac{12}{5}$.

12. If $\dfrac{7}{x+4} = \dfrac{5}{x+6}$, then $x =$

    F.   −11.   J.   7.

    G.   −7.   K.   11.

    H.   5.

13. If $\dfrac{\frac{3}{4}}{g} = (7 - a)g$, then $a =$

    A. $\dfrac{3}{4}$.   D. $\dfrac{25}{4}$.

    B. $\dfrac{16}{3}$.   E.   17.

    C.   5.

14. If $|\,2x - 5\,| = 3$, then $x =$

    F. $-2\dfrac{1}{2}$ or 3.   J.   1 or 4.

    G. $2\dfrac{1}{2}$ or 4.   K.   0 or −3.

    H.   1 or 3.

15. Find all the roots of the equation $(x + 1)\,(x^2 + 4x - 5) = 0$.

    A. $\{-1, 4, -5\}$ D. $\{1, 4, 5\}$

    B. $\{1, 2, 3\}$ E. $\{-1, 2, 3\}$

    C. $\{-5, -1, 1\}$

16. If $f(x) = 3x + 5$ and $3 < x < 5$, then $f(x)$ is between

    F.   10 and 16.   J.   16 and 22.

    G.   12 and 18.   K.   18 and 24.

    H.   14 and 20.

17. Simplify $8x^2 - [7x - (x^2 - x + 5y)] + (2x - 3y)$.

    A. $9x^2 - 6x + 2y$ B. $8x^2 - x + 2y$

C. $x^2 + 2$ D. $7x^2 + 2 + 3y$

E. 0

18. How many integers are in the solution set of $|2x - 6| < 3$?

F. None   J. Three

G. One   K. Four

H. Two

19. The fraction $\dfrac{\dfrac{2}{b^2 a^2}}{\dfrac{1}{b^2 - 2b}}$ may be expressed more compactly as

A. $\dfrac{2a}{b}$.   D. $\dfrac{b - a}{a}$.

B. $\dfrac{b - 4}{b}$.   E. $\dfrac{2b - 4}{ba^2}$.

C. $\dfrac{ab}{b^2 - a}$.

20. If $xy \neq 0$, then $\dfrac{\dfrac{1}{x} - \dfrac{1}{y}}{\dfrac{1}{x^2} - \dfrac{1}{y^2}} =$

F. $\dfrac{xy}{x + y}$.   J. $\dfrac{-xy}{x - y}$.

G. xy.   K. $\dfrac{xy}{x - y}$.

H. $\dfrac{1}{x + y}$.

21. The solution set of $\dfrac{7}{x^2 + 8x + 23} = 1$ is

A. $\{8\}$.   D. $\{4, -4\}$.

B. $\{8, -4\}$.   E. $\{16, 1\}$.

C. $\{-4\}$.

22. If $\dfrac{a}{b} = 4$, then what is $a^2 - 16b^2$?

    F.   −16   J.   4

    G.   −4   K.   16

    H.   0

23. If $\dfrac{x}{y} = \dfrac{2}{5}$, then $25x^2 - 4y^2 =$

    A.   −5.   D.   2.

    B.   −2.   E.   5.

    C.   0.

24. If $abc \neq 0$, then $\dfrac{3b^3a^2}{33a^3b^6(cb)^4} =$

    F. $\dfrac{11b}{a^3}$.   J. $\dfrac{1}{11ab^7c^4}$.

    G. $\dfrac{11}{ab^8c^4}$.   K. $\dfrac{1}{11a^3b^6c^4}$.

    H. $\dfrac{b^3a}{11c^4}$.

25. Solve the equation $I = \dfrac{E}{R}(1 - e^{-\frac{Ri}{L}})$ for t.

    A. $t = \dfrac{-R\log_e(1 - \frac{E}{RI})}{R\log e}$ D. $t = \dfrac{L}{R}\log_e\left(\dfrac{RI}{E}\right)$

    B. $t = -\dfrac{L}{R}\log_e\left(1 - \dfrac{RI}{E}\right)$ E. $t = \log_e\left(\dfrac{1 + RI}{E}\right)$

    C. $t = -\dfrac{R}{L}\log_e\left(\dfrac{RI + 1}{E}\right)$

26. If $2^{(6x-8)} = 16$, then $x =$

    F.   2.   G.   4.

H. 10. J. 1.

K. 6.

27. If $f(x) = x + 1$, $g(x) = 2x - 3$ and an operation $*$ is defined for all real numbers a and b by the equation $a * b = 2a + b - ab$, then $f(3) * g(4) =$

A. -9. D. 0.

B. -7. E. 5.

C. -1.

28. $\dfrac{\dfrac{2x-8}{x+1}}{\dfrac{3x^2-12x}{x^2-1}} =$

F. $\dfrac{2}{x^2}$. J. $\dfrac{2(x-1)}{3x}$.

G. $\dfrac{3x^2}{2}$. K. $\dfrac{x-5}{6x}$.

H. $\dfrac{2}{3}(16-x)$.

29. If $\log 2 + 2\log x = \log(4x - 2)$, then $x =$

A. -4. D. 1.

B. -2. E. 2.

C. 0.

30. If $x^{2a} = (2x)^a$ and $a = -1$, then $x =$

F. 0. J. 2.

G. -2. K. 3.

H. 1.

31. The solution of $\dfrac{2x+1}{x^2-4} > 0$ is

A. $x > 2$. B. $x > 1$.

C. $x > 2$ or $x < \dfrac{1}{2}$.

D. $x > 2$ or $-2 < x < -\dfrac{1}{2}$.

E. $x > 2$ or $x < -2$.

32. What is the solution to the pair of equations

$$\begin{cases} x - 3y = 1 \\ 2x + y = 2 \end{cases}?$$

F. $x = 1$ and $y = 0$

J. $x = 0$ and $y = 1$

G. $x = 2$ and $y = 0$

K. $x = 0$ and $y = 2$

H. $x = 3$ and $y = 1$

33. If $\dfrac{1}{a} = \dfrac{1}{\frac{1}{b}}$ and $2 < a < 5$, then

A. $\dfrac{1}{2} > b > \dfrac{1}{5}$.

D. $\dfrac{-1}{5} > b > \dfrac{-1}{2}$.

B. $2 > b > \dfrac{1}{2}$.

E. $\dfrac{-1}{2} > b > -2$.

C. $5 > b > 2$.

34. The diagonal of a square has endpoints $(3, 8)$ and $(-1, 2)$. What is its area?

F. 10

J. 32

G. 13

K. 40

H. 26

35. Line A passes through point $P(-6, 5)$ and makes a 45° angle with the x-axis. The equation of a perpendicular line passing through point P is

A. $y = x - 11$.

D. $y = x - 3$.

B. $y = -x + 11$.

E. $y = -x - 11$.

C. $y = -x - 1$.

36. At what point do the lines $y = 7x$ and $3y = 4x + 7$ intersect?

F. $(7, 17)$

G. $(17, 56)$

H.   (0, 7)

J. $\left(\dfrac{7}{17}, \dfrac{49}{17}\right)$

K. $\left(\dfrac{7}{17}, \dfrac{1}{17}\right)$

37. If $y = 3x$ lies in Quadrants I and III, then $y = |3x|$ lies in Quadrants

A.   III and IV.

D.   I, II, and III.

B.   I and II.

E.   I only.

C.   I and III.

38. The coordinates of the vertices of a right triangle are (1, 3), (5, 3), and (1, 6). Find the slope of its hypotenuse.

F. $-\dfrac{3}{4}$

J. $-\dfrac{1}{4}$

G. $-\dfrac{5}{3}$

K. -2

H. $\dfrac{4}{3}$

39. If point P has coordinates (3, –6) and point Q has coordinates (15, 5), the coordinates of the midpoint of the line segment between the two points is

A. $\left(9, -\dfrac{1}{2}\right).$

D. $\left(-\dfrac{1}{2}, 1\right).$

B. $\left(18, \dfrac{1}{2}\right).$

E. $\left(15, -\dfrac{1}{2}\right).$

C.   (15, 3).

40. What is the distance between the line $y = 4x + 9$ and the point (10, 4)?

F. $\dfrac{8}{15}$

J. $\dfrac{85}{19}$

G.   8

K. $\dfrac{45}{\sqrt{17}}$

H. $\dfrac{52}{\sqrt{15}}$

41. In which quadrants does the solution of the system

$$\begin{cases} y < -x + 3 \\ y < x - 3 \end{cases}$$

lie?

A. III and IV.   D. I and II.

B. I, III, and IV.   E. II and III.

C. II and IV.

42. In the system

$$\begin{cases} ax + by = 20 \\ bx + ay = 16 \end{cases}$$

the solution is $x = 2$ and $y = 1$. What are the coefficients a and b?

F. $a = 2$
   $b = 1$
     J. $a = 7$
   $b = 14$

G. $a = 8$
   $b = 7$
     K. $a = 9$
   $b = 4$

H. $a = 8$
   $b = 4$

43. A circle whose center is at $C(-4, 1)$ passes through the point $D(-2, 2)$. Find the length of the radius.

A. $\sqrt{3}$ D. $\sqrt{10}$

B. $\sqrt{7}$ E. $\sqrt{13}$

C. $\sqrt{5}$

44.

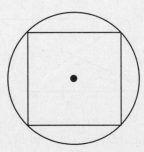

A square is inscribed in a circle. The area of the circle is π. What is the area of the square?

F. $\dfrac{\pi}{2}$ J. 2

G. $\dfrac{3\pi}{4}$ K. $\dfrac{\pi}{\sqrt{2}}$

H. $\sqrt{2}$

45.

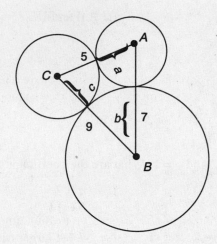

Circles A, B, and C are tangent to one another. Find the radius of circle A if $AB = 7$, $AC = 5$, and $BC = 9$.

A. 1   D. $\dfrac{11}{2}$

B. 2   E. $\dfrac{3}{2}$

C. $\dfrac{7}{2}$

46.

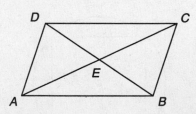

$ABCD$ is a parallelogram; $AE = 7x - 1$, and $EC = 5x + 5$. Find AC.

F.   40   J.   25

G.   20   K.   10

H.   30

47. A triangle has angles measuring x, y, and $x + y$. The triangle must be

A.   isosceles.   D.   equilateral.

B.   scalene.   E.   obtuse.

C.   right.

48. A square has diagonal of length r. A second square has twice the area of the first square. What is the perimeter of the second square?

F. r^2 J. $2r$

G. $r^2\sqrt{2}$ K. $4r$

H. $r\sqrt{2}$

49. Two triangles are similar. The larger one is four times larger in area than the smaller one. The length of the sides of the larger triangle are equal to the length of the sides of the smaller triangle multiplied by

A. $\sqrt{3}$.   D.   4.

B. $\sqrt{2}$.   E. $\sqrt{5}$.

C.   2.

50. In the accompanying figure of a circle centered about point O, the measure of arc $\overset{\frown}{AB}$ is $\dfrac{\pi}{5}$ radians. Find $\angle OBA$.

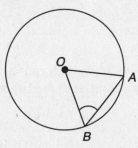

F.   36°   J.   72°

G.   144°   K.   17°

H.   90°

51. The ratio of the areas of two circles is 25:16. What number, when multiplied by the smaller diameter, will give the larger diameter?

A. $\dfrac{5}{4}$ D. $\dfrac{25}{4}$

B. $\dfrac{5}{2}$ E. 4

C. 5

52. The greatest area that a rectangle whose perimeter is 52 m can have is

F. 12 m².   J. 168 m².

G. 169 m².   K. 52 m².

H. 172 m².

53. The vertices of $\triangle ABC$ are $A(-3, 0)$, $B(3, 0)$, and $C(0, 2)$. The triangle ABC is therefore

A. equilateral.

B. isosceles.

C. scalene.

D. right angular.

E. Cannot be determined, due to insufficient information.

54.

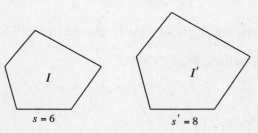

$s = 6$ $s' = 8$

Corresponding sides of two similar polygons are 6 and 8. If the perimeter of the smaller is 27, find the perimeter of the larger.

F. 29   J. 40

G. 36   K. None of the above.

H. 48

55.

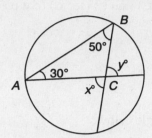

In the above figure, two chords of the circle intersect, making the angles shown. What is the value of $x + y$?

A. 40°   D. 160°

B. 50°   E. 320°

C. 80°

56. The set of points with the property that the distances from each point to two fixed points has constant difference is a

F. circle.   J. parabola.

G. ellipse.   K. pair of parallel lines.

H. hyperbola.

57. For the triangle below, determine sin 2α.

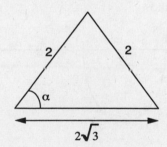

A. $\dfrac{1}{2}$ D. $\dfrac{-2}{\sqrt{2}}$

B. 0   E. $\dfrac{\sqrt{3}}{2}$

C. $\dfrac{\sqrt{2}}{2}$

58. The product $(\sin \alpha)(\cos \alpha)(\tan \alpha)(\sec \alpha)(\cot \alpha)$ is equivalent to

F. $\sin \alpha$.

G. $\tan \alpha$.

H. $\cot \alpha$.

J. $\cos \alpha$.

K. $\csc \alpha$.

59. Find the area of the triangle below.

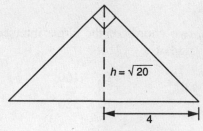

A. $2\sqrt{5}$

B. $20\sqrt{20}$

C. $2\sqrt{3}$

D. $9\sqrt{5}$

E. $10\sqrt{20}$

60. Which of the following is a sketch of $y = |\sin x|$?

F.

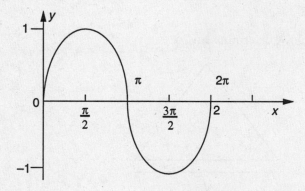

G.

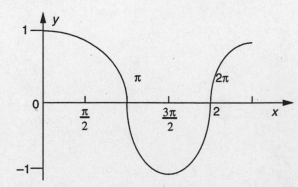

H.

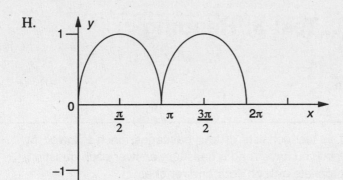

J.

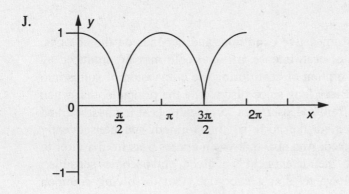

K.

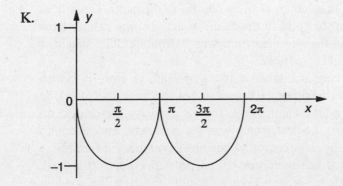

THIS IS THE END OF TEST 2.

Test 3: Reading

TIME: 35 Minutes
40 Questions

DIRECTIONS: This test consists of four passages, each followed by ten questions. Once you have read a passage, answer each question, and fill in the appropriate oval on your answer sheet.

Passage I

Cold is a negative condition, and depends on the absence, or privation, of heat. Intense artificial cold may be produced by the rapid absorption of heat during the conversion of solids into liquids. Dr. Black long since discovered the principle, that when
5   bodies pass from a denser to a rarer state, heat is absorbed and becomes latent in the body so transformed, and consequently cold is produced. And also that when bodies pass from a rarer to a denser state, their latent heat is evolved, and becomes sensible.

It is known to almost everyone, that dissolving common
10 salt in water, particularly if the salt is fine, will render the water so cold, even in summer, as to be painful to the hand. The salt, as it passes from the solid to the liquid state, absorbs caloric from the water, and thus the heat that was before sensible, becomes latent, and cold is produced.

15 On the contrary, when a piece of lead, or iron, is beaten smartly with a hammer, it becomes hot, because the metal, in consequence of the hammering, has its capacity for caloric reduced, and thus the heat which was before latent, now becomes sensible. For the same reason, when air is compressed forcibly in
20 a tube, or as it is sometimes called, in a *fire-pump*, the heat, which was before latent, becomes sensible, because the condensation lessens its capacity for caloric.

The principle on which all freezing mixtures act is therefore the change of state which one or more of the articles em-
25 ployed undergo, during the process, and this change consists in an enlarged capacity for caloric. The degree of cold will then depend on the quantity of caloric which passes from a free to a latent state, and this again will depend on the quantity of substance liquefied, and the rapidity of the liquefaction.

30 The substances most commonly employed for this purpose are those originally used by Fahrenheit, to produce the zero of his thermometric scale; viz. common salt and snow, or pounded

ice. For this purpose the salt should be fine, and the ice, which must always be used in summer, is to be reduced to small par-
35 ticles in a cold mortar.

The vessel to contain the substance to be frozen may be made of tin, and of the shape represented by the figure below. It is simply a tall vessel, holding a few pints, with a close cover, and a rim round the top, for the con-
40 venience of handling it. For common purposes, this may be set into any convenient wooden vessel (having first introduced the substance to be frozen) and then surrounded by the freezing mixture. The only care to be taken in this part of the process is
45 to see that the freezing mixture in the outside vessel reaches as high as the contents of the internal one. With two or three pounds of fine common salt, and double this weight of pounded ice, three or four pints of iced cream may be made in this
50 way, during the warmest days of summer. The process requires two or three hours, and while it is going on, the vessel should be set in a cellar, or covered with a flannel cloth, as a bad conductor of the external heat.

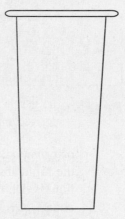

From J.L. Comstack, *Elements of Chemistry*.

1. After reading the above passage, the reader could correctly infer that dissolving sugar in hot tea will

    A. lower the temperature of the hot tea.

    B. cause the temperature of the tea to become even warmer just as beating a piece of lead with a hammer will raise its temperature.

    C. lower the temperature of hot tea so that if it were placed about cream in a tin container, the cream would freeze within two to three hours.

    D. reduce the temperature of the hot tea to such a low temperature as to be painful to the hand.

2. The drop in temperature which occurs when sugar is added to coffee is the result of

    I.   sugar passing from a solid to a liquid state.
    II. sugar absorbing caloric from the water.
    III. heat becoming latent when it was sensible.

    F. I only.   H. I, II, and III.

    G. I and II.   J. I and III.

3. Which is the best example of Dr. Black's discovery as outlined in the article?

    A. To gargle in warm salt water, one should start with water cooler than one desires and then add the salt.

    B. To gargle in warm salt water, one should start with salt and then pour water which is cooler than that desired over the salt.

    C. To gargle in warm salt water, one should adjust the temperature of the tap water to the temperature desired and then add fine salt; the fineness of the salt will prevent any change in the water temperature.

    D. To gargle in warm salt water, one should start with water warmer than desired and then add the salt.

4. The narrator seems to base this article on

    F. a sociological study.   H. scientific procedures.

    G. trial-and-error methods.   J. historical research.

5. The word "mortar" as used in this article can be best interpreted to mean

    A. that which can fix or hold together, as mortar holds bricks.

    B. a weapon, a piece of artillery, or a small cannon.

    C. a container used for grinding or mixing.

    D. a mixture; for example, the particles should be made smaller by combining with other ingredients in a mixture.

6. The writer does not make use of

    F. descriptions.   H. mathematics.

    G. interviews.   J. experiments.

7. In pumping up a basketball, one can infer from this article that the metal needle going into the ball

    A. will become warm.

    B. will not be affected by the process since metal is strong.

    C. will become cooler.

    D. will quickly reach a freezing temperature.

8. The writer can be best described as

    F. concerned with literary form and stylistic devices.

G. subjective in his writing.

H. objective.

J. presenting facts which are new to most scientists in the late twentieth century.

9. A positive condition depending on the absence of cold is

A. Fahrenheit.

B. intense artificial cold.

C. heat.

D. a rarer state, according to Black.

10. Black found that when bodies pass from a rarer to a denser state, their latent heat is evolved, and becomes sensible. "Sensible" can be interpreted to be

F. knowledgeable, making sense.

G. logical.

H. evolving.

J. perceptible.

Passage II

"Good evening to you, honored sir," said he, making a low bow, and still retaining his hold of the skirt. "I pray you tell me whereabouts is the dwelling of my kinsman, Major Molineux."

The youth's question was uttered very loudly; and one of
5   the barbers, whose razor was descending on a well-soaped chin, and another who was dressing a Ramillies wig, left their occupations, and came to the door. The citizen, in the meantime, turned a long-favored countenance upon Robin, and answered him in a tone of excessive anger and annoyance. His two sepulchral hems,
10   however, broke into the very centre of his rebuke, with most singular effect, like a thought of the cold grave obtruding among wrathful passions.

"Let go my garment, fellow! I tell you, I know not the man you speak of. What! I have authority, I have—hem, hem—au-
15   thority; and if this be the respect you show for your betters, your feet shall be brought acquainted with the stocks by daylight, to-morrow morning!"

Robin released the old man's skirt, and hastened away, pursued by an ill-mannered roar of laughter from the barber's shop.
20   He was at first considerably surprised by the result of his ques-

tion, but, being a shrewd youth, soon thought himself able to account for the mystery.

"This is some country representative," was his conclusion, "who has never seen the inside of my kinsman's door, and lacks
25 the breeding to answer a stranger civilly. The man is old, or verily—I might be tempted to turn back and smite him on the nose. Ah, Robin, Robin! even the barber's boys laugh at you for choosing such a guide! You will be wiser in time, friend Robin."

He now became entangled in a succession of crooked and
30 narrow streets, which crossed each other, and meandered at no great distance from the waterside. The smell of tar was obvious to his nostrils, the masts of vessels pierced the moonlight above the tops of the buildings, and the numerous signs, which Robin paused to read, informed him that he was near the centre of
35 business. But the streets were empty, the shops were closed, and lights were visible only in the second stories of a few dwelling-houses. At length, on the corner of a narrow lane, through which he was passing, he beheld the broad countenance of a British hero swinging before the door of an inn, whence proceeded the
40 voices of many guests. The casement of one of the lower windows was thrown back, and a very thin curtain permitted Robin to distinguish a party at supper, round a well-furnished table. The fragrance of the good cheer steamed forth into the outer air, and the youth could not fail to recollect that the last remnant of his
45 travelling stock of provision had yielded to his morning appetite, and that noon had found and left him dinnerless.

"Oh, that a parchment three-penny might give me a right to sit down at yonder table!" said Robin, with a sigh. "But the Major will make me welcome to the best of his victuals; so I will
50 even stop boldly in, and inquire my way to his dwelling."

He entered the tavern, and was guided by the murmur of voices and the fumes of tobacco in the public-room. It was a long and low apartment, with oaken walls, grown dark in the continual smoke, and a floor which was thickly sanded, but of no
55 immaculate purity. A number of persons—the larger part of whom appeared to be mariners, or in some way connected with the sea—occupied the wooden benches, or leather-bottomed chairs, conversing on various matters, and occasionally lending their attention to some topic of general interest. Three or four
60 little groups were draining as many bowls of punch, which the West India trade had long since made a familiar drink in the colony. Others, who had the appearance of men who lived by regular and laborious handicraft, preferred the insulated bliss of an unshared potation, and became more taciturn under its influ-
65 ence. Nearly all, in short, evinced a predilection for the Good

Creature in some of its various shapes, for this is a vice to which, as Fast Day sermons of a hundred years ago will testify, we have a long hereditary claim. The only guests to whom Robin's sympathies inclined him were two or three sheepish countrymen,

70 who were using the inn somewhat after the fashion of a Turkish caravansary; they had gotten themselves into the darkest corner of the room, and heedless of the Nicotian atmosphere, were supping on the bread of their own ovens, and the bacon cured in their own chimney-smoke. But though Robin felt a sort of broth-

75 erhood with these strangers, his eyes were attracted from them to a person who stood near the door, holding whispered conversation with a group of ill-dressed associates. His features were separately striking almost to grotesqueness, and the whole face left a deep impression on the memory. The forehead bulged out

80 into a double prominence, with a vale between; the nose came boldly forth in an irregular curve, and its bridge was of more than a finger's breadth; the eyebrows were deep and shaggy, and the eyes glowed beneath them like fire in a cave.

While Robin deliberated of whom to inquire respecting his

85 kinsman's dwelling, he was accosted by the innkeeper, a little man in a stained white apron, who had come to pay his professional welcome to the stranger. Being in the second generation from a French Protestant, he seemed to have inherited the courtesy of his parent nation; but no variety of circumstances was

90 ever known to change his voice from the one shrill note in which he now addressed Robin.

"From the country, I presume, sir?" said he, with a profound bow. "Beg leave to congratulate you on your arrival, and trust you intend a long stay with us. Fine town here, sir, beautiful

95 buildings, and much that may interest a stranger. May I hope for the honor of your commands in respect to supper?"

"The man sees a family likeness! the rogue has guessed that I am related to the Major!" thought Robin, who had hitherto experienced little superfluous civility.

100 All eyes were now turned on the country lad, standing at the door, in his worn three-cornered hat, gray coat, leather breeches, and blue yarn stockings, leaning on an oaken cudgel, and bearing a wallet on his back.

From *My Kinsman, Major Molineux* by Nathaniel Hawthorne.

11. Of all the people in the room, Robin would be most inclined to strike up a conversation with the

A. mariners.   C. countrymen.

B. day laborers.   D. persons standing near the door.

12. From all indications, which of the following is probably true of the men eating their home-cooked food?

    I.   They are from the countryside.
    II.   They are uncomfortable being in the tavern.
    III. They are resented by the rest of the men in the tavern.

    F.   I only.   H.   III only.

    G.   II only.   J.   I and II only.

13. Taken in context of the passage, the best interpretation of "Nearly all, in short, evinced a predilection for the Good Creature" (lines 65–66) is that nearly all the

    A.   mariners are celebrating a successful voyage to the West Indies.

    B.   people in the tavern are drinking an alcoholic beverage.

    C.   people in the tavern had been reformed by turning to religion.

    D.   men in the tavern were known for seeking out the enjoyable things in life.

14. To what does the author say "we have a long hereditary claim"?

    F.   Seafaring   H.   Smoking

    G.   Drinking   J.   Gossiping

15. The tone of the citizen who responded to Robin can best be described as

    A.   jovial and light-hearted.   C.   interested and helpful.

    B.   disdainful and aloof.   D.   passionate and gloomy.

16. The statements "your feet shall be brought acquainted with the stocks" can be interpreted as

    F.   first-hand contact with farm animals.

    G.   personal attention to investment.

    H.   punishment that could result from the youth's behavior.

    J.   a reference to a dance step familiar to the common people.

17. "As a result of drink, some of the tavern occupants became more taciturn;" this can be interpreted to mean that they were

    A.   unreticent.   C.   boisterous.

    B.   talkative.   D.   uncommunicative.

18. Compare and/or contrast the citizen at the barber shop and the innkeeper.

    F. The innkeeper and the citizen were courteous.

    G. The innkeeper and the citizen were inhospitable.

    H. The innkeeper was courteous; the citizen was inhospitable.

    J. The citizen was hospitable; the innkeeper was discourteous.

19. Which of the following quotations best indicates the reception Robin received?

    A. "...a predilection for the Good Creature..."

    B. "...after the fashion of a Turkish caravansary..."

    C. "...little superfluous civility..."

    D. "...insulated bliss of an unshared potation..."

20. Robin did not eat at the tavern because

    F. food was not served there.

    G. he expected to eat with the Major.

    H. the tavern keeper was inhospitable.

    J. no places were available.

Passage III

I have noticed in the course of my psychoanalytic work that
the state of mind of a man in contemplation is entirely different
from that of a man who is observing his psychic processes. In
contemplation there is a greater play of psychic action than in the
5   most attentive self-observation; this is also shown by the tense
attitude and wrinkled brow of contemplation, in contrast with the
restful features of self-observation. In both cases, there must be
concentration of attention, but, besides this, in contemplation one
exercises a critique, in consequence of which he rejects some of
10   the ideas which he has perceived, and cuts short others, so that
he does not follow the trains of thought which they would open;
toward still other thoughts he may act in such a manner that they
do not become conscious at all—that is to say, they are sup-
pressed before they are perceived. In self-observation, on the
15   other hand, one has only the task of suppressing the critique; if
he succeeds in this, an unlimited number of ideas, which otherwise would have been impossible for him to grasp, come to his

consciousness. With the aid of this material, newly secured for the purpose of self-observation, the interpretation of pathologi-
20 cal ideas, as well as of dream images, can be accomplished. As may be seen, the point is to bring about a psychic state to some extent analogous as regards the apportionment of psychic energy (transferable attention) to the state prior to falling asleep (and indeed also to the hypnotic state). In falling asleep, the
25 "undesired ideas" come into prominence on account of the slackening of a certain arbitrary (and certainly also critical) action, which we allow to exert an influence upon the trend of our ideas; we are accustomed to assign "fatigue" as the reason for this slackening; the emerging undesired ideas as the reason
30 are changed into visual and acoustic images. In the condition which is used for the analysis of dreams and pathological ideas, this activity is purposely and arbitrarily dispensed with, and the psychic energy thus saved, or a part of it, is used for the attentive following of the undesired thoughts now coming to the
35 surface, which retain their identity as ideas (this is the difference from the condition of falling asleep). "Undesired ideas" are thus changed into "desired" ones.

The suspension thus required of the critique for these apparently "freely rising" ideas, which is here demanded and which
40 is usually exercised on them, is not easy for some persons. The "undesired ideas" are in the habit of starting the most violent resistance, which seeks to prevent them from coming to the surface. But if we may credit our great poet-philosopher Friedrich Schiller, a very similar tolerance must be the condition of poetic
45 production. At a point in his correspondence with Koerner, for the noting of which we are indebted to Mr. Otto Rank, Schiller answers a friend who complains of his lack of creativeness in the following words: "The reason for your complaint lies, it seems to me, in the constraint which your intelligence imposes upon your
50 imagination. I must here make an observation and illustrate it by an allegory. It does not seem beneficial, and it is harmful for the creative work of the mind, if the intelligence inspects too closely the ideas already pouring in, as it were, at the gates. Regarded by itself, an idea may be very trifling and very adventurous, but it
55 perhaps becomes important on account of one which follows it; perhaps in a certain connection with others, which may seem equally absurd, it is capable of forming a very useful construction. The intelligence cannot judge all these things if it does not hold them steadily long enough to see them in connection with
60 the others. In the case of a creative mind, however, the intelligence has withdrawn its watchers from the gates, the ideas rush in pell-mell, and it is only then that the great heap is looked over

65 and critically examined. Messrs. Critics, or whatever else you may call yourselves, you are ashamed or afraid of the momentary and transitory madness which is found in all creators, and whose longer or shorter duration distinguishes the thinking artist from the dreamer. Hence your complaints about barrenness, for you reject too soon and discriminate too severely" (Letter of December 1, 1788).

70 And yet, "such a withdrawal of the watchers from the gates of intelligence," as Schiller calls it, such a shifting into the condition of uncritical self-observation, is in no way difficult.

Most of my patients accomplish it after the first instructions; I myself can do it very perfectly, if I assist the operation by 75 writing down my notions. The amount, in terms of psychic energy, by which the critical activity is in this manner reduced, and by which the intensity of the self-observation may be increased, varies widely according to the subject matter upon which the attention is to be fixed.

From Sigmund Freud, *The Interpretation of Dreams*, trans. A. A. Brill.

21. Which are characteristics of contemplation, according to the author of this article?

I. A greater play of psychic action than in the most attentive self-observation.
II. A tense attitude, a wrinkled brow, and a concentration of attention.
III. A suppression of some thoughts before they are perceived.
IV. A critique in which one rejects some of the ideas and cuts short others.

A. I only.   C. I, II, and III only.

B. I and II only.   D. I, II, III, and IV.

22. Which are characteristics of self-observation?

I. Restful features and a suppressing of the criticism.
II. Less play of psychic action and a concentration of attention.
III. An interpretation of pathological ideas and dream images.

F. I only.   H. I, II, and III.

G. I and II only.   J. I and III only.

23. In sleep

A. no psychic energy is available for the attentive following of undesired thoughts.

B. fatigue causes the slackening of a certain arbitrary and often critical action, according to most people's way of thinking.

C. undesired and desired ideas are not modified.

D. the watchers of the gates of intelligence have not withdrawn.

24. The writer states that shifting into the condition of uncritical self-observation

F. is impossible.

G. can be done perfectly by the writer's patients.

H. is difficult in many ways.

J. is a feat the writer of the article maintains he can do perfectly.

25. The lack of creativeness lies in the constraints imposed upon the imagination by the intelligence, according to

A. Freud.   C. Schiller.

B. Rank.   D. Koerner.

26. A trifling and very adventurous idea

F. is usually important in itself.

G. should be considered in isolation.

H. should not be held long in the mind to make room for other ideas.

J. may become important because of an idea which follows.

27. Uncritical self-observation

A. is difficult to perform since we are all biased toward ourselves.

B. should not be encouraged if creative thinking is to result.

C. is inherent, not learned.

D. requires one to be unashamed or unafraid of the momentary and transitory madness.

28. In a creative mind

F. each idea is examined critically and individually as it is received.

G. ideas enter in a systematic manner.

H. a heap of ideas are examined critically at one time.

J. rejection comes soon and discrimination must be severe at all times.

29. According to Schiller

    A. the tolerance of undesired ideas must be eliminated.

    B. freely rising ideas must be critically examined.

    C. the suspension of freely rising ideas is necessary.

    D. a tolerance for undesired ideas is a necessary condition.

30. The author notes that psychic energy, by which the critical activity is reduced and by which the intensity of the self-observation may be increased, varies according to

    F. the time of day at which the activity occurs.

    G. the subject matter upon which the attention is fixed.

    H. whether the intelligence has withdrawn its watchers from the gate.

    J. whether the idea is trifling or constructive.

Passage IV

Vaulting played a great part—perhaps the greatest, though certainly not the only part in developing Gothic architecture; but it will not do to define it as simply the expression of scientific vaulting. The Roman were masters of the art of vaulting
5 long before; they used—probably invented—the cross-vault, and understood the concentration of thrusts on isolated points. It was from them, and from the Eastern Rome as well, that the Romanesque builders learned how to make their stone roofs, and they in their turn passed the art on to their Gothic succes-
10 sors, who improved and developed it in their own way, making in the end almost a new art of it. But it must be remembered that most of the problems of scientific vaulting had presented themselves before their time, and had been partially at all events solved by their predecessors, though not so completely.
15 Nor is it correct to regard vaulting as an essential feature of the style, however great its influence may have been on the structure of great churches. In England except on a grand scale it is exceptional; and yet if Westminster Hall with its stupendous timber covering, and the Fen churches with their glorious
20 wooden roofs, and the splendid ceiling of the nave at St David's are not Gothic what are they? And what else can we call the countless village churches, gems of modest art, that stud our country far and wide, and constitute one of its greatest charms, though it is only here and there that they aspire to the dignity of a
25 vaulted ceiling?

Again if the test of Gothic is to be the logical expression of a vaulted construction what becomes of domestic architecture both here and abroad, in which vaulting certainly does not play an important part? Are the townhalls of Brussels, Ypres, and 30 Louvain not Gothic, nor the Broletto of Como, the pontifical palace at Viterbo, or that of the popes at Avignon, or the ducal palace at Venice?

Still less is Gothic architecture, as it has appeared to the ordinary layman, a matter of quatrefoils and trefoils, of cusps 35 and traceries, of crockets and finials, pinnacles and flying buttresses. These are but the accidents of the style, though no doubt they resulted naturally from the application of certain principles behind them. But they might all fly away and yet leave a Gothic building behind them. Many an old tithe barn of rough timber 40 framework is as truly a piece of Gothic architecture as York Minster or Salisbury Cathedral.

If then none of these attempted definitions are really coextensive with the Gothic style of architecture, for a building may be Gothic and yet have none of these characteristics, how are we 45 to define it?

The true way of looking at Gothic art is to regard it not as a definite style bound by certain formulas—for it is infinitely various—but rather as the expression of a certain temper, sentiment, and spirit which inspired the whole method of doing things dur- 50 ing the Middle Ages in sculpture and painting as well as in architecture. It cannot be defined by any of its outward features, for they are variable, differing at times and in different places. They are the outward expression of certain cardinal principles behind them, and though these principles are common to all 55 good styles—Gothic among them—the result of applying them to the buildings of each age, country, and people will vary as the circumstances of that country, that age, and that people vary.

From Sir Thomas Graham Jackson, *Gothic Architecture in France, England & Italy.*

31. Which statement is most accurate?

A. The Gothic forms were predecessors to the Romanesque builders.

B. The Romanesque builders were successors to the Gothic builders.

C. The Romanesque builders had partially solved many of the problems of scientific vaulting before their Gothic successors.

D. In developing Gothic architecture, vaulting played only a minor role.

32. The author believes that

    F. vaulting is an essential feature of Gothic architecture.

    G. Gothic architecture had no influence in churches, because, "…it is only here and there that they [the village churches] aspire to the dignity of a vaulted ceiling."

    H. Gothic architecture might still exist even without quatrefoils, trefoils, cusps, traceries, pinnacles, flying buttresses, and finials.

    J. Gothic architecture is a definite style bound by certain formulas.

33. Gothic art

    I.   is to be regarded as a definite style bound by certain formulas.
    II. is the expression of a certain temper, sentiment, and spirit which inspired sculpture and painting.
    III. cannot be defined by any of its outward features since they are variable.

    A. I only.   C. II and III only.

    B. I and II.   D. I, II, and III.

34. The writer believes that Gothic art

    F. is a thing of the past.

    G. will be applied to buildings of each age and country exactly as in the past.

    H. will be applied with some variation to buildings of each age and country.

    J. does not follow the principles common to all good styles.

35. The central purpose of the article is to

    A. define Gothic architecture.

    B. give the characteristics of Gothic architecture.

    C. present "the true way of looking at Gothic."

    D. disparage Gothic architecture.

36. "Vaulting" in this article refers to

    F. a way of leaping high, as in popularity.

    G. a way of styling similar to that of vaults, or places where bodies are interred.

H. a way of producing high ceilings without visible support.

J. a way of drawing and producing plans on paper.

37. A "pontifical palace" may be best interpreted as

   A. a place of happiness and merriment.

   B. a place of rest and relaxation.

   C. a place which seems friendly.

   D. a place which seems dignified.

38. Quatrefoils, according to the article, are

   F. not accidents of style.

   G. not results of applications of principles.

   H. essential to Gothic buildings.

   J. results of the natural application of certain principles.

39. The author regards Gothic art as

   A. a definite style bound by certain formulas.

   B. having styles which are similar in all expressions.

   C. the expression of infinitely various temper, sentiment, and spirit.

   D. defined by outward features.

40. The author says Gothic art is NOT

   F. a whole method of doing things during the Middle Ages.

   G. an influence on architecture, painting, and sculpture.

   H. defined by its features.

   J. an outward expression of certain cardinal principles.

THIS IS THE END OF TEST 3.

Test 4: Science Reasoning

TIME: 35 Minutes
40 Questions

> **DIRECTIONS:** This test consists of seven passages, each followed by several questions. Once you have read a passage, answer each question. Then fill in the appropriate oval on your answer sheet.

Passage I

The study of oxygenated hydrocarbons has been of great interest for many years. As an analytical chemist, you must take several different types of measurements and combine the results to get a factual picture of what is really occurring. You perform several experiments to determine the chemical and physical properties of these compounds.

Experiment 1

A 5.00 g sample of an unknown compound, containing only carbon, hydrogen, and oxygen, is burned completely in oxygen yielding 9.55 g CO_2 and 5.86 g water. You determine that the empirical formula of the compound is C_2H_6O. The molecular formula may be an integer multiple of the empirical formula.

Experiment 2

A 5.00 g sample of the same unknown compound is dissolved in 100 g of water. The measured freezing point is depressed by 2.02°C. Also, the temperature of the solution was recorded as the sample was dissolved. The temperature was found to increase by 5.27°C.

Experiment 3

Carbon (graphite) is reacted with $H_{2(g)}$ and $O_{2(g)}$ to yield the standard enthalpy of formation (ΔH_f) of the unknown compound. The measured $\Delta H°_f = -278$ kJ/mol and the standard entropy of formation ($\Delta S°_f$) = −346 J/(K mol).

All of the reactants (carbon as graphite, hydrogen gas, and oxygen gas) are placed into a bomb calorimeter which has a heat capacity of 6.11×10^4 J/C. The initial temperature of the calorimeter is set at 25.00°C. After the reaction, the temperature is 29.55°C.

From this data, you calculated the standard Gibbs Free Energy of Formation ($\Delta G°_f$) from the relationship:

$$\Delta G°_f = \Delta H°_f - T\Delta S°_f$$

You found it to be −175 kJ/mol at 25°C. If the Gibbs Free Energy of a reaction is greater than zero, the reaction will not proceed spontaneously forward. If the $\Delta G°_f$ is less than zero, the reaction will proceed spontaneously, and if it is equal to zero, the system is at equilibrium.

1. Based on the results of Experiment 2, if the freezing point of water is 0.00°C, what was the freezing point of the solution?

   A. 2.02°C

   B. −2.02°C

   C. ±2.02°C

   D. 0.00°C

2. What must the relationship of ΔH_f and $T\Delta S_f$ be in order for a reaction to be in equilibrium?

   F. $\Delta H_f > T\Delta S_f$

   G. $\Delta H_f < T\Delta S_f$

   H. $\Delta H_f = T\Delta S_f$

   J. $\Delta H_f + T\Delta S_f = 0$

3. A chemist determined experimentally the molecular formula for the oxygenated hydrocarbon. Which formula would most likely represent this compound?

   A. $C_3H_7O_2$

   B. $CH_3O_{1.5}$

   C. $C_4H_{12}O$

   D. $C_6H_{18}O_3$

4. What information concerning the reactants in Experiment 3, which could affect the results, is assumed?

   F. The temperature of the reactants is the same as the calorimeter.

   G. The amounts of the reactants are in a specific ratio.

   H. The reactants are all gases.

   J. The reactants have the same heat capacities as the calorimeter.

5. Which of the following property(ies) of an oxygenated hydrocarbon would be most useful for its identification?

   A. Its molecular formula

   B. Its empirical formula

   C. Its freezing point in water

   D. Its enthalpy of formation and Gibbs Free Energy of formation

6. Which diagram shown would be the most efficient design of the calorimeter used in Experiment 3?

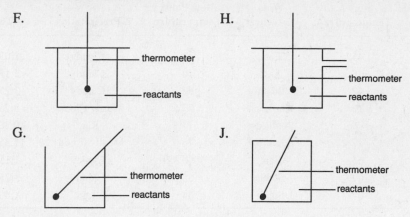

F.

H.

G.

J.

Passage II

A front is a transition zone between two different air masses. These air masses have distinguishing characteristics. Temperature, humidity, and wind direction are all properties that differ between the air masses. Depending on the type of frontal passage, several events may occur: the temperature will rise or fall, the barometric pressure (millibar, mb) will change, precipitation may occur, the wind direction will change, and the humidity will rise or fall.

Experiment 1

A warm front (Figure 1) is a specific front where warm air replaces cool air. It is associated with a low pressure system and usually moves from a southerly direction to the north. A warm front passage can be depicted by an increase in temperature and humidity (higher dew point temperatures), a decrease in the air pressure, a wind change to a southerly direction, and the likelihood of precipitation. A series of weather observations were taken for Boston, Atlanta, and Trenton (Table 1 on the following page).

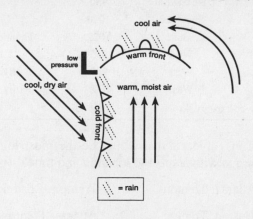

Figure 1

Table 1

Location	Temperature	Wind Direction	Dew Point Temperature	Precipitation	Time
Boston	45	East	40	Cloudy	1:05 pm
Boston	45	East	40	Cloudy	2:15 pm
Boston	62	South	62	Cloudy	3:25 pm
Atlanta	72	Northeast	72	Mostly Cloudy	8:25 am
Atlanta	78	Southeast	77	Rain	10:30 am
Atlanta	77	Southeast	76	Mostly Cloudy	11:35 am
Trenton	65	East	50	Cloudy	1:15 pm
Trenton	67	South	64	Cloudy	1:25 pm
Trenton	67	South	64	Rain	1:30 pm

Experiment 2

A cold front (Figure 1) is another specific front which is also associated with a low pressure system. During a cold front, cold air replaces warm air. A cold front usually moves from a northerly direction southward. A cold front can be depicted by rapidly falling temperatures and barometric pressure, a wind shift to the north or west, and a moderate chance of precipitation. The barometric pressure, after falling, usually rises very sharply after the passage of a cold front. Table 2 contains a series of weather observations for Columbus, Houston, and Mobile.

Table 2

Location	Temperature	Wind Direction	Barometric Pressure	Precipitation	Time
Columbus	80	South	1010	Cloudy	3:05 pm
Columbus	80	South	1000	Cloudy	3:30 pm
Columbus	63	Northwest	950	Clear	3:35 pm
Houston	94	Southeast	1020	Clear	5:00 pm
Houston	93	South	1022	Thunderstorms	5:15 pm
Houston	78	West	955	Clear	5:30 pm
Mobile	85	West	988	Partly Cloudy	8:10 pm
Mobile	84	West	1005	Partly Cloudy	8:25 pm
Mobile	83	West	1010	Clear	8:40 pm

7. Using the data in Table 1, what would be the most logical sequence of a warm front passage with respect to location and time?

A. Boston, Atlanta, Trenton

B. Atlanta, Boston, Trenton

C. Trenton, Boston, Atlanta

D. Atlanta, Trenton, Boston

8. What types of weather observations would be most accurate in determining when a warm front passage occurred?

    F. Temperature, wind direction, and precipitation

    G. Wind direction, dew point temperature, and precipitation

    H. Precipitation, dew point, and wind direction

    J. Temperature, wind direction, and dew point

9. What would be the most likely times of a cold front passage at Columbus and Houston?

    A. 3:35 pm and 5:30 pm   C. 3:35 pm and 5:00 pm

    B. 3:05 pm and 5:00 pm   D. 3:30 pm and 5:15 pm

10. What would be the most accurate meteorological description about what occurred in Mobile?

    F. There was no passage of a cold front.

    G. There was a passage of a cold front, but it occurred before the earliest observation was made.

    H. A warm frontal passage occurred.

    J. A cold front passage occurred followed by a warm front passage.

11. If a meteorologist received the computer data in the following table, what would be the best temperature forecast for Sunday afternoon?

Table 3

Time	Wind Direction	Barometric Pressure	Precipitation
Saturday Night	Southwest	1005	Cloudy
Sunday Morning	Northwest	974	Showers
Sunday Afternoon	Northwest	1020	Clearing

    A. Much warmer   C. Colder

    B. Colder, then warmer later   D. No temperature change

12. Based on the information in this passage, what would be the best explanation why the temperatures fall during the passage of a cold front?

F.   Clouds will form over the area, decreasing the amount of solar radiation reaching the surface.

G.   A warm air mass is moving into the area, displacing the cold air.

H.   A cold air mass is moving into the area, displacing the warm air.

J.   Low pressure is moving in the area, cooling the temperatures.

Passage III

Cell membranes function in the regulation of materials passing into and out of the cell. They consist of a lipid bilayer containing associated integral and peripheral proteins. Lipid-soluble substances can pass through the membrane by dissolving in the membrane lipids. Although the inner portion of the lipid bilayer is hydrophobic, water and water-soluble materials are able to cross the membrane and enter the cell. One mechanism by which such hydrophilic substances cross the membrane is through aqueous pores within the membrane. For a given group of homologous compounds, rates of membrane penetration are inversely related to molecular size, suggesting that the size of a pore must be at least as large as the molecule passing through it.

Table 1

Permeant	ΔH (kcal/mole)	Number of Hydrogen Bonds
Glycerol	24	6
Ethylene glycol	18.5	4
Diethylene glycol	18.5	4
Triethylene glycol	20.5	4
1,2, - Propandiol	19.5	4
1,3, - Propandiol	19	4
Propanol	4.5	2
Thiourea	13.5	4

Movement of molecules across cell membranes occurring in response to a concentration gradient is termed "passive transport" and implies that the membrane does not expend any energy. "Passive transport" is misleading. A molecule with high lipid solubility easily enters a cell membrane from the aqueous extracellular space. However, transport of the molecule from the membrane into the aqueous cytoplasm is more difficult because the cohesive bonds formed between the lipid molecules of the membrane must be broken before the molecule can leave the membrane. The passage of lipophilic molecules from one aqueous phase into the lipid phase and then from the lipid phase into the second aqueous phase occurs only if the molecules have appropriate energy of activation to overcome the lipid barrier.

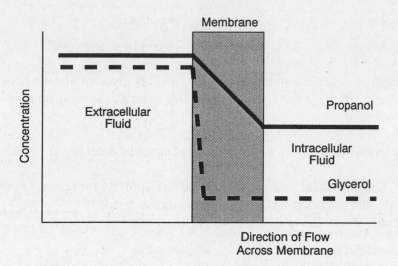

Figure 1

13. From the data given in Table 1, the energy of activation (ΔH) of the substances

    A. increases as the number of hydrogen bonds increases.

    B. decreases as the number of hydrogen bonds increases.

    C. is independent of the number hydrogen bonds.

    D. cannot be determined from these data.

14. Refer to Figure 1, which illustrates the concentration of substances on either side of a lipid membrane separating two aqueous compartments. which of the following statements explains why propanol has a higher concentration than glycerol across the cell membrane?

    F. Propanol is lipid-insoluble and crosses the membrane via aqueous channels.

    G. Glycerol is lipid-soluble and remains solubilized within the membrane rather than entering the aqueous phase.

    H. Choices F and G are both true.

    J. Neither choice F nor choice G is true.

15. Refer to Table 1 and Figure 1. Assume that the concentrations of propanol and 1,3-propanediol are equal in the left compartment. Compared to propanol, the concentration of 1,3-propanediol in the right compartment would be

A. higher. C. the same.

B. lower. D. cannot be determined.

16. Compared to water-soluble substances, such as glycerol and ethylene glycol, penetration of ethers, ketones, and aldehydes across lipid membranes

F. is faster. H. is at the same rate.

G. is slower. J. Cannot be determined.

17. For lipophilic substances which cross lipid membranes passively, the amount of energy needed to break cohesive bonds is _____ that of hydrophilic substances.

A. greater than C. equal to

B. less than D. Cannot be determined.

Passage IV

In a study of the conditions for static equilibrium in a body acted upon by concurrent forces, a physicist suspended a 100 kg ball using two ropes, as shown in the following figure.

$(\sin 30° = 0.500; \cos 30° = 0.866)$

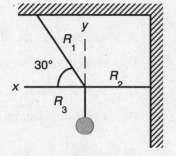

The physicist was able to calculate the various forces acting on the ball. These values were then determined experimentally using spring balances inserted along the ropes.

Figure 1

The weight of the ball was varied and the forces were recalculated and reported in Table 1. Later another rope was added R_3 and the forces were recalculated.

Table 1—Forces on Rope Supports

Mass	R_1	R_2	R_3
100 kg	200 N	177.2 N	—
50	100	86.7	—
200	400	354.4	—
100	200	100	77.2 N
50	100	0	86.7
200	400	100	254.4

18. Which of the following statements was assumed in the designing of the experiment?

    F. Concurrent forces do not depend on their respective angles.

    G. Concurrent forces are constant.

    H. Concurrent forces are in motion.

    J. Forces due to the spring balances are negligible.

19. In the first three trials, the reason that R_1 carries a greater force than R_2 is

    A. R_1 is at a greater angle to the ball than R_2.

    B. R_1 is at a lesser angle to the ball than R_2.

    C. R_1 is a stronger rope than R_2.

    D. the force of R_1 is the result of two vectors.

20. According to the data provided, the forces on the rope supports are proportional to the

    F. angle of the ropes to the ball.

    G. shape of the ball.

    H. mass of the ball.

    J. spring balances.

21. According to the data in Table 1, if the mass of the ball is held constant and the number of ropes varies from two to three, the forces on the ropes are dependent on

    A. the number of ropes attached to the ball.

    B. the distance of the ball from the ropes.

    C. the angle of the ropes to the ball.

    D. the lengths of the ropes attached to the ball.

22. From the data presented, it can be concluded that

    F. concurrent forces are dependent on the distance of the ball from the rope.

    G. concurrent forces are negligible.

    H. concurrent forces are distributive.

    J. concurrent forces are in static equilibrium.

Passage V

Geologists use many different tests to identify minerals. The most obvious is the color of the mineral itself. Some minerals have unique coloring, but many have similar coloration.

Two of the easiest tests to perform are the hardness test and the streak test. The hardness test uses common items or a known mineral to compare the hardness of minerals. Each mineral is scratched by a known item or another mineral to determine the hardness of the mineral.

The streak test determines the color of the powder of a mineral. It is determined by striking the mineral across an unglazed white porcelain tile. This gives the geologist an idea of the true color of the mineral in the rock.

A geologist found two dark-colored minerals. In order to identify them, he performed a series of experiments. The results of the hardness test and streak test are given below.

Experiment 1

Mineral A scratched the glass plate. The steel file did not scratch Mineral A.

Mineral B was scratched by the steel file. It scratched the glass plate. Mineral B was scratched by Mineral A.

Hardness Scale

Fingernail	2.5
Copper penny	3.0
Window glass	5.5
Steel file	6.5

Experiment 2

Mineral A had no streak produced when scraped across the porcelain tile.

Mineral B had a reddish-brown streak produced on the porcelain tile.

Dark Minerals Streak Chart

Hornblende	Green-gray
Labradorite	No streak
Hematite	Red-brown
Magnetite	Black
Flint	No streak
Black mica	No streak

23. Mineral A is probably

    A. labradorite.

    B. magnetite.

    C. flint.

    D. Not able to be determined by the information.

24. Mineral B is probably

    F. hornblende.   H. labradorite.

    G. hematite.   J. magnetite.

25. Mineral A probably has a hardness of

    A. 4.   C. 6.

    B. 5.   D. 7.

26. The best method of identifying minerals is

    F. to use the color of the mineral.

    G. to use only the hardness test and the scratch test.

    H. to use an identification book to look up the mineral and compare it to the pictures.

    J. to use a combination of many tests.

27. A streak test is performed on a third mineral. It has a black streak. The mineral is probably

    A. hornblende.   C. black mica.

    B. magnetite.   D. not on the chart.

28. Mineral C is compared to minerals A and B. It was scratched by both A and B, but not by the copper penny. The mineral probably has a hardness

    F. of 4.0.   H. greater than 6.5.

    G. of 5.5.   J. between 3.0 and 6.0.

Passage VI

An eclipsing binary consists of two stars in orbit around one another, thus causing a variation in the total apparent brightness, or magnitude of the system. By definition, apparent brightness is the perceived brightness of a celestial object at any given distance from Earth. However, objects at the arbitrary reference distance of ten parsecs (32.6 light years) are also said to shine with an absolute brightness.

It is important to note that lower numerical values for brightness correspond to brighter objects (i.e., the lower the brightness number, the brighter the star).

Table 1—Apparent and Absolute Brightness of Stars

Star	Apparent Brightness	Absolute Brightness	Distance in Parsecs
(A) Alpha	+10	+13	3
(B) Beta	+ 3	+ 3	10
(C) Gamma	+ 1	− 1	100
(D) Delta	+ 2	0	250

The brightness fluctuations in eclipsing binary systems are not caused by changes in distance but by the temporary blockage of one star's light. These fluctuations in apparent brightness can only be observed when an observer's line of sight is aligned with the orbital plane of an eclipsing binary system. That is, the orbit of the two stars must be observed edge-on and not face-on. The brighter star of an eclipsing binary is called the primary and the fainter one is called the secondary. A graph showing the change in apparent brightness as a function of time is called a light curve.

Observation 1

Light from an eclipsing binary system is seen to diminish twice during a complete cycle; and two points of unequal minimal brightness are observed. When the brighter star passes behind the fainter one, light from the brighter one is blocked and primary minimum is said to have occurred. This represents the greatest decrease in total brightness. When the brighter star passes in front of the fainter one, light from the fainter is blocked and secondary minimum has occurred. The maximum apparent brightness of an eclipsing binary system is shown by the top horizontal portions of its light curve.

Light Curve

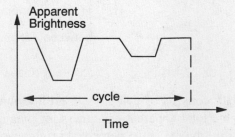

Figure 1

Table 2 below lists a few examples of eclipsing binaries. (Note: pc = parsecs, AU = astronomical units, M. = mass of the sun.)

Table 2—Eclipsing Binaries

Eclipsing Binaries	Primary		Secondary	
	Distance (pc)	Mass (M.)	Separation from primary (in AU)	Mass (M.)
Coronae Borealis	22	2.5	0.19	0.9
Algol (β Persei)	27	3.7	0.73	0.8
β Aurigae	27	2.4	0.08	2.3
ε Aurigae	1350	15	35	14

Observation 2

An astronomer makes the following observations on an eclipsing system. She determines that one star moves in a circular orbit at 100 km/s, and the time it takes to pass behind the other star (eclipse duration) is 3 hours, or 10,800 seconds. She then reports the diameter of the larger and obscuring star to be approximately one million kilometers (100 km/s × 10,800 s = 1,800,000 km). This is an example of one method for determining a star's diameter.

Eclipsing Binary System

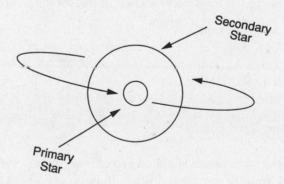

Figure 2

29. Apparent brightness cannot be determined at a distance of

    A.   10 parsecs.   C.   farther than 10 parsecs.

    B.   closer than 10 parsecs.   D.   Distance doesn't matter.

30. In Table 1, the star with the greatest apparent magnitude and the star with the greatest absolute magnitude are, respectively,

    F. A and A.   H. B and A.

    G. C and C.   J. C and D.

31. Which of the following statements is supported by the data in Table 2?

    A. Algol is the closest eclipsing binary system to Earth.

    B. Algol is the largest star of any eclipsing binary system known.

    C. The secondary member of an eclipsing binary must always have a mass larger than that of the sun.

    D. The primary star of an eclipsing binary system has a mass larger than that of the secondary star.

32. According to the light curve shown here, maximum apparent brightness is at

    F. Point 1.

    G. Point 2.

    H. Point 4.

    J. Both G and H.

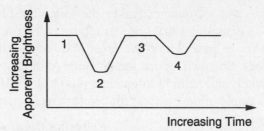

33. Which point along the light curve shown in question 32 corresponds to the configuration seen in the figure here?

    A. Point 1

    B. Point 2

    C. Point 4

    D. Both Point 2 and Point 4.

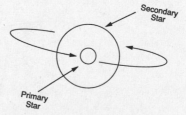

34. An astronomer makes observations of an eclipsing binary system and determines that the smaller star takes 4 hours to pass behind the larger one, and that it moves in a circular orbit at 150 km/s. The diameter of the larger star must be approximately

    F. 2 million kilometers.   H. 1 million kilometers.

    G. 0.5 million kilometers.   J. 4 million kilometers.

35. A star has an absolute magnitude of 0. At a distance of 32.6 light years, its apparent magnitude will appear

    A. brighter.

    B. dimmer.

    C. to remain the same.

    D. Answer cannot be determined due to insufficient data.

Passage VII

To study the immune response of mice, their immune systems must first be eliminated without killing them. This is often accomplished by irradiation. Figure 1 shows the percent of survival of mice after varying the radiation dose.

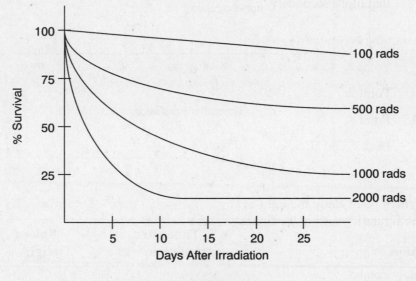

Figure 1

Mice, 11 weeks of age, were given 800 rads of X-irradiation. Half of the mice were then inoculated with 2×10^6 fetal liver cells from a $12\frac{1}{2}$- to $13\frac{1}{2}$-day gestation mouse embryo. This was given within a few hours after irradiation. The graph below shows the number of B cells found in the spleen at various times after irradiation. The remaining mice received no further treatment after irradiation. The number of B cells found in their spleen is also shown on the graph. The total spleen weight is shown in Table 1.

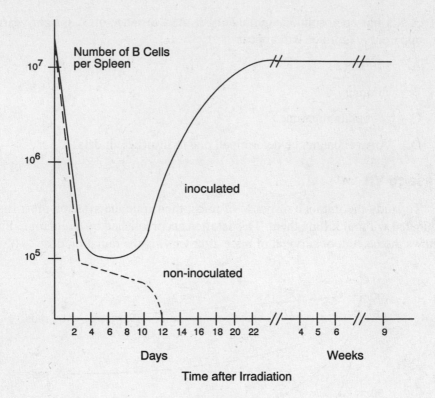

Figure 2

Table 1

Condition	Time after irradiation, wks	Spleen weight, g
Irradiated, Inoculated	1	12
	2	13
	3	29
Irradiated, Non-inoculated	1	12
	2	8
	3	10
Non-irradiated	1	18
	2	20
	3	21

36. For the experiment, 800 rads was the dose chosen. Which of the following statements was NOT helpful in making that choice?

    F.   It could be expected that about 50 percent of the mice would be alive for three weeks after irradiation at 800 rads.

    G.   800 rads was roughly in the middle of the doses tested.

    H.   100 rads did very little harm.

    J.   2,000 rads quickly killed most of the mice.

37. B cells play an important role in immunity. In the experiment, irradiation of mice with 800 rads resulted in

    A.   massive destruction of B cells within two weeks.

    B.   disappearance of antibodies within two weeks.

    C.   death of the mice within two weeks.

    D.   All of the above.

38. According to the results shown in Figure 2, after three weeks the irradiated mice inoculated with liver cells

    F.   had normal spleens.

    G.   had a normal number of B cells.

    H.   had normal livers.

    J.   None of the above.

39. The liver cells used in the experiment were taken from fetal mice. From your general understanding of biology, what might be the reason?

    A.   Mice multiply rapidly, so there is a large supply of fetal livers.

    B.   Fetal liver cells are not fully differentiated.

    C.   Liver cells contain iron, which helps counter the effects of irradiation.

    D.   None of the above.

40. Which data were helpful in determining that 800 rads affected the immune systems of the mice?

    F.   The data in Figure 1   H.   Choices F and G are both correct.

    G.   The data in Table 1   J.   Neither choice F nor choice G is correct.

THIS IS THE END OF TEST 4.

ACT ASSESSMENT
EXAM I

ANSWER KEY

Test 1: English

1.	(D)	20.	(F)	39.	(D)	58.	(J)
2.	(G)	21.	(B)	40.	(F)	59.	(D)
3.	(A)	22.	(J)	41.	(D)	60.	(G)
4.	(G)	23.	(D)	42.	(J)	61.	(C)
5.	(B)	24.	(J)	43.	(B)	62.	(H)
6.	(F)	25.	(B)	44.	(F)	63.	(B)
7.	(D)	26.	(J)	45.	(C)	64.	(H)
8.	(G)	27.	(C)	46.	(H)	65.	(C)
9.	(D)	28.	(J)	47.	(C)	66.	(G)
10.	(J)	29.	(A)	48.	(G)	67.	(A)
11.	(B)	30.	(G)	49.	(B)	68.	(F)
12.	(H)	31.	(C)	50.	(G)	69.	(C)
13.	(B)	32.	(J)	51.	(D)	70.	(G)
14.	(F)	33.	(B)	52.	(H)	71.	(D)
15.	(B)	34.	(J)	53.	(B)	72.	(H)
16.	(H)	35.	(C)	54.	(J)	73.	(C)
17.	(C)	36.	(J)	55.	(A)	74.	(J)
18.	(H)	37.	(D)	56.	(F)	75.	(C)
19.	(B)	38.	(G)	57.	(B)		

Test 2: Mathematics

1.	(B)	5.	(E)	9.	(C)	13.	(D)
2.	(K)	6.	(G)	10.	(F)	14.	(J)
3.	(E)	7.	(D)	11.	(E)	15.	(C)
4.	(G)	8.	(K)	12.	(F)	16.	(H)

17.	(A)	28.	(J)	39.	(A)	50.	(J)
18.	(J)	29.	(D)	40.	(K)	51.	(A)
19.	(E)	30.	(J)	41.	(A)	52.	(G)
20.	(F)	31.	(D)	42.	(H)	53.	(B)
21.	(C)	32.	(F)	43.	(C)	54.	(G)
22.	(H)	33.	(A)	44.	(J)	55.	(D)
23.	(C)	34.	(H)	45.	(E)	56.	(H)
24.	(J)	35.	(C)	46.	(F)	57.	(E)
25.	(B)	36.	(J)	47.	(C)	58.	(F)
26.	(F)	37.	(B)	48.	(K)	59.	(D)
27.	(B)	38.	(F)	49.	(C)	60.	(H)

Test 3: Reading

1.	(A)	11.	(C)	21.	(D)	31.	(C)
2.	(H)	12.	(J)	22.	(H)	32.	(H)
3.	(D)	13.	(B)	23.	(B)	33.	(C)
4.	(H)	14.	(G)	24.	(J)	34.	(H)
5.	(C)	15.	(D)	25.	(C)	35.	(A)
6.	(G)	16.	(H)	26.	(J)	36.	(H)
7.	(A)	17.	(D)	27.	(D)	37.	(D)
8.	(H)	18.	(H)	28.	(H)	38.	(J)
9.	(C)	19.	(C)	29.	(D)	39.	(C)
10.	(J)	20.	(G)	30.	(G)	40.	(H)

Test 4: Science Reasoning

1.	(B)	11.	(C)	21.	(C)	31.	(D)
2.	(H)	12.	(H)	22.	(H)	32.	(F)
3.	(D)	13.	(A)	23.	(D)	33.	(C)
4.	(G)	14.	(H)	24.	(G)	34.	(F)
5.	(A)	15.	(B)	25.	(D)	35.	(C)
6.	(F)	16.	(J)	26.	(J)	36.	(G)
7.	(D)	17.	(A)	27.	(B)	37.	(A)
8.	(J)	18.	(J)	28.	(J)	38.	(G)
9.	(A)	19.	(A)	29.	(D)	39.	(B)
10.	(G)	20.	(F)	30.	(G)	40.	(G)

DETAILED EXPLANATIONS OF ANSWERS

Test 1: English

1. **(D)** Choice (D) is correct because the singular pronoun "this" correctly agrees with the single appointment of the first architect. Furthermore, the plural verb "were" agrees with its plural subject "appointments." "Such as this" is simply an adjectival phrase describing "appointments" and as such cannot contain a subject. Because choice (A) offers a singular verb not in agreement with the plural subject, it is incorrect. Choice (B) is correct in the singularity of its verb but not in the plurality of its pronoun; and choice (C) suggests not only an incorrect plural pronoun, but the present tense verb "are," which is inconsistent with the past tense of the passage.

2. **(G)** Choice (G) is correct as the commas completely enclose the function word "however." This term acts as a means of changing the perspective of the passage and must either be surrounded by commas on both sides or have no commas whatsoever. Choice (F) uses a semicolon, which incorrectly presents the words preceding it, "The...has," as an independent clause. However, that group of words lacks a verb and, therefore, cannot be any kind of clause. Choice (H) places the semicolon after the word "however," thus implying "been...date" is an independent clause. Again, this is incorrect as that group of words lacks a subject. By failing to enclose the function word "however" on both sides by commas, choice (J), too, is incorrect.

3. **(A)** The correct answer (A) places the possessive apostrophe before the "s" in "offices," thus denoting that the term is singular, as the office of the architect is. Choices (B) and (D) incorrectly place the possessive apostrophe after the "s," indicating that the office is plural. Choice (C) correctly punctuates "office's," but the additional words do nothing to further the more concisely worded choice (A).

4. **(G)** The correct choice presents the correctly conjugated present perfect form of the verb "change." Choice (F) is improperly conjugated, as is choice (J), since both lack the necessary final "d." Choice (H), too, is incorrect as "changes" cannot be accompanied by an auxiliary verb such as "have."

5. **(B)** Choice (B) is the correct answer as its plural verb "were" is in agreement with the plural subject "duties." Choice (A) incorrectly presents a singular verb; and choice (C) jumps into a future tense which is not in keeping

with the tense of the rest of the passage. Omitting the underlined portion, as choice (D) suggests, would leave the clause without a verb and thus make it lack sense.

6. **(F)**   The correct answer is the original, choice (F), because a semicolon should separate two independent clauses. Choice (G) suggests a semicolon, but it is incorrectly placed after the coordinating conjunction "however." Choice (H) punctuates with only a comma, thus committing a comma splice error; and choice (J) also incorrectly places the semicolon after the coordinating conjunction.

7. **(D)**   Choice (D) is the correct answer here as it is tightly worded and the intervening phrase "for...building" is not marred by inappropriately placed commas. Either commas must appear at both ends of such a long adjectival phrase or at neither end.   Choice (A) is correct in its comma enclosure but wordy in its presentation. Both choices (B) and (C) incorrectly have only one comma each instead of the necessary enclosing two.

8. **(G)**   Choice (G) is the correct answer as it uses words economically and exhibits correct comma placement surrounding the parenthetical expression "amended occasionally." Choice (F) is wordy in its presentation, while choice (H) is both wordy and grammatically incorrect. By creating a dependent clause through the use of the subordinating conjunction "which," choice (H) has, in turn, created an incomplete sentence as no dependent clause follows.   Finally, choice (J) improperly places a comma following the verb when that comma should be at the end of the parenthetical expression ending with "time." Further, "occasionally" is a more economical way of saying "from time to time."

9. **(D)**   Because choice (D) links the act of 1876, the topic of Paragraph 3, with the variety of duties of the Architect, it offers the best transition between the two paragraphs. Choice (A) makes no reference to Paragraph 3's topic, and choice (B) changes the factual tone of the essay to one of complaining. As choice (C) mentions only the focus of Paragraph 3 and makes no reference to Paragraph 4's topic, it is also a poor choice for transition.

10. **(J)**   The correct choice is (J), omission of the underlined portion. The use of the term "more" implies something that preceded or follows is to form a basis of comparison. However, nothing is offered to compare. For the lack of a basis of comparison, choices (F), (G), and (H) are also incorrect.

11. **(B)**   Choice (B) is the correct answer because it is worded concisely and lacks unnecessary punctuation. Choice (A) is redundant in its use of the two versions of authority, and choice (C), "those," indicates a noun reference which isn't there. Choice (D) looks fine at first; however, the final comma incorrectly separates the phrase from the following prepositional phrase.

12. **(H)**   Because of the comma placed between two items in a simple list of three or more items ("maintenance, and improvements") and because of its fresh, straight-forward language, choice (H) is the correct answer. Choice (F) is incorrect because of the cliché "spruced up," while choice (G)'s use of "nor" doesn't make sense as its tandem term "neither" is not present. Finally, choice (J) is inappropriate with the cliché and incorrect as the comma should precede the coordinating conjunction "and" rather than follow it.

13. **(B)**   Choice (B) is the correct answer because it avoids the slang "perk" of choice (C) and choice (A). It is also more economical in its language. Choice (D) is incorrect because it changes the factual tone of the passage to one of dissatisfaction by the use of "burdened."

14. **(F)**   By excluding a comma before the essential adjectival phrase "as...time" and thus not separating it from the noun "buildings," which it modifies, choice (F) is the correct answer. Choice (G) is incorrect because of the intervening comma, and (H)'s use of the semicolon (which denotes an independent clause to come) is incorrect, as well, because no independent clause immediately follows. Choice (J) also is incorrect because the newly created sentence beginning with "As" is not truly a sentence; it lacks a subject.

15. **(B)**   Choice (B) makes the best closure as it ties together the paragraph's main ideas of current projects and the planning and constructing of buildings. Choice (A) elaborates on the current projects but doesn't lend an air of conclusion or finality to the paragraph. Choice (C) again simply elaborates on the current projects. Choice (D) doesn't belong in the paragraph at all as it focuses on issues other than building construction.

16. **(H)**   Choice (H) is the correct answer because it appropriately separates two independent clauses with a comma and the coordinating conjunction, "for." Choices (F), (G), and (J) all simply insert a comma between the independent clauses, thus committing a comma splice error.

17. **(C)**   Because it clearly defines what is being molded/shaped rather than vaguely and ambiguously offering the pronoun "it," choice (C) is the correct answer. Choices (A), (B), and (D) are all guilty of vague or ambiguous pronoun reference, as "it" could refer to several nouns in the previous sentence: "life," "era," or "refinement." By specifically stating the reference, the sentence is made much clearer.

18. **(H)**   Choice (H) is the correct answer. It avoids the clichés of choices (F) and (G) and is correctly followed by a comma separating the modifying phrase "and...Quakers." An additional error in choice (F) is its use of the semicolon

rather than the comma since the semicolon separates independent clauses. Choice (J) is incorrect in that it presents the transitive verb "authorized," which demands a direct object. *Something* must be authorized, and this something isn't present in (J)'s version. Choice (H)'s "dominated" does not require a direct object because the sentence implies other religious groups were dominated.

19. **(B)** The correct choice is (B) because it places a comma after the introductory phrase "Especially...colonies," not a period as does choice (A). This period of (A) results in the sentence fragment "Especially...colonies." Choice (C)'s insertion of the subordinate conjunction "where" causes the remainder of the clause to be dependent; thus the use of the semicolon following that dependent clause incorrectly identifies the clause as independent. Again, semicolons are used to separate two *independent* clauses. Finally, choice (D) places a possessive apostrophe after the plural "colonies" but fails to include a noun which "colonies" possesses. Further, it lacks the clarifying comma that sets off the introductory phrase from the rest of the sentence.

20. **(F)** Choice (F) is the correct answer since it is the most economical in language. Choices (G), (H), and (J) all offer essentially the same information but are much more wordy in doing so.

21. **(B)** Choice (B) is the correct answer for its brevity and clarity of language. Choice (A), the original, is wordy and unnecessarily inserts a comma before the coordinating conjunction "nor." A comma should precede a coordinating conjunction when that conjunction joins two independent clauses or when the conjunction separates the last item in a list of three or more items, neither of which is the case here. Because of its wordiness and its incorrect verb ("perceives" agrees with the singular subject "other"), choice (C) is incorrect. Choice (D) also fails because of wordiness and an incorrect verb, as "perceive" correctly agrees with "both." In a "neither/nor," "either/or" sentence, the verb agrees in number with the noun/pronoun following the "nor" or the "or." The plurality or singularity of the noun/pronoun following "neither" or "either" is immaterial.

22. **(J)** The use of the semicolon and the comma is at issue in this question. Choice (J) is the correct answer because it separates the introductory dependent clause "Because...England" from the following independent clause by a comma. Choice (F) incorrectly uses the semicolon, reserved for separating two independent clauses; and choice (G) fails to present the necessary comma. Choice (H) also incorrectly treats the beginning dependent clause as an independent one by using the semicolon.

23. **(D)** Choice (D) is the correct answer as the simple past tense "passed" is necessary to be consistent with the verb tense of the passage. Choice (A),

"past," can be used as a noun, an adverb, or an adjective, but not as a verb. Choice (B) is also incorrect because it makes no sense. Finally, choice (C) does not work because the auxiliary verb "have" must have a plural subject for agreement in number, and "colony" is singular.

24. **(J)**   Because of its economical language, which sacrifices no meaning, choice (J) is correct. All the other choices, (F), (G), and (H), are wordy and offer no additional necessary information.

25. **(B)**   By including the main idea from Paragraph 3, the religious element in Northern education, and the main idea of Paragraph 4, the secular education of the South, choice (B) makes the best transition from Paragraph 3 and the best introduction to Paragraph 4. Choice (A) mentions the North and the South, but the topic of legal precedents is not an issue in Paragraph 4; therefore, choice (A) is not the best answer. The "Deluder Satan" law, indeed, is an issue in Paragraph 3, but not in Paragraph 4; thus, choice (C) is inappropriate. Choice (D) does not work well as it fails to include a link to the Northern issue of education and, instead, focuses entirely on the South.

26. **(J)**   Choice (J) is the correct answer because only a comma is necessary to separate the independent clause and the dependent clause beginning with "who." Choice (F) creates a comma splice by using a comma incorrectly to separate the two independent clauses. Choice (G), too, is incorrect because it uses a semicolon between the first independent clause and the dependent clause created by the addition of the subordinate conjunction "who." The semicolon correctly acts to separate two independent clauses. Choice (H) presents an awkwardly worded phrase, "among whom they," which is much more directly said in choice (J)'s "who."

27. **(C)**   Here the correct choice is (C). It appropriately treats the two clauses as independent, creating a sentence out of each by the use of the period. Further, it necessarily separates the adjectival phrase "established..." from the rest of the sentence by a comma, thus clarifying the sentence. Choice (A) fuses the two independent clauses together by incorrectly inserting a comma between them. Choice (B) is correct in its use of the semicolon but incorrect in failing to insert a comma before "established" to clarify the sentence's meaning. Choice (D)'s problem is the comma splice between "founded" and "one," resulting in a sentence fusion.

28. **(J)**   Choice (J) is the correct answer because it has the necessary coordinating comma offsetting the appositive phrase "William and Mary" and refers to the college by the relative pronoun "which," a pronoun which refers to an object rather than a person. Choice (F) is incorrect because by inserting a period between "Mary" and "Which," the fragment beginning with the latter is incorrectly identified as a complete sentence. Choice (G) commits a fusion error by creating an

independent clause, "it...charter," without a coordinating conjunction (and semicolon or comma) between it and the previous independent clause. Choice (H) correctly uses the comma but incorrectly refers to the *institution*, William and Mary University, by the personal relative pronoun "who," reserved for people.

29. **(A)** Choice (A) is correct as the counterpart phrases in the sentence are parallel in grammatical construction, each being separated by a comma and each consisting of an adjective and a noun. Choice (B) is not parallel in construction, nor are choices (C) and (D). Further, choice (C) incorrectly uses the hyphen between items in a list and separates the adjectives from the modified noun by a comma. It also misuses the semicolon by placing it before the "and" in a simple list. Choice (D)'s use of semicolons to separate items in a simple list is unnecessary as the commas will suffice.

30. **(G)** Choice (G) is the best answer. Although witchcraft would draw the interest of the reader, the introductory paragraph should introduce the general topic of the essay, not the specific subtopics of the body paragraphs to follow; therefore, (F) is not the best choice. (H) is not the best choice either, as placing each different piece of interesting information in a separate paragraph would lead to an essay with a series of underdeveloped paragraphs. Yes, it is good to leave the reader with an important image; however, that image should add a sense of closure or summary overview, neither of which the witchcraft references do as they are too narrow to encompass the entire scope of the passage. Consequently, choice (J) is not the best answer.

31. **(C)** Choice (C) works best as it gives specific information on this topic. Choice (A) fails to deal with religion, the main focus of the passage; and choice (B) deals with biography, but the passage offers no biographical data on any person. The colonial era is mentioned in choice (D), but nothing about the printing press is present in the essay, thus making this answer an inappropriate choice.

32. **(J)** The correct answer is (J) as the subject "materials" and the simple verb "are" are both plural. Choice (F) has a singular verb "is," which disagrees in number with the subject. Choice (G) unnecessarily and awkwardly employs the auxiliary verb "being," and (H) exhibits the same agreement problem between subject and verb as choice (F).

33. **(B)** Choice (B) correctly places no unnecessary punctuation between the introductory independent clause and the following essential dependent clause. Choice (A) incorrectly places a semicolon reserved for separation of independent clauses between the independent and the dependent clauses. Choice (C) not only incorrectly uses the semicolon but begins the attached clause with a capital letter. And finally, choice (D) misuses the semicolon, and, with the addition of "yet, because," yields a dependent clause which makes no sense.

34. (J) Because (J) is the only answer which clarifies the issue of concern, "organic and chemical labels," it is the correct choice. Choices (F), (G), and (H) all offer extremely vague pronoun references to unspecified noun antecedents. One must be very careful, especially at a paragraph's beginning, to establish antecedent references for all pronouns.

35. (C) By using a comma before the coordinating conjunction "but," which separates the two independent clauses, choice (C) becomes the correct answer for this question. Choice (A) does not provide the necessary comma and, therefore, is incorrect. Choice (B) substitutes the conjunction "however," but this term, when used to separate two independent clauses, must be preceded by a semicolon. Without the semicolon, the sentence is fused. Choice (D) makes the error of using a semicolon before the subordinating conjunction "because." "Because" begins a dependent clause, and therefore, should not be separated by a semicolon, which is used to separate two independent clauses.

36. (J) The correct answer is (J) because the relative pronoun "which" refers to an object (soil). Because this antecedent "soil" is an object, it cannot be followed by the pronoun "whose," which is meant to refer to a person. It is for this reason that choice (F) is incorrect. (G) is incorrect because of the personal relative pronoun "who" but also because "who's" is the contraction for "who is," the use of which makes no sense in the given sentence. Choice (H) offers "whos," which is not a word at all.

37. (D) Because it is consistent with the first person plural voice of the passage, "we" and "our," choice (D) is correct. Choice (A) is incorrect because of its use of the third person singular and because the possessive apostrophe showing ownership of "meat" is absent. Choice (C) offers "its," which shows possession but has no object antecedent and is inconsistent with the controlling voice of the passage. Choice (B) is also inconsistent with the voice of the passage, although it does have the possessive apostrophe.

38. (G) The precise, non-colloquial, and fresh use of the word "commercial" makes choice (G) the correct choice. (F)'s term, "store-bought," is colloquial, and thus does not reflect standard English. Nor does (H)'s slogan "over-the-counter" work, as it is a cliché. (J)'s slogan "customer-ready" suffers from the same problem as (H).

39. (D) The most precise and nonrepetitive manner offered for this situation is choice (D). "Accurate" and "exact" are synonyms, and thus one is sufficient. For this reason, choices (A), (B), and (C), which use both synonyms, are incorrect.

40. (F) Because choice (F) links the paragraphs together by making reference to Paragraph 2's topics of organic and inorganic foods and Paragraph 3's means of food growth, it is the correct choice for transition and introduction. Choice (G) refers to an idea only in Paragraph 2, the definitions, leaving out Paragraph 3's concepts entirely. Choice (H) brings up businessmen and business-women, topics which are not present in either Paragraph 2 or 3. Finally, choice (J) narrowly deals with humus and organic plants, one specific subtopic in Paragraph 3, while both paragraphs clearly deal with inorganic plants, as well. Further, this choice fails to mention the issue of definition which forms the topic of Paragraph 2.

41. **(D)** Omitting the underlined portion, choice (D), is correct. All the other choices offer terms which necessitate a point of comparison for "more" (A), "much more" (B), and "inasmuch" (C). We are left with the questions, "More or much more than what?" and "Inasmuch as what?"

42. **(J)** Choice (J) is correct as it separates the independent clauses by a semicolon, suggests the correct singular pronoun "it" to refer to the singular antecedent "plant," and uses the conjunction "yet," which signals a change or contrast in perspective from that which just preceded. Choice (F) suggests a subordinate conjunction ("when") which then begins a dependent clause; how-ever, by allowing this dependent clause to act as a complete sentence, (F) is in error. Further, the use of "when" is illogical, as clearly a word that contrasts the unaware and the demanding plant is necessary. Choice (G) is incorrect for the use of "when." It also misidentifies the ensuing dependent clause as a complete sentence by preceding the "when" clause by a semicolon. Choice (H), too, is incorrect not because of clause misidentification problems but because the plural pronoun "they" is used to refer to the singular antecedent "plant."

43. **(B)** Because of its succinct and clear wording, choice (B) is the correct answer. Both (A) and (C) are unnecessarily wordy, and choice (D) simply makes no sense, for cells do not possess plants, but rather the reverse.

44. **(F)** For essay unity, choice (F) is the best answer. It links Paragraph 4's successful plant synthesis of inorganic/organic nutrients and leads the reader back to the initial problem presented in Paragraph 1, humans' difficulty in mak-ing sense of the inorganic/organic issue. Choice (G) centers only on the plant's synthesis of Paragraph 4 and fails to come back to the human issues of Paragraph 1, and choice (H) centers only on the human need for clarity in labels of Para-graph 1 and ignores the issues of Paragraph 4. The issue of meat products, introduced by choice (J), is really an issue primarily of Paragraph 3, and even if it fit uncomfortably with the Paragraph 4 coverage of plant synthesis, it does not deal with the human concerns of Paragraph 1 at all.

45. **(C)** Choice (C) is the most logical place as no other paragraph deals specifically with this consumer issue. The majority of this essay is quite techni-

cal, and so logically choice (A) is incorrect; but moreover, a paragraph's organization is not based on writing style but rather on content matter. The purpose of this essay is to clarify terms about which people are confused; therefore, it is only logical to include careful definitions of those terms. Thus, choice (B) is incorrect. Trends in consumer buying have not been discussed in this essay, and new information such as these trends certainly can't be considered as summary, for summary means an overview of what has gone before. Thus, choice (D) is also incorrect.

46. **(H)**   Because the suggested sentences list the typical organic feeds that Paragraph 3 generally mentions, these details act as topic support; thus, choice (H) is the correct answer. If all important information were to be introduced immediately in the first paragraph, there would be little need ever to read beyond that paragraph; therefore, choice (F) is incorrect. If each bit of important information were to be in a separate paragraph, paragraphs would be short, overwhelming in number, and underdeveloped; thus, answer (G), too, is incorrect. Yes, essays need to have strong endings, as choice (J) suggests, but those endings need to add closure or a sense summary to the ideas presented in the writing. The suggested sentences certainly don't have these qualities because they are too specific and too closely related to certain subtopics appearing earlier in only one paragraph in the essay. Placing these sentences at the end would be illogical.

47. **(C)**   Because of the correct use of the semicolon to divide two independent clauses, the logic of "yet" to signify a change in perspective, and the lack of redundancy in its usage, as opposed to choice (A)'s presentation of "because," choice (C) is the correct answer. Choice (B) commits a comma splice error in the separation of the independent clauses by a comma, and choice (D) fails to place a necessary comma preceding the coordinating conjunction "and" separating the two independent clauses.

48. **(G)**   The adverbial phrase "just beneath the surface" may be correctly punctuated in two ways: either by placing commas at both ends of it or by eliminating the commas altogether. Choice (G) uses the total elimination method. Choice (F) is incorrect because of the second comma's absence, and choice (H) incorrectly mixes punctuation by using a dash. Were the phrase separated, however, on both ends by the dash, this means of punctuation, too, would be acceptable. Placing a period after "find," as suggested by choice (J), leaves the transitive verb "find" without its necessary direct object "assumptions" in the same sentence. Choice (J) renders both of its "sentences" incomplete.

49. **(B)**   Using the superlative form "old*est*" when making a comparison between three or more objects is the correct choice, as indicated by choice (B). (A), (C), and (D) incorrectly use the comparative form "older," signifying a comparison

between two objects. The previous sentence has clearly stated that three horror types are in question: the Interplanetary Monster, the Atomic Beast, and the Mad Doctor. In addition to the comparative/superlative error, choice (D) unnecessarily inserts off-setting commas around the prepositional phrase "of the three," thus chopping up the sentence flow.

50. **(G)**   By correctly employing the comma to offset the lengthy appositional phrase "a figure...oppression" and by using economical language, choice (G) is the right answer. Choice (F) incorrectly places a semicolon between a clause and a mere phrase, and choices (H) and (J) are wordy.

51. **(D)**   Because choice (D) includes the second comma of the set separating the appositive "Dr. Frankenstein" from the rest of the sentence, retains past tense verb consistency with the use of "was," and is economical in word choice, it is the correct answer. (A) and (B) lapse into future perfect tense, and (C) not only lacks the second off-setting comma but is inconsistent in its use of the present tense "is."

52. **(H)**   The essential dependent clause "that...spirits" should not be separated by commas from the noun "black arts" which it modifies. Consequently, choice (H) is the correct answer. Choice (F)'s insertion of the period makes fragments of the words both preceding and following that mark. That a comma is inserted after "spirits," as suggested in choice (G), means a previous comma must appear to offset the clause; yet, that initial comma of the set is nonexistent. Thus, choice (G) is incorrect. Just as the period of choice (F) incorrectly indicates two complete sentences, the semicolon of choice (J) incorrectly indicates two independent clauses.

53. **(B)**   For unity and logical coherence, placing Sentence 5 after Sentence 3, choice (B), is the best answer. Sentence 3's reference to the Jews and to the superstition that a clay figure could lead them from oppression forms a logical basis for Sentence 5's phrases of "religious overtones and superstitions." This same phrase, then, leads to Sentence 4's reference back to "These religious and superstitious tones." The original order, choice (A), illogically places the obvious reference to a past comment, "These religious and superstitious tones," before that comment has even been made. Placing Sentence 5 after Sentence 6 interrupts the logical comparison between old and new movies that the coupled sentences, 6 and 7, make; thus, choice (C) is wrong. Finally, placing Sentence 5 after Sentence 7, as indicated by choice (D), makes little sense as Sentences 7 and 8 are set up to show the parallelism between Faustus' black magic and Frankenstein's research medicine, "test tubes and electrical equipment." Interrupting the pair with Sentence 5, concerned with "medieval flavor," would further place the sentence out of chronological sequence.

54. **(J)** Correctly referring to the singular antecedent "play" with the singular pronoun "it," choice (J) is the right answer. Further, placing the comma after a lengthy introductory phrase to separate it from the subject, as does choice (J), is also correct. Choice (F) is incorrect in its pronoun agreement, referring to the singular "play" with the plural "them." A common pronoun error is committed when the reader simply seeks to make the pronoun agree with the last noun, for example "movies," which logic does not necessarily dictate as the noun to which that pronoun refers. Choice (G) suffers because of pronoun disagreement, as well as the missing comma, and choice (H) is incorrect, again because of a pronoun agreement problem.

55. **(A)** Because of its fresh, non-idiomatic language, choice (A) is correct. Choices (B), (C), and (D) all use clichés which fail to inspire the images they once did. They also do not fit the tone of the passage.

56. **(F)** Here we have a short adverbial phrase, "as well," which can be correctly punctuated either by commas on both sides or by eliminating the commas entirely on each end. The comma key is *both* or *none*. Choice (F) chooses the latter, making that answer correct. Had a choice been suggested with the enclosing commas, that, too, would have been correct. Choice (G) suggests only one comma of the set, making this answer incorrect. Choice (H) suggests a different and acceptable adverb, but only one comma of the necessary off-setting pair is present. The same is the case with choice (J), thus making both (H) and (J) incorrect.

57. **(B)** Wordiness is the issue of this question. As long as contextual meaning is not sacrificed, the briefest and most succinct wording is usually the best in this type of expository writing. Thus, choice (B) is the best answer. Not only are (A), (C), and (D) unnecessarily wordy, but (D) inserts the objective case "whom" instead of the correct subjective/nominative case "who." "Who" takes an object, whereas "whom" is the object taken.

58. **(J)** Punctuation is of concern here. Because choice (J) correctly places a comma before the participial phrase "victimizing…violence," it is the right answer. Choice (F) creates a comma splice error by separating two independent clauses with a mere comma rather than a semicolon. (G) unnecessarily and incorrectly uses the semicolon with the coordinating conjunction "and" when a *comma* plus that conjunction is the grammatical choice. Finally, choice (H) lacks the coordinating conjunction and the subject which would grammatically correct the incomplete phrase following the comma.

59. **(D)** Nothing in this sentence is offered as a basis of comparison justifying the comparative terms "more," "greater," or "most," as suggested incorrectly

by choices (A), (B), and (C). Thus, the omission of the underlined portion as stated by choice (D) is the correct answer.

60. **(G)**   Through its concise wording and correct usage of verb tense, choice (G) is correct. Choice (F) is both wordy and ungrammatical because it creates a split infinitive error by separating the infinitive phrase "to comfort" with the adverb "fully." No word should interrupt an infinitive. Choice (H) suffers from wordiness, and choice (J) uses the transitive verb "lay," meaning "to place" which necessitates an object to place. No object is present.

61. **(C)**   Sacrificing human needs is certainly evil, and examples of Frankenstein doing just that would prove him as a villain, thus making choice (C) correct. The readers have nothing to do with the evil of the character; so choice (A) is an unacceptable answer. Again, it is Frankenstein's *evil* that is at issue; neither his detractors nor their looks have anything to do with the character's evil; for these reasons, choice (B), too, is incorrect. Showing Frankenstein's kindness to humans is directly opposed to proving his villainy, thus making (D) an incorrect answer as well.

62. **(H)**   By using the simple present tense verb "have" and by being consistent in voice with the pronoun "you," as is accomplished in the beginning of the sentence, choice (H) is correct. Simply because choices (F), (G), and (J) use the present perfect form of the verb, inserting the "got" into the sentence, a logical error results. The "have/has got" form is reserved to mean that one has obtained something and now has it in his/her possession. Additionally, choice (J) is incorrect as it switches voices to second person plural "we," rather than consistently using the second person *singular* "you."

63. **(B)**   Voice is again an issue here. Choice (B) correctly uses the second person singular "you," while choices (A) and (D) switch unnecessarily to second person plural. Choice (C) is in error both by incorrectly using the semicolon to separate an independent from a dependent clause and by switching to third person singular voice.

64. **(H)**   Because of its economy of language and consistent verb tense, choice (H) is correct. Although brief, choice (F) changes from the passage's primary present verb tense for no logical reason. Choices (G) and (J) are quite wordy, and the verbiage adds nothing to the content stated more succinctly in choice (H).

65. **(C)**   Choice (C) is correct here because the subordinate conjunction "as" indicates a clear comparison is to follow, the seemingly long day and its actual state. Choice (A) indicates a change in perspective, as in "while it really is not,"

and thus does not work logically. Choice (B) makes the same error. Choice (D) leaves the reader hanging, waiting for the point about time to be completed, as in "when it is in the summer."

66. **(G)**   Wordiness is the concern in this question. Choice (G) is both succinct and grammatically correct, and thus is the right answer. Choice (F) unnecessarily inserts the empty phrase "to the point," and choice (H) is simply verbose. Although it is certainly brief, choice (J) is incorrect as it leaves the adverb "tiringly" without a word to modify.

67. **(A)**   Choice (A) correctly omits punctuation between an independent and a following essential dependent clause. By beginning a new sentence with "When," choice (B) creates a fragment. A dependent clause cannot stand alone as a complete sentence. Choice (C) is in error because of unnecessary commas, and choice (D) commits an error similar to choice (B)'s. The semicolon indicates the following clause is independent, which it is not.

68. **(F)**   By using the nominative/subjective form "who," the relative pronoun meant to refer to people, choice (F) is correct. "Who" acts as the subject of the clause it begins and acts with the verb "concludes." Choice (G) incorrectly uses the relative pronoun "which," meant to refer to objects or things, not people. Choice (H) makes the error of indicating the dependent clause "Who...tomorrow" is a complete sentence, but this "sentence" doesn't make sense when separated from the independent clause which precedes it. Finally, choice (J) inserts the objective form "whom," which should act as the recipient of an action, not the one committing the action.

69. **(C)**   Because the verb for the second sentence is present in the contraction "There's" (There is) and the apostrophe is correctly placed to show the dropped letter "i," choice (C) is the correct answer. The original choice (A) presents a fragment lacking a verb. Because of the apostrophe lacking in "theres" to indicate a verb, choice (B) is incorrect, as well. Choice (D) doesn't work because there is no real association provided to show the relationship between "logical" and "that."

70. **(G)**   Succinct wording and parallel grammatical structure of similar parts of the sentence makes choice (G) the correct answer. Note how the sentence is given force and clarity by reducing each descriptor to a simple adjective modifying "programs." Choice (F) has a problematic repetition of the word "programs," and choice (H) mixes grammatical forms of similar sentence elements. "News reports" (adjective-noun), "programs on education" (noun-preposition-noun), and "exercising" (noun) do not reflect that similar parts-of-speech structure of choice (G). Choice (J), too, is guilty of mixed grammatical forms in what should be a

parallel series. It suggests a noun plus a prepositional phrase, an adjective and a noun, and a noun and a participial phrase.

71. **(D)** Passage focus is the problem of concern in this sentence. The passage as a whole deals only with fat or lean people; height is not at issue. Thus, choice (D), omitting the underlined section, is correct. Choices (A), (B), and (C) are off the topic when they mention "tall people."

72. **(H)** The present tense consistency indicated in choice (H)'s use of the verb "implies" renders this the correct answer. Choice (F) suggests the past tense "implied"; yet there is no logical reason to veer from the passage's overall use of present tense verbs. Choice (G) replaces "schedules" with "scheduling," implying a "scheduling *session*," which makes no sense. Further, choice (G) switches unnecessarily to the past tense "implied." Tense inconsistency is the problem with choice (J) as well when the past perfect verb "has implied" appears.

73. **(C)** The possessive second person pronoun "your" is the correct answer as indicated by choice (C). It modifies the noun "arteries" and is consistent with the second person references surrounding that phrase. Choice (A)'s suggestion of "you're," the contraction for "you are," makes no sense as a modifier for "arteries." Even if a contraction were appropriate in this case, choice (B)'s "your'e" misplaces the apostrophe intended to replace the missing letter "a." Because "one's" indicates an illogical switch to third person, choice (D), too, is incorrect.

74. **(J)** The use of "you" is appropriate in this passage because, as choice (J) states, this is an informal narrative spoken in a voice that seeks to be friendly, almost to conspire with the reader, to make the writer and his/her audience comrades. Choice (F) incorrectly asserts that the writer must know his/her reader to use the second person. Choice (G) incorrectly states that it is not valid to use the second person "you" in personal, informal writing. In more scholarly, formal—academic, if you will—writing, often this second person usage should be avoided. There is no absolute rule demanding the use of "you" in informal, personal writing; thus, choice (H) is incorrect.

75. **(C)** Undeniably, this passage is humorous as suggested by choice (C). The author is not hopeless, as choice (A) indicates; rather, the writer humorously derides the lean for their efficiency and lack of joy. Never does the author assert that leanies are smarter, as choice (B) suggests. In contrast to anger, the author quite good-naturedly explains that the fat people and the leanies simply have a different perspective of "smart." We, as readers, are not presented with a litany of hardships that might cause a note of sadness, as choice (D) implies. Lacking a television schedule and having a dirty cup for coffee are not presented as problems but as situations attacked in different manners by both fat and lean people equally.

Test 2: Mathematics

1. **(B)**
$$2 - \{5 + (2-3) + [2-(3-4)]\} = 2 - \{5 + (2-3) + [2-(-1)]\}$$
$$= 2 - \{5 + (-1) + [2+1]\}$$
$$= 2 - \{5 + (-1) + 3\}$$
$$= 2 - \{4 + 3\}$$
$$= 2 - 7$$
$$= -5$$

2. **(K)** I. An odd integer times two will become an even integer. An even integer times any number will remain even. The sum of two even numbers is also an even number. Therefore, $2x + 3y$ must be even.

II. An even integer times any number will remain even. Therefore, xy must be even.

III. The sum of an odd integer and an even integer is odd. An odd integer minus one will become even. Therefore, $x + y - 1$ must be even.

3. **(E)** $x^{-2} - 9 = 0, \quad x^{-2} = 9$

Therefore, $\left(x^{-2}\right)^{-\frac{1}{2}} = 9^{-\frac{1}{2}}$

$$x = \left(\pm 3^2\right)^{-\frac{1}{2}} = \pm 3^{-1}$$

Therefore, $x = \pm \dfrac{1}{3}$.

4. **(G)** We can express odd integers as:

$a = 2x + 1$ and $b = 2y + 1$

where x and y are integers.

I. $\dfrac{a+b}{2} = \dfrac{(2x+1)+(2y+1)}{2} = \dfrac{2x+2y+2}{2} = x+y+1$

which is not necessarily even.

II. $ab - 1 = (2x+1)(2y+1) - 1$
$$= (4xy + 2x + 2y + 1) - 1$$
$$= 2(2xy + x + y)$$

which is always even.

III. $\dfrac{ab+1}{2} = \dfrac{(4xy + 2x + 2y + 1) + 1}{2}$

$\qquad = 2xy + x + y + 1$

which is not necessarily even.

Hence, only II must be even.

5. **(E)** $\qquad \dfrac{\frac{1}{b}}{3} = \dfrac{1}{4}$ (cross multiply)

$\qquad \dfrac{b}{3} = 4$ (cross multiply)

$\qquad b = 12$

6. **(G)** Each box of pens costs \$7.20 and contains 12 pens. Therefore, each pen costs \$7.20 ÷ 12 = \$.60. Each box of pencils costs \$4.00 and contains 16 pencils. Therefore each pencil costs \$4.00 ÷ 16 = \$.25. Three pens cost 3(.60) = \$1.80. Three pencils cost 3(.25) = \$.75. The total cost is therefore \$2.55.

7. **(D)** $\qquad \dfrac{2}{\frac{x}{3}} = \dfrac{3}{7}$

$\qquad 14 = x$ (cross multiply)

8. **(K)** $\qquad \dfrac{7}{x+3} = \dfrac{8}{x+5}$

$\qquad 7x + 35 = 8x + 24$ (cross multiplied)

$\qquad \quad 35 = x + 24$ (subtracted 7x from both sides)

$\qquad \quad 11 = x$ (subtracted 24 from both sides)

9. **(C)** If $a < c$ and $b < d$, then $a + b$ must be less than $c + d$; thus q implies p.

Note if we allow $a = 3$, $b = 2$, $c = 1$, and $d = 8$, then indeed $3 + 2 < 1 + 8$ or $5 < 9$ but 3 is not less than 1. Therefore, p does not imply q.

10. **(F)** $\qquad \dfrac{2}{3}x = 1$

$\qquad \quad x = \dfrac{3}{2}$

$\qquad \dfrac{3}{4} + x = \dfrac{3}{4} + \dfrac{3}{2} = \dfrac{9}{4}$

11. **(E)** $\dfrac{1}{2x} + \dfrac{1}{3y} - \dfrac{2xy}{3x+2y} = \dfrac{1}{2(3)} + \dfrac{1}{3(-2)} - \dfrac{2(3)(-2)}{3(3)+2(-2)}$

$$= \dfrac{1}{6} - \dfrac{1}{6} - \dfrac{-12}{9-4}$$

$$= \dfrac{12}{5}$$

12. **(F)** $\dfrac{7}{x+4} = \dfrac{5}{x+6}$ (cross multiply)

$$7x + 42 = 5x + 20$$
$$2x = -22$$
$$x = -11$$

13. **(D)** $\dfrac{\frac{3}{4}}{g} = (7-a)g$

Multiply left side by $\dfrac{g}{g}$.

$$\dfrac{3}{4}g = (7-a)g$$

Divide equation by g.

$$\dfrac{3}{4} = (7-a)$$
$$a = 7 - \dfrac{3}{4} = \dfrac{25}{4}$$

14. **(J)** $|2x-5| = 3$

$\begin{array}{ll} 2x-5 = 3 & 2x-5 = -3 \\ 2x = 8 & 2x = 2 \\ x = 4 \quad\text{or} & x = 1 \end{array}$

Therefore, $x = 1$ or 4 is the solution to the given equation.

15. **(C)** $(x+1)(x^2+4x-5) = 0$

$x = -1$ or $x^2 + 4x - 5 = 0$

$$(x+5)(x-1) = 0$$
$$x = -5 \text{ or } x = 1$$

Therefore, $-5, -1$, and 1 are the roots of the equation.

16. **(H)**   For $x = 3, f(3) = 14$.
      For $x = 5, f(5) = 20$.

17. **(A)**   Where a succession of arithmetic operations is involved, appropriate grouping symbols indicate clearly how these algebraic operations are to be performed; that is, we perform them before other operations. In this problem, we also have grouping symbols within grouping symbols. Therefore, we perform the operation in the innermost parentheses first. Hence, multiply the terms in the first set of parentheses by minus one in order to remove the parentheses. Furthermore, the parentheses around $2x - 3y$ can be removed, since they serve no purpose.

$$8x^2 - [7x - (x^2 - x + 5y)] \quad + (2x - 3y)$$
$$= 8x^2 - [7x - x^2 + x - 5y] + 2x - 3y$$

Removing the brackets by multiplying the terms inside by minus one gives

$$8x^2 - 7x + x^2 - x + 5y + 2x - 3y$$

Now group like terms. Then perform the indicated operations from left to right. Thus, we obtain:

$$8x^2 + x^2 - 7x - x + 2x + 5y - 3y$$
$$= 9x^2 - 6x + 2y.$$

18. **(J)** $|2x - 6| < 3$
      $-3 < 2x - 6 < 3$
      $3 < 2x < 9$ (added 6 to each expression)
      $1.5 < x < 4.5$

Therefore, the solution set contains only three integers: 2, 3, and 4.

19. **(E)**   The fraction is a complex fraction. To simplify, we must multiply both the numerator and denominator by $b^2 - 2b$:

$$\frac{\dfrac{2}{a^2 b^2}}{\dfrac{1}{b^2 - 2b}} \times \frac{b^2 - 2b}{b^2 - 2b} = \frac{2(b^2 - 2b)}{a^2 b^2}$$

Multiplying through in the numerator:

$$= \frac{2b^2 - 4b}{a^2 b^2}$$

The numerator is factored and like terms are cancelled:

$$= \frac{b(2b - 4)}{a^2 b^2} = \frac{2b - 4}{a^2 b}$$

20. **(F)** $\dfrac{\dfrac{1}{x}-\dfrac{1}{y}}{\dfrac{1}{x^2}-\dfrac{1}{y^2}}=\dfrac{\left(\dfrac{y-x}{xy}\right)}{\dfrac{y^2-x^2}{x^2y^2}}$

Dividing by a fraction is the same as multiplying by its reciprocal. The expression thus becomes

$$\left(\frac{y-x}{xy}\right)\left(\frac{x^2y^2}{y^2-x^2}\right)$$

$$=\left(\frac{y-x}{xy}\right)\left(\frac{x^2y^2}{(y+x)(y-x)}\right)$$

$$=\frac{xy}{y+x} \qquad \text{(cancelled factors from numerator and denominator)}$$

$$=\frac{xy}{x+y} \qquad \text{(rearranged denominator)}$$

21. **(C)** $\dfrac{7}{x^2+8x+23}=1 \qquad$ (multiply both sides by $x^2+8x+23$)

$x^2+8x+23=7 \qquad$ (subtract 7 from both sides)

$x^2+8x+16=0 \qquad$ (factor)

$(x+4)(x+4)=0$

Solution set $\{-4,-4\}$

22. **(H)** $\dfrac{a}{b}=4 \qquad\qquad$ (multiply both sides by b)

$a=4b$

$a^2-16b^2=(4b)^2-16b^2 \qquad$ (substitute $a=4b$)

$=0$

23. **(C)** $\dfrac{x}{y}=\dfrac{2}{5}$

$x=\dfrac{2}{5}y$

Substitute $x = \frac{2}{5}y$ into the equation:

$$25\left(\frac{2}{5}y\right)^2 - 4y^2 = 25\left(\frac{4y^2}{25}\right) - 4y^2$$
$$= 4y^2 - 4y^2 = 0$$

24. **(J)** $\dfrac{3b^3a^2}{33a^3b^6(cb)^4}$

Multiplying out, and cancelling factors from numerator and denominator.

$$\frac{3}{33}\frac{a^2}{a^3}\frac{b^3}{b^6b^4}\frac{1}{c^4} = \frac{1}{11ab^7c^4}$$

25. **(B)** $\dfrac{RI}{E} = 1 - e^{-\frac{Rt}{L}}$ or

$$e^{-\frac{Rt}{L}} = 1 - \frac{RI}{e}$$
$$\log_e e^{-\frac{Rt}{L}} = \log_e\left(1 - \frac{RI}{E}\right)$$
$$\frac{-Rt}{L} = \log_e\left(1 - \frac{RI}{E}\right)$$
$$t = \frac{-L}{R}\log_e\left(1 - \frac{RI}{E}\right)$$

26. **(F)** $2^{(6x-8)} = 16$

$2^{(6x-8)} = 2^4$ (rewrote 16 as 2^4)

Equating exponents gives:

$6x - 8 = 4.$

Solve for x.

$6x = 12$ (added 8 to both sides)

$x = 2$ (divided both sides by 6)

27. **(B)**

$$f(3) = (3) + 1$$
$$= 4$$
$$g(4) = 2(4) - 3$$
$$= 5$$
$$f(3) * g(4) = 4 * 5$$
$$= 2(4) + 5 - (4)(5)$$
$$= -7$$

28. **(J)**

$$\dfrac{\dfrac{2x - 8}{x + 1}}{\dfrac{3x^2 - 12x}{x^2 - 1}}$$

Invert the denominator and multiply by the numerator:

$$= \left[\frac{2x - 8}{x + 1}\right]\left[\frac{(x+1)(x-1)}{3x^2 - 12x}\right]$$

$$= [2(x - 4)]\left[\frac{(x - 1)}{3x(x - 4)}\right]$$

$$= \frac{2(x - 1)}{3x}$$

29. **(D)**

$$\log 2 + 2\log x = \log(4x - 2)$$
$$\log 2 + \log x^2 = \log(4x - 2)$$
$$\log[(2)(x^2)] = \log(4x - 2)$$
$$2x^2 = 4x - 2$$
$$x^2 = 2x - 1$$
$$x^2 - 2x + 1 = 0$$
$$(x - 1)^2 = 0$$
$$x = 1$$

30. **(J)**

$$x^{2a} = (2x)^a$$
$$x^{-2} = (2x)^{-1} \qquad \text{(substituted } -1 \text{ for } a)$$
$$x^{-2} = 2^{-1}x^{-1}$$
$$\frac{1}{x^2} = \frac{1}{2x}$$
$$\frac{1}{x} = \frac{1}{2}$$
$$x = 2$$

31. **(D)** If $\dfrac{2x+1}{x^2-4} > 0$, then either:

$$2x+1 > 0 \quad \text{and} \quad x^2-4 > 0 \qquad \text{(Case I)}$$

$$\text{or}$$

$$2x+1 < 0 \quad \text{and} \quad x^2-4 < 0 \qquad \text{(Case II)}$$

Case I: $2x+1 > 0$ and $x^2-4 > 0$ must be solved individually for x. The solution for Case I will be the set of x-values which satisfy both $2x+1 > 0$ and $x^2-4 > 0$ (that is, the intersection of their individual solution sets).

Solve $2x+1 > 0$ for x.

$$2x+1 > 0$$
$$2x > -1$$
$$x > -\frac{1}{2} \tag{1}$$

Solve $x^2-4 > 0$ for x.

$$x^2-4 > 0$$
$$x^2 > 4$$
$$x > 2 \quad \text{or} \quad x < -2 \tag{2}$$

The graphs of solution sets (1) and (2) are shown below.

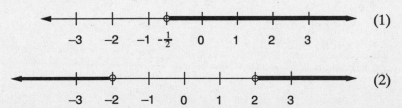

The intersection set consists only of those x-values which are darkened on *both* graphs. Therefore, the solution for Case I is all x-values greater than 2 ($x > 2$).

Case II: Now, we will find the intersection of the solution sets for $2x+1 < 0$ and $x^2-4 < 0$.

Solve $2x+1 < 0$ for x.

$$2x+1 < 0$$
$$2x < -1$$
$$x < -\frac{1}{2} \tag{3}$$

Solve $x^2 - 4 < 0$ for x

$$x^2 - 4 < 0$$
$$x^2 < 4$$
$$-2 < x < 2 \tag{4}$$

The graphs of solution sets (3) and (4) are shown below.

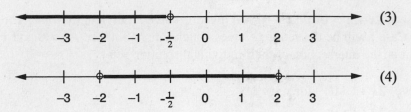

$$(3)$$

$$(4)$$

The intersection of solution sets (3) and (4) is thus $-2 < x < -\dfrac{1}{2}$ (solution for Case II).

Combining the results from Case I and Case II gives $x > 2$ or $-2 < x < -\dfrac{1}{2}$.

32. **(F)** $\begin{cases} x - 3y = 1 \\ 2x + y = 2 \end{cases}$ $\begin{matrix}(1)\\(2)\end{matrix}$

Add equation (1) to three times equation (2).

$$\begin{cases} x - 3y = 1 \\ 2x + y = 6 \end{cases}$$
$$\overline{7x + 0y = 7}$$

$$7x = 7$$
$$x = 1$$

Substitute $x = 1$ into equation (1) to find y.

$$1 - 3y = 1$$
$$3y = 0$$
$$y = 0$$

So $x = 1$, $y = 0$, and the answer is (F).

33. **(A)**
$$\frac{1}{a} = \frac{1}{\frac{1}{b}}$$

$$a = \frac{1}{b}$$

Substitute $a = \dfrac{1}{b}$ into the given inequality:

$$2 < a < 5$$

$$2 < \frac{1}{b} < 5$$

$$\frac{1}{2} > b > \frac{1}{5}$$

34. **(H)** The area of a square is the square of its side. When the diagonal is known, the side can be found by the relation:

$$2s^2 = d^2 \quad \text{(by Pythagorean Theorem)}$$
$$s^2 = \frac{d^2}{2}$$

Since $A = s^2$, we can say: $A = \dfrac{d^2}{2}$.

The length of the diagonal d is found by the distance formula:

$$d = \sqrt{(x_2 - x_1)^2 + (y_2 - y_1)^2}$$

Substituting the two endpoints:

$$d = \sqrt{(3 - (-1))^2 + (8 - 2)^2} = \sqrt{(4)^2 + (6)^2}$$
$$d = \sqrt{16 + 36} = \sqrt{52}$$

Squaring: $d^2 = 52$

Solving for the area: $A = \dfrac{d^2}{2} = \dfrac{52}{2} = 26$

35. **(C)** Use the point-slope form for the equation of a line:

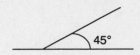

627

$$(y - y_1) = m(x - x_1)$$

The inclination is given as 45°. The slope m is defined as: $m = \tan 45° = 1$. The equation of line A is:

$$(y - 5) = 1(x + 6)$$

or $y = x + 11$.

A line perpendicular to A must satisfy the relation for the slopes of two perpendicular lines: i.e., $m_1 m_2 = -1$. The slope of $A = 1$, therefore, the slope of the line perpendicular to $A = -1$. This line passes through $P(-6, 5)$. The equation of this line is $(y - 5) = -1(x + 6)$ or $y = -x - 1$.

36. **(J)** Equate y's: $7x = \dfrac{4}{3}x + \dfrac{7}{3}$

Solve for x: $\dfrac{17}{3}x = \dfrac{7}{3}$

Multiply both sides by $\dfrac{3}{17}$:

$$x = \frac{7}{17}$$

We may now substitute this x value into any one of the given equations. Note that the best choice would be the first equation since it involves only one operation.

$$y = 7\left(\frac{7}{17}\right) = \frac{49}{17}$$

37. **(B)**

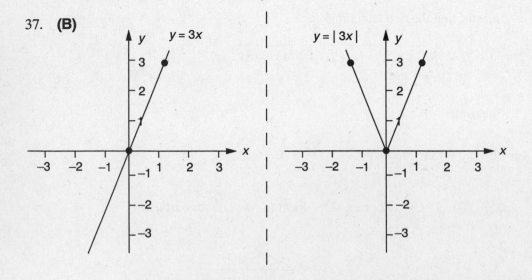

When taking the absolute value of a function, all negative function values are made positive. Positive y values are defined for Quadrants I and II. Negative values are in Quadrants III and IV. Therefore, the defined function must lie in Quadrants I and II only.

38. **(F)** The first thing we do is draw a sketch on the coordinate axes:

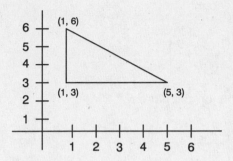

We see that the endpoints of the hypotenuse are (1, 6) and (5, 3). The slope is defined as:

$$m = \frac{y_2 - y_1}{x_2 - x_1}$$

$$m = \frac{3-6}{5-1} = \frac{-3}{4}$$

39. **(A)** $P(x_1, y_1), Q(x_2, y_2)$

From the equation for midpoint:

$$x_m = \frac{1}{2}(x_1 + x_2) = \frac{1}{2}(3 + 15) = 9$$

$$y_m = \frac{1}{2}(-6 + 5) = -\frac{1}{2}$$

Thus, the midpoint is:

$$P_{mid} = \left(9, -\frac{1}{2}\right)$$

40. **(K)** The relation that gives the distance between a point with coordinates (x_1, y_1) and a straight line of the form $ax + by + c = 0$ is:

$$d = \left| \frac{ax_1 + by_1 + c}{\sqrt{a^2 + b^2}} \right|$$

We are given both the point $(x_1, y_1) = (10, 4)$ and the line $y = 4x + 9$, but we must get this in the proper form: $ax + by + c = 0$. Subtracting $4x$ and 9 from both sides:

$$y - 4x - 9 = 0$$
$$\text{or,} \quad -4x + y - 9 = 0$$

In this equation, $a = -4$, $b = 1$, and $c = -9$. Substituting these values back into the distance formula, we obtain:

$$d = \left| \frac{(-4)(10) + (1)(4) - 9}{\sqrt{(-4)^2 + (1)^2}} \right|$$

Multiplying through on top and bottom:

$$\left| \frac{-40 + 4 - 9}{\sqrt{16 + 1}} \right| = \left| \frac{-45}{\sqrt{17}} \right|$$

which is equivalent to $\dfrac{45}{\sqrt{17}}$

41. **(A)** $y < -x + 3$
$\quad\quad\quad\quad y < x - 3$

Solve by graphing.

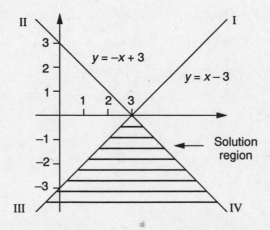

Note that the solution to the system of inequalities lies in Quadrants III and IV.

42. **(H)** Substitute the given values for x and y in order to solve for the unknown coefficients a and b.

Substituting $x = 2$ and $y = 1$:

$$\begin{cases} 2a + b = 20 \\ 2b + a = 16 \end{cases} \qquad \begin{array}{l}(1)\\(2)\end{array}$$

We can solve for b by using Equation (1)

$$b = 20 - 2a.$$

Substituting this into Equation (2) yields

$$2(20 - 2a) + a = 16.$$

Simplifying:

$$40 - 4a + a = 16$$
$$40 - 3a = 16$$
$$-3a = -24$$
$$3a = 24$$
$$a = 8$$

Substituting 8 for a in Equation (1), we obtain:

$$2(8) + b = 20$$
$$16 + b = 20$$
$$b = 4$$

Thus, $a = 8$, $b = 4$.

43. **(C)**   The length of the radius is the distance between points C and D.

The distance between two points is given by:

$$d = \sqrt{(x_2 - x_1)^2 + (y_2 - y_1)^2}.$$

Let $C = (x_1, y_1)$ and $D = (x_2, y_2)$; hence, we have:

$$d = \sqrt{[(-2) - (-4)]^2 + (2-1)^2} = \sqrt{4+1} = \sqrt{5}.$$

44. **(J)**

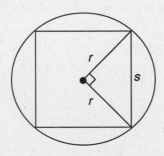

Area of a circle $= \pi r^2$. Since the area of our circle is given as π, $r = 1$ for our circle. Area of a square is given by $A = s^2$. From the diagram and the Pythagorean Theorem, $s^2 = r^2 + r^2 = 2r^2$. Thus, $A = s^2 = 2r^2 = 2$ (substituted 1 for r, since the radius equals 1).

45. **(E)**   We obtain the three equations:

$$a + c = 5 \qquad\qquad\qquad (1)$$
$$a + b = 7 \qquad\qquad\qquad (2)$$
$$b + c = 9 \qquad\qquad\qquad (3)$$

Solve for a in Equation (2): $a = 7 - b$

Substitute $a = 7 - b$ into Equation (1), and add the resulting equation to Equation (3).

$$(7 - b) + c = 5$$
$$+ \quad \underline{(b + c = 9)}$$
$$7 + 2c = 14$$

Or, $2c = 7$.

Thus, $c = \dfrac{7}{2}$.

Substitute $c = \dfrac{7}{2}$ into Equation (1)

$$a + c = 5$$
$$a + \frac{7}{2} = 5$$
$$a = \frac{3}{2} \quad (a \text{ is the radius of circle A})$$

46. **(F)** $AC = AE + EC$; therefore, $AC = (7x - 1) + (5x + 5)$.

We know that the diagonals of a parallelogram bisect each other. As such, $AE = EC$. This provides us with a method to solve for x and determine the total length AC.

$$AE = EC.$$

By substitution, $7x - 1 = 5x + 5$
$$2x = 6$$
$$x = 3$$

Returning to the equation for AC, and substituting, we obtain:

$$AC = (7(3) - 1) + (5(3) + 5) = 20 + 20 = 40.$$

47. **(C)**   The angles of a triangle must add up to 180°. Following this theorem with the angles given:

$$(x) + (y) + (x + y) = 180°$$

Adding like terms: $2x + 2y = 180°$

Dividing the equation by 2:

$$x + y = 90°$$

Since there is a 90° angle, this must be a right triangle.

48. **(K)**

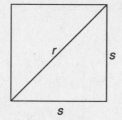

The first square has diagonal of length r; the length of its side is determined from the Pythagorean Theorem:

$$s^2 + s^2 = r^2 \text{ or } 2s^2 = r^2,$$

$$s = \frac{r}{\sqrt{2}}$$

So the area of the first square is $s^2 = \dfrac{r^2}{2}$. The second square thus has area $= r^2$ which implies that the second square has side of length r. The perimeter is thus $4r$.

49. **(C)**   If two triangles are similar, then the ratio of their areas is equal to the square of the ratio of their corresponding sides. That is:

$$\frac{A_2}{A_1} = \frac{s_2^2}{s_1^2} \tag{1}$$

if s_1 and s_2 are corresponding sides. It is given that triangle 2 is 4 times bigger in area than triangle 1. Thus:

$$\frac{A_2}{A_1} = \frac{4}{1} \tag{2}$$

The sides of triangle 1 must be multiplied by some number, let's say x, to equal the corresponding sides of triangle 2. That is:

$$s_2 = xs_1 \tag{3}$$

Substituting Equations (2) and (3) into (1), we obtain

$$\frac{4}{1} = \frac{x^2 s_1^2}{s_1^2}$$

Solving for x: $x^2 = 4$
$$x = \sqrt{4} = 2$$

The sides of triangle 2 are twice those of triangle 1.

50. **(J)**   From a theorem, we know that a central angle is equal in measurement to the arc it intercepts. The arc measurement is given as:

$$m\overset{\frown}{AB} = \frac{1}{5}\pi \text{ radians.}$$

Converting this to degrees, we obtain:

$$\left(\frac{1}{5}\pi\right)\left(\frac{180}{\pi}\right) = 36°.$$

Note that points A, O, and B form a triangle. Two sides of this triangle are equal to the radius of the circle. Thus, they are equal sides, and $\triangle AOB$ is isosceles (we know that the base angles of an isosceles triangle are equal). The vertex angle is 36° and there are 180° in a triangle. The relation that is set up is:

$$36° + 2(\text{base angle}) = 180°.$$

Solving for the base angle:

$$\text{base angle} = \frac{180° - 36°}{2} = 72°$$

Thus, $\angle OBA = 72°$.

51. **(A)**   Ratio: $\dfrac{25}{16} = \dfrac{\pi r_1^2}{\pi r_2^2}$; $\dfrac{25}{16} = \dfrac{r_1^2}{r_2^2}$

Taking the square root: $\dfrac{5}{4} = \dfrac{r_1}{r_2}$

Multiply both sides by r_2:

$$r_1 = \frac{5}{4}(r_2)$$

Double both sides: $\qquad 2r_1 = \dfrac{5}{4}(2r_2)$

$d_1 = \dfrac{5}{4}d_2 \Rightarrow d_1$ is $\dfrac{5}{4}$ as large as d_2.

52. **(G)** In order for a rectangle to encompass the greatest area, all of its sides must be equal. If this is the case, its perimeter $p = 4S$; and its area $A = S^2$. We were given that its perimeter $p = 52$ m. Substituting, we get $4S = 52$ m or $S = 13$ m. Substituting into the area formula, we get $A = (13 \text{ m})^2 = 169 \text{ m}^2$.

53. **(B)**

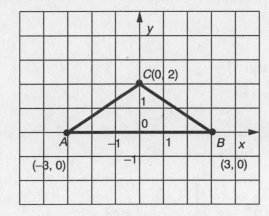

Use the distance formula to find the length of each of the sides of $\triangle ABC$.

$$d = \sqrt{(x_2 - x_1)^2 + (y_2 - y_1)^2}$$

length of $\overline{AC} = \sqrt{[0 - (-3)]^2 + (2 - 0)^2} = \sqrt{9 + 4} = \sqrt{13}$

length of $\overline{BC} = \sqrt{(0 - 3)^2 + (2 - 0)^2} = \sqrt{9 + 4} = \sqrt{13}$

length of $\overline{AB} = \sqrt{[3 - (-3)]^2 + (0 - 0)^2} = \sqrt{6^2} = 6$

Since two sides of $\triangle ABC$ are congruent ($\overline{AC}$ has the same length as $\overline{BC}$), this is an isosceles triangle.

54. **(G)** Find p', the perimeter of the larger polygon, by applying the following principle:

In similar polygons, the ratio of the perimeters equals the ratio of any two corresponding sides.

Hence, $\dfrac{\text{perimeter of } I'}{\text{perimeter of } I} = \dfrac{s'}{s}$.

Substitute 27 for the perimeter of I, 8 for s', and 6 for s.

$$\frac{p'}{27} = \frac{8}{6}$$

Multiply each side by 27.

$$p' = 27\left(\frac{8}{6}\right)$$
$$= 36$$

55. **(D)** $x = \angle CBA + \angle CAB$
$\qquad = 50° + 30°$
$\qquad = 80°$

$x = y$ (vertically opposite angles)

Therefore, $x + y = 2(80°) = 160°$.

56. **(H)**   The given description defines a hyperbola. The two fixed points are the foci.

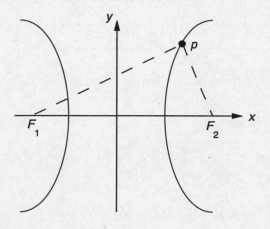

$\overline{F_1 P} - \overline{F_2 P}$ = constant, where P is any point on the hyperbola. F_1 and F_2 are fixed.

57. **(E)**   Since the two sides have the same measure, this is an isosceles triangle and, therefore, the altitude bisects the base.

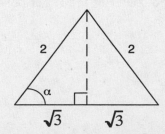

So we conclude that $\cos \alpha = \dfrac{\sqrt{3}}{2}$, or $\alpha = 30°$. Thus,

$$\sin 2\alpha = \sin 60° = \dfrac{\sqrt{3}}{2}$$

58. **(F)**   We must remember our trigonometric identities to solve this problem:

$\tan \alpha$ may be expressed as $\dfrac{\sin \alpha}{\cos \alpha}$,

$\sec \alpha$ may be expressed as $\dfrac{1}{\cos \alpha}$, and

$\cot \alpha$ may be expressed as $\dfrac{\cos \alpha}{\sin \alpha}$.

We now multiply and cancel like terms:

$$(\sin \alpha)(\cos \alpha)\left(\dfrac{\sin \alpha}{\cos \alpha}\right)\left(\dfrac{1}{\cos \alpha}\right)\left(\dfrac{\cos \alpha}{\sin \alpha}\right) = \sin \alpha.$$

59. **(D)**   We can demonstrate that for the given triangle $h^2 = mn$:

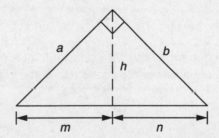

$$\begin{cases} \text{(I)} \ \ (m+n)^2 = a^2 + b^2 \\ \text{(II)} \ \ h^2 + n^2 = b^2 \\ \text{(III)} \ h^2 + m^2 = a^2 \end{cases}$$

If we substitute (II) and (III) into (I), we can obtain:

$$(m+n)^2 = h^2 + m^2 + h^2 + n^2$$

$$m^2 + 2mn + n^2 = h^2 + m^2 + h^2 + n^2$$

$$2mn = 2h^2$$

$$mn = h^2$$

$$\left.\begin{array}{r} h = \sqrt{20} \\ n = 4 \end{array}\right\} \Rightarrow \quad \begin{array}{c} (\sqrt{20})^2 = 4m \\ m = 5 \end{array}$$

$$\text{Area} = \frac{b \times h}{2} = \frac{(4+5)\sqrt{20}}{2} = \frac{9 \times 2\sqrt{5}}{2} = 9\sqrt{5}$$

60. **(H)**   The sketch of $y = \sin x$ is as follows:

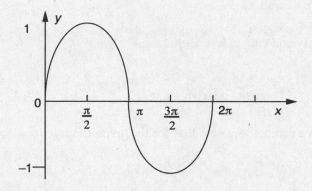

The absolute value function represents the magnitude of a particular function at a point. If we sketch the magnitude of the above curve, the graph will look like:

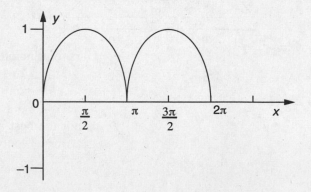

Test 3: Reading

1. **(A)** (A) is the best answer since, as stated in the third sentence of the passage, changing the solid to liquid will lower the temperature of the hot tea. Because changing the sugar to liquid will not raise, but rather lower, the temperature of the tea, (B) should not be selected. The temperature of the hot tea will not be lowered to such an extent that it will freeze cream (C) or cause the hand to be painful from the cold (D). Both (C) and (D) are unacceptable.

2. **(H)** The best answer is (H) since it includes three correct statements. The sugar does pass from a solid to a liquid state, the sugar does absorb caloric from the water, and the heat does become latent when it is sensible. Since I, II, and III are all causes of the drop of temperature when sugar is added to coffee, all three must be included when choosing an answer. (F) states that sugar passes from a solid to a liquid state (I), but no other information is given. (G) includes two true statements (I and II), but it does not include all the information since there is no mention of heat becoming latent when it was sensible (III). (J) is not a proper answer since it excludes statement II—that sugar absorbs caloric from the water. While (F), (G), and (J) each contain one or more of these statements, none contains all three; subsequently, each of these choices is incorrect.

3. **(D)** The best answer is (D). Answer (D) states that one should take into consideration that dissolving the salt in the water will lower the temperature of the water and that one should start with water that is warmer than is desired. One should not start with water that is cooler than one desires; (A) is not the best answer. The order of adding the salt and then the water or the water and then the salt will make little difference; the temperature will be lowered in both instances; (B) is not the best answer. The salt will lower the temperature of the water; (C) suggests that this will not happen if the salt is fine, so (C) is not an acceptable choice.

4. **(H)** The writing seems scientific since it refers to principles, causes and effects, and measures of heat and cold; (H) is the best answer. The writing is not sociological since there is little description of people and their relationships; consequently, (F) should not be chosen. Because the narrator reports scientific facts and there is no trial-and-error reporting, (G) is not the best answer. Since the information is not reported as historical research with references, footnotes, or dates of previous discoveries, (J) should not be chosen.

5. **(C)** The best choice is (C); paragraph five shows that in this case a mortar is a container used for pounding, pulverizing, and/or mixing. As employed in the last sentence of the fifth paragraph, the use of the mortar is not to fix or hold together; (A) should not be chosen. A mortar can be a weapon (B), but

that would not be used to reduce ice to small particles; therefore, (B) is not an acceptable choice. The word does not fit into the sentence; the mixture is to be that of salt and ice which must be contained somewhere. Choice (D) would not be practical.

6. **(G)**   The best choice is (G). The only device that the writer does not record is that of interviews. The other items—descriptions (F), mathematics (H), and experiments (J)—are used; the question, however, asks what items are NOT used.

7. **(A)**   One can infer that the metal needle will become warm when the basketball is being pumped up by the air pump. The reason is that the article states, "...air is compressed forcibly in a tube...the heat, which was before latent, becomes sensible..."; (A) is the correct answer. Choice (B) states that the needle will not be affected; (B) should not be chosen since the quotation from the passage states that there will be an effect, rather than no effect. (C) is also incorrect because it states that the needle will become cooler, not warmer. (D) is an incorrect choice; it incorrectly states that the needle will become freezing cold.

8. **(H)**   The writer is objective in his writing and offers no opinions of his own; (H) is the best answer. The writer's main concern is not literary form or stylistic devices; (F) is not acceptable. The writer is objective and does not offer his own opinions; since he is not subjective, (G) is not the best answer. Since the facts presented in the article are not new, (J) is not the best answer.

9. **(C)**   Since heat is a positive condition depending on the absence of cold, (C) is the best answer. Fahrenheit is a measure of temperature, not a condition; therefore, (A) is an incorrect choice. Heat is the opposite of intense artificial cold; (B) is not acceptable. Black states that it is "...when bodies pass from a rarer to a denser state that their latent heat is evolved..."; (D) is incorrect because it says that, "A positive condition depending on the absence of cold is a rarer state according to Black."

10. **(J)**   In this case, the word "sensible" means perceptible; (J) is the best answer. "Sensible" can mean knowledgeable (F), but the definition does not make sense in this case. The meaning of "sensible" can be logical (G), but that particular meaning does not fit the sentence or passage here. "Evolving" (H) is not an acceptable answer because it does not seem to fit the context; (H) should not be chosen.

11. **(C)**   The correct choice is (C) because the author states that the "two or three sheepish country men" are the "only guests to whom Robin's sympathies

inclined him." The mariners of choice (A) and the day laborers of choice (B) would not interest Robin and they are incorrect. Although the man at the door does draw Robin's attention, he does not seem like the type of person to start a conversation with; choice (D) is incorrect.

12. **(J)** Statements I and II best describe the diners, so choice (J) is correct. The author states that they are "countrymen" who are eating in the "darkest corner of the room;" that indicates that they do not wish to bring attention to themselves. There is no sign of hostility from the other men in the tavern; therefore, Statement III is invalid and cannot be a part of the correct answer; choice (H) is incorrect. Choices (F) and (G) are incorrect as they are incomplete.

13. **(B)** Almost all the tavern's patrons are drinking an alcoholic beverage of some kind, making choice (B) the correct one. The "Good Creature" is the punch "long since made a familiar drink in the colony." Also, some men prefer the "insulated bliss of an unshared potation"; "potation" is an alcoholic beverage. Where the mariners have returned from is not mentioned, so choice (A) should not be selected. The men have obviously not turned toward religion because they were still imbibing heavily; choice (C) is incorrect. Although drinking alcohol was most likely considered an enjoyable activity for the patrons, it was not described as such within the text; choice (D) is also incorrect.

14. **(G)** Choice (G) should be selected because the author states, "We have a long hereditary claim (to the) vice" of drinking. Seafaring is hardly a vice; choice (F) is incorrect. Although smoking (choice (H)) and gossiping (choice (J)) could be considered vices, the author does not describe them as such and therefore these are incorrect selections.

15. **(D)** Choice (D) is the best answer. The citizen was passionate in his response and threats to Robin. The citizen was also described as being "sepulchral"; passionate and gloomy best describe him. The citizen was not jovial and light-hearted but rather angry and annoyed; choice (A) is incorrect. The citizen, while disdainful, was not aloof; choice (B) should not be selected. The citizen was neither interested nor helpful, so choice (C) is also incorrect since he denied his knowledge of the kinsman.

16. **(H)** Choice (H) is the acceptable answer; this quote from the passage refers to feet being locked in a pillory for punishment—the threat issued when the youth clutches the citizen's clothing. Even though the word "stock" can refer to animals, that is not the meaning in this case; choice (F) is not the best answer. While the dictionary offers "stocks" as one definition of investments, that meaning does not fit this passage; choice (G) should not be chosen. While feet are mentioned, it is not in relation to a dance step; choice (J) is incorrect.

17. **(D)** "Tactiturn" means quiet, silent, and uncommunicative; choice (D) is correct. The tavern occupants were often reticent or reluctant to talk when they were under the influence of potation; therefore, they were not unreticent; choice (A) should not be chosen. The occupants were less talkative; choice (B), which states that they were talkative after drinking, should not be selected. Since there is nothing in the passage to support a choice of boisterous, choice (C) is not an acceptable answer.

18. **(H)** Choice (H) is the best answer since the innkeeper behaved in a hospitable manner but the citizen did not. The innkeeper and the citizen were not courteous; choice (F) is incorrect. Since the innkeeper was inhospitable and this choice states BOTH the innkeeper and citizen were, choice (G) is incorrect. Choice (J) is incorrect since it reverses accurate descriptions of the characters' behavior; it was the citizen who was discourteous and the innkeeper who was hospitable.

19. **(C)** Choice (C) is the best answer since Robin certainly received little extra (superfluous) civil treatment. Choice (A) has nothing to do with Robin's treatment. Instead, it refers to the affinity of the occupants toward alcoholic beverages. Choice (B) refers to a custom among the Turks of eating in their own small groups; it has nothing of great significance to add to the treatment that Robin received, and so choice (B) should be avoided. Choice (D) also seems to be a reference to the consumption of beverages in the tavern, and is not germane to the question.

20. **(G)** Robin probably avoided eating at the tavern because he did not have the money and hoped that the Major would give him food. Choice (G) includes one of these answers and is the best choice. Food was not avoided simply because it was not served; choice (F) should not be selected. Since we already know the innkeeper was hospitable and he does invite Robin to stay (suggesting available places), both choices (H) and (J) are unacceptable answers.

21. **(D)** All the statements given in the question are true and are taken from the passage, but only (D) allows one to select I, II, III, and IV; therefore it is the correct answer. The passage states that in contemplation there is a greater play of psychic action than in the most attentive self-observation (I), a tense attitude, a wrinkled brow, and a concentration of attention (II), a suppression of some thoughts before they are perceived (III), and a critique in which one rejects some of the ideas and cuts short others (IV).

22. **(H)** (H) is the best answer since it includes three correct statements. The passage includes the statements that self-observation involves restful features and a suppressing of the criticism (I), less play of psychic action and a

concentration of attention (II), and an interpretation of pathological ideas and dream images (III). Answers (F), (G), and (J) do not allow the reader to include all the correct choices.

23. **(B)** The best answer is (B); according to the passage, most people believe that fatigue causes the slackening of a certain arbitrary and often critical action. According to the reading passage, even in sleep there is psychic energy available for the attentive following of undesired thoughts; (A) is false and should not be chosen. At the end of the first paragraph of the reading passage, Freud refers to undesired ideas being changed into desired ones during sleep; therefore, (C), which states "NOT modified," is incorrect. Since in sleep the watcher of the gates of intelligence may be withdrawn, (D) is not correct.

24. **(J)** The feat the writer, Freud, mentions is that he can perform self-observation perfectly; therefore, (J) is the correct answer. Because the writer states that self–observation is possible, (F) is incorrect. The writer maintains that he, not the patients, can perform self-observation perfectly; hence, (G) should not be chosen. While the writer believes that self-observation can be taught; he does not make the statement that self-observation is difficult in many ways; (H) should not be selected.

25. **(C)** The passage states that the lack of creativeness lies in the constraints imposed upon the imagination by the intelligence, according to Schiller; therefore, (C) is the best answer choice. It is neither Freud (A), Rank (B), nor Koerner (D) who is directly quoted in the reading passage and credited with this statement.

26. **(J)** (J) is the best choice because, according to Schiller's correspondence, a trifling, very adventurous idea may become important because of another idea which follows it. The trifling idea is not usually important in itself; it is when the idea is followed by another that it may become important; hence, (F) should *not* be chosen. The trifling idea should not be considered in isolation in most cases, but rather it should be considered in connection with others; (G) is not the best selection. The trifling, adventurous idea should be held in the mind for a while; (H) suggests the opposite and is not acceptable.

27. **(D)** Uncritical self-observation requires one to be unashamed or unafraid of the momentary madness; (D) is the best answer. The writer tells the reader that uncritical self-observation is in no way difficult. Since (A) suggests that such self-observation is difficult, (A) should not be chosen. (B) suggests that self-observation should *not* be encouraged; (B) is an incorrect choice. The author of the passage states that uncritical, self-observation can be learned; (C), which suggests the opposite, should not be selected.

28. **(H)**   In a creative mind, a heap of ideas will be collected and examined critically at a later time; (H) is the best choice. A creative mind collects the ideas; it does not try to examine each critically and individually at the time they are collected; therefore, (F) is an incorrect answer. Because ideas enter in random order at times, there may not be a systematic way of collecting the ideas; (G) is not a good choice. According to Schiller's letter, it is the "withdrawal of the watchers (i.e., rejection and discrimination) from the gates of intelligence" which identifies the creative mind; since (J) suggests the opposite, it is another incorrect choice.

29. **(D)**   Schiller suggests that in order to be creative, one must learn to accept even undesired ideas as a possibility; (D) suggests this very idea and is, therefore, the best answer. (A) suggests that the tolerance must be eliminated, which is the opposite of what Schiller states, and, thereby, causes (A) to be incorrect. According to Schiller's letter in the reading passage, one should not critically examine freely rising ideas as they occur; (B) should be rejected. Schiller states that one must allow freely rising ideas to occur and the suspension of these ideas in not acceptable; therefore, (C) should not be selected.

30. **(G)**   The author suggests that the subject matter upon which the attention is fixed can affect psychic energy and intensity; (G) is the best answer. Neither time of day (F), watchers from the gate (H), nor the idea being trifling or constructive (J) can be the answer since none of these choices is supported in the passage as being the cause of variation in psychic energy. While (H) and (J) are mentioned in the passage, it is in reference to the creative mind, rather than psychic energy.

31. **(C)**   Since the Romanesque builders had partially solved many of the problems of scientific vaulting before their Gothic successors, (C) is the best answer. Since the Romanesque builders were predecessors to the Gothic forms (not the other way around), (A) is false. The Romanesque builders were predecessors (not successors) to the Gothic builders; therefore, (B) should not be chosen. Vaulting played a great part in Gothic architecture; (D) is false.

32. **(H)**   Gothic architecture might still exist even without quatrefoils, trefoils, cusps, traceries, pinnacles, flying buttresses, crockets, and finials; therefore, (H) is the best answer. Since vaulting is not essential to Gothic architecture, (F) is false. Gothic architecture had an influence in churches even if only here and there the village churches "…aspire to the dignity of a vaulted ceiling." (G) should not be chosen. Gothic architecture cannot be described as a definite style with certain formulas; (J) is incorrect.

33. **(C)**   (C) is the best answer since it includes both II (Gothic art is the expression of a certain temper, sentiment, and spirit which inspired sculpture and

painting) and III (Gothic art cannot be defined by any of its outward features since they are variable). Both II and III are correct, but I, which states that Gothic art is bound by certain formulas, is not true. Since (A), (B), and (D) all include I, only (C) is correct.

34. **(H)**   The best answer is (H); it states that the writer believes Gothic art will be applied with some variation to buildings of each age and country. (F), which states that Gothic art is a thing of the past, is false. Choice (G) states that Gothic art will be applied to buildings of each age and country exactly as in the past; (G) is inaccurate due to the inclusion of the words "exactly as in the past." Gothic art follows the principles common to all good styles; (J) states that Gothic art does not follow the principles common to all good styles. Since (J) is refuted by the last sentence of the passage, it is incorrect as an answer.

35. **(A)**   The best choice is (A); it states that the central purpose of the article is to define Gothic architecture, which is an accurate statement. Since the characteristics of Gothic architecture vary so much, (B) should not be chosen since a comprehensive analysis of the article does not give characteristics of Gothic architecture. (C) is incorrect since there is no true way of viewing Gothic architecture. (D) is inaccurate since the writer seems to value Gothic architecture and this answer suggests the opposite.

36. **(H)**   Since vaulting is a way of producing high ceilings without visible support, (H) is the correct answer by inference from the reading passage. (F) is incorrect since no mention of leaping is made in the passage. (G) is also incorrect since vaulting is part of a style rather than a style. (J) is incorrect since neither drawing nor producing plans on paper is mentioned or alluded to in the reading passage.

37. **(D)**   (D) is the best answer since "pontifical" is used to describe palaces in this reading passage; "pontifical" means dignified. Such a place is not necessarily a happy, merry place; (A) should not be chosen. A "pontifical palace" is not necessarily a place of rest and relaxation; (B) should not be selected. (C) should not be chosen since it suggests that a "pontifical palace" necessarily involves a place which is friendly.

38. **(J)**   Quatrefoils are the result of the natural application of certain principles; (J) is the best answer. By referring to the passage, it can be ascertained that (F), (G), and (H) are all opposites of what the author writes; therefore, all are incorrect.

39. **(C)**   Gothic art is the expression of infinitely various temper, sentiment, and spirit; (C) is the best choice. It is perhaps easier to define, first of all, what

Gothic architecture is not. It is not bound by formulas (A); it is not characterized by similar styles (B); and it is not defined by outward features (D).

40. **(H)** Choice (H)—Gothic art is not defined by its features—is not mentioned in the passage. Since the reader is searching for a statement which is not true, (H) should be selected. In perusing the passage, statements (F), (G), and (J) will be found; the author says that Gothic art is a whole method of doing things during the Middle Ages (F), an influence on architecture, painting, and sculpture (G), and an outward expression of certain cardinal principles (J). None of these answers should be chosen.

Test 4: Science Reasoning

1. **(B)** Based on the results of Experiment 2, the freezing point was lowered (depressed), indicating a negative (–) or lower than zero value; so (A) is an incorrect choice. Choice (B) is correct: since water freezes at 0.00° C and, according to the results of Experiment 2, the freezing point was lowered by 2.02° C, the freezing point of the solution was $0.00 - 2.02 = -2.02°$ C. (C) is incorrect, because no information was given showing the freezing point to have a range or value (+). Choice (D) is false, 0.00° C is the freezing point of pure water, not that of the solution, as asked for in the question.

2. **(H)** You can eliminate choice (F). Experiment 3 indicates that ΔG_f is equal to zero when the system is at equilibrium. Thus, if ΔH_F is greater than $T\Delta S_f$, then ΔG_f would be positive (using $\Delta G_f = \Delta H_f - T\Delta S_f$). Choice (G) is also incorrect, since if ΔH_f is less than $T\Delta S_f$, ΔG_f would be negative, indicating a spontaneous reaction. Choice (H) is correct because if ΔH_f equals $T\Delta S_f$, then $\Delta H_f - T\Delta S_f$ would equal zero and indicate equilibrium. (J) is false. Setting the sum of ΔH_f and $T\Delta S_f$ to equal zero states that $\Delta H_f = {}^-T\Delta S_f$.

3. **(D)** Experiment 1 reveals the molecular formula must be an integral multiple of the empirical formula (C_2H_6O). $C_3H_7O_2$ is not a multiple of C_2H_6O; so (A) is incorrect. Here, each subscript was merely increased by one. Choice (B) is false. As explained above, the molecular formula must be an integral multiple of the empirical formula. As 1, 3, and 1.5 are not integral multiples of 2, 6, and 1, respectively, $CH_3O_{1.5}$ cannot be the answer. Choice (C) is incorrect, because the O should have a subscript of 2 to be a multiple of C_2H_6O. Choice (D) is correct, because $C_6H_{18}O_3$ is an integral multiple by a factor of 3 of C_2H_6O.

4. **(G)** The information given in Experiment 3 does not indicate any relationship between the temperature of the reactants and that of the calorimeter with respect to its influence on results; so (F) is an incorrect answer. Choice (G) is the

best choice, because if the amounts of the reactants are arbitrary, compounds with undesired empirical and molecular formulas could be formed. These compounds could have a different enthalpy of formation (ΔH_f) than the intended product. (H) is false, since carbon (graphite) is a solid; thus all the reactants are not gases. (J) is incorrect since the experiments suggest no relationship between the heat capacities of the reactants and that of the calorimeter.

5.   **(A)**   The correct choice is (A), because the molecular formula gives the actual number of elements present in the compound and would specifically identify it. Choice (B) is incorrect. Many compounds could have the same empirical formula but different molecular formula, e.g., C_2H_6O, $C_4H_2O_2$ or $C_6H_8O_3$. Choice (C) is false. While the freezing point of the compound alone could identify it, the freezing point of a water solution containing it would not. Choice (D) is incorrect. Knowing the enthalpy of formation and the Gibbs Free Energy of formation would not be useful for identication since both are dependent upon temperature and pressure. Fluctuation in either of these parameters would affect the results.

6.   **(F)**   The best choice is (F). This design is closed to the outside (air), allowing no escape of heat, ensuring a more accurate temperature reading. Choice (G) is incorrect, because this design is completely open to the atmosphere, allowing the heat from the reaction to escape. (H) is incorrect. A tube is present in the design allowing some heat to escape, thus giving an inaccurate temperature reading. Choice (J) is also incorrect, because it is still open to the atmosphere.

7.   **(D)**   The correct choice is (D). The characteristics of a warm frontal passage are a rise in temperature and dew point, a wind shift to a southerly direction, and possible precipitation. By using Table 1, the frontal passage time was 10:30 am in Atlanta, 1:25 pm in Trenton, and 3:25 pm in Boston.

8.   **(J)**   The correct choice is (J). There is always a temperature change, wind shift, and rise in dew point during a warm front passage. Although it usually rains, precipitation is not a good indicator because it does not always rain during a warm front passage.

9.   **(A)**   Based on the changes of directions in the wind, the temperature drop, and fall in barometric pressure just preceding the cold front passage, the most accurate time of frontal passage would be 3:35 pm for Columbus and 5:30 pm for Houston. Therefore, the best answer is (A).

10.   **(G)**   The answer is (G). After a cold front passes, a sharp rise in barometric pressure takes place. Since the wind direction is from the west and a rapid rise in pressure took place at the time of the initial observation, it is very likely

that a cold front passed through Mobile before the earliest observation. There is no indication from temperature or wind direction of a warm front passage, so (H) and (J) have to be wrong.

11. **(C)** The correct answer is (C). The first step is to determine the type of frontal passage that is taking place, if any. The winds are shifting from the southwest to the northwest during Sunday morning. This is the first indication of a cold front. The next indication is the drop, followed by a sharp rise in barometric pressure. A warm front could not have passed because there would not have been a sharp rise in pressure nor a wind shift to the northwest. Since it has been determined that a cold front will be passing through Sunday afternoon, the temperatures will be colder.

12. **(H)** The correct choice is (H). Clouds may form over the area slightly decreasing temperatures, but this may also occur prior to a warm front. (G) is describing what takes place during a warm front passage. Low pressure (J) is associated with both warm and cold fronts; so the temperatures may not necessarily decrease.

13. **(A)** The correct answer is (A). Glycerol has six hydrogen bonds and propanol has two. ΔH for glycerol is 24 kcal/mole while ΔH for propanol is 4.5 kcal/mole. Intermediate numbers of hydrogen bonds have intermediate values for ΔH. Answer (B) is incorrect: ΔH becomes higher as the number of hydrogen bonds increases. Answer (C) is incorrect: Table 1 shows an inverse relationship between the ΔH and the number of hydrogen bonds (i.e., they are not independent). Answer (D) is incorrect: The energies of activation *are* given in the table of data.

14. **(H)** Answer choice (F) is true. Propanol is aqueous soluble. It passes through the lipid bilayer membrane via aqueous channels at some rate, dependent on its relative concentrations inside and outside the membrane, and passes into the intracellular aqueous phase. Answer (G) is also true. Glycerol is lipid–soluble. It enters the lipid layer easily, but it does not leave it easily. It needs to overcome the energy of activation. Therefore, (H) is the best answer, since it allows you to choose both correct answers. Since (H) is true, (J) is false.

15. **(B)** 1,3-propanediol is less hydrophilic than propanol and more lipophilic. The concentration of 1,3-propanediol in the right compartment would be lower than that of propanol, because to enter the right compartment, its higher energy of activation would have to be overcome. Therefore, choice (B) is correct. Choice (A) is incorrect, because of the reasoning for choice (B). Choice (C) is incorrect. Their energies of activation are not the same. Choice (D) is false, since the information needed can be obtained from Table 1 and Figure 1.

16. **(J)**   None of the data presented here discusses the rate of transport across cell membranes, only the concentration gradients and potential mechanisms of membrane transit. The correct answer, therefore, is (J). Since (J) is true, (F), (G), and (H) cannot be the right answers.

17. **(A)**   The best answer is (A). Hydrophilic substances do not form cohesive bonds with lipid membranes. They pass through the lipid layer via aqueous channels. Since (A) is true, choices (B), (C), and (D) are not correct.

18. **(J)**   The correct answer is (J). Choices (F) and (H) are false; and while (G) is true, it is not assumed.

19. **(A)**   The best answer is (A). According to Table 1, if the mass is held constant and the number of ropes increases, the amount of force applied to each rope changes. Choices (B) and (C) are false, and although (D) may be correct, it is not supported by the data in the table.

20. **(F)**   According to the diagram, R_1 is at a 120° angle while R_2 is only at a 90° angle. The best answer is (F). (G), (H), and (J) are all incorrect choices.

21. **(C)**   Choices (A) and (B) are false. Although choice (D) is a true statement, it is not a conclusion drawn from the data. From looking at the table, one can see that the correct choice is (C).

22. **(H)**   According to Table 1, as mass increases, the forces on the ropes increase. Thus, choices (F), (G), and (J) are false. (H) is the correct answer.

23. **(D)**   The best answer is (D). Since there are three minerals with no streak, Mineral A cannot be identified with the information given.

24. **(G)**   Since only hematite in the streak chart has a streak of reddish-brown, then Mineral B must be hematite. The answer is (G).

25. **(D)**   Since the steel file could not scratch Mineral A, then Mineral A must be harder than the steel file. The steel file has a hardness of 6.5; so Mineral A must have a hardness of about 7.

26. **(J)**   Many different tests must be used to identify minerals. With just the streak test, hardness test, and color identification, no close identification could be made of Mineral A. Therefore, further tests would be necessary to identify Mineral A. The correct answer, therefore, is (J).

27. **(B)**   Magnetite is the only mineral that has a black streak on the chart. (B) is the correct choice.

28. **(J)** Since Mineral C was scratched by both Minerals A and B, it has a hardness of less than 6.0. Mineral C was not scratched by the copper penny, indicating it has a hardness greater than 3.0. Therefore, Mineral C has a hardness between 3.0 and 6.0; so (J) is the correct answer.

29. **(D)** The passage states that apparent brightness is the perceived brightness at any given distance from Earth; therefore, distance doesn't matter. Answer choice (D) is correct.

30. **(G)** The passage states that "lower numerical values for brightness correspond to brighter objects." Therefore, you need to find the star with the lowest apparent brightness (or apparent magnitude) number to determine the brightest star. +1 is the lowest value; therefore, star C is the brightest. Similarly, −1 is the lowest value of absolute magnitude; therefore, C is also the star with the largest absolute magnitude. Answer choice (G) is the only answer choice that allows you to select these correct answers.

31. **(D)** The only statement supported is that the primary star has a mass larger than that of the secondary star (D). This can be seen by comparing the mass of the primary star to that of the secondary star in any of the four binaries listed in Table 2. (A) is wrong because the closest binary system to Earth is the one with the shortest distance, which is Coronae Borealis. (B) is not supported by Table 2 and is likely to be wrong since the larger the star is, the more massive it is. Aurigae is the most massive one and probably the largest. Finally, (C) is not true because the table shows all primary stars having larger masses than their secondary stars.

32. **(F)** The passage states that the maximum apparent brightness is shown by the horizontal portions of the light curve. On this curve, this is only point 1 or point 3, and only point 1 (F) is given as an answer choice. Therefore, (F) must be correct.

33. **(C)** The passage states that when the brighter primary star passes in front of the fainter secondary star, as shown in the figure for this question, secondary minimum has occurred. The passage also states that the greatest decrease in total brightness occurs at primary minimum. Therefore, point 4 on the light curve (see figure for question 32), which shows a slighter decrease in total brightness than point 2 does, indicates the secondary minimum. Hence, answer choice (C) is correct.

34. **(F)** As shown in Observation 2 in the passage, the diameter of the larger star is obtained as the product of the speed times the duration of the eclipse: 150 km/s × 3,600 sec/hr × 4 hr = 2,160,000 km, or approximately 2 million kilometers. Answer choice (F) is correct.

35. **(C)**   The apparent magnitude will remain the same (C). Absolute magnitude is determined at 10 parsecs, which is 32.6 light years according to the passage. Therefore, the apparent magnitude will not change because the distance has not changed from the point at which magnitude is determined.

36. **(G)**   Answer choice (G) is not helpful because the "doses tested" could have been all too high or too low; in these cases, the "middle" dose also would have been too high or too low. (F) is helpful because we are looking for a dose that will damage the immune system without destroying the mouse population. A 50 percent survival rate by the end of the experiment (about three weeks) would assure survivors to study and could be expected to yield results in terms of damage to the mice. (H) and (J) tell us that 100 rads was too low a dose and that 2,000 rads was too high a dose, respectively. This was helpful information.

37. **(A)**   The dotted line in Figure 2 shows that the numbers of B cells per spleen drops from 10^7 to 10^4 in 12 days in the irradiated but non-inoculated mice. Choice (B) is false; although antibodies are an immune response, this experiment did not measure them. Choice (C) is false because Figure 1 shows that it took 2,000 rads to kill approximately 75 percent of the mice in two weeks (14 days). Since (B) and (C) are false, (D) must be false. (A) is the correct answer.

38. **(G)**   The solid curve of Figure 2 shows that after 21 days, the number of B cells per spleen had risen to about 10^7, the same number seen at the time of the irradiation (i.e., before the effect of the irradiation). The best answer is (G). Choice (F) is wrong because Figure 2 does not tell us that the spleens are normal. Choice (H) is wrong because Figure 2 does not tell us about the livers of the mice. Since (G) is true, (J) must be false.

39. **(B)**   The best answer is (B). Liver cells from fetal mice are undifferentiated; when injected into the peritoneum of a mouse whose immune system has been damaged, these cells can develop into B cells. Choice (A) is not the reason because a large supply would not be useful unless they were undifferentiated. Choice (C) is incorrect; although liver is known as a source of dietary iron, iron does not protect against the effects of irradiation. Since (B) is true, (D) is false.

40. **(G)**   The data in Table 1 show that the spleens (where immune cells are formed) of irradiated, non-inoculated mice are half the weight of spleens from normal mice after three weeks. It might be suspected then that the irradiation affected the immune system. Choice (G) is, therefore, the best answer. Choice (F) is false because the data in Figure 1 shows that mouse survival was dropping at 21 days, but the figure does not give information about their immune systems. Choice (H) is false because (F) is false; (J) is false because (G) is true.

PRACTICE
EXAM II

ACT ASSESSMENT PRACTICE EXAM II

(An answer sheet for this test appears in the back of this book.)

Test 1: English

TIME: 45 Minutes
75 Questions

DIRECTIONS: This test consists of five passages. In each passage, certain words and phrases have been underlined and numbered. The questions on each passage consist of alternatives for these underlined segments. Choose the alternative that follows standard written English, most accurately reflects the style and tone of the passage, or best relays the idea of the passage. Choose "NO CHANGE," if no change is necessary.

In addition, you will also encounter questions about part of the passage, or the passage as a whole. These questions are indicated by a number in a box at the end of the section, rather than an underlined portion.

Once you have selected the best answer, fill in the appropriate oval on the answer sheet for the correct choice.

Passage I

[1]

While we can trace drama, as we know it since its emergence from the so-called Dark Ages, from its origin in the church, theater's move into secular circles was indeed significant. The earliest plays outside the church probably dates back to the twelfth century; the first certain date of any such performance that we have is 1204. But an even more important question revolves around the

reason <u>for dramas exit</u> from liturgical surroundings into the lives of ordinary
      3

people. We might assume the clergy opposed the condition into which drama had

settled<u>, buffoonery abounded</u> in the productions as plays that began with reli-
       4

gious foundations <u>focuses</u> on colorful antics of demons and devils, much to the
        5

delight of peasant audiences. Then, too, the productions may well have interfered

with regular liturgical services. After all, mounting a sizable production would

have required <u>no small effort and</u> would have levied much imposition on church
         6

facilities and personnel. Finally, the productions simply outgrew the churches;

they had to move outside.

[2]

<u>The festival of Corpus Christi was a gala event falling somewhere between</u>
          7

<u>May 23 and June 24.</u> We have few plays from the transitional period between
    7

theater's tenure within the church and <u>its</u> subsequent home outside the church.
          8

However, we can be certain of changes that ensued as a result of the move.

Spring and summer became "the season" of sorts, since the weather was best at

those times. Craft cycle plays or "cosmic" drama developed, covering biblical

themes from the Creation to Judgment Day. Instead of presenting all plays in a

central location like the church, the actors took the plays to the people on pageant

wagons in <u>"cycles," during which depicted</u> the story of Adam and Eve, Abraham
        9

and Isaac, Noah and the Flood, and <u>other biblical characters'</u> from the Old and
         10

New Testaments. One of the most important changes involved the switch from

<u>the use of Latin which was the language of liturgical dramas, to the use of the</u>
        11

<u>vernacular, the language of the people.</u> At first, the plays mixed the <u>two, *Play of*</u>
    11   12

<u>*Adam,*</u> for instance, mixed Latin with French. This important change not only
  12

introduced nonclerical actors to the <u>drama and</u> changed the nature of the drama
                                          13
from international to national. By the <u>final end</u> of the fourteenth century, the
                                          14
change from liturgical to secular drama was fairly complete. Secular theater was

<u>on a roll</u>.
   15

1. A. NO CHANGE

    B. Drama found its origin in the church at the end of the Dark Ages, and
        its move from the church into secular circles was indeed significant.

    C. Although today's drama began in the church at the end of the Dark
        Ages, its move into secular circles was indeed significant.

    D. Finding its beginnings and origins in the church of the so-called Dark
        Ages, drama, as we know it, moved significantly into secular circles.

2. F. NO CHANGE   H. probably date

    G. , probably dates   J. in all probability dates

3. A. NO CHANGE   C. for drama's exit

    B. ; for drama's exit   D. , for drama's exit,

4. F. NO CHANGE

    G. , which buffoonery abounded

    H. , buffoonery has been abounding

    J. ; buffoonery abounded

5. A. NO CHANGE   C. will have been focusing

    B. focused   D. is focusing

6. F. NO CHANGE   H. great effort, and

    G. great effort and   J. no great effort, and

7. A. NO CHANGE

    B. A gala event falling between May 23 and June 24, the festival of
        Corpus Christi was celebrated.

C. Somewhere between May 23 and June 24 the gala event of the festival of Corpus Christi was celebrated.

D. OMIT the underlined portion.

8. F. NO CHANGE   H. it's

    G. its'   J. it is

9. A. NO CHANGE

    B. "cycles" depicting

    C. "cycles"; depicting

    D. "cycles" in which were depicted

10. F. NO CHANGE

    G. characters' of biblical import

    H. other biblical characters

    J. characters of other biblical people

11. A. NO CHANGE

    B. Latin, the language of liturgical dramas, to the vernacular, the language of the people.

    C. the use of the language of liturgical dramas which was Latin, to the use of the language of the people, which was their vernacular.

    D. the use of Latin the language of liturgical dramas to the language of the people, their vernacular.

12. F. NO CHANGE   H. two, *Play of Adam*; for

    G. two *Play of Adam*, for   J. two; *Play of Adam*, for

13. A. NO CHANGE   C. drama; however

    B. drama, and   D. drama, but

14. F. NO CHANGE   H. end conclusion

    G. end   J. concluding end,

15. A. NO CHANGE   C. established.

    B. going strong.   D. in clover.

Passage II

[1]

Myth has it that a person either has or has not a mathematical mindset. While we might conclude that research of a complex nature require such traits as math-
16
ematical imagination and intuition; people whom can perform college-level func-
17
tions in other areas should be able to handle math as well. True, one may learn faster or slower than another; the pressure of time may affect some than others; low
18
self-esteem may hamper a few at times. However, we'd be hard-pressed to find evidence that says a "mathematical mind" is a necessity to learn math.

[2]

[1] The effect of this "math myth" is reasonably evident. [2]They uninten-tionally pass along the negative mindset. [3] Supposedly, only a handful of us possess the required necessary intelligence for math that means the rest of us are
19   20
living on "borrowed time" till we make an error and reveal our mathematical incompetency to the rest of the world. [4] Or parents, especially girls' parents, assume that their offspring will experience as much difficulty in learning math;
21
as they did themselves. 22
21

[3]

If we find ourselves examining the differences in girls' and boys' abilities
23
in math, we might consider several additional interesting tidbits of information: 1. Girls are being better at computation than boys from elementary school on. 2.
24
Word problems, long considered girls area of achievement, are solved better by
25
boys than girls from about age thirteen on. 3. Girls develop a hate for math at an earlier age than boys. Obviously these observations reveal problems with tradi-

tional <u>views, the</u> standard arguments that girls excel in word problems while boys
      26
excel in math do not always hold true.

[4]

The search for concrete, biological reasons for the differences between
boys' and girls' abilities in math <u>continues but few</u> results surface. But as we
                                          27
consider that only seven percent of all mathematics Ph.D's go to women, we
have to conclude that either <u>these women have</u> genes, hormones, or brain <u>organi-</u>
                                  28   29
<u>zation, that differs</u> from those of other women, or that these women have not had
      29
the negative experiences with math other women have. Can we conclude then
that males and females are different in a mathematical sense?

16. F.   NO CHANGE   H.   nature was required

    G.   natures require   J.   nature requires

17. A.   NO CHANGE

    B.   , and intuition, people who

    C.   and intuition, people whom

    D.   and intuition, people who

18. F.   NO CHANGE   H.   some more than others

    G.   one that others   J.   some, than others

19. A.   NO CHANGE   C.   required, necessary

    B.   required   D.   required and necessary

20. F.   NO CHANGE   H.   math; that means

    G.   math that mean   J.   math, that means

21. A.   NO CHANGE   C.   math as they

    B.   math as she   D.   math. As she

22. For the sake of unity and coherence, Sentence 2 should be placed

    F.   where it is now.

    G.   at the beginning of Paragraph 2.

    H.   after Sentence 3.

    J.   at the end of Paragraph 2.

23. A.   NO CHANGE   C.   When we do examine

    B.   As examining   D.   While examining

24. F.   NO CHANGE   H.   are more better

    G.   are best   J.   are better

25. A.   NO CHANGE   C.   our girl's area

    B.   the area of the girls'   D.   girls' area

26. F.   NO CHANGE   H.   views; the

    G.   views; and   J.   views; when

27. A.   NO CHANGE   C.   continues, few

    B.   continue, but few   D.   continues, but few

28. F.   NO CHANGE   H.   this woman has

    G.   this women have   J.   these woman has

29. A.   NO CHANGE   C.   organization. That differs

    B.   organization that differs   D.   organization, that differ

---

Items 30 and 31 pose questions about Passage II as a whole.

---

30. Which of the following sentences, if added to the end of Paragraph 4, would best relate Paragraph 4 to Paragraph 1 in order to tie together the passage as a whole?

    F.   It is difficult to determine through research a way of locating math ability in the human body.

    G.   Clearly, the study of genetics is not the key.

H. More doctorates in math should be awarded to women.

J. Whether by biology or experience, it seems women are at least different from men in their mathematical mindsets.

31. If you were putting together a collection of essays for high school seniors, it would be most appropriate to include this passage in a section containing essays on

A. education for fun and relaxation.

B. famous mathematicians in history.

C. gender issues in education.

D. modern religion's link to ancient mythology.

Passage III

[1]

Most people are a bit apprehensive about going to the <u>dentist, some are</u>
          32
positively panic-stricken. The prospect of sitting helplessly in a large mechanical

chair while at the mercy of the dentist keeps some people away. These especially

fearful people cancel appointments and delay getting checkups, ignoring the

possible future consequences of missed dental exams. <u>For a painful toothache,</u>
          33

<u>the dentist seems much more frightening alone than dealing with the pain of the</u>
          33

<u>toothache for some.</u> Some of these people suffer from a dental <u>phobia, they have</u>
   33   34

<u>an irrational fear of the dentist,</u> and avoid the dentist for a lifetime.
    34

[2]

Such sophisticated equipment and techniques <u>does not help</u> to calm all
         35
fears; therefore, dentists have adopted additional techniques for soothing patients.

Some dentists give patients headphones for listening to music during treatment.

Others use hypnosis <u>to relax his</u> patients. Having the patients perform relaxing
      36
exercises for <u>one's body</u> at the beginning of appointments may also work. Some-
   37

one who fears dental treatment should tell the dentist of <u>their</u> apprehension.

38

The dentist can then explain the treatment step-by-step in order to reduce some

of the fear.

[3]

Avoidance of the dentist because of the fear of pain is not a very logical

solution <u>to this fear</u>. Some people fail to realize that a twice-yearly dental clean-

39

ing and exam <u>is a relatively easy way</u> to avoid more serious and painful compli-

40

cations. <u>Since cavities</u> that are discovered early can be filled much less painfully

41

than if they are not discovered until they cause pain.

[4]

No one can promise that a visit to the dentist will be painless; however,

modern technology has made dental treatment much more <u>comfortable. Thanks</u> in

42

large part to the advent of anesthetics and updated equipment. Many people fear the

pain of the needle that delivers the anesthetic. Now some anesthetics can be in-

jected into the gums on a jet of air. The old image of a leering dentist with a huge

drill is a common one. <u>Today's dentists; however,</u> use high-speed, water-cooled

43

drills which are fast and virtually painless.

32. F. NO CHANGE   H. dentist, more is

     G. dentist; and some   J. dentist; some are

33. A. NO CHANGE

     B. Having a painful toothache, the dentist offers a poor alternative to simply ignoring the pain for some frightened people.

     C. For some frightened people, putting up with a painful toothache seems a better alternative than seeing the dentist.

D. Seeing the dentist for some frightened people for a painful toothache seems far worse than putting up with the pain the tooth is causing alone.

34. F. NO CHANGE

G. phobia, an irrational fear of the dentist,

H. phobia irrationally fearing the dentist, and

J. phobia an irrational fear of the dentist

35. A. NO CHANGE   C. doesn't help

B. help not   D. do not help

36. F. NO CHANGE   H. to relax their

G. to better relax his   J. for relaxing his or her

37. A. NO CHANGE   C. ones body

B. their body   D. their bodies

38. F. NO CHANGE   H. my

G. our   J. his or her

39. A. NO CHANGE   C. to that fear.

B. to the problem of fear.   D. OMIT the underlined portion.

40. F. NO CHANGE   H. is relatively easy

G. are relatively easy ways   J. is easy

41. A. NO CHANGE   C. Cavities

B. When cavities   D. Whereas cavities

42. F. NO CHANGE

G. comfortable; thanks

H. comfortable and lots of thanks go

J. comfortable, thanks

43. A. NO CHANGE

B. Today's dentists, however

C. Today's dentist, however,

D. Todays' dentists, however

Items 44-46 pose questions about Passage III as a whole.

---

44. For the sake of unity and coherence, Paragraph 2 should be placed

F. where it is now. H. before Paragraph 4.

G. before Paragraph 1. J. after Paragraph 4.

45. Suppose the writer wished to add the following sentences to the passage:

> Another fear many share about seeing their dentists is that of cost. Certainly the expense of extensive work as a result of years avoiding the dentist can be costly; however, if one regularly visits the dentist for modestly priced sessions, the larger costs can often be avoided.

The new sentences would most logically be placed in which of the following paragraphs?

A. Paragraph 1, because everything of importance must be first introduced at the beginning.

B. Paragraph 3, because it is painful to consider spending money.

C. Paragraph 4, because one is more comfortable with more money.

D. A separate paragraph, because although cost is a fear, it is not the same fear of physical hurt as in other paragraphs.

46. The writer wants to support the assertion in Paragraph 1 that there are future consequences of missing dental appointments. Which one of the following strategies would best accomplish that goal?

F. Listing the positive rewards of regular cleaning

G. Comparing techniques of various dentists

H. Citing specific examples of dental decay and gum disease resulting from infrequent dental work.

J. Explaining how to clean your teeth regularly

Passage IV

[1]

When they see how little respect and understanding <u>people, in general have</u>
<u>47</u>
for the animal kingdom, most environmentalists agree with the English poet
William Wordsworth: "Little that we see in nature is ours." That is, the public
may not always see the parallels between <u>we</u> humans and the animal kingdom.
<u>48</u>
Anyone with a <u>backyard; however,</u> can observe natural habitats and discern
<u>49</u>
correspondences with human lifestyles.

[2]

<u>There are among the inhabitants a scheme of balancing acts that take place</u>
<u>50</u>
<u>called an ecosystem.</u> Creatures depend upon each other for their own <u>existence</u>
<u>50</u>   <u>51</u>
<u>that is the</u> habits of one species enable another species to exist. With respect for
<u>51</u>
the environment, all can survive.

[3]

Animals do little towards destroying their environments. Unlike humans,
animals seem to realize that they are reliant upon nature for their survival. <u>Since</u>
<u>52</u>
<u>humans</u> held their environment in such reverence, perhaps solutions to the prob-
<u>52</u>
lems of pollution, the destroying of part of the earth, <u>would be found.</u>
<u>53</u>

[4]

In addition to teaching humans respect for their environment, nearly all
creatures could teach humans <u>about cooperation a lesson that many humans</u>
<u>54</u>
<u>sorely need.</u> For example, most people know that raccoons are fastidious about
<u>54</u>

their <u>food intake, carrying it</u> to a stream to wash it well before eating. Do they
₅₅

also know that raccoons can actually work together to accomplish a task? Two

raccoons have been known to work together to help each other reach places

neither could reach on <u>their</u> own.
₅₆

[5]

[57] Warfare is virtually unheard of in the animal kingdom; animals only

kill other animals when they know they are going to eat them. No creatures

engage in purposeless violence just for the sake of violence. Human cruelty <u>is</u>
₅₈

<u>something that is not</u> found in nature. Not just cruelty, but greed and dishonesty
₅₈

are also absent from the animal kingdom. Humankind should look to nature to

understand the importance of cooperation and perhaps learn something from the

<u>animals they</u> will teach them without a <u>pennies worth</u> of charge.
₅₉   ₆₀

47. A. NO CHANGE   C. people, in general, have

    B. people in general, had   D. people, in general, has

48. F. NO CHANGE   H. they're

    G. us   J. their

49. A. NO CHANGE   C. backyard, however,

    B. backyard, however;   D. backyard; however

50. F. NO CHANGE

    G. Among the inhabitants there are a scheme of balancing acts that take
        place called an ecosystem.

    H. There are a scheme of balancing acts called an ecosystem that takes
        place among the inhabitants.

    J. A scheme of balancing acts called an ecosystem takes place among the
        inhabitants.

51. A. NO CHANGE   C. existence; that is, the

     B. existence and that is the   D. existence, that is the

52. F. NO CHANGE   H. If humans would of

     G. Because humans   J. If humans

53. A. NO CHANGE

     B. which one might be able to find

     C. which we could find

     D. OMIT the underlined portion.

54. F. NO CHANGE

     G. a sorely needed cooperation lesson about humans that many need.

     H. a lesson about cooperation that many humans sorely need.

     J. a cooperative lesson about which many human beings sorely need.

55. A. NO CHANGE

     B. food intake, carrying food

     C. table manners, carrying it

     D. eating habits, carrying food

56. F. NO CHANGE   H. its'

     G. its   J. they're

57. Which of the suggested sentences makes the best introduction to Paragraph 5 and the best transition from Paragraph 4?

     A. Raccoons are, indeed, clever creatures.

     B. And who has ever heard of creatures intentionally harming each other?

     C. Because animals have learned to cooperate better than humans, their relationships are not marred by senseless and selfish cruelty, as human relationships often are.

     D. Cruelty, selfishness, and greed are often the earmarks of human relationships in today's increasingly violent world.

58. F. NO CHANGE   H. is not

     G. is that which is not   J. is something, that is not

59. A. NO CHANGE   C. animals, they

     B. animals; they   D. animals; in which

60. F. NO CHANGE   H. pennies' worth

     G. pennys worth   J. penny's worth

Item 61 poses a question about Passage IV as a whole.

---

61. The writer wishes to strengthen the assertion that cruelty, dishonesty, and greed exist among humans. Which of the following strategies would best accomplish that goal?

     A. Listing evidence that cruelty, dishonesty, and greed are not characteristics of animals.

     B. Contrasting carnivores with herbivores to show evidence of cruelty and passivity.

     C. Citing specific examples of cruelty, dishonesty, and grief within humankind.

     D. Explaining how we, as humans, can be less cruel, greedy, and dishonest.

Passage V

[1]

[1] A century ago, the typical family was an extended one with uncles, aunts, grandparents, parents, and children all under one <u>roof but</u>
                                                      62
today's typical family is a nuclear one with parents and perhaps only one child. [2] According to surveys and interviews, many young people today say that they want no children or that <u>they wanted</u> to postpone having a child until
                                                 63
their late thirties or even forties. 64 [3] Most women work outside the home, apparently because <u>of choice, rather than necessity</u>. The idea of a woman staying
                                   65

in the home and raising a family while her husband earns a living has become an anachronism. Living on one income is not even a possibility for many couples.

[2]

Once a couple lives on two salaries, the partners become accustomed to a higher <u>income, and having</u> children is put off until much later. If the couple later
66
decides to have a child, they may find that their biological clocks have run down. In addition to ignoring purely biological <u>considerations. Many</u> couples fail to
67
realize that they may want to slow down once they reach their forties; these same couples may not even consider the difficulties of raising a teenager when <u>one is</u>
68
<u>approaching</u> old age.
68

[3]

Some young people now put off marriage until much later than did <u>their parents generation</u>. Between 1950 and 1970, the median age for a male to
69
marry the first time was about 23; by 1987 the median age was 26, almost <u>as high</u>
70
<u>than</u> in 1890. Many men now <u>choosing</u> to stay single.
70   71

[4]

With the increase in maturity and financial security, one would think that <u>the current trend that includes two-income partners toward later</u>
72
<u>marriages would lower the divorce rate.</u> The old saying that "money doesn't
72
buy happiness" must still be true. Today, more than one out of five children live in a one-parent home, and although divorce is extremely difficult on both parents, <u>children are still the real losers in a divorce.</u> The family becomes torn apart, and
73

the relationship with the parent who is no longer in the home often becomes strained.

62. F. NO CHANGE
    G. roof. But

    H. roof, however
    J. roof, and when

63. A. NO CHANGE
    B. they are wanting

    C. we want
    D. they want

64. Which of the following sentences makes the best transition between Sentence 2 and Sentence 3?

    F. For some, even forty is too young to begin their family, and, because our life spans are relatively long, middle age for many is really the mid-forties.

    G. Often today's woman no longer finds herself solely a homemaker, and most women are unhappy about being forced to earn a living outside the home.

    H. Many men are satisfied to remain childless until their fifties, and, if they have married significantly younger women, they can become fathers at that time.

    J. Waiting until early middle age to have children allows women to leave the traditional role as homemakers and join the commercial workplace.

65. A. NO CHANGE

    B. of a choice of their own and not because of necessity.

    C.   choice than necessity.

    D. she chose to rather than had to.

66. F. NO CHANGE
    G. income, having

    H. income and having
    J. income, since

67. A. NO CHANGE
    B. considerations, for many

    C. considerations, many
    D. considerations; yet many

68. F. NO CHANGE
    G. they are approaching

    H. they were approaching
    J. he is approaching

69. A. NO CHANGE

    B. the generation of their parents'

    C. there parent's generation

    D. their parents' generation

70. F. NO CHANGE   H. higher later

    G. as high as if   J. as high as

71. A. NO CHANGE   C. were choosing

    B. choose   D. have chose

72. F. NO CHANGE

    G. the current trend toward later marriages would lower the divorce rate that includes two-income partners.

    H. the current trend toward later marriages that include two-income partners would lower the divorce rate.

    J. the current trend would lower the divorce rate that includes two-income partners toward later marriages.

73. A. NO CHANGE

    B. children still find themselves the real losers in a divorce.

    C. children are still the real losers.

    D. children still be the real losers.

Items 74 and 75 pose questions about Passage V as a whole.

---

74. If you were assembling a book of essays into chapters, which would be the most appropriate chapter title for this essay?

    F. "Childraising Practices of the Eighteenth Century"

    G. "Raising the High Achiever"

    H. "Changing Family Structures"

    J. "How to Plan for Retirement"

75. If the writer wanted to strengthen the aspect of the passage relating to the place of the confirmed bachelor in society, it would be most logical to put this new material in

A.   Paragraph 1, because all important information has to be introduced immediately.

B.   a separate paragraph, because no other paragraph deals with single men.

C.   Paragraph 3, because that paragraph mentions single men.

D.   Paragraph 4, because it sums up the points made earlier.

THIS IS THE END OF TEST 1.

Test 2: Mathematics

TIME: 60 Minutes

60 Questions

DIRECTIONS: Solve the following problems and fill in the appropriate ovals on your answer sheet. Do not use a calculator.

Unless otherwise indicated:

1. Figures may not have been drawn to scale.

2. All geometric figures lie in a plane.

3. "Line" refers to a straight line.

4. "Average" refers to arithmetic mean.

---

1. $\sqrt{16} + 3\sqrt{12} - 5\sqrt{3} =$

   A. $4 + \sqrt{3}$.

   B. 0.

   C. $3\sqrt{2} - \sqrt{3}$.

   D. $4\sqrt{3}$.

   E. $6\sqrt{3}$.

2. Simplify $x = a + 2[b - (c - a + 3b)]$.

   F. $2a + b + c$

   G. $a - b - c$

   H. $-2a + b + c$

   J. $a - 2c + b$

   K. $3a - 2c - 4b$

3. If $5 < a < 8$ and $6 < b < 9$, then

   A. $45 < ab < 48$.

   B. $30 < ab < 45$.

   C. $30 < ab < 72$.

   D. $54 < ab < 72$.

   E. $5 < ab < 72$.

4. If p and q are prime numbers greater than two, which of the following must be true?

   I. $pq + 1$ is also a prime number.

   II. $pq - 1$ is also a prime number.

III. p and q do not have a common factor (other than the number 1).

F.   I only.

G.   II only.

H.   III only.

J.   I and II only.

K.   I and III only.

5.   If $\dfrac{\frac{1}{b}}{3} = \dfrac{1}{5}$, then $b =$

A.   3.

B.   5.

C.   15.

D.   21.

E.   27.

6.   Find the smallest positive integer which is divisible by both 12 and 15.

F.   36

G.   48

H.   60

J.   80

K.   90

7.   Simplify $\dfrac{\frac{2}{3} + \frac{1}{2}}{\frac{3}{4} - \frac{1}{3}}$.

A. $\dfrac{6}{12}$

B. $\dfrac{14}{5}$

C. $\dfrac{11}{6}$

D. $\dfrac{7}{4}$

E. $\dfrac{3}{4}$

8.   If $a + \dfrac{1}{a} = 2$, then $a =$

F.   −1.

G.   0.

H.   1.

J.   2.

K. $\dfrac{3}{2}$.

9. For the following sequence of numbers, $\frac{1}{2}, \frac{1}{12}, \frac{1}{30}, \ldots,$ the next number will be

A. $\frac{1}{36}$.

D. $\frac{1}{56}$.

B. $\frac{1}{27}$.

E. $\frac{1}{72}$.

C. $\frac{1}{48}$.

10. If $\frac{3}{a+2} = \frac{5}{a+4}$, then $a =$

F. $\frac{1}{2}$.

J. $\frac{3}{2}$.

G. 1.

K. 2.

H. $\frac{5}{4}$.

11. If $\frac{2}{3}a = 2$, then $a - \frac{2}{3} =$

A. $-\frac{1}{3}$.

D. $\frac{7}{3}$.

B. 0.

E. 3.

C. $\frac{1}{3}$.

12. If $x = (a-3)^2$ and $a = -2$, then $x =$

F. 1.

J. 25.

G. 4.

K. 36.

H. 9.

13. If x and y are positive integers, which of the following must be a positive integer?

I. $x + y$

II. $x - y$

III. xy

A. I only.

D. I and III only.

B. II only.

E. I, II, and III.

C. I and II only.

14. If $9 - k$ and $17 - k$ are equal but have opposite signs, then $k =$

F. 11.

J. 17.

G. 13.

K. 19.

H. 15.

15. If $\dfrac{a}{b} = \dfrac{2}{3}$, then $9a^2 - 4b^2 =$

A. -6.

D. 4.

B. -4.

E. 6.

C. 0.

16. If $x = \sqrt{3}$ and $y = \sqrt{2}$, then $(2x + 3y)(x + y) =$

F. $6 + \sqrt{6}$.

J. $10 + 5\sqrt{6}$.

G. $6 + 3\sqrt{6}$.

K. $12 + 5\sqrt{6}$.

H. $9 + 2\sqrt{6}$.

17. If $a = 4$ and $b = 7$, find the value of $\dfrac{a + \dfrac{a}{b}}{a - \dfrac{a}{b}}$.

A. $\dfrac{5}{7}$

D. $\dfrac{4}{3}$

B. $\dfrac{3}{7}$

E. $\dfrac{1}{2}$

C. 1

18. Find the solution set of $\dfrac{|x+2|}{|x-1|} = 3$.

F. $\left\{\dfrac{5}{2}, \dfrac{1}{4}\right\}$ J. $\left\{\dfrac{1}{2}, 1\right\}$

G. $\left\{-\dfrac{2}{5}, -\dfrac{1}{2}\right\}$ K. $\left\{\dfrac{1}{2}, 2\right\}$

H. $\{-2, 2\}$

19. Perform the indicated operation:

$$\dfrac{3a - 9b}{x - 5} \times \dfrac{xy - 5y}{ax - 3bx}.$$

A. $\dfrac{a - 3b}{x - 5}\left(\dfrac{y}{x}\right)$ D. $\dfrac{a - b}{x - 5}$

B. $\dfrac{3y}{x}$ E. $\dfrac{3a - b}{a - 3}$

C. $\dfrac{y}{x}$

20. Simplify $3a - 2\{3a - 2[1 - 4(a - 1)] + 5\}$.

F. $-19a + 10$ J. $10a + 12$

G. $-11a + 9$ K. $19a + 1$

H. $-6a + 7$

21. Which equation expresses the relationship that the height (h) varies inversely as the square of the base (b)?

A. $h = \dfrac{b^2}{k}$ D. $kh = b^2$

B. $kb^2 = h$ E. $h = \dfrac{k}{b}$

C. $h = \dfrac{k}{b^2}$

22. Combine $a + b - \dfrac{2ab}{a + b}$.

F. $\dfrac{1}{a + b}$ G. $\dfrac{a^2 - b^2}{a + b}$

H. $\dfrac{a}{a+b}$ J. $\dfrac{a^2+b^2}{a+b}$

K. $\dfrac{a-b}{a+b}$

23. Evaluate $3s - [5t + (2s - 5)]$.

A. $2s + t + 5$ D. $5s + 3t + 3$

B. $s + 3t + 5$ E. $5s - 5t + 5$

C. $s - 5t + 5$

24. Perform the following division: $\dfrac{\dfrac{1}{x+y}}{x^2}$.

F. $x^2(x + y)$ J. $\dfrac{x^2}{x+y}$

G. $x + y$ K. $\dfrac{x+y}{x^2}$

H. $x^3 + y$

25. Find x and y if $(4^x)(6^y) = (2^4)(3^2)$.

A. $x = 1$ and $y = \dfrac{1}{2}$ D. $x = \dfrac{5}{2}$ and $y = 2$

B. $x = 1$ and $y = 2$ E. None of the above.

C. $x = \dfrac{5}{2}$ and $y = \dfrac{1}{2}$

26. If $\log_3(x + 7) = 2$, then $x =$

F. -1.   J. 4.

G. 2.   K. 6.

H. 3.

27. If $10^x = 31.4$, then $x =$

    A. 0.

    B. 1.

    C. 1.5.

    D. 3.14.

    E. 31.4.

28. If $-9 < x < -4$ and $-12 < y < -6$, then

    F. $0 < xy < 12$.

    G. $108 < xy < 112$.

    H. $24 < xy < 108$.

    J. $10 < xy < 24$.

    K. $4 < xy < 12$.

29. Find the solution set of the inequality $2x + 5 > 11$.

    A. $x < 6$

    B. $x > 3$

    C. $x = 3$

    D. $x < -3$

    E. $x > 6$

30. Given $\log_{10} 33! = 37$, $\log_{10} 37! = 43$ and $\log_{10} 51! = 66$, evaluate N, if

$$N = \frac{33! \, 37!}{51!}.$$

    F. 10^{14}

    G. e^{14}

    H. e^{-14}

    J. $33 + 37 - 51$

    K. Indeterminate

31. If $x \neq 0$, then $(2^{4x})(8^{2x}) -$

    A. 16^{3x}.

    B. 2^{10x}.

    C. 4^{4x}.

    D. 2^{16x}.

    E. 16^{2x}.

32. Find x and y which will satisfy the following pair of equations:

$3x + 5y = 6$
$2x - y = 4$

    F. $x = 2$ and $y = 0$

    G. $x = 1$ and $y = 1$

    H. $x = 0$ and $y = 2$

    J. $x = 0$ and $y = 4$

    K. $x = -1$ and $y = 1$

33. If $2^{3x} = 64$, then $x =$

    A. 0.

    B. 1.

    C. 2.

    D. 3.

    E. 4.

34. Which of the following is the graph of the equation $y = 2x + 1$?

    F.

    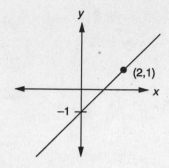

    G.

    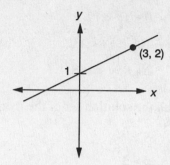

    H.

    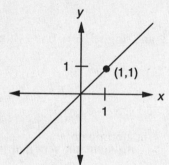

    J.

    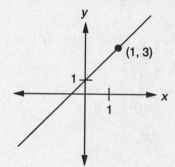

    K.

    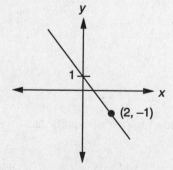

35. Consider the graph shown below. The graph represents a sketch of the equation

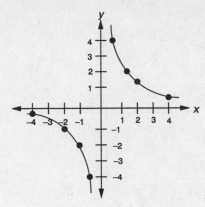

A. $y = \dfrac{1}{x^2}$.

B. $y = 2x^2$.

C. $y = \dfrac{2}{x}$.

D. $y = \log_{10} x$.

E. $y = 10^x$.

36. The equation $x = 3y + 8$ has a y-intercept of

F. $\dfrac{1}{2}$.

G. 8.

H. $-\dfrac{8}{3}$.

J. -8.

K. 16.

37. What is the equation of the line which is parallel to $6x + 3y = 4$ and has a y-intercept of -6?

A. $y = -2x + \dfrac{4}{3}$

B. $y = 2x + \dfrac{4}{3}$

C. $y = -2x - \dfrac{4}{3}$

D. $y = -2x - 6$

E. $y = -2x + 6$

38. Consider the function $P(x) = \sqrt{1-x^2}$ shown below and indicate which graph represents $P_{(x)}^{-1}$. $\{-1 \le x \le 0\}$

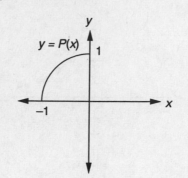

F.

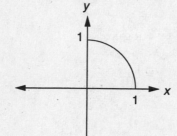

G.

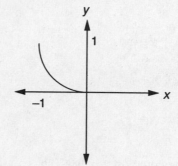

H.

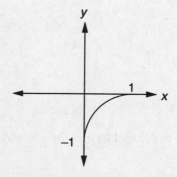

J.

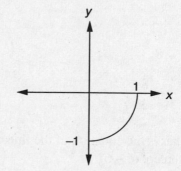

K. None of the graphs presented is correct.

39. If $f(x) = \dfrac{x}{5} - 3$ and the domain is the interval $-5 < x < 15$, then the range of $f(x)$ is

A. $-5 < f(x) < 15.$

B. $0 < f(x) < 10.$

C. $-5 < f(x) < 7.$

D. $-3 < f(x) < 3.$

E. $-4 < f(x) < 0.$

40. If $f(x) = 3x + 4$ for all x, then the slope of the line $y = f(x + 3)$ is

    F. 3.   J. 6.

    G. 4.   K. 9.

    H. 5.

41. Find the coordinates of the intersection of the following two lines: $x + 2y = 5$ and $2x + 3y = 2$.

    A. (−12, 6)   D. (10, 10)

    B. (−11, 8)   E. (11, 12)

    C. (−10, 9)

42. Which are the coordinates of the midpoint M of the segment joining the pair of points: (1, 2) and (5, 8)?

    F. $M\left(6, \dfrac{5}{2}\right)$ J. (6, 10)

    G. $M(3, 5)$ K. (6, 5)

    H. $M\left(3, \dfrac{5}{2}\right)$

43.

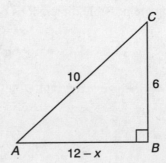

In the right triangle ABC, if $\overline{AC} = 10$, $\overline{AB} = 12 - x$, and $\overline{BC} = 6$, then $x =$

    A. 0.   D. 4.

    B. 1.   E. 6.

    C. 2.

44. If $y = 3t + 8$ and $x = 9t$, at what value of x will the graph of this function, in the $x - y$ plane, cross the x-axis?

F.   20

G.   –8

H.   –24

J.   16

K.   48

45.

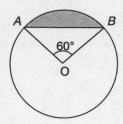

In the figure, if $\angle AOB = 60°$ and O is the center of the circle with radius = 6, then the area of the shaded region is

A. 6π.

B. $6\pi - 2\sqrt{3}$.

C. $6\pi - 4\sqrt{3}$.

D. $6\pi - 6\sqrt{3}$.

E. $6\pi - 9\sqrt{3}$.

46. A rectangular piece of metal has an area of 35m² and a perimeter of 24m. Which of the following are possible dimensions of the piece?

F. $\dfrac{35}{2}$ m × 2m

G.   5m × 7m

H.   35m × 1m

J.   6m × 6m

K.   8m × 4m

47.

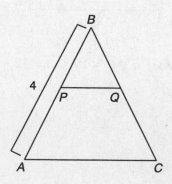

In the figure, $\triangle ABC$ is equilateral and points P and Q are, respectively, the midpoints of sides $\overline{AB}$ and $\overline{BC}$. If $\overline{AB} = 4$, what is the area of $APQC$?

A. 8

D. 4

B. $\dfrac{\sqrt{3}}{2}$

E. $8\sqrt{3}$

C. $3\sqrt{3}$

48.

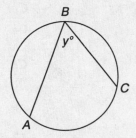

If $m\overset{\frown}{ABC}$ is $\dfrac{3}{2}\pi$ radians, then y is equal to

F. 90°.

J. 53°.

G. 72°.

K. 45°.

H. 36°.

49. In the figure, $\sin \angle BCD = \dfrac{1}{2}$, $\overline{BC} = 8$, $\angle BDC = 90°$. The ratio of the area of $\triangle ABD$ to $\triangle DBC$ is

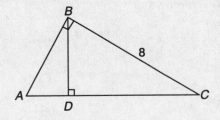

A. $\dfrac{2}{3}$.

D. $\dfrac{1}{2}$.

B. $\dfrac{4}{5}$.

E. $\dfrac{1}{3}$.

C. $\dfrac{1}{4}$.

50. In the figure, if $BD \parallel AE$, then which of the following must be true?

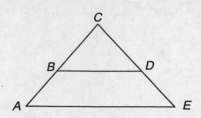

F. $\angle CBD = \angle CDB$

J. $\dfrac{\overline{CD}}{\overline{CE}} = \dfrac{\overline{BD}}{\overline{AE}}$

G. $\angle CAE = \angle CEA$

K. $\dfrac{\overline{CB}}{\overline{BD}} = \dfrac{\overline{CD}}{\overline{CA}}$

H. $\dfrac{\overline{CB}}{\overline{CA}} = \dfrac{\overline{CD}}{\overline{AE}}$

51.

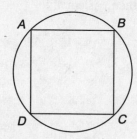

In the figure, if the square $ABCD$ has a side of length 3, then the circumference of the circumscribed circle is

A. 12π.

D. $6\pi\sqrt{2}$.

B. $4\pi\sqrt{3}$.

E. $3\pi\sqrt{2}$.

C. $2\pi\sqrt{10}$.

52.

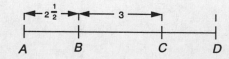

In the figure, if $\dfrac{\overline{AB}}{\overline{BD}} = \dfrac{1}{2}$, then the length of $\overline{CD}$ is

F. $\dfrac{1}{2}$.

J. $2\dfrac{3}{4}$.

G. 2.

K. 3.

H. $2\dfrac{1}{2}$.

53.

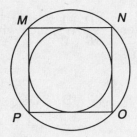

In the figure, if *MNOP* is a square with $\overline{MN} = x$, then the ratio

$$\dfrac{\text{circumference of circumscribed circle}}{\text{circumference of inscribed circle}} =$$

A. 2.

D. $2\sqrt{2}$.

B. $\sqrt{2}$.

E. $\dfrac{1}{2}$.

C. $\dfrac{1}{\sqrt{2}}$.

54.

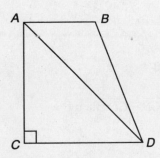

In the figure, $\overline{AB} \parallel \overline{CD}$ and $\triangle ACD$ is a right isosceles triangle. If $\overline{CD} = 6$ and $\overline{AB} = 4$, what is the area of $\triangle ABD$?

F. 2

J. 8

G. 4

K. 12

H. $4\sqrt{2}$

55.

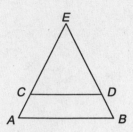

In the figure, $\overline{CD} \parallel \overline{AB}$ and $\dfrac{\overline{CD}}{\overline{AB}} = \dfrac{1}{2}$, then what is the ratio of the area of $\triangle CED$ to the area of $\triangle AEB$?

A. $\dfrac{1}{8}$ D. 2

B. $\dfrac{1}{4}$ E. 4

C. $\dfrac{1}{2}$

56.

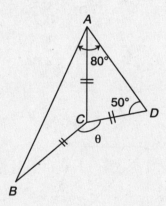

In the figure, if $\overline{AC} = \overline{CB} = \overline{CD}$, then $\theta =$

F. 40°.   J. 200°.

G. 120°.   K. 220°.

H. 160°.

57. Given $2\tan^2 x + \sec^2 x = 2$, what is $\tan x$?

A. $\dfrac{1}{2}\sqrt{3}$ B. $\dfrac{1}{\sqrt{3}}$

C. $\pm\dfrac{1}{\sqrt{3}}$ D. $2\sqrt{3}$

E. $\pm\sqrt{3}$

58.

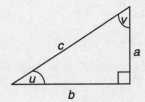

If $u + v = \dfrac{\pi}{2}$, find the value of $\sin^2 u + \sin^2 v$. (Use the figure above.)

F. $\sqrt{2}$

G. 1

H. $\dfrac{1}{\sqrt{2}}$

J. $2\sqrt{2}$

K. Cannot be determined from given information.

59. Use the diagrams below to find the value of $\cos\dfrac{1}{12}\pi$.

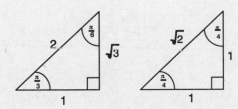

A. $\dfrac{\sqrt{2}}{4}\left(1+\sqrt{3}\right)$ D. $\dfrac{\sqrt{3}}{\sqrt{2}}$

B. $\dfrac{1}{2}\left(1+\sqrt{3}\right)$ E. $\dfrac{1}{2}\left(1-\sqrt{3}\right)$

C. $\left(1+\sqrt{3}\right)$

60.

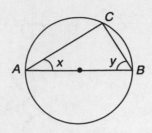

$\overline{AB}$ is the diameter of the circle, C is a point on the circle, and $\sin x = \dfrac{1}{3}$.

Evaluate $\sin y$.

F. $\dfrac{1}{\sqrt{2}}$

J. $\dfrac{4}{5}$

G. $2\sqrt{2}$

K. $\dfrac{3}{5}$

H. $\dfrac{2\sqrt{2}}{3}$

THIS IS THE END OF TEST 2.

Test 3: Reading

TIME: 35 Minutes
40 Questions

DIRECTIONS: This test consists of four passages, each followed by ten questions. Once you have read a passage, answer each question and fill in the appropriate oval on your answer sheet.

Passage I

An ancient Sage boasted, that, tho' he could not fiddle, he knew how to make a *great city* of a *little one*. The science that I, a modern simpleton, am about to communicate, is the very reverse.

5   I address myself to all ministers who have the management of extensive dominions, which from their very greatness are become troublesome to govern, because the multiplicity of their affairs leaves no time for *fiddling*.

In the first place, gentlemen, you are to consider, that a

10   great empire, like a great cake, is most easily diminished at the edges. Turn your attention, therefore, first to your *remotest* provinces; that, as you get rid of them, the next may follow in order.

That the possibility of this separation may always exist, take special care the provinces are never incorporated with the

15   mother country; that they do not enjoy the same common rights, the same privileges in commerce; and that they are governed by *severer* laws, all of *your enacting*, without allowing them any share in the choice of the legislators. By carefully making and preserving such distinctions, you will (to keep to my simile of

20   the cake) act like a wise gingerbread-baker, who, to facilitate a division, cuts his dough half through in those places where, when baked, he would have it *broken to pieces*.

Those remote provinces have perhaps been acquired, purchased, or conquered, at the *sole expence* of the settlers, or their

25   ancestors, without the aid of the mother country. If this should happen to increase her *strength*, by their growing numbers, ready to join in her wars; her *commerce*, by their growing demand for her manufactures; or her *naval power*, by greater employment for her ships and seamen, they may probably suppose some merit

30   in this, and that it entitles them to some favour; you are therefore to *forget it all, or resent it*, as if they had done you injury. If they happen to be zealous Whigs, friends of liberty, nurtured in revolution principles, *remember all that* to their prejudice, and re-

solve to punish it; for such principles, after a revolution is thor-
35 oughly established, are of *no more use*; they are even *odious* and
abominable.

However peaceably your colonies have submitted to your
government, shewn their affection to your interests, and patiently
borne their grievances; you are to *suppose* them always inclined
40 to revolt, and treat them accordingly. Quarter troops among
them, who by their insolence may *provoke* the rising of mobs,
and by their bullets and bayonets *suppress* them. By this means,
like the husband who uses his wife ill *from suspicion*, you may
in time convert your *suspicions* into *realities....*

45 If, when you are engaged in war, your colonies should vie
in liberal aids of men and money against the common enemy,
upon your simple requisition, and give far beyond their abilities,
reflect that a penny taken from them by your power is more
honourable to you than a pound presented by their benevolence;
50 despise therefore their voluntary grants, and resolve to harass
them with novel taxes. They will probably complain to your
parliaments, that they are taxed by a body in which they have no
representative, and that this is contrary to common right. They
will petition for redress. Let the Parliaments flout their claims,
55 reject their petitions, refuse even to suffer the reading of them,
and treat the petitioners with the utmost contempt. Nothing can
have a better effect in producing the alienation proposed; for
though many can forgive injuries, *none ever forgave contempt....*

Lastly, invest the General of your army in the provinces,
60 with great and unconstitutional powers, and free him from the
controul of even your own Civil Governors. Let him have troops
enow under his command, with all the fortresses in his possession; and who knows but (like some provincial Generals in the
Roman empire, and encouraged by the universal discontent you
65 have produced) he may take it into his head to set up for himself?
If he should, and you have carefully practised these few *excellent
rules* of mine, take my word for it, all the provinces will immediately join him; and you will that day (if you have not done it
sooner) get rid of the trouble of governing them, and all the
70 *plagues* attending their *commerce* and connection from hence-
forth and for ever.

From Benjamin Franklin, *The Ambassador of Political Reason.*

1. The author's purpose is

   A. to communicate the wisdom of an ancient sage.

   B. to advise ministers of churches who do not take time for fun and
   fiddling.

    C.   to describe how a little country can make itself a great one.

    D.   to tell how a great city may be reduced to a small one.

2.   The author compares

    F.   an empire to a cake.

    G.   a country to a gingerbread baker.

    H.   a minister to a cake.

    J.   a religious minister to a gingerbread baker.

3.   The passage was

    A.   to give advice to all rulers of small countries.

    B.   a tongue-in-cheek article.

    C.   from the viewpoint of a religious minister.

    D.   to inspire ministers to take time to "fiddle," or smell the roses.

4.   The best interpretation of the clause, "Let him [the General] have troops enow under his command..." is

    F.   let the General keep the troops in tow.

    G.   let the General have enough soldiers to command.

    H.   let the General have troops endowed with skill under his control.

    J.   let the General have captured troops to control.

5.   The author's reason for writing this passage is that he

    A.   hopes to help the ministers rid themselves of the trouble of governing the provinces.

    B.   hopes to help the ministers build their powers and increase the provinces.

    C.   is proposing new ideas on increasing the provinces of a country since this article was written only a few years ago.

    D.   is presenting the viewpoint of the colonies and the provinces to the mother country.

6.   Which of the following actions is least advisable in order to keep a large country intact?

    F.   Limit the General of the army of the large country to constitutional powers.

G. Give the citizens of the provinces the same rights as the citizens of the mother country.

H. Suppose the provinces to be always ready to revolt and treat them as if you expect revolt.

J. Do not require taxation without representation.

7. Which of the following actions by Parliaments toward the provinces is most advisable?

A. Flaunt their claims.

B. Allow petition for redress.

C. Refuse to suffer the reading of claims.

D. Take the necessary monies from your colonies by requisition and not benevolence.

8. How can one expect a great empire to be diminished most easily?

F. From within   H. At the edges

G. From without   J. From the ministers

9. To ensure separation of the provinces:

A. incorporate the provinces with the mother country.

B. do not give common rights.

C. allow them the right to enact their own laws.

D. allow them to choose legislators.

10. If there are zealous Whigs and friends of liberty in the provinces, the empire will be least likely to be reduced to a small one if

F. they are remembered in their prejudice by the empire.

G. they are punished for their principles by the empire.

H. they are punished by the empire after a revolution is already established.

J. the mother empire remembers that after the revolution is already established it may be too late to change.

Passage II

Though it is generally recognized from philosophic investigations extending over many years that heat is one manifestation of energy capable of being transformed into other forms such as mechanical work, electricity, or molecular arrangement, and de-
5 rivable from them through transformations, measurements of quantities of heat can be made without such knowledge, and were made even when heat was regarded as a substance. It was early recognized that equivalence of heat effects proved effects proportional to quantity; thus, the melting of one pound of ice
10 can cool a pound of hot water through a definite range of temperature, and can cool two pounds through half as many degrees, and so on. The condensation of a pound of steam can warm a definite weight of water a definite number of degrees, or perform a certain number of pound-degrees heating effect in water. So
15 that taking the pound-degree of water as a basis the ratio of the heat liberated by steam condensation to that absorbed by ice melting can be found. Other substances such as iron or oil may suffer a certain number of pound-degree changes and affect water by another number of pound-degrees. The unit of heat quan-
20 tity might be taken as that which is liberated by the condensation of a pound of steam, that absorbed by the freezing of a pound of water, that to raise a pound of iron any number of degrees or any other quantity of heat effect. The heat unit generally accepted is, in metric measure, the calorie, or the amount to raise one kilo-
25 gram of pure water one degree centigrade, or the B.T.U., that necessary to raise one pound of water one degree Fahrenheit.

All the heat measurements are, therefore, made in terms of equivalent water heating effects in pound-degrees, but it must be understood that a water pound-degree is not quite constant.
30 Careful observation will show that the melting of a pound of ice will not cool the same weight of water from 200° F to 180° F, as it will from 60° F to 40° F, which indicates that the heat capacity of water or the B.T.U. per pound-degree is not constant. It is, therefore, necessary to further limit the definition of the heat
35 unit, by fixing on some water temperature and temperature change, as the standard, in addition to the selection of water as the substance, and the pound and degree as units of capacity. Here there has not been as good an agreement as is desirable, some using 4° C = 39.4° F as the standard temperature and the
40 range one-half degree both sides; this is the point of maximum water density. Others have used one degree rise from the freezing point 0° C or 32° F. There are good reasons, however, for the most common present-day practice which will probably become universal, for taking as the range and temperatures, freezing-

45 point to boiling-point and dividing by the number of degrees. The heat unit so defined is properly named the mean calorie or mean British thermal unit; therefore,

$$\text{Mean calorie} = \frac{1}{100} \text{ (amount of heat to raise 1 Kg. water}$$

from 0° C to 100° C)

50 $$\text{Mean B.T.U.} = \frac{1}{100} \text{ (amount of heat to raise 1 lb. water}$$

from 32° F to 212° F)

From Charles Edward Lucke, *Engineering Thermodynamics*.

11. According to the author, which of the following is NOT true?

    A. Heat is capable of being transformed into mechanical work.

    B. Heat is derivable from molecular arrangement.

    C. Heat should be regarded as a substance.

    D. Measurements of quantities of heat can be made without knowledge of heat being derivable from mechanical work, electricity, or molecular arrangement.

12. The calorie and the B.T.U. are similar in that they both relate to

    F. one pound of water.

    G. the amount of heat necessary to raise the temperature one degree.

    H. the metric system.

    J. a pound of iron.

13. The author denies which of the following?

    A. The equivalence of heat effects proves proportional to quantity.

    B. The melting of one pound of ice can cool a pound of hot water through a definite range of temperature and can cool two pounds through twice as many degrees.

    C. The melting of one pound of ice can cool a pound of hot water through a definite range of temperature and can cool two pounds through half as many degrees.

    D. The condensation of a pound of steam can warm a definite weight of water a definite number of degrees.

14. The author states that

    F. a water pound-degree is constant.

G. the melting of ice will cool the same weight of water from 60° to 40° Fahrenheit as it will from 200° to 180° Fahrenheit.

H. the heat capacity of water or the B.T.U. per pound-degree is constant.

J. the heat capacity of water or the B.T.U. per pound-degree is not constant.

15. The author indicates a point of disagreement among scientists; this point of contention is

A. whether the melting point of ice will not cool the same amount of water from 200° to 180° Fahrenheit as it will from 60° to 40° Fahrenheit.

B. whether the heat capacity of water is constant.

C. whether the equivalence of heat effects proved effects proportional to quantity.

D. how to best limit the definitions of the heat unit.

16. The author appears to

F. be a proponent of the metric system.

G. be a proponent of the customary system.

H. be an opponent of the use of the mean calorie.

J. suggest that there are good reasons for taking the freezing-point to boiling-point as the range.

17. The purpose of the passage is to

A. advocate mean calories.

B. advocate mean British thermal units.

C. oppose mean calories and B.T.U.

D. advocate both mean calories and mean thermal units.

18. The author predicts

F. the universal adoption of the B.T.U.

G. the universal adoption of the calorie.

H. the universal calorie of the mean B.T.U. and the mean calorie.

J. the demise of the calorie and the universal adoption of the mean B.T.U.

19. The author would like to limit the definition of the heat unit by

    I.   fixing on some water temperature.

    II.   fixing on some temperature change.

    III. selecting water as the substance.

    IV.   using the pound as the unit of capacity.

    A.   I only.   C.   IV only.

    B.   II only.   D.   I, II, III, and IV.

20. The author's argument for limiting the definition of the heat unit is

    I.   to create an agreement within the scientific community regarding the heat unit.

    II.   to explain the inconsistencies found when melting a pound of ice to cool the same weight of water 20° F when heated to different temperatures.

    III. not fully explained in this passage.

    F.   I only.   H.   I and II only.

    G.   II only.   J.   I, II, and III.

Passage III

What, then, is the cause of the difference between Japanese painting and that of the Occident? Some say that the difference in the colouring matter and the brushes used has caused a wide divergence in the tone of Oriental and of Occidental painting.
5   This opinion is, however, far from conclusive. For, looking deeper into the matter, the question arises, "What has brought about all these differences in the pigments and the brushes, as well as in the technique adopted by artist of the East and of the West?" In my opinion here lies the key to the whole problem. In
10   the first place, Eastern and Western painters hold somewhat different views concerning the primary object of art, and from these results their disagreement in technique and other details. In order to understand the real source of the differences between Eastern and Western painting it is therefore requisite to study closely
15   their contents, which differ to some extent in essentials.

Painting should have for its object the expression of ideas, and as such "it is invaluable, being by itself nothing." In art an idea may be expressed in ways which differ, principally according to the two modes, the subjective and the objective. To state
20   the matter more explicitly, a painter may use the object he delineates chiefly for expressing his own thought, instead of revealing

the idea inherent in the object itself. On the contrary, another painter strives to bring out the spirit of the object he portrays, rather than to express ideas of his own that may arise in associa-
25 tion with the object. In general, Western painters belong to the latter class, while those of Japan to the former; the one laying stress on objective, and the other on subjective ideas. This distinction discloses the fundamental differences between Eastern and Western painting, which causes wide dissimilarities in con-
30 ception and execution.

Take for instance their subjects. Here one cannot fail to notice a marked contrast between Japanese and European pictures. In Western painting, where special importance is attached to objective qualities, the portraiture of human figures naturally
35 receives the foremost attention, as though it were nobler and grander than other themes. It is not because in man, unlike the lower creations, there exists a spirit, the interpretation of which, in its different manifestations, affords a rare scope for the artist's talent? Accordingly, in Occidental painting in which the expres-
40 sion of the spirit externally manifest in the object is made the chief point, human portraiture necessarily claims the first consideration. The same holds true not only of painting, but almost every other art. Conversely in Japanese pictures, flowers, birds, landscapes, even withered trees and lifeless rocks, are esteemed
45 as highly as God's highest creation—human being. The reason is not far to seek; it is simply this: landscapes, birds, flowers, and similar things may be devoid of soul, but the artist may turn them into nobler objects, as his fancy imparts to them the lofty spiritual attributes of man.
50 Anyone with an extensive knowledge of our pictures cannot fail to discern this common characteristic of composition, namely, that the centre of a picture is not found in any single individual object, for the guiding principle of the synthesis is expressed in the mutual relations of all the objects treated. In
55 other words, in Japanese painting no serious attempt is made to give all-exclusive prominence to any one particular object, but, instead, the effect of the whole is considered the point of prime importance. Hence in the minds of our painters, not each and every portion of a picture need be accurate, but the picture as a
60 whole should be microcosmically complete. Such is but the inevitable outcome of stress laid almost exclusively on subjective ideas.

From Sei-ichi Taki, *Three Essays on Oriental Painting*.

21. The term "Occidental art" refers to

    A.   accidental, or unintentional, art.

B. Western art.

C. non-Western art.

D. Oriental art.

22. The purpose of the article is to

F. contrast the paintings of the Japanese and the Occident.

G. compare the paintings of the Japanese and the Occident.

H. compare the contents of the paintings of the Occident and of the Japanese.

J. compare the composition of the paintings of the Japanese and the Occident.

23. A main difference between the Occidental and the Japanese paintings is

A. differing views concerning the primary object of art.

B. differing views on technique.

C. differing views of details.

D. differences in pigments and brushes.

24. The author's area of expertise appears to be primarily

F. Occidental painting.　　H. Oriental painting.

G. Japanese painting.　　J. Asian painting.

25. The Japanese painter can be said to

A. use the object he delineates to express his own thoughts.

B. express ideas of his own that may arise in association with the object.

C. stress objective ideas.

D. stress the spirit of the object being portrayed.

26. The painters of the pictures in Western art

F. give foremost attention to the human figure.

G. do not believe the human figure is grander than other themes.

H. accept the expression of the spirit.

J. esteem God's creations highly.

27. Japanese artists

    A. esteem rocks, trees, and flowers on the canvas as highly as human beings.

    B. see birds and flowers as having a soul.

    C. are not able to give landscapes, birds, and flowers lofty spiritual attributes.

    D. are not able to impart, through their fancy, spiritual attributes to non-human matter.

28. The author explains that in

    F. Japanese art the viewer can find a single individual object in the center of a picture.

    G. Japanese art there are mutual relations of all objects treated in a picture.

    H. Western art no one particular object receives all-exclusive prominence.

    J. Japanese painting a serious attempt is made to give all-exclusive prominence to any one particular object.

29. The author's primary purpose is to

    A. persuade the reader that Japanese art is superior to Western art.

    B. persuade the reader that Western art is superior to Japanese art.

    C. explain objectively some differences between Japanese and Western art.

    D. present the points in favor of Japanese art over Occidental art.

30. The reader should interpret the phrase, "...the picture as a whole should be microcosmically complete..." to mean

    F. Japanese paintings should be complete in every detail.

    G. every portion of the canvas should be completely covered with pigment so that, even if examined under a microscope, no area is without cover.

    H. everything on a canvas does not have to be accurate but rather the relations should be complete.

    J. the emphasis is placed on completion in objective terms.

Passage IV

It was there that, several years ago, I saw him for the first time; and the sight pulled me up sharp. Even then he was the most striking figure in Starkfield, though he was but the ruin of a man. It was not so much his great height that marked him, for the
5   "natives" were easily singled out by their lank longitude from the stockier foreign breed: it was the careless powerful look he had, in spite of a lameness checking each step like the jerk of a chain. There was something bleak and unapproachable in his face, and he was so stiffened and grizzled that I took him for an old man
10   and was surprised to hear that he was no more than fifty-two. I had this from Harmon Gow, who had driven the stage from Bettsbridge to Starkfield in pre-trolley days and knew the chronicle of all the families on his line.

"He's looked that way ever since he had his smash-up; and
15   that's twenty-four years ago come next February," Harmon threw out between reminiscent pauses.

The "smash-up" it was—I gathered from the same informant—which, besides drawing the red gash across Ethan Frome's forehead, had so shortened and warped his right side that it cost
20   him a visible effort to take the few steps from his buggy to the post-office window. He used to drive in from his farm every day at about noon, and as that was my own hour for fetching my mail I often passed him in the porch or stood beside him while we waited on the motions of the disturbing hand behind the grating. I noticed
25   that, though he came so punctually, he seldom received anything but a copy of the *Bettsbridge Eagle*, which he put without a glance into his sagging pocket. At intervals, however, the post-master would hand him an envelope addressed to Mrs. Zenobia—or Mrs. Zeena—Frome, and usually bearing conspicuously in the upper
30   left-hand corner the address of some manufacturer of patent medicine and the name of his specific. These documents my neighbour would also pocket without a glance, as if too much used to them to wonder at their number and variety, and would then turn away with a silent nod to the post-master.

35   Harmon drew a slab of tobacco from his pocket, cut off a wedge and pressed it into the leather pouch of his cheek. "Guess he's been in Starkfield too many winters. Most of the smart ones get away."

Though Harmon Gow developed the tale as far as his men-
40   tal and moral reach permitted there were perceptible gaps between his facts, and I had the sense that the deeper meaning of the story was in the gaps. But one phrase stuck in my memory and served as the nucleus about which I grouped my subsequent inferences: "Guess he's been in Starkfield too many winters."

45   Before my own time there was up I had learned to know
what that meant. Yet I had come in the degenerate day of trolley,
bicycle and rural delivery, when communication was easy between the scattered mountain villages, and the bigger towns in
the valleys, such as Bettsbridge and Shadd's Falls, had libraries,
50   theatres and Y.M.C.A. halls to which the youth of the hills
would descend for recreation. But when the winter shut down on
Starkfield, and the village lay under a sheet of snow perpetually
renewed from the pale skies, I began to see what life—or rather
its negation—must have been in Ethan Frome's young manhood.
55   I had been sent up by my employers on a job connected with
the big power-house at Corbury Junction, and a long-drawn carpen-
ters' strike had so delayed the work that I found myself anchored at
Starkfield—the nearest habitable spot—for the best part of the winter. I chafed at first, and then, under the hypnotizing effect of rou-
60   tine, gradually began to find a grim satisfaction in the life. During
the early part of my stay I had been struck by the contrast between
the vitality of the climate and the deadness of the community. Day
by day, after the December snows were over, a blazing blue sky
poured down torrents of light and air on the white landscape, which
65   gave them back in an intenser glitter. One would have supposed that
such an atmosphere must quicken the emotions as well as the blood;
but it seemed to produce no change except that of retarding still
more the sluggish pulse of Starkfield. When I had been there a little
longer, and had seen this phase of crystal clearness followed by long
70   stretches of sunless cold; when the storms of February had pitched
their white tents about the devoted village and the wild cavalry of
March winds had charged down to their support; I began to understand why Starkfield emerged from its six months' siege like a
starved garrison capitulating without quarter. Twenty years earlier
75   the means of resistance must have been far fewer, and the enemy in
command of almost all the lines of access between the beleaguered
villages; and, considering these things, I felt the sinister force of
Harmon's phrase: "Most of the smart ones get away." But if that
were the case, how could any combination of obstacles have hin-
80   dered the flight of a man like Ethan Frome?

From Edith Wharton, *Ethan Frome.*

31.   From the author's description of Ethan Frome, the reader can infer that he
was NOT

   A.   imposing.   C.   a ruin.

   B.   striking.   D.   approachable.

32. The reader can interpret the passage as saying

    I.   the inhabitants are more predictable than the winter.

    II. the inhabitants and the climate of Starkfield were volatile.

    III. the people were hypnotized by the routine weather.

    IV. the sluggishness of the people continued year round.

    F. I only.   H. I, II, and III only.

    G. I and II only.   J. I, II, III, and IV.

33. The narrator believes that

    A. it was easy to leave Starkfield 20 years before writing.

    B. Harmon was correct in saying, "Most of the smart ones get away."

    C. the resistance to leaving Starkfield has increased with time.

    D. the reasons for Ethan Frome's hindered flight from Starkfield were evident from his actions.

34. Ethan Frome can best be described as

    F. erratic.

    G. predictable.

    H. limited in "neutral and moral reach."

    J. drug-addicted.

35. Ethan Frome's physical destruction came

    A. when he was an impetuous man in his early twenties.

    B. when he was several years shy of 30.

    C. when he was a reckless teenager.

    D. when he was in his prime at 30.

36. The narrator of the passage can best be described as

    F. repelled by the stiffened, grizzled figure of Ethan Frome.

    G. satisfied with Harmon Gow and his information about Ethan Frome.

    H. an outsider, amused and entertained by Starkfield, and its residents.

    J. curious about Ethan Frome.

37. The phrase "checking each step like the jerk of a chain" (line 7) is best interpreted to mean that Ethan

    A. had served time on a chain gang.

    B. moved about with uncertainty and timidity.

    C. dragged along the dead weight of his injured leg.

    D. had a stocky build.

38. The phrase "singled out by their lank longitude" (line 5) evokes the

    F. tall stature of the town "natives."

    G. sailing history of the townfolk.

    H. animosity shown toward the "natives" by the foreigners in town.

    J. "natives" superiority over the foreign breed.

39. In context, which of the following supports Harmon Gow's observation, "Guess he's been in Starkfield too many winters" (lines 36–37) ?

    A. Ethan's striking figure

    B. Ethan's careless, powerful look

    C. Ethan's bleak and unapproachable face

    D. Ethan's awareness of Gow's opinion of him

40. It can be inferred from the passage that

    F. the narrator remained a stranger to the villagers.

    G. modern life had continued to pass the village by.

    H. the severe winters strengthened the bonds of the community.

    J. unusual circumstances compelled Ethan to stay there.

THIS IS THE END OF TEST 3.

Test 4: Science Reasoning

TIME: 35 Minutes
      40 Questions

DIRECTIONS: This test consists of seven passages, each followed by several questions. Once you have read a passage, answer each question. Then fill in the appropriate oval on your answer sheet.

Passage I

German astronomer Johannes Kepler (1571-1630) established three laws of planetary motion based on the following observations:

Kepler's First Observation

All planets revolve around the common center-of-mass of the Sun-planet system along closed orbits in the shape of ellipses. Both the Earth and Sun revolve around this common point in a period of one year. An ellipse is an eccentric (elongated) circle specifying two axes that intersect one another at right angles through their midpoints. The longer axis is called the major axis and the shorter one is called the minor axis. Equidistant from the midpoint on the major axis are two distinct points called the foci (plural of focus).

Kepler's Second Observation

The rotating vector of a planet moves across equal areas of its orbit in equal intervals of time. This rotating vector is a straight line that joins the center-of-mass of the Sun-planet system with the planet. At one point this vector is at maximum length and the planet is farthest from the common center-of-mass and the Sun. At an opposing point, the position vector is at a minimum length and the planet is closest to these points. As the position vector decreases in length, the planet's orbital speed increases, and vice versa. As a result, a planet's position vector covers equal areas of space in equal intervals of time.

Kepler's Third Observation

The square of a planet's orbital period is directly proportional to the cube of its semimajor axis. A planet's orbital period is the length of time required for it to complete one trip around the Sun. The semimajor axis of a planet's orbit is one-half the major axis, which is the average distance between the Sun and the planet. Therefore, the more distant a planet is from the Sun, the larger its orbit and the longer its path around the Sun.

1. Of the following orbital speeds, which one is representative of a planet closest to the Sun?

    A.   18 km/s   C.   35 km/s

    B.   30 km/s   D.   13 km/s

2. Which of the following semimajor axes represents the planet having the second fastest orbital speed?

   F.   778,000,000 Km   H.   414,000,000 Km

   G.   1,427,000,000 Km   J.   4,497,000,000 Km

3. Which of the following orbital eccentricities does not belong to an orbiting planet?

   A.   0.007

   B.   0.207

   C.   Exactly zero (circular)

   D.   Cannot be determined from the data supplied.

4. Of the following planetary periods, which one is representative of the planet closest to the Sun?

   F.   29.46 years   H.   0.241 years

   G.   16.48 years   J.   0.615 years

5. Which of the following statements is false?

   A.   There is a direct relationship between a planet's orbital period and distance from the Sun.

   B.   Planets move in circular and elliptical orbits.

   C.   The change in area with respect to time is constant for each planet.

   D.   Choices B and C are both correct.

6. The semimajor axis is equal to

   F.   twice the semiminor axis.

   G.   the sum of the planet's minimum and maximum distance from the Sun.

   H.   half of the sum of the planet's minimum and maximum distance from the Sun.

   J.   the sum of the semiminor and major axes.

Passage II

The number of snails in a random population decreases exponentially for twenty days. Afterwards, the number of snails decreases linearly until about sixty days, when the last death occurs. The death rate is influenced by the genetic composition of the organism. Figure 1 shows the number of snails remaining in a random population as a function of time expressed as a percentage of the population at time = 0.

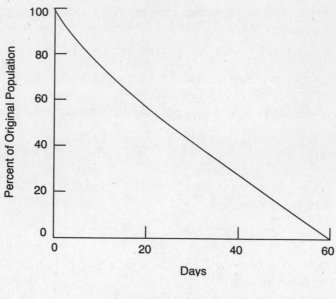

Figure 1

Experiment 1

A scientist collected snails for a genetic experiment. First, she collected snails with a single black stripe on their shells. These snails, designated X207, had a linear mortality rate. She also collected snails with no stripe. These she called wild type. She then mated the wild-type snails with the X207 snails and recorded the mortality data.

Table 1—Life span of progeny (X207 × wild type)

Marking	% of population	Age when 50% are dead
no stripe	52.7	16 days
one stripe	47.3	30 days

The scientist noted that when X207 snails were allowed to mate among themselves, snails with two stripes appeared in the population.

Table 2—Life span of progeny (X207 × X207)

Marking	% of population	Age when 50% are dead
no stripe	23.7	17 days
one stripe	58.7	31 days
two stripes	17.6	44 days

Experiment 2

Another study has suggested that the life span of the wild-type snail is dependent upon the temperature of the water in which they live. It is also known that the dissolved oxygen content of the water is dependent upon the temperature. Thus, the oxygen content of the water varied with temperature. In all cases, the water was obtained from the same source and its chemical composition was analyzed. The nutrient contents of the different water samples were deemed to be equivalent.

Table 3—Life span of wild-type snail

Water Temp	Dissolved O_2	Age when 50% are dead
20	100	15
20	70	15
20	50	14
23	100	10
23	70	17
23	50	20
25	100	19
25	70	20
25	50	25

7. From the data in Tables 1 and 2, one would expect that in a population of X207 snails with a single stripe, all snails would be dead within

   A. 20 days.   C. 52.5 days.

   B. 40 days.   D. 65 days.

8. The data in Tables 1 and 2 suggest that each stripe adds increased life expectancy to the described species of snail. From the data in Table 2, the approximate increase in half-life of the snail per stripe is:

   F. 5 days.   H. 15 days.

   G. 10 days.   J. 25 days.

9. Using the data in Tables 1 and 2, calculate the percentage of single-striped snails that would be expected from matings within a population that initially has a distribution of 100% wild-type snails.

   A. 49%   C. 24%

   B. 0.06%   D. 0%

10. Refer to the data in Table 3. At higher temperatures, reducing the dissolved oxygen content in the snails' environment causes life expectancy to

    F. increase.

    G. decrease.

    H. remain unchanged.

    J. Cannot be determined from these data.

11. Refer to Figure 1. These data can best be explained by

    A. the presence of two different populations of snails in the test environment.

    B. the toxic condition of the environment .

    C. additional availability of a required nutrient during the early phase of data collection.

    D. All of the above.

12. Refer to the data in Table 3. As the water temperature of the snails' environment decreases, life expectancy of the snail tends to

    F. increase.

    G. decrease.

    H. remain unchanged.

    J. Cannot be determined from these data.

Passage III

A hurricane is an intense storm of tropical origin with winds of at least 64 knots. Hurricanes occur when thunderstorms develop over warm water in the Atlantic and Pacific oceans. These thunderstorms organize and become hurricanes when the surface winds begin to converge and the system starts to rotate. The center of the storm is known as the eye. The eye of the storm exhibits calm winds and skies are clear to partly cloudy. Around the circumference of the eye is the eye wall. The eye wall is an area of dense thunderstorms and is the most intense part of the storm. The Saffir-Simpson Scale (Table 1) was developed to classify the strength of hurricanes.

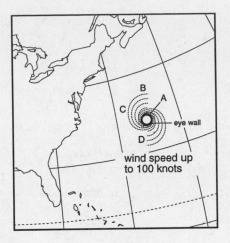

Figure 1

Table 1—Saffir-Simpson Hurricane Scale

Scale Category	Barometric Pressure (mb)	Wind Speed (knots)	Storm Surge (meters)	Damage
1	>980	64-82	<1.5	light
2	965-979	83-95	2.0-2.5	moderate
3	945-964	96-113	2.5-4.0	extensive
4	920-944	114-135	4.0-5.5	major
5	<920	>135	>5.5	severe

13. What scale category would the hurricane in Figure 1 be classified under?

A. Category 1

B. Category 2

C. Category 3

D. Category 4

14. What type of damage would be expected if a hurricane was reported to have a barometric pressure of 933 mb and a storm surge of 5.0 meters?

F. Severe

G. Extensive

H. Light

J. Major

15. What conclusion could be made if a hurricane with a maximum wind speed of 64 knots and a barometric pressure of 980 mb suddenly lost strength?

A. It would become a Category 2 hurricane.

B. It would no longer be considered a hurricane.

C. It would cause extensive damage.

D. The eye wall of the hurricane would intensify.

16. Regarding Figure 1, which area of the hurricane would have a wind speed of 100 knots?

F. Location A

H. Location C

G. Location B

J. Location D

17. Given the following data, which storm(s) would be considered a hurricane?

Storm Number	Maximum Wind Speed (knots)	Lowest Barometric Pressure (mb)	Area of Storm Formation
1	84	970	Canadian Mountains
2	98	955	Atlantic Ocean over warm water
3	55	968	Pacific Ocean over warm water

A. Storms 1, 2, and 3.

C. Storm 2 only.

B. Storms 2 and 3.

D. Storm 3 only.

Passage IV

The diagram below shows a Fenn-Winterstein Respirometer.

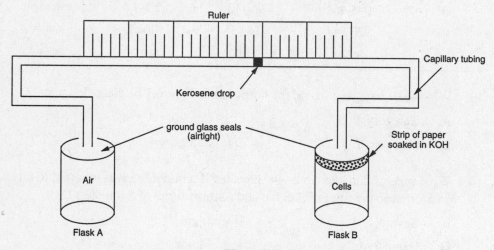

Figure 1

Living cells are sealed in Flask B, along with a strip of paper soaked in potassium hydroxide. As the cells consume oxygen, the kerosene drop moves. If the diameter of the capillary tube is known, the amount of oxygen consumed can be calculated.

This apparatus can be used to measure the respiration or metabolic rate of different cell types. Table 1 shows the distance the kerosene drop moved after 30 minutes and after 2 hours.

Table 1

Flask	Cell type	# cells/ml	Doubling time	Distance (0.5 h)	Distance (2 h)
1	*E. coli*	1×10^6	20 min	2 mm	6 mm
2	CHO	1×10^6	48 hr	0	0
3	HeLa	1×10^6	24 hr	0	0.5
4	H2B7	1×10^7	1 hr	1	1.5
5	H2B7	1×10^6	1 hr	1	2

18. To calculate the amount of oxygen consumed per hour, we need to know

   F. the volume of the capillary tube.

   G. the distance the kerosene drop moved per hour and the volume of the capillary tube.

   H. the distance the kerosene drop moved per hour, the volume of Flask A, and the volume of the capillary tube up to the drop.

   J. the distance the kerosene drop moved per hour and the diameter of the capillary tube where it lies along the ruler.

19. The CHO cells have not consumed oxygen in two hours. We might conclude that

   A. they have probably died.

   B. the KOH paper has absorbed the oxygen before it could get to the cells.

   C. the cells haven't multiplied enough to use measurable oxygen.

   D. there were too few cells of this strain to begin with.

20. Which of the following statements is best?

   F. A lower doubling time results in greater oxygen consumption.

   G. Without the KOH paper, CO_2 production would influence the movement of the kerosene drop.

   H. Both of the above.

   J. None of the above.

21. If the flasks were sealed with cotton instead of ground glass, we could expect

    A. the kerosene drop to move to the right.

    B. the kerosene drop to move to the left.

    C. the cell culture to become contaminated.

    D. the kerosene drop not to move.

22. A possible explanation for the fact that Flask 4 of H2B7 cells moved the drop only 1.5 mm after two hours (while the cells in Flask 5 moved it 2 mm) is that

    F. the growth of the cells in Flask 4 was beginning to slow down in two hours.

    G. there were fewer cells in Flask 4 to begin with.

    H. increased CO_2 production saturated the KOH, which resulted in a lowering of the pH in the flask.

    J. None of the above.

Passage V

As an electro-analytical chemist, you are testing new combinations of components to design batteries. In electrolytic cells the cathode, which is negatively charged because it is attached to the negative terminal of the battery, provides electrons to the electron-deficient species in the cathode compartment. Consequently, reduction takes place at the cathode. At the anode oxidation takes place so that electrons are released at the anode. Some means of maintaining the electrical neutrality in the cell must be provided. A salt bridge is one such device that allows ions to flow back and forth between the two solutions.

Experiment 1

In an electrolytic cell, you placed a solution of $CuSO_4$, a cathode, and an anode. A current of 5.0 A was passed through the solution for 6.0 hours.

Experiment 2

In another experiment a Ni/Cu galvanic cell is constructed by placing a 1 M $NiSO_4$ in one side of a two-chambered cell, with a 1 M $CuSO_4$ solution in the other chamber. A copper electrode is placed in the chamber with the Cu^{2+} solution, and a nickel electrode is placed in the side with the Ni^{2+} solution. The cell potential is measured using a voltmeter and is found to be 0.59 V. The volume of 1 M $NiSO_4$ solution varied and the potential and duration of the current flow between the cells is measured.

Table 1—Battery lifetime

Volume of 1 M $NiSO_4$	Potential , V	Time (min)
10 ml	+0.59	0.2
30	+0.59	1.0
50	+0.59	5.0
70	−0.59	5.0
100	−0.59	5.0

Table 2—Cell potential vs. temperature

Temperature	$[Sn^{2+}]$ solution	$[Ni^{2+}]$ solution	Potential
25	1.0 M	1.0 M	+0.1100 V
50	1.0	0.5	0.1196
10	1.0	0.2	0.1296
25	2.0	1.0	0.1189
50	2.0	0.5	0.1293
10	2.0	0.2	0.1381
25	0.5	1.0	0.1011
50	0.5	0.5	0.1100
10	0.5	0.2	0.1212

23. Which of the following diagrams would represent a Ni/Cu galvanic cell used in Experiment 2?

A.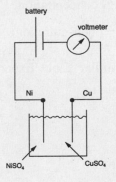

B.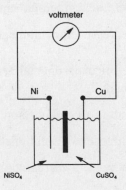

C. 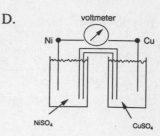 D.

24. According to Table 1, at 70 ml of 1 M $NiSO_4$ solution, what can be concluded about the direction of movement of the electrons in the cell compared to that at lower volumes?

   F.   There is no movement of electrons.

   G.   The electrons have reversed direction.

   H.   The electrons are moving in the same direction.

   J.   The electrons are moving back and forth.

25. Based on the results of the experiments, what is the main function of an electrolytic cell?

   A.   To produce electrical energy

   B.   To produce a current

   C.   To consume electrical energy

   D.   To produce a potential

26. What could an electro-analytical chemist do in order to increase the cell potential at a constant $[Sn^{2+}]$ concentration in Table 2?

   F.   Increase $[Ni^{2+}]$ concentration.

   G.   Decrease $[Ni^{2+}]$ concentration.

   H.   Increase temperature and decrease $[Ni^{2+}]$ concentration.

   J.   Decrease temperature and increase $[Ni^{2+}]$ concentration.

27. In terms of experimental set-up, what is similar about Experiment 1 and Experiment 2?

   A.   Both use a cathode and an anode.

   B.   Both use two solutions in the cell.

   C.   Both pass a current through the solution.

   D.   Both have the same temperature for the solutions.

28. What type of cell was used to generate the data in Table 2?

    F. An electrolytic cell, since two different solutions are used

    G. An electrolytic cell, since a potential was produced

    H. A galvanic cell, since a potential was produced

    J. A galvanic cell, since the temperature is changing

Passage VI

Physicist 1

A solar corona is a halo of glowing gases surrounding the star. It can reduce the gravitational pull of the star and extends far into space solely by maintaining a temperature that is over 200 times hotter than the surface, or several million degrees Kelvin. The existence of the corona contradicts standard thermodynamics principles, which state that the temperature should decrease with increasing distance from the star's core. The star's core produces the energy.

Most physicists believe that the corona is formed by mechanical means. The mechanical energy of the churning from the Sun's outer layers gets pumped up into the corona. The major mechanism of this churning is through bundles of magnetic field lines that arch over the Sun's surface. Small pockets of turbulence in these bundles may generate heat. These sparklike releases of magnetic energy, "nanoflares," heat the corona by spewing high energy particles.

The footprints of the magnetic bundles shuffle around on the surface of the star. Hence, the field lines in the bundles can be stretched and twisted like rubberbands resulting in a build up of magnetic energy. When adjacent field lines reconnect, energy is released and tension is reduced. Several reconnections occur every second, and thus immense quantities of heat are released. Using this mechanism, the corona then has the potential for being much hotter than the surface.

Physicist 2

The energy released by the nanoflares is not sufficient to heat the corona. Since these energy fluxes have never been recorded on high resolution x-ray movies, their energy release is not significant. Instead, the corona is heated by strong electrical currents which are forced along the bundles by the magnetic activity on the surface.

Images of solar coronas show the slim tubular appearance of the magnetic bundles. The explanation for these shapes is the assumption of current. The electric current would generate spiraling magnetic fields which wrap around the bundles and prevent them from bulging. Thin gases are heated by the electrical resistance. The principle is similar to heating the air in a toaster by the toaster filaments. If any instabilities occur in the magnetic field, they would be incorporated into the tubular shape and increase the current. This results in additional heat production.

29. Which of the following statements would support the hypothesis of Physicist I?

   A. Spiraling electric fields create nanoflares which heat the corona.

   B. Churning from the sun's outer layers increases the currents and results in heat production.

   C. Turbulence in the magnetic field bundles cause the corona to be over 200 times hotter than the surface.

   D. Electrical resistance heats thin gases that make up the corona.

30. Suppose that energy fluxes were recorded on high resolution x-ray film. How would this new information affect the two theories?

   F. It would refute Physicist II because the energy release from nanoflares would be significant.

   G. It would refute Physicist I because electrical fluxes prevent spiraling magnetic fields from bulging.

   H. It would support Physicist I because adjacent field lines reconnect and energy is released.

   J. It would refute Physicist II because instabilities within the magnetic field would reduce the current.

31. Which of the following statements is inconsistent with the theory that the corona is heated by electric currents?

   A. Solar coronas show the thin tubular appearance of the magnetic bundles.

   B. The mechanical energy of churning from the sun's outer layers gets pumped into the corona.

   C. Electric currents generate spiraling magnetic fields.

   D. Thin gases are heated by electrical resistance.

32. According to the information available, as field lines in the bundles are stretched and twisted

   F. adjacent field lines reconnect.

   G. instabilities occur in the magnetic field.

   H. encrgy is released and tension is reduced.

   J. magnetic energy builds up.

33. The existence of the corona is an atypical phenomenon because

   A. the temperature of the corona decreases with increasing distance from the core.

   B. the temperature of the corona increases with increasing distance from the core.

   C. magnetic bundles appear as slim tubules.

   D. footprints of magnetic bundles shuffle around the surface of the star.

34. According to the passage, both physicists agree that

   F. the formation of the corona is by mechanical means.

   G. the formation of the corona is by electrical means.

   H. the magnetic activity on the surface of the star is important in the formation of the corona.

   J. the energy released by nanoflares is important in the formation of the corona.

35. Which of the following conclusions is supported by Physicist II?

   A. Thin gases are heated by magnetic repulsion, a principle similar to heating the air in a toaster.

   B. The presence of electric currents cause the corona to be over 200 times hotter than the surface.

   C. Churning from the Sun's outer layers creates mechanical energy.

   D. Nanoflares heat the corona by spewing high energy particles.

Passage VII

To test the validity of global warming, scientists have investigated the average temperature and rainfall over the past one hundred years. To obtain data for the last millennium, researchers have examined the widths of tree rings of either redwoods or petrified samples. From the dark rings, relative changes in average seasonal temperature and rainfall were deduced. The lighter rings only reflected changes in rainfall. Combining these data sets, the scientists have been able to determine whether current climate changes have resulted from natural phenomena or have been induced by human interference.

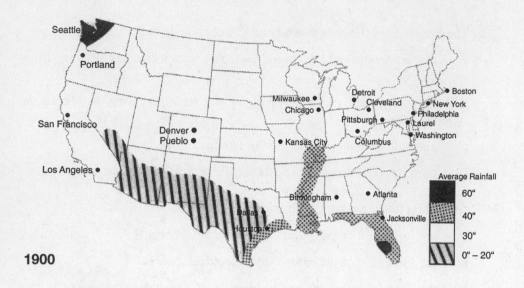

1900

1980

Figure 1—Average Rainfall 1900 and 1980 Compared

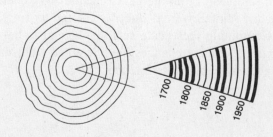

Figure 2

Table 1

Year	Region	Average Temperature
1900	Northeast	52.5° F
	Midwest	61.2
	Alaska	23.5
1920	Northeast	50.4
	Midwest	60.3
	Alaska	20.4
1940	Northeast	48.2
	Midwest	63.4
	Alaska	21.4
1960	Northeast	51.3
	Midwest	65.5
	Alaska	20.2
1980	Northeast	55.3
	Midwest	67.2
	Alaska	19.9

36. The change in rainfall of the Northeast between 1900 and 1980 is

    F.   10-20 inches decrease.   H.   50-60 inches decrease.

    G.   10-20 inches increase.   J.   50-60 inches increase.

37. The average temperature change in the Midwest from 1920 to 1960 was

    A.   63.4.   C.   3.1.

    B.   5.2.   D.   65.5.

38. The population has increased in the United States from 1900 to 1980. From the data given in Table 1, it can be inferred that

    F.   there is a definite human influence on the weather.

    G.   there is no significance in the changes in temperature in the United States.

    H.   the Midwest must have had a large population increase.

    J.   no inference can be made between the population and temperature changes.

39. Over the last 100 years, there has been

    A. a change in temperature only.

    B. a change in rainfall only.

    C. a change in rainfall and temperature.

    D. no changes in rainfall or temperature.

40. The largest temperature change from 1900 to 1980 occurred in

    F. the Northeast.   H. Alaska.

    G. the Midwest.   J. the West.

THIS IS THE END OF TEST 4.

ACT ASSESSMENT EXAM II

ANSWER KEY

Test 1: English

1. (C)	20. (H)	39. (D)	58. (H)
2. (H)	21. (C)	40. (F)	59. (B)
3. (C)	22. (J)	41. (C)	60. (J)
4. (J)	23. (D)	42. (J)	61. (C)
5. (B)	24. (J)	43. (B)	62. (G)
6. (G)	25. (D)	44. (J)	63. (D)
7. (D)	26. (H)	45. (D)	64. (J)
8. (F)	27. (D)	46. (H)	65. (A)
9. (B)	28. (F)	47. (C)	66. (F)
10. (H)	29. (B)	48. (G)	67. (C)
11. (B)	30. (J)	49. (C)	68. (G)
12. (J)	31. (C)	50. (J)	69. (D)
13. (D)	32. (J)	51. (C)	70. (J)
14. (G)	33. (C)	52. (J)	71. (B)
15. (C)	34. (G)	53. (A)	72. (H)
16. (J)	35. (D)	54. (H)	73. (C)
17. (D)	36. (H)	55. (D)	74. (H)
18. (H)	37. (D)	56. (G)	75. (C)
19. (B)	38. (J)	57. (C)	

Test 2: Mathematics

1. (A)	5. (C)	9. (D)	13. (D)
2. (K)	6. (H)	10. (G)	14. (G)
3. (C)	7. (B)	11. (D)	15. (C)
4. (H)	8. (H)	12. (J)	16. (K)

17.	(D)	28.	(H)	39.	(E)	50.	(J)
18.	(F)	29.	(B)	40.	(F)	51.	(E)
19.	(B)	30.	(F)	41.	(B)	52.	(G)
20.	(F)	31.	(B)	42.	(G)	53.	(B)
21.	(C)	32.	(F)	43.	(D)	54.	(K)
22.	(J)	33.	(C)	44.	(H)	55.	(B)
23.	(C)	34.	(J)	45.	(E)	56.	(H)
24.	(J)	35.	(C)	46.	(G)	57.	(C)
25.	(B)	36.	(H)	47.	(C)	58.	(G)
26.	(G)	37.	(D)	48.	(K)	59.	(A)
27.	(C)	38.	(J)	49.	(E)	60.	(H)

Test 3: Reading

1.	(D)	11.	(C)	21.	(B)	31.	(D)
2.	(F)	12.	(G)	22.	(F)	32.	(F)
3.	(B)	13.	(C)	23.	(A)	33.	(B)
4.	(G)	14.	(J)	24.	(G)	34.	(G)
5.	(D)	15.	(D)	25.	(D)	35.	(B)
6.	(H)	16.	(J)	26.	(F)	36.	(J)
7.	(B)	17.	(D)	27.	(A)	37.	(C)
8.	(H)	18.	(H)	28.	(G)	38.	(F)
9.	(B)	19.	(D)	29.	(C)	39.	(C)
10.	(J)	20.	(J)	30.	(H)	40.	(J)

Test 4: Science Reasoning

1.	(C)	11.	(A)	21.	(D)	31.	(B)
2.	(F)	12.	(G)	22.	(F)	32.	(J)
3.	(C)	13.	(C)	23.	(D)	33.	(B)
4.	(H)	14.	(J)	24.	(G)	34.	(H)
5.	(B)	15.	(B)	25.	(C)	35.	(B)
6.	(H)	16.	(F)	26.	(G)	36.	(G)
7.	(D)	17.	(C)	27.	(A)	37.	(B)
8.	(H)	18.	(J)	28.	(H)	38.	(J)
9.	(D)	19.	(C)	29.	(C)	39.	(C)
10.	(F)	20.	(H)	30.	(F)	40.	(G)

DETAILED EXPLANATIONS OF ANSWERS

Test 1: English

1. **(C)** Because choice (C) is clearly and directly stated, it is the correct answer. It doesn't exhibit the confused and repetitive working of Dark Age "origin" and church "emergence," nor does it include the unnecessary phrase "so-called," as does choice (A). Further, (A)'s use of "so-called" implies the author will make a point about the possible inaccuracy of the term "Dark Ages," which he does not. The repetition of the phrase "the church" slows the sentence's forward momentum, making (B) a poor choice. Because choice (D) contains the redundant "beginnings" and "origins" and the misleading "so-called," it, too, is incorrect.

2. **(H)** Subject-verb agreement comes into play in each choice here. As the plural subject "plays" correctly takes the plural verb "date," choice (H) is the correct grammatical answer. (F) incorrectly uses the singular "dates," and choice (G) compounds the error by adding an unnecessary comma. (J)'s error is in the poor subject-verb agreement and in its wordy phrase "in all probability." A common error in verb agreement is seeking to identify a subject within a prepositional phrase which intervenes between the real subject and the verb. A subject will never appear within a prepositional phrase such as "outside the church." Being familiar with a large variety of prepositions will help avoid this mistake.

3. **(C)** The correctly placed possessive apostrophe in "drama's" and the absence of the comma which allows a close logical link between the prepositional phrase "for drama's exit" and the term it modifies, "reason," makes (C) the right answer. Choice (A) lacks the necessary possessive apostrophe, while choice (B)'s misuse of the semicolon indicates incorrectly that the phrase "for drama's...man" is an independent clause. Choice (D) inserts commas to offset the prepositional phrase "for drama's exit" and thus interrupts the logical flow of the sentence.

4. **(J)** Because of the grammatical use of the semicolon to separate two independent clauses and because the verb "abounded" is consistent with the past tense of the rest of the passage, choice (J) is correct. Choice (F) is guilty of placing a comma between two independent clauses, thus committing a comma splice error. Even with the insertion of the term "in" before "which," as logic demands, the remaining sentence becomes so convoluted that it makes little sense; thus, choice (G) is incorrect. A comma splice also occurs in choice (H), an error which is compounded by the unnecessary switch from past to present perfect tense.

5. **(B)**   Because of its simple past tense in keeping with the rest of the passage, choice (B) is correct. (A) unnecessarily switches to present, (C) to future perfect, and (D) to present perfect. If the logic of the passage demands a change in verb tense (for example, if the passage is generally in the present and the writer makes reference to actions in the past), switching tense is correct. Otherwise, tense should remain consistent.

6. **(G)**   Choice (G)'s straightforward wording makes it the correct answer. It avoids (F)'s negative and confusing idiom of "no small effort" by substituting "great" in place of "no small." It also eliminates the comma preceding "and" evident in choice (H). Generally, a comma should precede "and" when the conjunction joins two independent clauses or when it precedes the last item in a list of three or more. Choice (J) is guilty of the same sort of negative and confusing working of choice (F) because "no great" simply translates into "small" and compounds the error by inserting an unnecessary comma.

7. **(D)**   Because the festival of Corpus Christi is not related to the history of drama presented in this passage, the underlined section should be entirely omitted, as suggested by choice (D). Thus, choices (A), (B), and (C), which rephrase the reference to the festival, are all incorrect.

8. **(F)**   The necessary possessive form "its," choice (F), modifying the noun "home," is the correct answer. "Its'" is not a word at all, so choice (G) is incorrect. Choice (H), "it's," is the contraction for "it is" and when used in this manner, makes no sense. Nor does (J)'s phrase "it is" make sense when inserted in place of the possessive form.

9. **(B)**   Due to its direct wording and the lack of the unnecessary comma used to separate the participial phrase "depicting...Testaments" from the word it modifies, "cycles," choice (B) is correct. Choice (A) lacks a subject for the dependent clause introduced by the subordinating conjunction "during which." "They" would appropriately complete the clause, but it is missing. Choice (C) misuses the semicolon, misleading the reader into thinking the participial phrase is indeed an independent clause. A clause must have a subject and a complete verb, which the phrase does not. Wordiness is the error of choice (D).

10. **(H)**   Because of its economy of language and lack of unnecessary punctuation, choice (H) is correct. Choice (F) places a redundant possessive apostrophe after "character," but the possession is already established by the earlier phrase "story *of*." Choice (G) misuses the possessive apostrophe and inserts the wordy phrase "of biblical import," said more directly with the simple adjective "biblical" preceding 'character." (J) suffers from similar wordiness, with verbiage that does nothing to improve upon the content and succinct language of choice (H).

11. **(B)** The direct, precise wording of choice (B) coupled with its correctly placed commas surrounding the fairly lengthy appositive phrases, "the language of liturgical dramas" and "the language of the people," makes this the correct answer. Choice (A) is quite wordy because of the unnecessary phrases "the use of" and "which was." It is the wordy and redundant phrase "which was" that makes (C) a poor choice as well. Choice (D) lacks the necessary offsetting commas around the lengthy appositive phrases and is not parallel in is sentence structure because "their vernacular" should precede "the language of the people." It is best to keep comparative parts of a sentence in similar grammatical structure and order. In this manner, the sentence will be more direct and forceful.

12. **(J)** Due to its correct use of the semicolon to separate two independent clauses, choice (J) is the right answer. Choice (F) creates a comma splice error in connecting these independent clauses by a mere comma. Choice (G) fuses the two independent clauses by omitting any grammatical means of connection, and choice (H) creates a comma splice with the comma following "two" and an incorrect placement of the semicolon.

13. **(D)** The phrase "not only" demands a later accompanying segment prefaced by "but." Because choice (D) is the only selection that provides this option, it is the correct answer. "[A]nd," as suggested by choice (A), does not fulfill the implied "not just, but more" meaning set up by the "not only" phrase. Choice (B) not only makes the previous error but incorrectly inserts an unnecessary comma. A conjunction joining two phrases, such as the verb phrases "introduced..." and "changed...," is not preceded by a comma. Placing a semicolon between "drama" and "changed," as does choice (C), incorrectly indicates the words following the semicolon are a sentence; yet, they lack a subject.

14. **(G)** The simplicity and direct wording of choice (G) recommend it as the correct answer. All of the other choices are redundant, as "final," "conclusion," and "concluding" are all fairly synonymous. Choice (J) compounds its redundancy error by incorrectly placing a comma after "end," implying that the phrase "of the fourteenth century" is to be set off by commas. Not only would the offsetting disrupt the logic of the sentence by indicating that another century was in question, but the companion comma is not present.

15. **(C)** The only use of fresh language occurs in (C). Thus, it is the correct choice. (A), (B), and (D) use clichés, which by overuse have lost any imagery they might initially have inspired. It is generally better to use one's own imagery or language that the worn-out phrases of others.

16. **(J)** The clear subject-verb agreement in choice (J) makes it the correct choice. The singular subject "research" takes the singular verb "requires." Choice

(F) incorrectly suggests the plural verb "require" as does choice (G). Pluralizing "nature," the object of the preposition "of," does not affect "require," and thus choice (G) is incorrect. Subjects for verbs are not located within prepositional phrases. Choice (H) is incorrect, as it changes the transitive verb "requires," which acts upon the direct object "traits," into the intransitive form "was required." Intransitive verbs take no direct object; yet, the direct object remains in the sentence, thus making (H) a poor choice.

17. **(D)** Because of the correctly placed comma separating an introductory dependent clause from the following independent one and because of the correct subjective/nominative case form of "who," choice (D) is the right answer. Note that the relative pronoun "who" acts as the subject of the dependent clause it begins, "who can perform college-level functions in other areas," thus necessitating the subjective/nominative case. Choice (A)'s use of the semicolon incorrectly indicates that an independent clause precedes it and another follows it; however, the first clause cannot stand on its own and make sense, thus making it dependent. Further, the case of "who" is incorrect. The incorrect placement of the comma preceding "and" is choice (B)'s problem. In a list of just two items, simply the conjunction is sufficient; the comma becomes redundant. Choice (C) exhibits the incorrect case of "whom."

18. **(H)** Choice (H) is correct because it provides the necessary comparative term "more" left out in choices (F), (G), and (J). Without this term to define the relationship between "some" and "others," the sentence makes no sense. "That," of choice (G), does not clarify the point of the comparison either.

19. **(B)** Due to directness of wording, choice (B) is the correct answer. It does not exhibit the redundancy of "required" and "necessary," terms which mean essentially the same thing. It is this redundant usage that makes choices (A), (C), and (D) incorrect.

20. **(H)** Because it correctly separates two independent clauses by a semicolon, choice (H) is correct. Choice (F) fuses the independent clauses by providing neither the semicolon nor the comma and coordinating conjunction. Choice (G) commits a subject-verb agreement error by suggesting the plural verb "mean" coordinate with the singular subject "that." Finally, choice (J) exhibits a comma splice error by placing the comma between the two independent clauses.

21. **(C)** Choice (C) is correct because it inserts no unnecessary punctuation between the independent clause and the following essential dependent clause. Further, choice (C) correctly uses the plural pronoun "they" to refer to the plural antecedent "parents." Choice (A) incorrectly places a semicolon between the independent clause and the dependent one. Choice (B) converts the second inde-

pendent clause to dependent through its use of the subordinating conjunction "as," thus eliminating the need for a semicolon, but it commits a pronoun agreement error by referring to the plural antecedent "parents" by the singular, gender-specific pronoun "she." Finally, choice (D) incorrectly treats the dependent clause as a complete sentence and makes the pronoun agreement error.

22. **(J)**   Because of its clear reference to "parents" of Sentence 4 and the pattern of logic between the parents' difficulty in learning math (Sentence 4) and the negative mindset toward math (Sentence 2), Sentence 2 should be placed at the end of Paragraph 2, after Sentence 4, as choice (J) correctly indicates. Choices (F) and (G) fail to provide an antecedent reference for Sentence 2's "they," and therefore are poor choices. Choice (H) not only fails to provide that antecedent for "they" but additionally presents a different voice, the first person plural "us" and "we," thus resulting in a most confusing passage were it chosen.

23. **(D)**   Direct wording qualifies choice (D) as the correct answer. Choice (A) unnecessarily repeats the pronouns "we" and "ourselves," and choice (B) implies a comparison is to be made; yet, this comparison fails to materialize. The wordy inclusion of "we" and the ponderous introductory dependent clause of choice (C) simply cannot compete with the economy of language of choice (D).

24. **(J)**   Because the correct linking verb "are" and the comparative term "better" are employed to show a relationship between two groups (girls and boys), choice (J) is correct. Choice (F) adds the superfluous and thus incorrect linking verb "being," and choice (G) uses the superlative "best," reserved for comparison of three or more things. As Choice (F) was superfluous in its inclusion of the second linking verb, so choice (H) is in the unnecessary "more." "Better" does the job alone.

25. **(D)**   The placement of the possessive apostrophe following the plural "girls" and the economy of language makes (D) the correct answer. Although possessive apostrophe placement is correct in choice (B), the phrase is wordy, and thus is not the correct answer. Because the passage deals with girls in general, not one girl in particular, the possessive apostrophe in "girls" must reflect that plurality, and choice (C) does not. Further, choice (C) suggests a voice change to second person plural; yet, nowhere in this section is that familiar relationship presented.

26. **(H)**   Because it separates the two independent clauses with a semicolon, choice (H) is correct. By separating them with a comma, choice (F) commits a comma splice error. The correct method of separating independent clauses is with a semicolon *or* with a comma and a coordinating conjunction.

The *semicolon* and coordinating conjunction render choice (G) incorrect. Choice (J) converts the second independent clause to a dependent clause by the use of the subordinating conjunction "when," but a dependent clause is not separated from an independent clause by a semicolon but by, at most, a comma. Thus, choice (J) is incorrect as well.

27. **(D)**   Because of the agreement between the singular verb "continues" and the singular subject "search" and the correct separation of two independent clauses by a comma and a coordinating conjunction, choice (D) is correct. Choice (A) fails to include the necessary comma between the independent clauses and instead fuses them together. Choice (B) correctly separates the clauses but exhibits a subject-verb agreement error. A common error is to seek the subject within a prepositional phrase and make the verb agree with that "subject." However, subjects are not found in prepositional phrases, even if they are long phrases or a series of phrases, as is the case here. A series of prepositional phrases begins with "for concrete" and does not end until "...in math." A comma splice is choice (C)'s error.

28. **(F)**   Because in choice (F), the original, both the plural pronoun "these" and plural verb "have" agree with the plural subject "women," it is the correct answer. Choice (G) incorrectly employs the singular pronoun reference "this," and choice (H) inconsistently switches to a singular "this woman" when the study involves many women. Choice (J) commits multiple errors by illogically changing to the singular "woman" yet using the plural pronoun "these" to refer to her.

29. **(B)**   Because choice (B) offers no unnecessary punctuation between the independent clause and the essential dependent clause "that differs..." which follows it, and because the verb "differs" agrees with the singularity of the last term ("brain organization") in a series of items separated by "or," it is the correct choice. Choice (A) inserts an unnecessary comma between the independent and dependent clauses, and choice (C) incorrectly treats the dependent clause as independent by indicating it is a complete sentence. Choice (D) inserts an unnecessary comma and commits a subject-verb agreement error between "organization" and "differ."

30. **(J)**   Because choice (J) includes the topics of Paragraph 4, women's biological makeup and life experience as applied to math, and the topic of Paragraph 1, differences in mathematical mindsets, it qualifies as the best means of unifying the entire passage. Choices (F) and (G) focus only on the biological and genetic issues, and choice (H) only elaborates on the very specific issues of Ph.D.'s mentioned briefly in Paragraph 4. A unifying sentence must bring the ideas of *two* parts together and not focus on just one.

31. **(C)**   This passage deals with males and females on the issue of math education; thus "gender issues in education," choice (C), is clearly the best answer. Although education is a passage focus, fun and relaxation are never mentioned, eliminating choice (A) as a possibility. As no famous mathematicians are mentioned in the passage, choice (B) can also be eliminated. Yes, the myth of gender and math is discussed in the passage, but certainly not religion or ancient mythology. Thus, choice (D) is incorrect.

32. **(J)**   The correct placement of the semicolon between two independent clauses and the agreement between the plural subject "some" and the plural verb "are" make choice (J) the right answer. Choice (F) uses a comma to separate the two independent clauses, thus committing a comma splice error. The superfluous and therefore incorrect use of the semicolon *with* the coordinating conjunction "and" to separate two independent clauses makes choice (G) incorrect. Not only is choice (H) guilty of a comma splice error, but of a subject-verb agreement error as well.

33. **(C)**   Because of its direct organization and economy of language, choice (C) is correct. Choice (A) is confusing, particularly in the placement of the phrase "for some," which would be more clearly situated after "frightening alone." By following the participial phrase "Having...toothache" by "the dentist," choice (B) misleads the reader into thinking the dentist has the toothache when logic requires it be the patient with the offending tooth. The wordiness of choice (D) precludes it from being the correct choice. The sequence of the two lengthy prepositional phrases beginning with "for," for example, is awkward and slows the cadence of the sentence.

34. **(G)**   By offsetting with commas the entire appositional phrase, "an irrational...dentist," (G) becomes the correct choice. Choice (F) commits a comma splice error when it places the comma between two independent clauses. The failure to enclose the appositive entirely by commas (the first of the set should be located between "phobia" and "irrationally" but is missing) renders choice (H) incorrect. Generally, when an appositive is over three or four words, it must be enclosed by commas to give the sentence clarity. Choice (J) fails to add either enclosing comma and thus is incorrect.

35. **(D)**   Subject-verb agreement is the basic concern in this case. Choice (D) is the only answer which correctly provides a plural verb to coordinate with the plural subject "equipment and technology." Choice (A) is incorrect in is use of the singular verb "does not help" for the plural subject. Choice (B)'s "help not" is both awkward in its reversal of the adverb and verb and incorrect in its plural subject-singular verb relationship. Finally, choice (C) exhibits a subject-verb disagreement problem similar to that of choice (A). The only difference between the two is that choice (C) makes the contraction "doesn't" out of "does not."

36. **(H)**   As the infinitive phrase "to relax" is not interrupted by any other term and thus is intact and the plural pronoun "their" accurately relates to the plural antecedent "Others," choice (H) is the correct answer. Choice (F) incorrectly suggests a singular pronoun "his" to refer to a plural antecedent, and choice (G) not only splits the infinitive phrase by inserting the adverb "better" between "to" and its verbal object "relax" but provides the singular pronoun "his" to refer to the plural antecedent "Others." Although choice (J) is correct in its presentation of two singular pronouns, "his" or "her," the grammatical issue is singularity and plurality, and the plural antecedent remains in need of a plural pronoun reference. Thus, choice (J) is also incorrect.

37. **(D)**   By employing the plural pronoun "their" and the plural noun "bodies" (as several persons do not inhabit just one body), choice (D) is correct. Choice (A) offers the singular pronoun "one's" and the single noun "body" to refer to a plural antecedent "patients," and thus is logically and grammatically incorrect. Choice (B) fails to provide the necessary plural "bodies," incorrectly substituting the singular "body." Compounding the singularity error with both the pronoun and the noun, choice (C) even fails to insert the necessary possessive apostrophe between "one" and "s."

38. **(J)**   Pronouns ending in "one," such as "someone," are considered to be in the third person singular form. Because choice (J)'s reference to "someone" is the third person singular pronoun "his" or "her," it is the correct answer. Choice (F) lapses into third person *plural* and choice (G) is in *second* person plural; therefore, both are incorrect. The first person singular case of "my" works no better, and so choice (H) is wrong.

39. **(D)**   Due to redundancy of the term "fear," already established earlier in the sentence as a cause of avoiding the dentist, the entire underlined portion should be omitted, as suggested correctly by choice (D). Because (A), (B), and (C) all incorporate similar redundancies with the term "fear," they are all incorrect.

40. **(F)**   The article "a" preceding "twice-yearly dental cleaning and exam" denotes this procedure is meant to be considered a single process, and all verbs, then, should conform to its singularity. Because the singular verb "is" does just that, and because the noun "way" provides the necessary noun to be modified by the following adverbial phrase "to avoid...complications," choice (F) is correct. The plural "are" is not in agreement with the singular "exam," nor is the noun "ways"; therefore, choice (G) is incorrect. Although the verb agrees in number with the subject in choice (H), "way" is missing, thus leaving the infinitive phrase "to avoid..." with nothing to modify. As a result, the sentence suggested by this last choice makes no sense.

41. **(C)**   By capitalizing "cavities" and making it begin a new sentence, choice (C) has correctly created and identified an independent clause. The insertion of the subordinate conjunction "since" renders this group of words a dependent clause, which, despite the presence of a clear subject and verb, cannot stand alone as a sentence and make sense. It depends on an independent clause for logic. Thus, choice (A), a fragment, is incorrect. It is this same use of subordinating conjunctions ("when" and "whereas") that causes choices (B) and (D) to be fragments as well.

42. **(J)**   The simple, direct, and complete wording of choice (J) makes it the correct answer. Choice (F) incorrectly indicates that the phrase "thanks...equipment" is a complete sentence; yet, it lacks both a subject and a verb. Choice (G) similarly indicates that the phrase is an independent clause by the use of the semicolon, but, of course, it is not, for the same reasons it is not a complete sentence. Choice (H) is incorrect because of its wordiness.

43. **(B)**   Because of the correctly placed possessive apostrophe before the "s" in the singular possessive "today's," the plural subject "dentists" which agrees with the later plural verb "use," and the correct use of the commas to offset the adverbial conjunction "however," choice (B) is the right answer. Not only does choice (A) lack the possessive apostrophe for "todays," an apostrophe necessary as an ownership relation exists between that term and "dentists," but it misuses the semicolon, reserved for separating independent clauses. An independent clause has a subject and a verb and can stand on its own as a complete sentence, if necessary. The phrase following "however" provides the verb for the subject "dentists" and has no subject of its own; thus, choice (A) is incorrect. Choice (C) is out of agreement with the plural verb "use" by providing a singular subject "dentist." Finally, choice (D) incorrectly places the possessive apostrophe after the "s" in "todays," illogically indicating there is more than one "today."

44. **(J)**   Paragraph 2 is correctly placed after Paragraph 4, as indicated by choice (J). Paragraph 4 introduces the advanced technology used in dental offices, providing the earlier reference the first sentence in Paragraph 2 demands when it states, "Such sophisticated equipment and techniques." This logical link is lacking in all the other choices.

45. **(D)**   Choice (D) is correct. The fear that cost may be painful exists, but not in the same sense of physical pain as the original passage depicts, and thus it should go into a separate paragraph. Choice (A) is incorrect in its presumption that everything of importance should be introduced in the beginning. Choice (B), too, is incorrect, for Paragraph 3's pain is, again, pain of the body. Money has nothing to do with Paragraph 4, but rather modern technology; thus, choice (C) is incorrect.

46. **(H)**   "Consequences" is the key to this question. The only answer which deals with consequences is choice (H), where "dental decay and gum disease" are the *consequences* of poor dental care. Listing the "rewards" for good dental care, as suggested by choice (F), is completely counter to the results of poor dental care. Comparing dentists, as choice (G) offers, may be interesting, but it doesn't address the consequences of missed appointments. Finally, choice (J)'s explanation may give the reader a method to avoid the consequences but still doesn't state what those consequences are, as the writer requires.

47. **(C)**   Because the expression "in general" is entirely offset by commas, suggests the verb "have," which agrees in number with the plural subject "people," and is consistent with the present tense of the passage, choice (C) is correct. Choice (A) is incorrect because it places the comma only at the beginning of the adjectival phrase. The basic rule is that commas must either entirely surround the word or phrase or be absent altogether. Choice (B) exhibits two errors: the presence of only one comma in conjunction with "in general" and a lapse into past tense with "had." By incorrectly supplying the singular verb "has" to coordinate with the plural subject "people," choice (D) becomes a poor choice.

48. **(G)**   The correct choice here is (G), for it suggests the objective case pronoun "us," which acts as the object of the preposition "between." The nominative/subjective case "we," as presented in choice (F), is incorrect because the pronoun does not act as the subject of a clause. Not only is "they" a nominative case pronoun but coupled with "'re" becomes the contraction for "they are," which renders the remainder of the sentence nonsense. Thus, choice (H) is incorrect. The illogical use of the possessive pronoun "their" indicates that the public owns the humans, thus making choice (J) wrong, as well.

49. **(C)**   In this sentence, "however" acts as an adverb meaning "in whatever way," not as a conjunction meaning "but." As a conjunction joining two independent clauses, "however" is generally preceded by a semicolon, but when used as an adverb, the semicolon is incorrect. Consequently, choice (C)'s punctuation with commas is correct. In (A), (B), and (D), the semicolon is in error.

50. **(J)**   Because of its economical language and the correct subject-verb agreement of the singular subject "scheme" with the singular verb "takes," choice (J) is correct. Not only is choice (F) excessively wordy, but the verb "are" takes a plural subject, and the subject of the sentence, "scheme," is singular. Thus, (F) is in error. A good rule to remember is not to be misled by a sentence beginning with "There." In such sentences, one should generally expect the subject to follow the verb, and in this case it does, with an intervening prepositional phrase "among the inhabitants" thrown in. One would also do well to ignore prepositional phrases when seeking a subject, for a subject will never appear in such a

place. Choices (G) and (H), too, exhibit the same subject-verb disagreement as (F), and therefore are incorrect, as well.

51. **(C)** Because of its correct use of the semicolon to separate two independent clauses and its clarifying comma following "that is," choice (C) is correct. Choice (A) fuses the two independent clauses together by offering no means of punctuation. The proper coordinating conjunction "and" is present in choice (B), but the conjunction must be preceded by a comma to avoid sentence fusion. Because it is not, choice (B) is a poor answer. Further, it lacks the clarifying comma following "that is." Finally, choice (D) commits a comma splice error by seeking to separate the two independent clauses by just a comma.

52. **(J)** The directness of the simple verb "held" works best and needs no auxiliaries. Adherence to this point and the logical use of the subordinate conjunction "If," denoting that a possibility is being suggested rather than a statement of fact, recommend choice (J) as the correct answer. Choices (F) and (G) illogically use the subordinate conjunctions "Since" and "Because," respectively. These conjunctions are synonymous, and both incorrectly indicate that humans do treat their environment with respect. Thus, (F) and (G) are poor choices. (H) suffers by the use of "of," commonly mistaken for "have." "Of" is certainly illogical, and even if correctly stated as "have," would exhibit a tense switch from the sentence's simple subjunctive past to past perfect. (H), too, is then incorrect.

53. **(A)** The original choice (A) is correct as it provides a verb to complete the subject "solutions" of the independent clause beginning with "perhaps." The main error of choices (B) and (C) is that in introducing a new dependent clause beginning with "which," both eliminate the verb necessary for the previous subject "solutions." The omission of the underlined portion suggested by choice (D) would also result in this absence of a verb for the subject "solutions."

54. **(H)** Because of its logical and straightforward presentation, (H) is the correct choice. Choice (F) lacks a comma after "cooperation," a mark of punctuation that would greatly clarify the sentence and correctly separate the rather lengthy appositive "as lesson...need" from the noun ("cooperation") it renames/defines. Choice (G) is incorrect due to logic error. "[A] cooperation lesson about humans" makes little sense. Choice (J) suggests a "cooperative lesson," indicating that creatures and humans will join together in the classroom, as it were. Certainly, this isn't the passage's intent, and thus choice (J) is incorrect.

55. **(D)** Because of its clear and non-redundant wording in the differentiation of "eating habits" and "food," (D) is logical in defining what is being carried and therefore is the correct choice. Grammatically, the pronoun "it," as used in

choice (A), refers to the noun "intake," not to the adjective "food," which describes *what kind* of intake. Logically, one cannot carry "food intake," and thus choice (A) is incorrect. Choice (B) suffers the redundancy of "food," and is therefore incorrect as well. "It," as used in choice (C), has no logical antecedent, for "table manners" cannot be carried. Consequently, choice (C) is a poor answer.

56. **(G)**   The singular possessive form "its" correctly refers to the singular references "each other" and "neither," as in "neither *one* nor *the other*." (F) incorrectly indicates the plural possessive. One must be careful to make the pronoun agree with its most recent antecedent. A common error, in this case, would be to refer to the earlier plural antecedent "raccoons." There is no such word as choice (H)'s "its'." Finally, the contraction "they're" ("they are") makes no sense when included in the sentence ("...neither could reach places on *they are* own."), so choice (J) is incorrect.

57. **(C)**   By logically linking Paragraph 4's topic of cooperation to Paragraph 5's focus on cruelty, choice (C) makes the best transition from Paragraph 4 and the best introduction to Paragraph 5. Choice (A) fails to introduce Paragraph 5's topic, settling rather on just the cleverness of raccoons as mentioned in Paragraph 4; thus (A) offers no connection between the paragraphs. Choice (B) focuses on the harm suggested in Paragraph 5 but shows no connection to the ideas of Paragraph 4 and thus makes a poor transition. Choice (D) also focuses solely on the issues of violence, cruelty, selfishness, and greed presented in Paragraph 5, totally ignoring the issues of cooperation presented in Paragraph 4, and thus is not the best choice for transition.

58. **(H)**   The economical and direct wording of (H) recommends it as the correct choice. Choice (F) inserts the empty phrase "something that is," qualifying this answer as too wordy. Similarly, choice (G) inserts even more empty verbiage with the dependent clause "that which is." (J) is guilty of the same wordiness and compounds the error by inserting an unnecessary comma separating the relative pronoun from its antecedent "something."

59. **(B)**   By correctly separating the two independent clauses by a semicolon, choice (B) is the right answer. Choice (A) presents no punctuation between these independent clauses and thus commits a fusion error. Creating a comma splice by separating the independent clauses by a comma, choice (C) too, is incorrect. Choice (D) incorrectly uses the semicolon and, by eliminating the pronoun "they," leaves the following clause without a subject.

60. **(J)**   The article "a" indicates that "penny" is to be treated as singular. Because ownership is the relationship between "penny" and "worth," a posses-

sive apostrophe must be added. Consequently, choice (J)'s singular possessive "penny's" is the correct answer. Choice (F) is incorrect due to the lack of the possessive apostrophe and the plural form of "pennies." Although the singular form "penny" is correct in choice (G), the possessive apostrophe is missing. That possessive apostrophe is present in choice (H), but "pennies" is in its plural form, not following the singular dictate of the article "a."

61. **(C)**   The purpose is to establish that humankind does, indeed, possess now the negative qualities of cruelty, greed, and dishonesty. What better way to establish this fact than to give specific instances of these characteristics, as choice (C) correctly does? Although choice (A) deals with negative characteristics, it doesn't pursue these in humans and thus is incorrect. A contrast between meat-eaters and plant-eaters does not give the necessary focus to humans that the author wishes, and therefore, choice (B) is a poor answer. Giving suggestions to rectify the problems in humans, as does choice (D), is quite admirable, but, again, does little to establish first that these problems are actually present, as the author hopes. Thus choice (D) is not the best strategy to achieve the author's purpose.

62. **(G)**   Two independent clauses meet at the conjunction of "roof" and "but." Because both are independent, it is grammatically correct to make the latter into a separate sentence as does choice (G). However, presenting neither punctuation nor coordinating conjunction between the two independent clauses, as does choice (F), creates a grammatical flaw of sentence fusion. By separating the clauses by a mere comma, choice (H) commits a comma splice error. Choice (J)'s insertion of the coordinating conjunction "and" indicates a coordinate part of the previous clause is to follow; however, what follows is a new dependent clause beginning with the subordinate conjunction "when." The "and" is still missing its coordinate part, and thus the sentence is incomplete.

63. **(D)**   As the pronoun "they" clearly relates in plurality and third person voice to "young people" and as the verb "want" logically remains in the present tense, choice (D) is correct. Because of the illogical switch to the past tense "wanted," choice (A) is incorrect. Again, tense switching is the problem as choice (B) moves unnecessarily to the wordier "are wanting." Although the present tense of choice (C) is both consistent and logical, the voice has illogically switched to the second person "we" when the third person "young people" is clearly the antecedent reference.

64. **(J)**   By logically linking Sentence 2's issue of middle age with Sentence 3's topic of women working outside the home, choice (J) offers the best transition sentence of those presented. Choice (F) makes no reference to women, the focus of Sentence 3, and is therefore a poor choice. The point of choice (G), that women are forced unhappily to work outside the home, is a direct contradiction of Sentence 3, which notes that women *choose* to work in the business sector. Thus, choice (G) is

incorrect. Although choice (H) does present the issue of starting a family relatively late in life, as does Sentence 2, it makes no reference to women in the outside work force and so provides insufficient transition to make it a good answer.

65. **(A)**   Choice (A)'s direct, correct, and economical language recommends it as the best answer. Although grammatically correct, choice (B) is stylistically wordy and therefore is not the correct choice. Grammatically incorrect because of the absence of the necessary linking preposition "of" and the conjunctive adverb "than," choice (C) makes no sense. The problem with choice (D) is the incorrect use of the singular pronoun "she" in reference to the plural antecedent "women."

66. **(F)**   Correctly punctuated by a comma preceding the coordinating conjunction "and," which serves to join the two independent clauses, choice (F), the original, is the right answer. Often, verbal phrases such as "Having children," act as nouns, and in this specific case, the verb phrase, or gerund, takes the subject position in the sentence. Simply because a word has a verbal ending such as "ed" or "ing" does not mean that it can act only as a verb. Confusion on this issue sometimes results in punctuation errors. The punctuation error evident in choice (G) is the comma inserted between the two independent clauses, resulting in a comma splice. Lacking separating punctuation at all, choice (H) is guilty of a fusion error. By inserting the subordinating conjunction "since," choice (J) implies a dependent clause is to follow, which is fine; however, the elimination of the gerund "having" leaves the subject of the clause as the plural noun "children," which doesn't agree in number with the singular verb "is." Thus, choice (J) is incorrect.

67. **(C)**   Choice (C) correctly inserts a comma between the dependent phrase ending with "considerations" and the independent clause beginning with "many." By placing a period after "considerations," choice (A) incorrectly indicates the initial phrase is an independent clause; yet, of course, it lacks a subject and a verb. The insertion of the comma and the conjunction "for," as suggested in choice (B), results in an illogical sentence. "For" indicates a cause-and-effect relationship between the idea preceding the conjunction and the idea following it. However, the relationship has already been established as one of providing further information, as indicated by the use of "In addition," which begins the sentence. Choice (D), "; yet," results in an illogical sentence, as did (B).

68. **(G)**   Because of its consistent and clear plural pronoun "they," which refers to the plural "couples," choice (G) is correct. The original version, choice (F), inserts the singular pronoun "one," which refers, illogically, to the immediately preceding noun "teenager." This choice has the teenager approaching old age. Choice (H) unnecessarily and illogically switches to the past tense "were" when the sentence is set up in present. Again, because of an illogical pronoun,

"he," choice (J) suggests the parents have difficulty when the teenager approaches old age. Of course, it is the problem of the aging parents dealing with a teenager that is the topic under discussion.

69. **(D)**   The plural possessive pronoun "their" coupled with the plural possessive "parents'" makes choice (D) the correct answer. Choice (A) fails to include the necessary possessive apostrophe to demonstrate ownership between the parents and their generation and thus is incorrect. Choice (B) is both wordy and includes an unnecessary possessive apostrophe after the "s" in "parents." Ownership between the parents and their generation has already been established by the use of "of," and thus the apostrophe is superfluous. Two errors occur in choice (C). First, the adverbial "there," indicating location, is illogically used instead of the logical possessive "their." Second, "parent's" is treated as singular possessive by the apostrophe placement; yet, the antecedent is clearly plural, as biology dictates all people originally have two parents.

70. **(J)**   The logical use of the comparative term "as" makes (J) the correct answer. The median age in 1987 for men to marry the first time is placed in comparison to the median age in 1890. Choice (F)'s use of "than" indicates an uneven comparison (a contrast); yet, the term "high" is not adjusted to "high*er*." "If," as used in choice (G), implies that we don't know the statistics of 1890, but the logic of the sentence acknowledges that we do; otherwise, the comparison would be meaningless. Choice (H)'s inclusion of the adverb "later" results in a blunder in logic; 1890 is earlier, not later, than the present.

71. **(B)**   The clear use of the present tense verb "choose" recommends (B) as the correct choice. Choice (A) lacks the necessary auxiliary verb "are" to make the verb complete, and choice (C) switches to past participial form. Unless logic demands, verb tense should remain consistent. The incorrect formation of the main verb "chose" causes (D) to be a poor choice. When linked with "have," the single main verb must be "chosen."

72. **(H)**   The logical placement of modifying phrases and clauses of choice (H) makes it the correct answer. Choice (F) illogically places the clause "that includes two-income partners" after "trend." "[T]oward later marriages" is the trend and should be placed as close as possible to that modified term. Choice (G)'s clause "that includes two-income partners," needs to be placed closer to "marriages," the term it modifies. Both of the aforementioned clauses are separated from the words they modify, as exhibited in choice (J), and thus the resulting sentence is quite confusing.

73. **(C)**   Because of its economical and grammatically correct formation, choice (C) is the right answer. Choices (A) and (B) suffer from the redundant

usage of "in a divorce," and choice (D) exhibits the non-standard and thus incorrect verb "be."

74. **(H)**   The most appropriate title for the essay is (H), "Changing Family Structures," for the different changes in marriages, child-bearing, and working wives over the past century are reviewed. Neither the methods of raising a child nor the eighteenth century are covered in the passage, thus negating (F) as a viable choice. Issues concerning high achievers are not mentioned, thus eliminating (G) as a possibility. Retirement planning is not even alluded to in this essay, and so choice (J), too, is an inappropriate chapter heading.

75. **(C)**   Paragraph 3 is the only section in which single men and marriage patterns are mentioned. Because of this connection, choice (C) is the most logical choice to deal with confirmed (lifelong) bachelors. All important material need not be mentioned in the first paragraph, counter to choice (A)'s assertion. If the assertion were true, no one would ever read more than one paragraph of any given text. Choice (B) falsely asserts that no other paragraph mentions single men, and so it is an inappropriate choice. Certainly commentary about confirmed bachelors is but a specific support in this essay, not a topic which could summarize the primary issues dealing with the trend for marriages and family to come later in life. Consequently, choice (D) is incorrect.

Test 2: Mathematics

1.   **(A)** $\sqrt{16} + 3\sqrt{12} - 5\sqrt{3} = 4 + 3(\sqrt{4} \times \sqrt{3}) - 5\sqrt{3}$

$$= 4 + 3(2\sqrt{3}) - 5\sqrt{3}$$
$$= 4 + 6\sqrt{3} - 5\sqrt{3}$$
$$= 4 + \sqrt{3}$$

2.   **(K)**   When working with several groupings, we perform the operations in the innermost parenthesis first, and work outward. Thus, we first subtract $(c - a + 3b)$ from b:

$$x = a + 2[b - (c - a + 3b)] = a + 2(b - c + a - 3b)$$

Combining terms, $= a + 2(-c + a - 2b)$

Distributing the 2, $= a - 2c + 2a - 4b$

Combining terms, $= 3a - 2c - 4b$

To check that $a + 2[b - (c - a + 3b)]$ is equivalent to $3a - 2c - 4b$, replace a, b, and c by any values. Letting $a = 1$, $b = 2$, $c = 3$, the original form

$$
\begin{aligned}
a + 2[b - (c - a + 3b)] &= 1 + 2[2 - (3 - 1 + 3 \times 2)] \\
&= 1 + 2[2 - (3 - 1 + 6)] \\
&= 1 + 2[2 - 8] \\
&= 1 + 2\,(-6) \\
&= 1 + (-12) \\
&= -11
\end{aligned}
$$

The final form, $3a - 2c - 4b = 3(1) - 2(3) - 4(2) = 3 - 6 - 8$

$$= -11$$

Thus, both forms yield the same result.

3. **(C)**   If $5 < a < 8$ and $6 < b < 9$, then ab will be bounded by (5×6) and (8×9).

4. **(H)**   If we want to prove a statement false, we only have to give a counter example.

Let $p = 3$ and $q = 5$.

$pq + 1 = 16$ (not prime)

$pq - 1 = 14$ (not prime)

Therefore, I and II are false. Since p and q are prime, they cannot possibly have a common factor. Thus, III is true.

5. **(C)**

$$\frac{\dfrac{1}{b}}{3} - \frac{1}{5}$$

$$\frac{b}{3} = 5$$

$$b = 15$$

6. **(H)** $12 = 2 \times 2 \times 3$

$15 = 3 \times 5$

LCM $(12, 15) = 2 \times 2 \times 3 \times 5 = 60$

7. **(B)**   A first method is to just add the terms in the numerator and denominator. Since 6 is the least common denominator of the numerator, $\left(\dfrac{2}{3} + \dfrac{1}{2}\right)$, we

convert $\dfrac{2}{3}$ and $\dfrac{1}{2}$ into sixths:

$$\frac{2}{3} = \frac{2}{3} \times 1 = \frac{2}{3} \times \frac{2}{2} = \frac{4}{6} \text{ and } \frac{1}{2} = \frac{1}{2} \times 1 = \frac{1}{2} \times \frac{3}{3} = \frac{3}{6}$$

Therefore, $\dfrac{2}{3} + \dfrac{1}{2} = \dfrac{4}{6} + \dfrac{3}{6} = \dfrac{7}{6}$

Since 12 is the least common denominator of the denominator, $\left(\dfrac{3}{4} - \dfrac{1}{3}\right)$, we

convert $\dfrac{3}{4}$ and $\dfrac{1}{3}$ into twelfths:

$$\frac{3}{4} = \frac{3}{4} \times 1 = \frac{3}{4} \times \frac{3}{3} = \frac{9}{12} \text{ and } \frac{1}{3} = \frac{1}{3} \times 1 = \frac{1}{3} \times \frac{4}{4} = \frac{4}{12}$$

Therefore, $\dfrac{3}{4} - \dfrac{1}{3} = \dfrac{9}{12} - \dfrac{4}{12} = \dfrac{5}{12}$

Thus, $\dfrac{\dfrac{2}{3} + \dfrac{1}{2}}{\dfrac{3}{4} - \dfrac{1}{3}} = \dfrac{\dfrac{7}{6}}{\dfrac{5}{12}}$

Division by a fraction is equivalent to multiplication by the reciprocal; hence,

$$\frac{\dfrac{7}{6}}{\dfrac{5}{12}} = \frac{7}{6} \times \frac{12}{5}$$

Canceling 6 from the numerator and denominator:

$$= \frac{7}{1} \times \frac{2}{5} = \frac{14}{5}$$

8. **(H)**
$$a + \frac{1}{a} = 2$$
$$\frac{a^2 + 1}{a} = 2$$
$$a^2 + 1 = 2a$$
$$a^2 - 2a + 1 = 0$$
$$(a - 1)^2 = 0$$
$$a = 1$$

9. **(D)** To determine the next number, we look for a pattern among the previous terms. Only the denominators differ. We note by inspection that each denominator is equal to the product of two successive integers. For example,

the first term: $\dfrac{1}{2} = \dfrac{1}{1 \times 2}$

the second term: $\dfrac{1}{12} = \dfrac{1}{3 \times 4}$

the third term: $\dfrac{1}{30} = \dfrac{1}{5 \times 6}$

Thus, the next term in the sequence can be expected to be

$\dfrac{1}{7 \times 8}$ or $\dfrac{1}{56}$.

10. **(G)** $\dfrac{3}{a+2} = \dfrac{5}{a+4}$ (cross multiply)

$$3(a+4) = 5(a+2)$$
$$3a + 12 = 5a + 10$$
$$2a = 2$$
$$a = 1$$

11. **(D)** $\dfrac{2}{3}a = 2$

$$a = 3$$
$$a - \dfrac{2}{3} = 3 - \dfrac{2}{3} = \dfrac{7}{3}$$

12. **(J)** $x = (a-3)^2$

$$= (-2-3)^2$$
$$= (-5)^2$$
$$= 25$$

13. **(D)**   I. The sum of two positive integers is always a positive integer. Therefore, $x + y$ is a positive integer.

II. If x is less than y, then $x - y$ is negative.

III. The product of two positive integers is always a positive integer.

14. **(G)**
$$9 - k = -(17 - k)$$
$$9 - k = k - 17$$
$$2k = 26$$
$$k = 13$$

15. **(C)**
$$\frac{a}{b} = \frac{2}{3}$$
$$a = \frac{2b}{3}$$

Substitute $a = \frac{2}{3}b$ into the given expression :

$$9a^2 - 4b^2 = 9\left(\frac{2}{3}b\right)^2 - 4b^2$$
$$= 9\left(\frac{4}{9}b^2\right) - 4b^2$$
$$= 4b^2 - 4b^2 = 0$$

16. **(K)**
$$(2x + 3y)(x + y) = 2x^2 + 2xy + 3xy + 3y^2$$
$$= 2x^2 + 5xy + 3y^2$$
$$= 2(\sqrt{3})^2 + 5(\sqrt{3})(\sqrt{2}) + 3(\sqrt{2})^2$$
$$= 2(3) + 5\sqrt{6} + 3(2)$$
$$= 12 + 5\sqrt{6}$$

17. **(D)**   By substitution, $\dfrac{a + \dfrac{a}{b}}{a - \dfrac{a}{b}} = \dfrac{4 + \dfrac{4}{7}}{4 - \dfrac{4}{7}}$.

In order to combine the terms, we convert 4 into sevenths:

$$4 = 4 \times 1 = 4 \times \frac{7}{7} = \frac{28}{7}.$$

Thus, we have:

$$\frac{\dfrac{28}{7}+\dfrac{4}{7}}{\dfrac{28}{7}-\dfrac{4}{7}}=\frac{\dfrac{32}{7}}{\dfrac{24}{7}}$$

Dividing by $\dfrac{24}{7}$ is equivalent to multiplying by $\dfrac{7}{24}$. Therefore,

$$\frac{4+\dfrac{4}{7}}{4-\dfrac{4}{7}}=\frac{32}{7}\times\frac{7}{24}$$

Now, the 7 in the numerator cancels with the 7 in the denominator. Thus, we obtain $\dfrac{32}{24}$. Dividing the numerator and denominator by 8, we obtain: $\dfrac{4}{3}$.

Therefore $\dfrac{a+\dfrac{a}{b}}{a-\dfrac{a}{b}}=\dfrac{4}{3}$ when $a=4$ and $b=7$.

18. **(F)** First we note that for any two real numbers we have:

$$\frac{|a|}{|b|}=\left|\frac{a}{b}\right|$$

Hence, if in the above equality, we put $a=x+2$, $b=x-1$, we will have:

$$\frac{|x+2|}{|x-1|}=\left|\frac{x+2}{x-1}\right|=3$$

Also, according to the definition of the absolute value of a number, we know that if $|y|=c>0$, then y can be either c or $-c$.

Hence, setting $y=\dfrac{x+2}{x-1}$ and $b=3$ in the above equality, we have:

$$\frac{x+2}{x-1}=3 \quad \text{or} \quad \frac{x+2}{x-1}=-3$$

From the first equation, we obtain: $x+2=3(x-1)$

$$5=2x$$

$$x=\frac{5}{2}$$

From the second equation, we have: $x + 2 = -3(x - 1)$
$$-1 = -4x$$
$$x = \frac{1}{4}$$

The solution set is thus $\left\{\frac{5}{2}, \frac{1}{4}\right\}$.

19. **(B)** According to our definition of multiplication, we need only to write the product of the numerators over the product of the denominators.

$$\frac{3a - 9b}{x - 5} \times \frac{xy - 5y}{ax - 3bx} = \frac{(3a - 9b)(xy - 5y)}{(x - 5)(ax - 3bx)}$$

The only remaining step is that of reducing the fraction to lowest terms by factoring the numerator and denominator of the answer and simplifying the result.

Factor out 3 from $(3a - 9b)$, and y from $(xy - 5y)$. Also, factor out x from $ax - 3bx$.

$$= \frac{3(a - 3b)y(x - 5)}{(x - 5)x(a - 3b)}$$

Group the same terms in the numerator and the denominator.

$$= \frac{3y}{x} \times \frac{a - 3b}{a - 3b} \times \frac{x - 5}{x - 5}$$

Cancel like terms.

$$= \frac{3y}{x} \times 1 \times 1$$
$$= \frac{3y}{x}$$

This procedure could have been abbreviated in the following manner:

$$\frac{3a - 9b}{x - 5} \times \frac{xy - 5y}{ax - 3bx} = \frac{3(a - 3b)}{x - 5} \times \frac{y(x - 5)}{x(a - 3b)} = \frac{3y}{x}$$

20. **(F)** When working with several sets of brackets and/or parentheses, we work from the inside out. That is, we use the distributive property throughout the expression, starting with the innermost parentheses, and working our way out. In the expression we have: $2\{3a - 2[1 - 4(a - 1)] + 5\}$. We note that $(a - 1)$ is the innermost parenthesis, so our first step is to distribute the (-4). Thus, we obtain:

$$3a - 2[3a - 2(1 - 4a + 4) + 5]. \tag{1}$$

We now find that $(1 - 4a + 4)$ is the innermost parentheses. Combining terms, we obtain:

$$(1 - 4a + 4) = (5 - 4a) \tag{2}$$

$$3a - 2[3a - 2(1 - 4a + 4) + 5] = 3a - 2[3a - 2(5 - 4a) + 5].$$

Since $(5 - 4a)$ is the innermost parentheses, we distribute the (-2), obtaining:

$$3a - 2(3a - 10 + 8a + 5). \tag{3}$$

We are now left with the terms in our last set of parentheses, $(3a - 10 + 8a + 5)$. Combining like terms, we obtain:

$$(3a - 10 + 8a + 5) = (11a - 5). \tag{4}$$

Substituting from Equation (4) into Equation (3) gives:

$$3a - 2(3a - 10 + 8a + 5) = 3a - 2(11a - 5).$$

Distributing the (-2),

$$= 3a - 22a + 10.$$

Combining terms,

$$= -19a + 10.$$

Hence,

$$3a - 2\{3a - 2[1 - 4(a - 1)] + 5\} = -19a + 10.$$

21. **(C)** If x and y vary inversely as each other and k is the constant of variation, then $xy = k$. So if height (h) varies inversely as the square of the base (b^2) then $hb^2 = k$. Solving for h, we divide both sides of the equation $hb^2 = k$, by b^2 as follows:

$$\frac{hb^2}{b^2} = \frac{k}{b^2}$$

$$h = \frac{k}{b^2}$$

Answer (A) is incorrect because h varies directly as the square of the base,

$$h = \frac{b^2}{k};$$

if h increases then b^2 must also increase. Answer (D) is incorrect because it takes the same form as answer (A) so the reasons are the same.

$$kh = b^2$$

$$h = \frac{b^2}{k}$$

Answer (B) does not allow us to use the correct formula, and answer (E) does not involve the square of the base; both those choices are incorrect.

22. **(J)** In order to combine fractions, we must transform them into equivalent fractions with a common denominator. In our case, we will use $a + b$ as our least common denominator (LCD). Thus,

$$
\begin{aligned}
a + b - \frac{2ab}{a+b} &= \frac{a+b}{a+b}\left(\frac{a+b}{1}\right) - \frac{2ab}{a+b} \\
&= \frac{(a+b)(a+b)}{a+b} - \frac{2ab}{a+b} \\
&= \frac{a^2 + 2ab + b^2}{a+b} - \frac{2ab}{a+b} \\
&= \frac{a^2 + 2ab + b^2 - 2ab}{a+b} \\
&= \frac{a^2 + b^2}{a+b}
\end{aligned}
$$

23. **(C)** We always evaluate the expression within the innermost parentheses first, when working with a group of nested parentheses. Thus,

$$
\begin{aligned}
3s - [5t + (2s - 5)] &= 3s - [5t + 2s - 5] \\
&= 3s - 5t - 2s + 5 \\
&= 3s - 2s - 5t + 5 \\
&= s - 5t + 5
\end{aligned}
$$

24. **(J)** Division by a fraction is equivalent to multiplication by that fraction's reciprocal. Hence,

$$\frac{1}{\dfrac{x+y}{x^2}} = 1 \times \frac{x^2}{x+y} = \frac{x^2}{x+y}.$$

25. **(B)** Convert the left side of the equation, $(4^x)(6^x)$, to a form consistent with the right side of the equation, i.e. (2 raised to some power) $\times$ (3 raised to some power):

$$(4^x)(6^y) = (2^2)^x((2)(3))^y$$
$$= 2^{2x} \times 2^y \times 3^y$$
$$= 2^{2x+y}3^y$$

Since $(4^x)(6^x) = (2^4)(3^2)$,

$$2^{2x+y}\, 3^y = (2^4)(3^2).$$

Equate the exponents on both sides of the equations:

$$y = 2 \tag{1}$$

$$2x + y = 4 \tag{2}$$

Substitute $y = 2$ into equation (2):

$$2x + 2 = 4$$
$$2x = 2$$
$$x = 1$$

Thus, $x = 1$, and $y = 2$.

26. **(G)** $\log_3(x + 7) = 2$
$$x + 7 = 3^2$$
$$x + 7 = 9$$
$$x = 2$$

27. **(C)**   Because $10 < 31.4 < 100$, we must have $1 < x < 2$. Hence, without a calculator, and assuming one of the given answers is correct, we determine that (C) 1.5 is the correct answer.

28. **(H)** $(-4)(-6) < xy < (-9)(-12)$
$$24 < xy < 108$$

29. **(B)** $2x + 5 > 11$
$$2x > 6$$
$$x > 3$$

30. **(F)** $N = \dfrac{33!\,37!}{51!}$

$$\log_{10} N = \log_{10} 33! + \log_{10} 37! - \log_{10} 51!$$
$$= 37 + 43 - 66 = 14$$

Since $\log_{10} N = 14$

then $N = 10^{14}$

31. **(B)** $(2^{4x})(8^{2x}) = (2^{4x})(2^3)^{2x}$
$$= (2^{4x})(2^{6x})$$
$$= 2^{4x+6x}$$
$$= 2^{10x}$$

32. **(F)** $3x + 5y = 6$ (1)

$2x - y = 4$ (2)

Multiply the second equation by 5, and add this to the first equation.

$$\begin{array}{rcl} 3x + 5y &=& 6 \\ 10x - 5y &=& 20 \\ \hline 13x &=& 26 \\ x &=& 2 \end{array}$$

Substitute $x = 2$ into Equation (2):

$$2(2) - y = 4$$
$$y = 0$$

Thus, $x = 2$, and $y = 0$.

33. **(C)** $2^{3x} = 64$

$(2^3)^x = 64$

$8^x = 64$

$x = 2$

34. **(J)** $y = 2x + 1 \rightarrow y$–intercept $= (0, 1)$, so we may eliminate F and H.

We may also eliminate K since the slope of y is 2 which is positive. Graph G indicates that the point $(3, 2)$ is on the graph, but if we substitute these values into the given equation, we find the statement false. The only possibility therefore is Graph J.

35. **(C)** $Y = \dfrac{2}{x}$ is the only one of the given choices whose graph will be in Quadrants I and III. (You can verify this by substituting several numbers for x, and plotting the (x, y) pairs.) In the equation $Y = \dfrac{2}{x}$, x and y are inversely proportional: as x increases, y decreases, except for a discontinuity at $x = 0$. For the sake of comparison, the remaining equations are also plotted below.

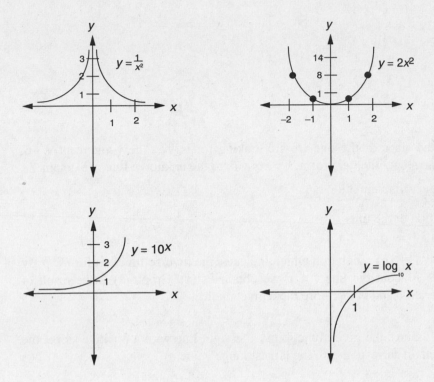

36. **(H)**   The simplest way to solve this is to get the equation into slope-intercept form: $y = mx + b$, where m is the slope and b is the y-intercept. The given equation is:

$$x = 3y + 8$$

Subtracting 8 from both sides:

$$3y = x - 8$$

Dividing by 3:

$$y = \frac{1}{3}x - \frac{8}{3}$$

From this and the slope-intercept form, $b = -\frac{8}{3}$. Thus, the y-intercept is $-\frac{8}{3}$.

37. **(D)**   We employ the slope-intercept form for the equation to be written, since we are given the y-intercept. Our task is then to determine the slope.

We are given the equation of a line parallel to the line whose equation we wish to find. We know that the slopes of two parallel lines are equal. Hence, by finding the slope of the given line, we will also be finding the unknown slope. To find the slope of the given equation $6x + 3y = 4$, we transform the equation $6x + 3y = 4$ into slope-intercept form.

$$6x + 3y = 4$$
$$3y = -6x + 4$$
$$y = -\frac{6}{3}x + \frac{4}{3}$$
$$y = -2x + \frac{4}{3}.$$

Therefore the slope of the line we are looking for is –2. The y–intercept is –6. Applying the slope-intercept form, $y = mx + b$, to the unknown line, we obtain,

$$y = -2x - 6$$

as the equation of the line.

38. (J) $P^{-1}{}_{(x)}$ is a notation which indicates the inverse function for $P(x)$. By reflecting $P(x)$ about the line $y = x$, we obtain $P^{-1}(x)$. Graph (J) is the result of such an operation and is therefore the correct choice.

39. (E)   Since the given function is a straight line with a positive slope, the smallest domain corresponds to the largest range value.

$$f(-5) = \frac{-5}{5} - 3 = -4$$
$$f(15) = \frac{15}{5} - 3 = 0$$

Therefore, the range of $f(x)$ is $-4 < f(x) < 0$.

40. (F)
$$\begin{aligned} y &= f(x + 3) \\ &= 3(x + 3) + 4 \\ &= 3x + 9 + 4 \\ &= 3x + 13 \end{aligned}$$

Therefore, the slope of the line is 3.

41. (B) $\begin{cases} x + 2y = 5 \\ 2x + 3y = 2 \end{cases}$ (1)
(2)

Multiply Equation (1) by 2 and subtract Equation (2):

$$\begin{array}{r} 2x + 4y = 10 \\ -(2x + 3y = 2) \\ \hline y = 8 \end{array}$$

Substitute $y = 8$ into Equation (1):

$$x + 2(8) = 5$$
$$x = -11$$

Therefore, $(-11, 8)$ is the intersection point of the given pair of lines.

42. **(G)**   The midpoint $M(x, y)$ of the line segment is given by the relations:

$$x = \frac{1}{2}(x_1 + x_2), \quad y = \frac{1}{2}(y_1 + y_2)$$

Thus, the coordinates of the midpoint are:

$$x = \frac{1}{2}(1 + 5) = 3, \quad y = \frac{1}{2}(2 + 8) = 5$$

Therefore $(x + y) = (3, 5)$.

43. **(D)**
$$(12 - x)^2 + 6^2 = 10^2 \quad \text{(Pythagorean Theorem)}$$
$$(12 - x)^2 = 100 - 36$$
$$(12 - x)^2 = 64$$
$$x = 4 \text{ or } 20$$

We reject the value $x = 20$ because that would imply $\overline{AB} = -8$, but $\overline{AB}$ cannot be negative.

44. **(H)**   We first have to obtain y as a function of x. Substituting $t = \frac{x}{9}$ gives:

$$y = 3t + 8 = 3\left(\frac{x}{9}\right) + 8 = \frac{1}{3}x + 8.$$

Setting y to 0, and solving for x,

$$0 = \frac{1}{3}x + 8$$
$$-8 = \frac{1}{3}x$$
$$x = -24$$

45. **(E)** $\overline{OA} = \overline{OB} \Rightarrow \angle OAB = \angle OBA.$

$$\angle OAB + \angle OBA + \angle AOB = 180° \qquad \text{(sum of interior } \angle\text{s of a } \Delta\text{)}$$
$$2\angle OAB + 60° = 180°$$
$$\angle OAB = 60°$$

Therefore, ΔAOB is equilateral and $\overline{AB} = 6$.

$$\text{Area of shaded region} = \frac{60}{360} \times \pi(6)^2 - \frac{1}{2} \times 6 \times 6 \, \sin 60°$$

$$= 6\pi - 18\frac{\sqrt{3}}{2} = 6\pi - 9\sqrt{3}$$

46. **(G)** The shape given is a rectangle. Its area is equal to the length multiplied by the width.

The perimeter is twice the length plus twice the width.

Let x = length, y = width. The relevant equations are:

$$xy = 35 \tag{1}$$

$$2x + 2y = 24 \tag{2}$$

Rewriting equation (1): $y = \dfrac{35}{x}$.

Substituting for y in Equation (2):

$$2x + 2\left(\frac{35}{x}\right) = 24.$$

Multiplying by x: $2x^2 + 70 = 24x$.

Subtracting $24x$ from both sides:

$$2x^2 - 24x + 70 = 0.$$

Dividing all terms by 2: $x^2 - 12x + 35 = 0$.

This can be factored into: $(x - 5)(x - 7) = 0$.

From this we get: $x - 5 = 0$ or $x - 7 = 0$.

Two possible lengths: $x = 5m$, $x = 7m$.

Substituting back into Equation (1):

$$5y = 35 \Rightarrow y = 7$$

$$7y = 35 \Rightarrow y = 5$$

Thus, the possible dimensions are:

5m × 7m and 7m × 5m.

5m × 7m are the only dimensions that correspond to the choices.

47. **(C)**

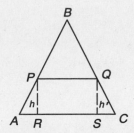

The region $APQC$ is a trapezoid. Its area is therefore given by: $A = \dfrac{1}{2}h(b_1 + b_2)$, where b_1 and b_2 are the two bases and h is the altitude.

Since $\overline{AB} = 4$ and ΔABC is equilateral, $\overline{AC} = 4$. So $b_1 = \overline{AC} = 4$.

$\angle ABC = \angle PBQ$ since ABC and PBQ are different ways of naming the same angle. $\angle BPQ = \angle BAC$ since lines $\overline{AC}$ and $\overline{PQ}$ are parallel the line $\overline{AB}$ which transverses them forms equal angles with them. Similarly, $\angle PQB = \angle ACB$. Note that $\angle ABC = \angle BCA = \angle CAB$. Therefore, $\angle PBQ = \angle BQP = \angle QPB$ so ΔBPQ is equiangular and therefore an equilateral triangle. Since P is the midpoint of $\overline{AB}$ and $\overline{AB} = 4$, $\overline{PB} = 2$; so $\overline{PQ} = 2$ since ΔBPQ is equilateral. So $b_2 = \overline{PQ} = 2$.

If we drop a perpendicular h from the point P to the line $\overline{AC}$ and name the point where h intersects $\overline{AC}$ R, then the length of PR can be found by using the Pythagorean Theorem,

$$(\overline{AP})^2 = (\overline{AR})^2 + (\overline{PR})^2,$$

since $\angle ARP$ is a right angle.

We know that $\overline{AB} = 4$ and that P is the midpoint of $\overline{AB}$; therefore, $\overline{AP} = 2$.

If we drop a perpendicular, h', from point Q to $\overline{AC}$, and name the point where h' intersects $\overline{AC}$ S, then $\overline{RS} = \overline{PQ} = 2$. We can also show that

$$\Delta PAR \cong \Delta QCS,$$

so that $\overline{AR} = \overline{SC}$. However,

$$\overline{AR} + \overline{RS} + \overline{SC} = 4.$$

Substituting we arrive at

$$\overline{AR} + 2 + \overline{SC} = 4$$

But $\overline{AR} = \overline{SC}$ so
$$2\left(\overline{AR}\right) = 2$$
$$\left(\overline{AR}\right) = 1$$

Substituting into
$$\left(\overline{AP}\right)^2 = \left(\overline{AR}\right)^2 + \left(\overline{PR}\right)^2$$
$$(2)^2 = (1)^2 + \left(\overline{PR}\right)^2$$
$$4 - 1 = \left(\overline{PR}\right)^2$$
$$3 = \left(\overline{PR}\right)^2$$
$$\sqrt{3} = PR = h$$

Recall:
$$A = \frac{1}{2}h(b_1 + b_2)$$

Substituting:
$$A = \frac{1}{2}\sqrt{3}\,(4 + 2)$$
$$A = 3\sqrt{3}$$

48. **(K)** From a theorem we know that the measure of an inscribed angle is equal to $\frac{1}{2}$ the intercepted arc.

We are told that $m\overset{\frown}{ABC}$ is $\frac{3}{2}\pi$ radians. There are 2π radians in a circle.

Therefore, the intercepted arc is the remaining $\frac{\pi}{2}$ radians.

Converting to degrees:
$$\left(\frac{\pi}{2}\right)\left(\frac{180}{\pi}\right) = 90°.$$

The angle y is half of this
$$y = \frac{90°}{2} = 45°$$

49. **(E)** The sine of angle C is $\frac{1}{2}$. The altitude of $\overline{BD}$ is thus:

$$\overline{BD} = \overline{BC}\sin C = 8\left(\frac{1}{2}\right) = 4.$$

Length $\overline{DC}$ is found from the Pythagorean Theorem: $a^2 + b^2 = c^2$:

$$\left(\overline{DC}\right)^2 = \left(\overline{BC}\right)^2 - \left(\overline{BD}\right)^2$$
$$\left(\overline{DC}\right)^2 = (8)^2 - (4)^2 = 48$$
$$\overline{DC} = 4\sqrt{3}$$

Area of $\Delta DBC = \dfrac{1}{2}\left(\overline{DC}\right)\left(\overline{BD}\right) = \dfrac{1}{2}(4\sqrt{3})(4) = 8\sqrt{3}$. Angle C must be 30°, since

its sine is $\dfrac{1}{2}$. Therefore, angle A is 60°. We must first find side $\overline{AB}$:

$$\sin 60° = \frac{\overline{BD}}{\overline{AB}} = \frac{4}{\overline{AB}}$$
$$\overline{AB} = \frac{4(2)}{\sqrt{3}} = \frac{8\sqrt{3}}{3}$$

Length $\overline{AD} = \left(\overline{AB}\right)(\cos 60°) = \left(\dfrac{8\sqrt{3}}{3}\right)\left(\dfrac{1}{2}\right) = \dfrac{4\sqrt{3}}{3}$

Area $\Delta ABD = \dfrac{1}{2}(\text{base})(\text{altitude}) = \dfrac{1}{2}\left(\overline{AD}\right)\left(\overline{BD}\right)$

$$= \frac{1}{2}\left(\frac{4\sqrt{3}}{3}\right)(4) = \frac{8\sqrt{3}}{3}$$

The ratio of the two areas is:

$$\frac{\text{Area } \Delta ABD}{\text{Area } \Delta DBC} = \frac{\dfrac{8\sqrt{3}}{3}}{8\sqrt{3}} = \frac{1}{3}$$

50. **(J)**   We are told that segments $\overline{BD}$ and $\overline{AE}$ are parallel. This implies that $\angle CBD = \angle CEA$ and $\angle CDB = \angle CEA$ (corresponding angles formed by parallel lines cut by a transversal are congruent).

$\angle ACE = \angle BCD$ (same angle)

Thus, ΔBCD and ΔACE are similar triangles. From a theorem, we know that the sides of similar triangles that correspond to each other are proportional. Sides $\overline{CD}$ and $\overline{CE}$, and $\overline{BD}$ and $\overline{AE}$ are corresponding sides and are thus proportional:
$\dfrac{\overline{CD}}{\overline{CE}} = \dfrac{\overline{BD}}{\overline{AE}}$.

51. **(E)**

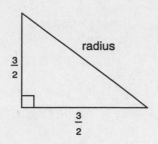

radius

$$\text{radius} = \sqrt{\left(\frac{3}{2}\right)^2 + \left(\frac{3}{2}\right)^2}$$

$$= \sqrt{\frac{18}{4}}$$

$$= \frac{3\sqrt{2}}{2}$$

$$\text{circumference} = 2 \times \pi \times \frac{3\sqrt{2}}{2}$$

$$= 3\pi\sqrt{2}$$

52. **(G)**

$$\frac{\overline{AB}}{\overline{BD}} = \frac{1}{2}$$

$$\overline{BD} = 2\overline{AB}$$

$$\overline{BD} = 2\left(2\frac{1}{2}\right)$$

$$\overline{BD} = 5$$

$$\overline{CD} = \overline{BD} - \overline{BC}$$

$$= 5 - 3$$

$$= 2$$

53. **(B)** The diameter of the inscribed circle is x. Therefore, the circumference of the inscribed circle $= x\pi$.

The diameter of the circumscribed circle is $\sqrt{x^2 + x^2} = x\sqrt{2}$.

Therefore its circumference is $x\pi\sqrt{2}$.

The ratio: $\dfrac{\text{circumference of circumscribed circle}}{\text{circumference of inscribed circle}}$

$$= \frac{x\pi\sqrt{2}}{x\pi} = \sqrt{2}$$

54. **(K)** $\overline{AC} = \overline{CD} = 6$ (because ΔACD is right isosceles)

Area of $\Delta ABD = \dfrac{1}{2} \times \overline{AB} \times \overline{AC}$

$\qquad\qquad\quad = \dfrac{1}{2} \times 4 \times 6$

$\qquad\qquad\quad = 12$

55. **(B)**   Since $\overline{CD} \| \overline{AB}$, $\Delta CED \sim \Delta AEB$. If two triangles are similar, then the ratio of their areas is equal to the square of the ratio of their sides. Therefore,

$$\frac{\text{area of } \Delta CED}{\text{area of } \Delta AEB} = \left(\frac{\overline{CD}}{\overline{AB}}\right)^2 = \left(\frac{1}{2}\right)^2 = \frac{1}{4}$$

56. **(H)** $\angle CAD = \angle CDA = 50°$ (as ΔACD is isosceles)

$\qquad \angle ACD = 180° - 2 \times 50°$ (sum of interior angles of a Δ)

$\qquad\qquad\quad = 80°$

$\qquad \angle CAB = 80° - \angle CAD$

$\qquad\qquad\quad = 80° - 50°$

$\qquad\qquad\quad = 30°$

$\qquad \angle CAB = \angle CBA = 30°$ (as ΔACB is isosceles)

$\qquad \angle ACB = 180° - 2 \times 30°$ (sum of interior angles of a Δ)

$\qquad\qquad\quad = 120°$

$\qquad \theta + \angle ACD + \angle ACB = 360°$

$\qquad\quad\; \theta + 80° + 120° = 360°$

$\qquad\qquad\qquad\quad\; \theta = 160°$

57. **(C)**   We are given $2\tan^2 x + \sec^2 x = 2$. Using the fact that $\sec^2 x = 1 + \tan^2 x$, we have

$2\tan^2 x + (1 + \tan^2 x) = 2$ or $3\tan^2 x = 1$

$\Rightarrow \tan x = \pm \dfrac{1}{\sqrt{3}}.$

58. **(G)**

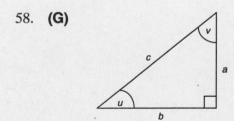

We know the following trigonometric identity, $\sin^2 u + \cos^2 u = 1$.

Now, if $u + v = \dfrac{\pi}{2}$, these angles are complementary, that is, the sum of these angles is $90° = \dfrac{\pi}{2}$. From the accompanying figure, it is seen that

$$\sin v = \frac{b}{c} = \cos u$$

Substitute this relation into the identity to obtain:

$$\begin{aligned}
\sin^2 u + \cos^2 u &= (\sin u)^2 + (\cos u)^2 = 1 \\
&= (\sin u)^2 + (\sin v)^2 = 1 \\
&= \sin^2 u + \sin^2 v = 1
\end{aligned}$$

59. **(A)**

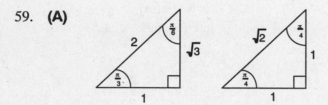

Express $\cos \dfrac{\pi}{12}$ in terms of angles whose values of the trigonometric functions are known.

$$\begin{aligned}
\cos \frac{1}{12}\pi &= \cos\left(\frac{4}{12}\pi - \frac{3}{12}\pi\right) \\
&= \cos\left(\frac{1}{3}\pi - \frac{1}{4}\pi\right) \\
&= \cos\left(\frac{\pi}{3} - \frac{\pi}{4}\right)
\end{aligned}$$

Now apply the difference formula for the cosine of two angles, α and β. $\cos(\alpha - \beta) = \cos \alpha \cos \beta + \sin \alpha \sin \beta$.

In this example, $\alpha = \dfrac{1}{\dfrac{\pi}{3}}$ and $\beta = \dfrac{1}{\dfrac{\pi}{4}}$.

$$\cos\left(\frac{1}{\dfrac{\pi}{3}} - \frac{1}{\dfrac{\pi}{4}}\right) = \cos\frac{1}{\dfrac{\pi}{3}}\ \cos\frac{1}{\dfrac{\pi}{4}} + \sin\frac{1}{\dfrac{\pi}{3}}\ \sin\frac{1}{\dfrac{\pi}{4}}$$

See the accompanying diagrams to find the values of these angles. We find:

$$\cos\frac{\pi}{3} = \frac{1}{2}$$

$$\cos\frac{\pi}{4} = \frac{1}{\sqrt{2}}$$

$$\sin\frac{\pi}{3} = \frac{\sqrt{3}}{2}$$

$$\sin\frac{\pi}{4} = \frac{1}{\sqrt{2}}$$

Thus, $\cos\left(\dfrac{1}{\dfrac{\pi}{3}} - \dfrac{1}{\dfrac{\pi}{4}}\right) = \dfrac{1}{2} \times \dfrac{1}{\sqrt{2}}\left(\dfrac{\sqrt{2}}{\sqrt{2}}\right) + \dfrac{\sqrt{3}}{2} \times \dfrac{1}{\sqrt{2}}\left(\dfrac{\sqrt{2}}{\sqrt{2}}\right)$

$$= \frac{\sqrt{2}}{4} + \frac{\sqrt{2}\sqrt{3}}{4} = \frac{1}{4}\sqrt{2}(1+\sqrt{3})$$

60. **(H)**   A triangle formed with the two endpoints of a diameter of a circle and any other point on the circle is a right triangle. Since $\sin x = \dfrac{1}{3}$, we can label the triangle as follows:

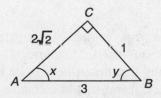

$\overline{AC}$ is determined from the Pythagorean Theorem:

$$\overline{AC}^2 = 3^2 - 1^2 = 8$$
$$\overline{AC} = \sqrt{8} = 2\sqrt{2}$$

So from the triangle we determine $\sin y = \dfrac{2\sqrt{2}}{3}$.

Test 3: Reading

1.   **(D)**   (D) is the best answer. The author is actually advising empires of the causes of revolutions and unrest. Even though the first sentence refers only to the wisdom of an ancient sage, more recent information is also imparted. Therefore, (A) is not the best answer. The advice is offered to rulers, not church ministers, so (B) should not be selected. Even though the first sentence states the passage is about how to make a little city into a great one, the second sentence clearly states the author is going to explain how to do the reverse. Therefore, (C) should not be chosen.

2.   **(F)**   The best answer is (F). The author compares an empire to a cake. (G) is incorrect, as it is a minister, not the country, who is compared to a gingerbread baker. It has already been ascertained that it is a minister being compared to a gingerbread baker so (H) is not the best answer. (J) is incorrect because it is not a religious minister who is compared to a gingerbread baker, but rather, a minister who has the "management of extensive dominions."

3.   **(B)**   The best answer is (B) since the article is tongue-in-cheek. Even though the suggestion is that Franklin is going to tell the reader how to make a little city of a great one, the author (who is not a simpleton) is actually giving advice. (A) is incorrect since Franklin addresses himself to ministers of "extensive" or large dominions rather than small countries. (C) is incorrect since the advice is being given to governmental ministers rather than being received from religious ministers. (D) is also incorrect since the word "fiddle" is used only as a vehicle for the satire of the passage and is not to be taken literally.

4.   **(G)**   In the last paragraph of the reading passage, the writer states that the General needs enough troops under his command. Therefore, (G) is the best choice. Since the paragraph is not suggesting that troops need to be kept in tow, (F) should not be chosen. Even though the General should certainly be lucky to have troops endowed with skill under his control, there is no support in the passage for this answer, so (H) should not be chosen. Because the clause has nothing to do with captured troops, (J) should not be chosen.

5.   **(D)**   (D) is the best choice because the article is written by Benjamin Franklin, who was a friend of the colonists and is writing to advise the mother country on how to behave. Franklin is not writing to help rid the ministers of their troubles; therefore, (A) should not be selected. The writer is not hoping to help the ministers build their powers and increase their provinces, so (B) should not be chosen. Since the article was written by Benjamin Franklin, it could not have been written only a few years ago nor does it contain new ideas to help increase the provinces, so (C) should not be chosen.

6. **(H)** The reader should note that the answer looked for is the one which is *least* advisable. (H) is the answer which is least advisable since a minister should *not* treat the provinces as if he/she expects them to revolt and as if he/she supposes them to be always ready to revolt. To keep a large country intact, the General of the army should be limited to the constitutional powers, so (F) is *not* an answer which is *least* advisable. The provinces should be given the same rights as those in the mother country; thus, (G) is an advisable answer and should not be chosen. A mother country should not require taxation without representation, just as (J) says. Since (J) is true, it should not be selected. (F), (G), and (J) are incorrect since they are extremely advisable actions to take for keeping a large country intact and the question asks for the least advisable action.

7. **(B)** The reader should note that in this case he/she is to give the answer which is *most* advisable. (B) is the best answer since the Parliaments should allow petition for redress and (B) is the only advisable action offered among the choices. Flaunting claims (A), refusing to read the claims (C), and allowing taxation without representation (D) are not to be chosen since they all are *not* advisable.

8. **(H)** One can expect a large empire to be diminished (according to the author of this article) from the edges, therefore, (H) should be selected. In the third paragraph of this reading passage, Franklin warns the ministers to, "Turn your attention, therefore, first to your remotest provinces...." The remotest provinces are those at the edges of the country. Once the information concerning the remotest provinces is located in the passage, it is clear that (F), (G), and (J) cannot be the answer since they offer incorrect choices.

9. **(B)** The reader is asked to give the answer which is most likely to ensure *separation* from the mother country. (B) is the answer most likely to ensure separation since if the mother country does not give common rights, separation is ensured, according to the fourth paragraph of the passage. On the other hand, incorporating the provinces (A), allowing them to enact their laws (C), and allowing them to choose legislators (D) are all actions which can unite or draw the provinces to the mother country. Therefore, they should not be accepted.

10. **(J)** The question asks which answer will *least* likely reduce an empire to a small country. The best answer is that if the revolution is already established, it may be too late to change. Therefore, (J) should be chosen. If the mother country remembers their prejudice (F), punishes provinces for their principles (G), and punishes the provinces after the revolution is already established (H), the empire may likely be reduced. Therefore, the reader should not select the incorrect answers (F), (G) and (H).

11. **(C)**   The item that the writer contends is *not* true is (C), since the first sentence of the reading passage uses the words "even when," implying that heat is no longer regarded as a substance. The other items (A), (B), and (D) are all items the writer states as being true in the first paragraph. None of them should be chosen.

12. **(G)**   The best answer is (G) since the calorie and B.T.U. both relate to the amount of heat necessary to raise the temperature one degree. Because one unit relates to a kilogram (2.2 pounds) and one relates to a pound of water, (F) should not be chosen since it relates to one pound of water only. One unit relates to the customary system and one to the metric system, not both to the metric system. Since both do not relate to the metric system, (H) cannot be chosen. Since only the B.T.U. relates to a pound of iron, (J) is incorrect.

13. **(C)**   The best answer is (C) because the melting of one pound of ice can cool a pound of hot water through a definite range of temperature and can cool two pounds of water through half as many degrees. (B) cannot be chosen since it says twice as many degrees instead of half as many degrees. Neither (A) nor (D) can be the correct answer because they are stated, not denied, by the author in the first paragraph of the reading passage.

14. **(J)**   Due to the author's stating that the heat capacity of water or the B.T.U. per pound-degree is not constant, (J) is the best answer. The author does not state that a water pound-degree is a constant; therefore, (F) should not be chosen. Since the temperature does make a difference, (G) should not be chosen. (H) is exactly opposite of the correct answer (J) and should not be selected.

15. **(D)**   The best choice is (D). The disagreement concerns how to limit and define the heat unit. Since the passage states without any indication of doubt or negation that the melting of a pound of ice will not cool the same weight of water from 200° Fahrenheit to 180° Fahrenheit as it will from 60° to 40° Fahrenheit, (A) is not the best answer. As the opening sentence of the second and last paragraph states, there is general agreement that a water pound-degree is not quite constant; thus, (B) should not be chosen. There is no point of disagreement among scientists as to whether the equivalence of heat effects proved effects proportional to quantity. Consequently, (C) is not the correct answer.

16. **(J)**   The best answer is (J). The author appears to suggest that there are good reasons for taking the freezing-point to the boiling-point as the range by including the words "which will probably become universal"—interesting, but not totally necessary, information that leads the reader to believe the author readily accepts this as a range. Both the metric and the customary systems are mentioned without preference for either system. Therefore, neither (F) which

indicates a predilection for the metric system nor (G) which indicates a predilection for the customary system is the correct answer. Since the author precedes his mention of the mean calorie with the words "properly named," he is indicating his approval of, rather than his opposition to, the mean calorie; hence, (H) is another incorrect choice.

17. **(D)**　As explained in the (H) section of the answer to question 16, the author is advocating mean calories. The same words, "properly named," are applied to the mean British Thermal Unit in the last sentence of the reading passage and make (D), which includes both mean calories and mean British Thermal Units, the correct choice. Neither (A) nor (B) is correct because each of these answers is only one-half of the correct answer. Since we already know that (D) is the correct answer, we can see that (C) is incorrect because there is no support for such opposition in the passage.

18. **(H)**　The author predicts the universal acceptance of the mean B.T.U. and the mean calorie as mentioned toward the end of the reading passage; hence, (H) is the best answer. (F) should not be selected since it mentions the universal adoption of the B.T.U. alone. (G) mentions the universal adoption of the calorie alone and should not be accepted. Since the author predicts not the demise, but the universal adoption of the calories, (J) is incorrect.

19. **(D)**　All the Statements I, II, III, and IV are a necessary part of the definition of the heat unit. Only (D) allows for all these parts. (A), (B), and (C) are all incorrect since each omits some part or parts of the correct four-part answer.

20. **(J)**　According to the passage, the author seems to be striving towards a "universality" of the heat unit (I), and would also like to find an explanation for the inconsistencies found when melting a pound of ice to cool the same weight of water 20°F when heated to different temperatures (II). The passage does end, however, before the author has completely stated his argument (III). (F), (G), and (H) only allow the reader to choose part of the complete answer and are incorrect. Only (J) allows the reader to select all the correct statements, and therefore should be selected.

21. **(B)**　The best answer is (B) because, in the first sentence, the author opposes the terms "Japanese" and "Occident." Later in the same paragraph, he opposes the terms "Oriental" and "Occidental" which effectively eliminates (D). Since there is no support for (A) in the passage, the reader is able to infer that this is incorrect. Assuming the reader knows that both Japan and the Orient are part of the East, (C) is incorrect since "non-Western" infers "Eastern." By a process of elimination, the reader can determine that only (B) can be the correct choice.

22. **(F)** The best answer is (F) since the author contrasts, or shows the differences between, the painting of the Japanese and the Occident. Since the author discusses differences, rather than similarities (comparisons), between the two types of painting, (G) is an incorrect answer. (H) and (J) are incorrect because the author writes about contrasts, rather than comparisons. In addition, (H) mentions only content, whereas the author also mentions the stress—objective or subjective ideas—in the painting.

23. **(A)** The best answer is (A), because the main difference between Occidental and Japanese painting is the differing views concerning the primary object of art, as is explained toward the end of the second paragraph of the reading passage. While (B), (C), and (D) are mentioned, there is no in-depth analysis of any of these answers. Since the question asks for the *main* difference, (B), (C), and (D) are all incorrect answers.

24. **(G)** Sei-ichi Taki's area of expertise is Japanese painting; therefore, (G) is the best answer. (F) is incorrect since the writer's area is not Occidental (Western) painting but Oriental painting, although he is able to make many comparisons between the two. The article does not cover the broad expanse of Oriental painting (H) or Asian painting (J), but concentrates on Japanese painting. Hence, (H) and (J) should not be selected.

25. **(D)** (D) is the best choice. The Japanese painter can be said to bring out the spirit of the object being portrayed, as stated by the author in the second paragraph. Since the correct answer (D) refers to the spirit of the object being portrayed, it is logical that neither the painter's own thought, ideas, or objective ideas can be the answer. Consequently, (A), (B), and (C) are incorrect choices.

26. **(F)** (F) is the best answer since the reader is asked to identify what the painters of Western art do. The author states near the beginning of the third paragraph of the reading passage the painters of Western art give their foremost attention to the human figure. Since in Western art the human figure is given much attention, (G) should not be chosen since it is exactly the opposite of what the author states. The painters of Western art are not greatly concerned with the expression of the spirit but rather with the human figure; (H) should not be chosen. The painters in Western art are not concerned with showing high esteem for God's creations, but rather with objective qualities; (J) should not be chosen.

27. **(A)** As discussed by the author in the third paragraph, Japanese artists are different from Western artists in that they esteem rocks, trees, and flowers on the canvas as highly as they do human beings; therefore, (A) is the correct answer. Since the author states that birds and flowers may be devoid of, rather than possess, souls, (B) is incorrect. Japanese artists do give landscapes, birds,

and flowers lofty spiritual attributes; thus, (C) is false and should not be selected. (D) is incorrect, as the author states precisely the opposite of the answer choice, as was also the case with (C).

28. **(G)**   The author explains that in Japanese art mutual relations of all objects treated in a picture are important; this makes (G) the best answer. As the author explains in the last paragraph, there is no one individual object in the center of Japanese pictures; consequently, (F) should not be chosen. In Western art, one particular object receives all-exclusive prominence. (H) says just the opposite and should not be chosen. (J) directly opposes the author's statement that in Japanese painting no serious attempt is made to give all-exclusive prominence to any one particular object and should not be chosen.

29. **(C)**   The writer presents objectively information about Western and Japanese art. He is not seeking to put one form above the other. Therefore, (C) is the best answer. Since the author is being objective in his writing, neither (A) nor (B) can be the answer as both contain the words "persuade" and "superior." (D) cannot be chosen since it suggests, by using the word "favor," that the writer presents one type of art as superior to another type.

30. **(H)**   The best answer is (H) since the author states in the first sentence of the last paragraph that the relations should be complete. "Microcosmically complete" does not mean that every detail must be in order. (F) should not be selected because it states the opposite of that which the author explains. Since the amount of pigment on the canvas is not mentioned anywhere in the passage, (G) is incorrect. (J) is incorrect since the emphasis is placed on completion in subjective, not objective, terms.

31. **(D)**   The correct answer is (D) because the author writes, "There was something bleak and unapproachable in his face..." when describing Ethan Frome. The question asks which choice does *not* apply to Ethan Frome. Choices (A), (B), and (C) can all be used to describe Frome and are incorrect by process of elimination.

32. **(F)**   The best choice is (F) since the author refers to the "sluggish pulse of Starkfield" in discussing the winter. Choice (G) is incorrect because it suggests that the people *and* the climate, rather than solely the climate, were volatile. Choices (H) and (J) are not acceptable answers because they, too, include Statement II, which indicates that the people are volatile.

33. **(B)**   The best answer is (B). In the last paragraph, the narrator agrees that the smart ones would leave a town like Starkfield. Choice (A) is not an acceptable answer since the narrator believes it was more difficult to leave

Starkfield 20 years earlier as evidenced by his references to "means of resistance far fewer" and "the enemy in command of almost all lines of access." Choice (C) is incorrect since the writer suggests that it was easier to leave in this day and time. Choice (D) is incorrect because the narrator wonders in the last line of the passage what "combination of obstacles" hindered Ethan Frome from leaving.

34. **(G)**   Ethan is very predictable in his behavior, as is shown by his daily routine at the post office; therefore, (G) should be chosen. Since Frome is predictable, (F) is incorrect because it suggests the opposite. Since there is no inference or reference to these unsupported choices in the passage, (H) and (J) are both incorrect.

35. **(B)**   Since the writer indicates that Frome is 52 and the accident occurred 24 years ago, then the accident occurred when he was 28. Choice (B) is the best choice since it states that the accident occurred before Frome turned 30. The age of 28 is far older than the age choices that (A) and (C) infer, and younger than the age choice that (D) indicates.

36. **(J)**   The primary thrust of the passage is the interest that the narrator shows in Frome as shown by his taking note of Frome's behavior at the post office and his pondering of Gow's statement about Frome: "Guess he's been in Starkfield too many winters." Choice (J) is the best answer. There is no evidence in the passage that the narrator is repelled by Frome. (F) is incorrect. Choice (G) is also incorrect because the narrator wonders in the last sentence of the passage why Frome is still in Starkfield. Also, the narrator voices his concern that the most interesting parts of Gow's tale "were in the gaps." Choice (H) is, perhaps, the second best answer, but it is Frome—not the other citizens—who commands the narrator's attention.

37. **(C)**   Choice (C) is the best answer because Ethan's physical handicap creates a noticeable contrast with his "careless, powerful look." Choice (A) is an incorrect interpretation of the simile. "(L)ike the jerk of a chain" was not meant to be taken literally. Choice (B) does not follow the narrator's previous observation of Ethan's "careless, powerful look." Because Ethan has been identified as one of the taller "natives," choice (D) is incorrect.

38. **(F)**   Choice (F) is the only correct interpretation of the figurative expression "lank longitude." The "natives" are being compared to the shorter and heavier "foreign breed" who have recently settled in Starkfield. Choice (G) interprets "longitude" in a sailing context which is clearly inappropriate and incorrect. Choices (H) and (J) hold no relevance to this passage and are incorrect.

39. **(C)**   Choice (C) is correct because the look on Ethan Frome's face is a direct result of his personal history. Choice (A) is incorrect because Ethan's physical appearance has to do with genetics and his "smash-up," not with the time he has spent in Starkfield. Despite his personal history, Ethan retains his "careless, powerful look," so choice (B) is incorrect. Choice (D) has no basis within the passage and is therefore incorrect.

40. **(J)**   Choice (J) is the only one that has any basis in the passage and is correct. The narrator struck up some sort of relationship with Herman Gow, therefore choice (F) is incorrect. The power house, the trolley, the bicycle, and the rural delivery were mentioned demonstrating that modern life had not passed the village by, making choice (G) incorrect. Choice (H) is incorrect because it is contradicted by the text when the narrator mentions "the deadness in the community" and the exodus of the "smart ones."

Test 4: Science Reasoning

1.   **(C)**   Kepler's second observation stated that as the position vector decreases in length, a body's orbital speed increases. Therefore, the body having the fastest velocity must have the shortest position vector, making it closer to the Sun and center-of-mass of the system. (C) is the correct choice.

2.   **(F)**   Again, using Kepler's second observation, you know that the body having the fastest velocity must have the shortest position vector. Choice (F) is correct.

3.   **(C)**   Kepler's first observation stated that all planets move across orbits in the shape of ellipses, which are eccentric circles. An eccentricity of zero would describe a circle; therefore, choice (C) would not describe an orbiting planet.

4.   **(H)**   Kepler's third observation stated that the square of a planet's orbital period is directly proportional to the cube of its semimajor axis. In other words, the greater the distance to the Sun (and center-of-mass of the system), the longer the period. Therefore, (H) is correct, because it represents the shortest period of time, and the closest planet to the Sun of the choices given in this question.

5.   **(B)**   Choice (B) is false, since it states that planets move in circular and elliptical orbits. From the discussion of Kepler's first observation in the passage, you know that all planets move in elliptical orbits.

6. **(H)** The semimajor axis is equal to the sum of a planet's minimum and maximum distance from the Sun (and center-of-mass) divided by two (H). Kepler's third observation stated that the semimajor axis is the average distance between the Sun and planet. (H) is the only choice that gives an average value.

7. **(D)** (D) is the correct answer: the variants of the X207 snails described in Table 1 all have linear mortality rates. Thus, snails with one stripe have a decrease in their initial population by 50% in 30 days. In the next 30 days, the remaining 50% would die. Choice (A) is not correct because the X207 snails, with one stripe and with a linear mortality rate, are only 50% dead in 30 days, so they will not be 100% dead in 20 days. (B) and (C) are incorrect choices because the population will require another 30 days for the remaining 50% to die, so 40 and 52.5 days are not sufficient.

8. **(H)** Refer to the column headed "Age when 50% are dead." Note that one stripe increases the half-life of the snail from 17 to 31 days, and in snails with two stripes, the half-life increases from 31 to 44 days. This increase is about 15 days per stripe. Therefore, (H) is right, (F) and (G) are too low, and (J) is too high.

9. **(D)** The distribution of stripe data as a percentage of the population suggests that the phenotype of stripe could be related to a single gene, with the number of stripes related to the number of genes (0, 1, 2) present. The mating of snails, each of which has no gene for stripe, would produce offspring, 0% of which would have one stripe. Therefore, (D) is the correct answer. (A), (B), and (C) are all too high.

10. **(F)** The correct answer is (F). The data for life expectancy as a function of dissolved oxygen demonstrate that at the higher temperatures of 23 and 25 degrees, the half-life (i.e., the life expectancy) increases as the dissolved oxygen content decreases. Therefore, (G) and (H) are false, and since the data show (F) to be true, (J) is also false.

11. **(A)** The best answer is (A). The data are suggestive of two different populations of snails, one whose death rate is proportional to the number of snails present (a first order process) and a second whose death rate is linear. (B) is not a good choice because Figure 1 shows that the snail population is decreasing from 100% to 0% over 60 days. This abrupt change is not a result of the state of the environment. (C) is not a good choice because additional availability of a nutrient would not be expected to increase the death rate. Since (B) and (C) are not correct choices, (D) must be false.

12. **(G)** Life expectancy decreases as water temperature falls from 25 to 20 degrees for 50 and 70 mm Hg of dissolved oxygen. Therefore, answer (G) is

correct. It does not increase, so (F) is false. It does change, so (H) is false, and the change can be determined from this data, so (J) is false.

13. **(C)**   See Table 1. The correct answer is (C). Based solely on the maximum wind speed, the hurricane in Figure 1 would be classified as a Category 3 hurricane.

14. **(J)**   The answer is (J). The first step is to determine the category of the hurricane. Since the pressure is 933 mb and the storm surge is 5.0 meters, it is a Category 4 hurricane. Major damage is associated with a Category 4 hurricane.

15. **(B)**   The correct answer is (B). According to the information provided and the Saffir-Simpson Hurricane Scale, a storm has to have a maximum wind speed of 64 knots. Since the storm in the example is on the threshold of this value, the loss of strength would cause it to lose its label as a hurricane. The answer could not be (A) or (C) because it would have to increase in strength for it to become a Category 2 storm or to cause extensive damage. (D) is incorrect because even though the eye wall of the hurricane is the most intense area of the storm, it too would weaken as the rest of the hurricane weakens.

16. **(F)**   According to the passage, the strongest part of the hurricane is located at the eye wall. Since the figure states that the maximum winds are 100 knots, it can be deduced that the wind speed at Location A is 100 knots. Therefore, the correct answer is (F). The other locations are not near the eye of the storm, and therefore the winds would be significantly less than at Location A.

17. **(C)**   Storm 2 is the only storm with sufficient winds, has low pressure, and is formed over warm ocean waters. Therefore, the answer would be (C). Storm 1, although very strong, did not form over warm ocean waters; it formed over land. Thus, Storm 1 cannot be a hurricane. Storm 3, although it did form over warm ocean water, does not have the required minimum wind speed to be a hurricane. This eliminates choices (A), (B) and (D).

18. **(J)**   The best answer is (J). Oxygen gas is part of the air in the capillary tube. As it is consumed, the kerosene drop moves to the right. The volume of gas consumed is the volume of a cylinder, which is equal to the distance the drop moves times the diameter of the capillary tube. Choices (F) and (G) are both false because the volume of the whole capillary tube is not needed, only the volume within the distance the drop moved. Choice (H) is wrong because the volume of Flask A is not needed; it is presumed to be more than ample to supply the oxygen needed.

19. **(C)** Since it takes 48 hours for the population of CHO cells to double, very little growth has occurred after only two hours. (The cells would still be in the log phase of growth.) Answer (C) is best. Oxygen consumption would be minimal in that amount of time, so (A) is incorrect, although it might be our first thought. A look at the doubling time of 48 hours shows that two hours is not enough time for significant oxygen consumption to have occurred, therefore answer (B) is wrong. The function of the KOH paper is to absorb the carbon dioxide, not the oxygen. Answer (D) is false since the cell concentration is no smaller than in the other cultures.

20. **(H)** A low doubling time, such as 20 minutes, means that the cells rapidly enter the log phase of growth and consume oxygen early; therefore, answer (F) is true. Answer (G) is true, since without the KOH paper to neutralize the production of CO_2, there would be pressure on the kerosene drop to move to the left. Therefore, answer (H) is the best choice. If (F) and (G) are true, answer (J) is wrong.

21. **(D)** The kerosene drop would not move because the system would not be airtight. Air from outside the system would equalize any pressure (positive or negative) created. Choice (D) is correct. Therefore, both (A) and (B) are incorrect. (C) is false because sterile cotton is sufficient to prevent contamination.

22. **(F)** Since the cell concentration in Flask 4 at the start of measuring was already 10 times higher than the concentration in Flask 5, it would indeed be possible for the culture to be nearing the end of its logarithmic phase of growth in under two hours with resultant reduced metabolism. Thus, (F) is the best answer. (G) is false because there were *more* cells in Flask 4 than in Flask 5. Choice (H) is false because the KOH-soaked paper would be more than sufficient to neutralize all the CO_2 produced. Choice (J) is false because (F) is true.

23. **(D)** The design in (A) is for an electrolytic cell with a battery. Two separate chambers are not present. Therefore, (A) is not a correct response. (B) is incorrect, since there must be two separate chambers with a salt bridge connecting them. (C) is also not correct because this cell has two chambers but no salt bridge. (D) is correct, based on Experiment 2, two separate chambers with two different solutions are joined by a salt bridge and connected to a voltmeter to allow for the reading of the potential.

24. **(G)** The detection of a potential indicates that electrons are flowing, so (F) is incorrect. Choice (G) is the best choice, because from 50 ml to 70 ml of $NiSO_4$, the sign of the potential changes from (+) to (−), indicating a change of direction of electrons. (H) is false, because the change of sign in the potential indicates some change in the direction of flow has occurred. (J) is incorrect.

There is no data in Table 1 to show an alternating flow of electrons. At a given volume, electrons flow in only one direction.

25. **(C)**   Choice (A) is incorrect because based on the design of the cell in Experiment 1, a battery is used, which supplies energy that is consumed or used by the solution. (B) is false, because the cell itself does not produce a current, only the battery establishes the current rate of supply of charge. (C) is correct since the cell uses the electrical energy produced by the battery as indicated in Experiment 1. (D) is incorrect, since an electrolytic cell consumes or uses up electrical energy and does not produce a potential. A potential is produced by a galvanic cell.

26. **(G)**   According to Table 2, to increase the cell potential, one would decrease the $[Ni^{2+}]$ concentration, so (F) is incorrect. (G) is correct, because if the $[Ni^{2+}]$ concentration is decreased at constant $[Sn^{2+}]$ concentration, the cell potential would increase. (H) is incorrect, because the data in Table 2 reveals an increase in cell potential. (J) is false as explained in choice (H).

27. **(A)**   The correct answer is (A). The cells in Experiments 1 and 2 both must use a cathode and an anode to function. (B) is incorrect, because only a galvanic cell; as explained in Experiment 2, uses two solutions. (C) is incorrect; only an electrolytic cell, as described in Experiment 1, uses a battery to pass current through a solution. (D) is false, since Experiment 1 gives no data on temperature and thus there is no basis for comparison.

28. **(H)**   Since it is a galvanic cell that uses two different solutions, (F) is incorrect. (G) is false, since only a galvanic cell produces a potential. (H) is correct. A galvanic cell produces a cell potential based on the results of Experiment 2. (J) is incorrect. A galvanic cell was used, not because the temperature was changed, but because a potential was produced.

29. **(C)**   The only statement made by Physicist 1 is (C). Statements (A) and (B) are false, while (D) is supported by Physicist 2.

30. **(F)**   Physicist 2 hypothesized about electrical currents because the evidence of nanoflares was not significant. If this data changed, the theory would be refuted. (F) is the correct answer. All other statements are false.

31. **(B)**   All statements agree with the hypothesis of Physicist 2 except statement (B). Therefore, (B) is the correct answer.

32. **(J)**   The information given in answer choices (F), (G), and (H) conflicts with the information presented in the passage. Therefore, (J) is the correct answer.

33. **(B)**   The existence of the corona violates standard thermodynamic principles and is therefore uncommon and atypical. Answer choice (B) is the correct answer. (A) is false, and while (C) and (D) are true, they are not atypical.

34. **(H)**   This is the only statement both physicists support. Physicist 1 only supports (F) and (J), while Physicist 2 supports (G).

35. **(B)**   The presence of electric currents causes the corona to be heated. Therefore, (B) is the correct answer. Conclusion (A) is a false statement, and (C) and (D) are conclusions of Physicist 1.

36. **(G)**   The rainfall changed from approximately 30 inches to approximately 40 inches. The difference between these is 10 inches. The correct answer is (G).

37. **(B)**   The average temperature in 1920 was 60.3° F. In 1960, the average temperature was 65.5° F. The temperature change would be 5.2°; therefore, (B) is the correct answer.

38. **(J)**   Since the exact location of population increases are unknown, there is not enough information to make a correlation between the changes in weather and the changes in information; therefore, (J) is correct.

39. **(C)**   There has been an increase of 10 to 20 inches in rainfall and there has been a change in temperature for most regions of the United States according to Figure 1. The correct answer is (C).

40. **(G)**   There was a change of 6.0 increase in the Midwest. In the Northeast and Alaska, the changes were 2.8 and 3.6, respectively. No information was given regarding the West. The largest change, therefore, is in the Midwest. Therefore, using the information given, (G) is the correct answer choice.

ACT
ASSESSMENT
with
REA's Interactive **TEST***ware*®

PRACTICE
EXAM III

Exam III is also provided in our special interactive ACT TEST*ware*®. It is highly recommended that you first take this exam on computer. You will then have the additional study features and benefits of enforced timed conditions, individual diagnostic analysis, and instant scoring. See page 4 for guidance on how to get the most out of our ACT book and software.

ACT ASSESSMENT PRACTICE EXAM III

(An answer sheet for this test appears in the back of this book.)

Test 1: English

TIME: 45 Minutes
75 Questions

DIRECTIONS: This test consists of five passages. In each passage, certain words and phrases have been underlined and numbered. The questions on each passage consist of alternatives for these underlined segments. Choose the alternative that follows standard written English, most accurately reflects the style and tone of the passage, or best relays the idea of the passage. Choose "NO CHANGE," if no change is necessary.

In addition, you will also encounter questions about part of the passage, or the passage as a whole. These questions are indicated by a number in a box at the end of the section, rather than an underlined portion.

Once you have selected the best answer, fill in the appropriate oval on the answer sheet for the correct choice.

Passage I

[1]

People of every civilization throughout history have celebrated the transmutation of life from one state to another. <u>Our wedding, the arrival of our adulthood, our funeral, completions of our education at various levels, birth</u>—each of these
1

significant <u>stages' is</u> proclaimed in some ceremonial fashion, always public, veri-
2

fied by the witness of others, testifying to the perpetualness of some sequence of

human history. Validating the uniqueness of the rite of <u>passage, its'</u> separateness
3
from the day's other occurrences, these rituals normally demand <u>pageantry,</u>
4
<u>elaborate dress, the giving of gifts, and eating and drinking.</u> Funerals ask <u>for my</u>
4 5
dark apparel, christenings and birthdays ask for our <u>gifts and</u> bar mitzvahs make
6
gluttons of us all. Yet, of birth, marriage, and death, oddly enough, only one can

claim our conscious attendance completely <u>and fully. The wedding, humankind's</u>
7
most vital rite of passage. And so it is that this indelible imprint is found en-

graved in civilization's foundation.

[2]

The wedding ceremony itself, <u>who</u> prepares an individual's move from one
8
stage in life to another, is organic to <u>the society from which</u>
9
<u>the individual comes.</u> In certain African tribes, a young adolescent male <u>finding</u>
9 10
himself hurled headlong into a wilderness where he is expected to kill a lion with

nothing but his bare hands and intellect. His society judges his <u>value, as a man</u> on
11
the basis of his success in meeting that challenge. In an odd way, the American

newlywed experiences a similar <u>rite as they enter</u> a consumer society; the proce-
12
dures of wedding hoo-hah <u>testifies</u> to commercial, mercantile values, especially in
13
the giving of gifts. Brides buy for the grooms, grooms for the brides, brides for

bridesmaids, ushers for grooms, and on the procedure <u>goes. Rehearsal</u> dinners, last-
14
fling dinners, showers, the spiraling carnival of splish-splash around the wedding

itself. The American wedding celebrates in a raucous fashion a frenzied gluttonous

revelry unparalleled by any future event in the life of the American couple.

1.   A. NO CHANGE

     B. The completion of various levels of our education, our funeral, wed-
        ding, adulthood's arrival, our birth

C. Our birth, the completion of our education at various levels, the arrival of adulthood, our wedding, our funeral

D. Our funeral, the arrival of adulthood, our birth, our wedding, the completion of our education at various levels

2. F. NO CHANGE   H. stages are

   G. stage is   J. stages is

3. A. NO CHANGE   C. passage, it's

   B. passage its'   D. passage, its

4. F. NO CHANGE

   G. appropriate pageantry, elaborate dress, various gifts, and requisite repasts.

   H. pageantry, dressing to the nines, an overflow of gifts, food and drink.

   J. elaborate dress, displays of pageantry, gift giving, and repasts that will be remembered.

5. A. NO CHANGE   C. with my

   B. for their   D. for our

6. F. NO CHANGE   H. gifts since

   G. gifts because   J. gifts, and

7. A. NO CHANGE

   B. fully, the wedding. Humankind's

   C. fully: the wedding, humankind's

   D. fully, the wedding, humankinds

8. F. NO CHANGE   H. in which

   G. which   J. OMIT the underlined portion.

9. A. NO CHANGE

   B. their society

   C. the society of the individual

   D. his/her society

10. F.   NO CHANGE   H.   finds

    G.   , finding   J.   found

11. A.   NO CHANGE   C.   value as a man,

    B.   value as a man   D.   value—as a man

12. F.   NO CHANGE   H.   rite as they both enter

    G.   rite as he or she enters   J.   rite when they enter

13. A.   NO CHANGE   C.   testified

    B.   testimonied   D.   testify

14. F.   NO CHANGE   H.   goes: Rehearsal

    G.   goes: rehearsal   J.   has gone. Rehearsal

15. Which organizational strategy best describes Paragraph 2?

    A.   Defining a series of unfamiliar terms

    B.   Explaining the process of becoming a man

    C.   Comparing an African and an American rite of passage

    D.   Arguing that American weddings are better than African lion hunts

Passage II

[1]

Survivors are always extraordinary people, seeming to possess qualities that humans in their finest hour have. One particular group of wanderers from <u>Vung Tau Vietnam, fall</u> into this category. Originally natives of Southeast Asia, they were part of an exodus from their homeland, finally ending up in the United States. Consisting mainly of fishermen and their families, altogether they number about 1,300 <u>in all</u>. Their most outstanding trait is their ability to survive after having to flee their home. They have done so with unity and togetherness. [18]

16 (under "Vung" and "Tau Vietnam, fall")

17 (under "in all")

[2]

Originally, these fishermen lived in North Vietnam. Because of the threat of communism they fled their homes in 1954 and settled in South Vietnam; when
19
the Vietnam War broke out, once again these people found themselves in a dangerous position. With the fall of South Vietnam comes the need to relocate
20
once more. In 1975 the group moved. This time halfway around the world to the
21
Mississippi Gulf Coast. Although they were newcomers with a chance to begin fresh, their troubles were not over. They found themselves in the process of
22
facing a war of not being accepted by Americans.
22

[3]

One particular source of opposition has been the American fisherman. The reason for this bone of contention is simple. Competition for jobs. The Vietnam-
23   24
ese people were glad to be here that they would work at any job. A few have
25
managed to survive here. As of 1981, some Vietnamese—like boat owner Ba
26
Ban Nguyen, actually owned part of a shipyard.
26

[4]

Today the wanderers from Vung Tau want more than menial labor along the
27
docks, they want to compete as fishermen. Gradually, these people have enabled
27
themselves to compete as commercial fishermen. But in the process, they have angered American fishermen who, while simply minding their own business,
28
were crowded by the Vietnamese moving into established fishing areas. After all, the Americans said, it is difficult to buy and sell their catch with so many more fishermen around.

[5]

29 Verbal confrontations are common, and, increasingly, physical harassment has occurred. Along the Texas coast, an American fisherman was killed, supposedly by a Vietnamese. Additionally, fishing styles differ. The Vietnamese fish from north to south while Americans fish from east to west. 30

16. F.   NO CHANGE   H.   Vung Tau Vietnam falls
     G.   Vung Tau, Vietnam, falls   J.   Vung Tau, Vietnam, fall

17. A.   NO CHANGE   C.   in total.
     B.   combined.   D.   OMIT the underlined portion.

18. Which of the following strategies would best support the assertion made in Paragraph 1, that the fishermen's survival was accomplished through unity and togetherness?

     F.   Discussing routes of travel, because group dynamics is unimportant to the reader

     G.   Discussing the history of communism, because dates make points clearer

     H.   Discussing group members conferring with each other and coming to unanimous decisions, because examples clarify an issue

     J.   Discussing irreconcilable disagreements and conflicts among group members that exemplify the fishermen's problems, because this issue is lacking in the passage

19. A.   NO CHANGE   C.   communism, they
     B.   communism; they   D.   communism, and they

20. F.   NO CHANGE   H.   Vietnam came
     G.   Vietnam, comes   J.   Vietnam, come

21. A.   NO CHANGE   C.   moved, this
     B.   moved; this   D.   is moving, this

22. F.   NO CHANGE
     G.   The Americans did not accept them.

H. They faced a war of not never being accepted by Americans.

J. They faced not being accepted by Americans who seemed at war with them.

23. A. NO CHANGE   C. resistance

    B. foul-up   D. glitch

24 F. NO CHANGE

    G. simple: competition

    H. simple and it is competition

    J. simple. Its competition

25. A. NO CHANGE   C. , were so grateful

    B. were ecstatic   D. were so glad

26. F. NO CHANGE

    G. Vietnamese–like boat owner Ba Ban Nguyen,

    H. Vietnamese, like boat owner Ba Ban Nguyen,

    J. Vietnamese like boat owner Ba Ban Nguyen,

27. A. NO CHANGE   C. docks; however, they

    B. docks; they   D. docks, yet, they

28. F. NO CHANGE   H. whom

    G. which   J. OMIT the underlined portion.

29. Which of the suggested sentences make the best introduction to Paragraph 5 and the best transition from Paragraph 4?

    A. The Vietnamese fishermen are proud of their expertise.

    B. Americans' incomes are suffering.

    C. Still more problems exist.

    D. The market value of fishing is dropping.

Items 30 and 31 pose questions about Passage II as a whole.

---

30. Which of the following sentences, if added to the end of Paragraph 5, would best relate Paragraph 5 to Paragraph 1 to tie together the passage as a whole?

F.   Now and then, signs pop up with slogans such as "Vietnamese Go Home."

G.   These all add up to even more problems for the wanderers from Vung Tau.

H.   The Vung Tau have traveled many miles to reach the United States.

J.   The journey through Southeast Asia was a harrowing one.

31. Which of the following sentences best expresses the author's opinion of the Vietnamese fishermen and their families?

A.   The Vietnamese fishermen and their families are to be admired for their persistence and determination in the face of adversity.

B.   The Vietnamese fishermen and their families will give up when challenged by American fishermen.

C.   The Vietnamese fishermen and their families are bullies because they pushed American fishermen around.

D.   The Vietnamese fishermen and their families are people whose familial fighting will destroy their culture.

Passage III

[1]

For centuries people have needed to live in cities and towns to find jobs; yet
                                                                          32
have desired the greenery, the cleaner air, and the opportunity to garden that are

available only in rural or suburban fringe areas.

[2]

Living space has always been at a premium in cities and towns; there has

been little green space—and even less space for gardens. During the Middle

Ages, when cities were walled for protection, houses and sheds were packed like
                                                                              33
sardines within the city walls and because of little inner-wall spaces, gardens
33
flourished in front of city gates.

[3]

Similar crowded conditions occurred several hundred <u>years later if</u> the in-
34
dustrial revolution forced rapid city growth. Ground space was at a premium so

that <u>there was, squeezed</u> together side by side, houses and townhomes. As condi-
35
tions worsened, these dwellings were pushed into alleys and inner courtyards or

forced upwards—into five- and six-story buildings with several apartments on

each floor.

[4]

Many rooms <u>have</u> no outside light. Ventilation was almost nonexistent.
36
Added to this were other poor health conditions, including a general lack of

sanitary facilities, inadequate heating, and meager and unwholesome food—<u>all of</u>
37
<u>which were compounded</u> by the terrible crowding as the workers and their fami-
37
lies swarmed into the cities. <u>Lack of air, lack of sunlight, and unsanitary, over-</u>
38
<u>crowded conditions</u> were a way of life for most working people.
38

[5]

 39 <u>One of the measures provided to relieve people living in such un-</u>
40
<u>healthy conditions in England</u> was a law in 1819 that provided for leasing land
40
for small gardens to the poor and unemployed. Later other countries in Europe

promulgated laws regarding provision of small-garden areas for city people.

[6]

Gardens for working people, the poor, and the unemployed were provided

as a health measure by <u>citys' governments</u>, philanthropists, and some factory
41
owners. Gardens also became a way <u>to better help</u> ensure stability by providing a
42

link to the countryside that the workers had left and a means of improving the quality of life.

[7]

By the mid-1800's the small-garden movement had appeared in most European <u>countries, neither</u> as an independent effort to meet the local conditions or
<u>43</u>
influenced by work in neighboring countries. The movement not only continued to grow into the early twentieth <u>century. It thrived.</u>
44

32. F.   NO CHANGE
    G.   jobs yet
    H.   jobs; yet,
    J.   jobs; and, yet

33. A.   NO CHANGE
    B.   snug as a bug in a rug
    C.   packed like cats and dogs
    D.   tightly packed together

34. F.   NO CHANGE
    G.   years later, if
    H.   years later when
    J.   years later when,

35. A.   NO CHANGE
    B.   there was squeezed
    C.   there was, squeezing
    D.   there were, squeezed

36. F.   NO CHANGE
    G.   had
    H.   will have
    J.   didn't have

37. A.   NO CHANGE
    B.   all compounded
    C.   all by
    D.   being that they were all compounded

38. F.   NO CHANGE
    G.   Lack of air, lack of sunlight, and lack of unsanitary and overcrowded conditions
    H.   Lack of air, sunlight, sanitation, and space
    J.   Air, sunlight, sanitation and overcrowding

39. Which of the following sentences would provide the best introduction to Paragraph 5 and the best transition from Paragraph 4?

    A. As a result of space demands, Europe created a series of laws.

    B. These workers were often paid poorly.

    C. The lack of sunlight was caused by heavy fogs.

    D. In 1989, the Clean Air Act was implemented in the United States.

40. F. NO CHANGE

    G. One of the measures which was provided to relieve the English living in such unhealthy living conditions in England

    H. One measure to alleviate unhealthy living conditions in England

    J. Measuring unhealthy living conditions in England

41. A. NO CHANGE   C. governments citys'

    B. city governments   D. governments of the city's

42. F. NO CHANGE   H. to help

    G. to really help   J. to perhaps help

43. A. NO CHANGE   C. countries; neither

    B. countries, either   D. countries; nevertheless

44. F. NO CHANGE   H. century; since it thrived.

    G. century, it thrived.   J. century and it thrived.

Items 45-46 pose questions about Passage III as a whole.

---

45. If you were grouping essays for a book, under what chapter heading would this essay fall?

    A. The Best Plants for Your Garden

    B. The Evolution of European City Gardens

    C. Architectural Design in Medieval England

    D. Methods of Keeping Gardens Pest Free

46. Suppose the writer wanted to support the assertion in Paragraph 5 that other European countries created laws to provide garden areas for city people.

Which of the following statements would best accomplish this goal?

F.   Explaining why a garden is an important nutritional aspect for mankind

G.   Comparing England's overcrowding to Spain's

H.   Citing some specific examples of non-English European laws providing garden space

J.   Listing a variety of beautiful gardens to visit in London

Passage IV

[1]

A rock-solid consensus of <u>opinion exist</u> in urban-industrial society regarding the correct means of measuring our progress beyond the <u>primal. The</u> period
₄₇
₄₈
when human civilization was in its infancy. The prevailing conclusion is that we measure progress by examining how artificial our environment becomes, either by ridding ourselves of <u>natures</u> presence <u>than</u> by controlling natural forces. Without much doubt, the human environment must always maintain an artificial flair about it. In fact, we might almost say that the human space is destined to possess a <u>"Artificial</u> naturalness" in that <u>each person spontaneously fills their</u> universe with artifacts and human-made, non-natural institutions. Humans invent and scheme, devising an intricate finished product: culture, a buffer zone conceived by and intended for humans where people may live as legitimately as plants and animals inhabit their environment of instinct, reflex, and roteness.

[2]

But, as we acknowledge human <u>culture; we</u> must also acknowledge the
₅₃
natural environment—the mountain and the shore, the fox and its flora, the heavenly bodies—and the close relationship primitives had with this natural habitat

for millennia. Then, people <u>are using</u> as their clocks the seasonal rhythms and
54
timed their own activities to these smooth, organic cycles. <u>They spoke to and</u>
55
<u>worshipped the surrounding plants and animals and thus learned from them.</u>
55
Primitives considered their destiny tied inherently to the non-humans—allies and
foes alike—and created places of honor for them in their culture.

[3]

We cannot possibly exaggerate the importance of this intimacy between human and nature to the growth of human awareness. This inadequate, sterile <u>term,</u>
56
<u>"nature"</u> that we use to categorize the non-human world has regretfully lost <u>its</u>
56   57
impact through the simple connotation we give it today: a designated area of random physical things and events outside and other than ourselves. Nature, however, has brought us into existence and will outdistance <u>us from them</u> we have
58
learned of our destiny. Whatever our culture produces <u>that severs humans</u> from a
59
vibrant tie with nature, that removes us from or alienates nature, is—strictly speaking—a delusion. What culture produces unmindful of the natural world doesn't merely lack ecological soundness; more alarmingly <u>it lacks</u> psychological com-
60
pleteness. It remains devoid of a truth our primitive counterparts learned from an infant world of nature: the reality of spiritual being.

47. A. NO CHANGE
    B. opinion exists
    C. opinions exist
    D. opinions existing

48. F. NO CHANGE
    G. primal the
    H. primal; yet,
    J. primal, the

49. A. NO CHANGE
    B. natures'
    C. nature's
    D. Mother Natures'

50. F. NO CHANGE   H. then
    G. when   J. or

51. A. NO CHANGE   C. an "artificial
    B. an artificial D. a artificial

52. F. NO CHANGE
    G. each person spontaneously fill their
    H. anyone spontaneously fills their
    J. all people spontaneously fill their

53. A. NO CHANGE   C. culture we
    B. culture. We   D. culture, we

54. F. NO CHANGE   H. use
    G. will use   J. used

55. A. NO CHANGE
    B. They learned from the plants and animals that surrounded them, spoke with them, worshipped them.
    C. From the plants and animals they learned, surrounded them, spoke with them that worshipped them.
    D. The plants and animals that surrounded them worshipped them, spoke with them and learned from them.

56. F. NO CHANGE   H. "term, nature"
    G. term, "nature," that   J. term" , "nature

57. A. NO CHANGE   C. it's
    B. its'   D. his

58. F. NO CHANGE   H. us and from him
    G. us; from them   J. us; from it

59. A. NO CHANGE   C. that sever's humans
    B. , that severs' humans   D. that severs

60. F.   NO CHANGE   H.   they lacked

     G.   they lack   J.   it had lacked

Item 61 poses a question about Passage IV as a whole.

---

61. Suppose the writer wished to add the following sentences to the passage:

Archeologists have discovered various sites where primitive cultures honored natural forces: the Aztec sun pyramids, the monuments of Stonehenge marking nature's cycles, the ancient Incan temples glorifying nature's powers. Additionally, sacred sculptures, such as the cats and falcons of ancient Egypt, attest to this worship of non-human creatures.

In which of the following paragraphs would the new sentences most logically be placed?

   A.   Paragraph 1, because all vital information must be told at first

   B.   Paragraph 2, because that is where worship of nature is discussed

   C.   In Paragraph 3's place, because that paragraph is just social philosophy and therefore irrelevant

   D.   In a separate paragraph following Paragraph 3, because it sums up the points made earlier

Passage V

[1]

Early in the nineteenth century, Napoleon sat across a chessboard from a robot swathed in the robes of a Turk. Napoleon moved his chessmen into battle,
                                                                            62
the Turk did the same. Then, when Napoleon blundered three times in succes-
62
sion, the audacious machine sweeps the board clean with an iron hand.
                                   63

[2]

The chess-playing Turk had been carefully slapped together by Baron Von
                                              64
Kempelen; who took all comers until Edgar Allan Poe deduced that beneath the
       65
Turk's chess table resided a diminutive chess expert who manipulated and ma-
                                                             66

neuvered <u>the variety of different</u> controls that gave life to the machine. Those
                66
were the innocent times when people believed that technology could build any-

thing—not the least of which was a chess-playing robot.

[3]

Indeed, humans have always been fascinated by robots—machines that do

their work and often look like them. Many of those fascinated are the basement

inventors <u>which have</u> built machines that walk and talk like people but cannot
                67
think or control themselves intelligently. <u>It is in science fiction that the ultimate</u>
                                                                      68
<u>robots find themselves dwelling.</u> These sleek robots are <u>computerized; and, thus</u>
                68   69
have some ability to think. They are also autonomous—that is, they need not be

controlled directly by humans. The ultimate robot of fiction, superior in physical

strength and mental capacity, <u>run the world for their</u> human creators.
                                                  70

[4]

The ultimate robot is a long way off. However, this fact should not dissuade

<u>them</u> from building machines that can help humans: machines that can take
 71
people's place in mind-dulling industrial <u>jobs. In</u> all the dirty and dangerous tasks
                                                          72
that still must be done by somebody or something. ⏥73⏥

62. F. NO CHANGE   H. battle; since the

    G. battle the   J. battle; the

63. A. NO CHANGE   C. having swept

    B. swept   D. will sweep

64. F. NO CHANGE   H. constructed

    G. thrown together   J. run up

65. A. NO CHANGE
    B. Kempelen; whom
    C. Kempelen; it
    D. Kempelen they

66. F. NO CHANGE
    G. manipulated the various
    H. maneuvered and manipulated the different
    J. maneuvered the various different

67. A. NO CHANGE
    B. who has
    C. who have
    D. which has

68. F. NO CHANGE
    G. Dwelling in science fiction, the ultimate robots find themselves.
    H. It is in the science fiction stories that the ultimate robots seem to dwell.
    J. The ultimate robots dwell in science fiction.

69. A. NO CHANGE
    B. computerized and thus
    C. computerized. And thus
    D. computerized; thus

70. F. NO CHANGE
    G. runs the world for their
    H. run the world for its'
    J. runs the world for its

71. A. NO CHANGE
    B. we
    C. us
    D. him

72. F. NO CHANGE
    G. jobs and in
    H. jobs; however, in
    J. jobs since

73. Which of the following sentences makes the best introduction to Paragraph 4 and the best transition from Paragraph 3?

    A. We can all remember the metal monsters of comic book fame.

    B. In many of these wild tales, these arrogant machines take over the planet.

    C. Stimulating as science fiction is, it is not reality.

    D. Computerized automatons are often seen in the manufacturing of automobiles.

Items 74-75 pose questions about Passage V as a whole.

74. Which of the following sentences, if added to the end of Paragraph 4, would best relate Paragraph 4 to Paragraph 1 to tie together the passage as a whole?

    F. Robots evolved from science fiction.

    G. Whether in games or work, robots can indeed be humans' allies.

    H. Consequently, robots are machines only of the past.

    J. The Turkish are quite an inventive and clever people.

75. The writer wants to support the assertion in Paragraph 2 that nineteenth-century technologists thought they could build anything. Which of the following strategies would best accomplish that goal?

    A. Comparing Edgar Allan Poe to famous Turkish writers

    B. Explaining various chess strategies

    C. Citing some specific examples of far-reaching experiments and inventions then in progress

    D. Discuss the economic feasibility of becoming an inventor

THIS IS THE END OF TEST 1.

Test 2: Mathematics

Time: 60 Minutes
60 Questions

DIRECTIONS: Solve the following problems, and fill in the appropriate ovals on your answer sheet.

Unless otherwise indicated:

1. Figures may not have been drawn to scale.

2. All geometric figures lie in a plane.

3. "Line" refers to a straight line.

4. "Average" refers to arithmetic mean.

---

1. Simplify $4[-2(3 + 9) \div 3] + 5$.

   A. -20
   B. 11
   C. -27
   D. 27
   E. 0

2. $\sqrt{8} + 3\sqrt{18} - 7\sqrt{2} =$

   F. $\sqrt{2}$.
   G. 2.
   H. $3\sqrt{2}$.
   J. $4\sqrt{2}$.
   K. $7\sqrt{2}$.

3. The number 120 is separated into two parts. The larger part exceeds three times the smaller by 12. The smaller part is

   A. 27.
   B. 33.
   C. 15.
   D. 39.
   E. 29.

4. If $f(x) = 3x^2 - x + 5$, then $f(3) =$

   F. 15.
   G. 17.
   H. 23.
   J. 27.
   K. 29.

5. If $\dfrac{3}{2}x = 5$, then $\dfrac{2}{3} + x =$

    A. $\dfrac{10}{3}$.
    D.   8.

    B.   4.
    E.   12.

    C. $\dfrac{15}{2}$.

6. If $y = 2(x - 3)^2$ and $x = -1$, then $y =$

    F.   4.
    J.   32.

    G.   8.
    K.   48.

    H.   16.

7. If $\dfrac{3}{x + 2} = \dfrac{5}{x + 7}$, then $x =$

    A. $\dfrac{7}{2}$.
    D. $\dfrac{13}{2}$.

    B. $\dfrac{9}{2}$.
    E. $\dfrac{15}{2}$.

    C. $\dfrac{11}{2}$.

8. Solve for x, when $|5 - 3x| = -2$.

    F. $x = \dfrac{7}{3}$
    J.   1

    G. $\dfrac{-7}{3}$
    K.   No solution

    H. -1

9. If $a^2 b^3 = 3^7$ and $a = 9$, then $b =$

    A.   1.
    D.   3.

    B.   2.
    E. $3\sqrt{3}$.

    C. $\sqrt{3}$.

10. If $a = 5$ and $b = 8$, then $\dfrac{a + \dfrac{a}{b}}{a - \dfrac{a}{b}} =$

F. $\dfrac{5}{8}$.

J. $\dfrac{9}{7}$.

G. $\dfrac{7}{9}$.

K. $\dfrac{8}{5}$.

H. -1.

11. If $x = 1$ and $y = -2$, then $3x^2y - 2xy^2 + 5xy =$

A. 6.

D. -12.

B. 9.

E. -15.

C. -24.

12. If $xy - x = 27$ and $y - 1 = 3$, then $x =$

F. 27.

J. 0.

G. 9.

K. -3.

H. 3.

13. Simplify $\dfrac{\dfrac{1}{2} + \dfrac{1}{3}}{\dfrac{1}{6}}$.

A. 5

D. 2

B. 3

E. $\dfrac{3}{4}$

C. 4

14. If $g(x) = x^2 + 5x - 3$, then $g(-7) =$

F. -7.

J. 9.

G. -5.

K. 11.

H. 7.

15. If $f(x) = -x^3 - 2x^2 + 4x - 8$, what is $f(-2x)$?

    A. $8x^3 - 8x^2 - 8x - 8$

    B. $-8x^3 + 8x^2 - 8x - 8$

    C. $8x^3 - 4x^2 - 8x - 8$

    D. $-8x^3 - 4x^2 - 8x - 8$

    E. $8x^3 - 6x^2 - 6x - 8$

16. If the functions f, g, and h are defined by $f(x) = x^3$, $g(x) = x - 2$, and $h(x) = \dfrac{x}{2}$, then $f(g(h(8))) =$

    F. 0.

    G. 4.

    H. 8.

    J. 27.

    K. 62.

17. What is the remainder when $2x^2 - 4x + 5$ is divided by $x + 1$?

    A. 9

    B. 11

    C. 13

    D. 15

    E. 16

18. If $f(x) = 1 + 3x - 2kx^2$ and $f(-\dfrac{1}{2}) = 0$ then $k =$

    F. 0.

    G. $\dfrac{1}{2}$.

    H. 1.

    J. -1.

    K. 5.

19. Solve for x: $\log(40x - 1) - \log(x - 1) = 3$.

    A. $\dfrac{333}{320}$

    B. $\dfrac{333}{960}$

    C. 999

    D. $\dfrac{1001}{960}$

    E. Cannot be determined.

20. If $\dfrac{5}{9}a = 1$, then $\dfrac{5}{9} + a =$

    F. $\dfrac{106}{45}$.

    G. $\dfrac{9}{5}$.

797

H.   1.

J. $\dfrac{5}{9}$.

K.   0.

21.   If $\dfrac{2}{x+5} = \dfrac{6}{x+3}$, then $x =$

A.   –6.

D.   3.

B.   –3.

E.   6.

C.   –1.

22.   If "Δ" is an operator that transforms a,b according to the rule $a \,\Delta\, b = a - b$, determine $(a \,\Delta\, b) \,\Delta\, ((a \,\Delta\, a) \,\Delta\, b)$.

F. $a - 2b$

J. $2a$

G. $2b$

K. a

H. $2a - b$

23.   Simplify: $\dfrac{x + \dfrac{1}{y}}{x - \dfrac{1}{y}}$.

A. $\dfrac{1}{x+y}$

D. $\dfrac{yx+1}{yx-1}$

B. $\dfrac{yx-1}{yx+1}$

E. $\dfrac{x-2}{x+3}$

C. $\dfrac{2}{3}$

24.   Add $\dfrac{2}{x-3}$ and $\dfrac{5}{x+2}$.

F. $\dfrac{1}{x+2}$

J. $\dfrac{x+2}{x-3}$

G. $\dfrac{3}{x-3}$

K. $\dfrac{5}{2}$

H. $\dfrac{7x-11}{(x-3)(x+2)}$

25. Write the expression $(x + y^{-1})^{-1}$ without using negative exponents.

    A. $x + y$

    B. $\dfrac{1}{x + y}$

    C. $\dfrac{y}{x}$

    D. $\dfrac{x}{y}$

    E. $\dfrac{y}{yx + 1}$

26. What is the value of $(0.0081)^{-\frac{3}{4}}$?

    F. $\dfrac{81}{27}$

    G. $\dfrac{1000}{27}$

    H. $\dfrac{27}{81}$

    J. $\dfrac{8.10 \times 10^{-2}}{4}$

    K. $\dfrac{8.10 \times 10^{-2}}{0.27}$

27. One solution of the equation $27^{x^2 + 1} = 243$ is

    A. $\sqrt{5}$.

    B. $\dfrac{3}{2}$.

    C. $-\sqrt{\dfrac{2}{3}}$.

    D. $\dfrac{-5}{2}$.

    E. 5.

28. Let n be an integer greater than 1. Which of the following values is greater than 1?

    F. $-(n)^3$

    G. $(n)^{-\frac{1}{3}}$

    H. $-(-n)^3$

    J. $-(n + 1)^3$

    K. $(-n + 1)^5$

29. If $\dfrac{1}{2x} = \dfrac{1}{\dfrac{1}{y}}$ and $1 < x < 5$, then which of the following is true?

    A. $0.1 < y < 0.5$

    B. $0.1 < y < 1$

C. $1 < y < 5$ D. $0.5 < y < 2$

E. $0.5 < y < 5$

30. If $\log_R N = \dfrac{2}{3}$ what is the value of N?

F. 2   J. 10

G. 4   K. 12

H. 8

31. If $x \neq 0$, then $(125^{2x})(5^x) =$

A. 5^{3x}.   D. 5^{7x}.

B. 5^{4x}.   E. 5^{9x}.

C. 5^{5x}.

32. If $2^{3x} = 64$, then $x =$

F. 1.   J. $\dfrac{5}{2}$.

G. $\dfrac{3}{2}$.   K. 3.

H. 2.

33. Find the solution set of the following pair of equations

$\begin{cases} 3x + 4y = -6 \\ 5x + 6y = -8 \end{cases}$

A. $\{(1,2)\}$ D. $\{(2,-3)\}$

B. $\{(1,3)\}$ E. $\{(3,-3)\}$

C. $\{(2,3)\}$

34.

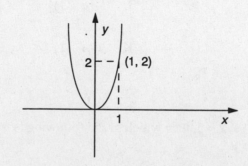

Which of the following equations corresponds to the graph above?

F. $y = x^2$ J. $y = 2(x^2 + 1)$

G. $y = 2x^2$ K. $y = 2(x^2 - 1)$

H. $y = 2x^2 + 1$

35. What is the distance between the points $(-2, 1)$ and $(3, 4)$?

A. $\sqrt{34}$ D. 17

B. 7   E. $\sqrt{43}$

C. $\dfrac{1}{3}$

36. An equation for the circle that has its center at the point $(1, 2)$ and passes through the origin is

F. $x^2 + (y - 2)^2 = 4.$ J. $(x - 2)^2 + y^2 = 5.$

G. $x^2 + (y - 1)^2 = 5.$ K. $(x - 1)^2 + (y - 2)^2 = 5.$

H. $(x - 1)^2 + y^2 = 4.$

37. A straight line is formed by $(1, 4)$ and $(3, 2)$; find the y-intercept of the line.

A. -1 D. 5

B. 2   E. 7

C. 3

38. Find the equation for the line passing through $(3, 5)$ and $(-1, 2)$.

F. $4x + 3y = 12$ J. $3x - 4y = -11$

G. $3x - 4y = 11$ K. $3x - 2y = -\dfrac{11}{2}$

H. $-3x - 4y = 11$

39. The coordinates of the point of intersection of the lines having equations $7x + 2y = 5$ and $2x + y = -2$ are

A. $(3, -8).$ D. $(0, 0).$

B. $(3, -6).$ E. $(1, -8).$

C. $(-8, 3).$

40. If a line contains the points (–3, 5) and (3, 7), then the slope of this line is

    F. –1.

    G. $-\dfrac{1}{3}$.

    H. 0.

    J. $\dfrac{1}{3}$.

    K. $\dfrac{5}{7}$.

41. Which of the following is a graph of the solution of the inequality $-x^2 + 5x - 6 < 0$?

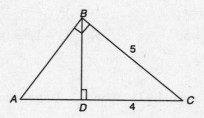

    A.

    B.

    C.

    D.

    E.

42.

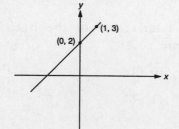

    In the figure, $BC = 5$ and $DC = 4$, what is the length of AC?

    F. $\dfrac{3}{2}$

    G. $\dfrac{25}{4}$

    H. $\dfrac{13}{6}$

    J. 7

    K. $5\sqrt{2}$

43. Which of the following represents the graph of the equation $x = |y - 2|$?

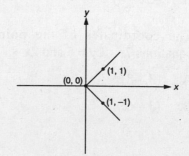

    A.

    B.

C.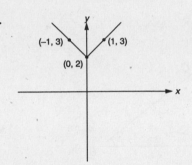

D.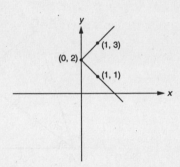

E.   None of the above

44. In the figure below of a regular hexagon inscribed within a circle with center O, line segment $\overline{AB} = 7$. What is the area of the circle?

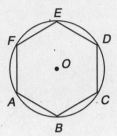

F. $\left(\dfrac{7}{6}\right)^2 \pi$

J. 21π

G. 7π

K. 49π

H. $\left(\dfrac{7}{2}\right)^2 \pi$

45.

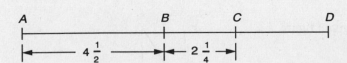

In the figure above, if B bisects the segment AD, then the length of segment CD is

A. $1\dfrac{3}{4}$.

D. $2\dfrac{3}{4}$.

B. $2\dfrac{1}{4}$.

E. $3\dfrac{1}{2}$.

C. $2\dfrac{1}{2}$.

46.

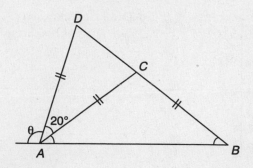

In the figure, if $AD = AC = BC$, then $\theta =$

F.   35.   J.   115.

G.   75.   K.   120.

H.   105.

47.

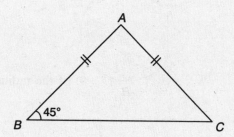

In the figure, if $AB = AC = 3$, then $BC =$

A. $2\sqrt{2}$.   D. $2\sqrt{3}$.

B. $3\sqrt{2}$.   E. $3\sqrt{3}$.

C.   3.

48.   In the given figure, $k =$

F.   5.

G.   3.

H.   2.

J.   1.

K.   –1.

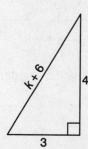

49. In the given figure, PQ is the diameter of the circle, R is a point on the circle, and $PR = 3$, $QR = 4$. What is the area of the circle?

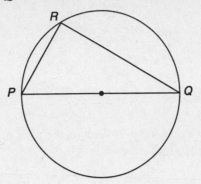

A. 25π

B. $\dfrac{7}{2}\pi$

C. 10π

D. 5π

E. $\dfrac{25}{4}\pi$

50. A square circumscribes a circle. The ratio of the radius of the circle to the perimeter of the square is

F. $\dfrac{1}{8}$.

G. $\dfrac{1}{4}$.

H. $\dfrac{1}{16}$.

J. $\dfrac{1}{2}$.

K. $\dfrac{1}{12}$.

51.

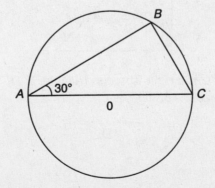

In the figure, if $\angle BAC = 30°$ and AC is a diameter of the circle with radius r, then $BC =$

A. $\frac{1}{2}r.$

D. $r.$

B. $\frac{\sqrt{2}}{2}r.$

E. $\frac{3}{2}r.$

C. $\frac{\sqrt{3}}{2}r.$

52. In the figure, $AB = 8$ and $BC = 2$. What is the area of region $BCDE$, if $\triangle ABE$ and $\triangle ACD$ are equilateral?

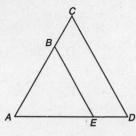

F. $\frac{\sqrt{3}}{2}$

J. $9\sqrt{3}$

G. 18

K. $\frac{35\sqrt{2}}{2}$

H. 50

53.

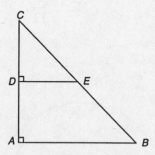

In the figure, $\triangle ABC$ is a right isosceles triangle. If $DE = 3$ and $AB = 5$, what is the area of trapezoid $ABED$?

A. 2

D. $\frac{16}{21}$

B. $\frac{16}{5}$

E. $\frac{16}{2}$

C. $\frac{43}{5}$

54.

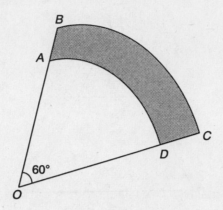

In the figure, *AOD* and *BOC* are sectors of concentric circles. If *OA* = 7 and *AB* = 2, then the area of the shaded region is

F. π.

G. 2π.

H. $\frac{7}{2}\pi$.

J. $\frac{13}{3}\pi$.

K. $\frac{16}{3}\pi$.

55. In the figure, 0 is the center of the circle. If arc *ABC* has length 2π, what is the area of the circle?

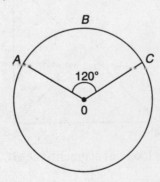

A. 3π

B. 6π

C. 9π

D. 12π

E. 15π

56.

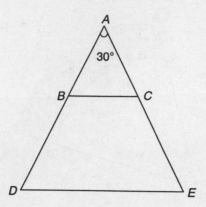

In the figure, if $BC \parallel DE$ and $\dfrac{BC}{DE} = \dfrac{1}{3}$, then the ratio of the area of $\triangle ABC$ to the area of $\triangle ADE$ is

F. $\dfrac{1}{9}$.

G. $\dfrac{1}{6}$.

H. $\dfrac{1}{3}$.

J. $\dfrac{1}{2}$.

K. $\dfrac{3}{2}$.

57.

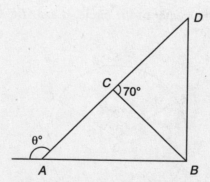

In the figure, C is the midpoint of segment AD, $BC = CD$, and $\angle BCD = 70°$, then $\theta =$

A. 110°.

B. 125°.

C. 130°.

D. 145°.

E. 160°.

58.

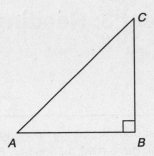

In right triangle ABC in the figure, if $\cos A = \dfrac{12}{13}$, and $AB = 12$, then the length of BC is

F. 1.

J. $5\sqrt{3}$.

G. 5.

K. 2.

H. $2\sqrt{5}$.

59. $\sin(45° + x) + \sin(45° - x) =$

A. $2 \cos x$.

D. $\sqrt{2} \cos x$.

B. $\cos 2x$.

E. $\sqrt{2x} \cos x$.

C. $\cos \sqrt{2x}$.

60. If $\dfrac{2\sin \dfrac{5\pi}{6} + \cos x}{\tan \dfrac{\pi}{2} + \cos \dfrac{2\pi}{3}} = 0$ and $0 \le x \le \pi$, then $x =$

F. $\dfrac{\pi}{2}$.

J. π.

G. $\dfrac{2\pi}{3}$.

K. $\dfrac{5\pi}{6}$.

H. $-\dfrac{\pi}{2}$.

THIS IS THE END OF TEST 2.

Test 3: Reading

TIME: 35 Minutes
40 Questions

Passage I

Whatever has the air of a paradox, and is contrary to the first and most unprejudic'd notions of mankind is often greedily embrac'd by philosophers, as shewing the superiority of their science, which cou'd discover opinions so remote from vulgar

5 conception. On the other hand, any thing propos'd to us, which causes surprize and admiration, gives such a satisfaction to the mind, that it indulges itself in those agreeable emotions, and will never be perswaded that its pleasure is entirely without foundation. From these dispositions in philosophers and their disciples

10 arises that mutual complaisance betwixt them; while the former furnish such plenty of strange and unaccountable opinions, and the latter so readily believe them. Of this mutual complaisance I cannot give a more evident instance than in the doctrine of infinite divisibility, with the examination of which I shall begin this

15 subject of the ideas of space and time.

'Tis universally allow'd, that the capacity of the mind is limited, and can never attain a full and adequate conception of infinity: And tho' it were not allow'd, 'twou'd be sufficiently evident from the plainest observation and experience. 'Tis also

20 obvious, that whatever is capable of being divided *in infinitum*, must consist of an infinite number of parts, and that 'tis impossible to set any bounds to the number of parts, without setting bounds at the same time to the division. It requires scarce any induction to conclude from hence, that the *idea*, which we form

25 of any finite quality, is not infinitely divisible, but that by proper distinctions and separations we may run up this idea to inferior ones, which will be perfectly simple and indivisible. In rejecting the infinite capacity of the mind, we suppose it may arrive at an end in the division of its idea; nor are there any possible means

30 of evading the evidence of this conclusion.

'Tis therefore certain, that the imagination reaches a *minimum*, and may raise up to itself an idea, of which it cannot conceive any sub-division, and which cannot be diminished

without a total annihilation. When you tell me of the thousandth
35   and ten thousandth part of a grain of sand, I have a distinct idea
of these numbers and of their different proportions; but the images, which I form in my mind to represent the things themselves, are nothing different from each other, nor inferior to that
image, by which I represent the grain of sand itself, which is
40   suppos'd so vastly to exceed them. What consists of parts is
distinguishable into them, and what is distinguishable is separable. But whatever we may imagine of the thing, the idea of a
grain of sand is not distinguishable, nor separable into twenty,
much less into a thousand, ten thousand, or an infinite number of
45   different ideas.

   'Tis the same case with the impressions of the senses as
with the ideas of the imagination. Put a spot of ink upon paper,
fix your eye upon that spot, and retire to such a distance, that at
last you lose sight of it; 'tis plain, that the moment before it
50   vanish'd the image or impression was perfectly indivisible. 'Tis
not for want of rays of light striking on our eyes, that the minute
parts of distant bodies convey not any sensible impression; but
because they are remov'd beyond that distance, at which their
impressions were reduc'd to a *minimum*, and were incapable of
55   any farther diminution. A microscope or telescope, which renders them visible, produces not any new rays of light, but only
spreads those, which always flow'd from them; and by that
means both gives parts to impressions, which to the naked eye
appear simple and uncompounded, and advances to a *minimum*,
60   what was formerly imperceptible.

From *A Treatise of Human Nature*.

1.   Philosophers are characterized as

   I.   embracing the paradox.
   II.   approving of what is contrary to the accepted notions.
   III. taunting the superiority of their science.
   IV.   discovering opinions remote from vulgar conceptions.

   A.   I only.   C.   I, II, and III only.

   B.   I and II only.   D.   I, II, III, and IV.

2.   The author denies that

   F.   the capacity of the mind is limited.

   G.   the idea is not infinitely divisible.

   H.   the mind may arrive at an end in the division of its ideas.

   J.   the imagination is unable to raise an idea.

3.   The author's impression of philosophers is

   A.   that they are valuable.

   B.   that they do not confirm our beliefs and loyalties.

   C.   that they receive the respect of others in many occupations.

   D.   that he agrees with them — particularly on the doctrine of infinite divisibility.

4.   The reader can infer that the author believes

   F.   that something which consists of parts is distinguishable into parts.

   G.   that which is distinguishable is always separable.

   H.   that which one imagines of a thing is always separable.

   J.   that disciples of philosophy are least likely to accept the doctrine of infinite divisibility.

5.   The author

   A.   contrasts ideas of the imagination with impressions of the senses.

   B.   contrasts philosophers with their disciples.

   C.   compares ideas of the imagination with impressions of the senses.

   D.   sees a spot of ink as an example of a divisible image.

6.   A spot of ink vanishes at a distance

   F.   because of a want of light rays striking our eyes.

   G.   because the parts are not removed beyond the distance at which their impressions are reduced to a minimum.

   H.   because the parts are removed beyond the distance at which their impressions are reduced to minimum.

   J.   because the parts are removed beyond that distance at which light rays strike their impression.

7.   Which of the following describe the work of a telescope? The telescope

   I.   renders the parts visible by producing new rays of light.
   II.   renders the parts visible by spreading rays of light.
   III. gives parts to impressions.
   IV. advances the imperceptible to a minimum.

   A.   I only.   C.   II, III, and IV only.

   B.   II only.   D.   II and III only.

8. The phrase "...by that means both...," found in the last paragraph of the reading passage is used

   F. to refer to the rays of light, mentioned earlier.

   G. with *and* as a conjunction to join "...give parts..." and "...advances to a minimum...."

   H. to refer to the microscope and the telescope.

   J. to the spreading of the rays of light and the new rays of light.

9. Philosophers generally

   I. disagree with what is accepted.

   II. do not accept that which causes most people satisfaction and admiration.

   III. furnish unaccountable opinions which their followers accept.

   A. I only.   C. II and III only.

   B. I and II only.   D. I, II, and III.

10. The author suggests that philosophy is widely accepted

   I. because it causes surprise and admiration.
   II. because it gives satisfaction to the mind.
   III. because it indulges itself in agreeable emotions.

   F. I only.   H. I, II, and III.

   G. I and II only.   J. III only.

Passage II

In earlier years during the Industrial Revolution, personnel practices of business and industry were mostly confined to hiring enough people to do the work, close supervision of employees to see that they did the work, and firing people if they
5   did not abide by management guidelines. Labor had little influence on the system in the private sector. The management system was simple. In contrast, today personnel practices of business and industry have become complex and subject to influence of labor and government. Changes have occurred because
10 society expects leaders in the private and public sectors to be sensitive to a number of social issues and to resolve difficulties that arise in the workplace.

Toward the end of the nineteenth century and early in the twentieth century, social issues were rarely considered part of the

15   decision making process of employers. On occasion, constituents
      would press state or federal legislators to pass laws which would
      protect the health and/or morals of employees. Immediately the
      laws would be challenged in court. For example, a 1923 case dealt
      with a law that established a board authorized among other things,
20   to determine minimum wages of female and child workers. In that
      case, the Supreme Court majority stated that "adult women... are
      legally as capable of contracting for themselves as men." The law
      was struck, and employer personnel practices continued to dis-
      criminate against women and children. If in the late 1880s and
25   early 1900s the Supreme Court felt that the legislature had over-
      stepped constitutional boundaries, those laws were made void, and
      management continued its harsh management policies, not only
      toward women and children, but also toward men.

         Among the first of several court cases during the hectic years
30   of the Industrial Revolution in America, comparison of policies
      showed that legislative and judicial branches were rarely unified in
      legal philosophy, setting national goals, and what could or could
      not be regulated. In a major case in 1918, the Supreme Court
      struck a federal law that penalized industry when it failed to abide
35   regulations that specified ages and working hours of child employ-
      ees. The children continued to work long hours. In 1923, a reporter
      interviewed the young man who was a child plaintiff in the land-
      mark case. At the time of interview, the respondent was a young
      man who was married. The toll of working in a cotton mill long
40   hours for many years had affected Reuben Dagenhart's growth
      and denied him the opportunity to be educated. His mood was
      somber when he told the reporter: "It would have been a good
      thing for all the kids in the state if that law they passed had been
      kept." Had Reuben read the dissenting opinion when his case was
45   reported by the Supreme Court in 1918, he would have found that
      four justices also felt that the child labor law should have not been
      struck. They concurred that Congress does indeed have a role in
      protecting the national welfare and in enforcing policy designed to
      "benefit... the nation as a whole." In contrast, the majority of the
50   court prevailed with a different interpretation of the Constitution
      and decried Congress's ulterior motive "to standardize the ages at
      which children may be employed...."

         Today the role of business and government in solving so-
      cial problems remains a controversial topic. Children no longer
55   work in factories. Working hours for both men and women are
      regulated by government. Some observers feel that New Deal
      legislation sponsored by President Franklin D. Roosevelt pro-
      vided the major thrust for governmental regulation of private
      sector personnel practices that were too long within the exclusive

60   jurisdiction of industry and business management. At first the Supreme Court struck Roosevelt-initiated statutes. But the sentiment of the country and appointment of men politically sensitive to the political goals of the President led to judicial support of laws designed to deal with social ills in the country. In the 1930s

65   and early 1940s, Congress followed the leadership of the top executive who proposed such legislation as Social Security, workers' compensation, and mandatory minimum wages. At that time a desire for change was ripe due to economic chaos caused by the Great Depression. Business and industry managers were

70   suddenly cast into a different role when Congress and the Supreme Court became allies in authorizing governmental intrusion into the private sector's arena. Swift changes led to new professional expertise required for interpretation of law, additional paperwork, and implementation of personnel policies.

75   By the 1950s, long-standing racial discrimination was challenged. Congress had remained too long aloof and generally ignored problems associated with inequality. The NAACP bypassed the legislative branch and took its case to the judicial branch. By the 1960s, President Lyndon Johnson influenced Congress to take

80   bold steps that eventually called for changes in the workplace. Title VII was passed, and a reduction of inequities was expected. However, NAACP director of labor, Joann Aiggs, said in 1987 that racial discrimination remains, but federal legislation "does provide an avenue people can use to seek redress."

11. Which statement best illustrates personnel management in American history?

    A. Since the beginning of the twentieth century, Congress and state legislatures have had wide latitude in correcting social ills in the private sector of business and industry.

    B. Personnel practices have been fairly stable with little change after 1901.

    C. During the years of the Industrial Revolution "big business" was highly respected by sociologists for its grave concern for the welfare of children and women employees — especially standardization of working hours.

    D. Personnel management of business and industry has become increasingly complex as ideas change about social welfare.

12. Which statement describes some of the problems that have occurred in personnel management?

    F. The author proposes that the health of employees is a private matter and that government should keep out of the personal lives of employees.

G.   The author applauds the early twentieth century Supreme Court because it was a staunch advocate of equal rights for children and females by striking laws that provided special protections in the workplace.

H.   Mood and attitude of ordinary workers toward personnel practices have not changed very much since 1900.

J.   The Supreme Court's legal and social philosophy in two cases cited above were aligned with industry's management theories and social philosophy.

13. What values are reflected in the narrative provided by the author?

A.   The author is apparently a religious person because of his emphasis on moral issues.

B.   The author unfairly criticizes capitalism in the United States and is therefore a socialite.

C.   The author unfairly criticizes justices who write dissenting opinions and therefore leaves law unsettled.

D.   The author's choice of historical facts might lead the reader to consider motives of business and industry — such as profits — that led to hiring small children.

14. How would students of history describe the plight of women in the workplace toward the end of the nineteenth century?

F.   An opportunity to get away from the children

G.   Happy to have freedom to make contracts with their bosses

H.   Competitive for higher positions usually held by men

J.   Repressive

15. In the early twentieth century, what was the role of government in determining wages of women who worked in factories, hospitals, and other businesses?

A.   The Supreme Court majority felt that government should not set minimum wages for private employers.

B.   The legislature was filled with men whose wives did not work; thus, they were insensitive to the needs of working women.

C.   Presidents finally bargained with industrial owners who caved in and established a business board that established minimum wages.

D.   Some legislators tried to protect economic welfare and morals of women by establishing an agency with authority to set minimum wages, but courts abolished the law and the agency.

16. How would one evaluate the judicial process and its influence on the economic and/or social realm of society?

    F. The Supreme Court became a cohesive group of judges when considering the plight of child labor and the attempt to regulate personnel practices in the private sector.

    G. Within a few years after his case was decided, the child plaintiff realized that his case proved detrimental to the welfare of large numbers of children in his state.

    H. The majority opinion vividly portrayed a conscientious group of judges who were dedicated to the improvement of working conditions in factories and mills.

    J. In the choice of a respondent for interview purposes, the reporter was obviously trying to cast governmental regulation in a poor light.

17. Which observation is the most appropriate conclusion that can be drawn from the author's text?

    A. Some of the justices on the Supreme Court had difficulty in persuading most of the justices that legislation should be upheld when social welfare of the nation is at stake.

    B. Congressional leaders failed to persuade most of the members of the House and the Senate that legislation should be passed in order to protect the social welfare of the nation.

    C. The passage above is an excellent illustration of how the legislative branch and the judicial branch can lose their identities in the face of strong voter appeal in working class neighborhoods.

    D. Young Reuben's case was first filed in the trial court in 1918 and was not decided until 1923, too late to help the child laborer.

18. Where was political leadership lodged in the mid-twentieth century?

    F. It is evident that the author felt that President Roosevelt as chief executive should have stayed out of the legislative process and relied more on the judicial process.

    G. The author explained how President Roosevelt changed the direction of government by showing a stronger social orientation than national leaders of judicial and executive branches in earlier years.

    H. Although new legislation was passed, the laws more or less left business and industry personnel policies intact by the 1940s.

    J. At first President Roosevelt had to rely more on the courts than on stubborn legislators in order to pass laws designed to deal with social problems.

19. What kinds of changes occurred due to strong leadership from the Oval Office?

    A. One can gather that bills sponsored by Roosevelt were successful in Congress because they were supported by the effective lobbying influence of business and industry.

    B. The reader can assume that when the Roosevelt administration enforced new laws described above, the manufacturing and business labor expenditures increased accordingly.

    C. Organizations representing the interests of business most likely welcomed changes in Supreme Court personnel appointed by Roosevelt.

    D. Roosevelt's keen interest lay in ending racial discrimination through passage of the Special Security Act.

20. Although observers may argue about what really happened during Roosevelt's term of office, interpret the factual information presented by the author by selecting the best description below.

    F. New Deal legislation received its name from the deals the President made with business and industry for the purpose of pulling the rug out from under Congress, so to speak.

    G. Evolution and transformation of labor policies increased at a rapid pace during the Roosevelt administration.

    H. The author has inferred that historically the name "Great Depression" was a phrase that caught on after the press disclosed Roosevelt's mood when the Supreme Court struck the first three social welfare bills passed by Congress.

    J. Strange alliances are often formed in the political arena. Unorganized labor and their representatives in the legislature were seldom impressed with promises of reforms which would lead to a welfare state.

Passage III

    Knowing that Mrs. Mallard was afflicted with a heart trouble, great care was taken to break to her as gently as possible the news of her husband's death.

    It was her sister Josephine who told her, in broken sentences, veiled hints that revealed in half concealing. Her husband's friend Richards was there, too, near her. It was he who had been in the newspaper office when intelligence of the railroad disaster was received, with Brently Mallard's name leading the list of "killed." He had only taken the time to assure himself of its truth by a second telegram, and had hastened to forestall any less careful, less tender friend in bearing the sad message.

She did not hear the story as many women have heard the same, with a paralyzed inability to accept its significance. She wept at once, with sudden, wild abandonment, in her sister's

15 arms. When the storm of grief had spent itself she went away to her room alone. She would have no one follow her.

There stood, facing the open window, a comfortable, roomy armchair. Into this she sank, pressed down by a physical exhaustion that haunted her body and seemed to reach into her soul.

20 She could see in the open square before her house the tops of trees that were all aquiver with the new spring life. The delicious breath of rain was in the air. In the street below a peddler was crying his wares. The notes of a distant song which some one was singing reached her faintly, and countless sparrows were

25 twittering in the eaves.

There were patches of blue sky showing here and there through the clouds that had met and piled above the other in the west facing her window.

She sat with her head thrown back upon the cushion of the

30 chair quite motionless, except when a sob came up into her throat and shook her, as a child who has cried itself to sleep continues to sob in its dreams.

She was young, with a fair, calm face, whose lines bespoke repression and even a certain strength. But now there was a dull

35 stare in her eyes, whose gaze was fixed away off yonder on one of those patches of blue sky. It was not a glance of reflection, but rather indicated a suspension of intelligent thought.

There was something coming to her and she was waiting for it, fearfully. What was it? She did not know; it was too subtle

40 and elusive to name. But she felt it, creeping out of the sky, reaching toward her through the sound, the scents, the color that filled the air.

Now her bosom rose and fell tumultuously. She was beginning to recognize this thing that was approaching to possess her,

45 and she was striving to beat it back with her will — as powerless as her two white slender hands would have been.

When she abandoned herself a little whispered word escaped from her slightly parted lips. She said it over and over under her breath: "Free, free, free!" The vacant stare and the look

50 of terror that had followed it went from her eyes. The stayed keen and bright. Her pulses beat fast, and the coursing blood warmed and relaxed every inch of her body.

She did not stop to ask if it were not a monstrous joy that held her. A clear and exalted perception enabled her to dismiss

55 the suggestions as trivial.

She knew that she would weep again when she saw the kind, tender hands folded in death; the face that had never looked save with love upon her, fixed and gray and dead. But she saw beyond that bitter moment a long procession of years to come
60 that would belong to her absolutely. And she opened and spread her arms out to them in welcome.

There would be no one to live for during those coming years; she would live for herself. There would be no powerful will bending her in that blind persistence with which men and
65 women believe they have a right to impose a private will upon a fellow-creature. A kind intention or a cruel intention made the act seem no less a crime as she looked upon it in that brief moment of illumination.

And yet she had loved him — sometimes. Often she had
70 not. What did it matter! What could love, the unsolved mystery, count for in face of this possession of self-assertion which she suddenly recognized for the strongest impulse of her being.

"Free! Body and soul free!" she kept whispering.

Josephine was kneeling before the closed door with her lips
75 to the keyhole, imploring for admission. "Louise, open the door! I beg; open the door — you will make yourself ill. What are you doing, Louise? For heaven's sake open the door."

"Go away. I am not making myself ill." No; she was drinking in a very elixir of life through that open window.
80 Her fancy was running riot along those days ahead of her. Spring days, and summer days, and all sorts of days that would be her own. She breathed a quick prayer that life might be long. It was only yesterday she had thought with a shudder that life might be long.

85 She arose at length and opened the door to her sister's importunities. There was a feverish triumph in her eyes, and she carried herself unwittingly like a goddess of Victory. She clasped her sister's waist, and together they descended the stairs. Richards stood waiting for them at the bottom.

90 Some one was opening the front door with a latchkey. It was Brently Mallard who entered, a little travel-stained, composedly carrying his gripsack and umbrella. He had been far from the scene of accident, and did not even know there had been one. He stood amazed at Josephine's piercing cry; at Richards' quick
95 motion to screen him from the view of his wife.

But Richards was too late.

When the doctors came they said she had died of heart disease — a joy that kills.

From Kate Chopin, *The Story Of An Hour*.

21. Mrs. Mallard's initial reaction to news of her husband's death can best be described as

    A. hypocritical.   C. uncomprehending.

    B. sincere grief.   D. calculated to deceive others.

22. The details in the fifth paragraph (lines 20–25) suggest

    F. sorrow.   H. rebirth.

    G. triviality.   J. death.

23. Mrs. Mallard's joy over becoming free is first presented as something that she

    A. has long desired.   C. believes is monstrous.

    B. resists.   D. is ashamed of.

24. Which of the following LEAST accurately describes Brently Mallard?

    F. Faithful   H. Filled with good intentions

    G. Abusive   J. Loving

25. In her "brief moment of illumination," (line 68) Mrs. Mallard's criticism is chiefly directed at

    A. Brently Mallard.   C. herself.

    B. the bonds of marriage.   D. society's expectations of widows.

26. Mrs. Mallard thinks that her love for her husband was irrelevant because

    F. death had separated them forever.

    G. her new sense of self makes her past life with him seem insignificant.

    H. he had never made it clear to her whether he loved her.

    J. love is a mystery which can never be solved.

27. Mrs. Mallard's most important discovery is

    A. that she is capable of living without Brently.

    B. that she never loved Brently.

    C. that people do not understand her.

    D. her need for self-assertion.

28. Which of the following statements about the last sentence of the story is LEAST accurate?

F. The author implies that Mrs. Mallard's death is just punishment for the "monstrous joy" she experienced earlier.

G. Mrs. Mallard has experienced great joy that intensifies her shock at seeing Brently alive.

H. The doctors are wrong in believing that Mrs. Mallard died of joy from seeing Brently alive.

J. The effectiveness of the last sentence depends on the reader understanding events more completely than the other characters who witness them.

29. The ending of the story can best be described as

A. humorous.   C. ironic.

B. hyperbole.   D. word play.

30. The clause, "...she was drinking in a very elixir of life..." refers to

F. the quaff Mrs. Mallard was given to drink for medicinal purposes.

G. the alcoholic beverage Louise drank alone.

H. the feeling of freedom Louise was experiencing.

J. the poison that Louise took when she was told of her husband's death.

Passage IV

Before entering on the subject of this chapter I must make a few preliminary remarks to show how the struggle for existence bears on natural selection. It has been seen in the last chapter that among organic beings in a state of nature there is some indi-
5   vidual variability: indeed I am not aware that this has ever been disputed. It is immaterial for us whether a multitude of doubtful forms be called species or sub-species or varieties; what rank, for instance, the two or three hundred doubtful forms of British plants are entitled to hold, if the existence of any well-marked
10   varieties be admitted. But the mere existence of individual variability and of some few well-marked varieties, though necessary as the foundation for the work, helps us but little in understanding how species arise in nature. How have all those exquisite adaptations of one part of the organization to another part, and to
15   the conditions of life and of one organic being to another being, been perfected?

Again, it may be asked, how is it that varieties, which I
have called incipient species, become ultimately converted into
good and distinct species, which in most cases obviously differ
20   from each other far more than do the varieties of the same species? How do those groups of species, which constitute what are
called distinct genera and which differ from each other more
than do the species of the same genus, arise? All these results, as
we shall more fully see in the next chapter, follow from the
25   struggle for life. Owing to this struggle, variations, however
slight and from whatever cause proceeding, if they be in any
degree profitable to the individuals of a species, in their infinitely
complex relations to other organic beings and to their physical
conditions of life, will tend to the preservation of such individu-
30   als, and will generally be inherited by the offspring. The offspring, also, will thus have a better chance of surviving, for, of
the many individuals of any species which are periodically born,
but a small number can survive. I have called this principle, by
which each slight variation, if useful, is preserved, by the term
35   natural selection, in order to mark its relation to man's power of
selection. But the expression often used by Mr. Herbert Spencer,
of the Survival of the Fittest, is more accurate, and is sometimes
equally convenient. We have seen that man by selection can
certainly produce great results, and can adapt organic beings to
40   his own uses, through the accumulation of slight but useful
variations, given to him by the hand of Nature. But Natural Selection, we shall hereafter see, is a power incessantly ready for
action, and is as immeasurably superior to man's feeble efforts as
the works of Nature are to those of Art.
45   Nothing is easier than to admit in words the trust of the
universal struggle for life, or more difficult — at least I found it
so — than constantly to bear this conclusion in mind.

From Charles Darwin, *Origin of Species.*

31. Which of the following are characteristics of the groups of species?

    I.   They constitute distinct genera.
    II. They differ from each other more than do the species of the same
        genus.
    III. They follow from the struggle for life.

    A.   I only.   C.   I, II, and III

    B.   I and II only.   D.   II and III only.

32. In explaining natural selection, the author

    F. is adamant about the importance of distinguishing among species, sub-species, and varieties.

    G. has attempted to define species, sub-species, and varieties.

    H. does not think it important to identify a form as species, sub-species, or variety.

    J. clearly outlines the distinction among species, sub-species, and varieties.

33. According to the author,

    A. distinct genera follow from the struggle for life.

    B. the struggle for existence is separate from natural selection.

    C. he coined the term "natural selection."

    D. the struggle for existence is not important to natural selection.

34. As a result of the struggle for life, which of the following are true?

    I. Variations will occur.
    II. Groupings of species differ from each other more than do the species of the same genus.
    III. Variations follow from the struggle for life.
    IV. Variations may occur from many causes.

    F. I only.   H. I, II, and III only.

    G. I and II only.   J. I, II, III, and IV.

35. Offspring having variations

    A. may have a better chance of surviving.

    B. will survive in large numbers.

    C. will not pass these variations to their offspring.

    D. have nothing to do with the struggle for life.

36. The principle by which slight variation, if useful, is preserved

    F. is called "natural selection" by the author.

    G. is called "Survival of the Fittest" by the author.

    H. is called by the inaccurate term "Survival of the Fittest" by Herbert Spencer.

    J. is called by the inconvenient term "Survival of the Fittest" by the author.

37. Which of the following does the author believe?

    I.   People can produce great results by selection.
    II. People can adapt organic beings to their own uses through variation.
    III. Nature provides people with the variations.
    IV. Natural selection can be controlled by human beings.

    A. I only.   C. I, II, and III only.

    B. I and II only.   D. I, II, III, and IV.

38. Natural selection is

    F. a power which is at times ready for action.

    G. inferior to the powers of human beings.

    H. as superior to human efforts as Art is to Nature.

    J. as superior to the efforts of human beings as Nature is to Art.

39. Which of the following is generally accepted?

    A. There is individual variability among organic things.

    B. It is easy to keep in mind the truth of the universal struggle for existence.

    C. It is difficult to admit that the struggle for existence exists.

    D. One can understand the whole economy of nature quite easily without keeping the struggle for existence in mind.

40. The author's purpose is

    F. to define the struggle for existence and stress its importance.

    G. to describe Herbert Spencer's Survival of the Fittest and stress its importance.

    H. to describe evolution in nature.

    J. to discuss the evolution "...we see...everywhere and in every part of the organic world."

THIS IS THE END OF TEST 3.

Test 4: Science Reasoning

TIME: 35 Minutes
40 Questions

DIRECTIONS: This test consists of seven passages, each followed by several questions. Once you have read a passage, answer each question. Then fill in the appropriate oval on your answer sheet.

Passage I

When openings are found between soil particles, the soil is said to have the property of porosity: the more separated the soil particles, the more porous the soil. Permeability is the ability of soil to transmit water through the soil.

An accepted hypothesis is that the more porous a soil, the more permeable the soil. In order to test this hypothesis, three experiments are performed. Each uses a quart jar half filled with a different type of dry soil. Fifty milliliters of water is then poured into the jar over the soil. The process of water passing through the soil is then observed for 60 minutes.

Experiment 1

Into jar one is placed very porous dry sand. Water is then poured over the sand. The water passes quickly through the sand, becoming evenly dispersed throughout. After ten minutes, some water seeps to the bottom of the jar. The soil becomes damp throughout with water.

Experiment 2

A limestone rich soil, which is almost nonporous, is placed into jar two. Fifty milliliters of water is poured over the limestone. After about 20 minutes, water begins to travel through the limestone in streams. It takes about 30 minutes for some of the water to pass through the soil to the bottom of the jar. There is still some water on top of the soil, which does not pass through the soil. The soil does not become damp throughout. Only the holes formed transmit the water.

Experiment 3

A soil with a very high percentage of clay is nonporous and is placed in jar three. The water placed on top of the soil stays on top, not passing through. By the end of the 60 minutes, the top portion of the soil has begun to become moist, but the water has not passed through to the bottom of the jar. The major portion of the clay soil is dry.

1. The hypothesis is not proven by

   A. Experiment 1.

   B. Experiment 2.

   C. Experiment 3.

   D. any of the experiments.

2.   By using the experiments, which soil is the most permeable?

   F.   Sand   H.   Clay

   G.   Limestone   J.   They are equally permeable.

3.   These three experiments

   A.   completely prove the hypothesis.

   B.   do not prove the hypothesis.

   C.   somewhat prove the hypothesis.

   D.   disprove the hypothesis.

4.   In Experiment 3, the water will probably

   F.   not go any further.

   G.   eventually pass to the bottom of the jar.

   H.   travel only through half of the soil.

   J.   There is not enough evidence to make an assumption about the water.

5.   Experiment 2 indicates that a soil

   A.   must be porous to be permeable.

   B.   must be permeable to be porous.

   C.   may be porous, but not permeable.

   D.   may be permeable, but not porous.

6.   If a small fish pond were being made, the best type of soil to use as a water barrier, according to these three experiments, would be

   F.   sand.   H.   clay.

   G.   limestone.   J.   any of the soils.

Passage II

Humidity is the term used to describe the amount of moisture content in the air. There are several methods of expressing humidity. Absolute humidity (g/m^3) (the density of water in the atmosphere) is defined as the mass of water vapor per volume of air. However, relative humidity (%) is the most common method of expressing moisture in the atmosphere. It is the ratio of water vapor in the air compared to the amount the air can hold at a specific temperature (°F) and pressure.

Experiment 1

Weather observations were taken for five areas across the country (Table 1). The temperature, relative humidity, and absolute humidity were measured.

Table 1

Location	Temperature	Relative Humidity	Absolute Humidity
Phoenix, AZ	110	22	17
Newark, NJ	65	85	7
Orlando, FL	76	94	16
Nome, AK	24	90	2
San Diego, CA	45	54	4

Experiment 2

At higher temperatures, the atmosphere can hold larger amounts of water, making it feel warmer than the actual temperature. The Humiture Index (Table 2) combines the temperature and humidity to determine an apparent temperature. Actual temperatures were measured across Colorado and are plotted as isotherms (equal lines of temperature) on the map in Figure 1.

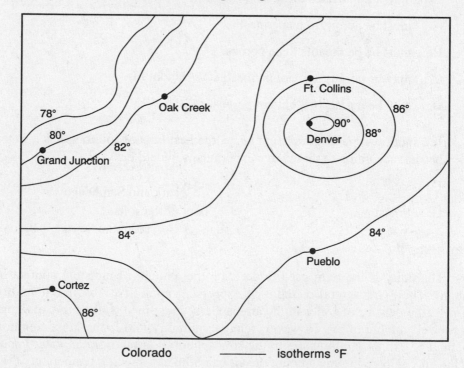

Figure 1

Table 2

Temperature	Relative Humidity %									
	10	**20**	**30**	**40**	**50**	**60**	**70**	**80**	**90**	**100**
104	90	98	106	112	120					
102	87	95	102	108	115	123				
100	85	92	99	105	111	118				
98	82	90	96	101	107	114				
96	79	87	93	98	103	110	116			
94	77	84	90	95	100	105	111			
92	75	82	87	91	96	101	106	112		
90	73	79	84	88	93	97	102	108		
88	70	76	81	85	89	93	98	102	108	
86	68	73	78	82	86	90	94	98	103	
84	66	71	76	79	83	86	90	94	98	103
82	63	68	73	76	80	83	86	90	93	97
80	62	66	70	73	77	80	83	86	90	93
78		63	67	70	74	76	79	82	85	89
76		60	63	67	70	73	76	79	82	85

7. Which location in Table 1 has the greatest amount of water vapor in the atmosphere?

    A. Phoenix, AZ

    B. San Diego, CA

    C. Orlando, FL

    D. Nome, AK

8. At which two locations would the poorest rate of evaporation occur?

    F. Phoenix and Orlando

    G. Nome and San Diego

    H. Nome and Orlando

    J. Newark and San Diego

9. Determine the Humiture Index for Denver, Colorado and Cortez, Colorado using the following humidity data:

Table 3

Location	Relative Humidity
Denver, Colorado	40
Cortez, Colorado	80

A. 40 and 80   C. 88 and 98

B. 90 and 86   D. 108 and 82

10. Based on the passage, what conclusion could be made about the effect of temperature on the humidity?

F. The temperature does not affect the humidity.

G. The temperature affects only the relative humidity.

H. The temperature affects only the absolute humidity.

J. The temperature affects both the absolute and relative humidity.

11. Based on the passage, what would happen to the relative humidity and absolute humidity if the temperature increased and the amount of water vapor in the air remained constant?

A. The relative humidity would decrease and the absolute humidity would remain constant.

B. The absolute humidity would decrease and the relative humidity would remain constant.

C. Both would remain constant.

D. Both would increase.

12. At which place would the highest amount of water vapor most likely be located?

F. On a cool beach in autumn

G. In a blizzard

H. In an office building

J. In a hot, humid desert in the summer

Passage III

A man pulls a crate at a constant speed of 2 m/s up a hill using a rope inclined at 25° with respect to the 30° incline. The force of friction between the crate and the slope varies with the roughness of the surface over the 20 m long slope. The rope is assumed not to stretch as it is pulled. However, the tension may vary. Table 1 shows the tension in the rope and the roughness of various portions of the surface.

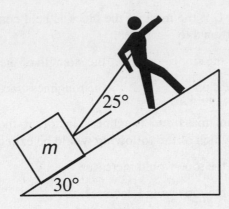

Figure 1

Table 1

Mass of block, kg	Distance, m	Roughness factor	Tension, N
10	5	0.001	2.5
	10	0.203	17.3
	12	0.013	3.7
	17	0.001	2.3
	20	0.072	9.2
25	5	0.001	6.3
	10	0.203	35.5
	12	0.013	9.3
	17	0.001	5.8
	20	0.072	2.3
50	5	0.001	12.5
	10	0.203	rope broke
	12	0.013	18.5
	17	0.001	11.5
	20	0.072	46.0

13. According to the experimental data, if the distance along the slope is constant, the tension in the rope is proportional to

    A. the tension of the man.   C. the roughness of the slope.

    B. the mass of the block.   D. the angle of the slope.

14. According to Table 1, if the mass of the block is held constant, the tension in the rope is proportional to

    F. the distance of the slope.   H. the strength of the man.

    G. the angle of the slope.   J. the roughness factor.

15. Assuming a constant mass and roughness factor, if the distance of the slope is increased, which of the following would be expected to occur?

    A. The tension of the rope would increase.

    B. The tension of the rope would decrease.

    C. The tension of the rope stays the same.

    D. The rope breaks.

16. Which of the following was assumed in the designing of the experiment?

    F. The length of the rope will influence the tension in the rope.

    G. The length of the rope will not influence the tension in the rope.

    H. The mass of the block will not influence the tension in the rope.

    J. The tension depends on how hard the man pulls.

17. Which of the following statements summarizes the results of the experiment?

    A. On a surface which is uniformly rough, tension is proportional to mass.

    B. Roughness is proportional to distance.

    C. Mass is proportional to distance.

    D. Tension is proportional to distance.

Passage IV

A genetic trait has been identified as the cause of a new disease. Geneticists are trying to determine how the disease is passed from parent to child. The pedigree for one family is shown in Figure 1. Squares represent males and circles represent females. Members of the family with the disease are shaded. Genes can be sex-linked (occurring on the X- or Y-chromosome) or autosomal (occurring on any chromosome *except* the sex chromosomes).

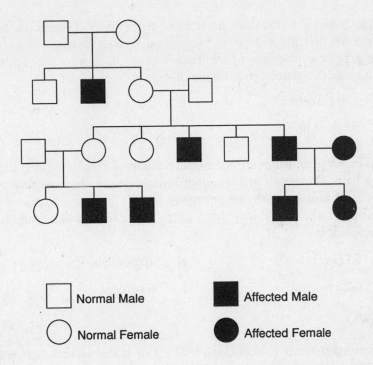

Normal Male   Affected Male

Normal Female   Affected Female

Figure 1

18. Transmission of this disease is consistent with the classic genetic pattern which reflects

    F. an autosomal dominant gene.

    G. an autosomal recessive gene.

    H. a sex-linked dominant gene.

    J. a sex-linked recessive gene.

19. A recessive autosomal gene for a disease has a frequency of 0.05 (1/20) in the population. Two parents both have the gene, but not the disease. The probability that any one of their children would have the disease is

    A. 50 percent.   C. 25 percent.

    B. 4 percent.   D. 0.05 percent.

20. For the disease described in question 19, all affected individuals die during infancy. The expected incidence of the disease in the population would be

    F. 0 percent.   H. 0.06 percent.

    G. 4 percent.   J. 2.5 percent.

21. A rare disease is found in an isolated community. Geneticists are able to determine that the disease is transmitted as an autosomal dominant gene. The expected incidence of the disease in children who are born of parents who are both heterozygous for the disease is

A. 100 percent.

C. 50 percent.

B. 75 percent.

D. 25 percent.

22. In cats, the gene for color-point is an autosomal recessive, as is the gene for long hair. The genes are inherited independently. In a mating between a male and female, each heterozygous for the genotype for long hair and color-point, the probability that a kitten in the litter will be long haired and color-point is

F. 25 percent.

H. 10 percent.

G. 6.25 percent.

J. 0 percent.

Passage V

75 grams of fresh potatoes and 500 ml of water were homogenized in a blender. Three drops of this "potato juice" were each added to plain water, a dextrose solution, a sodium chloride solution, and a solution of pyrocatechol. After five minutes, all of the solutions remained colorless, except for the pyrocatechol, which had turned yellow.

Experiment 1

Three solutions of pyrocatechol, of the same concentration, were kept either at 0°C, at room temperature (25°C), or in boiling water (100°C). Keeping them at these temperatures and adding three drops of the above "potato juice" to each solution gave the following results in five minutes:

Table 1

Solution Temperature °C	Color after 5 min	Color after 30 min
0	faint yellow	yellow
25	yellow	bright yellow
100	colorless	colorless

Experiment 2

Solutions of equal concentrations of pyrocatechol were adjusted to have pH values of 4, 7, or 10. When three drops of the above "potato juice" were added (at room temperature) to each solution, within five minutes the solution at pH 4 was dark yellow; the solution at pH 7 was faint yellow; and the solution at pH 10 was still colorless. Four test tubes were set up containing a pyrocatechol solution at the same concentration. Phenylthiourea was added to each tube as shown in Table 2. Then several drops of the "potato juice" were added. After 5 minutes, the color of each tube was recorded.

Table 2

Phenylthiourea	Potato juice	Color – 5 min	Color – 30 min
20 drops	3 drops	bright yellow	bright yellow
10	3	faint yellow	yellow
1	3	very faint yellow	faint yellow
0	3	colorless	colorless
20	5	bright yellow	bright yellow
10	5	yellow	bright yellow
1	5	faint yellow	bright yellow
0	5	colorless	colorless
20	1	faint yellow	yellow
10	1	very faint yellow	faint yellow
1	1	colorless	very faint yellow
0	1	colorless	colorless

23. What is the temperature of the solutions tested in the passage experiment?

    A. 0°C

    B. 25°C

    C. 100°C

    D. Between 0°C and 25°C

24. Given the results of Experiment 1 and Experiment 2, at what combination of temperature and pH would a potato juice and pyrocatechol solution remain light yellow after 5 minutes?

    F. T = 0°C, pH = 7

    G. T = 25°C, pH = 7

    H. T = 100°C, pH = 10

    J. T = 0°C, pH = 10

25. Which of the following factors, if investigated by a chemist, could affect the color of the solutions tested?

    A. Vary the temperature above 100°C.

    B. Observe the colors after 60 minutes of standing.

C.   Vary the concentrations of pyrocatechol.

D.   Vary the pH values above 10.

26. To improve the accuracy of the data in Experiment 2, one should know which of the following conditions?

F.   The concentration of the pyrocatechol solution

G.   The temperature of the pyrocatechol solution

H.   The concentration of the potato juice

J.   The pH of the pyrocatechol solution

27. Which statement concerning the initial design of all of the experiments is assumed?

A.   Pyrocatechol does not mix with water.

B.   The pyrocatechol solution has a pH of 7.

C.   Potato juice is yellow in color.

D.   Pyrocatechol is colorless.

28. If a chemist wanted to achieve the most dramatic change in color over time of the pyrocatechol solution, which combination of drops of phenylthiourea and potato juice would be added?

F.   20 drops phenylthiourea, 1 drop potato juice

G.   10 drops phenylthiourea, 5 drops potato juice

H.   1 drop phenylthiourea, 5 drops potato juice

J.   10 drops phenylthiourea, 3 drops potato juice

Passage VI

Environmentalist 1

When a consumer is given the choice between paper and plastic bags to package purchases, he/she should choose paper because it is better for the environment. Paper is made from trees, which are a renewable resource. The newer technologies use hemp and other grasses to make paper and thus further reduce the strain on the environment. Paper also easily degrades, and thus reduces waste in the landfills. Plastic bags can take decades to degrade; and when they do degrade, the small plastic pieces are eaten by birds and other small animals. The plastic blocks their digestive tracts, causing illness and even death.

Even in the production process, paper is cleaner. Paper pulp does not emit toxic fumes, as petroleum by-products do. With the newer processing techniques, the bleaching steps no longer employ chlorinated compounds, further reducing toxic waste. One must also keep in mind that most paper bags are readily recycled, thus saving millions of trees. Recycled paper products have strength equivalent to that of virgin products and require less processing. Therefore, since paper is manufactured from a renewable resource, is less toxic to produce, and has endless recycling options, it is the best choice of material from which to make bags.

Environmentalist 2

Contrary to popular opinion, plastic bags are actually environmentally safer than paper. Plastic bags are stronger and thus fewer are required to carry the same weight. While they are fabricated from petroleum, the process is cleaner than paper making.

The paper industry uses thousands of acres of trees each year to produce grocery bags. Replacing these trees requires decades of careful tending and soil management. Even new paper methods will result in soil erosion and loss of homes for countless species of animals. Meanwhile, very little petroleum is needed for plastic, and in most cases, plastic is made from the petroleum by-products. These by-products are the remnants after gasoline and kerosene have been removed.

Plastic is more suitable for recycling than paper. It can be reused to make furniture, automobile parts, and stuffing for toys, among countless other products. The newer plastics are made to be easier to degrade, sometimes even faster than paper; so if the bags are found in landfills, they will readily be incorporated into the soil and pose no threat to the residential wildlife. Based on the cleaner manufacturing processes and numerous recycling options, plastic bags should be the consumer's choice.

29. Environmentalist 1 claims that paper bags are preferable partly because trees are a renewable resource. Environmentalist 2 directly counters this statement with the argument that

    A.   the process of fabricating plastic bags is cleaner than the process of paper-making.

    B.   harvesting trees destroys bird and animal habitats and results in soil erosion.

    C.   Choices A and B are both correct.

    D.   Neither choice A nor choice B is correct.

30. Recycling is mandated by law in many communities. Which environmentalist would recommend his/her favorite bags because of recycling options?

    F.   Environmentalist 1   H.   Both environmentalists

    G.   Environmentalist 2   J.   Neither environmentalist

31. Although they reach different conclusions, both environmentalists appeal to our concerns

   A.   for wildlife.

   B.   for waste disposal.

   C.   for cleanliness in production.

   D.   for the issues in A, B, and C.

32. The reason Environmentalist 2 states that in most cases, plastics are by-products of petroleum production is to assure us that

   F.   the production of plastics creates less air pollution than the production of paper products.

   G.   the production of plastics doesn't increase the amount of resources consumed.

   H.   Choices F and G are both correct.

   J.   Neither choice F nor choice G is correct.

33. You are a member of the "Defenders of Wildlife." You should advocate the use of

   A.   paper bags, according to Environmentalist 1.

   B.   plastic bags, according to Environmentalist 2.

   C.   reusable canvas bags, according to both environmentalists.

   D.   Choices A and B are both correct.

34. You are the director of a municipal landfill. You should advocate the use of

   F.   paper bags, according to Environmentalist 1.

   G.   plastic bags, according to Environmentalist 2.

   H.   incineration to eliminate burnable items from landfills, according to Environmentalist 2.

   J.   Choices A and B are both correct.

35. According to Environmentalist 2, all of the following are reasons to use plastic bags EXCEPT

   A.   plastic bags are stronger than paper bags.

   B.   since plastics are petroleum by-products, their production does not use additional energy.

   C.   newer plastic bag material degrades faster than paper.

   D.   plastic can be recycled into many products.

Passage VII

A spectroscopic binary consists of two stars which orbit around each other, but telescopically appear as one. The binary nature of such a system can only be determined by analyzing the starlight through an instrument called a spectroscope. For simplicity, we will examine the motion of only one of the stars and consider the other as stationary. We can measure the change in the wavelength of the light from a star and determine its radial velocity. This change in wavelength, called the Doppler effect, is observed whenever an object is approaching or receding from an observer. Radial velocity is defined as an object's speed of recession or approach and is assigned a positive or negative value, respectively. Approaching objects show a blue Doppler shift and receding objects show a red Doppler shift. Figure 1 shows a binary star system in a elliptical orbit and Figure 2 shows the radial velocity of the orbiting star as obtained from the Doppler shift and as a function of time. Table 1 relates the orbital points in Figure 1 to the radial velocity points in Figure 2.

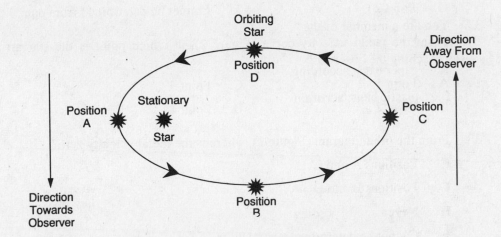

Figure 1—Elliptical Orbit of Binary Star System

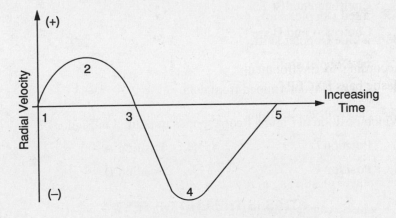

Figure 2—Radial Velocity of Orbiting Star

Table 1

Corresponding Points Between Figures 1 and 2				
Positions Along Fig. 1 Orbit Diagram	A	B	C	D
Points in Fig. 2 Radial Velocity Curve	4	1	2	3

36. From the radial velocity curve (Figure 2), at which point is the orbiting star moving fastest?

    F. Point 1
    G. Point 2

    H. Point 4
    J. Cannot be determined from data.

37. From the radial velocity curve (Figure 2), at which point is the star approaching the observer?

    A. Point 1
    B. Point 2

    C. Point 3
    D. Point 4

38. From the orbit diagram (Figure 1), where is the radial velocity zero?

    F. Positions A and C
    G. Positions B and D
    H. Never
    J. Cannot be determined from data.

39. From the orbit diagram (Figure 1), position C shows

    A. a red Doppler shift.
    B. a blue Doppler shift.
    C. no Doppler shift.
    D. Cannot be determined from data.

40. Which position in Figure 1 corresponds to point 5 in Figure 2?

    F. Position D
    G. Position C

    H. Position A
    J. Position B

THIS IS THE END OF TEST 4.

ACT ASSESSMENT
EXAM III

ANSWER KEY

Test 1: English

1.	(C)	20.	(H)	39.	(A)	58.	(J)
2.	(J)	21.	(C)	40.	(H)	59.	(A)
3.	(D)	22.	(G)	41.	(B)	60.	(F)
4.	(G)	23.	(C)	42.	(H)	61.	(B)
5.	(D)	24.	(G)	43.	(B)	62.	(J)
6.	(J)	25.	(D)	44.	(F)	63.	(B)
7.	(C)	26.	(H)	45.	(B)	64.	(H)
8.	(G)	27.	(B)	46.	(H)	65.	(C)
9.	(D)	28.	(F)	47.	(B)	66.	(G)
10.	(H)	29.	(C)	48.	(J)	67.	(C)
11.	(B)	30.	(G)	49.	(C)	68.	(J)
12.	(G)	31.	(A)	50.	(J)	69.	(B)
13.	(D)	32.	(G)	51.	(C)	70.	(J)
14.	(G)	33.	(D)	52.	(J)	71.	(C)
15.	(C)	34.	(H)	53.	(D)	72.	(G)
16.	(G)	35.	(D)	54.	(J)	73.	(C)
17.	(D)	36.	(G)	55.	(A)	74.	(G)
18.	(H)	37.	(B)	56.	(G)	75.	(C)
19.	(C)	38.	(H)	57.	(A)		

Test 2: Mathematics

1.	(C)	5.	(B)	9.	(D)	13.	(A)
2.	(J)	6.	(J)	10.	(J)	14.	(K)
3.	(A)	7.	(C)	11.	(C)	15.	(A)
4.	(K)	8.	(K)	12.	(G)	16.	(H)

17. (B)	28. (H)	39. (A)	50. (F)
18. (J)	29. (A)	40. (J)	51. (D)
19. (A)	30. (G)	41. (D)	52. (J)
20. (F)	31. (D)	42. (G)	53. (E)
21. (A)	32. (H)	43. (B)	54. (K)
22. (K)	33. (D)	44. (K)	55. (C)
23. (D)	34. (G)	45. (B)	56. (F)
24. (H)	35. (A)	46. (K)	57. (D)
25. (E)	36. (K)	47. (B)	58. (G)
26. (G)	37. (D)	48. (K)	59. (D)
27. (C)	38. (J)	49. (E)	60. (J)

Test 3: Reading

1. (D)	11. (D)	21. (B)	31. (C)
2. (J)	12. (J)	22. (H)	32. (H)
3. (B)	13. (D)	23. (B)	33. (A)
4. (F)	14. (J)	24. (G)	34. (J)
5. (C)	15. (D)	25. (B)	35. (A)
6. (H)	16. (G)	26. (G)	36. (F)
7. (C)	17. (A)	27. (D)	37. (C)
8. (H)	18. (G)	28. (F)	38. (J)
9. (D)	19. (B)	29. (C)	39. (A)
10. (H)	20. (G)	30. (H)	40. (F)

Test 4: Science Reasoning

1. (B)	11. (A)	21. (B)	31. (D)
2. (F)	12. (J)	22. (G)	32. (G)
3. (C)	13. (B)	23. (B)	33. (D)
4. (J)	14. (J)	24. (F)	34. (J)
5. (D)	15. (C)	25. (C)	35. (B)
6. (H)	16. (G)	26. (G)	36. (H)
7. (A)	17. (A)	27. (D)	37. (D)
8. (H)	18. (J)	28. (H)	38. (G)
9. (C)	19. (C)	29. (B)	39. (A)
10. (J)	20. (H)	30. (H)	40. (J)

DETAILED EXPLANATIONS OF ANSWERS

Test 1: English

1. **(C)** By organizing the stages of life into chronological order, thus developing a clear and orderly structure, choice (C) provides the correct answer. This logical progression from birth to death is much more effective than the funeral preceding the birth, say, of choice (A) or preceding both the wedding and the birth of choice (B). (D), likewise, places the funeral before other stages in life and birth before the wedding. Only in choice (C) is time order consistent and therefore logical.

2. **(J)** Correct agreement of the singular subject "each" and the singular verb "is" is achieved by choice (J). Choice (F) incorrectly suggests the plural possessive "stages'," which is not followed by a necessary object to possess. The term "these" indicates that a plural noun is to follow as the object of the preposition "of"; however, choice (G) supplies the *singular* noun "stage" and is therefore in error. The plural verb "are" presented by choice (H) fails to agree with the singular subject "each" and is thus incorrect. It is a common error to seek a verb's subject within the nearest preceding set of words; however, when these words form a prepositional phrase, they cannot "hold" that subject. One must then look further for the correct subject.

3. **(D)** Because it places the necessary comma following an introductory participial phrase, in this case "Validating…passage," and because of the possessive construction of "its" completed by the modified object "separateness," choice (D) is the right answer. Choice (A) presents a nonexistent word "its'," as does choice (B), but (B) furthers the error by failing to include the comma after "passage." Although the correct comma is present in choice (C), "it's" is the contraction for "it is" and, as such, makes no sense, for there is no logical antecedent reference for "it."

4. **(G)** Parallelism is the issue in this sentence. Sentences achieve clarity, force, and smoothness when their similar parts are expressed in similar patterns. Note that the correct choice, (G), places the list of direct objects in a consistent adjective-noun order ["appropriate" (adjective)-"pageantry" (noun), etc.]. No clear pattern emerges in (F)'s presentation of its list (noun, adjective-noun, gerund-prepositional phrase, gerund, gerund). Nor is a clear pattern achieved by (H)'s noun, gerund-prepositional phrase (cliché), noun-prepositional phrase order. (J)'s adjective-noun, noun-prepositional phrase, adjective noun, and noun organization is no better.

5. **(D)** Because of the consistency of "our" with the first person plural voice of the passage, choice (D) is correct. Note that the author makes reference to "*our* birth" and "*our* attendance," indicating that we are all in this process together. Choice (A)'s use of the singular first person pronoun "my" excludes the rest of us and is inconsistent with the passage's voice. "Their," as suggested by choice (B), excludes the author and us, as that pronoun is in third person plural. "My" is incorrectly used in choice (C) just as it was in choice (A), but the addition of "with" creates an error of logic. "For" is the logical connector.

6. **(J)** The placement of the comma before the logical coordinating conjunction "and," joining two independent clauses, makes choice (J) correct. Without the comma, as choice (F) offers, the sentence is fused. Making the second of the two independent clauses dependent *via* the subordinating conjunctions "because" and "since," as do choices (G) and (H), corrects the fusion problem; however, the cause and effect relationship suggested by these conjunctions does not exist. A bar mitzvah's gluttony does not make us buy birthday gifts.

7. **(C)** The colon is synonymous with "the following" and is correctly employed in this manner by choice (C). The "one" that "can claim our conscious attendance" is the following, "the wedding." Separating the antecedent "wedding" from its fairly lengthy appositive "humankind's...," is the necessary comma found in (C). Further, choice (C) correctly places a possessive apostrophe in "humankind's," indicating a relationship of possession with "most vital rite of passage." "The wedding...passage" is an appositive lacking a subject and verb, not a complete sentence, as choice (A) incorrectly presents. Within this appositive exists another appositive, "humankind's...passage" that cannot be a complete sentence, as choice (B) suggests. Finally, choice (D) fails to punctuate the possessive "humankind's" correctly by leaving out the possessive apostrophe.

8. **(G)** Choice (G) correctly employs the relative pronoun "which," used in reference to the non-human term "wedding ceremony." The relative pronoun "who" is reserved for reference to humans, and therefore choice (F) is incorrect. The inclusion of the phrase "in which" of choice (G) sets the reader up for something or someone to "prepare an individual's move." Because the expectation is unfulfilled by a subject for the verb "prepares," the construction is incomplete and therefore incorrect. Omitting the relative pronoun, as (J) suggests, leaves the sentence with an unnecessary comma between "itself" and the verb "prepares." A comma would only be appropriate here if one preceded "itself" as well, indicating the author's intention of treating the word as a parenthetical expression.

9. **(D)** As the singular pronoun "his/her" agrees with the singular reference "individual," choice (D) is correct. Stylistically wordy with "from which" and redundant in its use of "individual," (A) is a poor choice. Because of its plural pronoun "their" used in reference to a singular noun "individual," choice (B) is

not grammatically correct. Excessive verbiage with the prepositional phrase and repetitious use of "individual" are the downfalls of choice (C).

10. **(H)** Agreeing with the present tense of the passage and supplying the verb necessary for the subject "male," "finds" of choice (H) is correct. Choices (F) and (G)'s "finding" and ", finding" both begin a participial phrase modifying "male," a phrase which doesn't end until "intellect." As a consequence, no verb exists, making the sentence incomplete. (J) exhibits an illogical and unnecessary tense switch to the past.

11. **(B)** Consistent punctuation of a brief modifying phrase is at issue in this question. Brief adjectival phrases have either no enclosing punctuation *or* the same punctuation on both ends. Choice (B) meets the grammatical criteria by absenting itself of enclosing punctuation entirely. Choice (A) shows inconsistent comma usage as the companion comma at the end of the phrase is missing. Choice (C), too, lacks a companion comma. In (D), the companion dash is absent.

12. **(G)** The singular "newlywed" forms the antecedent for the singular pronouns "he or she," as choice (G) correctly indicates. (F), (H), and (J) all incorrectly supply the plural pronouns "they," "they both," and "they," respectively.

13. **(D)** Providing the plural verb "testify" for the plural subject "procedures" qualifies (D) as the correct choice. (A) incorrectly offers the singular verb "testifies." One should not be misled into seeking a subject within a prepositional phrase intervening between the subject and the true verb. The singular "hoo-hah" of the phrase is only a prepositional object, not a subject. The verbal form of "testimony" is "testify," not the noun "testimony" with a verbal ending such as "testimonied." No such term exists, and thus choice (B) is incorrect. Inconsistency of verb tense is (C)'s error, as "testified" is in the past tense form and the passage is in present.

14. **(G)** Preceding a list with a colon, as does choice (G), is correct as that colon means "the following." The items in the list have no verb and no subject and therefore cannot be considered a complete sentence, as choices (F) and (J) suggest. (J) is incorrect in its use of the past tense in a consistently present tense passage. Finally, capitalizing "rehearsal" is incorrect because neither is it a proper noun, nor does it begin a sentence; therefore, (H) is a poor choice.

15. **(C)** Like the African rite of lion-killing, which prepares a young adolescent man for adulthood, the American rite of marriage prepares the newlywed couple for adult consumerism; thus, choice (C)'s comparison of American and African rites of passage is correct. No definitions are really necessary nor provided in this paragraph, thereby making choice (A) incorrect. The African male's process

of becoming a man is explained, but the American rite involves men and *women*, and thus choice (B) is incorrect in its narrowness. In no place is a contest over the superiority of one rite explored. Consequently, choice (D), too, is incorrect.

16. **(G)**   Choice (G) correctly places commas between both the region and the country and after the country. However, had the passage stated only the region ("Vung Tau") or the country ("Vietnam"), no commas would be needed whatsoever. Choice (G) also correctly uses the singular "falls," corresponding with the singular subject "group." Choices (F) and (J) incorrectly use the plural "fall," which is wrong because "wanderers" is the object of a prepositional phrase and not the subject of the sentence. Choices (F) and (H) are incorrect because they fail to use commas properly.

17. **(D)**   "Altogether" is synonymous with "in all" (A), "combined" (B), and "in total" (C); therefore, (A), (B), and (C) are redundant in meaning. Consequently, (D), the omission of the underlined phrase, is the correct answer.

18. **(H)**   Providing examples is an excellent means of proving a premise, as long as the examples clearly relate and support that same premise. This is the case in choice (H) as conferring and unanimity both indicate a sense of "unity and togetherness." Choice (F)'s travel routes have nothing to do with unity. (G) makes no indication that the discussion of the political philosophy of communism will be connected to the unity the fishermen exhibited. Irreconcilable disagreements and conflicts, as suggested by choice (J), are contrary to unity and togetherness. A unified group would reconcile differences.

19. **(C)**   By following an introductory non-essential dependent clause by a comma, choice (C) is correct. (A) lacks this mandatory comma, and (B) and (D) treat the dependent clause as if it were independent. A semicolon in (B) separates two *independent* clauses, as does a comma plus a conjunction such as "and," in (D).

20. **(H)**   The smooth sentence delivery, uninterrupted by unnecessary commas, and the consistent past tense of "came" make (H) the correct choice. By illogically switching to the present tense verb "come," choice (F) is in error. The comma (G) inserts between "Vietnam" and "comes" slows the forward movement of the sentence and is thus a poor choice. (J) combines the errors of tense inconsistency and unnecessary comma placement.

21. **(C)**   The adverbial phrase modifying "moved" should be joined to the preceding independent clause by a comma, as is accomplished in choice (C). Treating the phrase, which lacks a subject and a verb, as a complete sentence, as does choice (A), results in a sentence fragment. Choice (B)'s use of the semico-

lon indicates the phrase is an independent clause, but, of course, it lacks the subject and verb. Although the punctuation is correct in choice (D), the tense is illogically in present perfect when the passage is written in past.

22. **(G)**   The straightforward, economically worded, active-voice presentation of choice (G) is the correct choice. Note that the subject "Americans" performs the actions, thus eliminating much of the unnecessary verbiage of choices (F), (H), and (J). The general wordiness of (H) is made more problematical by the double negative "not never," which really means "always."

23. **(C)**   This passage is formal in its wording; thus, the formal term "resistance" of choice (C) is in keeping with the writing style. A cliché such as that used by choice (A) should be avoided for clichés are worn-out phrases that no longer inspire the vivid images they originally did when first composed. Both (B)'s "foul-up" and (D)'s "glitch" are slang and thus are inconsistent with the formality of the writing.

24. **(G)**   Correctly employing the colon to mean "the following," choice (G) succinctly presents the reason with "competition for jobs." Treating the noun phrase as a complete sentence, as does choice (F), is incorrect for no verb is present. The wordiness of choice (H) is a problem, as is the fusion error that results because of the absence of the comma, which should precede a coordinating conjunction ("and") linking the now-two independent clauses. "Its competition for jobs" lacks a verb; so it cannot be treated as a complete sentence as (J) indicates.

25. **(D)**   The completed construction of the "so...that" relationship is achieved in choice (D), the correct answer. Choices (A) and (B) fail to add the necessary "so," and choice (C) places an unnecessary comma before the verb, thus disrupting the smooth momentum of the sentence.

26. **(H)**   The consistent use of commas to enclose the comparative adjectival phrase "like boat owner Ba Ban Nguyen" recommends (H) as the correct choice. Hyphenating "Vietnamese-like" makes no sense for it acts as an adjective modifying Ba Ban Nguyen, who now is defined as *not* Vietnamese but merely *like* a Vietnamese. The rest of the sentence logically crumbles with this interpretation for the passage is about the survival of actual Vietnamese. The dash coupled with the comma to enclose the adjectival phrase reveals an inconsistent use of punctuation, and therefore (G) is a poor choice. Finally, the placement of only one of the necessary companion commas results in sentence confusion, as illustrated by choice (J). The reader would probably have to reread the sentence to make sense of it, whereas if the commas were correctly placed, the sentence would be clear upon the first reading.

27. **(B)** By separating the two independent clauses by a semicolon, choice (B) is correct. A comma between the two clauses results in a comma splice, illustrated by choice (A). (C)'s punctuation is correct, but its use of "however" is illogical. "However" signifies a change or contrast from that which precedes, but the following clause reiterates and defines what was stated in the first independent clause. More than continuing as *menial laborers*, the Vietnamese want to become *fishermen*. In addition to the comma splice, choice (D) presents "since," which falls victim to the same logical error as "however."

28. **(F)** The pronoun "who" correctly refers to people, "American fishermen," and is correctly in the nominative/subjective case as it acts as the subject for the verb "were crowded." Thus, choice (F) is correct. Choice (G) uses the pronoun "which," reserved for reference to objects, not people. (H) is incorrect because of its objective case "whom." An objective case pronoun acts as just that, a direct object, an indirect object, or the object of a prepositional phrase. It cannot take the subject position. Omitting the underlined portion, as choice (J) suggests, results in confusion as to who was "minding their own business."

29. **(C)** Because of its general reference to the problems which both Paragraph 4 and Paragraph 5 discuss, choice (C) offers the best transition between the paragraphs. The issue of pride, as indicated in choice (A), is nonexistent in either paragraph and is thus an inappropriate point of transition. Linking existing ideas together is the purpose of good transition. That Americans' incomes are suffering is indeed strongly implied in Paragraph 4, but this is too narrow a focus for transition as it fails to mention the other side of the issue, the Vietnamese needs and the main development of the resulting violence of Paragraph 5. Therefore, choice (B) is a poor answer. The market value of fishing is mentioned in neither paragraph, and thus (D) is inappropriate for transition, as well.

30. **(G)** By linking the problems listed in Paragraph 5 with the term "wanderers from Vung Tau" from Paragraph 1, choice (G) successfully unifies the composition as it skillfully reminds the readers of these new Americans' journey. Choice (F)'s "Vietnamese Go Home" leaves the reader with the violent tone of Paragraph 5, but fails to unify that paragraph with the positive sense of mission established in Paragraph 1. Focusing only on the journey of Paragraph 1 and not on the achieved destination and its problems of Paragraph 5, choices (H) and (J) offer poor transition between the sections.

31. **(A)** Through the use of such positive terms as "extraordinary" and "outstanding" in the characterization of the Vietnamese, the evidence of their escape from communism and the Vietnam War, and the discussion of their persistence in establishing themselves through hard work as successful fishermen, the author reveals his admiration for these people, as suggested in choice (A). According to the passage, the Vietnamese never gave up and are still fighting the challenge of

American fishermen; thus, choice (B) fails to reflect the author's perspective. Basically, the author exposes a clash between Vietnamese and American methods of fishing. He further presents the Vietnamese as survivors whose marketable skills were fishing. There is no indication of the Vietnamese intentionally "bullying" the Americans. There are simply too many people in the same small area who want to accomplish the same task. Thus, choice (C) doesn't truly reflect the author's perspective. "Unity and togetherness" are the characteristics of the Vietnamese, according to the author. "Familial fighting" and cultural destruction are counter to this unity, thus making (D) a poor choice for the author's point of view.

32. **(G)** This sentence's subject, "people," is completed by the compound verb "have needed" and "have desired." Even though these verbs are quite far apart in the sentence, there is no grammatical need to separate them by a comma or semicolon before the adverb "yet." Thus, choice (G) is correct. In all other choices, the semicolon inappropriately divides the sentence. When the semicolon appears before the adverbial conjunction "yet," it signifies the juncture of two independent clauses, each having a subject and a verb. This is not the case in this sentence as the verb in the segment after the semicolon has its subject in the preceding independent clause.

33. **(D)** The clarity and freshness of language in (D) recommends it as the correct answer. Choices (A) and (B) are clichés, which, because of overuse, can no longer impart the visual imagery they originally inspired. Choice (C) offers an adjusted cliché [("raining) like cats and dogs"], substituting "packed" for "raining." In either case, the image is illogical.

34. **(H)** Because of the logical use of the subordinating conjunction "when," relating to the time of "several hundred years later," and because this conjunction is not separated from the subject of the clause it begins by a comma, choice (H) is correct. Choices (F) and (G) present the tentative conjunction "if," indicating a state of possibility rather than one of actuality, as the previous verb "occurred" demands. By unnecessarily placing a comma after "when," choice (J) is incorrect.

35. **(D)** Subject-verb agreement is the issue in this question. Because the subject of the *plural* verb "were" is the compound and thus *plural* "houses and townhouses," choice (D) is correct. In all the other choices, the singular "was" is indicated as the common verb, but it fails to agree in number with the plural subject and, therefore, is incorrect. A common error is to choose a verb that sounds right with the adverb "there" rather than seek the true subject of the sentence. "There" is rarely the subject of a clause.

36. **(G)** This passage is written primarily in the past tense. Only if logic demands should the verb tense switch. As there is no logical reason to switch from the past tense in this sentence, choice (G)'s past tense "had" is correct. (F)

switches to present tense, (G) to future, and (J) to past perfect, and all are therefore incorrect.

37. **(B)**   Because of its logical and economical language, choice (B) is correct. In its brevity, it sacrifices neither grammar nor content nor style and therefore is superior to choice (A)'s wordy "which" construction, choice (C)'s illogical "all by" phrase that fails to show the relationship between the "poor health conditions" and the "crowding," and choice (D)'s awkward "being that."

38. **(H)**   Logic and economy here, too, are the qualities that recommend (H) as the correct answer. Note how the clear, direct, parallel phrasing of (H) forcefully makes the point. The confused construction of choice (F) muddles the point. The rules of parallel structure are totally ignored here, as the similar sentence elements are arranged in unsimilar patterns (noun-prepositional phrase, noun-prepositional phrase, adjective-adjective-noun). Although (G) is closer to this parallelism, the repetition of the "lack of" phrase renders the sentence unnecessarily wordy. Further, the phrase "lack of unsanitary and overcrowded conditions," in truth, illogically means *sanitary* and *roomy* conditions. Logic is also lacking in choice (J)'s coupling of "overcrowding" with "air, sunlight, and sanitation."

39. **(A)**   By linking Paragraph 4's topic of overcrowded space with Paragraph 5's focus on laws to alleviate the problem, choice (A) provides the best transition. The workers' pay is mentioned in neither paragraph, and thus (B) is an inappropriate choice to link logically the two paragraphs. Not only does (C) present an incorrect fact, that the lack of sunlight was caused by fog (rather than the crowded buildings), but it fails to make any tie to Paragraph 5. In both paragraphs, the setting is the Industrial Age of the 1800's in Europe, not the late 1900's in the United States. Certainly, this anachronism precludes choice (D) from being correct.

40. **(H)**   The logical and economical language of (H) makes it the correct choice. Without losing meaning, it presents a clear, easily comprehensible observation. By the time the reader finally wades through all of (F)'s prepositional phrases to reach the verb "was," he/she quite possibly has forgotten the subject. Because of the excessive phrases and dependent clause intervening between the subject and verb of choice (G), the reader wonders, "What *was* the subject?" Logically, the law would not measure "unhealthy living conditions," but rather seek to alleviate them. The illogic of choice (J) eliminates it as a possibility.

41. **(B)**   Correctly establishing possession is a concern of this question. By simply using the adjective-noun format of "city government," choice (B) logically and grammatically makes the point. (A) places a possessive apostrophe after the "s" in "city"; however, the correct possessive of the singular "city" is

"city's." Choice (C) compounds the error of "citys'" by allowing this incorrect possessive no possessed object. Further, it is "governments" which grammatically should be possessive; yet, even so, the government does not "own" the city. The "of" construction already establishes possession in choice (D), making the possessive "city's" ungrammatically redundant.

42. **(H)** An infinitive is formed by joining "to" and a verb. Grammar dictates that nothing should come between the two. Only in choice (H) does the infinitive retain its integrity as "to help." Choices (F), (G), and (J) split the infinitive with the adverbs "better," "really," and "perhaps," respectively, and are therefore incorrect.

43. **(B)** The positive implications of the verb "had appeared" and the later use of the conjunction "or" indicate that (B)'s "either" is the appropriate choice to complete this sentence. Choice (A)'s "neither" is logically coupled with "nor," not the positive "or," and thus cannot be correct. Not only is (C) incorrect as to this last issue, but the semicolon incorrectly indicates that at the juncture two independent clauses are joined. Following the semicolon is an *adverbial phrase* modifying "had appeared." (D) also incorrectly uses the semicolon and compounds its error by the use of "nevertheless." "Nevertheless" sets the reader up for an independent clause to follow the phrase "as…countries"; yet, the clause fails to materialize.

44. **(F)** By correctly indicating that two complete sentences meet here, choice (F), the original, is correct. A common error is to judge a very short sentence as incomplete simply based on its brevity. However, if a subject and a verb are present, and the result makes sense alone, it is a sentence, no matter how short. Hence, "It thrived" works. Placing a comma between the two independent clauses, as does (G), results in a comma splice. (H) suffers for two reasons. First, the semicolon is incorrectly coupled with a now-dependent clause as a result of the subordinate conjunction "since." Second, the use of "since" makes no sense as a cause and effect relationship does not exist between "growth" and "thrive." These two terms are simply different degrees of the same thing. In failing to provide a comma before the coordinating conjunction "and," choice (J) creates a sentence fusion.

45. **(B)** In grouping essays for a book, the best chapter heading for this passage is (B), "The Evolution of European City Gardens," for the history of these gardens from their origin to the early twentieth century is the essay's focus. Choice (A)'s focus on specific plants is not addressed at all in the essay and thus is an inappropriate answer. Although Medieval England marked the beginning of city gardening, this heading is far too narrow to encompass the time period presented in the essay, and thus choice (C) is a poor answer. Choice (D) is no better as garden pests are not considered at all in the essay.

46. **(H)**   Providing examples involving the topics of other European countries, laws, and gardens is an excellent means of support, and thus choice (H) is correct. Although interesting, "nutritional aspects" have nothing to do with law or with other European countries; so (F) is an inappropriate choice. Spain is another European country, but gardens and laws are not mentioned in (G); thus it is a poor choice for topic support. Finally, choice (J) fails to address laws or other European countries and thus is not correct.

47. **(B)**   Because the singular verb "exists" agrees with the singular subject "consensus," choice (B) is correct. When seeking the subject of a verb, one should never be misled by prepositional phrases, such as "of opinion," intervening between that subject-verb combination. Subjects do not appear within prepositional phrases. Choices (A) and (C) are incorrect because they supply the plural verb "exist." In choice (D), "existing" begins a participial phrase modifying the noun "consensus," and, since the rest of the sentence completes the participial phrase, the subject "consensus" is left without a verb. A lengthy fragment is the result.

48. **(J)**   A comma correctly separates the lengthy appositive, "the period...infancy," from "primal," the word it modifies, making choice (J) the right answer. Choice (F) incorrectly treats this appositive as a complete sentence; however, it is composed of just the noun "period" and a dependent clause. The absent comma of choice (G) makes the sentence confusing and disregards the grammatical necessity of punctuating lengthy appositives. Finally, (H) treats the appositive as an independent clause by using the semicolon and falls into the same grammatical error as did choice (F).

49. **(C)**   "Nature" is a singular noun, and when used as a possessive for "presence" is correctly punctuated with the apostrophe before the "s," as indicated by choice (C). The possessive relationship is ignored in choice (A), and choices (B) and (D) incorrectly place the possessive apostrophe after the "s," signifying that "nature"/"Nature" is plural.

50. **(J)**   Completing the "either-or" construction set up earlier in the sentence by supplying the necessary "or," choice (J) is correct. None of the other choices fulfill the demand that "either" makes on the sentence.

51. **(C)**   The article "an" precedes words beginning with a vowel, as choice (C) correctly indicates. Further, (C) supplies the first quotation mark to complete the pair surrounding the term "artificial naturalness." Choice (A) is incorrect in suggesting "a," which precedes words beginning with consonants. Further, it capitalizes a common noun; only proper nouns (names of people, places, things, or ideas) should be capitalized. By failing to supply the first of the quotation mark pair, choices (B) and (D) are incorrect. (D) compounds the error by placing "a" before the vowel.

52. **(J)**   The plural noun "people" agrees in number with its plural reference "their" and makes choice (J) correct. Choices (F) and (G)'s singular noun, "each person," is not in agreement with its plural pronoun reference "their"; thus these choices are incorrect. "Anyone" of choice (H), too, is incorrectly referred to by the plural "their." "Anyone" can be interpreted to mean any *one* person and therefore is singular.

53. **(D)**   A comma is necessary after an introductory non-essential dependent clause, as correctly illustrated by choice (D). By placing a semicolon between the dependent clause and the independent clause, choice (A) incorrectly indicates both clauses are independent. (B), too, makes this error by treating the dependent clause as a complete sentence. Choice (C) simply fails to include the mandatory comma.

54. **(J)**   "Then" signifies a logical switch to the past experiences of the primitives and thus necessitates a switch in verbs from the primarily present tense to past. (J) correctly provides the past tense "used"; however, (F) switches illogically to present perfect. (G) moves to future, and (H) remains in present.

55. **(A)**   The direct, non-repetitive wording of choice (A) results in clear syntax easily understood by the reader. The repetitive "them" and the illogical assertion that the plants worshipped the primitives make choice (B) incorrect. (C) and (D) suffer from the same repetitive wording; yet, (D) commits the additional logic error of asserting that the plants spoke.

56. **(G)**   By supplying both the entire set of quotation marks around the term "nature" and offsetting the appositive with commas on both sides, choice (G) is correct. Consistency is the issue with short appositives. One is correct in supplying both commas or in supplying none. One comma will not do. Choices (F), (H), and (J) are incorrect in the one comma they supply. They are also incorrect in their placement of the quotation marks. It is "nature," as a term, that is being considered, and as a term, it must be surrounded by quotation marks. "Term" is not the term being considered as such and thus requires no quotation marks at all.

57. **(A)**   The singular possessive "its" agrees in number with the singular noun "term" and shows a possessive relationship with the noun "impact." Thus, choice (A) is correct. Choice (B) supplies a nonexistent word, as "its" is never followed by an apostrophe. Using 'it's," the contraction of "it is," as choice (C) indicates, yields a sentence that makes no sense. Finally, the personal pronoun "his" is intended for reference to a person, not an object such as "nature."

58. **(J)**   By correctly using the semicolon to join two independent clauses and by employing the singular pronoun "it" in reference to the singular "nature,"

choice (J) is the correct answer. Choice (F) fuses the two clauses by failing to provide the necessary semicolon as does choice (G), which refers to the singular "nature" with the plural "them." Fusion is also the error of choice (H) as the comma preceding the coordinating conjunction "and" is missing. Additionally, "him" refers to a person, not objects such as "nature."

59. **(A)** "Severs" is a transitive verb and as such must take an object. The original choice (A) supplies this direct object ("humans") and therefore is the correct answer. Choices (B) and (C) incorrectly treat this verb as a possessive noun, and choice (D) provides no object for "severs" to act upon.

60. **(F)** "What" is the singular subject of the first independent clause and is correctly referred to in the second independent clause by the singular pronoun "it." Thus, choice (F) is correct. Choices (G) and (H) incorrectly supply the plural pronoun "they," and choice (J), although correct in the pronoun, is incorrect in the unnecessary tense switch from past to past perfect.

61. **(B)** Specific, concrete examples of glorified nature, such as sculptures and buildings, offer excellent support for the general plants and animals that Paragraph 2 notes the primitives worshipped. Thus, choice (B) is correct. Although a general overview is often present and correct in a first paragraph, not all important information must be placed here, as (A) mistakenly asserts. Rather, it can be specifically developed later in the paper. Further, if the important information just appeared in the first paragraph, why would anyone write or read more than this first section? Humanity's social development in conjunction with nature is a key theme throughout the essay, but especially in Paragraph 3, which therefore cannot be deleted, as choice (C) suggests. Furthermore, the new sentences are much better suited to act as support for Paragraph 2. The specificity of these new sentences is not appropriate for a concluding paragraph, as suggested by choice (D). They do not summarize what has gone on before, but merely support a specific assertion within a earlier paragraph.

62. **(J)** A semicolon is correctly placed between the two independent clauses in choice (J). The comma which appears between the two clauses in choice (F) creates a comma splice error, and the absence of punctuation exhibited in choice (G) results in sentence fusion. By inserting the subordinate conjunction "since," choice (H) make a dependent clause out of the original second independent clause, thus making the semicolon unnecessary.

63. **(B)** As the passage is written in past tense, and no logical reason exists to change from this tense, choice (B)'s consistent past tense "swept" is correct. Choice (A) exhibits tense inconsistency by switching to present, just as choice (D) errs in changing to future. "Having," as appears in choice (C), creates a participial

phrase modifying "machine." Constructed in this manner, "machine" becomes a subject lacking a verb, and thus choice (C) creates a sentence fragment.

64. **(H)**   Diction, or word choice, is the issue in question. As the passage is written in a formal style, slang is inappropriate and inconsistent. Choice (H)'s standard "constructed" meets this formal style and renders this the correct choice. The term "carefully" is contrary to (F) and (G)'s nonstandard terms "slapping together" and "thrown together," thus making these incorrect choices. Not only is choice (J)'s "run up" nonstandard English, but the verb should be correctly conjugated as "ran."

65. **(C)**   Because of the correct use of the semicolon to join two independent clauses and because of the singular pronoun "it" used in reference to the singular "Turk," choice (C) is correct. Because "who...comers" is a dependent clause, choice (A)'s use of the semicolon is incorrect, for a semicolon doesn't connect an independent and a *dependent* clause. Although (B)'s punctuation is correct, "whom" is an objective case pronoun, not a subjective/nominative case as it should be to take the subject position in a clause. Finally, the absence of punctuation between the two independent clauses of choice (D) results in sentence fusion.

66. **(G)**   The clear, direct, and economical syntax of choice (G) recommends it as the correct choice. "Manipulated" and "maneuvered" are synonymous and thus redundant when used together, making choices (F) and (H) incorrect. Additionally, "various" and "different" synonyms, and their tandem use in choices (F) and (J) results in unnecessary verbiage.

67. **(C)**   The personal pronoun "who" in reference to people, "the inventors," and the plural verb "have," which corresponds in number with these inventors, make (C) the correct answer. Choice (A)'s "which" refers to objects, not people, and choice (B)'s singular "has" does not agree in number with the plural "inventors." (D) combines both the singular verb and the nonpersonal pronoun errors, making it a poor choice.

68. **(J)**   Sacrificing no meaning, the clear, direct, and economical syntax of choice (J) makes it the appropriate choice. Note the wordiness of choices (F) and (G)'s "find themselves" and the insertion of the noun clause "that...dwell" of choice (H). None of these constructions improves upon the simplicity of choice (J).

69. **(B)**   The concern here is the punctuation. No mark of punctuation is necessary between the compound verb "are computerized" and "have," as choice (B) correctly indicates. Choice (A)'s semicolon incorrectly asserts, as does choice (D), that it joins two independent clauses. By separating the second of the compound verbs and treating the resulting segment as a sentence, choice (C) creates a fragment which lacks a subject for the verb "has."

70. **(J)** The singular subject "robot" agrees in number with the singular verb "runs" and the singular possessive pronoun "its," thus making (J) the correct choice. (F) and (H)'s plural "run" fails to agree with the singular subject, and (F) and (G) incorrectly supply the plural possessive pronoun "their." (H) further indicates a nonexistent term, "its'," as a possibility.

71. **(C)** Providing clear pronoun reference in the correct (objective) case, as demanded by its direct object position, is choice (C)'s "us." Both (A) and (D) suggest the vague pronouns "them" and "him," respectively; however, no prior antecedent reference exists, thus making these choices incorrect. The nominative/subjective case pronoun "we" cannot legitimately act in a direct object position, and thus choice (B) is incorrect as well.

72. **(G)** Two prepositional phrases meet at the intersection in question. Although they are somewhat lengthy, no punctuation is grammatically necessary when they are correctly linked by the simple coordinating conjunction "and," as occurs in choice (G). A prepositional phrase cannot be a complete sentence as choice (F) mistakenly indicates; nor can two such phrases be independent clauses as choice (H)'s semicolon implies. The subordinate conjunction suggested by choice (J) renders the words following it fragmented because the resulting subject "tasks" lacks a verb.

73. **(C)** Because it relates by contrast the science fiction element of robots established in Paragraph 3 and the reality of robots in industry as discussed in Paragraph 4, choice (C) provides the best transition between the paragraphs. Choice (A)'s focus is solely the fictive element within Paragraph 3 as is choice (B)'s, and thus they provide no logical relationship between the paragraphs. As choice (D)'s focus is solely the real-life applications of robots as mentioned in Paragraph 4 alone, it provides no logical reference to Paragraph 3 and thus fails as a transitional device.

74. **(G)** For unity of the passage, choice (G) offers the best route. It links the work role of today's robots mentioned in Paragraph 4 to the early chess-playing robot of Paragraph 1. Thus, the chronological cycle is closed, and the passage is unified. (F) fails to unify as it deals not at all with the Turk of Paragraph 1, nor with the reality of robots of Paragraph 4. Really, this sentence would be better placed in Paragraph 3, which deals with robots in fiction. As Paragraph 4 proves, robots are not just machines of the past, (H)'s suggestion. The inaccuracy of this choice discounts the modern information supplied in the passage and thus does not unify the essay. Although "Turkish" is a word signaling a connection with Paragraph 1, choice (J) fails to deal with the robot, which was not Turkish, but simply costumed accordingly. In addition to this inaccuracy, choice (J) mentions nothing of the industrial world of robotics discussed in Paragraph 4 and thus does nothing to unify the passage.

75. **(C)**   Supplying specific examples of a general assertion is an excellent strategy, as suggested by choice (C). Certainly, experiments and inventions conducted during the 19th century would prove the self-confidence these inventors felt in relation to their technology. By comparing Poe to Turkish writers, literary analysis might be served, but certainly not the required support of nineteenth-century technology. The various chess strategies really have nothing to do with the development of scientific technology; thus, choice (B) is off topic. Off the topic as well is choice (D); discussing financing is not the same as supporting the self-confidence these inventors felt to experiment and build anything.

Test 2: Mathematics

1.   **(C)**   To simplify means to find the simplest expression. We perform the operations within the innermost grouping symbols first. That is $3 + 9 = 12$.

Thus, $4[-2(3 + 9) \div 3] + 5 = 4[-2(12) \div 3] + 5$

Next we simplify within the brackets:

$$= 4[-24 \div 3] + 5$$
$$= 4 \times (-8) + 5$$

We now perform the multiplication, since multiplication is done before addition:

$$= -32 + 5$$
$$= -27$$

Hence, $4[-2(3 + 9) \div 3] + 5 = -27$.

2.   **(J)** $\sqrt{8} + 3\sqrt{18} - 7\sqrt{2}$

$$= 2\sqrt{2} + 3(\sqrt{9})(\sqrt{2}) - 7\sqrt{2}$$
$$= 2\sqrt{2} + 9\sqrt{2} - 7\sqrt{2}$$
$$= 4\sqrt{2}.$$

3.   **(A)**   Let x = larger number

y = smaller number

$x + y = 120$ (1)

$x = 3y + 12$ (2)

We need to solve for y in this system of equations.

Substituting the expression for x from Equation (2) into Equation (1):

$$(3y + 12) + y = 120$$
$$4y = 108$$

Dividing by 4: $y = 27$

4. **(K)** $\quad f(3) = 3(3)^2 - (3) + 5$
$\quad\quad\quad\quad = 27 - 3 + 5$
$\quad\quad\quad\quad = 29$

5. **(B)** $\quad \dfrac{3}{2}x = 5$

$$x = \frac{(5)(2)}{3}$$

$$x = \frac{10}{3}$$

$$\frac{2}{3} + x = \frac{2}{3} + \frac{10}{3}$$

$$= \frac{12}{3}$$

$$= 4$$

6. **(J)** $\quad y = 2(x-3)^2$
$\quad\quad\quad = 2(-1-3)^2$
$\quad\quad\quad = 2(-4)^2$
$\quad\quad\quad = 32$

7. **(C)** $\quad \dfrac{3}{x+2} = \dfrac{5}{x+7}$
$\quad\quad 3x + 21 = 5x + 10 \quad\quad$ (cross multiplied)
$\quad\quad\quad\quad 11 = 2x$

$$x = \frac{11}{2}$$

8. **(K)** This problem has no solution, since the absolute value can never be negative.

9. **(D)** $\quad a^2 b^3 = 3^7$
$\quad\quad 9^2 b^3 = 3^7$
$\quad\quad 3^4 b^3 = 3^7$
$\quad\quad\quad b^3 = 3^3$
$\quad\quad\quad b = 3$

10. **(J)** Substitute $a = 5$ and $b = 8$ into the given expression:

$$\frac{5 + \dfrac{5}{8}}{5 - \dfrac{5}{8}}$$

$$= \frac{\dfrac{40}{8} + \dfrac{5}{8}}{\dfrac{40}{8} - \dfrac{5}{8}}$$

$$= \frac{\dfrac{45}{8}}{\dfrac{35}{8}}$$

$$= \frac{45}{8} \times \frac{8}{35}$$

$$= \frac{45}{35}$$

$$= \frac{9}{7}$$

11. **(C)** $3x^2y - 2xy^2 + 5xy$
$= 3(1)^2(-2) - 2(1)(-2)^2 + 5(1)(-2)$
$= -6 - 8 - 10$
$= -24$

If we simplify the expression first, we will need fewer computations:

$$3x^2y - 2xy^2 + 5xy = xy(3x - 2y + 5)$$
$$= (1)(-2)(3 + 4 + 5)$$
$$= (-2)(12) = -24$$

12. **(G)**
$$xy - x = 27$$
$$x(y - 1) = 27 \qquad \text{(factored)}$$
$$x(3) = 27$$
$$x = 9 \qquad \text{(substituted 3 for } y - 1)$$

13. **(A)** Since division by a fraction is equivalent to multiplication by its reciprocal:

$$\frac{\dfrac{1}{2} + \dfrac{1}{3}}{\dfrac{1}{6}} = \left(\frac{1}{2} + \frac{1}{3}\right) \times \frac{6}{1}.$$

By the distributive law:

$$\left(\frac{1}{2}+\frac{1}{3}\right) \times 6 = \left(\frac{1}{2}\right)(6)+\left(\frac{1}{3}\right)(6)$$
$$= \frac{6}{2}+\frac{6}{3}$$
$$= 3+2$$
$$= 5.$$

14. **(K)** $g(-7) = (-7)^2 + 5(-7) - 3$
$$= 49 - 35 - 3$$
$$= 11$$

15. **(A)** $f(-2x) = -(-2x)^3 - 2(-2x)^2 + 4(-2x) - 8$
$$= -(-8x^3) - 2(4x^2) - 8x - 8$$
$$= 8x^3 - 8x^2 - 8x - 8$$

16. **(H)**   Start with the inner set of parentheses and work outwards.

Find $h(8)$:

$$h(8) = \frac{8}{2} = 4$$

Substitute 4 for $h(8)$:

$$f(g(h(8))) = f(g(4))$$

Find $g(4)$:

$$g(4) = 4 - 2 = 2$$

Substitute 2 for $g(4)$:

$$f(g(4)) = f(2)$$

Find $f(2)$:

$$f(2) = 2^3 = 8$$

Thus, $f(g(h(8))) = f(2) = 8$.

17. **(B)**   Use synthetic division:

$$
\begin{array}{r}
2x - 6 \\
x + 1 \overline{\big)\; 2x^2 - 4x + 5} \\
-\;\;\underline{(2x^2 + 2x)} \\
-6x + 5 \\
\underline{-(-6x - 6)} \\
11
\end{array}
$$

The remainder is 11.

18. **(J)**
$$f\left(-\frac{1}{2}\right) = 1 + 3\left(-\frac{1}{2}\right) - 2k\left(-\frac{1}{2}\right)^2 = 0,$$

$$1 - \frac{3}{2} - 2k\left(\frac{1}{4}\right) = 0$$

$$\frac{2}{2} - \frac{3}{2} - \frac{k}{2} = 0$$

$$-\frac{1}{2} - \frac{k}{2} = 0$$

$$\frac{k}{2} = -\frac{1}{2}$$

$$k = -1 \qquad \text{(multiplied both sides by 2)}$$

19. **(A)** Using the law for the logarithm of a quotient $\left(\log\frac{a}{b} = \log a - \log b\right)$, we find $\log(40x - 1) - \log(x - 1) = \log\frac{40x - 1}{x - 1} = 3$. Since no base is written, it is understood that we are using $\log_{10}$. Hence, $\log_{10}\frac{40x - 1}{x - 1} = 3$. By the definition of a logarithm, if $\log_b N = x$, then $b^x = N$.

Therefore, $\log_{10}\frac{40x - 1}{x - 1} = 3$ means $10^3 = \frac{40x - 1}{x - 1}$. Thus $1000 = \frac{40x - 1}{x - 1}$. Multiply both sides by $(x - 1)$:

$$(x - 1)1000 = (x - 1)\left(\frac{40x - 1}{x - 1}\right)$$

$$(x - 1)1000 = 40x - 1.$$

Distributing, $1000x - 1000 = 40x - 1$. Subtract $40x$ from both sides to obtain:

$$960x - 1000 = -1.$$

Add 1000 to both sides to obtain:

$$960x = 999.$$

Divide both sides by 960:

$$x = \frac{999}{960} = \frac{333}{320}.$$

20. **(F)**
$$\frac{5}{9}a = 1$$

$$a = \frac{9}{5}$$

$$\frac{5}{9} + \frac{9}{5} = \frac{25 + 81}{45} = \frac{106}{45}$$

21. **(A)**

$$\frac{2}{x+5} = \frac{6}{x+3}$$

$2(x+3) = 6(x+5)$ (cross multiplied)

$2x+6 = 6x+30$

$4x = -24$

$x = -6$

22. **(K)** According to the rule given and solving within the parentheses first:

$(a \Delta b) \Delta ((a \Delta a) \Delta b)$

$(a - b) \Delta (0 \Delta b)$

$(a - b) \Delta (-b)$

$(a - b) + b = a - b + b = a.$

23. **(D)** Use y as the common denominator.

$$\frac{x + \dfrac{1}{y}}{x - \dfrac{1}{y}} = \frac{\dfrac{y(x)}{y} + \dfrac{1}{y}}{\dfrac{y(x)}{y} - \dfrac{1}{y}} = \frac{\dfrac{yx+1}{y}}{\dfrac{yx-1}{y}}$$

Dividing by a fraction is the same as multiplying by its reciprocal:

$$\frac{\dfrac{yx+1}{y}}{\dfrac{yx-1}{y}} = \left(\frac{yx+1}{\cancel{y}}\right)\left(\frac{\cancel{y}}{yx-1}\right) = \frac{yx+1}{yx-1}$$

24. **(H)** Change these fractions to fractions with a common denominator, then add fractions by adding numerators and placing them over the common denominator. Neither of the denominators is factorable; therefore, the LCD is the product of the denominators. $LCD = (x - 3)(x + 2)$. To change $\dfrac{2}{x-3}$ to an equivalent fraction with $(x - 3)(x + 2)$ as its denominator, multiply by the unit fraction $\dfrac{(x+2)}{(x+2)}$. To change $\dfrac{5}{x+2}$ to an equivalent fraction with the LCD as its denominator, multiply by $\dfrac{x-3}{x-3}$. Then add the resulting fractions as follows:

$$\frac{2}{x-3}+\frac{5}{x+2}=\frac{2(x+2)}{(x-3)(x+2)}+\frac{5(x-3)}{(x-3)(x+2)}$$

$$=\frac{2(x+2)+5(x-3)}{(x-3)(x+2)}$$

$$=\frac{2x+4+5x-15}{(x-3)(x+2)}$$

$$=\frac{7x-11}{(x-3)(x+2)}$$

The numerator is not factorable; so the result cannot be reduced.

25. **(E)**   Since $x^{-a}=\dfrac{1}{x^{a}},\ \ y^{-1}=\dfrac{1}{y^{1}}=\dfrac{1}{y},$

$$\left(x+y^{-1}\right)^{-1}=\left(x+\frac{1}{y}\right)^{-1}$$

$$=\frac{1}{x+\dfrac{1}{y}}$$

Multiply numerator and denominator by y in order to eliminate the fraction in the denominator,

$$\frac{y(1)}{y\left(x+\dfrac{1}{y}\right)}=\frac{y}{yx+\dfrac{y}{y}}=\frac{y}{yx+1}.$$

Thus $\left(x+y^{-1}\right)^{-1}=\dfrac{y}{yx+1}.$

26. **(G)** $(0.0081)=(.3)^{4}$

Hence

$$(.0081)^{-\frac{3}{4}}=(.3^{4})^{-\frac{3}{4}}=(.3)^{-3}$$

$$=\frac{1}{.3^{3}}=\frac{1}{.027}=\frac{1}{\dfrac{27}{1000}}=\frac{1000}{27}.$$

27. **(C)** $27^{x^{2}+1}=243$ (given)

Rewriting 27 as 3^{3}, and 243 as 3^{5}, we obtain

$$\left(3^3\right)^{x^2+1} = 3^5$$

$$3^{3x^2+3} = 3^5$$

Equating exponents gives

$$3x^2 + 3 = 5$$

$$3x^2 = 2$$

$$x^2 = \frac{2}{3}$$

$$x = \pm\sqrt{\frac{2}{3}}.$$

Thus, one solution is $-\sqrt{\frac{2}{3}}$, which is answer (C).

28. **(H)**   Answer (H) is always greater than 1, by the following reasoning:

(a) n is any positive integer (except 1).

(n = 2, 3, 4, 5 ...)

(b) $(-n)$ will therefore be any negative integer (except -1).

(c) $(-n)^3$ must be negative, since a negative number raised to an odd power is negative.

(d) $-(n)^3$ will always be positive, since the negative of a negative number is positive. It will also be greater than 1, since n cannot equal 1, and also cannot be a fraction less than 1.

29. **(A)** $\dfrac{1}{2x} = \dfrac{1}{\dfrac{1}{y}}$

$$\frac{1}{2x} = y$$

For $x = 1$, $y = \dfrac{1}{2}$

for $x = 5$, $y = \dfrac{1}{10}$.

Therefore, $0.1 < y < 0.5$.

30. **(G)**   Since $\log_8 N = \dfrac{2}{3},\quad N = 8^{\frac{2}{3}}.$

$N = \sqrt[3]{8^2} = \sqrt[3]{64} = 4$

31. **(D)** $(125^{2x})(5^x) = (5^3)^{2x}(5^x)$
$$= (5^{6x})(5^x)$$
$$= 5^{6x+x} = 5^{7x}$$

32. **(H)** $2^{3x} = 64$
$$(2^3)^x = 64$$
$$(8)^x = 64$$
$$x = 2$$

33. **(D)** $\begin{cases} 3x + 4y = -6 \\ 5x + 6y = -8 \end{cases}$ (1)
                                                                    (2)

Subtract 2 times Equation (2) from 3 times Equation (1):

$$9x + 12y = -18$$
$$-(10x + 12y = -16)$$
$$-x = -2$$
$$x = 2$$

Substitute $x = 2$ into (1):

$$3(2) + 4y = -6$$
$$4y = -12$$
$$y = -3$$

Therefore the solution set is $\{(2,-3)\}$.

34. **(G)**   The general equation of a parabola with vertex at the origin and symmetrical about the y–axis is

$y = ax^2$.

Use the point $(1,2)$ to find a:

$$2 = a(1)^2$$
$$a = 2$$

865

Therefore the equation should be $y = 2x^2$.

35. **(A)**   distance $= \sqrt{(3-(-2))^2 + (4-1)^2}$

$= \sqrt{25+9}$

$= \sqrt{34}$

36. **(K)**   radius $= \sqrt{(1-0)^2 + (2-0)^2} = \sqrt{5}$

Therefore, the equation is $(x-1)^2 + (y-2)^2 = 5$.

37. **(D)** $\dfrac{y-4}{x-1} = \dfrac{4-2}{1-3}$

$\dfrac{y-4}{x-1} = -1$

$y - 4 = -x + 1$

$y = -x + 5$

Therefore, the y–intercept is 5.

38. **(J)**   We use the two–point form with $(x_1, y_1) = (3,5)$ and $(x_2, y_2) = (-1,2)$. Then

$\dfrac{y - y_1}{x - x_1} = m = \dfrac{y_2 - y_1}{x_2 - x_1}$

$\dfrac{y_2 - y_1}{x_2 - x_1} = \dfrac{2-5}{-1-3}$ thus $\dfrac{y-5}{x-3} = \dfrac{-3}{-4}$.

Cross multiply, $-4(y-5) = -3(x-3)$.

Distributing, $-4y + 20 = -3x + 9$

$3x - 4y = -11$.

39. **(A)**   (1)

(2) Multiply Equation (2) by 2, and subtract the resulting Equation from Equation (1).

$7x + 2y = 5$

$2x + y = -2$

$7x + 2y = 5$

$-\quad \underline{4x + 2y = -4}$

$3x \qquad = 9$

$x = 3$

Substitute $x = 3$ into (2):

$$2(3) + y = -2$$
$$6 + y = -2$$
$$y = -8$$

Thus, the coordinates are $(3, -8)$.

40. **(J)**   slope $= \dfrac{7-5}{3-(-3)}$

$= \dfrac{2}{6}$

$= \dfrac{1}{3}$

41.   **(D)**   In order to solve the inequality, we can first solve the equation

$-x^2 + 5x - 6 = 0,$

as shown below:

$$x = \frac{-(5) \pm \sqrt{(5)^2 - 4(-1)(-6)}}{-2}$$

so $x = \dfrac{-5-1}{-2} = 3$ or $\dfrac{-5+1}{-2} = 2$

The graph of the function $y = -x^2 + 5x - 6$ is

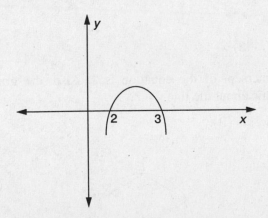

Since we need the values of x that will make the function become negative, the solution is represented below:

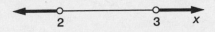

42. **(G)**   From the quantities that are given, the quickest way to solve the problem is to use the relation:

(1) $AD \times DC = DB^2$

DC is known. DB can be obtained by applying the Pythagorean Theorem to triangle DBC. Doing this:

$$DB^2 + DC^2 = BC^2$$

Rearranging: $DB^2 = BC^2 - DC^2$

Taking square roots: $DB = \sqrt{BC^2 - DC^2}$

Substituting for BC and DC: $DB = \sqrt{5^2 - 4^2}$
$$DB = \sqrt{25 - 16}$$
$$DB = \sqrt{9} = 3.$$

Equation (1) can now be used to find AD.

$$AD = \frac{DB^2}{DC}$$

Substituting for DB and DC:

$$AD = \frac{3^2}{4} = \frac{9}{4}$$

Side AC is the sum of $AD + DC$.

Adding: $AC = AD + DC = \dfrac{9}{4} + 4 = \dfrac{25}{4}$

43. **(B)**   Substitute $x = 0$ into the given equation to obtain the y–intercept:

$$x = |y - 2|$$
$$0 = |y - 2|$$
$$y = 2$$

Therefore, the y–intersept of the equation is 2. Also, the graph of the given equation is symmetric about the line $y = 2$.

Thus, the answer is (B).

44. **(K)**

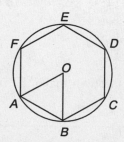

In order to find the area of the given circle, we need to know how large its radius is, so we can use the formula for the area of a circle, $A = \pi r^2$.

Recall that since ABCDEF is a regular hexagon, the measure of the central angle $AOB = \dfrac{360°}{6} = 60°$. Since $\overline{AO} \cong \overline{BO}$, $\angle OAB = \angle OBA$. The points O, A, and B describe a triangle and the sum of the interior angles of a triangle must add up to 180°,

$$180° = \angle AOB + \angle OAB + \angle OBA.$$

Substituting the fact that $\angle AOB = 60°$ and $\angle OAB = \angle OBA$, we obtain:

$$180° = 60° + 2\angle OAB \quad \text{or}$$
$$120° = 2\angle OAB \quad\quad \text{or}$$
$$60° = \angle OAB$$

So now we know that $\angle OAB = 60°$ and therefore $\angle OBA = 60°$. Therefore all three angles are 60°. So $\triangle AOB$ is equiangular and therefore equilateral. Since $\overline{AB} = 7$, $\overline{AO} = 7$, but this is the radius of the given circle.

Recall that $A = \pi r^2$. Substituting $r = 7$, we obtain $A = 49\pi$.

45. **(B)** Since B is the midpoint of AD, $AB = BD$. Thus, we can replace BD in Equation (1) with AB.

$$CD = BD - BC$$
$$CD = AB - BC$$
$$CD = 4\frac{1}{2} - 2\frac{1}{4}$$
$$CD = 2\frac{1}{4}.$$

46. **(K)** $\angle ACD = \angle ADC$ $\quad$ ($\triangle ADC$ is isosceles)

$$\angle ACD = \frac{180° - 20°}{2} = 80°$$
$$\angle ACD = \angle CAB + \angle CBA$$
$$\angle ACD = 2\angle CAB \quad\quad \text{(Since } \triangle CAB \text{ is isosceles)}$$
$$\angle CAB = \frac{80°}{2}$$
$$\angle CAB = 40°$$

$$\theta° + \angle DAC + \angle CAB = 180° \quad \text{sum of angles on a straight line}$$
$$\theta° + 20° + 40° = 180°$$
$$\theta° = 120°$$

47. **(B)** $\angle ACB = \angle ABC = 45°$ because $AB = AC$ (isosceles triangle)

$$\angle CAB = 180° - \angle ABC - \angle ACB$$
$$= 180° - 90°$$
$$= 90°$$

Therefore, $\triangle ABC$ is a right triangle. Use the Pythagorean theorem:

$$BC = \sqrt{AB^2 + AC^2}$$
$$= \sqrt{3^2 + 3^2}$$
$$= 3\sqrt{2}$$

48. **(K)**   The given figure is a right triangle. Therefore,

$$3^2 + 4^2 = (k+6)^2$$
$$9 + 16 = (k+6)^2$$

Taking the square root of both sides gives

$$\sqrt{9+16} = k+6$$
$$\sqrt{25} = k+6$$
$$5 = k+6$$

Solving for k:

$$k = 5 - 6$$
$$k = -1$$

(Although k is negative, the length of the hypoteneuse is positive, as it must be $k + 6 = -1 + 6 = 5$.) The answer is $k = -1$.

49. **(E)**   Since the hypoteneuse of the triangle is the diameter of the circle, $\triangle PQR$ must be a right triangle.

$$(Diameter)^2 = (PR)^2 + (RQ)^2$$
$$= 3^2 + 4^2 = 9 + 16 = 25$$
$$\Rightarrow \quad Diameter = \sqrt{25} = 5$$
$$Radius = \frac{5}{2}$$
$$Area\ of\ circle = \pi\left(\frac{5}{2}\right)^2 = \frac{25}{4}\pi$$

50. **(F)** The best way to solve this problem is by means of a figure describing the situation.

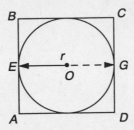

Let *ABCD* be the square which circumscribes the circle centered at point *O*. Let *r* be the radius of the circle. Therefore 2*r* is the diameter of the circle. The diameter is any line segment which intersects the center and has endpoints on the circle. We can simply choose $\overline{EG}$ to be the diameter of the circle. $\overline{EG}$ is parallel to $\overline{BC}$.

Note that $\overline{AB}$ is tangent to the circle at point *E*. Likewise $\overline{CD}$ is tangent at *G*. Therefore $BC = EG = 2r$.

The perimeter of $ABCD = 4s = 4\overline{BC} = 4(2r) = 8r$, since *ABCD* is a square.

Therefore, the ratio of the radius of the circle to the perimeter of the square is

$$\text{ratio} = \frac{r}{8r} = \frac{1}{8}.$$

51. **(D)** $\angle ABC = 90°$ (Since a diameter subtends $\angle ABC$)

$AC = 2r$ (Since *AC* is a diameter)

$$\sin 30° = \frac{BC}{AC}$$

$$BC = AC \sin 30°$$

$$BC = 2r\left(\frac{1}{2}\right)$$

$$BC = r$$

52. **(J)**   Since $\triangle ACD$ is equilateral, it is also equiangular. Therefore each angle is equal to 60°.

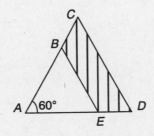

Area $\triangle ACD = \dfrac{1}{2}(AC)^2 \times \sin 60°$ (used base $= AC$, and height $= AC \sin 60°$)

$$= \dfrac{1}{2}(10)^2 \times \sin 60°$$

$$= \dfrac{100}{2} \times \dfrac{\sqrt{3}}{2}$$

$$= 25\sqrt{3}$$

Area $\triangle ABE = \dfrac{1}{2}(AB)^2 \times \sin 60°$ (used base $= AB$, and height $= AB \sin 60°$)

$$= \dfrac{1}{2}(8)^2 \times \sin 60°$$

$$= \dfrac{64}{2} \times \dfrac{\sqrt{3}}{2}$$

$$= 16\sqrt{3}$$

Area $BCDE$ = Area $\triangle ACD$ – Area $\triangle ABE$

$$= 25\sqrt{3} - 16\sqrt{3} = 9\sqrt{3}$$

53. **(E)** $AB = AC$, since $\triangle ACB$ is an isosceles triangle.

Area of $\triangle ACB = \dfrac{1}{2}(AB)(AC)$

$$= \dfrac{1}{2}(5)(5)$$

$$= \dfrac{25}{2}$$

Since $\triangle ACB$ is an isosceles right triangle,

$$\angle ABC = \angle ACB = 45°$$

Therefore, $\angle DCE = \angle DEC = 45°$

so that $\triangle DCE$ is an isosceles triangle.

So $DE = DC$.

Area of $\triangle DCE = \dfrac{1}{2}(DE)(DC)$

$$= \dfrac{1}{2}(3)(3)$$

$$= \dfrac{9}{2}$$

Area of *ABED*   = Area of $\triangle ABC - \triangle DCE$

$$= \frac{25}{2} - \frac{9}{2}$$

$$= \frac{16}{2}$$

54. **(K)**   Area of shaded region $= \frac{60°}{360°}\pi OB^2 - \frac{60°}{360°}\pi OA^2$

$$= \frac{\pi}{6}((7+2)^2 - 7^2)$$

$$= \frac{\pi}{6}(81-49) = \frac{16\pi}{3}$$

55. **(C)** $\frac{2\pi}{120°} = \frac{2\pi r}{360°}$

$r = 3$

Area $= \pi r^2 = 9\pi$.

56. **(F)**   Since $BC \parallel DE$, $\triangle ABC \sim \triangle ADE$

ratio of areas $=$ (ratio of sides)^2

$$= \left(\frac{1}{3}\right)^2$$

$$= \frac{1}{9}$$

57. **(D)** $\triangle ACB$ is isosceles because $AC = CD = BC$. Then

$\angle BCA = 180° - 70° = 110°$

The sum of the 2 remaining angles in $\triangle ACB$ is $180° - 110° = 70°$.

$$\angle ABC = \frac{1}{2}(70°) = 35°$$

$$\theta = 110° + 35° = 145°.$$

58. **(G)**
$$\cos A = \frac{AB}{AC} = \frac{12}{13}$$
$$BC = \sqrt{AC^2 - AB^2}$$
$$= \sqrt{13^2 - 12^2}$$
$$= \sqrt{25}$$
$$= 5$$

59. **(D)** Use the formula for the sine of the sum and difference of two angles.

$$\sin(A + B) = \sin A \cos B + \cos A \sin B \qquad (1)$$

$$\sin(A - B) = \sin A \cos B - \cos A \sin B \qquad (2)$$

Add Equation (1) to Equation (2) to get

$$\sin(A + B) + \sin(A - B) = 2 \sin A \cos B$$

Substitute $A = 45°$ and $B = x$

$$\sin(45° + x) + \sin(45° - x) = 2 \sin 45° \cos x$$
$$= \frac{2\sqrt{2}}{2} \cos x \qquad \left(\text{since } \sin 45° = \frac{\sqrt{2}}{2} \right)$$
$$= \sqrt{2} \cos x$$

60. **(J)** We need $2 \sin \dfrac{5\pi}{6} + \cos x = 0$. $\qquad (1)$

Substitute $\sin \dfrac{5\pi}{6} = \dfrac{1}{2}$ into Equation (1) to obtain

$$2\left(\frac{1}{2} \right) + \cos x = 0$$
$$1 + \cos x = 0$$
$$\cos x = 1$$
$$x = \pi$$

Test 3: Reading

1. **(D)** By perusing the opening paragraph of the reading passage, the reader finds that all are correct: since only (D) includes I, II, III, and IV, (D) is the correct answer. (A), (B), and (C) do not include all the correct answers; these answers should not be chosen.

2. **(J)** In the next paragraph, the author states (F), (G), and (H) rather than denying them. Since he would agree with—and not deny—each of these items, only (J) remains to be the correct answer by process of elimination.

3. **(B)** (B) is the best answer since the author believes that the philosopher does not confirm our beliefs and loyalties; in fact, he believes that they take great pleasure in causing surprise as is evidenced by the second sentence of the passage. The author would disagree that philosophers are valuable as indicated by his sarcastic tone in the first paragraph; (A) should not be chosen. Neither respect nor other occupations is mentioned; without validation from the passage, (C) becomes an incorrect answer. The author does not always agree with philosophers as his arguments in the last two paragraphs prove; therefore, (D) should not be selected.

4. **(F)** The author states that which consists of parts is divisible into parts; (F) is the best answer. The author believes that which is distinguishable is not always separable as demonstrated by his "grain of sand" explanation; (G) should not be chosen. Those things which one imagines are not always separable; (H) should not be chosen. Disciples of philosophy are likely to follow the doctrine of infinite divisibility; (J) states that they are least likely to follow it. (J) should not be selected.

5. **(C)** The author compares ideas of the imagination with impressions of the senses in the ink spot illustration; (C) is the best choice. The author does not contrast, but compares, ideas of the imagination with impressions of the senses; (A) should not be selected. The author sees a similarity, not a contrast, between disciples and their followers; (B) should not be chosen. The author discusses the spot of ink and says that just before it disappears from sight, the spot was "...perfectly indivisible," not divisible; (D) is not the best answer.

6. **(H)** (H) is the best answer since the reason the spot disappears is that the parts are removed beyond the distance at which their impressions are reduced to a minimum. (G) should not be selected since it says just the opposite. (F) is not the best answer; as the author states, the spot of ink does not disappear because of a want of light rays striking on our eyes. (J) should not be selected; the reason the object disappears is not because the parts are removed beyond that distance at which light rays strike their impression.

7. **(C)**   II, III, and IV are all correct; (C) is the best choice since it allows the reader to select all three answers. (A) is incorrect because the telescope does not produce new rays of light. (B) and (D) do not include all of the correct answers and should not be selected.

8. **(H)**   *Both* refers to the microscope and the telescope; therefore (H) is the best answer. *Both* does not refer to the rays of light (F), or the rays of light and the new ray of light (J); so these answers are both incorrect. *Both* is not used as a conjunction; therefore, (G) should not be selected.

9. **(D)**   All the answers (I, II, and III) are part of philosophers' beliefs; since only (D) includes all these parts, it is the correct choice. (A), (B), and (C) should not be selected since each is missing one of the parts of philosophers' beliefs.

10. **(H)**   All the answers (I, II, and III) are part of why philosophy is widely accepted; hence (H) is the best answer. Each of the other choices excludes one or more parts of the complete answer as stated in the first paragraph of the reading passage; consequently (F), (G), and (J) cannot be correct.

11. **(D)**   Answer D concisely summarizes how management practices have had to change in order to take into consideration laws, agency rules, and court decisions. Answer (A) is incorrect. As the author explains, courts often struck laws designed to eradicate unhealthy and unfair practices. Answer (B) fails to take into account major changes, especially after the Supreme Court changed its interpretation of the Constitution. Answer (C) has missed the point of the author, who pointed out that profit motives often led to harsh working conditions for children and women.

12. **(J)**   Answer (J) certainly reflects how management, which did not want interference from government, was most delighted with Supreme Court decisions that struck laws. Answer (F) has misinterpreted the author's intent as he provides information about the history and philosophy that lay behind court decisions. Answer (G) has confused the role of the court in the early 1900s and the fact that its decisions, which protected contracts, actually failed to protect women and children. Although there is room for improvement, answer (H) did not take into consideration how poor working conditions in earlier years would depress workers much more than present-day work environments.

13. **(D)**   Answer (D) is correct. The author has apparently chosen a topic that shows how profit motives can lead to poor personnel practices. Answer (A) is a narrow assessment of the author's values because morality is not confined to persons of the cloth. Answer (B) is wrong. One of the great freedoms in America

is the ability to observe and express freely opinions about the way government operated over the years. Critics are not necessarily socialites or socialists. Answer (C) offers the reader an opportunity to make a personal judgment on fairness. Actually, the author finds no problems when dissenting opinions are adopted by later courts in an effort to protect workers from poor working conditions.

14. **(J)** Answer (J) correctly identifies how women were under repressive working conditions. While some mothers may have been happy to get away from children and/or happy to agree to work long hours in unsanitary and unsafe conditions, most women were most likely miserable under the early policies of the private sector. Answers (F) and (G) therefore, are incorrect. Answer (H) is incorrect since it is reasonable to assume that women, caught in the lowest positions without power under court decisions and laws to change their poor conditions, offered no competition to the men in higher positions.

15. **(D)** Answer (D) discusses the 1923 case described in the passages. It should be recalled that the court justified its decision to strike the minimum wage law by stating: "adult women ... are legally as capable of contracting for themselves as men." Answer (A) incorrectly reports early court decisions that struck laws governing wages of workers. Answer (B) is only partially true. However, enough male legislators voted approval of laws protecting female workers to discount the conclusion that all males were insensitive to needs of female employees. Answer (C) is wrong. The author offered no evidence that presidents played an active role in influencing private sector owners to increase wages through such agencies as an industrial board.

16. **(G)** Answer (G) is correct. After the young man married, Dagenhart expressed regret about the Supreme Court decision that "protected" him as a child laborer from governmental regulations. Answer (F), as the author shows, is incorrect in that Supreme Court decisions on laws governing working conditions were not unanimous opinions. Answer (H) may have correctly described the Supreme Court judges as being conscientious men, but most of the judges' dedication was aimed at protecting free enterprise, not the workers. Answer (J) expresses a wrong opinion. Press exposure of Dagenhart's negative remarks about how his health suffered made both industry and the court appear callous.

17. **(A)** Answer (A) reaches the correct conclusion about how disagreement among judges on the high bench indicated that the persuasive abilities of the minority judges were ineffective during those years. Answer (B) has incorrectly assessed the role of legislative leaders required to secure passage of controversial laws in years when industrial and business elite were economically and politically powerful. Answer (C) has erroneously concluded, without evidence in the paragraphs above, that blue collar workers exercised political power at the polls. In Answer (D), the dates are incorrect.

18. **(G)**   Answer (G) is correct. Although President Roosevelt was powerless when the Supreme Court made void several new laws, he persisted. Under other presidents, Congress had earlier passed laws to protect the safety and health of children. It is the proper conclusion that Roosevelt's record showed that he was indeed more social welfare oriented while in the Oval Office than earlier presidents. Answer (F) tries to figure out the author's preferences. His analysis of the judicial process does not indicate that he favored the judicial over the executive. Answer (H) is wrong. The pre-1950 laws initiated tremendous change in governmental regulation of management practices previously left to the private sector. Answer (J) deals with chronology. Reviewing the text above, the reader will find that the judicial branch resisted change wanted by both Congress and the President.

19. **(B)**   Answer (B) correctly assumes that such benefits as higher wages and fewer working hours would increase expenditures of manufacturing and business. Answer (A) requires review of how federal legislation attempted to change management/labor relations and improve the lot of the workers. Executive-sponsored bills described by the author were challenged in courts of law by business and industry. Answer (C) does not consider how new justices' legal philosophy would radically increase the amount of government regulation, much to the detriment of freedom to make decisions in the private sector. Answer (D) is wrong. Check the paragraphs again, and note that the author correctly gave no credit to Roosevelt for aggressive leadership in civil rights. There is no such act.

20. **(G)**   Answer (G) correctly concludes that although Congress had tried in earlier years to make great differences in labor policies, it was not until the Supreme Court interpretation changed during Roosevelt's term of office that new labor laws were rapidly passed and enforced. Answer (F) is wrong. The author does not imply that the term New Deal originated from such bizarre circumstances. Answer (H) is wrong. The Great Depression dealt with the economic situation; the author did not suggest any other definition. Rather, he writes of economic problems. Answer (J) has misinterpreted the author's analysis. Since the welfare state seeks to assure minimum standards for all people, both workers and their representatives agreed that labor conditions and wages should be improved.

21. **(B)**   Choice (B) is the correct answer. Mrs. Mallard's reaction was an immediate sadness from the news she had received. There is no evidence in the story that Mrs. Mallard was hypocritical; thus choice (A) is incorrect. Nor did she have the time to "calculate" a deception; so choice (D) is incorrect. Choice (C) is incorrect for the simple reason that if she had not comprehended the news, she would not have been crying; she would have taken the news with "the paralyzed inability to accept its significance."

22. **(H)**   Paragraph five uses symbols to indicate rebirth—new spring life, trees reviving from the winter, sparrows twittering, etc.; so choice (H) is correct

and, for these same reasons, choice (J) is wrong. The experience is far from sorrowful; it is uplifting and so choice (F) is incorrect. Choice (G) is wrong because an experience such as the one Louise had is far from trivial.

23. **(B)**   Choice (B) is correct because the text states "she was striving to beat it back with her will." However, it does not go so far as to say that she believed that it was monstrous; choice (C) is incorrect. There is no indication that anything that Mrs. Mallard went through was premeditated; therefore choice (A) is incorrect. Additionally, there is no basis in the text to show that she was ashamed of anything she went through; choice (D) is incorrect.

24. **(G)**   Choice (G) is the only choice that was NOT demonstrated in the text as one of Mr. Mallard's qualities and therefore should be chosen as the correct answer. Choices (F) and (J) are mentioned in (lines 57–58); choice (H) is demonstrated in (lines 66–68).

25. **(B)**   Mrs. Mallard's criticism is directed at marriage in general as shown through the general language she uses. "Men and women" and "fellow-creature" demonstrate that she is not speaking specifically; this makes choice (B) correct and choices (A) and (C) incorrect. Mrs. Mallard does not make mention of society anywhere in her thoughts; choice (D) is also incorrect.

26. **(G)**   Choice (G) is correct because she thinks things like, "what did it matter" and "what could love…count for." The author does not address the other choices at all with the intent of having the reader being caught up with Mrs. Mallard and her newfound freedom. Choices (F), (H), and (J) are incorrect because they are somewhat irrelevant.

27. **(D)**   Choice (D) is correct because it acknowledges the fact that Mrs. Mallard's discovery that the need for "self-assertion" was the "strongest impulse of her being" outweighs all the other options. Whether she loved Brently, whether she can live comfortably without him, and whether people understand her are secondary issues which make choices (A), (B), and (C) incorrect.

28. **(F)**   The author never implies that Mrs. Mallard's death is justified; therefore choice (F) is the correct answer because it is the LEAST accurate. Choice (G) is accurate because, had Mrs. Mallard not gone through her revelation, seeing Brently would not have been so traumatic. Choices (H) and (J) are also accurate as they demonstrate the irony to be found in the passage's ending.

29. **(C)**   The passage is one with a surprise ending—one which is just the opposite of that which the reader expected. The passage is ironic; (C) is the best answer. This story of death is not one which could be described as humorous; (A)

should not be chosen. The story is not an exaggeration, or hyperbole; (B) is not the best choice. Since there is no word play at the end of the story, although there is an opposition in the two possible causes of death, choice (D) is also incorrect.

30. **(H)**   The clause "...she was drinking in the very elixir of life..." refers to the emotion that Louise was experiencing when she realized her husband was dead; choice (H) is the best answer. Since there is no mention of Louise drinking anything in the passage, neither (E), (F), nor (G) can be the correct answer.

31. **(C)**   In the middle of the reading passage, the author states that characteristics of the groups of species include the fact that they constitute distinct genera (I), differ from each other more than do the species of the same genus (II), and follow from the struggle for life (III). The correct answer is (C); it includes I, II, and III. The other items [(A), (B), and (D)] do not include all the correct answers and should not be chosen.

32. **(H)**   In the third sentence of the passage, the author states, "It is immaterial for us whether a multitude of doubtful forms be called species or sub-species or varieties..."; hence (H) is the best answer. The author is not adamant about the importance of distinguishing among species, sub-species, and varieties; (F) should not be selected. The author has not attempted to define species, sub-species, and varieties; (G) is not the best choice. The author does not clearly outline the distinction among species, sub-species, and varieties; (J) is not an appropriate choice.

33. **(A)**   The best answer is (A), since the author states in the second paragraph that distinct genera follow from the struggle for life. Since the author believes that the struggle for existence is relative to, rather than separate from, natural selection, (B) should not be selected. It was not the author, but Herbert Spencer who coined the term *natural selection*; (C) is not a good choice. The struggle for existence is important to natural selection—and vice versa as the author suggests in the middle of the reading passage; (D) should not be chosen.

34. **(J)**   As the reading passage shows, all the answers given are a result of the struggle for life and are all true. (J) should be chosen since it allows the reader to choose all the choices. The other choices [(F), (G) and (H)] do not allow the reader to choose all four choices.

35. **(A)**   The author states that offspring having variations may have a better chance of surviving; (A) is the best choice. The author does not believe that offspring having variations will survive in large numbers; he, in fact, states that "...of the many individuals of any species which are periodically born, but a small number can survive." (B) is not a good choice. The author thinks that

"...slight variation, if useful, is preserved..."; since (C) states the opposite, it should not be selected. The author thinks the variation is preserved by natural selection, which affects the struggle for life; (D) should not be selected.

36. **(F)** The best answer is (F); the author states that the principle by which slight variation, if useful, is preserved is called "natural selection." Herbert Spencer—not the author—uses the term "Survival of the Fittest;" (G) should not be selected. The author describes the term "Survival of the Fittest" as accurate—not inaccurate; (H) should not be chosen. The author calls the phrase "Survival of the Fittest" convenient, rather than inconvenient; (J) should not be selected.

37. **(C)** Near the end of the reading passage, the author refers to control of nature as "power of selection"; this sentence indicates that statement IV is false because IV refers to natural selection. The sentence following the previous reference proves that statements I, II, and III are true. Since (C) includes statements I, II, and II, but not IV, it is the correct answer. (A) and (B) are not possible answers since they each lack one or more of the three correct statements. (D) is an incorrect answer since it includes statement IV which is false.

38. **(J)** (J) is the best analogy; as stated in the closing sentences of the passage, natural selection is as superior to the efforts of human beings as Nature is to Art. Since natural selection is at ALL times ready for action, (F) should not be chosen since it states that natural selection is "at times," meaning sometimes, ready for action. Natural selection is superior—not inferior—to the powers of humans; (G) should not be chosen. The author believes that Nature is superior to Art—not the reverse; (H) is incorrect and should not be selected.

39. **(A)** The best answer is (A); there is individual variability among organic things, as the author states in the opening sentences of the passage. It is NOT easy to keep in mind the truth of the universal struggle for existence as stated in the last sentence of the passage; (B) should not be selected. The author thinks it is easy to admit the struggle for existence; since (C) says the reverse, it should not be selected. The struggle for existence is a part of the whole economy of nature; since (D) states otherwise, (D) is false and should not be chosen.

40. **(F)** The author seeks to define the struggle for existence and stress its importance; (F) is the best choice. The author is not seeking mainly to describe Herbert Spencer's "Survival of the Fittest" and to stress its importance, although he does mention the term; (G) should be chosen. Both (H) and (J) are incorrect answers since it is not evolution, but selection, which is the focus of the reading passage.

Test 4: Science Reasoning

1. **(B)** Limestone is not a very porous soil; according to the hypothesis, water should not have passed easily through the soil. However, water did pass through the soil by producing holes in the soil, in Experiment 2. (B) is the correct answer.

2. **(F)** Since water passed through the sand quickly, sand (F) is the most permeable of the three soil samples.

3. **(C)** Experiments 1 and 3 prove the hypothesis. However, the limestone in Experiment 2 should not have had the water pass through so quickly. This experiment causes the hypothesis to be only somewhat proven; (C) is the correct answer.

4. **(J)** Since the process was observed for only one hour, an assumption cannot be made (J). The experiment would need to be observed for a longer period of time in order to make an assumption.

5. **(D)** Since the limestone is considered almost nonporous, but the water passed through it, an assumption of permeability for limestone can be made. This indicates that a soil can be permeable, yet not porous (D).

6. **(H)** Since the clay (H) did not allow water to pass through to the bottom of the jar, it is the least permeable and would therefore make the best fish pond.

7. **(A)** The answer is (A) Phoenix because although the relative humidity is the highest in Orlando, the absolute humidity is the highest in Phoenix. Relative humidity is the percentage of water vapor present for a given temperature and pressure. So, Orlando has a very high percentage of water vapor relative to the temperature. But, Phoenix has a much higher temperature and the atmosphere can hold more water vapor. The density of water vapor (absolute humidity), or the exact quantity of water vapor per volume, is highest in Phoenix.

8. **(H)** The correct answer is (H) because Nome and Orlando have the highest relative humidity; thus poor evaporation would take place. Evaporation would be at a minimum because the atmosphere is already holding a great deal of moisture (for those temperatures) and is virtually unable to evaporate and hold any more water vapor.

9. **(C)** The correct answer is (C) because using Figure 1, the temperature for Denver and Cortez can be found, 90 and 86 degrees. Then, using the

relative humidity data from Table 3, the Humiture Index can be found using Table 2. The temperature would feel cooler in Denver because it is drier than in Cortez, even though the actual temperature is higher in Denver.

10. **(J)**   The temperature has a strong influence on the absolute and relative humidity. The answer is (J). The relative humidity is a measurement of how much water vapor the atmosphere can hold at a certain temperature. The absolute humidity is a measurement of water vapor per volume in the air. The amount of water vapor per volume will be determined by the temperature. Higher temperatures can hold more water vapor.

11. **(A)**   The answer is (A). The absolute humidity would remain constant, because even though the temperature was higher, the amount of water vapor remained constant. This seems to contradict question 4 in the previous passage, but just because the temperature *can* hold more water vapor, it does not mean it *will*. The relative humidity would go down because the temperature had increased; the atmosphere can hold more moisture, so the relative humidity is not as high as it was.

12. **(J)**   The answer is (J) because a cool beach in autumn and an office building would not have too much moisture. A blizzard, although very wet and having a high relative humidity, contains very little water vapor due to the cold temperatures. Remember, the relative humidity does not measure the amount of water vapor; it only measures the percentage of moisture present at a certain temperature.

13. **(B)**   If you look carefully at the data and hold distance to be constant, you can see that as mass increases, tension does also; therefore answer (B) is correct. The statements in (A) and (D) are false, while from (C) it is clear that if distance is constant, then roughness will be also.

14. **(J)**   According to the table, tension increases with the roughness factor; therefore, (J) is the correct answer. Choices (F), (G), and (H) are false.

15. **(C)**   The correct answer is (C). As long as the angle of the slope remains the same, the magnitude of the force of kinetic friction will equal the tension at constant speed. Tension would only depend on the mass of the crate and the roughness factor, not the distance.

16. **(G)**   Answer choices (H) and (J) are incorrect; so the choice comes down to (F) and (G). The reason (G) is correct: the length of the rope does not matter; only the angle does.

17. **(A)** Choices (B), (C), and (D) are all incorrect. According to the data of the experiment, only (A) is a correct answer.

18. **(J)** In generations 1-3, there are only affected males. The absence of phenotypically affected females suggests an x-linked gene that is recessive. A recessive gene on an x-chromosome will produce affected males whenever it appears in a male, because there is no second x-chromosome to provide a dominant gene. (J) is therefore correct. It will produce affected females only when the recessive trait appears also in the female's second x-chromosome. The mating of an affected female with an affected male results in both males and females with the disease. (F) and (H) are false because if the gene were dominant, the trait would be visible in at least one parent of any affected progeny. The pattern of affected males suggests that (G) is false: An autosomal recessive gene will not produce affected progeny, male or female, unless the recessive gene from each parent is present.

19. **(C)** For a recessive autosomal gene, the maximal probability that the disease would be present would be the product of the gene frequencies in the parents (0.5×0.5) or 25 percent; (C) is the correct answer. (The gene frequency in each parent is 0.5, or 1/2, when the parent has the gene on only one chromosome.) This means that one in four progeny may be affected, not 4 percent; so (B) is incorrect. (D) is incorrect because the frequency in the general population is not relevant. (A) is incorrect because 50 percent is the percent of the progeny who will carry the gene, but be unaffected.

20. **(H)** Answer choice (H) is correct. The gene frequency is 0.05, or 1/20. The gene is an autosomal recessive gene. The probability that both parents would both have the gene is 1/400. 25% of their children would have the disease, which is 1/1600 of the general population, or 0.06%. Answer choice (F) is incorrect: Although the affected children die in infancy, the disease is still counted. (G) and (J) are also incorrect.

21. **(B)** For autosomal dominant genes, heterozygous individuals have one chromosome with the trait and one without, and they demonstrate the phenotype. 25% of the progeny (D) would be homozygous for the trait and 50% (C) would be heterozygous. But all 75% [correct answer (B)] would demonstrate the phenotype. Choice (A) is incorrect: the remaining 25% of the progeny lack the gene for the disease.

22. **(G)** The genes are inherited independently. The genes are recessive; so the progeny must be homozygous for each particular trait in order to demonstrate it. 25% (1/4) of the kittens will be homozygous for color paint and 25% (1/4) will be homozygous for long hair. The probability that any one kitten will be homozy-

gous for both traits is the product of the probabilities for both traits, or 6.25% (1/16). (G) is the correct choice. (F) is incorrect: It is the percent of kittens likely to show either one of the traits, not both. (H) and (J) are incorrect.

23. **(B)** Based on Table 1, (A) is incorrect; the color of a pyrocatechol/potato juice solution is yellow after 5 min. at a temperature of 25°C. A faint yellow color would occur at 0°C. (B) is correct, because according to the passage, after 5 min. a pyrocatechol/potato juice solution turned yellow. According to Table 1, a yellow color after 5 min. occurred at 25°C. Choice (C) is incorrect, because at T = 100°C, the pyrocatechol/potato juice solution would be colorless after 5 min., according to Table 1. (D) is incorrect, because a temperature range is not indicated by the given data, rather only specific temperatures.

24. **(F)** The correct answer is (F); Table 1 (Experiment 1) reveals that after 5 min. the pyrocatechol/potato juice solution would be light (faint) yellow at 0°C. Experiment 2 shows that a potato juice/pyrocatechol solution of pH = 7 is faint yellow. Choice (G) is incorrect. While it is true that a potato/pyrocatechol solution is faint yellow at pH = 7, according to Table 1, the solution would be faint yellow after 5 min. at a temperature of 0°C rather than at 25°C. Choice (H) is incorrect because according to Table 1 a solution at 100°C would be colorless, as would a solution at pH = 10, according to Experiment 2. (J) is incorrect because based on Experiment 2, the higher the pH becomes, the lighter the solution becomes, until it is colorless at a pH = 10.

25. **(C)** The question asks which factor could alter the data; temperature above 100°C would reveal colorless solutions, as was shown in Experiment 1. (A) is, therefore, incorrect. (B) is also incorrect. Even though the experiments showed that color changes with time, after 30 min., the solutions had already undergone their most significant color change. Choice (C) is the best answer, because none of the experiments varied the concentration of pyrocatechol. This could affect solution color when potato juice is added. Choice (D) is incorrect, because the results of Experiment II revealed solutions of pH = 10 remained colorless; and there is no data to indicate the color of the solution will change.

26. **(G)** Choice (F) is incorrect, because the same concentrations of pyrocatechol were used in each tube in Experiment 3. Choice (G) is the correct answer. Experiment 2 indicates that the temperature affects the color of the pyrocatechol/potato juice solutions. If the temperature in Experiment 3 were allowed to vary, the results could be influenced. The accuracy of the experiment would be enhanced if the temperature at which it was conducted were known. Choice (H) is incorrect, because only one potato juice mixture was used and it must be assumed the concentration was constant. (J) is incorrect, because there is no experimental results to indicate that pH affects color when phenylthiourea is added to the pyrocatechol/potato juice solutions. This would represent a separate experiment.

27. **(D)** Choice (A) is incorrect. Pyrocatechol solutions were used in the experiments. Unless otherwise indicated, the term solution generally means an aqueous one; pyrocatechol must therefore be soluble in and mix with water. (B) is also incorrect, since based on Experiment 2, the pH values of the solutions were adjusted. The pH of pyrocatechol is likely closer to 10. (C) is false, because if potato juice was initially yellow in color, the experimental results could be flawed. (D) is the correct choice, because the experiment in the passage indicated that all of the solutions were colorless initially.

28. **(H)** Answer (F) may be eliminated because this combination of phenylthiourea and potato juice shows a color change of faint yellow to yellow based on Table 2. (G) is incorrect, since this combination indicates a change of yellow to bright yellow. (H) is correct. The combination of 1 drop of phenylthiourea and 5 drops of potato juice shows a dramatic color change of faint yellow to bright yellow. Choice (J) is incorrect, because this combination results in a color change from faint yellow to yellow.

29. **(B)** Environmentalist 2 does not deny that trees are a renewable resource, but he points out that when a forest is cut, there are consequences (soil erosion and habitat loss) that occur before the forest can be renewed. Choice (A), although correct, does not *directly* answer the claim of Environmentalist 1. Since (A) is wrong and (B) is correct, both (C) and (D) must be wrong.

30. **(H)** Choice (H) is best because Environmentalist 1 says that paper bags are readily recycled, and Environmentalist 2 says that plastic can be re-used for countless products. Choice (J) is therefore incorrect.

31. **(D)** Answer (D) is the best choice. Answer (A) is true: Environmentalist 1 worries about wildlife eating partially-degraded plastic; Environmentalist 2 worries about habitat loss. Answer (B) is true: Environmentalist 1 says paper easily degrades; Environmentalist 2 says the newer plastics sometimes degrade even faster than paper. Answer (C) is true: Environmentalist 1 says production of paper bags is cleaner; Environmentalist 2 says production of plastic bags is cleaner. Therefore, answer (D) is the best.

32. **(G)** Environmentalist 2 claims that very little petroleum is used in the production of plastic bags, in contrast to the thousands of acres of trees used to produce paper bags; answer (G) is true. Choice (F) is incorrect: Environmentalist 2 does not discuss how much pollution is created to convert the petroleum by-products into plastic bags. Since (F) is incorrect and (G) is correct, both (C) and (D) are incorrect choices.

33. **(D)** Answer choice (A) is true: Environmentalist 1 says that degrading plastic bags are harmful to wildlife when eaten. (B) is true: Environmentalist 2 says that cutting down forests for paper destroys wildlife habitats. Therefore, (D) is the correct answer. (C) is incorrect: neither environmentalist suggests canvas bags.

34. **(J)** Answer (J) is the best choice. (F) is true: Environmentalist 1 claims that paper degrades easily, thus reducing volume in the landfills. (G) is also true: Environmentalist 2 claims that some plastics degrade faster than paper and are readily incorporated into the soil. Choice (H) is wrong: neither environmentalist advocates incineration.

35. **(B)** Petroleum by-products are not produced without use of additional energy, and Environmentalist 2 does not try to claim so. Choice (A) is true: Environmentalist 2 says that since plastic bags are stronger, fewer are needed to carry more. (C) is true: he says newer plastics degrade faster than paper. (D) is also true: he says that plastic has numerous recycling options. So (B) is the only false statement.

36. **(H)** Point 4 has the greatest vertical distance from the zero reference line. This vertical distance represents the magnitude of the radial velocity along the radial velocity axis. The positive and negative signs indicate direction of travel. Therefore, at point 4 the orbiting star is moving the fastest, and answer (H) is correct.

37. **(D)** The passage states that an object's speed of approach is assigned a negative value. It can be seen in Figure 2 that point 4 is the only position below the zero reference line; therefore, at that point, the star is approaching the observer (D).

38. **(G)** The passage states the radial velocity is an object's speed of recession or approach. At point B and D in Figure 1, the orbiting body is moving across the line of sight and therefore has no radial velocity. (G) is the correct choice.

39. **(A)** The passage states that receding objects exhibit a red Doppler shift. At position C in Figure 1, the star's orbit is away from the observer; therefore, (A) is the correct answer.

40. **(J)** You must combine information from both figures and the table to answer this question. Figure 2 shows that point 5 indicates a radial velocity of zero. Figure 1 indicates a radial velocity of zero at only two positions, B and D. According to Table 1, position D in Figure 1 corresponds to point 3 in Figure 2; so the next instance of zero radial velocity has to be at position B. (J) is the correct choice.

ACT
ASSESSMENT
with
REA's Interactive TEST*ware*®

PRACTICE
EXAM IV

Exam IV is also provided in our special interactive ACT TEST*ware*®. It is highly recommended that you first take this exam on computer. You will then have the additional study features and benefits of enforced timed conditions, individual diagnostic analysis, and instant scoring. See page 4 for guidance on how to get the most out of our ACT book and software.

ACT ASSESSMENT PRACTICE EXAM IV

(An answer sheet for this test appears in the back of this book.)

Test 1: English

TIME: 45 Minutes
75 Questions

DIRECTIONS: This test consists of five passages. In each passage, certain words and phrases have been underlined and numbered. The questions on each passage consist of alternatives for these underlined segments. Choose the alternative that follows standard written English, most accurately reflects the style and tone of the passage, or best relays the idea of the passage. Choose "NO CHANGE," if no change is necessary.

In addition, you will also encounter questions about part of the passage, or the passage as a whole. These questions are indicated by a number in a box at the end of the section, rather than an underlined portion.

Once you have selected the best answer, fill in the appropriate oval on the answer sheet for the correct choice.

Passage I

[1]

Modern technology has enabled scientists to learn a great deal about the human brain. Using the most modern equipment, <u>discoveries have been made of</u>
<u>1</u>
important information about how we learn, how the brain affects the way we feel, <u>memory, and the aging of the brain.</u> Of course, much of the brain is still a
<u>2</u>
mystery, but scientists have made some amazing discoveries about this organ.

Contrary to popular opinion, intelligence is determined not by the size of the brain, but by the number and complexity of dendrites it contains.

[2]

These dendrites form connections with nerve <u>cells; thus</u> enabling the brain
                                     3
to receive and use information. Researchers estimate that the human brain functions at only a fraction of <u>its</u> potential. Scientists have not been able to under-
                           4
stand why we use so little of our brain <u>capacity, nor</u> have they found ways of
                           5
tapping into the brain's unused potential. Having lost a portion of the brain through injury or illness, some people are still able to function quite effectively.

[3]

 6 (1) <u>Acting as a producer of chemicals,</u> the brain produces and secretes
                         7
chemicals which affect intelligence, mood, and memory. (2) Scientists have been able to isolate and reproduce many of these substances. 8 (3) Many mental illnesses are now at least partially treatable with drugs; still, quite a few brain disorders <u>are still</u> beyond the grasp of researchers.
          9

[4]

Because brain function deteriorates with <u>age. Some people believe</u> that
                                       10
<u>a persons</u> ability to learn also declines with age. However, older people who
  11
engage in intellectual activity or regularly pursue a "learning" activity, according to recent studies, actually show little or no loss of learning ability. Therefore, to keep the brain functioning for a <u>lifetime; a person</u> should continue to learn new
                                     12
things and be involved in stimulating activities. It is useful to think of the brain as a muscle; if one does not exercise the brain by engaging in intellectual

activity, we will atrophy, and learning ability will decrease. Yet, if the brain is
13

kept in shape, it continued to function quite effectively. ⬚15⬚
14

1. A. NO CHANGE

    B. discoveries of a sort has been made of

    C. researchers have discovered

    D. researchers discovering

2. F. NO CHANGE

    G. how memory works, and how the brain ages.

    H. memory, and brain aging.

    J. memory, and the aging brain.

3. A. NO CHANGE   C. cells, and thus they

    B. cells; and thus   D. cells, thus

4. F. NO CHANGE   H. it's

    G. its'   J. their

5. A. NO CHANGE   C. capacity, nor

    B. capacity; nor   D. capacity neither

6. Which of the following sentences makes the best introduction to Paragraph 3 and the best transition from Paragraph 2?

    F. Strokes and high fevers are major causes of brain cell loss.

    G. Scientists are developing synthesized brain chemicals for various purposes.

    H. The brain's potential is also affected by the chemicals it emits and those created by health scientists.

    J. Even though able to function with brain injury or impairment, these individuals often have difficulty learning new concepts.

7. A. NO CHANGE

    B. Producing chemicals, the

    C. As a chemical producer, the

    D. OMIT underlined passage.

8. Which of the following sentences provides the best transition between Sentence 2 and Sentence 3?

    F. But between these dendrites are gaps called synapses.

    G. Developed by skilled pharmacologists, then, these substances are used to medicate patients.

    H. However, the cost of this research has been astronomical.

    J. Unfortunately, mental illness seems to be escalating, or perhaps it is simply being identified more frequently.

9. A. NO CHANGE   C. remain

    B. still is   D. remaining

10. F. NO CHANGE

    G. age some people believe

    H. age; yet some people believe

    J. age, some people believe

11. A. NO CHANGE   C. a individual's

    B. a person's   D. an individuals'

12. F. NO CHANGE   H. lifetime; we

    G. lifetime; one   J. lifetime, one

13. A. NO CHANGE   C. activity it

    B. activity, they   D. activity, it

14. F. NO CHANGE

    G. , and it continued

    H. ; it would have continued

    J. , it will continue

15. In relating the brain function to muscle exercise, the writer is

    A. demonstrating the differences of the two so the reader will not be misled.

    B. arguing that one process is superior to the other so the reader can make a choice.

C.   proving that one process is much like the other and that both yield similar effects.

D.   revealing that the first process causes the second process to occur.

Passage II

[1]

Dr. Robert H. Goddard, at one time a physics professor at Clark <u>University</u>
<u>in Worcester, Massachusetts was</u> largely responsible for the sudden interest in
                     16
rockets in the 1920s. When Dr. Goddard first started his experiments with
<u>rockets, there were no related technical information available</u>. From a virtually
                                        17
unexplored territory, he developed a <u>new science, industry and field of engineering</u>.
                                                    18
Through his scientific experiments, he pointed the way to the development of

rockets as we know them today. From his experiments, he wrote a brief essay titled

<u>"A Method of Reaching Extreme Altitudes" in which,</u> he outlined a space rocket on
                                    19
the step (multi-stage) principle, theoretically capable of reaching the moon.

[2]

Goddard <u>discovers that</u> with a properly shaped, smooth, tapered nozzle he
                  20
could increase the ejection velocity eight times with the same amount of <u>fuel he</u>
                                                                                    21
<u>would use</u> for a less aerodynamic shape. This would not only drive the rocket eight
     21
times faster but 64 times farther, according to his theory. Early in his experiments,

he found that solid-fueled rockets would give him neither the high power nor the

duration of <u>power. Which he needed</u> for a dependable supersonic motor capable of
                      22
extreme altitudes. On March 16, 1926, Dr. Goddard successfully fired a liquid-

fueled rocket into the air for the first time in history. It attained an altitude of 184

feet and a speed of 60 mph. <u>Seemingly weak when compared</u> to present-day speeds
                                          23

and heights of missile flights, <u>but, instead of trying to achieve speed or altitude at</u>
<u>this time, Dr. Goddard sought to develop a dependable rocket motor.</u>
24

[3]

25 Dr. Goddard later was the first to fire a rocket that reached a speed faster than the speed of sound. He was the first to develop a gyroscopic steering apparatus for rockets. And <u>they were</u> the first to patent the idea of a step rocket.
26
After proving on paper and in actual tests that a rocket can travel in a <u>vacuum; he</u>
27
developed the mathematical theory of rocket propulsion and flight, including designs for long-range rockets. Not until <u>close to nearing the final end</u> of World
28
War II in 1945 did we start intense work on rocket-powered missiles, using <u>Dr. Goddard and the American Rocket Societys</u> experiments and developments.
29

16. F. NO CHANGE

    G. University, in Worcester Massachusetts was

    H. University in Worcester, Massachusetts, was

    J. University in Worcester Massachusetts, was

17. A. NO CHANGE

    B. rockets, no related technical information was available.

    C. rockets; there were no related technical information available.

    D. rockets, there weren't any related technical information available.

18. F. NO CHANGE

    G. new trajectory science, space industry, and engineering field.

    H. engineering field, field of trajectory science, and new space industry.

    J. new space industry, field of engineering, and science of rocket trajectory.

19. A. NO CHANGE

    B. <u>A Method of Reaching Extreme Altitudes</u> in which,

C. A Method of Reaching Extreme Altitudes, in which

D. "A Method of Reaching Extreme Altitudes," in which

20. F. NO CHANGE   H. will discover that

    G. discovered, that   J. discovered that

21. A. NO CHANGE   C. fuel; he would have used

    B. fuel. He would of used   D. fuel he use

22. F. NO CHANGE   H. power; which was necessary

    G. power needed   J. power; that he needed

23. A. NO CHANGE

    B. Comparatively weaker when compared

    C. Weak when compared

    D. This seems weak when compared

24. F. NO CHANGE

    G. ; yet Dr. Goddard at this time was seeking to find rocket motor dependability rather than speed and altitude.

    H. ; however, at this moment, rather than trying to achieve speed or altitude, trying to develop a dependable rocket motor was more important to Dr. Goddard at this time.

    J. ; since a dependable rocket motor rather than speed or altitude was the goal Dr. Goddard sought to achieve at this time.

25. Which of the following sentences would provide the best transition from Paragraph 2 and the best introduction to Paragraph 3?

    A. In addition to being a scientist, Dr. Goddard was a respected author.

    B. Dr. Goddard was recognized by the public too late to enjoy his fame.

    C. Dr. Goddard's innovative experiments yielded him a series of "firsts."

    D. World War II finally offered Dr. Goddard a chance to prove his ideas.

26. F. NO CHANGE   H. we were

    G. they're   J. he was

27. A. NO CHANGE   C. vacuum when he

     B. vacuum, he   D. vacuum; since he

28. F. NO CHANGE   H. close to the end

     G. close to nearing the end   J. almost to the very end

29. A. NO CHANGE

     B. Dr. Goddards' and the American Rocket Societys

     C. Dr. Goddard's and the American Rocket Societies

     D. Dr. Goddard and the American Rocket Society's

Items 30 and 31 pose questions about Passage II as a whole.

---

30. If you were putting together a group of essays for high school seniors, it would be most appropriate to include this passage in a section containing essays on

     F. biological experiments of the early twentieth century.

     G. military strategy in the Roaring '20s.

     H. engineering for fun and profit.

     J. history of rocket development.

31. Which of the following sentences, if added to the end of Paragraph 3, would best relate Paragraph 3 to Paragraph 1 in order to tie together the passage as a whole?

     A. For 25 years, Dr. Goddard's experiments taught the world about rockets.

     B. Weapons escalation is a result of Dr. Goddard's experimentation.

     C. Missiles offer protection in times of war.

     D. Gyroscopic steering influenced the missiles of today.

Passage III

[1]

An ancient use for honey was in medicine as a dressing for wounds and inflammations. Today, medicinal uses of honey are largely confined to folk

medicine. <u>However, as milk can carry some diseases, honey, too, was suspected</u>
32

<u>to be a disease carrier.</u> Some years ago this idea was examined by adding nine
32

common pathogenic bacteria to honey. All the bacteria died within a few hours or

<u>days. Proving honey</u> is not a suitable medium for bacteria for two reasons.
33

<u>Its fairly acidic</u> and too high in sugar content for growth to occur. | 35 |
34

[2]

The presence of inhibine, the antibacterial activity in honey, was first reported about 1940 and confirmed in several laboratories. Since then, a variety of
papers have been published on this subject. Generally, most investigators agree
that inhibine is sensitive to heat and light. The effect of the inhibine content of
many honey types <u>were studied</u> in the past few years by several investigators.
36
Apparently, heating honey sufficiently to reduce markedly or to destroy its
inhibine activity <u>would deny him</u> a market as first-quality honey in several Euro-
37
pean countries. The use of <u>sucrase, and inhibine assays together</u> was proposed to
38
determine the heating history of commercial honey.

Until 1963, when White showed that the inhibine effect was attributable to
hydrogen peroxide produced and accumulated in diluted <u>honey; its'</u> identity re-
39
mained unknown. This material, well known for antiseptic properties, is a
byproduct of the formation of gluconic acid by an enzyme that occurs in honey,
glucose oxidase. The peroxide can inhibit the growth of certain bacteria in the
diluted honey. <u>Honey makes an ideal sweetener for today's baking.</u> Since perox-
40
ide is destroyed by other honey constituents, an equilibrium level of peroxides
<u>occurs</u> in diluted honey, its magnitude depending on many factors such as en-
41

zyme activity, oxygen availability, and amounts of peroxide-destroying materials in the honey.

[4]

A chemical assay method has been developed that rapidly measures peroxide accumulation in diluted honey by this procedure, different honey's have been
<u>42</u>   <u>43</u>
found to vary widely in the sensitivity of their inhibine to heat. In general, the sensitivity is about the same as or greater then that of invertase and diatase in
<u>44</u>
honey.

32. F. NO CHANGE

     G. On the other hand, some milk can be a carrier of some diseases, putting two and two together, some thought likewise of honey.

     H. Yet, since milk can carry disease, honey once, likewise, was thought to be a carrier.

     J. However, like milk, honey was once suspected to carry disease.

33. A. NO CHANGE

     B. days; yet proving honey

     C. days, proving honey

     D. days, and proving that honey

34. F. NO CHANGE   H. It's fairly acidic

     G. Its' fairly acid   J. Its quite acidic

35. Which of the following sentences would best unify and introduce Paragraph 1?

     A. Honey cannot harbor bacteria.

     B. Bacteria destroys honey's sugar and acid content.

     C. Honey is dangerous to our health.

     D. Honey has long been associated with our health.

36. F. NO CHANGE   H. was studied

    G. have been studied   J. are studied

37. A. NO CHANGE   C. would deny it

    B. will deny wc   D. would of denied it

38. F. NO CHANGE

    G. sucrase and inhibine assays together

    H. sucrase and inhibine assays, together

    J. sucrase, and inhibine assays, together

39. A. NO CHANGE   C. honey, since its identity

    B. honey. Its' identity   D. honey, its identity

40. F. NO CHANGE

    G. For today's baking, honey makes an ideal sweetener.

    H. Honey, an ideal sweetener, works well for today's baking.

    J. OMIT the underlined passage.

41. A. NO CHANGE   C. have occurred

    B. occur   D. are occurring

42. F. NO CHANGE

    G. honey, by this procedure,

    H. honey, by this procedure

    J. honey. By this procedure,

43. A. NO CHANGE   C. honeys have

    B. honeys' have   D. honey have

44. F. NO CHANGE   H. as greater then

    G. as great than   J. greater than

> **Items 45 and 46 pose questions about Passage III as a whole.**

45. Supposing the writer of this passage wanted to discuss the costs involved in manufacturing and packaging honey, in which of the following paragraphs should he/she most logically place the information?

   A. Paragraph 1, because all vital information must be introduced immediately

   B. In Paragraph 3's place, because the study of chemical composition is irrelevant

   C. A separate paragraph, as it would be the only one dealing solely with business finances

   D. Paragraph 4, because every essay must end in summary

46. Suppose the writer wanted to add the following sentences to the passage:

   > The killing of bacteria by high sugar content is called osmotic effect. It seems to function by literally drying out the bacteria, thus rendering the honey an unsatisfactory carrier of infection.

   The new sentences would most logically be placed in which of the following paragraphs?

   F. Paragraph 1, because that is where disease and sugar are discussed

   G. Paragraph 2, because that paragraph needs a human note to make it important

   H. A separate paragraph, because all important new material must be placed alone so it stands out

   J. Paragraph 4's place, because that paragraph is just more about chemicals and thus redundant

Passage IV

[1]

One of the most wonderful things about North America, our fascinating
                                                              47
continent is its diversity. And one of the most unusually extreme aspects of this
      47
diversity is found in South Dakota: the Badlands National Park located in a semi
                                                                  48

arid area, this wonder of nature goes through long periods of drought followed by storms raining cats and dogs. The result is erosion that continually shapes the
49
landscape. The rain-swollen rivers spread mud, sand, and gravel on the flatlands, which in turn are eroded to create the spectacular scenery we see in South Dakota.

[2]

The geological history of the Badlands' fascinating. Millions of years ago
50
on these plains, erosion took place much more slow than the deposits accumu-
51
lated. However, time has reversed the process.

[3]

Today, the buildup of these same deposits occur at a much slower rate than
52
the rate of erosion. The by-products of this wearing away are spires, pinnacles, and ridges that give the suggestion of castles in the clay. And today the heart of this picturesque site was the Badlands National Park.
53

[4]

(1) Like the ever-changing face of sand dunes along the seashore, since the
54
complexion of the Badlands doesn't stay the same. (2) One may find an ancient tool from an earlier stage of man, a tooth from a now-extinct animal. (3) Rain constantly eats away at surfaces, changing the shapes and reducing sizes. (4) Old layers of sediment deposits peel off to reveal new sights. (5) Fossils are among them. (6) For we scientists, it is thrilling to find saber-toothed cats, especially the
55
Hyaenodon. (7) This wolf-like creature was the size of a black bear. 56

Today the Badlands National Park protects the land, the <u>animals; and</u> the
57
fossils alike. This protection can help to restore partially what has been lost in the

past to early American settlers and <u>miners. Who</u> inhabited the area when the
58
country was younger. However the land has not always been protected. President

Franklin Roosevelt did erect a Badlands National <u>Monument, but</u> a national park
59
was not established until 1978. <u>As far as wild game is concerned, a resurgence in</u>
60
<u>the number of the species has taken place.</u> In 1963, for example, twenty-eight
60
bison were introduced into the area as well as twelve Rock Mountain bighorn

sheep. Since that time a wide variety of animals has flourished under the protec-

tion of the Badlands National Park.

47. A. NO CHANGE
    B. America—our fascinating continent,
    C. America our fascinating continent,
    D. America, our fascinating continent,

48. F. NO CHANGE
    G. Park, located
    H. Park. Located
    J. Park which is located

49. A. NO CHANGE
    B. raining cats and dogs.
    C. torrential rains.
    D. terrible dry spells.

50. F. NO CHANGE
    G. Badlands is
    H. Badlands
    J. Badland

51. A. NO CHANGE
    B. more slower than
    C. slowly than
    D. more slowly than

52. F. NO CHANGE
    G. deposit occurs
    H. deposits occurs
    J. deposit occur

53. A. NO CHANGE
    B. is
    C. were
    D. are

54. F.   NO CHANGE
    G.   seashore; since

    H.   seashore since
    J.   seashore,

55. A.   NO CHANGE
    B.   us scientists,

    C.   they, scientists
    D.   we as scientists,

56. For paragraph unity and logic, Sentence 2 should be placed

    F.   where it is now.
    G.   before Sentence 1.

    H.   after Sentence 3.
    J.   after Sentence 5.

57. A.   NO CHANGE
    B.   animals,

    C.   animals and,
    D.   animals, and

58. F.   NO CHANGE
    G.   miners who

    H.   miners whom
    J.   miners whose

59. A.   NO CHANGE
    B.   Monument but

    C.   Monument, however,
    D.   Monument, yet;

60. F.   NO CHANGE

    G.   However, there has been a resurgence in the number of species of wild game.

    H.   Nevertheless, the number of wild game species has resurged.

    J.   Nevertheless, wild game has resurged in the number of different game animals.

Item 61 poses a question about Passage IV as a whole.

---

61. Suppose the writer wished to add the following sentences to the passage:

    One such important find in the Badlands is the oredont, a pig-shaped mammal. Other fossils, such as those of early antelope, wolves, and sheep, indicate South Dakota was a main passageway for prehistoric mammal migration.

    The new sentences would be most logically placed in which of the following paragraphs?

A.   Paragraph 1, because all important information comes in the introduction

B.   Paragraph 2, because that paragraph needs more than just geological history

C.   In Paragraph 3's place, since it is simply description and therefore irrelevant

D.   Paragraph 4, because that is where fossil discovery is discussed

Passage V

[1]

Established firmly in popular culture is the notion that each of the two hemispheres of the brain <u>have</u> specialized functions. The left hemisphere, insist
<u>62</u>
proponents of this <u>theory, controls language, and</u> logic; espousers claim the right
<u>63</u>
hemisphere as the <u>most creative</u> and intuitive half. Many proponents try to clas-
<u>64</u>
sify a person as "right-brained" or "left-brained," suggesting that the two hemispheres do not work together in the same person <u>and; thus,</u> can be considered
<u>65</u>
independent. "Right-brained" individuals are the creative, intuitive persons (artists, for instance) of <u>society, "left-brained"</u> persons are the verbal, language-
<u>66</u>
oriented, logical individuals of civilization.

[2]

Opponents of the split-brain theory dispute the <u>premise. That</u> the hemi-
<u>67</u>
spheres operate independently simply because of the specialized functions. They state that the very fact that the two hemispheres differ in purpose <u>indicated</u> that
<u>68</u>
they must integrate activities. These split-brain theory opponents <u>base their argu-</u>
<u>69</u>
<u>ments on the fact</u> that when surgery is performed to disconnect the two sides,
<u>69</u>
each can still function <u>good (but not perfect).</u> They also argue that when a person
<u>70</u>

writes an original story, the left hemisphere works to produce a logical composition, but the right hemisphere helps with creativity. The third argument notes that if a patient has right hemisphere damage, major logical disorders are manifested <u>in their thinking;</u> in fact, more logical disorders appear in this instance than if the
71
left hemisphere suffers damage. The opponents to split-brain theory state <u>that its</u>
72
impossible to educate one side of the brain <u>than</u> educating the other. They state
73
that there is no evidence that one can be purely right-brained or left-brained.

62. F. NO CHANGE   H. hold

     G. retain   J. has

63. A. NO CHANGE

     B. theory controls language, and

     C. theory, controls language and

     D. theory controls language and

64. F. NO CHANGE   H. more creative

     G. greatest creative   J. most creatively

65. A. NO CHANGE   C. ; and, thus

     B. and, thus,   D. and, thus;

66. F. NO CHANGE   H. society's "left-brained"

     G. society; "left-brained"   J. society and "left-brained"

67. A. NO CHANGE   C. premises; requiring that

     B. premise. In that   D. premise that

68. F. NO CHANGE   H. indicates

     G. indicating   J. were indicative

69. A. NO CHANGE

     B. argue

C. formulate their arguments based on the fact

D. base his argument

70. F. NO CHANGE   H. well (but not perfect).

     G. good (but not perfectly).   J. well (but not perfectly).

71. A. NO CHANGE   C. in his/her thinking

     B. in our thinking   D. in it's thinking

72. F. NO CHANGE   H. thats'

     G. that it's   J. that its'

73. A. NO CHANGE   C. without

     B. then   D. rather

Items 74–75 pose questions about Passage V as a whole.

---

74. Which of the following sentences, if added at the end of Paragraph 2, would best relate Paragraph 2 to Paragraph 1 in order to tie together the passage as a whole?

F. Education must address both brain hemispheres.

G. The integrated-brain and split-brain theorists continue the debate on brain function.

H. The left hemisphere structures civilized society.

J. Surgery is a key means of discerning brain function.

75. If you were assembling essays for an anthology, you would include this passage most appropriately in a section entitled

A. How Our Bodies Function.

B. The Battle of the Sexes.

C. Our Cultural Heritage.

D. Techniques in Microsurgery.

THIS IS THE END OF TEST 1.

Test 2: Mathematics

TIME: 60 Minutes
60 Questions

DIRECTIONS: Solve the following problems, and fill in the appropriate ovals on your answer sheet.

Unless otherwise indicated:

1. Figures may not have been drawn to scale.

2. All geometric figures lie in a plane.

3. "Line" refers to a straight line.

4. "Average" refers to arithmetic mean.

---

1. If $\dfrac{2}{x-5} = \dfrac{3}{x+7}$, then $x =$

    A.   3.
          D.   15.

    B.   6.
          E.   29.

    C.   8.

2. If $xy - 3x = 20$ and $y - 3 = 5$, then $x =$

    F.   20.
          J.   4.

    G.   15.
          K.   3.

    H.   5.

3. If $x = 1$ and $y = -2$, then $3x^2y - 2xy^2 + 5xy =$

    A.   -36.
          D.   6.

    B.   -24.
          E.   12.

    C.   -1.

4. If there exist positive integers a and b such that $8a + 12b = c$, then c must be divisible by

    F.   3.
          J.   24.

    G.   4.
          K.   96.

    H.   18.

5. $\sqrt{8} + 3\sqrt{18} - 7\sqrt{2} =$

   A. $3 - 3\sqrt{2}$ D. $4\sqrt{2}$

   B. 0   E. $10\sqrt{2}$

   C. $6\sqrt{2} - 4\sqrt{3}$

6. If $xy - 2x = 16$ and $y + 4 = -2$, then $x =$

   F. -2.   J. 1.

   G. -1.   K. 2.

   H. 0.

7. If $ab - 3 = 7$ and $b - 2 = 3$, then $a =$

   A. -1.   D. 4.

   B. 2.   E. 5.

   C. 3.

8. Simplify the following expression: $1 - \dfrac{1}{2 - \dfrac{1}{3}}$.

   F. $\dfrac{2}{5}$ J. $\dfrac{4}{3}$

   G. $\dfrac{2}{3}$ K. $\dfrac{3}{2}$

   H. $\dfrac{1}{2}$

9. The sum of the digits of a two-digit number is 9. The number is equal to 9 times the units digit. Find the number.

   A. 36   D. 54

   B. 45   E. 72

   C. 63

10. The sum of four consecutive even integers is 68. What is the value of the smallest one?

F.   12

G.   14

H.   7

J.   18

K.   None of the above.

11. If $\frac{2}{3}x = 0$, then $\frac{2}{3} + x =$

A. $\frac{4}{9}$.

B. $\frac{2}{3}$.

C.   1.

D. $\frac{4}{3}$.

E.   2.

12. If $\dfrac{2}{\dfrac{y}{3}} = \dfrac{1}{4}$, then $y =$

F.   6.

G.   8.

H.   12.

J.   16.

K.   24.

13. If the sum of three consecutive odd numbers is 51, then the first odd number of the sequence is

A.   11.

B.   13.

C.   15.

D.   17.

E.   19.

14. If a is an even integer and b is an odd integer, which of the following must be an even integer?

I. ab

II. $2(a + b)$

III. $\dfrac{ab - 2}{2}$

F.   I only.

G.   II only.

H.   I and II.

J.   II and III.

K.   I, II, and III.

15. Simplify $\dfrac{\dfrac{2}{x} + \dfrac{3}{y}}{1 - \dfrac{1}{x}}$.

A. $\dfrac{1 + xy}{x - 1}$

D. $\dfrac{3y + 2x}{x(y - 1)}$

B. xy

E. $\dfrac{xy}{x - 1}$

C. $\dfrac{2y + 3x}{y(x - 1)}$

16. Find the minimum value of the function $f(x) = (x - 1)^2 + 3$.

F. 0

J. 3

G. 1

K. -2

H. 2

17. If $\dfrac{2}{3}y = 0$, then $\dfrac{4}{3} + y =$

A. 0.

D. $\dfrac{5}{3}$.

B. $\dfrac{3}{3}$.

E. $\dfrac{4}{3}$.

C. 2.

18. $\dfrac{3 + 4i}{2 + i}$ (where $i = \sqrt{-1}$) is the same as

F. $\dfrac{10}{3} + \dfrac{5}{3}i$.

J. $2 + i$.

G. $\dfrac{2}{3} + \dfrac{5}{3}i$.

K. $2 - i$.

H. $\dfrac{3}{2} + 2i$.

19. If $\dfrac{a}{b} = 3$, then $a^3 - 27b^3 =$

    A. −27.   D. 26.

    B. −26.   E. 27.

    C. 0.

20. If $f(x) = 3x + 2$ and $g(f(x)) = x$, then $g(x) =$

    F. $\dfrac{x-2}{3}$.   J. $3x - 2$.

    G. $\dfrac{x}{3} - 2$.   K. $4x + 9$.

    H. $3x$.

21. What is $2x^2 + 5x - 12$ divided by $x + 4$?

    A. $x^2 + 2x - 1$ D. $2x - 8$

    B. $2x^2 - 8x + 1$ E. $2x - 3$

    C. $2x + 3$

22. What is the value of b if $\log_b \dfrac{1}{25} = -2$?

    F. 2   J. 25^2

    G. $\pm\sqrt{2}$ K. 5

    H. 2^{25}

23. If $\log_2(x - 1) + \log_2(x + 1) = 3$, then $x =$

    A. −1.   D. 3.

    B. 1.   E. 4.

    C. 2.

24. If $i = \sqrt{-1}$ and $(a + bi)(1 - i) = 2 - 4i$ then $a =$

    F. 0.   J. 4.

    G. −1.   K. −4.

    H. 3.

25. If $f(x) = 7x - 8$ and $-5 \le x \le 8$, what is the range of $f(x)$?

    A. $-25 \le y \le 15$ D. $-15 \le y \le 20$

    B. $-43 \le y \le 0$ E. $-43 \le y \le 48$

    C. $-30 \le y \le 12$

26. What is the range of values for which $|6x - 5| \le 8$ is satisfied?

    F. $-\dfrac{1}{2} \le x \le \dfrac{1}{2}$ J. $-\dfrac{1}{2} \le x \le \dfrac{13}{6}$

    G. $0 \le x \le \dfrac{5}{6}$ K. $-\dfrac{1}{2} \le x \le \dfrac{1}{3}$

    H. $-1 \le x \le \dfrac{1}{2}$

27. The fourth term of $(1 - 2x^2)^9$ is

    A. $24x^3$.   D. $4x^6$.

    B. $-223x^5$.   E. $-672x^6$.

    C. $1249x^6$.

28. If $27^x = 9$ and $2^{x-y} = 64$ then $y =$

    F. -5.   J. $-\dfrac{11}{3}$.

    G. -3.   K. $-\dfrac{16}{3}$.

    H. $-\dfrac{2}{3}$.

29. The simplest expression for $\dfrac{a^2 - 3ab + 2b^2}{2b^2 + ab - a^2}$ is

    A. 1.   D. $a - b$.

    B. $a + b$.   E. $\dfrac{b - a}{b + a}$.

    C. $\dfrac{2a + b}{b - a}$.

30. If $abc \neq 0$, then $\dfrac{3a^2bc^3 + 9a^3b^2c}{27ab^2c + 15a^2b^2c^3} =$

    F. $\dfrac{ab(c^2 + 3)}{c(9 + 5a)}.$　　　　　　J. $\dfrac{c^2 + 3ab}{9 + 5ac^2}.$

    G. $\dfrac{a(c^2 + 3ab)}{b(9 + 5ac^2)}.$　　　　　K. $\dfrac{a}{b(9 + 5ac^2)}.$

    H. $\dfrac{a(c^2 + 3ab)}{c(9 + ac^2)}.$

31. $\dfrac{\sqrt[3]{-16}}{\sqrt[3]{-2}} =$

    A.   2.　　　　　　　　D. $\sqrt[3]{2}.$

    B.   −2.　　　　　　　E. $\sqrt[3]{-2}.$

    C.   an imaginary number.

32. The solution to the pair of equations

$$\begin{cases} ax + by = 8 \\ bx + ay = 10 \end{cases}$$

is $x = 2$, $y = 1$. Find a and b.

    F. $a = 3$　　　　　　G. $a = 3$
            $b = 4$　　　　　　　　　　$b = 3$

    H. $a = 2$　　　　　　J. $a = 2$
            $b = 3$　　　　　　　　　　$b = 4$

    K. $a = 4$
            $b = 4$

33. If $Y(t) = \dfrac{(t^2 + 3)}{(t^3 - 4)}$ and $x = t + 2$, what is the expression for $Y(t)$ in terms of x?

    A. $\dfrac{3x^2 + 4x + 8}{x^3 + 8x^2 + 3x + 5}$　　　　B. $\dfrac{x^2 + 8x + 14}{x^3 + 5x^2 + 12x + 8}$

C. $\dfrac{t^2 + 4t + 7}{t^3 + 6t^2 + 12t + 4}$ D. $\dfrac{x^2 - 4x + 7}{x^3 - 6x^2 + 12x - 12}$

E. $\dfrac{t^2 + 3}{t^3 - 4}$

34.

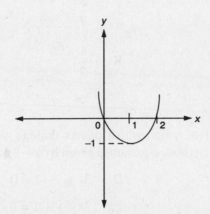

If the above figure represents the graph of a quadratic equation, what are the roots of the equation?

F.   −1 and 0   J.   0 and 2

G.   −1 and 2   K.   1 and 2

H.   −1 and 1

35. What is the equation of the line which has a slope equal to 2 and passes through the point (−1,1)?

A. $2x - y + 3 = 0$ D. $x - 2y + 1 = 0$

B. $2x - y + 1 = 0$ E. $x - y + 3 = 0$

C. $x - 2y + 3 = 0$

36. Find the distance between the points $A(4, 6)$ and $B(−1, 2)$.

F.   4   J. $\sqrt{41}$

G.   5   K. $\sqrt{53}$

H.   6

37. Find the coordinates of the midpoint of the points $A(3, 4)$ and $B(−3, 6)$.

A.   (−3, 5)   B.   (−3, 4)

C.   (0, 5)   D.   (0, 6)

E.   (0, 10)

38. If $f(x) = 7x - 4$ for all x, then the x-intercept of the line given by $y = f(x + 3)$ is

F. $-\dfrac{19}{7}$.   J. $\dfrac{3}{7}$.

G. $-\dfrac{17}{7}$.   K. $\dfrac{4}{7}$.

H.   0.

39. What is the equation of a line which passes through the point $(-1, 2)$ and perpendicular to a line whose equation is given by $x - 3y + 2 = 0$?

A. $x - 3y + 1 = 0$ D. $3x + y - 1 = 0$

B. $x - 3y = 0$ E. $3x + y + 1 = 0$

C. $3x + y - 2 = 0$

40. At how many points do the curve $y = x^3$ and the line $y = x$ intersect?

F.   1   J.   4

G.   2   K.   0

H.   3

41. Find the midpoint of the segment from $P(-2, 4)$ to $Q(4, -6)$?

A. $(-2, 6)$ D. $(1, 2)$

B. $(-1, 2)$ E. $(1, -1)$

C. $(-1, 3)$

42. A chord, 16 inches long, is 6 inches from the center of a circle as shown below. Find the length of the radius of the circle.

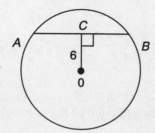

F.   10

G.   8

H.   6

J.   12

K.   Cannot be determined.

43. Which of the following represents the graph of the equation $y = |x - 2|$?

A.

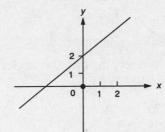

D.

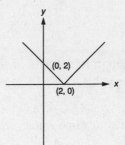

B.

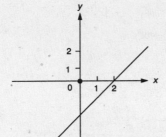

E.

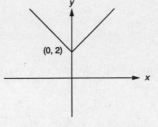

C.

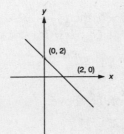

44.

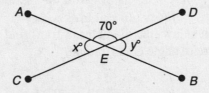

In the figure, two line segments $\overline{AB}$ and $\overline{CD}$ intersect at E, making the angles shown. What is the value $x + y$?

F.   140

G.   165

H.   180   J.   200

K.   220

45.

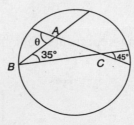

In the figure, three chords of the circle intersect making the angles shown.
What is the value of θ?

A.   35°   D.   75°

B.   45°   E.   80°

C.   60°

46.

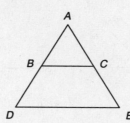

In the figure, if $BC \parallel DE$ and if $AE = a$ and $AC = b$, then $\dfrac{BC}{DE} =$

F. $\dfrac{b}{a}$.   J. $a - b$.

G. $1 - \dfrac{b}{a}$.   K.   None of the above.

H. $1 + \dfrac{b}{a}$.

47.   For the circle given below (the diameter is 10m) find the measure of arc AB
in meters if measure of angle C is 1 radian.

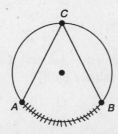

A. 10

B. 5

C. 20

D. 180

E. 105

48. A right triangle has legs of length 6 and 8 inches. $\overline{CD}$ bisects the right angle. Find the lengths of $\overline{AD}$ and $\overline{DB}$.

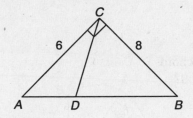

F. $\overline{AD} = \dfrac{21}{10}$, $\overline{DB} = \dfrac{79}{10}$

G. $\overline{AD} = \dfrac{25}{10}$, $\overline{DB} = \dfrac{45}{10}$

H. $\overline{AD} = 5$, $\overline{DB} = 5$

J. $\overline{AD} = 4$, $\overline{DB} = 6$

K. $\overline{AD} = \dfrac{30}{7}$, $\overline{DB} = \dfrac{40}{7}$

49. If A_T is the area of the triangle below and A_C is the area of the circle, then the ratio of $\dfrac{A_T}{A_C}$ is

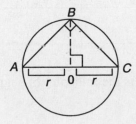

A. $\dfrac{\sqrt{3}}{2\pi}$.

B. $\dfrac{\sqrt{3}}{\pi}$.

C. $\dfrac{1}{\pi}$.

D. $\dfrac{\sqrt{2}}{2\pi}$.

E. $\dfrac{\sqrt{2}}{\pi}$.

50. If $\triangle ABC \sim \triangle A'B'C'$, $A'C' = kAC$ and area of $\triangle ABC = \frac{1}{2}ah$, what is the area of $\triangle A'B'C'$ in terms of k, a, and h?

F. $\dfrac{kah}{2}$ J. $\dfrac{k^2ah}{4}$

G. $\dfrac{k^2ah}{2}$ K. $\dfrac{ah}{2k^2}$

H. $\dfrac{ah}{2k}$

51.

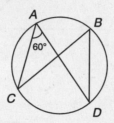

In the above figure, if $\angle CAD = 60°$, then $\angle CBD =$

A. 30°.   D. 120°.

B. 60°.   E. 135°.

C. 90°.

52.

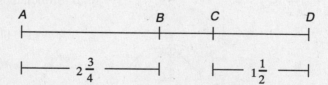

In the above figure, if B is the midpoint of segment AD, then the length of segment AC is

F. $3\dfrac{1}{2}$.   J. $4\dfrac{1}{4}$.

G. $3\dfrac{3}{4}$.   K. 5.

H. 4.

53.

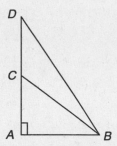

In the above figure, $\triangle ABC$ is a right isosceles triangle. If $AD = 7$ and $AB = 4$, what is the area of $\triangle DCB$?

A. 2   D. 8

B. 4   E. 10

C. 6

54.

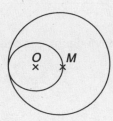

In the figure, if M and O are the centers of the larger and smaller circles respectively, then the ratio

$$\frac{\text{circumference of larger circle}}{\text{circumference of smaller circle}} =$$

F. $\dfrac{1}{4}$.   J. 4.

G. $\dfrac{1}{2}$.   K. 8.

H. 2.

55. In the figure, if $AC \| DF$ and if $DE = a$ and $EF = b$, then $\dfrac{AB}{AC} =$

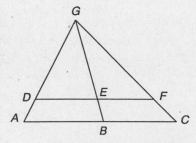

A. $\dfrac{a}{b}$.

D. $\dfrac{b}{a}$.

B. $\dfrac{a}{a+b}$.

E. $\dfrac{b}{a}-1$.

C. $\dfrac{a}{b}-1$.

56.

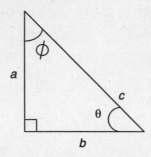

In the right triangle in the above figure, c is equal to which of the following?

I. $\sqrt{a^2+b^2}$

II. $\dfrac{b}{\cos\theta}$

III. $\dfrac{b}{\sin\phi}$

F.   I only.

J.   I and III.

G.   II only.

K.   I, II, and III.

H.   III only.

57. If $0 \le x \le \pi$, then the set of all x satisfying $\sin 2x - \sqrt{2}\,\sin x = 0$ is

A. $\left\{0, \dfrac{\pi}{4}, \pi\right\}$.

D. $\left\{\dfrac{\pi}{2}, \dfrac{\pi}{4}\right\}$.

B. $\{0\}$.

E. $\{0, \pi\}$.

C. $\left\{0, \dfrac{\pi}{2}\right\}$.

58. In the right triangle in the figure below, tanθ is equal to which of the following?

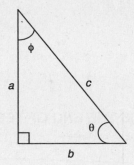

I. $\dfrac{\sin\theta}{\cos\theta}$

II. $\dfrac{\cos\phi}{\sin\phi}$

III. $\dfrac{a}{b}$

F. I only.

G. II only.

H. III only.

J. I and II only.

K. I, II, and III.

59. Express cos(arctan x) without trigonometric functions.

A. $\sqrt{1+x^2}$

B. $\dfrac{1}{\sqrt{1+x^2}}$

C. $\dfrac{1}{x}$

D. $\dfrac{x}{\sqrt{1-x^2}}$

E. $\dfrac{1}{\sqrt{1-x^2}}$

60.

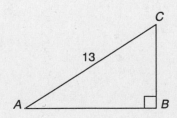

In right triangle ABC in the figure on the previous page, if $\cos C = \dfrac{5}{13}$ and $AC = 13$, then the length of BC is

F.   5.

G.   7.

H.   9.

J.   12.

K.   13.

THIS IS THE END OF TEST 2. .

Test 3: Reading

TIME: 35 Minutes
40 Questions

DIRECTIONS: This test consists of four passages, each followed by ten questions. Once you have read a passage, answer each question, and fill in the appropriate oval on your answer sheet.

Passage I

Whatever may be thought of the evidence bearing upon the question of the former gaseous condition of our world, it is generally admitted that the evidence of former igneous fluidity is somewhat conclusive. Our earth was once a self-luminous star.

5   At the temperature which would fuse the mass of the rocks, all the more volatile substances could only exist in the form of an elastic vapor surrounding the earth. All the carbon in the world must have existed in the form of carbonic acid; all the water as an invisible elastic vapor, extending out beyond the limits of the

10   present atmosphere. There could hence be upon the earth no vegetation, no animals, no salt, no water. All that we now behold must have been represented by a glowing, liquid nucleus, enveloped in a dense atmosphere of burning acrid vapors. This orb must have revolved upon its axis and performed its revolutions around the

15   sun. The sun and moon (if the latter existed) must have raised the fiery ocean to a tidal wave which rolled around the globe. An ocean of fire sent up to the nocturnal heavens a glare that was more fearful than the poisoned ray of feebly-shining sun. Here was chaos. Here was the death and silence of the primeval ages, when

20   the Uncreated alone looked on, and saw order, and beauty, and life germinating in the heart of universal discord.

     In obedience to the law of thermal equilibrium, the high temperature of the earth gradually subsided through radiation into external space. A crystallization of the least fusible elements

25   and simple compounds eventually took place in the superficial portions of the molten mass. This process continued till a crystalline crust had been formed, resting upon the liquid mass which still constituted the chief bulk of the globe.

     It has sometimes been objected to this view that the solidi-

30   fied materials would possess superior density, and would, accordingly, sink into the liquid portions. If this were so, the solidification of such a molten mass would either commence at the center, or a uniform refrigeration would proceed till the whole

35 world would suddenly be consolidated. It is the general belief that the central portions of the earth still remain in a molten condition, while the habitable exterior is but a comparatively thin crust. If this belief is well founded, the first solidified portions did not descend toward the centre. Moreover, we know that, in the case of water and several other substances, the newly-solidi-

40 fied parts are less dense, and float upon the liquid portions. This apparent exception to the law of expansion by heat is accounted for by supposing that, when the molecules of a solidifying fluid arrange themselves in a regular crystalline manner, they inclose certain minute spaces, so that the resulting crystal is a little more

45 bulky than the unarranged molecules from which it was constructed. If this law applies to the refrigeration of water, iron, and other substances, we may reasonably infer it to be a general law of matter. We should expect, then, that crystals of quartz would float upon molten quartz, just as solid iron floats upon molten

50 iron. We have, therefore, not only evidences of the fact of a forming crust, but also a probable means of accounting for it.

From Alexander Winchell, *Sketches of Creation.*

1. The author believes

   I. that solidified materials in the earth's formation would possess superior density and would sink into the liquid portions.

   II. that the solidification of the earth would begin at the center.

   III. that a uniform refrigeration proceeded until the whole world was consolidated.

   IV. that the earth's crust is thin and its center is molten.

   A. I only.   C. I, II, and III.

   B. I and II.   D. IV only.

2. The existence of an igneous fluid condition of the earth, according to this passage, is

   F. probably a myth.

   G. probably an actuality.

   H. not relevant to this reading passage.

   J. inconclusive, with little supporting evidence.

3. The author's opinion as to whether there existed a former gaseous condition of the earth is

   A. inconclusive.   C. negative.

   B. favorable.   D. an essential part of this passage.

4. During the time the earth was a self-luminous star

    F. the moon did not exist.

    G. there was no carbonic acid.

    H. there was a liquid core surrounded by burning acrid vapors.

    J. it did not emit a glow as bright as that of our sun.

5. The author's purpose is

    A. to present his view of the gaseous condition of the world and the following period of igneous fluidity.

    B. to describe a view of the earth from its stage of igneous fluidity until the stage when solidification of the crust began.

    C. to describe a view of the formation of the earth and the expansion of heat.

    D. to describe the law of thermal equilibrium.

6. The author admits some skepticism about

    F. the crystallization of materials to form the earth's crust.

    G. the existence of a sun at the time the igneous fluid condition existed.

    H. whether chaos existed before the earth was formed.

    J. whether solid iron will float upon molten iron.

7. Crystallization occurred first

    I.   among the least fusible elements.
    II. among simple compounds.
    III. in superficial portions of molten mass.
    IV. near the core.

    A. I only.   C. II, III, and IV.

    B. II only.   D. I, II, and III.

8. The author thinks that when newly-solidified parts are less dense than the unsolidified parts,

    F. this is an apparent exception to the law of expansion by heat.

    G. they will descend toward the center.

    H. this action will begin at the center.

    J. the action will continue until the whole is consolidated.

9. The author infers

   A. that less-dense, newly-formed crystals are less bulky than unarranged molecules.

   B. that crystals of quartz would float on molten quartz as solid iron floats on molten iron.

   C. that newly-formed crystals are more dense than the unarranged molecules because they inclose certain minute spaces.

   D. that newly-formed crystals are not likely related to the formation of the earth's crust.

10. The author would deny

   F. the igneous fluidity of the earth.

   G. that our earth was a self-luminous star.

   H. that the moon could have raised the fiery ocean to a tidal wave.

   J. that there is no probable means of accounting for the formation of the crust.

Passage II

My master added that he was daily pressed by the Houyhnhnms of the neighborhood, to have the assembly's exhortation executed, which he could not put off much longer. He doubted it would be impossible for me to swim to another country; and therefore wished I would contrive some sort of a vehicle,

5 resembling those I had described to him, that might carry me on the sea; in which work I should have the assistance of his own servants, as well as those of his neighbors. He concluded, that for his own part, he could have been content to keep me in his service as long as I lived; because he found I had cured myself of some

10 bad habits and dispositions, by endeavoring, as far as my inferior nature was capable, to imitate the Houyhnhnms.

I should here observe to the reader, that a decree of the general assembly in this country is expressed by the word *hnhloayn*, which signifies an exhortation, as near as I can render it:

15 for they have no conception how a rational creature can be compelled, but only advised, or exhorted; because no person can disobey reason, without giving up his claim to be a rational creature.

I was struck with the utmost grief and despair at my master's discourse; and being unable to support the agonies I

20 was under, I fell into a swoon at his feet. When I came to myself he told me that he concluded I had been dead; for these people

are subject to no such imbecilities of nature. I answered in a faint
voice that death would have been too great a happiness; that
although I could not blame the assembly's exhortation, or the
25 urgency of his friends; yet, in my weak and corrupt judgment, I
thought it might consist with reason to have been less rigorous.
That I could not swim a league, and probably the nearest land to
theirs might be distant above a hundred. That many materials
necessary for making a small vessel to carry me off, were wholly
30 wanting in this country; which, however, I would attempt, in
obedience and gratitude to his honor, although I concluded the
thing to be impossible, and therefore looked on myself as already
devoted to destruction. That the certain prospect of an unnatural
death was the least of my evils; for, supposing I should escape
35 with life by some strange adventure, how could I think with
temper of passing my days among *yahoos*, and relapsing into my
old corruptions for want of examples to lead and keep me within
the paths of virtue? That I knew too well upon what solid reasons
all the determinations of the wise Houyhnhnms were founded,
40 not to be shaken by arguments of mine, a miserable *yahoo*; and
therefore, after presenting him with my humble thanks for the
offer of his servants' assistance in making a vessel, and desiring
a reasonable time for so difficult a work, I told him I would
endeavor to preserve a wretched being; and if ever I returned to
45 England, was not without hopes of being useful to my own species, by celebrating the praises of the renowned Houyhnhnms,
and proposing their virtues to the imitation of mankind.

My master, in a few words, made a very gracious reply;
allowed me the space of two months to finish my boat; and or-
50 dered the sorrel nag, my fellow servant (for so at this distance I
may presume to call him), to follow my instruction, because I told
my master that his help would be sufficient, and I knew he had a
tenderness for me. When all was ready, and the day came for my
departure, I took leave of my master, and lady, and the whole
55 family, my eyes flowing with tears, and my heart quite sunk with
grief. But his honor, out of curiosity, and perhaps (if I may speak it
without vanity) partly out of kindness, was determined to see me
in my canoe; and got several of his neighboring friends to accompany him. I was forced to wait above an hour for the tide, and then
60 observing the wind very fortunately bearing towards the island to
which I intended to steer my course, I took a second leave of my
master; but as I was going to prostrate myself to kiss his hoof, he
did me the honor to raise it gently to my mouth. I am not ignorant
how much I have been censured for mentioning this last particular.
65 For my detractors are pleased to think it improbable that so illustri-
ous a person should descend to give so great a mark of distinction

to a creature so inferior as I. Neither have I forgotten how apt some travelers are to boast of extraordinary favors they have received. But, if these censurers were better acquainted with the

70 noble and courteous disposition of the Houyhnhnms, they would soon change their opinion.

I paid my respects to the rest of the Houyhnhnms in his honor's company; then getting into my canoe, I pushed off from the shore.

From Jonathan Swift, *Gulliver's Travels*.

11. The phrase "to have the assembly's exhortation executed" can be interpreted to mean

   A. to have a person executed or killed.

   B. to carry out an execution order of the assembly.

   C. to carry out an order of the assembly.

   D. to speak before the assembly.

12. The master was pleased with his servant because the servant

   I. could swim.

   II. could build a boat.

   III. had cured himself of bad habits and dispositions.

   IV. had imitated the Houyhnhnms.

   F. I only.   H. III only.

   G. I and II only.   J. III and IV.

13. The phrase "imbecilities of nature" refers to

   A. the intelligence of the Houyhnhnms.

   B. the lack of intelligence of the servant.

   C. the intelligence of the servant.

   D. the occasions when the body does not function properly.

14. The narrator of this article is

   F. the master.   H. a Houyhnhnm.

   G. a yahoo.   J. a servant.

15. The servant had his master to see him off because

   A. his master was grieved to see him go.

    B.   his master was curious about the craft.

    C.   his master wanted to make sure he really left.

    D.   his master was curious and kind.

16. The "sorrel nag" can be interpreted to mean

    F.   a red horse.   H.   the master.

    G.   a tool.   J.   the narrator.

17. The narrator wants to

    I.   return to France.

    II.   propose the ways of the Houyhnhnms to others.

    III. swim the hundred leagues.

    IV. build a craft to sail.

    A.   I and II.   C.   II and IV.

    B.   I and III.   D.   I and IV.

18. The narrator's attitude toward his master might be inferred to be that of

    F.   submission.   H.   exhortation.

    G.   arrogance.   J.   grief.

19. The Houyhnhnms

    A.   have no conception of compelling others.

    B.   have no conception of advising a person to do something.

    C.   are not rational creatures.

    D.   can best be described as those who disobey reason.

20. To be a rational creature

    F.   one must disobey reason.   H.   one must be exhorted.

    G.   one must be compelled.   J.   one must obey reason.

Passage III

    1. Having shown that the periodical resistance on the part of the working men against a reduction of wages, and their periodical attempts at getting a rise of wages, are inseparable from the wages system, and dictated by the very fact of labor being
5   assimilated to commodities, and therefore subject to the laws

regulating the general movement of prices; having furthermore, shown that a general rise of wages would result in a fall in the general rate of profit, but not affect the average prices of commodities, or their values, the question now ultimately arises, how

10 far, in this incessant struggle between capital and labor, the latter is likely to prove successful.

I might answer by a generalization, and say that, as with all other commodities, so with labor, its *market price* will, in the long run, adapt itself to its *value*; that, therefore, despite all the

15 ups and downs, and do what he may, the working man will, on an average, only receive the value of his labor, which resolves into the value of his laboring power, which is determined by the value of the necessaries required for its maintenance and reproduction, which value of necessaries finally is regulated by the

20 quantity of labor wanted to produce them.

But there are some peculiar features which distinguish the *value of the laboring power, or the value of labor*, from the values of all other commodities. The value of the laboring power is formed by two elements—the one merely physical, the other

25 historical or social. Its *ultimate limit* is determined by the *physical* element, that is to say, to maintain and reproduce itself, to perpetuate its physical existence, the working class must receive the necessaries absolutely indispensable for living and multiplying. The *value* of those indispensable necessaries forms, there-

30 fore, the ultimate limit of the *value of labor*. On the other hand, the length of the working day is also limited by ultimate, although very elastic boundaries. Its ultimate limit is given by the physical force of the laboring man. If the daily exhaustion of his vital forces exceeds a certain degree, it cannot be exerted anew,

35 day by day. However, as I said, this limit is very elastic. A quick succession of unhealthy and short-lived generations will keep the labor market as well supplied as a series of vigorous and long-lived generations.

Besides this mere physical element, the value of labor is in

40 every country determined by a *traditional standard of life*. It is not mere physical life, but it is the satisfaction of certain wants springing from the social conditions in which people are placed and reared up. The important part which historical tradition and social habitude play in this respect, you may learn from Mr.

45 Thornton's work on *Over-population*, where he shows that the average wages in different agricultural districts of England still nowadays differ more or less according to the more or less favorable circumstances under which the districts have emerged from the state of serfdom. But as to *profits*, there exists no law which

50 determines their *minimum*. We cannot say what is the ultimate

limit of their decrease. And why cannot we fix that limit? Because, although we can fix the *minimum* of wages, we cannot fix their *maximum*. We can only say that, the limits of the working day being given, the *maximum* of profit corresponds to the *physi-*
55 *cal minimum of wages*; and that wages being given, the *maximum of profit* corresponds to such a prolongation of the working day as is compatible with the physical forces of the laborer. The maximum of profit is therefore limited by the physical minimum of wages and the physical maximum of the working day. It is
60 evident that between the two limits of this *maximum rate of profit* an immense scale of variations is possible. The fixation of its actual degree is only settled by the continuous struggle between capital and labor, the capitalist constantly tending to reduce wages to their physical minimum, and to extend the work-
65 ing day to its physical maximum, while the working man constantly presses in the opposite direction.
The matter resolves itself into a question of the respective powers of the combatants.

2. As to the *limitation of the working day* in England, as in
70 all other countries, it has never been settled except by *legislative interference*. Without the working man's continuous pressure from without that interference would never have taken place. But at all events, the result was not to be attained by private settlement between the working men and the capitalists. This very
75 necessity of *general political action* affords the proof that in its merely economic action capital is the stronger side.

21. The writer believes the wage system

    I.   necessarily involves laborers resisting a raise in wages.

    II.   necessarily involves workers resisting a reduction in wages.

    III. involves workers attempting periodically to get a raise in wages.

    A.   I only.   C.   II and III.

    B.   I and II.   D.   I, II, and III.

22. The writer denies that a rise in wages

    F.   would result in the fall of the general rate of profit.

    G.   would affect the average price of commodities.

    H.   would not affect the average price of commodities.

    J.   would not affect the value of commodities.

23. The author would not agree that

    A. the market price of labor will adapt to its value.

    B. the working man will only receive the value of his labor.

    C. one's laboring power is determined by the value of the necessities.

    D. that the values of one's necessaries are separate and apart from the quantity of labor wanted to produce them.

24. What is the ultimate limit of the length of the working day?

    F. A limit determined by historical events.

    G. A limit determined by the social environment in which the worker resides.

    H. A limit determined by the physical limitation of the worker.

    J. A limit determined by the ruling class.

25. The author's purpose is to

    A. present the struggle between capital and labor and its results.

    B. present the meaning of labor, value, and national standard.

    C. present the importance of legislative interference.

    D. show the importance of money in society.

26. The author believes that

    F. the market price of labor will adapt to its value.

    G. the market price of labor must be controlled by legislative action.

    H. the value of commodities is determined by the physical strength of a person.

    J. the laborer works for a maximum day and a minimum of wages.

27. The value of the laboring power is

    I.   distinguished from the value of all other commodities.
    II. formed by two elements—one physical and one mental.
    III. limited by the value of the necessities.

    A. I and III.   C. III only.
    B. II only.   D. II and III.

28. The limitation of the working day is a result of

    I.   legislative action.

    II. pressure from the laborers.

    III. private settlement.

    F. I only.   H. I and II.

    G. II only.   J. I, II, and III.

29. The writer would deny that

    I.   in its merely economic action, laborers are stronger than capital.

    II. in its merely economic action, capital is stronger than laborers.

    III. general political action gives proof that capital is stronger than laborers.

    A. I only.   C. II and III.

    B. II only.   D. I and III.

30. The content can be best summarized in the title

    F. "The Struggle."   H. "Capitalism."

    G. "Reaching Consensus." J. "Laborers."

Passage IV

Unjust laws exist: shall we be content to obey them, or shall we endeavor to amend them, and obey them until we have succeeded, or shall we transgress them at once? Men generally, under such a government as this, think that they ought to wait
5   until they have persuaded the majority to alter them. They think that, if they should resist, the remedy would be worse than the evil. But it is the fault of the government itself that the remedy *is* worse than the evil. *It* makes it worse. Why is it not more apt to anticipate and provide for reform? Why does it not cherish its
10 wise minority? Why does it cry and resist before it is hurt? Why does it not encourage its citizens to be on the alert to point out its faults, and *do* better than it would have them? Why does it always crucify Christ, and excommunicate Copernicus and Luther, and pronounce Washington and Franklin rebels?
15 One would think that a deliberate and practical denial of its authority was the only offence never contemplated by government; else, why has it not assigned its definite, its suitable and proportionate, penalty? If a man who has no property refuses but once to earn nine shillings for the State, he is put in prison for a
20 period unlimited by any law that I know, and determined only by the discretion of those who placed him there; but if he should

steal ninety times nine shillings from the State, he is soon permitted to go at large again.

If the injustice is part of the necessary friction of the machine
25 of government, let it go, let it go: perchance it will wear smooth—
certainly the machine will wear out. If the injustice has a spring, or
a pulley, or a rope, or a crank, exclusively for itself, then perhaps
you may consider whether the remedy will not be worse than the
evil; but if it is of such a nature that it requires you to be the agent
30 of injustice to another, then, I say, break the law. Let your life be a
counterfriction to stop the machine. What I have to do is to see, at
any rate, that I do not lend myself to the wrong which I condemn.

Under such a government which imprisons any unjustly, the
true place for a just man is also prison. The proper place today, the
35 only place which Massachusetts has provided for her freer and less
desponding spirits, is in her prisons, to be put out and locked out of
the State by her own act, as they have already put themselves out by
their principles. It is there that the fugitive slave, and the Mexican
prisoner on parole, and the Indian come to plead the wrongs of his
40 race should find them; on that separate, but more free and honorable
ground, where the State places those who are not *with* her, but
against her—the only house in a slave State in which a free man can
abide with honor. If any think that their influence would be lost
there, and their voices no longer afflict the ear of the State, that they
45 would not be as an enemy within its walls, they do not know by how
much truth is stronger than error, nor how much more eloquently
and effectively he can combat injustice who has experienced a little
in his own prison. Cast your whole vote, not a strip of paper merely,
but your whole influence. A minority is powerless while it conforms
50 to the majority; it is not even a minority then; but it is irresistible
when it clogs by its whole weight. If the alternative is to keep all just
men in prison, or give up war and slavery, the State will not hesitate
which to choose. If a thousand men were not to pay their tax-bills
this year, that would not be a violent and bloody measure, as it
55 would be to pay them, and enable the State to commit violence and
shed innocent blood. This is, in fact, the definition of a peaceable
revolution, if any such is possible. If the tax-gatherer, or any other
public officer, asks me, as one has done, 'But what shall I do?' my
answer is, 'If you really wish to do anything, resign your office.'
60 When the subject has refused allegiance, and the officer has re-
signed his office, then the revolution is accomplished. But even
suppose blood should flow. Is there not a sort of blood shed when
the conscience is wounded? Through this wound a man's real manhood and immortality flow out, and he bleeds to an everlasting
65 death. I see this blood flowing now.

From Henry David Thoreau, *Civil Disobedience*.

31. The author believes the only offense never contemplated by government is

    I.   being unfair to the taxpayer.

    II. denying its authority.

    III. putting one in prison for tax evasion.

    A. I only.   C. I, II, and III.

    B. II only.   D. III only.

32. Most people think

    F. they should be content to obey unjust laws.

    G. they should transgress unjust laws.

    H. they should amend unjust laws and obey them until they are altered.

    J. they should ignore unjust laws.

33. The author would agree that

    A. injustice should not be eliminated since it is a necessary part of government.

    B. one should not be an agent of injustice even if it means breaking the law.

    C. one should not stop the machines of government.

    D. one might, at times, find it necessary to do the wrong that one condemns.

34. The author would

    F. oppose a just man being in prison.

    G. oppose a government which imprisons others.

    H. suggest the place for a just man is in prison if a government imprisons unjustly.

    J. oppose a government which imprisons people unjustly.

35. A just person should be in prison

    A. because a government should imprison unjustly.

    B. to represent those who are against an unjust government.

    C. to represent the principles of other people.

    D. to represent the only house in a free state where a slave can abide with honor.

36. In prison a just person's

    F. influence is lost.

    G. voice is lost to the State.

    H. ability to combat injustice can be exercised.

    J. appearance would be as a friend within its walls.

37. A minority

    A. is powerless within a state.

    B. is powerful if it adheres to the majority.

    C. is powerless if it adheres to the majority.

    D. is resistible to the State.

38. Violence is represented by

    F. a thousand people not paying their taxes.

    G. a thousand people paying their taxes.

    H. a thousand people paying their taxes to a State that sheds innocent blood.

    J. friction in the machinery of government.

39. The author sees a loss of one's person when

    A. there is violence.

    B. the conscience is wounded.

    C. there is a war.

    D. taxes are not paid.

40. The reason the place of a just person should be in prison is because

    I.   Massachusetts has provided this place for her freer and less desponding spirits.
    II. the State has locked persons out by its own act.
    III. the persons have put themselves out of the State by their own actions.
    IV. the State places persons there who are against the State.

    F. I only.   H. I, II, and III.

    G. I and II.   J. I, II, III, and IV.

THIS IS THE END OF TEST 3.

Test 4: Science Reasoning

TIME: 35 Minutes
40 Questions

DIRECTIONS: This test consists of seven passages, each followed by several questions. Once you have read a passage, answer each question. Then fill in the appropriate oval on your answer sheet.

Passage I

A 10 mL sample of blood was drawn from a patient and several experiments, as outlined below, were done on subsamples of this blood.

Experiment 1

The concentration of calcium in the blood was determined by adding oxalate ions to the blood subsample to precipitate calcium oxalate according to the equation:

$$Ca^{++} \text{ (in blood)} + C_2O_4^= \text{ (aq)} \rightarrow CaC_2O_4 \text{ (s)}$$

The solid calcium oxalate was separated from the blood, dissolved in acid, and titrated with standardized potassium permanganate solution according to the equation:

$$2MnO_4^- \text{ (aq)} + 5C_2O_4^2 \text{ (aq)} + 16H^+ \text{ (aq)} \rightarrow 2Mn^{++} \text{ (aq)} + 10CO_2 \text{ (g)} + 8H_2O$$

The calcium in a 5.00 mL blood sample was precipitated as CaC_2O_4. After separation, the calcium oxalate was dissolved in 6.0 M HCl and titrated with 11.63 mL of 0.00100 M potassium permanganate solution.

Experiment 2

Using another blood subsample and a glass microelectrode, the pH of the blood was determined (pH = 7.45). The pH of blood is determined almost entirely by the combination of the various carbonate species (H_2CO_3, HCO_3^-, and CO_3^{2-}) present in the blood. The Henderson-Hasselbach equation in the form below relates the pH to the concentrations of bicarbonate and carbonic acid (dissolved carbon dioxide):

$$pH = 6.1 + \log\left\{\left[\frac{[HCO_3^-]}{[H_2CO_3]}\right]\right\}$$

where 6.1 is the pK_a of carbonic acid. The total carbonate species in the blood was determined by reacting the bicarbonate ion with acid, converting the carbonic acid to carbon dioxide gas, and collecting the resulting CO_2 gas. A microgasometer was used to collect the carbon dioxide from a 0.0300 mL sample of blood; it occupied a volume of 0.200 mL at 67.0 mm Hg pressure and 21° C.

Experiment 3

The pH determined in Experiment 2 was 7.45; it was considered to be slightly higher than normal. One possibility may be that the patient has been suffering from a liver disease. To test this hypothesis, a sample was separated into plasma and cellular fractions by centrifugation. The plasma was analyzed for liver proteins. The number of cells was also counted and found to be elevated from normal. One liver protein, found to be elevated, sometimes increases blood cell production.

1. Based on the results of all the experiments, which of the following species, if present, could affect the pH of blood?

    A. Ca^{2+}
    B. $C_2O_4^{2-}$
    C. CO_2
    D. H_2O

2. What is the purpose of dissolving calcium oxalate in acid solution instead of water for the titration procedure in Experiment 1?

    F. The water does not dissolve MnO_4^-.
    G. The water does not dissolve calcium oxalate.
    H. Acid solution removes the Ca^{2+} from $C_2O_4^{-2}$.
    J. No purpose; either acid or water could have been used.

3. Using the experimental procedures given above, which species, if measured quantitatively, would indicate the concentration of calcium present in blood?

    I. MnO_4^-
    II. $C_2O_4^{2-}$
    III. H_2O

    A. I only.
    B. II only.
    C. I and II only.
    D. I, II, and III.

4. In the titration described in Experiment 1, if a 0.0100 M concentration of potassium permanganate solution were used in place of the 0.00100 M concentration, how would the amount of calcium detected and volume (mL) of potassium permanganate solution needed for the titration be affected, if at all?

    F. A larger volume of $KMnO_4$ would be needed and the amount of calcium would increase.
    G. A larger volume of $KMnO_4$ would be needed, but the amount of calcium would not change.
    H. A smaller volume of $KMnO_4$ would be needed and the amount of calcium would decrease.
    J. A smaller volume of $KMnO_4$ would be needed, but the amount of calcium would not change.

5. Given the results of Experiment 3, what is the cause and effect relationship between blood pH, liver protein levels, and blood cell count?

    A. The presence of a particular liver protein increases blood cell production which causes a higher pH.

    B. The presence of a particular liver protein increases pH which causes an increase in blood cell production.

    C. The number of blood cells increase which causes a particular protein to form and increase the pH.

    D. The increased pH level causes a particular protein to form and increase blood cell production.

6. What experimental procedure was used directly to determine the pH of a blood sample?

    F. No experimental procedure was used. The pH must be calculated.

    G. The number of blood cells present was counted.

    H. A glass microelectrode was used.

    J. A microgasometer was used.

Passage II

A chemist is studying the reaction of three compounds and the products they form. This reaction is known to be reversible. Previously all three compounds were placed into a beaker and mixed. After 4 hours, equilibrium was assumed to have been established. The amounts of the reactants were varied and the initial rate of the forward reaction was measured. The preliminary data is shown in Table 1.

Table 1

	$2A + B + 3C \leftarrow \rightarrow$ Products		
Initial Rate	[A]	[B]	[C]
3	1	1	1
6	2	1	1
27	1	1	3
3	1	4	1

Experiment 1

The chemist placed known concentrations of A, B, and C into a beaker. The concentrations of B and C were kept constant throughout the experiment. The concentration of A was observed over time. The rate of the reaction was proposed to be dependent upon the concentration of A. The results are shown in Table 2.

Table 2

Time, min	[A]
0	0.400
10	0.300
20	0.200
30	0.150
40	0.100
50	0.075
60	0.050

Experiment 2

The overall rate law of the reaction was found to be equal to $k[A][C]^2$. The mechanism was proposed to be a one-step termolecular collision. To determine the rate constant, k, a given set of concentrations of A, B, and C were mixed at different temperatures. The relationship between the rate constant and temperature was initially assumed to follow the Arrhenius equation: $K = Ae^{-x}$ where $x = \dfrac{E_a}{RT}$. The figure below shows the experimental results.

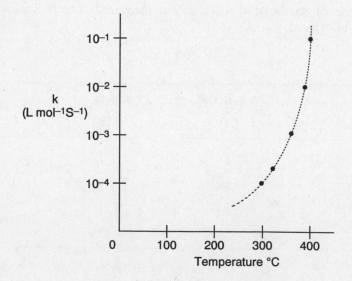

Figure 1

7. Based on the data from the experiments and the passage, which compound, if any, does NOT affect the rate of the reaction?

    A. Compound A

    B. Compound B

    C. Compound C

    D. All the compounds affect the rate of reaction.

8. Which graph best illustrates the relationship between the concentration of A with time, based on the data in Table 2?

    F.
    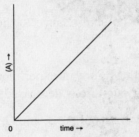

    H.
    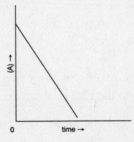

    G.
    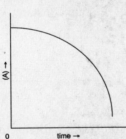

    J.
    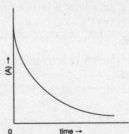

9. Which of the following statements is true concerning the amounts of reactants and products present at equilibrium?

    A. Both reactants and products are present, but the amounts cannot be determined from the information given.

    B. Both reactants and products are present in equal amounts.

    C. Only reactants are present.

    D. Only products are present.

10. To improve the experimental design of the experiments performed in the passage, a chemist should

    F. determine the concentrations of the products formed.

    G. find a method to ensure equilibrium has been established.

H.   perform the same experiment with the reverse reaction.

J.   only vary the amounts of two reactants instead of three.

11. Given the reaction in the passage $2A + B + 3C \leftarrow \rightarrow$ products, what is the significance, if any, of the numbers in front of the reactants A, B, and C with regards to how fast each is used up during the reaction?

A.   Reactant A is used up twice as fast as reactant B.

B.   Reactant C is used up three times as fast as reactant B.

C.   Reactant B is used up twice as fast as reactant A and three times as fast as reactant C.

D.   The results of the experiments reveal no significance to the numbers and rate.

12. Given the results of the experiments and the figure in experiment 2, what happens to the rate of the reaction as the temperature is decreased?

F.   It would depend on the initial concentrations of A, B, and C.

G.   No effect, since temperature affects only the rate constant.

H.   The rate of reaction decreases.

J.   The rate of reaction increases.

Passage III

If a solid object is in equilibrium but is subjected to forces that tend to stretch, shear, or compress it, the shape of the object changes. When an object is subjected to forces that tend to compress it rather than stretch it, the stress is called compressive stress. For some materials, the compressive stress is the same as the tensile stress. If the tensile or compressive stress is too great, the object breaks. The stress at which breakage occurs is called the tensile strength, or in the case of compression, the compressive strength. Approximate values of the tensile and compressive strengths for various materials are listed in Table 1. In Figure 1, a force is applied tangentially to the top of a book. This is an example of a compressive force. The ratio of the compressive force, F, to the area is equal to the compressive stress.

Table 1

Material	Tensile strength MN/m^2	Compressive strength MN/m^2
Aluminum	90	—
Bone		
Tensile	200	—
Compressive	—	270
Brass	370	—
Concrete	2	17
Copper	230	—
Iron (wrought)	390	—
Lead	12	—
Steel	520	520

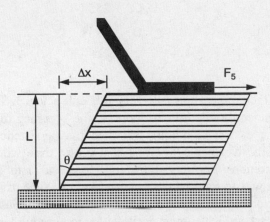

Figure 1

13. If a force of 72 N is applied to the top of the book in Figure 1, and the compressive stress is equal to 6 N/m^2, which of the following are possible dimensions of the book?

    A. 4×2 C. 4×3

    B. 3×3 D. 5×1

14. A small child is running on the playground. The child trips over a rock and breaks her arm when she lands. What was the tensile force with which the child landed?

    F. 270 MN/m^2 H. 390 MN/m^2

    G. 200 MN/m^2 J. 90 MN/m^2

15. If a force is applied tangentially to the top of the book in Figure 1, at what point will the binding of the book break?

    A. When compressive force equals compressive stress

    B. When tensile force equals compressive stress

    C. When tangential force equals compressive force

    D. When compressive strength equals compressive stress

16. According to Table 1, which material has a low tensile strength, but will not break under any compressive stress?

    F. Aluminum   H. Iron

    G. Copper   J. Lead

17. A photo album with the dimensions of 8×4 has a compressive strength of 8 N/m^2. What is the maximum force that can be applied to the top of the book without breaking it?

    A. 190 N   C. 255 N

    B. 356 N   D. 89 N

Passage IV

Accurate weather forecasting is a very difficult science. There are several techniques that a meteorologist uses to increase the accuracy of his or her forecast (Table 1). The easiest technique is called the persistence forecast. This method states that the weather conditions at a future time will be the same as present weather conditions. For very short range forecasts (1 to 3 hours), this can be a highly accurate way to forecast the weather. Another type of forecast uses past climatological data to predict current or future weather conditions. This is called a climatological forecast and is the most accurate for forecasting long range weather conditions (several months in the future). The most technologically advanced technique is the probability forecast and often utilizes computers. This method is the most accurate for medium range predictions (1 to 3 days in the future).

Table 1—Temperature Predictions for Phoenix, AZ

Time/ Date	Persistence Forecast	Climatological Forecast	Probability/ Computer Forecast
Afternoon, July 6	112 degrees	108 degrees	107 degrees
Night, March 12	85 degrees	88 degrees	90 degrees

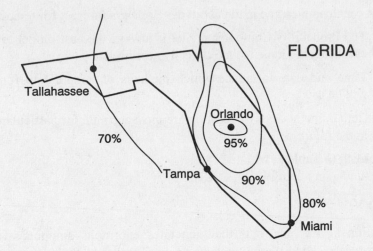

Figure 1—Computer Generated Forecast of the Probability of Thunderstorms

18. Using the computer generated forecast in Figure 1, which city in Florida has the lowest probability of having a thunderstorm on August 5?

    F. Orlando   H. Tallahassee

    G. Tampa   J. Miami

19. If the current date is July 6, it is late morning, and 109° F, what would the most accurate temperature forecast be for the afternoon of July 6 for Phoenix, AZ?

    A. 112°F   C. 107°F

    B. 108°F   D. 85°F

20. If the current date is January 1, which method(s) of forecasting would be the most accurate in forecasting for September 1?

    F. Persistence forecasting

    G. Climatological forecasting

    H. Computer/Probability forecasting

    J. Both F and H.

21. If the current date is March 10, what would be the most accurate temperature forecast for the night of March 12 for Phoenix, AZ?

    A. 112°F   C. 85°F

    B. 88°F   D. 90°F

22. What conclusion can be made about developing a forecast for temperatures?

   F. The Probability/Computer model is always the best model to use because it is the most technologically advanced.

   G. Time and date influence which methods of temperature forecasting will be used.

   H. Certain methods of forecasting are most accurate for particular periods in the future.

   J. Both G and H.

Passage V

The Sun is a typical star that generates enormous amounts of energy through a process called thermonuclear fusion. Through a chain reaction series, atomic nuclei are fused into ordinary helium nuclei ($_2^4H$). This results in a series of mass defects (mass losses) which cause the release of nuclear binding energies. Thermonuclear fusion in the Sun is principally accomplished through two different chains. The first is called the proton-proton chain and the second is called the carbon-nitrogen-oxygen cycle. Nuclear equations are useful in expressing these chain reactions. Elements that initiate a specific reaction (reactants) are found to the left of the reaction arrow, and those that are produced (reaction products) are found to the right. Note that ν stands for a neutrino particle and γ stands for a gamma ray photon.

Experiment 1: The Proton-Proton chain

In this reaction, protons interact to eventually form ordinary helium. The proton-proton chain has three possible branches, but it is primarily completed in the three step branch shown in Table 1. Here, you see each one of the step reactions, the energy released by each reaction, and the time scale (how fast or slow) of the reaction:

Table 1—The proton-proton chain

Reaction	Energy Released	Time Scale
$_1^1H + _1^1H \rightarrow _1^2D + e^+ + \nu$	1.441 MeV	14 billion years
$_1^2D + _1^1H \rightarrow _2^3He + \gamma$	5.494 MeV	6 seconds
$_2^3He + _2^3He \rightarrow _2^4He + _1^1H + _1^1H$	12.859 MeV	1 million years

Since the third reaction uses two He particles, the creation of one He nucleus necessitates that the first and second reactions each occur twice. The proton-proton reaction is the dominant source of energy in stars with core temperature less than about 15 million Kelvin.

Experiment 2: The Carbon Cycle (Carbon-Nitrogen-Oxygen Cycle)

In stars where the interior temperature is higher than about 15 million Kelvin, another reaction series dominates energy production. It is an alternative way of converting hydrogen into helium, and consists of six reactions as shown in Table 2.

Table 2—The carbon cycle

Reaction	Energy Released	Time Scale
$^{12}_{6}C + ^{1}_{1}H \rightarrow ^{13}_{7}N + \gamma$	1.943 MeV	13 million years
$^{13}_{7}N \rightarrow ^{13}_{6}C + e^{+} + \gamma$	2.221 MeV	7 minutes
$^{13}_{6}C + ^{1}_{1}H \rightarrow ^{14}_{7}N + \gamma$	7.551 MeV	2.7 million years
$^{14}_{7}N + ^{1}_{1}H \rightarrow ^{15}_{8}O + \gamma$	7.297 MeV	320 million years
$^{15}_{8}O \rightarrow ^{15}_{7}N + ^{12}_{6}e^{+} + ^{4}_{2}He$	2.753 MeV	82 seconds
$^{15}_{7}N + ^{1}_{1}H \rightarrow ^{12}_{6}C + ^{4}_{2}He$	4.966 MeV	110,000 years

Note that it is the last step which makes the carbon cycle a true cycle by reproducing $^{12}_{6}C$ so that the net effect of the whole cycle is to produce one helium nucleus out of four hydrogen nuclei, just as the proton-proton chain.

23. In the proton-proton chain, how many hydrogen nuclei are consumed in producing a nucleus of ordinary helium?

    A. Two

    B. Three

    C. Four

    D. Six

24. The total energy released by the proton-proton chain (neglecting neutrino ions) is approximately

    F. 19.78 MeV

    G. 26.71 MeV

    H. 21.22 MeV

    J. 25.27 MeV

25. The production of a neutrino is due to the weak force which is a fundamental interaction in nature. Which of the following statements is true about this force?

    A. It slows down the first step of the proton-proton chain.

    B. It makes the second step of the proton-proton chain go fast.

C. It slows down the first step of the carbon chain.

D. It makes the second step of the carbon cycle go the fastest in the whole cycle.

26. What is the common feature shared by the proton-proton chain and the carbon cycle?

    F. They both take more than 13 billion years to proceed.

    G. They produce the same number of neutrinos.

    H. They both convert hydrogen into helium.

    J. They both are equally important when the temperature at the center of the star is higher than 15 million Kelvin.

27. Which of the following is a lone reactant that breaks down to form reaction products?

    A. Carbon-12   C. Oxygen-15

    B. Nitrogen-14   D. Both B and C.

28. A catalyst is something necessary to initiate a reaction but is not consumed. Which element acts as a catalyst in the carbon-nitrogen-oxygen cycle?

    F. Hydrogen   H. Oxygen-15

    G. Carbon-12   J. Nitrogen-13

Passage VI

The formation of mountains has long been a curiosity to scientists. Many theories have been stated over time concerning mountain formation. One theory even stated that gravity pulled the heavy rocks down and forced the lighter rocks up to produce a mountain. Most theories of the last one hundred years use the idea of the asthenosphere being a fluid with the crust on top. The crust is then manipulated in different ways depending on the theory.

The type of mountains most common on the earth's surface is folded mountains. Examples of folded mountains are the Alps, the Himalayas, and the Appalachians. Folded mountains have thick layers of sedimentary rock with fossils of marine organisms embedded within the layers. This indicates that folded mountains are made from materials that were once found in the oceans.

In the 1870s James D. Dana proposed a theory of mountain formation. The Dana theory states that the heating and subsequent cooling of the earth causes wave formation. The wave formation is due to a thin crust with liquid rock underneath. This allows the flexible crust to be pushed up as a wave. The waves cool forming mountains and valleys.

The heating and cooling of the rock beneath the earth's crust also causes earthquakes and volcanoes to be more prevalent in mountainous areas around the oceans. This process of wave formation occurred during the early formation of the earth.

Dana also viewed the formation of the ocean basins as due to the weight of sediment on the ocean floor. The sediment is pulled down by the gravity of the earth. This would not allow the ocean floor to build above the ocean's water.

A more recent theory, the theory of plate tectonics, offers a different view of mountain formation. The theory of plate tectonics states that the earth's crust is divided into many moving plates. These plates float on a layer of liquid rock. The earth's plates collide forcing one plate under the other plate. This pushes the top plate up forming mountains. The oceanic plates meet the continental plates forcing the ocean plates down producing the ocean basin. This process also causes earthquakes and volcanoes to be more prevalent around the plate boundaries.

According to plate tectonics, much of this process is continuing today. An example of the continuation is that the Himalayas are still increasing in height each year.

29. The Dana theory agrees with the theory of plate tectonics by

   A. stating that there exists a solid core.

   B. stating that there exists a liquid crust.

   C. stating that there exists a liquid asthenosphere.

   D. stating that plates move to produce mountains.

30. A difference between the two theories is

   F. the Dana theory states that waves produce mountains.

   G. the theory of plate tectonics states that gravity produces the ocean basin.

   H. the theory of plate tectonics states that the crust moves the asthenosphere.

   J. None of the above.

31. The force of the liquid asthenosphere produces mountains is a summary of

   A. the theory of plate tectonics.

   B. the Dana theory.

   C. Both theories.

   D. Neither theory.

32. Some evidence giving the theory of plate tectonics validity is

    F. that marine fossils are found in folded mountains.

    G. that volcanoes and earthquakes occur near oceans.

    H. Choices F and G are both correct.

    J. Neither choice F nor choice G is correct.

33. There exists an area around the Pacific Ocean called the ring of fire. It is on this ring of fire that a large number of earthquakes and volcanoes occur. This tends to give validity to

    A. Dana's theory.

    B. the theory of plate tectonics.

    C. Choices A and B are both correct.

    D. Neither choice A nor choice B is correct.

34. The belief of some modern geologists that the processes of today have been continuous throughout earth's history best correlates with

    F. Dana's theory.

    G. the theory of plate tectonics.

    H. Choices F and G are both correct.

    J. Neither choice F nor choice G is correct.

35. Which of the following causes Dana's theory to be least likely to be accepted?

    A. The crust is manipulated to form mountains.

    B. The asthenosphere is a liquid.

    C. Earthquakes and volcanoes occur mostly around oceans.

    D. Marine fossils are found in the sedimentary rock of folded mountains.

Passage VII

The owners of a greenhouse wish to optimize the light and watering schedules for their plants. They have a choice of three light bulbs. These bulbs emit different intensities at different wavelengths as shown in Figure 1. They examine the growth of four plants with each of these lights; the results are shown in Figure 2.

The plants are subjected to watering schedules, continuous and intermittent at different intervals. Plant characteristics are recorded and shown in Table 1.

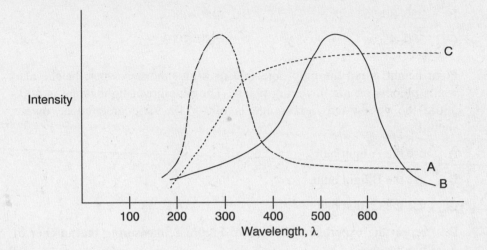

Figure 1

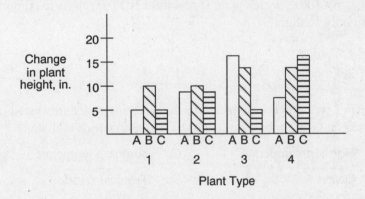

Figure 2

Table 1

Water schedule for plant type #2	Change in height	No. new branches	No. new leaves
continuous	1.2"	45	176
once a day	–"	3	114
twice a day	6"	14	95
4 times a day	6"	26	121

36. If the greenhouse owners can choose only one light bulb type, the one they choose to achieve the best possible growth of all four plant types, without sacrificing any one, has a high intensity in the range

    F. 250–300λ.   H. 450–600λ.

    G. 300–450λ.   J. 550–700λ.

37. Plant height is not the only objective of a greenhouse owner; he/she also wants blooms on his flowering plants. The blue-green light range is 400–500λ, the yellow-red light range is 600–700λ. The greenhouse owner should

    A. use the A light bulb.

    B. use the B light bulb.

    C. use the C light bulb.

    D. repeat the experiment that led to Figure 2, measuring the number of blooms.

38. Sunlight produces visible light over a wide range of wavelengths, from ~350λ to ~700λ. Which plant type would NOT reach its maximum height if it had only sunlight?

    F. 1   H. 3

    G. 2   J. 4

39. Plants of type 2 were subjected to the watering schedules listed in Table 1. These plants might be expected to be native to which climate?

    A. Northern temperate   C. Southern temperate

    B. Desert   D. Tropical rain forest

40. In Table 1, the change in height data for plant type 2 receiving water once a day were lost. Which figure is most likely to be correct?

    F. 6   H. ≤6

    G. ≥6   J. Impossible to predict.

THIS IS THE END OF TEST 4.

ACT ASSESSMENT EXAM IV

ANSWER KEY

Test 1: English

1.	(C)	20.	(J)	39.	(D)	58.	(G)
2.	(G)	21.	(A)	40.	(J)	59.	(A)
3.	(D)	22.	(G)	41.	(A)	60.	(H)
4.	(F)	23.	(D)	42.	(J)	61.	(D)
5.	(C)	24.	(F)	43.	(C)	62.	(J)
6.	(H)	25.	(C)	44.	(J)	63.	(C)
7.	(D)	26.	(J)	45.	(C)	64.	(H)
8.	(G)	27.	(B)	46.	(F)	65.	(B)
9.	(C)	28.	(H)	47.	(D)	66.	(G)
10.	(J)	29.	(D)	48.	(H)	67.	(D)
11.	(B)	30.	(J)	49.	(C)	68.	(H)
12.	(J)	31.	(A)	50.	(G)	69.	(B)
13.	(D)	32.	(J)	51.	(D)	70.	(J)
14.	(J)	33.	(C)	52.	(H)	71.	(C)
15.	(C)	34.	(H)	53.	(B)	72.	(G)
16.	(H)	35.	(D)	54.	(J)	73.	(C)
17.	(B)	36.	(H)	55.	(B)	74.	(G)
18.	(G)	37.	(C)	56.	(J)	75.	(A)
19.	(D)	38.	(G)	57.	(D)		

Test 2: Mathematics

1.	(E)	5.	(D)	9.	(B)	13.	(C)
2.	(J)	6.	(F)	10.	(G)	14.	(H)
3.	(B)	7.	(B)	11.	(B)	15.	(C)
4.	(G)	8.	(F)	12.	(K)	16.	(J)

17. (E)	28. (K)	39. (E)	50. (G)
18. (J)	29. (E)	40. (H)	51. (B)
19. (C)	30. (G)	41. (E)	52. (H)
20. (F)	31. (A)	42. (F)	53. (C)
21. (E)	32. (J)	43. (D)	54. (H)
22. (K)	33. (D)	44. (K)	55. (B)
23. (D)	34. (J)	45. (E)	56. (K)
24. (H)	35. (A)	46. (F)	57. (A)
25. (E)	36. (J)	47. (A)	58. (K)
26. (J)	37. (C)	48. (K)	59. (B)
27. (E)	38. (G)	49. (C)	60. (F)

Test 3: Reading

1. (D)	11. (C)	21. (C)	31. (B)
2. (G)	12. (J)	22. (G)	32. (H)
3. (A)	13. (D)	23. (D)	33. (B)
4. (H)	14. (J)	24. (H)	34. (H)
5. (B)	15. (D)	25. (A)	35. (B)
6. (F)	16. (F)	26. (F)	36. (H)
7. (D)	17. (C)	27. (A)	37. (C)
8. (F)	18. (F)	28. (H)	38. (H)
9. (B)	19. (A)	29. (A)	39. (B)
10. (J)	20. (J)	30. (F)	40. (J)

Test 4: Science Reasoning

1. (C)	11. (D)	21. (D)	31. (C)
2. (G)	12. (H)	22. (J)	32. (H)
3. (C)	13. (C)	23. (C)	33. (C)
4. (J)	14. (G)	24. (G)	34. (G)
5. (A)	15. (D)	25. (A)	35. (D)
6. (H)	16. (J)	26. (H)	36. (H)
7. (B)	17. (C)	27. (C)	37. (D)
8. (J)	18. (H)	28. (G)	38. (H)
9. (A)	19. (A)	29. (C)	39. (D)
10. (G)	20. (G)	30. (F)	40. (H)

DETAILED EXPLANATIONS OF ANSWERS

Test 1: English

1.   **(C)**   By providing the introductory participial phrase, "Using the most modern equipment," with an immediate and logical word to modify, "researchers," choice (C) is the correct answer. Choice (A) follows the participial phrase with "discoveries," which is illogical as the discoveries didn't use the equipment. (B) commits this same dangling modifier error and compounds it by incorrectly suggesting that the singular verb "has been made" agrees with the plural subject "discoveries." By inserting "discovering" after researchers, choice (D) creates an incomplete sentence. When used in the manner of choice (D), "discovering" acts as a participle modifying "researchers." It answers the question, "Which researchers?" However, it leaves "researchers" without a clear verb, leading one to ask the question, "The researchers who made discoveries about the brain *did what*?"

2.   **(G)**   Because of its parallel structure, choice (G) is correct. Note that the important information learned by researchers all falls into a "how-subject-verb" pattern ("how we learn," "how the brain affects," etc.) When presenting lists, one achieves a stylistically stronger sentence by adhering to this parallel construction of grammatical elements. None of the other choices are parallel in form and thus are incorrect.

3.   **(D)**   Because of its direct wording and its use of the comma for sentence clarity, choice (D) is correct. Choice (A) incorrectly uses the semi-colon, which is reserved for joining two independent clauses. As the remainder of the sentence which follows (A)'s semi-colon has no subject, it certainly cannot be considered an independent clause. Choice (B), too, incorrectly uses the semi-colon as the words following it still do not form an independent clause. Although the comma in choice (C) adds a measure of clarity, "and thus they enabling" lacks the necessary auxiliary verb "are" to give the sentence sense. Yet, even with "are enabling," (C) would be guilty of switching tense from simple present to present perfect. Verb tenses should remain consistent unless logic demands otherwise.

4.   **(F)**   The original choice (F) is correct as "its" is the singular possessive form of "it" referring to the singular antecedent "brain." "It" possesses "potential." Choice (G) suggests "its'," but no such word exists. Choice (H) offers "it's," the contraction for "it is," which makes the sentence illogical ("a fraction of *it is* potential). Finally, choice (J) is incorrect as it offers the plural possessive "their" in reference to a singular antecedent.

5. **(C)** By joining two independent clauses by a comma and a coordinating conjunction, choice (C) is correct. Without punctuation between the two independent clauses, as is suggested by choice (A), the sentence becomes fused. Choice (B) suggests a semi-colon *and* a conjunction, but grammatically, just the semi-colon, or just the comma and the conjunction, is correct. The conjunction becomes incorrect and superfluous when joined by the semi-colon. Just as (A) resulted in fusion by the absence of punctuation between the independent clauses, so does choice (D), and thus both are incorrect.

6. **(H)** Because choice (H) joins the ideas of both paragraphs into one, it is the correct answer. Note that (H) includes the brain potential of Paragraph 2 and the chemicals of Paragraph 3. Choice (F) is not as good a choice because it focuses only on Paragraph 2's issue of brain cell loss because of illness. Choice (G) refers only to the scientifically created chemicals, a support found only in Paragraph 3, and therefore does not logically link the two paragraphs. Focusing on the brain injury point of Paragraph 2, choice (J) fails to link this paragraph to Paragraph 3 and thus makes a poor choice for transition.

7. **(D)** By avoiding the redundancies of "producer/produces" and "chemicals," choice (D), to omit the underlined portion, is correct. The underlined phrase adds no information to the sentence that is not already there and therefore can be left out. All the other choices include these redundant terms in various patterns, but they are redundant nonetheless and therefore quite expendable.

8. **(G)** Transition requires one idea to be logically linked to another. Choice (G) does that when it includes both the "substances" mentioned in Sentence 2 and the "patients" of Sentence 3. The logical connection is that the substances provide the means for patient medication. (F) is an incorrect choice because it fails to refer to Sentence 3 but rather focuses on the scientific explanation of brain cell reception, as discussed solely in Paragraph 2. Choice (H) is completely unconnected to Paragraph 2 or 3, as funding is not an issue in either. That mental illness is not an issue at all in Paragraph 3, and only briefly discussed in Paragraph 3, precludes choice (J) from providing any strong, logical link between the two sections.

9. **(C)** For three reasons, choice (C) is the correct answer. First, the plural verb "are" agrees with the plural subject "disorders." Second, the present tense verb is consistent with the verb tense of the rest of the passage, and, third, the redundant "still" is absent. Because of this redundant use of "still," which is already present in the sentence, choices (A) and (B) are poor choices. (B) compounds the error by suggesting the singular verb "is," not in agreement with the plural subject. Finally, choice (D) offers the verb "remaining" which needs the auxiliary "are" to be complete. Even if it were complete, the verb tense would then be inconsistent with the rest of the passage.

10. **(J)**   Correctly following the introductory dependent clause by a comma to separate it from the following independent clause and to clarify the sentence, choice (J) is the right answer. (F) incorrectly treats the beginning dependent clause as a complete sentence; however, that clause does not make sense unless connected to the independent clause. The lack of comma following the initial dependent clause makes the sentence confusing, and thus (G) is a poor choice. By placing the semi-colon between the two clauses, choice (H), too, incorrectly indicates the first dependent clause is independent, for semi-colons are used to join independent clauses.

11. **(B)**   Since it correctly places the possessive apostrophe before the "s" in "person's" indicating that "person" is singular, as indicated in the article "a" which precedes it, (B) is the correct choice. Choice (A) suggests the plural possessive "persons," which doesn't agree with the author's intention as indicated by the "a," noting just one person. Choice (C) is ungrammatical as the article "a" precedes nouns beginning with consonants, and, of course, "individual" begins with a vowel. Although the article is correct in (D), it still indicates the singular possessive is necessary, not the plural as indicated in this choice.

12. **(J)**   After the relatively lengthy introductory infinitive phrase, a comma correctly appears for sentence clarity and grammatical integrity, as indicated by the correct choice (J). Additionally (J) is correct as it supplies the third person pronoun "one," which agrees with its third person references in the rest of the passage. The semi-colon supplied by choice (F) incorrectly indicates that the introductory phrase is an independent clause, having a subject and a verb and able to stand alone as a complete sentence. However, a subject will never be found within an infinitive phrase (defined as "to" plus a verb and any associated modifiers), as one cannot be found in this sentence's introductory phrase "to keep...." (G), too, makes the mistake of indicating the introductory phrase is an independent clause by inserting the semi-colon, while (H) adds to the semi-colon error by introducing a first person plural pronoun in an otherwise consistently third person singular essay.

13. **(D)**   With the clarifying comma following the introductory dependent clause and with the singular pronoun "it" in agreement with the singular antecedent "brain," (D) is the correct choice. The plural pronoun "we" of choice (A) illogically indicates that if we don't exercise our brains, we will physically waste away, or atrophy. This might be true of muscles, but it is not necessarily true of brains, for many people who fail to learn new things or be involved in stimulating activities remain physically fit. Not only does choice (A) suffer because of a logic error, but it also suffers from an inconsistency in pronoun usage by introducing the first person plural "we" when all other references are in the third person singular form. Choice (B) leaves the reader wondering to whom "they" refers, as no plural third person antecedent is nearby. Thus, (B) is incorrect.

Although (C) includes the logical pronoun "it," it fails to follow the introductory dependent clause by the clarifying comma and therefore is incorrect.

14. **(J)**   The "if" clause implies that an event which has not yet happened may, indeed, happen, contingent upon meeting certain requirements. Choice (J)'s "will continue" logically, then, meets the implication of the clause, for this verb is in the future tense. Further indicating (J) is the correct choice is the effectively placed comma following the introductory dependent clause. Choice (F) doesn't meet the "if" criterion. "If" implies the action has not yet happened, but (F)'s inclusion of the past tense "continued" illogically states that action has already taken place. Both (G) and (H) fall prey to this same past tense illogic and are therefore incorrect.

15. **(C)**   The analogy between the muscles and the brain presented in choice (C) works well. If one does not exercise the muscles, they will atrophy. Similarly, if one does not exercise the brain, it will atrophy. As the passage only explores the similarities between the brain and the muscles, choice (A)'s reference to the differences is completely unfounded and therefore incorrect. The passage doesn't ask the reader to choose either to exercise his/her muscles or to exercise his/her brain. It simply compares the two processes, and thus choice (B) is incorrect. Although the brain function may lead one to exercise one's muscles, this passage does not entertain this particular sequence. Consequently, (D) is a poor choice.

16. **(H)**   It is mandatory that a comma appears between a city and its state, as exhibited correctly in answer (H). Additionally a comma should separate relatively lengthy appositives from the surrounding sentence. In this sentence, "Dr. Goddard" is the antecedent for the appositive phrase, "at one time...Massachusetts." Note the comma preceding the phrase and, in choice (H), the companion comma correctly following it. Choice (F) fails to include this second companion comma to the set and so is incorrect. Unnecessarily, choice (G) places a comma between "University" and the prepositional phrase which modifies it, but, of even more significance, it forgoes the necessary comma separating city from state, as does choice (J).

17. **(B)**   Subject-verb agreement is the issue of concern here. Choice (B) correctly suggests the singular verb "was" to agree with the singular subject "information." However, choice (A) offers the plural verb "were," which doesn't agree in number with the singular "information." One often makes the common error of choosing a verb because it sounds good with "there," which precedes the verb as the subject commonly does, rather than ascertaining the true subject. Choices (C) and (D) commit this error and thus incorrectly suggest the plural verb "were[n't]."

18. **(G)** Due to its parallel structure, choice (G) is the correct answer. Basically, parallelism demands that similar parts of a sentence be phrased in similar grammatical patterns, thus resulting in clearer and more forceful sentences. Notice the adjective-noun, adjective-noun, adjective-noun pattern evident in Goddard's developments as stated in (G). No pattern is established in any of the other answers as choice (F) presents an adjective-noun-prepositional phrase, adjective-noun, and noun-prepositional phrase mix; choice (H) presents a mixture of adjective-noun, noun-prepositional phrase, and adjective-noun; and (J) presents an adjective-noun, noun-prepositional phrase, and noun-prepositional phrase combination.

19. **(D)** Because it correctly surrounds with quotation marks the title of a brief text, in this case, an essay, choice (D) is correct. Underlining (or italicizing) a title should be reserved for long works, such as books or plays. Both (B) and (C) incorrectly underline the title; however, choice (B) is additionally in error because like (A) it incorrectly inserts a comma between the subordinate conjunction "which" and the subject of its dependent clause, "he."

20. **(J)** Because of its tense consistency and its lack of superfluous commas, choice (J) is correct. The majority of the passage is in past tense, as is (J)'s "discovered." (F) illogically switches to the present with "discovers" and (H) switches to future with "will discover." Unless logic demands, verb tense should remain constant. Although (G) is in the correct past tense, an unnecessary comma appears before "that," thus making the cadence of the sentence rather awkward and halting. As a result, (G) is a poor choice.

21. **(A)** The correct verb and the absence of unnecessary punctuation recommends choice (A), the original, as the right answer. Choice (B) incorrectly treats the dependent clause, "[that] he would use...shape," which modifies "fuel" as a complete sentence. In addition, choice (B) illogically uses "of" instead of "have." Choice (C) also incorrectly treats the dependent clause as independent as indicated by the semi-colon. Choice (D) is incorrect as it fails to include the necessary auxiliary verb "have."

22. **(G)** Unencumbered by an unnecessary dependent clause, as are the other choices, the direct wording of choice (G) makes it the correct answer. Not only do the other choices include this dependent clause, but they commit additional grammatical errors. Choice (F) treats the dependent clause beginning with "Which" as an independent clause, incorrectly making it a sentence. Choice (H) and (J) similarly indicate by the semi-colon that the dependent clauses, beginning with "which" and "that" respectively, are independent clauses. Of course, "which" and "that" are subordinated conjunctions which introduce dependent clauses.

23. **(D)**   Who or what is weak is the issue in this question. Choice (D) is the only right answer which provides a logical answer, "This" of course referring to the height and altitude of Goddard's first liquid-fueled rocket. Illogically worded, choice (A) indicates that Dr. Goddard was weak. One must disregard intervening dependent clauses and prepositional phrases (in this case, "when...time") between a modifier ("seemingly weak") and the next "unattached" noun or pronoun ("Dr. Goddard") which it, indeed, modifies. Choices (B) and (C) commit this same error, yet choice (B) adds to it by the redundant wording of "Comparatively" and "compared."

24. **(F)**   The direct and non-redundant wording of (F), the original, recommends it as the correct choice. Choice (G)'s "was seeking to find" is certainly repetitive in its meaning, for what other reason would one be seeking if not to find? "[T]o find" is quite expendable. The choppy structure (because of several phrases offset by commas) and the redundant phrases of "at this moment" and "at this time" make choice (H) a poor answer. Choice (J) incorrectly uses the semi-colon to join the dependent clause beginning with the subordinating conjunction "since" with the preceding independent clause. Semi-colons join *independent* clauses.

25. **(C)**   Because choice (C) logically links Paragraph 2's topic of "innovative experiments" with Paragraph 3's focus on "firsts," it is the correct answer. Choice (A) is incorrect as it concerns Goddard's authorship, a fact mentioned only in Paragraph 1 and not at all in the two paragraphs under examination. Choice (B)'s topic of posthumous fame is not mentioned in the entire passage, and therefore this answer is incorrect. Finally, choice (D) only deals with the content of Paragraph 3, making it a poor transition between paragraphs. Transitions provide logical means of connecting two parts together. To do this, one part cannot be left out.

26. **(J)**   The antecedent reference for "he" of choice (J) is obviously the "he" of the previous sentence, which in turn refers to "Dr. Goddard" of the first sentence in the paragraph. This logical pronoun reference and the consistent past tense of the verb "was" of (J) makes this choice correct. Choice (F) is incorrect because of the plural pronoun "they" used in reference to the singular antecedent "he." Compounding this pronoun agreement error with an illogical verb tense switch to the present tense "are" ("they're" = "they *are*"), choice (G), too, is incorrect. Pronoun disagreement is the problem with choice (H), as well, in that "we" is plural and the antecedent "he" is singular.

27. **(B)**   For sentence clarity, lengthy non-essential introductory elements should be separated from the following independent clause by a comma. The lengthy introductory adjectival phrase and accompanying dependent clause, "After proving...vacuum," are correctly followed by a comma, as indicated in choice (B). Choice (A) makes the error of treating the introductory elements as an

independent clause by following them by a semi-colon; however, these elements cannot stand alone as a complete sentence, and therefore are not an independent clause. By changing the original independent clause into a dependent one through the use of the subordinate conjunction "since," choice (C) creates an incomplete sentence as it now lacks an independent clause. Compounding the semi-colon error of choice (A) and the independent clause change of choice (C), choice (D) is doubly in error.

28. **(H)** The economical wording of choice (H) recommends it as the correct answer. Note that choice (F) exhibits two redundancies: "close" and "nearing," and "final" and "end." Choice (G) suggests the former redundancy, and choice (J) employs the idiomatic "very end." The end is just that—the end.

29. **(D)** Joint ownership and the placement of the possessive apostrophe are the issues in this question. When two or more show joint rather than individual ownership of an item, the possessive apostrophe occurs only with the last in the list of owners, as is the case with choice (D). Note further that the apostrophe correctly indicates that there is only one "Society" by appearing after the singular "Society" and before the "s." Choice (A) is incorrect as it lacks a possessive apostrophe. Choice (B) incorrectly indicates that more than one Dr. Goddard possess the "experiments and developments." Further, it fails to show possession by the Society. Conversely, choice (C) gives Goddard possession but fails to do so with the Society. Additionally, (C) mistakenly pluralizes "Society."

30. **(J)** The passage's chronological approach and historical perspective to rocket development make (J), "the history of rocket development," the best choice. Although the twentieth century is the correct time period, as suggested by choice (F), biology, the study of living things, is not the focus, and thus this choice is incorrect. Yes, military issues are mentioned in the passage, but not as a main focus; nor is the Roaring '20s the entire period. Therefore, (G) is incorrect. Because "fun and profit" are not mentioned in the passage, (H) is a poor choice.

31. **(A)** Because it links Paragraph 3's focus on Goddard's rocket experiments up to the end of World War II to Paragraph 1's discussion of his work of the 1920s, a period of about 25 years, choice (A) is the best answer for passage unity. The passage does not deal with the theory of "weapons escalation," as choice (B) suggests; thus this choice cannot serve as a unifier. That missiles protect in war is a feature only of Paragraph 3; hence, choice (C) is too limited in scope to unify the passage. This narrowness is the problem with choice (D), as well, for "gyroscopic steering" is but a subpoint of Paragraph 3.

32. **(J)** Because of its straightforward and smooth presentation, choice (J) is correct. Choice (F), repetitious in its use of "disease," is also quite wordy and

accomplishes no more than does the briefer (J). Repetition is also a characteristic of (G), as exemplified by the use of "some." In addition to repetition, choice (G) uses the cliché "putting two and two together." Because of overuse, clichés no longer inspire in the reader the literal images they did when first coined; hence, they are wasted words. The awkward choppiness of choice (H) makes it a poor choice as well. Note how the excessive number of short phrases offset by commas in (H) causes the sentence to bump along rather than move relatively smoothly to its end.

33. **(C)** The adjectival phrase beginning with "proving" is separated from the preceding independent clause by a comma in choice (C), the correct answer. Choice (A) mistakenly treats this phrase as an independent clause by indicating it is a complete sentence. However, this group of words makes no sense when standing alone. Choice (B) makes the same error of indicating the phrase is independent by joining it to the preceding independent clause with a semi-colon. (D) is also in error. The coordinating conjunction "and" normally links two equal parts of a sentence together. A coordinate part to the independent clause is missing as is a coordinate part to the phrase; thus, choice (D) does not work.

34. **(H)** Because (H) uses the contraction "it's," meaning "it is," a subject and verb are provided to make the sentence complete. Therefore, (H) is the correct answer. Incorrectly, choices (F) and (J) employ the possessive pronoun "its" and offer no object to be possessed. Further, the sentences are rendered incomplete as they are left without subjects and verbs. Choice (G) uses a non-existent word, "its'," and therefore is incorrect as well.

35. **(D)** Broad enough to include ancient beliefs and modern chemical truths, all of which relate to our health, choice (D) best unifies and introduces Paragraph 1. Choice (A) is too narrow in its coverage, for it fails to incorporate room for ancient beliefs. An error in logic eliminates choice (B) as it is the honey's sugar and acid that preclude bacteria's development, not the reverse. Even if choice (B) correctly interpreted the relationship between bacteria and honey's sugar and acid, it would still be too narrow a sentence to encompass the whole passage. Choice (C) is simply disproven by Paragraph 1, which, in contrast, presents honey as a poor medium for disease-carrying bacteria.

36. **(H)** Because of the logical use of the past tense for studies conducted in the last few years and because the singular verb "was" agrees in number with the singular subject "effect," choice (H) is correct. This agreement in number is not evident in choice (F), as "were" is plural. Both (G) and (J) make this same subject-verb agreement error as the verbs "have" and "are" are plural, as well. Additionally, the present tense of choice (J) is illogical as the investigations were in the past.

37. **(C)**   Because of the logical singular pronoun "it," referring to the singular act of "heating honey sufficiently," choice (C) is correct. No singular male antecedent exists for choice (A)'s pronoun "him," thus making it a poor choice. The pronoun "we" of choice (B) is in the nominative case when the subjective case "us" should take the position of direct object for the transitive verb "will deny." Even so, the introduction of the first person plural pronoun "us" is inconsistent with the rest of the passage, written strictly in a scientifically impersonal third-person style. Finally, choice (D) makes the common mistake of substituting "of" for the necessary auxiliary verb "have." When casually speaking, we often seem to say "of" for "have"; yet, to be grammatically appropriate, "have" is the correct choice.

38. **(G)**   No unnecessary commas interrupt the smooth phrasing of choice (G), the correct answer. The comma preceding "and" of choice (F) incorrectly separates a list of two brief prepositional objects. The conjunction itself is sufficient. Only in lists of three or more should the comma precede the conjunction (in this case "and") appearing before the final item. "Together" must either be offset by commas on both sides or be totally void of commas. With only the comma preceding it, as indicated by choice (H), "together" implies "together with something else," and the "something else" is absent. Thus, choice (H) is incorrect. (J) commits this same error and that of choice (F).

39. **(D)**   By following a nonessential introductory dependent clause with a comma and by the correct use of the possessive pronoun "its," signifying a possessive relationship with "identity," choice (D) is correct. Choice (A) misidentifies the first clause as independent by following it with a semi-colon. Note that this clause would make no sense standing alone, a key test of an independent clause. Further, (A) and (B) incorrectly employ a nonexistent word, "its'." Choice (B), like (A), treats the dependent clause as an independent clause by indicating it is a complete sentence. Dependent clauses are still the issue in choice (C), which turns the independent clause into a dependent one by the use of the subordinating conjunction "since." The incorrect result is two dependent clauses masquerading as a complete sentence, when, indeed, they are but a fragment.

40. **(J)**   Paragraph 3 concerns peroxide and the inhibine effect, not honey for baking. For this reason, the entire underlined portion should be omitted as it is off the topic, as choice (J) indicates. As choices (F), (G), and (H) deal with baking, they are incorrect.

41. **(A)**   In keeping with the logical present tense of the section and in agreement with the singular subject "level," the singular verb "occurs" of choice (A) is correct. A common error is to choose the verb based on a noun found in an immediately preceding prepositional phrase which intervenes between the true subject and that verb. "[P]eroxides" is the object of the preposition "of" and as such cannot act as a subject. Choice (B) falls victim to this common error.

Choices (C) and (D) both present plural verb forms as indicated by "are" and "have" respectively. Further complicating this error is the tense switch to present perfect that both exhibit. There is no logical reason to switch from the present tense established by the preceding verb "is."

42. **(J)**   Sentence structure is at issue in this case. The two independent clauses are correctly identified by their appearance as two separate sentences, as indicated in choice (J). Without punctuation between these clauses, they become fused, as demonstrated by choice (F). Both (G) and (H) commit the same mistake of uniting the clauses by a comma, thus creating a comma splice error. The comma following "procedure" is optional, depending on the way the author wishes the sentence to be read.

43. **(C)**   The plural "honeys" with the plural verb "have" is the correct answer, as indicated in choice (C). Making a possessive of "honey," as does choice (A), is incorrect as no object exists to be possessed. For the same reason, choice (B)'s "honeys'" is a poor choice. Choice (D) makes the error of providing the plural verb "have" as a complement to the singular subject "honey."

44. **(J)**   Because of its economical language and correct use of the comparative "than," choice (J) is correct. "Then" is an adverb signifying time and is therefore incorrectly used in choices (F) and (H). "[A]s great" signifies an equal relationship while "than" signifies an unequal relationship. Putting these two contrasting terms together in one phrase, as does choice (G), is completely illogical.

45. **(C)**   Choice (C) correctly indicates that the most logical place for the development of a new subtopic, in this case, "financing," is in a separate paragraph. Not all vital information must appear in the first paragraph as choice (A) advises; otherwise, why would we ever read beyond that? Chemical composition is the heart of this passage and therefore cannot be discounted as choice (B) suggests. Essays need not end in summaries, as choice (D) asserts, and even if they did, "finance" would certainly not serve to summarize the passage as it would be but a subtopic.

46. **(F)**   Paragraph 1, as indicated by choice (F), offers the most logical placement for the new sentences. Paragraph 2 is already important without a "human" note, as choice (G) suggests, for the inhibine effect is a key to understanding the relationship of honey and bacteria, the topic of the entire essay. Furthermore, the new sentences are more related logically to the topics of disease and sugar in Paragraph 1 than to the inhibine of Paragraph 2. If new information logically is associated with ideas in an already existing paragraph, it is perfectly acceptable to put that information there. If doesn't necessarily demand a separate paragraph, as choice (H) asserts. Paragraph 4 is an important offshoot of the

chemical processing of honey and involves a different aspect than the chemical process suggested in the new sentences. Thus, the information is not redundant, nor should Paragraph 4 be removed to make room for the new information, as suggested by choice (J).

47. **(D)** Because of its companion commas offsetting the appositive phrase, "our fascinating continent," from the rest of the sentence, choice (D) is correct. Choice (A) only has the first of the necessary set of two commas and therefore is incorrect. Choice (B) is incorrect as well in that it is inconsistent in these marks, mixing a dash with a comma. Because choice (C) lacks one of the necessary set of two commas, it, too, is a poor choice.

48. **(H)** Two independent clauses meet at the junction of "Park" and "located." Each independent clause can act as a complete sentence, as choice (H) correctly indicates. By presenting no mark of punctuation between the clauses, however, choice (F) commits a fusion error. However, joining the two by a comma, as choice (G) does, results in a comma splice. Choice (J) restructures the second independent clause into a dependent one, but this action causes a comma splice to occur between "area" and "this wonder" in the now quite elongated and very confusing sentence.

49. **(C)** For its fresh, logical phrasing, choice (C) is correct. Choices (A) and (B) are cliches and should be avoided for they no longer inspire fresh images in the readers' minds. Choice (D) is illogical in its redundancy. A "drought" is a "dry spell"; one cannot follow the other if they both are the same.

50. **(G)** Choice (G) is the only option which results in a complete sentence. The provided verb "is" completes the subject "history." Choice (F) fails for two reasons. First, the possessive "Badlands" has no possessed object. Second, the subject "history" has no verb, resulting in a sentence fragment. Both (H) and (J) lack verbs and are fragments.

51. **(D)** Because it presents the comparative adverb "more" necessitated by the comparative conjunction "than" and because the adverb "slowly" is correctly used to modify the verb "took," choice (D) is correct. Incorrectly, choice (A) suggests that an adjective "slow" modify the verb. Adjectives modify only nouns or pronouns. Choice (B), too, is incorrect. The comparative degree is already established by the use of "more." Placing "slow" in the comparative form "slower," as does (B), is incorrect in its redundancy. Choice (C) has some problems as well. The word "much," which precedes the underlined section, when coupled with the comparative term "than," indicates that an uneven comparison is to be made. However, choice (C) fails to provide "more" and thereby leaves this phrase incomplete.

52. **(H)** Because the singular subject "buildup" agrees in number with the singular verb "occurs" and the plural noun "deposits" meets the expectations that the plural adjective "these" sets up, choice (H) is correct. Choice (F), however, is incorrect as the verb presented is plural. Verb choice will never be based upon the object in a prepositional phrase that intervenes between that verb and the true subject of a sentence. Choice (G) incorrectly provides the singular "deposit" when "these" clearly indicates a plural term is necessary. Compounding the subject-verb agreement error of choice (F) and the "deposit" error of choice (G), (J) is doubly incorrect.

53. **(B)** "Today" demands that the verb be in the present tense, as choice (B) indicates. But choice (B) is correct for an additional reason; in its singularity, the verb "is" agrees with the singular subject "heart." By illogically switching to past tense, choice (A) is incorrect, as is choice (C); however, (C) also commits the error of suggesting a plural verb to go with a singular subject. Choice (D) continues this error with the plural verb "are." One should not be misled by prepositional phrases intervening between the true subject and verb for a subject will never be the object of a preposition.

54. **(J)** Choice (J) is correct for two reasons. It provides a noun, "complexion," for the adjectival phrase "Like...seashore" to modify, and it separates this lengthy introductory phrase from the following independent clause by a comma. By including the subordinate conjunction "since," choice (F) makes the independent clause dependent, and a phrase plus a dependent clause only results in a fragment. Thus, choice (F) is incorrect. (G) compounds (F)'s error by placing a semi-colon between the phrase and the dependent clause. Semi-colons join two *independent clauses*. Eliminating punctuation between the phrase and the dependent clause does not solve the fragment problem either, as choice (H) indicates. Still, there is just a phrase and a dependent clause.

55. **(B)** Correctly using the objective pronoun "us" as the object of the preposition "for," choice (B) is the right answer. All the other choices incorrectly supply nominative case pronouns reserved for the subject position in a clause.

56. **(J)** The logical placement for Sentence 2 is after Sentence 5, as indicated by choice (J). The paragraph is arranged in a spatial-chronological order, taking the reader down through the processes of erosion to the ancient artifacts that process reveals. Because of this order, it is logical that after the fossils, in general, are mentioned in Sentence 5, the specific types, the tool and tooth of Sentence 2, should follow. This tooth is then made more specific in Sentence 6 as perhaps belonging to the saber-toothed cats. Retaining Sentence 2 in its original position, as indicated by choice (F), interrupts the geological erosion sequence that changes the complexion of the Badlands (Sentence 1) by rain (Sentence 3). In order to appear before Sentence 1, as indicated by choice (G),

Sentence 2 would have to offer some transition from the previous paragraph, which it does not. If placed after Sentence 3, as suggested by choice (H), Sentence 2 would again interrupt the sequence of rain eating away the surfaces (Sentence 3) that results in the deposits peeling off (Sentence 4).

57. **(D)**   A comma precedes the coordinating conjunction separating the last two items in a list of three or more items. Choice (D) does just that and therefore is correct. Choice (A) incorrectly uses a semi-colon for this purpose, and choice (B) fails to provide the conjunction, thus making the sentence cadence incomplete. Finally, choice (C) is incorrect because of the comma appearing after the conjunction when it should appear before it.

58. **(G)**   By using the nominative case pronoun "who," which acts as the subject of that dependent clause, choice (G) is correct. A dependent clause cannot act as a complete sentence, as choice (F) incorrectly indicates. Choice (H) suggests the objective case "whom" act as the subject of the dependent clause, but grammar demands that the nominative case take the subject position. Using the possessive pronoun "whose," as suggested by choice (J), inspires one to ask,"Whose what?" Thus, choice (J) indicates an incomplete construction.

59. **(A)**   The separation of two independent clauses by a comma and a conjunction is grammatically correct, and thus choice (A) is the right answer. Without punctuation, the clauses become fused, as is the case with choice (B). The comma separating the independent clauses results in a comma splice error, evident in Choice (C), and choice (D) incorrectly places the semi-colon after the conjunction "yet" when its place is before that conjunction.

60. **(H)**   Because of its direct and economical use of language, choice (H) is correct. Conversational as it may be, choice (F)'s introductory dependent clause adds nothing to the more direct choice (H). Neither does the preponderance of prepositional phrases illustrated in choice (G) result in any added information. Finally, the repetitive "wild game" and "game animals" makes (J) an uneconomical choice.

61. **(D)**   The most logical placement of information on specific fossils is in Paragraph 4, where fossil discovery is discussed, as choice (D) correctly indicates. Not all important information comes in the introduction, otherwise nothing but introductions would be written or read. Thus, choice (A) is incorrect. Paragraph 2 provides transition between the past geological history of Paragraph 1 and the present state of the Badlands and furthermore has nothing specifically to do with particular mammal fossils and prehistoric migratory routes. Finally, Paragraph 3 certainly cannot be discounted as irrelevant, as choice (C) suggests, for it gives a concrete picture of this modern park, a picture necessary for us to be able to envision the effects of erosion.

62. **(J)** Because the singular verb "has" agrees in number with the singular subject "each," choice (J) is correct. "[H]ave," "retain," and "hold" of choices (F), (G), and (H), respectively, are all plural verbs and therefore don't agree with this singular subject. Often prepositional phrases which intervene between the subject and the verb will mislead one into an incorrect verb choice. "[E]ach" is the subject of the dependent clause beginning with "that," and "of the two hemispheres" and "of the brain" are merely prepositional phrases. It is wise to remember that a subject for a verb will never be found in a prepositional phrase. It is also wise to be able to recognize prepositions.

63. **(C)** The correct use of commas makes choice (C) the right answer. First, "insist the proponents of this theory" is a parenthetical expression, signaled by the first of a necessary set of two enclosing commas which appears before "insist." The mandatory companion comma is present after the phrase, as indicated in choice (C). Second, in lists of just two items, a comma does not precede the connective conjunction, in this case "and." Lists of three or more can have this preceding comma. As just two items are listed in this underlined portion, the comma is correctly absent, as choice (C) suggests. Choices (A) and (B) mistakenly place the comma before "and." Additionally, choice (B) fails to include the comma after the parenthetical expression, as does choice (D).

64. **(H)** Comparing two items requires an adjective or adverb of the comparative degree, as choice (H)'s selection of the adverb "more" correctly demonstrates. "[M]ost" and "greatest" of choices (F), (G), and (J) are all in the superlative degree and therefore are incorrect. Choice (J) compounds the error by suggesting the adverb "creatively" rather than the adjective "creative." An adverb cannot modify "half," a noun; an adjective can.

65. **(B)** Because choice (B) correctly foregoes punctuation before "and" as this conjunction is neither separating the last in a list of three or more items nor joining two independent clauses. The adverb "thus," as used in this sentence can be correctly punctuated in a variety of manners, depending on where the author would like the reader to pause while reading. Commas can surround "thus," be entirely absent, or appear on either one side or the other. At issue is the semicolon. In none of the choices is it necessary as it doesn't separate two independent clauses, and it isn't needed to clarify long lists of groups of items. Thus, choices (A), (C), and (D) are incorrect.

66. **(G)** Choice (G) correctly uses the semi-colon to join two independent clauses. By placing a comma at this juncture, choice (F) commits a comma splice error. Choice (H)'s presentation of the possessive "society's" renders the sentence nonsensical. First, the only object for "society" to possess is the "'left-brained' persons," but if these people are possessive objects, then "are" of the next set of words is left without a subject. The absence of punctuation between the two inde-

pendent clauses, as choice (J) indicates, creates a fused sentence, and thus this choice is incorrect.

67. **(D)** "[T]hat...functions" is a dependent clause having a subject and a verb but unable to stand alone and make sense. Choice (D) is the only selection that treats it as such. Note that no mark of punctuation is required between an independent clause and the essential dependent clause which follows. A dependent clause cannot act as a complete sentence, as choice (A) indicates, nor does choice (B)'s addition of "In" alter the essential problem. Still, in (C), the dependent clause incorrectly is made to stand alone. A semi-colon joins two independent clauses; however, since the words following the semi-colon in choice (D) cannot stand alone and make sense, they do not form an independent clause, thereby making this choice incorrect.

68. **(H)** The present tense singular verb "indicates" of choice (H) agrees in number with the singular subject "fact" and is consistent with the present tense of the rest of this passage. Hence, (H) is correct. Choice (F)'s "indicated" illogically switches to the past tense, and (G)'s "indicating" hints at present perfect tense, except that it lacks the necessary auxiliary verb "is." At any rate, the verb tense of choice (G) is in error. (J) both switches into past with "were" and makes plural what should be a singular verb.

69. **(B)** Because of economical language without loss of content, choice (B)'s "argue" is correct. (A)'s "on the fact that" says nothing and therefore is wasted wording. (C) suffers similar wordiness. Although not as excessively wordy as either (A) or (C), choice (D) suffers from illogical pronoun agreement. "[H]is" has no male antecedent.

70. **(J)** Adjective and adverb usage is the concern in this question. Adverbs modify verbs, adjectives, and other adverbs, and adjectives can only modify nouns. "[C]an still function" is the modified *verb* phrase, requiring therefore an adverb modifier. Choice (J) correctly supplies the adverbs "well" and "perfectly." Choice (F) incorrectly employs the two adjectives "good" and "perfect," and (G) fails with "good." (H) fails with "perfect."

71. **(C)** Pronoun reference is the issue here. Because the person who possesses the "thinking" is the third person singular noun "patient," the following pronoun reference must be third person singular, as well. Choice (C), "his/her" is just that. Choice (A) incorrectly suggests the third person *plural* "their," and choice (B) reverts to the *first* person *plural* "our." Choice (D) presents the contraction for "it is" and makes no sense at all.

72. **(G)** Because it supplies both the subject "that" and the verb "is" (in the contraction form "that's") for the dependent clause "that's...other," choice (G) is

correct. The possessive pronoun "its" offered by choice (F) neither has an object to possess nor is able to supply the necessary subject and verb to make the clause complete. No such words exist as (H)'s "thats" or (J)'s "its'," and thus these choices are incorrect.

73. **(C)** Choice (C)'s "without" functions correctly in the sentence by fulfilling the negative expectation set up with "impossible." (A)'s use of "than" shows no logical relationship between educating and not educating. Even more illogical is (B)'s adverb "then," for time is not an issue. Finally, choice (D) lacks a term which functions in comparison, a word such as "than"; however, even with the idiomatic phrase "rather than" complete, the sentence still does not fulfill the expectation of "without."

74. **(G)** Passage unity is best achieved by choice (G), which makes a general observation that a debate between two factions exists concerning brain function. The two factions are introduced in Paragraph 1, and their specific perspectives are developed in Paragraph 2. Choice (F)'s focus on education is too narrow as it applies only to Paragraph 2. Choice (H) is also too narrow a focus as it applies to the definition of the right-hemisphere abilities found only in Paragraph 1. Surgery to determine brain function, choice (J), is not discussed at all in the passage and therefore certainly cannot unify the existing paragraphs.

75. **(A)** Because the brain is part of the body and because this organ's functioning is at the heart of this passage, choice (A) is the best answer. Nowhere in the passage is gender an issue, and so choice (B)'s "Battle of the Sexes" is inappropriate. In Paragraph 1 a small allusion to civilization is made in connection with "left-brained" people; however, it is not enough to classify the entire passage, as choice (C) does, under "Cultural Heritage." This term implies a historical study of society's patterns and customs, certainly not the focus of this quite scientific debate. Surgical techniques are not a part of the passage either, and thus choice (D) is a poor selection for a section title.

Test 2: Mathematics

1. **(E)** $\dfrac{2}{x-5} = \dfrac{3}{x+7}$ (cross multiply)

$2x + 14 = 3x - 15$

$x = 29$

2. **(J)**

$$xy - 3x = 20$$
$$x(y - 3) = 20 \quad \text{(factored)}$$
$$x(5) = 20 \quad \text{(substituted } (y - 3) = 5)$$
$$x = 4 \quad \text{(divided both sides by 5)}$$

3. **(B)**

$$3x^2y - 2xy^2 + 5\,xy = xy(3x - 2y + 5)$$
$$= (1)(-2)[3(1) - 2(-2) + 5]$$
$$= -2[3 + 4 + 5]$$
$$= -24$$

4. **(G)**

$$8a + 12b = c$$
$$4(2a + 3b) = c \quad \text{(only 4 can be factored out)}$$

5. **(D)**

$$\sqrt{8} + 3\sqrt{18} - 7\sqrt{2} = \sqrt{4} \times \sqrt{2} + 3\sqrt{9} \times \sqrt{2} - 7\sqrt{2}$$
$$= 2\sqrt{2} + 9\sqrt{2} - 7\sqrt{2}$$
$$= 4\sqrt{2}$$

6. **(F)**

$$y + 4 = -2$$
$$y = -6$$

Substitute $y = -6$ into $xy - 2x = 16$:

$$x(-6) - 2x = 16$$
$$-6x - 2x = 16$$
$$-8x = 16$$
$$x = -2$$

7. **(B)**

$$b - 2 = 3$$
$$b = 5$$
$$ab - 3 = 7$$
$$5a - 3 = 7$$
$$5a = 10$$
$$a = 2$$

8. **(F)** In order to combine the denominator, $2 - \dfrac{1}{3}$, we must convert 2 into

thirds. $2 = 2 \times 1 = 2 \times \dfrac{3}{3} = \dfrac{6}{3}$. Thus

$$1 - \cfrac{1}{2 - \cfrac{1}{3}} = 1 - \cfrac{1}{\cfrac{6}{3} - \cfrac{1}{3}} = 1 - \cfrac{1}{\cfrac{5}{3}}.$$

Since division by a fraction is equivalent to multiplication by that fraction's reciprocal,

$$1 - \frac{1}{\frac{5}{3}} = 1 - (1)\left(\frac{3}{5}\right) = 1 - \frac{3}{5} = \frac{5}{5} - \frac{3}{5} = \frac{2}{5}$$

$$1 - \frac{1}{2 - \frac{1}{3}} = \frac{2}{5}.$$

9.   **(B)**   The problem may best be solved by setting up a system of simultaneous equations. Since there are two unknowns, namely the units digit and the tens digit, two equations are needed to solve for these variables, u and t, respectively.

One equation can be obtained from the fact that the sum of the digits is 9. Thus

$$t + u = 9. \tag{1}$$

The other condition states that the number itself (which can be expressed as $10t + 1u$ since the number has t 10's and u units) is equal to 9 times the units digit. Therefore we obtain:

$$10t + u = 9u. \tag{2}$$

Solving Equation (1) for t we have $t = 9 - u$. Now substituting this value of t into Equation (2) we obtain:

$$9u = 10(9 - u) + u$$

Simplifying we obtain:

$$9u = 90 - 10u + u,$$
$$9u = 90 - 9u,$$
$$18u = 90,$$
$$u = \frac{90}{18},$$
$$u = 5.$$

Substituting this value of u into Equation (1) we obtain 4 as the value of t, therefore the required number is 45.

10.   **(G)**   Four consecutive even integers can be represented by $2n$, $2n + 2$, $2n + 4$, and $2n + 6$.

$$(2n) + (2n + 2) + (2n + 4) + (2n + 6) = 68$$

$$8n + 12 = 68$$
$$8n = 56$$
$$2n = 14.$$

Therefore, the value of the smallest one is 14.

11. **(B)** $\frac{2}{3}x = 0 \Rightarrow x = 0$

Therefore, $\frac{2}{3} + x = \frac{2}{3}.$

12. **(K)** $\frac{2}{\frac{y}{3}} = \frac{1}{4}$

$8 = \frac{y}{3}$ (cross multiplied)

$y = 24$ (multipled both sides by 3)

13. **(C)** Let x be the first odd number. Then,

$$x + (x + 2) + (x + 4) = 51$$
$$3x + 6 = 51$$
$$3x = 45$$
$$x = 15$$

14. **(H)** When an even integer is multiplied by another integer, the result will be even, i.e. it will be divisible by 2.

I satisfies this. (a is even)

II satisfies this. (The sum $a + b$ is multiplied by 2, which is even.)

III can be even or odd (when we divide an even number by 2, the result can be either odd or even, e.g. $\frac{6}{2} = 3$ but $\frac{8}{2} = 4$).

Thus, (H) is the correct choice.

15. **(C)** A first method is to just add the terms in the numerator and denominator, obtaining

$$\frac{\dfrac{2}{x}+\dfrac{3}{y}}{1-\dfrac{1}{x}}=\frac{\dfrac{2y}{xy}+\dfrac{3x}{xy}}{\dfrac{x}{x}-\dfrac{1}{x}}=\frac{\dfrac{2y+3x}{xy}}{\dfrac{x-1}{x}}.$$

Since dividing by a fraction is equivalent to multiplying by its reciprocal,

$$=\frac{2y+3x}{xy}\times\frac{x}{x-1}=\frac{2y+3x}{y(x-1)}.$$

A second method is to multiply both numerator and denominator by the least common denominator of the entire fraction, in this case xy:

$$\frac{\dfrac{2}{x}+\dfrac{3}{y}}{1-\dfrac{1}{x}}=\frac{xy\left(\dfrac{2}{x}+\dfrac{3}{y}\right)}{xy\left(1-\dfrac{1}{x}\right)}.$$

Distributing, $\quad=\dfrac{xy\left(\dfrac{2}{x}\right)+xy\left(\dfrac{3}{y}\right)}{xy(1)-xy\left(\dfrac{1}{x}\right)}$

Cancelling like terms,

$$=\frac{2y+3x}{xy-y}$$

Using distributive law,

$$=\frac{2y+3x}{y(x-1)}.$$

16. **(J)** Since $(x-1)^2 \geq 0$ for all x, the minimum value occurs when $(x-1)^2 = 0$. Hence, $f(x) = 0 + 3 = 3$ is the minimum value. This conclusion can also be made by considering the graph of the function, which is a parabola.

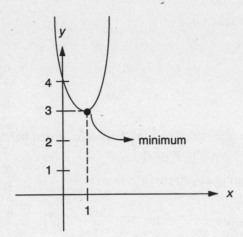

17. **(E)** $\quad \frac{2}{3}y = 0 \qquad$ (multiply both sides by $\frac{3}{2}$)

$\qquad y = 0$

$\qquad \frac{4}{3} + y = \frac{4}{3} + 0 \qquad$ (substitute $y = 0$)

$\qquad\qquad = \frac{4}{3}$

18. **(J)** $\quad \dfrac{3+4i}{2+i}\dfrac{2-i}{2-i} = \dfrac{6-4i^2+5i}{4-i^2}$

$\qquad\qquad = \dfrac{6+4+5i}{4+1} \qquad$ (substituted -1 for i^2)

$\qquad\qquad = \dfrac{10+5i}{5}$

$\qquad\qquad = 2+i$

19. **(C)** $\quad \dfrac{a}{b} = 3 \Rightarrow a = 3b$

$\qquad a^3 - 27b^3 = (3b)^3 - 27b^3$

$\qquad\qquad\quad = 27b^3 - 27b^3$

$\qquad\qquad\quad = 0$

20. **(F)** Since $g(f(x)) = x$, $f(x)$ and $g(x)$ must be inverse functions. To find the inverse function for $f(x)$, first solve $f(x) = y = 3x + 2$ for x:

$\qquad x = \dfrac{y-2}{3}.$

Then interchange (switch) x and y:

$$y = \frac{x-2}{3}.$$

This is $g(x)$.

21. **(E)**   If we notice that the given polynomial can be factored into $(x + 4)$ $(2x - 3)$, we have the answer immediately.

Otherwise we can use synthetic division:

$$
\begin{array}{r}
2x - 3 \\
x + 4 \enclose{longdiv}{2x^2 + 5x - 12} \\
-\ \ (2x^2 + 8x) \\
\hline
-3x - 12 \\
-\ \ (-3x - 12) \\
\hline
0
\end{array}
$$

22. **(K)**   Since the statement,

$$\log_b \frac{1}{25} = -2$$

is equivalent to

$$b^{-2} = \frac{1}{25} \text{ and}$$

$$b^{-2} = \frac{1}{b^2}, \text{ we know}$$

$$\frac{1}{b^2} = \frac{1}{25}.$$

Cross multiply to obtain the equivalent equation,

$$b^2 = 25.$$

Take the square root of both sides, to find

$$b = \pm 5.$$

You must discard the negative root, since the base must always be positive, therefore

$$b = +5.$$

23. **(D)** $\log_2 (x - 1) + \log_2 (x + 1) = 3$

$$\log_2 (x - 1)(x + 1) = 3$$
$$(x - 1)(x + 1) = 2^3$$
$$x^2 - 1 = 8$$
$$x^2 = 9$$
$$x = 3 \quad \text{(again, discard the negative root, since you cannot take the log of a negative number)}$$

24. **(H)**   To simplify the left side of the equation, note that $i^2 = -1$:

$$(a + bi)(1 - i) = a - ai + bi - bi^2$$
$$= (a + b) + (b - a)i = 2 - 4i.$$

The corresponding real and imaginary parts must be equal:

$a + b = 2$ and $b - a = -4.$

Solve these equations simultaneously, rewriting second as

$-a + b = -4.$

$$a + b = 2$$
$$\underline{- (-a + b = -4)} \qquad \text{(subtract equations)}$$
$$2a = 6$$
$$a = 3.$$

25. **(E)**   We are given the domain of $f(x)$ as $-5 \le x \le 8$. This domain corresponds, on a one-to-one basis, to a particular range of values. Given $f(x)$, we substitute the minimum and maximum values of the domain to find the required range (this method is correct here because the function $f(x) = 7x - 8$ is a straight line with a positive slope).

Function: $f(x) = 7x - 8$

Substituting -5 for x:

$f(-5) = 7(-5) - 8 = -35 - 8 = -43$

-43 is the lower limit.

Substituting 8 for x:

$f(8) = 7(8) - 8 = 56 - 8 = 48$

48 is the upper limit.

Therefore the range is:

$-43 \le y \le 48.$

26. **(J)**   When given an inequality with an absolute value, recall the definition of absolute value:

$$|x| \equiv \begin{cases} x \text{ if } x \geq 0 \\ -x \text{ if } x < 0 \end{cases}$$

$6x - 5 \leq 8$ if $6x - 5 \geq 0$.

$-6x + 5 \leq 8$ if $6x - 5 < 0$.

$-6x + 5 \leq 8$ can be written as $6x - 5 \geq -8$.

We can set up both of these equations as follows:

$$-8 \leq 6x - 5 \leq 8.$$

adding 5: $-3 \leq 6x \leq 13$

dividing by 6: $-\dfrac{1}{2} \leq x \leq \dfrac{13}{6}.$

So the values of x which satisfy $|6x - 5| \leq 8$ are $\left[-\dfrac{1}{2}, \dfrac{13}{6} \right]$.

27. **(E)**   A general term is given by the expression:

$$\sum_{r=0}^{n} \frac{n!}{r!(n-r)!} a^{n-r} b^r$$

For the fourth term, $r = 3$ (not 4) and $n = 9$.

By substitution we obtain:

$$\frac{9!}{3!6!}(1)^6(-2x^2)^3 = -672x^6.$$

28. **(K)** $27^x = (3^3)^x = 3^{3x}$

$\quad\quad\quad\quad 9 = 3^2$

Thus we have $3^{3x} = 3^2$. Equating exponents gives $3x = 2$ or $x = \dfrac{2}{3}$. Now $2^{x-y} = 64 = 2^6$ so $x - y = 6$ or $\dfrac{2}{3} - y = 6$. Hence, $y = \dfrac{2}{3} - 6 = -\dfrac{16}{3}$.

29. **(E)**   To solve we must factor both numerator and denominator of the given expression to lowest terms.

Expression: $\dfrac{a^2 - 3ab + 2b^2}{2b^2 + ab - a^2}$.

Factoring the numerator:

$$a^2 - 3ab + 2b^2 = (a - 2b)(a - b).$$

Factoring the denominator:

$$2b^2 + ab - a^2 = (2b - a)(b + a).$$

Rewriting the expression:

$$\frac{(a - 2b)(a - b)}{(2b - a)(b + a)} = \frac{a - 2b}{2b - a} \times \frac{a - b}{b + a}.$$

We note that $a - 2b = -1(2b - a)$. Therefore,

$$\frac{a - 2b}{2b - a} = -1.$$

The expression reduces to

$$-1\left(\frac{a - b}{b + a}\right) = \frac{b - a}{b + a}.$$

30. **(G)** $\dfrac{3a^2bc^3 + 9a^3b^2c}{27ab^2c + 15a^2b^2c^3} = \dfrac{3a^2bc(c^2 + 3ab)}{3ab^2c(9 + 5ac^2)}$

$$= \frac{a(c^2 + 3ab)}{b(9 + 5ac^2)}$$

31. **(A)** $\dfrac{\sqrt[3]{-16}}{\sqrt[3]{-2}} = \dfrac{\sqrt[3]{(-2)8}}{\sqrt[3]{-2}} = \dfrac{\sqrt[3]{-2}\sqrt[3]{8}}{\sqrt[3]{-2}} = \sqrt[3]{8} = 2$

Note that since 3 is an odd number, $\sqrt[3]{-2}$ is defined to be a real number and is not imaginary.

32. **(J)** Substitute $x = 2$ and $y = 1$ into the given pair of equations to obtain:

$2a + b = 8$ (1)

$a + 2b = 10$ (2)

Multiply the second equation by -2 and add it to the first equation to solve for b.

$$2a + b = 8$$
$$-2a - 4b = -20$$
$$\overline{}$$
$$-3b = -12$$
$$b = 4$$

Substituting 4 back into equation (1) yields:

$$2a + 4 = 8$$
$$2a = 4$$
$$a = 2.$$

33. **(D)** $Y(t) = \dfrac{(t^2 + 3)}{(t^3 - 4)}$, but in order for us to express this in terms of x, we

must note that $x = t + 2$ or $t = x - 2$. Substituting we have

$$\frac{[(x-2)^2 + 3]}{[(x-2)^3 - 4]}$$

$$= \frac{[(x^2 - 4x + 4) + 3]}{[(x^3 - 6x^2 + 12x - 8) - 4]}$$

$$= \frac{(x^2 - 4x + 7)}{(x^3 - 6x^2 + 12x - 12)}.$$

34. **(J)** From the graph, when $y = 0$, $x = 0$ or $x = 2$. Therefore, $\{0,2\}$ are the roots of the quadratic equation.

35. **(A)** The equation of the line is obtained from the point-slope equation:

$$\frac{y - 1}{x - (-1)} = 2$$
$$\frac{y - 1}{x + 1} = 2$$
$$y - 1 = 2x + 2$$
$$2x - y + 3 = 0.$$

36. **(J)** $AB = \sqrt{[4 - (-1)]^2 + (6 - 2)^2}$

$$= \sqrt{5^2 + 4^2}$$
$$= \sqrt{41}$$

37. **(C)** $x\text{-coordinate} = \dfrac{3+(-3)}{2} = 0$

    $y\text{-coordinate} = \dfrac{4+6}{2} = 5$

38. **(G)** $y = f(x + 3)$
    $= 7(x + 3) - 4$
    $= 7x + 21 - 4$
    $= 7x + 17.$

Set $y = 0$: $7x + 17 = 0$
    $x = \dfrac{-17}{7}.$

Therefore, the x-intercept is $\dfrac{-17}{7}$.

39. **(E)**   If two lines are perpendicular, the slope of one line is the negative reciprocal of the slope of the other. We can rewrite the equation of the line given so that it appears in slope-intercept form. That is,

$$x - 3y + 2 = 0$$
$$x + 2 = 3y$$
$$\frac{1}{3}x + \frac{2}{3} = y.$$

In this form the coefficient of the x variable is the slope of the given line. Therefore the slope of the line which is perpendicular to it is -3.

   Since we know a point on the line and the slope of the line, the obvious choice for the form of the equation is the point-slope form: $y - y_0 = m(x - x_0)$, where m is the slope and (x_0, y_0) is the given point.

Substituting yields: $y - 2 = -3(x - (-1))$

    $y - 2 = -3x - 3$

    $y = -3x - 1.$

Adding $3x + 1$ on both sides, we obtain

    $3x + y + 1 = 0.$

40. **(H)**

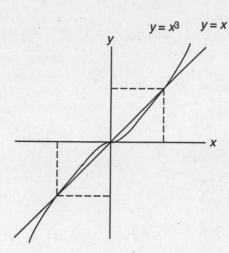

If we solve $x^3 = x$ we find that $x = 0$ is one solution. If $x \neq 0$ we can divide by x to get $x^2 = 1 \Rightarrow x = \pm 1$. Hence the three points of intersection are

$$\{(0,0), (-1,-1), (1,1)\}.$$

41. **(E)** The midpoint of a line segment from (x_1, y_1) to (x_2, y_2) is given by

$$\left(\frac{x_1 + x_2}{2}, \frac{y_1 + y_2}{2} \right).$$

$$\left(\frac{-2 + 4}{2}, \frac{4 + (-6)}{2} \right)$$

Therefore, $(1,-1)$ is the midpoint of PQ.

42. **(F)** The segment $\overline{OC}$, in addition to being perpendicular to $\overline{AB}$, intersects chord $\overline{AB}$ at its midpoint. Hence,

$$\overline{AC} = \overline{BC} = 8 \text{ in.}$$

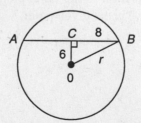

We have

$$r^2 = 6^2 + 8^2$$
$$r^2 = 100$$
$$r = 10.$$

The length of the radius is 10 inches.

43. **(D)** The quickest method is to find some (x, y) pairs by substituting values for x.

If $x = 2$, $y = |2 - 2| = |0| = 0$, so the point $(2,0)$ must be on the graph.

If $x = 0$, $y = |0 - 2| = |-2| = 2$, so the point $(0,2)$ must be on the graph.

Only graphs (C) and (D) meet both these requirements.

However, only (D) has the characteristic shape of an absolute value graph, so the answer is (D).

44. **(K)** $x° = y°$ (therefore vertically opposite angles)
$x° + 70° = 180°$ (therefore supplementary angles)
$x° = 110°$

Therefore, $x + y = 220.$

45. **(E)** $\angle ACB = 45°$ (vertically opposite angles)
$\theta = \angle ABC + \angle ACB$
$= 35° + 45°$
$= 80°$

46. **(F)**   Since $BC \parallel DE$, $\triangle ABC$ is similar to $\triangle ADE$. Therefore,

$$\frac{AB}{AD} = \frac{BC}{DE} = \frac{AC}{AE} = \frac{b}{a}.$$

Thus, $\dfrac{BC}{DE} = \dfrac{b}{a}.$

47. **(A)**   If $\angle C = 1$ rad then $\overset{\frown}{AB} = 2$ radians. Now we use the formula $S = r\theta$, where S = arc length (in meters, for this problem), r = length of radius, and θ = measure of intercepted arc in radians. $S = r\theta = \left(\dfrac{10}{12} \text{ meters}\right)(2) = 10$ meters.

Note that the central angle corresponds to twice the measure of an inscribed angle if both of them intercept the same arc.

48. **(K)**   A bisector of one angle of a triangle divides the opposite side so that the lengths of its segments are proportional to the lengths of the adjacent sides. Thus,

$$\frac{6}{8} = \frac{\overline{AD}}{\overline{DB}}$$

Since $\dfrac{8}{8} = \dfrac{\overline{DB}}{\overline{DB}}$ is always true, by adding to the above proportion, we obtain:

$$\frac{6+8}{8} = \frac{\overline{AD}+\overline{DB}}{\overline{DB}}.$$

But, $\overline{AD}+\overline{DB}=\overline{AB}$, the hypotenuse of a right triangle. Applying the Pythagorean theorem, $a^2 + b^2 = c^2$, where $a = 6$, $b = 8$, we obtain:

$$6^2 + 8^2 = c^2$$
$$36 + 64 = c^2$$
$$100 = c^2$$

Thus, $c = 10$ or hypotenuse $\overline{AB} = 10$. Substituting we obtain:

$$\frac{6+8}{8} = \frac{\overline{AD}+\overline{DB}}{\overline{DB}}$$
$$\frac{14}{8} = \frac{\overline{AB}}{\overline{DB}}$$
$$\frac{14}{8} = \frac{10}{\overline{DB}}$$
$$14\overline{DB} = 8 \times 10$$
$$\overline{DB} = \frac{80}{14} = \frac{40}{7}, \overline{AD} = \overline{AB} - \overline{DB} = 10 - \frac{40}{7} = \frac{30}{7}$$
$$\overline{AD} = \frac{30}{7} \quad \text{and} \quad \overline{DB} = \frac{40}{7}.$$

49. **(C)**   A triangle (inscribed in a circle) that has one side as the diameter of the circle is a right triangle. The base of the triangle, $\overline{AC}$, equals $2r$ and the height, $\overline{OB}$, equals r. The area of a triangle is $\dfrac{1}{2} \times$ base $\times$ height. The area of a circle is πr^2.

$$\frac{A_T}{A_C} = \frac{\frac{1}{2} \times 2r \times r}{\pi r^2} = \frac{r^2}{\pi r^2} = \frac{1}{\pi}$$

50. **(G)** Area of $\Delta A'B'C' = \dfrac{1}{2}a'h'$.

Since the triangles are similar,

$$a' = ka \tag{1}$$
$$h' = kh \tag{2}$$

Substituting from (1) and (2) gives:

$$\text{Area of } \Delta A'B'C' = \frac{1}{2}(ka)(kh)$$
$$= \frac{1}{2}k^2 ah$$
$$= \frac{k^2 ah}{2}.$$

51. **(B)** $\angle CAD = \angle CBD$ since angles inscribed in the same or congruent arcs are congruent.

52. **(H)**
$$AC = AD - CD$$
$$= 2AB - CD \qquad (\text{as } AD = 2AB)$$
$$= 2 \times 2\frac{3}{4} - 1\frac{1}{2}$$
$$= \frac{22}{4} - \frac{6}{4}$$
$$= \frac{16}{4}$$
$$= 4$$

53. **(C)** $AB = AC = 4$ because ΔABC is an isosceles triangle.

$$\text{Area of } \Delta ABC = \frac{1}{2}(4)(4)$$
$$= 8$$

$$\text{Area of } \Delta ADB = \frac{1}{2}(4)(7)$$
$$= 14$$

$$\text{Area of } \Delta DCB = \text{ area of } \Delta ADB - \text{ area of } \Delta ABC$$
$$= 14 - 8$$
$$= 6$$

54. **(H)** Let r be the radius of the smaller circle. Then the radius of the larger circle is $2r$.

$$\text{Ratio} = \frac{2\pi(2r)}{2\pi r} = 2$$

55. **(B)** $\Delta DEG \sim \Delta ABG$, $\quad \Delta GEF \sim \Delta GBC$ and $\Delta GDF \sim \Delta GAC$.

Therefore,

$$\frac{AB}{AC} = \frac{DE}{DF} = \frac{DE}{DE + EF} = \frac{a}{a+b}.$$

56. **(K)** I. From Pythagoras' theorem, $c = \sqrt{a^2 + b^2}$

II. $\cos\theta = \dfrac{b}{c}$

$\quad c = \dfrac{b}{\cos\theta}$

III. $\sin\phi = \dfrac{b}{c}$

$\quad c = \dfrac{b}{\sin\phi}$

Therefore, I, II, and III are true.

57. **(A)** $\sin 2x - \sqrt{2}\,\sin x = 0$

$\quad 2\sin x \cos x = \sqrt{2}\,\sin x$

$x = 0$ and $x = \pi$ are solutions, for we obtain 0=0. If $x \neq 0$ and $x \neq \pi$ then we can divide by $\sin x$:

$$2\cos x = \sqrt{2}$$

$$\cos x = \frac{\sqrt{2}}{2} \Rightarrow x = \frac{\pi}{4}.$$

58. **(K)** I. From trigonometric identity:

$$\tan\theta = \frac{\sin\theta}{\cos\theta}$$

II. $\cos \phi = \sin(90° - \phi) = \sin \theta$

Similarly, $\sin \phi = \cos(90° - \phi) = \cos \theta.$

Thus, $\dfrac{\cos \phi}{\sin \phi} = \dfrac{\sin \theta}{\cos \theta} = \tan \theta.$

III. $\tan \theta = \dfrac{\text{opposite side}}{\text{adjacent side}} = \dfrac{a}{b}$

Therefore, all of the above expressions are equal to $\tan \theta$.

59. **(B)**   Let $\theta = \arctan x$. Then $\tan \theta = x$. We can construct a right triangle with $\tan \theta = x$:

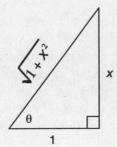

The length of the hypotenuse is obtained by the Pythagorean Theorem to be $\sqrt{1 + x^2}$. Thus $\cos(\arctan x) =$

$$\cos \theta = \frac{1}{\sqrt{1 + x^2}}.$$

60. **(F)** $\cos C = \dfrac{BC}{AC} = \dfrac{5}{13}$

$BC = AC\left(\dfrac{5}{13}\right)$

$BC = 13\left(\dfrac{5}{13}\right)$

$BC = 5$

Test 3: Reading

1. **(D)** As stated in the fourth paragraph of the reading passage, the author believes that the earth's crust is thin and its center is molten; IV reflects this belief. (D) is the only means by which answer IV alone can be selected; therefore, (D) is the correct answer. The author believes that solidified materials float on the surface and do not sink; statement I cannot be selected. (A), (B), and (C) cannot be chosen because all include I. The author does not believe that the solidification of the earth would begin at the center; the author believes solidification begins at the crust of the earth. Since both (B) and (C) include II, (B) and (C) should not be selected. The author does not believe that the whole world is consolidated; III cannot be selected. Since (C) includes III, the reader, again, should not select (C).

2. **(G)** The best answer is (G); the author believes that the condition was probably an actuality, as evidenced by his use of the words "somewhat conclusive" in discussing this concept. Because a myth is the opposite of an actuality, (F) is not the correct answer. The author does think the igneous fluid condition is relevant to this reading passage; the use of the word NOT causes (H) to be incorrect, so (H) should not be chosen. The author does believe that there is supporting evidence for the igneous fluid condition; (J) is incorrect due to the prefix "in," meaning "not," before the word conclusive. (F), (H), and (J) all indicate the opposite of that which the author presents in the reading passage.

3. **(A)** (A) is the best answer because the author does not venture any opinion as to whether the former gaseous condition existed. Since the author ventures no opinion of the theory, this non-existent opinion can neither be favorable, negative, nor essential; consequently, (B), (C), and (D) are all incorrect.

4. **(H)** During the time the earth was a self-luminous star, there was a liquid core surrounded by burning acrid vapors, according to the statement in the middle of the second paragraph; (H) is the best answer. The passage questions, rather than denies, the existence of the moon at this time; hence, (F) is not correct. There was carbonic acid, according to the second sentence of the second paragraph ; (G) is false and should not be selected. (J) is another incorrect answer since the author states that the glow of the earth was "more fearful than the poisoned ray of feebly-shining sun."

5. **(B)** The author's purpose is to describe a view of the earth from its stage of igneous fluidity until the stage when solidification of the crust began; (B) is the best answer since these are the parameters of the passage. The author presents a view of the gaseous condition of the world, but not necessarily his; (A) should not be chosen. The purpose of the article is not really to describe a view

on the expansion of heat; (C) places too much emphasis on this view and should not be chosen. The main purpose of the article is not to describe the law of thermal equilibrium; (D) should not be selected because the law of thermal equilibrium is only mentioned, not elaborated upon in any great depth.

6. **(F)**   The author admits some skepticism about the crystallization of materials to form the earth's crust; (F) is the best answer. (G) should not be chosen since it denies the existence of a sun and the author refers to the existence of the sun at the time the igneous fluid condition existed. Because the author states, rather than questions, that chaos existed at that time, (H) is not an acceptable answer. The author also states, rather than questions, that solid iron will float upon molten iron; (J) should not be selected.

7. **(D)**   I, II, and III are correct as all of these choices are stated in the third paragraph; (D) includes all three correct answers. (A) and (B) cannot be chosen since they do not include all the correct choices. IV is incorrect since crystallization began at the crust, not the core, of the earth; therefore, (C) is incorrect since it includes IV.

8. **(F)**   The best answer is (F), since the author, near the end of the fourth paragraph, expresses the view that newly-solidified parts are less dense than the unsolidified parts—an exception to the law of expansion by heat. Since the author believes that the newly-solidified parts will float, rather than sink or descend toward the center, (G) should not be chosen. The author writes that "the central portions of the earth still remain in a molten condition," which negates any suggestion that (H) is true and makes (H) another incorrect answer. The author does not think the whole will be consolidated but, rather, recognizes the liquid core; (J) is, therefore, an incorrect choice.

9. **(B)**   In the last paragraph the author infers that the crystals of quartz would float; (B) is the best choice. Because the newly-formed crystals are a little more, not less, bulky, (A) cannot be the answer. According to the passage, they are less, not more, dense; therefore, (C) is also incorrect. The author does believe, as evidenced by the final sentence of the passage, that the crystals are related to the formation of the earth's crust; (D), which states the opposite, should not be selected.

10. **(J)**   The question asks which answer the author would deny; the implication is that he states what he accepts. Since the author spends the entire passage accounting for this crust, (J) is the correct choice since it indicates that there is probably no means of accounting for the formation of the crust. The author does not deny, but rather discusses, the igneous fluidity of the earth (F), the earth as a self-luminous star (G), and the possibility that the moon could have raised the fiery ocean to a tidal wave (H); neither (F), (G), nor (H) are correct answers.

11. **(C)**   The correct answer is (C); the author means that an order (exhortation) of the assembly will be carried out as given. In this case the word "executed" means carried out, not with ending a life; (A) should not be chosen. Again the word "execution" means to carry out, not to kill, in this instance; (B) is not the best choice. The phrase in this case does not mean to speak before the assembly because there is no reference to this in this reading passage; (D) is an incorrect choice.

12. **(J)**   The master is particularly pleased with the servant because he has cured himself of bad habits (III) and has sought to imitate the Houyhnhnms (IV) as is stated at the end of the first paragraph; (J) allows the reader to choose both answers. (H) includes only one of these and should not be selected. While the servant is able to swim (I) and build a boat (II), the master does not express pride in these two actions; answers (F) and (G) include these two items and should not be chosen.

13. **(D)**   The best answer is (D); the phrase refers to a swoon or faint during which the body does not function properly. In this case, the word "imbecilities" relates to foolishness, rather to intelligence. Neither (A), (B), nor (C) should be chosen since all refer to intelligence.

14. **(J)**   The narrator of the article is the servant as is indicated by "My master," the first words of the reading passage, and later references to the narrator being "in his service"; (J) is the best answer. Once one has ascertained that (J) is the correct answer, (F) must be incorrect since one cannot be the master and the servant at the same time. (H) is also incorrect since the narrator continually refers to the Houyhnhnm with respect and deference while referring to himself as "miserable," or lowly. The narrator is not literally an animal; the reference he makes to himself as an animal is only figurative language; (G) is an incorrect answer.

15. **(D)**   The master came to see him off for two reasons: he was kind and curious as stated in the next to the last paragraph of the passage; (D) is the best answer. Because the passage makes no reference to either grieving by the master (A) or the need for the master to make certain that the narrator really left (C), (A) and (C) are incorrect answers. (B) contains only part of the answer: curiosity; since it does not include the kindness, (B) should not be chosen.

16. **(F)**   The "sorrel nag" is a reference to a horse; (F) is the best choice. The reader can figure this out by the process of elimination. The red sorrel is ordered to help the narrator; since one would not order a tool to help, (G) is not the correct answer. The master orders the red sorrel to help; since the red sorrel cannot, therefore, be the master, (H) is incorrect. The narrator is telling the story so the narrator himself cannot be the red sorrel (J).

17. **(C)** The correct answer is (C); the narrator wants both to propose the ways of the Houyhnhnms to others (II) and to build a craft to sail (IV) as stated in the third paragraph. There is no reference to wanting to return to France (I) so the reader should not choose (A), (B), and (D), which involve answer (I). Neither does the servant want to swim the hundred leagues; since (III) is in answer (B), the reader should not choose (B).

18. **(F)** (F) is the best answer since the narrator seems to be in submission to his master; the narrator demonstrates this by prostrating himself to kiss his master's hoof. The narrator is not arrogant as the reader can tell from the narrator's description of himself as "a miserable yahoo"; (G) is not a good answer. (H) is an incorrect answer since the master is the one exhorting the narrator, rather than vice-versa as this choice suggests. The narrator does not have grief toward the master, but rather at the thought of leaving the master; (J) should not be chosen.

19. **(A)** The Houyhnhnms have no conception of compelling others to do something as is stated in the second paragraph; therefore, (A) is the best answer. Since this same paragraph explains that the Houyhnhnms advise (B) is not the correct answer since it claims the opposite. One may infer from the narrator's discussion of hnhloayn that the Houyhnhnms are rational creatures; since (C) suggests otherwise, (C) is not a correct answer. The Houyhnhnms obey—and do not disobey—reason as the last part of this discourse about hnhloayn explicates; (D) should not be chosen.

20. **(J)** The narrator declares, "...no person can disobey reason, without giving up his claim to be a rational creature."; conversely, a rational person obeys reason which makes (J) the correct answer. (F) is incorrect since it states the opposite of (J). A rational creature does not have to be compelled but rather advised; hence (G) is false. According to the text, a rational creature does not have to be told what to do or exhorted; consequently, (H) is not a good choice.

21. **(C)** The best answer is (C), since both II and III are stated in the opening sentence of the reading passage and (C) allows the reader to choose both of these answers. (A), (B), and (D) cannot be chosen since each includes I, which is incorrect since laborers attempt to get, rather than resist, a raise in wages.

22. **(G)** The reader is looking for the false statement; since a raise in wages would NOT necessarily affect the average price of commodities, (G) is false and should be selected. The other statements, (F), (H), and (J) are all true, as can be verified by referring to the passage; since the question asks for a false statement, each of these is an incorrect answer.

23. **(D)**   Again the test-taker is looking for the false answer—the one that the author would not agree with, according to the passage. In this case (D) is the false answer and should be selected, since the author would not agree with the statement that the value of one's necessaries are separate and apart from the amount of labor needed to produce them. The author states that the market price of labor will adapt to its value (A), that the working man will receive only the value of his labor (B), and that the laboring power is determined by the value of the necessaries (C); answers (A), (B), and (C) are true and should not be selected.

24. **(H)**   The ultimate length of the working day is determined by the physical limitation of the worker, as the author explains in the third paragraph of the reading passage; (H) is the correct answer and should be selected. The length of the work day is not ultimately determined by historical events (F), the social environment (G), or the ruling class (J). All three are incorrect choices since each is mentioned in relation to the value of labor rather than the ultimate limit of length of the working day; neither (F), (G), nor (J) should be selected.

25. **(A)**   The author's purpose is to present the struggle between capital and labor and its results; since this purpose is evident in his statement that "...this incessant struggle between capital and labor...." in the last sentence of his opening paragraph, (A) is the best answer. (B) is incorrect since the author does discuss labor and value at length but barely mentions national standards. Because legislative interference is mentioned only once, it cannot be the author's purpose in writing the passage; subsequently, (C) is also incorrect. The author deals with the manipulations of getting, rather than the importance of, money in society causing (D) to be another incorrect answer.

26. **(F)**   The best answer is (F) since the author states in paragraph two that the market price of labor will adapt to its value. It is the limitation of the working day, rather than the market price of labor, which must be controlled by legislative action; consequently, (G) is not the correct answer. Because it is the value of labor, not commodities, which is determined by the physical strength of a person, (H) is not the correct answer. (J) is incorrect because of the erroneous placement of the nouns; it is the minimum DAY and the maximum of WAGES for which the laborer works.

27. **(A)**   Since both I and III are stated by the author, they are both true. II is untrue since it is physical and historical, not mental elements which form the value of the laboring power. (A) is the correct answer since it includes both I and III. (B) is incorrect since it gives only the incorrect answer II. (C) is incorrect since it excludes one of the two correct statements. (D) is incorrect; although it includes the correct answer III, it also includes the incorrect statement II.

28. **(H)** In the last paragraph of the passage, the author states both I and II. Since, in the same paragraph, the author states that the limitation of the working day is NOT a result of private settlement (III), III is a false statement. (H), which includes both I and II, is the correct answer. (F) and (G) are both incorrect since each includes only one of the two true statements. Although (J) includes the two true statements, it also includes (III) which is incorrect; therefore, (J) should not be selected.

29. **(A)** I is false since the author states, "...the capitalist constantly tending to reduce wages to their physical minimum, and to extend the working day to its physical maximum...."; he is denying that laborers are the stronger in economic action. This same quote proves II to be a true statement. III is also a true statement according to the closing sentence of the passage. (A) is the correct answer since it incorporates only the false statement which the author would deny. (B) is incorrect since it incorporates only a true statement which the author would deny. (C) is incorrect because it includes both true statements while the question asks for the false statement. While (D) does include a true statement, it also includes a false statement; Therefore, (D) cannot be the correct choice.

30. **(F)** The best title for the passage involving the struggle between capital and labor is "The Struggle" (F); the author makes numerous and constant references to the struggle between laborers and capitalists. Since the author sees the two as constantly at odds, "Reaching Consensus" (G) is not a feasible title. The passage deals with more than just "Capitalism" (H) or just "Laborers" (J); (H) and (J) are incorrect choices.

31. **(B)** The correct answer is (B) because the author believes the only offense never contemplated by the government is denying its authority. Since the "injustice" or unfairness mentioned in the first sentence of the third paragraph refers to the treatment of taxpayers, choice I, which states the opposite, is incorrect; answers (A) and (C) are not correct thanks to their inclusion of I. Because the inclusion of choice III in answer (D), (D) is incorrect in view of the example in the second paragraph. This reasoning further supports (D) as an incorrect answer.

32. **(H)** According to the second sentence of the text, (H) is the best answer. (G) is an incorrect answer since the third sentence in the passage states that retaliation for resistance of "transgression" of unjust laws is feared, which is the opposite of what this answer suggests. Neither (F) nor (J) can be correct answers since being content with or ignorant of the law is not the same as amending and obeying unjust laws until they are altered.

33. **(B)** (B) is the best answer since the author believes that one should not be an agent of injustice even if it means breaking the law; this is stated in the second

paragraph. Because the author thinks that injustice should, rather than should not, be eliminated, (A) is an incorrect answer. (C) is also incorrect since the author favors the stopping of the machines of government, rather than not stopping them. The author argues that it is not necessary to do the wrong one condemns, rather than agreeing that one should do it; subsequently, (D) is also incorrect.

34. **(H)**   Because the author suggests a just man go to prison if the government imprisons unjustly in the first sentence of the fourth paragraph, (H) is the best answer. (F) is incorrect since it states the opposite of (H). Because of the author's seeing prison as a place to demonstrate against injustice, (G) is also incorrect. The author confines himself to opposing a government which imprisons people unjustly, not justly; consequently (J) is incorrect.

35. **(B)**   The author asserts in the beginning of paragraph four that a just person should be in prison to represent those who are against an unjust government as he; (B) is the best answer. A just person should be in prison because a government does, not should, imprison unjustly; (A) should not be chosen. A just person should not be in prison to represent the principles of other people but rather his or her own principles; (C) is not correct. A just person should not be in prison to represent the only house in a free state where a slave can abide with honor, but may choose to be there, to protest the only house in a slave state where a slave can abide with honor; hence, (H) is not the right answer.

36. **(H)**   The best answer is (H), since the last paragraph implies that in prison a just person's ability to combat injustice can be exercised. In prison a just person's influence is not lost; (F) should not be selected. In prison a just person's voice is not lost to the State; (G) is an incorrect choice. A just person's appearance in prison would be as an enemy—not a friend—within the walls; therefore, (J) is not the correct answer.

37. **(C)**   The correct answer is (C), since a minority is powerless if it adheres to the majority; it then becomes consumed and a member of the majority as the author explains in the closing paragraph. A minority is not necessarily powerless within a state UNLESS it adheres to the majority; (A) is not a good choice. A minority may become less powerful and may be consumed if it adheres itself to the majority; (B) should not be chosen since it states the opposite of that which the author argues. The article attests a "minority is irresistible [not resistible] if it clogs by its own weight"; (D) should not be chosen.

38. **(H)**   As he declares in the last paragraph, the author thinks that violence can be represented by a thousand people paying their taxes to a State that sheds innocent blood; (H) should be chosen. Violence is not a thousand people not paying (F) or paying (G) their taxes alone; (F) and (G) are incorrect. Violence is

not necessarily represented by friction in the machinery of government; (J) is a poor choice.

39. **(B)**   The author asserts near the end of the text that the loss of one's person comes when the conscience is wounded; (B) is the best choice. While violence (A), war (C), and unpaid taxes (D) all are mentioned in the author's exhortation, none is considered to be the cause of the loss of one's person; accordingly, (A), (C), and (D) are all incorrect answers.

40. **(J)**   All the answers [(I), (II), (III), and (IV)] are correct as can be verified by looking for each in the closing paragraph of the reading passage; only one answer—(J)—allows the reader to choose all the answers. The other choices [(F), (G), and (H)] omit one or more of the correct answers and are therefore, incorrect answers.

Test 4: Science Reasoning

1.   **(C)**   No data in the experiments indicate a relationship between Ca^{2+} and pH of the blood; (A) is incorrect. (B) is not correct because there are not experimental results to show a relationship between oxalate ion and pH of blood. Choice (C) is correct according to experiment 2. It states that carbonic acid (H_2CO_3) is produced from dissolved carbon dioxide (CO_2) and that the concentration of H_2CO_3 is directly related to the pH of the blood. The Henderson-Hasselbach equation shows the relationship between the concentration of H_2CO_3 and pH. (D) is an incorrect answer, because the data in experiment 2 gives no relationship of water (H_2O) to the pH of blood.

2.   **(G)**   Answer choice (F) is not correct because experiment 1 indicates that MnO_4^- is in a water or aqueous solution. Choice (G) is the correct choice, The equation in experiment 1 shows calcium oxalate, as a precipitate, indicating that it does not dissolve in water. It dissolves in acid and must be dissolved to perform the titration. (H) is incorrect because the experiments give no indication that the acid specifically removes Ca^{2+}. Choice (J) is false as the acid was necessary to dissolve the acid prior to titration.

3.   **(C)**   Choice (A) is incorrect. While it is true that MnO_4^- can be used to indicate the concentration of Ca^{2+} as is demonstrated by the titration, $C_2O_4^{2-}$ may also be used to measure Ca^{2+} concentration as it combines stoichiometrically with Ca^{2+} to form CaC_2O_4. Choice (B) is incorrect because as explained in (A), the amount of MnO_4^- used in the titration is an indicator of Ca^{2+}. Oxalic acid ($HC_2O_4^-$) reacts with MnO_4^- as shown in the equation in experiment 1. Choice (C) is correct

as both MnO_4^- and $C_2O_4^{2-}$ may be used to measure Ca^{2+} concentration for the reasons given above. Choice (D) is not correct, because, even though H_2O appears in the titration experiment as a product, the solutions are aqueous so that measuring the amount of water would tell nothing about the concentration of calcium.

4.   **(J)**   A smaller volume of potassium permanganate would be required, and the amount of calcium detected in the titration would not increase, as a given quantity of blood contains a constant amount of calcium. (F) is incorrect. Choice (G) is also incorrect. While it is true that the amount of calcium detected would not change, as in choice (F), a more concentrated solution means that there are a larger number of moles per unit volume, and thus a smaller volume is required to stoichiometrically react in the titration. Choice (H) is incorrect, while it is true that smaller volume of the more concentrated solution is necessary for the titration, the amount of calcium detected will always remain constant for a given sample of blood. (J) is the correct choice, since the more concentrated solution dictates that a smaller volume of potassium permanganate is required for the titration since the calcium level for a given sample of blood must remain constant.

5.   **(A)**   The best choice is (A). The question asks for the cause and effect among blood pH, liver proteins, and the number of blood cells produced. The passage in experiment 3 reveals that the presence of a particular liver protein increases blood cell production. This in turn causes the pH to be elevated. (B) is incorrect because the liver protein causes increased blood cell production directly. The increase in pH is due to the elevated cell count. (C) is incorrect because the reverse is true, the liver protein increases blood cell production and it is the blood cells that increase the pH. (D) is also incorrect because the increase in pH is the result of increased blood cell production caused by an elevated level of a particular liver protein.

6.   **(H)**   Experiment 2 indicated a glass microelectrode can be used to determine pH, so (F) is incorrect. While according to the equation given in experiment 2, one could calculate the pH if the concentrations of bicarbonate and carbonic acid were known, the question asks for an experimental procedure. (G) is false because according to the information given, the number of blood cells present is not related to a specific pH value. (H) is correct. Based on the information given in Experiment 2, a glass microelectrode could be used directly to determine the pH value. (J) is incorrect because a microgasometer measures only the volume of CO_2 in a sample of blood and does not directly measure pH.

7.   **(B)**   Answer choice (A) is incorrect because the data in the passage and experiment 2 (rate = $k[A][C]^2$) indicated [A] does affect the reaction rate. Choice (B) is correct. The rate law in experiment 2 does not include [B] and also the data in the passage experiment shows [B] does not affect the reaction. When the concentration of [B] is quadrupled at constant [A] and [C], the rate of reaction is

not affected. (C) is incorrect because experiment 2 includes [C] in the rate law. (D) is also incorrect, because [B] does not affect the reaction rate as explained in response (B).

8. **(J)** The data in Table 2 of Experiment 1 shows a decrease of [A] with time which is not proportional or linear; this graph shows an increase in [A] with time. Therefore (F) is not correct. (G) is incorrect, because although [A] does decrease with time, this decrease is not proportional as revealed in Table 2. (H) is also incorrect because this graph shows a linear decrease in [A]. The decrease is sharp at the beginning. (J) is the correct response. The data in Table 2 reveals a sharp decrease at the start, then a slow, gradual decrease at the end with time.

9. **(A)** According to the information presented in the passage, (A) is the best response. Some reactants and products are present at equilibrium, but no information is given with regards to a comparison. (B) is false, based on the results of the experiments and passage. No data is shown to conclude equal amounts of reactants and products are present at equilibrium. (C) is incorrect since the equation shown in the passage has products included in it. Choice (D) is incorrect. The absence of any reactants would imply that the system was not at equilibrium and that the reaction went to completion.

10. **(G)** The question addresses improving experimental design, knowing the concentrations of the products (F) would not change this. (G) is the best answer. Based on the passage, the concept of equilibrium is an assumed position of a reaction. A procedure used to verify that equilibrium has been established would improve the accuracy of the results. (H) is incorrect because the same experiment being performed with products to reactants would just prove the reaction was reversible which already was stated in the passage. (J) is incorrect because only varying the amounts of two reactants instead of three would exclude pertinent information. One would not know if one reactant affected the rate of the reaction.

11. **(D)** Responses (A), (B), and (C) are all incorrect because the data and results of the experiments reveal no relationship of these coefficients to how fast each is used up during the reaction. The numbers in the amounts in the experiment in the passage have no relation to the coefficients of the letters in the equation. Choice (D) is the correct response because there is no data to support any other conclusion.

12. **(H)** Since varying the initial concentrations of the reactants with different temperatures was not tested, (F) is incorrect. This statement is merely assumed with no data to support it. Choice (G) is false. Thus, as the temperature affects the rate constant as shown in the figure, it affects the rate of reaction as

well. (H) is correct. Since k and the rate of reaction are proportional, a decrease in temperature would decrease k (rate constant) and thus decrease the rate of reaction. (J) is incorrect, because based on the rate law, a decrease in temperature lowers k (rate constant) and decreases, not increases, the reaction rate.

13. **(C)** The ratio of $\dfrac{F}{A}$ is equal to the compressive stress. Therefore, $\dfrac{72}{x} = 6$ and $x = 12$. The only possible dimension is 4×3. The correct choice is (C).

14. **(G)** The correct choice is (G). According to Table 1, the tensile strength of bone is $200 \ MN/m^2$. Answer (F) refers to the compressive strength of bone while (H) and (J) refer to the tensile strength of other materials.

15. **(D)** The correct choice is (D). According to the passage, the stress at which breakage occurs is called compressive strength. Therefore, when the compressive stress equals the compressive strength, the binding will crack. Answers (A), (B), and (C) are incorrect.

16. **(J)** Although all the materials listed as answer choices will not break under compressive stress, lead has the lowest tensile strength. The correct answer, therefore, is (J).

17. **(C)** The correct choice is (C). The area of the book is $32m^2$ and the compressive strength is $8 \ \dfrac{N}{m^2}$. The force at which the book will break is 256 N. Therefore, the maximum force that can be applied is 255 N.

18. **(H)** The answer is (H). Based on the figure, Orlando has a 100% probability of having a thunderstorm, Tampa has a 90% chance, and Miami has a 80% chance. However, Tallahassee only has a 70% chance of getting a thunderstorm and therefore (H) is the correct answer.

19. **(A)** The correct answer is (A). As stated in the passage, persistence forecasting is often the most accurate method of predicting the weather for very short range periods. (B) would not be a good choice because climatological forecasts are not very accurate short range indicators of the weather. (C) is not a bad choice but if the computer forecasted 107° and the temperature is already 109°, the computer is already inaccurate for that day.

20. **(G)** According to the passage, the most accurate forecast for long range time periods is the climatological forecast. (G) is the best answer. Persistence

forecasting (F) would not be useful because it is only accurate for a few hours into the future. (H) would not be a good choice because computer models forecast medium range conditions most accurately. Thus, (J) is eliminated as well.

21. **(D)**   The answer is (D). The first step is to determine which method of forecasting would be most accurate in this situation. Probability/computer forecasting is the best for medium range forecast and 90 degrees is the value correlated to that method. (B) and (C) would not be correct because those values are associated with forecasting methods not prolific for medium range forecasting.

22. **(J)**   Answer choice (F) is incorrect because it is not always best to use a probability/computer forecast. (G) is correct because depending on how far in the future the forecast is for, different forecasting techniques would be employed. (G) is correct for the same reason in (F). Thus, (J) is the correct answer.

23. **(C)**   In the equations in Table 1, steps 1 and 2 show a total of three protons to begin with. Steps 1 and 2 must occur twice, which gives a total of 6 protons. Finally, step 3 shows two protons left over which means that only 4 were consumed.

24. **(G)**   In order to obtain the correct answer, (G) 26,73 MeV, one needs to take into account the fact that steps 1 and 2 in the proton-proton chain must be repeated before step 3 can take place. Thus, the total energy released is 2 (1.442 + 5.494) + 12.859 = 26.731 MeV 26.73 MeV.

25. **(A)**   The correct answer is (A). Since the neutrino (ν) is *not* produced in the second step of the proton-proton chain nor in the first step of the carbon cycle, the weak force cannot effect these two reactions, and answers (B) and (C) are wrong. Neutrinos are produced in the carbon cycle in the second and fifth steps only, and the last step is faster (82 seconds) than the first step (7 minutes), thereby proving answer choice (D) is incorrect. Step 1 of the proton-proton chain is the slowest reaction, and this is due to the weak force creating a neutrino.

26. **(H)**   The common feature shared by the proton-proton cycle and the carbon chain is that they both convert hydrogen into helium (H). The net effect of both cycles can be summarized as $4 {}_1^1 H \rightarrow {}_1^4 He$ + energy. (F) and (G) are obviously wrong, as can be seen from the different time scales and numbers of neutrinos produced. (J) is wrong because, as stated in the passage, the proton-proton cycle dominates when the temperature is less than 15 million Kelvin, while the carbon cycle takes over when the temperature is higher than 15 million Kelvin.

27. **(C)**   From the reactions in the carbon cycle, the fifth equation clearly shows that oxygen-15 breaks down to produce nitrogen-15, a positron, and a neutrino.

28. **(G)**   From the table showing the carbon cycle, the first and sixth steps show carbon-12 to be an initial reactant and a final reaction product, respectively. (G) is the correct answer.

29. **(C)**   Both theories state that the crust is manipulated by the liquid rock beneath. This liquid rock is called the asthenosphere. Answer (C) is correct.

30. **(F)**   The Dana theory (F) states that waves are produced in the asthenosphere which cool and produce mountain ranges.

31. **(C)**   The theory of plate tectonics states that one plate moves beneath another plate to produce mountains. The Dana theory states that the liquid asthenosphere forms waves to push the crust up to produce mountains. The Dana theory indicates that the liquid asthenosphere produces waves which become solid to form mountains. The best answer is (C).

32. **(H)**   According to the theory of plate tectonics, the crust is pushed up to produce mountains. This would cause marine fossils (F) to be forced up with the crust. Since earthquakes and volcanoes occur at plate boundaries where oceans are located (G), they would also support the theory of plate tectonics. (H) is the best answer choice.

33. **(C)**   The Dana theory (A) states that the ocean basins are pulled due to gravity; this would have caused a formation of earthquakes. The Dana theory also states that where mountains exist, waves are occurring under the crust. These waves cause earthquakes. Since there must be liquid rock to produce the waves, it is reasonable to assume that volcanoes would also be prevalent in the area. The theory of plate tectonics (B) states that wherever plate movement is occurring, there are volcanoes and earthquakes. So, the ring of fire would indicate that the area has a great deal of plate movement. The best answer is (C).

34. **(G)**   The theory of plate tectonics (G) is based on the idea that the processes seen today are a continuation of the processes that began with the beginning of the earth. The Dana theory (F) states that the majority of the processes ended after the earth formed. It states that there is no continuous process of mountain building. Since (G) is correct and (F) is incorrect, neither (H) nor (J) is a correct answer choice.

35. **(D)**   Since Dana's theory states that oceans are sinking due to gravity pulling down the sediment, no marine fossils would be found in the folded mountains. (D) is the best answer.

36. **(H)**   Combining information from figures 1 and 2 we see that light bulb B, wavelength 450–600λ, is the only bulb that does not give the least "change in plant height" for any one of the four plant types. Therefore, (H) is the correct answer. Choice (F) the range 250–300λ belongs to bulb A, which produces the least change in plant growth for plant types 1 and 4 (although good for plant 3). Choice (G) is wrong because none of the bulbs has a high intensity in this range. Choice (J) is wrong because bulb C (range 550–700λ) is poor for plant types 1 and 3.

37. **(D)**   The information given in these experiments is not related to bloom production, so a new experiment would have to be conducted (D). Choice (A), (B), and (C) are all incorrect because the color ranges of the spectrum are not related to flower colors.

38. **(H)**   Plant type 3 (H) reached its maximum height with light bulb A whose greatest intensity was at about 250λ, which is below the sunlight range. Choices (F), (G), and (J) are not correct because plant types 1, 2, and 4 reached their maximum heights under bulbs B and C whose maximum intensities are in the 350–700λ range, which is duplicated by sunlight.

39. **(D)**   Plants of type 2 (D) responded with best growth to a schedule that provided continuous moisture, as in a rain forest. Choices (A), (B), and (C) are climates that provide less moisture than a continuous watering schedule, so they could be expected to result in less change in height and fewer new branches and new leaves.

40. **(H)**   Plants whose best growth was made under conditions of continuous moisture, and whose growth was less satisfactory when watered two or four times a day, could be expected to grow no higher than those on the twice a day schedule (H). Choice (F) is wrong because watering once a day *could* produce less change in height than twice a day if continuous is optimal. Choice (G) is wrong because we would not expect once a day to be better than twice a day if continuous is optimal. Since we can predict (H), (J) is incorrect.

ACT Assessment – Diagnostic Exam
ANSWER SHEET

Scoring Key*

English	**Mathematics**	**Reading**
UM = Usage/Mechanics	EA = Pre-Algebra/Elementary Algebra	SS = Social Studies/Science
RH = Rhetorical Skills	AG = Intermediate Algebra/Coordinate Geometry	AL = Arts/Literature
	GT = Plane Geometry/Trigonometry	

TEST 1

English

1. Ⓐ Ⓑ Ⓒ Ⓓ UM
2. Ⓕ Ⓖ Ⓗ Ⓙ UM
3. Ⓐ Ⓑ Ⓒ Ⓓ UM
4. Ⓕ Ⓖ Ⓗ Ⓙ UM
5. Ⓐ Ⓑ Ⓒ Ⓓ UM
6. Ⓕ Ⓖ Ⓗ Ⓙ RH
7. Ⓐ Ⓑ Ⓒ Ⓓ UM
8. Ⓕ Ⓖ Ⓗ Ⓙ RH
9. Ⓐ Ⓑ Ⓒ Ⓓ RH
10. Ⓕ Ⓖ Ⓗ Ⓙ UM
11. Ⓐ Ⓑ Ⓒ Ⓓ RH
12. Ⓕ Ⓖ Ⓗ Ⓙ UM
13. Ⓐ Ⓑ Ⓒ Ⓓ RH
14. Ⓕ Ⓖ Ⓗ Ⓙ UM
15. Ⓐ Ⓑ Ⓒ Ⓓ UM
16. Ⓕ Ⓖ Ⓗ Ⓙ UM
17. Ⓐ Ⓑ Ⓒ Ⓓ UM
18. Ⓕ Ⓖ Ⓗ Ⓙ UM
19. Ⓐ Ⓑ Ⓒ Ⓓ UM
20. Ⓕ Ⓖ Ⓗ Ⓙ RH
21. Ⓐ Ⓑ Ⓒ Ⓓ UM
22. Ⓕ Ⓖ Ⓗ Ⓙ UM
23. Ⓐ Ⓑ Ⓒ Ⓓ RH
24. Ⓕ Ⓖ Ⓗ Ⓙ UM
25. Ⓐ Ⓑ Ⓒ Ⓓ UM
26. Ⓕ Ⓖ Ⓗ Ⓙ UM
27. Ⓐ Ⓑ Ⓒ Ⓓ UM
28. Ⓕ Ⓖ Ⓗ Ⓙ UM
29. Ⓐ Ⓑ Ⓒ Ⓓ RH
30. Ⓕ Ⓖ Ⓗ Ⓙ UM
31. Ⓐ Ⓑ Ⓒ Ⓓ RH

32. Ⓕ Ⓖ Ⓗ Ⓙ RH
33. Ⓐ Ⓑ Ⓒ Ⓓ UM
34. Ⓕ Ⓖ Ⓗ Ⓙ UM
35. Ⓐ Ⓑ Ⓒ Ⓓ RH
36. Ⓕ Ⓖ Ⓗ Ⓙ UM
37. Ⓐ Ⓑ Ⓒ Ⓓ UM
38. Ⓕ Ⓖ Ⓗ Ⓙ UM
39. Ⓐ Ⓑ Ⓒ Ⓓ RH
40. Ⓕ Ⓖ Ⓗ Ⓙ UM
41. Ⓐ Ⓑ Ⓒ Ⓓ RH
42. Ⓕ Ⓖ Ⓗ Ⓙ UM
43. Ⓐ Ⓑ Ⓒ Ⓓ UM
44. Ⓕ Ⓖ Ⓗ Ⓙ RH
45. Ⓐ Ⓑ Ⓒ Ⓓ RH
46. Ⓕ Ⓖ Ⓗ Ⓙ RH
47. Ⓐ Ⓑ Ⓒ Ⓓ UM
48. Ⓕ Ⓖ Ⓗ Ⓙ UM
49. Ⓐ Ⓑ Ⓒ Ⓓ RH
50. Ⓕ Ⓖ Ⓗ Ⓙ RH
51. Ⓐ Ⓑ Ⓒ Ⓓ UM
52. Ⓕ Ⓖ Ⓗ Ⓙ UM
53. Ⓐ Ⓑ Ⓒ Ⓓ UM
54. Ⓕ Ⓖ Ⓗ Ⓙ UM
55. Ⓐ Ⓑ Ⓒ Ⓓ RH
56. Ⓕ Ⓖ Ⓗ Ⓙ UM
57. Ⓐ Ⓑ Ⓒ Ⓓ UM
58. Ⓕ Ⓖ Ⓗ Ⓙ UM
59. Ⓐ Ⓑ Ⓒ Ⓓ UM
60. Ⓕ Ⓖ Ⓗ Ⓙ RH
61. Ⓐ Ⓑ Ⓒ Ⓓ RH
62. Ⓕ Ⓖ Ⓗ Ⓙ UM
63. Ⓐ Ⓑ Ⓒ Ⓓ RH
64. Ⓕ Ⓖ Ⓗ Ⓙ RH

65. Ⓐ Ⓑ Ⓒ Ⓓ UM
66. Ⓕ Ⓖ Ⓗ Ⓙ UM
67. Ⓐ Ⓑ Ⓒ Ⓓ UM
68. Ⓕ Ⓖ Ⓗ Ⓙ UM
69. Ⓐ Ⓑ Ⓒ Ⓓ RH
70. Ⓕ Ⓖ Ⓗ Ⓙ RH
71. Ⓐ Ⓑ Ⓒ Ⓓ UM
72. Ⓕ Ⓖ Ⓗ Ⓙ UM
73. Ⓐ Ⓑ Ⓒ Ⓓ UM
74. Ⓕ Ⓖ Ⓗ Ⓙ RH
75. Ⓐ Ⓑ Ⓒ Ⓓ RH

TEST 2

Mathematics

1. Ⓐ Ⓑ Ⓒ Ⓓ Ⓔ EA
2. Ⓕ Ⓖ Ⓗ Ⓙ Ⓚ AG
3. Ⓐ Ⓑ Ⓒ Ⓓ Ⓔ AG
4. Ⓕ Ⓖ Ⓗ Ⓙ Ⓚ EA
5. Ⓐ Ⓑ Ⓒ Ⓓ Ⓔ EA
6. Ⓕ Ⓖ Ⓗ Ⓙ Ⓚ EA
7. Ⓐ Ⓑ Ⓒ Ⓓ Ⓔ EA
8. Ⓕ Ⓖ Ⓗ Ⓙ Ⓚ AG
9. Ⓐ Ⓑ Ⓒ Ⓓ Ⓔ AG
10. Ⓕ Ⓖ Ⓗ Ⓙ Ⓚ EA
11. Ⓐ Ⓑ Ⓒ Ⓓ Ⓔ AG
12. Ⓕ Ⓖ Ⓗ Ⓙ Ⓚ AG
13. Ⓐ Ⓑ Ⓒ Ⓓ Ⓔ EA
14. Ⓕ Ⓖ Ⓗ Ⓙ Ⓚ EA
15. Ⓐ Ⓑ Ⓒ Ⓓ Ⓔ EA
16. Ⓕ Ⓖ Ⓗ Ⓙ Ⓚ EA
17. Ⓐ Ⓑ Ⓒ Ⓓ Ⓔ AG
18. Ⓕ Ⓖ Ⓗ Ⓙ Ⓚ AG
19. Ⓐ Ⓑ Ⓒ Ⓓ Ⓔ AG

*Note that the Science Reasoning Test has no subscores and thus is not coded.
See pp. 7–11 for details on scoring.

20.	Ⓕ Ⓖ Ⓗ Ⓙ Ⓚ EA
21.	Ⓐ Ⓑ Ⓒ Ⓓ Ⓔ EA
22.	Ⓕ Ⓖ Ⓗ Ⓙ Ⓚ EA
23.	Ⓐ Ⓑ Ⓒ Ⓓ Ⓔ EA
24.	Ⓕ Ⓖ Ⓗ Ⓙ Ⓚ AG
25.	Ⓐ Ⓑ Ⓒ Ⓓ Ⓔ AG
26.	Ⓕ Ⓖ Ⓗ Ⓙ Ⓚ AG
27.	Ⓐ Ⓑ Ⓒ Ⓓ Ⓔ AG
28.	Ⓕ Ⓖ Ⓗ Ⓙ Ⓚ AG
29.	Ⓐ Ⓑ Ⓒ Ⓓ Ⓔ AG
30.	Ⓕ Ⓖ Ⓗ Ⓙ Ⓚ AG
31.	Ⓐ Ⓑ Ⓒ Ⓓ Ⓔ AG
32.	Ⓕ Ⓖ Ⓗ Ⓙ Ⓚ EA
33.	Ⓐ Ⓑ Ⓒ Ⓓ Ⓔ AG
34.	Ⓕ Ⓖ Ⓗ Ⓙ Ⓚ AG
35.	Ⓐ Ⓑ Ⓒ Ⓓ Ⓔ AG
36.	Ⓕ Ⓖ Ⓗ Ⓙ Ⓚ AG
37.	Ⓐ Ⓑ Ⓒ Ⓓ Ⓔ AG
38.	Ⓕ Ⓖ Ⓗ Ⓙ Ⓚ GT
39.	Ⓐ Ⓑ Ⓒ Ⓓ Ⓔ AG
40.	Ⓕ Ⓖ Ⓗ Ⓙ Ⓚ AG
41.	Ⓐ Ⓑ Ⓒ Ⓓ Ⓔ EA
42.	Ⓕ Ⓖ Ⓗ Ⓙ Ⓚ EA
43.	Ⓐ Ⓑ Ⓒ Ⓓ Ⓔ GT
44.	Ⓕ Ⓖ Ⓗ Ⓙ Ⓚ AG
45.	Ⓐ Ⓑ Ⓒ Ⓓ Ⓔ GT
46.	Ⓕ Ⓖ Ⓗ Ⓙ Ⓚ GT
47.	Ⓐ Ⓑ Ⓒ Ⓓ Ⓔ GT
48.	Ⓕ Ⓖ Ⓗ Ⓙ Ⓚ GT
49.	Ⓐ Ⓑ Ⓒ Ⓓ Ⓔ GT
50.	Ⓕ Ⓖ Ⓗ Ⓙ Ⓚ GT
51.	Ⓐ Ⓑ Ⓒ Ⓓ Ⓔ GT
52.	Ⓕ Ⓖ Ⓗ Ⓙ Ⓚ GT
53.	Ⓐ Ⓑ Ⓒ Ⓓ Ⓔ GT
54.	Ⓕ Ⓖ Ⓗ Ⓙ Ⓚ GT
55.	Ⓐ Ⓑ Ⓒ Ⓓ Ⓔ GT
56.	Ⓕ Ⓖ Ⓗ Ⓙ Ⓚ AG
57.	Ⓐ Ⓑ Ⓒ Ⓓ Ⓔ GT
58.	Ⓕ Ⓖ Ⓗ Ⓙ Ⓚ GT
59.	Ⓐ Ⓑ Ⓒ Ⓓ Ⓔ GT
60.	Ⓕ Ⓖ Ⓗ Ⓙ Ⓚ GT

TEST 3
Reading

1.	Ⓐ Ⓑ Ⓒ Ⓓ AL
2.	Ⓕ Ⓖ Ⓗ Ⓙ AL
3.	Ⓐ Ⓑ Ⓒ Ⓓ AL
4.	Ⓕ Ⓖ Ⓗ Ⓙ AL
5.	Ⓐ Ⓑ Ⓒ Ⓓ AL
6.	Ⓕ Ⓖ Ⓗ Ⓙ AL
7.	Ⓐ Ⓑ Ⓒ Ⓓ AL
8.	Ⓕ Ⓖ Ⓗ Ⓙ AL
9.	Ⓐ Ⓑ Ⓒ Ⓓ AL
10.	Ⓕ Ⓖ Ⓗ Ⓙ AL
11.	Ⓐ Ⓑ Ⓒ Ⓓ AL
12.	Ⓕ Ⓖ Ⓗ Ⓙ AL
13.	Ⓐ Ⓑ Ⓒ Ⓓ AL
14.	Ⓕ Ⓖ Ⓗ Ⓙ AL
15.	Ⓐ Ⓑ Ⓒ Ⓓ AL
16.	Ⓕ Ⓖ Ⓗ Ⓙ AL
17.	Ⓐ Ⓑ Ⓒ Ⓓ AL
18.	Ⓕ Ⓖ Ⓗ Ⓙ AL
19.	Ⓐ Ⓑ Ⓒ Ⓓ AL
20.	Ⓕ Ⓖ Ⓗ Ⓙ AL
21.	Ⓐ Ⓑ Ⓒ Ⓓ SS
22.	Ⓕ Ⓖ Ⓗ Ⓙ SS
23.	Ⓐ Ⓑ Ⓒ Ⓓ SS
24.	Ⓕ Ⓖ Ⓗ Ⓙ SS
25.	Ⓐ Ⓑ Ⓒ Ⓓ SS
26.	Ⓕ Ⓖ Ⓗ Ⓙ SS
27.	Ⓐ Ⓑ Ⓒ Ⓓ SS
28.	Ⓕ Ⓖ Ⓗ Ⓙ SS
29.	Ⓐ Ⓑ Ⓒ Ⓓ SS
30.	Ⓕ Ⓖ Ⓗ Ⓙ SS
31.	Ⓐ Ⓑ Ⓒ Ⓓ SS
32.	Ⓕ Ⓖ Ⓗ Ⓙ SS
33.	Ⓐ Ⓑ Ⓒ Ⓓ SS
34.	Ⓕ Ⓖ Ⓗ Ⓙ SS
35.	Ⓐ Ⓑ Ⓒ Ⓓ SS
36.	Ⓕ Ⓖ Ⓗ Ⓙ SS
37.	Ⓐ Ⓑ Ⓒ Ⓓ SS
38.	Ⓕ Ⓖ Ⓗ Ⓙ SS
39.	Ⓐ Ⓑ Ⓒ Ⓓ SS
40.	Ⓕ Ⓖ Ⓗ Ⓙ SS

TEST 4
Science Reasoning

1.	Ⓐ Ⓑ Ⓒ Ⓓ
2.	Ⓕ Ⓖ Ⓗ Ⓙ
3.	Ⓐ Ⓑ Ⓒ Ⓓ
4.	Ⓕ Ⓖ Ⓗ Ⓙ
5.	Ⓐ Ⓑ Ⓒ Ⓓ
6.	Ⓕ Ⓖ Ⓗ Ⓙ
7.	Ⓐ Ⓑ Ⓒ Ⓓ
8.	Ⓕ Ⓖ Ⓗ Ⓙ
9.	Ⓐ Ⓑ Ⓒ Ⓓ
10.	Ⓕ Ⓖ Ⓗ Ⓙ
11.	Ⓐ Ⓑ Ⓒ Ⓓ
12.	Ⓕ Ⓖ Ⓗ Ⓙ
13.	Ⓐ Ⓑ Ⓒ Ⓓ
14.	Ⓕ Ⓖ Ⓗ Ⓙ
15.	Ⓐ Ⓑ Ⓒ Ⓓ
16.	Ⓕ Ⓖ Ⓗ Ⓙ
17.	Ⓐ Ⓑ Ⓒ Ⓓ
18.	Ⓕ Ⓖ Ⓗ Ⓙ
19.	Ⓐ Ⓑ Ⓒ Ⓓ
20.	Ⓕ Ⓖ Ⓗ Ⓙ
21.	Ⓐ Ⓑ Ⓒ Ⓓ
22.	Ⓕ Ⓖ Ⓗ Ⓙ
23.	Ⓐ Ⓑ Ⓒ Ⓓ
24.	Ⓕ Ⓖ Ⓗ Ⓙ
25.	Ⓐ Ⓑ Ⓒ Ⓓ
26.	Ⓕ Ⓖ Ⓗ Ⓙ
27.	Ⓐ Ⓑ Ⓒ Ⓓ
28.	Ⓕ Ⓖ Ⓗ Ⓙ
29.	Ⓐ Ⓑ Ⓒ Ⓓ
30.	Ⓕ Ⓖ Ⓗ Ⓙ
31.	Ⓐ Ⓑ Ⓒ Ⓓ
32.	Ⓕ Ⓖ Ⓗ Ⓙ
33.	Ⓐ Ⓑ Ⓒ Ⓓ
34.	Ⓕ Ⓖ Ⓗ Ⓙ
35.	Ⓐ Ⓑ Ⓒ Ⓓ
36.	Ⓕ Ⓖ Ⓗ Ⓙ
37.	Ⓐ Ⓑ Ⓒ Ⓓ
38.	Ⓕ Ⓖ Ⓗ Ⓙ
39.	Ⓐ Ⓑ Ⓒ Ⓓ
40.	Ⓕ Ⓖ Ⓗ Ⓙ

ACT Assessment – Practice Exam I
ANSWER SHEET

Scoring Key*

English

UM = Usage/Mechanics

RH = Rhetorical Skills

Mathematics

EA = Pre-Algebra/Elementary Algebra

AG = Intermediate Algebra/Coordinate Geometry

GT = Plane Geometry/Trigonometry

Reading

SS = Social Studies/Science

AL = Arts/Literature

TEST 1
English

1. Ⓐ Ⓑ Ⓒ Ⓓ UM
2. Ⓕ Ⓖ Ⓗ Ⓙ UM
3. Ⓐ Ⓑ Ⓒ Ⓓ UM
4. Ⓕ Ⓖ Ⓗ Ⓙ UM
5. Ⓐ Ⓑ Ⓒ Ⓓ UM
6. Ⓕ Ⓖ Ⓗ Ⓙ RH
7. Ⓐ Ⓑ Ⓒ Ⓓ UM
8. Ⓕ Ⓖ Ⓗ Ⓙ RH
9. Ⓐ Ⓑ Ⓒ Ⓓ RH
10. Ⓕ Ⓖ Ⓗ Ⓙ UM
11. Ⓐ Ⓑ Ⓒ Ⓓ RH
12. Ⓕ Ⓖ Ⓗ Ⓙ UM
13. Ⓐ Ⓑ Ⓒ Ⓓ RH
14. Ⓕ Ⓖ Ⓗ Ⓙ UM
15. Ⓐ Ⓑ Ⓒ Ⓓ UM
16. Ⓕ Ⓖ Ⓗ Ⓙ UM
17. Ⓐ Ⓑ Ⓒ Ⓓ UM
18. Ⓕ Ⓖ Ⓗ Ⓙ UM
19. Ⓐ Ⓑ Ⓒ Ⓓ UM
20. Ⓕ Ⓖ Ⓗ Ⓙ RH
21. Ⓐ Ⓑ Ⓒ Ⓓ UM
22. Ⓕ Ⓖ Ⓗ Ⓙ UM
23. Ⓐ Ⓑ Ⓒ Ⓓ RH
24. Ⓕ Ⓖ Ⓗ Ⓙ UM
25. Ⓐ Ⓑ Ⓒ Ⓓ UM
26. Ⓕ Ⓖ Ⓗ Ⓙ UM
27. Ⓐ Ⓑ Ⓒ Ⓓ UM
28. Ⓕ Ⓖ Ⓗ Ⓙ UM
29. Ⓐ Ⓑ Ⓒ Ⓓ RH
30. Ⓕ Ⓖ Ⓗ Ⓙ UM
31. Ⓐ Ⓑ Ⓒ Ⓓ RH
32. Ⓕ Ⓖ Ⓗ Ⓙ RH
33. Ⓐ Ⓑ Ⓒ Ⓓ UM
34. Ⓕ Ⓖ Ⓗ Ⓙ UM
35. Ⓐ Ⓑ Ⓒ Ⓓ RH
36. Ⓕ Ⓖ Ⓗ Ⓙ UM
37. Ⓐ Ⓑ Ⓒ Ⓓ UM
38. Ⓕ Ⓖ Ⓗ Ⓙ UM
39. Ⓐ Ⓑ Ⓒ Ⓓ RH
40. Ⓕ Ⓖ Ⓗ Ⓙ UM
41. Ⓐ Ⓑ Ⓒ Ⓓ RH
42. Ⓕ Ⓖ Ⓗ Ⓙ UM
43. Ⓐ Ⓑ Ⓒ Ⓓ UM
44. Ⓕ Ⓖ Ⓗ Ⓙ RH
45. Ⓐ Ⓑ Ⓒ Ⓓ RH
46. Ⓕ Ⓖ Ⓗ Ⓙ RH
47. Ⓐ Ⓑ Ⓒ Ⓓ UM
48. Ⓕ Ⓖ Ⓗ Ⓙ UM
49. Ⓐ Ⓑ Ⓒ Ⓓ RH
50. Ⓕ Ⓖ Ⓗ Ⓙ RH
51. Ⓐ Ⓑ Ⓒ Ⓓ UM
52. Ⓕ Ⓖ Ⓗ Ⓙ UM
53. Ⓐ Ⓑ Ⓒ Ⓓ UM
54. Ⓕ Ⓖ Ⓗ Ⓙ UM
55. Ⓐ Ⓑ Ⓒ Ⓓ RH
56. Ⓕ Ⓖ Ⓗ Ⓙ UM
57. Ⓐ Ⓑ Ⓒ Ⓓ UM
58. Ⓕ Ⓖ Ⓗ Ⓙ UM
59. Ⓐ Ⓑ Ⓒ Ⓓ UM
60. Ⓕ Ⓖ Ⓗ Ⓙ RH
61. Ⓐ Ⓑ Ⓒ Ⓓ RH
62. Ⓕ Ⓖ Ⓗ Ⓙ UM
63. Ⓐ Ⓑ Ⓒ Ⓓ RH
64. Ⓕ Ⓖ Ⓗ Ⓙ RH
65. Ⓐ Ⓑ Ⓒ Ⓓ UM
66. Ⓕ Ⓖ Ⓗ Ⓙ UM
67. Ⓐ Ⓑ Ⓒ Ⓓ UM
68. Ⓕ Ⓖ Ⓗ Ⓙ UM
69. Ⓐ Ⓑ Ⓒ Ⓓ RH
70. Ⓕ Ⓖ Ⓗ Ⓙ RH
71. Ⓐ Ⓑ Ⓒ Ⓓ UM
72. Ⓕ Ⓖ Ⓗ Ⓙ UM
73. Ⓐ Ⓑ Ⓒ Ⓓ UM
74. Ⓕ Ⓖ Ⓗ Ⓙ RH
75. Ⓐ Ⓑ Ⓒ Ⓓ RH

TEST 2
Mathematics

1. Ⓐ Ⓑ Ⓒ Ⓓ Ⓔ EA
2. Ⓕ Ⓖ Ⓗ Ⓙ Ⓚ AG
3. Ⓐ Ⓑ Ⓒ Ⓓ Ⓔ AG
4. Ⓕ Ⓖ Ⓗ Ⓙ Ⓚ EA
5. Ⓐ Ⓑ Ⓒ Ⓓ Ⓔ EA
6. Ⓕ Ⓖ Ⓗ Ⓙ Ⓚ EA
7. Ⓐ Ⓑ Ⓒ Ⓓ Ⓔ EA
8. Ⓕ Ⓖ Ⓗ Ⓙ Ⓚ AG
9. Ⓐ Ⓑ Ⓒ Ⓓ Ⓔ AG
10. Ⓕ Ⓖ Ⓗ Ⓙ Ⓚ EA
11. Ⓐ Ⓑ Ⓒ Ⓓ Ⓔ AG
12. Ⓕ Ⓖ Ⓗ Ⓙ Ⓚ AG
13. Ⓐ Ⓑ Ⓒ Ⓓ Ⓔ EA
14. Ⓕ Ⓖ Ⓗ Ⓙ Ⓚ EA
15. Ⓐ Ⓑ Ⓒ Ⓓ Ⓔ EA
16. Ⓕ Ⓖ Ⓗ Ⓙ Ⓚ EA
17. Ⓐ Ⓑ Ⓒ Ⓓ Ⓔ AG
18. Ⓕ Ⓖ Ⓗ Ⓙ Ⓚ AG
19. Ⓐ Ⓑ Ⓒ Ⓓ Ⓔ AG

20. Ⓕ Ⓖ Ⓗ Ⓙ Ⓚ EA	**TEST 3**	**TEST 4**
21. Ⓐ Ⓑ Ⓒ Ⓓ Ⓔ EA	**Reading**	**Science Reasoning**
22. Ⓕ Ⓖ Ⓗ Ⓙ Ⓚ EA	1. Ⓐ Ⓑ Ⓒ Ⓓ AL	1. Ⓐ Ⓑ Ⓒ Ⓓ
23. Ⓐ Ⓑ Ⓒ Ⓓ Ⓔ EA	2. Ⓕ Ⓖ Ⓗ Ⓙ AL	2. Ⓕ Ⓖ Ⓗ Ⓙ
24. Ⓕ Ⓖ Ⓗ Ⓙ Ⓚ AG	3. Ⓐ Ⓑ Ⓒ Ⓓ AL	3. Ⓐ Ⓑ Ⓒ Ⓓ
25. Ⓐ Ⓑ Ⓒ Ⓓ Ⓔ AG	4. Ⓕ Ⓖ Ⓗ Ⓙ AL	4. Ⓕ Ⓖ Ⓗ Ⓙ
26. Ⓕ Ⓖ Ⓗ Ⓙ Ⓚ AG	5. Ⓐ Ⓑ Ⓒ Ⓓ AL	5. Ⓐ Ⓑ Ⓒ Ⓓ
27. Ⓐ Ⓑ Ⓒ Ⓓ Ⓔ AG	6. Ⓕ Ⓖ Ⓗ Ⓙ AL	6. Ⓕ Ⓖ Ⓗ Ⓙ
28. Ⓕ Ⓖ Ⓗ Ⓙ Ⓚ AG	7. Ⓐ Ⓑ Ⓒ Ⓓ AL	7. Ⓐ Ⓑ Ⓒ Ⓓ
29. Ⓐ Ⓑ Ⓒ Ⓓ Ⓔ AG	8. Ⓕ Ⓖ Ⓗ Ⓙ AL	8. Ⓕ Ⓖ Ⓗ Ⓙ
30. Ⓕ Ⓖ Ⓗ Ⓙ Ⓚ AG	9. Ⓐ Ⓑ Ⓒ Ⓓ AL	9. Ⓐ Ⓑ Ⓒ Ⓓ
31. Ⓐ Ⓑ Ⓒ Ⓓ Ⓔ AG	10. Ⓕ Ⓖ Ⓗ Ⓙ AL	10. Ⓕ Ⓖ Ⓗ Ⓙ
32. Ⓕ Ⓖ Ⓗ Ⓙ Ⓚ EA	11. Ⓐ Ⓑ Ⓒ Ⓓ AL	11. Ⓐ Ⓑ Ⓒ Ⓓ
33. Ⓐ Ⓑ Ⓒ Ⓓ Ⓔ AG	12. Ⓕ Ⓖ Ⓗ Ⓙ AL	12. Ⓕ Ⓖ Ⓗ Ⓙ
34. Ⓕ Ⓖ Ⓗ Ⓙ Ⓚ AG	13. Ⓐ Ⓑ Ⓒ Ⓓ AL	13. Ⓐ Ⓑ Ⓒ Ⓓ
35. Ⓐ Ⓑ Ⓒ Ⓓ Ⓔ AG	14. Ⓕ Ⓖ Ⓗ Ⓙ AL	14. Ⓕ Ⓖ Ⓗ Ⓙ
36. Ⓕ Ⓖ Ⓗ Ⓙ Ⓚ AG	15. Ⓐ Ⓑ Ⓒ Ⓓ AL	15. Ⓐ Ⓑ Ⓒ Ⓓ
37. Ⓐ Ⓑ Ⓒ Ⓓ Ⓔ AG	16. Ⓕ Ⓖ Ⓗ Ⓙ AL	16. Ⓕ Ⓖ Ⓗ Ⓙ
38. Ⓕ Ⓖ Ⓗ Ⓙ Ⓚ GT	17. Ⓐ Ⓑ Ⓒ Ⓓ AL	17. Ⓐ Ⓑ Ⓒ Ⓓ
39. Ⓐ Ⓑ Ⓒ Ⓓ Ⓔ AG	18. Ⓕ Ⓖ Ⓗ Ⓙ AL	18. Ⓕ Ⓖ Ⓗ Ⓙ
40. Ⓕ Ⓖ Ⓗ Ⓙ Ⓚ AG	19. Ⓐ Ⓑ Ⓒ Ⓓ AL	19. Ⓐ Ⓑ Ⓒ Ⓓ
41. Ⓐ Ⓑ Ⓒ Ⓓ Ⓔ EA	20. Ⓕ Ⓖ Ⓗ Ⓙ AL	20. Ⓕ Ⓖ Ⓗ Ⓙ
42. Ⓕ Ⓖ Ⓗ Ⓙ Ⓚ EA	21. Ⓐ Ⓑ Ⓒ Ⓓ SS	21. Ⓐ Ⓑ Ⓒ Ⓓ
43. Ⓐ Ⓑ Ⓒ Ⓓ Ⓔ GT	22. Ⓕ Ⓖ Ⓗ Ⓙ SS	22. Ⓕ Ⓖ Ⓗ Ⓙ
44. Ⓕ Ⓖ Ⓗ Ⓙ Ⓚ AG	23. Ⓐ Ⓑ Ⓒ Ⓓ SS	23. Ⓐ Ⓑ Ⓒ Ⓓ
45. Ⓐ Ⓑ Ⓒ Ⓓ Ⓔ GT	24. Ⓕ Ⓖ Ⓗ Ⓙ SS	24. Ⓕ Ⓖ Ⓗ Ⓙ
46. Ⓕ Ⓖ Ⓗ Ⓙ Ⓚ GT	25. Ⓐ Ⓑ Ⓒ Ⓓ SS	25. Ⓐ Ⓑ Ⓒ Ⓓ
47. Ⓐ Ⓑ Ⓒ Ⓓ Ⓔ GT	26. Ⓕ Ⓖ Ⓗ Ⓙ SS	26. Ⓕ Ⓖ Ⓗ Ⓙ
48. Ⓕ Ⓖ Ⓗ Ⓙ Ⓚ GT	27. Ⓐ Ⓑ Ⓒ Ⓓ SS	27. Ⓐ Ⓑ Ⓒ Ⓓ
49. Ⓐ Ⓑ Ⓒ Ⓓ Ⓔ GT	28. Ⓕ Ⓖ Ⓗ Ⓙ SS	28. Ⓕ Ⓖ Ⓗ Ⓙ
50. Ⓕ Ⓖ Ⓗ Ⓙ Ⓚ GT	29. Ⓐ Ⓑ Ⓒ Ⓓ SS	29. Ⓐ Ⓑ Ⓒ Ⓓ
51. Ⓐ Ⓑ Ⓒ Ⓓ Ⓔ GT	30. Ⓕ Ⓖ Ⓗ Ⓙ SS	30. Ⓕ Ⓖ Ⓗ Ⓙ
52. Ⓕ Ⓖ Ⓗ Ⓙ Ⓚ GT	31. Ⓐ Ⓑ Ⓒ Ⓓ SS	31. Ⓐ Ⓑ Ⓒ Ⓓ
53. Ⓐ Ⓑ Ⓒ Ⓓ Ⓔ GT	32. Ⓕ Ⓖ Ⓗ Ⓙ SS	32. Ⓕ Ⓖ Ⓗ Ⓙ
54. Ⓕ Ⓖ Ⓗ Ⓙ Ⓚ GT	33. Ⓐ Ⓑ Ⓒ Ⓓ SS	33. Ⓐ Ⓑ Ⓒ Ⓓ
55. Ⓐ Ⓑ Ⓒ Ⓓ Ⓔ GT	34. Ⓕ Ⓖ Ⓗ Ⓙ SS	34. Ⓕ Ⓖ Ⓗ Ⓙ
56. Ⓕ Ⓖ Ⓗ Ⓙ Ⓚ AG	35. Ⓐ Ⓑ Ⓒ Ⓓ SS	35. Ⓐ Ⓑ Ⓒ Ⓓ
57. Ⓐ Ⓑ Ⓒ Ⓓ Ⓔ GT	36. Ⓕ Ⓖ Ⓗ Ⓙ SS	36. Ⓕ Ⓖ Ⓗ Ⓙ
58. Ⓕ Ⓖ Ⓗ Ⓙ Ⓚ GT	37. Ⓐ Ⓑ Ⓒ Ⓓ SS	37. Ⓐ Ⓑ Ⓒ Ⓓ
59. Ⓐ Ⓑ Ⓒ Ⓓ Ⓔ GT	38. Ⓕ Ⓖ Ⓗ Ⓙ SS	38. Ⓕ Ⓖ Ⓗ Ⓙ
60. Ⓕ Ⓖ Ⓗ Ⓙ Ⓚ GT	39. Ⓐ Ⓑ Ⓒ Ⓓ SS	39. Ⓐ Ⓑ Ⓒ Ⓓ
	40. Ⓕ Ⓖ Ⓗ Ⓙ SS	40. Ⓕ Ⓖ Ⓗ Ⓙ

ACT Assessment – Practice Exam II
ANSWER SHEET

TEST 1
English

1. Ⓐ Ⓑ Ⓒ Ⓓ UM
2. Ⓕ Ⓖ Ⓗ Ⓙ UM
3. Ⓐ Ⓑ Ⓒ Ⓓ UM
4. Ⓕ Ⓖ Ⓗ Ⓙ UM
5. Ⓐ Ⓑ Ⓒ Ⓓ UM
6. Ⓕ Ⓖ Ⓗ Ⓙ RH
7. Ⓐ Ⓑ Ⓒ Ⓓ UM
8. Ⓕ Ⓖ Ⓗ Ⓙ RH
9. Ⓐ Ⓑ Ⓒ Ⓓ RH
10. Ⓕ Ⓖ Ⓗ Ⓙ UM
11. Ⓐ Ⓑ Ⓒ Ⓓ RH
12. Ⓕ Ⓖ Ⓗ Ⓙ UM
13. Ⓐ Ⓑ Ⓒ Ⓓ RH
14. Ⓕ Ⓖ Ⓗ Ⓙ UM
15. Ⓐ Ⓑ Ⓒ Ⓓ UM
16. Ⓕ Ⓖ Ⓗ Ⓙ UM
17. Ⓐ Ⓑ Ⓒ Ⓓ UM
18. Ⓕ Ⓖ Ⓗ Ⓙ UM
19. Ⓐ Ⓑ Ⓒ Ⓓ UM
20. Ⓕ Ⓖ Ⓗ Ⓙ RH
21. Ⓐ Ⓑ Ⓒ Ⓓ UM
22. Ⓕ Ⓖ Ⓗ Ⓙ UM
23. Ⓐ Ⓑ Ⓒ Ⓓ RH
24. Ⓕ Ⓖ Ⓗ Ⓙ UM
25. Ⓐ Ⓑ Ⓒ Ⓓ UM
26. Ⓕ Ⓖ Ⓗ Ⓙ UM
27. Ⓐ Ⓑ Ⓒ Ⓓ UM
28. Ⓕ Ⓖ Ⓗ Ⓙ UM
29. Ⓐ Ⓑ Ⓒ Ⓓ RH
30. Ⓕ Ⓖ Ⓗ Ⓙ UM
31. Ⓐ Ⓑ Ⓒ Ⓓ RH

32. Ⓕ Ⓖ Ⓗ Ⓙ RH
33. Ⓐ Ⓑ Ⓒ Ⓓ UM
34. Ⓕ Ⓖ Ⓗ Ⓙ UM
35. Ⓐ Ⓑ Ⓒ Ⓓ RH
36. Ⓕ Ⓖ Ⓗ Ⓙ UM
37. Ⓐ Ⓑ Ⓒ Ⓓ UM
38. Ⓕ Ⓖ Ⓗ Ⓙ UM
39. Ⓐ Ⓑ Ⓒ Ⓓ RH
40. Ⓕ Ⓖ Ⓗ Ⓙ UM
41. Ⓐ Ⓑ Ⓒ Ⓓ RH
42. Ⓕ Ⓖ Ⓗ Ⓙ UM
43. Ⓐ Ⓑ Ⓒ Ⓓ UM
44. Ⓕ Ⓖ Ⓗ Ⓙ RH
45. Ⓐ Ⓑ Ⓒ Ⓓ RH
46. Ⓕ Ⓖ Ⓗ Ⓙ RH
47. Ⓐ Ⓑ Ⓒ Ⓓ UM
48. Ⓕ Ⓖ Ⓗ Ⓙ UM
49. Ⓐ Ⓑ Ⓒ Ⓓ RH
50. Ⓕ Ⓖ Ⓗ Ⓙ RH
51. Ⓐ Ⓑ Ⓒ Ⓓ UM
52. Ⓕ Ⓖ Ⓗ Ⓙ UM
53. Ⓐ Ⓑ Ⓒ Ⓓ UM
54. Ⓕ Ⓖ Ⓗ Ⓙ UM
55. Ⓐ Ⓑ Ⓒ Ⓓ RH
56. Ⓕ Ⓖ Ⓗ Ⓙ UM
57. Ⓐ Ⓑ Ⓒ Ⓓ UM
58. Ⓕ Ⓖ Ⓗ Ⓙ UM
59. Ⓐ Ⓑ Ⓒ Ⓓ UM
60. Ⓕ Ⓖ Ⓗ Ⓙ RH
61. Ⓐ Ⓑ Ⓒ Ⓓ RH
62. Ⓕ Ⓖ Ⓗ Ⓙ UM
63. Ⓐ Ⓑ Ⓒ Ⓓ RH
64. Ⓕ Ⓖ Ⓗ Ⓙ RH

65. Ⓐ Ⓑ Ⓒ Ⓓ UM
66. Ⓕ Ⓖ Ⓗ Ⓙ UM
67. Ⓐ Ⓑ Ⓒ Ⓓ UM
68. Ⓕ Ⓖ Ⓗ Ⓙ UM
69. Ⓐ Ⓑ Ⓒ Ⓓ RH
70. Ⓕ Ⓖ Ⓗ Ⓙ RH
71. Ⓐ Ⓑ Ⓒ Ⓓ UM
72. Ⓕ Ⓖ Ⓗ Ⓙ UM
73. Ⓐ Ⓑ Ⓒ Ⓓ UM
74. Ⓕ Ⓖ Ⓗ Ⓙ RH
75. Ⓐ Ⓑ Ⓒ Ⓓ RH

TEST 2
Mathematics

1. Ⓐ Ⓑ Ⓒ Ⓓ Ⓔ EA
2. Ⓕ Ⓖ Ⓗ Ⓙ Ⓚ AG
3. Ⓐ Ⓑ Ⓒ Ⓓ Ⓔ AG
4. Ⓕ Ⓖ Ⓗ Ⓙ Ⓚ EA
5. Ⓐ Ⓑ Ⓒ Ⓓ Ⓔ EA
6. Ⓕ Ⓖ Ⓗ Ⓙ Ⓚ EA
7. Ⓐ Ⓑ Ⓒ Ⓓ Ⓔ EA
8. Ⓕ Ⓖ Ⓗ Ⓙ Ⓚ AG
9. Ⓐ Ⓑ Ⓒ Ⓓ Ⓔ AG
10. Ⓕ Ⓖ Ⓗ Ⓙ Ⓚ EA
11. Ⓐ Ⓑ Ⓒ Ⓓ Ⓔ AG
12. Ⓕ Ⓖ Ⓗ Ⓙ Ⓚ AG
13. Ⓐ Ⓑ Ⓒ Ⓓ Ⓔ EA
14. Ⓕ Ⓖ Ⓗ Ⓙ Ⓚ EA
15. Ⓐ Ⓑ Ⓒ Ⓓ Ⓔ EA
16. Ⓕ Ⓖ Ⓗ Ⓙ Ⓚ EA
17. Ⓐ Ⓑ Ⓒ Ⓓ Ⓔ AG
18. Ⓕ Ⓖ Ⓗ Ⓙ Ⓚ AG
19. Ⓐ Ⓑ Ⓒ Ⓓ Ⓔ AG

20. Ⓕ Ⓖ Ⓗ Ⓙ Ⓚ EA	**TEST 3**	**TEST 4**
21. Ⓐ Ⓑ Ⓒ Ⓓ Ⓔ EA	**Reading**	**Science Reasoning**
22. Ⓕ Ⓖ Ⓗ Ⓙ Ⓚ EA	1. Ⓐ Ⓑ Ⓒ Ⓓ AL	1. Ⓐ Ⓑ Ⓒ Ⓓ
23. Ⓐ Ⓑ Ⓒ Ⓓ Ⓔ EA	2. Ⓕ Ⓖ Ⓗ Ⓙ AL	2. Ⓕ Ⓖ Ⓗ Ⓙ
24. Ⓕ Ⓖ Ⓗ Ⓙ Ⓚ AG	3. Ⓐ Ⓑ Ⓒ Ⓓ AL	3. Ⓐ Ⓑ Ⓒ Ⓓ
25. Ⓐ Ⓑ Ⓒ Ⓓ Ⓔ AG	4. Ⓕ Ⓖ Ⓗ Ⓙ AL	4. Ⓕ Ⓖ Ⓗ Ⓙ
26. Ⓕ Ⓖ Ⓗ Ⓙ Ⓚ AG	5. Ⓐ Ⓑ Ⓒ Ⓓ AL	5. Ⓐ Ⓑ Ⓒ Ⓓ
27. Ⓐ Ⓑ Ⓒ Ⓓ Ⓔ AG	6. Ⓕ Ⓖ Ⓗ Ⓙ AL	6. Ⓕ Ⓖ Ⓗ Ⓙ
28. Ⓕ Ⓖ Ⓗ Ⓙ Ⓚ AG	7. Ⓐ Ⓑ Ⓒ Ⓓ AL	7. Ⓐ Ⓑ Ⓒ Ⓓ
29. Ⓐ Ⓑ Ⓒ Ⓓ Ⓔ AG	8. Ⓕ Ⓖ Ⓗ Ⓙ AL	8. Ⓕ Ⓖ Ⓗ Ⓙ
30. Ⓕ Ⓖ Ⓗ Ⓙ Ⓚ AG	9. Ⓐ Ⓑ Ⓒ Ⓓ AL	9. Ⓐ Ⓑ Ⓒ Ⓓ
31. Ⓐ Ⓑ Ⓒ Ⓓ Ⓔ AG	10. Ⓕ Ⓖ Ⓗ Ⓙ AL	10. Ⓕ Ⓖ Ⓗ Ⓙ
32. Ⓕ Ⓖ Ⓗ Ⓙ Ⓚ EA	11. Ⓐ Ⓑ Ⓒ Ⓓ AL	11. Ⓐ Ⓑ Ⓒ Ⓓ
33. Ⓐ Ⓑ Ⓒ Ⓓ Ⓔ AG	12. Ⓕ Ⓖ Ⓗ Ⓙ AL	12. Ⓕ Ⓖ Ⓗ Ⓙ
34. Ⓕ Ⓖ Ⓗ Ⓙ Ⓚ AG	13. Ⓐ Ⓑ Ⓒ Ⓓ AL	13. Ⓐ Ⓑ Ⓒ Ⓓ
35. Ⓐ Ⓑ Ⓒ Ⓓ Ⓔ AG	14. Ⓕ Ⓖ Ⓗ Ⓙ AL	14. Ⓕ Ⓖ Ⓗ Ⓙ
36. Ⓕ Ⓖ Ⓗ Ⓙ Ⓚ AG	15. Ⓐ Ⓑ Ⓒ Ⓓ AL	15. Ⓐ Ⓑ Ⓒ Ⓓ
37. Ⓐ Ⓑ Ⓒ Ⓓ Ⓔ AG	16. Ⓕ Ⓖ Ⓗ Ⓙ AL	16. Ⓕ Ⓖ Ⓗ Ⓙ
38. Ⓕ Ⓖ Ⓗ Ⓙ Ⓚ GT	17. Ⓐ Ⓑ Ⓒ Ⓓ AL	17. Ⓐ Ⓑ Ⓒ Ⓓ
39. Ⓐ Ⓑ Ⓒ Ⓓ Ⓔ AG	18. Ⓕ Ⓖ Ⓗ Ⓙ AL	18. Ⓕ Ⓖ Ⓗ Ⓙ
40. Ⓕ Ⓖ Ⓗ Ⓙ Ⓚ AG	19. Ⓐ Ⓑ Ⓒ Ⓓ AL	19. Ⓐ Ⓑ Ⓒ Ⓓ
41. Ⓐ Ⓑ Ⓒ Ⓓ Ⓔ EA	20. Ⓕ Ⓖ Ⓗ Ⓙ AL	20. Ⓕ Ⓖ Ⓗ Ⓙ
42. Ⓕ Ⓖ Ⓗ Ⓙ Ⓚ EA	21. Ⓐ Ⓑ Ⓒ Ⓓ SS	21. Ⓐ Ⓑ Ⓒ Ⓓ
43. Ⓐ Ⓑ Ⓒ Ⓓ Ⓔ GT	22. Ⓕ Ⓖ Ⓗ Ⓙ SS	22. Ⓕ Ⓖ Ⓗ Ⓙ
44. Ⓕ Ⓖ Ⓗ Ⓙ Ⓚ AG	23. Ⓐ Ⓑ Ⓒ Ⓓ SS	23. Ⓐ Ⓑ Ⓒ Ⓓ
45. Ⓐ Ⓑ Ⓒ Ⓓ Ⓔ GT	24. Ⓕ Ⓖ Ⓗ Ⓙ SS	24. Ⓕ Ⓖ Ⓗ Ⓙ
46. Ⓕ Ⓖ Ⓗ Ⓙ Ⓚ GT	25. Ⓐ Ⓑ Ⓒ Ⓓ SS	25. Ⓐ Ⓑ Ⓒ Ⓓ
47. Ⓐ Ⓑ Ⓒ Ⓓ Ⓔ GT	26. Ⓕ Ⓖ Ⓗ Ⓙ SS	26. Ⓕ Ⓖ Ⓗ Ⓙ
48. Ⓕ Ⓖ Ⓗ Ⓙ Ⓚ GT	27. Ⓐ Ⓑ Ⓒ Ⓓ SS	27. Ⓐ Ⓑ Ⓒ Ⓓ
49. Ⓐ Ⓑ Ⓒ Ⓓ Ⓔ GT	28. Ⓕ Ⓖ Ⓗ Ⓙ SS	28. Ⓕ Ⓖ Ⓗ Ⓙ
50. Ⓕ Ⓖ Ⓗ Ⓙ Ⓚ GT	29. Ⓐ Ⓑ Ⓒ Ⓓ SS	29. Ⓐ Ⓑ Ⓒ Ⓓ
51. Ⓐ Ⓑ Ⓒ Ⓓ Ⓔ GT	30. Ⓕ Ⓖ Ⓗ Ⓙ SS	30. Ⓕ Ⓖ Ⓗ Ⓙ
52. Ⓕ Ⓖ Ⓗ Ⓙ Ⓚ GT	31. Ⓐ Ⓑ Ⓒ Ⓓ SS	31. Ⓐ Ⓑ Ⓒ Ⓓ
53. Ⓐ Ⓑ Ⓒ Ⓓ Ⓔ GT	32. Ⓕ Ⓖ Ⓗ Ⓙ SS	32. Ⓕ Ⓖ Ⓗ Ⓙ
54. Ⓕ Ⓖ Ⓗ Ⓙ Ⓚ GT	33. Ⓐ Ⓑ Ⓒ Ⓓ SS	33. Ⓐ Ⓑ Ⓒ Ⓓ
55. Ⓐ Ⓑ Ⓒ Ⓓ Ⓔ GT	34. Ⓕ Ⓖ Ⓗ Ⓙ SS	34. Ⓕ Ⓖ Ⓗ Ⓙ
56. Ⓕ Ⓖ Ⓗ Ⓙ Ⓚ AG	35. Ⓐ Ⓑ Ⓒ Ⓓ SS	35. Ⓐ Ⓑ Ⓒ Ⓓ
57. Ⓐ Ⓑ Ⓒ Ⓓ Ⓔ GT	36. Ⓕ Ⓖ Ⓗ Ⓙ SS	36. Ⓕ Ⓖ Ⓗ Ⓙ
58. Ⓕ Ⓖ Ⓗ Ⓙ Ⓚ GT	37. Ⓐ Ⓑ Ⓒ Ⓓ SS	37. Ⓐ Ⓑ Ⓒ Ⓓ
59. Ⓐ Ⓑ Ⓒ Ⓓ Ⓔ GT	38. Ⓕ Ⓖ Ⓗ Ⓙ SS	38. Ⓕ Ⓖ Ⓗ Ⓙ
60. Ⓕ Ⓖ Ⓗ Ⓙ Ⓚ GT	39. Ⓐ Ⓑ Ⓒ Ⓓ SS	39. Ⓐ Ⓑ Ⓒ Ⓓ
	40. Ⓕ Ⓖ Ⓗ Ⓙ SS	40. Ⓕ Ⓖ Ⓗ Ⓙ

ACT Assessment – Practice Exam III
ANSWER SHEET

TEST 1
English

1. (A) (B) (C) (D) UM
2. (F) (G) (H) (J) UM
3. (A) (B) (C) (D) UM
4. (F) (G) (H) (J) UM
5. (A) (B) (C) (D) UM
6. (F) (G) (H) (J) RH
7. (A) (B) (C) (D) UM
8. (F) (G) (H) (J) RH
9. (A) (B) (C) (D) RH
10. (F) (G) (H) (J) UM
11. (A) (B) (C) (D) RH
12. (F) (G) (H) (J) UM
13. (A) (B) (C) (D) RH
14. (F) (G) (H) (J) UM
15. (A) (B) (C) (D) UM
16. (F) (G) (H) (J) UM
17. (A) (B) (C) (D) UM
18. (F) (G) (H) (J) UM
19. (A) (B) (C) (D) UM
20. (F) (G) (H) (J) RH
21. (A) (B) (C) (D) UM
22. (F) (G) (H) (J) UM
23. (A) (B) (C) (D) RH
24. (F) (G) (H) (J) UM
25. (A) (B) (C) (D) UM
26. (F) (G) (H) (J) UM
27. (A) (B) (C) (D) UM
28. (F) (G) (H) (J) UM
29. (A) (B) (C) (D) RH
30. (F) (G) (H) (J) UM
31. (A) (B) (C) (D) RH

32. (F) (G) (H) (J) RH
33. (A) (B) (C) (D) UM
34. (F) (G) (H) (J) UM
35. (A) (B) (C) (D) RH
36. (F) (G) (H) (J) UM
37. (A) (B) (C) (D) UM
38. (F) (G) (H) (J) UM
39. (A) (B) (C) (D) RH
40. (F) (G) (H) (J) UM
41. (A) (B) (C) (D) RH
42. (F) (G) (H) (J) UM
43. (A) (B) (C) (D) UM
44. (F) (G) (H) (J) RH
45. (A) (B) (C) (D) RH
46. (F) (G) (H) (J) RH
47. (A) (B) (C) (D) UM
48. (F) (G) (H) (J) UM
49. (A) (B) (C) (D) RH
50. (F) (G) (H) (J) RH
51. (A) (B) (C) (D) UM
52. (F) (G) (H) (J) UM
53. (A) (B) (C) (D) UM
54. (F) (G) (H) (J) UM
55. (A) (B) (C) (D) RH
56. (F) (G) (H) (J) UM
57. (A) (B) (C) (D) UM
58. (F) (G) (H) (J) UM
59. (A) (B) (C) (D) UM
60. (F) (G) (H) (J) RH
61. (A) (B) (C) (D) RH
62. (F) (G) (H) (J) UM
63. (A) (B) (C) (D) RH
64. (F) (G) (H) (J) RH

65. (A) (B) (C) (D) UM
66. (F) (G) (H) (J) UM
67. (A) (B) (C) (D) UM
68. (F) (G) (H) (J) UM
69. (A) (B) (C) (D) RH
70. (F) (G) (H) (J) RH
71. (A) (B) (C) (D) UM
72. (F) (G) (H) (J) UM
73. (A) (B) (C) (D) UM
74. (F) (G) (H) (J) RH
75. (A) (B) (C) (D) RH

TEST 2
Mathematics

1. (A) (B) (C) (D) (E) EA
2. (F) (G) (H) (J) (K) AG
3. (A) (B) (C) (D) (E) AG
4. (F) (G) (H) (J) (K) EA
5. (A) (B) (C) (D) (E) EA
6. (F) (G) (H) (J) (K) EA
7. (A) (B) (C) (D) (E) EA
8. (F) (G) (H) (J) (K) AG
9. (A) (B) (C) (D) (E) AG
10. (F) (G) (H) (J) (K) EA
11. (A) (B) (C) (D) (E) AG
12. (F) (G) (H) (J) (K) AG
13. (A) (B) (C) (D) (E) EA
14. (F) (G) (H) (J) (K) EA
15. (A) (B) (C) (D) (E) EA
16. (F) (G) (H) (J) (K) EA
17. (A) (B) (C) (D) (E) AG
18. (F) (G) (H) (J) (K) AG
19. (A) (B) (C) (D) (E) AG

20.	Ⓕ	Ⓖ	Ⓗ	Ⓙ	Ⓚ EA
21.	Ⓐ	Ⓑ	Ⓒ	Ⓓ	Ⓔ EA
22.	Ⓕ	Ⓖ	Ⓗ	Ⓙ	Ⓚ EA
23.	Ⓐ	Ⓑ	Ⓒ	Ⓓ	Ⓔ EA
24.	Ⓕ	Ⓖ	Ⓗ	Ⓙ	Ⓚ AG
25.	Ⓐ	Ⓑ	Ⓒ	Ⓓ	Ⓔ AG
26.	Ⓕ	Ⓖ	Ⓗ	Ⓙ	Ⓚ AG
27.	Ⓐ	Ⓑ	Ⓒ	Ⓓ	Ⓔ AG
28.	Ⓕ	Ⓖ	Ⓗ	Ⓙ	Ⓚ AG
29.	Ⓐ	Ⓑ	Ⓒ	Ⓓ	Ⓔ AG
30.	Ⓕ	Ⓖ	Ⓗ	Ⓙ	Ⓚ AG
31.	Ⓐ	Ⓑ	Ⓒ	Ⓓ	Ⓔ AG
32.	Ⓕ	Ⓖ	Ⓗ	Ⓙ	Ⓚ EA
33.	Ⓐ	Ⓑ	Ⓒ	Ⓓ	Ⓔ AG
34.	Ⓕ	Ⓖ	Ⓗ	Ⓙ	Ⓚ AG
35.	Ⓐ	Ⓑ	Ⓒ	Ⓓ	Ⓔ AG
36.	Ⓕ	Ⓖ	Ⓗ	Ⓙ	Ⓚ AG
37.	Ⓐ	Ⓑ	Ⓒ	Ⓓ	Ⓔ AG
38.	Ⓕ	Ⓖ	Ⓗ	Ⓙ	Ⓚ GT
39.	Ⓐ	Ⓑ	Ⓒ	Ⓓ	Ⓔ AG
40.	Ⓕ	Ⓖ	Ⓗ	Ⓙ	Ⓚ AG
41.	Ⓐ	Ⓑ	Ⓒ	Ⓓ	Ⓔ EA
42.	Ⓕ	Ⓖ	Ⓗ	Ⓙ	Ⓚ EA
43.	Ⓐ	Ⓑ	Ⓒ	Ⓓ	Ⓔ GT
44.	Ⓕ	Ⓖ	Ⓗ	Ⓙ	Ⓚ AG
45.	Ⓐ	Ⓑ	Ⓒ	Ⓓ	Ⓔ GT
46.	Ⓕ	Ⓖ	Ⓗ	Ⓙ	Ⓚ GT
47.	Ⓐ	Ⓑ	Ⓒ	Ⓓ	Ⓔ GT
48.	Ⓕ	Ⓖ	Ⓗ	Ⓙ	Ⓚ GT
49.	Ⓐ	Ⓑ	Ⓒ	Ⓓ	Ⓔ GT
50.	Ⓕ	Ⓖ	Ⓗ	Ⓙ	Ⓚ GT
51.	Ⓐ	Ⓑ	Ⓒ	Ⓓ	Ⓔ GT
52.	Ⓕ	Ⓖ	Ⓗ	Ⓙ	Ⓚ GT
53.	Ⓐ	Ⓑ	Ⓒ	Ⓓ	Ⓔ GT
54.	Ⓕ	Ⓖ	Ⓗ	Ⓙ	Ⓚ GT
55.	Ⓐ	Ⓑ	Ⓒ	Ⓓ	Ⓔ GT
56.	Ⓕ	Ⓖ	Ⓗ	Ⓙ	Ⓚ AG
57.	Ⓐ	Ⓑ	Ⓒ	Ⓓ	Ⓔ GT
58.	Ⓕ	Ⓖ	Ⓗ	Ⓙ	Ⓚ GT
59.	Ⓐ	Ⓑ	Ⓒ	Ⓓ	Ⓔ GT
60.	Ⓕ	Ⓖ	Ⓗ	Ⓙ	Ⓚ GT

TEST 3
Reading

1.	Ⓐ	Ⓑ	Ⓒ	Ⓓ AL
2.	Ⓕ	Ⓖ	Ⓗ	Ⓙ AL
3.	Ⓐ	Ⓑ	Ⓒ	Ⓓ AL
4.	Ⓕ	Ⓖ	Ⓗ	Ⓙ AL
5.	Ⓐ	Ⓑ	Ⓒ	Ⓓ AL
6.	Ⓕ	Ⓖ	Ⓗ	Ⓙ AL
7.	Ⓐ	Ⓑ	Ⓒ	Ⓓ AL
8.	Ⓕ	Ⓖ	Ⓗ	Ⓙ AL
9.	Ⓐ	Ⓑ	Ⓒ	Ⓓ AL
10.	Ⓕ	Ⓖ	Ⓗ	Ⓙ AL
11.	Ⓐ	Ⓑ	Ⓒ	Ⓓ AL
12.	Ⓕ	Ⓖ	Ⓗ	Ⓙ AL
13.	Ⓐ	Ⓑ	Ⓒ	Ⓓ AL
14.	Ⓕ	Ⓖ	Ⓗ	Ⓙ AL
15.	Ⓐ	Ⓑ	Ⓒ	Ⓓ AL
16.	Ⓕ	Ⓖ	Ⓗ	Ⓙ AL
17.	Ⓐ	Ⓑ	Ⓒ	Ⓓ AL
18.	Ⓕ	Ⓖ	Ⓗ	Ⓙ AL
19.	Ⓐ	Ⓑ	Ⓒ	Ⓓ AL
20.	Ⓕ	Ⓖ	Ⓗ	Ⓙ AL
21.	Ⓐ	Ⓑ	Ⓒ	Ⓓ SS
22.	Ⓕ	Ⓖ	Ⓗ	Ⓙ SS
23.	Ⓐ	Ⓑ	Ⓒ	Ⓓ SS
24.	Ⓕ	Ⓖ	Ⓗ	Ⓙ SS
25.	Ⓐ	Ⓑ	Ⓒ	Ⓓ SS
26.	Ⓕ	Ⓖ	Ⓗ	Ⓙ SS
27.	Ⓐ	Ⓑ	Ⓒ	Ⓓ SS
28.	Ⓕ	Ⓖ	Ⓗ	Ⓙ SS
29.	Ⓐ	Ⓑ	Ⓒ	Ⓓ SS
30.	Ⓕ	Ⓖ	Ⓗ	Ⓙ SS
31.	Ⓐ	Ⓑ	Ⓒ	Ⓓ SS
32.	Ⓕ	Ⓖ	Ⓗ	Ⓙ SS
33.	Ⓐ	Ⓑ	Ⓒ	Ⓓ SS
34.	Ⓕ	Ⓖ	Ⓗ	Ⓙ SS
35.	Ⓐ	Ⓑ	Ⓒ	Ⓓ SS
36.	Ⓕ	Ⓖ	Ⓗ	Ⓙ SS
37.	Ⓐ	Ⓑ	Ⓒ	Ⓓ SS
38.	Ⓕ	Ⓖ	Ⓗ	Ⓙ SS
39.	Ⓐ	Ⓑ	Ⓒ	Ⓓ SS
40.	Ⓕ	Ⓖ	Ⓗ	Ⓙ SS

TEST 4
Science Reasoning

1.	Ⓐ	Ⓑ	Ⓒ	Ⓓ
2.	Ⓕ	Ⓖ	Ⓗ	Ⓙ
3.	Ⓐ	Ⓑ	Ⓒ	Ⓓ
4.	Ⓕ	Ⓖ	Ⓗ	Ⓙ
5.	Ⓐ	Ⓑ	Ⓒ	Ⓓ
6.	Ⓕ	Ⓖ	Ⓗ	Ⓙ
7.	Ⓐ	Ⓑ	Ⓒ	Ⓓ
8.	Ⓕ	Ⓖ	Ⓗ	Ⓙ
9.	Ⓐ	Ⓑ	Ⓒ	Ⓓ
10.	Ⓕ	Ⓖ	Ⓗ	Ⓙ
11.	Ⓐ	Ⓑ	Ⓒ	Ⓓ
12.	Ⓕ	Ⓖ	Ⓗ	Ⓙ
13.	Ⓐ	Ⓑ	Ⓒ	Ⓓ
14.	Ⓕ	Ⓖ	Ⓗ	Ⓙ
15.	Ⓐ	Ⓑ	Ⓒ	Ⓓ
16.	Ⓕ	Ⓖ	Ⓗ	Ⓙ
17.	Ⓐ	Ⓑ	Ⓒ	Ⓓ
18.	Ⓕ	Ⓖ	Ⓗ	Ⓙ
19.	Ⓐ	Ⓑ	Ⓒ	Ⓓ
20.	Ⓕ	Ⓖ	Ⓗ	Ⓙ
21.	Ⓐ	Ⓑ	Ⓒ	Ⓓ
22.	Ⓕ	Ⓖ	Ⓗ	Ⓙ
23.	Ⓐ	Ⓑ	Ⓒ	Ⓓ
24.	Ⓕ	Ⓖ	Ⓗ	Ⓙ
25.	Ⓐ	Ⓑ	Ⓒ	Ⓓ
26.	Ⓕ	Ⓖ	Ⓗ	Ⓙ
27.	Ⓐ	Ⓑ	Ⓒ	Ⓓ
28.	Ⓕ	Ⓖ	Ⓗ	Ⓙ
29.	Ⓐ	Ⓑ	Ⓒ	Ⓓ
30.	Ⓕ	Ⓖ	Ⓗ	Ⓙ
31.	Ⓐ	Ⓑ	Ⓒ	Ⓓ
32.	Ⓕ	Ⓖ	Ⓗ	Ⓙ
33.	Ⓐ	Ⓑ	Ⓒ	Ⓓ
34.	Ⓕ	Ⓖ	Ⓗ	Ⓙ
35.	Ⓐ	Ⓑ	Ⓒ	Ⓓ
36.	Ⓕ	Ⓖ	Ⓗ	Ⓙ
37.	Ⓐ	Ⓑ	Ⓒ	Ⓓ
38.	Ⓕ	Ⓖ	Ⓗ	Ⓙ
39.	Ⓐ	Ⓑ	Ⓒ	Ⓓ
40.	Ⓕ	Ⓖ	Ⓗ	Ⓙ

ACT Assessment – Practice Exam IV
ANSWER SHEET

Scoring Key*		
English	**Mathematics**	**Reading**
UM = Usage/Mechanics	EA = Pre-Algebra/Elementary Algebra	SS = Social Studies/Science
RH = Rhetorical Skills	AG = Intermediate Algebra/Coordinate Geometry	AL = Arts/Literature
	GT = Plane Geometry/Trigonometry	

TEST 1
English

1. Ⓐ Ⓑ Ⓒ Ⓓ UM
2. Ⓕ Ⓖ Ⓗ Ⓙ UM
3. Ⓐ Ⓑ Ⓒ Ⓓ UM
4. Ⓕ Ⓖ Ⓗ Ⓙ UM
5. Ⓐ Ⓑ Ⓒ Ⓓ UM
6. Ⓕ Ⓖ Ⓗ Ⓙ RH
7. Ⓐ Ⓑ Ⓒ Ⓓ UM
8. Ⓕ Ⓖ Ⓗ Ⓙ RH
9. Ⓐ Ⓑ Ⓒ Ⓓ RH
10. Ⓕ Ⓖ Ⓗ Ⓙ UM
11. Ⓐ Ⓑ Ⓒ Ⓓ RH
12. Ⓕ Ⓖ Ⓗ Ⓙ UM
13. Ⓐ Ⓑ Ⓒ Ⓓ RH
14. Ⓕ Ⓖ Ⓗ Ⓙ UM
15. Ⓐ Ⓑ Ⓒ Ⓓ UM
16. Ⓕ Ⓖ Ⓗ Ⓙ UM
17. Ⓐ Ⓑ Ⓒ Ⓓ UM
18. Ⓕ Ⓖ Ⓗ Ⓙ UM
19. Ⓐ Ⓑ Ⓒ Ⓓ UM
20. Ⓕ Ⓖ Ⓗ Ⓙ RH
21. Ⓐ Ⓑ Ⓒ Ⓓ UM
22. Ⓕ Ⓖ Ⓗ Ⓙ UM
23. Ⓐ Ⓑ Ⓒ Ⓓ RH
24. Ⓕ Ⓖ Ⓗ Ⓙ UM
25. Ⓐ Ⓑ Ⓒ Ⓓ UM
26. Ⓕ Ⓖ Ⓗ Ⓙ UM
27. Ⓐ Ⓑ Ⓒ Ⓓ UM
28. Ⓕ Ⓖ Ⓗ Ⓙ UM
29. Ⓐ Ⓑ Ⓒ Ⓓ RH
30. Ⓕ Ⓖ Ⓗ Ⓙ UM
31. Ⓐ Ⓑ Ⓒ Ⓓ RH

32. Ⓕ Ⓖ Ⓗ Ⓙ RH
33. Ⓐ Ⓑ Ⓒ Ⓓ UM
34. Ⓕ Ⓖ Ⓗ Ⓙ UM
35. Ⓐ Ⓑ Ⓒ Ⓓ RH
36. Ⓕ Ⓖ Ⓗ Ⓙ UM
37. Ⓐ Ⓑ Ⓒ Ⓓ UM
38. Ⓕ Ⓖ Ⓗ Ⓙ UM
39. Ⓐ Ⓑ Ⓒ Ⓓ RH
40. Ⓕ Ⓖ Ⓗ Ⓙ UM
41. Ⓐ Ⓑ Ⓒ Ⓓ RH
42. Ⓕ Ⓖ Ⓗ Ⓙ UM
43. Ⓐ Ⓑ Ⓒ Ⓓ UM
44. Ⓕ Ⓖ Ⓗ Ⓙ RH
45. Ⓐ Ⓑ Ⓒ Ⓓ RH
46. Ⓕ Ⓖ Ⓗ Ⓙ RH
47. Ⓐ Ⓑ Ⓒ Ⓓ UM
48. Ⓕ Ⓖ Ⓗ Ⓙ UM
49. Ⓐ Ⓑ Ⓒ Ⓓ RH
50. Ⓕ Ⓖ Ⓗ Ⓙ RH
51. Ⓐ Ⓑ Ⓒ Ⓓ UM
52. Ⓕ Ⓖ Ⓗ Ⓙ UM
53. Ⓐ Ⓑ Ⓒ Ⓓ UM
54. Ⓕ Ⓖ Ⓗ Ⓙ UM
55. Ⓐ Ⓑ Ⓒ Ⓓ RH
56. Ⓕ Ⓖ Ⓗ Ⓙ UM
57. Ⓐ Ⓑ Ⓒ Ⓓ UM
58. Ⓕ Ⓖ Ⓗ Ⓙ UM
59. Ⓐ Ⓑ Ⓒ Ⓓ UM
60. Ⓕ Ⓖ Ⓗ Ⓙ RH
61. Ⓐ Ⓑ Ⓒ Ⓓ RH
62. Ⓕ Ⓖ Ⓗ Ⓙ UM
63. Ⓐ Ⓑ Ⓒ Ⓓ RH
64. Ⓕ Ⓖ Ⓗ Ⓙ RH

65. Ⓐ Ⓑ Ⓒ Ⓓ UM
66. Ⓕ Ⓖ Ⓗ Ⓙ UM
67. Ⓐ Ⓑ Ⓒ Ⓓ UM
68. Ⓕ Ⓖ Ⓗ Ⓙ UM
69. Ⓐ Ⓑ Ⓒ Ⓓ RH
70. Ⓕ Ⓖ Ⓗ Ⓙ RH
71. Ⓐ Ⓑ Ⓒ Ⓓ UM
72. Ⓕ Ⓖ Ⓗ Ⓙ UM
73. Ⓐ Ⓑ Ⓒ Ⓓ UM
74. Ⓕ Ⓖ Ⓗ Ⓙ RH
75. Ⓐ Ⓑ Ⓒ Ⓓ RH

TEST 2
Mathematics

1. Ⓐ Ⓑ Ⓒ Ⓓ Ⓔ EA
2. Ⓕ Ⓖ Ⓗ Ⓙ Ⓚ AG
3. Ⓐ Ⓑ Ⓒ Ⓓ Ⓔ AG
4. Ⓕ Ⓖ Ⓗ Ⓙ Ⓚ EA
5. Ⓐ Ⓑ Ⓒ Ⓓ Ⓔ EA
6. Ⓕ Ⓖ Ⓗ Ⓙ Ⓚ EA
7. Ⓐ Ⓑ Ⓒ Ⓓ Ⓔ EA
8. Ⓕ Ⓖ Ⓗ Ⓙ Ⓚ AG
9. Ⓐ Ⓑ Ⓒ Ⓓ Ⓔ AG
10. Ⓕ Ⓖ Ⓗ Ⓙ Ⓚ EA
11. Ⓐ Ⓑ Ⓒ Ⓓ Ⓔ AG
12. Ⓕ Ⓖ Ⓗ Ⓙ Ⓚ AG
13. Ⓐ Ⓑ Ⓒ Ⓓ Ⓔ EA
14. Ⓕ Ⓖ Ⓗ Ⓙ Ⓚ EA
15. Ⓐ Ⓑ Ⓒ Ⓓ Ⓔ EA
16. Ⓕ Ⓖ Ⓗ Ⓙ Ⓚ EA
17. Ⓐ Ⓑ Ⓒ Ⓓ Ⓔ AG
18. Ⓕ Ⓖ Ⓗ Ⓙ Ⓚ AG
19. Ⓐ Ⓑ Ⓒ Ⓓ Ⓔ AG

20. Ⓕ Ⓖ Ⓗ Ⓙ Ⓚ EA
21. Ⓐ Ⓑ Ⓒ Ⓓ Ⓔ EA
22. Ⓕ Ⓖ Ⓗ Ⓙ Ⓚ EA
23. Ⓐ Ⓑ Ⓒ Ⓓ Ⓔ EA
24. Ⓕ Ⓖ Ⓗ Ⓙ Ⓚ AG
25. Ⓐ Ⓑ Ⓒ Ⓓ Ⓔ AG
26. Ⓕ Ⓖ Ⓗ Ⓙ Ⓚ AG
27. Ⓐ Ⓑ Ⓒ Ⓓ Ⓔ AG
28. Ⓕ Ⓖ Ⓗ Ⓙ Ⓚ AG
29. Ⓐ Ⓑ Ⓒ Ⓓ Ⓔ AG
30. Ⓕ Ⓖ Ⓗ Ⓙ Ⓚ AG
31. Ⓐ Ⓑ Ⓒ Ⓓ Ⓔ AG
32. Ⓕ Ⓖ Ⓗ Ⓙ Ⓚ EA
33. Ⓐ Ⓑ Ⓒ Ⓓ Ⓔ AG
34. Ⓕ Ⓖ Ⓗ Ⓙ Ⓚ AG
35. Ⓐ Ⓑ Ⓒ Ⓓ Ⓔ AG
36. Ⓕ Ⓖ Ⓗ Ⓙ Ⓚ AG
37. Ⓐ Ⓑ Ⓒ Ⓓ Ⓔ AG
38. Ⓕ Ⓖ Ⓗ Ⓙ Ⓚ GT
39. Ⓐ Ⓑ Ⓒ Ⓓ Ⓔ AG
40. Ⓕ Ⓖ Ⓗ Ⓙ Ⓚ AG
41. Ⓐ Ⓑ Ⓒ Ⓓ Ⓔ EA
42. Ⓕ Ⓖ Ⓗ Ⓙ Ⓚ EA
43. Ⓐ Ⓑ Ⓒ Ⓓ Ⓔ GT
44. Ⓕ Ⓖ Ⓗ Ⓙ Ⓚ AG
45. Ⓐ Ⓑ Ⓒ Ⓓ Ⓔ GT
46. Ⓕ Ⓖ Ⓗ Ⓙ Ⓚ GT
47. Ⓐ Ⓑ Ⓒ Ⓓ Ⓔ GT
48. Ⓕ Ⓖ Ⓗ Ⓙ Ⓚ GT
49. Ⓐ Ⓑ Ⓒ Ⓓ Ⓔ GT
50. Ⓕ Ⓖ Ⓗ Ⓙ Ⓚ GT
51. Ⓐ Ⓑ Ⓒ Ⓓ Ⓔ GT
52. Ⓕ Ⓖ Ⓗ Ⓙ Ⓚ GT
53. Ⓐ Ⓑ Ⓒ Ⓓ Ⓔ GT
54. Ⓕ Ⓖ Ⓗ Ⓙ Ⓚ GT
55. Ⓐ Ⓑ Ⓒ Ⓓ Ⓔ GT
56. Ⓕ Ⓖ Ⓗ Ⓙ Ⓚ AG
57. Ⓐ Ⓑ Ⓒ Ⓓ Ⓔ GT
58. Ⓕ Ⓖ Ⓗ Ⓙ Ⓚ GT
59. Ⓐ Ⓑ Ⓒ Ⓓ Ⓔ GT
60. Ⓕ Ⓖ Ⓗ Ⓙ Ⓚ GT

TEST 3
Reading

1. Ⓐ Ⓑ Ⓒ Ⓓ AL
2. Ⓕ Ⓖ Ⓗ Ⓙ AL
3. Ⓐ Ⓑ Ⓒ Ⓓ AL
4. Ⓕ Ⓖ Ⓗ Ⓙ AL
5. Ⓐ Ⓑ Ⓒ Ⓓ AL
6. Ⓕ Ⓖ Ⓗ Ⓙ AL
7. Ⓐ Ⓑ Ⓒ Ⓓ AL
8. Ⓕ Ⓖ Ⓗ Ⓙ AL
9. Ⓐ Ⓑ Ⓒ Ⓓ AL
10. Ⓕ Ⓖ Ⓗ Ⓙ AL
11. Ⓐ Ⓑ Ⓒ Ⓓ AL
12. Ⓕ Ⓖ Ⓗ Ⓙ AL
13. Ⓐ Ⓑ Ⓒ Ⓓ AL
14. Ⓕ Ⓖ Ⓗ Ⓙ AL
15. Ⓐ Ⓑ Ⓒ Ⓓ AL
16. Ⓕ Ⓖ Ⓗ Ⓙ AL
17. Ⓐ Ⓑ Ⓒ Ⓓ AL
18. Ⓕ Ⓖ Ⓗ Ⓙ AL
19. Ⓐ Ⓑ Ⓒ Ⓓ AL
20. Ⓕ Ⓖ Ⓗ Ⓙ AL
21. Ⓐ Ⓑ Ⓒ Ⓓ SS
22. Ⓕ Ⓖ Ⓗ Ⓙ SS
23. Ⓐ Ⓑ Ⓒ Ⓓ SS
24. Ⓕ Ⓖ Ⓗ Ⓙ SS
25. Ⓐ Ⓑ Ⓒ Ⓓ SS
26. Ⓕ Ⓖ Ⓗ Ⓙ SS
27. Ⓐ Ⓑ Ⓒ Ⓓ SS
28. Ⓕ Ⓖ Ⓗ Ⓙ SS
29. Ⓐ Ⓑ Ⓒ Ⓓ SS
30. Ⓕ Ⓖ Ⓗ Ⓙ SS
31. Ⓐ Ⓑ Ⓒ Ⓓ SS
32. Ⓕ Ⓖ Ⓗ Ⓙ SS
33. Ⓐ Ⓑ Ⓒ Ⓓ SS
34. Ⓕ Ⓖ Ⓗ Ⓙ SS
35. Ⓐ Ⓑ Ⓒ Ⓓ SS
36. Ⓕ Ⓖ Ⓗ Ⓙ SS
37. Ⓐ Ⓑ Ⓒ Ⓓ SS
38. Ⓕ Ⓖ Ⓗ Ⓙ SS
39. Ⓐ Ⓑ Ⓒ Ⓓ SS
40. Ⓕ Ⓖ Ⓗ Ⓙ SS

TEST 4
Science Reasoning

1. Ⓐ Ⓑ Ⓒ Ⓓ
2. Ⓕ Ⓖ Ⓗ Ⓙ
3. Ⓐ Ⓑ Ⓒ Ⓓ
4. Ⓕ Ⓖ Ⓗ Ⓙ
5. Ⓐ Ⓑ Ⓒ Ⓓ
6. Ⓕ Ⓖ Ⓗ Ⓙ
7. Ⓐ Ⓑ Ⓒ Ⓓ
8. Ⓕ Ⓖ Ⓗ Ⓙ
9. Ⓐ Ⓑ Ⓒ Ⓓ
10. Ⓕ Ⓖ Ⓗ Ⓙ
11. Ⓐ Ⓑ Ⓒ Ⓓ
12. Ⓕ Ⓖ Ⓗ Ⓙ
13. Ⓐ Ⓑ Ⓒ Ⓓ
14. Ⓕ Ⓖ Ⓗ Ⓙ
15. Ⓐ Ⓑ Ⓒ Ⓓ
16. Ⓕ Ⓖ Ⓗ Ⓙ
17. Ⓐ Ⓑ Ⓒ Ⓓ
18. Ⓕ Ⓖ Ⓗ Ⓙ
19. Ⓐ Ⓑ Ⓒ Ⓓ
20. Ⓕ Ⓖ Ⓗ Ⓙ
21. Ⓐ Ⓑ Ⓒ Ⓓ
22. Ⓕ Ⓖ Ⓗ Ⓙ
23. Ⓐ Ⓑ Ⓒ Ⓓ
24. Ⓕ Ⓖ Ⓗ Ⓙ
25. Ⓐ Ⓑ Ⓒ Ⓓ
26. Ⓕ Ⓖ Ⓗ Ⓙ
27. Ⓐ Ⓑ Ⓒ Ⓓ
28. Ⓕ Ⓖ Ⓗ Ⓙ
29. Ⓐ Ⓑ Ⓒ Ⓓ
30. Ⓕ Ⓖ Ⓗ Ⓙ
31. Ⓐ Ⓑ Ⓒ Ⓓ
32. Ⓕ Ⓖ Ⓗ Ⓙ
33. Ⓐ Ⓑ Ⓒ Ⓓ
34. Ⓕ Ⓖ Ⓗ Ⓙ
35. Ⓐ Ⓑ Ⓒ Ⓓ
36. Ⓕ Ⓖ Ⓗ Ⓙ
37. Ⓐ Ⓑ Ⓒ Ⓓ
38. Ⓕ Ⓖ Ⓗ Ⓙ
39. Ⓐ Ⓑ Ⓒ Ⓓ
40. Ⓕ Ⓖ Ⓗ Ⓙ

ATTACKING THE ACT WRITING TEST

DESCRIPTION OF THE WRITING TEST

An optional writing test is being included as part of the ACT Assessment beginning in February 2005. This portion of the exam has been devised to complement the ACT's English Test. It has been designed so that postsecondary institutions have the opportunity to determine whether an applicant has the writing skills necessary to succeed at select colleges and universities. Since not every school requires a writing sample produced under time constraints, ACT has decided to offer the Writing Test as an option.

The ACT Writing Test has been structured to measure those skills indispensable for cogent and persuasive writing, including punctuation, grammar, sentence structure, organization, and style. A single prompt will be provided on the Writing Test; the examinee will have to create a response within 30 minutes that either supports or does not support a given argument, or one that provides an opinion about a particular issue or topic. No knowledge of any specific discipline is required; this portion of the exam assesses only a person's writing ability.

Because it is optional, there is an additional fee for the ACT Writing Test. You'll be able to take the ACT Writing Test at the same place and time at which you opt to take the ACT Assessment. For more information about the ACT Writing Test, visit the official ACT Web site at www.act.org.

WRITING TEST STRATEGIES

Here are some strategies for mastering the ACT Writing Test:

1. **Keep a close eye on your time.** You should spend five to 10 minutes collecting and outlining your thoughts rather than planning on the fly.

2. **Don't overload your essay with too many ideas,** and be sure to develop each concept thoroughly.

3. **Don't let good ideas be undermined by poor transitions.** For example, you may want to present your argument and then examine another point of view. Transitions like "conversely" and "on the other hand" will lend a smoothness and coherence to your prose. Likewise, if you're pointing to a result or effect, transitions such as "consequently" or "thus" will help you state your case. Use them with precision and you'll boost your score.

4. **Set aside five minutes at the end to copyedit and proofread your work—** and then proofread it again.

SCORING THE ESSAYS

The essay is evaluated on a six-point scale. The essay is scored by two separate graders, each of whom will grade it on a scale of 1 to 6; the two graders' ratings are then combined to yield a total score for the Writing Test. As you may already have deduced, the highest score possible on the ACT Writing Test is a 12. Your performance on the Writing Test will *not* affect your subject-area scores on the ACT Assessment or your composite score.

The ACT Writing Test follows this scoring system:

6 — Outstanding

5 — Strong

4 — Adequate

3 — Limited

2 — Seriously Flawed

1 — Fundamentally Deficient

0 — Illegible, Off-Topic

ESSAY WRITING REVIEW

The ACT Writing Test contains one writing exercise. You will have 30 minutes to plan and write an essay on a given topic. You must write on only that topic. Because you will have only 30 minutes to complete the essay, efficient use of your time is essential.

Writing under pressure can be frustrating, but if you study this review, practice and polish your essay skills, and have a realistic sense of what to expect, you can turn problems into possibilities. The following review will show you how to plan and write a logical, coherent, and interesting essay.

PRE-WRITING/PLANNING

Before you begin to actually write, there are certain preliminary steps you need to take. A few minutes spent planning pays off—your final essay will be more focused, well-developed, and clearer. For a 30-minute essay, you should spend five to ten minutes on the pre-writing process.

Understand the Question

Sometimes a student fails to understand the question the essay is meant to address. The resulting answer may be very well written, but if it fails to address the issue correctly, it will not receive a high score. Read the essay question very carefully and ask yourself the following questions:

- What is the meaning of the topic statement?

- Is the question asking me to persuade the reader of the validity of a certain opinion?

- Do I agree or disagree with the statement? What will be my thesis (main idea)?

- What kinds of examples can I use to support my thesis? Explore personal experiences, historical evidence, current events, and literary subjects.

Consider Your Audience

Essays would be pointless without an audience. Why write an essay if no one wants or needs to read it? Why add evidence, organize your ideas, or correct bad grammar? The reason to do any of these things is because someone out there needs to understand what you mean or say.

What does the audience need to know to believe you or to come over to your position? Imagine someone you know listening to you declare your position or opinion and then saying, "Oh, yeah? Prove it!" This is your audience—write to them. Ask yourself the following questions so that you will not be confronted with a person who says, "Prove it!"

- What evidence do I need to prove my idea to this skeptic?

- What would s/he disagree with me about?

- What does he or she share with me as common knowledge? What do I need to tell the reader?

WRITING YOUR ESSAY

Once you have considered your position on the topic and thought of several examples to support it, you are ready to begin writing.

Organizing Your Essay

Decide how many paragraphs you will write. In a 30-minute exercise, you will probably have time for four or five paragraphs. In such a format, the first paragraph will be the introduction, the next two or three will develop your thesis with specific examples, and the final paragraph should be a strong conclusion.

The Introduction

The focus of your introduction should be the thesis statement. This state-ment allows your reader to understand the point and direction of your essay. The statement identifies the central idea of your essay and should clearly state your attitude about the subject. It will also dictate the basic content and organization of your essay. If you do not state your thesis clearly, your essay will suffer.

The thesis is the heart of the essay. Without it, readers won't know what your major message or central idea is.

The thesis must be something that can be argued or needs to be proven, not just an accepted fact. For example, "Animals are used every day in cosmetic and medical testing," is a fact—it needs no proof. But if the writer says, "Using animals for cosmetic and medical testing is cruel and should be stopped," we have a point that must be supported and defended by the writer.

The thesis can be placed in any paragraph of the essay, but in a short essay, especially one written for evaluative exam purposes, the thesis is most effective when placed in the last sentence of the opening paragraph.

Consider the following sample question:

ESSAY TOPIC:

"That government is best which governs least."

ASSIGNMENT: Do you agree or disagree with this statement? Choose a specific example from current events, personal experience, or your reading to support your position.

After reading the topic statement, decide if you agree or disagree. If you agree with this statement, your thesis statement could be the following:

"Government has the right to protect individuals from harm, but no right to extend its powers and activities beyond this function."

This statement clearly delineates your opinion in a direct manner. It also serves as a blueprint for the essay. The remainder of the introduction should give two or three brief examples that support your thesis.

When writing under time constraints, your essay may take a turn you hadn't quite expected when you began. During proofreading, if you discover that your thesis statement is no longer accurate, go back and revise your statement to reflect the essay that you have, in fact, written.

Supporting Paragraphs

The next two or three paragraphs of your essay should elaborate on the supporting examples you gave in your introduction. Each paragraph should discuss only one idea. Like the introduction, each paragraph should be coherently organized, with a topic sentence and supporting details.

The topic sentence is to each paragraph what the thesis statement is to the essay as a whole. It tells the reader what you plan to discuss in that paragraph. It has a specific subject and is neither too broad nor too narrow. It also establishes the author's attitude and gives the reader a sense of the direction in which the writer is going. An effective topic sentence also arouses the reader's interest.

Although it may occur in the middle or at the end of the paragraph, the topic sentence usually appears at the beginning of the paragraph. Placing it at the beginning is advantageous because it helps you stay focused on the main idea.

The remainder of each paragraph should support the topic sentence with examples and illustrations. Each sentence should progress logically from the previous one and be centrally connected to your topic sentence. Do not include any extraneous material that does not serve to develop your thesis.

Conclusion

Your conclusion should briefly restate your thesis and explain how you have shown it to be true. Because you want to end your essay on a strong note, your conclusion should be concise and effective.

Do not introduce any new topics that you cannot support. If you were watching a movie that suddenly shifted plot and characters at the end, you would be disappointed or even angry. Similarly, conclusions must not drift away from the major focus and message of the essay. Make sure your conclusion is clearly on the topic and represents your perspective without any confusion about what you really mean and believe. The reader will respect you for staying true to your intentions.

The conclusion is your last chance to grab and impress the reader. You can even use humor, if appropriate, but a dramatic close will remind the reader you are serious, even passionate, about what you believe.

EFFECTIVE USE OF LANGUAGE

Clear organization, while vitally important, is not the only factor the graders of your essay consider. You must also demonstrate that you can express your ideas clearly, using correct grammar, diction, usage, spelling, and punctuation. For rules on grammar, usage, and mechanics, consult the English Language Skills Review in this book.

Point of View

Depending on the audience, essays may be written from one of three points of view:

1. *First Person* Point of View (Subjective/Personal):

    "I think . . ."

"I believe cars are more trouble than they are worth."

"I feel . . ."

2. *Second Person* Point of View (We . . . You; I . . . You):

"If *you* own a car, *you* will soon find out that it is more trouble than it is worth."

3. *Third Person* Point of View (focuses on the idea, not what "I" think of it):

"*Cars* are more trouble than *they* are worth."

It is very important to maintain a consistent point of view throughout your essay. If you begin writing in the first-person ("I"), do not shift to the second- or third-person in the middle of the essay. Such inconsistency is confusing to your reader and will be penalized by the graders of your essay.

Tone

A writer's tone results from his or her attitude toward the subject and the reader. If the essay question requires you to take a strong stand, the tone of your essay should reflect this.

Your tone should also be appropriate for the subject matter. A serious topic demands a serious tone. For a more light-hearted topic, you may wish to inject some humor into your essay.

Whatever tone you choose, be consistent. Do not make any abrupt shifts in tone in the middle of your essay.

Verb Tense

Stay with the same verb tense with which you begin your essay. If you start in the past, stay there—unless you have a compelling reason to switch tense to make an already well-supported point. Staying in the same verb tense improves the continuity and flow of ideas. Avoid phrases such as "now was," a confusing blend of present and past. Consistency among temporal references is essential to the reader's understanding.

Transitions

Transitions are like the links of a bracelet, holding the "beads," or major points, of your essay together. They help the reader follow the smooth flow of your ideas and show a connection between major and minor ideas. Transitions are used either at the beginning of a paragraph, or to show the connections among ideas within a single paragraph. Without transitions, you will jar the reader and risk distraction from your theme. For a list of helpful transitional words and phrases, see pg. 197.

Common Writing Errors

The four writing errors most often made by beginning writers are run-ons (also known as fused sentences), fragments, lack of subject-verb agreement, and incorrect use of objects:

1. **Run-ons**: "She swept the floor it was dirty" is a run-on, because the pronoun "it" stands as a noun subject and starts a new sentence. A period or semicolon is needed after "floor."

2. **Fragments**: "Before Jimmy learned how to play baseball" is a fragment, even though it has a subject and verb (Jimmy learned). The word "before" fragmentizes the clause, and the reader needs to know what happened before Jimmy learned how to play baseball.

3. **Problems with subject-verb agreement**: "Either Maria or Robert are going to the game" is incorrect because either Maria is going or Robert is going, but not both. The sentence should say, "Either Maria or Robert is going to the game."

4. **Incorrect objects**: Probably the most common offender in this area is saying "between you and I," which sounds correct, but isn't. "Between" is a preposition that takes the objective case "me." The correct usage is "between you and me."

Test graders also cite lack of thought and development, misspellings, incorrect pronouns or antecedents, and lack of development as frequently occurring problems. Finally, keep in mind that clear, coherent handwriting always works to your advantage. Readers will appreciate an essay they can read with ease.

Five Words Weak Writers Overuse

Weak and beginning writers overuse and otherwise misuse the pronouns *you, we, they, this,* and *it,* often without explaining who or what the pronoun represents. Vagueness can sap the life out of your writing, driving your reader to distraction, or at least a good bit of head-scratching. Here are some telltale signs that your prose may need a tune-up:

1. Shifting to second-person *you* when you actually mean "a person." This shift confuses readers and weakens the flow of the essay. We grant you that "you" is commonly accepted in creative writing, journalism, and other arenas—including *this book,* because we (i.e., the author and publishers) know exactly who's reading this, and the very point of much of we're writing is to address you directly! However, in a brief, formal essay, it is best to avoid it altogether.

2. Don't slip into the use of *we* without explicitly establishing to whom you are referring. If by "we" the writer means "Americans," "society,"

or some other group, then he or she should say so.

3. *They* is often misused in essay writing, perhaps because it is overused in casual conversation. How often have you heard or been heard to say something like this? "I went to the doctor, and they told me to take some medicine." Tell the reader who "they" are, and if it turns out not to be the proper pronoun for the number of people to whom you're referring, use the pronoun that is.

4. *This* is usually used incorrectly without a referent: "She told me she received a present. This sounded good to me." This what? This idea? This news? This present? Be clear—don't make your readers guess what you mean. The word "this" should be followed by a noun or referent.

5. *It* is a common leaning post among weak writers. To what does "it" refer? Readers don't appreciate having to struggle to grasp vague prose, so take the time to be clear, logical, and complete when you express yourself.

Use Your Own Vocabulary

Is it a good idea to use big words that look good in the dictionary or thesaurus, but that you don't typically use or even fully understand?

No!

So whose vocabulary should you use? Your own, because you will be most comfortable with your own level of vocabulary.

This "comfort zone" doesn't give you license to be informal in a formal setting or to violate the rules of standard written English, but if you try to write in a style that is not yours, your writing will be awkward and lack genuineness.

You should certainly improve and build your vocabulary at every opportunity, but don't try to change your vocabulary level at this point.

Avoid the Passive Voice

When you write, prefer the active voice; it will lend *oomph* to your prose. A weak, passive verb leaves the doer unknown or seemingly unimportant. The passive voice, however, is essential (1) when the action of the verb is more important than the doer, (2) when the doer is unknown, or (3) when the writer wishes to place the emphasis on the receiver of the action rather than on the doer.

PROOFREADING

Make sure to leave yourself enough time at the end to read over your essay for errors such as misspellings, omitted words, or incorrect punctuation. You will not have enough time to make large-scale revisions, but take this chance to make any small changes that will strengthen your essay. Consider the following when proofreading your work:

- Are all your sentences really sentences? Have you written any fragments or run-on sentences?

- Are you using vocabulary correctly?

- Did you leave out or garble any punctuation? Did you capitalize correctly?

- Are there any misspellings, especially of difficult words?

If you have time, read your essay backwards, from the last paragraph to the first. By doing so, you may catch errors that you missed reading it serially.

ACT WRITING TEST

SAMPLE ESSAY PROMPT NO. 1*

TIME: 30 Minutes
1 Essay

DIRECTIONS: You have 30 minutes to plan and write an essay on the topic below. You may write only on the assigned topic. You may take either one of the two positions given, or you may present another point of view that speaks to the question. Give specific reasons and examples to support your thesis.

There is ongoing debate and discussion of the question, "Is human culture incompatible with wilderness?" Thoughtful people have a great deal to say about this issue. Speak to the issue, taking a stand that supports (1) the notion that the two are basically incompatible or (2) that the two can coexist. You may base your stance on knowledge or your life experiences, or a combination of both.

SAMPLE ESSAY PROMPT NO. 2*

It has been suggested that it would be beneficial for students to take a year off after graduating high school before they begin attending college. Do you agree or disagree with this statement?

* The actual ACT Writing Test features one essay. We show two examples for practice purposes only.

ACT WRITING TEST

Sample Essays with Detailed Analyses

Sample 1 Responses

Sample Essay Response Scoring 5–6

Can wilderness and human culture coexist? I think so, although such coexistence can be horrendously challenging. There is a real question about whether human beings will have the wisdom to know how important wilderness is to them.

At this point, humans are encroaching on wilderness at a very frightening rate. For instance, great swaths of the rainforest are being destroyed every year, and yet we know that the is a rainforests is repository of all sorts of animal species and may hold important plants that may some day hold the key to curing terrible diseases like cancer. I believe that wilderness and human culture not only can, but must, coexist.

One way to make sure that humans understand that they must get along with wilderness is to experience it. Certainly no one who has ever spent time backpacking in the Rocky Mountains or watching the Sandhill Crane migration on the Platte River in Nebraska would not want to preserve the wilderness.

We need to make sure that we continue to preserve what we have. So much of our land is developed that we must be sure to take great care of what we have left. By driving in vehicles that don't burn a lot of gas, we can help keep the air clean, and clean air is an important part of wilderness. A lot of species of plants and animals cannot thrive in dirty air and water. We have a duty to help wild nature to survive.

Our country has been a world leader in preserving the wilderness. The first national park in the world was Yellowstone. The national parks are enjoyed by a large number of people from all over the world every year, and yet they are protected and are safe habitat for wild animals and plants. Our national parks system is proof that when we want to, we can preserve the wilderness. By being careful of how we live and how we use the resources we have, wilderness and human culture can coexist.

Analysis of Sample Essay Response Scoring 5–6

This paper has a good introduction, and it is written using a variety of grammatical sentences. Words like "horrendously" are casual, and talking about "the rainforest" is not correct. If the writer is talking about the world's rainforests, the term needs to be in the plural. There is some repetition ("may hold . . . may hold") The second and third body paragraphs are strong and well developed. The concluding paragraph is less strong. It would work better if the author used a transition such as, "The United States has shown that it is possible to preserve portions of wilderness while growing and developing," and then go on to talk about the national parks system, etc.

Sample Essay Response Scoring 3–4

There has been much written about wilderness. Can it be preserved as our world grows larger and as we use natural resources at an ever growing pace? I believe that wilderness is doomed. Whole miles of rainforest are cut down practically every day, and the carbon dioxide layer gets worse and worse. I think human culture and wilderness are entirely incompatible.

When people were simple hunters, they were in tune with nature. They hunted animals and respected the wild. As soon as they started to plant crops and live in towns, they started to harm the environment.

They dirtied the water and dug the land up and maybe they didn't know about fertilizing the land. It has been said that the Sahara Desert was once a more fertile place where people lived and grew crops. One day the whole world may be like that.

As civilizations grew and developed, people dug minerals out of the earth and cut down trees and never thought about replacing things that they used. Now we are just doing that on a huge scale and we have probably gotten to a point where we cannot put back things back the way they were. One time, I heard somebody say that we can make a species go extinct, but we cannot make a species. I think people should think about that before they do any more taking of natural resources and killing off wild animals

Although it is sad to say, I really think that there is no way human culture and wilderness can coexist.

Analysis of Sample Essay Scoring 3–4

This essay starts out strongly, and the second paragraph shows nice development. The third paragraph tends to ramble, and the writing, although grammatical, has several vague pronouns "be like that," "just doing that," and "people should think about that." The final paragraph, while it restates the writer's opinion, is too brief. The writer probably was rushed and didn't have time to complete the essay.

Sample Essay Response Scoring 2

Wilderness is a hard thing to talk about. People who live in or near it have one idea, and people who live in big cities don't ever get close, all they know is going to the zoo or watching Crocodile Hunter on TV. But they really have never gone out day after day to try and make a living in the wilderness.

My aunt lives in a town in the mountains, and the deer are always coming into her yard and eating all her trees and flowers and she can't even grow nice flowers. And she worries about skunks and cougars (the cougars would kill her little dog if she let him run around) and it isn't easy for her. So it's hard to be a human and have a human culture and get along with the wilderness. But what if she had to really make a living by growing crops on her property? Would she just let the deer come in and eat them, or would she have to shoot the deer?

I don't think people and wilderness really get along. Maybe if all you do is go out and have a day in the mountains it's nice, in fact it is nice, but if you have to go and deal with the wilderness all the time, it's not so easy. So no, people and wilderness can't get along together.

Analysis of Sample Essay Response Scoring 2

This writer states a clear opinion, but the essay tends to wander. Several topics are brought up in the first paragraph: (1) people who live near the wilderness; (2) people whose only contact with the wilderness is through television or very controlled experiences such as zoos; and (3) people who have to make a living from the wilderness. Each is a valid point, but none is really developed. The second paragraph gives some details, but again, the writing tends to ramble. For instance, the third sentence in the paragraph should be the concluding sentence of that paragraph. The final paragraph also rambles; it's as if the writer is thinking "out loud" on paper. The grammar is fine, but beginning sentences with "so" is not advisable.

Sample Essay Response Scoring 1

Wilderness and human culture can't really get along. Ever since the dawn of time, man has been screwing up the wilderness. Maybe once upon a time the Indians only hunted as much game as they needed, nowadays we just kill and take anything we think we need, even if we dont and we have so much stuff that we don't really need. We could do without a lot of the stuff we have, and maybe if we did, then wilderness wouldn't be so screwed up.

Analysis of Sample Essay Response Scoring 1

Although the writer takes a stance, this essay is much too short. There is a run-on sentence, a typo (don't), and "screwing up" is a slang term not appropriate for a formal essay, while the word "stuff" is too vague. This essay needs a lot of development and correction.

Sample 2 Responses

Sample Essay Response Scoring 5–6

I don't believe you can speak for all students when you have to answer a question like this, because the answer completely depends on the individual. There are students who would profit greatly from taking a year off, and there are others who would suffer if they were forced to stay away from college.

Some students have been waiting practically their entire life for a chance to attend college. They may have developed a love for a particular field in grade school, even. I know people who have been going to special science programs at local colleges for the past three years, and they can't wait to get to college. Highly motivated students have been taking college prep classes since before the 9th grade, and they spent the spring break of their junior year visiting college campuses. They are like a long-distance runner who sights the finish line. To make them stop or stay away for a year would be cruel.

On the other hand, there are students who have been pushed and pushed by their parents or other people to go to college. They are like a racer who has depleted all of his or her energy, and although they may make it to the finish line, the race has just about killed them. If they were forced to take a year out to explore some other parts of life, maybe take an internship in a local business or hospital or travel around, and if they could still get admitted to a college at the end of that time, they would greatly profit from having a break.

There are still other students who do not have a clue about what they want to do when they grow up, but they have pressure from their family to go to college. When people like this go to college sometimes all they do is party and not study and get into trouble, and they have spent a lot of time and money that has all been wasted. If they spent a year at some sort of boring job, it might really motivate them to get serious about studying, and also they might get a clue about how hard it is to make a living.

There is no "one size fits all" answer to a question such as deciding if staying out of school for a year would be beneficial for students. Some students would benefit from such a scheme, and others would not. This is a question that has to be evaluated for each student.

Analysis of Sample Essay Response Scoring 5–6

A good thoughtful essay. It demonstrates that although you are encouraged to take a side and defend it when answering an either-or question, if you truly believe that there is not a single answer to a question, and you can defend your stance, you can create a successful essay. The body paragraphs discuss aspects of the issue in some detail, and the conclusion reiterates the writer's position. There is even the use of an extended simile (a race) to help make the point. However, there is incorrect usage of "they" and "their" for third person singular (the racer). One fault is that the development is not parallel. The introductory paragraph speaks first of students who would suffer from staying out of college, then of students who would benefit, but the first body paragraph discusses how some students would suffer, then of how some would benefit. An essay is stronger when each point follows the order presented in the introduction.

Sample Essay Response Scoring 3–4

Should a student stay out of school for a year before they on to college? On the whole, I believe this is a good idea. Our world is so complicated, and there are so many facets to it, that most students would benefit from doing something other than studying for a year.

Most students have spent 12 whole years doing nothing but going to school. What do they know about the world outside the classroom? In most cases, not a whole lot.

There would be some kids who would take off and travel. Maybe they could spend a year going around Europe and visiting museums and stuff. Think of all the exposure they would have to art and when they came back they would appreciate a lot of things about the world that is beyond the little world they know from high school.

Other people might work for a year. They might have to for financial reasons, but it would still be a good thing for them to do to have to go off to work every day and then maybe they would have an apartment and they would have to learn how to live on a budget and that would make them appreciate it more when they got back in school.

There would have to be some sort of deal set up where students could still get into college after their year off, but if that was taken care of, I think that letting students "out" to do something else for a year is a great idea.

Analysis of Sample Essay Response Scoring 3–4

The essay lacks a strong conclusion, and in fact brings up a new issue, which is not a good idea for a conclusion. There is development in the body paragraphs, but the student tends to write rather casually, using terms like "kids" and "stuff," for instance. The grammar is mostly all right, but there is an error in singular-plural verb agreement (it should be "a lot of things . . . that are"). There is variety in the type of sentence structures used, but some sentences ramble.

Sample Essay Response Scoring 2

On the issue of kids staying out of school for a year before they go to college, there are some good things and some bad things about the idea.

A good thing is that kids would learn about other things out here in the world besides school. They might have to go off and live by themselves, and their parents would probably like to watch them have to pay rent and cook, and learn about how to get along. Which is not such a darn bad idea, when you think about it.

On the other hand, there might be kids who would get in a lot of trouble if they were not in school. There is enough partying, and drugs going on that if people weren't in a safer place, like college they might just be partying all the time.

And then again, there could be people who were going to go to college but when they took a year off they never applied to college and they never got around to going and, they might wind up in a pathetic job and that would be really sad.

So all in all, I think people should probably go ahead and go to college right out of high school, because they could get in a lot of trouble if they don't.

Analysis of Sample Essay Response Scoring 2

This essay begins without a strong opinion, and the student comes to a conclusion in the process of writing. Thus, the organization suffers. There is not a strong introduction, and the paragraphs, while they address different issues, are more a discovery process than a focused essay. There are problems with rambling sentences and misplaced commas and there is a sentence fragment. Using "kids" and phrases like "a darn bad idea" sets a more casual tone than is needed in a formal essay.

Sample Essay Response Scoring 1

I think it is a very bad idea to have kids stay out of school for a year. We have waited for so long to get to college, and to make us wait one more year would be really mean and it would be stupid to just hang around for a year and what would you do, anyway? I guess you could spend a year flipping hamburgers but I that was the whole reason to go to school, so you wouldn't have to spend whole life saying "do you want cheese with that" or such lame job.

Making people not go to college is horrible. And what about when they wanted to go? What college would want them if they hadn't been in school for a whole year? This idea doesn't make any sense.

Analysis of Sample Essay Response Scoring 1

This essay has an opinion, but the arguments are poorly developed. There is not a strong conclusion; the final paragraph restates the writer's opinion and then brings up another issue. There are rambling sentences and a couple of missing words ("I ___ that was the whole reason" and "spend ___ whole life"). The writer should have gone back to proofread the essay.

APPENDIX

List of 125 Most Common and Important Prefixes, Suffixes, and Roots in Content Areas

	Prefix	Meaning	Word
1.	a-	not, without	asexual
2.	ad-	to	adhesive
3.	ambi-	both	ambidextrous
4.	ante-	before	antecedent
5.	anti-	against	antidote
6.	apo-	away from	apostle
7.	archae-	ancient	archaeological
8.	auto-	self	automation
9.	be-	throughout	bespeak
10.	bene-	well, good	benign
11.	bi-	two	bilingual
12.	biblio-	book	bibliophile
13.	bio-	life	biodegradable
14.	capt-	take, seize	captivated
15.	cata-	down	catacombs
16.	cent-	one hundred	centennial
17.	circum-	around	circumstances
18.	co-, com-	together	cohesive
19.	con-, contra-	against	contradictory
20.	de-	down	delineate
21.	deci-	one-tenth	decimate
22.	dia-	cross, through	diametric
23.	dis-	within	dissonance
24.	en-	in, on	entymology
25.	epi-	on, upon, over	epitaph
26.	eu-	well, good	eugenics
27.	ex-	out	expatriot
28.	hemi-	half	hemisphere

	Prefix	Meaning	Word
29.	**hetero-**	other	heterogeneous
30.	**hyper-**	over	hyperbole
31.	**hypo-**	under	hypochondria
32.	**il-**	not	illogical
33.	**in-**	in, into, on	inure
34.	**inter-**	between	interfere
35.	**intro-**	inside	introversion
36.	**iso-**	same	isometric
37.	**mal-**	bad	malevolent
38.	**mis-**	error, defect	misconstrue
39.	**mono-**	one	monopoly
40.	**multi-**	much, many	multitude
41.	**non-**	not	nonconformist
42.	**ob-**	in front of	obnoxious
43.	**over-**	over, above	overwrought
44.	**pan-**	all, every	pandemic
45.	**para-**	beside	paraprofessional
46.	**poly-**	many	polytheism
47.	**post-**	after	posterior
48.	**photo-**	light	photogenic
49.	**pre-**	before	prefix
50.	**pro-**	forward	procure
51.	**re-**	again	relapse
52.	**retro-**	backward	retrospect
53.	**semi-**	half, partly	semiskilled
54.	**sub-**	under, below	submerge
55.	**super-**	over, beyond	superimpose
56.	**syn-**	together	synthesis
57.	**tele-**	far off	telecommunication
58.	**trans-**	across	transcend
59.	**ultra-**	beyond	ultramodern
60.	**un-**	not	unceasing
61.	**uni-**	one	unitary

	Suffix	Meaning	Word
1.	**-able**	fit for	amenable
2.	**-ac**	resembling	insomniac
3.	**-age**	rate of	dosage
4.	**-al**	relating to	thermal
5.	**-an**	characteristic of	partisan
6.	**-ance**	quality, state	severance
7.	**-ant**	personal, impersonal agent	vagrant
8.	**-ary**	place of, for	aviary
9.	**-ate**	action in a specified way	alleviate
10.	**-dom**	quality, condition, domain	fiefdom
11.	**-ence**	action, process	reference
12.	**-ent**	personal, impersonal	decadent
13.	**-er**	one who performs a specified action	necromancer
14.	**-escent**	beginning to be, slightly	adolescent
15.	**-esque**	in the style of, manner of	grotesque
16.	**-ism**	doctrine, quality of	agrarianism
17.	**-ive**	tending toward, an indicated action	furtive
18.	**-less**	not having	guileless
19.	**-ment**	object of a specified action	detriment
20.	**-ness**	state, quality, degree	garishness
21.	**-or**	one who does a specified thing	ardor
22.	**-ous**	full of, resembling	ludicrous
23.	**-y**	like that of	homey

	Root	Meaning	Word
1.	**anim**	life, mind	animation
2.	**anthrop**	man, human	anthropomorphic
3.	**auto**	self	autonomous
4.	**bio**	life	biography
5.	**cap**	take, hold	caprice
6.	**chrom**	color	chromatic
7.	**chron**	time	chronometer

	Root	Meaning	Word
8.	cycle	circle	cyclone
9.	dem	people	democracy
10.	eu	happy	euphoric
11.	fac	make	facsimile
12.	fer	carry, bring, bear	ferment
13.	fin	end	finite
14.	flex	bend	flexible
15.	gamy	marriage	allogamy
16.	gen	produce	generate
17.	gnos	knowledge	agnostic
18.	grade	go, take steps	retrograde
19.	graph	write	graphology
20.	leg	law, legal	legalize
21.	log	word, speech, science	logogram
22.	loq, loqy	speech	loquacious
23.	meter	measure	odometer
24.	mit	send, throw	mitigate
25.	mov, mot	move	motile
26.	ped	foot	pediform
27.	ped	boy	pediatrics
28.	phil	love	philanthropy
29.	phon	sound	phonogram
30.	reg	rule	regimen
31.	rupt	break	rupture
32.	soph	wise	sophisticate
33.	scrib	write	script
34.	spect	look	introspective
35.	stat	stable	static
36.	tang, tact	touch	tangible
37.	ten	hold	tenure
38.	tract	draw, drag	detract
39.	vert, vers	to turn	avert
40.	vid	see	provident
41.	voc	to call	advocate

Index

Carbon cycle, 482
Carbon dioxide, volcanoes and, 487
Cardiac muscles, 440
Cartesian coordinate plane, 309
Catalyst, 451
Celestial equator, 503
Celestial latitude, 503
Celestial longitude, 503
Celestial meridian, 504
Celestial sphere, 503–504
Cell membrane, 423
Cells, 423–435
Cellular respiration, 432–433
Cell wall, 424
Celsius, 467
Cenozoic era, 436
Central angle, 305
Centrioles, 424
Charles' Law, 459
Charts, 387–388
Chemical bond, 450
Chemical kinetics, 453
Chemical processes of weathering rock, 496
Chemical property, 449
Chemistry, 447–457
Chloroplasts, 424, 431
Chord, of circle, 304
Chromosomes, 424, 434
Circles, 303–307
Circuits, 470–471
Circulatory system, 440
Circumscribed circles, 306
Classification, 437–439
Clastic rock, 494
Cleavage, 495
Climate, 486
Climatology, 486
Clouds, 513
Coefficient, 249
Cohesion in Rhetorical Skills, 198–199
Collective nouns
  pronoun agreement, 183
  subject-verb agreement, 177
Collision hypothesis, 493
Colloid, 449
Colon, 164–166
Coma, 505
Combustion, 451
Comets, 477, 505
Comma, 157–162
Common denominator, 223
Common gender, pronoun agreement and, 184
Commutative law, 249, 250
Comparatives, 181
Comparisons

of adjectives, 181
of ideas and parallel structure, 179
in sentences, 180
Complete the square, quadratic equations, 269
Complex fraction, 225
Complimentary angle, 282
Composite score, 8
Compound, chemical, 452–453
Compound sentences
  comma and, 159
  semicolon use, 166–168
Compound subject
  pronoun agreement, 183
  subject-verb agreement, 177
Compression, 459
Concentric circles, 306
Concoidal, 495
Conditional inequality, 274
Conduction, 467
Conductors, 467, 470
Cone of depression, 498
Conflicting viewpoints, 414–418
  format of ACT and overview of, 4, 6–7
  strategies for, 414
Congruent angle, 282
Congruent circles, 306
Conjunctions, correlative and parallel structure, 179
Connecting words, compound sentences and comma, 159
Consecutive angles, parallelogram, 298
Consecutive integers, 218
Conservation, 489–490
  of energy, 459
  Law of Conservation of Energy, 460
  Law of Conservation of Matter or Energy, 448
  Law of Conservation of Mechanical Energy, 460–461, 466
  Law of Conservation of Momentum, 460
Constant, 249
Constellations, 478, 506
Continental divide, 499
Continental drift, 481
Continental shelves, 481
Contour lines, 497
Contractions, apostrophe use and, 169
Contrasting elements
  comma use and, 162
  semicolon use and, 167

Controls, in research summaries, 401
Convection, 467
Convergence, 513
Coordinate axes, 309
Coordinate geometry, 309–311
Coriolis effect, 514–515
Coriolis force, 514–515
Correlative conjunctions, parallel structure, 179
Corrosion, 449
Covalent bonds, 450
Covalent compound, 453
Creation Theory, 477
Crystal, 495
Crystalline Substance, 495
Cumulus stage of thunderstorm, 513
Currents
  electrical, 470–471
  Lenz's Law, 461
  Ohm's Law, 461
  water, 489
Cytology, 423
Cytoplasm, 423
Dalton, Thomas, 447
Darwin, Charles, 436
Dashes, 172–173
Data representation, 385–400
Date, comma use, 162
Decimals, 230–237
Declination, 498, 503
Definite Composition, Law of, 452–453
Denominator, 222
  lowest common, 223
Dependent equations, 262–263
Depression
  cone of, 498
  contour maps, 498
Dermis, 441
Diameter, of circle, 304
Diction errors, words and idioms commonly misused, 191–194
Differentiation process, 493
Diffraction, 469
Digestion, cells, 431
Digestive system, 439
Dip-slip fault, 496
Direct address, comma and, 160
Direct current (DC), 470–471
Direct quotations, comma use and, 162
Disk spiral, 507
Dissipating stage of thunderstorm, 513, 514
Distributive laws, 249

INSTALLING REA's TEST*ware*®

System Requirements
14-inch monitor or larger, CD-ROM drive

Macintosh: Any Macintosh with a 68020 or higher processor or Power Macintosh, 4 MB of RAM minimum, System 7.1 or later. At least 5 MB of hard-disk space available.

Windows: Any PC with at least 4 MB of RAM and 5 MB of hard-disk space available.

MACINTOSH INSTALLATION
1. Insert the ACT TEST*ware*® CD-ROM into the CD-ROM drive.
2. Double-click on the REA ACT INSTALLER icon. If you choose the standard installation, the installer will automatically place the program—containing both the ACT TEST*ware*® and the ACT Verbal Builder—into a folder entitled "REA ACT." (If you choose the custom installation, you will have a choice of installing either or both applications.) If the name and location are suitable, click the INSTALL button. If you want to change this, type over the existing information, and then click INSTALL.
3. Start the ACT TEST*ware*® or ACT Verbal Builder applications by double-clicking on their respective icons.

WINDOWS INSTALLATION
1. Insert the ACT TEST*ware*® CD-ROM into the CD-ROM drive.
2. From the Start Menu, choose the RUN command. When the RUN dialog box appears, type d:\setup (where D is the letter of your CD-ROM drive) at the prompt and click OK.
3. The installation process will begin. The standard (typical or compact) installation will install both the ACT TEST*ware*® and the ACT Verbal Builder. If you choose the custom installation, you will have a choice of installing either or both applications. A dialog box proposing the directory "REA_ACT" will appear. If the name and location are suitable, click OK. If you wish to specify a different name or location, type it in and click OK.
4. Start the ACT TEST*ware*® or ACT Verbal Builder applications by double-clicking on their respective icons.

TECHNICAL SUPPORT

REA TEST*ware*® is backed by customer and technical support. For questions about **installation or operation of your software**, contact us at:

Research & Education Association
Phone: (732) 819-8880 (9 a.m. to 5 p.m. ET daily)
Fax: (732) 819-8808
Website: http://www.rea.com
E-mail: info@rea.com

USING REA's INTERACTIVE ACT TEST*ware*®

REA's ACT TEST*ware*® is **EASY** to **LEARN AND USE**. To achieve maximum benefits, we recommend that you take a few minutes to go through the on-screen tutorial on your computer. The "screen buttons" are also explained here to familiarize you with the program.

Program Help and Test Directions

To get help at any time during the test, choose the **Program Help** button which reviews basic functions of the program. The **Test Directions** button allows you to review the specific exam directions during any part of the test.

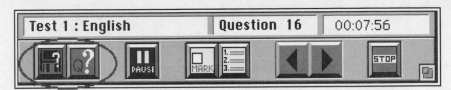

Stop Test

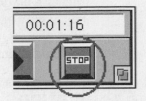

At any time during the test or when you are finished taking the test, click on the **Stop** button. The program will forward you to the following screen.

Once you leave this test, without suspending the exam, you will not be able to return to this test.

| GO TO NEXT TEST | SUSPEND EXAM | RETURN TO WHERE I WAS |

This screen allows you to go to the next test section, suspend or quit the test, or return to the last question accessed prior to clicking the **Stop** button.

Arrow Buttons

When an answer is selected, click on the **Right Arrow** button or press the **Return** key to proceed to the next question.

Mark Questions

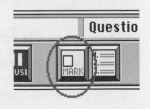

If you are unsure about an answer to a particular question, the program allows you to mark it for later review. Flag the question by clicking on the **Mark** button.

Table of Contents

To review all marked questions, review answer choices, or skip to any question within a test section, click on the **Table of Contents** button.

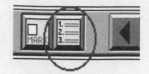

Results

Review and analyze your performance on the test by clicking on the **Results** button.

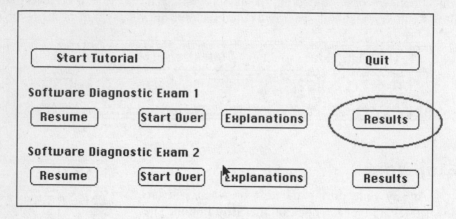

Explanations

In Explanations mode, click on the **Explanation** button to pop up a detailed explanation to any question. At the end of every explanation is a page reference to the appropriate review section in the book.

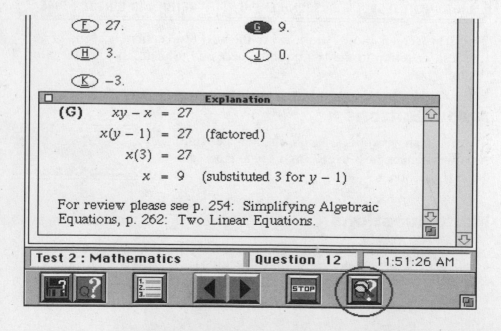